OREGON
HANDBOOK

D0048629

OREGON
HANDBOOK
FOURTH EDITION

STUART WARREN & TED LONG ISHIKAWA

MOON
TRAVEL
HANDBOOKS

OREGON HANDBOOK
FOURTH EDITION

Published by
Moon Publications, Inc.
P.O. Box 3040
Chico, California 95927-3040, USA

Printed by
Colorcraft Ltd.

ISBN: 1-56691-113-3
ISSN: 1080-3394

Editor: Diane Wurzel
Map Editor: Gina Wilson Birtcil
Copy Editors: Diane Wurzel, Asha Johnson
Production & Design: Carey Wilson
Cartography: Chris Folks, Mike Morgenfeld, and Bob Race
Index: Karen Bleske

Front cover photo: © Rich Schafer, Crater Lake National Park. Summer storms leave the lake turquoise in color. Summer. Klamath County.

Distributed in the United States and Canada by Publishers Group West
Printed in China

Please send all comments,
corrections, additions,
amendments, and critiques to:

**OREGON HANDBOOK
MOON TRAVEL HANDBOOKS
P.O. BOX 3040
CHICO, CA 95927-3040, USA
e-mail: travel@moon.com
www.moon.com**

Printing History
1st edition—1991
4th edition—April 1998
5 4 3 2

To Mr. Ed Hardy,
who always said we could.

CONTENTS

SPECIAL TOPICS

THE HIGH CASCADES 398-489

SPECIAL TOPICS

SOUTHEASTERN OREGON 490-506

MAPS

MAP SYMBOLS

	WATERFALL
	WATER
	SKI AREA
■	POINT OF INTEREST
	N.W.R. NATIONAL WILDLIFE REFUGE
	N.P. NATIONAL PARK
	S.P. STATE PARK

| | INTERSTATE HIGHWAY |
| U.S. HIGHWAY |
| STATE HIGHWAY |
O	LARGE CITY
o	SMALL CITIES & TOWNS
▲	MOUNTAIN

| | FREEWAY |
| MAIN HIGHWAY |
| SECONDARY ROAD |
| UNPAVED ROAD |
| FOOT PATH, TRAIL |
| STATE BORDER |
| OTHER BORDER |
| TUNNEL |
| PASS |
| RAILROAD |
| BRIDGE |

ABBREVIATIONS

AYH—American Youth Hostel

AARP—American Association of Retired People

BLM—Bureau of Land Management

CCC—Civilian Conservation Corps

F—Fahrenheit

FSR—Forest Service Road

MAX—Metropolitan Area Express

mph—miles per hour

NRA—National Recreation Area

NWR—National Wildlife Refuge

OMSI—Oregon Museum of Science and Industry

ORE (plus number)—state highway

POVA—Portland Oregon Visitors Association

RV—recreational vehicle

US (plus number)—federal highway

WISTEC—Willamette Science and Technology Center

IS THIS BOOK OUT OF DATE?

We strive to keep our books as up to date as possible and would appreciate your help. If you find that a resort is not as we described or discover a new restaurant or other information that should be included in our book, please let us know. Our mapmakers take extraordinary effort to be accurate, but if you find an error, let us know that as well.

We're especially interested in hearing from female travelers, RVers, outdoor enthusiasts, expatriates, and local residents. We are always interested in hearing from the tourist industry, which specializes in accommodating visitors to Oregon. Happy traveling! Please address letters to:

Oregon Handbook
Moon Publications, Inc.
P.O. Box 3040
Chico, CA 95927-3040, USA

e-mail travel@moon.com

ACKNOWLEDGMENTS

Oregon Handbook began in Alaska when Moon's editor-in-chief emeritus and esteemed author Deke Castleman grabbed Stuart and said, "Oregon needs a good book. Just get it down, man." We're also indebted to Rhys Thomas and Theo Trimmell for their wise and witty sidebar about the Oregon Country Fair. Special thanks to Anne Long Larsen for artistic brilliance, Jennifer and Elliot Gehr for their help on the prehistory section, and to Bill and Dierdre Dant for their insightful comments about Portland and the north coast, which prevented those sections from reading like a telephone directory. Dave Johnson, prehaps the most respected environmental journalist in the state did the same on the eastern side of the mounatins Kudos to Phineas Warren, Rhys and Maria Thomas, Bruce Bush, Henning Larson, Hatsuko Ohashi, and Adam Long for help in bringing the project to fruition.

Technical expertise was added by Jim Pollack of the Portland Office of the National Forest Service and Brian Litt, a commissioner in the Columbia Gorge Scenic Area. Doug Bloch receives our gratitude for hiking tips. Steve Trimmell and Aline Maguire deserve special mention for their input and hospitality during the final push to bring out the fourth edition. Sue McGuire's photos and travel experience were also invaluable contributions.

In addition to the "Beast of the East," we thank Number 95, "Old Blue," for schoolin'; The Bob, The Big Man, and Larry for being straight shooters; Duke Dunnell for esprit de corps; Bowl-of-Rice for teaching us how to avoid black holes; and The Prez for sage advice. We'd also be remiss if we didn't give a nod to the college boys and overly articulate Bill for "inducing a more sanguine outlook," and to Ralph and April, looking hopefully over our shoulders as we wrote. In this vein, we dole out a special medal of honor to Sawako Ishikawa, who read the text more than anyone should ever have had to, and who took photos while riding shotgun on our roadtrips. Last but not least, our gratitude goes out to our parents for their unwavering encouragement, which sustained us through many long months of work.

ANNIE LONG LARSEN

INTRODUCTION

Theodore Winthrop, a mid-19th-century adventurer and novelist from New England, made the following observation at the end of his journey to the Oregon Territory:

Our race has never yet come into contact with great mountains as companions of daily life, nor felt that daily development of the finer and more comprehensive senses which these signal facts of nature compel. . . . These Oregon people, in a climate where being is bliss—where every breath is a draught of vivid life—these Oregon people, carrying to a newer and grander New England of the West a full growth of the American Idea . . . will elaborate new systems of thought and life.

What this boils down to in the language of today is that "these Oregon people" know how to live. Modern travelers to the state will tell you that nowhere else in the country has civilization meshed so peacefully with the environment. Recycling and mass transit maintain a benefi-

cent quality of life in the state's largest cities, and vast tracts of preserved land attest to Oregonians' appreciation of their gemlike coastline and snowcapped mountain ranges. In short, we live in a place that is still environmentally and socially intact compared to elsewhere.

Most of these trophies of the good life didn't come easily. Just as it took Oregon Trail pioneers many months to cross 2,000 miles of forbidding deserts and treacherous mountain passes to reach the promised land, Oregonians have sacrificed much to blaze trails in the thickets of environmental legislation and jurisprudence. And while the dilemma of one person's conservation being another's unemployment has been a continuous fact of life here, the debate has never raged more fiercely than it does at present. Inevitably, the outcome will bring more change and the regrettable passing of a way of life for many. But as the millennium approaches, one fact becomes clear—if Oregon has erred on the side of conservation, it has at least preserved an increasingly valuable and vanishing commodity: its natural resources. The proof is here for you to see.

THE LAND

GEOGRAPHY

The Overview

If Oregon were part of a jigsaw puzzle of the U.S., it would be a squarish piece with a dip in the center of its top. To the west is the Pacific Ocean; to the east is the Snake River and Idaho. Up top, much of the northern boundary between Oregon and Washington is defined by the Columbia River; the southern border is comprised of the state lines of California and Nevada.

If this puzzle also depicted the vertical relief of topographic features, it would show the broad columns of mountains dividing the coast from the inland valleys, as well as peaks cutting off western Oregon from the central and eastern parts of the state. East of the highest central range the Columbia Plateau predominates, broken up in the northeast where mountainous features reassert themselves. In the southeast, many lakes fill the landscape in the least mountainous expanse of the state. The Great Basin desert—characterized by rivers that evaporate, peter out, or dis-appear into underground aquifers—makes up the bottom third of eastern Oregon. Here, the seven-inch annual rainfall of the Alvord Desert seems more at home in southeastern Nevada and California than in a state better known for blustery rainstorms.

The Peak Experience in Western Oregon

Moving west to east, let's consider the major ranges, beginning with the Coastal and Klamath mountains. The Klamaths comprise the lower quarter of the state's westernmost barrier to the Pacific; the eastern flank of this range is generally referred to as the Siskiyous. As we move north, the Oregon Coast Range, a younger volcanic range, replaces the Klamaths. The highest peaks in each of these cordilleras barely top 4,000 feet and stand in between coastal plateaus on one side and such agricultural centers as the Willamette and the Rogue valleys on the other. East of these valleys are dormant (as of this writing) volcanoes. Known collectively as the Cascades, five of the peaks top 10,000 feet above sea level.

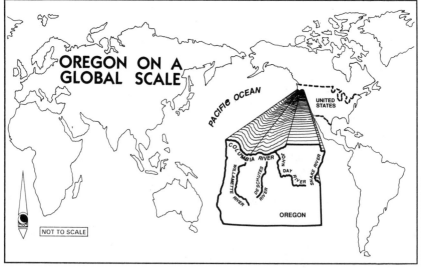

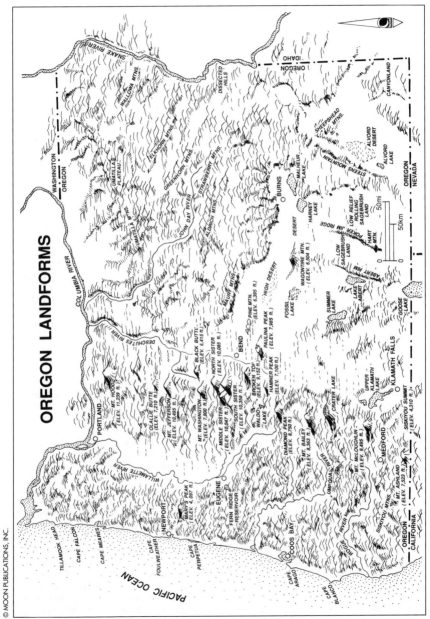

OREGON LANDFORMS

Contrasts in Eastern Oregon

Beyond the Cascades' eastern slope, one finds semiarid high-desert conditions contrasting with the Coast Range rainforests and the mild, wet maritime climate which characterizes much of western Oregon. The contrast is repeated in the northeast, where the 10,000-foot elevation of the snowcapped Wallowas lies less than 50 miles from a subtropical enclave—the hot, dry floor of Hells Canyon, about 1,300 feet above sea level.

In addition to Hells Canyon, America's biggest hole in the ground (7,900 feet maximum depth), Oregon also boasts the continent's deepest lake: Crater Lake, with a depth of 1,962 feet.

Last of the Red-Hot Lavas

In each part of the state, there are other well-known remnants of Oregon's cataclysmic past. Offshore waters here feature 1,477 volcanic islands. Lava fields dot the approach to the High Cascades. East of the range a volcanic plateau supports cinder cones, lava caves, and lava-cast forests in the most varied array of these phenomena outside of Hawaii.

Seismic events may not be just a thing of the past, according to research which took place on the north Oregon coast in 1990. Scientists unearthed discontinuities in both rock strata and tree rings here, indicating that Tillamook County has experienced major tremors every several hundred years. They estimate that the next one could come within our lifetimes and be of significant magnitude. In this vein, Japanese scientists maintain that a 9.0 quake struck the Northwest coast in 1700, based on tsunami records indicating 6-9 foot high tidal waves hitting Japan's coastline. This date is also consistent with Indian oral histories and geologic evidence. These coastal quakes are caused by what geologists call subduction. This process occurs when one of the giant plates that make up the earth's crust slides under another as they collide (see the "Introduction" in The High Cascades chapter for more on plate tectonics). In Pacific Northwest coastal regions, this takes place when the Juan de Fuca plate's marine layer is pushed under the continental North American plate. With virtually every part of the state possessing seismic potential that hasn't been released in many years, the pressure along the fault lines is increasing. The fact that Oregon building codes have not yet acknowledged this became evident in March of 1993 when a quake centered 30 miles south of Portland and registering 5.7 on the Richter scale accounted for several million dollars worth of damage. In September of that year, two Klamath Falls tremblors averaging nearly 6.0 on the Richter scale compounded the impression that the earth's internal burners are heating up again. The Klamath Falls quakes were the largest recorded in the state since 1873.

A few north coast towns take the possibility of seismic occurrences seriously. In Rockaway and other parts of Tillamook County, you'll note evacuation signs with arrows pointing the way to higher ground, acknowledging the imminent danger of a 30-foot tidal wave. Farther north, Seaside and Cannon Beach have warning sirens. Whenever there's a big quake in Alaska or Japan, you might hear one of these sirens. Ever since a tidal wave unleashed by Alaska's Good Friday quake in '64 resulted in five casualties in Seaside and over a million dollars in damage, local authorities have made seismic preparedness a priority. The highest officially measured tsunami wave from the Alaska quake of '64 was 14.2 feet at the mouth of the Umpqua River, indicating that the tidal wave threat in Oregon is not just restricted to the north coast.

The Great Meltdown

However pervasive the effects of volcanism here, they must still share top billing with the big Ice Age in Oregon's topographic grand epic.

At the height of the most recent major glaciation, the world's oceans were lower by 300 to 500 feet, North America and Asia were connected by a land bridge at the Bering Strait, and the Oregon coast was far west of where it is today. The Columbia Gorge extended out past present-day Astoria. As the glaciers melted, the sea rose.

When that glacial epoch's final meltdown 12,000 years ago unleashed water dammed up by thousands of feet of ice, great rivers were spawned and existing channels were enlarged. A particularly large inundation was the Missoula Flood, which began with an ice dam breaking up in present-day Montana. Before it subsided, it carved out the contours of what are now the Columbia River Gorge and the Willamette Valley. Other glacial floodwaters found their outlet westward to the sea, digging out silt-ridden estuaries in the process. Pacific wave action washed this debris back up onto the land, helping to create dunes and beaches.

Metes and Bounds

Oregon's 3.2 million people live in the 10th-largest state in the U.S., some 62 million acres, an area of 97,073 square miles. Two counties in eastern Oregon, Harney and Malheur, are bigger than eight other states. Harney County alone could hold Rhode Island eight times. With only 7,000 people and 100,000 head of cattle in the county, that wouldn't be too hard.

Over two-thirds of the state's population lives in Portland or within a 30-mile radius of the city; only 12.8% of the population lives east of the Cascades. As for land ownership, Uncle Sam has controlling interest in 55% of the territory (so-called "public lands"); state and local government get a three percent cut; and private and corporate concerns divvy up what's left.

CLIMATE

The Rain Shadow

Oregon's weather system is best understood as a series of valley microclimates set apart from each other by mountain ranges. Moving west to east, each of these valley zones records progressively lower rainfall levels until one encounters a desert on the eastern side of the state.

It all begins when moisture-laden westerlies off the Pacific slam into the Coast and Klamath ranges. As the clouds climb higher they drop their moisture in the form of rain or snow. That is because rising air cools three degrees Fahrenheit every 1,000 feet, and cooler air can't hold as much moisture as warm air. As a consequence, coastal rainfall often exceeds 80 inches a year, while the Willamette and other inland valleys on the other side of the mountains usually record half that total. The rain shadow effect is repeated when the Cascades catch precipitation from eastward-moving cloud masses; consequent-

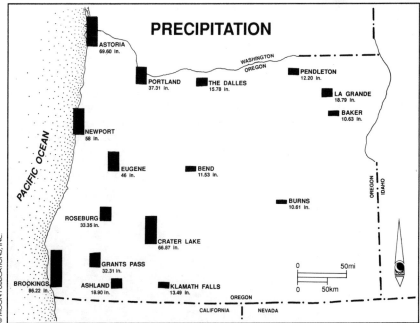

PRECIPITATION

ASTORIA 69.60 in.

PORTLAND 37.31 in.   THE DALLES 15.78 in.

WASHINGTON / OREGON

PENDLETON 12.20 in.

LA GRANDE 18.79 in.

BAKER 10.63 in.

NEWPORT 58 in.

PACIFIC OCEAN

EUGENE 46 in.   BEND 11.53 in.

BURNS 10.61 in.

ROSEBURG 33.35 in.

CRATER LAKE 66.87 in.

GRANTS PASS 32.31 in.

OREGON / IDAHO

0   50mi
0   50km

BROOKINGS 86.22 in.   ASHLAND 18.90 in.   KLAMATH FALLS 13.49 in.

OREGON
CALIFORNIA   NEVADA

ly, the other side of this range often records annual rainfall totals below 10 inches. This dryness is contrasted by the climate of the western Cascades and Coast Range, where precipitation commonly exceeds 100 inches.

Anyone driving through the Coast Range sees evidence of the "siege mentality," which sets in with each winter monsoon season. Giant TV satellite discs and stacks of covered firewood are common lawn ornaments here in the rainiest part of the state.

Western Oregon

Oregon's location equidistant from the equator and the North Pole subjects her to weather from both tropical and polar air flows. This makes for a pattern of changeability in which calm often alternates with storm, and extreme heat and extreme cold seldom last long. Of the 10 different climate zones in the world, Oregon hosts seven. (Coastal conditions are treated in detail in that region's chapter.)

If there is one constant in western Oregon, it is cloudiness. Portland and the Willamette Valley receive only about 45% of maximum potential sunshine; more than 200 days of the year are cloudy and rain falls an average of 150 days. While this might sound bleak, consider that the cloud cover helps moderate the climate by trapping and reflecting the earth's heat. Daily fluctuations in temperature average only 15° F here; the difference between the average temperatures of the warmest month, July, and the cold-

est one, January, is only about 20°. Best of all, on average, less than 30 days of the year record temperatures below freezing. Thus, the region, despite being on a more northerly latitude than parts of Canada, has a milder climate. Except in mountainous areas, snow usually isn't a force to be reckoned with here. Another surprise is that the average annual rainfall of 40 inches is often less than totals recorded in New York, Miami, and Chicago.

While Portland and the rest of the Willamette Valley share mild climates, with wintertime highs of 45° F and average summertime mercury readings between 65° and 75°, their weather differences are worth noting. Portland is affected by icy winds coming out of the Columbia River Gorge, originally derived from frigid Rocky Mountain air. At these times, the otherwise mild Portland climate experiences uncharacteristic frosts. The stereotype of Portland as having a cold climate derives from a location 150 north of Green Bay, Wisconsin on the same latitude as England. The warming influence of the Japanese current, however, mitigates the effects of Portland having such a northerly location.

The rest of the Willamette Valley is affected by temperature inversions. In winter, for example, warm air above the valley walls holds in the colder air below, resulting in enduring, but not endearing, fogs. In the southern valleys, fog helps to counterbalance the region's long dry season: Ashland and Medford sometimes record only half the yearly precipitation of their neighbors to

the painted hills of John Day Fossil Beds National Monument

OREGON TOURISM DIVISION

the north, as well as higher winter and summer temperatures. At the same time, these inversions can cause unwelcome pollution to linger.

In much of western Oregon, the day-night differences in temperature are seldom extreme because of cloud cover and vegetation. Both act to keep the air cool and moist during the day and trap heat at night. Still, east coast travelers will be struck by how much more Oregon cools down at night than locales in the mid-Atlantic states.

While it's difficult to predict daily weather patterns in western Oregon, there are definite seasonal climatic shifts here. In winter, arctic and tropical air masses collide over the Pacific, producing much of the state's rain. During the summer the clashes are less frequent. At that time, Oregon weather is more affected by Pacific Ocean temperatures and air pressure differences between inland and coastal areas.

Eastern Oregon

By contrast, the scorching deserts of eastern Oregon can give way to cold temperatures at night. This is because clear skies and a dearth of vegetation facilitate the escape of heat. Consider that on May 2, 1968, the difference between the high and low temperatures at Juniper Lake, north of the Alvord Desert in southeastern Oregon, was 81°.

Mountain areas also experience extreme diurnal temperature fluctuations. Thin mountain air does not filter out ultraviolet radiation as effectively as the denser air at lower elevations, so the sun's force is accentuated at higher elevations. At night, chill spreads quickly through this thin air.

Choose Your Poison

What eastern and western Oregonians have in common is a tendency to poke fun at each other's climates. West of the Cascades, the reigning opinion seems to be that it's so dry in the Oregon desert that the jackrabbits pack canteens. In like measure, the dry-siders will assure you that people in western Oregon don't tan, they rust. A quick look at the extremes of rain, heat, and cold will set the record straight.

As the rainiest places in the state don't have weather stations, we'll have to accord the dubious distinction for precipitous precipitation to a "noncommunity." West of Salem, nestled high in the Coast Range, is Valsetz, a tiny lumber town that once was. Until the town's demise in 1985, its 129.9 inches yearly average was the highest in the state, although rainfall in the surrounding mountains and over maritime locations commonly exceeds 150 inches. Then, too, the typical winter storm season on the coast usually sees 100-mile-per-hour gales and 12-foot waves near Cape Blanco, Cape Foulweather, and at the mouth of the Columbia River near Astoria. Oregon's percentage of sunny days is only 48% (ranking it 49th in the nation), thanks largely to the persistent cloud cover west of the Cascades. In 1996-1997, record rainfall totals were racked up from Medford to Portland. Eugene and Portland about doubled their average totals and a new "rain king" was crowned in the Coast Range east of Lincoln City. Laurel Mountain sustained 204 inches (far exceeding its 120 inch annual average). But high totals were not only recorded in uninhabited mountaintops in the Coast Range. The town of Mapleton had over 138 inches and the floods and slides made western Oregon a dangerous place to be for two straight winters (1996 and 1997), lending credence to meterologists who forsee the onset of a several decade "wet cycle."

Statistics from the other side of the mountains make it clear that the sectional debate over whose climate is worse can best be summed up by the phrase, "choose your poison." To wit, Pendleton and Prineville have both recorded 119° F days. Two other eastern Oregon communities, Seneca and Ukiah, share the distinction for the lowest temperature, -54° F.

Such statistics should be viewed in their proper context. These climatic aberrations are not the reality that most Oregonians experience. In fact, the extremes of wind, rain, heat, and cold affect less than one percent of the population, leaving the vast majority in mild, temperate conditions.

FLORA

Trees

Oregon is known for its forests. The mixed-conifer ecosystem of western Oregon boasts such record specimens as the 329-foot high, 11.5-foot diameter **Doerner fir** in the Coast

Range outside Coquille, rated the nation's largest Douglas fir by the American Forestry Association based on height, diameter, and crown size. Jumbo-sized western hemlock and Sitka spruce also exist in between Oregon's shoreline and the mid-Cascades. Within this region, the evergreen forest of the wet lowlands is the most productive belt of conifers in the world. This woodland carries up to 1,000 tons of plant matter per hectare and sometimes more.

Oregon has the record ponderosa pine outside Bend, the world's tallest Sitka spruce off US 26 near Cannon Beach, the world's largest Monterey cypress in Brookings, and a bevy of similar distinctions (over 40 "champion" trees statewide. See this Internet site for directions and additional information: http://www.odf.state.or.us.bigtrees/btreg.htm, might also rate a nod from the *Guinness Book of World Records*. With only seven percent as much rainfall as the Coast Range forests, 20 million acres of eastern Oregon's desert is largely rabbitbrush, cheatgrass, sagebrush, and juniper. In the John Day backcountry of eastern Oregon, you can find even hedgehog cactus.

Tree lovers will also be taken by such arboreal aberrations as southern Oregon's redwood groves, the huge ponderosa pines in the middle of Christmas Valley desert, and fall color in Portland and Willamette Valley towns from deciduous trees planted by early pioneers. A particularly striking natural display along the McKenzie River mixes red vine maple and sumacs with golden oaks and alders against an evergreen backdrop.

Trees to Know in Oregon, published by the Oregon State University Extension Service in Corvallis, is an excellent aid to tree identification as well as a compendium of useful facts. Oregon schoolchildren first learn to distinguish between fir, spruce, hemlock, and ponderosa pine by a mnemonic device. The needles of a **f**ir are **f**lat, **f**lexible, and **f**riendly. **S**pruce needles are **s**quare, **s**tiff and will **s**tick you. **H**emlock needles have a **h**ammocklike configuration, and the crown of the tree is curved like it's tipping its **h**at. Finally, the **p**onderosa **p**ine's **p**latelike bark is also distinctive.

Old Growth Trees

Naturalists describe an old-growth forest as a mixture of trees, some of which must be at least 200 years old, and a supply of snags or standing dead trees, nurse logs, and streams with downed logs. Throughout this book, reference will be made to old-growth groves that are noteworthy for size, age, beauty, ecological significance, or ease of access. Of all the venues mentioned in this volume, **Opal Creek** (see Salem) most spectacularly embodies all of the above. Its recent incorporation into a protected wilderness is significant given the fact that of the 19 million acres of old-growth that once proliferated Oregon and Washington, only 10% survive. An easy-to-pack source for hiking tips is an annotated map series distributed by **Old Growth Day Hikes,** Box 11288, Eugene, OR 97405.

Flowers and Fruits

The state of Oregon has forever been associated in the public mind with such sobriquets as the "Emerald Empire" and the "Chlorophyll Commonwealth." While giant conifers and a profuse understory of greenery do in fact surround the state's most populous areas, this ecosystem represents only the most visible part of Oregon's bountiful botany. In between the mist-covered mountains and the deserts exist other worlds.

While not as visually arresting as the evergreens of western Oregon, the several varieties of blackberries in the state are no less pervasive. Found mostly from the coast to the mid-Cascades, blackberries favor clearings, burned-over areas, and people's gardens. Some Oregonians swear that they've seen this hardy vine growing on the fenders of cars! It also takes root in the woods alongside wild strawberries, salmonberries, thimbleberries, currants, and salal. Within this edible realm, wild food connoisseurs especially seek out the thin-leafed huck-

BOB RACE

Pseudotsuga menziessi, *Douglas fir*

leberry found in the Wallowa, Blue, Cascade, and Klamath ranges. Prime snacking season for all these berries ranges from midsummer to midfall. During the fall, U-pick orchards are also popular. Apples in the Hood River Valley and on Sauvie Island, pears outside of Medford, and all of the above throughout the Willamette Valley are choice pickin's.

Autumn is also the season for those who covet chanterelle, matsutake, and morel mushrooms, particularly after the first rains until the onset of frosts. The Coast Range September through November is the prime picking area for chanterelles—a fluted orange or yellow mushroom in the tall second-growth Douglas fir forests. If you plan to sell what you find, you will need to purchase a permit from the National Forest Service for a nominal fee. After picking, don't put them in plastic bags. Use waxed paper or a basket, and leave them uncovered unless it's raining. Of late, fungus fever has reached epidemic proportions, largely due to a matsutake mushroom shortage in Japan, where it is prized for medicinal and spiritual qualities as well as a soup garnish. From 1993 to 1996, matsutakes fetched up to $500/pound in Japan, a fact which precipitated violence in northern Klamath County Forests and other areas that were saturated with pickers during the fall harvest. This mycological harvest, along with the cutting of ferns, beargrass, and other ornamental greenery, helps many residents of forest communities make ends meet. Maidenhair ferns command an especially high price from florists.

Exempt from exploitation but no less prized are the rare plant communities of the Columbia River Gorge and the Klamath/Siskiyou region. A quarter of Oregon's rare and endangered plants are found in the latter area, a portion of which is in the valley of the Illinois River, a Wild and Scenic tributary of the Rogue. One of these anomalies, *Kalmiopsis leachiana,* even has a wilderness named after it. Whole volumes have been dedicated to Oregon's singular ecosystems, such as *Rare Plants of the Columbia Gorge* by Russ Jolley (Portland: Oregon Historical Society Press, 1990).

Motorists will treasure such springtime floral fantasias (both wild and in roadside nurseries and orchards) as the dahlias and irises near Canby off I-5; tulips near Woodburn; irises off ORE 213 outside Salem; the Easter lilies along US 101 near Brookings; blue lupines alongside ORE 97 in central Oregon; apple blossoms in the Hood River Valley near the Columbia Gorge; pear blossoms in the Bear Creek Valley near Medford; beargrass, columbines, and Indian paintbrush on Cascades thoroughfares; as well as Scotch broom, rhododendrons, and fireweed along the coast. And on some of the busiest highways in the state, Willamette Valley daffodils chart a springtime yellow brick road through the heart of the Emerald Empire.

Wildflower lovers will notice that in the country east of the Cascades the undergrowth is often more varied than the ground cover in the damp forests on the other side of the mountains. This is because sunny openings in the forest permit room for more species and for plants of different heights. And, in contrast to the white flowers that predominate in the shady forests in western Oregon, "dry-side" wildflowers generally have brighter colors. These blossoms must attract color-sensitive pollinators like bees and butterflies. On the opposite flank of the range, the commonly seen white trillium relies on beetles and ants for propagation, lessening the need for eye-catching pigments.

The hand of man has brought Oregon's horticultural highlights to the notice of flower lovers everywhere. Such world-famous displays as the **Hendricks Park Rhododendron Garden** in Eugene, Brookings's **Azalea State Park,** and the **International Rose Test Garden** in Portland all peak in mid-June. Not surprisingly, nationally known seed companies and nurseries proliferate in the western part of the state.

There is no shortage of good flower books about each specific section of Oregon. Powell's Books on Burnside St. in Portland has a good collection. Since the color plates in many of these books make them expensive, you'll appreciate the fact that Powell's sells used editions at a discount.

FAUNA

Wildlife

Oregon's creatures great and small comprise an excitingly diverse group, especially in so developed a country as the United States. Oregon's low population density, abundance of wildlife refuges and nature preserves, as well as biomes running the gamut from rainforest to desert, explain this variety.

Let's begin our overview from the ground up, with the venerable Oregon slug. There are few places on earth where these snails-out-of-shells grow as large and in such numbers. The reason is western Oregon's climate: moister than mist but drier than drizzle. This balance and calcium-poor soil enables the native banana slug and the more common European black slug to thrive while being the bane of Oregon gardeners. When these three-to-ten-inch squirts of slime are not eating plants, you'll see them moving along at a snail's pace on some sidewalk or forest trail. The eight species of nonnative slugs that have established themselves in the Northwest tend to prey on crops and gardens. Native species generally confine themselves to forests and eat indigenous plants.

It's altogether fitting that the continent's fastest land mammal, the pronghorn antelope, also walks the earth here . . . when it's not running, that is. Able to log over 60 miles per hour in short bursts, pronghorns prefer open country east of the Cascades. The low brush there suits their excellent vision, which enables them to spot predators. The most dangerous predator of all is kept at a distance by the boundaries of the **Hart Mountain National Antelope Refuge** (see "Sights: La Pine to Lakeview," under "Lake County" in the Southeastern Oregon chapter).

Felis concolor,
mountain lion

Eutamias townsendi,
chipmunk

In like measure, such tracts as the **South Slough Estuary,** the **Malheur Bird/Wildlife Refuge,** the **Jewell Preserve for Roosevelt Elk,** and the **Finley Bird and Wildlife Preserve** provide safe havens for both feathered and furry friends.

While the dominant animals in each of the state's ecosystems are profiled in the relevant chapters, there are certain species whose ubiquitous presence demands an in-depth treatment.

Small Scavengers

Many of the most frequently sighted animals in Oregon are small scavengers. Even in the most urban parts of the state, it's possible to see raccoons, skunks, chipmunks, squirrels, and opossums. All are frequently encountered in woodsier neighborhoods, often around garbage cans, in parks, and near picnic areas. Urban gardens attract moles and pocket gophers.

West of the Cascades, the dark-colored Townsend's chipmunks are among the most commonly encountered mammals; east of the Cascades, lighter-colored pine chipmunks and golden mantled ground squirrels proliferate in drier interior forests. The latter two look alike but can be distinquished from each other because the chipmunk has stripes on the side of its head. Expect to see the dark brown, cinnamon-bellied Douglas squirrel on both sides of the Cascades.

Urban jungles, suburbs, and bush communities throughout Oregon have seen an infestation of opossums. These docile nocturnal marsupials are usually sighted during twilight hours and often as road kills. Brought by a contingent of rural folk from Arkansas as a food source back in the '30s and '40s, their numbers have increased exponentially. In fact, people are becoming so used to North America's only marsupial that the opossum is taking on a new life as a domesticated household pet. They can't get rabies or distemper because their body temperatures are too low, and their ability to grasp objects with their tail and the presence of opposable thumbs make opossums fascinating to watch. Just catch them when they're awake. These nearly-blind fruit and carrion eaters spend most of their lives asleep.

Raccoons are not so agreeable. These deceptively cute critters are really vicious scavengers who've earned a dubious distinction as dog-killers. Though no match for many canines on land, they can even the odds by luring a family pet to water. Be especially careful of potentially rabid mothers near cubs.

Eastern Oregon Critters
When talking about this desert region, it should first be noted that marine fossils dating back 225 million years were found in eastern Oregon creekbeds. These crustaceans were discovered in present-day Lake County, which today is home to such diverse wildlife as pronghorn antelope and wild mustangs. Since 99% of desert animals are nocturnal, it's difficult to see many of them. Nonetheless, their variety and exotic presences should be noted. Horned lizards, kangaroo rats, red-and-black ground snakes, kit foxes, and four-inch-long greenish yellow-hairy scorpions are some of the more interesting denizens of the desert east of the Cascade mountains. Should you ever have the chance to witness the intelligence of coyotes on the hunt or the nimble-footed bighorn sheep dancing along a precipitous ridge here, you'll never forget it.

Big Game
Sportspeople and wildlife enthusiasts alike appreciate Oregon's big-game herds. Their habitats differ dramatically from one side of the Cascades to the other, with Roosevelt elk and black-tail deer in the west and Rocky Mountain elk and mule deer east of the Cascades. The Columbian whitetail deer is a seldom-seen endangered species that populates western Oregon. Prong-

Servus canadensis, elk

ANNIE LONG LARSEN

horn reside in the high desert country of southeastern Oregon.

While sightings are rare, the state boasts cougar and wild horse populations. The nocturnal stalking behavior of the cougar and wild horse habitat in the remote draws of the Great Basin make any encounter with these creatures memorable.

"Kiger" mustangs, descendants of horses that the Spanish conquistadores brought to America centuries ago, are identified by their hooked ears, thin dorsal stripes, two-toned manes, and faint zebra stripes on their legs. Narrow trunks and a short back are other distinguishing physical characteristics. They sometimes can be identified from a distance by the herding instinct bred into them by the Spanish. The Kigers constitute a small percentage of the 2,000 wild mustangs in the state. For information on viewing the Steens Mountain herd, contact the BLM Burns District Office, HC 74-125339, Hwy 20 W., Hines 97738, tel. 573-5241.

Beavers in the Beaver State
Castor canadensis, the Americas' largest rodent, has long been Oregon's mascot. For good reason: it was the beaver that inspired the fur brigades and spurred the initial exploration and settlement of the state. Apart from its role in bringing Europeans into the wilderness, the

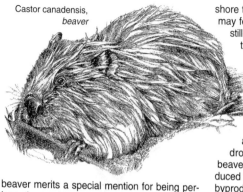

Castor canadensis,
beaver

ANNIE LONG LARSEN

beaver merits a special mention for being perhaps the most important animal in Oregon's forest ecosystem. Contrary to popular conception, the abilities of Mother Nature's carpenter extend far beyond the mere destruction of trees to dam a waterway. In fact, the activities associated with lodge construction actually serve to maintain the food chain and the health of the forest.

When a mated pair (beavers mate for life) packs sticks and mud to dam a river or stream, the resulting pool of deeper water in which they build their lodge protects these ungainly creatures from predation. The dam also reduces the stream's current and potential flooding of the lodge. The beavers' chances for survival are aided by their ability to enter the lodge underwater and to stay beneath the surface for as long as 20 minutes. Ear flaps and retractable membranes that protect their eyes enable them to dive comfortably, and a flat rudderlike tail helps them to swim. With a pair of long, sharp middle teeth beavers are perfectly equipped to cut trees into sticks of exact specifications and float them to the construction site. If river conditions don't permit a dam spanning two shorelines, beavers will build their lodge into a bank.

The resulting lodge, together with the dammed beaver pond, creates a fertile web of life. Aged trees killed by the intrusion of a pond into a forest become homes for millions of insects, which provide food for woodpeckers and many other birds. Fish, turtles, frogs, and snakes soon inhabit the pond and its surrounding environment, and herons, muskrats, otters, and raccoons arrive later as part of the newly emerging ecosystem. Bears, birds of prey, and deer may come to the shore to drink or feed on smaller animals. Fish may feed on mosquito larvae deposited in the still waters. After the beavers have exhausted the nearby food supply and have moved on, the pond may eventually drain and become a fertile meadow and home to yet other creatures.

The presence of beavers has other positive implications for the nearby human population. In early times, pioneers coveted the fertile soil left from a drained beaver pond. Floods and droughts are tempered in the long run by beaver activities; control of soil erosion and reduced numbers of forest fires are other positive byproducts. All of these benefits result from a beaver complex built of trees that are considered trash species by lumbermen—willow, birch, alder, vine maple, and certain kinds of pine.

The beaver's belated recognition from scientists as Oregon's forest manager comes along with an increased respect for the complexity of its social order. Despite the traditional rodent propensity for violence when living in close quarters, the beaver is distinguished by a peaceable demeanor. Even though the mating pair and their litter (kits) may be crammed into a small lodge, their ability to cooperate is notable. This seems to be due to touching and territoriality. Their instinct to groom one another has a soothing behavioral effect, and information conveyed by imparting their scent to sticks in the pond can serve to ward off other trespassing beavers. The beaver's extra-long lifespan of 25 years enables the rodent to socialize its young for several years, thus perfecting an intricate behavioral repertoire.

Beavers are widespread throughout the state, though they're most commonly sighted in second-growth forests near marshes after sunset. Fall is a good time to spot beavers as they gather food for winter. Oregon's estimated population of 174,000 beavers could be reduced in the future if the state pays heed to complaints from Christmas-tree farmers and orchard owners. To protect their trees, they are requesting that the state mascot become a "marked mammal." Whether or not these concerns are valid, a beaver hunt would be an ironic turn in the Beaver State—a region whose exploration and settlement were dependent on this animal.

Bears

Black bears, *Ursus americanus,* proliferate in remote mountain forests of Oregon. The state's Department of Fish and Wildlife estimates that 14,000 to 19,000 black bears roam the western Cascades and the Coast Range. Adults average between 200 and 500 pounds and have dark coats. Despite Washington Cascades sightings of the feared grizzly—a species twice the size of the black bear, with three-inch claws, sharper teeth, and a meaner disposition—no encounters have been reported in the Oregon wilderness since 1931.

Black bears shy away from people except when provoked by the scent of food, when cornered or surprised, or upon human intrusion into territory near their cubs. Female bears tend to have a very strong maternal instinct that may construe any alien presence as an attack upon their young. Authorities often counsel hikers unfortunate or foolish enough to come between mama bear and her cub to lie down and play dead if she charges. Bears can run faster than the fastest human on steroids can sprint, and their retractable claws enable black bears to scramble up trees like squirrels. Furthermore, bears tend to give chase when they see something running.

ANNIE LONG LARSEN

Ursus americanus, *black bear*

So if you see a bear at a distance, try to stay upwind and back away slowly. Remember, bears are omnivorous, eating fruits and greens as readily as meat, but it is worth noting that human flesh has no appeal to them. In fact, some studies suggest that our body scent is abhorrent to bears.

Despite their strong sense of smell, bears possess very poor eyesight, which makes an attack by mistake a possibility, particularly when a human on the run resembles the bear's prey. Bears can remove a human limb with one swipe of the paw, so an encounter should be avoided at all costs. To this end, campers should place all food in a sack tied to a rope and suspend it 20 feet or more from the ground.

About every third year the female gives birth to cubs. Her one or two young, born blind and helpless (usually in February), stay with her through the first summer and commonly den up with her the following winter. Humans tend to first see the cubs in the spring, when they are five months old, having no idea that at birth the cubs were small enough to fit into teacups.

Salmon

Note: Dwindling Pacific salmon stocks have prompted bans on many forms of commercial fishing in order to restore threatened and endangered species. The following paragraphs envision a time when this ban and other salmon-saving measures have helped restore a measure of health to this ecosystem. For more information about fishing restrictions, contact the Oregon Department of Fish and Wildlife, tel. (541) 229-5403.

"To everything there is a season," and spring and fall are prime times to savor the fate as well as the flavor of the Pacific salmon. During these seasons, some of Oregon's rivers and streams become choked with spawning fish returning to the exact site of their conception, where they mate and die. As with the eruptions of Old Faithful geyser and the return of the swallows to Capistrano, this poignant dance of death affords a look at one of Mother Nature's time clocks.

The salmon's life cycle begins in a freshwater stream when the female deposits her eggs on some coarse sand and the male fertilizes them in vitro. Their bodies then deteriorate to become part of the food chain for young fish. Prior to their death, the adults starve themselves during their journey upriver from the ocean. The resulting weight loss acts as a deterrent to predators along the way. Thus, the optimum time for a fisherman to reel in something fit for dinner is prior to spawning.

Each species varies in the number of years it remains away from its home stream. The largest species, known as king or chinook, can spend as many as seven years away from its nesting (and ultimately its resting) place. For smaller species like chum, it is less than half that. Theories about how the salmon's miraculous homing instinct works range from electromagnetic impulses in the earth to celestial objects in the sky, but one thing has been established with certainty—"the nose knows." When salmon's olfactory orifices were stuffed with cotton and petroleum jelly, they were unable to find their spawning streams. The current belief is that baby salmon imprint the odor of their birth stream, enabling them to find their way home years later.

The salmon's traditional predators like the sea lion, squaw fish, harbor seal, black bear, and herring gull pale in comparison to the threats posed by modern civilization. Everything from phosphates to nuclear waste have polluted Oregon waters, and until recently dams and hydroelectric turbines threatened to block Oregon's all-important Columbia River spawning route. This was remedied somewhat when the U.S. Army Corps of Engineers built the fish ladders, a series of concrete baffles, at Bonneville Dam to divert the fish from turbine blades that would chop them to bits. These facilities, together with subterranean fish-viewing windows, offer a special perspective on the spawning phenomenon.

While viewing the salmon's life cycle in various rivers and streams in the fall and spring can be inspiring, most people's interests extend beyond food for the soul. Hence, let's briefly survey what's on the menu:

King or **chinook** salmon—the largest, sometimes weighing in at over 60 pounds. Touted as the best-tasting salmon when caught fresh (especially the spring chinook caught off the Rogue River estuary).

Silver or **coho** salmon— Known as a fighting fish among anglers despite a weight around ten

Oncorhynchus tshawytscha,
chinook salmon

pounds. In 1994, the El Niño warming current inhibited coho reproduction enough to bring about a total ban on harvesting this species. In 1997, the state of Oregon lobbied to forgo Federal Endangered Species status for this fish so that state government and private industry could conduct rehabilitation efforts instead. The rationale was that a pro-active approach (the timber industry pledged to enact salmon-friendly logging practices as well as streamside rehabilitation efforts) would serve both fish as well as human economic needs. Time will tell.

Sockeye or **red** salmon—the "money" fish. Canned sockeye is popular, but this fish is also smoked and eaten fresh, commanding a hefty price. This fish can weigh in at 15 pounds.

Chum salmon—known derogatorily as "dog salmon" because Canadian and Alaskan native people thought them worthy only of being fed to their dog teams. (Be aware that Oregon salmon contain a microorganism poisonous to dogs.) Today, this misconception has been replaced by the realization that these fish can be enjoyed canned or smoked.

Another variety, called **pink** salmon, is not caught south of Washington waters, but it is sold in Oregon stores. Among canned varieties, its tastiness rates below sockeye and coho but above chum.

As for fresh fish, you'll notice a variance in price based on how the salmon was caught. Troll salmon (usually chinook and coho in Oregon) are landed in the ocean by hook and line, one at a time. This method permits better handling than the net salmon, which are caught in large groups as they come upriver from the ocean to spawn. Thus, you'll pay more for troll salmon, but you can taste the difference. Currently as efforts are undertaken to restore the species in The Northwest, most grocery-store salmon and some in restaurants come from Alaska or fish farms in Chile. There are limited stocks of Oregon-caught salmon available, however, and it pays to be sensitive to nuances of harvest and preparation.

The results of a study by Swedish scientists complete our gustatory perspective on the Pacific

ANNIE LONG LARSEN

THE SPOTTED OWL—A BIRD IN THE HEADLINES

The Northwest spotted owl is spoken of so passionately in Oregon that newcomers to the state might have the impression that every other person on the street is an ornithology buff. To the environmentalist, the bird represents the "indicator" species of the old-growth Douglas fir forest, an animal whose health and survival is synonymous with an ecosystem that took centuries to develop. To the loggers, the bird is the scourge of the timber industry, a species whose protection will tie up millions of acres of valuable trees, resulting in tens of thousands of lost jobs. To Oregon legislators in Washington, the bird represents a knotty problem, that of balancing the mandates of the 1972 Endangered Species Act and the interests of a public increasingly sensitive to environmental issues with the needs of almost 80,000 people who work in the state's forest-products industries. In other words, with 52% of Oregon's land owned by the federal government, the Endangered Species Act has especially far-reaching consequences.

The points of contention between the two constituencies are better understood when we examine the spotted owl's habits and habitat. In a 150-year-old Douglas fir forest, hollowed-out trees provide ideal nesting areas for these birds, while voles, snowshoe hares, flying squirrels, and other prey provide an abundant food supply. A mated pair needs 1,000 acres of old-growth forest to feed and reproduce, so the survival of several thousand mated pairs might require that logging of the few remaining ancient stands be stopped. The fact that these forests contain several times more biomass than any other forests in the world makes scientists covet them as a laboratory to study this crucial part of the food chain. They point out that destroying the old-growth forests is like playing dice with Mother Nature. The counterargument contends that one person's conservation is another person's unemployment.

Old-growth Douglas fir makes straight-grained lumber with no knots. It is prized around the world as a building material par excellence. With lumber prices up worldwide and demand expected to increase 300% by the 21st century, the wood represents an economic bonanza. However dire the consequences to the spotted owl, sustained-yield forestry and the environment must be balanced against the consequences of reduced logging: destruction of families, communities, and the state's economy.

If the tangible concerns seem to cast spotted owl defenders as selfish ideologues, consider that an overall shortage of trees and automation in the mills will phase out logging revenues and employment drastically within the decade anyway. In the long run, it's possible that extending the life of the spotted owl will extend the life of the logging industry.

salmon. These researchers found that wild salmon had three times the fat content of hatchery-raised fish. What's significant about this is that fat is what gives this species its flavor and, surprisingly, its healthful properties. The latter owes to the concentration of omega-three fatty acids, a proven inhibitor of heart disease. In addition to food value and flavor, wild salmon possess more vigor to survive the elements than do their hatchery-raised cousins, compelling a reassessment of aquaculture's domination of the current fish population's gene pool. In the Columbia River, for example, only about 25% of the returning salmon spawn in the wild, leaving the majority to mate in fish hatcheries. The best exhibit on the process takes place at the McNary dam hatchery, located in Umatilla near the junction of I-84 and US 395. Portions of the first and third floors are devoted to visitor exhibits. A fourth-floor skywalk overlooks a fish sorting and handling area.

BOB RACE

Branta canadensis,
Canada goose

BOB RACE

Birds

Oregon is rapidly gaining a reputation as one of the best birding states. Seasonal variance in populations is often dramatic. Birdwatchers present during the changing of seasons are best able to appreciate the diversity of the influx. For example, in the winter and summer the outskirts of Klamath Falls become inundated with more bald eagles than anyplace else in the lower 48; other times of year, many of these birds are in Alaska. But southern Oregon hunting season byproducts such as deer carcasses, road kills, and wounded waterfowl provide a ready food source for migrating carnivorous birds.

Birds of prey, or raptors, abound all over the state. Northeast of Enterprise and near Zumwalt are perhaps the best places to see hawks. Species commonly sighted include the ferruginous, red-tailed, and Swainson's hawks. Along I-5 in the Willamette Valley, look for red-tailed hawks on fenceposts, and American kestrels, North America's smallest falcons, sitting on phone wires. Farther south, turkey buzzards circle the dry areas during the warmer months. Vultures are commonly sighted above the Rogue River. Along the lower Columbia east of Astoria, over a hundred bald eagles have chosen to winter during the past few years; in 1989 the Twilight Eagle Sanctuary was established in this estuary. The upper McCord Creek spur of the Elowah Falls Trail (see "Hikes" under "Cascade Locks" in the Portland and Vicinity chapter) has a cliffside overlook into a canyon that has

been home to a family of osprey for years. In central Oregon, osprey are frequently sighted off the Cascades Lakes Highway south of Bend, nesting atop hollowed-out snags near water (especially Crane Prairie Reservoir).

Those motoring on Sauvie Island near Portland will be treated to an amazing variety of birds. The northern third of this island is a protected wildlife refuge. More than 200 bird species come through here on the Pacific Flyway, feeding in grassy clearings.

The best inland locations to take in an array of migratory species are wildlife preserves such as Finley and Malheur. The latter is Oregon's premier bird retreat, a stopover for large groups of Canada and snow geese, whistling swans, and pintail ducks. It's also home to the rare sandhill crane.

Apart from great flocks of geese, gulls, and other shorebirds, the species most travelers notice are Clark's nutcracker and the Steller's jay, whose grating voice and large size (for a jay) often command the most attention. Mountain hikers are bound to share part of their picnic lunch with these birds. At high elevations, the quieter gray jay (also known as The Canada jay or "camp robber") will more likely be your guest. The seven-foot wingspan of the great blue heron is also unforgettable.

Unfortunately, the western meadowlark, the state bird, has nearly vanished from western Oregon due to loss of habitat, but thanks to natural pasture east of the Cascades you can still hear its distinctive song. Just look for this bird's brown plumage with buff and black markings. The meadowlark also is distinguished by a yellow underside with a black crescent pattern across the breast and white outer tail feathers.

Birding Information

In terms of sheer numbers and variety, the coast's mudflats at low tide and the tidal estuaries are the best birding environments. Rare species like tufted puffins and the snowy plover enjoy special protection here, along with other types of migratory waterfowl. A good bird identification tool are the laminated color monographs illustrating the major species from *Mac's Field Guides* (Seattle Mountaineers Press, 1990). These and other guides are available at Portland's Audubon Bookstore, 5151 S.W. Cornell Rd., tel. (503) 292-6855.

The zeal of **Oregon Birders,** P.O. Box 10373, Eugene 97440, is evident from their monthly publication, *Oregon Birds.* In addition to articles on various species and sightings, phone numbers for each part of the state are included for the **Oregon Rare Bird Telephone Network.** Should you see a particular bird of note, you can participate. You can also call the Portland Audubon Society, tel. (503) 292-0661, to find out what has recently been sighted.

The U.S. Fish and Wildlife Service has established viewpoints for wildlife- and birdwatching at 12 Oregon national wildlife refuges. You can obtain specific information from these branches: Hart Mountain, Room 308, Post Office Bldg., Lakeview 97630, tel. (541) 947-3315; Malheur, P.O. Box 245, Princeton 97721, tel. (541) 494-2323 or 494-2364; Umatilla, P.O. Box 239, Umatilla 97882, tel. (541) 922-3232, which serves McKay Creek and Cold Springs; and William L. Finley, Route 2, Box 208, Corvallis 97333, tel. (541) 757-7236, which serves Ankeny, Cape Meares, Oregon Islands, Three Arch Rocks, and Bandon Marsh.

Also of interest to serious birders and naturalists is the excellent *Oregon Wildlife Viewing Guide,* put together by Defenders of Wildlife and published by Falcon Press, P.O. Box 1718, Helena, MT 59624. Not only does this highly regarded resource list wildlife sites and nearby accommodations, but its detailed state and regional maps and several guided nature trails offer independent readers the means to design their own wildlife adventure. Proceeds from the book go toward wildlife site maintenance and publications put out by Defenders of Wildlife.

Oregon's state bird, the western meadowlark, can often be seen in fields or perched on fences.

BOB RACE

HISTORY

NATIVE PEOPLES

Early Days

Long before the white man came to this hemisphere, native peoples thrived for thousands of years in the region of present-day Oregon. A popular theory concerning their origins maintains that their ancestors came over from Asia on a land/ice bridge spanning what is now the Bering Strait. Along with archaeological evidence, shipwrecks of Oriental craft on the Pacific coast also support the theory that Native Americans had Asian roots. This contention has been further substantiated by facial features and dental patterns common to both peoples, as well as isolated correspondences in ritual, music, and dialect.

Despite common ancestry, the tribes on the rain-soaked coast and in the Willamette Valley lived quite differently from those on the drier eastern flank of the Cascade Mountains. Tribes west of the Cascades enjoyed abundant salmon, shellfish, berries, and game. Great broad rivers facilitated travel, and thick stands of the finest softwood timber in the world ensured that there was never a dearth of building materials. A mild climate with plentiful food and resources allowed the wet-siders the leisure time to evolve a startlingly complex culture. This was perhaps best evidenced in their artistic endeavors, theatrical pursuits, and in such ceremonial gatherings as the traditional potlatch, where the divesting of one's material wealth was seen as a status symbol. Dentalia and abalone shells, woodpecker feathers, obsidian blades, and hides were especially coveted. Later on, Hudson's Bay blankets were added to this list.

After contact with traders, Chinook, an amalgam of Indian tongues with some French and English thrown in, was the common argot among the diverse tribes that gathered in the Columbia Gorge during solstice. It was at these powwows that the coast and valley dwellers would come into contact with their poorer cousins east of the Cascades. These dry-siders led a semi-nomadic existence, following the game and avoiding the climatic extremes of winter and summer in their region. In the southeast desert of the Great Basin, seeds and roots added more protein to their diet. Subsistence needs were thus pushed to the fore in their cultures while recreational endeavors were limited.

The introduction of horses in the mid-1700s made hunting, especially for large bison, much easier. In contrast to their west-of-the-Cascade counterparts, who lived in 100- by 40-foot longhouses, extended families in the eastern tribes inhabited pit houses when not hunting. Hunting necessitated caves or crude rock shelters.

Twelve separate nations populated Oregon. Although these were further divided into 80 tribes, the primary allegiance was to the village. The "nation" status referred to language groupings such as Salish and Athabascan. Tribal names such as Calapooya, Alsea, or Shasta Costa were usually derived from a word in the local argot for "The People," or from what the neighboring tribe called "Them." On occasion, white explorers be-

an Umpqua Indian

ANNIE LONG LARSEN

The bicentennial wagon train retraced the pioneers' journey along the Oregon Trail.

OREGON TOURISM DIVISION

stowed a name upon the particular native grouping. An example of this was the "Rogue" Indian appellation. According to one theory, this name came from French fur trappers who referred to the troublesome thieves as *"les coquins,"* which was translated as "the rogues." Another theory was that "Rogue" was inspired by the ocher riverbed, described as "rouge" by French trappers and subsequently misspelled. Across the region, many Indians were united in their worship of Spilyai, the coyote demigod. Spilyai, as well as many other figures animal and human, formed the subject of a large body of folk tales which explain the origins of the land in ways that are both entertaining and insightful.

White Settlers

The coming of white settlers meant the usurpation of tribal homelands, exposure to European diseases like smallpox and diphtheria, and the passing of a way of life. Violent conflicts ensued on a large scale with the influx of settlers seeking missionary work and government land giveaways in the 1830s and '40s. In the 1850s, mining activity in southern Oregon and on the coast incited the Rogue River Indian Wars, adding to the strife brought on by annexation to the United States.

All these events compelled the federal government to send in troops and to eventually set up treaties with Oregon's first inhabitants. The attempts at arbitration in the 1850s added insult to injury. Tribes of different, indeed often incompatible, backgrounds were rounded up and grouped together haphazardly on reservations, often far from their indigenous surroundings. In the century that followed, the evils of modern civilization destroyed much of the ecosystem upon which these cultures were based. An especially regrettable result of settlement was the decline of the Columbia River salmon runs due to overfishing and loss of habitat through pollution. This not only weakened the food chain but treated this spiritual totem of the many tribes along the Columbia as an expendable resource.

For a while, there was an attempt to restore the balance. In 1924, the government accorded citizenship to Indians. Ten years later, the Indian Reorganization Act provided for tribal guards and prohibited the sale of land to non-Indians. A decade later a court of treaty claims was established. In the 1960s, however, the government, acting on the premise that the Indians needed to assimilate into white society, terminated several reservations.

Recent government reparations have accorded many native peoples preferential hunting and fishing rights, monetary/land grants, and the restoration of tribal status to certain disenfranchised groups. In Oregon, there are now nine federally recognized tribes and five reservations: Warm Springs, Umatilla, Burns Pauite, Siletz, and Grand Ronde. Nonetheless, most of the 40,000 native people of the region feel they can never regain their birthright. In an attempt to repay this irrevocable debt, Indian gaming came to Oregon in the mid-nineties. There are now eight casinos here. This volume mentions several of these establishments for dining or location, but the reader should consult the Oregon State Tourism Commission for detailed information on this new presence in the state.

Archaeological Perspectives

To help measure what we've lost by the passing of the traditional ways, archaeologists have unearthed all manner of native artifacts. One that has evoked considerable controversy is a site found at Fort Rock, east of the Cascades near Bend. Charcoals from a hearth there are thought to be over 13,000 years old, exceeding earlier estimates of the period of human presence in the region by about 3,500 years. A sandal found at the same site dated at 9,500 years old had been the previous standard-bearer. Another significant find is a gallery of 5,000-year-old petroglyphs on the walls of a cave in the foothills just east of the Willamette Valley. The valley itself boasts perhaps the best-known excavation in the state, due to its location on the site of the Oregon Country Fair near Eugene. Relics there have been dated at 8,000 to 10,000 years of age. Other recent finds include coastal and Rogue Valley digs where 9,000-year-old artifacts have been unearthed. Finally, in 1997, an obsidian flaked in the Clovis style indicates that Ice Age people roamed the Rogue Valley as long as 11,000 years ago. The distinctive grooves in the obsidian mark it as a product of the Clovis big game hunter culture.

In terms of written history, a manuscript found in a Chinese monastery could have the distinction of being the first written account of a voyage to our continent. A Chinese navigator, Hee-li, was spirited from offshore Cathay waters by a violent storm. Both captain and crew survived the storm but were thrown off course during their return voyage by a cockroach lodged underneath a compass needle. Hee-li persisted in following the cockeyed compass in the direction he thought was west, despite sunsets appearing on the opposite horizon. After miles and miles of open ocean, the ship docked in a country of forests towering around a vast inlet, which the mariners explored. The manuscript, which supposedly dates to 217 B.C., was found 21 centuries later in the archives at Shensi Province by

an American missionary to China. In it, a reference to towering trees and red-faced men could well have referred to the Pacific Northwest. In any event, Chinese and Japanese shipwrecks along the Oregon coast have been dated as early as the 5th century A.D. Potsherds and other ceramic artifacts found along the Columbia River also point to early contact with the Orient.

When you look at this evidence, it is clear that while east may be east and west may be west, the two probably *did* meet in the Oregon Country.

The only in-depth overview of Oregon's prehistory currently in print is *Oregon Archaeology,* by Melvin Aikens, obtainable for a nominal fee through the Department of the Interior, BLM, Oregon State Office, P.O. Box 2965-825, N.E. Multnomah St., Portland 97208. The book describes tools and prehistoric weapons used by Native Americans in Oregon. Aikens separates the state into five regions, showing how individuals and groups adapted to the various environments.

EXPLORATION, SETTLEMENT, AND GROWTH

One theory of how Oregon got its name goes back to an encounter between the native peoples and the Spanish mariners who plied West Coast waters in the 17th and 18th centuries. Upon seeing the abalone shell earrings of the coastal Salish Indians, the sailors exclaimed, *"Orejon!"* ("What big ears!"). This was later anglicized to Oregon. Others have pointed out the name's similarity to those of such Spanish locales as Aragon and Obregon (in Mexico). A less fanciful explanation has it that the state's name was inspired by the English word *origin,* conjuring the image of the forest primeval. The French word *ouragan* (hurricane) has also been suggested as the source of the state's name, courtesy of French Canadian fur trappers who became the first permanent white settlers in the region during the early 19th century. It was recently noted that "Oregonon" and "Orenogonia," two Greek words pertaining to mountainous locales, were seen on old navigator's maps marking the area between northern California to British Columbia. Given that the famous Pacific Northwest explorer Juan de Fuca was actually Greek (born Valerianos) and that many navigators were schooled in Greece, perhaps Oregon's name originated in the Mediterranean. In any case, Spanish, English, and Russian vessels came to offshore waters here in search of a sea route connecting the Atlantic with the Pacific. Accounts differ, but the first sightings of the Oregon coast have been credited to either Juan Cabrillo (in 1543) or the English explorer Sir Francis Drake (in 1579). Other voyagers of note included Spain's Vizcaíno and de Alguilar (in 1603) and Heceta (in 1775), and England's Cook and Meares during the late 1770s, as well as Vancouver (in 1792).

In 1807, Meriwether Lewis and William Clark arrived in Oregon along with their Corps of Discovery.

In 1996, a front page story in the *London Times* proclaimed Sir Francis Drake the first European to set foot on the coast (previously Heceta was credited with the first landing) on the basis of an archeological find in Little Whale Cove south of Depoe Bay. Timbers from a stockade left by Drake who is known to have beached for repairs were purportedly found, leading to this speculation.

Sea otter and beaver pelts added impetus to the search for a trade route connecting the two oceans. While the Northwest Passage turned out to be a myth, the fur trade became a basis of commerce and contention between European, Asian, and eventually American governments. The pattern was repeated inland when the English beaver brigades eventually moved down from Canada to set up headquarters on the Columbia near present-day Portland.

American Expansion in Oregon

The Americans first came into the area when Robert Gray sailed up the Columbia River in 1792. The first American overland excursion into Oregon was made by the Corps of Discovery in 1804-07. Co-captained by Lewis and Clark, the expedition trekked across the continent to the mouth of the Columbia and back to St. Louis.

Dispatched by Thomas Jefferson to explore the lands of the Louisiana Purchase and beyond, the expedition threw down the gauntlet for future settlement and eventual annexation of the Oregon Territory by the United States.

Lewis and Clark's exploration and mapping of Oregon wasn't the only impetus to America becoming a two-ocean power. The expedition also initially secured good relations with the Indians, thus establishing the preconditions to trade and the missionary influx. In fact, several decades after the coming of the expedition, the Nez Percé Indians sent a delegation to William Clark in St. Louis to ask for "The Book of Heaven," as well as teachers of the Word.

But before the missionaries came west, there were years of wrangling over America's right to settle in the new territory. John Jacob Astor's Pacific Fur Company was a case in point. The mere threat of British gunboats on the Columbia caused the quick departure of Astor's company during the War of 1812. It wasn't until the Convention of 1818 that the country west of the Rockies, south of Russian America, and north of Spanish America was open for use by American citizens as well as British subjects. The following year, the U.S. and Spain signed a treaty which fixed the present southern border of Oregon. With the Monroe Doctrine in 1824 opposing European expansion in this hemisphere, another blow was struck toward removing the shackles of British rule in the Northwest.

During the 1820s, the Hudson's Bay Company continued to hold sway over Oregon country by means of Fort Vancouver, on the north shore of the Columbia. Over 500 people settled here under the charismatic leadership of John McLoughlin, who oversaw the planting of crops and the raising of livestock.

Despite the establishment of almost half a dozen Hudson's Bay outposts, several factors harbingered the inevitable demise of British influence in Oregon. Most obvious was the decline of the fur trade as well as England's difficulty in maintaining her far-flung empire. Less apparent but equally influential was the lack of white females in a land populated predominantly by white trappers and explorers. If the Americans could attract settlers of both genders, they'd be in a position to create an expanding population base which could dominate the region. The first step in this process was the arrival of the missionaries. In 1834, Methodist soul-seekers led by Jason Lee settled near the Columbia River. Two years later Marcus and Narcissa Whitman's missions started up on the upper Columbia in present-day Washington (until 1853, the Washington area was considered a single entity with Oregon). The missionaries brought alien ways and diseases for which the Indians had no immunity. As if this weren't enough to provoke a violent reaction, the Indians would soon have their homelands inundated by thousands of settlers lured by government land giveaways.

But it wasn't just the Organic Act's 640 free acres that each adult white male could claim in the mid-1840s that fueled the march across the frontier. The westward expansion that Americans regarded as their "manifest destiny" leapt to the fore as a ready solution to the problems of the 1830s. During this decade, the country was in its worst depression yet, with land panics, droughts, and an unstable currency. Despite ignorance of western geography and the hardships it held, the Oregon Trail, a 2,000-mile frontier thoroughfare, was viewed with covetous eyes, especially in Missouri. (By 1840, 400,000 settlers had arrived there, tripling the population in 10 years.) Around Independence, Missouri, the trees thinned, the settlements ended, and the Oregon Trail began.

Over 53,000 people traversed the trail between 1840 and 1850 en route to western Oregon. In 1850, the Land Donation Law cut in half the acreage of the Organic Act, reflecting diminishing availability of real estate. But although a single pioneer man was now entitled to only 320 acres, and single women were totally excluded from land ownership, as part of a couple they could also own an additional 320 free acres. This promoted marriage, and in turn families, and helped to fulfill Secretary of State John C. Calhoun's prediction that American families could outbreed the single Hudson's Bay Company trappers, thus winning the battle of the West in the bedroom.

The Land Donation Act also stipulated that nonwhites could not own any part of the Oregon Territory, enabling the pioneers to seize native people's lands. The act impeded the growth of towns and industries, too, as large parcels of land were given away to relatively small numbers of people, which kept the population geographically distant from one another. This was one reason why urbanization was slow in coming to the Northwest.

The Applegate Trail

Another route west was the Applegate Trail pioneered by brothers Lindsay and Jesse Applegate in the mid-1840s. When the borthers reached Fort Hall, Idaho, they veered south from the Oregon Trail across northern Nevada's Black Rock Desert, traversing the northeast top of California to enter Oreon near present-day Klamath Falls. A southern Oregon gold rush in the 1850s drew thousands across this route. As you drive I-5 in southern Oregon, Territorial Rd. between Cheshire and Veneta (west of Eugene) and other thoroughfares from the lower Willamette Valley (the trail ended at Dallas west of Salem) south, you'll see signs denoting this trail.

Early Government and Statehood

Nevertheless, there was enough unity among American settlers to organize a provisional government in 1843. Then, in 1848, the federal government decided to accord Oregon territorial status. With migration increasing exponentially from 1843 on, there was little doubt in Congress about Oregon's viability. Still, it took frontiersman Joe Meek to coalesce popular opinion. He had first performed this role in Champoeg, at the northern end of the Willamette Valley, in 1843, when he boomed out the rallying cry for regional confederation, "Who's for a divide?" In equally dramatic fashion, he strode into the halls of Congress fresh from the trail in mountain-man regalia to state the case for territoriality.

The Oregon Territory got off to a rousing start thanks to the California gold rush of 1849. The rush occasioned a housing boom in San Francisco and a need for lumber, and the dramatic

OREGON—HOTBED OF BIOREGIONALISM

O regonians have a well-deserved reputation for embodying the maverick spirit. Oregon's politicians, for example, don't always vote with a party majority, and even the state's motto, "She flies with her own wings," expresses this outlook. In addition, the state holds unofficial status as a haven to social, religious, and cultural groups who eschew convention. Therefore, it is altogether fitting to find here the only serious American secessionist movement outside of the Southern Confederacy.

At various times since the 1850s, the people of Oregon and northern California have tried to establish a new state. With common interests transcending state boundaries, inhabitants of this region attempted to secede in each of the years 1852-1854, and more recently, in 1941. This last drive, for an independent state of Jefferson (the name of the third president of the United States was chosen because of his vision of America as a self-sufficient agrarian country), was dramatized by a blockade of highway ORE 99 at the Oregon-California border. The movement got as far as inaugurating an acting governor, but the U.S. entry into WW II several days later preempted further action.

These days, southern Oregon is once again a hotbed of bioregional revolt. The 1973 book *Ecotopia,* by Ernest Callenbach, added fuel to the fire by proposing that northern California break off from the rest of the state to join with Oregon as a single republic based on environmental imperatives. Another bioregional manifesto, *The Nine Nations of North America,* divided the continent into nine bioregions on the basis of their cultural, historical, ethnic, economic, and environmental interests. The region north of San Francisco to Vancouver was identified once again as "Ecotopia."

In recent years the Ashland-Jacksonville area and the surrounding Rogue and Applegate valleys have carried the torch for bioregionalism, often invoking as a rallying cry the name of the late great state-that-never-was, Jefferson. With a constituency ranging from survivalists and radical environmentalists to folks just tired of big government and bureaucracy, this activist region coalesces the spirit of Jefferson throughout the state.

To keep up on the politics and the patrimony of Jefferson, send for the newsletter of the Siskiyou Regional Education Project, P.O. Box 220, Cave Junction, OR 97523.

---

population influx created instant markets for the agriculture of the Willamette Valley. Portland was located at the north end of the valley and 110 miles upriver from the Pacific on the Columbia, near the world's largest supply of accessible softwood timber. The young city was in a perfect position to channel goods from the interior to coastal ports. So great was the need in California for food that wheat from eastern Oregon was declared legal tender. The exchange rate started around one dollar a bushel and went as high as six dollars. The economic benefits from the gold rush notwithstanding, Oregon lost two-thirds of her adult male population to gold fever. Many of the emigrants returned when the news of gold discoveries in southwestern Oregon came out between 1850 and 1860. The resulting influx helped establish the Rogue Valley and coastal population centers.

However, strategic importance and population growth alone do not explain Oregon becoming the 33rd state in the Union. It was no accident that shortly before statehood, the Dred Scott decision had become law in 1857. This had the effect of opening the territory to slavery. While slavery didn't lack for adherents in Oregon, the prevailing sentiment was that this controversial institution was neither necessary nor desirable. Because territorial status would be a potential liability to a Union on the mend, the congressional majority saw an especially compelling reason to open its doors to this new member. When nonslavery status was assured, Oregon entered the Union on Valentine's Day, 1859.

Economic Growing Pains

During the years of the Civil War and its aftermath, internal conflicts were the order of the day within the state. By 1861, good Willamette Valley land was becoming scarce, so many farmers moved east of the Cascades to farm wheat, where they ran into violent confrontations with Indians over land. Between 1862 and 1934 the Homestead Act land giveaways helped fuel these fires of resentment. In the 1870s, cattlemen came to eastern Oregon, followed by sheep ranchers, whose presence precipitated range wars with the cattlemen. Just when it appeared that eastern Oregon land was ripe for agricultural promoters and community planners, the bottom fell out. Overproduction of wheat, uncertain markets, and two severe winters were the culprits. In the early 20th century a population influx created further problems by draining the water table. Thus, the glory that was gold, grass, and grain east of the Cascades was short-lived. Many eastern Oregon towns grew up and flourished for a decade, only to fall back into desert, leaving nary a trace of their existence.

Unlike the downturn east of the Cascades, boom times were ahead for the rest of the state as the 20th century approached. In the 1860s and '70s, Jacksonville to the south became the commercial counterpart to Portland, owing to its proximity to the Rogue Valley and south coast goldfields as well as the California border. During this period, transportation links began to consolidate, in part due to the efforts of stagecoach magnate Ben Holladay. The first stagecoach, steamship, and rail lines moved south from the Columbia River into the Willamette Valley; by the 1880s, Portland was joined to San Francisco and the east by railroad. Henry Villard was the prime mover in this effort, eventually dominating all commerce in the Northwest by channeling freight and passengers through Portland and along the Columbia. In 1900, Union Pacific magnate James J. Hill picked up where Villard left off. By selling 900,000 acres of timberland to lumber baron Frederic Weyerhaeuser at $6 an acre (with the stipulation that Weyerhaeuser build his mills close by Union Pacific tracks), he hitched the destinies of the region to the iron horse.

Progressive Politics

In the modern era, Oregon also blazed trails in the thicket of governmental legislation and reform. The so-called Oregon system of initiative, referendum, and recall was first conceived in the 1890s, coming to fruition in the first decade of this century. The system has since become an integral part of the democratic process.

In like measure, Oregon's extension of suffrage to women in 1912, a 1921 compulsory education law, as well as the first large-scale union activity in the country during the '20s, were red-letter events in American history. This tradition of reform continues to this day with Oregon's bottle bill and progressive land-use statutes. More recently, the Oregon Health Plan has extended health care coverage to the state's working poor by expanding the procedures covered by Medicaid. The plan's costs are controlled by prioritizing various services, an idea which could set the precedent for a future federal health insurance plan.

The 1930s were exciting years in the Northwest. Despite widespread poverty, the foundations of future prosperity were laid during this decade. New Deal programs such as the Works Projects Administration and the Civilian Conservation Corps undertook many projects around the state. Building roads and hydroelectric dams created jobs and improved the quality of life in Oregon, in addition to bolstering the country's defense during wartime. Hydroelectric power from the Bonneville Dam, completed in 1938, enabled Portland's shipyards and aluminum plants to thrive. Thanks to Henry Kaiser's mass production techniques, 10,000 workers were employed in the Portland shipyards. Such well-known liberty ships as the *Star of Oregon* were born here, making the state an integral part of the war effort. Low utility rates encouraged more employment and settlement, while the Columbia's irrigation water enhanced agriculture.

War Years

In addition to laying the foundations for future growth, the war years in Oregon and their immediate aftermath were full of trials for state residents. Vanport, a city of 18,000 (at one time, 45,000) that grew up in the shadow of Kaiser aluminum plants and the shipyards north of Portland, was washed off the map by a Columbia River flood. Tillamook County forests, which supplied Sitka spruce for airplanes, endured several massive fires which destroyed 500 square miles of trees. Along with these natural disasters, Oregon was the only state among the contiguous 48 to have a military installation (Fort Stevens in Astoria) shelled by a Japanese submarine, to endure a Japanese bombing mission on the mainland (on Mt. Emily, near Brookings), and to suffer civilian casualties when a balloon bomb exploded near the Gearhart Mountain Wilderness Area in Lake County. While California also sustained an attack when a Japanese surface submarine put a shell into a Southern Pacific Daylight train near Goleta, only Oregon experienced all three wartime mishaps. See the appropriate travel chapters for more details.

The Modern Era

With the perfection of the chainsaw in the 1940s, the timber industry could take advantage of the postwar housing boom. Today, Oregon's resource-based economy has followed a boom-bust cycle. The timber and fishing industries have been especially hard hit by the current era of limits.

Politically, the late '60s and '70s brought environmentally ground-breaking measures spearheaded by Governor Tom McCall. The bottle bill and the clean-up of the Willamette River were part of this legacy. In the decades to follow, Senator Mark Hatfield's national prominence attracted federal monies to the state, funding key projects in transportation, education, research, and tourism.

The 1990s have seen the Oregon economy flourish and relocation figures top the nation. This has been fueled by the establishment of computer hardware and software companies here as well as a real estate market favorable to California retirees. The latter has had sociological ripple effects with many longtime state residents feeling displaced by the transformed economy and living standards. The legalization of gambling (there could be a dozen Indian gaming casinos by the year 2000), drastic cuts in education, and re-criminalization of marijuana have provoked controversy on all sides of the political spectrum. A retreat from longstanding legislative commitments reflects the demographics of Oregon's new arrivals as well as its changing economic climate.

While Oregon's traditionally humanistic outlook and environmental advocacy have been somewhat tempered by these tensions of late, the state still enjoys a reputation for being both progressive and pristine.

ECONOMY

The leading industries within the state are agriculture (including forest products), followed by high-tech enterprises and tourism. But these rankings only tell part of the story; the scenario for every sector of Oregon's economy should change dramatically in the coming years.

The ripple effects from the decline in timber will affect many aspects of society in the Northwest. Weyerhaeuser, Georgia Pacific, and other wood-products giants are bracing for a reduction in the allowable cut as well as export restrictions. More timber from private holdings, as opposed to government lands, will be harvested, and jobs will shift to the manufacture of secondary wood products such as doors, window frames, laminated beams, and furniture parts.

In agriculture, specialty products have become the fastest-growing business in Oregon. These products include nursery crops (Monrovia is the nation's largest nursery and Oregon is the number one Christmas tree state) as well as wine grapes, herbs and organic produce, gourmet mushrooms, goat cheese, and other fare prized by "foodies." At the same time, large-scale agribusiness is thriving with the booming food-processing and -packing industries proliferating the lower Willamette Valley and Eastern Oregon.

High-tech industries and tourism are often mentioned as the engines of economic growth that'll carry the state into the next century. Both owe their rosy reputation to being in the right place at the right time. The region's pure water and low utility rates are ideal for computer chip manufacture; low production costs and a high quality of life have also helped attract the computer industry. Thanks to jobs created by high-tech expansion and an exodus from California's high real estate costs and increasing urbanization, Oregon has been among the nation's prime destinations for relocation since the beginning of the decade.

In the winter of 1994, *U.S. News and World Report* singled out Portland as having one of the nation's top three housing markets. According to Atlas and Allied moving companies,

In the past, Oregonians depended heavily on a resource-based economy.

BUREAU OF LAND MANAGEMENT

Oregon was the most moved-into state in 1992, and California the most moved out of. In 1996 Oregon was still ranked among the top three relocation destinations by Allied Van Lines. The Germans and Japanese are also expected to come here to take advantage of world-class *kulturfests* and nature on a grand scale.

High Profile Industries

There are certain industries in Oregon that exert a presence beyond a healthy bottom line. For instance, who hasn't heard of Pendleton shirts or Jantzen swimwear? Two of the top shoe manufacturers are headquartered in Portland—Nike and Adidas. River City also has an impressive creative community, including one of America's most successful ad agencies, Wieden-Kennedy, as well as prominent animators, multimedia publishers, filmmakers, and a thriving music industry. Production of "infomercials" is a particulary active sector of this market. In addition, a varied environment that can simulate Cape Cod to California brings in tens of millions of dollars a year from Hollywood studios filming on location in Oregon. Prominent movies shot in Oregon include *One Flew Over the Cuckoo's Nest* (filmed at the Oregon Penitentiary in Salem and Depoe Bay), *Mr. Holland's Opus* (shot at Portland's Grant High School), and *The Shining* (parts filmed at Timberline Lodge on Mt. Hood). In 1997, Kevin Costner filmed *The Postman* at diverse locales including Smith Rock, Paulina Lake (both in central Oregon), and Estacada (near the base of Mt. Hood). Since the early nineties, film revenues have dropped markedly in Oregon due to production companies choosing to do location shots in Vancouver, B.C. due to a favorable exchange rate.

LUMBER

Until recently, logging and wood products have been the most important industries to Oregon in terms of jobs provided and revenue produced. Despite recent declines, tens of thousands of workers are still employed in logging, sawmills, and paper production, contributing billions of dollars annually to Oregon's gross state product. It is still the leading supplier of wood products in the nation, providing one-fifth of the country's softwood lumber.

Throughout its history, the Oregon logging industry has been dogged by controversy. In the 1920s, shoddy treatment of workers resulted in the first large-scale unionization in the country and inspired the spadework for the AFL-CIO.

Currently, the forestry and economic practices which are the basis of the industry are being questioned. The National Forest Service administers most of the lands slated for timber harvest and has been scrutinized for what some critics charge are policies not in keeping with healthy forest ecosystems. Some of these purported excesses have been reined in, resulting in the reduction of the allowable cut and devastating losses in employment and revenue. Regardless of the imminent ban on logging in spotted owl habitats and the like, the industry will face a slowdown in the '90s simply because of the lack of trees to cut. Nonetheless, timber products should continue to be a major force in the state. This becomes clear when we look at

"the tale of the tape." Consider that because of these environmental restrictions and shortfalls, Oregon produced 6.2 billion less board feet of timber in 1993 than in 1992. But since lumber wholesale prices rose during this period, Oregon still ranked number one in the country in timber revenues. Given projected profits from the

MUSHROOM PICKING FOR PROFIT

Pioneer fortune seekers who took to the woods in search of a lucky strike came for timber or gold. Laden only with their dreams and the tools of their trade, they imbued Oregon's resource-based economy with a vitality that continues to this day. By contrast, the latest rainbow chasers swarming Oregon's wilderness come without gold pans, saws, or implements of any kind, relying instead on sharp eyes and their own two hands to pull a future out of the ground.

Despite the low-tech nature of the wild mushroom industry, Oregon pocketed a record 60 million dollars in 1992 from the sale of gourmet fungus. Most of the harvest is exported to Europe and Japan, with the latter country accounting for the largest market share; the '92 bonanza resulted from Japan's particularly bad matsutake harvest that year. While profits from this crop will never approach the take from Oregon's gold rushes or from her annual cut of softwood sawtimber, mushrooms produce a consistent yearly yield with no apparent environmental shortcomings. Oregon's mild climate, offering the right amount of dampness and a ground resistant to freezing, generally ensures a long mushroom season, and the state's varied topography yields a multiplicity of species. These facts, along with a growing demand, explain projections of a 10-12% annual increase in profits.

Beyond the monetary concerns, mushroom picking is the lifestyle of choice for a significant number of Asian, Hispanic, and Russian immigrants, as well as scores of laid-off timber workers and others who prefer the forest to the urban working world. Be that as it may, the woods during the various harvest times can be dangerous. Harvesters gathering morels in the Blue mountains and matsutakes in the Cascades wear bright colors to alert fall hunters. Chanterelle pickers in the Coast Range and the Siskiyous might run into a booby-trapped patch of marijuana. Sometimes interracial flare-ups erupt into violence, a byproduct not only of competition

but locals' allegations that foreign pickers harvest more with an eye to efficiency than to maintaining the fragile topsoil or the mushroom-to-tree mycelial network. Add an easily abused government permit system and a cash-and-carry relationship between picker and broker that's difficult to regulate, and it's conceivable that mushroom patches could become a breeding ground for other crimes against humans and the environment.

Despite these concerns, a drive along the quarter-mile strip of US 30 southeast of La Grande during the fall morel harvest is more likely to evoke the romance of the gold rush than anything unsavory. The half dozen brokers here flash wads of cash in the shadow of Quonset huts or pickup trucks serving as temporary offices. In front of these makeshift storefronts, you sometimes hear picking crews speaking to each other in several languages while questioning a transaction at the weighing scale. During the bumper crop years that generally occur in the aftermath of forest fires, local bars echo with outlandish stories of thousand-dollar paydays and wanton violence.

Nonetheless, picking edible fungus in Oregon forests can be a safe and satisfying way to appreciate the region's bounty. The **Mt. Mazama Mushroom Association,** 4017 Garfield St., Medford 97501, **Willamette Valley Mushroom Society,** 20610 Nob Hill S.E., Salem 97302, and **Lincoln County Mycological Society,** tel. (541) 765-4326, can share useful tips and point recreational pickers in the direction of patches closely supervised by the Forest Service. Be sure to bring along a mushroom identification book such as *Mushrooms Demystified* by David Arora (Berkeley: Ten Speed Press, 1988) to avoid picking poisonous look-alikes. To cap off your experience, *Oregon Cuisine of the Rain* by Karen Brooks (New York: Addison Wesley, 1993) contains recipes by the state's master chefs to inspire your own use of these tasty morsels in salads, stir-fry dishes, and omelettes.

harvest of a huge forest that was replanted in the wake of the Tillamook Burn over half-a-century ago, this trend should become more pronounced into the next century. Be that as it may, Big Timber will assume a lower profile.

The new forestry orientation has created job opportunities for tree-planters, since the law mandates that for every one tree cut on federally owned land, at least nine must be replanted. It has also resulted in significant gains for private timber owners who are currently significant players in the new Oregon economy.

AGRICULTURE

In the 1930s a Woody Guthrie song extolled the "pastures of plenty" in the Northwest. Six decades later, the pastures are still plentiful, only more so. Oregon leads the nation in the production of such varied agricultural commodities as filberts, peppermint, blackberries, rhubarb, several kinds of grass seed, and Christmas trees. The Willamette Valley boasts the most diversified farming region on the planet; the Bing and maraschino cherries and elephant garlic were developed here, and the Valley's legendary fertility inspired tens of thousands of Oregon Trail emigrants.

An oft-heard refrain in pioneer days was "Crops never fail west of the Cascades." The Oregon Trail migration and government land giveaways resulted in the settlement of most of the Willamette's good agricultural land by the mid-1850s. In the 1860s, gold-rush activity put a premium on eastern Oregon's wheat. Later on, alfalfa, sheep, and livestock diversified farmers' options on the dry side of the mountains. Today, this region's food-processing plants have enjoyed a boom, particularly with the potato crop; McDonald's gets most of its spuds for french fries from Eastern Oregon, as do several of the leading potato-chip and frozen-food manufacturers. Oregonians themselves look to the east side toward Hermiston for the best melons and potatoes in the state.

The golden age of Oregon agriculture began with the tapping of the Columbia River for irrigation water, enabling large-scale farming to get started. At about the same same time, World War II compelled Oregon to develop her own flower-bulb industry, instead of relying upon Japan. Today, Oregon is a leader in nursery crops, ornamental flowers, and flower seed production (number three is nursery crops in the U.S.).

If you're interested in roadside agriculture, certain highways have signs identifying crops and some livestock operations. Look for these signs in Hermiston, Pendleton, The Dalles, Hood River, Madras, Redmond, Medford, Ashland, and Brookings. Agricultural operations are also labeled along I-5 and ORE 99 in the Willamette Valley, the Sunset Highway between Portland and the coast, ORE 34 from Corvallis to the coast, and ORE 211 out of Molalla.

Oregon grows about 200 different commercial commodities. Only California ranks ahead of Oregon in crop diversity. Agriculture-related employment accounts for 300,000 jobs, with four out of 10 Oregonians involved in getting food from the farm to market.

Perennial leaders among vegetable crops in the state are onions, sweet corn, potatoes, beets, mint, and snap beans. The top corporate agricultural revenue producers include such giants as Tillamook Cheese, Norpac (the state's largest farmer-owned food processor), and Smith's Frozen Foods (peas, corn, and carrots—the largest private employer in Umatilla County). While beef, nursery stock, hay, grass seed, dairy products, and wheat traditionally have been the leading economic entities in the state's several-billion-dollar farm economy, specialty crops and processing currently enjoy the fastest rates of growth. With changing forestry policies, sales of logs from small, nonindustrial woodlots have rocketed to the top of Oregon's leading revenue producers. In addition, Oregon wineries garner top honors in international competitions, with the bulk of the prizes going to the pinot noir and chardonnay varietals from Yamhill and Washington counties.

GOLD AND MINERALS

Although not a major economic force in the modern era, gold mining played a pivotal role in the early growth of towns throughout the state. In the decade following the California gold rush of 1849, thousands of miners came into southern Oregon because of gold finds in the Rogue Valley and

miners at the Greenhorn Mine, circa 1913

on the south coast. The boomtown of Jacksonville was created in 1851 near a gold-bearing creek, and the Applegate Trail became the low-road alternative to the Oregon Trail for cross-country emigrants. Baker, Jacksonville's eastern Oregon counterpart, was located near the main spur of the Oregon Trail. Both places were reputed to be among the wildest towns west of Chicago during the mid-19th century. In any case, Oregon gold production helped the Union win the Civil War. One stretch of Canyon Creek near Canyon City in the John Day area of eastern Oregon yielded $28 million in gold for Union coffers.

In addition to the Canyon City strike, there was other activity that compounded the impression that 1860 was a golden decade. During that era, gold finds launched Jacksonville as a center of commerce. In addition, gold was reported in the foothills surrounding Cottage Grove, near the southern tip of the Willamette Valley. This latter discovery by James "Bohemia" Johnson (so named because of his heritage) in 1863 lay virtually dormant until the early 20th century, due to insufficient technology to mine the million-dollar deposits.

The Bohemia mining country also generated a story, perhaps apocryphal, that part of Cottage Grove was paved with gold-rich gravel from the Row River. So far, no one has been willing to rip up the streets and check. To the south 150 miles, the "streets of gold" story was rehashed

with a new twist during the Depression, when residents unearthed tens of thousands of dollars from old claims in their back yards.

In the 1990s, a process that involves the cyanide leaching of gold-laden soils is slated for large-scale implementation in southeastern Oregon, despite the protests of ranchers and environmentalists. Throughout the state, gold is still in "them thar hills," but its price on the world market has to be high enough to make it financially feasible to extract. Moreover, mining companies wanting to break ground in Oregon, need to keep bird watchers, ranchers, and state regulatory agencies happy. This was seen from the resistance to proposed cyanide leaching of gold-laden soils in southeastern Oregon during the nineties.

Southwestern Oregon is often touted as the part of the state with the most mineral wealth. The only producing nickel mine and smelter in the U.S. is still operating in Riddle, a small Douglas County town off of I-5. In addition to gold and nickel, deposits of copper, chromium, platinum, manganese, asbestos, mercury, iron, molybdenum, zinc, coal, and limestone have been mined in the region. South coast offshore-oil and mineral-mining leases have been proposed, but environmental restrictions make such operations more likely off the central coast near Newport.

But when all is said and done, the most mundane minerals and aggregates make the most money. Sand, gravel, and limestone for the manufacture of cement account for half of the revenues in the state's 153-million-dollar-a-year mining economy.

FISHING

The exploitation of Oregon's fishing resources has been an enduring aspect of life in the region for thousands of years. Salmon has always been the most valued species. Native Americans on both sides of the Cascades have depended upon it, and commercial fishermen have viewed it as a mainstay for over a century. This, unfortunately, is changing.

The advent of commercial salmon fishing was late in coming due to the pioneer preoccupation with mining, logging, and agriculture. Canning technology and fishing methods first perfected in Alaska made their way down to

Oregon in the 1860s in time to meet the demands of emerging domestic and foreign markets. In the modern era, Oregon salmon fisheries grew into a megabusiness until a decline in the '90s.

Still, the future is troubling to contemplate, given the evolution of the industry. At first, fish wheels depleted rivers once so choked with spawning fish that a pioneer pitchfork stuck haphazardly into the water would often yield a salmon. Dam construction and pollution joined overfishing to further reduce the catch. Watersheds have been compromised by clearcuts, denuding slopes of erosion breaks to inhibit siltation of spawning streams and reducing shaded riparian environments for the coldwater-loving salmon. Cattle grazing has also impacted spawning areas with collapsed stream banks and polluted water. In recent years, Asian drift nets have emerged as the most virulent scourge of all. Northwest fishermen say the 30-mile-long, 50-foot-deep driftnets rake off millions of pounds annually of baby salmon that would otherwise have returned to waters in the American Northwest.

The salmon shortfall and other outgrowths of the drift-net debacle have spawned alternative ocean fisheries. Bottom fishing for black ling cod and rockfish, together with the harvest of such long-ignored species as hake, whiting, and pollock have increased in proportion to the decline of salmon, flounder, albacore tuna, smelt, and halibut. Growing out of the pollock fishery has been the development of a successful surimi (artificial crab) industry supplying Asian and U.S. markets. Clam, oysters, shrimp, and crab continue to be strong facets of the industry, despite occasional pollution problems. Recently unearthed shellfish middens (mounds) dating back to ancient Indian times indicate that these species were the most enduring part of the Northwest diet.

opossum

SCOTT TEEPLE

BOB RACE

ON THE ROAD
OUTDOOR ACTIVITIES

Sea Level to Ski Level

Oregon's outdoor recreation bounty is not restricted to one corner of the state. Whether it's climbing some of the most highly rated ascents in the world at Smith Rock in central Oregon, hiking from wilderness lodges a day's walk from each other along the Rogue River Trail, or fishing for steelhead and chinook on the Willamette River a stone's throw from downtown Portland, Oregonians and fellow travelers can take their pick of golden moments. Ever since Mt. Bachelor was selected by *Ski Magazine* as one of the top five resorts in the country, and no fewer than six state golf courses were voted by *Golf Digest* as among the nation's best, the word has gotten out. However, there are still some well-kept secrets: scuba diving off Port Orford; surfing near Cannon Beach and Seaside; mountain biking outside Oakridge near Eugene; the best night skiing in America an hour away from Portland, Eugene and Medford; hut-to-hut skiing in the Wallowas; hunting game birds and spelunking in eastern Oregon; and hang gliding in the high desert town of Lakeview. Lovers

of life on the wild side will discover that, in Oregon, their greatest problem is narrowing down the countless recreational opportunities.

Windsurfing near the town of Hood River is a perfect example. Other than the San Francisco Bay Area, there's no other place in the continental U.S. boasting summertime air flows as consistently strong as those in the Columbia River Gorge. Championship events and top competitors have coalesced around the shores of the river here, 60 miles from Portland. Water temperatures between 55-65° and wind currents that occasionally exceed 40 miles per hour allow windsurfers to "rig up" from spring until fall at the Hood River Marina and Riverfront Park in The Dalles. Since the great river of the West runs in the opposite direction of the air flows, windsurfers can maintain their positions relative to the shore. In short, the area offers the perfect marriage of optimum conditions and scenic beauty.

But when conditions are too placid, many windsurfers take to the hills of 11,235-foot Mt. Hood. Summer snow skiing at Timberline Lodge, commonly a practice venue for the U.S. Olympic team, is an hour away. But it's area hiking and camping that attract most people. The Columbia River Gorge boasts over 70 waterfalls in as many miles, and one of the greatest range of plant habitats in the world. Mt. Hood's Fuji-like contours tower over ancient forests and alpine meadows choked with wildflowers.

For more information on other world-class recreational opportunities around the state, see the travel chapters.

CAMPING AND HIKING

Oregon has more state parks than almost any other place in the country, as well as a natural environment suited to all manner of recreational activities. With a coastline that is largely owned by the public, the nation's first scenic highway in the Columbia Gorge, and the country's fifth national park at Crater Lake, the land ethic was given eloquent voice early here. In

FESTIVAL HOPPING

O regon loves to fête its heritage, as well as its artistic and gastronomic bounty. The following seasonal sampler highlights some of the festivals and celebrations throughout the state.

In spring, two coastal gourmet affairs of note are the **Newport Seafood and Wine Festival** and the **Astoria Crab Feed and Seafood Festival.** Also around this time, Florence's **Rhododendron Festival** and Brookings **Azalea Festival,** both on the coast, attract blossom connoisseurs.

Such world-class kulturfests as Ashland's **Oregon Shakespeare Festival,** Eugene's **Bach Festival,** and the **Mt. Hood Festival of Jazz** coincide with the glories of summer. The same holds true for Oregon's pageants of patrimony such as the **Lewis and Clark** play in Seaside, the **Oregon Trail** play in Oregon City, as well as living-history presentations at The Dalles and Astoria's Fort Clatsop. If you have kids in tow, take advantage in June of the parades, carnival rides, air shows, and floral splendor of Portland's **Rose Festival** or the **Cannon Beach Sandcastle Festival.** You could fill up July and August with such varied musical talents as the new vaudeville acts of **The Oregon Country Fair,** the gold-record performers at Jacksonville's **Peter Britt Music Festival,** virtuosi at the **Cascade Head Chamber Music Festival** and Portland's **Chamber Music Northwest,** not to mention the blues icons who appear at the **Waterfront Blues Festival** in Portland, the West Coast's largest.

During this time, festival-goers can toast their appreciation of Oregon at Portland's **Oregon Brewer's Festival,** where over 60 microbreweries are showcased, and the **Annual International Pinot Noir Festival** in McMinnville, attracting master vintners from around the world. Summer festivalhoppers might also want to take in **Da Vinci Days** in Corvallis, uniting the community's scientific and artistic elements, and Portland's **Literuption** and **The Bite,** featuring the best in books and food, respectively. The **Salem Art Fair and Festival** and high-quality but free music-in-the-park programs in Roseburg and Eugene are other summertime highlights.

. In the fall and winter, the leading events west of the Cascades include Mt. Angel's **Oktoberfest,** the **Eugene Celebration,** the **Corvallis Fall Festival,** and Thanksgiving open houses in the wine country. Those who really want to savor this time of year take the scenic train ride through foliage and orchard country during the **Hood River Harvest Fest.** At Christmastime the leading events are Albany's **Caroling** and **Victorian Parlour tours,** Portland's **Christmas Ships,** and light displays all over the state.

While most of Oregon's celebrations take place west of the Cascades, there are notable exceptions to the rule. Birdwatchers relish the **Klamath Basin Bald Eagle Conference** in February, and the springtime **John Scharff Migratory Waterfowl Conference** in Burns. Highbrows can take in the summertme literary festival at **Fishtrap** in the Wallowas or the **Sunriver Music and Arts Festivals** in central Oregon. Rockhounds flock to summer mineral shows in the central Oregon hamlets of Madras and Prineville. Rodeo fans can whoop and holler at the venerable **Pendleton Round-up** in September. Such celebrations of ethnicity as Portland's Cinco de Mayo (largest celebration of this kind in the nation) and Scandanavian Festivals in Astoria and Junction City express the state's diversity.

Add such arcane events as the **Rogue River Rooster Crow** and couch races at Silverton's **Homer Davenport Days,** and you have a picture of a state that plays as hard as it works.

BOB RACE

With the most state parks in the nation, Oregon offers great odds of finding the perfect campsite.

order to keep Oregon the way it is, here are some suggestions:

• Stay on the trails so you do not increase the rate of erosion or destroy such fragile vegetation as alpine wildflowers.

• Use established campsites, and avoid digging tent trenches or cutting vegetation.

• Camp several hundred feet from water sources.

• Bring a tool to dig a latrine, and make it four to six inches deep.

• As for trash, if you pack it in, pack it out. Leave nothing but footprints.

• Avoid feeding wild animals so you do not inhibit their natural instinct to fend for themselves.

Camping in State Parks
Despite charging the highest camping fees in the West, Oregon's 224 state parks are still the most heavily used (per state park acre) in the country—a tribute to their excellence. To help manage the influx, the state has created an information phone (800) 551-6949 and a reservation line (800) 452-5687. Peak season (spring and summer) hours are Mon.-Fri. 8 a.m.-8 p.m. Otherwise, winter and fall service hours are 8 a.m.-5 p.m. In addition to tentsites and RVs, some parks offer yurt camping, teepees, cabins, and houseboats. Reservations may be made up to 11 months in advance. The reservation fee is $6.

The Reservations Northwest center is located on the ground floor of the **Oregon Dept. of Fish and Wildlife,** 2501 S.W. 1st Ave., Portland. Visitors can get an Oregon hunting or fishing li-

cense, or purchase an Oregon state park day-use permit (no camping reservations are accepted in person). There's usually a 14-day limit on overnight stays. At more popular parks like Rooster Rock, Ecola Park, Cape Lookout, and Shore Acres, there's a $3 day-use fee.

For camping-related agencies such as the U.S. Forest Service and Dept. of Fish and Wildlife, etc., see "Information" later in this chapter.

Stay in a Fire Lookout
A relatively new and romantic option for campers is the opening-up of fire-lookout stations for overnight stays. We say "campers" because most of these places have wood heat, no electricity, and an outhouse. Bring matches, water, a lantern or flashlight, garbage bags, and a first-aid kit. Since lookouts usually sleep four, bring an air mattress if your party exceeds that. Although there are sometimes furnishings, you have to bring your own bedding, and getting there sometimes can involve an uphill hike of several miles. In some cases, cross-country skis or snowshoes are required to get to your hideaway. To reserve one of these ultimate rooms-with-a-view, contact the Forest Service ranger districts that maintain these facilities, most of which are either out-of-service or out-of-season lookouts. Rent per night is usually in the $25-40 range.

Several ranger districts with lookouts are currently available for overnights, but there are many more in the process of restoration. The program has proved so popular that weekends are usually booked up well in advance, but weekdays are frequently open. Acker Rock lookout exemplifies this unique type of lodging. With propane-powered stoves, a refrigerator, and 360-degree views, the place is often booked up to a year in advance. The $40 per night rent is upscale compared to the $25 charge at Goodman Ridge, which has remote location 60 miles east of La Grande and is in less demand. In addition to the places listed below, you can get updates on new lookouts by writing to the **PNW Region,** P.O. Box 3623, Portland 97208-3623. The best in-depth source is *Renting a Fire Lookout in the Pacific Northwest* by Foley and Steinfeld (Foghorn Press, 1996).

Here are some ideas for those of you interested in this kind of getaway: Ludlum House, Snow Camp, and Packers Cabin on the south coast, c/o Chetco Ranger Station, 555 5th St., Brookings 97415, tel. (541) 469-2196; Acker Rock, c/o Tiller Rock Ranger Station, 27812 Tiller Trail, Tiller 97484, tel. (541) 825-3201, in southwestern Oregon; the Warner Mt. lookout in the Willamette National Forest, c/o Willamette National Forest, P.O. Box 14109, Oakridge 97463, call Frank Carson, tel.(541) 782-2283; Five Mile and Flag Point lookouts in the Cascade foothills, c/o Barlow Ranger District, P.O. Box 67, Dufur 97021, tel. (541) 467-2291; and Goodman Ridge lookout in eastern Oregon, Umatilla National Forest, 2517 S.W. Haily Ave., Pendleton 97809, tel. (541) 276-3814. In contrast to the summertime availability of their counterparts, the Barlow lookouts are available November through May. If the skies are clear here,

you can see north to Mt. Adams, Mt. St. Helens, and Mt. Rainier, with Mt. Hood to the west.

Yurts, which you will find detailed in the "Introduction" in the Oregon Coast chapter, are another recent camping alternative expected to be put into use all over the state. These can be reserved at selected locations through the state parks reservation number: (800) 452-5687.

Hiking Permits and Trail Fees

In 1997, it was announced that trail park fees would be charged, $3/day or $25 for an annual pass per vehicle, to park at certain trailheads. This is in response to major reductions in timber harvests and cutbacks in federal money. The resulting revenue shortfall has made it hard to keep up trails and campgrounds at a time when the region's population has put more demand on this facilities. Due to unavailability of information on which trails would be designated for fee collection and how this policy would be administered, we can only advise readers of the fourth edition to stay tuned.

What to Take

As you may know, clothing in layers of polypropylene, wool, and Gore-Tex are the best choices on most Oregon camping trips. Lightweight down vests are always appreciated for their warmth, and they make great pillows. Those camping in the Columbia Gorge as well as the Coast and Klamath ranges during early spring might bring along rain pants. Danner

on the trail through the Green Lakes Basin

OREGON TOURISM DIVISION

boots, made right in Oregon, are tailored specifically to the state's rainforest, alpine, and desert regions. Get discount prices at the factory outlet, 12722 N.E. Airport Way, Portland, tel. (503) 251-1111. Whatever brand of boot you buy, it's a safe bet that waterproofing will be useful here. Athletic shoes at a bargain can be procured at the **Nike Outlet Store,** 3044 N.E. Martin Luther King Blvd., Portland, tel. (503) 281-5901.

Lightness, durability, and water-resistance are also the predominant criteria in choosing tents and sleeping bags. Neophyte hikers are reminded that tents and bags should be as compact as possible. These considerations compel the selection of down as the preferable "fill" for sleeping bags, even though these bags can be faulted for becoming useless when wet. Nonetheless, their lightness, warmth, and compressibility supersede the higher resistance to moisture of synthetic fill. (The best synthetic fill, according to some, is Quallofil by Du Pont.) To make sure down retains its advantages, bring along a foam mat or Therm-a-Rest inflatable pad in a Gore-Tex stuff bag (or a plastic bag— both waterproof and cheap). The pad provides extra insurance for a comfortable night on the damp, uneven terrain in many locales.

While it cools down significantly at night almost everywhere in Oregon during the June to October peak hiking season, the diurnal temperature variations are the most pronounced in the high Cascades and in the Wallowas, necessitating heavier fill in your sleeping bag. Among popular camping areas, coldest of all during the summer could well be Steens Mountain, frequently recording subfreezing nocturnal temperatures. By contrast, the Willamette and southern Oregon valleys along the I-5 corridor sometimes experience daytime heat continuing into the night; at such times a down bag becomes a sweat lodge. Regardless of the kind of bag you choose, it should have a waterproof cover.

In like measure, tents should have rainflies. Dome tents are the best choice, given their ease of setup and lightweight construction; waterproof ones go for a little over $100. Probably the best selection in the state is available at the **REI Co-op** in Portland's Jantzen Beach Mall, 1798 Jantzen Beach Center, Portland 97217, tel. (503) 283-1301, just off I-5 near the Columbia River. There is also an outlet in Tualatin, 7410 S.W. Bridgeport Rd., tel. (503) 624-8600; take exit 290 off of I-5, and one in downtown Eugene, 306 Lawrence Street. All of these stores have helpful staff as well as pamphlets on what to look for when buying gear.

Discount prices are available at **Andy and Bax,** 324 S.E. Grand, Portland, tel. (503) 234-7538. Everything from U.S. Army reissue coolers and other G.I. surplus to a wide variety of camping equipment is available here. Specialty items such as Metsker Oregon County maps and whitewater guidebooks will also be appreciated by the outdoors person.

As long as we're on the subject of camping-gear outfitters, we should mention that Oregon is one of the best places in the world to purchase equipment. First of all, Portland, Bend, and the two college towns of Eugene and Corvallis boast many stores and equipment manufacturers that cater to the Oregonian love affair with the outdoors. Since these purchases tend to run into higher figures wherever you shop, Oregon's comparatively low overhead and lack of sales tax help keep costs down. Look for markdowns on items with "blems" or cosmetic defects, as well as "annex" stores selling the same or closeout items. If you need a high level of sophistication in your gear, chances are you'll find state-of-the-art hardware within the Beaver State.

One item many travelers might have to purchase on-site will be fuel for cookstoves, since its transport is prohibited on commercial airlines. White gas is the best, but for flexibility, bring a stove that uses a variety of fuels. Propane rates highly with many campers because of its low cost and compatibility with other camping implements. Nonetheless, its volatility makes it potentially hazardous. Stoves are very important to have on many treks because of the shortage of dry firewood.

Flashlights or lanterns are essential for comfort and safety. Common sense items like water-purification tablets, sunscreen, a canteen, a Swiss army knife, cooking and eating utensils, freeze-dried food, maps and compasses, plastic bags, and nylon twine will also ensure a bon voyage. Certain trips will also require mosquito repellent and wooden matches dipped in nail polish or wax (for waterproofing). Finally, a safety kit containing iodine, lip balm or Chapstick, diarrhea medication, aloe vera, aspirin, antibiotics, and bandages or Band-Aids is also a good idea; add eye drops and antihistamine and/or allergy medicine if you're camping in or near the Willamette Valley from April till July. Carry some baking soda in a film cannister for bee and yellow jacket stings. It helps to pull out the poison, and it can also double as toothpaste in a pinch. The Red Cross recommends first-aid kits containing tweezers, cotton, adhesive-bandage tape, hydrogen peroxide, antiseptic, ipecac syrup (or something to induce vomiting), elastic bandages, scissors, sterile gauze pads, two rolls of gauze, tongue depressors, and a cold compress. Pre-made kits are available at drugstores if you don't want to put these items together yourself.

Camping and Hiking Information

In addition to the earlier section on Oregon State Park camping information and reservations, we offer some more resources for those interested in sleeping under the stars and hitting the trails.

Oregon Outdoors, P.O. Box 10841, Eugene 97440, tel. (541) 683-9552, has the scoop on outfitting just about any kind of adventure you can imagine. Whether you want to pack llamas into the Kalmiopsis Wilderness, shoot the rapids of Hells Canyon, or take to the Cascades on horseback, you'll find a listing here for something interesting to do in Oregon.

The **National Forest Service,** tel. (800) 280-CAMP, Mon.-Fri. 7 a.m.-4 p.m., has a nationwide reservation and information center. There is a reservation fee in addition to regular campground fees, $6 for reserving family sites, $10 for reserving group sites. Campsites can be booked up to 120 days in advance for single family sites and 360 days in advance for group sites. Campgrounds in the Willamette, Umpqua, and Siuslaw national forests are Oregon's bailiwicks covered in this program.

The **Northwest Interpretive Association,** 83 King St. ste 212 Seattle, WA 98104, tel. (206) 553-7958, has a free catalogue of their interpretive publications relating to Oregon national forests. Their Campground Information Guide is especially recommended.

The State Highways Division completed *The Oregon Campground Guide* in 1992. It includes state parks system, Forest Service, and BLM sites. All of the campgrounds are indicated on an accompanying map, and the free directory lists user fees and the kinds of facilities available.

The **Oregon Parks and Recreation Division,** 525 Trade St., Salem 97310, tel. (503) 378-6305, the **U.S. Bureau of Land Management,** 1515 S.W. 5th., Portland, tel. (503) 952-6001, and the **U.S. Forest Service,** 333 S.W. 1st, Portland, tel.(503) 326-2971, have free information and maps on specific recreation areas and preserves under their respective auspices. Hikers can benefit from *An Oregonian's Trail Sourcebook,* published by the Oregon Student Public Interest Research Group, or OSPIRG, 1536 S.E. 11th, Portland 97214, tel.(503) 231-4181.

Skiers can benefit from information put out by the **Pacific Northwest Ski Association,** P.O. Box 34481, Kirkland, WA 98083, tel. (206) 822-1770.

In northeast Portland the state-sponsored **Nature of The Northwest Information Center,** 800 N.E. Oregon St., Suite 177, Portland 97232, tel. (503) 731-4444, makes available the gamut of publications having to do with Oregon outdoors. Much of this is free thanks to the departments of forestry, agriculture, wildlife, tourism, state parks, etc.; U.S. Geological Survey, Forest Service, and BLM maps, as well as reprints of research papers done by various agencies, are on sale also. The hours are Mon.-Fri. 10 a.m.-5 p.m.

Locating this important information resource isn't easy for those unfamiliar with Portland. At the end of an obscure street, the center sits a few blocks due east from the Oregon Convention Center and south of Lloyd Center on the bottom floor of a nine-floor state office building. To get there from I-5 driving north, take exit 302A (Coliseum/Broadway/Weidler), go right on Weidler, right on Martin Luther King Blvd., and then left on Oregon Street. Driving south on I-5, take the Coliseum/City Center exit and veer left toward Vancouver. Turn left on Weidler, right on Martin Luther King Blvd., and then left on Oregon Street.

The **Pacific Crest Trail Association,** P.O. Box 2514, Lynwood, WA 98036, publishes an eight-page bimonthly newsletter. The 2,638-mile Pacific Crest Trail runs from Canada to Mexico, traversing Oregon along the Cascades at high elevations. Such scenic access routes and offshoots as the Eagle Creek Trail in the

Columbia Gorge and Ramona Falls on the lower slopes of Mt. Hood beckon further exploration. Other popular entry points include Big Lake Campground off US 20, and McKenzie Pass off ORE 242. The free publication has articles about events along the trail as well as accounts of trips taken on it.

U.S.G.S. Maps

Mountain bikers and hikers on Oregon trails will appreciate the 911 Oregon maps published by the U.S. Geologic Survey. They can be purchased in bookstores and outdoor stores for about $3 each. A few hints might help first-time users. First, the fine squiggly lines covering the map are called "contour lines." When you see them close together, expect steep slopes. Conversely, kinder, gentler terrain is indicated by larger spaces between contour lines.

By molding a pipe cleaner in the pattern of a trail, then straightening it out and superimposing it on the mileage scale at the bottom of the map, you can find out the distance you'll be covering.

FISHING AND HUNTING

If you are interested in fishing, contact the **Oregon Department of Fish and Wildlife,** 2501 S.W. 1st Ave. Portland, tel.(503) 872-5275. Nonresident fishing licenses are $8.25 (for one day), $15.50 (two days), $22.75 (three days), $34.25 (seven days) or $48 (year). The cost for a one-year license for residents is $20.50 for adults, $6.25 for ages 14-17. Residents can purchase a combination fishing and hunting license for $32.50. You can pick up licenses at Ticketmaster outlets or many sporting goods stores.

The **Oregon Coast Charterboat Association,** P.O. Box 494, Newport, OR 97365, offers a resource guide that helps in selecting a charterboat and skipper, and deciding when to fish and what to bring. It also lists which outfits do sightseeing and whalewatching charters. These days expect to pay around $15 for a coastal charter that goes out for sea bass, ling cod, and other bottomfish.

Anglers can dial (800) ASK-FISH to keep up-to-date on Beaver State fishing conditions. Callers with touch-tone phones can choose from a varied menu of recorded information, including data on campgrounds, wheelchair access, and important state regulations.

Hunting licenses are available at the same address, hunting tel. 872-5275. A nonresident license is $100.50, deer tags are $75.50, and elk tags are $165.50. Game tags are needed prior to the first day of hunting season. Apply early, since availability is limited.

The most efficient way to get a fishing or hunting license is to use the state computer available in many sporting goods stores. The agent there asks for all the "specs" (age, address, etc.) and enters them along with the requests for licenses, tags, and stamps. Your new forms are then issued by the computer. All the necessary documents come out on a single sheet of paper. Tags and stamps that you need to attach to the kill are also issued. The information is kept in the system to facilitate renewal the following year.

RAFTING

Oregon's world-class whitewater rafting proves that the winter rain clouds here have a silver lining. With 90,000 river miles in the state and hundreds of outfitters to choose from, however, neophyte rafters may have the problem of sorting out an embarrassment of riches. To help navigate the tricky currents of brochure jargon and select the experience that's right for you, here's a list of rivers to run and questions to ask before going.

The famous **Rogue River** reaches its whitewater crescendo at the green forested canyons of the Klamath Mountains in southwestern Oregon. Come June through September to see abundant birds and wildlife and avoid the rainy season. This run is characterized by gentle stretches broken up by abrupt and occasionally severe dropoffs as well as swift currents. In fact, Blossom Bar (where Meryl Streep braved the elements in "The River Wild") is often cited as the state's consummate test of skill for rafters. Water turbulence on the Rogue is often intensified by constricted channels created by huge boulders. At day's end, superlative campsites give repose and allow you to savor your adventures.

Despite the dryness and isolation of Oregon's southeast corner, the **Owyhee River** has become a prime destination for whitewater enthusiasts. The reasons include the red-rock canyons, lava flows, and high desert panoramas which line its course. The 53 miles from Rome to the Owyhee Reservoir has two sections of exceptionally heavy rapids, but the many pools of short, intense whitewater alternating with easy drifts make for a well-paced trip. Stay alert even along stretches of placid water and such eye-catching diversions as a 10-mile gorge lined by 1,000-foot-high walls, because sharp rocks abound along the Owyhee's course. The best times to come are during May and June. Before going, check conditions with the National Weather Service in Portland, tel. (503) 249-0666, and the Vale BLM District office, tel. (541) 473-3144, because the Owyhee can only be run in high snow-melt years. Acess to rafting put-in points in this part of the state is greatly facilitated by a four-wheel drive vehicle.

The **John Day River** in northeastern Oregon offers an even-flowing current as it winds through unpopulated rangeland and scenic rock formations. Below Clarno, the grade gets steep, creating the most treacherous part of the state's longest river (275 miles). The 157-mile section of the John Day that rafters, canoeists, and kayakers come to experience also has falls near the mouth which require a portage. The special charm of this Columbia tributary is the dearth of company you'll have here even during the river-running seasons of late March to May and then again in November. Just watch out for rattlesnakes along the bank and remember that the siltload in this undammed river reduce it to an unboatable trickle in summer months. Contact the Prineville Bureau of Land Management, tel. (541) 447-4115, for more information.

Unlike the John Day and the Owyhee rivers, the **Deschutes** rapids aren't totally dependent on snowmelt. As with the Rogue, river runners enjoy superlative conditions even in the driest of years. As a result, it has become the busiest vacation waterway in the state. The 44 miles between Maupin and the Columbia River contain sage-covered grasslands and wild rocky canyons where you might see bald eagles, pronghorns, and other wildlife. If there's a good run of salmon you might also encounter plenty of powerboats. Expect most of the thrills and spills near the mouth of this 250 mile river. Heavy winds might also whip up in the final quarter of the journey. With an average of 310 days of sunshine annually, weather is seldom a problem except for excessively hot summer days.

Oregon River Tours, by John Garren (Garren Publishing, 1008 S.W. Comus, Portland 97219, gives a blow-by-blow description of these and other rivers in the state. A good selection of in-depth guides focusing on each river individually is available at Andy and Bax, 324 S.E. Grand, Portland 97214, tel. (503) 234-7538. Up-to-the-minute conditions are provided by the National Weather Service in Portland, tel. (503) 249-0666.

Knowing the contours and characteristics of the river you want to float does not alone ensure a good trip. Choosing an outfitter who can meet your "specs" on cost, style, safety, and the degree of your own participation is integral to an enjoyable experience. Procure *The Oregon Outdoors Directory,* P.O. Box 10841, Eugene 97440, tel. (541) 683-9552. This publication's long roster of whitewater raft trip operators lists the address/phone of each company and their itineraries. Chambers of commerce and phone books are other good sources. For example, the Portland Yellow Pages lists four columns of ads under Rafts and River Trips. Typical outfitter services include gourmet meals, wetsuits or rain gear, and inflatable rafts and kayaks. Should you consult commercial backpacking magazines and newspaper sports and travel sections (also check the *Oregonian*'s "Outdoors" section on Thursday), chances are that the blurbs might include adjectives like "participatory" (i.e., you paddle and perhaps help set up camp) and "deluxe" (i.e., you don't paddle if you don't want to, fancy equipment, and good eats provided). Guided raft trips begin at $45 for a half-day trip and increase to $150 a day for longer trips. There are volume discounts for groups.

However, detailed as these listings may be, they mean little without some follow-up. For example, if "gourmet meals" are advertised, find out what they include. To ensure an intimate wilderness experience, ask about the number of people in a raft and how many rafts on the river at one time. Are there any hidden costs such as camping gear rental or added transfer charges? What is the cancellation policy? Another consideration is the training and experience of the guides. Can he or she be expected to give commentary about history, geology, and local color? You might also want to check about

APPROXIMATE DIFFICULTY OF RAPIDS		SKILL LEVEL
Class 1	Easy	Beginner
Class 2	Requires Care	Intermediate
Class 3	Difficult	Experienced
Class 4	Very Difficult	Highly Skilled
Class 5	Exceedingly Difficult	Expert Crew
Class 6	Unnavigable	Get Life Insurance

the company's willingness to customize its trips to special interests like photography, birdwatching, or hiking. Finally, a discussion of safety may be facilitated by a knowledge of the system used to classify river rapids, see chart, above.

The Oregon whitewater enthusiast's cup runneth over, thanks to the state's securing federally designated Wild and Scenic status for thousands of river miles within its boundaries. Oregon's environmental leadership helped create the Wild and Scenic Rivers Act, which now inhibits dam building and regulates land use along more river frontage here than anywhere else in the nation.

Willamette River Recreation
The **State Parks Dept.** has put out a free guide to the Willamette, arguably Oregon's most important river. History, wildlife refuges, fishing, boating, navigation rules, hazards, car ferries, biking, hiking, state parks, and annotated maps are all covered in this publication. The guide is available at many Willamette Valley Visitor and Convention Bureaus, or can be obtained by calling (800) 551-6949.

Recreation Information for Travelers with Disabilites
The following numbers will serve disabled outdoor recreationists with specific information on their many options in Oregon. The U.S. Forest Service, tel. (503) 872-2750, the Bureau of Land Management, tel. (503) 375-5646, the U.S. Fish and Wildlife, tel. (503) 231-6214, and the Oregon Dept. of Fish and Wildlife, tel. (503) 229-5403.

ROCKHOUNDING

Hunting for semiprecious stones is a popular form of outdoor recreation here. Geode-like thunder eggs, agates, jasper, Oregon sandstone (a feldspar crystal), obsidian, gold, and fossils are some of the possibilities. A free brochure, *Oregon's Geologic Treasures,* gives a comprehensive overview of where to prospect. This publication is available at the Nature of Oregon Information Center, 800 N.E. Oregon St., Suite 177, Portland 97232, tel. (541) 731-4444.

SHOPPING

In 1992, *Money* magazine considered Oregon second only to New York as the state with the heaviest tax burden. This might be true for folks with high incomes such as those in the magazine's survey, but the lack of sales tax here, cheap car-registration fees, and comparatively low real estate prices are boons to the average wage earner. In fact, the U.S. Census Bureau places Oregon in the middle of the pack in its tax burden survey. Those passing through needn't be concerned with the state's income tax. Instead, they can revel in the shopping opportunities here, which include an abundance of craft fairs, auctions, and garage sales.

The profusion of locally made objets d'art available in **Made in Oregon** shops in the state's larger cities deserves special mention, as does the potlatch of creations at the Portland and Eugene Saturday markets (for more details, see those cities' chapters). Coastal and mountain resort areas also purvey the work of nationally known potters, woodworkers, painters, jewelers, and glass artisans from Oregon. These homemade items often go for quite a bit less than would be charged in out-of-state markets for work of comparable quality. While these "arts" cottage industries don't have the "bottom line" of timber and agriculture, they are one of the more visible and appreciated forms of economic activity. The best guide to shopping for indigenous items is *Where to Find Oregon in Oregon,* written and published by

Bridget Beattie McCarthy, 7277 S.W. Barnes Rd., Portland 97225.

Throughout the Northwest you'll encounter Fred Meyer, the region's leading retailer. In addition to offering good buys on merchandise, this company maintains the state's environmental ethic. Its boycott of drift-net tuna, support of a regional ban on phosphates, and assurance of pesticide-free produce bespeaks this commitment.

ACCOMMODATIONS AND FOOD

ACCOMMODATIONS

Cutting Costs

Oregon lodging prices are for the most part significantly lower than those of neighboring California and Washington. Nonetheless, Cascade mountain and coastal resort areas can put a strain on the pocketbook. Fortunately, state park and national forest campgrounds proliferate in these areas, offering low-cost overnight lodgings in attractive settings. As if by design, the highest percentage of Oregon's 200 state parks surround the high-ticket areas, with sites usually priced around $16-20 a night. Most of these have showers. National forest campgrounds usually cost less but offer more primitive facilities; many of them are chosen for their proximity to swimming holes and/or scenic appeal.

If creature comforts are a priority, state parks and RV parks are often available with such amenities as firewood, laundromats, and showers. All you need is a tent. If you don't have a tent, there are yurts—furnished and heated tent cabins in selected camping areas. However, private RV campgrounds and their expensive Kampgrounds of America counterparts tend to be crowded with people and vehicles, inhibiting the enjoyment of nature. Government campgrounds charge less and often feature more aesthetic surroundings.

Regarding the costs of campgrounds, there's good news and there's bad news. The bad news is fees at state park campgrounds have gone up 30% in the past few years. The good news is they are not expected to go up much more. For information and reservations, call the **Campsite Information Center** tel. (800) 452-5687 to reserve, (800) 551-6949 for information. Reservations can be made up to eleven months in advance and must be paid for by mail with check, money order, or credit card. In addition to the campsite fee, a $6 processing fee is charged. Reservations can be faxed at (503) 378-6308. By the time this volume goes to press there should also be e-mail and a Web site. During winter, hours are Mon.-Fri. 8 a.m.-5 p.m. The rest of the year, hours are Mon-Fri. 8 a.m.-9 p.m., Saturday 8 a.m.-5 p.m.

"Off-season" specials are another way to beat the crowds and the costs. For example, one often sees room rates cut in half on the coast during the February storm-watching season. The cost-conscious traveler should also keep in mind that there is no shortage of large condos and vacation homes that rent out to large parties who can split costs.

The final word on beating the high cost of lodging may go to youth hostels (see Ashland, Astoria, Bandon, Bend, Corvallis, Eugene, Newport, Portland, and Seaside) and Elderhostels (see "Practicalities" under "Ashland" in the Southern Oregon chapter) with rates generally between $10-20. Motel 6 promises the lowest rates, $20-40, with rooms that pass our cleanliness tests. Their rooms feature cable TV, the motels often have swimming pools and are usually close to restaurants. Rooms sleep four, with $6 charged for additional adults (kids stay free). Motel 6 has outlets in Coos Bay, Eugene-Springfield, Grants Pass, Klamath Falls, Medford, Ontario, Pendleton, Portland, and Salem. Perhaps the best deal of all are college dorm rooms occasionally rented out during summer session (see "Accommodations" under "Practicalities" in the Portland and Vicinity chapter). We just list one such alternative but the grapevine tells us that cash-strapped colleges will be resorting to this arrangement more and more in summers to come.

If you're looking for a romantic spot for that special occasion or just a place to get away from it all, there are many hotels with aesthetic locations as well as a high level of comfort and service. A compendium of these is published every few years by Graphic Arts of Portland, Oregon, and is aptly entitled *Special Places*.

Finally, keep in mind that a hotel reservation at many lodgings *does not* guarantee exactly what you reserved. Regardless of how far in advance you reserve or even if you gave them your credit card number, all you are really guaranteed is a room. Especially during peak season, this may translate to the whole family piling onto a king-size bed for a dubious night's rest, sleeping in a foul-smelling smoker's den, or perhaps bedding down in a dingy closet-sized cell instead of the suite you requested. Nonsmoking rooms, bed configuration, and preferred room styles are often given out to confirmed-reservation guests on a first-come, first-serve basis. To avoid problems, clarify exactly your room and the check-in time when you make the reservation, and schedule an early check-in (most hotels have midafternoon vacancies available) which may be followed up by an afternoon activity.

Bed and Breakfasts

These bits o' Britain provide a homey alternative to the typical hotel room. Ashland and the coast lead the state in bed and breakfast establishments, but the idea seems to be catching on everywhere. And why not? Whether it's a glass of sherry by a crackling fire to warm up Ashland theatergoers or a huge picture window on a Pacific storm, these retreats can impart that extra-special personal touch to the best the state has to offer.

If a turn-of-the-century Victorian or an old farmhouse doesn't give a bed and breakfast an extra measure of warmth, the camaraderie of the guests and the host family usually will. Most bed and breakfasts restrict kids, pets, and smoking in deference to what are often close quarters. Private baths are also sometimes in short supply. Offsetting any potential intrusions on privacy is an included full or continental breakfast, sometimes in bed. And in Oregon, it has become customary to see homemade jams and breads as well as a complimentary glass of a local wine for a nightcap. For complete free listings of B&Bs in Oregon write to the **Oregon Bed and Breakfast Directory**, 230 Red Spur Dr., Grants Pass 97527.

Elderhostels

Oregon is blessed with dynamic elderhostel programs featuring education experiences and low-cost accommodations with outlets in Lakeview, Corvallis, Ashland, and Sandy. The adventuresome senior can choose from a range of offerings such as a Shakespeare theater program in Ashland or a comparative religion class at a retreat center in Sandy. In-state contact, tel. (541) 552-6677, otherwise contact **Elderhostel,** 75 Federal St., Boston, MA 02110-1941 or (617) 426-8056, for registration and details.

FOOD AND DRINK

Oregon Cuisine

What will the newcomer to Oregon notice most on his or her plate? It all depends on where you happen to be. From the Basque food in southeastern Oregon to Portland's purveyors of pan-Asian cuisine (restaurants where you'll see Chinese, Thai, and Vietnamese dishes on one menu), you'll be surprised to find no shortage of exotic offerings in a state more famous in the public mind for salmon and jumbo pears.

As for humbler fare, jo-jos (refried baked potato spears encased in spices), the patented Gardenburger (Portland's own version of the vegetarian hamburger), and marionberry jams, jellies, and pies are foodstuffs most likely to confound out-of-staters.

The marionberry is a dark maroon berry whose tarter-than-blackberry taste and small seeds make it ideal for dessert fare, especially marionberry ice cream. Higher up on the food chain, world-class Oregon lamb and the seasonally available, excellent, fresh sturgeon, venison, and game birds are other little-known taste treasures here. The frequent use of locally grown herbs, exotic mushrooms, and organic produce in regional restaurants will also catch your taste buds by surprise. Award-winning dairy products, berry products coveted by gourmet ice cream makers, and hazelnuts in demand all over the world are other palate-pleasers in Oregon's horn of plenty.

All of the above can be washed down by world-class pinot noir, gourmet coffee, and microbrews. In addition to quality spirits accompanying your meal, fresh-squeezed juices and old-fashioned style root beer (notably Widmer's and Henry Weinhard's) provide quality nonalcoholic refreshments. In short, while there is not a defined substratum of cuisine that is quintessentially Oregon, uniqueness and variety combine here to satisfy even the most jaded palate.

Oregon's abundance of fresh produce, seafood, and other indigenous ingredients prompted America's apostle of haute cuisine, James Beard, to extol the restaurants and cooking of his home state. In his autobiography, *Delights and Prejudices,* he implies that Oregon strawberries, Seaside peas, Dungeness crab, and other local fare became his standards by which to judge the culinary staples of the world. This horn of plenty is the basis of a regional cuisine emphasizing fresh natural foods cooked lightly to preserve flavor, color, and texture.

Nonetheless, it *is* possible to have a bad meal in this state. In fact, the quality of the cuisine in some remote eastern Oregon towns is a source of self-deprecating humor for the locals. And as many Yankees will tell you, there is no shortage of bland New England-style clam chowder on the Oregon coast.

Still, it's easy to dine well at an affordable price throughout most of the state. This does not have to mean McDonald's, either. Because Oregon abounds in places with genuine ambience and home cooking at a good value, fast-food listings will be kept to a minimum in this book. Budget travelers might want to bring their own food to expensive resort environments.

Throughout Oregon there are also stores purveying locally made food products, which make excellent gifts. In both the Portland and Eugene airports, for example, are mini-malls selling Oregon jams, smoked salmon, hazelnuts, wines, and similar products.

The restaurant recommendations in this book were made with the traveler in mind who would prefer to have some cash left over at the end of a meal to take advantage of a raft trip or a museum. At the same time, we recognize that one of the most pleasurable ways to get to know a locale is at the dinner table. Thus, "justifiable splurges" will occasionally supplant "dollar-value" orientation, especially when the locale would lend itself to gourmet dining such as in Ashland and the wine country. Throughout the Food sec-

tions of the book, adjectives like "reasonably priced, affordable, moderate, budget, and pricey/expensive" might beg clarification. Given some amount of geographic variance, look at a tab at breakfast and lunch in the $5-8 range and $10-15 for dinner (minus tax, tip, and alcohol) as average meal costs in Oregon.

Liquor and Microbreweries

Note Oregon's liquor laws: liquor is sold by the bottle in state liquor stores open Monday through Saturday. Beer and wine are also sold in grocery stores and retail outlets. Liquor is sold by the drink in licensed establishments between 7 a.m. and 2:30 a.m. The minimum drinking age is 21.

Another related development throughout the Northwest is the popularity of "microbreweries" and pubs serving their own beers. Technically, the term "microbrewery" in Oregon refers to an establishment that sells beer on the premises in limited quantities—less than 20,000 barrels a year. However, this term connotes more than mere quantitative distinctions. Microbrews are handcrafted beers minus preservatives or chemical additives to enhance head or color. Instead of the rice or corn used by the big outfits, the micros just use barley, malt, hops, yeast, and water. The end result is a more full-bodied, tastier brew with a distinct personality. The trend is so pervasive in Portland that this metropolis is already being touted as "the city that made Milwaukee nervous."

The reason for Oregon being awash in gourmet suds owes much to the availability of top-notch ingredients—hops, barley, and clear water. Almost a third of the world's hops is produced here in the Northwest. The Willamette Valley alone cultivates over a dozen varieties. Add Cascade Mountain water, malt barley from the Klamath basin, and Hood River-grown yeast cultures and you can figure out why there are more breweries and brewpubs per capita in Oregon than anywhere else in the U.S.

Some big names in the custom brew scene include Portland Brewing Co., 1339 N.W. Flanders, Portland, tel. (503) 222-7150; Brewery Taproom, 2730 N.W. 31st, Portland, tel. (503) 226-7623, whose McTarnahan's Scottish Ale won a gold medal at the 1992 Great American Beer Festival in Denver; Bridgeport Brewing Co., 1313 N.W. Marshall St., (541) tel. 241-7179, a pioneer on the microbrew circuit and famous for Blue Heron Ale; Full Sail Ale Co., The White Cap Brewpub, 506 Columbia St., tel.386-2247; and The Pilsner Room, 6307 Montgomery, Portland—you'll find Full Sail Amber widely distributed all over the state; McMenamin's Pubs (with numerous outlets in western Oregon); Widmer Brewery whose hefeweizen is Oregon's most popular microbrew (served at Heathman Pub as well as the Widmer Gasthaus in Portland—see Portland food) and one of Oregon's largest microbreweries; and Rogue Brewing Company (Rogue Bayfront Brewery in Newport), the Oregon coast's finest. For more information on the preceding microbreweries, please refer to the applicable travel chapters.

In late July or early August in Portland's Tom McCall Waterfront Park, the **Oregon Brewer's Festival** takes place with 60-80 breweries in attendance. Admission is free but to sample the product of dozens of brewers, you must buy a mug for $2, $1 beer tokens are good for a half glass each. According to noted beer expert Michael Jackson, no other cities can compete with the quality and quantity of microbrews put out in Seattle and Portland. A few rounds at the Brewer's Festival would tend to make most anyone a believer.

GETTING THERE AND GETTING AROUND

TOURS

While not for everybody, group travel is the fastest-growing aspect of a fast-growing industry. Those inclined to "do" Oregon by package tour can recline in the air-conditioned comfort of a Mercedes-like motorcoach as it rolls past the many-splendored landscapes of Oregon. A knowledgeable guide gives you the scoop on what you're seeing in addition to building your anticipation for cliffside coastal grandeur, a jet-boat ride on the Rogue, or a play at Ashland's Shakespeare Festival. Sound idyllic? If so, touring Oregon by motorcoach could well be the mode of travel for you.

Many of these packages may seem expensive, but if you compare the price of meals, lodgings, and other services to what you'd pay independently, it's a good dollar value for the upscale traveler. In addition to volume discounts, the tour companies provide the services of a guide to spare you the hassles associated with the logistics and practicalities of travel.

Despite the togetherness that comes from sharing a positive experience with others, younger folks can sometimes feel alienated from the predominantly older clientele and/or constraints imposed by a schedule. On the other hand, there is no better way to survey Oregon in style with a limited amount of time.

The advantages of Oregon tour travel are made manifest by looking at the package put together by **Tauck Tours,** 11 Wilton Rd., Westport, CT 06880, tel. (800) 468-2825. Their itinerary features a loop from Portland, taking in the best of the coast, the Willamette Valley, a jet-boat trip on the Rogue River, a Shakespeare play in Ashland, Crater Lake, and a Cascades Mountain resort as well as the Columbia River Gorge. Along the way, four- and five-star hotels and restaurants give you the luxurious repose to savor your experiences. To book a tour or request additional information, contact the companies or see a travel agent.

Tour season in Oregon begins in late May and can run until the end of September. Before or after that, you're playing dice with the weather. In general, during tour season, prepare for warm and pleasant days all over the state, morning coastal fog, and cool mountain nights.

The Portland and Bend chapters detail touring options out of these cities. Foremost among the latter in terms of quality and variety are those of **Evergreen Grayline of Portland,** tel. (800) 422-7042, and **Wanderlust Tours** of Bend, tel. (800) 962-2862. Such Grayline daytrips as the Columbia Gorge-Mt. Hood Loop and the north coast supplement the company's city tours. Trips to the state's popular events like the Pendleton Roundup and the Hood River Blossom Festival are also available. Finally, each August, Grayline usually offers a four-day loop showcasing all the land forms of the state (except for the coast) with special emphasis on Crater Lake. Wanderlust tours specializes in

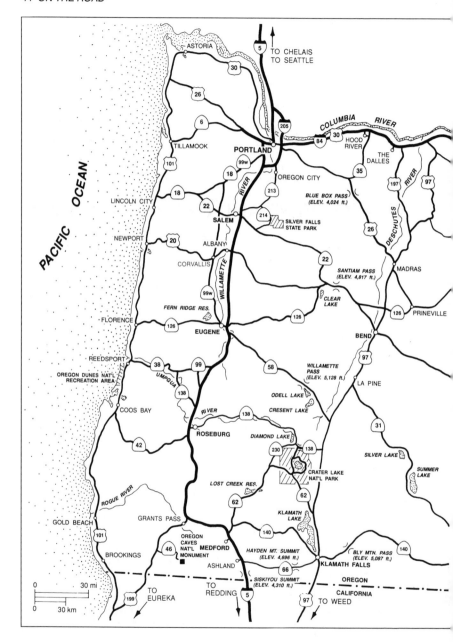

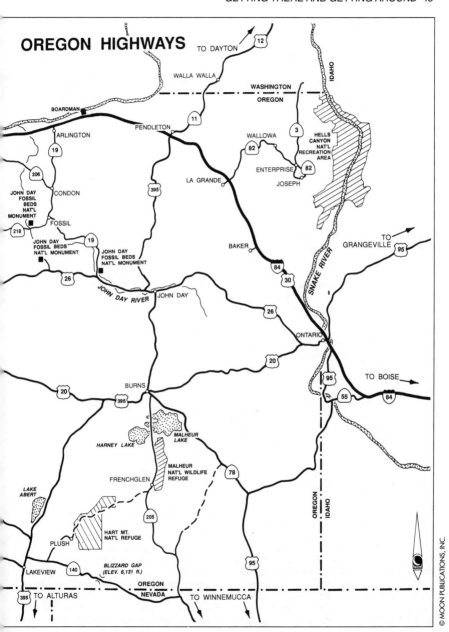

OREGON HIGHWAYS

daytrips taking in America's most varied array of volcanic phenomena outside Hawaii, Crater Lake, and other daytrips nearby Bend. The company's ecotourism packages featuring everything from snow camping to old growth forest ecology are especially recommended. These are geared to the average person's budget. Consult the appropriate travel chapter for more details.

BY AIR

It is a simple enough matter getting to and getting around Oregon by air. If there is a break in the weather, the views are breathtaking. The main point of entry is Portland International Airport (PDX), which is serviced by over a dozen airlines. Your travel agent can help you find the best current bargains, and a good weekly overview of airfares is printed in the Sunday travel section of the *Oregonian*. According to a recent study, the average fare in Portland is $77 less than the average fare from Eugene to the same destinations due to its hub status.

Horizon Air, tel. (800) 547-9308, the commuter-league farm club of Alaska Airlines, connects with a half-dozen smaller airfields in the state. Horizon operates commuter prop planes with 10-40 seats. If you are sensitive to loud noises and pressure change, ask for earplugs when you check in for your boarding pass. Astoria, Bend/Redmond, Eugene/Springfield, Klamath Falls, Medford, North Bend/Coos Bay, and Salem all enjoy Horizon service. United Express, tel. (800) 241-6522, also serves several smaller Oregon markets.

If your final destination is Astoria, Baker, La Grande, Newport, or Pendleton, many private flying outfits connect with these five municipal airports. Just check the yellow pages or the PDX information booth on the first floor.

Finally, the entry of Southwest Airlines, tel. (800) 435-9792, into Portland's array of domestic carriers warrants special attention. While there are not a lot of frills, you'd be hard-pressed to beat Southwest's Supersaver-like fares.

Plans are also in the works for "code-sharing" of routes between domestic and foreign airlines, facilitating the flow of foreign travelers into Portland International Airport. Likely partnerships

AIRLINES	
Air Canada	(800) 776-3000
Alaska	(800) 426-0333
American	(800) 433-7300
America West	(800) 235-9292
Continental	(800) 323-3273
Delta	(800) 221-1212
Hawaiian Airlines	(800) 367-5320
Horizon	(800) 547-9308
Mark	(800) 627-5247
Northwest	(800) 225-2525
Reno Air	(800) 736-6247
Southwest	(800) 435-9792
TWA	(800) 221-2000
United	(800) 241-6522

include Lufthansa with United, ANA (All Nippon Air) and China Southern Airlines with Delta, and British Air with US Air. Currently, Portland's direct access to Europe comes courtesy of a Delta flight to Frankfurt (with a stop in Cincinnati).

A little advice about cutting costs will help air travelers to and from Portland. As with most major hubs, advance purchase (at least seven days) and weekend stayovers are the key to saving up to 60% on your airfare. In like measure, many resorts have low promotional weekend rates. Incidentally, low-cost airlines, while giving you a better "shake" than the big outfits on a consistent basis, do not vary much from weekday to weekend fares (5-10% savings).

BY TRAIN

Amtrak
Amtrak has recently cut all Oregon service except for the *Coast Starlight* which runs between Los Angeles, California, and Seattle, Washington with such stops in Oregon as Klamath Falls, Chemult, Oakridge, Eugene, Salem, and Portland.

Getting a sleeper on the Coast Starlight, for example, requires reservations 5-11 months in advance any time of the year. Those who take this route northbound from California will see why when the train crosses into Oregon. After riding all night from the San Francisco Bay Area, passengers wake up to sunrise over alpine lakes and the snowcapped Cascades. As the tracks take you higher, you can see thousands of treetops in the foreground of dramatic peaks, especially if you're on the right-hand side of the car. From Cascade Summit, you head down into Eugene along the beautiful McKenzie River. Commentary over the loudspeaker and on the complimentary handbills enhances your sense of place. By the year 2000, an extension of this service to Vancouver B.C. is envisioned, if budget cuts don't preclude it.

The Empire Builder which leaves Portland en route to Chicago shows off the Columbia River Gorge to good advantage in ultramodern, bilevel Superliner coaches. With a trackbed on the Washington side of the Columbia, you get a distant perspective on the waterfalls and mountains across the river.

The trains on these routes are Superliners. These bilevel trains are replete with such people spaces as full-service dining cars and sightseers' lounges. Farther along, Christmas tree farms, llama ranches, and other pastoral landscapes will also make you glad to forgo the interstate. The wraparound windows in these cars and a smooth ride are conducive to passenger interaction. Gourmet food (prices range from $4 for eggs and hash browns to $12.95 for steak or salmon filet) in the dining cars bring back the good old days of rail travel. Budget travelers should pack their own, but the local bounty of each region on the menu rates at least one justifiable splurge. Microbrews and Oregon pinots can add to the fun.

Such amenities as reclineable seats (with leg rests) and a sightseers' lounge with swivel seats by picture windows are added pleasures. Should you be fortunate to get a "sleeper," they come equipped with air conditioning, light panels, piped-in music, and vanities. Fresh flowers are an appreciated extra in these units and a parlor car spares folks the hassle of competing with coach passengers for scarce space in the lounge car. Travelers can enjoy books, games, snacks (showcasing regional products), and complimentary wine and cheese in the Pacific Parlor car.

Trains are usually more expensive than buses but cheaper than planes. However, as with buses, special airfares occasionally undercut Amtrak.

Kids 2-11 travel half fare; children under two ride free. There are other discounts for groups, seniors, the disabled, and students. The company also advertises special holiday packages. The best buy for extended rail travel is a program called All Aboard America, which is operational year-round. For information and reservations, call (800) 872-7245, or obtain Amtrak's local station number through directory assistance.

Amtrak Fun

A nice introduction to Amtrak is the special Eugene-to-Klamath Falls roundtrip accompanied by a Forest Service interpreter. Trains leave Eugene Sun.-Fri. at 5:41 p.m. As the train begins its 110-mile, 4,500-foot ascent to Cascade Summit near Odell Lake, head to the left side of the observation car. This way you'll face east, toward the most scenic snowcapped peaks. As you climb up and out of the Willamette Valley, you pass from rural farms and timber communities through forest-fire burns and alpine vistas until the final downhill leg, which passes one of the largest lakes in Oregon—Klamath Lake. En route, Native American lore, pioneer history, forest management, and remarks about wildlife enhance the mile-by-mile commentary. The next morning, the Coast Starlight leaves Klamath Falls at 7:02 a.m. and arrives in Eugene at 11:16 a.m. One-way coach fare on this run is $43. A limited number of roundtrip excursion fares are offered daily for $65, which is $21 off the regular roundtrip ticket.

Other Trains

If the mystique of a lonely train whistle and vintage rail cars appeals to you, the following trips should avail some golden moments. The **Mt. Hood Railroad,** 110 Railroad Ave., Hood River 97031, tel. (503) 386-3556, was originally built in 1906 to bring lumber out of the Mt. Hood National Forest to Hood River mills. But since 1988 it has been carrying passengers in restored early-1900s coaches through the scenic Hood River Valley to Parkdale. The "blossom tours" in April and the "foliage trips" in October are particularly popular, as the trains wind through colorful cherry, apple, and pear orchards on their way up the valley. The chance to snap a photo of the classic train backdropped by Mt. Hood, buy fall fruit direct from the farmer at the Parkdale station, and

explore the National Historic Landmark depot at Hood River are other highlights. The 44-mile, four-hour roundtrip (call for prices and schedule updates) departs Hood River at 10 a.m. and gives you an hour to stretch your legs and shop in Parkdale before retracing its route and returning around 2 p.m. An afternoon train runs 3-7:15 p.m. The June-Sept. schedule offers trips Tuesday through Saturday. In the spring and fall the schedule is abbreviated, so call or write for the brochure that details blossom and foliage tours and other special events.

On December weekends, special Christmas tree trains offer a traditional holiday dinner at the Parkdale Grange and a chance to buy a Christmas tree and bring it back to Hood River by train. Saturday and Sunday, a luxuriously appointed dinner train is available for dinner and brunch respectively. Most tour packages cost less than $20. The dinner train is a pricier affair. Take exit 63 off I-84 to get to the station or walk down from the Hood River Hotel on Oak Street.

The **Crooked River Dinner Train,** O'Neil Road, Redmond 97756, tel. (541) 548-8630 after March, shows off the broad vistas of central Oregon's high desert as well as the state's indigenous delicacies and local wines. The 2.5-hour, 38-mile route through the Ochoco River Valley goes from Redmond to Prineville, offering Sunday champagne brunches, murder mystery theatre, and western theme dinners from mid-June till October. Call for prices and schedule updates. This is deluxe service that can run over $60 per person.

One of the attractions of the Sumpter area is the **Sumpter Valley Railroad Excursion,** P.O. Box 389, Baker City 97814, tel. (541) 894-2268. Passengers ride in two observation cars pulled by a wood-burning, narrow-gauge steam engine originally used to haul logs and ore in addition to people. There is also a restored 1920 car and an 1890 caboose. The seven-mile run from Phillips Reservoir to Sumpter only costs in the $10 range. The railroad is open from Memorial Day weekend through the last weekend in September with four runs daily at 10 a.m., noon, 2 p.m., and 4 p.m. Call or write the railroad to find out about special moonlight rides featuring live entertainment and hobo stew. Construction of a depot within Sumpter Valley Dredge State Park is in the planning stages. The railroad will make a 1.5 mile loop around the dredge. The depot will feature a museum and an auditorium. With the possible exception of the dredge in Fox, Alaska, this is the longest and most accessible gold dredge in the country.

BY BUS

Greyhound

Greyhound and its offshoots have regular connections to most population centers in Oregon. "Its offshoots" refers to the slew of smaller companies created in the wake of deregulation and Greyhound cost-cutting. In terms of the consumer experience, all this means is that you might have a bus with a different paint job that uses Greyhound terminals and fare structures. Pierce Pacific Stages, Porter, Valley Retriever, and other smaller companies operate on former Greyhound routes and have information on their schedules available from Greyhound personnel. If present trends continue, Greyhound will soon be operating mostly along I-5 in western Oregon. For an update on local carrier service, write to the State Tourism Division, 775 Sumner St., Salem 97310, for the Oregon passenger services pamphlet.

Since routes are continually being dropped and added, it's imperative to call the local Greyhound information number to supplement any printed schedule. The lack of terminals in remote locations is another reason to plan your bus trip carefully.

As for comfort, a ride on an MCI (the bus most commonly used) is both good news and bad news. First, the good news: on the West Coast, buses are usually no more than 10 years old, which means you can enjoy footrests, reclinable seats, and air-conditioning. The majority of folks will also appreciate the fact that no smoking is permitted on mass transit while in Oregon. And, should the bus on your route fill up, rest assured that the company will put another bus into service. In fact, this extra departure will often run as an express instead of a local, assuming there's a preponderance of passengers with a common destination.

The bad news is not that bad. Too much air-conditioning in summer and too much heat in winter can be dealt with by dressing accordingly. The unappetizing fare in many of the terminals can be avoided by bringing your own food.

The ticket prices, while usually twice the cost of driving, are still not out of line. Even though a special airline fare might occasionally undercut the bus on longer interstate routes, for the most part the 'Hound costs less than air tickets. Consider too that half-fare discounts are available to kids 5-11 and to the disabled traveling with an attendant. Another potential discount is the **Ameripass.** Discounts are available for 7, 15, and 30 days. Call Greyhound, tel. (800) 231-2222, for details and prices. It's cost-effective only if you're doing lots of travel in a short time. Also keep an eye out for various promotions which feature low-cost long-distance travel, particularly during the summer. The Ameripass and promotional fares are honored by most of the Greyhound franchises, but all connections should be clarified upon purchase.

A few hints about seating will ensure a smooth trip. The first and last seats on the bus can be a boon or a bane to your traveling comfort, depending on your needs. If a footrest and the ability to recline your seat are important, avoid these locations. The front seats are generally the only seats that lack footrests, and the back ones don't recline. Worse yet, restrooms are in the rear of the coach, which inevitably results in an unpleasant odor on longer trips for those seated close by. Despite these shortcomings, the views out the front windshield are the best to be had, and the back row of three seats offers the most stretching room.

Green Tortoise

One commonly hears the Green Tortoise, Green Tortoise Alternative Travel, P.O. Box 24459, San Francisco, CA 94127, tel. (800) 867-8647, referred to as "the hippie bus." Lest this conjure a seedy anachronism from the '60s, an update is in order. While the Tortoise is not exactly the Orient Express of two-lane blacktop, this mode of travel comes as close to a hotel on wheels as exists in this country. First, imagine a recycled Greyhound with the seats taken out. In their place are foam-rubber mattresses on elevated platforms behind a lounge area in the front of the bus. The chairs and tables here are converted to another sleeping area at night. Just bring your sleeping bag.

In Oregon, the fare is usually about 30% less than Greyhound's and might include such amenities as a stop for a home-cooked meal, $3-4 extra, and a soak in a hot spring. Passengers also have the option to pool money for groceries or eat at the restaurants near Tortoise stops. The clientele are a diverse group with surprisingly many Europeans and Australians. It's a rare Tortoise trip that doesn't turn into a party, although alcohol is prohibited. You can also bring your favorite cassettes to listen to on the Tortoise stereo. Another way Tortoise differs from Greyhound is in its policy of stopping at any freeway exit to pick up or drop off passengers (who are charged an extra $10 for this service). Kids shorter than four feet nine inches travel half price (one child per family) with an adult. Always reserve trips in advance.

The Tortoise heads southbound Sunday and Thursday, and northbound Monday and Friday traveling I-5 between Portland and Ashland. Established stops include Portland, Eugene, and Ashland. In addition, there are "flag stops" which necesitiate a call in advance, tel. (800) 847-8647. Pay the driver on departure with cash, travelers check, or money-order—no credit cards or personal checks are accepted.

BY CAR

The automobile remains the vehicle of choice for exploring the state. Oregon is blessed with good roads and light traffic on many thoroughfares. Consider that 141,000 miles of roads and 2.3

million registered cars works out to about 16 cars per mile. But before you jam down on the accelerator, keep in mind that the Man is equipped with the latest in radar technology and sometimes lies in wait out in the middle of nowhere.

Technically, you can only open up to 65 mph on sections of I-5 and I-84. The rest of the roads in the state have a 55 mph maximum speed limit. However, most people here seem to cruise at 5-10 miles above the speed limit and usually appear successful in avoiding trouble with the law. One final consideration is that speeding fines in Oregon are among the highest in the nation.

Nowadays Oregon roads are often depicted in TV automobile commercials—the inviting places replete with mountains majesty or cliffside coastal grandeur. The Columbia River Gorge Highway near Vista House and the Thomas Creek Bridge north of Brookings are two prime time TV auto ad locations, but there's beauty all over the state. The magnificent scenery prompted the construction of the first federally designated scenic highway in the Columbia River Gorge (rated by AAA among the country's top 10 most scenic roads) as well as the longest one, the 362 mile Oregon Coast Highway. Compounding the impression that Oregon is King of the roads was the 1996 designation of the Cascade Lakes Scenic HIghway outside of Bend as one of the top four scenic byways, denoted by the Scenic American Association for its "exceptional scenic, historic, and recreational value." In short, welcome to Car Country, where toll roads are the exception, the traffic is light, and the pavement is in generally good condition.

While the roads are beautiful and largely unfettered by rush-hour bottlenecks, the motorist must be sensitive to the nuances of the weather. Frequent cloudbursts can cause cars to hydroplane all over the road, thick palls of fog that hang over the Willamette Valley can cause multicar pileups, and the icy mountain roads of the Cascades and eastern Oregon also claim their share of victims.

Winter Driving
From late fall to early spring, expect snow on the Cascade mountain passes and I-5 through the Siskiyous; snow tires and/or chains are often required. Another thing to remember in the winter Cascades is your **snow park permit.** Without the daily sticker or season pass in your left-hand window, a car left in a snow park area will also receive a hefty ticket. This permit is essentially a duty levied by the state to pay for the upkeep of parking and rest areas in the mountains. Pick these up at the local DMV (Department of Motor Vehicles) for a few bucks prior to setting out, $1.50/day, $2.50 three consecutive days, and $9/season. They apply to travel November 15-April 15. It's often possible to buy them on-site at an area ski shop or other commercial establishment.

Another consideration for drivers is the fact that the road signs found throughout the state are sometimes less than explicit. Whether it's a turn sign coming up a half mile after the fact or directional markers obscured from view, this state seems to have more than its share of unwanted surprises for motorists.

Finally, keep in mind that in winter, the roads are bound to be covered with sand and gravel in places because the state does not use salts or other chemicals to melt snow and ice. The ground-up pumice from nearby lava deposits comes in many colors and provides great traction, but it sure can scratch up the paint on your car if you tailgate. Also, give oncoming trucks a wide berth to avoid the sandblasting likely to follow in their wake. Statewide road conditions, 24 hours a day from anywhere in Oregon, can be obtained by calling (503) 889-3999.

Fuel
Gas is readily available on the main western routes, but finding it can be a little trickier proposition on the more remote east side, especially after 5 p.m. Oregon's small-town gas stations are disappearing all over the state due to legislation mandating costly replacements of old gas tanks, which are prone to seepage. In other words, fill up before you leave the city. Another thing to remember is that Oregon is one of the few states that do not have self-service gasoline outlets, one reason why the state has some of the highest gas prices in the country. Another reason is the gas tax levied to help pay for Oregon's roads.

Rentals
Renting a car is no problem, assuming you have a credit card. The rental chains (Avis, Alamo,

Budget, Dollar, National, and Thrifty) have outlets in Portland and many other population centers. You can also flip through the yellow pages and try to save some bucks with an independent operator. But while *you* may not care about the way the Rent-a-Dents and Ugly Duckling Rent-a-Cars look, they're not the vehicles of choice to impress your date. Another thing to consider is that the major chains have more service centers to assist you in the event of any mechanical problems. And while it costs a little more, it is always a good idea to make certain that you're adequately insured.

Finally, members of American Automobile Association (AAA) are eligible for guidebooks, maps, and special tow/repair/insurance services. In Portland, call (503) 222-6734

BY BICYCLE

If you like to pedal on your own two wheels, Oregon is user-friendly to bicyclists. With special bike routes in cities like Eugene, Medford, and Portland, Oregon has given the right of way to cyclists. In the wake of the oil shocks of the 1970s, the Oregon legislature allocated one percent of the state highways budget to develop bike lanes and encourage energy-saving bicyclists. In addition to establishing routes throughout the state with these funds, many special parks were developed with bicycle and foot access specifically in mind. For example, minutes away from Eugene's downtown is the Willamette River Greenway bike-path system, which winds through a string of parks. Oxygen-rich air from the vegetation and the peaceful gurgling of the Willamette make a pleasant change from the fumes and roar of traffic. A decent biker could easily beat a car across town during rush hour using the bicycle network.

A similar respect has been granted to the cyclist on the open road. According to the Oregon *Motor Vehicles Handbook,* a bicycle has the right of way, which means that cars and trucks are not supposed to run you off the road. Nonetheless, remember that there are always motorists whose concepts of etiquette vis-à-vis bikers were formulated elsewhere. Play it safe out there: wear a helmet and reflective clothing, keep close to the right of the road, and al-

ways use a light at night. While most of the drivers will give you a wide berth and slow down if necessary in tight spots, rush hours, traffic patterns, and circumstance can change that.

The *Oregon Bicycling Guide,* distributed by the Oregon Department of Transportation, State Highways Division, Salem 97310, is a good pamphlet to have around to help plan a bike trip. This publication includes statewide maps of bike trails and routing suggestions as well as listings for rental/repair shops and bike touring groups. Be aware that transporting your own machine cross-country can sometimes be a problem, as every carrier has its own set of rules and regulations. Check with the bus, train, or plane company to make sure that you are within the allowable parameters.

Mountain bike enthusiasts might want to write the Mt. Hood Ski Bowl Bike Shop, 87000 E. US 26, Government Camp 97028, tel.(503) 272-3206, for a free bike trail map and information on using the chairlift to transport you and your bike to these pathways. Rentals are available.

Fortunately, there are some companies that offer pre-planned group bicycle trips, with everything from the bicycle to the meals and lodging included. **Tour Oregon Style,** P.O. Box 987, Oregon City 97045, tel. (503) 655-2831, has a deluxe seven-day coastal bicycle trip that traverses spectacular US 101. All you have to do is pedal; they take care of the rest. The cost is $299 per person, and a small discount is given to groups. **Bicycle Adventures,** Dept. K, P.O. Box 7875, Olympia, WA 98507, tel. (206) 786-0989, offers a longer Oregon/Washington package.

Oregon is user-friendly to bicyclists.

BOB RACE

HEALTH AND SAFETY

EMERGENCY SERVICES

Throughout Oregon, dial 911 for medical, police, or fire emergencies. Isolated rural areas often have separate numbers for all three, and they're listed under "Information and Services" in each section of this book. Then, too, one may always dial 0 to get the operator. Most hospitals offer a 24-hour emergency room. Oregon's larger cities maintain switchboard referral services as well as hospital-sponsored free advice lines. Remember that medical costs are high here, as in the rest of the U.S.; emergency rooms are the most expensive. However, low-cost inoculation and testing for certain infectious diseases is available through the auspices of county health departments in major cities.

HEALTH HAZARDS

Hypothermia

In this part of the country, the hiker should be alerted to problems with hypothermia—when your body loses more heat than can be recovered and shock ensues. Eighty-five percent of hiking-related fatalities are due to this malady. In fact, the damp chill of the Northwest climate poses more of a hypothermia threat than do colder climes with low humidity. In other words, it doesn't have to be freezing in order for death from hypothermia to occur; wind and wetness often turn out to be greater risk factors. Remember that a wet human body loses heat 23 times faster than a dry one. Even runners who neglect to dress in layers in the cold fog of western Oregon often contract low-level symptoms during the accelerated cooling-off period following a workout.

The affliction sets in when the core temperature of the body drops to 95° F or below. One of the first signs is a diminished ability to think and act rationally. Speech can become slurred, and uncontrollable shivering usually takes place. Stumbling, memory lapses, and drowsiness also tend to characterize the afflicted. Unless the body temperature can be raised several degrees by a knowledgeable helper, cardiac arrhythmia and/or arrest may occur. Getting out of the wind and rain into a dry, warm environment is essential for survival. This might mean placing the victim into a prewarmed sleeping bag, which can be prepared by having a healthy hiker strip and climb into the bag with his or her endangered partner. Ideally, a groundcloth should be used to insulate the sleeping bag from cold surface temperatures. Internal heat can be generated by feeding the victim high-carbohydrate snacks and hot liquids. Placing wrapped heated objects against the victim's body is also a good way to restore body heat. Be careful not to raise body heat too quickly, which could also cause cardiac problems. If body temperature doesn't drop below 90°, chances for complete recovery are good; with body temperatures between 80° and 90°, victims are more likely to suffer some sort of lasting damage. Most victims won't survive a body temperature below 80°.

Measures you can take to prevent hypothermia include eating a nutritious diet, avoiding overexertion followed by exposure to wet and cold, and dressing warmly in layers of wool and polypropylene. Wool insulates even when wet, and because polypropylene tends to "wick" moisture away from your skin, it makes a good first layer. Gore-Tex and its counterparts like Helly-Tech or other new "miracle" fabrics make for more comfortable rain gear than nylon because they don't become cumbersome and hot in a steady rain. Finally, wear a hat: more radiated heat leaves from the head than from any other part of the body.

Frostbite

This is not generally a major problem until the combined air and windchill temperature falls below 20° F. Outer appendages like fingers and toes are the most susceptible, with the ears and nose running a close second. Frostbite occurs when blood is redirected out of the limbs to warm vital organs in cold weather, and the exposed parts of the face and peripherals cool very rapidly. Mild frostbite is characterized by extremely pale skin with random splotchiness; in more severe cases, the skin will take on a gray, ashen look and feel numb. At the first signs of suspected frostbite, you should gently warm the afflicted area. In more aggravated cases, immerse hands and feet in warm water between 108-113° F. Do not massage or risk further skin damage. Warming frostbitten areas against the skin of another person is suitable for less serious frostbite. The warmth of a campfire cannot help once the skin is discolored. As with hypothermia, it's important to avoid exposing the hands and feet to wind and wetness by dressing properly.

Poison Oak
Neither the best intentions nor knowledge from a lifetime in the woods can spare the western Oregon hiker at least one brush with poison oak. In this writer's experience, 90% of the afflicted campers knew to look out for the three shiny leaves, but still woke up the next morning looking like a pepperoni pizza.

Since the plant seems to thrive in hardwood forests, it's always a good idea to wear long pants, shirts, and other covering on excursions to this ecosystem. Major infestations of the plant are seldom encountered in the Coast Range. In the fall, the leaves are tinged with red, giving the appearance of Christmas decorations. Unfortunately, this is one gift that keeps giving long after the holidays. Even when the plant is totally denuded in winter, the toxicity still remains a threat. Whatever the season, fair-skinned people tend to be more prone to severe symptoms. Direct contact is not the only way to get the rash. Someone else's clothing or a pet can transmit the oils; you can even get it by inhaling smoke if the shrub is in a burning pile of brush.

When you know that you've been exposed, try to get your clothes off before the toxic resin permeates your garments. Follow up as soon as possible with a cold bath treated with liberal amounts of baking soda or bleach, or a shower

Rhus diversiloba,
*the infamous
poison oak*

BOB RACE

with lots of abrasive soap (Fels Naptha or Boraxo). Don't use hot water because it opens up the pores and can aggravate the condition. If this doesn't stop the symptoms, cooling the inflamed area with copious applications of aloe vera or calamine lotion, which draws out the contaminants, is another recourse. Clay is also considered effective in expelling the poison. In emergency situations, cortisone cream might kill a poison oak rash but can take lots of healthy cells along with it, too. Some tree-planters build up their immunity by eating poison-oak honey and drinking milk from goats who graze on the weed. Health-food stores now sell a poison oak extract that, if taken over time prior to exposure, is said to mollify the symptoms.

Scientists in Oregon might have come up with the best answer of all. Tech Laboratories, P.O. Box 1958, Albany 97321, tel. (541) 926-4577, has developed a pre-exposure lotion, a cleanser to remove toxic plant oils from the skin, and a chemical agent to deal with the itch. All products are sold at Wal-Mart outlets throughout the state.

Allergies
Even if you come out of the forests unscathed, Willamette Valley-bound travelers during springtime might have to confront another pernicious health hazard: perennial allergic rhinitis. With the world's highest volume of grass seed produced between Salem and Eugene, allergy-susceptible visitors should expect some sneezing and wheezing as well as itchy eyes during the June-July pollination season. In addition to grass seed, the earlier bloom of various ornamentals throughout western Oregon might occasion such discomfort.

As allergy shots are not always practical, antihistamines are often resorted to as a short-term remedy for those passing through. Unfortunately, such side effects as depression and sleepiness have been attributed to them. Lately, many Willamette Valley doctors have been prescribing Allegra, an asthma medicine. This prescription drug (available over the counter in

Canada) combats allergic reactions without side effects. Regular chiropractic adjustments have helped some residents build their own natural resistence to the pollens. Many health-food stores offer herbal remedies, but these both usually fall short of the quick-fix relief demanded by travelers. Finally, honey from the area of the offending allergen taken regularly several months prior to the allergy season is often mentioned as a folk remedy.

Beaver Fever

Folk remedies just won't do it for that other hiker headache, "beaver fever." Medically known as giardiasis, this syndrome afflicts those who drink water contaminated by *Giardia lamblia* parasites. Even water from cold, clear streams can be infested by this microorganism, which is spread throughout the backcountry by beavers, musk-

rats, livestock, and other hikers. Boiling water for 20 minutes is the most common prevention to spare you endless hours as king or queen of the throne during and after your trip. (At higher elevations, it's a good idea to boil water longer than 20 minutes.) Should that prove inconvenient, try better living through chemistry: apply five drops of chlorine, or preferably iodine, to every quart of water and let it sit for a half hour. Also available are water pumps that filter out *giardia* and other organisms, but they cost about $20 and up. First-Need is a filter/pump device that costs about $35. Potable water is also achieved by purification pills like Potable Aqua, iodine-based tablets that cost about a nickel each. However, these chemical approaches are less reliable than boiling. Whatever method you choose, try to avoid major rivers or any creek that runs through a meadow as your source of water.

WHAT TO TAKE

Without belaboring commonsensical considerations, a few comments are in order regarding the proper apparel for Oregon's rainforest-to-desert diversity. To begin, remember that this region places a premium on practical and informal dress. A predilection for the outdoors as well as a lack of pretense explain the relative dearth of ties and haute couture even in somewhat formal urban settings.

The Old West is still alive and well east of the Cascades. In the Oregon desert regions, boots are like a second skin. This isn't so much tradition as good sense. It's always advisable to wear boots around horses and when walking in desertlike areas. Durable footwear certainly makes being stepped on or bitten less annoying.

Another concern in the desert is keeping cool. Carry water and wear a shade hat in summer. Cowboy hats work exceptionally well and are in vogue in this region. To avoid dehydration, Gatorade, 7-Up, or good old H_2O might be your best recourse; it's even better than salt tablets or beer for restoring evaporated sodium rates because alcohol depletes the body's water by accelerating perspiration and elimination.

Whether it's the subzero temperatures of the desert melting you or the western Oregon mist

cutting through your clothes, spare yourself needless discomfort by being prepared. Despite goose down's superior insulating qualities when dry, it's almost useless when wet because it clumps up and no longer traps air. The synthetic down imitators insulate well and do much better than down when wet but have a stiffness that bothers active wearers. Nonetheless, given the pervasiveness of moisture here, coats with Thinsulate and/or synthetic fleece are becoming more popular than down. A good test of the garment's suitability for vigorous movement is to put it on and quickly raise your fist to your shoulder in an arm-flexing motion. In a better-quality parka, you shouldn't feel insulation material restricting motion at your elbow.

Finally, a word for those who find the lightweight lofting and warming qualities of down hard to kick. These days Eddie Bauer, a well-known Northwest outfitter, has married Gore-Tex to down, so you have a waterproof shell covering a warm insulation layer. Recommended down care for diehards is nothing more than throwing the garment in the washer with powdered detergent, then drying it with sneakers to beat the pockets of down into shape. Do this twice a year to maintain the loft.

INFORMATION AND SERVICES

INFORMATION

Maps

For a full list of books, maps, and pamphlets on Oregon national parks and forests write to: **Northwest Interpretive Association,** Forest Service/Park Service Outdoor Recreation Information, 83 South King St., Suite 212, Seattle, WA 98104, tel. (206) 553-7958. Another good source of useful information is the **Explorers Map of Oregon,** available at Exclusive Maps, Ltd., Suite 369, 1430 Willamette St., Eugene 97401, tel. (541) 935-7499, $7.50. This map depicts hot springs, fossil beds, caves, gold-mining areas, remote beaches, wild areas, Indian village sites, artifact sites, abandoned historical places, petroglyph and pictograph locations, gem, mineral, and precious metal sites, stage and immigrant routes, 19th-century fort locations, Indian travel routes and battlegrounds, anomalies and curiosities, and notes on the state's history and prehistory. The best all-in-one collection of topo maps, entitled *Oregon Atlas and Gazeteer,* is available from **DeLorme Mapping,** P.O. Box 298, Freeport ME 04032.

Another local mapmaker, **Raven Maps,** 34 N. Central, Medford 97501, tel. (541) 773-1436 or (800) 237-0798, is esteemed among the cartographic cognoscenti. Based on U.S. Geological Survey maps, these computer-enhanced topographic projections depict vertical relief (by shading) and three-dimensionality. Many of Raven's offerings are large enough to cover a dining-room table, with costs commonly in the $15-20 range. All Raven maps are printed in fade-resistant inks on fine-quality 70-pound paper and are also available in vinyl-laminated versions suitable for framing.

The Forest Service's primary walk-in sales outlet for topographical maps in Portland is **Nature of the Northwest,** 800 N.E. Oregon St., Room 177, tel. (503) 731-4444. Other places in Portland to buy outdoor recration maps on-site include REI and Andy and Bax (see "Outdoor Activities" for addresses). Procuring free state highway maps in-preson can be done at visitor information entities such as the ones listed in the chart Ask Us, or you can get one mailed directly from the State Tourism Commission, tel. (800) 547-7842. Other places to get maps include the U.S. Forest Service, 333 S.W. 1st Ave., Portland 97208, tel. (503) 326-2877, the Oregon Dept. of Forestry, Graphics Division, 2600 State St., Bldg. E, Salem 97310, tel. (503) 945-7336, the Oregon Dept. of Geology, 5375 Monuent Dr., Grants Pass 97526,

ASK US

The following information centers can be called toll free, and each has a wide variety of information available on its respective locale.

Bay Area Chamber of Commerce, 50 E. Central St., P.O. Box 210, Coos Bay 97420, tel. (800) 824-8486.

Eugene/Springfield Convention and Visitors Bureau, 115 W. 8th Ave. Suite 190, Eugene 97401, tel. (800) 547-5445.

Gold Beach Chamber of Commerce, 1225 S. Ellensburg St., Gold Beach 97444, tel. (800) 525-2334.

Grants Pass Visitor and Convention Bureau, P.O. Box 970, 1510 N.E. 6th, Grants Pass 97526, tel. (800) 547-5927.

Lincoln City Visitor and Convention Bureau, 801 S.W. US 101, Lincoln City 97367, tel. (800) 452-2151.

Pendleton Chamber of Commerce, 25 S.W. Dorion St., Pendleton 97801, tel. (800) 547-8911.

Portland Visitor Information Association (POVA), 26 S.W. Salmon St. Portland, OR 97208, tel. (800) 345-3214

Southern Oregon Reservation Center, P.O. Box 477, Ashland 97522, tel. (800) 547-8052.

Seaside Chamber of Commerce, P.O. Box 7, 7 N. Roosevelt St., Seaside 97138, tel. (800) 444-6740.

tel. (541) 476-2496, and Oregon Dept. of Geology, 1831 1st St., Baker City, 97815, tel. (541) 523-3133.

A 28- by 38-inch relief map and brochure produced by **Emerald Imagery,** send $5.50 to P.O. Box 3429, Eugene 97403, is perhaps the best linear introduction to the area of southeastern Oregon. Entitled *Visitors Guide to Oregon High Desert Wilderness,* it demarcates the region's mountains, deserts, and grasslands, as well as boundaries of wildlife refuges, national parks, preserves, monuments, BLM wilderness, and the country inside the proposed Oregon High Desert Protection Act. Fans of annotated pictographic maps should contact **Nutshell Maps,** Box 230998, Tigard, OR, 97281, tel. (800) 779-7056, for maps of central Oregon and the Oregon coast.

Finally, you can visit the virtual visitor center operated by the Oregon Dept. of Geology and Mineral Industries and the USDA Forest Service, http://www.naturenw.org/index.html, for maps as well as information on the geology and national forests of Oregon.

Accommodations and Chambers of Commerce

The **Oregon Tourism Commission,** 775 Summer St. N.E., Salem 97310, tel. (800) 547-7842, will send you a full list of local chambers of commerce and tourist information offices upon request. They also feature many well-produced free pamphlets on different regions, seasons, and activities. Especially recommended are their winter/fall activities booklets and regional loop tour brochures. See the chart Ask Us for a list of helpful information centers. The **Oregon Lodging Association,** 12724 S.E. Stark St., Portland 97233, tel. (503) 255-5135, has a good set of lodging listings across the state. The **Oregon Tourism Web site,** http://www.traveloregon.com, can help plan trips with a search menu keyed to regions of the state or activity, with links to specific sites giving details (including phone numbers) of resorts, motels, B&Bs, and attractions.

MONEY

Although the prices listed for hotels, meals, and attractions were current at press time, they will undoubtedly increase due to inflation. But while the rates are not absolute, they should nonetheless prove useful in comparing prices between establishments.

In any case, you'll need Uncle George or plastic to make your transactions in Oregon, and foreign currency can be exchanged at most major banks throughout the state. Canadian coins in particular are considered by many merchants as the bane of existence, and they will not accept them. Banks also turn up their noses at Canadian silver, because it costs them more in shipping and handling than it is worth. The major exceptions to this are Hood River businesses that cater to Canadian windsurfers.

But the presidents on your greenbacks aren't the only ones smiling, because Oregon is one of a handful of states in the country that *does not* have a sales tax. Many visitors take advantage of Oregon's generally low prices and lack of sales tax to purchase big-ticket items to take home. On the other hand, you will find that room taxes range about 5-12%, depending on the locale.

MEASUREMENTS

Oregon—like the rest of the U.S.—has been slow to join the world community and adopt the metric system. You may see some aberrations now and then, like a bank sign giving the temperature in Celsius, or perhaps liter-sized containers at the supermarket, but basically Oregon clings to the English system. To aid the traveler not familiar with the English system, we have included a conversion chart in the back of the book.

COMMUNICATIONS

Mail

Most post offices open between 7-9 a.m., and close between 5-6 p.m. In some of the larger cities, you will find main branches open on Saturday. Sometimes drugstores or card shops have a postal substation open on weekends and holidays when the government operations are closed. If it happens to be Sunday and the post office is closed, you can also get stamps from grocery stores and hotels, with little or no markup. Oregon also has many Federal Express, UPS, and other private shipping companies operating across the state to complement government services.

Telephone

Oregon has two area codes: **503** for the greater Portland metropolitan area including Mt. Hood and most of the Columbia River Gorge, as well as Astoria to Lincoln City on the coast, and Portland to Salem in the Willamette Valley; **541** for the rest of the state. Refer to the area code map if you are not sure of the long distance prefix. For long-distance calls within the state, dial 1 before the correct area code and then the seven-digit telephone number. For directory assistance dial 1, the appropriate area code for the locale you are searching, and then 555-1212.

Media

The two largest-circulation dailies in the state come out of the most populous cities, Portland and Eugene. Both the *Oregonian* and the *Eugene Register Guard* have gained a bevy of Pulitzers and other awards. In general, the *Guard* has fewer columns generated by wire services and stringers than does the *Oregonian*. The result is a big-town paper with a charming small-town feel.

As for the *Oregonian,* there are several special sections of interest to the traveler. On Wednesday, the "Outdoors" section offers a digest of activities for the active traveler—be it hiking trail suggestions, fishing, hunting, and skiing tips or news about a natural history museum. In like measure, the Wednesday "Science" section might have a geology article explaining part of Oregon's landscape. On Friday, "Arts and Entertainment" outlines a full cultural calendar with news and reviews of movies, plays, concerts, literary readings, gallery openings, and restaurants.

The *Oregonian* is distributed statewide, while the *Guard* is carried in newspaper dispensers as far away as the south coast of Oregon. The editorial content of each paper is mostly middle of the road but can be activist on environmental issues. While this last assessment would be challenged by residents of different parts of this politically diverse state, an equal number of letters to the editor from the extreme right and the extreme left each day indicates a measure of balance.

Portland and Eugene also dominate the broadcast media, serving far-flung rural communities by means of electronic translators. What is especially noteworthy throughout the state is tremendous support of listener-subscriber public TV and radio. Many Oregon-generated shows, news blurbs, and features are carried by out-of-state public radio outlets.

Warm Springs Indian Reservation's KWSO 91.9 FM is a progressive country radio station spiced with elders chanting in the morning and topical discussions of native issues by younger tribemembers.

Even though regional monthlies like *Northwest Travel* and **Sunset** do not have a strictly Oregon focus, there are usually several destination pieces about the state in each edition of these magazines.

Oregon Parks and *Oregon Coast* magazines confine their coverage to subjects closer to home. All these periodicals can be obtained at newsstands throughout the state.

BOB RACE

THE OREGON COAST
INTRODUCTION

The Oregon coast is one of those blessed corners of the earth where you come upon a little piece of paradise wherever you go. The south coast is a world apart, with a landscape dominated by dense evergreen forest, parting to reveal black-sand beaches and exceptional rock formations. One often gets the feeling here that sheep and cattle outnumber people.

The central coast is a land of superlatives, boasting such features as the largest ocean-front dunes in the world, the highest coastal viewpoint accessible by car, and the only mainland sea lion rookery located in the lower 48 states. In addition, *The Guinness Book of World Records* recognizes Oregon's other coastal claims to fame, like the smallest navigable harbor and the shortest river in the world.

The north coast can be billed as "the real end of the Oregon Trail." Although that famous frontier wagon road ends inland, the pioneering spirit that it connotes is on display here by the sea. Lewis and Clark, John Jacob Astor, and the legions of settlers who conquered the wilderness are commemorated in the landmark buildings and historical placards of Astoria, the oldest U.S. city west of Missouri. In like measure, many works in north coast galleries draw inspiration from these same historical antecedents.

While each part of the coast possesses a distinct regional flavor, together they have one thing in common. Whether it's virgin beachfront, a lofty promontory, or simply a cozy bed and breakfast, each section of Oregon's seascape will leave you hungering for more.

THE LAND

The Oregon coast includes 362 miles of rainforest, sand dunes, high-rise basalt headlands, and tidal pools, showcasing marine worlds in miniature. This scenery is broken up by over a dozen major rivers, which flow past mountain barriers to the sea. The estuaries of these rivers

OREGON COAST

WASHINGTON
COLUMBIA RIVER
ASTORIA
101
30
SEASIDE
CANNON BEACH
26
NEHALEM RIVER
TILLAMOOK BAY
6
WILSON RIVER
TILLAMOOK
SIUSLAW NATIONAL FOREST
18
LINCOLN CITY
22
DEPOE BAY
GLENEDEN BEACH
NEWPORT
101
20
WALDPORT
34
YACHATS
ALSEA RIVER
SIUSLAW NATIONAL FOREST
FLORENCE
126
SIUSLAW RIVER
OREGON DUNES NATIONAL RECREATION AREA
REEDSPORT
WINCHESTER BAY
38
GOLDEN & SILVER FALLS STATE PARK
NORTH BEND
CHARLESTON
COOS BAY
COOS RIVER
UMPQUA RIVER
BANDON
425
COQUILLE
42
5
PORT ORFORD
SISKIYOU
ROGUE RIVER
NATIONAL
FOREST
GOLD BEACH
KALMIOPSIS
WILDERNESS
5
101
199
BROOKINGS
SMITH RIVER
REDWOOD NATIONAL PARK
MIDDLE FORK SMITH RIVER
SMITH RIVER NATIONAL RECREATION AREA
SMITH RIVER
CRESCENT CITY

PACIFIC OCEAN

0   20 mi
0   20 km

© MOON PUBLICATIONS, INC.

offer resting places for migratory waterfowl as well as a thoroughfare for spawning fish. They cut through the Klamath Mountains in the southern quarter of the region and bisect parts of the Coast Range in the north.

Of the two ranges, the Klamaths are much older, dating back 225 million years. By contrast, the Coast Range, beginning near Coos Bay, emerged from the sea between 20 and 50 million years ago. The mountains of each of these coastal cordilleras rarely exceed several thousand feet in elevation. The uplifts that created both the Klamaths and the Coast Range also left black-sand beaches and offshore volcanic plugs, as well as headlands made of erosion-resistant basalt.

A look at the globe offers a bird's-eye view of this dramatic meeting of rock and tide: the 6,000 miles of water lying between Oregon and Japan are largely unfettered by archipelagoes and reefs—the longest stretch of open ocean on earth. This impression of remoteness and isolation is compounded by the fact that Cape Blanco stands as the westernmost point in the contiguous United States. Finally, this extraordinary region is roughly equidistant from the equator and the north pole. It all adds up to a complex interplay of climatic and geologic forces that have orchestrated nature on a grand scale.

Land Use Crisis

Oregon's Beach Bills of 1967 and 1972 were written to guarantee public access to the state's gem of a coastline. In recent years, however, certain sections of this "publicly owned" paradise have increasingly become exclusive bailiwicks of the wealthy with gated communities cutting off access to certain beaches. Astute lawyers have used "grandfather clauses" and other dodges to undermine the vision of public beaches first enunciated by Governor Oswald West in 1913. The decline of the resource-based economy and the higher standards of living brought in by newly arrived retirees has also displaced many loggers and fishermen who had traditionally been the bedrock of the coastal population. And in upscale tourist towns like Cannon Beach, police, tradespeople, and hotel/restaurant workers frequently commute from out of town. Widened traffic corridors, and polluted runoff water from drain fields are other outgrowths of the "discovery" of

LINCOLN CITY VISITOR AND CONVENTION BUREAU

the view from Cascade Head: a picture-perfect slice of the Oregon Coast

the Oregon Coast. At the same time, there are enough tracts of preserved land and small towns away from coastal access roads here to sustain the impression of a bucolic time warp.

CLIMATE

Coastal rain or shine begins with the Japanese current. This offshore system of tepid water evaporates up into billowy cloud masses which are blown inland by the Pacific westerlies. If these clouds don't drop their moisture over the water or on the shoreline, chances are good that the Coast Range's lower temperatures will create condensation and rain. This translates into a 166-inch annual maritime rainfall, with a 150 inch average over the mountains. (In the winter of 1996-97, Laurel Mountain in the Coast range near Lincoln City sustained 204 inches, Oregon's record). In between, the strip of land near sea level often sees half of these totals.

But generalized regional precipitation totals tell only part of the story. On the south coast, Port Orford receives an average of 108 inches of rain annually. Coos Bay, a few towns to the north, often gets half this amount. If this sounds foreboding, remember that almost all of these totals are racked up during the winter months. Keep in mind, too, that in the midst of this gloom, midwinter dry spells with 60°-plus temperatures commonly occur. These respites also serve to thaw coastal habitués used to temperatures in the 40s . . . not that they need it! With infrequent freezes and rarely recorded snowfall, Old Man Winter definitely pulls his punches here. In fact, Coos Bay is often touted as having the mildest (in terms of absence of extremes) year-round climate in the United States.

Here's a little tip for those looking to take advantage of midwinter lulls in the gray wetness which hangs over much of western Oregon. Should you be inland during a rainy spell, keep an eye on satellite photos on TV or in the paper. By the time a major storm reaches the interior, there is often a respite between fronts at the coast. By anticipating the approach of a "blue hole," you can time your visit to coincide with the arrival of clear weather, short-lived as it may be.

In general, count on good traveling weather mid-April through mid-September, with a preponderance of daytime highs in the 60s. Within this period, there might be enough June gloom to dismay travelers accustomed to simmering southland beaches, but storm-watching is an acquired taste. An added plus is that when summertime inversions drive temperatures up east of the Coast Range, the heat will draw cooler maritime air to the shore. The mountains often lock in these welcome fronts, though they also can cause coastal fog and overcast conditions to linger. Nonetheless, respite from the characteristic morning fog banks in summer is often only minutes away upriver on one of the many tidal estuaries. As a general rule, September is the most reliable month for clear coastal weather. However, it's helpful to remember the local adage, "little boys who tell lies grow up to be Oregon weathermen."

Finally, newcomers to the region should know that the icy temperatures of the coastal waters (as low as 40-45°) make the beaches more valued for beachcombing than for swimming. Even in the hottest days of summer, water temperature doesn't exceed 62°. Ironically, 20-30 miles offshore, the warming effects of the Kuroshio current create subtropical conditions.

FLORA AND FAUNA

Sandwiched between the mountains and the sea are mixed conifer forests of Douglas fir, spruce, cedar, and hemlock. Due to the construction industry's penchant for Douglas fir, which they replant assiduously, this tree predominates. The conifers are broken up by pockets of alder, oak, vine maple, and myrtle trees. A largely edible understory of thimbleberry, salmonberry, blackberry, and salal are interspersed among the ferns and mosses that carpet the forest floor. In addition to Brookings's Azalea Festival and Florence's Rhododendron Festival, coast-bound travelers come to take in such horticultural highlights as the insect-eating Darlingtonia plant and the myrtle tree, said to be native only to the Holy Land and southern Oregon. Serious botanists might search out the pine mushroom, exclusive to the Oregon dunes and Japan, or explore the Kalmiopsis Wilderness near the south coast, habitat to many rare plants.

Such eclecticism is paralleled in the animal kingdom. Consider, for example, the nutria and the boomer. The nutria was brought to Oregon in the 1930s from South America to be raised for its fur. After numerous escapes, this furry rodent was able to breed in the wild and establish a niche in the woodlands of the Coast Range. The boomer is another distinctive resident of this ecosystem. Similar in appearance to a beaver (minus the flat tail), the predilection of this primitive squirrel species for eating Douglas fir seedlings has made it the scourge of the timber industry. Currently an open season encourages hunting of both these varmints.

By contrast, biologists find the boomer a fascinating object of study because it evolved independently of other rodents for at least 40 million years, and possibly 100 million. In this vein, a species of tailed toad considered to be among the most primitive in the world also stimulates interest. Because the species apparently diverged from other frogs and toads during the Jurassic period 150 million years ago, biologists at the 1994 American Association for the Advancement of Science Convention consider its preservation (and that of the boomers) more important than that of the spotted owl.

Other coastal critters include muskrat, raccoon, Roosevelt elk, black-tailed deer, bald eagles, and an impressive array of anadromous fish, shore birds, and migratory waterfowl. Regional estuaries and the Oregon dunes are the best places to take in this wildlife show. Another distinctive resident of coastal forests is the giant Pacific salamander. This stout, mottled creature grows to a length of more than one foot . Sightings are rare, but hikers occasionally encounter them around stagnant pools in the Kalmiopsis. This is the largest salamander in the world.

Oregon's Seal and Sea Lion Species

Pacific harbor seals, California sea lions, and Steller sea lions are frequently sighted in Oregon waters. Look for Pacific harbor seals in colder waters such as the Columbia River estuary during the winter. It's easy to distinguish them from sea lions because they have no ear flaps and, at 300 pounds, are much smaller.

California sea lions are the animals you might have seen in circuses. These 1,000-pound mammals are characterized by small ear flaps. Like seals, they have flippers, but only in front, unlike their pinniped cousins. They also lack the underfur of seals and prefer warmer waters.

Steller sea lions are seen frequently at the Sea Lion Caves near Florence (see "Sights" under "Florence and Vicinity" later in this chapter). They also breed on reefs off Gold Beach and Port Orford. They are the largest sea lion species, sometimes weighing over a ton. Their coats tend to be more gray than the black-coated California sea lion. They also differ from their California coun-

rhododendron

BOB RACE

terparts in that they are comfortable in cold water.

Finally, the most northerly breeding colony of elephant seals established themselves on Shell Island off Cape Arago in 1993. Since that time, they've returned every year. The species were so named because the male's snout looks like a squat elephant trunk.

HISTORY

Native Peoples

No one knows when the first inhabitants took up residence on the Oregon coast. Archaeological dig sites at Yaquina Head and Cape Perpetua yielded implements 4,000-5,000 years old, some of the oldest found on the coast. But the sea level rose significantly before that time, inundating earlier remains. In fact, the oldest dig site at the coast, Tahkenitch Landing, has been dated at 9,000 to 8,630 B.C. Recent finds near Cape Perpetua and in Curry County also point to a longer period of human occupation on the coast. Willamette Valley archaeological sites dating back 8,000 to 10,000 years and the Applegate Valley excavation in southern Oregon that unearthed projectile points 10,000 years old also corroborate this theory.

What is clear is that by the time the white explorers and settlers came here, Indian culture was a patchwork of languages and cultural traits as diverse as the topography. Most native coastal communities typically included a dozen or more small bands linked by a common dialect. These bands or villages consisted of perhaps an extended family in one or two houses, or a larger grouping under a headman. The linguistic and lifestyle divisions between native communities were maintained by mountains, an ocean too rough for canoes, and other geographic barriers.

In the aftermath of the Rogue Indian Wars in the 1850s, the Chetco, Coquille, Coos, Umpqua, Siuslaw, Alsea, Yaquina, Nestucca, and Tillamook peoples were grouped together with the Rogue River tribes and forced to live on the 1.1-million-acre Siletz Reservation, and so the culture and heritage of many indigenous peoples were lost forever. More tragic than the watering down of cultural distinctiveness was the huge mortality rate resulting from natives being "removed" to the Siletz Reservation.

Over the years, whatever wealth the Siletz tribes had left was stripped as a result of the United States not honoring a multitude of treaties. The final indignity came in 1951 with the termination of the Siletz Reservation. The divestiture of tribal status meant the loss of health services, educational support, tax exemptions, and other benefits. Predictably, this last in a long line of forced transitions brought about alcoholism and despair in many native peoples. In 1977, Senator Mark Hatfield and Congressman Les AuCoin helped push a bill through Congress for tribal restoration. This has resulted in the tribe getting the wherewithal to flourish economically in everything from logging and construction projects to such enterprises as the Siletz Tribal Smokehouse in Depoe Bay (see "Practicalities" under "Depoe Bayand Vicinity" later in this chapter). The latter endeavor has been accompanied by an interest in the old ways and a renewed sense of pride in native identity.

The Coming of the White Man

In 1542, Juan Rodríguez Cabrillo sailed into what are now southern Oregon waters. Sixty years later, Sebastiáno Vizcaíno came to the same area, but he also failed to lay claim for the armada. A succession of Spanish, English, American, and Russian explorers followed in search of whales, sea otter and beaver pelts, and hides for the tallow trade. But the major impetus for exploring this coast was the quest for the mythic Northwest Passage—a sea route connecting the Pacific with the Atlantic. While written histories vary as to the exact dates and locations of these excursions, hundreds of shipwrecks remain as evidence of the exploratory zeal of past centuries. At the northern edge of this rock-studded graveyard for ancient mariners, the fur-trading center of Astoria was established in 1811. Several decades later, gold mining near the Rogue River drew more settlers to the south coast. It was a later gold rush, however, that had the greatest implications for the development of the region.

In 1849, the influx of prospectors into California's Sierra Nevada occasioned a housing boom in San Francisco, port of entry to the goldfields. The demand for Coast Range timber and foodstuffs from Oregon's inland agricultural valleys caused downriver Pacific ports like Astoria and Newport to flourish. As a result, the coastline of California's friendly neighbor to the north was able to develop the necessary economic base for it to prosper and endure.

The exploitation of coastal resources was so successful that Governor Oswald West had to spearhead legislation restricting beachfront development in 1913. This set the tone for future preservationist measures in the state. Today, Oregon has more state parks than anyplace else in America, with the majority of these located on the coast.

WHALEWATCHING

Whalewatching trips serve each part of the coast from December into the early spring. Wherever and whenever you go, dress warmly, take precautions against seasickness, and expect to get wet if you go out on deck. By land or by sea, early morning hours are best because winds cause whitecaps later in the day. This inconvenience can be made up for the instant you see one of these benign monsters come up for air. The sight of a mammal as long as a Greyhound bus breaking water has a way of emptying the mind of mundane concerns. Wreathed in seaweed and sporting barnacles and other parasites on its back, a 40-foot-long, 40-ton California gray whale would look more like the hull of a ship were it not for its expressive eyes.

Further empathy might be engendered upon learning of these mammals' humanlike propensities. Some whale birthings have been observed, for example, which included the help of whale "midwives" pushing mama above the surface of the water so that baby could be born into the air.

Though the latter tendencies might endear these cetaceans to some people, it is their homing instinct that makes it possible to enjoy whalewatching on the Oregon coast. Coastal headlands and beaches provide excellent vantage points from which to spy on the 12,000-mile roundtrip December-to-May migration of the California gray whale, particularly in midwinter. This yearly pilgrimage ranges between Baja and the Arctic, the longest migratory movement by land or sea of any animal. Along the way, the whales search for tiny shrimplike crustaceans, their major food, and other zooplankton. The southward migration along the Oregon coast lasts until early February, although the migration peaks the last week in December. Whales migrating northward can be sighted off Oregon from March through May. Some locals swear that many whales have foresaken migration to take up permanent residency in Oregon waters in recent years.

The following listing gives a cross section of excursions from each part of the coast. Booking information is also available from local Greenpeace chapters in Portland, Eugene, and other major cities. Greenpeace, in conjunction with Newport's **Marine Science Center,** has helped stimulate whalewatching awareness. The Marine Science Center is an extension of Oregon State University, which supplies trained volunteers to staff vantage points 10 a.m.-1 p.m. each day, Dec. 26-Jan. 1. Look for the big sign that says Whalewatching Spoken Here. For additional information, contact Hatfield Marine Science Center, Newport 97365, tel. (541) 867-3011, ext. 226. On the envelope write "Attention: Whales" and include a self-addressed, stamped envelope. You'll receive a list

gray whale

BOB RACE

of charter operators as well as background information.

By Land

Cape Arago State Park, west of Coos Bay, has a promontory with a commanding view of the ocean that is excellent for whalewatching.

The Reedsport Chamber of Commerce, located where ORE 38 and US 101 intersect, offers directions to the whalewatching platform across the road from the **Umpqua Lighthouse** in Winchester Bay. The two-tiered platform overlooks the Umpqua River estuary, where whales are often sighted. Seven placards here describe whale habits and habitat. Two jetties provide reference points for directing the observer's gaze.

Rockwork, a pullout just north of the Sea Lion Caves, offers a magnificent view of Heceta Head, as well as frequent spottings of whales, sea lions, and an assortment of seabirds.

Three miles south of Yachats, immediately after Devil's Churn, there is a sign for **Cape Perpetua Drive.** Follow the steep and windy road up the highest coastal drive in Oregon to the parking lot on top of Cape Perpetua. From there, take the quarter-mile hike on the famous **Trail of the Whispering Spruce** to the old Coast Guard lookout. On a clear day, you can see 150 miles north, south, and west. If there are whales out there, this is one of the best places to spot them.

Nearby is **Cape Perpetua Visitor Center,** where you can whalewatch and stay dry behind picture windows. Locals say that sightings of these leviathans can occur any time of year. This has been the case since the mid-'80s between Cape Perpetua and Otter Crest. Five miles north of Newport, there's a road to Yaquina Head Lighthouse where a resident "mini-pod" of whales can be observed throughout most of the year. The conventional wisdom concerning migratory patterns and observation has been denied here for reasons not yet entirely clear to scientists.

At **Depoe Bay,** in addition to the natural blowholes in the lava rock that shoot up a 30- to 50-foot fountain of water when the tide is right, the lucky visitor is often treated to the sight of whales coming up for air just offshore.

Cape Meares State Park lies 10 miles west of Tillamook on a headland that features a lighthouse built in 1896, as well as great views. If you happen to get rained out, take a look at the Octopus Tree, a Sitka spruce of gargantuan proportions located a short walk away from the parking lot.

South of **Port Orford** are kelp beds where younger bulls sometimes move close in to shore during spring.

By Sea

Dick's Sporthaven Marina, 16372 Lower Harbor Rd., P.O. Box 2215, Harbor 97415, tel. (541) 469-3301, offers two-hour trips beginning in January. Reservations necessary.

Betty Kay Charters, P.O. Box 5020, Charleston 97420, tel. (541) 888-9021, features three-hour trips on weekends Dec.-Jan. and during part of the spring. Reservations are essential. **Bob's Sport Fishing,** 7960 Kingfisher Rd., P.O. Box 5457, Charleston 97420, tel. (541) 888-4241, hosts three- to four-hour trips in December and January. Reservations required, five-person minimum, and discounts for seniors and kids. **Charleston Charters,** P.O. Box 5032, Charleston 97420, tel. (541) 888-4846, runs three-hour trips, beginning in December. Reservations recommended.

Cape Perpetua Charters, 839 S.E. Bay Blvd., Newport 97365, tel. (541) 265-7777, has daily two-hour trips beginning in mid-December, depending upon weather and the number of passengers. **South Beach Charters,** P.O. Box 1446, Newport 97365, tel. (541) 867-7200, operates two-hour trips daily from mid-December to May, reservations required. **Newport Tradewinds,** 653 S.W. Bay Blvd., Newport 97365, tel. (541) 265-2101, offers two-hour trips Dec.-June. **Newport Sportfishing,** 1000 S.E. Bay Blvd., Newport 97365, tel. (541) 265-7558, runs daily two-hour trips departing at 10 a.m. and 1 p.m. from mid-December through May, reservations are recommended.

Oregon Natural Resources Council from Portland, Attn: Michael Carigan, 522 S.W. 5th Ave., Suite 1050, Portland 97204, tel. (503) 223-9001, or from Eugene, 1161 Lincoln St., Eugene 97401, tel. (541) 344-0675, is a coalition of 90 conservation organizations that has put together a series of two-hour trips. Beginning in mid-December and continuing each weekend through mid-April, these charters depart from Newport at 10 a.m. and 1 p.m. A naturalist gives an informative and entertaining presentation before sailing. Advanced registration is required.

Dockside Charters near the Coast Guard station, P.O. Box 1308, Depoe Bay 97341, tel. (541) 765-2545 or (800) 733-8915, has hourly trips daily, year-round depending upon sightings. **Oregon Museum of Science and Industry,** 4015 S.W. Canyon Rd., Portland 97221, tel. (503) 222-2828, offers two-hour tours departing from Depoe Bay, depending upon availability of boats, weather, and number of people. A naturalist is on hand to give a presentation, reservations required. Arguably the best company on the coast is **Marine Discovery Tours,** 345 S.W. Bay Blvd, tel. (800) 903-BOAT. They offer one and two hour whalewatching trips with expert narration.

By Air

The **Astoria Flight Center** offers a 40-minute flight in a Cessna 150 for $40. Two or three people can charter a Cessna 172 for $65. Departures are from the Port Astoria airport in Warrenton. Call (541) 861-1222 for information.

Aurora Aviation, tel. (503) 222-1754 in Portland or (541) 678-1217 in Aurora, offers charters from Aurora, south of Portland, at $89 an hour (minimum of three passengers) or $260 an hour (minimum of six passengers). Flying time to the coast is approximately 45 minutes.

McKenzie Flying Service in Eugene, tel. (541) 688-0971, has whalewatching flights that begin and end in Newport, with departures also from Eugene or North Bend. Hourly rates, excluding flight time to the coast, are $65 per person in a Cessna 172, $47 in the C-206, $73 in the C-182, and $105 in the C-340.

BEACHCOMBING

The Beach: Contours and Character

For most Oregon visitors who travel west of the Coast Range, life is a beach. Despite Pacific temperatures cold enough to render swimming an at-your-own-risk activity, the cliffside ocean vistas, wildlife, and beachcombing make the coast the state's number-one attraction. With rare exception, all beaches in Oregon below mean high tide are owned by the public. These beaches are generally separated by basaltic headlands, volcanic plugs which remain after wind and sea erosion have worn away the softer surrounding earth.

Black sand, high in iron and other metals, is common on the coast, particularly south of Coos Bay. There was also enough gold in the black

OREGON TOURISM DIVISION

Beachcombers should take advantage of Hug Point State Park at low tide.

sands to spur a flurry of gold-mining activity on the south coast 130 years ago. These days, mining companies are eyeing the shelf off the south coast for possible exploitation of ilmenite, magnetite, chromite, zircon, garnet, gold, and platinum. Scientists have known for decades of the placer deposits of heavy minerals washed ashore on prehistoric beaches thousands of years ago when ocean levels were much lower. These beach sands now lie submerged. Despite a study indicating a significant presence of precious metals in the offshore sands of Rogue River and Cape Blanco, incipient prospecting ventures were abandoned.

Speaking of sand, the Oregon coast has 40 miles of dunes (about 32,000 acres), the largest oceanfront collection in North America. Some hills top out at several hundred feet high. Oregon's Sahara is located between Coos Bay and Florence. Many coastal travelers will notice European beachgrass covering the sand wherever they go. Originally planted to inhibit dune growth, the beach grass has solidified into a ridge behind the shoreline, which blocks the windblown sand from replenishing the rest of the beach. In some places, highways are in danger of being engulfed by the dunes.

Throughout your coastal travels, you'll notice names like Oswald West, Samuel Boardman, and Henry B. Van Duzer adorning the names of state parks and highways. These state government officials were the prime movers in preserving the land, building the highways, and establishing the state park system.

Flotsam and Jetsam

Among the first things a newcomer to the Oregon coast notices are the huge piles of driftwood on the beach. Closer inspection usually reveals other treasures. Beachcombers particularly value agates and Japanese glass fishing floats. The volume and variety of flotsam and jetsam here come courtesy of the region's unique geography. Much of the driftwood, for instance, originates from logging operations located upriver on the many waterways which empty into the Pacific. In addition, storms, floods, rockslides, and erosion uproot many trees which eventually wash up on shore.

The Japanese fishing floats are swept into Oregon waters when the Kuroshio current takes a southerly turn. These balls of ornate green and blue glass sometimes require over a decade to reach the Oregon coast after breaking free from fishnets thousands of miles across the sea. In addition to driftwood and floats, shells, coral, sand dollars, starfish, and other seaborne trophies can be best culled from the intertidal zone on south coast beaches. Unfortunately, the more settled and accessible north coast has slimmer pickin's due to the larger population of resident beachcombers and the higher visitor influx. March is the best time to find floats, especially after two-day storms from the northwest, west-southwest, or due west. December to April are the best months to find agates, jaspers, petrified wood, and a variety of fossils. At that time, the gravel bars covered by sand in summer are exposed. Clamming in the tidal flats and crabbing in the estuaries are also popular, but check carefully for conditions.

On the north coast, the best beachcombing is on the Nehalem, the Netarts, and the Nestucca sandspits. Ten Mile Creek south of Yachats and Agate Beach north of Newport are the central coast's best places to look. In the south, the Coos Bay sandspit, Bandon's beachfront, the beaches on the western side of Humbug Mountain, and the isolated shorelines of Boardman State Park are choice treasure hunting spots.

Consult a tidal chart any time you anticipate an extended beachcombing excursion. Half a dozen people perish here yearly from being washed off a beach, jetty, or outcropping. Tide charts are usually available from chambers of commerce as well as from sport and bait shops.

While you may not always come across a 100-foot-long kelp or a message in a bottle, you'll probably find beachcombing on the Oregon coast to be its own reward.

Crabbing

Prime time for crabbing along the coast is late spring and early summer. At that time, the crabs are about to shed their shells for new ones and they're at their meatiest. Bait shops and marinas can instruct you on how to catch dinner. Boats and crab pots are usually available to rent at these places. If boats are unavailable, crabbing from piers is an alternative. Some of the best crabbing spots are the estuaries of the following rivers: the Coos, Siuslaw, Yaquina, lower Tillamook, Netarts, and Nehalem rivers.

OREGON TOURISM DIVISION

The trick to successfully negotiating US 101 along Oregon's coast can be summed up in two words: slow down.

PRACTICALITIES

Accommodations

Coastal accommodations run the gamut from humble fishing lodges to bona fide five-star resorts. In between are condominiums rented as guest rooms, bed and breakfasts, and conventional motels. Air-conditioning is a rarity in these establishments, as is direct access to the beach. The latter is due to the strict land-use statutes against building on the beach. Getting to the beach, however, seldom involves more than a five-minute walk. Rates tend to be much lower in the winter, with special weekend-getaway packages quite common during the February stormwatching season. Rather than give several seasonal rate changes, coastal accommodations listings will instead indicate a range. A dollar-wise option for large groups of families is to contact local realty companies that rent out houses. Several such concerns are listed in the Yachats, Manzanita, and Waldport sections later in this chapter.

Also check out the yurts available at eight of the coast's campgrounds. The yurts are canvas-walled, wood-floored, and equipped with fold-out beds, heaters, and lamps. They sleep five and are available for $27-42 per night. For more information, and to make reservations, call the **Oregon Parks and Recreation Department's Campsite Information Center** at (800) 452-5687. The center can reserve yurts at Fort Stevens, Nehalem Bay, Cape Lookout, Beverly Beach, South Beach, Honeyman State Park, Bullards Beach, and Harris Beach.

Food

Oregon coast cuisine boasts such delicacies as Dungeness crab, razor clams, Yaquina Bay oysters and bay shrimp, as well as world-famous salmon.

Let's start with the bay shrimp as an appetizer. While a hasty visual appraisal of an Oregon shrimp cocktail might prompt an unfavorable comparison to the larger Gulf prawns, these savory morsels prove that good things come in small packages. Expect them to be in season during August. Another coveted crustacean is the Dungeness crab. The firm texture of this species in peak season (March or October) has been compared to that of Maine lobster.

Speaking of which, those used to *Homarus americanus* from the East Coast will be disappointed by the oversized crayfish passed off as lobster on some menus. Freshwater "crawdads" here are another distant cousin. Among non-ambulatory shellfish, Oregon's Yaquina Bay oysters are considered gourmet fare. If you want them fresh, avoid the summer months and wait until the weather is cooler. Razor clams are another indigenous shellfish—an acquired taste for many. Once you get past their rubbery consistency, however, you might enjoy this local favorite. Local mussels and albacore tuna near the end of July are also worth a try.

Spring chinook salmon (May) from the Rogue River estuary seems to be a "can't miss" item for almost everyone. While red snapper would normally also merit such an assessment, this is not always the case in Oregon, due largely to a case of mistaken identity. In contrast to the red snapper found on southern and eastern menus, this Pacific version is a bottomfish. The brown widow rockfish and its several counterparts which receive the red snapper designation out here have a similar consistency but more of a fishy taste than their East Coast cousin.

Nightlife

Big name talent comes to the coast for Lincoln City's Chinook Winds Casino line up of country music all-stars including Merle Haggard, George Jones, and Kenny Rogers. Be that as it may, with the exception of an occasional big-name rock band playing in Lincoln City, Newport, or Astoria, there are only taverns and lounges for those interested in stepping out after dark. Taverns sell beer, often cheaply, and are frequented by the locals. Hard liquor, beer, wine, and live music characterize the lounges. Outside of happy hours, prices are much higher than elsewhere, and when many of the bartenders in these establishments pour, they seem to miss the glass. Nonetheless, a picture window on the Pacific or the Coast Range can make up for a multitude of sins.

Publications

Oregon Coast magazine, P.O. Box 18000, Florence 97439-1030, is an excellent bimonthly about life on Oregon's western edge. It is sold all over the state.

Alternative papers *The Upper Left Edge* and *Inkfish* out of Cannon Beach and Waldport respectively, are the liveliest community-based monthlies in the state. Frequent coverage of environmental issues are interpersed with cultural listings, reviews, and commentary in these publications.

Bus Service

Greyhound sold off many of its coastal routes in the early nineties making for a patchwork quilt of mass transit providers on the western edge of the state. Add a dearth of city buses and only two airports serving Oregon's shoreline and you can understand why it's especially difficult if you're not traveling by car. Only Coos Bay and Newport currently have staffed bus stations, making convenience stores the most frequently seen bus pick-up fronts. The fact that there isn't any bus service between Cannon Beach and Lincoln City compounds summertime traffic jams.

Currently, Pierce Pacific Stages (call Greyhound, tel. (800) 231-2222 for schedule information) operates a beach loop that leaves Portland Greyhound each day at 10:40 a.m., hitting Astoria, Seaside, and Cannon Beach before returning to the city at 6:05 p.m. In like measure, service to the interior cities of the lower Willamette Valley are served by subcontractors. Greyhound does have Portland-to-San Francisco buses which access the coast at ORE 18, hitting Lincoln City, Newport, and Yachats several times daily in either direction. With the only depot on the central coast, Newport is a pivotal stop as detailed in the travel chapters. This can be best appreciated when you consider that a Valley Retriever bus goes from Newport to Corvallis where it makes a timely connection with a Greyhound to Bend.

Lincoln County's **Central Coast Connectors,** tel. (541) 265-4900, offers weekday intercity transit between Newport-Lincoln City and Newport-Yachats.

Driving US 101, the Oregon Coast Highway

The motorist heading up the coast from California should keep in mind that few major vehicular routes access the population centers of Oregon's interior for the coast highway's first 100 miles. One characteristic of US 101 is heavy summer traffic; you'll have a better chance of passing a slow-moving log truck or a lumbering Winnebago on the four-lane main drag of many coastal cities than on the two lanes of US 101. In any case, be prepared to modify your schedule to accommodate the breathtaking scenery surrounding the road. Also, save time and money by stocking up on groceries and filling up on gas inland before encountering the higher prices endemic to the coast's tourist economy. It also pays to be careful of log trucks doing twice the speed limit on circuitous coastal access roads, as well as bicycles attempting to share hairpin turns with large vehicles. Beach loops are often less traveled and offer some good scenery. Finally, keep in mind that the majority of the communities on the coast are "strip towns" along US 101. As such, their simple layout usually renders maps of them unnecessary.

By Bicycle

While not for everybody, biking the Oregon coast is the surest way to get on intimate terms with this spectacular region. Before going, get a free copy of *The Oregon Coast Bike Route Map*, Dept. of Transportation, Salem 97310, or from coastal information centers and chambers of commerce. This brochure features strip maps of the route, noting services from Astoria to the California border. With information on campsites, hostels, bike-repair facilities, temperatures, and wind speed, this pamphlet does everything but map the ruts in the road. Since the prevailing winds are from the northwest, cycle south on US 101 to take advantage of a steady tailwind. You'll also be riding on the ocean side of the road with better views and easier access to turnouts.

By Foot

The **Oregon Coastal Trail** goes 360 miles through some of the most beautiful landscape anywhere. At this writing, about 60% of the trail is completed. The north portion of the trail is in the best condition, while the central and southern sections are still in the process of development. A free map and directory are available by calling (800) 551-6949 and requesting the *Oregon Coast Trail Guide*. This pamphlet makes it clear where this trail crosses open beaches, forested headlands, the shoulder of 101, and even city streets in some coastal villages. Bring water on northerly sections of the trail as much of the trek here is on beachfront away from a potable supply.

By Air

Despite a dozen airports on the coast, only the North Bend field near Coos Bay and the Astoria Airport south of town in Warrenton enjoy commercial service. **Horizon,** an offshoot of Alaska Airlines, flies in from Eugene and Portland to Coos Bay daily. They fly to these same cities, with occasional through-flights to Seattle and isolated stopovers in Salem. Horizon has four nonstop flights to Astoria daily.

BROOKINGS AND VICINITY

If you cross the California-Oregon state border on US 101 in early summer, the welcome mat of Easter lily blossoms often lines the way into Oregon's gateway city of Brookings (population 3,400). While the lilies may not carpet these roadsides so extravagantly during the rest of the year, the coast-bound traveler can still look forward to being greeted by mild temperatures and colorful bouquets, even in winter. Enough 60° days occur during February in this south coast "banana belt" town that over 50 species of flowering plants thrive here, along with retirees, sportsmen, and beachcombers. With two gorgeous state parks virtually part of the city and world-class salmon and steelhead fishing nearby, only the lavish winter rainfall that often exceeds 80 inches a year can cool the ardor of local outdoor enthusiasts.

Brookings sits on a coastal plain overlooking the Pacific, split by US 101 (Chetco Ave.).

The ocean and the Klamath Mountains east of town are linked up by the Chetco River. This river drains part of the nearby **Siskiyou National Forest** and the **Kalmiopsis Wilderness,** renowned for their rare flowers and trees and for possessing some of the wildest country in the United States. Quite fittingly, the Kalmiopsis area is named for the flowering plant that grows nowhere else on earth. This area enjoys strict federal protection, safeguarding the northernmost stand of giant redwoods as well as the coveted Port Orford cedar. The latter species of strong but pliable lumber can fetch $10,000 for a single tree.

But you don't have to trek miles into the backcountry to enjoy the natural beauty of Brookings and vicinity. Just make your way past the somewhat honky-tonk main drag to **Samuel Boardman State Park** north of town, where 11 of the most scenic miles of the Oregon coast

BROOKINGS TO PORT ORFORD

PORT ORFORD
BATTLE ROCK S.P.
HUMBUG MTN. S.P.
HUMBUG MTN.
(ELEV. 1,756 FT.)

TO COOS BAY
TO POWERS
ROAD TO AGNESS

PACIFIC OCEAN

101
AGNESS
OPHIR
ROGUE RIVER
WEDDERBURN
TO GRANTS PASS
GOLD BEACH

CAPE SEBASTIAN S.P.
BIG CRAGGIES (ELEV. 4,489 ft.)

PISTOL RIVER S.P.
ROAD TO KALMIOPSIS WILDERNESS
KALMIOPSIS WILDERNESS

SAMUEL BOARDMAN S.P.
THOMAS CREEK BRIDGE
HOUSE ROCK
CAPE FERRELO
LITTLE REDWOOD CAMPGROUND
AZALEA S.P.
POLLYWOG BUTTE (ELEV. 2,682 ft.)
HARRIS BEACH S.P.
GOAT ISLAND
LOEB S.P.
CHETCO PEAK (ELEV. 4,648 ft.)
BROOKINGS HARBOR

CHETCO RIVER

0   10 mi
0   10 km

TO CRESCENT CITY AND EUREKA
101

© MOON PUBLICATIONS, INC.

await you. Or for a total escape, head down to the harbor to enjoy some of the safest offshore navigation conditions in the region. In short, Brookings is the perfect place to launch an adventure by land or by sea.

HISTORY

What is now the shopping hub of rural Curry County started out as a factory town for the Brookings Box Company in 1914. In the years that followed, lumber, fishing, and tourism became established. Architect Bernard Maybeck (famous for the Palace of Fine Arts in San Francisco) was recruited to design a utopian company town, a vision later gutted by the state highway. Several examples of his craftsmanship are still visible around town (see South Coast Inn). If we omit the speculation that the offshore waters here were visited by Cabrillo (in 1542) and the English explorer Sir Francis Drake (in 1579), the local event with the most historical significance was the Japanese bombing incident in 1942. On September 9 of that year, a

Japanese air raid scorched the treetops of near-by Mt. Emily in what the Brookings Chamber of Commerce calls the only wartime air bombing mission against the U.S. mainland.

Ironically, this frightful episode had two positive outgrowths of enduring significance. First, it sounded the death knell of a secessionist uprising comprised of southern Oregonians and northern Californians. During the '30s, these people wanted to break off from the Union to set up the self-sufficient agrarian state of Jefferson (see the special topic "Oregon—Hotbed of Bioregionalism" in the Introduction chapter). Secondly, the bombing encouraged the local lily industry to expand in an effort to make up for the imminent cutoff of Japanese flowers. Today, the area produces 90% of the world's Easter lily crop.

SIGHTS

Chetco Valley Historical Society Museum
The **Chetco Valley Historical Society Museum**, 5461 Museum Rd., Brookings 97415, tel. (541) 469-6651, is in an older red-and-white house built on a hill overlooking US 101 two miles south of the Chetco River. Open Tues.-Sat. 2-6 p.m., Sunday noon-6 p.m. From November to mid-May hours are Fri.-Sun. 9 a.m.-5 p.m. Admission is $1 for adults, 50 cents for children under 12, and donations are always welcome. The structure dates back to the mid-1800s and was used as a stagecoach way station and trading post before Lincoln was president.

Even if you are not one for museums, several exhibits here stand apart from the traditional collections of pioneer wedding dresses, Indian baskets, and spinning wheels. These include a small trunk which came around Cape Horn in 1706, a patchwork quilt dating back to 1844, and an Indian dugout canoe. Should these fail to inspire, an iron casting of a woman's face might do the trick—especially in light of the speculation that this relic was left by an early undocumented landing on the Oregon coast, perhaps by Sir Francis Drake. Drake has been commonly suggested because of the mask's likeness to Queen Elizabeth.

The **World Champion Cypress Tree** is located on the hill near the museum. The 99-foot-tall tree has a trunk circumference of more than

27 feet and has been home to a pair of owls for years.

Quail Prairie Lookout

If you've always romanticized mountain fire lookout stations but have never seen an operating one, visit the Quail Prairie Lookout, 17 air miles northeast of Brookings. This is one of the few remaining outposts still staffed each summer during the fire season. As negotiating the Forest Service roads just west of the Kalmiopsis Wilderness can be tricky, get exact directions to 3,000-foot Quail Prairie Mountain from the Chetco Ranger Station in Brookings, tel. (541) 469-2196. You can also find out about renting a night in several out-of-operation fire lookouts in the area.

Brookings—Home to Winter Flowers

Camelias bloom at Christmas and the flowering plums add color the next month. Daffodils, grown commercially on the coastal plain south of Brookings, bloom in late January and into February. Magnolia shrubs, some early azaleas, and rhododendrons also bloom in late winter.

Carpenterville Road

The current roadbed of US 101 was laid in southern Oregon in 1961. The previous coastal route still exisits along Carpenterville Rd., which can be picked up near Harris Beach (inquire at the State Welcome Center located nearby). It comes out near the Pistol River where it descends in a series of switchbacks. It's highest point is 1,700 feet above sea level at Burnt Hill. Views of the Siskiyous to the east and the Pacific panoramas to the west make the sometimes rough road worth the effort. In very clear weather, it's possible to look back toward the southeast at Mt. Shasta between the ridgelines. This route is best appreciated going south.

HIKES AND BEACHCOMBING

Harris Beach State Park

You're driving north along the first 20 miles of scenic US 101 in Oregon, but instead of stopping to take out the camera, you're asking yourself, "So where's the Oregon coast?" It's easy to have second thoughts after a half-hour drive through the "Twilight Zone" of small-town America, with only a few fleeting glimpses of the ocean. And then, at the northern limits of Brookings, across from the State Information Center on US 101, you find your lost picture postcard at Harris Beach State Park. One look at the 24 miles of rock and tide visible from the parking-lot promontory should quell any misgivings. The effect can be described as Gibraltar-like and then some.

Besides stunning views, this state park offers many incoming travelers from California their first chance to actually walk on the beach in Oregon. You can begin directly west of the park's campground, where a sandy beach strewn with boulders often becomes flooded with intertidal life and driftwood. The early morn-

Harris Beach

ing hours, as the waves crash through a small tunnel in a massive rock onto the shoreline, are the best time to look for sponges, umbrella crabs, solitary corals, and starfish. Offshore, Goat Island, Oregon's largest seabird rookery, dispatches squadrons of cormorants, pelicans, and other waterfowl who divebomb the incoming waves for food.

In addition to beachcombing, you can picnic at tables above the parking lot, loll about in the shallow waters of nearby Harris Creek, or cast the tidewaters for perch.

Mill Beach is the southernmost part of the Harris Beach area. Locals prefer the beach access from downtown, which is easy to miss. To get there, drive toward the ocean on Center Street in downtown Brookings, make a right at the plywood mill, and stop next to a small ballpark. An unimproved road leads to a hillock from which trails take you down to a beach full of driftwood. Residents say that Japanese fishing floats occasionally roll up onto the beach after a storm.

The Kalmiopsis Wilderness/Vulcan Lake

The lure of untrammeled wilderness attracts intrepid hikers to the Kalmiopsis, despite the summer's blazing heat and winter's torrential rains. In addition to enjoying the isolation of Oregon's largest (180,000 acres) and probably least-visited wilderness, they come to take in the pink rhododendron-like blooms of *Kalmiopsis leachiana* (in June) and other rare flowers. The area is also home to such economically valued species as Port Orford cedar and *cannabis sativa*. The illicit weed is the leading cash crop in the state, and its vigilant protection by growers might inspire extra care for those hiking here during the late fall harvest season. The potential for violence associated with the mushroom harvest (see "Economy" section of the general Introduction) also mandates a measure of caution.

In any case, the Forest Service prohibits plant collection *of any kind* to preserve the region's special botanical populations. These include the insect-eating Darlingtonia plant and the Brewer's weeping spruce. The forest canopy is composed largely of the more common Douglas fir, canyon live oak, madrone, and chinquapin. Stark peaks top this red-rock forest, whose understory is choked with blueberry, manzanita, and dense chaparral. Many of the Kalmiopsis species

survived the glacial epoch because the glaciers from that era left the area untouched. This, combined with the fact that the area was an ancient offshore island, has enabled the region's singular ecosystem to maintain its integrity through the millennia. You'd think that federal protection, remoteness, and climatic extremes would ensure a sanguine outlook for this ice-age forest, but an active debate still rages over the validity of some logging claims.

Even if you don't have the slightest intention of hiking the Kalmiopsis, the scenic drive through the **Chetco Valley** is worth it. From Brookings, turn off US 101 at the north end of the Chetco River Bridge, follow County Roads 784 and 1736 along the Chetco River for six miles, and then turn right and follow County Rd. 1909 to its end. Here, a one-mile-long trail leads to **Vulcan Lake** at the foot of Vulcan Peak, the major jumping-off point for trails into the wilderness. Hikers should watch out for the three shiny leaves of poison oak, as well as for rattlesnakes, which are numerous here. Black bears also populate the area, but their lack of contact with humans makes them more shy than their Cascade counterparts.

Streams here in the water-deficient Kalmiopsis are often too warm to quench a thirst. This high temperature can be better appreciated at one of the preserve's many secluded swimming holes.

Here's what to expect on the way to Vulcan Lake. Road 1909 takes off up the mountains past Pollywog Butte and Red Mountain Prairie. The open patches in the Douglas fir reveal a kaleidoscope of Pacific Ocean views and panoramas of the Chetco Valley and the Big Craggies. For the botanist in search of rare plants, however, the real show is on the trail. No matter how expert you might consider yourself, bring along a good plant guide to help you identify the many exotic species here. On the final leg of the hike, sadler oak, manzanita, Jeffrey pine, white pine, and azalea precede the sharp descent to the lake. Despite steep spots, the walk from County Rd. 1909 to Vulcan Lake is not a difficult one.

If you backtrack from the lake to Spur 260 on the trail, you can make the steep ascent over talus slopes and brush to Vulcan Peak. At the top, from an old lookout, a view of Kalmiopsis treetops and the coast awaits. Before going, check with the Forest Service in Brookings to see if the road to Vulcan Lake trailhead is open, since weather-related closures occasionally occur.

ACCOMMODATIONS

Camping

Campers should pick up literature on fishing and a **Siskiyou Forest Service** map and at the ranger station in town (see "Information and Services," below). In addition to printed matter about Siskiyou and Kalmiopsis trails for hikers, the rangers there can tell you where to find some good fishing holes on the nearby Chetco River, noted for its good fall salmon runs and winter steelhead.

Harris Beach State Park, two miles north of town on US 101, 1655 Hwy. 101, Brookings 97415, tel. (541) 469-2021, $15-17, is open all year, but reservations are definitely necessary from Memorial Day through Labor Day. There are 69 tent sites, 87 trailer/motor-home sites (up to 50 feet long), and a special camping area for hikers and bicyclists, $4. Picnic tables and fire grills are provided. Flush toilets, electricity, piped-in water, sewer hookups, sanitary service, showers, firewood, and a laundromat are also available. Whalewatching is particularly good here in January and May.

Loeb State Park is eight miles northeast of Brookings on North Bank Road along the Chetco River. For information call (541) 469-2021 or write c/o Harris Beach State Park. The park is open mid-April to late October, but camping is allowed only during the summer; no reservations necessary. The rate is $16-20 per night, with 53 sites for trailers/motor homes (50 feet maximum), as well as a special campground for bicyclists and hikers. Electricity, piped water, and picnic tables are provided; flush toilets and firewood are available. The campground is located in a secluded myrtlewood grove on the east bank of the Chetco River. This grove, the state's largest collection of old growth of this species, imparts a special fragrance to the campsite. A quarter-mile north of Loeb Park is the northernmost stands of coastal redwoods. One tree here is estimated to exceed 800 years in age and 33 feet in girth. Within the grove are specimens

over 500 years old, measuring 5-8 feet in diameter, towering more than 300 feet above the forest floor. When the south coast is foggy and cold on summer mornings, it's often warm and dry in upriver locations such as this one.

Beyond Loeb State Park is the more primitive **Little Redwood Campround,** which for the price can't be beat. To get there, go one-half mile south of Brookings on US 101 to County Rd. 784, then go northeast for seven miles. At Forest Service Rd. 376 turn northeast and drive six miles to the campground. Contact **Chetco Ranger District,** P.O. Box 730, Brookings 97415, tel. (541) 469-2196, for information. Open late May to mid-September; no reservations necessary. Bargain-priced at $9 per night per family, there are 16 sites for tents, trailers, or motor homes (16 feet maximum). Picnic tables and grills are on-site; pit toilets and firewood are available. Though it lacks showers and other amenities, Little Redwood is located on the main access route to the Kalmiopsis Wilderness, 20 miles away, and is a good spot for fishing during the winter steelhead run.

Bed and Breakfasts

Holmes Sea Cove Bed and Breakfast, 17350 Holmes Dr., Brookings 97415, tel. (541) 469-3025, $80-100, is a year-round retreat located two miles north of Brookings, turn onto Dawson Rd. from US 101. Along with lushly landscaped grounds and continental breakfast in bed, the Holmeses offer two bedrooms on the lower level of their home and a guesthouse. Below is a private park with picnic tables along a creek by a beach.

Located right on the beach is **Oceancrest House B&B,** 15510 Pedrioli Dr., tel. (541) 469-9200 or (800) 769-9200, http://www.bestinns.net/usa/or/ocean.html, e-mail, inkeep@wave.net. Here you'll find two rooms with queen size bed, microwave, refrigerator, VCR/TV (with an extensive video library), and private bath. Other nice touches are the beachtowels, thongs, and binoculars as well as a basket of fresh seasonal fruit waiting for you in your room. With the hot tub on the deck overlooking the water and a good Continental breakfast, you have all the makings of a romantic getaway worth the $96 a night.

Another gem is the **South Coast Inn B&B,** 516 Redwood St., tel. (541) 469-5557 or (800)

525-9273; e-mail, scoastin@wave.net. This 1917 Craftsman building was the home of lumber baron William Ward, and was designed by famed architect Bernard Maybeck. Situated in the heart of old Brookings and blocks away from the beach and shopping, this 4,000-square foot B&B offers three rooms ranging $79-89, and a guest cottage that also has a kitchen, for $89. All rooms have VCR/TV (and access to the Inn's video library), private bath, and other amenities. An indoor spa with a sauna and hot tub, and an included breakfast featuring a health-conscious menu are additional enticements to book space early. Ask the innkeepers about other Maybeck structures in town as well as bicycle/walking treks they conduct June-October.

Surrounded by water on three sides, the **Chetco River Inn,** 21202 High Prairie Rd., Brookings 97415, tel. (800) 327-2688, $95-105, is also an intimate alternative. Located just 16 miles from Brookings on the periphery of the Kalmiopsis, it's easy to feel as if you're in your own private forest. Its location near prime fishing river frontage makes this place especially popular during the steelhead season on the Chetco. In addition to an included gourmet breakfast, picnic lunches and dinners are available upon request. There is an option to pay $120 and have a four-course dinner included in the price of the room. The welcome mat here is laid out in the form of thick oriental carpets partially covering floors of green and black marble. Tasteful antiques also decorate this reasonably priced first-class lodging.

Motels

At around $50, the **Spindrift Motor Inn,** 215 Chetco Ave., tel. (541) 469-5345, is a good dollar value. Soundproofed walls blunt traffic noise from US 101 and there are ocean views you'd expect to find at higher-priced lodgings. Up a rung in the $70 range, the **Best Western Brookings Inn,** 1143 US 101, tel. (541) 469-2173 or (800) 822-9087, may be about a mile from the ocean, but it has a pool and jacuzzi, a comfy myrtlewood panelled lounge, and a very good on-site restaurant.

For the full oceanfront experience, head south to the town of Harbor. Here, **Best Western Beachfront Inn,** 16008 Boat Basin Rd., tel. (541) 469-7779 or (800) 468-4081, offers a window on a colorful port. All units feature private decks, microwaves, and refrigerators. Kitchenettes as well as suites with oceanview hot tubs are available here. Rates range from $80-170, depending upon the season and the room configuration.

PRACTICALITIES

Food

Brookings has a profusion of family-friendly restaurants that serve large portions at a good dollar value with enough creativity to suit the most finicky eater. At the north end of town in a small building which gives the appearance of a drive-in is **Rubio's,** 1136 Chetco, tel. (541) 469-4919, one of the better Mexican places along US 101. This will be apparent upon tasting the house salsa and the chiles rellenos. The house specialty, seafood à la Rubio, throws together prawns, ling cod, and scallops in a butter, garlic, wine, and jalapeño sauce. Rubio's can be spotted on the east side of the highway across from the Flying Gull. Just look for a low-slung wooden building painted yellow and red. (Dinner entrees $8-13.)

Chives, 1025 Chetco, tel. (541) 469-4121, greets arrivals from California with the kind of upscale restaurant they might encounter in Marin County but at Oregon prices. For lunch consider steamer clams in white wine and garlic butter broth for $7, or marinated and grilled lamb loin chops with a risotto, $7.25. Dinner entrees run $10-17. We recommend the baked King salmon with oysters in pesto cream. The restaurant is closed Monday and Tuesday.

Wild River Pizza, 16279 US 101, tel. (541) 469-7454, has a menu similar to its outlet in Cave Junction (see "Grants Pass"), highlighting pizza and microbrews. Look for it on the east side of the highway about a mile south of the Brookings Harbor Bridge at the four-way stoplight. While the food is good and inexpensive, this large restaurant tends to fill up with families on weekends. In other words, go elsewhere for an intimate Saturday night dinner.

With pig sun symbols, pig cups, and pig dolls, **Hog Wild Cafe,** west side US 101, 1 mile south of Brookings Harbor Bridge, tel. (541) 469-8869, will probably first strike you as a theme restaurant run amok. While this level of continuity doesn't quite extend to the breakfast menu, each dish evidences a taste-pleasing creative touch. The omelette with spinach, basil, green onion, cilantro, and cream cheese, $6.25, breakfast fajitas, $6, and fresh berry Belgium waffles, $5.25, will wake you up with flavors interesting enough to divert your attention from the decor. Espresso drinks and an intriguing lunch and dinner menu might encourage a return visit later in the day.

Events

The **Beachcomber's Festival,** held every March, features exhibits, demonstrations, and slide shows as well as an art competition for the best works wrought from indigenous materials like driftwood, agates, and other beachcomber treasures.

azalea

BOB RACE

The **Azalea Festival** is an unforgettable floral fantasia that takes place each Memorial Day weekend. Among the activities are a parade, flower display and crafts fair, a five-kilometer run, seafood luncheon, and beef barbecue. Much of the activity revolves around Azalea State Park. This WPA-built enclave features 20-foot-high azaleas (several hundred years old) and hand-hewn myrtlewood picnic tables. Wild cherry and crabapple blooms, wild strawberry blossoms, and purple and red violets round out the bouquet. Butterflies, bees, and birds all seem to concur with locals that this array smells sweetest around graduation time in mid-June.

Easter in July celebrates the blooming of the Easter lilies on July 1. Brookings holds this event in conjunction with nearby Smith River, California, where many of the festivities are conducted.

Shopping

Of the many stores on the Oregon coast purveying items made of myrtlewood, a local hardwood famed for its fine grain and durability, **Stateline Myrtlewood,** 14377 US 101 South, located 25 feet from the California border, open 8:30 a.m.-5:30 p.m. every day except Thanksgiving, Christmas, and New Year's Day, tel. (541) 469-

2307, and its parent store, **The House Of Myrtlewood,** P.O. Box 457, Coos Bay 97420, tel. (541) 267-7804, both deserve special mention. Factory tours and an array of quality items ranging from cranberry candy to smoked salmon complement the myrtlewood clocks, bowls, and other handicrafts. Best of all, the friendly staff at both of these stores will gladly answer any questions as well as volunteer all manner of helpful information.

Getting Around

Greyhound, tel. (541) 469-3726, stops twice daily at the corner of Cottage and Pacific. The fare to Portland is $32.

If you are planing to head inland to southern Oregon via US 199, consult the Grants Pass chapter for useful tips and information.

Information and Services

The **post office,** 711 Spruce St., Brookings 97415, tel. (541) 469-2318, is open Mon.-Fri. 9 a.m.-5 p.m.

Wondering about offshore **weather** conditions? The Coast Guard hotline, tel. (541) 469-2242, has the answers. For some fun in the sun, cruise down Easy Street to **Bud Cross City Park** for some **tennis** or a dip in the **outdoor pool.**

For laundry, the **Old Wash House,** corner of Shopping Center Ave. and Grodendorst Lane, tel. (541) 469-3975, is clean and convenient.

Before you embark on the country's longest (341 miles) designated scenic highway, US 101, stop off at the **Oregon Welcome Center** just north of town, 1630 US 101, Brookings 97415, tel. (541) 469-4117. The facility is open Monday, Wednesday, and Friday 9 a.m.-5 p.m.; Tuesday and Thursday 8 a.m.-6 p.m., May-November, and has brochures covering the state. For additional information pertinent to Brookings and environs, backtrack from the state facility to the south side of the bridge. Here you'll find the town's **chamber of commerce,** 16330 Lower Harbor Rd., Brookings 97415, tel. (541) 469-3181, www.brookings-harbor.com.

Recreational information, including forest and trail maps, is available at the **Chetco**

Samuel Boardman State Park, the first leg of the "fabulous 50 miles"

OREGON TOURISM DIVISION

Ranger Station, 555 5th St., Brookings 97415, tel. (541) 469-2196. The station's advisories include information on the Siskiyou National Forest and the Kalmiopsis Wilderness. It's open Mon.-Fri. 7:30 a.m.-4:30 p.m. but is closed on holidays.

Tours
Strahm's Lilies Farm, 15723 Oceanview Dr., Brookings 97415, tel. (541) 469-3885, offers self-guided tours free of charge 8:30 a.m.-6 p.m. from late June to Labor Day. To get there, turn off of US 101 about a mile south of the Chetco Bridge onto Benham Lane, which curves south onto Ocean View Drive. Look for signs that lead to the greenhouses. The Strahms' friendly presence and their literature should pave the way for a memorable walk down the garden path.

Fishing
Fishing on the Chetco was once one of southern Oregon's best-kept secrets. The word has gotten out about the river's October run of huge chinook as well as a superlative influx of winter steelhead. And should river traffic ever become too heavy, the late-summer ocean salmon season out of Brookings may be the best in the Northwest.

Five-hour salmon and bottom-fishing trips may be arranged through **Leo's Sporthaven Marina,** P.O. Box 2215, Harbor 97415, tel. (541) 469-3301.

NORTH TO GOLD BEACH

The stretch of highway from Brookings to Port Orford is known as the "fabulous fifty miles." Some consider the section of coastline just north of Brookings to be the most scenic in Oregon— and one of the most dramatic meetings of rock and tide in the world. The offshore rock formations and winding roadbed hundreds of feet above the surf invite comparison to Europe's Amalfi Drive. This sobriquet is perhaps most apt in the first dozen miles north of Brookings, known as **Samuel Boardman State Park.** Of the 11 named viewpoints that have been cut into the highway's shoulder here, the following are especially recommended (all viewpoints are marked by signs on the west side of US 101 and are listed in order of appearance).

House Rock
House Rock was the site of a WW II air-raid sentry tower that sits hundreds of feet above whitecaps pounding the rock-strewn beaches. To the north, you'll see one of the highest cliffs on the coast, Cape Sebastian. A steep, circuitous trail lined with salal (a tart blueberry) goes down to the water. The path begins behind the Samuel Boardman monument on the west end of the parking lot. The sign to the highest viewpoint in Boardman Park is easy to miss, but look for the turnout which precedes House Rock, called Cape Ferrelo (for Cabrilho's

FRANK LONG

Natural Bridges, south of Gold Beach

navigator, who sailed up much of the West Coast in 1543).

Thomas Creek Bridge

The highest bridge in Oregon (345 feet above the water), as well as the highest north of San Francisco, Thomas Creek Bridge has been used for many TV commercials. A parking lot at the south end of the bridge marks a trailhead down. Do not take the path you see closest to the bridge because it's too steep. At the south end of the lot, the true trail eventually leads down to a view of the bridge on one side and miles of coast on the other. The offshore rock formations here are especially interesting. From here some hikers access the Indian Sands Trail, ending up in pine-rimmed dunes and a sandstone bluff high above the sea.

A few miles down the highway, the **Natural Bridges Cove** sign seems to front just a forested parking lot. However, the paved walkway

at the south end of the lot leads to a spectacular overlook. Below, several rock archways frame an azure cove. This feature was created by the collapse of the entrance and exit of a sea cave. A steep trail through giant ferns and towering Sitka spruce and Douglas fir winds down for a closer look. Thimbleberries (a sweet but seedy raspberry) are sometimes plentiful. Here as in similar forests on the south coast, it's important to stay on the trail. The rainforest-like biome is exceptionally fragile, and the soil erodes easily when the delicate vegetation is damaged.

Natural Bridge's counterpart is near the north end of Boardman Park. A short walk down the hillside trail leads you to the **Arch Rocks** viewpoint to see an immense boomerang-shaped basalt archway about a quarter mile offshore. This site has picnic tables within view of the monolith.

Cape Sebastian

Beyond Boardman Park and seven miles south of Gold Beach is Cape Sebastian. This spectacular windswept headland was named by Sebastián Vizcaíno, who plied offshore waters here for Spain in 1602 along with Manuel d'Alguilar. At least 700 feet above the sea, Cape Sebastian is possibly the highest south coast overlook reachable by paved public road. On a clear day, visibility extends nearly 50 miles in either direction. A trail zigzags through beautiful springtime wildflowers down the south side of the cape for about two miles until it reaches the sea. In April and May, Pacific paintbrush, Douglas iris, orchids, and snow queen usher you along. In addition, Cape Sebastian supports a population of large-headed goldfields, a summer-blooming, daisylike yellow flower found only in coastal Curry County.

In 1942, a caretaker here heard Japanese voices through the fog. When the mist lifted he looked down from Cape Sebastian trail to see a surfaced submarine. This sighting, together with the Japanese bombing at Brookings and the incendiary balloon spotted over Cape Blanco, sent shock waves up the south coast. But the potential threat remained just that, and local anxiety eventually subsided.

GOLD BEACH/ROGUE RIVER ESTUARY

Despite the name "Gold Beach," this town is one part of the coast where the action is definitely away from the ocean. To lure people from Oregon's superlative ocean shores, the nearby Rogue River estuary has been bestowed with many blessings. First, it was the gold-laden black sands which were mined in the 1850s and '60s. While this era gave Gold Beach its name, the arrival of Robert Hume, later known as the "Salmon King of the Rogue," had greater historical significance. By the turn of the century, Hume's canneries had established the river's image as a leading salmon and steelhead stream, a reputation which was later enhanced by the writings of Zane Grey *(Rogue River Feud)*. Over the years, Herbert Hoover, Winston Churchill, Ginger Rogers (who had a home on the Rogue), Clark Gable, Jack London, George Bush, and Jimmy Carter have come here to try their luck. During the last several decades, whitewater rafting and jetboat tours focusing on the abundant wildlife, scenic beauty, and fascinating lore of the region have hooked other sectors of the traveling public.

Today, Gold Beach is a town of 1,500 and the Curry County seat. Besides serving as the south coast tourism hub, a pulp mill and commercial fishing industry make up the local economy here. The seasonal nature of many local businesses creates serious wintertime unemployment. This fact, combined with torrential rains, drastically reduces the population of Gold Beach from Thanksgiving until spring. Thereafter, the wildflowers and warm weather transform this town into a vacation mecca.

SIGHTS

Driving through town on US 101, just before the road gives way to the bridge, the harbor comes into view on the left. Salmon trawlers, jetboats, pelicans, and seals bobbing up and down will be there to greet you. Across the Oscar Patterson Bridge is **Wedderburn,** a baby sister to Gold Beach. Named for the Scottish birthplace of Robert Hume, its major claim to fame is that it's

the home port of the Mailboat, which has been the mail carrier to upriver residents on the Rogue since 1895.

At the **Curry County Historical Museum,** 920 S. Ellensburg, Gold Beach 97444, tel. (541) 247-6113, the local historical society has assembled a small collection of exhibits on Indian and pioneer life, mining in the region's golden age, logging, fishing, and agriculture. It's located at the county fairgrounds at the south edge of town. Particularly interesting are a realistic reconstruction of a miner's cabin, vintage photos, and Indian petroglyphs. Open May 15-Sept. 30, Mon.-Sun. 1-5 p.m.; Oct. 11-May 15, Fri.-Sat. noon-4 p.m. Admission is free.

Jetboat Trips

The best way to take in the mighty Rogue is on a jetboat ride from Gold Beach harbor. Several different companies run this trip, and they all provide comparable service and prices. It's a relaxing and interesting look at the varied flora and fauna along the estuary as well as the changing moods of the river. Most of the estimated 50,000 people per year who "do" the Rogue in this way take the 64-mile roundtrip cruise. This and the more adventurous 104-mile cruise include a stop for a sumptuous lunch at one of several secluded fishing lodges upriver. The pilots/commentators usually have grown up on the river, and their evocations of the diverse ecosystems and Indian and gold-mining history adds greatly to your enjoyment. Bears, otters, and beavers may be sighted en route, and anglers will generally hold up "a big one" to show off. Ospreys, snowy egrets, eagles, mergansers, and kingfishers are also seen with regularity in this stopover for migratory waterfowl.

In the first part of the journey, idyllic riverside retreats dot the hillsides, breaking up stands of fir and hemlock. Myrtle, madrone, and impressive springtime wildflower groupings also vary the landscape. Both the 64- and 104-mile trips focus on the section of the Rogue protected by the government as a Wild and Scenic River. Only the longer trips take you into the pristine Rogue Wilderness, an area that motor launches from

cruising the Rogue River, jetboat style

Grants Pass do not reach either. The 13 miles of this wilderness you see from the boat have canyon walls rising 1,500 feet above you. Geologists say that this part of the Klamaths is composed of ancient islands and sea floor that collided with North America. To deal with the rapids upstream, smaller, faster boats are used that are able to skim over the boulders with just six inches of water between hull and rock surface.

Remember that chill and fog near the mouth of the estuary are replaced by much warmer conditions upstream. These tour outfits have wool blankets available on cold days as well as complimentary hot beverages. Also keep in mind that the upriver lodges can be booked for overnight stays and your trip may be resumed the following day. The following three suppliers offer 64- and 104-mile trips; rates range $30-75 for these itineraries (meals included in the cost of the 104 mile trip). Each has other specific offerings that you can inquire about.

Located just south of the bridge over the Rogue, west of US 101, is **Jerry's Rogue River Jetboats,** P.O. Box 1011, Gold Beach 97444, tel. (541) 247-4571 or (800) 451-3645. This heavily patronized company runs trips from May through October. Jerry's is noted for personable, well-informed guides. If you forgot a hat to buffer the winds at the mouth of the Rogue, stop in at Jerry's new gift shop. While you're there, check out the local jams and critically acclaimed fish prints of local artist Don Jensen. In the museum next door, centuries of natural and human

history along the south coast are depicted. In addition to geologic history, photos of pioneer families, arrowheads and other native artifacts, and a taxidermic collage of local critters will round out your introduction to the Rogue Valley. Perspectives from the museum on the local salmon industry in the 1920s and on early river travel are expanded upon in the jetboat guide's commentary. Museum photos of early river runs, hauling freight, passengers, and mail also can impart a sense of history to your trip upriver.

Rogue River Mailboats, P.O. Box 1165, Gold Beach 97444, tel. (541) 247-7033, 247-6225, or (800) 458-3511, is located a quarter mile upstream from the north end of the Rogue River bridge. Besides human cargo, this boat also carries mail sacks, ensuring a warm welcome in upriver locations.

Court's Whitewater Jetboat Trips, P.O. Box 1045, Gold Beach 97444, tel. (541) 247-4571, 247-6504, or (800) 367-5787, leaves from Jot's Resort at the north end of the Rogue River bridge, west of US 101. Court's pioneered the first whitewater trips here almost 30 years ago. A store connected to Jot's sells food and other supplies.

Beach Access/Auto Tour

Two miles south of Gold Beach there's easy access to a nice beach at **Hunter Creek.** The creek is just off the highway and marked by a sign. From Hunter's Creek you can pick up Hunter's Creek Rd., which loops north through the forest, finally following the course of the Rogue back into town. The three-hour drive goes past interpretive markers explaining "our national forest, land of many uses," and is mapped out in a free pamphlet available at the Gold Beach Ranger Station. This map shows locations of several picnic areas and campgrounds.

Other roads less traveled include the old coast highway, which you can pick up near Pistol River and Brookings; the Carpenterville Rd.; the Shasta Costa Rd. paralleling the Rogue from Gold Beach to Galice; and an unpaved road into the Rogue Wilderness from Agness (a town upriver on the Rogue) to Powers. Despite most of these routes being paved (except the last one), they are all narrow, winding, and not suitable for trailers or motor homes. Maps and directions to these back roads can be obtained from the Gold Beach Ranger Station.

RECREATION

Local Activities

The **Curry County Fair,** 920 S. Ellensburg, Gold Beach, 97444, tel. (541) 247-4541, usually takes place in early August. Highlights include Oregon's largest flower show and a lamb barbecue. Contact the chamber of commerce for more information. The chamber can also fill you in on the exact times for the **jetboat races** that take place July Fourth weekend. People line the river for the event.

To get to **Indian Creek Trail Rides,** P.O. Box 194 Wedderburn 97491, tel. (541) 247-7704, follow Jerry's Flat Rd. one-half mile. Ride along the Rogue on well-trained mounts (one hour $12, two hours $20, family and groups $10 per person).

Outdoor Pursuits

Curry County's only golf course, **Cedar Bend,** P.O. Box 1234, Gold Beach 97444, is located in nearby Ophir. Eleven miles north of Gold Beach, pick up Ophir Rd. off US 101. Follow it to Squaw Valley Rd., turn right at the Old Ophir Store and continue until you see the links. It costs $9 for nine holes, $12 for 18 holes.

Well-known **fishing guides** Bill McNair and Denny Hughson can be contacted through Jerry's Rogue River Jetboats (see above). Most lodgings can also set you up with a guide. For fishing and camping advice and equipment, try the **Rogue Outdoor Store,** 560 N. Ellensburg, Gold Beach 97444, tel. (541) 247-7142.

The 40-mile **Rogue River Trail** offers lodge-to-lodge hiking, which means you need little more in your pack than the essentials. The lodges here are comfortably rustic, serve home-style food in copious portions, and run $40-75. They are also comfortably spaced, so extended hiking is seldom a necessity.

Before you go, check with the Gold Beach Ranger Station on trail conditions and specific directions to the trailhead. Pick up the western end of the trail 35 miles east of Gold Beach,

*the Schrader
Old Growth Trail
near Gold Beach*

about one-half mile from Foster Bar, a popular boat landing (see "Rogue River Campsites," below). Park there and walk east and north on the paved road until you see signs on the left marking the Rogue River Trail. Go in spring before the hot weather and enjoy yellow Siskiyou iris and fragrant wild azaleas. The trail ends at Graves Creek, 27 miles northwest of Grants Pass. Be careful of rattlesnakes on the trail. Contact the chamber of commerce for more information on the upriver lodges.

Odds and Ends

Prehistoric Gardens, tel. (541) 332-4463, unfortunately stands out like a sore thumb on the otherwise unspoiled stretch of US 101, 15 miles north of Gold Beach. Imagine a group of dinosaurs built to exact scale amid giant ferns and towering evergreens. While the setting may be appropriate to the display, the reverse is not true unless you're a kid. Still, the explanatory signs and obvious hard work and care of the concessioner are easy for anyone to appreciate. Open daily 8 a.m. to dusk, admission $3.50 for adults, students 12-18 $3, children 5-11 $2.

PRACTICALITIES

Accommodations

As with most coastal cities, there is no shortage of places to stay along the main drag, Ellensburg Street (a.k.a. US 101). In fact, Gold Beach offers the largest number and widest range of accommodations on the south coast, with intimate lodges overlooking the Rogue as popular as the oceanfront motels: A discount of 20% or more on rooms is usually available during the winter here when 80 to 90 inches of rain can fall.

The cheapest place in town is probably the **Oregon Trail Lodge,** 550 N. Ellensburg, P.O. Box 721, Gold Beach 97444, tel. (541) 242-6030. For about $35-55 you get sanitized Motel 6-type accommodations with room to spare. The **River Bridge Inn,** 1010 Jerry's Flat Rd., Gold Beach 97444, tel. (541) 247-4533 or (800) 759-4533, has modern, comfy river view rooms for $50-90. Kitchenettes are available, as are spa suites.

Ireland's Rustic Lodge, 1120 S. Ellensburg, Gold Beach 97444, tel. (541) 247-7718, was started by two women who used to bring meals to the rooms. While this is no longer the case, the touch of home has not been lost. Many of the rooms have fireplaces, knotty-pine interiors, and distinctive decor. Best of all, the grounds are lovingly landscaped with pine trees, flowers, and ocean views. A sandy beach is a short stroll to the west. There are 27 motel units, nine old but well-kept cabins, and cottages which sleep eight each. The rates are $45-70. Ireland's opened an RV park in 1993 close by the lodge. Add ocean views and you have one of the best values in town.

Located on the Rogue River's north bank, **Jot's Resort,** 94360 Wedderburn Loop, P.O. Box J, Wedderburn 97491, tel. (541) 247-6676 or (800) FOR-JOTS, can host a full vacation in one compound featuring pool and spa, sports shop, private dock, rental boats, and an excellent restaurant across the street. The rooms here are at a premium in summer when the motorcoach tours come through, leaving other travelers with the rooms left over that tend to be marginally maintained. The rates are as follows: $90 for standard view rooms, riverfront condos big enough for six people at $200. The Rod 'n' Reel across the street features evening entertainment with low-stakes blackjack, a country music duo, and a Big Band dance on weekends.

Rogue River Campsites

Campsites east of town along the Rogue and off US 101 en route to Port Orford provide wonderful spots to bed down for the night. Those taking the road along the Rogue should be alert for oncoming log trucks, raft transport vehicles, and other wide-body vehicles.

Foster Bar, Siskiyou National Forest, Gold Beach Ranger Station, P.O. Box 548, 1225 S. Ellensburg, Gold Beach 97444, tel. (541) 247-6651, campground is located 30 miles east of Gold Beach on the south bank of the Rogue. Take Jerry's Flat Rd. east for 30 miles to the turnoff for Agness. Turn right on Illahe Agness Rd. and drive three miles to camp. There are 10 sites for tents and RVs. Picnic tables and fire rings are provided. Pit toilets and firewood are also available, but there is no drinking water. No reservations are necessary and the fee is $5 per night. The site is open March to late September. This is a popular spot from which to

TU TU TUN RESORT

Tu Tu Tun resort, 96530 N. Bank, tel. (541) 247-6664, (800) 864-6357; http://www.tututun.com, e-mail, tututun@AOL.com, open May 1-Nov. 1, emphasizes the tranquility of an evergreen coastal forest on prime river frontage. The latter actually makes you forget that Gold Beach and US 101 are only seven miles away. This feeling of blissful remoteness is reinforced by the absence of TV in the rooms (except in the suites and houses). While there is a TV in the cedar planked lodge, most guests prefer to take in the view of the river through the floor-to-ceiling windows or enjoy a good book from the lodge's library in front of the massive river rock fireplace.

As you sit on your patio overlooking the water along with two nearby resident bald eagles, only the sounds of an occasional passing boat may intrude upon your Rogue River reverie. The tranquility is reinforced by extra wall and ceiling insulation to block noise between rooms and "moonsoaker" hot tubs without jets so guests won't be deprived of the comforting sounds of nature. A heated pool and other recreational facilities, the lodge's beautifully appointed interiors, **Tu Tu Tun Lodge**

and delicious meals served family style are other appeals of this acclaimed retreat. Meals are available on an inclusive Modified American Plan, which includes hors d'oeuvres, a gourmet four-course dinner, and a bountiful breakfast buffet for $39.50 per person. And if you want to fish, fishing gear and tips to find some of the river's best fishing holes are available. With all this, it's no wonder that Tu Tu Tun has earned four-star and four-diamond awards for excellence as well as a place on the coveted *Conde Naste* Gold List.

Spring is the best time to be here, because much of the traveling public is still at home and the wildflowers are in their glory. Pink rhododendrons, native to Oregon, blossom at the edge of the forest in May. From early summer to late fall, a huge Dahlia garden at the lodge is in bloom. While autumn is also beautiful, business meetings in September and October necessitate that bookings be made well in advance for stays after Labor Day. The rates are as follows: $135-175 double, $185-195 suite, and $210-310 for a house.

---

embark on an eight-mile inner tube ride to Agness. The rapids are dangerous, so wear a life jacket. You are also within walking distance of the trailhead of the Rogue River Trail (see "Recreation," above).

Lobster Creek Campground, contact the Forest Service at address above, tel. (541) 247-7922, is nine miles up Jerry's Flat Rd., along the Rogue's south bank. This free campground is open year-round and has five camping sites, picnic tables, fishing, and flush toilets, but there is no drinking water. Ask the Forest Service for directions to the recently established old-growth trail nearby. It is a gentle one-mile walk through a rare and majestic ecosystem which is under siege in other forests throughout the state.

Oceanside Campgrounds

Honeybear Campground, P.O. Box 97, 134161 Ophir Rd., Ophir 97464, tel. (541) 247-2765 or (800) 822-4444, ext. 00, is nine miles

north of Gold Beach on US 101, then two miles north on Ophir Rd., but could just as well be in the Black Forest. The owners have built a large rathskeller with a dance floor. Six nights a week during the summer, there are dances here with traditional German music. Locals praise the Honeybear's on-site delicatessen for its homemade German sausage. There are 20 tent and RV sites, picnic tables, flush toilets, hot showers, firewood, a laundromat, and ocean views for $10-15. It's open May to October.

Arizona Beach Campground, P.O. Box 621, Gold Beach 97444, tel. (541) 332-6491, is a campground close by a beach with lots of driftwood. It has 31 tent sites and almost a hundred RV spaces. You can camp on the beach, in an adjoining meadow, or back in the woods by a tiny stream for $10-15. All the amenities are here, 15 miles north of Gold Beach on US 101, but the closely spaced sites lack privacy. Nonetheless, there are few better places for kids, due to the creek running though the site and the proximity of the Prehistoric Gardens (see "Recreation," above). It's open all year and in case it rains, there's a motel nearby (see Port Orford).

Food

You can't eat scenery, but Gold Beach restaurants charge you for it anyway. Still, this is one place where the oceanfront and riverside views are often worth it. Then, too, there's always the option of cheaper restaurants away from port. Spring chinook salmon, blackberry pie, and other indigenous specialties taste good anywhere.

The **Golden Egg,** 710 S. Ellensburg, Gold Beach, tel. (541) 247-7528, at last count offered 27 omelette combinations. Try their Western omelette (bacon, onion, green pepper, and cheese) for $4.75. In addition, pancakes and waffles round out the breakfast menu. Sandwiches and burgers are featured at lunch, with moderately priced steak and seafood the bill of fare at night.

As you enter the **Rod 'n' Reel,** on the north end of the Rogue River bridge across from Jot's Resort, Wedderburn, tel. (541) 247-6823, you'll read a sign that says, "You're a stranger here but once." The food and attractiveness of the restaurant as well as the congeniality of the Powers family and their staff make it so. Breakfast, lunch, and dinner are served here. Lunch is an especially popular meal, due in part to the restaurant's proximity to the jetboat docks. The more important reasons include the grilled crab or shrimp sandwiches with melted cheese, $5.95, real yummy, some of the best salmon (baked,

broiled, or poached for $8.50) you've ever tasted, an ample salad bar, and excellent pies—notably the blackberry and strawberry rhubarb. Dinner features fresh seafood and many Italian-accented dishes.

Information and Services

The **Gold Beach Chamber of Commerce,** 1225 S. Ellensburg, Gold Beach 97444, tel. (541) 247-7526 or (800) 525-2334, is open Mon.-Fri. 9 a.m.-5 p.m. and Sat.-Sun. 10 a.m.-4 p.m. They'll send you a good, comprehensive information folder upon request. The **Gold Beach Ranger District** office, 1225 S. Ellensburg, Gold Beach 97444, tel. (541) 247-6651, offers a free packet on camping and recreation in the district. It's open Mon.-Fri. 7:30 a.m.-5 p.m. The **post office,** Moore St., Gold Beach 97444, tel. (541) 247-7610, is open Mon.-Fri 8:30 a.m.-5:30 p.m.

The **Greyhound** station, 310 Colvin St., Gold Beach 97444, tel. (541) 247-7246, is a terminal case as far as the health hazards of nicotine are concerned—welcome to the tumor! Across the street is a modern building housing the public library. Comfy armchairs here would make this a perfect alternative waiting room to Greyhound, except for the lack of restrooms. Open Mon.-Thurs. 10 a.m.-8 p.m., Fri.-Sat. 10 a.m.-6 p.m. **Stonsell's Coin-Op Laundry** is located on US 101 near 8th Street.

Curry General Hospital, 220 E. 4th, Gold Beach 97444, tel. (541) 247-6621, is the only hospital in the county. It coordinates the "Mercy Flight," an air taxi service to Medford, should there be any cases it can't handle.

loon

PORT ORFORD AND VICINITY

As you come up US 101 into Port Orford, it's hard to ignore an immense rock promontory fronting the shoreline. Battle Rock was the focus of a conflict between the local Indians and the first landing party of white settlers in 1851. When Captain William Tichenor observed the hostility of the natives in the tidewater, he put nine men ashore on the rock fronting the beach due to its suitability as a battle position. These men defended this outpost long enough for Tichenor to return with reinforcements to carry the day. From such inauspicious beginnings, "Awford," as the locals call it, established itself as the first townsite on the south coast. Shortly thereafter, the town became the site of the first fort established on the coast during the Rogue Indian Wars. This conflict started when gold miners and settlers came into Indian lands. As a result of the clashes, hundreds of local natives were sent to the Siletz Reservation near Lincoln City in 1856.

Besides Indian conflicts, Port Orford has other claims to fame. By a quirk of geography, it is both the most westerly incorporated city in the contiguous U.S. and the center of the country, if you include Hawaii. What's more, *Forbes* magazine dubbed Port Orford the "sleeper" of the Oregon coast, ready to be awakened due to its "knockout" view, despite the fact that it's the rainiest burg on the coast—108 inches annually.

Impressive as some of these geographical calling cards may sound, they have not conferred any great prosperity on the region. Commercial fishing and cedar logging join tourism as the leading revenue producers. Lately, many other eclectic cottage industries have sprung up to supplement the boom/bust, resource-based economy. The outskirts of Port Orford host such diverse undertakings as an escargot-breeding farm, llama and sheep ranches, a goat-milk dairy, kelp harvesting, and commercial berry growers, as well as plots of land devoted to Christmas trees and exotic herbs. In addition, divers harvest sea urchins to supply the Japanese with a popular aphrodisiac and seafood delicacy. This business is northern Curry County's largest employer.

SIGHTS

Humbug Mountain

Some people will tell you that 1,756-foot-high Humbug Mountain, six miles south of Port Orford on US 101, is the highest mountain rising directly off the Oregon shoreline. Since the criteria for such a distinction varies as much as the tides, let's just say it's a special place. Once the site of native vision quests, today Humbug Mountain's shadow falls upon an Eden-like campground surrounded by myrtles, alders, and maples. Just north is a breezy black-sand beach. A three-mile trail to the top of Humbug will reward the hardy hiker with impressive vistas to the south of Nesika Beach and a chance to see rhododendrons 15 to 20 feet high. Rising above the rhodies and giant ferns are big leaf maple, Port Orford cedar, and Douglas and grand firs. The name Humbug derives from the gold miners who were drawn

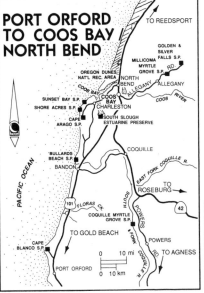

the coast south
of Port Orford

here in the 1850s by tales of gold in the black sands. These stories, of course, proved to be just "humbug." Perhaps more reliable is the Indian legend which says that if the top of the mountain can be seen, the weather will be good.

Battle Rock State Park
Port Orford has an ocean view from downtown that is arguably the most scenic of any city on the coast. A waterfront stroll lets you appreciate the cliffs and offshore sea stacks as well as the unique sight of commercial fishing boats being lowered by crane into the harbor. (The harbor is unprotected from southerly winds so boats can't be safely moored on the water.) Here too is the previously mentioned Battle Rock in its own state park. If you can make your way through driftwood and blackberry bushes surrounding its base, you can take the short trail to the top for a heightened perspective on the rockbound coast which parallels the town. You'll also notice the east-west orientation of the harbor. Once you get to the top of the rock, don't think that the battle is necessarily over. Bracing winds will often chill you, and high tides can sometimes render this huge coastal extension an island. The rock is also the focus of a **Fourth of July Jubilee Celebration** which reenacts the historic battle described above.

Downtown Walking Tour
A brochure from the information kiosk in the parking lot opposite Battle Rock details *Port Or-*

ford's History in Its Architecture and introduces you to homes from the last century in a nice 15-minute walk. Also at the kiosk you can find out about the famed fishing in the Elk and Sixes rivers north of town. Scuba divers can make inquiries at the information desk about the many protected coves with water temperatures as high as 50°—which is warm for Oregon's Pacific—and underwater visibility ranging 10-50 feet in summer.

The Heads
Another shoreline scene worth taking in is located up W. 9th St. at what the locals call "The Heads," featuring a striking panorama from north to south at Port Orford Head State Park, just a short hike away from the parking lot. If you go down the cement trail to the tip of a blustery headland, you look south to the mouth of Port Orford's harbor. To the north, many small rocks fill the water, along with boats trolling for salmon or checking crab pots. It's said that on clear days visibility extends from Cape Blanco to Humbug Mountain.

Cape Blanco State Park, Hughes House
Eleven miles north of Port Orford on US 101 is Cape Blanco, perhaps the westernmost point of land in the contiguous U.S. (although Californians and Washingtonians beg to differ). Whether or not it rates the nod, the remote appendages of this place will give you the feeling of being at the edge of the continent. From the

vantage of Cape Blanco, dark mountains sit behind you and forest almost abuts tidewater. Driftwood and 100-foot-long bull kelp on slivers of black-sand beach fan out from both sides of this earthy red bluff 245 feet above the ocean. Somehow, the Spaniards who sailed past it in 1603 viewed the cape as having a "blanco" (white) color. It's been theorized that perhaps they were referring to the fossilized shells on the front of the cliff.

Atop the headland is the oldest and highest lighthouse in continuous use in Oregon. This beacon still uses the same French-made lens that was originally installed in 1870, blinking out a signal every 30 seconds to points 20 miles out at sea. Call (541) 332-6774 for tour hours Thurs.-Mon.

Over the years a number of shipwrecks have occurred on the reefs near Cape Blanco. During WW II, Japanese submarines used the beacon as an orientation mark to aim planes loaded with incendiary bombs at the Coast Range. This effort to start forest fires was motivated by the existence of Port Orford cedar trees here, which were used to construct planes. Due to the perennial dampness, the results were negligible.

The vegetation along the five-mile-long state park road down to the beach will attest to the severity of winter storms in the area. One-hundred-mile-per-hour gales (the record winds were clocked at 184 mph) and horizontal sheets of rain have given some of the usually massive Sitka spruces the appearance of bonsai trees. An understory of salmonberry and bracken fern help evoke the look of a southeast Alaska forest.

Near Cape Blanco on a side road along the Sixes River is the **Hughes House,** a restored Victorian home built in 1898 for rancher and county commissioner Patrick Hughes. Owned and operated by the state of Oregon, the house serves as a museum and repository of antique furnishings. The Hughes House is open May 1-Sept. 30, daily except Tuesday and Wednesday 10 a.m.-5 p.m., Sunday noon-5 p.m. It's also open during the holiday season when punch and cookies are often served on the weekend before Christmas.

Seven miles east of the Cape Blanco turnoff, the **Grassy Knob Wilderness** showcases the Port Orford cedar; this majestic, fragrant tree is light, strong, and durable. Its use in planes during WW II and in Japanese construction has also made it highly valued, but a fungus fatal to it that is found on logging trucks that transport the logs currently accounts for its rarity and astronomically high stumpage price.

ACTIVITIES

Beachcombing for agates and fishing floats on nearby south coast beaches and searching for the lost Port Orford meteorite in the surrounding foothills typify the adventures available in the area. The meteorite was found in the 1860s by a government geologist, who estimated its weight at 22,000 tons. Unfortunately, he was unable to relocate the meteorite when he returned for another look.

Those in search of more conventional pursuits are advised to drive out 14th or 18th Streets to **Garrison Lake.** Boating, water-skiing, and trout fishing are available here. Nearby **Buffington Memorial City Park,** west of US 101, has a dock for fishing or swimming on the lake, plus playing fields, tennis courts, picnic areas, hiking trails, and a horse arena. North of the lake, look for agates on **Paradise Point Beach.** Garrison Lake State Wayside offers access to coastal dunes.

Stone Butte Stables, 46509 US 101 South, Langlois 97450, tel. (541) 348-2525, lets you ride into the sunset over Coast Range foothills ushered along by views of the Pacific and abundant wildlife. During early summer, the fields on Stone Butte are covered with wild irises and daisies. Later, purple foxglove and huckleberries proliferate. The rates are $12 for one hour, $15 for 1.5 hours, and $20 for the two-hour ride. It's open May-Sept., 10 a.m.-6 p.m. Look for the stables on the hillside eight miles north of Port Orford.

Between Port Orford and Bandon (just south of Langlois) is Floras Lake, which is becoming a mecca for coastal windsurfing. For more information, contact **Floras Lake Windsurfing School,** P.O. Box 1591, Bandon 97411, tel. (541) 347-9205. Close by is **Boice Cape Country Park** Drive three miles south of Langlois and follow the signs. From here north to Bandon, the most desolate beachfront on the coast can be found—ideal for beachcombing. Grasses, dunes, and shore pine will usher you the third of

THE SEA OTTERS OF CAPE BLANCO

Down on the beach below Cape Blanco, you might see the furry heads of sea otters peering out from above the whitecaps about 200 yards offshore. The progenitors of this colony were transported here courtesy of the Atomic Energy Commission in 1970. At that time, a planned bomb test in the Aleutians compelled the AEC to move 95 of these animals to this area. In addition to Cape Blanco, they've been sighted south of Port Orford.

Between 1775 and 1823, over 100,000 sea otters were killed for their pelts, many along the Oregon coast. They became the trappings of royalty, selling in Paris for as much as $1,000 apiece. After sea otters were declared extinct

BOB RACE

south of the Aleutians in 1911, they became a protected species.

The first accounts of the plunder of the sea otter should have brought about their protection long before the 20th century. An early 19th-century Spanish journal described the colony off of Monterey, California as playful and intelligent. It detailed how a typical otter would dive hundreds of feet down to pull an abalone off a rock; would reemerge on the surface on its back, shell in paw; and then, using its stomach for a table, would crack the shell open with a rock.

In addition to the Spanish chronicler's fascination with otter dining behavior, he noted another similarity to *Homo sapiens* when mama sea otter was observed putting baby in a cradle of kelp. The account went on to describe the mother's reaction upon returning with breakfast and finding her baby missing: she emitted humanlike cries for days on end, eventually starving herself to death.

---

a mile back to Bandon and chances are good you won't see a soul. Call (541) 247-7074 for more information.

PRACTICALITIES

Accommodations
Port Orford is the kind of place where a room with a view will not break your budget. The **Shoreline Motel,** P.O. Box 426, Port Orford 97465, tel. (541) 332-2903, is across the highway from Battle Rock, has an outstanding view, offers clean rooms, and accommodates pets for $35-45. Close by are the Golden Owl Deli and the Greyhound stop. **Castaway-by-the-Sea,** 545 W. 5th St., Port Orford, tel. (541) 332-4502, features ocean views from high on a bluff, fireplaces, and housekeeping units, and will allow pets; rates are $45-75. These rates go down 60% in the off-season. It's said that Jack London once stayed in an earlier incarnation of this place.

The **Seacrest Motel,** P.O. Box C, tel. (541) 332-3040, (888) 332-3040, features views of coastal cliffs and a garden from a quiet hillside on the east side of the highway. The rates are $42 for a single and $52 for a double. **Home-by-the-Sea,** P.O. Box 606, Port Orford 97465, tel. (541) 332-2855, includes a full breakfast at a rate of $75 a night for two. The dramatic hillside view of Battle Rock seascape makes for excellent stormwatching here.

As you drive by Humbug Mountain six miles south of Port Orford, you'll notice a small motel complex just off the road. The **Humbug Mt. Lodge,** between milepost 308-309, US 101, tel. (541) 332-1021, has kitchen units, 30 inch TVs (with cable for rainy days), microwaves, and refrigerators. There's a decent restaurant on the premises, a trout pond, and no shortage of peace and quiet. Excellent hiking is nearby on the Humbug Mountain Trail. They proclaim to have the lowest rates on the coast, with doubles going for less than $30 certain times of the year. While this may be cause for suspicion, rest assured that you are not getting the grunge tour, and that basic standards of cleanliness are met.

Campgrounds

Humbug Mountain State Park, six miles south of Port Orford, tel. (541) 332-6774, features 80 tent sites and 30 sites for trailers and motor homes, and wind-protected sites reserved for hikers and bikers at a buck a night. Flush toilets, showers, picnic tables, water, firewood, and a laundromat are available. The park is open April-Oct., $16-20 **Cape Blanco State Park,** P.O. Box 299, Sixes 97476, tel. (541) 332-2971, can be reached by driving four miles north of Port Orford on US 101, then heading northwest on the park road which continues five miles beyond to the campground. It features 58 sites for tents, trailers, and motor homes, as well as hiker/biker sites for $4 a night; picnic tables, water, showers, and a laundromat are available. No reservations are necessary, and a $16-20 fee is charged mid-April to late September.

Food

On first appearances **Sixes,** a rural burg of sheep ranches and cranberry bogs four miles north of Port Orford, may not conjure the idea of good restaurants, much less fine dining, but the **Sixes River Hotel,** US 101 and Sixes River Road, (look for the sign in the shape of a salmon) will make you sit down and take notice. Farm grown spring lamb with vegetables from the B&B's own garden is the specialty. Steak, chicken, seafood (main courses $11-15), and homemade desserts round out the menu at this bed and breakfast located a quarter mile east of US 101. Pork tenderloin in plum sauce, $13.95, also comes recommended. Reservations are a must here because of limited seating. It costs $75 a night for two to stay over in this gussied up version of Grandma's house.

Other than Sixes, food choices are pretty basic after massive restaurant closures in the mid-nineties. You're better off waiting to take advantage of Bandon's array of gourmet restaurants.

Information and Services

Begin your travels here at **Battle Rock Information Center** on the west side of US 101, tel. (541) 332-8055. The people here are especially friendly and helpful. The **post office,** turn north at Washington St. intersection, near Wells Fargo, then right one block, Port Orford 97465, is open 8:30 a.m.-5:30 p.m. **Greyhound** stops at a convenience store, 914 N. Oregon St., tel. (541) 332-3181. Two buses go in each direction up and down the coast. The library and city hall, 555 W. 20th St., are open weekdays 8 a.m.-5 p.m. Culture vultures can get their "hit" at **Grantland Mayfield Gallery,** 246 US 101, tel. (541) 332-6610, which features over 150 artists in a 2,000 square feet display area. There's also a gift boutique and a working glass studio.

BANDON AND VICINITY

In contrast to the glitzy tourist trappings of some of the larger coastal towns, Bandon-by-the-Sea is characterized by the style and grace of an earlier era. The glory that was Bandon is alive and well in Old Town, a picturesque collection of shops, galleries, restaurants, and historical memorabilia. A converted Coast Guard station houses the Coquille River Museum, whose placards tell the stories behind the scenes in this restored neighborhood.

The museum's exhibits also detail other aspects of the heritage of this quiet port city near the Coquille River. While logging, fishing, dairy products, and the harvest of cranberries have been the traditional mainstays of the local economy, in the early part of the century Bandon also enjoyed a brief tourism boom. In addition to being a summer retreat from the heat of the Willamette Valley, it was a port of call for thousands of San Francisco-to-Seattle steamship passengers. This era inspired such touristic venues as the Silver Spray dance hall and a natatorium housing a saltwater swimming pool.

The golden age which began with the advent of large-scale steamship traffic in 1900 came to an abrupt end following a devastating fire in 1936. The blaze was started by the easily ignitable gorse weed, imported from Ireland (as was the town's name) in the mid-1800s. Dramatic descriptions of the townspeople fighting the flames with their backs to the sea earned the incident a citation as one of the top ten news stories of the year.

The facelift given Old Town decades later and the subsequent tourist influx conjured for many the image of the mythical phoenix rising from its ashes to fly again. On the wings of the recovery, Bandon has established itself as a town rooted in the past with its eyes on the future.

Today Bandon is a curious mixture of provincial backwater, destination resort, and new-age artist colony. Backpack-toting travelers from all over the world have been flocking to this town of 3,000 in recent years because of its beaches, its cultural and recreational pursuits, and its European-style hostelry. They coexist happily with the large population of retirees, award-winning artisans, and locals who seem to have cornered the market on late-model pickups with gun racks.

SIGHTS

One of the most appealing things about Bandon is that most of its attractions are within walking distance of each other. In addition, on the periphery of town are a varied array of things to see and do.

West Coast Game Park

Six miles south of Bandon is the West Coast Game Park, P.O. Box 1330, Bandon 97411, tel. (541) 347-3106, the self-proclaimed largest wild-animal petting park in the world. There are 450 animals, including tiger cubs, chimps, camels, zebras, bison, and two snow leopards. Along with these exotics you'll also encounter such indigenous species as elk, bears, raccoons, and cougars. Park visitors may be surprised to see a lion and tiger caged together, or a fox and a raccoon sharing the same nursery. The park tries raising different species together and often finds that animals can live harmoniously with their natural enemies. Free-roaming animals include deer, seacock, pygmy goats, and llamas. An elk refuge is another popular area of the park. Even if you're not with a child, the opportunity to pet a pup, a cub, or a kit can bring out the kid in you. The park is open year-round but call during winter because of restricted hours of operation. The park is only open weekends December through February. Regular hours are 9:30 a.m.-dusk in summer, and 9:30 a.m.-4:30 p.m. in other seasons. Adult tickets cost $6, and kids 7-12 get in for $4.75.

Coquille River Museum

Also known as the Bandon Historical Society Museum, 1000 6th Ave. West, ground floor of Heritage Place, tel. (541) 347-2164, this museum first traces the history of the Coquille tribe and its forebears. The chronology continues with the steamers and the railroads that brought in white settlers. One room is devoted to Bandon's unofficial standing as the "Cranberry Capital of Oregon." Black-and-white blowups showing women stooping over in the bogs to harvest the ripe berries are captioned with such bon mots as this dubious one from an overseer: "I had 25 women picking for me, and I knew every one by her fanny." Color photos spanning five decades of cranberry festival princesses also adorn the walls.

Another room traces "Bandon's Resort Years, 1900-1931," when the town was called the "Playground of the Pacific." The most compelling exhibits in the museum deal with shipwrecks and the fires of 1914 and 1936. Open Tues.-Sat. noon-4 p.m.; the museum is often closed January and February. If the museum is closed, call (541) 347-2164 and a tour can usually be arranged. Admission is $1 for adults; children are admitted free.

Bandon Driftwood Museum, Old Town

Old town is four blocks of shops and cafes squeezed in between the boat basin and the highway. Another exposition is Bandon Driftwood Museum, a collection of natural sculptures from gnarly root balls to whole tree trunks. It is housed at Big Wheel Farm Supply store on 1st St. in Old Town, across from the boat basin. The hours are Mon.-Fri. 9 a.m.-5:30 p.m.; Saturday 9 a.m.-5 p.m.; Sunday 11 a.m.-5 p.m.

Preservation buffs should check out Masonic Hall, 2nd and Alabama, one of the few buildings to have survived both Bandon blazes. A photo in the museum shows the same building and surrounding structures on Alabama St. (then called Atwater) circa 1914. The photo depicts boardwalks leading to a woolen mill, old storefronts, a theater, and the Bandon Popular Hotel and Restaurant, outside which a horse and buggy await. This contrasts greatly with the contemporary scene. Today the Minute Cafe and a parking lot sit on the same spot as some of the structures in the photo. Nonetheless, a turn-of-the-century charm still pervades the architecture and ambience of the neighborhood. Housed within many of the Old Town shops and galleries are artisans pursuing such time-honored professions as glassblowing, leathercraft, and pottery.

Say "Cheese!"
The **Bandon Cheddar Cheese Plant,** on US 101 just north of Old Town, Bandon 97411, tel. (800) 548-8961, is the second-largest cheese factory in Oregon. The famous taste and texture of the Bandon's cheese are the results of hand-cheddaring by a master cheesemaker. You can watch the process through a window in the gift store and sample the results, including fresh, squeaky cheese curds, every day of the week except Sunday, 8 a.m.-5:30 p.m. Their jalapeño cheese is a pepper lover's delight.

Old Town Boat Basin
Walk off your cheese samples at the newly refurbished boat basin just north of Old Town. While strolling the docks you can watch locals land salmon, steelhead, and Dungeness crab. The commercial fleet steams into the Coquille River's estuary with holds full of salmon, tuna, or whitefish.

The Beach Loop
Since US 101 follows an inland path for more than 50 miles between Coos Bay and Port Orford, you'll want to leave the highway in Bandon and take the Beach Loop above the oceanfront on a bluff. There are several access roads that lead to Beach Loop Drive, each about onequarter mile from each other. Most of the traffic seems to head west on 1st St. along the Coquille. Another popular approach is from 11th St., which heads toward Coquille Point. On the beach itself are rock formations with such evocative names as Elephant Rock, Garden of the Gods, and Cat and Kittens Rocks. The most eye-catching of all is **Face Rock,** Bandon's answer to New Hampshire's Old Man of the Mountain. This basalt monolith resembles the face of a woman looking at the sky. Indian legends say that she was a maiden frozen by an evil sea spirit. The whole grouping of sea stacks looks like a surrealist chess set cast upon the waters. Look for the Face Rock turnout a quarter mile south of Coquille Point on the Beach Loop.

Despite this array, the beach is surprisingly deserted. Perhaps this is due to the long, steep trails up from the water along other parts of the beach. In any case, this dearth of people can make for great beachcombing. Agates, driftwood, and tidepools full of starfish and anemones are commonly encountered here, along with birdwatching opportunities galore. Elephant Rock has a reputation as the Parthenon of puffins, while murres, oystercatchers, and other species proliferate on the other offshore formations in varying concentrations.

The Bird Man of Bandon
In the movie *The Birdman of Alcatraz,* Burt Lancaster portrays an embittered convict who lifts his spirits by caring for birds. Dan Deuel is Bandon's bird man, a Vietnam veteran with shattered limbs who takes in injured sea lions, raptors, and shorebirds brought to him by beachcombers and government agencies. If you are interested in animal rehabilitation and Dan isn't too busy (call 541-347-3882 to check) you can get a life-affirming look at his flockon-the-mend. Particularly interesting are several resident owls.

Sometimes there aren't too many critters to look at since they are released back into the wild after being nurtured back to health, but Dan's wealth of knowledge about his charges is always edifying. The bird man's lair at 1185 Portland Ave., can be found by taking the Beach Loop and turning off at Gables Motel on Coquille Point. Dan's cliffside home is easy to spot since its adjoining yard is filled with pens housing the "patients." This heroic operation is largely selfsustaining, so please leave donations.

ACTIVITIES

Bandon Storm-watchers, P.O. Box 1693, Bandon 97411, tel. (541) 347-4721 or 347-3918, is a group that coordinates activities and natural history seminars.

Birdwatchers flock to the **Bandon National Wildlife Refuge** (a.k.a. the Bandon Marsh), especially in the fall, to take in what may be the prime birding site on the coast. Bar-tailed godwits and Mongolian plovers often join the usual assemblage of migrating shorebirds during October. Access is via unmarked trails off River Rd., bordering the Coquille River east of Bandon.

Bandon Beach Loop Stables, tel. (541) 347-9242, is located four miles south of Old Town, just past Crooked Creek State Park. They rent horses by the hour, $10, day, or week for beach trail rides, with lessons available to beginners. In addition, kids can enjoy 15 minutes on a pony for $2 here. Fishing guides and gear can be arranged through **Bandon Bait Shop,** 1st and Alabama, Bandon 97411, tel. (541) 347-3905, across from the boat basin. Clamming and crabbing information can also be procured from the youth hostel.

Just off the south end of Beach Loop Dr., **Bradley Lake** has good trout fishing and a boat ramp. It is protected from ocean winds by high dunes.

Winter River Books and Gallery, 170 2nd St., Bandon, tel. (541) 347-4111, has crystals, objets d'art, and an interesting selection of self-help books. A fine and wide-ranging assortment of travel titles, photo essays, fiction, and tapes also makes this the best bookstore on the south coast.

Artworks Gallery, Clocktower Gallery, and Second Street Gallery, clustered together on Second Street, are three high-quality shops worth a gander.

PRACTICALITIES

Accommodations

The expression "You can't go wrong" applies for price, view, cleanliness, and whatever else you're looking for in this town. Bandon bills itself as America's Storm-watching Capital, and special packages are often available October until March.

Sea Star Hostel

The hostel, 375 2nd St., tel. (541) 347-9632, has skylights, a natural wood interior, a wood stove, and a harbor-view courtyard. There is also one of of the better restaurants on the south coast. Private, couple, and family rooms are available. The latter are more likely found at the adjoining

Sea Star Guesthouse, 370 1st St., where you get the feel of a tasteful motel. Rates at the hostel are $13-16; at the guesthouse, $40-85.

Campgrounds

Bullards Beach State Park, P.O. Box 25, Bandon 97411, tel. (541) 347-2209, is a great place to spend the night, fish, crab, bike, fly a kite, windsurf, or picnic. The park has about 100 campsites with some hiker/biker spaces. To get there, drive north of town on US 101 for about a mile; just past the bridge on the west side of the highway is the park entrance. The beach itself is reached via a scenic two-mile drive paralleling the Coquille River. Look for jasper, agates, and driftwood here. There are campsites by the river. Electricity, picnic tables, and fire grills are provided. You'll also find a store, a cafe, a laundromat, horse riding/camping facilities, an inviting sandy beach, and hiking trails. The fee for camping at Bullards Beach along the Coquille is $16-20 a night.

A side road going out to the north jetty takes you to the octagonal **Coquille Lighthouse,** tel.

BANDON ACCOMMODATIONS

Bandon Beach Motel, 1110 11th St. S.W., tel. (541) 347-4430, $45-70, ocean view, restaurant, pets.

Caprice Motel, Route 1, Box 530, tel. (541) 347-4494, $40-65, kitchenettes, pets, near restaurants and shops.

Gorman Motel at Coquille Point, 1110 11th St. S.W., tel. (541) 347-4451, $60-90, oceanfront view, continental breakfast.

Inn at Face Rock, 3255 Beach Loop Rd., tel. (541) 347-9441 or (800) 638-9441, $60-135, pets, full-service resort, golf, stables.

La Kris Motel, US 101 and 9th St., tel. (541) 347-3610, $35-60, pets, restaurant, lounge.

Sea Star Guesthouse, 370 1st St., tel. (541) 347-9632, $50-100, restaurant, laundry. This is an extension of the hostel with nicer rooms facing the ocean and no chores.

Sunset Ocean Front Resort, 1755 Beach Loop Rd., tel. (541) 347-2453 or (800) 842-2407 $55-215, wheelchair access, selection of wood-paneled rooms, family suites, ocean views, houses, cabins, condos, restaurant.

Windermere, 3250 Beach Loop Rd., tel. (541) 347-3710, $60-100, ocean view, quiet, kitchenettes.

the lighthouse at
Bullards Beach

OREGON TOURISM DIVISION

(541) 347-2209, built in 1896. It was abandoned in 1939 but will be open for tours on a schedule that fluctuates with the seasons. Call ahead for hours when park staff and volunteers can open the lighthouse to show you around. Etchings of ships that made it across Bandon's treacherous bar, and those that didn't, greet you as you enter. Visitors during the next few years are likely to see a flurry of activity here as a luxury resort with several golf courses is going up near Bullard Beach.

Food

Bandon has quite a few restaurants that serve up specialty dishes that break the mold while not breaking your budget. **Wheelhouse Seafood Grill,** 1st and Chicago, Bandon, tel. (541) 347-7933, deep-fries their fish (they also grill and broil) with a beer batter that doesn't mask the taste of the food. **Andrea's Old Town Cafe,** 160 Baltimore, Bandon, tel. (541) 347-2111, features such items as fresh-caught local ling cod with Andrea's own tomato feta sauce. Lots of vegetarian items are offered in this longtime south coast favorite. Count on Andrea's for something special for breakfast, lunch, and dinner (main dinner courses are $10-19).

International flavors predominate at the **Sea Star Coffeehouse,** 375 2nd St., Bandon, tel. (541) 347-9533, with European breakfast plates, croissants, pita sandwiches, fruit dessert crepes, soups, salads, and espresso drinks. As with Andrea's, a premium is placed on fresh local

ingredients in a dinner menu which changes to conform to the seasonal catch or harvest. While the culinary components are indigenous, the recipes themselves have an international flair. Enjoy a Moroccan rack of lamb, or cod stuffed with scallop mousse en papillot. Omelettes here are so huge they'll sustain you until dinner (main dinner courses $12-15).

Bandon Boatworks, South Jetty Rd., Bandon, tel. (541) 347-2111, has fresh seafood and steaks for lunch and dinner. For a dinner appetizer, try their squid in the chef's secret-recipe batter. Other pre-dinner delectables include the cranberry bread and a sumptuous salad bar. The Boatworks has views of the Coquille Lighthouse and an intimate lounge with entertainment. Sunday brunch and Mexican food (dinner only) change the pace. The restaurant is closed Monday and goes into winter hibernation during January and February. Budget diners and smoked fish connoisseurs will appreciate the **Bandon Fish Market,** at the boat basin near the intersection of 1st and Chicago, tel. (541) 347-4282. Heartier appetites call for the market's excellent fish and chips. A picnic table outside by the harbor is the place to enjoy it all with a trip across the street to Cranberry Sweets for dessert.

South of downtown, **Lord Bennett's,** 1695 Beach Loop Dr., tel. 347-FOOD, cliffside aerie looks out over the breakers in what is easily Bandon's most dramatic restaurant view. Lunch and dinner do justice to these surroundings with elegantly rendered seafood dishes. Rec-

CRANBERRIES

From the vantage point of US 101 between Port Orford and ten miles north of Bandon, you'll notice what appears to be reddish-tinged ground in flood-irrigated fields. If you get close, you'll see cranberries, small evergreens that creep along the ground and send out runners that take root. Along the runners, upright branches six to eight inches long are formed, on which pink flowers and fruits develop.

These berries are cultivated in bogs to satisfy their tremendous need for water and to protect them against insects and winter cold. Bandon leads Oregon in this crop, with an output ranking third in the nation. Oregon berries are often used in juice production by Ocean Spray because of their deep red pigment and high vitamin-C content. The Bandon crop could well take on a higher profile nationally due to the nationwide demise of wild bees (over 90% of the population have been killed) who are the prinicpal cranberry pollinators. On the Oregon coast, domestic bees have taken up the breach left in the wake of their winged counterparts killed by a European mite infestation. (Incidentally, you can help save the wild bees by planting peppermint and spearmint at home. The natural oils imparted by these plants help the bees rid themselves of the deadly mites. Not only will you help an important endangered species survive, but you will play a significant role in maintaining the biodiversity of your area, as many plants specifically require these wild pollinators.)

It is possible to arrange a visit to see some of these bogs. The most interesting time is during the late autumn harvest. Write the **Cranberry Growers Alliance,** P.O. Box 1737, Bandon 97411, for more information on when and where to watch the harvest. A sweeter encounter can be found at **Cranberry Sweets,** 1st and Chicago Streets, Bandon 97411. Herein are confections ranging from cranberry fudge to cranberry truffles. Sugar fans will be glad to know it's open seven days a week, 9 a.m.-5 p.m.

Oregon bogs were producing wild cranberries when Lewis and Clark first traded with the Indians for them in 1805. Shortly thereafter, cultivated bogs were developed in Massachusetts, which like Oregon has acid soils with lots of organic materials conducive to berry production. By the California gold rush of 1849, East Coast growing and harvesting techniques had transformed Bandon's marshes into commercial cranberry bogs. In the years to come, much of the modern equipment for harvesting these bogs was developed in Bandon. Wet-picking, for instance, is facilitated by the water reel, which is rotated to create eddies on the bog to shake berries off the vines. After they float to the surface, the cranberries are pushed by long booms toward a submerged hopper. They are then transferred by conveyor belt onto trucks. Walking through the bogs without trampling the berries is made possible by fastening wooden platforms with short pegs to the soles of boots.

Without such innovations, Thanksgiving dinner wouldn't be the same. In order to bring the enormous annual volume of cranberries to the dinner table for the holidays, all these harvesting techniques as well as processing and packaging technology are called into play.

BOB RACE

ommended are the bouillabaisse and the blackened ahi (main dinner courses $12-16). Jazz in the lounge is another nice touch. Between Bandon and Port Orford on US 101, hit the brakes at **Misty Meadows** roadside stand for first-rate jams and jellies.

Events

The biggest annual celebratory weekend for Bandonians comes in mid-to-late October when the **Cranberry Festival** brings the whole town together in a parade, crafts fair, and the Bandon High Cranberry Bowl—in which the local footballers take on their traditional rivals, the team from Coquille High.

During the Christmas holiday season, the merchants of Old Town and fisherfolk deck their stores and boats with white lights in the traditional **Festival of Lights.** Particularly striking is the Coquille Lighthouse lit up like a Christmas tree.

On Memorial Day, the Bandon Storm-watchers organize the annual **Wine and Seafood Festival.** On the same weekend, competitors in the sandcastle contest create amazing sculptures out of sand, water, and imagination. This takes place on the beach off Beach Loop Dr. at Seabird Lane. Construction starts at 9 a.m.; judging is at 1 p.m. Call (541) 347-9616 for more information. A fish fry is the big event of Bandon's **Fourth of July.** Later, at dusk, fireworks are launched across the Coquille to burst above the river.

Fishing

In summer, anglers come to southern Oregon for salmon and bottomfish. Bandon is midway between such fishing meccas as the Elk and Sixes Rivers (25 miles south near Port Orford) and the Millicoma River (25 miles north near Coos Bay). The southerly rivers have salmon in November and December. The Millicoma and Bandon's own Coquille River have steelhead October to March.

Information and Services

The **Bandon Chamber of Commerce,** 2nd and Chicago, Bandon 97411, tel. (541) 347-9616, has an authoritative 63-page guide and a large annotated pictographic map of the town. Ask them about what they call "the best river fishing and crabbing docks on the coast." The **post office,** one block east of US 101, Bandon 97411, tel. (541) 347-3406, is open Mon.-Fri. 9 a.m.-5 p.m. The **Greyhound** bus stop is at McKay's Market at US 101 and 10th Street. **The Western World,** 1185 Baltimore St., P.O. Box 248, Bandon 97411, tel. (541) 347-2423, is a useful compendium of cultural/recreational goings-on. **Southern Coos General Hospital,** 640 W. 4th, Bandon, 97411, tel. (541) 347-2426, features an ocean view that in itself is therapeutic, as well as an emergency room and facilities for coronary/respiratory care.

NORTH TO CHARLESTON

You can escape the tedium of US 101's inland route to Coos Bay by taking the Seven Devils Beach route a few miles north of Bandon. This road will eventually get you to Coos Bay by way of Charleston, a fishing village which sits closer to the ocean than its larger neighbors to the east of US 101. En route, beaches, state parks, and an estuarine preserve make the drive interesting. The sights detailed in this chapter are expanded upon in "The Bay Area: Coos Bay, Charleston, North Bend" which follows.

Whisky Run

The first beach encountered is Whisky Run, whose ore-bearing sands spread gold fever down the south coast in the early 1850s. As many as 2,000 miners worked here until a storm washed away the deposit. Other forms of beachcombing at Whisky Run and on the beaches to the north are still thriving, however. Agate-hunting, after a season of winter storms, and clamming make these solitary shorelines ideal places to forget the cares of the world.

The lightly traveled northern route continues through heavily logged fir forests until you stop at an estuarine preserve, the coastal town of Charleston, or one of three spectacular state parks.

South Slough Estuarine Preserve

From the beaches, the road climbs northeastward toward the South Slough Estuarine Preserve, whose visitor-center displays and trails can make an hour pass profitably. Though it can be tricky to find, it is worth it. The center looks out over several estuarine arms of Coos Bay, the largest harbor between San Francisco Bay and the Columbia River. These vital wetlands nurture a vast web of life which is detailed by the placards captioning the center's exhibits. The coastal ecosystem is presented by the "10-minute trail" in back of the visitor center. The various conifers and the understory are clearly labeled along the gently sloping half-mile loop. Branch trails lead down toward the water for an up-close view of the estuary itself. Down by the slough, you may see elk grazing in marshy meadows and bald eagles circling above, while

Homo sapiens harvest oysters and shrimp in these waters of life.

Charleston

From South Slough, you drive four miles on Seven Devils Rd. into the little town of Charleston, which makes few pretensions of being anything other than what it really is—the third-largest commercial fishing port on the Oregon coast. Four processing plants here can or cold-pack tuna, salmon, crab, oysters, shrimp, and other kinds of seafood. The town might occasionally smell of fish, but the few restaurants and lodgings here are good dollar values. Moreover, a post office, a laundromat, and a visitor information center are all conveniently crammed together on the main street, the Cape Arago Highway (County Rd. 240).

Sunset Bay, Shore Acres, and Cape Arago State Parks

A portion of this road heads south and west of Charleston to some of the most idyllic beaches and interesting state parks on the coast. Pick up this stretch of highway close by the junction of Seven Devils Road (ORE 240). Among the several beaches on the road to Cape Arago, **Sunset Bay State Park** is the big attraction. This is because its sheltered shallow cove is warm and calm enough for swimming, a rarity in the Pacific north of Santa Barbara, California. In addition to swimmers, divers, surfers, and boaters, many people come here to watch the sunset. Near the park is one of three golf courses within a 10-mile radius. A four-mile cliffside trail from Sunset Beach south is the best way to appreciate the sea stacks and islands between here and Cape Arago.

Less than a mile south at **Shore Acres State Park,** the grandeur of nature is complemented by the hand of humankind. The park is set on the grounds of a lumber magnate's turn-of-the-century estate. Formal Oriental gardens here are in themselves compelling attractions, but the headland's rim is more dramatic. Whitecaps appear to hang suspended upon contact with the rock embankments at the base of Shore Acres' sandstone cliffs. The orange, brown, and buff strata of these escarpments heighten the visual effect.

Although the original Simpson mansion burned to the ground in 1921, the grounds are still kept up by the state, which was ceded the land by the family. A restored gardener's cottage with antique furnishings sits in back of the gardens. It is open for exhibition December 9-31, with music, entertainment, and refreshments. The history of the Simpsons is really the history of the Coos Bay/Charleston/North Bend area and is captioned beneath period photos in the observation tower and in a small enclosure at the west end of the floral displays. Also in the gardens, note the copper egret sculptures and the greenhouse for rare plants from warmer climes.

The bird sculptures are displayed at a pond to the rear of the gardens. If you bear right and follow the pond's contours toward the ocean, you'll come to a trail. Follow it north for cliffside views of the rock-studded shallows below. Southward, the trail goes downhill to a scene of exceptional beauty. From the vantage point of a small beach, you can watch waves crash into rocks with such force that the white spray appears to hang suspended in the air. Exploring tidepools and caves, as well as springtime swimming in a cove formed by winter storms on the south side of the beach, are pursuits for the active traveler here. In summer, thimbleberries and salal growing along the trail down to the beach can provide sustenance for these activities.

A few miles south is **Cape Arago State Park.** Locals have made much of the fact that it was a possible landing site of the English explorer Sir Francis Drake in 1579 and have put a plaque here commemorating him. Such speculation is not just confined to this part of the south coast. At any rate, beachcombers can make their own discoveries in the numerous tidal pools. Savvy wildlife watchers have a chance to make a siting of the most northerly breeding colony of elephant seals. At that time, these huge (By the time their mothers wean them after they are a month old, they weigh 300 to 400 pounds!) creatures can be seen on Shell Island just off Cape Arago. For more information on these parks see "The Bay Area: Coos Bay, Charleston, North Bend" following.

THE BAY AREA:
COOS BAY, CHARLESTON, NORTH BEND

The towns around the harbor of Coos Bay refer to themselves collectively as the "Bay Area." In contrast to its namesake in California, the Oregon version is not exactly the Athens of the state. Nonetheless, the visitor will be impressed by the area's beautiful beaches (including the largest oceanfront dunes in North America), as well as scenic and historic state parks. Because much of this natural beauty is on the periphery of the industrialized core of the Bay Area, it's easy to miss. All the motorist sees entering Coos Bay/North Bend on US 101 are the dockside lumber mills and foreign vessels anchored at the world's largest lumber port.

The historical antecedents for this scene were laid over a century ago when the region's mills supplied lumber to a gold rush-era housing boom in San Francisco. Heading up this effort was Simpson's lumber company, and later on, the family shipping concern. By the turn of the century, Simpson ships were hauling lumber to 11 nations. Also during that time, companies such as Weyerhaeuser were building their mills by the Union Pacific tracks here.

Today, the Bay Area, along with other western Oregon towns dependent upon timber, is in transition. The region's wealth of diversions and what is probably the mildest weather of any major city in Oregon are being promoted to draw tourists and retirees, and to recruit new businesses.

SIGHTS

Along The Coast

To many people, an estuary is just a place where you get stuck in the mud. More often than not, however, the interface of fresh water and salt water represents one of the richest ecosystems on earth, capable of producing five times more plant material than a cornfield of comparable size while supporting great numbers of fish and wildlife. The South Slough of Coos Bay is the largest such web of life on the Oregon coast. **The South Slough Estuarine Preserve Visitor**

Center, off Cape Arago Highway on Seven Devils Rd. in Charleston, tel. (888) 5558, will help you coordinate a canoe trip through the estuary and offers guided hikes as well. Paralleling the drive to the visitor center is the **estuary study trail,** the first of a large network of pathways you'll encounter here. The center is open daily in summer 8:30 a.m.-4:30 a.m. In the off-season, it operates Mon.-Fri. 8:30 a.m.-4:30 p.m., Sept.-May. The admission is free.

The jewel of the previously detailed "tremendous trio" of Oregon state parks about 12 miles southwest of Coos Bay is **Shore Acres.** This former estate of Louis J. Simpson began as a summer home and grew into a three-story mansion complete with an indoor heated swimming pool and large ballroom. Originally a Christmas present to his wife, Shore Acres became the showplace of the Oregon coast, with formal and Japanese gardens eventually added to the 743-acre estate. After a 1921 fire, a second, smaller (two stories high and 224 feet long) incarnation of Simpson's "shack by the beach" was built. This was acquired by the state in 1942 after it fell into disrepair. Because of the cost of upkeep, the latter had to be razed, but the gardens have been maintained. The international botanical bounty culled by Simpson clipper ships and schooners is still in its glory, complemented by award-winning roses, rhododendrons, and azaleas. It's open year-round till dusk, with a $3 fee charged for vehicles only in summer and on holiday weekends.

When there's a storm, it's not uncommon to feel the spray atop the 75-foot promontory at Shore Acres. And when conditions are calm, be sure to look for sea lions along this part of the coast.

Coos County Museum

The Coos County Museum is close to the Conde McCullough Bridge, one of several distinctive 1930s-era high-wire acts by Oregon's master bridgebuilder. The museum houses more than the usual bric-a-brac from earlier eras, thanks

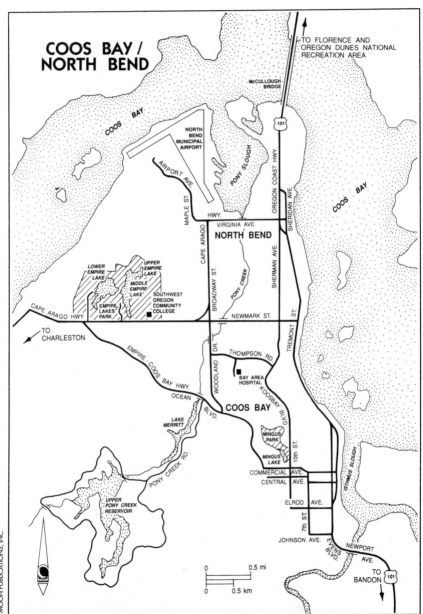

The Oregon coast is dotted with distinctive bridges.

OREGON TOURISM DIVISION

largely to the region's heritage as a shipping center. A turn-of-the-century Regina music box, a piano shipped around the Horn, miniature boat models, and a jade Chinese plaque, as well as Coos Indian beadwork/artifacts make this collection especially memorable. In summer, the museum is open Tues.-Sat. 10 a.m.-4 p.m., Sunday 1-4 p.m. From October till Memorial Day, it's open Tues.-Sat. 10 a.m.-4 p.m., charging a nominal admission. Outside the museum, old-time logging equipment and a 1920s steam train are also worth a look. Close by is a tourist information center.

Seaman's Center

From North Bend, head south into Coos Bay. The route follows unending dockside detritus of mills and foreign cargo ships, giving no hint where one city ends and the other begins. Park your car near the intersection of US 101 and the Coos Bay/Charleston turnoff. This is the center of town. Southbound travelers will notice a storefront on the right-hand side of the street with an orange model pagoda in the window. Seaman's Center, 171 N. Broadway, Coos Bay 97420, is a cafe/club where old salts mingle with foreign sailors and anyone else interested in a wealth of sea lore and camaraderie. Model ships made by retired seamen, oddities from the back alleys of Asian ports, and coins and curios from the harbor cities of the world fill this treasure chest of maritime memorabilia. What's more, matey, your ears will be filled with some

scintillating sagas. Since this center is also operated by an evangelical group, you might also hear the Gospel. The center is open every day after 5 p.m. when ships are in port. There is no admission fee. Across the street is a tourist information center.

The Harbor: Milling Around

Due to the decline in the supply of lumber and the subsequent mill closures, the Weyerhaeuser and other forest-product facility tours are currently not operating. But it's still fun to watch the ships docking and the portside wood-chip piles growing by dozens of feet overnight. Wood chips are Oregon's number-one forest-product export. What had been considered surfeit slivers can now be made into a low-grade paper with the addition of chemicals during processing aboard the Japanese factory ships in the harbor. What's left onshore is often enough "hog fuel" to provide sufficient BTUs to heat a mill. Given the return on these chips, locals call these piles the "million-dollar view." Another roadside perspective on the mills is the sight of "log broncs." These short, powerful boats are highly maneuverable. The broncs evoke the "little engine that could" as they move the floating logjams from the millpond to the conveyors into the mill.

The New Salmon Boom

In the fall of 1995, 150,000 spring chinook smolts were released in Coos Bay. In 1997 they returned as mature fish averaging 12-18 pounds, reviving the days of "combat fishing" when hundreds of anglers jostled each other along the bank as they vied for the best fishing spot. These "springers" sometimes exceed 30 pounds and are renowned as an unrivaled dining treat.

The Oregon Connection

To see something closer to a finished product, take the Oregon Connection, located just off US 101 at the south end of town, P.O. Box 457, Coos Bay 97420, tel. (541) 267-7804, factory tour. Myrtlewood carving is an Oregon folk art with a long history.

In 1869, the golden spike marking the completion of the nation's first transcontinental railroad was driven into a highly polished myrtlewood tie. Novelist Jack London was so taken by the beauty of the wood's swirling grain that he ordered an entire suite of furniture. Hudson's Bay trappers used myrtlewood leaves to brew tea as a remedy for chills.

During the Depression years, the city of North Bend issued myrtlewood coins after the only

Called both a California laurel and an Oregon myrtle, this tree is technically neither a laurel nor a myrtle. Crush a leaf to release the tree's distinctive camphor-like aroma.

BOB RACE

bank in town failed. The coins ranged from 50 cents to $10 and are still redeemable—though they are worth far more as collector items. The Oregon Connection's myrtlewood factory tour shows you how an uncut myrtlewood log gets fashioned into bowls, clocks, tables, and other utensils. No admission is charged for this 25-minute guided run through a working factory. After you're done, the store itself is a delight, with Oregon gourmet foods and crafts supplementing the quality woodwork.

Museums

The **Coos Art Museum,** 235 Anderson Ave., Coos Bay 97420, tel. (541) 267-3901, is the Oregon coast's only art museum, featuring paintings by Robert Rauschenberg, Larry Rivers, and Romare Bearden. Don't miss the Prefontaine Room on the second floor of the museum. Photos and videos of this native-son world-class runner bear out his credo of "I want to make something beautiful when I run." It's open Tues.-Fri. 11 a.m.-5 p.m., and on weekends noon-4 p.m.

Just south of here is the *Marshfield Sun Printing Museum,* 1049 N. Front St., Coos Bay 97420, tel. (541) 269-1363, at the junction of Front St. and US 101. This newspaper was in operation 1891-1944. In 1944, Marshfield became Coos Bay. From an old print shop on the first floor, proceed upstairs to vintage photos of early Marshfield and exhibits on printing and newspaper history. It's open June-Aug. Monday, Wednesday, and Friday 1-4 p.m., and the last Sunday of each month (except December). There is no charge.

Golden and Silver Falls State Park

Twenty-five miles northeast of Coos Bay in the Coast Range is Golden and Silver Falls State Park. Two spectacular waterfalls are showcased in this little-known gem of a park. Getting there involves driving east of Coos Bay along the Coos River, crossing to its north bank, and continuing along the Millicoma River through the community of Allegany. To find your way from Coos Bay, look for the Allegany/Eastside exit off US 101. Beyond Allegany, continue up the East Fork of the Millicoma River to its junction with Glenn Creek, which ultimately leads to the park. The narrow windy roads make this trip unsuitable for a wide-body vehicle. Ignore signs indicating that the bridge is out because the access is always passable.

You can reach each waterfall by way of two half-mile trails. Both 200-foot cataracts lie about a mile apart from one another, and although both are about the same height, each has a distinct character. For most of the year, Silver Falls is more visually arresting because it flows in a near semicircle around a knob near its top. During or just after the winter rains, however, the thunderous sound of Golden Falls makes it the more awe-inspiring of the two. Along the trails, look for the beautifully delicate maidenhair fern. En route, **Millicoma Myrtle Grove State Park** makes a fine prelude or appendix to a tour of the House of Myrtlewood.

Oyster lovers might want to visit **Quallman's,** 4898 Crown Point Rd., Charleston, tel. (541) 888-3145. Just look for the signs on the north side of the Charleston Bridge on the east side of the highway. It's open Mon.-Sat. 8:30 a.m.-5:30 p.m. and has fresh high-quality oysters for sale. Several other oyster purveryors make this delicacy available at other Bay Area outlets.

Big Tree Tour

Contact the BLM Coos Bay District, 1300 Airport Ln., North Bend, OR 97439, tel. (541) 756-0100, about the Big Tree Tour loop outside Coquille (southeast of Coos Bay), highlighted by the Doerner Fir, the world's largest Douglas fir at 329 feet in height, 11.5 feet in diameter. Call or write requesting the pamphlet *Growing Forest Driving Tour.* This is a 5-8 hour, 60-mile jaunt, so plan to make a day out of it. To this end, we've mention nearby cultural activities and a good restaurant in the pages to follow.

For those "winging it," here's how to get to the "big tree loop." To get to Fairview (a small town on the way to Coquille), which is the closest town to the loop, first drive US 101 south to ORE 42 east. Take a left on W. Central Blvd. toward downtown Coquille. Go about a mile and take a left toward Fairview Lavern Park. Follow for eight miles to the Fairview intersection. Follow the tree symbols from there. Station five on the tour is the Doerner Fir.

By the way, recent improvements to ORE 42 make it possible to get to Roseburg in 2 hours. Motorists should still be aware that this thoroughfare carries more truck traffic than any other interior-to-coast road in Oregon. But weekenders will encounter few trucks and light traffic to impede the enjoyment of the waysides, wineries, and historic buildings.

RECREATION AND EVENTS

There are two public golf courses in the Bay Area. One, the **Sunset Bay Golf Course,** 11001 Cape Arago Hwy., Charleston 97420, tel. (541) 888-9301, is a nine-holer and has been described as "one of the most interesting courses anywhere" by *Golf Oregon* magazine. The other is the 18-hole **Kentuck Golf Course,** Kentuck Inlet, North Bend 97459, tel. (541) 756-4464.

Fishing charters, bay cruises, whalewatching, and the like can be arranged through **Charleston Charters,** P.O. Box 5457, Charleston 97420, tel. (541) 888-4846; please call in advance.

The bulk of the Bay Area's special events fall in July and August. The first event of note in summer is the **Oregon Coast Music Festival,** P.O. Box 663, Coos Bay 97420, tel. (541) 267-0938, in mid-July. Coos Bay is the most common performance venue of these south coast classical, jazz, and folk concerts but Bandon, North Bend, Charleston and other neighboring burgs occasionally serve as performance venues. Tickets range $9-18.

In late August, the everpresent blackberry is celebrated with the **Blackberry Arts Festival.** Food and winetasting booths and street artists fill the downtown. Picking the fruit itself can best be enjoyed just south of Charleston on the Cape Arago Highway (but everyone has his or her own secret patch). Avoid picking near roads, as exhaust fumes and the possibility of herbicides sprayed along the road shoulder could mean unhealthy residues on (or in) the berries. Both the Himalaya blackberry and the Pacific blackberry (or dewberry) are found here. The latter is the only native Oregon blackberry, while the Himalaya variety took root in the wild after originally being a cultivated plant brought from Europe. The Himalaya's hooked thorns, heavy canes, and large leaves distinguish it from the dewberry's slender stems and diminished leaf presence. Both can be enjoyed midsummer to midfall.

In mid-September, perhaps the best-known Bay Area personality of this century, Steve Prefontaine, is honored with a 10-km race. Prefontaine was a world-class runner whose gutsy style of running and record performances made him a major sports personality until his death at 24 years of age in 1974. Many top-flight runners pay homage by taking part in the race. For more information on this and the previous listings, contact the chamber of commerce (see "Information and Services," below).

The major airport on the south coast hosts **North Bend's Air Show,** 1321-D Airport Way, North Bend 97459, tel. (541) 756-1723, at the beginning of August. The show itself occurs between noon-3 p.m., but the festival gets off the ground with a pancake feed at 8 a.m.

Culture in the Hinterland

A half-hour drive from Coos Bay, a small town theater boasting a quarter-century of melodrama tradition can be experienced weekends at the **Sawdust Theater,** tel. (541) 396-3947, in Coquille. Tickets can be purchased after 6 p.m. at the door if still available, or you can buy advance tickets at Bonnie's Drugs in the middle of town. With the big tree loop and a French bistro nearby (see Chez Claudine in the "Food" section), this detour can turn into an escape from the ordinary. For additional information, contact the Coquille Chamber of Commerce, 119 N. Birch St., Coquille, OR, 97423, tel. (541) 396-3414.

PRACTICALITIES

Accommodations

Some people take umbrage at the fact that many accommodations here face industrial sites. Nevertheless, there is no shortage of low-cost places at which to stay, and noise is seldom a problem.

Over in Charleston is a lodging within walking distance of fishing, charter boats, clamming, and dock crabbing. **Capt. John's Motel,** 8061 Kingfisher Dr., Charleston 97420, tel. (541) 888-4041, is clean, quiet, and has some units with kitchenettes. Close by is a special fish/shellfish-cleaning station and, with any luck, your dinner. Staying in Charleston also puts you close to state parks and within easy reach of laundry and postal services, as well as offering temper-

atures that are warmer than Coos Bay in winter and cooler in summer. The rates run $40-70 in summer and about $5 less in winter; reserve well in advance for July and August.

Situated at a high elevation out of the coastal wind and fog is the aptly named **Highland's Bed And Breakfast,** 608 Ridge Rd., North Bend 97459, tel. (541) 756-0300. The glass-and-cedar home has a huge deck which overlooks meadows, a river, and thousands of acres of the Coast Range. Breakfast on the deck is as much a feast for the eyes as it is for the palate. A few miles from US 101 and nearby sand dunes, beaches, and fine restaurants, Highland's still gives the feeling of being serenely remote. All rooms have antique furniture and private baths (one with a whirlpool tub). There is also an adjoining kitchen, and a family room with satellite TV and library. The rates are $63-90.

Another area bed and breakfast, **Coos Bay Manor,** 955 S. 5th St., Coos Bay 97420, tel. (541) 269-1224, offers the luxury of a renovated Georgian-style mansion for around $60. Large rooms with baths and feather beds, as well as homemade blackberry cobbler accompanying an excellent breakfast, also recommend this spot.

A spendier alternative is the **Coos Bay Doubletree,** 1313 Bayshore Dr., Coos Bay 97459, tel. (541) 267-4141. Large rooms with immense beds, thick pile carpet, and everything else in the way of little extras are characteristic of these units. The Coos Bay Doubletree is also distinguished by having one of the best restaurants in town, a lounge with quality entertainment, and a happy hour with complimentary hors d'oeuvres. The rates range $65-110.

Campgrounds

Cape Arago, south of Charleston, tel. (541) 888-5353, has a county park with a few hiker/biker sites with beautiful views. For reservations write 13030 Cape Arago Hwy., Coos Bay 97420, tel. (541) 888-4902, Even though crowds at **Sunset Bay State Park,** can make it seem like a trailer park in midsummer, the proximity of Oregon's only major swimming beach on the ocean keeps occupants of the 75 tent sites and 29 trailer sites here happy. There are also a laundromat and showers. Sites are $10-15, primitive hiker/biker sites are $4. This site, located three miles southwest of Charleston, is popular with fishermen who can cast into tidal pools for cabezon and sea bass. Good views of Cape Arago lighthouse (closed to the public) can be had here. Listen for its unique foghorn.

The first campsites encountered south of Charleston on the Cape Arago Highway are at **Bastendorff Beach County Park,** tel. (541) 888-5353. For $7, 25 tent sites and 30 trailer sites have drinking water, wood stoves, flush toilets, and hot showers (for an extra two bits). Fishing and hiking are the recreational attractions. Like the previously mentioned campgrounds on the Cape Arago Highway, it's open all year.

North of the Bay Area—2.5 miles north of the McCullough Bridge—is Jordan Cove Rd., a causeway west across the water leading to Forest Service Rd. 1099 and **Horsfall Dunes** campground. Eschew the main campground here with its crowds of noisy all-terrain vehicles and RVs for the privacy of **Bluebill Lake** campsites, call Oregon Dunes NRA Visitor Center at Reedsport for more information, tel. (541) 271-3611. Across the water bear right at the fork in the road on Forest Service Rd. 1099 and continue 2.5 miles to Bluebill's entrance on the left-hand side of the road. Equipped with picnic tables and bathrooms, the campground charges $9 a night and is open all year. No reservations required for the 18 tent/RV sites. Ask the campground hosts about area trails and nearby Clausen's Oyster Farm for the ultimate in campfire fare.

Food

Oregon's Bay Area abounds in places where your nutritional needs can be met, if not in fine style then at least at the right price. Oddly enough, prime rib is a recurring special in this coastal town. There is no shortage of seafood places along this part of the coast, but you'll find the freshest, cheapest maritime morsels close to where they're caught. **The Sea Basket,** Charleston Boat Basin, Charleston 97420, tel. (541) 888-5711, typifies the good seafood, fast service, and relatively low prices in these parts. Oysters are especially tasty in this restaurant, with two noted breeding farms close by. This and other fish dinners (halibut, scallops, prawns, etc.) with potatoes or rice and salad usually don't run you much more than $7-10. The fluorescent glare above the cafeteria-style

tables frequented by fishermen in work-blackened denims may not count much for atmosphere, but you'll leave satisfied.

The Portside, opposite Captain John's Motel, Charleston Boat Basin, Charleston 97420, tel. (541) 888-5544, close by has won Silver Spoon Awards from the Diners Club the past three years. Fine dining in Charleston might seem a contradiction in terms, but the chance to select your own lobsters and crabs out of a tank, along with the sight of the fleet unloading other dinners just outside the door, would wet the appetite of any gourmet. Reserve ahead for the Friday night all-you-can-eat seafood buffet at a low price. Main courses run $11-25.

Also near the boat basin, on the opposite side of Charleston near the bridge is **Cheryn's.** The price range and the menu are similar to the Sea Basket. Often-mentioned specials are broiled fresh Chinook in season and fresh Dungeness crab and cheese sandwich, homemade pies, clam chowder, clam fritters, oyster burgers, and fish and chips. Enjoy warm weather, wind-free dining on the enclosed patio.

Bank Brewing Company, 201 Central Ave., tel. (541) 267-0963, serves seven handcrafted brews from the tap as well as steaks, seafood, and gourmet pizza in a historic bank building. Prices are moderate.

Even though the **Blue Heron Bistro,** 110 W. Commercial, Coos Bay 97420, tel. (541) 267-3933, is located in the heart of downtown Coos Bay, it evokes dining experiences in the San Francisco Bay Area or some other place far from this logging port. This impression can come from opening the door to the restaurant, or opening the menu. The restaurant's tile floors, newspapers on library-style posts, and international posters adorning the walls are in keeping with a European-influenced bill of fare. The extensive menu's eclectic array ranges from Greek salad to Cajun-style blackened fish and emphasizes the freshest ingredients and a creative interpretation whenever possible. An impressive list of microbrews and imports as well as Oregon, California, and European wines will complement whatever dish you order. Expensive, I hear the reader thinking, but it's not really. For not appreciably more money than you'd pay on a high ticket at Denny's, you can enjoy an oasis of refinement in "Timbertown, U.S.A."

The dining room at the **Coos Bay Doubletree,** tel. (541) 267-4141, ext. 305, offers extra-thick cuts of prime rib and flambé items prepared tableside which are as much a treat to look at as to taste. This restaurant is an "in" place to eat out, so make reservations. We recommend the smoked prime rib.

Another prime rib special is featured on Tuesday night 4-6 p.m. at the **Mill Casino,** east side US 101, tel. (800) 953-4800. The restaurant's windows on Coos Bay make the $7 prime rib, salad, vegetables, dessert, and beverage taste even better. Even if you miss the prime rib special, you'll probably appreciate knowing that the restaurant is open 24 hours.

Natural food fans converge at **Coos Head Natural Foods,** 1960 Sherman, tel. (541) 756-7264, which has the largest selection of certified organic produce and food on the south coast.

Finally, for those heading inland to visit the Doerner Fir (see Big Trees Tour), we recommend the nearby town of Coquille (about 20 miles southeast of Coos Bay) for a dining stop. A drive through dairy country along ORE 42 will bring you into this sleepy hamlet (take the West Coquille exit) where you'll encounter, hard as it may be to believe, a French bistro. The proprietress of **Chez Claudine,** 1220 W. Central, tel. (541) 396-5312, is from France, a fact belied by the 99 cent burgers and breakfasts and the small-town cafe facade. One taste of the home-made crepes and croissants for breafast, however, as well as classic renditions of rabbit for dinner, you may start to think that this town's French-sounding name is not mere coincidence. The Raoul Dufy prints on the wall and the resemblance of the topography to parts of France will happily reinforce this illusion.

Information and Services

With over 16,000 people, the Bay Area is the population hub of the coast. As such, it has a large array of services available. **Coos Bay Chamber of Commerce,** 50 E. Central, Coos Bay 97420, tel. (541) 260-0215 or (800) 762-6278, is five blocks west from US 101 off Commercial Avenue. It's open Mon.-Fri. 9 a.m.-7 p.m., weekends 10 a.m.-4 p.m. From September to May hours are Mon.-Sat. 9 a.m.-5 p.m. (closed on Sunday). Inquire here about free tours of logging sites offered during the sum-

mer. For more information on the "Bay Area," call (800) 824-8486.

North Bend's **information center** is just south of the harbor bridge, 138 Sherman Ave., North Bend 97459, tel. (541) 756-4613. It's open Mon.-Fri. 8:30 a.m.-5 p.m., Saturday 10 a.m.-3 p.m., and Sunday 10 a.m.-4 p.m. From Labor Day to Memorial Day the center is not open on weekends. Another information resource is the **Oregon State Parks** office, 115 S. 5th, Coos Bay 97420, tel. (541) 269-9410.

Allen's Washtub, 255 Golden Ave., tel. (541) 267-2814, is Coos Bay's version of a fast-disappearing American institution—the all-night laundromat. The **Egyptian Theater,** 229 S. Broadway, tel. (541) 267-3456, is a movie house with a middle eastern motif goes back to the 1940s when many small towns took to emulating the opulence and foreign intrigue of such big city movie houses as Graumann's Chinese Theater in Hollywood. A selection of three first run movies are usually available here.

The **Greyhound** bus depot, 2007 Union Ave., North Bend, tel. (541) 756-4900, has arrivals from Portland and Lincoln City. There are also two buses between Coos Bay and Eugene. If Greyhound doesn't fit into your plans, consider the **North Bend Airport,** 1321-D Airport Way, North Bend 97459. Horizon, tel. (800) 547-9308, flies to or from Eugene and Portland almost every day of the week, and to Salem and Seattle on occasion. One way rates are $100-200, with discounts on early morning and weekend flights. To get to the airport, follow the signs on the road between Charleston and North Bend.

Within the city the **Shuttle,** tel. (541) 267-4521, offers low-cost transport and scenic/historical tours. There is no set schedule but it's on call 24 hours. Roundtrip within the city can be had for $5, and the fare to Shore Acres one way is $7.

The North Bend pool is a wonderful way to break up long coastal drives. Just ask for directions and schedule at the information center (located just south of the McCullough Bridge) to the high school. For a nominal fee you can enjoy the daily recreational swim in what has to be one of the nicest public pools in the state.

The Coos Bay Public Library, 525 W. Anderson, Coos Bay 97420, tel. (541) 267-1101, is open Mon.-Thurs. 1-4 p.m., Friday 10 a.m.-5 p.m., and Saturday noon-5 p.m. For **medical emergencies,** Tel-Med, 1775 Thompson Rd., Coos Bay 97420, tel. (541) 269-2313, and the ambulance, tel. (541) 269-1151, will get help fast. Help Line, tel. (541) 269-5910, gives re-ferrals. In what's considered a "big city" on the Oregon coast, you might occasionally need the **police,** tel. (541) 269-1151. The **post office,** 4th and Golden, Coos Bay 97420, tel. (541) 267-4514, is open Mon.-Fri. 8:30 a.m.-5 p.m.

REEDSPORT/WINCHESTER BAY

If you're about to go fishing or are coming back from a dunes hike, you'll appreciate a hot meal and a clean low-priced motel room in Reed-sport. Otherwise this town of several thousand people might seem like a strange mirage of cut-rate motels, taverns, and burger joints in the midst of the Oregon Dunes NRA.

It evolved because of the site's proximity to the Umpqua River. Jedediah Smith explored this country in the 1820s after the Hudson's Bay Company's Peter Skene Ogden theorized that the Umpqua River might be the fabled Northwest Passage. Even though it wasn't, this river is still one of the great fishing streams of the state. Zane Grey avoided writing about it, lavishing the publicity instead upon the Rogue to divert people from his favorite steelhead spots. At any rate, Winchester Bay's Salmon Harbor Marina has given the whole area new life in recent years, following hard times precipitated by the decline in timber revenues. Salmon Harbor sits at the mouth of the Umpqua, one of the largest rivers between San Francisco Bay and the Co-lumbia.

SIGHTS

Just south of Winchester Bay is **Umpqua Light-house State Park.** Even though the 1894 light-house isn't open to the public, there's a county museum, tel. (541) 271-4631, there with ma-rine and timber exhibits, open May-Sept., Wed.-Sat. 10 a.m.-11:30 a.m., and 1-4 p.m., Sunday 1-4 p.m. Directly opposite the lighthouse is a whalewatching platform. Huckleberries can be found in the area (in season), and, according to some books, the largest oceanfront dunes in the world. There's also campsite near Lake Maire with showers and drinking water, tel. (800) 452-5687, $16-20, call for reservation and details.

Close by the Oregon Dunes NRA headquar-ters on US 101 south of Reedsport is ORE 38, which takes you inland to Curtin and I-5. Ore-gon's "foremost motorcycle road" (according to Harley-Davidson) goes through pastoral country-side along the Umpqua on a well-maintained highway. One highlight is the **Dean Creek Elk Preserve** just outside of Reedsport. There are about 55 Roosevelt elk here, the largest species of this animal in the world. They graze the pre-serve's marshy pastures in full view of the high-way. Farther east are a number of historical plac-ards by landmarks in the one-time shipping cen-ter of **Scotsburg.** Cargo ships from this town supplied San Francisco markets with meat, milk, and produce between 1856 and the early 20th century. In Reedsport's Old Town on the south bank of the river, the **Umpqua Discovery Cen-ter,** 409 Riverfront Way, tel. (541) 271-4816, in-terprets regional human and natural history and offers tours on a retired Antarctic research vessel. Exhibits from the Umpqua steamboat era tell the story behind the scenery along ORE 38. Admis-sion is $5 adults, $2.50 children. Hours are Sun.-Fri. 10 a.m.-6 p.m., Saturday 10 a.m.-9 p.m. April-Sept., 10 a.m.-6 p.m. the rest of the year.

PRACTICALITIES

Accommodations
Bargain rooms are easy to find in Reedsport off US 101, but forget about ambience and seclusion. For the latter, check out the small towns close by.

Of the half-dozen motels that sit off of US 101 in Reedsport, the **Fir Grove Motel,** 2178 Winchester Ave., Reedsport 97467, tel. (541) 271-4848, is slightly less expensive but com-parable in comfort to the other lodgings. The rooms go for $34 for a single, $45 for a double, and about $10 less on each rate in winter.

OREGON TOURISM DIVISION

*Umpqua River
Lighthouse*

For about the same money, the **Winchester Bay Motel,** 4th and Broadway, Winchester Bay 97467, tel. (541) 271-4871, puts you next to the water. Reserve ahead of time in fishing season.

A few miles north of Reedsport in **Gardiner** is another lodging alternative with more character than motel row for not significantly more money. **The Gardiner Guest House,** 401 Front, P.O. Box 222, Gardiner 97441, tel. (541) 271-4005, is located in a cute, tranquil, paper-mill town which sits close by the confluence of the Smith and Umpqua rivers. The 1883 home was built by local bigwig and State Senator Albert Reed, for whom Reedsport was named. The recently remodeled home still has the Victorian feel, without lacking in modern comforts. Choose between a room with the facility down the hall for $35, $45 peak season, or a view room with private bath for $55, $65 peak. A large home-cooked breakfast is included in the rates.

Gardiner was created in the wake of a shipwreck. The *Bostonian* (owned by Mr. Gardiner) was dashed against the rocks at the mouth of the Umpqua in 1856 and from its remnants the first wooden structure in this area was built. It was soon joined by other white-painted homes and facilities for a port on the Umpqua. While this "white city by the sea" declined in importance when the highway elevated Reedsport to regional hub status, the homes still bear the same color scheme from the earlier era.

If you're interested in a get-away-from-it-all alternative, try **Salbasgeon,** 45209 ORE 38, tel. (541) 271-2025. With rooms on the Umpqua and a location near an elk preserve, this moderately priced, $60-98, lodging should fill the bill.

Food
There's places to eat in town, but try to stave off hunger pangs until Coos Bay.

Up the road in Winchester Bay, lunch and dinner at the **Seafood Grotto** also offer the touch of home. This family restaurant relies on the local fleet to supply the ingredients for home-made cioppino (at $5.45—a meal in itself), clam chowder, and what might be the best grilled salmon in Dune Country. The menu has a range of prices and selections to suit a variety of budgets and appetites.

Charters and Jetboats
Winchester Bay has what is probably the cheapest deep-sea-fishing outfitter in Oregon. **Main Charters,** 4th and Beach Streets, Winchester Bay 97496, tel. (541) 271-3800, charges around $30 for a full day of salmon or bottom fishing. Call the day before for reservations.

In Reedsport, you can tour the Umpqua's mouth from a newly developed harbor area or head upriver on **Umpqua Jet Adventures,** 423 Riverfront Way, tel. (541) 271-5694. The fare is $15, call for cruise times. This waterfront is an old town on the south bank of the Umpqua.

Information and Services
The Reedsport Chamber of Commerce **information kiosk,** tel. (541) 271-3352, is located at the junction of US 101 and ORE 38 just north of the NRA Visitor Center. It's open 10 a.m.-5 p.m. every day, but don't expect lots of help. The Forest Service personnel at the **Oregon Dunes NRA Visitor Center** just south on US

101, 855 Highway Ave., Reedsport 97467, tel. (541) 271-3611, should fill in any gaps. They maintain office hours Mon.-Fri. 8 a.m.-4:30 p.m., weekends 10 a.m.-5:30 p.m. From Labor Day to Memorial Day there are no weekend hours. Ask about guided visits to an archaeological dig site that was inhabited by the Coos Indians until about 3,000 years ago.

DUNE COUNTRY: NORTH TO FLORENCE

Even though the 47 miles of US 101 between Coos Bay and Florence does not overlook the ocean, your eyes will be drawn westward every few minutes. After all, it's not every day that you can see mountains of shifting sand that have swallowed up a giant conifer forest. The largest and most extensive oceanfront dunes in the world are found in this national recreation area. Halfway between Coos Bay and Florence in Reedsport is Oregon Dunes NRA headquarters. This town of 5,000 people and the nearby fishing village of Winchester Bay have carved out tourist identities as refueling and supply depots for excursions into Oregon's Sahara-by-the-Sea.

These forays can take several forms. While joyriding in noisy dune buggies and other off-road vehicles doesn't lack for devotees, the best way to appreciate the interface of ecosystems is on foot. Dunes exceeding 500 feet in height,

DUNE COUNTRY TO FLORENCE

wetland breeding grounds for animals and waterfowl, evergreen forests, and deserted beaches can be encountered in a march to the sea. En route you might also come upon the nearly extinct silver spot butterfly and the insect-eating Darlingtonia plant.

But the dunes themselves probably will claim most of your attention. How did they come to be in a coastal topography otherwise dominated by rocky bluffs? A combination of factors created this landscape over the past 12,000 years, but the principal agents are the Coos, Siuslaw, and Umpqua rivers. The sand and sediment transported to the sea by these waterways are deposited by waves on the flat shallow beaches. Prevailing westerlies move the particulate matter exposed by the tide eastward up to several yards per year.

Ancient forests lie beneath these dunes, a fact occasionally proven by hikers as they stumble upon the top of an exposed snag. The cross section of sandswept woodlands seen from US 101 demonstrates that this inundation is still occurring. Nonetheless, the motorist will have the impression that the trees are winning the battle, as the dunes are only intermittently visible from the road. A further inhibition to appreciating the range and size of Oregon's dunes is the limited or obscured access from US 101.

The Forest Service personnel at the Dunes NRA Visitor Center in Reedsport can direct you to the best points of entry as well as supply information on camping and hiking in this remarkable landform. One tip you're bound to hear is that the highest dunes can be reached from secluded trails and campsites south of Reedsport. If your interests extend to fishing, boating, and water-skiing, however, **Ten Mile Lakes** and other freshwater paradises encoun-

The dunes stretch for nearly 50 miles along US 101 between Coos Bay and Florence.

R.W. McLEAN

tered en route from Coos Bay (and later on, north of Florence) might divert you from playing in the sand. Many of these lakes were formed when advancing dunes trapped upland streams. Oceangoing anglers can enjoy the coast's saltwater sportfishing capital, Winchester Bay, six miles south of Reedsport.

The Dunes NRA is home to over 400 species of wildlife, but the only dangerous animal within this ecosystem is possibly the American teenager. This species migrates here during summer vacation to enact puberty rites or auditory assaults with large radios. Extreme caution is advised in parking lots or within earshot of dune buggies.

SIGHTS

Begin your travels at the visitor center, 855 Highway Ave., Reedsport 97467, tel. (541) 271-3611, where US 101 intersects ORE 38. In addition to the information on hiking, camping, and recreation, the Siuslaw Forest Service personnel are very helpful. Next door is a Reedsport tourism information kiosk which can complete an orientation. There's a $3 day use fee for the Dunes National Recreation Area.

Dune Access
The most spectacular dunes landscape can be found nine miles south of the visitor center at **Umpqua Dunes,** at North Eel Campground near Lakeside. After you emerge from a quarter-mile hike through coastal evergreen forest, you'll be greeted by dunes 300 to 400 feet high. It's said that dunes near here can approach 500 feet high and a mile long after a windblown buildup. According to some books, the area between here and the Umpqua Lighthouse encompasses some of the highest oceanfront dunes in the world. In any case, be it mountain or molehill, the view here is most photogenic. Since a regular trail through the dunes is impossible to maintain, you should only expect to find wooden posts spaced at irregular intervals west of the dunes to guide you to the beach. This trail can also be accessed from the Middle Eel Creek campground. Just look for grey posts about 10 feet high with a blue band at the top marking the trail.

Honeyman State Park, 10 miles south of Florence, also has a spectacular dunescape and then some. Come here in May when the rhododendrons bloom along the short, sinuous road heading to the parking lot. A minute's walk west of the lot brings you to a 150-foot-high dune overlooking Cleawox Lake. From the top of this dune, look westward across the expanse of sand, marsh, and remnants of forest at the blue Pacific.

Due to the fact that they are difficult to see from the highway, the most commonly asked question in the visitor center is "Where are the dunes?" To answer it for everybody, the National Forest Service opened **Oregon Dunes Overlook** about halfway between Reedsport and Florence south of Carter Lake at the point where the dunes come closest to US 101, about 10 miles south of Florence. In addition to four levels of railing-enclosed platforms connected by wooden walkways, there are trails down to the sand. It's only about a quarter mile to the dunes and, thereafter, a mile through sand and wetlands to the beach.

You can hike a loop beginning where the sand gives way to willows. Bear right en route to the beach. Once there, walk south 1.5 miles. A wooden post marks where the trail resumes. It then traverses a footbridge going through trees onto sand, completing the loop. If you go in February, this loop has great birdwatching potential. There is a small day-use fee here for cars. For more information, call (541) 271-3611.

HIKING

A hike through the dunes lets you star in your own *Lawrence of Arabia* flick and moonwalk in the earthbound Seas of Tranquility. The soundtrack can be provided by the 247 species of birds here—along with your heartbeat—as you scale these elephantine anthills. Deserted beaches and secret swimming holes are among the many rewards of the journey.

Getting Oriented

To ensure a bon voyage, it's important to understand this terrain. Carry plenty of water and dress in layers because of hot spots in dune valleys and ocean breezes at higher elevations. Expect cool summers and wet, mild winters. While rainfall here can average over 70 inches a year (with 75% of it falling March-Nov.), a string of dry, 50-60 degree days in February is not uncommon. Another surprise is summertime morning fog, brought in by hot weather inland. These fogs, together with the inevitable confusion caused by dunes that don't look much different from each other, make a compass necessary. The lack of defined trails also compels such measures as marking your return route in the sand with a stick. Binoculars help with visual orientation, not to mention the birdwatching opportunities galore. Finally, there are always the sounds of traffic and surf to help you determine the eastern and western extents of this bailiwick.

Prior to setting out, write for or pick up the *Hiking Trails Recreation Opportunity Guide* from the Siuslaw National Forest Service, Oregon Dunes National Recreation Area. This and their other publications will correct the superficial impression that the dunes are just a domain for all-terrain vehicles and campgrounds for day-hikers.

RECREATION

Riding across the dunes into the sunset on a trusty steed sounds like a fantasy, but you can do it, too, thanks to **C&M Stables,** 90241 US 101, Florence 97439, tel. (541) 997-7540. Rates work out to $20 per person for trips of from one to two hours (with discounts for larger parties). The stables are open daily Memorial Day through Labor Day. They operate Wed.-Sun. the rest of the year. With beach rides, dune trail excursions and sunset trips, there's something for everybody. Call for specific times and reservations.

Another option for those who fear to tread is **Dunes Frontier,** 83960 US 101, Florence 97439, tel. (541) 997-3544. This company rents vehicles for travel in specially designated areas within the Dunes NRA. Odysseys, small one-person dune buggies, go for $25 per hour and a $50 deposit. You must be strapped in with a helmet, stay within the marked territory, and be especially careful going uphill. If you lose power on an incline, it's possible to roll over when turning around to go back down. The 20-person dune buggy rides cost $5 for adults, $2.50 for children 6-10 years old, and kids under five ride for free. A four-seater goes for $45 per hour. Protective goggles are provided, along with a driver. Go in the morning when the sand tends to be blowing around less.

The **Dune Mushers Mail Run** is a noncompetitive endurance dogsled run held in March of each year. This is the world's longest organized dry-land run for dogsled teams. It goes most of the length of the dunes, from Horsefall Beach in the south, ending in Florence. Call (541) 269-0215 for more information.

CAMPGROUNDS

North Eel Creek

Set along Eel Creek near Eel Lake and Ten Mile Lakes is North Eel Creek Campground. The area boasts superlative hiking and aquatic sports as well as a favorite restaurant, the **Stable Cafe**, on neighboring Lakeside's Main St. close to Ten Mile Lakes, in case your breakfast rations run low. The camp is open June to late September at $8 per night with no reservations necessary. Picnic tables, fire grills, piped water, and flush and pit toilets service the 52 tent sites and RV spaces. It is near several other campgrounds 10 miles south of Reedsport. For more information on North Eel campground, contact **Oregon Dunes National Recreation Area,** 855 Highway Ave., Reedsport 97467, tel. (541) 271-3611.

Also ask about the **Tahkenitch Dunes Trail** close by. It's located 13 miles south of Florence (turn right six miles south of mile marker 203). Once in the Tahkenitch Dunes campground, follow the loop road to campsite 30 and the trailhead. Ancient conifers, gourmet mushrooms, and sand dunes await.

Nearby State Parks

Umpqua Lighthouse and **William A. Tugman** state parks, P.O. Box 94, Winchester Bay 97467, tel. (541) 271-4118, are five and eight miles south of Reedsport respectively, in the heart of Dune Country. The Umpqua beacon, which bears the name of the river whose mouth it illuminates, is a light in the forest for campers who like fishing, boating, swimming, and hiking. Trails from here lead to the highest dunes in the U.S. (elevation 545 feet), west of Clear Lake. From mid-April to late October, 41 tent sites and 22 trailer sites go for $16-19 per night. Firewood, flush toilets, a laundromat, picnic tables, electricity, and piped water are all included in the on-site facilities. Close by, the Visitor Center, 1020 Lighthouse Road, tel. (541) 271-4631, is a helpful resource. They can point the to way to dunes often cited as the highest in the world.

Tugman is a larger campground with 115 sites and a similar range of creature comforts, price, and recreation. It sits on the west shore of Eel Lake east of US 101 across from where the dunes reach their widest extent, two miles to the sea.

Steller's sea lion

BOB RACE

FLORENCE AND VICINITY

"Location, location, and location." This tenet of business success also explains the growing appeal of Florence for retirees and vacationers. Many people who could afford to live almost anywhere choose to do so here between the Oregon Dunes NRA and some of the most beautiful headlands on US 101. The fact that Florence is also situated halfway up Oregon's coastal route and a little over an hour's drive from shopping and culture in Eugene has made it a major beachhead of vacation-home development in the region. A mild climate, a modern health-care facility, award-winning Sand Pines Golf Course nearby, and lower housing prices than would be encountered elsewhere in a comparable setting also explain the influx. Plans to build a cultural venue will add another dimension to living here.

Florence began shortly after the California gold rush of 1849 put a premium on the lumber and produce upriver from the Siuslaw River estuary here. Several decades later, the town's name was inspired by a remnant from a shipwreck which floated ashore, bearing the ship's title, *Florence*. The townspeople either recognized an omen when they saw it or just figured they couldn't come up with anything better.

SIGHTS

Easy access to beach and dunes is offered by South Jetty Rd. just south of the Siuslaw River Bridge and Florence proper. While birdwatching opportunities abound in the marshy lakes en route to the beach at all times of the year, the chance to see tundra swans here November to January is a special treat. The six-foot wingspan of this majestic bird is best appreciated with binoculars, and waterproof boots are a must for comfortable hiking in the area.

Siuslaw River Bridge
If first and last impressions are enduring, Florence is truly blessed. As you enter the city from the south, a graceful bridge over the Siuslaw greets you. Shortly after you leave city limits to the north, US 101 climbs to dizzying heights above the ocean.

The Siuslaw River Bridge is perhaps the most impressive of Conde McCullough's WPA-built spans. The Egyptian obelisks and art deco styling characteristic of other McCullough designs are complemented by the views to the west of the sand dunes. To the east, the riverside panorama of Florence's Old Town beckons further investigation. Prior to making the turnoff several blocks beyond US 101, you can stop at the chamber of commerce on the highway. Old Town itself is a tasteful restoration, with all manner of shops and restaurants along the river. The absence of car traffic is conducive to a pleasant walk after lunch there. One place to stop if you're looking for regional titles is **Old Town Books,** 1340 Bay St., Florence, tel. (541) 997-6205. The friendly staff here will also gladly direct you to local attractions and answer any questions you might have about the region.

Museums
To fill in the missing captions on the original town site and get some notion of Indian and pioneer life, return to the highway for the **Siuslaw Pioneer Museum,** 85294 US 101, Florence 97439, tel. (541) 997-7884. You'll find it on the south side of the Siuslaw River on the west side of the highway in a converted church. Open year-round 10 a.m.-4 p.m. every day except Monday, the usual array of artifacts is accompanied by an account of how the U.S. government double-crossed the Siuslaw tribespeople, who sold their land to the feds and never received the promised recompense.

Another museum in town is the **American Museum of Fly Fishing,** 280 Nopal St., Florence 97439, tel. (541) 997-6102. Located three blocks north of the Old Town waterfront, thousands of fishing flies are attractively framed here. Next to the tufts of feathers and hair are fish paintings and lifelike wooden amphibian sculptures. This palace of Poseidon is open 10 a.m.-5 p.m. daily with an admission charge of $2.50 for adults; kids under 16 get in free.

Indian Forest

Four miles outside of town is the Indian Forest, 88493 US 101, Florence 97439, tel. (541) 997-3677. When you see a totem pole on the right-hand side of the road, pull into this exhibit of Native American dwellings. A Navajo hogan, an Ojibwa wigwam, a Sioux tipi, and other dwellings are on display here. A kitschy plastic horse and a herd of real buffalo gaze forlornly over this assemblage. It's open daily June-Aug. 8 a.m.-dusk. In May, September, and October, the exhibit is open 10 a.m.-4 p.m. The admission is $3, half that for kids below 18; under-fives get in free.

Fifteen miles east of Florence in the Mapleton area are several cascades on Kentucky Creek and the North Fork of the Smith River. Known collectively as **Kentucky Falls,** they are set in an old-growth forest on a trail kept up by the Mapleton Ranger Station of the U.S. Forest Service, 10692 ORE 126, Mapleton 97453, tel. (541) 268-4473. Contact this office for exact directions or see "Activities and Recreation—Off the Beaten Path" under "Eugene and Vicinity" in The Willamette Valley chapter for an in-depth discussion.

Darlingtonia Wayside

Several miles up the road from Florence in an area noted for dune access and freshwater lakes is the Darlingtonia Wayside. In a sylvan grove of spruce and alder are a series of wooden platforms that guide you through a bog overlooking the carnivorous Darlingtonia plants, which are shaped like serpent heads. Known alternatively as the pitcher plant, cobra orchid, or cobra lily, the sweet smell the plant produces invites insects to crawl into the top of the Darlingtonia's serpentlike extension.

Once inside, thin transparent "windows" allow light to shine inside the leaf, confusing the bug as to where the exit is. As the insect crawls around in search of an escape, downward-pointing hairs within the enclosure inhibit its movement to freedom. Eventually, the tired-out bug falls to the bottom of the stem, where it is digested. The plant needs the nutrients from the trapped insects to compensate for the lack of sustenance supplied by its small root system. If you still have an appetite after witnessing this carnage, you might want to enjoy lunch at one of the shaded picnic tables here.

Sea Lion Caves

Ten miles north of Florence, you'll have an opportunity to descend into the world's largest sea cave to observe the only mainland rookery of the Steller's sea lion in the lower 48. Sea Lion Caves, 91560 US 101, Florence, tel. (541) 547-3111, is home to several hundred of this species. These animals occupy the cave during the fall and winter, which are thus the prime visitation times. The Steller's sea lions you'll see at those times are cows, yearlings, and immature bulls. Otherwise, go a quarter mile past the concession entrance to the "rockwork" turnout, where the herd can often be witnessed on the rocky ledges several hundred feet below. Many people snap the picturesque **Heceta Head Lighthouse** across the cove to the north from the turnout. It's said that this is the most photographed beacon in the United States (For more on Heceta Head, see Yachats State Parks).

Enter Sea Lion Caves through the gift shop on US 101. To the right, tickets can be purchased 8 a.m.-7 p.m. in summer and 9 a.m.-4 p.m. in winter for $6. Kids 6-15 get in for $4, and those under five enter free. A steep downhill walk reveals stunning perspectives of the coastal cliffs as well as several kinds of gulls and cormorants which nest here. The final leg of the descent is facilitated by an elevator. After disembarking the lift into the cave, look for the sea lions to the left from behind a partition. You'll also note a set of stairs on the right. These lead up to a view of Heceta Head Lighthouse through an opening in the cave. Flash photography is forbidden in the cave, so bring high-speed film if you wish to take pictures inside. You have a better chance of seeing these animals inside during fall and winter.

The Steller's sea lions were referred to as *lobos marinos* (sea wolves) in early Spanish mariners' accounts of their 16th-century West Coast voyages, and their doglike yelps might explain why. You'll notice several shades of color in the herd, which has to do with the progressive lightening of their coats with age. Males can sometimes weigh over a ton and dominate the scene here with macho posturings to scare off rivals for harems of as many as two dozen cows. Their protection as an endangered species enrages many fishermen, who claim that the sea lions take a significant bite out of fishing revenues by preying on salmon. In any case, the sight of these huge sea mammals close-up in the cavernous enclaves of their natural habitat should not be missed . . . despite an odor that can be likened to sweat-soaked sneakers.

PRACTICALITIES

Accommodations

As in Reedsport, there are budget motels on the main drag here, but to experience the coast fully, try one of the romantic getaways between Florence and Yachats. Romantic B&Bs abound north of town, covered in detail in the Yachats and Vicinity chapter. Another alternative is renting a house out in the dunes through **Dolphin Property Management,** tel. (541) 997-7368.

FLORENCE ACCOMMODATIONS

Americana Motel, 3829 US 101, tel. (541) 997-7115, $45-55, kitchenettes, covered pool.

Best Western Pier Point Inn, 85625 U.S. 101, tel. (541) 997-7191 or (800) 4-FLORENCE, $60-100, bayview, continental breakfast, close to Old Town.

Driftwood Shores, 88416 1st Ave., tel. (800) 422-5091 or (541) 997-8263, $80-150, restaurant, lounge, indoor pool and spa, all rooms have ocean view.

Gull Haven on the Sea, 94770 US 101, (16 miles north of town), tel. (541) 547-3583, $40-90, sandy beach, seclusion, private bath, kitchen privileges, midweek discounts available, reserve early.

Holliday Inn Express, 2475 U.S. 101, tel. (541) 997-7797 or (800) HOLIDAY, $60-100, new facility, continental breakfast, laundry.

Johnson House Bed and Breakfast, 216 Maple St., tel. (541) 997-8000, $65-105 antiques in an old Victorian a block from the bayfront, full breakfast, afternoon tea, down comforters, separate cottages available.

Le Chateau Motel, 1084 US 101, tel. (541) 997-3481, $40-65, restaurant, pool, wheelchair access, laundromat.

Money Saver Motel, 170 US 101, tel. (541) 997-7131, $35-55, off-season discounts available, adjacent to Old Town.

Park Motel, 85034 US 101 South, tel. (541) 997-2634, $40-65, restaurant, pets, kitchenettes.

Silver Sands Motel, 1449 US 101 North, tel. (541) 997-3459, $50-70.

Campgrounds

Camping here offers recreational opportunities comparable to those at the Oregon Dunes NRA, with more varied scenery.

Carl G. Washburne State Park, c/o The Campground, Florence 97439, tel. (541) 238-7488, is popular with Oregonians due to its proximity to beaches, tidepools, Sea Lion Caves, and elk. The eight tent sites and 58 RV sites have such modern conveniences as showers, a laundromat, electricity, and piped water. It's located 14 miles north of Florence on US 101 (several miles past Sea Lion Caves), then one mile west on a park road. The fee is $16-20, $5 for hiker and biker spaces, and it's open all year. In addition, there are nearby forest pathways such as the **Hobbit Trail,** named after the furry-toed gnome-like characters in J.R.R. Tolkien's works. You'll probably feel like a hobbit when peering up at the high walls woven of roots, peat, and sand that loom above the trail cut deep into the forest floor here. The path winds through dense forest thickets of pine, fir, and rhododendrons down to the beach. Look for the turnout on the right side of the road just over the hill north of the Heceta Head curves on US 101. Ask the park personnel about this and China Creek Trail.

Heceta Head Lighthouse is within state park boundaries. According to some accounts, Heceta was the first European to set foot in Oregon (in 1774). Beyond Heceta Head is a trail down to the beach at adjoining **Devil's Elbow State Park.** Be conscious of tides here if you climb along the rocks adjoining the beach en route to the top of Heceta Head. Near these campgrounds, Devil's Elbow Tunnel on US 101 is a 600-foot cut through solid mountain.

Three miles south of Florence's McCullough Bridge and on both sides of US 101 is **Honeyman State Park,** tel. (541) 997-3851. This exceedingly popular campground gets very crowded in the

*Devil's Elbow State
Park north of Florence*

summer—reservations a must—but it empties out enough during spring and autumn to make a stay here worthwhile. There are 240 tent sites with the basics, a large number of RV spaces with all the amenities, and many hiker/biker spots as well (381 in total). Fishing, swimming, hiking, and dune buggies are available nearby, so there's always something to do. In spring, pink rhodies line the highway and park roads. Advance reservations are accepted here Memorial Day through Labor Day, call (800) 452-5687, and the sites cost $16-20. Finally, at **Honeyman Park Lodge,** tel. (541) 997-9143, west of US 101 on Cleawox Lake, the food is tasty and ample. Walk it off by climbing the dune fronting the opposite shore and trudging 1.5 miles to the sea. Ask about canoe rentals here to savor the serenity of Cleawox Lake.

An ideal place to escape from the summertime coastal crowds is the **North Fork of the Siuslaw** campground (write Siuslaw Forest, Mapleton Ranger District, Mapleton 97453, tel. (541) 268-4473. Chances are you'll see mostly locals here—if anybody. From Florence follow ORE 126 about 15 miles to Mapleton and the junction with ORE 36. The latter road will take you 13 miles to County Route 5070. Then it's a short drive to the riverside campsite, (or you can drive the North Fork Siuslaw River Road from Florence 14.5 miles). The fee is $4 between July and early September. Sheltered picnic tables, fire pits, and crawdads in the river are other reasons to come.

Close by is the **Pawn Old Growth Trail,** a half-mile pathway through several-hundred-year-old 100-inch diameter Douglas fir 275 feet tall and hemlock. The trailhead, located at the confluence of the North Fork of the Siuslaw and Taylor's Creek, is a good place to see salmon spawning in the fall and observe water ouzels (also called "dippers"). It follows the creek and offers interpretive placards along the way. At one point in the trail visitors walk through fallen Douglas fir logs 260 inches in diameter. Placards explain the science of tree rings. Consult the Mapleton Ranger District mentioned above to get exact directions.

By the way, nearby ORE 36 makes an interesting access road back to the Willamette Valley if you're not in a hurry. Its circuitous route passes through Deadwood and ends up in the Junction City area.

Food

A famous Zen master once said, "If you can make a cup of tea right, you can do anything." The same aphorism seems to apply to clam chowder in coastal restaurants, if three Florence eateries are any indication.

The local **Mo's,** 1436 Bay St., Old Town Florence, tel. (541) 997-2185, is the largest outlet of this famed Oregon chowderhouse, and its fresh fish, fast service, fair prices, and Siuslaw River frontage make it this neighborhood's most popular restaurant. Highly recommended are the dozen baked oysters (seasonal availability) with salad, chowder, or homemade bread for $8.95. Even if you don't eat here, you might want to stock up on Mo's clam chowder base packaged to go.

Another chowder fêted by the People's Choice Award as well as a 1990 *Oregon Coast* magazine poll is the creamy clam-filled concoction made by **The Blue Hen,** 1675 US 101, Florence, tel. (541) 997-3907, at the north end of town. Fourteen finely chopped items go into this orange-specked beige soup. However, as the name and the sign out front imply, chicken is the mainstay of this small cafe operating out of a home on the highway. You may be asked to share your table with the interesting cross section of travelers drawn to this Oregon coastal hub. It's open Mon.-Sat. 8 a.m.-8 p.m. You'll enjoy dining on the outdoor deck in summer. In 1997, *Sunset* selected the chowder at **Ruby Begonia,** tel. (541) 997-1827, as the best seafood chowder on the coast. This golden-hued soup has salmon, halibut, prawns, and clams. The homemade pie is good too.

The Bridgewater Seafood Restaurant and Oyster Bar, 129 Bay St., Old Town Florence, tel. (541) 997-9405, features exotic clam chowder with Indonesian clams, in keeping with a Banana Republic decor, and the only "fine dining" in Old Town. Of course, this also means the highest prices on the waterfront, $2.75 for a cup of chowder, but to be fair, you're getting what you pay for and then some. The Bridgewater was the recipient of a "People's Choice Award" for the best clam chowder in town several years back. Besides that, if you don't like it, the chowder's free. Fresh fish, often with a Cajun flair, is the star of a menu whose lunch entrees average around $6.50, twice that for dinner. A lower-priced option exists on Wednesday, winter through early spring, with the all-you-can-eat seafood dinner buffet in the $10 range.

Traveler's Cove, 1362 Bay St., Florence, tel. (541) 997-8194, manages to combine an import shop and gourmet cafe under the same roof. The cafe serves good lunches in the $7-10 range, worth a stop for the homemade clam chowder and interesting salads and sandwiches. Fresh Dungeness crab makes an appearance here with crab quiche, crab enchiladas, and "crabby" Caesar salad. Best of all, the patio out back provides riverfront views to enjoy along with your meal. The cafe is open 9 a.m.-7 p.m.

Another Old Town venue to satisfy your sweet tooth, albeit healthy, is **Crystal Wood Natural Foods,** 1263 Bay St., Florence, tel. (541) 997-4848. In addition to home-baked goodies, espresso drinks, microbrews, Oregon wines, and a natural foods market are other reasons to stop in. Close by, **International C-Food Market,** 1498 Bay St., Florence, tel. (541) 997-9646, gets good word-of-mouth from locals. This combination restaurant and retail market offers seafood right off the boat. Not only is the freshness of the fish exceptional, but prices are low, averaging $6 for lunch and $10-12 for dinner. The catch of the day and the smoked salmon pizza are both in the $8 range.

Up the road a few miles, it's a safe bet that you'll find the chowder and whatever else is ordered to your liking. That's because **The Windward Inn,** 3757 US 101, Florence, tel. (541) 997-8243, is one of the better restaurants in the state. Without belaboring the critical acclaim and kudos, let's just say it's good enough to make believers out of even jaded guidebook writers. Fresh-cut flowers, skylights, a wood-paneled interior, and four separate dining rooms set the stage for an imaginative and extensive menu. For the budget-conscious, the bistro dinners are lighter meals that might forestall your wallet losing too much weight here. A chicken-and-veal sausage known as *boudin blanc,* $8.50, also makes for an excellent lower-priced alternative to a full dinner. If you're into a full splurge, go with the fresh mussels broiled on the half shell with Oregon hazelnuts, Oregon peppered bacon, and Tillamook cheddar cheese, $14.75.

After dinner, have dessert at either of **BJ's Ice Cream Parlor**'s two locations, 2930 US 101 or 1441 Bay St., Florence, tel. (541) 997-7286. BJ's churns out 48 flavors famous all over Oregon. Full fountain service, ice cream cakes, cheesecakes, gourmet frozen yogurt, and pies complement the cones and cups.

Driving east on ORE 126 en route to Eugene from the coast lets you follow the Siuslaw past isolated farms and lush forests topped by clearcut ridges. Shortly after leaving Florence, you come to **Mapleton.** Set at the base of the Coast Range, it's one of the rainiest burgs in the whole state. It also has two restaurants which'll evoke remembrances of things past.

The Alpha Bit Crafts Cafe, 10780 ORE 126, Mapleton, (541) 268-4311, is only 11 miles outside of Florence, but it exists in a different time and space. Started by a commune in the nearby town of Deadwood, the restaurant serves a varied menu of good ol' American food and vegetarian fare (try the grainburger) at reasonable prices. The preparations frequently include produce grown on Alpha Farm, and the coffee for two bits puts the higher-priced coastal brews to shame. Also don't miss the home-baked cakes and pies, and the December 1991 *Life* magazine article about the commune, available upon request. Finally, the unusual local crafts and fine selection of books make Alpha Bit the cultural center of Mapleton.

A mile or two down ORE 126 is the **Gingerbread Village,** 12300 ORE 126, Mapleton, tel. (541) 268-4713. This is the kind of place your parents might have taken you when you were a kid . . . you know, a greasy spoon without the grease, serving simple, wholesome meals. While the food here is good enough to get you to Eugene, the gingerbread is unforgettable. Order it warm so the vanilla ice cream on top melts down decadently. Getting this dish to go costs a quarter more, $1.25, but the "boat" it comes in carries a disproportionately larger serving.

Shopping

A nice selection of Oregon food products and crafts is available down in Old Town Florence at **Incredible Edible Oregon,** 1350 Bay St., tel. (541) 997-7018.

Events and Recreation

During the third week of May, Florence celebrates the **Rhododendron Festival,** coinciding with the bloom of these flowers which proliferate in the area. A parade, boat and slug races, a carnival, a flower show, and a five-kilometer "rhody's run" highlight the festivities. Contact the chamber of commerce for more information.

On July 4 at 2 p.m., the **National Stilt Walking Championship** starts at the corner of Maple and Bay Streets in Old Town.

Ocean Dunes Golf Links, 3315 Munsel Lake Rd., Florence 97439, tel. (541) 997-3232, lets you tee off with sand dunes as a backdrop. The manicured 18-hole course has a driving range,

a full pro shop, and equipment rentals on-site. For the ultimate in golfing by the dunes, however, try **Sand Pines Golf Course,** 1050 35th St., tel. (800) (541) 497-1937. This was voted *Golf Digest*'s number one public course several years ago. To get there, go west off US 101 on 35th Street. In May and June rhododendrons line this drive, which heads into dune country as you move toward the sea. Follow the signs until you see a water tower not far from the mobile home currently housing the pro shop. Sand Pine's layout features fairways lined with Douglas fir and beach grass on gently undulating terrain. As with Salishan, that other Scottish links-style course by the sea, coastal winds can figure prominently in your shot selection. Greens fee is $35. A future resort here is in the planning stages.

The Harbor Theatre, 1368 Bay, Old Town Florence, tel. (541) 997-3361, charges $6 for first-run movies with discounts for seniors and kids. The showtime is 7 p.m.

For sternwheeler trips on the Siuslaw, the 65-foot *Westward Ho,* tel. (541) 997-9691, leaves from the Old Town docks. In addition to the succession of historic sites along the Siuslaw between Florence and Mapleton detailed in the 11 a.m. cruise, two other daily departures at 1 p.m. and 3 p.m. feature lunch and "lots of music and cool spirits," respectively. On Friday and Saturday there are dinner cruises. Weekday cruise fares are $12, and the dinner excursion is $29. Paddlewheelers along the Siuslaw were part of the two-day Eugene-to-Florence pilgrimage a century ago.

Huckleberry picking is another attraction just outside of town. Some prime pickin's are found about five miles north of Florence at the Sutton Creek Trail, which begins in the campground with the same name that's just off of US 101. During late summer or fall, these berries flourish below the dense canopy of shorepine here. Rhododendrons bloom in profusion mid-May to early June. In addition to these delights, you can hike through the dunes, which are broken up by several freshwater lakes. The Forest Service in Reedsport can answer your questions about the huckleberries and the trails and point the way to the new whalewatching vista overlooking dunes and ocean. (Day-use fee $3, overnight camping $10.)

Information and Services
The **Florence Chamber of Commerce,** 270 US 101, Florence 97439, tel. (541) 997-3128, is three blocks north of the Siuslaw River Bridge; open 9 a.m.-5 p.m. Close by the junction of ORE 126 and US 101 is the library. **Peace Harbor Hospital,** 400 9th St., Florence 97439, tel. (541) 997-3128, is open 24 hours, with a dozen specialists and an emergency room. The **post office,** 770 Maple St., Florence

97439, tel. (541) 997-2533, is open Mon.-Fri. 8 a.m.-5 p.m. The **Greyhound** bus stop, 75 Napal St., tel. (541) 997-1123, sees twice daily service from two different routes. In addition to two buses coming down from Portland via Lincoln City en route to San Francisco on US 101, there are two buses a day from Eugene. KCST 106.9 FM showcases live area talent every Thursday direct from various venues in and around Florence.

YACHATS AND VICINITY

Yachats (when "ya-hots," you're hot) is an Alsea Indian word meaning "at the foot of the mountain," which aptly describes this resort town of 600 people in the shadow of Cape Perpetua. While the native campfires are gone now, ceremonial clamshell middens have been found on area beaches. More importantly, the legacy of the Alsea will live on forever as long as people come here to gaze in wonder at sunsets and at the fury of winter storms.

SIGHTS

Cape Perpetua
The most notable sight near Yachats, indeed on the whole central coast, is the view from 800-foot-high Cape Perpetua. Oregon's highest paved public road this close to the shoreline af-

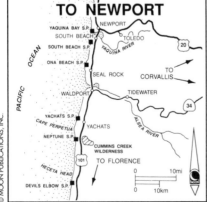

fords 150 miles of north-to-south visibility from the top of the headland. On a clear day, you can also see 37 miles out to sea. Prior to hiking the trail or driving to the top of Cape Perpetua, stop off at the **Siuslaw Forest Visitor Center,** Forest Service Rd. 55, mile marker 188.5, US 101, tel. (541) 547-3289, on the east side of the highway. A picture window framing a bird's-eye view of rockbound coast along with exhibits on forestry and marinelife begin your orientation to the region here. The center is open 10 a.m.-5 p.m. daily, except Christmas. Personnel at the desk have maps and pamphlets about such trails as Cook's Ridge, Riggin' Slinger, and Giant Spruce, as well as directions for the auto tour to the summit. In addition, they can point the way to tidepools and berry patches.

The awe-inspiring four-mile Saint Perpetua Trail to the cape's summit is of moderate difficulty. En route, placards explain the role of wind, erosion, and fire in forest succession in this mixed-conifer ecosystem. Historic events, such as the naming of the cape by England's Captain Cook on Saint Perpetua's Day in 1778 and the devastating Columbus Day storm of 1962, are also documented. The latter lasted several days and unleashed winds of 138 mph.

At the crest of Cape Perpetua the **Trail of the Whispering Spruce** begins, a quarter-mile loop through the grounds of a former WW II Coast Guard lookout built by the Civilian Conservation Corps in 1933. The southern views from the crest take in the highway and headlands as far as Coos Bay. Halfway along the path, you'll come to a WPA-built rock lean-to that makes a lofty perch for whalewatching. Beyond this ridgetop aerie the curtain of trees parts

Map: TO NEWPORT — YAQUINA BAY S.P., NEWPORT, SOUTH BEACH, TOLEDO, SOUTH BEACH S.P., YAQUINA RIVER, ONA BEACH S.P., SEAL ROCK, TO CORVALLIS, WALDPORT, TIDEWATER, YACHATS S.P., CAPE PERPETUA, YACHATS, ALSEA RIVER, NEPTUNE S.P., CUMMINS CREEK WILDERNESS, TO FLORENCE, HECETA HEAD, DEVILS ELBOW S.P., PACIFIC OCEAN, 0 10mi, 0 10km

© MOON PUBLICATIONS, INC.

to reveal fantastic views of the shoreline between Yachats and Lincoln City as far north as Cape Foulweather.

The two-mile drive up the cape is complicated by a not-so-prominent sign on US 101 indicating the turnoff onto Forest Service Rd. 55, and a junction in the road midway to the summit that can lead the unsuspecting on a wild ride in the opposite direction. To begin your auto ascent, drive a hundred yards north on US 101 from the visitor center and look for the steep winding spur road on the right. As you climb, you'll notice numbered roadside markers annotated with explanations about forest ecology. Halfway up, you'll come to a Y in the road. Take a hard left and follow the road another mile to the top of Cape Perpetua. If you miss the left turn here and go straight ahead, you'll soon find yourself on a 22-mile paved-over logging route to Yachats. Despite distant shorelines and mountaintops on the horizon, the butchered forests along this blacktopped "cat" trail and signposts bearing Forest Service rationalizations for same might leave you more worried than inspired. Recent clearcuts on the opposite side of this headland facing Yachats have prompted many disgruntled locals to refer to Cape Perpetua as "Cape Clearcut."

State Parks, Coastal Waysides

Between Heceta Head and Yachats, state parks and viewpoints abound with attractions. There's so much to see here that keeping your eyes on the road in this heavily traveled section becomes a challenge.

Heceta Lighthouse, built in 1893, is rated the strongest light on the Oregon coast, and can be seen 21 miles from land. It's open for tours daily noon-5 p.m. Close by is **Heceta House,** tel. (541) 547-3696, where the lighthouse keepers used to live. Today, it's a B&B as well as a window on the past for the general public. It's open for tours Memorial Day-Labor Day, Thurs.-Monday. Antique furnishings and vintage photos help recreate the lives of the keepers of the flame. Devil's Elbow Beach is nice for strolling and nearby Cape Creek has spawning salmon each fall.

On the way to Cape Perpetua, **Neptune State Park** has a beautiful beach and is near the 9,300-acre **Cummin's Creek Wilderness** east

of US 101. Scenic shorelines can also be found to the south of the cape at **Muriel O. Ponsler** and **Stonesfield Beach** waysides. Close by, there's a chance to explore tidepools and sometimes observe harbor seals at **Strawberry Hill.** The **Cape Perpetua Visitor Center,** tel. (541) 547-3289, is open 9 a.m.-5 p.m. in summer with twice-daily guided walks to give the visitor information about old growth, the plants, the animals, and the tidepools (reachable by a trail heading west from the parking lot). There's also the chance to see shell middens built up between 300 and 2,000 years ago. Mountain bike through an old growth forest at the top of Cape Perpetua (Cummin's Creek Trail). Ask at the Visitor Center front desk for directions.

Just north from the junction of the Cape Perpetua road and US 101 is **Devil's Churn.** Here, the tides have cut a deep fissure in a basalt embankment on the shore. While watching the whitewater torrents in this foaming cistern, beware of "sneaker waves," particularly if you venture beyond the boundaries of the **Trail of the Restless Waters.** The highlights here are the spouting horns where sea water is funneled between rocks and explodes into spray. All along this stretch of the coast, many trees appear to be leaning away from the ocean as if bent by storms. This illusion is caused by salt-laden westerlies drying out and killing the buds on the exposed side of the tree, leaving growth only on the leeward branches.

On the south bank of the Yachats River is a short but beautiful beach loop off US 101. The roadbed sits astride the landscaped grounds of beach houses and a foamy sea. Tidepools and blowholes on the bank by the river's mouth are a special treat. Ocean Drive along the opposite bank will also guide you to where the river meets the sea. It loops around wave-battered **Yachats State Park** and heads north along the ocean, where it becomes Marine Drive. After going through a residential community, it eventually takes an easterly turn to reconnect with US 101. In town the **Little Log Church Museum,** 3rd and Pontiac, sits a few blocks from US 101. Clothing and tools from pioneer days and a working pump organ are on display along with period furnishings. The hours of operation are variable, so check the chamber of commerce.

PRACTICALITIES

Accommodations

Yachats-area lodgings take full advantage of the dramatic setting in a town called "the Gem of the Oregon coast." For the ultimate in seclusion, **Oregon House**, 94288 US 101, Yachats 97498, tel. (541) 547-3329, nine miles south of Yachats, overlooks the Pacific from a high cliff. Seven suites with private baths and kitchens, some with fireplaces, as well as one bed-and-breakfast room take advantage of forested walking trails to the beach and a glass-enclosed whalewatching tower. Except in the case of the bed and breakfast room, there is an additional charge for full breakfasts. This is the kind of place that is especially cost-effective for groups, with a unit for four at $65 and more spacious units with kitchen, fireplace, dining room, etc., for larger parties costing $95. Ask the hotel proprietors about oceanfront grottoes between here and Sea Lion Caves.

A little closer to Yachats at the beginning of the beach loop (on the south bank of the Yachats River and west of US 101) are the **Shamrock Lodgettes**, P.O. Box 219, Yachats 97498, tel. (800) 845-5028 or (541) 547-3312. Shamrock's beautiful parklike landscape frames a selection of individual log cabins or more conventional rooms. Stone fireplaces, in-room movies, and ocean or bay views all contribute to a relaxed get-away-from-it-all feeling. The sauna and jacuzzi on the premises also enhance the "mellowing-out" process, which'll begin as soon as you set foot here. Reserve early the much-requested cabins that range $91-99 for two, $105-112 for four, while other units average $71-95—a small price for peace of mind. The more expensive rooms in the latter category have jacuzzis. There is also a health club on the premises with a redwood hot tub and sauna. Ask about midwinter specials.

For those looking for a budget place close to the center of town with some of the comforts of home, try **Rock Park Cottages** on W. 2nd, tel. (541) 547-3214 or 343-4382, two blocks from the chamber of commerce and a stone's throw from Yachats State Park. Consisting of five cabins right on the beach, Rock Park has to be considered one of the better bargains on the coast.

Should weather keep you inside, the wood-paneled walls hold bookshelves with reading matter and board games, and the kitchens are equipped with dishes. The price can be negotiated for multinight stays, but seems to average around $60 per night for a double, $10 less in winter. For reasonably priced beach cabins and new homes try **Barrett's Vacation Rentals**, P.O. Box 491, Yachats 97498, tel. (541) 547-4501.

The **Fireside Motel**, US 101, P.O. Box 313, Yachats 97498, tel. (541) 547-3636, and the imposing **Adobe Resort** (see "Food" following) both overlook Smelt Sands Beach. If you appreciate all services in one compound, from dining room to gift shop, the Adobe, $59-99, gets the nod, but for about the same money, $64-88, the Fireside's smallish rooms have more than enough amenities. In addition to ocean views, many of the rooms also have such extras as refrigerators and fireplaces. Perhaps the most appreciated little touch is the guidebook the management has put together for guest use. It can point the way to some of the area's natural attractions, including Smelt Sands and Cape Perpetua. A State Park trail behind both properties leads over rockbound coast to a driftwood-laden beach. Boundary disputes between private-property owners with land abutting the State Park here are currently in litigation. Ever since private property rights clashed with public beachfront at Whale Cove up the coast in the two previous decades, the central coast has seen such controversies. As the state's population increases, more pressures on the environment are inevitable.

The levelling of forests in 1997 for new homes near Cape Foulweather have put the private property rights versus public land controversy in the spotlight.

Eggs With Your Beacon

Heceta House, 92072 US 101, Yachats, tel. (541) 547-3696, lets you spend a night in the one-time home of the hardy souls who maintained the adjoining Heceta Head Lighthouse (established 1893). Three upstairs bedrooms for $95, $105, or $125, are furnished with antiques. Only one room has a private bath. Vintage photos of early lighthouse keepers add a historical dimension to the experience. The current caretakers maintain a flock of chickens on the grounds as did the actual lighthouse keepers of yesteryear. Your current hosts keep them as a source of fresh eggs to be used in the eight-course included breakfast.

Bed and Breakfasts

A few classic bed and breakfasts around Yachats rate a mention for those willing to spend a little more for comfort, location, and privacy. **Sea Quest,** 95354 US 101, Yachats, tel. (541) 547-3782 or (800) 341-4878, http://www.seaq.com, e-mail, seaquest@newportnet.com, is an antique-filled aerie above the pounding surf. Private entrances and a location adjacent to Ten Mile Creek in this contemporary cedar-and-glass inn make rates above $135 per night well worth it. Their exceptional service and attention to detail make every visitor feel special. From the fine cognac and wines in the evening, the fruit, scones, and popcorn in the commons, to the chocolates and bottled water in your room, the house is well stocked with quality goodies catering to your whim and pleasure. Breakfasts are delicacy-laden presentations superior to many hotel fine dining rooms. The wrap around deck affords superlative views of the beach, and telescopes and binoculars are always on hand for spotting whales and other marine life. Many guests return each year, so be sure to book well in advance.

In the same area and price range are **Ziggurat,** 95330 US 101, Yachats, tel. (541) 547-3925, a four-story pyramid with an abundance of sunlight and comforts; and the **Kittiwake,** 95368 US 101, Yachats 97498, tel. (541) 547-4470, a sprawling, contemporary, beachfront home. Look for all of them six miles south of Yachats at mile marker 171 near Ten Mile Creek. At all these establishments you might find such seasonal breakfast fare as local berries and smoked sturgeon. Unlike many of their counterparts elsewhere, at most Yachats-area bed and breakfasts you won't be required to share a bathroom. However, it's also worth noting that the welcome mats are seldom out for children and pets.

Campgrounds

Set along Cape Creek in the **Cape Perpetua Scenic Area,** Cape Perpetua Visitor Center, P.O. Box 274, Yachats 97498, tel. (541) 563-3211, the Forest Service campground here has 37 sites for tents, trailers, or motor homes up to 22 feet long. Picnic tables and fire grills are provided. Flush toilets, piped water, and sanitary services are available, no reservations are necessary, and the $12 fee applies mid-May to late September. The Forest Service rangers put on slide-illustrated campfire talks here and at Tillicum Beach during summer months.

Just south, **Neptune State Park** has several $4 beachfront hiker/biker sites, and four miles south you can turn east off US 101 and follow Forest Service Rd. 56 to get to **Ten Mile Creek.** With no reservations and no fee, this small secluded campground has four sites for tents and small RVs. You'll find fire grills, picnic tables, primitive sanitary facilities, but no piped water. It's just 15 minutes off the highway but feels more remote.

Several miles down Ten Mile Creek is **Rock Creek,** c/o Siuslaw Forest, Waldport Ranger District, Waldport 97394, tel. (541) 563-3211. For $6 a night you get a small out-of-the-way campground a quarter mile from the ocean. Most of the 16 sites are for tents, but a few accommodate small RVs. Fire grills and picnic tables provided; flush toilets and piped water are available.

If you're on a budget, try **Lanham Bike Camp,** which involves a hike in from Rock Creek but doesn't charge a fee. There's everything you need to make it through the night at the 10 primitive sites here, but bring your own water. Each place is open all year and doesn't require reservations.

Food

The eight restaurants in town are able to satisfy a variety of tastes and budgets. Right on the main highway is **La Serre,** 2nd and Beach, Yachats, tel. (541) 547-3420. A bright skylit restaurant with lots of plants creates an appropriate setting for cuisine that eschews deep-fat frying and is heavy on the whole wheat. This may not suggest gourmet continental fare, but somehow La Serre pulls it off. With entrees running the gamut from strawberry-ricotta crepes to charbroiled steaks, the menu manages to please the brie-and-chablis set as well as the health-conscious. Their crabcakes, Manhattan clam chowder, bouillabaisse and clam puffs appetizer please folks who just like good food. On chilly evenings, wash it all down with a coffee nudge. Main courses average $8-23.

The **Yankee Clipper,** 125 Ocean Dr., Yachats, tel. (541) 547-4004, is a tiny but charming sandwich shop overlooking the Yachats River estuary. Fresh ingredients and care go into soup and sandwich creations (try the shrimp melt) ideal for a lunch in the $5 range. Blustery days pack 'em in here for hot coffee, homemade desserts, and the angry beauty of the river meeting the sea.

Another place for a light bite and a long cup of coffee is the **New Morning Coffee House and Bookstore,** US 101 and 4th St., Yachats, tel. (541) 547-3848. Set on a hillside just west of US 101, it gives the appearance of an old beach house with modern architectural flourishes. You can sit downstairs near the bustling espresso counter or upstairs in the extravagantly windowed bookstore. On sunny days, kick back on the outside deck the restaurant shares with the **Back Porch Gallery,** (which displays paintings, sculpture, weaving, pottery, and porcelain dolls). Wherever you plop down, continental breakfast, black bean soup, homemade bread, and desserts ensure a happy landing.

Elaborate picnic fare is available from the **Yachats Crab and Chowder House** "To Go" shop, 131 US 101, Yachats, tel. (541) 547-4132. Pick up fresh half crab and garlic bread, rock cod and halibut fish and chips, as well as assorted breads, meats, and cheeses. **Orca Whole Foods,** 84 Beach Ave, Yachats, is a small natural foods grocery that can also help supplement an outing.

On a hill overlooking Smelt Sands Beach is the glass-enclosed **Adobe Resort,** 155 US 101, Yachats, tel. (541) 547-3141, with its semicircular dining room. The setting is a great place to start the day for breakfast or end it with a romantic evening repast. Adobe Sunday brunches, 9 a.m.-1 p.m., have eye-opening flair as demonstrated by stuffed grilled French toast, $9.25, or eggs Adobe style—two poached eggs on an English muffin with creamed bay shrimp garnished with artichoke bottoms and topped with hollandaise, $10. Later, bay shrimp fettucine, $8.25, and salmon ricotta, $17, are also guaranteed to satisfy, especially when followed by a drink in the Crows Nest Lounge looking out over the waves. If Adobe prices seem high, an "early bird" menu is available Sun.-Thurs. 5-6 p.m.

Events

During the Yachats **smelt fry** held the second week of July, up to 700 pounds of this sardine-like fish are served on the grounds of Yachats School. Yachats is one of the few (perhaps only) places in the world blessed with a run of oceangoing smelt. Information is available from the chamber of commerce.

The **Yachats Kite Festival** falls in November when the winds really kick up. Shamrock Lodgettes proprietor Robert Oxley has all the information. Contact him via the hotel or at P.O. Box 364, Yachats 97498.

Information and Services

The **Yachats Chamber of Commerce,** P.O. Box 174, Yachats 97498, tel. (541) 547-3530, has a central location on the highway (right across from the Coffee Merchants) and a loquacious staff. Ask them about fishing, rockhounding, birdwatching, and beachcombing in the area. Next door, **On the Rise** bakery offers grainy goodies to take with you on these journeys. The Yachats **post office,** Yachats 97498, is right behind La Serre.

The bus stop is also in the parking lot of the bakery/chamber of commerce/food market complex, US 101 and W. 2nd. Here you can catch **Central Coast Connections,** tel. (541) 265-4900, buses to Newport at 7 a.m. and 1 p.m. For connections to Corvallis and Eugene, contact **Valley Retriever,** tel. (541) 265-2253, for schedule information.

On the north end of Yachats on US 101 after the Texaco Station, **By-The-Sea Books,** tel. (541) 547-4455, can edify your curiosity about the area with region titles or supply the perfect page-turner for that rainy winter day by the woodstove. There are 10,000 used books here, and a large collection of new bestsellers. Browsers are encouraged with rocking chairs, coffee, cookies, and a corner dedicated to small children. Open every day 10 a.m.-5 p.m., except Tuesday.

WALDPORT AND VICINITY

Originally a stronghold of the Alsea Indians, Waldport also has had incarnations as a gold rush town and lumber port. In addition, almost two decades ago it gained notoriety for being a hotbed of environmental activism. When locals rallied against the spraying of dioxin-based defoliants in Coast Range forests, Waldport attracted national media attention. These chemicals were used by the lumber industry to eliminate blackberries, vine maples, and other vegetation that impede the growth of the Douglas fir. When the defoliants were linked to abnormally high numbers of birth defects and miscarriages, citizens rallied successfully for a government ban on the toxins.

This otherwise quiet town, whose name in German means "Forest Port," is today possessed of more mundane distinctions. A chamber of commerce flier touts Waldport's livability, suggesting that the town's "relative obscurity" has spared it the fate of more crowded tourist towns. This may also be explained by a nondescript main drag that gives no hint of surrounding beaches and prime fishing spots. A recent influx of retirees has spurred new homebuilding, but this place is still decidedly low-key. For those passing through, the town provides a low-cost alternative to the name destinations; in Waldport you won't have to fight for a parking spot or make reservations months in advance.

Dateline Waldport

It's hard to picture the quiet beach town of Waldport as the object of national media scrutiny, but it happened twice during the 1970s and again in 1997. During the 70s, a *Sixty Minutes* investigative team came here to document the link between dioxin-based defoliants used in the area timber stands to a high incidence of birth defects and miscarriages. This report and the ensuing government ban on this substance in Oregon forests took on national significance when soldiers exposed to ill-effects of the same chemical (Agent Orange) in Vietnam were denied compensation by the Pentagon.

But this wasn't the only occasion that Waldport basked in the hot glare of a national media spotlight during the seventies. A 1975 *New York Sunday Times* article described a bizarre UFO cult's recruitment of followers here to undertake a rendezvous with a spacecraft that'd transport them to a higher plane of existence. Walter Cronkite, John Chancellor and the like followed up with TV coverage. Their leader, Marshall Applewhite, exhorted the faithful to give up their possessions and depart Oregon for Colorado where the ascension was to take place.

The same Marshall Applewhite re-surfaced in 1997, this time in California when his cult's mass suicide prompted another media explosion with reverberations felt in Waldport. Broadcast media from *Dateline NBC* to *Good Morning America* interviewed locals here for impressions of the deceased, as a stunned and curious nation looked on.

The notoriety of this sportfishing haven rimming Alsea Bay is made especially unseemly by some of the most laidback, down-to-earth townspeople you'll encounter anywhere on the central coast. Despite the media hoopla worthy of a big city over the past few decades, Waldport is still the kind of place where "all the news that's fit to print" is more likely to be found on a laundromat bulletin board than on the front page of a national newspaper.

ACTIVITIES

Waldport's recreational raison d'être is fishing. World-class clamming and Dungeness crabbing in Alsea Bay and the Alsea River's famous salmon, steelhead, and cutthroat trout runs account for a high percentage of visits to the area.

The **Alsea Bridge Historical Information Center,** Alsea Bridge, tel. (541) 563-2133, in Waldport is open Wed.-Sun. 9 a.m.-4 p.m. Displays about transportation methods along the central coast since the 1800s, information on the Alsea tribe, and a telescope trained on the seals and waterfowl on the bay are worth a quick stop. Admission is free.

Seal Rock State Park, four miles north of town, attracts beachcombers and agate-hunters as well as folks who come to explore the tidepools and observe the seals on offshore rocks. The park's name derives from a seal-shaped rock in the cluster of interesting formations in the tidewater.

Seven miles east of Waldport are the nine square miles of **Drift Creek Wilderness.** Within this area are stands of old-growth forest. Here you can see hemlocks hundreds of years old. These trees are the "climax forest" in the Douglas fir ecosystem. They seldom reach old-growth status since the timber industry tends to replant only fir seedlings after logging operations. There is also perhaps the largest population of spotted owls in the state. Steep ridges and their drainages as well as small meadows make up the topography. The trailhead closest to Waldport is the **Harris Ranch Trail,** which descends 1,200 feet in two miles to a meadow near Drift Creek. The wilderness is administered by the Siuslaw National Forest—Waldport Ranger Station, tel. (541) 563-3211, which can supply specific directions to the different trailheads into this increasingly rare ecosystem (see "Information and Services" following). The local access to Harris Ranch and Horse Creek trails leaves ORE 34 at the Alsea River crossing seven miles east of Waldport. Here, pick up Risely Creek Rd. (Forest Service Rd. 3446).

PRACTICALITIES

Accommodations

"Cottage" is a word often heard between Yachats and Waldport. It may be a duplex or self-contained cabin-type lodging, generally by a beach. The price ranges between $60 and $75 for units with kitchen facilities, fireplaces, and oceanfront locations. Cottages with all of the above include **Deane's Oceanside Lodge,** 8800 S.W. US 101, Waldport 97374, tel. (541) 547-3321, **Terry-a-While Motel,** 7160 S.W. US 101, Waldport 97374, tel. (541) 563-3377, **Sea Stones Cottages,** 6317 S.W. US 101, Waldport 97374, tel. (541) 547-3118, the **Edgewater Cottages,** 3978 S.W. US 101, Waldport 97374, tel. (541) 563-2240, and **Cape Cod Cottages,** 4150 S.W. US 101, Waldport 97374, tel. (541) 563-2106. Cottage-dwellers looking for a good book to "hole-up" with on a rainy weekend can go to **Blue Iris Books,** 195 Maple, tel. (541) 563-5488.

Other lodging options are the rental houses of **Horizon Property,** tel. (541) 563-5151. Oceanfront digs are available and prices are extremely reasonable. For more information on all of the above call **The Central Oregon Coast Association,** (800) 767-2064.

Camping

Two premium campgrounds sit about four miles south of Waldport on US 101 along the beach. **Beachside State Park,** reserve at P.O. Box 1350, Newport 97365, tel. (541) 563-3023, is located near a half mile of beach not far from Alsea Bay and Alsea River. This is a paradise for rock fishermen, surfcasters, clammers, and crabbers. For $16-19 a night from mid-April to mid-October, there are 49 tent sites, 20 sites for RVs up to 30 feet long, and 12 hiker/biker sites. Beachside fills up fast, with such amenities as a laundromat and hot showers, so reserve early for space between Memorial Day and Labor Day.

A half mile down US 101, the Forest Service has comparable site offerings at **Tillicum Beach.** Set right along the ocean, the campground is open all year and doesn't require reservations. For $11 a night you have the full range of creature comforts plus ranger campfire programs in summer. Forest Service roads from here access Coast Range fishing streams, which are detailed in a Forest Service map. You'll also appreciate the strip of vegetation blocking the cool evening winds that whip up off the ocean here.

Should Beachside and Tillicum be filled to overflowing, you might want to set up a base camp in the Coast Range along ORE 34—especially if you have fishing or hiking in the Drift Creek Wilderness in mind. Just go east of Waldport 17 miles on ORE 34 to **Blackberry Campground,** Siuslaw National Forest, Alsea Ranger District, Alsea 97324, tel. (541) 487-5811. There are 33 sites open May-Sept. for tents and RVs, most of them on the river. A boat ramp, flush toilets, and piped water are on-site. (Prices were in transition at presstime.) The Kozy Kove Kafe (see "Food" following) is eight miles away.

Food

Forget fine dining in Waldport. This is an eat 'n' run town. Unless you want to drive to Yachats, **Bumps 'n' Grinds,** 225 Maple St., Waldport, tel. (541) 563-5769, is about the only place in the area for gourmet coffee. They also have bakery specialties, lunch (chicken enchiladas are good), and Alsea Bay views off the deck. For lunch and dinner, **At'sa Pizza,** Seastrand Mall, Waldport, tel. (541) 563-3232, is a favorite with the locals. Premium ingredients go into their pizza, calzone, and pasta dishes. The homemade garlic rolls and "grinders" (submarine or hero sandwiches) are great for picnics, and like everything else here are moderately priced. There is also an outlet in Newport, tel. (541) 265-6000.

At the south end of Waldport across from the Visitor Information Center is another local franchise. Like **Leroy's Blue Whale** in Yachats, tel. (541) 547-3397, the Waldport branch of this restaurant, tel. (541) 563-3445, is located right on US 101. These self-described "family restaurants" can be counted on for low prices and a varied menu of American food. Culinary flourishes are limited to seafood dishes such as squid rings and prawns sautéed in wine and butter. These places stay open in January when many of the other eateries in nearby Yachats close early or suspend operation for the month.

Also at the south end of town on US 101 is **Moby Dick's Waldport Seafoods,** tel. 563-HOOK. If you're holed up in a cottage with a kitchen or camping, you'll appreciate fresh fish at a good price. The cooked crab here is exceptional, attesting to Waldport's status as a leading Dungeness crab fishery, and the smoked fish also makes a great to-go snack.

If you're interested in a unique dining experience, follow ORE 34 along the Alsea River for nine miles to a most unlikely site for a good restaurant. Attached to a trailer court and convenience store is the **Kozy Kove Kafe,** 9464 ORE 34, Tidewater 97390, tel. (541) 528-3251 or (800) 388-KOVE. The dining room and lounge float on a bed of logs by a riverbank and are well placed to observe Australian black swans, elk, salmon jumping in September, and other wildlife. Breakfasts (three egg omelettes with ingredients like cajun smoked salmon and herb cream cheese, $5-10) are hearty, and lunch and dinner focus on fresh seafood, steak, and prime rib, $11-14. Clam chowder and strawberry shortcake are recommended accompaniments. There are also Mexican (try the "fajitas with the flame") and Italian entrees to add spice to this retreat.

Information and Services

At the south end of Waldport on the west side of US 101 is the **Visitor Information Center,** tel. (541) 563-2133. It's open 9 a.m.-4 p.m. daily during summer. The **Siuslaw National Forest—Waldport Ranger Station,** Waldport Ranger District, Waldport 97374, tel. (541) 563-3211, can provide information on area camping and hiking. A **post office,** Waldport 97374, tel. (541) 563-3011, can be found on ORE 34, one block east of US 101. Close by on ORE 34 is the **public library,** which is open Mon.-Fri. 1-4:30 p.m., Saturday 11 a.m.-2 p.m. ORE 34 itself is a scenic 60-mile access road to Corvallis.

Gene-O's Guide Service, P.O. Box 43, Waldport 97374, tel. (541) 563-3171, calls on four decades of experience to help you reel in salmon and steelhead. **Crestview Hills Golf Course,** 1680 Crestline Dr., Waldport 97374, tel. (541) 563-3020, has nine holes and a pro shop a mile south of town.

The **Greyhound,** tel. (800) 231-2222, and Central Coast Connection buses serve Waldport. Bus stops are at the Waldport Ranger Station, 1049 US 101, and the Waldport Senior Center, 265 Elsie Highway.

NEWPORT AND VICINITY

The discovery of a tiny sweet-tasting oyster in Yaquina Bay during the 1860s was the first major impetus to growth and settlement in Newport. These tasty morsels which delighted diners in San Francisco and at New York's Waldorf-Astoria Hotel are almost gone now, but their port of embarkation is still bustling with activity. New factories to process *surimi* (a fish paste popular in Japan) and whiting have provided hundreds of jobs here, and a state-of-the-art aquarium featuring Keiko the whale (from *Free Willy*) to bring in the tourist dollar. In this vein, new wildlife observation facilities and improved access to tidal pools north of town at Yaquina Head promise to make it a highlight of the coast. The shops, galleries, and restaurants along Newport's historic bayfront, together with the Performing Arts Center and quieter charm of Nye Beach, keep up a tourism tradition that goes back to when this town was the "honeymoon capital of Oregon." Today, Newport boasts more oceanfront hotel rooms than any place between San Francisco and Seattle, except perhaps for Lincoln City. This can make for traffic jams on holiday weekends, but it's a small price to pay for proximity to some of the coast's best agate-hunting beaches, cultural programs, and restaurants.

SIGHTS

Sea Gulch Trail
In addition to the diverse appeals of Newport, the area is also distinguished by a handful of attractions that skirt the line between tasteful and tawdry. This tightrope is skillfully walked at **Sea Gulch**, along US 101, tel. (541) 563-2727, a collection of chainsaw sculptures on the east side of the highway five miles north of Waldport. The creator of these red cedar Rodins has a light touch with his sawblades as well as a cartoonist's flair in his art. Western and fantasy themes are humorously hacked out on the quarter-mile Sea Gulch Trail, where anthropomorphic bears and bigfoot vie for attention with cowboys, gnomes, Rip Van Winkle, and Mother Goose. It's open daily 8 a.m.-7 p.m. in winter,

and closes an hour or two later in summer. The admission is $3.50, with discounts for seniors and kids.

Mark O. Hatfield Marine Science Center
Just prior to crossing the bridge into downtown Newport, head east on the road that parallels the bay to the Hatfield Marine Science Center, Marine Science Drive, Newport 97365, tel. (541) 867-0100; http://wwwhmsc.orst.edu/. At the door to greet you is an octopus in an open tank pointing the way to oceanography exhibits and a "hands on" area where you can experience the feel of starfish, anemones, and other sea creatures. The back hallway has educational dioramas and there's a theater showing marine-science films throughout the day. If you proceed left from the octopus tank, you'll see tanks with different sea ecosystems. Beyond the walls of the museum, the center's Seataugua program offers one- to three-day field trips various times of the year (check with the front desk for details). Admission is free and it's open daily 10 a.m.-6 p.m. in summer and Thurs.-Tues. 10 a.m.-4 p.m. the rest of the year. This facility is a low-key but interesting alternative to the Oregon Coast Aquarium, located less than a mile south. A $3 donation is suggested.

The Oregon Coast Aquarium
There are 6,000 miles of water between the Oregon coast and Japan—the largest stretch of open ocean on earth. Come hear our side of the story at the Oregon Coast Aquarium, 2820 S.E. Ferry Rd., P.O. Box 2000, Newport 97305, tel. (541) 867-3474. The aquarium features 40,000 square feet of galleries devoted to wetland communities, near-shore and marine ecosystems, and an environmental center.

In addition to all of the above, on Jan. 7, 1996, Keiko, a 7,720-pound, 32-foot-long orca who starred in *Free Willy* has joined these exhibits. Understandably, his presence has overshadowed four acres of sea lions, sea otters, tidepools, undersea caves, as well as the largest walk-in seabird aviary in the Americas. Housed in his own state-of-the-art pool (150 feet long, 75 feet wide, and 25 feet deep), Keiko spends a lot of time at the underwater viewing windows, watching the people watch him. While this spectacle is indeed absorbing, to spend all your time in a staring contest with a Leviathan is to forego an introduction to the other denizens of this fascinating ecosystem. Of the 200 species of Pacific Northwest fish, birds, and mammals on display here, don't miss the sea otters, spotted ratfish, wolf eels, leopard sharks, lion's mane jellyfish, and the tufted puffins. The younger set will enjoy the sea cave with simulated wave action, which houses a resident octopus.

Indigenous simulated ecosystems help articulate the region's biology. The centerpiece of the Wetland's Gallery, for example, is a cross section of the salt marsh subject to the periodic ebb and flow of tides. Another ecological niche is illustrated by a 4,730-gallon tank in the Sandy Shores exhibit. Here, you can see smelt, perch, and leopard sharks navigate amid human-made rocks and piers. The Rock Shores Gallery adds another dimension to the experience with an open tidal pool that allows visitors to handle starfish, sea anemone, and the like. In the outside aviary and sea mammal pools, latex molds of rocky outcroppings provide perches for birds, otters, and sea lions (many of these animals were rescued from such debacles as the Exxon Valdez oil spill).

FREE WILLY—TEMPEST IN A SEASPOT

The movie *Free Willy* entranced viewers with the notion of a captive orca eventually being set free from an aquarium and returning to the ocean. Whether life will imitate art in the actual re-introduction of this movie star into the wild is a leading question not only for the public and marine biologists, but for the town of Newport as well. Revenues from room taxes have soared as have tourism dollars from other area attractions since Keiko's arrival. The Oregon Coast Aquarium itself has seen its attendance double to 1.3 million visitors in 1996.

Economics notwithstanding, there is a sincere and focused mission on the part of the Oregon Coast Aquarium and the **Free Willy Keiko Foundation,** (800) 4-WHALES, http://www.freewilly.org who've collectively raised millions to bring Keiko here from substandard Mexican facilities to give this orca every possible chance to answer the call of the wild. Since he arrived in Newport, improved nutrition and an exercise regime have added considerable weight (a gain of nearly a ton every year and a half since coming to Oregon) and strength to his previously depleted physical condition. In addition, Keiko is being given live food as part of a training program to facilitate acculturation to life in a wild pod. There's also the possibility that Keiko will be moved to a bay pen in the Atlantic in 1998 as a step toward ultimate freedom.

As this goes on, an undercurrent of concern about Keiko's release has surfaced in the scientific community. Fear of the orca's papilloma virus (a skin disease) or other nonendemic maladies threatening the survival of wild orcas and other sea mammals is one cause for trepidation. Equally compelling arguments against release present themselves when we look at the hunting behavior of killer whales in the wild. Orcas from birth are instilled with a high level of cooperative hunting skills within their own pod. More than a decade ago, Keiko was a contributing member of such a pod in Iceland. Some scientists fear that even in the unlikely event that Keiko can find them and is taken back as one of their own, there'd still be resistance against an interloper whose muscles are slack from age and disuse. The possible impediments of forgotten hunting skills and loss of facility in the pod's dialect makes room for doubt about Keiko's survival—especially when you consider that orcas even in the prime of life are unable to avert starvation hunting solo. Scientists are also assessing if his vision, hearing, and echolocation abilities could hold up well enough to handle life in the Atlantic.

Despite these concerns, the training of Keiko and accompanying research have continued toward making him the first captive orca to ever be released in the wild. Underwater microphones monitor Keiko's sounds so that they may eventually be matched up with his birth pod.

Whatever happens, one thing is for certain— the primal urges of the human spirit to be free are embodied for million of people in this animal's contemplated re-introduction into the wild. As such, count on the unfolding real-life drama of "Free Willy" to stir up a tempest in a seaspot.

The research facilities of the nearby Hatfield Marine Science Center effectively complement the educational concerns of the Coast Aquarium. While the new facility's raison d'être is public outreach, it's more low-key than the "high-viz" floating zoos commonly associated with other aquariums. In other words, the interpretive placards, videos, and tape presentations are more essential to the experience here than at your typical undersea peep show.

In addition to leaving here with a heightened understanding of the coast biome, you might also come away with something from the museum shop's first-rate collection of regional books and oceanographic tomes or perhaps some crystals or gemstones. The Ferry Slip Cafe is also on-site, emphasizing such Oregon fare as Tillamook dairy products, seasonal fruits, and seafood. Outside in the summer, enjoy barbecued burgers and hot dogs and teriyaki shish-kebabs. The aquarium is open 10 a.m.-4:30 p.m. Oct.-March, 9 a.m.-6 p.m. the rest of the year. Prices are $8.50 for adults, $7.50 for students, $4.25 for kids 4-12, and those under four get in free. To get there going north on US 101, turn right on 32nd St. just before the Yaquina Bay Bridge and follow Ferry Slip Rd. to the parking lot.

Due to Keiko's presence, summertime visitors should avoid weekends and holidays to be spared the crush. In like measure, to best take in this suprisingly graceful creature, go late in the day if you happen to be at the aquarium during peak season.

Lincoln County Historical Society Museum

After crossing the bridge, a half-hour stop at the Lincoln County Historical Society Museum, 545 S.W. 9th St., Newport 97365, tel. (541) 265-7509, is recommended. It's located a half block east of the chamber of commerce on US 101. The logging, farming, and maritime exhibits (particularly Newport shipwrecks) are interesting, but the Siletz Indian baskets and other Native American artifacts steal the show.

The museum flier on coast historical sights details the hardships of inadequate housing, insufficient food, and poor medical facilities which plagued the diverse tribes that made up the Confederated Siletz Indian Reservation. These dozen tribes were defeated during the Rogue Indian Wars and other conflicts of the 1850s. In 1856, 2,000 of these coastal natives were marched to a north coast reservation site. En route, they were sometimes forced to stand shivering in freezing rain until the tide moved out, permitting them to cross a beach. It's no wonder that at the end of one year their numbers had dwindled to 600.

The museum is open Tues.-Sunday. Hours are 10 a.m-5 p.m. June-Sept., 11 a.m.-4 p.m. Oct.-May. Admission is free. Just north of the log cabin that houses the Lincoln County collection is the **Burrows House.** This is part of the museum and has the same hours but focuses exclusively on pioneer life. Antique buffs will especially enjoy these exhibits.

The Bayfront

The bayfront is easy to miss. After crossing the Yaquina Bay Bridge, look for the green marker pointing east at the intersection of US 101 and Hubert Street. Several right turns take you down the hill to Bay Blvd., the bayfront's main drag. Forget about parking anywhere here unless you arrive early. Spots close by the boulevard can often be found, however, along Canyon Way, the hillside access route to downtown. Just curb your wheels to inhibit rolling. One of the first things that'll strike you about the bayfront is that it's a working neighborhood. The cries of fishmongers purveying wharfside walkaway cocktails and the smells of fish-packing plants and canneries fill the air as you stroll the boulevard. On the waterfront, you can watch fisherfolk step off charter boats with their salmon catch and head to the cannery, or observe vessels laden with everything from wood products to whalewatchers out in the bay. Unfortunately, the severe catch limits and cost of equipment make this less of a working port every year. In deference to the Oregon commercial fisherman and other endangered species, wall-length murals memorialize fishing boats and whales here on the bayfront.

The facilities of Oregon's second-largest fishing port eventually give way to restaurants, shops, and galleries. **Ripley's Believe It or Not!, The Waxworks,** and **The Undersea Gardens** are worth a look should the other appeals of Newport pall.

Yaquina Bay Harbor, Newport—very much a working neighborhood

Yaquina Bay State Park

While it's difficult to get a bad meal on the bayfront and there is no shortage of true objets d'art sold here, sooner or later you'll want respite from crowds and commercialism. Relief is just a boat ride away, with at least a dozen reputable fishing charter and whalewatching excursion operators here to serve you. Landlubbers are advised to drive under the bridge to Yaquina Bay State Park for sweeping sea and bay views. There's also the old **Yaquina Bay Lighthouse,** tel. (541) 867-8451, built in 1871 and abandoned three years later. It seems materials intended for lighthouse construction at Otter Crest were mistakenly delivered to this location, which proved to be a poor site. The restored Yaquina Bay beacon, replete with period furniture, is open daily 11 a.m.-5 p.m. May-Sept.; the rest of the year it's just open 11 a.m.-4 p.m. In 1997, the government decided to turn Yaquina Bay's beacon back on. The chance to hear about the ghost here is alone worth the modest price of admission .

Better yet, pick up a reprint of the first written account (1899) of the ghost story at the Lincoln County Museum (see above), then round out your perspective with the century-old pictures on the lighthouse walls, which will convey the bleakness of the treeless, windswept cliff where this lighthouse was erected. This is important because the spit-and-polish facade of the restoration surrounded by stands of coastal pines would be an inappropriate setting for a ghost story.

Without ruining the tale for you, let's just say that if you stand outside the lighthouse on a dark, windy night and hear a maiden's wail, don't linger.

Finally, Yaquina Bay State Park is a good place to have a picnic, or you can descend the trails to the beach and dig for razor clams.

Nye Beach

Another breather from the rampant commercialism on the bayfront and along US 101's business district is Nye Beach. Located a mile north from the bayfront on the western side of US 101 (look for signs on the highway), this one-time favorite retreat for wealthy Portlanders has undergone a revival. Rough times and rougher weather had reduced luxurious beach houses here to a cluster of weatherbeaten shacks until a new performing arts center went up several years back. On the heels of the development of this first-rate cultural facility, the conversion of a 1910 hotel into a kind of literary hostel (see "Accommodations" following) encouraged other restorations. Culture vultures, beach lovers, and people-watchers will want to come to Nye Beach soon, before the shadows of nearby resort hotels grow larger over the Cape Cod cottages, aging hippies, artists and friendly fisherfolk.

Agate Hunting

Agate hunting after winter storms is a passion here. Prior to the ice ages, metals, oxides, and silicates were fused together to create this type of quartz. Red, amber, and blue tones sometimes form stripes or spots on these rocks. The best place to find these treasures is on the beach north of Hotel Newport, appropriately called **Agate Beach.** The beach north of Seal Rock as well as area estuaries and streambeds are also worth a look Oct.-May. Procure the free pamphlet *Agates: Their Formation and How to Hunt for Them* from the chamber of commerce before setting out.

Toledo and Sights North
Aficionados of antiquities can head six miles east of town on ORE 20 to Toledo, where "junque" shops abound. This small town's fortunes have risen and fallen with the timber cut. At one time, the world's largest spruce mill was here. In the era of big timber's swan song, dealers of collectibles have sprouted up to take advantage of coast-bound traffic from the Willamette Valley. Most of the antique shops are located on Main Street. Timber has enjoyed a resurgence here with the mill getting logs submerged at the bottom of Yaquina Bay during WW II.

North of Newport is **Yaquina Head Lighthouse.** It is Oregon's tallest lighthouse (1873). The **Yaquina Head Outstanding Natural Area,** tel. (541) 867-0100, http://www.blm.gov, is open during daylight hours, with an observation deck providing views of seals, sea lions, and shorebirds. Of late, this lookout has also had whale sightings throughout the summer. Low tide reveals sea stars, purple urchins, anemones, and hermit crabs in the tidal pools below. Tools dating back 5,000 years have been unearthed at Yaquina Head. Many were made from elk and deer antler and bone as well as stone. Clam and mussel shells from middens in the area evidence a diet rich in shellfish for the area's ancient inhabitants. Recently improved access to tidal pools (wheelchair friendly), a visitor center, and lighthouse with restored period furniture and paraphernalia also make this a "must" stop.

The center features a life-size replica of the Fresnel lens that shines from the top of the nearby lighthouse. A sea cave simulation with a life-size mural of a Calfornia Gray Whale (accompanied by an exhibit detailing its migratory pattern) as well as statues of birds and harbor seals also welcome visitors. Information on starfish, sea urchins, and other inhabitants of the tidal pools outside is also part of the center's inter-

pretive offerings. Open daily 10 a.m.-6 p.m. from mid-May to mid-Oct., day use fee is $3.

Beaches north of town include **Agate Beach,** famed for its gemstone-hunting opportunities, **Moolack Beach,** a favorite with kite flyers and agate hunters, and **Beverly Beach,** where 20-million-year-old fossils have been found in the sandstone cliffs above the shore. Beverly Beach also attracts waders, unique for Oregon's chilly waters. Offshore sandbars temper the waves and the weather so it's not as rough or as cold as many coastal locales.

In addition to gemstones, the contemplative appeals of Agate Beach inspired no less than Ernest Bloch, a noted classical music composer who died there in 1959. Famed violinist Yehudi Menuhin spoke of Bloch and the locale thusly: "Agate Beach is a wild forlorn stretch of coastline looking down upon waves coming in all the way from Asia to break on the shore, a place which suited the grandeur and intensity of Bloch's character." Each summer, the Ernest Bloch Music Festival (see "The Arts," below) pays tribute to the spirit of this man.

Birds of Yaquina Head
Of the half dozen varieties of shorebird who cluster on Colony Rock—a large monolith in the shallows 200 yards from the Yaquina Head Observation Deck—the tufted puffin is the most colorful. It's sometimes called a sea parrot because of its large yellow orange bill. Puffins arrive here in April and are most visible early in the day on the rock's grassy patches. The most ubiquitous presences here are common murres, pigeons guillemots, and cormorants. The murre's white breasts and bellies contrast with their darker bills and elongated backs. The guillemots resemble pigeons with white wing patches and bright red webbed feet. The cormorants look like prehistoric pelicans. For more local birding information, there is no better book than *Shorebirds of the Pacific Northwest* by Dennis Paulson (Seattle: University of Washington Press, 1994).

ACTIVITIES

Sampling Local Fare
On the road to Toledo about eight miles east of the bayfront, the **Oregon Oyster Company,** 6878 Bay Rd., tel. (541) 265-3078, is the only re-

maining commercial outlet of Yaquina Bay oysters, on sale 9 a.m.-4 p.m. daily. Visitors are welcome to observe the farming and processing of these succulent shellfish. Before you leave, try the smoked oysters on a stick.

Fishing Charters

Charter companies here are numerous. In addition to the whalewatching charters (average cost $20 for a two-hour trip) listed in this chapter's introduction, salmon and bottom fishing average $30-40 for a four-to-five-hour run. Some local outfits include **Sea Gull Charters,** 343 S.W. Bay Blvd., tel. (541) 265-7441, **Newport Sportfishing at the Embarcadero Dock,** 1000 S.E. Bay Blvd., tel. (541) 265-7558, and **Newport Tradewinds,** 653 S.W. Bay Blvd., tel. (541) 265-2101. Sea Gull and Tradewinds also offer whalewatching. The best company on the coast in terms of having state-of-the-art equipment and natural history interpretation is **Discovery Tours,** 345 S.W. Bay Blvd., tel. (800) 903-BOAT. Whalewatching, an oyster bed tour, estuary and ocean exploration, and a bayfront harbor tour exemplify their offerings. Call for prices and times.

Crabbing, Clamming, and Birdwatching

For those who prefer to take matters into their own hands, the **clamming** and **Dungeness crabbing** are superlative in Yaquina Bay. If you haven't done this before, a local tackle shop will rent crabpots or rings and offer instruction. The best time to dig clams is at an extremely low tide. Tide tables are available from the chamber of commerce and many local businesses.

And if you're the kind who just likes to watch, **Yaquina Birders and Naturalists,** tel. (541) 265-2965, welcomes newcomers on its free weekly hikes. This group sponsors monthly outings on the third weekend of the month except during July and August. To really get down, rent diving equipment, $50, and get tips from **Deep Sea John's,** South Jetty Rd., tel. (541) 867-3742. John can direct you to sheltered coves north of Depoe Bay. Whalewatching and scenic flights can be negotiated with **Bertea Aviation,** tel. (541) 867-7767, at Newport Airport, three miles south of the Yaquina Bay Bridge.

Sports

Swimming and **tennis** enthusiasts are not served only by resort facilities. The city of Newport operates an indoor swimming pool at N.W. 12th St., tel. (541) 265-7770. In addition, you can raise a racquet at six public outdoor tennis courts and several privately owned indoor courts. The public courts are located at N.E. 4th and Benton Streets and Bay Creek Rd., one block north of the public swimming pool. While its name might evoke visions of that other course on the 17-mile drive between Monterey and Carmel, California, the **Agate Beach Golf Course,** just north of Newport on US 101, tel. (541) 265-7331, is far from that category True devotees can go 17 miles north to **Salishan Lodge,** tel. (541) 764-3632, to play an 18-hole award-winning course set in the foothills of the Coast Range. The greens fee is $60, and club rental is $15. Keep in mind that this is a Scottish links course where the roughs are really rough.

The Arts

The **Newport Performing Arts Center,** 777 W. Olive, tel. (541) 265-9231, the coast's largest, hosts local and national entertainment in the 400-seat Alice Silverman Theatre and the smaller Studio Theatre. At the same address is the **Oregon Coast Council for the Arts,** which puts out a free monthly newsletter and has ticket information on the previously mentioned venues. It also has updates on the **Newport Visual Arts Center,** 239 N.W. Beach Dr., tel. (541) 265-5123, whose two floors of paintings, sculpture and the like often have a maritime theme. If you care to take in a flick, **Newport Cinema,** 5836 North Coast Hwy., and **Midway Theatre,** 453 South Coast Hwy., tel. (541) 265-2111, will do the trick.

Each summer, the **Ernest Bloch Music Festival,** tel. (541) 265-2787, is eagerly anticipated by classical music lovers. Usually, it takes place toward the end of July with revolving venues. These usually include Salishan, Newport, and Florence over the course of a week. The works of Schubert, Ravel, and other icons of classical music are performed by top musicians in acoustically superior halls. This event along with Lincoln City's **Cascade Head Chamber Music Festival** are considered the coast's preeminent classical music offerings. Call for schedule and rates.

A mural depicting the eyes of Robert De Niro from the movie *Cape Fear* catches your eye from the corner of US 101 and Hubert St. as you head down to the bayfront. **Cape Fear,** tel. (541) 265-7777, is the only coastal all-ages club where you can hear music between Coos Bay and Seattle. Bands from all over the Northwest, a breeding ground for alternative music, find a place to roost here as do kids just looking for a clean place to dance and hang out (for a small cover charge). As with all amplified music, foam earplugs modify decibel input to a reasonable level, and it's recommended you have a pair handy here.

PRACTICALITIES

Accommodations

The cliché "something for everybody" might literally be the case as far as places to stay in Newport go. A vast network of accommodations can be found in every price range here. Here's one worthy of special mention:

The **Sylvia Beach Hotel,** 267 N.W. Cliff, tel. (541) 265-5428, combines the camaraderie of a hostel with the intimate charm of a bed and breakfast. Built in the era when the Corvallis-to-Yaquina Bay train and seven-seater Studebaker touring cars from Portland ferried the newly wed and the nearly dead to Nye Beach, this hostelry was considered the height of luxury. Known as the Cliff House and later on as the Gilmore Hotel, even a "Honeymoon Capital of Oregon" sobriquet could not forestall it eventually being overshadowed by newer, more elaborate resorts.

Its rebirth as the Sylvia Beach Hotel was expedited by a National Historic Landmark designation and a literary theme that has attracted an enthusiastic following. The 20 guest rooms have been named after different authors and furnished with decor evocative of each respective literary legacy. The Edgar Allen Poe Room, for instance, has a pendulum guillotine blade, stuffed ravens, and who knows what else, given Poe's recurring theme of cementing family relations. The Tennessee Williams Room sets the stage with a ceiling fan, a glass menagerie, and mosquito netting, while the Agatha Christie Room drops such clues as shoes underneath the curtains and capsules marked poison in the medicine cabinet.

The Sylvia Beach would be just another cute idea were it not for an imaginative innkeeper who even facilitates guest interactions. This often comes to pass over the tasty $17.50 fixed priced dinner in the oceanfront restaurant, **Tables of Content,** thanks to a game called Two Truths and a Lie. Guests seated at long tables regale each other with several stories, the object being to distinguish which one is true. If this doesn't break the ice, there's hot spiced wine served in the library at 10 p.m., which often leads to conversations far into the night.

Most of the rooms run $68-99, with oceanfront suites featuring a fireplace and deck going for $145. Particularly recommended is the Mark Twain suite featuring an outside patio facing south. This exposure acts as a buffer to the north winds of summer. All these rates include a full breakfast and reflect double occupancy. Single patrons pay $10 less. The fact that no smoking, pets, young children, or radios are allowed on the premises should also be mentioned. And if you're looking for a budget room, Sylvia Beach features dormitory bunk beds for $20 per night. Even if you don't stay here, you're invited to come by for a look at unoccupied rooms whose doors are always left open for this purpose. If nothing else, have a meal at the Tables of Content. There's a nice view of the breakers, good company, and not overly expensive Northwest cuisine.

To get there, turn off US 101 on N.W. 3rd and follow it down to the beach, where N.W. 3rd and Cliff Streets meet. Then look for a large four-story dark green wooden structure with a red roof on a bluff above the surf.

Another retreat from the ordinary in this neighborhood is **The Nye Beach Hotel & Cafe,** 219 N.W. Cliff St., tel. (541) 265-3334. Here 18 guest rooms with all the modern amenities, $60 and up, feature fireplaces as well as willow loveseats on oceanview balconies. Add the whimsical decor evocative of the era when Newport was Oregon's self-proclaimed honeymoon capital, a bright airy restaurant with a creative, multi-ethnic menu as well as a sunset-friendly outside deck, and you have the perfect Valentine's Day getaway.

The **Brown Squirrel Hostel,** 44 S.W. Brook St., tel. (541) 265-3729, charges $15 per night for

NEWPORT ACCOMMODATIONS

Hallmark Resort, 744 S.W. Elizabeth, tel. (541) 265-2600 or (800) 448-4449, $90-200, wheelchair access, ocean view, restaurant/lounge, fireplaces, pets, kitchenettes.

City Center Motel, 538 S.W. Coast Highway 101, tel. (541) 265-7381 or (800) 628-9665, $40-70, pets, kitchenettes.

Embarcadero Resort Hotel, 1000 S.E. Bay Blvd., tel. (541) 265-8521 or (800) 547-4779, $100-145, bay view, laundry, restaurant/lounge, covered pool, kitchenettes.

The Hotel Newport, 3019 N. Coast Highway 101, tel. (541) 265-9411, $85-120, wheelchair access, ocean view, pool, restaurant/lounge, nonsmoking rooms, live entertainment.

Little Creek Cove, 3641 N.W. Oceanview Dr., tel. (541) 265-8587 or (800) 294-8025, $100-125, ocean view, fireplaces, kitchenettes.

Money Saver Motel, 861 S.W. Coast Highway 101, tel. (541) 265-2277, $35-65, kitchenettes, laundry, nonsmoking rooms.

Moolack Shores Motel, 8835 N. Coast Highway 101, tel. (541) 265-2326, $75-110, wheelchair access, ocean view, fireplaces, kitchenettes, small and secluded.

Newport Motor Inn, 1311 N. Coast Highway 101, tel. (541) 265-8516, $40-50, pets, nonsmoking rooms, restaurant/lounge.

Penny Saver Motel, 710 N. Coast Highway 101, tel. (541) 265-6631, $40-65, kitchenettes, nonsmoking rooms, complimentary continental breakfast.

Puerto Nuevo Inn, 544 S.W. Coast Highway 101, tel. (541) 265-5767 or (800) 999-3068, $45-100, wheelchair access, nonsmoking rooms, complimentary continental breakfast.

Shilo Inn, 536 S.W. Elizabeth, tel. (541) 265-7701 or (800) 222-2244, $105-160, wheelchair access, ocean view, pets, covered pool, laundry, restaurant/lounge, complimentary continental breakfast.

Surf 'n' Sand Motel, 8143 N. Coast Highway 101, tel. (541) 265-2215, $65-100, ocean view, fireplaces, pets, kitchenettes.

Sylvia Beach Hotel, 267 N.W. Cliff St., tel. (541) 265-5428, $70-1450, wheelchair access, ocean view, pool, restaurant/lounge, nonsmoking rooms.

Tides Inn, 715 S.W. Bay St., tel. (541) 265-7202, $40-65, ocean view, pets, kitchenettes.

Val-U Inn Motel, 531 S.W. Fall St., tel. (541) 265-6203 or (800) 265-7777, $65-130, wheelchair access, ocean view, laundry, restaurant/lounge, nonsmoking rooms, complimentary continental breakfast.

Viking's Cottages, 729 N.W. Coast St., tel. (541) 265-2477, $60-100, ocean view, fireplaces, pets, kitchenettes.

Waves Motel, 820 N.W. Coast Highway 101, tel. (541) 265-4661 or (800) 282-6993, $60-150, ocean view, nonsmoking rooms, complimentary continental breakfast.

Whaler Motel, 155 S.W. Elizabeth, tel. (541) 265-9261 or (800) 433-9444, $90-125, wheelchair access, ocean view, pets, kitchenettes, nonsmoking rooms, complimentary continental breakfast.

Willers Motel, 754 S.W. Coast Highway 101, tel. (541) 265-2241 or (800) 945-5377, $40-85, wheelchair access, ocean view, laundry, nonsmoking rooms.

a room with shared bath and bunk beds (take your sleeping bag). It's one block from the beach.

Campgrounds

Sites at **South Beach,** P.O. Box 1350, Newport 97365, tel. (541) 867-4715, and **Beverly Beach,** Star Route North, Box 684, Newport 97365, tel. (541) 265-7655, state parks could

well be the most popular places to stay of their kind on the Oregon coast. The absence of other camping in the area and the special features of each campground explain their appeal.

Beverly Beach's 152 tent sites, 127 RV spaces, and hiker/biker campground, $4, are set seven miles north of Newport on the east side of the highway in a mossy glade. Across the road is a tunnel leading to a beach., $16-20, **Devil's Punchbowl** and **Otter Crest** are one and two miles up the highway, respectively. All the amenities, including a cafe, are provided for $16-20 per night, and they're open all year.

South Beach State Park is located two miles south of town along the beach, with opportunities for fishing, agate hunting, and hiking. It has the full range of creature comforts, including a laundromat. It's open mid-April to late October at $16-20 per night (hiker and biker spaces $4).

Food

This is a town for serious eaters—folks who know good food and don't mind paying a tad more for it. It's also the kind of place where there are wharfside vendors as well as fast-food joints and a 24-hour Safeway, 220 US 101, tel. (541) 265-2930, to do it on the cheap. The **Oceana Natural Foods Co-op,** 159 S.E. 2nd St., tel. (541) 265-8285, is a place to stock up on bulk and organic foods if you're planning a picnic. There are also sandwiches, soups, salads, juices etc. served on-site here. Since you'll probably be spending most of your time at either Nye Beach or the bayfront, eateries in those neighborhoods highlight this section.

The bayfront is where Mohava Niemi, a Siletz Indian, opened the original **Mo's,** 622 S.W. Bay Blvd., tel. (541) 263-9411, several decades ago. When word got out about the good food and low prices, Mo's small homey place soon had more business than it could handle. In response to the overflow, **Mo's Annex,** tel. (541) 265-7512, was created across the street. While both establishments feature such favorites as oyster stew and peanut butter cream pie, the Annex bay window has the best view. Other ways to enjoy quality and quantity here include prime rib specials, $13.95 on Saturday, and an all-you-can-eat seafood buffet held the last Friday of every month, $6.95.

Rogue Ale Brewery and Tasting Room, 2320 Marine Science Dr., tel. (541) 862-3660, is a well-regarded establishment with national microbrew distribution open for tours and tastings daily 11 a.m.-6 p.m. (closed January). After crossing the bridge (heading south), take the first right which circles underneath the bridge to the brewery (located near the Aquarium). The brewery's restaurant, the **Rogue Ale's Public House,** 748 S.W. Bay Blvd., tel. (541) 265-3188, is across the Bay in Old Town, serving seafood, pasta, and pizza, $6-8. In addition to washing down all the above with renowned Rogue ales, there's Keiko Draft root beer, a creamy concoction laced with honey and vanilla.

Champagne Sunday brunch overlooking the bay at the **Embarcadero** dining room, 1000 S.E. Bay Blvd., tel. (541) 265-8521, lets you fill up on all the breakfast entrees, fresh seafood, and all the bubbly you can handle for $14. This is a good deal in what is otherwise a high-ticket restaurant. Reservations are recommended between 10 a.m. and 2 p.m.

Another fancy but flexibly priced alternative is a place that has earned critical accolade is **Canyon Way Bookstore and Restaurant,** 1216 S.W. Canyon Way, tel. (541) 265-8319. Instead of going the haute cuisine route, the budget-conscious might prefer to feast on homemade quiche and croissants from the carryout shop after browsing the wide-ranging selection of travel titles in the front room bookstore. These can be savored with a cup of espresso. In addi-

---

MO'S FISH SHANTY

Several decades ago Mo Niemi started up a humble fish shanty on the Newport bayfront. Locals extolled the tasty and reasonably priced seafood, especially the clam chowder. Knowledge became more widespread during the filming of *Never Give an Inch,* starring Paul Newman and Henry Fonda. Restaurant scenes from this movie (based on Ken Kesey's *Sometimes a Great Notion*) were filmed here, and the stars soon became restaurant devotees. Over the years other luminaries, ranging from Robert Kennedy to Bruce Springsteen, joined the club. Soon outlets at Coos Bay, Florence, Lincoln City, Otter Rock, and Cannon Beach opened up, along with an annex to handle the overflow in Newport. Menus are pretty much standard in each restaurant, with fresh fish, clam chowder, and burgers the main bill of fare. Long benches around the kind of tables you'd find in a logging camp cookhouse impart an air of informality to what has become an institution on the Oregon coast.

tion to the bakery selections in the carryout shop, there is other low-priced luncheon fare. In the evening, early dinners (available 5-6 p.m. only) almost halve the later menu prices, $20, for the same order. You'll also appreciate little extras such as an extensive wine and beer list, outdoor patio dining, and works by local artists adorning Canyon Way's walls.

The **Whale's Tale,** 452 S.W. Bay Blvd., tel. (541) 265-8660, is another bayfront restaurant that has great food at all meals, but is more cost-effective at breakfast and lunch. Eggs Newport, $7, will keep you going all day: local Oregon shrimp and two poached eggs on an English muffin topped with béarnaise sauce and accompanied with home fries. The poppyseed pancakes are also first-rate.

Night owls will be grateful for the **Pip Tide's Restaurant and Lounge,** 8365 S.W. Bay Blvd., tel. (541) 265-7797. Besides a 24-hour restaurant, they have low-stakes blackjack tables and live rock 'n' roll bands. The **Bayfront Brewery,** 7485 S.W. Bay Blvd., tel. (541) 265-3438, serves up the same quality suds as its parent brewery in Ashland. Before quaffing Rogue ales and enjoying pizza, visit the brewery itself (open daily 11 a.m.-7 p.m.) located in the South Marina building by the Coast Aquarium.

The **Cosmos Cafe & Gallery,** 740 W. Olive St. across from the Performing Arts Center, tel. (541) 265-7511, fits right in with the funky, laid-back, but stylish Nye Beach neighborhood. This combination coffeehouse restaurant and gallery specializes in vegetarian fare but has dishes to suit all tastes. Whether it's cajun chicken burritos, $6.25, or eggplant parmesan, $9, the food is evocative of a really good potluck. And like most potlucks, Cosmos is an order-at-the-counter, bus-your-own-table kind of place. The gallery features work for sale by artists and craftspeople. Work by visual artists and painters is exhibited throughout the cafe. In short, come here for an omelette in the morning or for coffee and dessert after the show (open till 11 p.m. Friday and Sunday; patio dining when sun is out).

Also in the neighborhood behind a painted Italian-flag facade is **Don Petrie's Italian Food Company,** 613 N.W. 3rd, Nye Beach, tel. (541) 265-3663. This place evokes San Francisco's North Beach pasta houses, offering filling manicotti and fettuccine dinners for $9-15. Try the specialty of

the house, seafood lasagna, $14.25. Their pesto adds much to certain dishes, and the huge pieces of crisp garlic bread that accompany every meal prove that first impressions are enduring.

It's open Wed.-Sun. 8 a.m.-11 p.m. **Yuzen,** US 101, Seal Rock, tel. (541) 563-4766, eight miles south of Newport, is a Japanese restaurant that is worth putting on the brakes for. Country-style Japanese food at moderate to expensive prices attracts crowds Tues.-Sat., so avoid peak dining hours. In addition to sushi and miso soup, less well-known fare like fish noodle soup, *yuza* (pork-minced rock shrimp with vegetables in a dumpling), and *syo-yaki* (a small whole broiled fish encrusted in salt) leave room for new discoveries. To enjoy a high-priced gourmet treat at a moderate price here, we recommend sharing an order of Shabu Shabu (paper thin beef, fresh vegetables, and tofu boiled in a pot and served with three gourmet sauces). With salad and dessert, three people could get away with paying less than $15 apiece.

Events
The biggest bash here is February's **Newport Seafood and Wine Festival,** which presents these palate pleasers, along with music and crafts, at the Newport Marina at South Beach (across Yaquina Bay from the bayfront). A huge tent joins the exhibition hall wherein festival goers wash down delights from the deep with Oregon vintages. The second event of note is **Loyalty Days and Sea Fair** in early May, focusing on sailboat races, a chicken feed, and a parade. Call the chamber for updates.

Outside of town, the **Siletz Powwow** takes place on the second weekend of August. It brings together tribes from all over the Northwest to nearby Siletz for a celebration of the reenfranchisement of the Siletz tribe and reservation. Crafts, food, and traditional dancing spice up this event. Siletz can be reached via ORE 20 (Bay Rd.), which will take you to Toledo. At the crossroads, follow ORE 229 eight miles to Siletz. Contact the Siletz Tribal Smokehouse (see "Food" under "Practicalities" under "Depoe Bay and Vicinity" later in this chapter) for more details.

Information and Services
The Newport Chamber of Commerce, S.W. US 101, Newport 97365, tel. (541) 265-8801 or

(800) 262-7844, has lots of literature available. The *Comprehensive Guide to Services* is the most helpful pamphlet of its kind made available by coastal cities. A booklet on agate hunting is also recommended. The office is open daily 8:30 a.m.-5 p.m., except Nov.-Jan., when there are no weekend hours. The **Central Coast Association,** tel. (800) 767-2064, can supplement the offerings of Newport, Yachats, Depoe Bay, Waldport, and Lincoln City information centers.

Greyhound, 956 W. 10th St., tel. (541) 265-2253, handles 'Hound service along US 101 and the **Valley Retriever,** tel. (541) 265-2253, feeder line service from the Willamette Valley along US 20. Access Valley Retriever buses here to Corvallis and Bend. Central Coast Connections buses to other towns on the central coast are also available. This is the only formal depot on the coast.

Given the size of this city, there's more likelihood of calling the city **police,** tel. (541) 265-5352, than in many other coastal locales. Other useful numbers include **Pacific Communities Hospital,** tel. (541) 265-2244, and the **ambulance** service, tel. (541) 265-3175. The Coast Guard **weather** phone is tel. (541) 265-5511. The **library,** 35 N.W. Nye St., tel. (541) 265-2153, is open Mon.-Thurs. 10 a.m.-8 p.m., Fri.-Sat. 1-6 p.m., and Sunday 1-4 p.m. The **post office,** 310 S.W. 2nd St., Newport 97365, tel. (541) 265-5542, is open Mon.-Fri. 8:30 a.m.-5 p.m. A National Public Radio station, KLCO, is located at 90.5 FM.

NORTH TO DEPOE BAY

The expanse of flat beaches and sandstone bluffs north of Newport takes on a more dramatic aspect after you leave the highway at the Otter Crest Loop six miles south of Depoe Bay.

At the swirling waters of **Devil's Punchbowl,** an urnlike sandstone formation has been sculpted by centuries of tidewater flooding what had been a cave until the roof collapsed. The inexorable process continues today, thanks to the ebb and flow of the Pacific through two openings in the wall of the cauldron. The state park viewpoint sits at a low elevation above the spectacle, giving you a ringside seat on this frothy confrontation between rock and tide. When the water recedes, you can see purple sea urchins and starfish in the **Marine Gardens** tidepools 100 feet to the north.

To the south of the Punchbowl vantage point are picnic tables and a wooden walkway down to the beach. In the parking lot in back of the overlook is a Mo's outlet where a seat occupied by "The Boss" himself, Bruce Springsteen, on June 11, 1987, is enshrined. Enjoy the cuisine that made this Oregon coast chain an institution, then go several doors down to the Otter Rock

Devil's Punchbowl

OREGON TOURISM DIVISION

Cafe and have the marionberry coffeecake for dessert. By the way, we vote Otter Rock's chowder the best on the coast.

Farther along the loop is the **Inn at Otter Crest,** a pricey condo resort whose **Flying Dutchman** dining room, tel. (541) 765-2111, faces 453-foot Cape Foulweather also known as Otter Crest) to the north. Classical cuisine is served here at dinnertime, and more reasonably priced sandwiches and salads can be enjoyed at lunch. The restaurant's bluffside aerie makes a great place to watch the sunset or look for whales. At the end of October, Jazz at the Inn at Otter Crest takes place. Call (541) 648-0179 for details and to be on the mailing list for this festival.

The visibility from atop the cape can extend down to Yaquina Head on a clear day. The view north is another photographer's fantasy of headlands, coves, and offshore monoliths. Bronze plaques in the parking lot tell of Captain Cook naming the 500-foot-high headland during a bout with storm-tossed seas in 1778. Comic relief from the coast's parade of historical plaques comes with a tablet bearing the inscription, "On this site in 1897, nothing happened."

The Lookout gift shop on the north side of the promontory is a good place to get Japanese fishing floats for a few bucks or to take advantage of the telescopes by the entrances. If the weather's blustery, the view from inside the shop is probably one of the more spectacular windows on the ocean to be found anywhere.

From the Otter Crest parking lot, continue north on the loop, whose dips and turns bring the view from the cape into sharper focus. Shortly after this road-less-traveled terminates, US 101 takes you past **Whale Cove.** The tranquility of the calendar-photo-come-to-life here is deceptive. During Prohibition, bootleggers used the rocky crescent-shaped shoreline as a clandestine port. In the 1980s, a court decision allowing property owners to restrict access to Whale Cove set a precedent undermining public ownership of other Oregon beaches. More recently, this trend was counteracted by another high court decision that prevented a Cannon Beach innkeeper from building on a public beach.

DEPOE BAY AND VICINITY

William Least Heat Moon in *Blue Highways* characterized Depoe Bay thusly: "Depoe Bay used to be a picturesque fishing village; now it was just picturesque. The fish houses, but for one seasonal company, were gone, the fleet gone, and in their stead had come sport fishing boats and souvenir ashtray and T-shirt shops."

To be fair, tourists have always come here since the establishment of the town. In fact, for all intents and purposes, the town didn't really exist until the completion of the Roosevelt Highway (US 101) in 1927, which opened the area up to car travelers. Prior to that time, the area had been mainly occupied by a few members of the Siletz Reservation. One of the group worked at the U.S. Army depot and called himself Charlie Depot. The town was named after him, eventually taking on the current spelling.

Depoe Bay also took on another incarnation as part of the so-called Twenty Miracle Miles, denoting the attractive stretch of rockbound coast near Depoe Bay north to the broad beaches of Lincoln City. Nowadays, the only thing miraculous about the commercial strip here is that dozens of gift shops selling the exact same merchandise next door to each other survive year after year.

Unwritten History
In the first months of 1996, the media exploded with stories raising the possibility that the tiny hamlet of Whale Cove, two miles south of Depoe Bay, could supplant Plymouth Rock as the birthplace of a nation. Rotting timbers from what is theorized to have been a stockade built by Sir Francis Drake in 1579 were unearthed in an area where stories have long circulated of the English pirate's landfall. These notions have been fueled by an unsigned ship log from Drake's voyage in a museum in England that identified 44 degrees latitude (same as Whale Cove) as a landing site, and an English shilling found on the central Oregon coast in 1982 dating from 1560; excavations of a nearby Indian village thought to have been buried in the year 1600 that turned up brass items, blades and Venetian beads; a

photo from the 1930s showing a local resident with a distinctly English sword he unearthed; a ship's cutlass found in Newport at the turn-of-the-20th-century bearing the markings of 16-century English arsenal. Since the initial blizzard of publicity, there has been no word from the archaeologists and historians involved in corroborating these claims. As most history books have placed New Albion, Drake's fabled lost settlement, near San Francisco, researchers will not be too quick to claim otherwise without years of research. In any case, given such stories of Drake's supposed landing and the area's legacy as a bootlegger's harbor during Prohibition, Whale Cove has to have the most interesting unwritten history on the Oregon coast.

SIGHTS

Depoe Bay is situated along a truly beautiful coastline that cannot be fully appreciated from

OTTER ROCK TO ROCKAWAY BEACH

an automobile. An especially nice perspective is offered alongside the **Channel House Bed and Breakfast** at the west end of Ellingson Street. Just go left up this road where US 101 passes the Channel Book Shop (see "Activities and Events" following). Perhaps the most all-encompassing overlook on the Bay itself is offered by the glass-enclosed rooftop lookout (open to the public) on top of the Made In Oregon store located on the western side of the bridge in Center City. From this perch, a viewing of this cross-section of the Pacific through the provided telescopes may eliminate the desire of a sightseeing charter.

East of the bridge, look down to your right to see the world's smallest navigable harbor. This distinction is announced by a sign citing the *Guinness Book of World Records* claim to fame (a tactic repeated later in Lincoln City with its "world's shortest river"). Despite the hype, this boat basin is unique because it's a harbor within a harbor. This topography is the result of wave action cutting into the basalt over eons until a 50-foot passageway leading to a six-acre inland lagoon was created. In addition to whalewatching, folks congregate on the bridge between the ocean and the harbor to watch boats maneuver into the enclosure. A blowhole can also be enjoyed from this vantage point when there is sufficient tide. Depoe Bay's Harbor was scenic enough to be selected as the sight from which Jack Nicholson commandeered a yacht for his mental patient crew in *One Flew Over the Cuckoo's Nest.*

North of town is **Boiler Bay,** so named because of the boiler remaining from the 1910 wreck of the *Marhoffer,* visible at low tide. This bay is a favorite spot for rock fishing and whale-watching.

PRACTICALITIES

Accommodations
Depoe Bay lodgings require advance reservations on weekends and holidays.

Food
The following restaurants represent a cross section of the old reliables in the region.

Two miles south of Depoe Bay the **Whale Cove Inn,** Star Route South, Box 1-X, Depoe

DEPOE BAY ACCOMMODATIONS

Agate Beach Motel, US 101 two miles north of town, tel. (541) 265-8746, $60-125, ocean view, beachfront pool, nonsmoking rooms.

Arch Rock Motel, P.O. Box 21, Depoe Bay, tel. (541) 765-2560, $45-60, ocean view, pets, kitchenettes.

Beachcombers Haven, 7045 Glen Ave., Gleneden Beach, tel. (541) 764-2252, $50-75, oceanfront, fireplaces, laundry.

Budget Motel, P.O. Box 66, Depoe Bay, tel. (541) 765-2287, $50-80, ocean view, pets, sundeck, cable TV/Showtime.

Channel House Bed and Breakfast, P.O. Box 56, Depoe Bay, tel. (541) 765-2140 or (800) 447-2140, $75-225, oceanfront, fireplaces, country inn with jacuzzi, full breakfast included.

Four Winds Motel, P.O. Box 423, Depoe Bay, tel. (541) 765-2793, $45-65, ocean view, pets, free coffee.

Gracie's Landing Inn, 235 S.E. Bay View Ave., (541) 765-2322 or (800) 228-0448, $80-115, fireplaces, overlooking harbor.

Holiday Surf Lodge, P.O. Box 9, Depoe Bay, tel. (541) 765-2133, $50-340, ocean view, motel and cabin units, health club, laundry.

Ocean West Motel, P.O. Box 414, Depoe Bay, tel. (541) 765-2789, $45-55, ocean view, pets.

Surfrider Oceanfront Resort, P.O. Box 219, Depoe Bay, tel. (541) 764-2311, $75-105, oceanfront, lounge, covered pool, sauna, and jacuzzi.

Whale Cove Inn, SRS Box 1-X, Depoe Bay, tel. (541) 765-2255, $65-125, ocean view, restaurant/lounge, jacuzzi.

Bay, tel. (541) 765-2255, has a dining room providing everything you could want in a restaurant in this part of the state. If fresh fish innovatively prepared at reasonable prices and a romantic sea coast view don't put a twinkle in your eye, perhaps the Friday night rib special and cozy lounge next door will. Start the day here with the Whale Cove omelette—a three-egg masterpiece with crab, shrimp, cheese, onions, peppers, and mushrooms. And don't forget the coast's biggest breakfast—a five egg omelette (spuds and toast included). Breakfast prices start at $5. Little touches like binoculars at your table and the friendliest waitresses on the coast also rate a thumbs-up.

The local favorite in Depoe Bay is the **Sea Hag,** 5757 US 101, Depoe Bay, tel. (541) 765-2734. Their seafood hors d'oeuvres (fried whitefish, scallops, oysters, smoked tuna, and boiled baby shrimp) give ample testimony to their claim of "seafood so fresh the ocean hasn't missed it yet." Another popular dish is salmon stuffed with crab and shrimp, baked in wine and herb butter. A lavish salad bar, a Friday night all-you-can-eat seafood buffet, and a recipe for clam chowder fêted by the *New York Times* has also generated good word of mouth. Expect dinner prices in the $11-14 range.

Two other restaurants north of the bridge also get good reports from locals. **Oceans Apart,** 177 N.W. US 101, tel. (541) 765-2513, and **Tidal Raves,** 279 N.W. US 101, tel. (541) 765-2995, boast the best views in town and a casual ambience. The resemblance ends there. Tidal Raves is open for lunch and dinner with tasty food at moderate prices. In addition to fresh fish and other seafood dishes like Thai prawns and oyster spinach bisque, the restaurant's pasta specialties are uniformly excellent. The Pasta Rave features crab, shrimp, ling cod, snapper, and more on a bed of linguine with pesto. For dessert don't miss warm chocolate chunk cookie with Tillamook Vanilla Bean ice cream. Price ranges for lunch are $5-9 and dinner $9-16.

Oceans Apart serves breakfast and lunch with a Hawaiian flair at a fraction of what would be charged in the islands. Consider such entrees as Paka Paka Keoni (sautéed red snapper with coconut topped with macadamia nuts) and the Island Boy's Dream (Portuguese sausage, two eggs, and rice or potatoes). Less adventuresome types can find salmon, Yaquina Bay oysters, a crab-broil sandwich, and the like. Whatever your tastes, you'll appreciate the hang-loose yet attentive waitstaff. Main courses at dinner range $8-12.

the narrow inlet to Depoe Bay, the world's smallest navigable harbor

OREGON TOURISM DIVISION

Finally, the **Siletz Tribal Smokehouse,** 272 US 101 South, P.O. Box 1004, Depoe Bay, tel. (541) 765-2286 or (800) 828-4269, at the south end of town should not be missed. In addition to native objets d'art, the fresh smoked salmon and smoked tuna, $12-13 a pound, are of exceptional quality. You can sample these traditional native delicacies prepared several different ways (try the honey-smoked fish) from the tray on the counter. Canned and vacuum-packed fish are also available for purchase. This is a good place to find out more about the Siletz tribe's August powwow (or call 800-922-1399). When you're done here, take your gourmet treats—which go well with Oregon microbrews—and drive two miles south on US 101 to Rocky Creek Wayside near Whale Cove. This has to be the coast's best ocean view with picnic tables

ACTIVITIES AND EVENTS

Book Browsing
The largest used-book emporium on the Oregon coast is the **Channel Book Shop,** tel. (541) 765-2352, located just south of the bridge, across from the chamber of commerce. The store's five rooms of romance novels, Westerns, travel books, and varied esoterica also function as the citadel of higher learning in Depoe Bay. In the front of the store, pick up the free map of used-book shops on the Oregon coast. **Oregon Books,** 52 N. Highway 101, tel. (800) 668-6105,

devotes its entire stock to titles concering Oregon, and books by Oregon authors. Oregon Books holds weekly book signings as well as readings. At presstime it looked as though the shop may be making a move to a larger venue.

Charters
With the ocean minutes from port here, catching a salmon or seeing a whale is possible as soon as you leave the harbor. On the way back into port you might see the **spouting horns,** 50-foot "geysers" of sea water that shoot through fissures in basalt when the tide is high. Charters are also popular because of reasonable prices. Fishing trips average around $45 for a five-hour run, and whalewatching excursions run about $10 per person per hour. Some companies are **Dockside Charters,** P.O. Box 1308, Depoe Bay 97341, tel. (541) 765-2545 or (800) 733-8915, **Deep Sea Trollers,** P.O. Box 513, Depoe Bay 97341, tel. (541) 765-2705, and **Depoe Bay Sportfishing,** P.O. Box 388, Depoe Bay 97341, tel. (541) 765-2382. Dockside Charters runs a four-hour eco-tour that takes in the scenic coast between Depoe Bay and Yaquina Head. The narration includes information on the area's history, shoreline, and sea life.

Joan-E Charters, 214 S.E. US 101, tel. (800) 995-3866, offers fishing trips and whalewatching excursions. The whalewatching cruises are aboard the 56-foot double-decked *Grande,* the largest boat in Depoe Bay. **Sunset Scenic Flights,** P.O. Box 427, Gleneden Beach 97388,

SALISHAN LODGE

We're often asked where is *the* place to stay on the Oregon coast. Of course, it depends on what you're looking for (and even then it's purely subjective), but if we had to select a place which best enhances the appreciation of the coast's spectacular scenery, recreational appeals, and regional cuisine, the choice is clear—Salishan. Seven miles south of Lincoln City on the east side of US 101 is a sign advertising the Salishan Lodge, tel. 764-3616 or (800) 452-2300. Named for a widespread native dialect in the Oregon Territory, this resort is one of a dozen properties in the nation that consistently receives a five-star as well as a five-diamond rating. In 1997, *Conde Nast Travel* magazine rated Salishan one of the top 15 resorts in the country.

Even if you don't stay here, the grounds and facilities are worth a look. The art gallery is free and features the best Oregon artists (also check out master woodcarver Leroy Setziol's bas-relief panels in the dining room). The forested trails behind the golf course (rated among the top 75 in the United States) showcase the rainforested foothills of the Coast Range. A breezeway behind the lobby displays interesting native artifacts and fossils, and the beautifully landscaped grounds look down on Siletz Bay in the distance. Across the street, the Salishan Marketplace features first-rate galleries and a good bookstore, Allegory Books.

Understated elegance and respect for natural surroundings are encountered at every turn—no high-rise schlocky beach architecture or neon signs here. This low-key approach at top-drawer prices, $150-250 in summer, attracts well-heeled nature lovers, corporate expense-account clientele, folks enjoying a special occasion, and serious golfers. You'll also find Mom 'n' Pop from Anywhere, U.S.A., and seminar attendees on winter weekend specials at half the summertime rates. Ask about multi-day packages for big savings on your room rate.

Despite the fact that the resort does not have ocean frontage or rooms appreciably larger or more ornate than those at many other upscale digs, the occupancy rate is high year-round. Why? Perhaps it's the fireplaces and cotton robes in the rooms or the little piece of coastal paradise your porch overlooks outside. For others, it's the objets d'art that decorate the public rooms or the forest/wetland/beach nature trail encircling the resort. While the diverse appeals of Salishan are too numerous to list, the theme of low-key elegance with respect for natural surroundings is everywhere extant. (If money is no object, the Lodge's Chieftain units with views of Siletz Bay are highly recommended.) With advance notice, you can even bring your dog with you. From attractive cedar-shaked self-contained units in the upper level of the complex to the smaller luxury motel rooms overlooking the golf course, you'll find nicely appointed interiors in earth colors with no trace of Naugahyde in sight.

In addition to the recreational and aesthetic appeals of the resort, the **Dining Room** is also responsible for Salishan's lofty reputation. Consistently touted as one of the top three restaurants in the state, it has become famous for its creative interpretations of seasonal Northwest delicacies and a 20,000-bottle wine cellar. The latter is open for tours, as are the grounds, whose plantlife is described by pamphlets available at the front desk. Fliers on area nature trails, art, and other topics are also available.

Salishan celebrated its 25th anniversary in 1990. The essence of its enduring popularity is perhaps best expressed in the words George Bernard Shaw used to describe another palace of poshness: "This is the way God would have done it if only he had the money."

SALISHAN LODGE
On the Oregon Coast

tel. (541) 764-3304, is located at Gleneden Beach Airport, a half mile southwest of Salishan Resort midway to Lincoln City. Whale-watching and scenic coastline flights of variable lengths depart from hangar number seven.

Events

The **Depoe Bay Salmon Bake** takes place on the third Saturday of September at Depoe Bay City Park, located just south and east of the bridge flanking the rear of the boat basin. Fresh ocean fish are caught and cooked on Indian style on alder stakes over an open fire and served with all the trimmings. Cost is $10 per person. The **Fleet of Flowers** happens each Memorial Day in the harbor to honor those lost at sea. Over 20,000 people come to witness a blanket of blossoms cast upon the waters.

Information and Services

Depoe Bay Chamber of Commerce, P.O. Box 21, Depoe Bay 97341, tel. (541) 765-2889, offers a lot of printed matter about the town as well as the central coast in general. What's really special about their office is a tranquil back patio overlooking the boat harbor where you can sit and recover from the shop-until-you-drop ambience along US 101.

The **Laundramat** [sic] is open 24 hours in the rear lower level of Mall 101 at the north end of town. Also at the north end of town is the **post office,** Depoe Bay 97341, next to the U.S. Bank. The Coast Guard **weather service,** tel. (541) 765-2122, can be contacted around the clock.

Three northbound and southbound **Greyhound,** tel. (800) 231-2222, buses hit Depoe Bay each day. The southbound stops at the Fire Hall on US 101 at the north end of town, whereas northbound coaches stop at Whistlestop Market, US 101 and Schoolhouse Rd., and Liberty Market,

466 N.E. US 101. There are also **Central Coast Connection,** tel. (541) 265-4900, buses servicing (except on weekends) other towns on the coast.

NORTH TO LINCOLN CITY

A Crafthouse

On Immonen Rd., **Alder House II** is a glass-blowing operation open to the public. The variety of shapes and colors produced are fascinating aspects of this ancient craft which the artisans here will explain to you. Alder House is open daily 10 a.m.-5 p.m. Their high-quality creations are on sale at bargain prices. The road to this establishment is indicated by signs on US 101 three miles south of Lincoln City, three-quarters of a mile east on Immonen Road.

Sometimes a Great Notion

Back on the coast route to Lincoln City, you'll come to the turnoff for ORE 229 along the Siletz River. If you drive down the north side of the river for a few miles, you'll note a Victorian house on the opposite shore that's built to last. A huge porch once fronted the riverbank, heavily reinforced against the elements. This was taken down in the decade following the movie version of Ken Kesey's *Sometimes a Great Notion,* but it lives on in the first pages of the novel.

The 1971 film, *Sometimes A Great Notion,* (renamed *Never Give A Inch* when it was shown on TV) starred Paul Newman, Lee Remick, Henry Fonda, and Michael Sarrazin. The plot concerns the never-say-die spirit of an anti-union timber baron, his not-always-supportive family, and life in the mythical Coast Range logging community of Wakonda. Much of this movie was shot in this area, with cafe scenes taking place at Mo's on Newport's bayfront.

LINCOLN CITY AND VICINITY

Several decades back, five towns that straddled seven miles of beachfront between the Siletz Bay and the Salmon River came together as Lincoln City. While the resulting sprawl and "zoned commercial" signs can be maddening at times, the most visited town on the coast must be doing something right. Perhaps it's the beach, broad and sandy, featuring superlative wildlife viewing near Siletz Bay. Or maybe it's the proximity of Devil's Lake State Park, a gem without equal among coastal freshwater playgrounds. Add prime kite-flying, mushroom-hunting, and bibliophilic and antiquing haunts, and it's clear that there's more to the area than the pull of saltwater taffy and outlet malls.

SIGHTS

Around Town
The **D River Wayside** is a state park property where you can watch what locals claim is the "world's shortest river" flow into the ocean. It traverses a 440-foot path from Devil's Lake and, despite its unspectacular appearance, was a cause célèbre when *Guinness* threatened to withdraw the D's claim to fame in favor of a Montana waterway. Local schoolkids rallied to its defense with an amended measurement, and perhaps the D's title will be restored. In addition to seeing D River flow from "D" Lake into "D" ocean, the beach here is great for kite-flying. The river itself is the point from which the street numbers of the city begin.

In commemoration of the establishment of Lincoln City, a 14-foot bronze statue was donated to the city by an Illinois sculptress. *The Lank Lawyer Reading in His Saddle While His Horse Grazes* originally occupied a city park (Governor Hatfield and actor Raymond Massey came for the dedication). Today the impressive statue is off in a nondescript lot at N.E. 22nd and Quay Avenue. Look for the sign on US 101 near the Dairy Queen pointing the way.

OREGON'S CIVIL WAR CONNECTION

Despite the haphazard patterns of growth here, the choice of Abraham Lincoln's name for the city was not made arbitrarily. Shortly after Oregon gained territorial status, Honest Abe was nominated as its first secretary. Even though he declined the nomination, his name was affixed to this north coast county in 1867. And when five smaller coastal communities decided to consolidate in 1965, the choice of the appellation "Lincoln City" was lent impetus by both the centennials of his passing and of the Civil War's conclusion.

This was also in keeping with Oregon's long-standing tradition of assigning Civil War-era place names to cities and counties. And why not? The major players in America's domestic theater of war had their first curtain calls out west. General George Pickett of Pickett's Charge fame at Gettysburg; General Edward Baker, who distinguished himself at the Battle of Balls Bluff in Maryland; Generals Phil Sheridan and William Tecumseh Sherman, whose marches across the Shenandoah Valley and Georgia were Confederate nightmares; General

George McClellan, who preceded Ulysses S. Grant as head of the Union Army; and Generals George Crook and Phil Kearney all served in Oregon. The Southern side was represented at Fort Vancouver near Portland with General Robert E. Lee and the "eyes and ears of the Confederacy," Jeb Stuart.

Primarily, these men were involved in protecting the Oregon Trail settlers, gold-mining areas, and trading posts from Indians. When the Civil War drew these men east, the area was left unprotected and incurred much damage. In 1981, Oregon symbolically and unsuccessfully lobbied for a $1.3 million reparation for the losses due to the lack of federal protection. In any case, the aforementioned Civil War generals' presence is still remembered in the names of the Oregon towns of Sheridan, Baker, and Grants Pass, as well as Crook and Sherman counties. Oregon's entry into the Union helped break a tie in Congress on the vote to abolish slavery. It's altogether fitting then that there would be a city named for the Great Emancipator, Abraham Lincoln.

LINCOLN CITY ACCOMMODATIONS

Anchor Motel and Lodge, 4417 S.W. US 101, tel. (541) 996-3810 or (800) 582-8611, $35-90, pets, kitchenettes, nonsmoking rooms, cable.

Bay West Motel, 1116 S.W. 51st St., tel. (541) 996-3549, $65-90, kitchenettes, fireplaces, cable, river view, ocean view.

Beachfront Garden Inn, 3313 N.W. Inlet Ave., tel. (541) 994-2324, $50-90, pets, kitchenettes, wheelchair access, fireplaces, ocean view.

Blue Heron Landing Motel/Marina, 4006 W. Devil's Lake Rd., tel. (541) 994-4708, $60-100, pets, kitchenettes, cable, nonsmoking rooms, river/lake view.

Brey's Oceanview Bed and Breakfast Inn, 3725 N.W. Keel, tel. (541) 994-7123, $70-135, wheelchair access, fireplace, cable, tennis, ocean view.

Captain Cook's Motel, 2626 N.E. US 101, tel. 994-2522 or (800) 994-2522, $345-85

City Center Motel, 1014 N.E. US 101, tel. (541) 994-2612, $35-50, pets, kitchenettes, cable.

Coho Inn, 1635 N.W. Harbor Ave., tel. (541) 996-3684 or (800) 848-7006, $80-100, pets, kitchenettes, fireplaces, cable, ocean view.

D Sands Motel, 171 S.W. US 101, tel. (541) 994-5244, $85-120, wheelchair access, covered pool, cable, nonsmoking rooms, ocean view.

Edgecliff Motel, 3733 S. US 101, tel. (541) 996-2055, $50-125, wheelchair access, fireplaces, cable, nonsmoking rooms, pets, ocean view.

Ester Lee Motel, 3803 S.W. US 101, tel. (541) 996-3606, $60-90, wheelchair access, fireplaces, ocean view.

Inn at Spanish Head, 4009 S. US 101, tel. (541) 996-2161 or (800) 452-8127, $120-200, wheelchair access, pool, restaurant/lounge, nonsmoking rooms, laundry, ocean view (particularly room 906)

Lincoln Lodge Ocean Front Motel, 2735 N.W. Inlet Ave., tel. (541) 994-5007 or (800) 423-6240, $50-80, kitchenettes, fireplaces, cable, ocean view.

Lincoln Shores Motel, 136 N.E. US 101, tel. (541) 994-8155, $40-90, wheelchair access, fireplaces, cable, nonsmoking rooms, ocean view.

With ORE 18 connecting Lincoln City to the Yamhill County wine country, it's not surprising to find several tasting rooms in town to pique your taste buds. **Honeywood Winery,** 30 S.E. US 101, Lincoln City 97367, tel. (541) 994-2755, sits across from the D River; try the blackberry wine from Oregon's oldest continuously operating winery. **Oak Knoll Winery,** 3521 S.W. US 101, Lincoln City 97367, tel. (541) 996-3221, presents its own varietals (try the 1985 pinot noir) along with award winners from other Oregon vintners. The hosts can help you plan a wine-country foray, and they sell cases at bulk discounts. **Chateau Benoit,** found in the Quality Factory Village on Devil's Lake Rd. at the south end of town, also has a place at which to sample some excellent pinots.

East on ORE 18

Heading east of Lincoln City on ORE 18 takes you on a road framed by the giant fir stands of the Van Duzer corridor. Just prior to heading over this pass through the Coast Range you cross the 45th parallel (it's just outside of Lincoln City by the Devil's Lake Golf Course on US 101, before its junction with ORE 18, indicated by a sign on the highway). At this point you are halfway between the equator and the north pole (every degree of latitude is 66 miles).

About a dozen miles east of town is the **Van Duzer Forest Wayside,** a prime spot on the Salmon River for a picnic. The site used to be a post office on an old stagecoach route. ORE 18 continues on through the Coast Range until the greenery of the tall firs gives way to drier orchard country wherein a major percentage of the world's filberts are grown. Roadside stands selling walnuts, cherries, and other crops dot the highway. You'll also see antique stores and tasting rooms as you ease into Yamhill Valley wine country (see "Day-Trips from Portland" in the Portland and Vicinity chapter).

Nendels Cozy Cove, 515 N.W. Inlet Ave., tel. (541) 994-2950, $45-115, wheelchair access, pool, fireplaces, complimentary continental breakfast, ocean view.

Nordic Motel, 2133 N.W. Inlet Ave., tel. (541) 994-8145 or (800) 452-3558, $75-95, kitchenettes, wheelchair access, fireplaces, covered pool.

Ocean Terrace Motel, 4229 S.W. Beach Highway 101, tel. (541) 996-3623 or (800) 648-2119, $50-110, wheelchair access, pool, restaurant/lounge, nonsmoking rooms, cable, ocean view.

Sailor Jack Ocean Front Motel, 1035 N.W. Harbor Ave., tel. (541) 994-3696 or (888) HEAVE-HO, $50-120, pets, wheelchair access, fireplaces, nonsmoking rooms, complimentary continental breakfast, ocean view.

Sandcastle Beachfront Motel, 3417 S.W. Anchor Ave., tel. (541) 996-3613, $55-110, kitchenettes, fireplaces, cable, ocean view.

Sea Echo Motel, 3510 N.E. US 101, tel. (541) 994-2575, $40-60, pets, kitchenettes, cable, ocean view.

Seagull Beach-Front Motel, 1511 N.W. Harbor Ave., tel. (541) 994-2948, $55-120, pets, kitchenettes, wheelchair access, nonsmoking rooms, ocean view.

Sea Horse Oceanfront Lodging, 2039 N.W. Harbor Dr., tel. (541) 994-2101 or (800) 662-2101, $50-115, pets, kitchenettes, fireplaces, covered pool, cable, ocean view, nonsmoking rooms.

Shilo Inn, 1501 N.W. 40th St., tel. (541) 994-3655 or (800) 222-2244, $80-180, pets, wheelchair access, covered pool, restaurant/lounge, nonsmoking rooms, laundry, ocean view.

Siletz Bay Inn, 861 S.W. 51st St., tel. (541) 996-3996, $45-150, wheelchair access, fireplaces, cable, ocean view.

Surftides Beach Resort, 2945 N.W. Jetty, tel. (541) 994-2191 or (800) 452-2159, $60-100, wheelchair access, covered pool, restaurant/lounge, live entertainment, ocean view.

Westshore Oceanfront Motel, 3127 S. Anchor Ave., tel. (541) 996-2001 or (800) 621-3187, $70-80, pets, kitchenettes, fireplaces, cable, ocean view.

Due to the state's increased population and the fact that ORE 18 serves as a major access road to two Indian gaming centers, this is one of the most dangerous roads to drive in the state.

PRACTICALITIES

Accommodations
Outside of Portland and Eugene, there aren't any cities in Oregon to rival Lincoln City for sheer volume of creature comforts. There are 1,800 hotel rooms here, and many face the ocean or are close to a beach. Peak traffic can result in 25,000 cars a day inching through town, so try to get locals to share their secret detours with you. We're sworn to secrecy about an alternative route involving a logging road around the east side of Devil's Lake that will take you across town during rush hour faster than US 101.

Campgrounds
Several wilderness retreats are worth noting in the Lincoln City area. One remote escape is at the previously mentioned **Van Duzer Wayside** on ORE 18. A dozen primitive hiker/biker sites (free) sit in a beautiful forest near the Salmon River.

More free rustic sites can be found about eight miles north of town and just south of Neskowin. To get there, just look for the "Scenic Drive" sign east of US 101 and follow County Rd. 12 for four miles. From there, travel about 100 yards west on Forest Service Rd. 12131 and you'll see the campground set along **Neskowin Creek.** To find out about the trails in the surrounding rainforest, call or write the Siuslaw National Forest, Hebo 97121, tel. (541) 392-3161. The campground is open mid-April to mid-October—bring your own water or water-purification kit. The nearby scenic drive continues up into an area of huge trees captioned by Forest Service placards explaining the ecology.

More elaborate camping is available at **Devil's Lake State Park,** write to reserve at 1542 N.E. 6th, Lincoln City 97367, tel. (541) 994-2002. Sixty-eight tent sites and 32 RV sites are serviced with all the amenities, including showers, a cafe, and a laundromat. The fee is $16-20 per night, $4 for hiker and biker spaces, mid-April to late October. This campground is just off US 101 at the northeast end of town.

Food

Lincoln City offers surprisingly many cost-effective and palate-pleasing dining options.

The best smoked fish in these parts can be had at **Barnacle Bill's Seafood Store,** 2174 US 101, tel. (541) 994-3022. The smoked sturgeon here is half the price it is on the East Coast, and although it's not thin-sliced New York deli style, it has a more delicate flavor. Look for a little storefront on the east side of the highway in the middle of town. Another place to graze is the **Safeway** at the northern edge of town in the Lincoln Plaza Mall. Stock up here, too, before heading north on the Three Capes Loop en route to Tillamook. A more upscale takeout place nearby is **The Salmon River Cafe,** North Lincoln City Plaza. Here you'll find Mediterranean-style salads, pastas, pastries, meats, cheeses, wines, and first-rate sandwiches, all at a fair price. In addition to the take-out deli, there is a spacious, simply furnished area for sit-down dining where breakfast is a highlight. Especially recommended is the marzipan brioche and the scrambled eggs with smoked salmon.

Mo's, 860 S.W. 51st St., tel. (541) 996-2535, as usual, can be counted on for good clam chowder and full fish dinners in the $6-9 range as well as good views of the Pacific. You'll find more of the same north of town off US 101 at **Dory Cove Restaurant,** 5819 Logan Rd., tel. (541) 994-5180, near Road's End State Park. The prices are a little higher than at Mo's, $9-16, but the range of broiled seafood entrees and cheeseburger fantasies make this place the favorite with locals. Another Lincoln City hot spot is **Kyllo's,** 1110 N.W. 1st St., tel. (541) 994-3179, specializing in broiled, sautéed, and baked seafood, plus excellent homemade desserts. The former can be washed down by Oregon microbrews and wines. Dinners are in the $15 range, and lunch is often about half

that. Locals say they've had good luck with the "specials" which are new and different every night. These can range from fresh char-broiled swordfish served with an herb curry spread to fish tostadas. Cajun-accented seafood preparations here also come highly recommended. End with deep dish marionberry cobbler or lemon lush pie for dessert. The restaurant is visible from US 101 as you drive by the D River wayside. With views of the water on all sides, this restaurant is a good place to linger. Since no reservations are taken avoid peak dining hours.

A place that appeals to everybody is the **Otis Cafe,** Otis Junction on ORE 18, Otis, tel. (541) 494-2813, whose innovative variations on American road food have been warmly embraced by everyone from local loggers to yuppies stopping off on the drive between Portland and the coast. Breakfast in this small, unpretentious cafe five miles northeast of Lincoln City is such an institution that long waits on the porch are the rule on weekend mornings. The reasons why include the thick-crusted molasses bread that comes with many orders, buttermilk waffles, and their legendary hash browns under melted Rogue Valley white cheddar (about $5). A half portion for one dollar less is the equivalent of all-you-can-eat fare, so walk the beach at Neskowin before tackling the unabridged version. Large portions, low prices, and a culinary touch that turns pork chops and rhubarb pie into epicurean delights are also in full evidence at lunch and dinner (Thurs.-Sun. till 9 p.m.).

Road food aficionados en route to or from Portland may also want to visit **Eyvette's Brookside Cafe** located midway through the Coast Range on ORE 18 six miles east of Grande Ronde and 15 miles east of US 101. You'll feel like you've stepped into an early 20th century log camp cookhouse here with prices to match. If a pot-bellied stove, antique tools adorning the walls, and a chainsaw sculpture greeting you at the door don't evoke lumberjack appetites, the breakfast of fried red taters and corned beef hash topped with two eggs will. Omelettes served 7 a.m.-3 p.m. daily, homemade soups, and a bakery counter showcasing the day's fresh-from-the-oven creations are also hard to pass up. To find it, keep an eye out for the red roof on the side of the highway.

The **Bay House,** 5911 S.W. US 101, Lincoln City, tel. (541) 996-3222, is a place food critics describe as "intimate" and "elegant." You might also add "expensive." Dinners can run over $30 a person, but you might want to come here just to enjoy select appetizers accompanied by a glass of wine. Particularly recommended is the Dungeness crab cocktail served with fresh tomato-wasabi (a hot Japanese mustard) and pickled ginger. If you're feeling less inclined to experiment, try the Umpqua Bay oysters with a soy vinaigrette sauce. A long-time favorite here is the creamy onion soup with bay shrimp. Have it during Walla sweet onion season (late spring) which coincides perfectly with local fresh bay shrimp season. A distinct Asian flavor pervades the menu supported by a wine list singled out in *The Wine Spectator.* The tab at the Bay House is definitely worth it—especially if you're fortunate to be dining in view of the sunset over Siletz Bay.

The reasonable prices at Salishan Lodge's **Sun Room** are a welcome surprise. This casual restaurant might be less elaborate than Salishan's five-star Dining Room, but its Northwest cuisine comes from the same kitchen. Breakfast, lunch, and dinner are served here overlooking the golf course, and you don't have to dress up or make reservations.

A good cup of coffee can be had at **Cap'n Bean's Espresso By the Sea,** 128 S.E. US 101, tel. (541) 994-7743. This Portland-based chain also has a wide variety of pastry and dessert items. It's located across from D River State Park on the north side of town. The **Lighthouse Brew Pub,** 4157 US 101 North, tel. (541) 994-7238, is a welcome rehash of the McMenamin formula so successful in the Willamette Valley. Just look for a lighthouse replica in a parking lot on the north side of US 101 across from McDonald's. Pizza bread, burgers, sandwiches, and chili can be washed down by McMenamin's own ales or some other quality brew, as well as hard cider and wine.

Cafe Roma Bookstore and Coffeehouse, 1437 N.W. US 101, tel. (541) 994-6616, brings an air of refinement to Lincoln City. Fresh home-baked pastries and desserts, fresh-roasted gourmet coffees and espresso drinks, as well as a collection of interesting books make this a wonderful retreat on a cold and drizzly day.

Hershey's Place, 815 S.W. 51st St., tel. (541) 996-9966, where Siletz Bay meets the ocean, offers a varied menu with such nightly dinner specials as blackened redfish, baked oysters, and homemade lasagna—averaging about $11. Low-cholesterol dishes are available for all three meals, compounding the impression of something for everyone. There's plenty to feast your eyes on, too, with a telescope available to focus on the multitude of seals, as well as eagles and over a hundred other species of birds.

Kernville Steak and Seafood House, 186 Siletz Hwy, Kernville, tel. (541) 994-6200, looks out on the river and surrounding hills through huge picture windows. Blue heron and deer are frequent dinner companions here, but the real attractions are the half-dozen nightly seafood specials (all in the $12-15 range) which often showcase fresh-caught shellfish. The other heavy hitters on the menu include prime rib and chicken and dumplings. You might couple your visit here with a look at the *Sometimes a Great Notion* film location (see "North to Lincoln City" under "Depoe Bay and Vicinity," above). In any event, finding this dinner house is tricky because its inconspicuous facade on the south side of the river displays no sign. Farther down ORE 229, the **Siletz Brewing Co. and Public House,** 267 Gaither St., Siletz, tel. (541) 444-7012, is an outpost of beer in the Coast Range.

Two Indian gaming casinos are located with 30 miles of one another and offer dining alternatives to the coast-bound traveler. Both **Chinook Winds,** 1777 N.W. 44th St., tel. (888) (541) 661-7469, and **Spirit Mountain,** 30 miles W of Salem on ORE 22 in Grande Ronde, tel. (800) 760-7977, have many dining options. Each offers generous full buffets for breakfast, lunch, and dinner and both have "fine-dining," full service restaurants offering moderate to expensive prices. The buffet prices at both casinos are roughly $4.25 for breakfast, $6 for lunch, and $9 for dinner. Chinook Winds also offers a Friday night seafood buffet and a Sunday champagne brunch for $13. Chinook Winds' ocean views are also worth noting. Both casinos have outlets for 24-hour dining.

Events and Activities

On the first and second weekends of February, and antique fair, quilt display, and bus tours (two hours long, $5) take place during **Lincoln Days.** The **Cascade Head Chamber Music Festival,** P.O. Box 145, Otis 97368, tel. (541) 994-5999, is another Oregon kulturfest that brings together world-class artists in an informal setting. Events are hosted at St. Peter the Fisherman Lutheran Church, 1226 S.W. 13th St., under the direction of Sergiu Luca, a famed violinist who draws on decades of international experience and the friendship of virtuosi who fly in from all corners of the globe to make music on the Oregon coast. Beethoven, Brahms, and the like are highlighted on July weekend concerts. To order tickets, contact the festival ticket office, tel. (541) 994-5333, or get them at the gallery in Salishan or the Lincoln City Visitor and Convention Bureau. Tickets runs around $15, and may not always be available at the door.

Several Lincoln City beaches have interesting **tidepools** to explore. Some of the best places in town are north of **Roads End State Park** and at S.W. 11th St. (Canyon Drive Park). There are also intertidal life zones at N.W. 15th St. and at 32nd. A few miles north of Lincoln City (off US 101) on the north bank of the Salmon River estuary is another set of pools to visit. Just follow Three Rocks Rd. (see "Neskowin Hiking," below). Public telescopes at S.W. 51st St. let you watch a colony of seals offshore.

Lincoln City calls itself the kite capital of the world, pointing to its position midway between the pole and the equator, which gives the area predictable wind patterns. The spring **Kite Festival** takes place Mother's Day weekend; the fall festival is held the last weekend in September. The event is famous for giant spin socks, some as long as 150 feet. The exact time depends on when the winds are right at the D River Wayside, site of the contest. Call (541) 994-3070 or (800) 452-2151 (in Oregon) for more information. When you come by the D River Wayside, go across US 101 to **Catch The Wind Kites,** tel. (541) 994-9500, for a shop that's bound to set your spirits soaring.

Devil's Lake is the recreation center of Lincoln City. In addition to windsurfing and hydroplaning, eight species of fish can be caught here. There's also good birdwatching at this lake, which Indians said held a sea monster that gobbled up unwary visitors. Devil's Lake Golf and Racquet Club and picnic tables grace the lake's shores, along with boat-launching facilities. Of the five points of access, East Devil's Lake Rd. off US 101 northeast of town is the best, offering a scenic route around the lake. Mountain bikes, canoes, and paddleboats can be rented at the **Blue Heron,** 4006 W. Devil's Lake Rd., Lincoln City 97367, tel. (541) 994-4708, and windsurfing rigs from **Windsurfing Oregon,** 4933 S.W. US 101, Lincoln City 97367, tel. (541) 996-3157, are also available for those who want to experience the lake more intimately. Also ask the visitor and convention bureau about the Blues Festival held at Devil's Lake each fall.

The **North Lincoln City Historical Museum,** 1512 S.E. US 101, has 2,000 items, including old-time logging machinery, homesteading tools, and exhibits on fishing, military life, and Indian history. Check out the early fashion mannequins and a WW II mine that was washed ashore. It's open Wed.-Sun. noon-4 p.m.; admission is free.

Tennis players can enjoy the public outdoor courts at N.W. 28th. If the weather is bad, play indoors at **Neptune Courts,** tel. (541) 994-8442, and at the **Surftides,** 2943 N.W. Jetty Rd., Lincoln City 97367, tel. (541) 994-2191. These are about half the price of **Salishan,** tel. (541) 764-3633, which averages about $15 per person for a 75-minute set. Another alternative is Salishan's early-morning or late-night rate of $7 per person (for more information see "North to Lincoln City" under "Depoe Bay and Vicinity," above). An outdoor court goes for $10.

Golfers can choose between two nine-hole courses at Neskowin, tel. (541) 392-4120 and 342-2377, 12 miles north of Lincoln City, or the 18 holes at the Devil's Lake Club. The small condo and beach house community of Neskowin also has **riding stables,** 48490 Hawk Rd., Neskowin 97149, tel. (541) 392-3277, and a scenic beach to explore. **Proposal Rock,** a high forested butte, sits impressively in Neskowin's tidewater, inviting an assault. Unfortunately, the thick underbrush and undeveloped trails impede in-depth exploration, but the slopes here still have some great hideouts.

At the **Lincoln City Community Pool,** tel. (541) 994-5208, you can swim for $1.50 and shower for 75 cents, and the **Bijou Theatre,** 1624 N.E. US 101, tel. (541) 994-8255, has first-run movies.

Information and Services

The helpful **Lincoln City Visitor and Convention Bureau,** 801 S.W. US 101, tel. (541) 994-8228 or (800) 452-2151, is open Mon.-Fri. 8 a.m.-5 p.m., Saturday 9 a.m.-5 p.m., and Sunday 10 a.m.-4 p.m. Ask for information on the town's impressive collection of antique and used-book shops. The factory-outlet mall (Quality Factory Village) located between Salishan and Lincoln City off US 101 is worth a gander, too, if only for Chateau Benoit's tasting room/espresso shop and steals on London Fog raincoats and American Tourister luggage. The **Traveler's Convenience Center,** 660 S.E. US 101, a mile south of the D River has a coin laundry. **Greyhound,** tel. (800) 231-2222, and **Central Coast Connections,** tel. (541) 265-9400, buses stop in town. The public **library** can be reached at (541) 996-2277, and the **post office,** Lincoln City 97367, tel. (541) 994-2128, is two blocks east of US 101 on E. Devil's Lake Road. It's open Mon.-Fri. 8:30 a.m.-5 p.m.

NESKOWIN HIKING

The tiny family-oriented vacation town of Neskowin (rhymes with "let's go in") has a quiet appeal based on a beautiful beach and two golf courses in the shadow of 1,500-foot-high Cascade Head. When you drive in off of US 101, a deli, a post office, and the **Hawk Creek Cafe,** tel. (503) 392-3838, greet you. Count on good breakfast, reliable pizza for lunch, and grilled fish for dinner here. Behind this small complex are the moderately priced Proposal Rock Inn and the Neskowin Resort.

Cascade Head Scenic Research Area

The previous statement is made manifest along the Cascade Head (two miles south of town) and Hart's Cove trails. The trails fall within the Cascade Head Scenic Research Area, the only region so designated in the United States. It was set aside by Congress in 1974, thanks to the efforts of the Nature Conservancy, and is today a mecca for 6,000 hikers annually. Rainforested pathways and wildflowered meadows give way to dramatic ocean views on Cascade Head and the Harts Cove trails. The trailheads can be reached on Forest Service Rd. 1861 (also called Cascade Head Rd.), an old gravel road west of US 101. Three miles down, there's a fork to a viewpoint where you should bear left. Three-quarters of a mile farther downhill on Rd. 1861, begin the hike to Cascade Head by a large Nature Conservancy sign and a highway guardrail.

The first part of the trail runs through arching red alder treetops and 250-year-old Sitka spruces with five-foot diameters. The understory of mosses and ferns is nourished by 100-inch rainfalls. In addition, a mind-boggling array of mushrooms comes out in the fall. Above the woods is a grassy hillside at the top of which you can look south over the mouth of the Salmon River, clear down to Siletz Bay (and

Old growth forest characterizes the flora in the Cascade Head Scenic Research Area near Neskowin.

sometimes to Cape Foulweather). This climb shouldn't take much more than 20 minutes. To the north you can see Cape Lookout. From this 1,300-foot perch, you can descend the long slope west toward the 500-foot-high **Pinnacle,** the headland's westernmost thrust. The Pinnacle is fenced off to protect endangered plants and species. The Forest Service and Nature Conservancy fear the onslaught of hiking boots obliterating several rare wildflowers common only to here and Cape Lookout. Originally, these barriers were built by farmers to keep their stock from going over the cliffs.

Indians purposely burned areas around Cascade Head to provide "browse" for deer and to reduce the possibility of larger, uncontrollable blazes. These human-made alterations were complemented by the inherent dryness of south-facing slopes that receive increased exposure to sun. In contrast to these grasslands, the northern part of the headland is the domain of giant spruces and firs because it catches the brunt of the 100-inch yearly rainfalls and lingering fogs.

Less than two miles from the Pinnacle is **Three Rocks Road.** En route you descend steep meadows and lose 800 feet in elevation, which might make the hike back a less-than-appealing proposition. The access to Three Rocks Rd. is several miles south of Forest Service Rd. 1861 on US 101. A midsummer trip to the area is enhanced by purple foxglove blooms breaking up the white yarrow, Queen Anne's lace, and daisies. So beautiful are these blooms, you might want to hike Cascade Head from Three Rocks Rd. during this season. To drive to the Three Rocks Rd. trailhead, go two miles through a rural residential community to Savage Road, go up the hill about a mile, passing the Ridge Road entrance to Sitka Center (see below). As you head down the hill you'll come to a curve on the shoulder, which is a parking lot big enough for a half-dozen cars. Beyond it is the trailhead, marked with a Nature Conservancy sign and a brochure box.

Around these parts, many will tell you that Cascade Head is the highest promontory on the Oregon coast rising directly off the shoreline. This is true as long as you accept the figure of 1,770 feet as its height. Because a height of just over 1,500 feet is just as often reported for Cas-

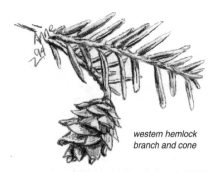

western hemlock branch and cone

ANNIE LONG LARSEN

cade Head, the south coast's 1,756-foot Humbug Mountain might get the nod. The north coast's Neahkahnie Mountain is also mentioned for its 1,700-plus-foot elevation. One thing is for certain: the silliness of such statistical preoccupations is immediately evident when you're surrounded by the grandeur of any of these headlands.

Hart's Cove

To the right of the Cascade Head trailhead on Forest Service Rd. 1861 is the beginning of the trail to Hart's Cove. This five-mile hilly loop can have plenty of mud, so boots are recommended as you tromp through the rainforest. You'll emerge on an oceanfront meadow overlooking Hart's Cove, where the barking of sea lions might greet you. For more information on these trails, write to **Hebo Ranger District,** c/o Siuslaw National Forest, Hebo 97122, tel. (503) 392-3161.

Sitka Center for Art and Ecology

The region in the shadow of Cascade Head can be explored in even greater depth thanks to the Sitka Center for Art and Ecology, P.O. Box 65, Otis 97368, tel. (541) 994-5485. From June through August, classes are offered in art and nature as an expression of the strong relationship between the two. Experts in everything from local plant communities to Siletz Indian baskets conduct outdoor workshops on the grounds of Cascade Head Ranch. Classes can last from a couple of days to a week, and fees vary as well. For complete information, write for a brochure or call the Sitka Center office between 10 a.m. and 5 p.m. during the period of instruction, or noon-4 p.m. other times of the year.

THE THREE CAPES LOOP

The Three Capes Loop, a 35-mile byway off US 101 between Neskowin and Tillamook, is considered by many to be the preeminent scenic area on the north coast. While the beauty of Capes Kiwanda, Lookout, and Meares justifies leaving the main highway, it would be a mistake to think of this drive as a thrill-a-minute detour on the order of the south coast's Boardman Park or the central coast's Otter Crest Loop. Instead of fronting the ocean, the road connecting the capes winds mostly through dairy country, small beach towns, and second-growth forest. What's special here are the three capes themselves, and unless you get out of the car and walk on the trails, you'll miss the aesthetic appeals and the distinctiveness of each headland's ecosystem. The wave-battered bluffs of Cape Kiwanda, the precipitous overlooks along the Cape Lookout Highway, and the bizarre octopus tree at Cape Meares are the perfect antidotes to the strip towns along US 101.

SIGHTS

US 101 north from Neskowin passes through pastoral settings befitting Tillamook County's nickname, "the Land of Cheese, Trees, and Ocean Breeze." If you've tasted Tillamook ice cream, touted by the *New York Times* as superior to Häagen-Dazs, or their extra premium aged sharp white cheddar (rated by the National Milk Producers in 1997 as the country's best cheese), chances are the mere sight of the cows grazing the lush grasses here will have you salivating. After thoughts of cheese, the realities of trees and ocean breeze will begin to take form on the Three Capes scenic drive turnoff about eight miles north of Neskowin.

Cape Kiwanda and Haystack Rock
Assuming you're not diverted by what some people consider to be the best fishing stream in the state, the **Nestucca River** (noted for chinook and coho salmon and steelhead), the next object of your prolonged gaze will be Haystack Rock. The sight of this 327-foot sea stack a half

mile offshore in Nestucca Bay will greet you after you make your way through tiny Pacific City. Your attention will probably then shift to the sandstone escarpment of Cape Kiwanda just to the north of the beach, especially if seas are rough. In storm-tossed waters, this cape is the undisputed king of rock and roll if you go by coffee-table books and calendar photos. While other north coast sandstone promontories have been reduced to sandy beaches by the pounding surf, it's been theorized that Kiwanda has endured thanks to the buffer of Haystack Rock. In any case, hang-gliding aficionados are glad that the cape is here. They scale its shoulder by climbing over hundreds of feet of deep sand in order to set themselves aloft off the north face.

Most people will probably be content just to look up the coast from here at the knockout view of Cape Lookout or south at the unique spectacle of American fishing dories being launched into the ocean off the beach. The lat-

ANNIE LONG LARSEN

Cape Kiwanda is the undisputed king of rock 'n' roll.

ter practice has been a tradition since the 1920s after commercial fishermen took these flat-bottomed boats out to sea when gill-netting was banned on the Nestucca River.

These days outboard motors have replaced oar power, enabling the dories to get 50 miles out to sea from the Pacific City shoreline. If you come here around 6 a.m., you can watch them taking off. The fleet's late afternoon return attracts a crowd which comes to see the dory operators skidding their crafts as far up on the beach as possible to the boat trailers. Other people meet the dories to buy salmon and tuna direct. In addition, this beach is besieged by surfers, who enjoy some of the longest waves on the Oregon coast. Other invasions are seen just north of Cape Kiwanda, where squadrons of dune buggies play king of the mountain outside the town of Sandlake. The sudden transition from the sand dunes here to the rainforested slopes on top of the nearby Cape Lookout also draws hikers to the area. In addition, those interested in beach, bay and dune horseback rides, $25 for 90 minutes, have come to the area for personalized guided excursions with **Into The Sunset,** call for reservations, (503) 965-6326. The "full moon ride" comes highly recommended.

Cape Lookout

While the appeals of Cape Kiwanda might be missed by the uninitiated or the sedentary, Cape Lookout can be appreciated by a glance out your car window on the way up to the cape or from beachside picnic tables at the state park in its shadow. However, the two plus-mile walk out to the tip of the cape should be attempted by anyone in reasonable health. The three-pronged trailhead has right and left offshoots that go down to the edge of the water. A large map delineating these trails sits at the trailhead for clarification. Follow the middle route halfway to reach the tip of the Cape. Even if you settle for a mere 15-minute stroll down the trailhead, you'll be able to look southward beyond Haystack Rock to Cascade Head. Right about where the trees open up permitting this view across the water, start to look for a bronze plaque commemorating the crash of a WW II plane (nearly a dozen casualties) embedded into the rock wall bordering the righthand side (north) of the

trail at eye-level. Giant spruces, western red cedars, and hemlocks surround the gently hilly trail to the tip of the cape. In late summer red huckleberries line the path. Halfway to the overlook, there are views north to Cape Meares over the Netarts sandspit. A bevy of wildflowers and birds can further enhance your march to the westernmost edge of this headland. Clear days in early April find hordes of whalewatchers scanning the horizon from atop this 500-foot cliff.

The Cape Lookout trail is marked only by a sign on the highway. What the views from Capes Sebastian and Perpetua are to the south and central coasts, the overlooks here are to the northern part of the region. But even if you're not able to make this pilgrimage, the views along the highway to Cape Meares and south to Cascade Head are exhilarating. To get to the campground and beach extension of this park, drive two and a half miles down the hill (north) from the trailhead parking lot and follow the signs on the Capes Loop Road. A trail beginning at the registration booth eventually leads to a ridge above the ocean. Another trail heads north through a variety of estuarine habitats along a five-mile sandspit separating Netarts Bay from the Pacific. The former is a popular site for agate hunters, clammers, and crabbers. There is a day use fee.

The road between Netarts and Cape Meares heads into the pricey beach-house community of Oceanside. Many of the homes are built into the cliff overlooking the ocean, Sausalito-style. This motif reaches its apex atop Maxwell Point. From the **House on the Hill** parking lot (see "Accommodations" following) you can peer several hundred feet down at **Three Arch Rocks Wildlife Refuge,** part-time home to one of the continent's largest and most varied collections of birds. A herd of sea lions also populates this trio of sea stacks from time to time.

Cape Meares

With stunning views, picnic tables, a lighthouse, and a uniquely contorted tree a short walk from the parking lot, Cape Meares State Park is the most user-friendly site on the Three Capes Loop. The park was named for English navigator John Meares, who mapped many points along this coast in a 1788 voyage. The famed octopus tree is less than a quarter mile up a forested hill. The tentacle-like extensions of this Sitka

OREGON TOURISM DIVISION

Cape Meares in a benign mood

spruce have also been compared to the arms of a candelabra. Another writer likened this tree to a gargantuan spider in a near-fetal position. The 10-foot diameter of its base supports five-foot-thick trunks, each of which by itself is large enough to be a single tree. An Indian legend about the spruce contends that it was shaped this way so that the branches could hold the canoes of a chief's dead family. Supposedly, the bodies were buried near the tree. This was a traditional practice among the tribes of the area, who referred to species formed thusly as "council trees." Scientists have propounded several theories for the cause of its unusual shape, including everything from wind and weather to insects damaging the spruce when it was young.

Beyond the tree you can look back at Oceanside and Three Arch Rocks Refuge. The sweep of Pacific shore and offshore monoliths makes a fitting finale to your sojourn along the Three Capes Loop, but be sure to also stroll the short paved trail down to the lighthouse, which begins at the parking lot and provides dramatic views of an offshore wildlife refuge, Cape Meares Rocks. Bring binoculars to see tufted puffins, pelagic cormorants, seals, and sea lions.

The restored interior of this 1890 lighthouse is open May-Sept., 11 a.m.-4 p.m. daily. This bea-

con was replaced as a functioning light in 1963 by the automated facility located behind it. The free tour is occasionally staffed by volunteers who might tell you about how the lighthouse was built here by mistake, and perhaps offer a peek into the prismatic Fresnel lenses. Before leaving the park, be sure to hike 200 yards east of the parking lot into the woods for a look at a giant Sitka spruce. Another giant Sitka is situated in the woods near the park's entrance.

PRACTICALITIES

Accommodations

The best deal in the area, if you're fortunate enough to get a reservation, is the **House on the Hill**, P.O. Box 187, Oceanside 97134, tel. (503) 842-6030, located on previously described Maxwell Point. For $75-110 you get the seclusion and cliffside ocean grandeur of this headland. Such a location for this price is an incredible bargain.

Another place with a nice view is the **Terimore Lodge by the Sea,** 5015 Crab Ave., Netarts, tel. (503) 842-4623 or (800) 635-1821, about two miles south of Oceanside, six miles west of Tillamook. Rates ranging $55-75 and units featuring kitchens and fireplaces make this a good base from which to explore the Three Capes. From November to April, if you stay two nights you get the third one free. We like the view from the deck near room 25. With pets allowed and a coin laundry available to wash off your beachcombing clothes, you'll feel right at home here.

Campgrounds

Campsites along the loop might offer greater proximity to the capes as well as increased cost-effectiveness for a protracted stay compared to a room at a motel. Two campgrounds between Cape Meares and Cape Lookout offer centralized locations, great views, and more than the usual run of campground creature comforts.

Cape Lookout State Park, 13000 Whiskey Creek Rd., West Tillamook 97141, tel. (503) 842-4981 or (800) 452-5687 in Oregon, has 197 tent sites and 53 trailer sites, as well as special camps for hikers and bikers. Showers, flush toilets, and a laundromat are available here. Reservations are required, so enclose a $14 deposit, desired dates, and desired specs for your site. Overnight fees from May to early October are $16-20 (off-season rates are $3 less). Hiker and biker spaces are also available for $4 per night.

Happy Camp, P.O. Box 52, 845 Happy Camp Rd. Netarts 97143, tel. (503) 842-4012, is a few miles away in Netarts. Stop in at the Schooner Restaurant (see below) along the Netarts spit just off the highway for complete directions. There are 30 tent sites and 38 RV sites. All the amenities are available at $15 a night. Reservations are accepted and it's open all year.

Food

A decent selection of roadside stands, moderately priced local hangouts, and fine dining are available along the Three Capes scenic drive. **Wee Willies Restaurant,** 6300 Whiskey Creek Rd., Netarts, tel. (503) 842-6869, has homebaked goodies and grilled-crab-and-Tillamookcheddar-cheese sandwiches. You can also get chili dogs, hot dogs, burgers, and the like. It's located a few miles north from the Cape Lookout trailhead. Just look for a drive-in secluded among the trees on the west side of the highway

As you come to the end of Netarts spit after driving the highway from Cape Lookout State Park, you'll see a turnout west of the road with two wide-body mobile homes attached to each other. There is no indication that this is the **Schooner Restaurant and Lounge,** tel. (503) 842-4988, until you come to a sign at the far end of the turnout. The Schooner caters most of the year to a lot of fixed-income retirees, as the restaurant's 1950s-style prices attest. In addition to run-of-the-mill diner food, there are local fish specialties (try the oyster burger, $3.75), homemade soup, and homemade bread pudding and carrot cake for dessert. Fresh cinnamon rolls and the cook's own biscuits and gravy are deliciously filling for breakfast. Gourmet it ain't, but geographically speaking, it's the best restaurant to be found for miles.

If hanging plants, a piano, and Nestucca River frontage don't make you feel at home, the apple pie and other wholesome fare at the **Riverhouse,** 34450 Brooten Rd., Pacific City, tel. (503) 965-6722, probably will. The seafood crepes, burgers, and open-face sandwich combinations are the perfect pick-me-ups after a morning of fishing or beachcombing along the Nestucca River estuary. Your bill should run around $6 for lunch and twice that for dinner (try the steamer clams simmered in vermouth). Finally, the somehow sweet blue cheese salad dressing has enough of a following throughout western Oregon to be sold in regional supermarkets. Weekends feature the eclectic offerings of live musicians on Saturday night and a wonderful Sunday brunch. Come early, as seating is limited in this small 11-table restaurant. Close by, at the **Grateful Bread Bakery,** 34085 Brooten Rd., Pacific City, the challah, carrot cake, and other homemade baked goods deserve special mention.

Another Pacific City hangout is the **Pelican Pub and Brewery,** 33180 Cape Kiwanda, tel. (503) 965-7007 or 965-7779. Microbrews and pub fare in view of Cape Kiwanda are an excellent combination. Inside, a warm ambiance rich in brick and wood can take the chill out of the sea air. We recommend the stormwatcher stout, $2.25/pint, to go with the panorama of sand and sea you'll enjoy from the pub's windows.

At first, the weatherbeaten cedar shakes outside **Roseanna's Cafe,** Pacific St., Oceanside, tel. (503) 842-7351, might lead you to expect an old general store, as indeed it was decades ago. Once inside, however, the ornate decor leaves little doubt that this place takes its new identity seriously. From an elevated perch above the breakers, you'll be treated to expertly prepared steak and seafood followed by sumptuous desserts. Dishes centered on local oysters and fresh salmon are the specialties frequently touted by the staff. The menu is surprisingly extensive, as is the wine list, but be forewarned—the bills can be high at Roseanna's, so you might just want to enjoy lunchtime gourmet sandwiches, $5-8. Better yet, come for blackberry cobbler dessert, $4.50; order it warm so the Tillamook Vanilla Bean ice cream on top melts down the sides, and watch the waves over a long cup of coffee.

Anchor Tavern, Pacific St., Oceanside, tel. (503) 842-2041, is the only alternative for food by the beach. Along with microbrews, specialties are smoked meats, BBQ ribs, clam chowder, pizza, and burgers. Hanging above the bar is a wide-angle photo of Hartford, Connecticut. The four-foot-long picture depicts the kind of urban sprawl that will make you glad you're here.

TILLAMOOK COUNTY

Without much sun or surf, what could possibly draw enough visitors to Tillamook to make it one of the top three tourism attractions (according to a state survey) in Oregon? Superficially speaking, a tour of a cheese factory in a town flanked by Tillamook Bay mudflats and rain-soaked dairy country shouldn't pull in over 750,000 tourists a year. But as anyone who has driven to Tillamook via the Three Capes Loop, or past Neahkahnie Mountain on US 101 can attest, those tasty morsels of jack and cheddar provide the perfect complement to the surrounding region's scenic beauty.

Aesthetic and gastronomic appeals notwithstanding, Captain Robert Gray was merely looking for safe harbor when he pulled into the area of present-day Garibaldi, just north of Tillamook, in 1788. Some historians cite this as the first American landing on Oregon soil. In any case, the region—whose name in Indian parlance means "Land of Many Waters"—has been written up in several other footnotes of history. Shortly after the turn of the 19th century, Tillamook Bay's sandspit was the site of a popular resort known as Bayocean. This complex was once envisioned as the Atlantic City of the Pacific Coast. Over the years, changes in ocean currents due to construction of a new jetty caused the sandspit to wash away and by 1953 nothing

remained of the three-story hotel, natatorium, cabins, private homes, and the world largest indoor swiming pool (with heated seawater). As any old-timer on the coast will tell you, "Woe betide those who build their castles on the sand." However, many people still choose to construct houses on unstable Oregon sandspits.

In 1933 the Tillamook Burn devastated forests in the Coast Range east of town in what was the worst disaster in the state's history. The blazes raged for four weeks, reducing massive acreage of old growth to rows of charred stumps. Fires in 1939 and 1945 further ravaged the area, leaving a total of 355,000 acres destroyed by the three blazes. The first fire generated a cloud of ash 40,000 feet into the air. Ashfall was recorded 500 miles out to sea and and as far away as Yellowstone National Park in Wyoming, while Oregon's upper left edge lived in semi-darkness for weeks. Seedlings planted by a community reforestation effort in the years that followed have produced an impressive stand of trees in these forests today.

A decade after the burn, the Tillamook blimp hangars, the two largest wooden structures ever built, according to *Guinness,* went up south of town. The hangars were built partially in response to a Japanese submarine firing on Fort Stevens in Astoria. Of the five stations on the Pa-

OREGON TOURISM DIVISION

Tillamook's namesake lighthouse is actually visible between Cannon Beach and Seaside.

cific coast, the Tillamook blimp guard patrolled the waters from northern California to the San Juan Islands and escorted ships into Puget Sound. Until 1946, when the blimps were decommissioned, naval presence here created a boomtown. Bars and businesses flourished and civilian jobs were easy to come by. After the war years, Tillamook County returned to the economic trinity of "trees, cheese, and ocean breeze" which has sustained the region to the present day.

Tillamook County—A Traveler's Advisory
In the floods of February 1996 downtown Tillamook streets were submerged under 10 feet of water and mud slides closed ORE 6, the Wilson River Highway, for several weeks. In addition over 1,000 cows died In the floods and mudslides throughout Tillamook County.

These events have thrust the imminent logging of the regenerated forests of the Tillamook Burn into the headlines. With billions of dollars of timber revenues at stake here, concern about logged-over hillsides left in unstable equilibrium (due to no tree cover to inhibit erosion) have created resistance to the proposed harvests. Tillamook State Forest officials have provided reassurances that clearcuts will not totally denude slopes of trees and erosion breaks. According to the Forestry Department, selective cutting will leave hillsides stabilized and fishing streams free of siltation.

Whatever happens, precipitation increases in the next 20 years are forecast by many meteorologists, mandating extra caution for those traveling in Tillamook County during winter and spring.

SIGHTS

Local Bounty
The traveler heading north toward Tillamook on US 101 encounters sights which might prove even more compelling than the ever-popular cheese factory. Start with a field of artichokes, a crop not usually seen in the United States outside of California. While California artichokes traditionally come into Oregon markets from March-June, artichokes grown around Tillamook have an August-October run. The variety grown in Oregon is meatier and slightly sweeter than the type grown in central California. Look for them at farmer's markets, Safeway, and Cub Foods. Eleven miles south of Tillamook on US 101, near Beaver Road in Hebo, is a fruit stand purveying the locally grown 'chokes as well as an astounding variety of herbs, perennials, and fruit. The cherries, marionberries, blackberries, and plums are also recommended, as are the homemade fruit jams. Even if you're not hungry, **Bear Creek Artichokes,** tel. (503) 398-5411; for information write 1604 5th St., Tillamook 97141, displays the creations of an enterprising horticulturist who'll be glad to share gardening tips with passersby.

Munson Creek Falls
Four miles north of the fruit stand on US 101 is a one-mile access road to the highest waterfall in the Oregon Coast Range. Munson Creek Falls drops 266 feet over mossy cliffs surrounded by an old-growth forest. A roadside marker on the east side of the highway just past the Pleasant Valley sign directs you up a steep road past a cluster of homes. A very narrow, bumpy dirt road then takes you to the parking lot at the base of the falls. A trail from the middle of the lot provides a good view with a minimum of exertion. This is a spectacle in all seasons, but come in winter when the falls pour down with greater fury.

The Blimp Hangar Museum
Farther north on US 101 you'll see a huge barn-like building east of the highway. The Blimp Hangar Museum, 4000 Blimp Blvd., Tillamook, tel. (503) 842-2413, is housed two miles south of ORE 6 in the huge (1,080 feet long, 300 feet wide, 195 feet high) hangar of the decommissioned Tillamook Naval Air Station (the other one burned down in 1992). The chance to look inside a structure big enough to hold a half-dozen football fields is justification enough to pull off the highway. You can learn about the big role the blimps played during wartime as well as how they are used today. In addition to historic and operational blimps on display, there's also a large collection of World War II fighter planes (many one-of-a-kind vintage models) as well as photos and artifacts from the naval air station. Be sure to check out the cyclo-crane, a

combination blimp/plane/helicopter. This was devised in the 1980s to aid in remote logging operations; it ended up an $8 million bust.

If possible, bring binoculars here to see the interesting latticework of rafters, and navy uniformed mannequins on the catwalks 20 stories up. The curators envision such additions as restaurant service, vintage planes, and blimp and biplane rides. To get there from downtown, take US 101 south a half mile, make a left at the flashing yellow light, and follow the signs. From a distance you can see a sign on the roof referring to historic aircraft. The museum is open 10 a.m.-5 p.m. daily. Admission is $6 adults, $4 children 13-17, $2.50 ages 7-12.

While all kinds of blimp stories abound in Tillamook bars, only one wartime encounter has been documented. Recently declassified records confirm that blimps were involved in the sinking of what was believed to be two Japanese submarines off Cape Meares. In late May 1943, two of the high-flying craft, assisted by U.S. Navy subchasers and destroyers, dropped several depth charges on the submarines, which are still lying on the ocean floor.

Tillamook County Pioneer Museum

West of the highway in the heart of downtown, Tillamook County Pioneer Museum, 2106 2nd St., Tillamook 97141, tel. (503) 842-4553, is famous for its taxidermic exhibits as well as memorabilia from pioneer households. Particularly intriguing are hunks of beeswax with odd inscriptions recovered from near Neahkahnie Mountain (see "Sights" under "Cannon Beach and Vicinity" following). Old photos are also worth the admission price. The old courtroom on the second floor has one of the best displays of natural history in the state. There are many beautiful dioramas, plus shells, inserts, nests eggs, and taxidermy. The Beals Memorial Room houses a famous rock and mineral collection along with fossils. The main floor and the basement highlight human history with antique kitchen tools, old-time logging equipment, Indian artifacts and basketry, historic modes of conveyance (from stagecoaches to cars), and simulated pioneer households. In short, this is probably Oregon's best pioneer history museum. It's open Mon.-Sat. 8 a.m.-5 p.m., and Sunday noon-5 p.m. April-September. In winter, the museum is closed Monday but the rest of the schedule remains the same. Admission is a dollar, $5 for families, and half price for those 12-17 years of age.

Tillamook Cheese Factory

The Tillamook Cheese Factory, 4175 US 101 North, Tillamook 97141, tel. (503) 842-4481, welcomes visitors with an imposing parking-lot

NORTH COAST FONDUE

Here's another way to enjoy the famous cheese, trees, and ocean breeze of Oregon's North Coast. When visiting the Tillamook Cheese Factory, purchase a 10 ounce bar of Tillamook extra sharp cheddar. They are often on special for under three dollars. These so-called "seconds" may look funky, but those cosmetic blemishes are actually an indication of additional aging that enrich the flavor, and can be easily trimmed. You might consider getting an extra bar or two to keep in your cooler to take home with you. You'll also need a bottle of beer. Every beer imparts its own distinctive finish. The Oregon ales in particular work best for this recipe (try Newport pale ale, Bridgeport blue heron, or Bridgeport coho). Finally, you'll need a good loaf of bread, preferably sourdough or some crusty baguette.

Rest assured that some fancy fondue pot with a denatured alcohol burner is not required to produce and enjoy this venerable dish. I've made it on a campfire in a well-blackened Boy Scout pot. A camp stove works quite well if you don't have access to a kitchen.

Begin by slicing the French bread into pieces about an inch square so that each piece has some crust to hold it together. Then cut up the entire 10 ounce cheese bar into small cubes and toss them into a saucepan. Add about a half cup of beer to start, you can add more later depending upon how thick or thin you like your fondue. Melt the cheese on low temperature, stirring to obtain a creamy texture. Season to taste with pepper. Grab a fork, stab a piece of bread, dip it in, and feast.

reproduction of the *Morning Star,* the ship that once transported locally made butter and cheese and now adorns the label of every Tillamook product. The quaint vessel symbolizing Tillamook cheesemaking's humble beginnings stands in stark contrast to the technology and sophistication that go into making this world-famous gourmet product today.

Inside the plant, a self-guided tour follows the movement of curds and whey to the "cheddaring table." Whey is drained from the curds, which are then cut and folded. These processes are coordinated by white-uniformed workers in a stadium-sized factory. As you look down on the antiseptic scene from the glassed-in observation area, it's hard to imagine this as the birthplace of many a pizza and grilled-cheese sandwich. If you can bring yourself to taste a few samples, however, the operation-room ambience will quickly be forgotten.

User-friendly informational placards and historical displays also inject a human touch to the proceedings. They recount Tillamook Valley's dairy history from 1851, when settlers began importing cows. The problem then was how to ship the milk to San Francisco and Portland. Even though salting butter to preserve it created some export revenue, there remained for ships the difficulty of negotiating the treacherous Tillamook bar. In 1894, Peter McIntosh introduced techniques here to make cheddar cheese, whose long shelf life enabled it to be transported overland.

In the early 1900s, the Tillamook County Creamery Association absorbed smaller operations and the modern plant opened in 1949. Today, Tillamook churns out tens of millions of pounds of cheese annually, including Monterey jack, Swiss, and multiple variations of their "American Milk Producer's Best Cheese in America" award winning cheddar. Pepperoni, butter, cheese soup, milk, and other products are also available at the ice-cream counter, gift shops, and deli. There's also a full-service restaurant here, but the big attraction is the ice cream counter. Have a double scoop chocolate peanut butter cone, worth every penny of the $2.50 charge. (If it's convenient, a packaged pint gives you more for the money). The Tillamook Cheese Factory and visitor center is open daily 8 a.m.-8 p.m. in summer and 8 a.m.-6 p.m. in winter.

Tillamook Bay
Five rivers, the Trask, Wilson, Tillamok, Kilchis, and Miami, flow into Tilamook Bay and carry with them silt that clogs the bag and changes the ecosystem. The Environmental Protection Agency has funded an estuary restoration program that will clean up the bay so that shellfish, oyster-harvesting, salmon, trout, and shorebirds can thrive.

PRACTICALITIES

Accommodations
Tillamook County has plenty of garden-variety places to stay. The best digs are in the northern part of the county in Manzanita. A good alternative to motels for families here are the rentals available from **Ribbon Realty,** 467 Laneda, P.O. Box 326, Manzanita 97130, tel. (503) 368-6754. Their free brochure features houses in all price ranges with some oceanfront homes. All are fully furnished and go for $55-175. If you're looking for an upscale-but-worth-it retreat, the **Inn at Manzanita,** 67 Laneda, P.O. Box 243, Manzanita 97130, tel. (503) 364-6754, has tree-top ocean views and private fireside spas in the $110 range.

Finally, just south of Manzanita is scenic **Nehalem Bay Campground,** write: 8300 3rd St., Nehalem 97130, tel. (503) 368-5943, a favorite with beginning windsurfers, beachcombers, and anglers. Sandwiched between the bay and a six-mile oceanfront stop are 292 sites going for $16-20, plus some bargain hiker/biker sites, $4, and hot showers. Park amenities include a laundromat, flush toilets, and piped water. No reservations are necessary (but it can get crowded during summer so reserve during July and August), and it's open mid-April to late October. Campers here often head over to the **Bunkhouse,** 36315 US 101, Nehalem, tel. (503) 368-6183, for ample and tasty breakfasts. The Bunkhouse has seven rooms to rent out if your camping trip gets rained out. Leaving Manzanita, you can get to Nehalem Bay State Park by turning south (right) at Bayshore Junction just before US 101 heads east into the town of Nehalem. The latter has developed quite a network of gift and antique shops in keeping with its new identity as a tourist town. Further south, the **Idle Nook Motel,** 141 N.W. 20th St., Pockaway Beach, tel. (503) 355-2007, is a little motel on the beach renting units for a good price. Each contain a living room, bedroom, kitchen, and bath. You can sleep five or six comfortably and kids and pets are welcome. It's a steal at $40-50, and the friendly management makes you feel welcome.

Food

While not always the height of haute cuisine, Tillamook restaurant fare can at least draw on the local bounty from the sea and surrounding farm country. Dungeness crab, bay shrimp, clams, and oysters are indigenous to the area, and a burgeoning number of wine and gourmet outlets throughout Tillamook County provide alternatives to the high-priced deli at the end of the creamery tour. Regarding high prices, it's worth spending a few extra bucks at Manzanita's (in north Tillamook County) restaurants; several establishments are of exceptional quality.

The **Blue Heron French Cheese Factory,** 2001 Blue Heron Dr., tel. (503) 842-8281, offers samples of its brie and Camembert cheese, picnic fixin's for sale, and winetasting from leading Oregon vineyards. Lunchtime sandwiches can be supplemented by locally raised and cured meat from **D's Sausage Factory,** tel. (503) 842-2622, located down the road in between the Blue Heron and the Tillamook Cheese Factory on the west side of US 101.

The **Muddy Waters Coffee** company, 1904 3rd St., tel. (503) 841-1400, makes the daily grind that much better for Tillamook folks and travelers in search of a decent cup. This place is one block off Main Avenue.

No one would figure tiny Bay City, eight miles north of Tillamook, as the continuation of your Tillamook County gourmet tour, but those in the know hit the brakes here for Artspace Cafe and Downie's. **Downie's Cafe,** 5th and C Streets, Bay City, is a favorite among anglers. Whether it's homemade buttermilk pancakes for breakfast or the famous oysterburger for lunch, you'll leave full and satisfied. Motoring through Bay City, you'll notice piles of oyster shells on the roadside destined to be ground up into chicken feed. Predictably, local menu entrees with bivalves—grilled Tillamook Bay oysters, steak and oysters—are a good bet. Finish off with a slice of homemade pie, especially pumpkin with Tillamook ice cream. To get to Downie's, look for

the dark facade of Artspace Cafe on the east side of US 101. Turn at Artspace onto 5th St. and drive two blocks to its intersection with C Street. **Artspace Cafe,** tel. (503) 377-2782, is another great place for oysters. Paintings by featured artists on the walls, and the chance to create your own courtesy of tableside crayons and paper, make for a cultural interlude.

Twenty-five miles north in **Garibaldi, Miller's Seafood Market,** tel. (503) 322-0355, sits on the left-hand side of US 101. Fresh salmon, ling cod, and bottom fish are the specialties here. Garibaldi is a fish-processing center, so Miller's selection is both low-priced and fresh (except for tired-tasting clam chowder). The town's fishing pier attracts hordes who want to catch their own. In addition to dock fishing, there's guide and charter service including salmon, birdwatching, and whalewatching excursions; call the **Pier of Garibaldi** at (503) 322-0333. Should there be a damper on salmon fishing, go for bottom fish here including halibut, cabezon rockfish, and sea perch. Cost is usually about $60 a trip. Kayaks also available. As for fishing from the pier, the best bet appears to be crab. In any event, the biggest challenge may be finding the place, despite the fact that it's within walking distance of Garibaldi's stores and restaurants. To get there heading north on U.S. 101, head to 12th St. When you see the large white headquarters of the Garibaldi U.S. Coast Guard Station on your right, head down the hill (left) across the highway to the bottom of the street, then turn right into the pier parking area.

North of Garibaldi on US 101 is the resort town of **Rockaway.** A walk along the seven miles of sandy beach here could well provide your only respite from 50 miles of inland towns between Tillamook and Neahkahnie Mountain if you're not an angler.

Look to Rockaway's **Pancake House,** 202 US 101, tel. (503) 355-2411, for big portions at moderate prices. Locals tout the chicken and dumplings. Other features include Mexican dishes, fresh oysters, and breakfast all day.

After eating your way up the coast, what could be more fitting than to wash it all down with a local wine? The **Nehalem** (pronounced "Knee-hail-em") **Bay Winery,** 34965 ORE 53, Nehalem, tel. (503) 368-5300, produces varietal wines as well as fruit and berry wines (pinot noir, gewürztraminer, and blackberry). This winery's welcoming milieu is reason alone to stop by. Or board the **Fun Run Express** excursion train that runs from Tillamook to the winery, for more information call (503) 355-8108. Tour the winery and picnic on the grounds 10 a.m.-5 p.m. daily. To get there, look for an ORE 53 sign on US 101 and follow it to the winery.

Shortly before leaving Tillamook County, gourmets pull off into the little hamlet of Manzanita. When adjacent coastal areas are fogbound, the seven-mile Manzanita Beach usually enjoys sunshine due to the shelter of Neahkahnie Mountain. It also has good windsurfing. Its single main drag, Laneda Avenue, is home to the **Blue Sky Cafe,** 154 Laneda Ave., tel. (503) 368-5712, and **Jarboe's** across the street, two of the better restaurants on the Oregon coast. Blue Sky's seasonally rotating menu uses organic vegetables, wild mushrooms, and fresh seafood to create elegant multi-ethnic dishes. A skylit art-filled interior and attentive service complement Blue Sky's culinary cutting edge. Jarboe's changing dinner menu typically includes mesquite-grilled meats and fresh seafood. Expect to pay around $13-18 for dinner in both places.

Even closer to the water, **Cassandras,** 60 Laneda Ave., tel. (503) 368-5593, serves up the coast's best slices of gourmet pizza (with, unfortunately, prices to match). Between Cassandra's near-beachfront location and the half-mile of Laneda to US 101, there are more places serving espresso drinks per capita here than any other town on the entire coast. Best of the lot is **Manzanita News and Espresso,** 500 Laneda, whose quiches, sandwiches, muffins, and remarkable selection of magazines and newspapers are also appreciated.

House renters, budget diners, and picnickers can take advantage of the excellent produce and impressive (for a coastal market) grocery section at **Manzanita Deli,** 2nd and Laneda. It's open till 8 p.m.

Recreation

Among Oregon anglers, Tillamook County is known for its salmon. Motorists along US 101 know that the fall chinook run has arrived when fishing boats cluster outside the Tillamook Bay entrance at Garibaldi. As the season wears on, the fish—affectionately called "hogs" since they sometimes weigh in at over 50 pounds—make their way as far inland as the Trask and Tillamook rivers. At their peak, the runs create such competition for favorite holes that the process of sparring for them is jocularly referred to as combat fishing. Smokehouses and gas stations dot the outer reaches of the bay to cater to this fall influx. **Bob Singley's Guide Service,** tel. (503) 641-6771 or (800) 466-1472, serves first-time anglers and features a 20-foot jet sled. In the event of salmon season restrictions, there's steelhead and bottom fishing available.

Along with birdwatching, crabbing, and salmon fishing in Tillamook Bay and angling in the area rivers, the Tillamook State Forest holds lots of other recreational opportunities. From a distance, the forest seems like a tree plantation, but hidden waterfalls, old railroad trestles from the days of logging trains, and moss-covered oaks in the Salmonberry River Canyon will convince you otherwise. Birdwatchers and mushroom pickers can easily penetrate this thicket thanks to 1,000 miles of maintained roads and old railroad grades. Two challenging trails off ORE 6, **King Mountain,** 25 miles east of Tillamook, and **Elk Mountain,** 28 miles east of Tillamook, climb through lands affected by the Tillamook Burn, but with scenic views throughout. Thanks to salvage logging in the wake of the disaster and subsequent replanting, myriad trails crisscross forests of Douglas and noble fir, hemlock, and red alder. A pamphlet entitled *Tillamook Forest Trails* is put out by the State Forestry Dept., Tillamook District, 4907 E. 3rd St., Tillamook, tel. (503) 842-2543. Birdwatchers flock to Tillamook Bay June to November to sight pelicans, sandpipers, tufted puffins, blue herons, and a variety of shorebirds. Prime time is before high tide, but step lively because this waterway was originally called "quicksand bay." Manzanita's hard flat sandy beach makes for a good landing area for windsurfers, a sport also popular at Nehalem Park.

Camping

Kilchis County Park, tel. (503) 842-8662, has cheap, $5, but primitive sites near a river with good steelhead and salmon fishing. To get there, go up Kilchis River Rd. about 10 miles northeast of Tillamook. The park is closed Sept.-May.

Campers are advised to wait till "Oz West" shortly after Tillamook County gives way to Clatsop County (see "Camping" under Canon Beach).

Information and Services
The **Tillamook County Chamber of Commerce,** 3705 US 101 North, Tillamook 97191, tel. (503) 842-7525, is located across the parking lot from the cheese factory. It's open Mon.-Fri. 9 a.m.-5 p.m., Saturday 1-5 p.m., Sunday 11 a.m.-2 p.m., mid-June through September.

The **post office,** 2200 1st St., Tillamook 97191, is open Mon.-Fri. 8:30 a.m.-5 p.m.

For local transportation between Tillamook and Seaside, call or write **Salt Water Shuttle Transit and Charter Service,** Nehalem 97131, tel. (503) 368-6711. Special stops are indicated on their schedule, featuring such diverse locations as the Tillamook Cheese Factory, Oswald West State Park, and Arch Cape. The drivers also respond to flag stops at unmarked locations where it's safe to pull over.

Other useful numbers include the **Tillamook Crisis and Resource Center,** tel. (503) 842-9486, **Tillamook Ambulance,** tel. (503) 842-4444, the county **sheriff,** tel. (503) 842-2561, and the **Alderbrook Golf Course,** Idaville Rd., tel. (503) 842-6413. The latter is located north of town and charges a $12 greens fee. Good regional titles can be found at **Rainy Day Books,** 2015 2nd St., tel. (503) 842-7766.

Events
The **Tillamook County Fair** takes place the second week of August and represents more than three-quarters of a century of tradition. Call the chamber of commerce for more information. The **Dairy Festival** takes place throughout June with rodeos, parades, and evocations of the Swiss-German roots of the region's settlers. Lederhosen, polka bands, sausages, and thousands of cheese-crazed tourists make this a lively celebration of the end of a long rainy season.

CANNON BEACH AND VICINITY

John Steinbeck in *Travels With Charlie* bemoaned how present-day Carmel, California, would be eschewed by the very people who gave the town the appealing sobriquet of "artist colony." This same thing could well happen to the Carmel of the Oregon coast, Cannon Beach, unless the growth which began in 1980 is slowed. Within a decade, the number of motel rooms here has doubled, as has the number of visitors on a busy weekend (now averaging 10,000-12,000).

Nonetheless, the broad stretch of beach highlighted by the impressive promontory Haystack Rock still provides a contemplative experience, although you might have to walk a couple of miles from your parking place to get to it. And if you're patient and resourceful enough to find a space for your wheels, the finest gallery-hopping, crafts, and shopping on the coast await. The city is zoned in such a way as to keep it small enough for strolling, and a location far removed from US 101 spares it the kind of blight seen on the main drags of other coastal tourist towns.

The hamlet got its name when a cannon from the wrecked USS *Shark* washed ashore south of the current city limits in 1846. The *Shark* met its end in the waves of the treacherous Columbia bar while monitoring a territorial dispute with a contingent of English merchant ships.

In 1873, stagecoach-and-railroad tycoon Ben Holladay helped create the first coastal tourist mecca, Seaside, while ignoring its attractive neighbor in the shadow of Haystack Rock. In the 20th century, Cannon Beach evolved into a bohemian alternative to the hustle and bustle of the more robust resort scene to the north. Before the recent era of development, this place was a quaint backwater attracting laid-back artists, summer-home residents, and the overflow from pricier digs in Seaside. Today, the low-key charm and atmosphere conducive to artistic expression are threatened by a massive visitor influx and price increases. While such vital signs as a first-rate theater, a good bookstore, and fine restaurants are still in ample evidence in Cannon Beach, your view of them from the other side of the street might be blocked by a convoy of Winnebagos.

SIGHTS

Neahkahnie Mountain, Oswald West State Park

South of Cannon Beach, north of Manzanita, is Neahkahnie Mountain. Sections of the coast highway here trace the mountain's outlines 700 feet above the Pacific. Nowhere along US 101 is the roadbed so high above an ocean view; soaring another thousand feet above you on the other side of the highway is the peak named for the Tillamook tribe's fire spirit. More homage is paid to this demigod at Neahkahnie Wayside, a turnout that offers a wonderful vantage point on the Nehalem Valley and across the water to Cape Meares. Nonetheless, keep your eyes on the road until you've parked your car. The area is full of hikers and, occasionally, at daybreak or dusk, Roosevelt elk and black-tailed deer. This WPA-built section was constructed by blasting through rocks and building a series of roads across ravines to highlight the dramatic meeting of rock and tide.

Scenic turnoffs abound, but take the half-mile trail from the main parking lot at Oswald West State Park (look for signs) to **Short Sands Beach.** This lot is on the east side of the road, where the trail winds down under a culvert beneath the highway. From Short Sands Beach you can pick up the three-mile old-growth-lined Cape Falcon Trail to the highway, or you might want just to linger at Smuggler's Cove. Spruce, hemlock, and cedar rainforests crowd the secluded boulder to boulder shoreline, and it's easy to believe local legends of Spanish pirates burying a treasure along this coast. One legend had the crew of a shipwrecked Manila galleon salvaging its cargo of gold and beeswax (a popular commodity in trade with the Orient) by burying it in the side of the mountain. To deter Indians from the site, the Spanish pirates killed a black man and buried him on top of the cargo. While this account taken from native histories has never been substantiated, a piece of crudely inscribed beeswax retrieved from the Neahkahnie region (on display at Tillamook's Pioneer Museum) keeps speculation alive.

In any case, there is real treasure here today for all who venture into this realm. We have Governor Oswald West's 1913 beach bill to thank

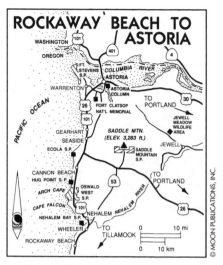

for Oregon's virgin shoreline. And a 1967 amendment to West's bill additionally protected the dry-sand area of the beach (from the high-tide line to the vegetation line). The spirit of the legislation is honored with the **Matt Kramer Memorial.** Kramer was a reporter whose detailed coverage of the 1967 legislative proceedings produced a groundswell of public support for the bill.

The memorial's location along this part of the coast is timely and appropriate, given 1969 and 1994 Supreme Court decisions. In both cases, Cannon Beach hotel owners unsuccessfully challenged Oregon statutes that established beaches as public property. The most recent decision ruled against the condo community's right to restrict access to parts of Whale Cove near Depoe Bay. Nonetheless, the spirit of the Beach Bill has unfortunately been eroded by societal forces.

Neahkahnie Mountain Summit Trail

Two miles north of the Manzanita turnoff is the access road to the Neahkahnie Mountain Summit Trail. The summit view south to Cape Meares and east to the Nehalem Valley ranks as one of the finest on the coast. As the trailhead access road on the east side of the highway is not well-marked, look for a subdivision on the golf course to the west. A realty office on the west side of US 101 is also nearby. Drive the gravel road up a quarter mile to the trailhead parking lot and begin a moderately difficult one-and-a-half-mile ascent. Allow about forty-five minutes to get to the top.

Entering Cannon Beach

Several miles up from Oswald West State Park's main parking lot is **Arch Cape Tunnel,** cut right into the mountain. This marks the end of the state park but not the beauty. On the way into Cannon Beach, views of **Hug Point State Park** and pristine beaches will have you lacing up your hiking boots again. Two miles south of the downtown area, park at **Tolovana Beach Wayside.** Picnic and restroom facilities aren't the only reasons to come here. This is an excellent base from which to walk south three miles to Hug Point (so named because wagons had to dash between the waves hugging the point to get around) or north two miles past Haystack Rock into town. If you are going to Hug Point, you'll appreciate how the knot of beachgoers thins out south of Tolovana. Time your trek to coincide with low tide, when all manner of marinelife in tidal pools will be exposed. At low tide, you'll also see remains of an 800-foot-long, Model-T-sized road blasted into the base of Hug Point, an early precursor to US 101. The cliffs at Hug Point are gouged with caves and crevasses which also invite exploring.

Heading into town on foot from Tolovana is a good idea on holiday weekends, when there's a dearth of parking spaces. As you head north, **Haystack Rock** will loom larger. This is the third-highest coastal monolith in the world, measuring 235 feet in height. Flanking the mountain are two rock formations known as **The Needles.** These skinny spires had two other counterparts at the turn of the century that were gradually leveled by weathering and erosion. Old-timers will tell you that a trail to the top of Haystack was dynamited by the government to keep people off this bird rookery and away from the intertidal life at its base. It also reduced the number of intrepid hikers trapped on the rock at high tide.

Today the area is designated an Oregon island national wildlife refuge and has wilderness status. During the summer, the **Haystack Rock Awareness Program** sponsors free interpretive programs here and evening programs in Cannon Beach; check the chamber of commerce for details. While these talks are interesting, the beach will also speak to you with its own distinctive voices. Don't miss the cacophony of shorebirds at sunset and the winter phenomenon of "singing sands" created by wind blowing over the beach.

The Beach Loop Into Town

Driving into town along the beach loop which branches off US 101, you'll pass such destination resorts as the Tolovana Inn, the Surfsand, and the Surfview. Thereafter, the town that greets you is more like Cape Cod and Carmel than any other town on the Oregon coast. Wood shingles and understated earth colors dominate the ar-

the view from Neahkahnie Mountain, overlooking the supposed spot of the as-yet-undiscovered treasure hidden by the crew of a wrecked Spanish galleon

OREGON TOURISM DIVISION

chitecture of tastefully rendered galleries, bookstores, and bistros. Throngs of walkers along Hemlock St., the main drag, also distinguish this burg from the typical coastal strip town whose heart and soul have been pierced by US 101. You have to go clear to the north end of Cannon Beach to find a gas station, and even then you're liable to bypass its stone-cottage facade.

Klootchy Creek and Saddle Mountain

From the north end of town, it's not far to the junction of US 101 and US 26. The latter goes 80 miles east to Portland, but many coastal travelers just travel two miles on US 26 to visit Klootchy Creek Park. In an old-growth spruce and fir forest you'll find the **world's tallest Sitka spruce.** Standing 216 feet high and 52 feet in circumference, it's believed to be over seven centuries old. To find the tree, look for signs on the north side of the highway shortly after leaving Cannon Beach. A wooden boardwalk protects the tree's root system and lets you approach the tree while sparing you the muddy terrain .

Another reason to head east from Cannon Beach is the hike up 3,283-foot **Saddle Mountain.** To get to the trailhead, take US 26 from its junction with US 101 for 10 miles and turn left on the prominently indicated Saddle Mountain Road. Although it's paved, this road is not suitable for RVs or wide-bodied vehicles. After seven twisting miles, you'll come to the trailhead of the highest peak in this part of the Coast Range. The trail itself is steep and gains over 1,600 feet in two and a half miles. Wet conditions can make the going difficult (allow four hours roundtrip) and the scenery en route is not always exceptional, but the view from the top is worth it.

On a clear day, hikers can see some 50 miles of the Oregon and Washington coastlines, including the Columbia River. Also possible are spectacular views of Mt. Rainier, Mt. St. Helens, Mt. Hood, and, unfortunately, miles of clearcuts. If you go between May and August you'll be treated to a wildflower display that'll surprise you. On the upper part of the trail, species that pushed south from Alaska and Canada during the last Ice Age thrive. The cool, moist climate here keeps them from dying out as they did at lower elevations. Some early blooms include pink coast fawn lily, monkey flower, wild rose, wood violet, bleeding heart, oxalis, Indian

paintbrush, and trillium. Cable handrails provide safety on the narrow final quarter-mile trail to the summit.

Down US 26 about one mile west of Elsie you can visit **Camp 18 Logging Museum,** P.O. Box 195, Seaside 97138, tel. (503) 755-2476. The chance to look at steam donkeys and other antique logging equipment breaks up the long drive to Portland. A restaurant serving American road food in a large log building might also add to your respite here. The 85-foot long ridgepole supporting the ceiling is the largest beam you're likely to see anywhere. Ax-handle doorknobs, crosscut saws, and other logging paraphernalia complete the motif. A walk downstairs to look at a bar created from one giant log and some oldtime logging pictures is also recommended. Family-style seating, specials catering to lumberjack appetites, and a gift shop purveying Northwest books and crafts are additional enticements.

Jewell Meadow Wildlife Area

Farther east down US 26, however, is the best place of all to see wildlife. Each fall and winter Roosevelt elk come to the Jewell Meadow Wildlife area. Elk-hunting season is in November, so come before October at dawn or dusk for the best viewing times. Black-tailed deer might show up in the spring and summer. To get there, take US 26 to the Jewell junction (about 20 miles east of Cannon Beach) then head north on an unmarked state road for nine miles to **Jewell.** Turn west and drive one mile on ORE 202 to parking spaces in close proximity to elk on Fishhawk Creek. If there are no elk in the first parking area or at headquarters, go on to the third lot and viewpoint. Three miles west is 100-foothigh Fishhawk Falls at Lee Wooden County Park. For more information, call (503) 755-0204.

Ecola State Park

Ecola State Park is just north of the Cannon Beach townsite. Thick conifer forests line the access road to Ecola Point. This forested cliff has many trails leading down to the water. The view south takes in Haystack Rock and the overlapping peaks of the Coast Range extending to Neahkahnie Mountain. This is probably the most photographed view on the coast. Out to sea, the sight of sea lions basking on surf-drenched rocks (mid-April through July) or migrating gray

the view from Ecola Point summit

REBECCA SINGER

whales (March) and orcas (May) are seasonal highlights. From Ecola Point, trails lead north to horseshoe-shaped **Indian Beach,** a favorite with surfers. Some prefer to drive there as a prelude to hiking up Tillamook Head, considered by Lewis and Clark to be the region's most beautiful viewpoint (see "Following Lewis and Clark" under "Seaside and Vicinity" following).

The name Ecola means "whale" in Chinook jargon and was first used as a place-name by William Clark, referring to a creek in the area. Lewis and Clark journals note a 105-foot beached whale found somewhere within present-day Ecola Park's southern border, Crescent Beach. This general area represents the southernmost extent of Lewis and Clark's Oregon coastal travels.

From Ecola Point, the historic **Tillamook Rock Lighthouse** sits a mile northwest out to sea. This beacon was operative 1881-1957, despite sustained 100-mile-per-hour gales that frequently pushed seas up and over the 130-foot height of the light. Today it serves as a depository for cremated human remains.

During summer weekends and other high usage times, there is a $3 admission fee at the park.

Les Shirley Park

A city park worth visiting is Les Shirley Park. In addition to being the probable location of the whale carcass observed by Lewis and Clark, this place has interpretive signs to explain the interaction of ocean and fresh water that occurs in Ecola Creek estuary. To reach the park after leaving town on the beach loop to US 101, turn left on 5th St. at the foot of the hill. Pass the sign for Ecola State Park; Les Shirley Park is a few more blocks ahead.

PRACTICALITIES

Camping

At **Oswald West State Park,** write: 8300 3rd St., Nehalem 97130, tel. (503) 368-5943 or 238-7488, you walk a half mile from a parking lot to campsites in a grove of old-growth conifers backdropped by high cliffs. In addition to Short Sands Beach, Smuggler's Cove, and the previously detailed hiking options, surfing and tidepooling can be enjoyed nearby. The State Parks Division supplies wheelbarrows to cart your gear from the parking lot to 36 primitive campsites. Camping is allowed mid-May to October and costs $9 a night. This campground is the only state park without electrical hookups.

Accommodations

If you're not willing to make stormwatching an acquired taste, do not reserve Cannon Beach lodgings from mid-January through early March. During this time much of the annual rainfall total of 80 inches is recorded. Should high room rates or crowds on weekends other times of the year be a deterrent, remember that Cannon Beach is only an hour and a half from Portland, perfect for a day-trip.

A nice oceanfront family-style lodge is the **Sea Sprite,** write for brochure to P.O. Box 66, Tolovana Park 97145, tel. (503) 436-2266. With a beachfront location just south of Haystack

*Short Sands Beach
at Oswald West
State Park*

OREGON TOURISM DIVISION

Rock, plus kitchens, TV, and spectacular views, it's not surprising that this place commands $60-150 rates during the regular season. What *is* surprising is the off-season discount of 50% of these rates, Oct.-May, Sun.-Thursday. These family-style beach cabins are a throwback to the Oregon coast of an earlier era. Inside you'll find such homey touches as fireplaces, games, books, periodicals, and rockers. Outside you have flowers, picnic tables, and the best of Cannon Beach shopping and beachcombing in close proximity. Two cabins are for two people, one cabin holds six, a two-bedroom cottage holds eight, and a couple lodgings sleep five people each. To get there take the Beach Loop (Hemlock St.) south of town and turn west at Nebesna Street. If the Sea Sprite is filled up, the same management will steer you to the **Hearthstone Inn,** Hemlock and Jackson Streets, tel. (503) 436-2266, $75-85, which also features off-season specials. While this lodging doesn't have the Haystack Rock views of the Sea Sprite, it's closer to downtown shopping.

Slightly lower in price are the studio units at the **Blue Gull,** 632 Hemlock St., tel. (503) 436-2714. These come with housekeeping facilities. A sauna and laundry room are on the grounds. Cottages for larger groups are also available. The **McBee Motel,** 888 S. Hemlock St., tel. (503) 436-2569, is less elaborate and less expensive, $30-130, but close enough to town and far enough from traffic to be worth considering. McBee accepts pets in its homey cot-

tages. **Hidden Villa,** 188 E. Van Buren, tel. (503) 436-2237, has six newly renovated pine cabins a few blocks from the beach, charging $85 in summer, $35 in the off-season. For somewhat more money than you'd pay at these places, you can get the intimacy and flavor of a bed and breakfast. In Cannon Beach the two-bedroom **Tern Inn,** 3663 S. Hemlock, tel. (800) 600-1528, is close enough to the beach for good views. Private baths, private entrances, and full breakfasts with home-baked goodies go for as low as $75 a night. Reserve a month in advance. The **Cannon Beach Hotel,** 1116 Hemlock St., tel. (503) 436-1392, is a 1910 converted loggers' boardinghouse with 30 rooms and a small cafe and restaurant on the premises. Full breakfasts are included in the $50-170-per-night rates, and lunch and dinner can be enjoyed here apart from the lodging package. The most expensive rooms have fireplaces, whirlpools, and partial ocean views. As with all Cannon Beach accommodations, be sure to reserve well in advance.

Given this book's emphasis on smaller lodgings with a home-grown flavor, the **Best Western Surfsand Resort,** Oceanfront and Gower Streets, tel. (503) 436-2274 or (800) 547-6100, is not your typical *Oregon Handbook* hotel recommendation, but you'd be hard-pressed to find a better combination of location and amenities in Cannon Beach. You can park your car upon arrival and walk to downtown galleries or enjoy Haystack Rock just outside your door. Other neighbors include the Wayfarer Restaurant (award-winning clam chowder and seafood) as well as Hane Bakery (a combination art gallery and first-rate bakery). The Surfsand's array of lodging options run the gamut from spacious oceanfront rooms, many with such features as kitchens, fireplaces, and spas to houses in the Coast Range. Such comforts and conveniences come with a price (rooms begin at $120), but Cannon Beach is one town whose many charms rate a deluxe treatment like this one.

Food

As you might expect, eating out can get expensive here. However, there are some ways to beat the costs, and, there are a few justifiable splurges.

The **Mariner Market**, 139 N. Hemlock St., tel. (503) 436-2412, is an antique-filled grocery that's fully stocked with fresh meat, fruit, and vegetables. The Mariner's prices beat the tab at several other markets in town and it's open 9 a.m.-9 p.m. Before you leave, check out the antique grocery paraphernalia, old-time bottles and containers, and the jewelry and crystal shop upstairs. **Ecola Seafoods**, 208 N. Spruce, tel. (503) 436-9130, features walk-away cocktails, $7-9, pricy-but-worth-it mounds of dungeness crab and bay shrimp as fresh as we've found. There's also smoked salmon and fish and chips as well as one of the few clam chowders, $2.75/cup, in Oregon that can stand up to East coast competition. You'll find it located across from the public parking lots and rest rooms.

The **Lazy Susan Cafe**, 126 N. Hemlock St., tel. (503) 436-2816, is set back from Hemlock Street in Coaster Square. Just look for Coaster Theater, 108 N. Hemlock St., on the west side of the street and go beyond it into the mall. Look for the sign near Cannon Beach Book Company. This is *the* place in town for breakfast and lunch. Homemade muffins, eggs Benedict, and the best coffee in town can fuel up or finish off an early morning beach walk. Homemade soups and sandwiches are the bill of fare at lunch. With prices not going too much beyond $5-7 for a good-sized meal, the lines can be long on weekend mornings. **Homegrown**, 3301 S. Hemlock, tel. (503) 436-1803, is one place guaranteed to satisfy even the most fire-and-brimstone of the lacto-ovo-vegan food police. Gourmet or-

ganic salads the size of a small car, $5 range, and Sunrise (organic spuds and range-free eggs with salsa and cheese, $7.50) even manage to taste pretty good too. In short, this friendly cafe with the sixties-tinged decor is the perfect antidote to the greasy jo-jos, saltwater taffy, fried corn dogs, ice creams cones, and other implements of dietary destruction that often accompany a visit to the beach.

Morris' Fireside Restaurant, 207 N. Hemlock, tel. (503) 436-2917, is an attractive log building where moderately priced steak and seafood are featured along with "logger" breakfasts. Portions are large and so is the selection. Try the oyster and bacon sandwich, $7.25, for lunch and the fresh seafood special for dinner. **Heather's**, 271 N. Hemlock, tel. (503) 436-9356, is a tiny cafe set back from the main drag across from the gas station at the north end of town. Just look for a green sign directing you back to a tiny cafe in back of a mini-mall. Exotic fare like African peanut soup and creative sandwiches let you enjoy a gourmet lunch in the $6-8 range.

Mo's at Tolovana, 3400 S. Hemlock, sits next to Tolovana Park and boasts a restaurant site once selected by *Pacific Northwest* magazine as having "the most romantic view on the Oregon coast." Add this to Mo's reliable formula of fresh fish and rich clam chowder at reasonable prices and you can't miss. Yaquina Bay oysters, crab cakes, and breakfast are new and notable here.

Several afterthoughts deserving of serious consideration are the chocolate-covered shortbread at **Cannon Beach Cookie Company**, 239 N. Hemlock, tel. (503) 436-2832, and the espresso drinks and ice cream across the street at **Osburn's Ice Creamery**, 240 N. Hemlock, tel. (503) 436-1470. The latter is adjacent to **Osburn's Deli**, tel. (503) 436-2234, which features $4.25 sandwiches that can make a meal for two. Summertime specials on local produce, and people-watching from old classroom chairs on Osburn's porch, are Cannon Beach traditions.

On your way to the beach via downtown's 2nd St. shoreline access, **Fultano's**, 200 N. Hemlock, tel. (503) 436-9717, sits unobtrusively off to the right near the corner of 2nd and Hemlock. If you're hungry, aromas of fresh cheese, garlic, and free-baked dough will draw you inside this brick enclave. Pizza by the slice with an array of toppings, $2-2.50, hefty salads for $6, an all-you-can-eat $5 salad bar, pasta dishes, and oven baked subs for $6, all hold their own with most establishments of this ilk in Oregon. Nonetheless, its competition, **Pizza Fetta,** located behind the Cannon Beach Cookie Company, gets the nod for pizza with the most creative combinations of ingredients.

Finally, there are several good bakeries in town, but **Hane Bakery,** 1064 Hemlock, rates the nod if you're looking for the touch of home combined with cosmopolitan flair. With first-rate coffee and fresh juices to wash down muffins, scones, and light meals, and an adjoining gallery devoted to local artists, this is a special spot. Hane's outdoor patio could well be the best spot in town for a coffee break.

Shopping and Galleries

Most of the Cannon Beach galleries and shops are on Hemlock Street. At the north end of town **White Bird Gallery,** tel. (503) 436-2681, displays a variety of arts and crafts worth a special look. Also on the northern part of Hemlock is a fine kite store, **Once Upon a Breeze,** tel. (503) 436-1112. In the middle of the block is **Cannon Beach Book Company,** tel. (503) 436-1301, one of the best bookstores on the coast. This is the place to pick up regional titles or a good novel for that rainy weekend.

Events

The half-dozen other **sandcastle contests** that take place on the Oregon coast are given nary a mention in this book, so much do they pale in comparison to the Cannon Beach event. Approaching its third decade, this is the state's first and most prestigious competition of its kind. Tens of thousands of spectators show up to watch 1,000-plus competitors fashion their creations with the aid of buckets, shovels, and squirt guns. This event is free to spectators, but entrants pay a fee. Recent winners included Egyptian pyramids and a gigantic sea turtle. The event usually coincides with the lowest-tide Saturday in late May. Call (503) 436-2623 to find out the exact date of this collapsible art show, which takes place a mile north of Haystack Rock. Building begins in the early morning; judging starts at noon.

The **Author Series** features notable regional writers reading from their works in spring and fall. Dates and locations are posted around town, or contact the chamber of commerce for additional information.

The **Stormy Weather Festival** in November brings out local artists, musicians, and their creations. Call the chamber of commerce for details. December heralds the annual **Dickens Festival.** Each Friday and Saturday Dec. 1-16, local thespians don traditional Victorian costumes and

THE GREAT NORTHWEST SHOE SWAP

Designer kites, Japanese glass fishing floats, berry jams, myrtlewood bowls, and objets d'art culled from galleries are among the gift-shopping treasures typically found on the Oregon coast. But in 1991, a unique event added a new wrinkle to the scene. It all started when a cargo of Nike athletic shoes washed up on north coast beaches, the result of the wreck of an Asian ship. The Japanese current swept the shoes down from the North Pacific to be deposited in Clatsop County beaches. Before long, beachcombers here were forming "shoe swap" clubs to match up sizes and styles in pairs. With extensive washing, these shoes were almost good as new, or at least good enough to sell for less than the $50-120 asking price at conventional outlets. From Cannon Beach north, the flotsam footwear was advertised on laundromat bul-

letin boards, in community newspapers, and by hawkers on the street. Nike, Beaverton's multibillion-dollar shoemaker, did nothing to spoil this party, reveling instead in the publicity generated by the incident.

In March 1996, another beachcombers bonanza hit the Oregon coast. This time, it was both athletic shoes and toys from a ship that burned in Asian waters 15 months before. These encounters with flotsam footwear have provided oceanographers with important data on ocean currents. Such incidents have also heartened proponents of "trans-oceanic diffusion," the theory that contends there were Asian boat migrations hundreds, maybe thousands of years ago in addition to the overland migration over a land-ice bridge in the area of the present-day Bering Strait.

perform a Dickensian Christmas play at the Coaster Theater, 108 N. Hemlock, tel. (503) 436-1242. Other related events such as teas and lamplighting ceremonies usher in the holiday season with a Dickensian or Victorian motif.

The Coaster Theater, for information or reservations write P.O. Box 643, Cannon Beach 97110, also features summer plays as well as local and out-of-town shows in winter.

Recreation

Sea Ranch Stables, at north entrance to Cannon Beach off US 101, rents horses 9 a.m.-5 p.m. for beach rides mid-May to Labor Day. **Mike's Bike Shop,** 248 N. Spruce St., Cannon Beach, tel. (503) 436-1266, has rentals for $3-6 per hour. Mike's specializes in mountain bikes, which can be returned at a Warrenton outlet.

Getting There

In addition to the **Salt Water Shuttle Transit and Charter Service,** tel. (503) 368-6711, which operates between Tillamook and Seaside, there is a free natural gas-powered Cannon shoppers' shuttle that runs 9 a.m.-6 p.m. daily with half-hour loops. The schedule is available at the chamber of commerce. If you're driving north on US 101, there's a choice of four entrances to the beach loop to take you into town. The most practical choice is the first one, Tolovana Park, which is connected to the Coast Highway by Warren Road. From Tolovana Park you follow the Beach Loop (part of the old Oregon Coast Highway and also known as US 101 Alternate) north into the downtown core. Along the way, gorgeous views of Haystack Rock and surfside lodging line the route. As the resort ambience gives way to shops, galleries, and restaurants, this beach loop is referred to as Hemlock St., the main drag of Cannon Beach. A beach loop bus operated by **Pierce Pacific Stages** out of Portland's Greyhound terminal (leaves Portland at 10:40 a.m. daily) drops off arrivals at Spruce St. every day at 2:05 p.m. It leaves for Portland at 2:40 p.m. and arrives back at the Portland Greyhound station at 6:05 p.m.

Information and Services

The **Cannon Beach Chamber of Commerce,** P.O. Box 64, 201 E. 2nd, Cannon Beach 97110, tel. (503) 436-2623, is open Mon.-Sat. 11 a.m.-5 p.m., Sunday 11 a.m.-4 p.m., and is occasionally closed on winter weekends. This facility is close by the public restrooms (2nd and Spruce), basketball, and tennis courts. The **post office,** 155 N. Hemlock, Cannon Beach 97110, tel. (503) 436-2822, is open Mon.-Fri. 9 a.m.-5 p.m. Artists and writers congregate in Cannon Beach for one- or two-week courses in the **Haystack Program for the Arts.** Call the arts office, tel. (503) 464-4812, of Portland State University for more details. **Sandpiper Medical Walk-in Clinic,** 171 N. Larch, tel. (503) 436-1142, offers quality medical care for the whole family and minor emergency services. It's located in Sandpiper Square behind the stores on the main drag.

SEASIDE AND VICINITY

Seaside is the quintessential family beach resort. The beach is long and flat, protected from ocean tides by scenic headlands; lifeguards are on duty weekends. In addition, Seaside has beachside playground equipment and the only West Coast boardwalk north of Santa Cruz, California. Atlantic City it's not, thank goodness, but the carny motif of the Jersey Shore is evoked by the cotton candy, Ferris wheel, arcades, and abundance of tourist facilities. South of town the presence of clammers and waders in the shallows and surfers negotiating the swells also recalls the liveliness of a southern California or Atlantic Ocean littoral instead of the remote peacefulness of many Oregon beaches. East Coast visitors often liken Cannon Beach to Provincetown, and Seaside to Coney Island—prior to their declines as destination resorts.

Located in the shadow of majestic Tillamook Head at the mouth of the Necanicum River, Seaside has attracted tourists since the early 1870s, when transportation magnate Ben Holladay sensed the potential of a hotel near the water. Train service from Portland helped realize that potential. Prior to being the first coastal resort in the state, Seaside's fame as the end of the Lewis and Clark Trail made it a national landmark. The dynamic duo came here in the

Frederic Remington's depiction of Lewis and Clark meeting an Indian

winter of 1805-06 and set about boiling seawater nonstop for seven weeks to produce four bushels of salt for the trip back east.

In recent years, the town has become more than just a retreat for Portland families. Oregon's apostle of haute cuisine, the late James Beard, used to hold a celebrated cooking class here each summer. This opened the door for writers' retreats, art classes, and business conventions. If these occasions or a family outing should bring you to Seaside, you'll enjoy the spirit of fun—just be prepared to swallow hard when you see the bill.

SIGHTS

Downtown Seaside

Sightseeing in Seaside means walking the **Prom.** This two-mile-long boardwalk, extending from V St. to 12th Ave., was constructed in 1921 to replace the rotten planks from an older walk and to protect ocean properties from the waves. Beaches along the way offer vantages from which to contemplate the sand, surf, and massive contours of 1,200-foot-high Tillamook Head. Along the Prom is the **Turnaround,** a small traffic circle framing a placard proclaiming this point the end of the trail for Lewis and Clark. Eight blocks south of here between Beach Dr. and the Prom is a replica of the Lewis and Clark salt cairn. Running east from the Turnaround, Broadway—Seaside's central traffic artery—goes a half mile to US 101 (Roosevelt) through a mind-numbing array of arcades, game rooms, gift shops, taverns, and a carousel.

If you tire of having a good time on Broadway, make your way to **Seaside Historical Museum,** 570 Necanicum Dr., tel. (503) 738-7065, whose Clatsop Indian artifacts will impart more of a sense of history than anything else in town. Exhibits on early tourism in Seaside are also interesting. It's open daily 10:30 a.m.-4:30 p.m.; admission is $2 for adults, $1 for children.

Along the shores of the Necanicum, you might also look for some fancy Victorian frame homes. Many of the old buildings that survived the 1912 fire, which destroyed much of the town, are concentrated in a four-block area running west of US 101 and bordered by the Necanicum River, 1st Ave., Broadway, and Avenue A.

Just because you're downtown doesn't mean you can't enjoy some of nature's bounty—anglers can reel in trout, salmon, and steelhead from the Necanicum River right in the center of downtown.

Seaside Aquarium

Right on the Prom north of the turnaround is the Seaside Aquarium, tel. (503) 738-6211. We recommend this only if you have kids who will be attracted by the sound of barking seals even before you enter this 60 year-old establishment. Back in the era of the Daddy Train (about 60 years ago, fathers would train back in from Portland to join their families on summer weekends), this place served as a natatorium. Today the pool is filled with the results of one of the best captive breeding programs for seals in the world. In addition, a hundred species of marine life including 20-ray sea stars, ferocious-looking wolf eels, green pipefish that swim almost vertically, and a white octopus that turns red should captivate kids from 9 to 99. Admission for ages 6-13 is $2.50, ages 14 and up is $5. Open daily 9 a.m.-5 p.m. in summer; Wed.-Sun. 9 a.m.-5 p.m. in winter.

Following Lewis and Clark

One block south of the prom are the reconstructed salt works of Lewis and Clark. The salt works and Fort Clatsop in Astoria are the only places besides Baltimore's Fort William McHenry to fly the flag that was this country's banner 1795-1818. The 15 stars and 15 stripes represent the original 13 states plus Vermont and Kentucky, states 14 and 15. It soon became clear that a stripe for every state would be unworkable, and in 1818 Congress decreed 13 stripes for the original colonies and one star for each state.

Just south of Seaside you can walk in the footsteps of Lewis and Clark to **Tillamook Head.** In January 1806, on a quest for a beached whale, Clark found the promontory. He was moved enough by the view to later write about it in his journal:

I beheld the grandest and most pleasing prospect which my eyes ever surveyed. Immediately in front of us is the ocean breaking in fury. To this boisterous scene the Columbia with its tributaries and studded on both sides with the Chinook and Clatsop villages forms a charming contrast, while beneath our feet are stretched the rich prairies.

Prior to setting out, arrange to have a friend drive down to **Indian Beach** to pick you up at the end of this seven-mile, three-hour pilgrimage. Or you can be picked up another mile south at the Ecola Point parking lot. To get to the trailhead, drive south of Seaside out Avenue U (Beach St.) past the golf course to Edgewood St., until you reach the parking lot at the end of the road. Nearby is an area known as **The Cove,** frequented by surfers (prevailing winds favor winter surfing rather than summer) and fisherfolk. As you head up the forested trail on the north side of Tillamook Head you can look back over the Seaside townsite. In about 20 minutes, you'll be looking down at the ocean from cliffs 1,000 feet above. Several hours later, you'll hike down onto Indian Beach, arriving near the restrooms.

PRACTICALITIES

Whatever your price range, you'll have to reserve ahead for a room in Seaside during the summer and spring break. (This holiday in Oregon takes place from the third week in March to the beginning of April and brings out high school cruisers en masse.) If you do, chances are you'll be able to find the specs you're looking for, given the area's array of lodgings; if you don't, come prepared to camp.

Bed and Breakfasts

One option especially worth considering in the so-called Sunset Empire is a stay at a bed and breakfast. In Seaside, the **Boarding House,** 208 N. Holladay Dr., tel. (503) 738-9055, overlooks the Necanicum River. The 1898 Victorian features fir tongue-and-groove walls and beamed ceilings. All rooms have private baths and go for $70-115 a night. Reserve two weeks in advance in summer. The **Riverside Inn,** 430 S. Holladay Dr., tel. (800) 826-6151, has separate four-room cottages (11 units in total) overlooking the river, with double occupancy rates ranging $55-95. Private baths, homemade breakfast, and special discount rates Sun.-Thurs. for stays of three days or more are available Oct.-June. During peak season, be sure to reserve a room a month in advance.

Budget Accommodations

The cheapest place in town is the **Seaside Inn and International Hostel,** 936 Holladay, tel. (503) 738-7911. Unlike the other hostels, it doesn't close down during the day, and the Necanicum River runs through the backyard. Close by is the Necanicum Estuary Park described later in this chapter. There are shared rooms with four to six bunks and private rooms

SEASIDE ACCOMMODATIONS

Ambassador by the Sea, 40 Ave. U, tel. (503) 738-6382 or (800) 641-4919, $60-150, cable TV, kitchenettes, laundry, pool, nonsmoking rooms, ocean view.

Best Western Ocean View Resort, 414 N. Prom, tel. (503) 738-3334 or (800) 234-8439, $85-230, wheelchair access, kitchenettes, fireplace, covered pool, laundry, nonsmoking rooms, complimentary continental breakfast, ocean view.

Coast River Inn, 800 S. Holladay Dr., tel. (503) 738-8474 or (800) 479-5191, $50-75, wheelchair access, cable TV, kitchenettes, laundry, nonsmoking rooms.

Colonial Motor Inn, 1120 N. Holladay Dr., tel. (503) 738-6295 or (800) 221-3804, $70-100, cable TV, laundry, nonsmoking rooms, river view.

Country River Inn, 1020 N. Holladay Dr., tel. (503) 738-8049 or (800) 605-3337, $50-80, wheelchair access, cable TV, restaurant, nonsmoking rooms, river view.

Driftwood Motel, 815 N. Holladay Dr., tel. (503) 738-5597 or (800) 738-5191, $65-100, small 10-unit property with a laundry.

Hillcrest Inn, 118 N. Columbia, tel. (503) 738-6273 or (800) 270-7659, $45-90, wheelchair access, cable TV, kitchenettes, laundry, nonsmoking rooms.

Hi-Tide Motel, 30 Ave. G, tel. (503) 738-8414 or (800) 621-9876, $85-150, cable TV, kitchenettes, pool, covered pool, nonsmoking rooms, ocean view.

Inn on the Prom, 361 S. Prom, tel. (503) 738-5241 or (800) 654-2506, $75-150, kitchenettes, fireplace, nonsmoking rooms, ocean view.

Lanai Condos Motel, 3140 Sunset Blvd., tel. (503) 738-6343 or (800) 738-2683, $45-95, cable TV, kitchenettes, pool, ocean view.

Oceanfront Motel, 50 1st Ave., tel. (503) 738-5661, $60-85, wheelchair access, ocean view.

Royale Motel, 531 Ave. A, tel. (503) 738-9541, $50-65, wheelchair access, river view.

Seaside Beach Club, 561 S. Prom, tel. (503) 738-7113 or (888) 733-7113, $95-175, wheelchair access, cable TV, kitchenettes, laundry, nonsmoking rooms, ocean view.

Seashore Resort, 60 N. Prom, tel. (503) 738-6368, $75-90, covered pool, ocean view.

Shilo Inn-Oceanfront, 30 N. Prom, tel. (503) 738-9571 or (800) 222-2244, $90-215, cable TV, kitchenettes, fireplace, covered pool, laundry, restaurant/lounge, nonsmoking rooms, ocean view.

Sundowner Motor Inn, 125 Ocean Way, tel. (503) 738-8301 or (800) 645-8678, $65-90, wheelchair access, cable TV, pets, kitchenettes, covered pool.

Tides Condos, 2316 Beach Dr., tel. (503) 738-6317 or (800) 548-2846, $60-120, cable TV, kitchenettes, pool, nonsmoking rooms, ocean view.

Tradewinds Motel, 1022 N. Prom, tel. (503) 738-9468 or (888) 738-9468, $70-90, pets, kitchenettes, ocean view.

for $15 a night. To get there from US 101, make a left at the city center sign and stay on Holladay. When you get to 9th Ave. look for the hostel on the left. There's no curfew here.

If you're in need of a budget motel room here, the **Mariner Holladay Motel,** 426 S. Holladay Dr., tel. (503) 738-3690, offers rooms in the $40-50 range and it's a 10-minute walk from the beach; there's a pool on the premises. A bit more upscale at $55-85 is the **River View Inn,** 555 Ave. G, tel. (503) 738-0670. In addition, some rooms have jacuzzis at this quiet lodging

four blocks from the beach. The **Seasider Motel,** 110 5th St., tel. (503) 738-7764, has fireplaces, laundry facilities, and ocean views, and allows pets, all for $50-75.

Upscale Digs

The **Shilo Oceanfront Resort,** 30 N. Prom tel. (503) 738-9571 or (800) 222-2244, is located right by the Prom turnaround and is a justifiable splurge. A first-rate restaurant, health club, and rooms with fireplaces and all the amenities make it worth the $100-plus nightly rate.

Camping

Saddle Mountain and Klootchy Creek parks (see "Cannon Beach," above), due east of Cannon Beach on US 26 (the Sunset Highway), make great camping spots.

Klootchy Creek Park, Clatsop County Parks, Astoria 97103, tel. (503) 325-2631, home of the giant spruce, is 300 yards off US 26. A boardwalk to the tree spares you the mud you might encounter in the campground. It has nine primitive sites that go for $6 a night —a small price to pay for proximity to a giant spruce grove, the beaches, and the civilized haunts of two nearby coastal cities. Add fishing (trout, steelhead, salmon) on the banks of the Necanicum River and surfing between Cannon Beach and Seaside and it's easy to ignore the lack of amenities.

Saddle Mountain State Park, Cannon Beach 97110, tel. (503) 861-1671, also has nine primitive sites with flush toilets and firewood available. Open from mid-April to late October, these campsites make good alternatives to beachfront parks on cloudy days. Sites go for $9 a night. No reservations are necessary at either campground.

On Tillamook Head north of Ecola State Park, there's a primitive campground, accessible to backpackers or all-terrain cyclists, a third of the way up the head from Indian Beach (the Cannon Beach side). It can be approached by using an abandoned logging road that runs parallel to the hiking trail from Indian Beach.

Food

While a stroll down Broadway might have you thinking that cotton candy, corn dogs, and saltwater taffy are the staples of Seaside cuisine, there are several eateries here which can satisfy taste and nutrition as well as the broad-based clientele of this beach town. For breakfast, the Swedish pancakes and crab-n-cheese omelettes at **Pig n' Pancake,** 323 Broadway, tel. (503) 738-7243, are tops. If you're seriously hungry there are Frisbee-sized cinnamon rolls. At last count, you could choose from 33 different breakfast variations at this place. Although you might think it's just another chain on the main drag, you can count on this place for three meals every day of the week (ditto with its Astoria outlet at 146 Bend St., tel. (503) 325-3144 and Cannon Beach outlet 223 N. Hemlock, tel. (503) 436-

2891, at night try the stir fry. For $8, you get a gargantuan portion of stir-fried veggies with a choice of steak, prawns, or chicken. Follow with marionberry pie for dessert.

The **Vista Sea Cafe,** 150 Broadway, tel. (503) 738-8108, is known for pies with ingredients like artichokes, feta, chorizo, and pesto, plus topnotch clam chowder with homemade beer bread. Its location one block from the turnaround makes it especially convenient.

Dooger's, 505 Broadway, Seaside, tel. (503) 738-3773, a chain with an outlet in Cannon Beach, 1321 N. Hemlock, tel. (503) 431-2225, has won acclaim for its clam chowder. Local clams and oysters, fresh Dungeness crab legs, sautéed shrimp, and marionberry cobbler are also the bases of Dooger's do-good reputation (main courses $10-21). Across the street is an excellent kite shop. **Cafe Espresso,** 600 Broadway, tel. (503) 738-6169, has coffee drinks, breakfast fare, and views of the Necanicum River. Another plus is its proximity to outdoor concerts on the public square. The cafe also does its part, as one of the only outlets of Seaside's nightlife, featuring musicians on weekend nights. To find this place, follow the walkway down from the bridge into the complex at 600 Broadway and look for no. 7.

Alternatives, 846 Ave. C., tel. (503) 738-5286, is the local outlet for fresh home-grown and organic groceries. For crab in a can, fresh tuna, and other tasty kippered treats, as well as sturgeon, and minced razor clams stop in at the **Bell Buoy Crab Co.,** 1800 Holladay. They make excellent razor clam chowder, and much of their seafood is brought in by their own fleet. **Premier Pasta,** 1530 S. Holladay Dr., tel. (503) 738-5062, lets you overlook the Necanicum River while you enjoy quality fresh-made pasta dishes, homemade soups, and sandwiches at prices anyone could afford. Soups, sandwiches, and some pasta dishes run $3-5. The most expensive meals cost $6 and include soup and salad. Especially recommended is tricolor linguine with pesto, feta, and olive lasagna. It's also a good idea to start with minestrone soup and end with the Italian dessert tiramisu.

Should the taste of weak coffee and the ambience of Seaside on a holiday weekend pall, try the **Pacific City Bakery and Cafe,** 601 Pacific Way, Gearhart, tel. (503) 738-0245. Gearhart is an appealing out-of-the-way place just north of Seaside, a half mile west of US 101. This is the area where famed food writer James Beard was raised. Beard himself would probably give Pacific City's croissants five stars, so flaky and buttery are these breakfast time mainstays. They take center stage again at lunch, providing the foundations for delectable sandwich fillings. Particularly recommended are the smoked salmon and cream cheese with thin-sliced red onion on croissant, the cioppino, and Caesar salad. Pasta and seafood dishes as well as crepes also pop up at lunchtime and dinnertime in the surprisingly urbane little cafe. If you decide to stay the night, the **Gearhart Ocean Inn,** 67 N. Cottage St., tel. (503) 738-7373, charges $40-90 (but offers off-season specials Oct.-April) for your choice of 11 New England-style cottages with comforters, wicker chairs, throw rugs, and a location close to the beach.

Shopping
The **Riverhouse Metaphysical General Store,** 2010 S. Holladay, tel. (503) 788-8370, specializes in historic and ethnic beads including those of the native Clatsops. Herbs, crystals, and books round out the array.

Events and Recreation
Seaside predates any other town on the Oregon coast as a place built with good times in mind. A zoo and racetrack were among Seaside's first structures. Today, the town hosts the likes of the **Miss Oregon Scholarship Pageant** in July at the Civic Center and the **World Cup Kite Competition** for stunt kite flyers at the Turnaround in October. Contact the chamber of commerce for information on these events.

The story of Lewis and Clark has always been an integral part of Seaside lore. Lately it is also the focus of the town's major summer event, the **Lewis and Clark Pageant,** 783 1st Ave., tel. (503) 738-0817 or (800) 444-6740. The pageant's staged "Journey to the Pacific" takes place in Broadway Park on the east side of town along the banks of Neawanna Creek, and tells the story from the time the expedition started in 1803 near St. Louis, Missouri, to its arrival in 1805 at Fort Clatsop. Showtime is 8 p.m. Thurs.-Sat. and 2 p.m. Sunday, July 29 through August 22. Tickets are $7.50 for adults, $6 for se-

niors, and $4.50 for students ages 8-16; kids under eight get in free.

Anglers don't only come to Seaside for the Necanicum River's steelhead, trout, and salmon. **Carnahan Park** on Cullaby Lake north of Seaside has crappies, bluegills, perch, catfish, and largemouth bass. Just west of Cullaby, **Sunset Lake** adds trout to the list. Boating, swimming, and water sports add to the appeal of Cullaby Lake. This is probably the only practical place to water-ski.

Golfers can escape to public courses south of Seaside, 451 Avenue U, tel. (503) 738-5261, and north in the small town of Gearhart, **Gearhart-by-the-Sea Resort,** Marion St., tel. (503) 738-5248. Greens fees are $7 for Seaside's nine holes and $14 for Gearhart's 18-hole course. Gearhart's "British links-style" course was built in 1892 making it the second oldest in the west. Gearhart boasts a quieter beach than Seaside and a bowling alley, Evergreen Lanes, west side of US 101 just north of the road to downtown, that reportedly serves the best hamburgers, halibut fish and chips, $8.50, and homemade pie around.

Despite the lifeguard stand, don't swim in Seaside unless you're used to the North Sea. Instead, head to **Sunset Pool,** 1140 E. Broadway, Seaside, tel. (503) 738-3311. Fees are $2 for adults, with discounts for children and seniors. Hours vary greatly, so call in advance.

The Turnaround is the starting point and finishing line for such famed races as the eight-mile **Across-the-Sand** beach run and the **Hood-to-Coast Relay,** in mid and late August, respectively. At the end of each February, the highly regarded **Trail's End Marathon** loops partway to Astoria and back to the Turnaround. Check with the chamber of commerce for details.

In Seaside, the high school, 1901 N. Holladay Dr., and **Broadway School,** 1120 Broadway, have free **tennis courts** with lights. There are also free public courts in Gearhart.

The surfing venues north of Tillamook Head, Indian Basin, and near Short Sands Beach in Oswald West State Park can be enjoyed with surfboard and equipment rentals from **Cleanline Surf Shop,** 719 1st Ave., Seaside, tel. (503) 738-7888. Boogie boards and surfboards go for $12.50, wetsuits, boots, and flippers cost $15, or you can spend $25 for the complete package.

The **Prom Bike Shop,** 622 12th Ave., Seaside, tel. (503) 738-8251, offers rentals for $3-6 per hour.

Birdwatchers revel in **Necanicum Estuary Park,** 1900 block of N. Holladay across the street from Seaside High School. Local students have built a viewing platform, stairs to the beach, a boardwalk, and interpretive signs. Great blue and green herons and numerous migratory species flock to the grassy marshes and slow tidal waters near the mouth of the Necanicum River. Occasionally, Roosevelt elk, black-tailed deer, river otters, beavers, minks, and muskrats can also be sighted.

Information and Services

The **Seaside Chamber of Commerce,** 7 N. Roosevelt St., Seaside 97138, tel. (503) 738-6391 or (800) 444-6740, is open from May to mid-September, Mon.-Fri. 8 a.m.-6 p.m., Saturday 10 a.m.-4 p.m., and Sunday noon-4 p.m. In the off-season, the hours are Mon.-Fri. 9 a.m.-5 p.m., Saturday 10 a.m.-3 p.m., and Sunday noon-3

p.m. This facility also functions as a welcome center with brochures ranging the state. **Pierce Pacific Stages,** 930 N. Holladay Dr., tel. (800) 231-2222, picks up on a beach loop bus that leaves Portland every day at 10:40 a.m., with stops at Astoria, here, and Cannon Beach.

A **laundromat** is located on 57 N. Holladay St. near 1st Avenue. It's open daily 6 a.m.-11 p.m. Beware, the **police,** 1090 S. Roosevelt Dr., tel. (503) 738-6311, have developed a hard edge due to violent crime and unruly behavior by young people during Spring Break. The **post office,** 300 Avenue A, Seaside 97138, tel. (503) 738-5462, is open Mon.-Fri. 8:30 a.m.-5 p.m. **Providence Seaside Hospital,** 725 S. Wahanna Rd., tel. (503) 738-8463, has 24-hour service and an emergency room. Public restrooms are located at the Turnaround and one block from the Prom at the intersection of 12th Ave. and Necanicum Drive. **Debra's Surplus,** 1725 N. Roosevelt, tel. (503) 738-9779, is the place to find fishing gear, a car battery, clothing, or hardware.

ASTORIA AND VICINITY

Many coastal travelers are aware of Astoria's legacy as the oldest permanent U.S. settlement west of the Mississippi, whose glory days are kept alive by museums, historical exhibits, and pastel-colored Victorian homes weathered by the sea air. This often creates the expectation of a Williamsburg of the West, where the portrayal of heritage is a focal point of the local identity. The reality of modern-day Astoria is more accurately captured in a locally popular bumper sticker that defiantly proclaims, "We Ain't Quaint!" The preserved pioneer past and attractive historic homes may soften these rough edges, but not enough to let anyone mistake Astoria for a tourist town. This city of 10,000 people is still rooted in a resource-based economy whose logging and fishing industries are in decline. The closing of the U.S. Naval station after WW II, and the disappearance of Bumble Bee tuna and several dozen other canneries from the waterfront, have had lasting effects here.

A maritime flavor dominates the local scene, with old salts filling many a smoky barroom with

stories of ships that didn't make it past the waves and weather of the Columbia bar. Where the River of the West meets the ocean offshore could well be the biggest widow-maker on the high seas, earning it the title Graveyard of the Pacific. Lewis and Clark referred to it as "that seven-shouldered horror" in a journal entry from the winter of 1805-06.

Another striking aspect of the town is the Scandinavian traditions like public steam baths, *lutefisk, smorrebrod* platters, and church services in Finnish. Nonetheless, Hollywood has chosen Astoria's picturesque neighborhoods to simulate the all-American city on at least a half-dozen occasions. Given its rich history, this is altogether fitting.

HISTORY

The Clatsop Indians lived in this area for thousands of years before Astoria's written history began. The region was first chronicled by Heceta, a Spanish explorer who sailed near the

Columbia's mouth but failed to enter. American presence on the Columbia began with Captain Robert Gray's discovery of the river in 1792, which he christened after his fur-trading ship. Thereafter, Lewis and Clark's famous expedition of 1803-1806, with its winter encampment at Fort Clatsop south of present-day Astoria, incorporated the Pacific Northwest as part of a new nation. In 1811, John Jacob Astor's agents built Fort Astoria—the first settlement west of the Mississippi. Despite temporary occupation by the British between 1813 and 1818, the fort and a shaky American presence were able to hold on until settlers came to farm the region during the Oregon Trail era of the 1840s.

From that time until the 1900s, emigrants of Scandinavian descent predominated. Commerce grew with the export of lumber and foodstuffs to gold rush-era San Francisco and the Far East. Shipwrecks became commonplace on the treacherous Columbia River bar despite Captain Flavel's pilot service in the 1850s. Later, Fort Stevens was built during the Civil War to guard against a Confederate naval incursion. Salmon canneries became the basis of Astoria's economy during the 1870s, helping it grow into Oregon's second-largest city—and a notorious shanghaiing port. Over the ensuing decades, logging, fishing, and shipbuilding coaxed the population up to 20,000 by WW II.

Near the end of the war, a Japanese submarine's shelling of Fort Stevens made it the only fortification on American soil to have sustained an attack in a world war (this fact is disputed by two locations in California). After the war, the region's fortunes rose and fell with the resource-based economy. In a 1966 attempt to supplement that economy with tourism, the State Highway Division built the 4.1-mile **Astoria Bridge,** connecting Oregon and Washington (according to *Guinness Book of World Records,* the world's longest three-span, continuous through-trusses bridge). The bridge provided the final link in 1,625-mile-long US 101. The modern era has also been characterized by the development of world-class museums and artful Victorian restorations.

Unfortunately, preserving Astoria's glory days could not make up for the closing of the canneries and the decline of logging and fishing.

Moves to make Astoria a major port of entry for Japanese cars and to begin large-scale tourist enterprises on the waterfront have been suggested as a means to improve the economic climate here. In this vein, movie shoots have come here on numerous occasions and Columbia-River-Gorge bound cruise ships have put in for shore excursions. Whether or not Astoria's ship ever comes in, let's hope the unpretentious charm of this hillside city-by-the-sea will not be lost in the process.

THE LAND

The view from **Astoria Column** on Coxcomb Hill (for directions see "Museums and Miscellany" following) orients you to the city and the north coast. To the north, note the freighters docked on the edge of Astoria's cityscape and the Astoria Bridge (to Megler, Washington) spanning the Columbia. Across Baker Bay to the northwest, on the Washington side of the six-mile channel that Robert Gray entered in 1792, is Cape Disappointment. Looking over Young's Bay south and west of Astoria, the Clatsop Plains extend to Tillamook Head. Although the 1840s settlers had no luck farming these sand traps, the relative flatness of the terrain lent itself to the building of the region's first road, which US 101 now parallels. The beaches west of the road contribute 95% of the state's harvest of razor clams. Farther south, the plains give way to a dense area of settlement around Seaside. Tillamook Head, the coast's northernmost headland, then defines a valley cut by the Necanicum River. Fairweather views reveal Saddle Mountain southeast of this lowland. Clear visibility also treats you to panoramas of Mt. St. Helens and Mt. Hood on the far eastern horizon. A visit to the information booth on top of the hill (open from Memorial Day to the second week of September) and a look at the annotated bronze relief map of the north coast should precede climbing the steps to the top of the column. The map is found on the entry walkway and notes the distances and directions to such landmarks as Mt. Rainier, Mt. St. Helens, Tillamook Head, and Saddle Mountain.

one of Astoria's many well-preserved Victorian homes

SIGHTS

In recent years, the Victorian homes and ocean view in Astoria's hillside neighborhood have backdropped such fanciful modern sagas as *Free Willy, Kindergarten Cop, Ninja Turtles,* and *Goonies.* However, the story lines of these movies pale against those of the timber and shipping magnates who occupied homes here for over a century. While not as polished as Albany's Monteith neighborhood in terms of signage and landscaping, there is a greater sense that real people live here.

Flavel House

Begin your walking tour at the Flavel House, 441 8th St., Astoria 97103, tel. (503) 325-2203, on the corner of 8th and Duane, a right turn off Marine Dr., which is an extension of ORE 30. This splendid Queen Anne-style Victorian mansion was built by George Flavel, whose guiding of vessels across the Columbia bar made him Oregon's first steamship captain and Astoria's earliest millionaire. The home's intricate woodwork, period furnishings, and art, along with its extravagantly rendered gables, cornices, and porches, rank it with the Carson Mansion in Eureka, California, as a Victorian showplace. From its fourth-story cupola, Captain Flavel could watch his own sailing fleet, and it's said that his wife would keep the light going in this perch when the captain was bringing in a ship.

The 14-foot ceilings, Persian rugs, and an international array of tiles are upstaged only by the fireplaces framed in exotic hardwoods in every room. Known locally as "the house with the red roof," it has withstood more than a century of storms off the Columbia River estuary. This landmark for incoming ships is now the foremost monument to Astoria's golden age as the leading port in the Northwest.

Flavel House is open daily May-Sept., 10 a.m.-5 p.m., and charges $4 for adults, $2.50 for seniors, and $2 for children 6-12. The admission price includes any two of the three museums operated by the Clatsop County Historical Society (see "Museums and Miscellany" following). Close by is **Shallon Tasting Room,** 1598 Duane St., tel. (503) 325-5978, open noon-6 p.m. daily, where you can sample this vineyard's specialty fruit wines. Try the chocolate-orange wine as well as other unique wines produced from whey. The winemaker is effusive and knowledgeable and will show you around while you sip. If the wine also has the locals in an effusive mood, try to get one to tell you the amazing story of the Flavel family, a saga depicted in gory detail by Calvin Trillin in *The New Yorker* in 1992.

Walking Tour

In addition to the Flavel House, Astoria is home to dozens of beautifully preserved 19th-century and early-20th-century houses. A walking tour of many of them is laid out in a guidebook written by a local historian and available for $3 at the **Her-**

itage Museum, 1618 Exchange Street. After the Flavel House tour, however, most people seem content to forgo the purchase and let the architectural scenery do the talking. Just start walking south on 8th St. and turn on Franklin Avenue. Continue east to 11th St., then detour south a block on 11th St. to Grand Ave., east on Grand, north on 12th St., and back to Franklin, continuing your eastward trek. Walk to 17th St., then south again to Grand, double back on Grand two blocks to 15th St., then walk north on 15th to Exchange St. and east on Exchange to 17th, where you'll be just two blocks from the Columbia River Maritime Museum. The route will take you past 74 historical buildings and sites. Toward the end of the tour, don't miss the Foard house, an 1892 Queen Anne with a gaudy paint job, rich in Victorian nuance. You can book a guided tour through **Historical Tours of Astoria,** 612 Florence Ave., tel. (503) 325-3005.

Doorways of Astoria
The ornate doorways of Astoria weave Victorian nuance and other architectural sensibilities together well enough to merit a special look, particularly at the following addresses: 1243 Franklin Ave., 1509 Franklin Ave., 1555 Franklin Ave., 1 2nd St., 10 6th St., 130 Bond St., and 441 8th Street. Walkers will also take note that the streets are alphabetical.

MUSEUMS AND MISCELLANY

The above walking tour makes for a very full morning. If you get an early start, however, you'll still have time to visit several other Astoria landmarks. Among these, Fort Clatsop, Fort Stevens, Astoria Column, and the Maritime Museum are must-see attractions.

Astoria Column
Astoria Column can be reached from downtown by following 14th Street south (uphill) to Jerome Ave. Turn east (left) one block and continue up 15th St. to the park entrance on Coxcomb Drive. It's also accessible by city bus (See "Information and Services" following). Once atop this 595-foot summit, walk the 166 steps up the 125-foot tower. A frieze depicting major historical events adorns the column's exterior, but the real at-

traction is the view of the surrounding countryside. This column was a joint project of the Great Northern Railroad and the descendants of John Jacob Astor to commemorate a 1926 cross-country rail excursion. As for the view, begin by focusing on the Astoria Bridge. Look to the right of the bridge's highest point then over to the opposite shore of the Columbia. You'll see Cape Disappointment, home of the Coast Guard station. At one o'clock is the Chinook village site where some of the earliest West Coast contact with white sailors occurred. The wide inlet at three o'clock on the far shore is where Captain Gray anchored in 1792 to claim discovery of the Columbia.

Uppertown Fire Fighters Museum
Back on Marine Drive is the Uppertown Fire Fighters Museum, 30th and Marine Dr., tel. (503) 325-2203, housed in an old brick and timber firehouse. This exposition contains hand-pulled, horse-drawn, and motorized fire-fighting vehicles in service 1877-1921. Such details as the six-foot-high wheels of an 1890s hand-drawn hose will give you pause. A 1921 fire is often cited by locals as the major factor in keeping Astoria from becoming another San Francisco or Seattle. In any case, the photos and information about Astoria's major blazes are fascinating. The museum is operated by the Clatsop County Historical Society. Hours are Fri.-Sat. 11 a.m.-4 p.m., Sunday 2-4 p.m. and charges $4 for adults, $2.50 for seniors, and $2 for children 6-12.

Heritage Museum
The Clatsop County Historical Society also operates the **Heritage Museum,** 1618 Exchange St., Astoria 97103, tel. (503) 325-2203. Housed in a vintage turn of the century building, it has several galleries with antiquities, tools, and old photographs depicting various aspects of life in Clatsop County. Gallery One deals with the natural history, geology, Native American artifacts, early immigrants and settlers in the region, as well as important natural events. Gallery Two portrays the development of commerce in such enterprises as fishing, fish packing, logging, and lumber. Gallery Two's focus on cannery life circa 1829 when salt-cured chinook were shipped to Boston is interesting. Gallery Three concentrates on the 22 ethnic groups who came to

Clatsop County in search of a better life. Swedish newspapers, Finnish confirmation booklets, and Chinese articles exhibit the town's rich ethnic history. Particularly sobering are the exhibits detailing Klu Klux Klan activity that resulted in a Klan-supported candidate becoming governor in the '20s. The Heritage Museum is open daily May-Sept., 10 a.m.-5 p.m., and charges $4 for adults, $2.50 for seniors, and $2 for children 6-12.

Oceanview Cemetery

This cemetery off US 101 on Ridge Road is noteworthy for the granite grave markers recording the diverse trades and passions of Astoria's townpeople. Log trucks, fishing trawlers, a Viking ship, elk, a knitting basket, and dogs are included in this assemblage. The work of Thompson Granite Works is also on display near the cemetery at De Laura Beach Road where a monument marks where the Japanese shells landed in June 1942. You also might want to explore the Astoria Pioneer Cemetery, 15th and Madison, near the Astoria Column. This cemetery was in use 1865-1900.

Fort Clatsop

To reach Fort Clatsop National Memorial, Route 3 Box 604FC, Astoria 97103, tel. (503) 861-2471, site of the Lewis and Clark encampment, from Marine Dr. head west across Youngs Bay, taking care to stay in the right lane to avoid getting sidetracked by US 101 Alternate. Lewis and Clark crossed this bay en route to the Fort Clatsop site after their original encampment on the Washington side proved too exposed to the elements. On the other side of the bay look for signs for the Fort Clatsop turnoff a quarter mile past the Fort Stevens State Park sign. Then turn left off the Coast Highway and follow the direction markers. This memorial sits six miles south of Astoria and three miles east of US 101 on the Lewis and Clark River. Although the expedition's story is nicely narrated here with displays, artifacts, slides, and films every day except Christmas, summertime "living history" reenactments are the main reason to come. The winter of 1805-06 put a premium on wilderness survival skills, some of which are exhibited here by rangers in costume, 9 a.m.-5:30 p.m. daily, Memorial Day to Labor Day. You can see

the tanning of hides, making of buckskin clothing and moccasins, and the molding of tallow candles and lead bullets. In addition, visitors may occasionally participate in the construction of a dugout canoe or try their luck at starting a fire by striking flint on steel.

Despite the discomfort, a visit on a cold, wet wintry day is an opportunity to better understand the travails of Lewis and Clark. The fort housed a lot of people for seven rooms. This group consisted of 30 people including one African American, one Native American, and a baby, all of whom spent the winter of 1805-06 here. The dynamic duo and party camped near the mouth of the Columbia River in November 1805 and wrote, "Ocian view! O! The joy!" The fort was built a month later and named for the Clatsop tribe. The party remained at this site for 106 days and began its trek east on March 23, 1806.

The hands-on experiences complement the following permanent features of Fort Clatsop: a log replica of the original fort (site of living history exhibits); a well-equipped visitor center (check for botanical walks on the bulletin board here); a beautifully landscaped picnic area; and

fishing boats at Astoria Dock

OREGON TOURISM DIVISION

trails that lead from the visitor center to the fort, to the canoe landing, and to a spring used by the expedition in 1805-06. Admission is $2 for visitors ages 17-61, all others free, and the ticket is good for seven days. The maximum charge is $4 per family. Gates to the memorial are open 8 a.m.-8 p.m. during the summer season and 8 a.m.-5 p.m. the rest of the year. Admission is free on winter weekends.

Fort Stevens

From Fort Clatsop, retrace the route back to US 101 and the sign pointing the way to Fort Stevens, Fort Stevens Historic Area, Hammond 97121, tel. (503) 861-2000. This Civil War-vintage outpost is situated 10 miles west of Astoria, 15 miles northwest of Seaside, on the northwest corner of the coast. To get there, drive through Warrenton en route to Pacific Dr. in Hammond, which leads to the Fort Stevens Historic Area and Military Museum. The fort was established shortly before the Confederates surrendered at Appomattox on April 9, 1865.

Its creation was not the only outgrowth of the Civil War on the West Coast. The year before, Lincoln had created the city of Port Angeles, Washington, for "lighthouse purposes." Given the subsequent creation of Fort Stevens shortly thereafter, it's a safe assumption that "lighthouse purposes" also meant being on the lookout for Confederate ships and the British, whom the Union feared would ally with the South. This seems more credible when you consider that the last shots of the war were fired by the *Shenandoah* on a fleet of Yankee whalers in the Bering Strait. The June 5, 1865 shelling occurred after the surrender because the Confederate skipper was unaware of the Appomattox treaty, signed two months before.

Though Fort Stevens was spared in the Civil War, it sustained an attack in another conflict. On June 21, 1942, a Japanese submarine fired 17 shells on Battery Russell (massive gun emplacements), making it the only U.S. fortification in the 48 states to be bombed by a foreign power since the War of 1812. No damage was incurred and the Army didn't return fire. Shortly after WW II, the fort was deactivated and all armaments were removed.

Today, the site features a memorial rose garden, old photos, weapons exhibits, and maps, as well as seven different batteries and other structures left over from almost a century of service. Exploring some of the gun batteries and climbing to the nearby commander's station for a scenic view of the Columbia River and South Jetty are popular visitor activities. During the summer months, guided tours of the underground Battery Mishler, $1.50, and a narrated tour of the fort's 37 acres on a two-ton U.S. Army truck, $2.50, are also available. The summer programs include Civil War reenactments and archaeological digs; consult the visitor center for schedules. The fort's hours are daily 10 a.m.-6 p.m., Memorial Day to Labor Day, and Wed.-Sun. 10 a.m.-4 p.m. during the rest of the year. Except for the tours, admission is free.

Eight miles of bike trails (See "Sports and Recreation" following for information on rentals) link the historic area to the rest of the park and provide access to Battery Russell and the 1906 wreck of the British schooner *Peter Iredale,* more remnants of the ship are displayed at the Maritime Museum). You can also bike to the campground one mile south of the Military Museum.

Parking is available at one of four lots about a mile apart from one another at the foot of the dunes. The beach runs north to the Columbia River, where excellent surf fishing, birdwatching, and a view of the mouth of the river await. South of the campground (east of the *Peter Iredale*) there's a self-guided nature trail around part of the two-mile shoreline of **Coffenberry Lake.** The lake also has two swimming beaches with bathhouses and fishing for trout and perch.

Columbia River Maritime Museum

About a half mile east of downtown Astoria, near the foot of 17th St. on the north side of Marine Dr. (US 30), the Columbia River Maritime Museum, 1792 Marine Dr., tel. (503) 326-2323, is hard to miss. The roof of the 37,000-square-foot museum simulates the curvature of a wave, and a gigantic 25,000-pound anchor from the U.S. battleship *Indiana* is also hard to ignore. This eye-catching facade is more than matched by what's inside. Even if the Columbia River could talk, it would be hard-pressed to surpass the eloquence of this museum's historical displays. The eras when Indian canoes plied the Columbia, Lewis and Clark camped on its shores, and dramatic shipwrecks occurred on its bar are recounted with scale models and miniatures of ships and paintings. The chance to peer through a periscope, walk the bridge of a WW II destroyer, or enter a Columbia River sternwheeler pilothouse imparts a hands-on aspect to your experience here. Local lighthouses, the evolution of boat design, and harpoons are the focus of other exhibits here. Scrimshaw, fishing and cannery artifacts, and sea charts dating as far back as 1587 also highlight your visit. Our favorite item is a small watercolor of the harbor by a crew member on Robert Gray's 1792 voyage of discovery.

At the end of your journey through maritime history, tour the 128-foot lightship *Columbia*. This vessel served as a floating lighthouse, marking the entrance to the mouth of the river and helping many ships navigate the dangerous waters. After almost three decades of service it was replaced in 1979 by an unstaffed 42-foot-high navigational buoy. The museum is open daily 9:30 a.m-5 p.m. and closed only on Thanksgiving and Christmas Day. Adults are $5, seniors $4, under 18 $2, and children under six get in free. The gift shop has a great collection of books on Astoria's wartime history.

Twilight Eagle Sanctuary

Six miles northeast of Astoria in the Burnside area is the new Twilight Eagle Sanctuary; for more information write the Twilight Eagle Sanctuary, c/o Oregon Eagle Federation, 5873 Estate Dr., Klamath Falls 97601. This 15-acre parcel hosts 50 eagles during the winter. In addition, there are ducks, Canada geese, wrens, songbirds, and on occasion, tundra swans. To get there, drive six miles east of town on US 30 and turn left at Burnside. Another left a half mile later will take you to the viewing platform.

SPORTS AND RECREATION

Fishing and River Watching

More than any other industry, commercial fishing has dominated Astoria throughout its history. Salmon canneries lined the waterfront at the turn of the century. Albacore and longline shark fishing put dinner on the table in the '30s and '40s. In the modern era, commercial fishing has turned to sole, rockfish, flounder, and less-well-

known bottom fish. If it's not enough to watch these commercial operations from the dock, **Tiki-Fleet,** 897 Pacific St., Hammond 97121, next to the coin laundry, tel. (503) 861-1201, and **Thunderbird Charters,** tel. (503) 325-7990, will show you where to drop your line for salmon, sturgeon, and bottom fish. Given the retail price of fresh salmon, you could theoretically pay for a charter trip by landing a single fish. Sports anglers can fish for salmon in either salt or fresh water (depending on time of year) or go after trout, bass, catfish, steelhead, and sturgeon in freshwater lakes, streams, and rivers. Ling cod, rockfish, surf perch, or other bottom fish can be pursued at sea, off jetties, or along ocean beaches.

While most of Astoria's waterfront is lined with warehouses, industry, and docks, there's a way to get right to the water's edge. The **6th Street Riverpark** is a local favorite at which to fish for Columbia River salmon and watch ships. At 10 6th St., there's also a farmers' market held every Saturday June-October. To get down to the 6th Street viewing station, turn toward the river near McDonald's. The platform is sheltered from the weather with glass windows.

Astoria Flight Center

Another way to avoid being landlocked is the Astoria Flight Center, tel. (503) 861-1222. One person is charged $40, groups of two or three are charged $65 for a 40-minute flight. See the whalewatching section in this chapter's introduction for information on similar options along the coast.

Oregon Coast Trail

More down-to-earth pursuits can be found along the Oregon Coast Trail. It extends from Fort Stevens Park to the area around Three Capes Lookout. The first stretch extends south along the beach for 14 miles to Gearhart. It's a flat, easy walk, and your journey could well be highlighted by a sighting of the endangered silverspot butterfly. It now frequents just six sites, including four in Oregon, with Clatsop County being one of them. The endangered status of this species protects it under law, and has stopped developers from building resorts on coastal meadows and dunes north of Gearhart. Look for a small orange butterfly with silvery spots on the undersides of its wings. You also might encounter cars on the beach. This section of shoreline is inexplicably the longest stretch of coastline open to motor vehicles in Oregon. Call the State Parks and Recreation Division for an up-to-date report on trail conditions before starting out, tel. (800) 551-6949.

Tapiola Pool, Tennis Courts

Outdoor recreationists will also appreciate Tapiola Pool, 901 W. Marine Dr., tel. (503) 323-7027, and tennis courts at three locations: 36th and Leif Erickson; 785 Alameda (the gray school); and 6th and Niagara. The latter facility is lit until 10 p.m. More courts with lights can be found in Warrenton at the corner of 2nd and Alder Streets.

Bike Rentals

Bike rentals are conveniently located next to Fort Stevens State Park Historic Area, 316 Russell Dr., Hammond, tel. (503) 861-0937. Tenspeeds, mountain bikes, and youth bikes may be rented by the day or by the hour. The 8.5 miles of trails here go through forests, by military gun batteries, over arched wooden bridges, past Coffenbury Lake, and up to the south jetty. Here you can watch ships confront the Columbia River Bar. Close by is a reminder of one that tried and failed. The *Peter Iredale,* an English sailing ship, washed up here in 1906.

PRACTICALITIES

As with the rest of the north coast, bed and breakfasts are the best way to go. This kind of lodging is all the more appealing in Astoria, with its picturesque hills framing Victorian neighborhoods. Homes of merchants, politicians, sea captains, and salmon canners number among Astoria's bed and breakfast offerings.

Fort Columbia Hostel

If a bed and breakfast is out of your budget range, try the Fort Columbia AYH Hostel, tel. (206) 777-8755, across the river in Chinook, Washington. Despite the typically low youth hostel rates, this is more than just another no-frills crash pad for backpackers. The rustic former Army hospital on a hill above the Columbia has rocking chairs and couches on a long porch, and a fire going on chilly evenings to bring together naturalists, historians, ornithologists, and beachcombers in homey communion. Outdoor barbecue pits on beautiful grounds become gathering spots on warm summer nights. Any misgivings you might have about dormitory-style rooms in a military infirmary are also tempered by 11-foot, tin-tile ceilings evocative of the turn of the century. One private room is available for couples. The hostel features an all-you-can-eat pancake breakfast for $1. Reservations are not necessary in this well-kept secret. On the grounds check out the exhibit buildings left over from the Coast Artillery Corps. The fort sits on a hill that was a navigator's landmark on the lower river for a least 100 years.

To get there, cross the Astoria Bridge, go two miles west on US 101, and look for signs to Fort Columbia State Park. A Pacific Transit bus goes there from the Greyhound station, 364 9th St., several times a day. Call before you go because the hostel closes for some months during the winter; however, the manager says the hostel will open to accommodate reservations. Regular hours are 5 p.m.-9 a.m. June to mid-September. Rates are $15 for nonmembers, and as with other AYH hostels, some chores are required.

Bed and Breakfasts

Franklin Street Bed and Breakfast, 1140 Franklin St., Astoria 97103, tel. (503) 325-4314, is an elegant turn-of-the-century Victorian. Five rooms with private baths and queen beds can accommodate 14 people here. Rich woodwork and local art are appreciated extras. It's within walking distance of downtown and a breakfast (a delicious spinach and cheese quiche) is included in the rates, $68-115 a night, double occupancy. A minimum two-night stay is required on weekends, and 10-day advance reservations have become necessary due to the popularity of this place.

The **Rosebriar Inn,** 636 14th St., Astoria 97103, tel. (503) 325-7427 or (800) 482-0224, is located on a quiet neighborhood street near the Maritime Museum. For $50-110 nightly (double occupancy) you have a choice of three rooms with baths or seven without (facilities down the hall). In this spacious turn-of-the-century former convent, a full breakfast on a family-style

*former home of Miss
Nellie Wilson and parrot*

dining table is also included. Reserve a week and a half in advance during summer.

The **Windover House Bed and Breakfast,** 550 W. Lexington Ave., Astoria 97103, tel. (503) 325-8093, is a stately older home offering a panoramic view of the mouth of the Columbia and a perspective on passing cargo ships. March 1-Oct. 30 take advantage of rooms with private baths for $65-90. Once a week, an authentic Danish breakfast is served. Two moderately priced hillside lodings on the eastside of town rate special mention. The **Astoria Inn,** 3391 Irving Ave., tel. (503) 325-8153, is a rambling 1890s National Historic Landmark perched on a hilltop with views of incoming ships. An interior decor evocative of the last century and a second floor library with comfy wing chairs also recommend this place. Good breakfasts such as sourdough French toast soaked in Grand Marnier are included in the $70-85 rate. A few dollars below this price range, the **Crest Motel,** US 30, tel. (800) 421-3141 or (503) 325-3141, offers river views, a coin-operated laundry, and a whirlpool set in a gazebo overlooking the river. They accept pets, too.

Camping
With 253 tent sites, 343 RV sites, and a special area for walk-in campers and bicyclists, **Fort Stevens State Park,** Hammond 94121, tel. (503) 861-1671, is the largest camping facility in the state. In addition to the usual amenities, you'll find a playground. To get there from Astoria, cross the Klaskanine River west on US 30 and take the Hammond exit four miles to the park. Five miles of ocean frontage and three miles of Columbia River frontage, as well as several small lakes, make this *the* place on the north coast for water sports. Add the park's amenities and other natural attractions and you have the perfect base camp from which to take advantage of the region. Avoid spring break (around March 20 to April 1) if you wish to be spared the rites of spring enacted here by Oregon teenagers. Reservations are accepted at (800) 452-5687, and a $17-20 fee is charged. Yurts can be had here for $27-42. The state park is open year-round.

Food
If you like good food with a minimum of expense and pretense you've come to the right place. Espresso fans will also be pleased to know that there are no fewer than 16 outlets for the stuff in town. But first, several retail outlets are deserving of mention.

The freshest produce in town is available Tues.-Sat. 9 a.m.-5:30 p.m. at **Columbia Farmers Market,** 6th and Bond, tel. (503) 325-4045. Just look for a ramshackle yellow house one block off Marine Drive. The outdoor **Astoria Farmer's Market,** 20th St. and Marine Dr., next to Maritime Museum, takes place Saturday 9 a.m.-4 p.m., May through late October. Another healthful alternative is the **Astoria Community Store,** 1389 Duane St., tel. (503) 325-0027. This place has lots of organic grocery items.

As you come into Astoria from the east after crossing the bridge on Marine Dr. (US 30), you'll see a nondescript storefront on the left among the bars and bait shops. Little would you suspect that one of Oregon's most esteemed purveyors of gourmet smoked fish conducts business here. **Josephson's Smokehouse,** 106 Marine Dr., tel. (503) 325-2190, produces a Scandinavian cold-smoked salmon without dyes or preservatives, so it is seldom sold through retail outlets. Instead, Josephson's caters to mail-order clientele, to order: P.O. Box 412, Astoria 97103, and fine restaurants which serve the product upon arrival. You can buy direct at a cheaper (but not cheap) price than the mail-order rates. Pickled salmon, salmon jerky, sturgeon caviar, and a variety of alder-smoked and canned fish are also sold here. On typically foggy days here in midwinter there's nothing finer than a cup of Josephson's clam chowder.

Oregon's number-one retail chain, **Fred Meyer,** 1451 US 101, Warrenton, tel. (503) 861-3003, has a deli that stocks salads, meats, cheeses, French bread, and other takeout items. This store is also known for good deals on clothes, camping equipment, and hardware.

Underneath the Astoria Bridge near the water, **Cafe Uniontown,** 218 W. Marine Dr., tel. (503) 323-8708, boasts an upscale menu with such seasonal offerings as salmon lasagna with pine nut cream sauce and spice-rubbed steak. (Entrees $13-20). Entrees are served with a variety of gourmet "greens" and a red pepper pesto spread for the bread. Check out the 1907-vintage bar in the restaurant's lounge, where weekend songfests can end your evening on a high note. On occasion, jazz artists of note perform here. It's open Tues.-Sat. for lunch and dinner. Nearby **Pacific Rim,** 229 W. Marine Dr., Astoria, tel. (503) 325-4481, can satisfy your hankerin' for pizza and burgers better and more cheaply than any other place in town. In addition, the low-priced and tasty Italian entrees at this drab cafe might also make you temporarily forget seafood.

If you have seafood on the brain, try the fish and chips, $8.50, at the **Ship Inn,** 1 2nd St., tel. (503) 325-0033. A state travel magazine selected this restaurant as the best pub in Oregon, and another regional publication gave it awards for seafood and business lunches. Even if you're not very hungry, you can always enjoy its scenic waterfront location while snacking on English cheeses, Cornish pasties, and imported brews. Jazz and bluegrass also provide conviviality here.

The **Columbian Cafe,** 1114 Marine Dr., tel. (503) 325-2233, is where the meatless '60s meet '90s Northwest cuisine. The good selection of pasta entrees, crepes, and fresh catch of the day are all expertly prepared and moderately priced. The chef here is also famous for Uriah's St. Diablo jelly, which comes in garlic, jalapeño, and red-pepper flavors. These jellies are available here and sold throughout the state. You may also enjoy the free-flowing political repartee with the staff and regulars in this cramped but friendly place. Breakfast is a highlight here. Dinners run $10-15, with most lunch and breakfasts coming in under $6.

Pier 11, 77 11th Ave., tel. (503) 325-0729, has a great view of the Columbia, and a wood-framed interior that conjures a shrine to the ancient mariner. Dinner entrees, $10-18, can run high, but few restaurants do razor clams, halibut, fish and chips, and clam chowder as well. You can also get steak and dine affordably at breakfast and lunch. It's one of the few places in town open Sunday.

Finding a good cup of joe in some coastal towns can seem like a search for the holy grail but salvation is waiting up the hill on Exchange Street. Here, **Lagniappe Cafe,** 847 Exchange St., adjacent to Clementine's B&B, whose name means "something special" in Louisiana Creole dialect, has cappuccino and homemade scones to make believers out of you. Open daily 7 a.m.-9 p.m.

Events and Entertainment

The biggest event in town is the **Astoria Scandinavian Festival,** P.O. Box 754, Astoria 97103, tel. (503) 325-6311, which takes place the weekend of June 21, Friday through Sunday. Local Danes, Finns, Icelanders, Norwegians, and Swedes come together to celebrate their heritage. Costumed participants dance around a flowered midsummer pole (a fertility rite), burn a bonfire to destroy evil spirits, and have tugs-of-war pitting Scandinavian nationalities against each other. Food, dancing, crafts, and a parade bring the whole town out to Astoria High School on West Marine Drive just off ORE 202. Admission is $5 for adults and $1 for children 6-12.

Flying Barney's, 1161 Marine Dr., fuses alternative music with the aesthetic sensibilities of an old beat coffeehouse. "Beat" in every sense of the word describes the mission store couches and funky furnishings of the high-ceilinged performance venue located in what had been an old hotel. Live alternative music, poets, folk singers, and revolving exhibits of alternative art give this place an appealing energy. Admission, $2-5, is charged Friday and Saturday (folk music night). Thursday is open-mike night, and there's no cover. Coffee, juices, and baked goods are available.

Another fête that might prove enjoyable is the **Great Astoria Crab Feed and Seafood Festival,** held the last weekend in April. Seafood, cookery, wines, crafts, a carnival, and a traditional crab dinner are featured. Admission is $3 for adults, $2 for seniors, and $1 for children 6-12; call (503) 325-6311 for more information.

The chamber of commerce offers a **Victorian homes tour** the second weekend in August. They also coordinate the **Astoria Regatta** in conjunction with this event.

Cultural stimulation can be found on 10th St. at **Parnassus Books,** 234 10th St., tel. (503) 325-1363, and the **Ricciardi Gallery,** 108 10th St., tel. (503) 325-5420. Ricciardi's opens at 7:30 a.m. weekdays for breakfast, making it the only art gallery opening this early. Around the corner from the bookstore is **Michael's Antiques and Art Gallery,** 1007 Marine Dr., tel. (503) 325-2350.

There are about a dozen antique stores in town as well as several other bookstores, notably **Godfathers Books and Espresso,** 105 Commercial. The latter is located in Phog Bounders Antique Mall and is the largest used bookstore on the north coast.

During the September **Astoria Art Festival** the above galleries together with the Maritime Museum's Kern Room Gallery have the meet-the-artists workshops and other activities. Call the Astoria Chamber of Commerce for additional details.

Theater

Those interested in a melodrama with historical antecedents might enjoy *Shanghaied in Astoria,* which is based on Astoria's dubious distinction as a notorious shanghai port during the late 1800s. A local theater troupe, the **Astor Street Opry Co.,** Elks Hall, 453 11th St., tel. (503) 325-6104, has shows Thurs.-Sat. night, mid-July through mid-August. Buy tickets in the lobby of the John Jacob Astor Apartments, a renovated 1920s hotel at 14th and Commercial St. or at the Elks Hall box office. Chase scenes, bar fights, and a liberal sprinkling of Scandinavian jokes will have you laughing, in between applauding the hero and booing the villain. Tickets run $5-12. First run movies can be seen at **Liberty Theater,** 1203 Commercial, tel. (503) 325-4191.

Information and Services

With 10,000 people, Astoria is the largest city and media hub of the north coast. The local newspaper, the *Daily Astorian,* is sold around town and is worth a look if only to get the editorial slant of Steve Forrester. This former Washington correspondent's witty commentary on events local, regional, and national pulls no punches. The *North Coast Times Eagle* is a politically activist monthly that holds forth coastal issues. It's sold around town and in Powells in Portland.

Throughout the north coast KMUN (91.9 FM Astoria and Seaside, 89.5 in Cannon Beach) is a public radio station with community-based programming that is especially diverse. Classical, jazz, rock, and folk music, public affairs, radio drama, literature readings and children's bedtime stories, and National Public Radio news will keep your dial glued to this frequency.

The **Astoria Chamber of Commerce,** 111 W. Marine Dr., tel. (800) 535-3637 or (503) 325-6311, will send you a free guidebook, (write: P.O. Box 176, Astoria 97103) to all the sites as well as maps, motel listings, and other visitor information. The facility itself also has generic north coast and southwest Washington materials. It's open daily 8 a.m.-8 p.m.; Oct.-April hours are Mon.-Fri. 8 a.m.-5 p.m. While there ask for directions to Young River Falls to see fall salmon migrations or to picnic in summer.

The **post office,** Astoria 97103, tel. (503) 325-2141, is located in the Federal Building at 8th and Commercial. It's open Mon.-Fri. 8:30 a.m.-5 p.m. The **library** is located at 458 10th Ave., tel. (503) 325-7323. **Clean Services Coin Laundry,** 823 W Marine Ave., tel. (503) 325-2027 will help you deal with any left-over mud you might have accumulated on your clothes from walking around Ft. Clatsop trails after a rainstorm.

Other useful numbers include the **county sheriff,** tel. (503) 225-2061, the **Coast Guard** and **airport** at Warrenton, tel. (503) 861-2242, and **Columbia Memorial Hospital,** 2111 Exchange St., tel. (503) 325-4321.

In town, public restrooms can be found at the corner of 1st and Downing as well as on Broadway and Ocean Way. The most scenic public restrooms can be found on the way to Astoria-Megler bridge near Lake Uniontown. Look for the WW I veterans memorial at the intersection of Marine Dr., Bond St., and Columbia Avenue. Underneath the doughboy statue you'll find the facilities.

Getting Around

Getting around Astoria can have its pitfalls for the unsuspecting. Remember that US 101 between Astoria and the other north coast towns is a one-laner much of the way and makes for slow going. Pedestrians should also take care crossing Astoria's wide streets where it's easy to misjudge the flow of traffic. Potentially troublesome for visitors is the city's layout of one-way streets and San Francisco-type hills. To understand this last reference, try going up 8th St. in a large vehicle (or save your rig undue duress and take our word for it). Holidays and summer weekends bring heavy traffic along US 30, a.k.a. Commercial St. and Marine Dr., Astoria's major traffic artery. In light of the foregoing, you might consider the following alternatives.

A Greyhound subcontractor, **Pierce Pacific Stages** packs up at the Minimart, 95 W Marine Dr., tel. (800) 231-2222, on Portland's beach loop bus that leaves Portland each day at 10:40 a.m. taking in Astoria, Seaside, and Cannon Beach. **Astoria Transit System,** tel. (503) 325-0563, provides service to Warrenton and to Seaside.

Finally, Horizon, tel. (503) 861-0241 or (800) 547-9308, has inaugurated service to Astoria with four nonstop flights daily. The Astoria airport is in Warrenton on Flightline Dr. off US 101 near Ft. Clatsop. One-way fares between Portland and Astoria range $40-90, depending mostly upon how early you book your flight.

BOB RACE

PORTLAND AND VICINITY

In shadows cast by 100-year-old trees and buildings, the new Northwest is taking shape in Portland, Oregon. Amid greenery seldom seen in an urban environment, high-tech business ventures, a full cultural calendar, and an activist community are carving out a vibrant image. A latticework of bridges over the Willamette River adds a distinctive profile, while parks, malls, and other people spaces give Portland a heart and a soul. The overall effect is more European than American, where the urban core is equal parts marketplace, cultural forum, and working metropolis.

Such a happy medium is the result of progressive planning and a fortunate birthright. Patterns of growth in this one-time Indian encampment at the confluence of the Willamette and Columbia rivers were initially shaped by the practical Midwestern values of Oregon Trail pioneers as well as by the sophistication of New England merchants. Rather than the boom-bust development which characterized Seattle and gold-rush San Francisco, Portland was designed to be user-friendly over the long haul. During the modern era, such utopian refinements as

the most advanced and extensive mass-transit systems in the U.S. and an urban plan that places strict limitations on the height of buildings and the space between them were added. In this vein, aesthetically pleasing and historic architecture has been spared during Portland's last decades of growth. Over time, the place that was once called "stumptown" has become the poster child for cities that work.

Another blessing is Portland's auspicious location. Even though it sits 110 miles from the Pacific Ocean on the Columbia River, the city's port is the leader in overall tonnage of foreign waterborne cargo on the West Coast and recognized as the second leading grain export site in the world. Timber and a remarkably diverse variety of agricultural produce from eastern Oregon, the Columbia River Gorge, and the Willamette Valley also depart the port of Portland, bound for Pacific Rim countries. In addition to this commerce on the Columbia, battleships, ocean liners, and other vessels go into dry dock here for repair and renovation.

Portland's waterways are her lifeblood in other ways. Mt. Hood's Bull Run watershed supplies

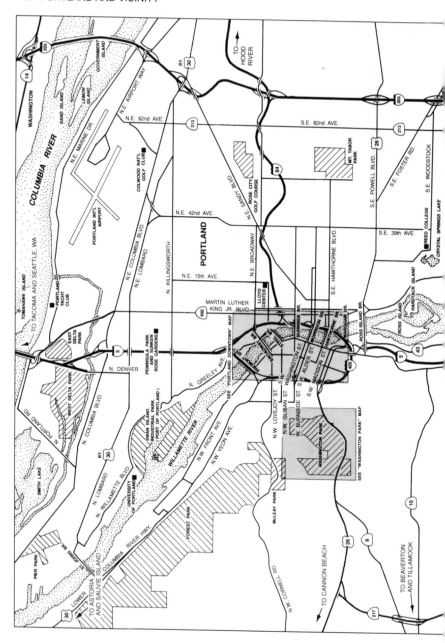

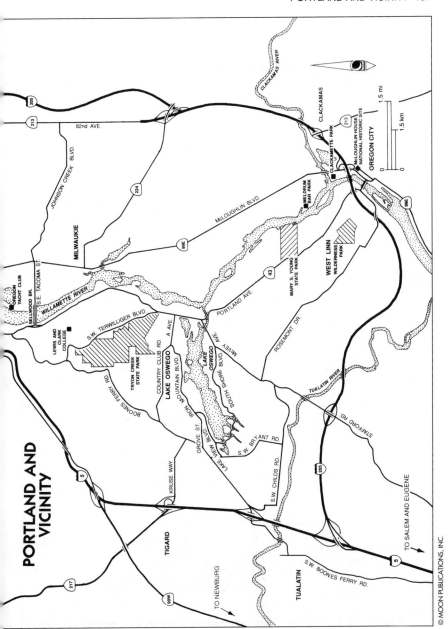

PORTLAND AND VICINITY

CLACKAMAS RIVER

CLACKAMAS

CLACKAMETTE PARK

McLOUGHLIN HOUSE NATIONAL HISTORIC SITE

OREGON CITY

1.5 mi

1.5 km

213

99E

82nd AVE.

JOHNSON CREEK BLVD.

224

McLOUGHLIN BLVD.

MELDRUM BAR PARK

MILWAUKIE

99E

43

WEST LINN

WILDERNESS PARK

MARY S. YOUNG STATE PARK

PORTLAND AVE.

ROSEMONT DR.

S.E. TACOMA ST.

OREGON YACHT CLUB

SELLWOOD BR.

WILLAMETTE RIVER

LEWIS AND CLARK COLLEGE

S.W. TERWILLIGER BLVD.

TRYON CREEK STATE PARK

COUNTRY CLUB RD.

A AVE.

LAKE OSWEGO

McVEY AVE.

SOUTH SHORE BLVD.

TUALATIN RIVER

STAFFORD RD.

BOONES FERRY RD.

IRON MOUNTAIN BLVD.

GROVE ST.

LAKE VIEW BLVD.

S.W. BRYANT RD.

S.W. CHILDS RD.

205

KRUSE WAY

5

TIGARD

217

99W

TO NEWBURG

TO SALEM AND EUGENE

5

S.W. BOONES FERRY RD.

TUALATIN

© MOON PUBLICATIONS, INC.

some of the purest drinking water anywhere in the U.S., and the printing, textile, papermaking, and high-tech industries (the Portland area has over 1,100 such companies) place a premium on Portland's clean-running aqueous arteries. Cheap and abundant power from the Willamette and Columbia rivers' hydro projects has also provided an incentive for many other industries to locate here.

The traveler will appreciate Portland's proximity to rural retreats. With scenic Columbia Gorge and year-round skiing on Mt. Hood to the east, and the Carmel of the Oregon Coast, Cannon Beach, to the west, relief from urban stress is little more than an hour away. Other nearby getaways include the wine country and the historic sites of Champoeg and Oregon City. Closer to home, Forest Park is the largest urban wilderness in the country. Washington Park's Japanese and Rose gardens are other internationally renowned places of beauty and contemplation.

The cultural offerings in this city of half-a-million people are noteworthy for their scope and excellence. Whether it's the wine, cheese, and camaraderie on first-Thursday-of-the-month gallery walks or the smorgasbord of live theater and state-of-the-art concert halls, Portland's music mavens and culture vultures enjoy a full table. In like measure, bibliophiles revel in one of the world's largest bookstores, Powell's, as well as many other outlets for rare editions. The Portland Symphony Orchestra under the baton of James De Priest has also gained an international reputation through its compact-disc recordings and world travels. As for popular music, top rock acts regularly hit Portland, while the local pub scene showcases many fine blues and jazz players.

On a smaller scale, readings by local literati Ursula Le Guin and Jean Auel, or equally prominent visiting authors, are a treat for Portland's book lovers. The flame of knowledge is kept burning by Portland's museums. The Portland Art Museum in the mid-nineties has risen to regional prominence with such coups as the only 1996 west coast appearance of the Imperial Tombs of China Exhibit. Such arcane exhibition halls as the Portland Police Museum and the American Advertising Museum complement the Oregon Museum of Science and Industry and the Washington Park Zoo. Adding to this array are more movie screens, radio stations, bookstores and dining spots than in any American city of comparable size.

Nonetheless, there are faint rumblings of trouble in River City. In recent years, Portland has not been exempt from the urban ills of gang warfare, escalating real estate prices, and a sizable homeless population. Locals will tell you that rush-hour traffic jams on the Banfield Expressway (I-84), the Sunset Highway (ORE 26), and the "Terwilliger Curves" portion of I-5 get worse each year. This is due to the fact that greater Portland's population doubled from 704,000 in 1950 to 1,403,000 in 1991 and is still climbing. Despite these problems, Portland's quality of life is still frequently touted by surveys and media as being unsurpassed by few, if any, major American cities. The *New York Times* at the end of 1996 selected Portland as the only city among the leading areas of growth in the country likely to weather the transition into the next century gracefully. *Newsweek* picked it as one of 10 hot spots for the 1990s, and Allied and United Van Lines have continually ranked it among the most moved-to cities during the final two decades of

A CITY THAT WORKS

Metro, a tri-county regional planning commission, has overseen efforts to ease Portland's growth-related stresses. The extension of the light rail transit system, the 1973 urban growth boundry, and citywide recycling are all overseen by Metro. The idea of the urban growth boundary is to stop leapfrog development across the open countryside by confining the new subdivisions and commercial enterprise to agreed-upon areas. Such progressive innovations have enabled Portland to place second in the country in *Utne Reader's* 1997 ranking of enlightened cities (first among large cities). With the approach of the 21st century, Metro is debating whether or not to make the city's first major land annexation (25 square miles in Clackamas County) in two decades. Portland had incorporated only 2 square miles over the last 20 years, counteracting the nationwide trend toward urban sprawl.

the 20th century. As such, the era of "small is beautiful" may soon be a thing of the past. Come now and see Portland in its Golden Age.

EARLY HISTORY

Sauvie Island, northwest of the current city limits, was the site of an Indian village whose name inspired William Clark to christen the nearby river the Willamette in 1805. Two decades later, England's establishment of Fort Vancouver across the Columbia brought French trappers into the area, some of whom retired around what would eventually become Portland. The city was formally born when two New Englanders, Pettygrove from Portland, Maine, and Lovejoy from Boston, Massachusetts, flipped a coin at a dinner party to decide who would give a name to a 640-acre claim they co-owned. The state-of-Mainer won and decided in the winter of 1844-45 to name it after his birthplace. The original claim is located in the vicinity of Southwest Naito Parkway (also known as Front Avenue).

The trade that grew up along the Willamette River and the so-called plank road south of the city enabled Willamette Valley produce and lumber from the interior to find an outlet to the sea at Portland's Columbia River port. This was especially important in the mid-nineteenth century because San Francisco needed these resources to sustain a housing boom fueled by the California Gold Rush. Portland was thus able to make the transition from a sleepy village called "Stumptown" to the major trade center and population vortex in the state, becoming incorporated in 1851. Another defining event was Portland being selected as the terminus of the Northern Pacific Railroad in 1883, linking the city to the eastern U.S.A. The single greatest impetus contributing to the emergence of Portland as Oregon's leading city however, was the Lewis and Clark Exposition in 1905. Two to three million people attended this centennial celebration of the famed expedition, establishing the city in the minds of the American business community as the gateway to the Orient as well as paving the way for significant population growth in the years following the fair. By 1910, a metropolis of almost a quarter million people had grown up at the confluence of the Columbia and Willamette rivers, almost tripling the town's population over a period of five years.

Moreover, the years between 1905 and 1912 saw the substantial expansion of railroads, farming, and livestock raising east of the Cascades, in part attributable to the growth of the Rose City as a commerical hub. The shift of America's timber industry from the Great Lakes states to the Northwest also occurred during this era. In response to this deluge of commodities, new wharves and factories were built at the northern end of the Willamette Valley. On the grounds of the original exposition site, northwestern Portland became a center of housing and commerce. Not surprisingly, city leaders have hopes for a bicentennial celebration of the Lewis and Clark expedition in 2005 to once again showcase the town in a beneficial way.

ECONOMY

A Harris poll at the end of 1991 ranked Portland the fifth-best city in the country in which to locate a business. In 1993, *World Trade* magazine rated Portland among its top ten cities for U.S.-based global companies. The CEOs polled in this survey probably recognized the fact that Portland is at a geographical crossroads with economic destiny. With the third leading port on the west coast, I-84 and three transcontinental railroads linking the city to the east, and I-5 providing connections north and south, Portland is perfectly located to take advantage of Pacific Rim trade as well as stateside business opportunities. As such, Portland is the second most active freight hauling and distribution center on the West Coast. Also facilitating the flow of commerce are 21 weekly flights heading to Tokyo, Osako, Nagoya, Taipei, Seoul, and Bangkok. Currently, the engine of economic growth in Portland is high tech. In 1995 alone, 13 billion dollars worth of investment by silicon wafer chip manufactureres were invested here. Intel, LSI, and other computer industry giants flocked to Portland to take advantage of tax incentives, availability of clean water (necessary for chip manufacture), and relatively inexpensive real estate. Today, Portland is the leading city in the world for the manufacture of silicon wafer chips and the site of such projects as Intel's two and a half billion dollar Hillsboro complex, the most costly plant in the world. Not surpisingly, Portland creates jobs three times as fast as Seattle and was ranked by INC. magazine as being the best U.S. city for small business at the end of 1996.

GETTING ORIENTED: PORTLAND NEIGHBORHOODS

Portland's revival picked up steam in the 1970s, turning a city mostly known for rain, roses, and run-down buildings into a showplace of eye-catching art and architecture. Included in this legacy were the renovation of the historic Old Town neighborhood and Pioneer Courthouse Square, as well as a law requiring that one percent of construction costs go toward public art projects.

Before getting started on your travels, here are a few things worth keeping in mind. Most Portlanders sleep east of the Willamette River. The business district, shopping areas, museums, and theaters west of the Willamette can be easily reached from east-of-the-river residential areas by mass transit. Buses and light rail are preferable to cars because of streets closed to traffic and the dearth of parking in the city. Once you're downtown, Portland's compact beauty invites strolling. In addition to parks, galleries, and shops which engage the eye, city blocks are half the size (200 feet) of those in most other cities. And the downtown landscape is basically flat, letting you log miles on foot relatively painlessly. In deference to the foregoing, the June 1996 edition of *Walking* magazine rated Portland among the top ten walking cities in the country. So ditch your car, put on your walking shoes, and ride the bus to its point of origin, **Transit Mall**, on 5th and 6th Avenues. This strip of 11 blocks is banned to vehicular traffic other than Tri-Met buses. Bus and light-rail travel is free throughout much of downtown (see "Mass Transit Buses and Light Rail" under "Getting There and Getting Around" in the "Practicalities" section following). Bus commuters and pedestrians on the go appreciate the variety of street carts (purveying burritos, bentos, and the like) in the heart of the bus mall around S.W. 5th and Stark.

Finding Your Way

Helpful information sources throughout the downtown core are the **Portland Guides**, tel.

(503) 295-0912. Their distinctive green baseball caps make it easy to spot these free walking information centers.

If you cannot find one, the following observations will help you get the lay of the land. The line of demarcation between north and south in addresses is Burnside St.; between east and west it's the Willamette River. These give a reference point for the address prefixes southwest, southeast, north, northwest, and northeast.

Another useful thing to keep in mind is that avenues run north-south and streets run east-west. Many street names on one side of the river continue across to the other. Twelve bridges connect east to west. Almost every downtown address will carry a southwest or northwest prefix.

Other aids to orientation include the fact that Naito Parkway (S.W. Front Ave.) is the road nearest the Willamette River downtown and Water Ave. is the nearest on the east side. Thereafter, numbered avenues begin.

The city's major thoroughfares are Grand Ave., Martin Luther King Jr. Blvd. (formerly Union Ave.), Sandy Blvd., US 26, and S.E. 82nd Avenue. Expect most streets downtown to run one way, alternating with the next going in the opposite direction. Streets in the Northwest District are named alphabetically (i.e., Burnside, Couch, on through Wilson). Ankeny St. precedes Burnside but by definition is in the Southwest District. The only exceptions to this ordering system are Roosevelt and Seed Streets, which are substituted for the "X" and "Y" Streets, respectively.

Finally, addresses increase by 100 each block, beginning at the Willamette River for streets and Burnside for avenues. More information is provided at chapter's end.

Portland Bridges

Of all the metro areas in the U.S.A., Portland is arguably the City of Bridges. With a dozen bridges on the Willamette and two on the Columbia, the

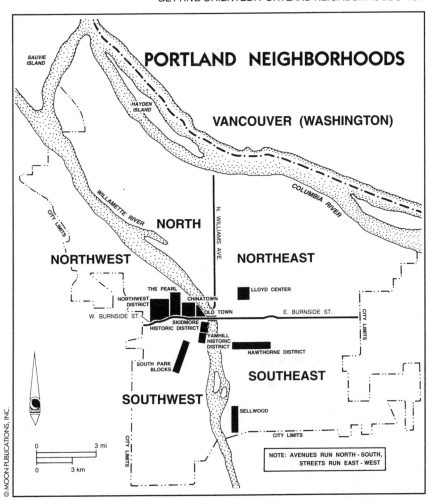

© MOON PUBLICATIONS, INC.

spans are both numerous and diverse. The three oldest were built prior to World War I. Bridge-o-philes can also revel in broad array of bridge types presented here that were designed by the pre-eminent engineers of their day. Many of the Willamette River crossings are illuminated by strategically placed floodlights at night, adding yet another pleasing visual dimension. Downtown bridges are located a third of a mile from each other and are, for the most part, safe and ac-

cessible for bicyclists and pedestrians (only the I-5 Marquam and I-405 Fremont bridges are off-limits to nonmotorized vehicles and pedestrians).

DOWNTOWN PORTLAND

The following introduction to Portland neighborhoods is intended to give an idea of how the city is laid out. Obviously, you can't do all of the

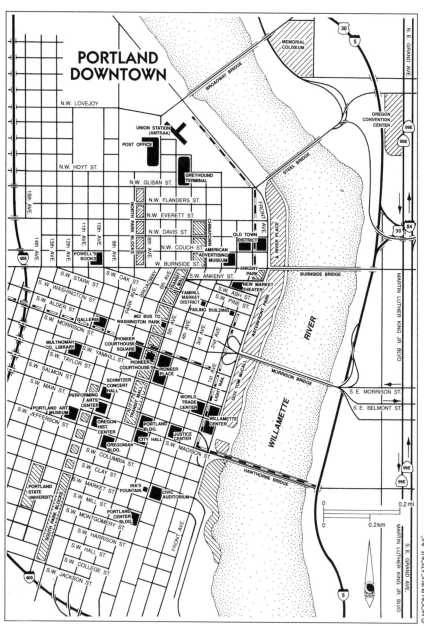

PORTLAND DOWNTOWN

N.W. LOVEJOY

UNION STATION (AMTRAK)

POST OFFICE

N.W. HOYT ST.

GREYHOUND TERMINAL

N.W. GLISAN ST.

N.W. FLANDERS ST.

N.W. EVERETT ST.

N.W. DAVIS ST.

CHINATOWN

N.W. COUCH ST.

OLD TOWN DISTRICT

AMERICAN ADVERTISING MUSEUM

W. BURNSIDE ST.

15th AVE.

14th AVE.

13th AVE.

12th AVE.

11th AVE.

10th AVE.

9th AVE.

8th AVE.

NORTH PARK BLOCKS

POWELL'S BOOKS

S.W. STARK ST.

S.W. WASHINGTON ST.

S.W. ALDER ST.

S.W. MORRISON ST.

GALLERIA

MULTNOMAH CO. LIBRARY

S.W. TAYLOR ST.

S.W. SALMON ST.

S.W. MAIN ST.

PERFORMING ARTS CENTER

PORTLAND ART MUSEUM

S.W. JEFFERSON ST.

OREGON HIST. CENTER

OREGONIAN BLDG.

S.W. COLUMBIA ST.

S.W. CLAY ST.

PORTLAND STATE UNIVERSITY

S.W. MARKET ST.

S.W. MILL ST.

S.W. MONTGOMERY ST.

S.W. HARRISON ST.

S.W. HALL ST.

S.W. COLLEGE ST.

S.W. JACKSON ST.

SOUTH PARK BLOCKS

S.W. OAK ST.

PARK AVE.

BROADWAY

6th AVE.

TRANSIT MALL

S.W. ANKENY ST.

YAMHILL MARKET DISTRICT

FAILING BUILDING

#63 BUS TO WASHINGTON PARK

PIONEER COURTHOUSE SQUARE

S.W. YAMHILL ST.

PIONEER COURTHOUSE

PIONEER PLACE

SCHNITZER CONCERT HALL

5th AVE.

4th AVE.

3rd AVE.

2nd AVE.

TRANSIT MALL

WORLD TRADE CENTER

PORTLAND BLDG.

JUSTICE CENTER

CITY HALL

1st AVE.

LIGHT RAIL

S.W. ANKENY ST.

S.W. ASH ST.

S.W. PINE ST.

NEW MARKET THEATER

ANKENY PARK

WILLAMETTE CENTER

S.W. MADISON ST.

IRA'S FOUNTAIN

CIVIC AUDITORIUM

PORTLAND CENTER BLDG.

FRONT AVE.

FRONT AVE.

GOV. TOM McCALL

WATERFRONT PARK

ANKENY PARK

RIVER PLACE

BROADWAY BRIDGE

STEEL BRIDGE

BURNSIDE BRIDGE

MORRISON BRIDGE

HAWTHORNE BRIDGE

WILLAMETTE

RIVER

MEMORIAL COLISEUM

30

5

OREGON CONVENTION CENTER

99E

99E

30

84

N. E. GRAND AVE.

MARTIN LUTHER KING JR. BLVD.

S. E. MORRISON ST.

S. E. BELMONT ST.

99E

99E

MARTIN LUTHER KING JR. BLVD.

S. E. GRAND AVE.

405

405

5

0   0.2 mi

0   0.2km

© MOON PUBLICATIONS, INC.

different portions of this tour in one day, so slow down and savor each part of town. After reading the capsule descriptions of sights in the walking tour, you can find out the hours, costs, and other details in the sections which follow. The bus stops of the most far-reaching and cost-effective inner-city transportation system in the nation (according to the American Transit Association) feature brick-inlaid promenades and glass-canopied pavilions garlanded with floral displays. But the aesthetics don't stop there. These waiting areas have so many ornate statues and fountains that former Portland Mayor Bud Clark exhorts you to "expose yourself to art" here. A famous poster depicts hiz' honor flashing the female nude statue *Kvinneakt,* on 5th Ave. between S.W. Washington and S.W. Stark, underscored by the aforementioned invitation.

Portland Building

The best-known statue in the city is Raymond Kaskey's ***Portlandia,*** which ranks right behind the Statue of Liberty as the nation's largest cop-

THEO TRIMMEL

Portlandia beckons passersby.

per sculpture. Located outside Michael Graves's postmodern Portland Building, S.W. 5th Ave. between S.W. Main and S.W. Madison, the golden-hued female figure holding a trident recreates the Lady of Commerce on the state seal. Locals refer to it as "Queen Kong," and sometimes practical jokers from Portland State University will dangle a giant yo-yo from her outstretched finger. Inside the Portland Building on the second floor is the **Metropolitan Center for Public Art,** 1120 S.W. 5th Ave., where you can pick up a brochure annotating a walking tour of the city's murals, fountains, sculptures, and other art forms. This profusion of statues and other public art pieces comes from the "one percent for art" program. This began in the early eighties, allocating a percentage of construction costs for the purchase and display of public art. Downstairs in the Portland Building basement is an excellent Thai food cafeteria, **Suriya,** 1101 S.W. 4th Ave., tel. (503) 228-1509.

More graphic evocations of the region are rendered by the simulated cascades at **Ira's Fountain.** To get to the fountain, walk down S.W. 4th Ave. to Clay Street. From the block-long fountain complex, retrace your steps back down 4th to Yamhill Street. If you turn left on Yamhill and go west a block, the Northwest motif is maintained by small bronzed beavers, bears, ducks, and sea lions congregating near a series of pools around the Pioneer Courthouse.

Pioneer Courthouse Square

You are now on the north side of Pioneer Courthouse, 555 S.W. Yamhill, the oldest public building in the state, constructed between 1869 and 1873. The classic contours of this gray granite structure contrast with the blue-tiled, mauve-and-beige tuxedo-patterned facade you saw at the Portland Building. On the first floor of the Hall of Justice is a post office with historic photos on the wall. Period furniture and brass lamps line the hallways on the way to the Ninth Circuit Court of Appeals, located upstairs in room 204. If court is not in session, ask a security guard to let you in, 8:30 a.m.-5 p.m. weekdays, to see the Victorian courtroom. Also, from the cupola atop the courthouse peer out the same window from which President Rutherford B. Hayes viewed the city in 1880. Afterwards, budget gourmets can enjoy a quick bite at two of

Portland's premier food cars. Both **Pasta From Venus** and **Full Moon Fajita,** located on either side of the courthouse buidling, serve up epicurean eats at fast food prices (along with sociopolitical commentary free of charge).

One block west, outside the front door of the building, is **Pioneer Courthouse Square,** bordered by Yamhill, Morrison, 6th Ave., and Broadway, the cultural vortex of the city. On the south side of the square is *Allow Me,* a life-sized statue of a businessman with an umbrella hailing a cab. Also within the amphitheaterlike confines of the square is **Powell's Travel Bookstore,** 701 S.W. 6th Ave., at S.W. Yamhill St., tel. (503) 228-1108.

Diagonally across the square is a 25-foot column known as the **weather machine.** Every day at noon the forecast is delivered by one of three creatures: a dragon if it's stormy, a blue heron in overcast weather, or a sun figure. As if that's not enough, the machine also emits a small cloud accompanied by a fanfare while colored lights display temperature and air quality.

All roads lead to Pioneer Courthouse Square.

TED LONG ISHIKAWA

The red-bricked square in summer hosts jazz, folk, and other types of music every Tuesday through Thursday from noon till 1 p.m. at the **Peanut Butter and Jam.** On Monday summer evenings, 5-7 p.m., you'll find another free concert series here, **Starbucks by Starlight.** On warm spring and summer nights the music and crowds return, augmented by symphony-goers departing the **Performing Arts Center** just up Broadway. The Birkenstocks and Gore-Tex of casual Northwest attire mingle easily with business suits here.

Should you tire of people-watching, inspect the bricks on the square, each of which bears the name of one of the 50,000 donors who anted up $15-30 for the privilege. From the northeast corner of the square gaze up at the white-brick and terra-cotta clock tower of the Jackson Tower on S.W. Yamhill and Broadway, and over at the copper sheathing of the Guild Theater building on 9th and Salmon to experience the glory that was Portland in the early part of this century.

Another part of the Pioneer Courthouse Square experience can be had in the middle of the amphitheater located on the northwest corner of the square. Here you might notice people talking to themselves. If you follow suit, you'll be treated to a perfect echo bouncing back at you.

Downtown Shopping

East of the courthouse is **Pioneer Place,** an upscale shopping atrium with such shops as The Sharper Image, The Nature Company, The Museum Company, Godiva Chocolates, Eddie Bauer, and Banana Republic. Downstairs is a food court with dozens of quality concession stands purveying an array of cuisines. Especially recommended is Wazwan, an Indian food place where you can have an exotic dinner for less than $5. Shoppers might also want to note the Pendleton shop, 900 S.W. 5th Ave., tel. (503) 242-0037, near the corner of 4th and S.W. Salmon. If the famous retailer of quality wool blankets and clothing is too pricey, have them direct you to their outlet and factory across the Columbia River in Washougal, Washington.

The South Park Blocks

Paralleling Broadway and the square to the west are the Park Blocks, created in 1842 and comprising a 25-block spread between Park and

THEO TRIMMEL

*fall foliage at the South
Park Blocks*

9th Avenues. Come to the South Park blocks in the fall and you can sense Portland's New England heritage. One-hundred-year-old elm trees with their bright yellow leaves line a series of small parks down the middle of the South Park blocks. These sentinels tower above cast-iron benches, bronze statues, and neatly trimmed grass fronting the **Portland Art Museum** and the **Oregon Historical Society.** Be sure to check out the murals portraying Lewis and Clark, Sacajawea, fur traders, and Oregon Trail pioneers on the south and west walls of the Historical Center on Main Street. **Portland State University** is at the end of the South Park Blocks. Sandwiched in between the South Park Blocks and Broadway is the heart of the theater district, with the **Performing Arts Center, Schnitzer Concert Hall,** and several smaller theaters nearby. On S.W. Salmon St. and Park Ave., note the four Simon Benson (see "Hotel Dining Rooms" under "Practicalities" following) drinking fountains put in by early 20th century lumber magnate Simon Benson to promote a teetotaling outlook among his workers. In the same block is the Italianesque Shemanski Fountain with its *Rebecca At the Well* statue. Several years ago, the city increased the number of brighter period-style lampposts here to make it more inviting after dark. To further help the neighborhood realize its potential, there are plans to forge mass-transit links to the Greyhound/Amtrak terminals at Union Station. This would provide easy access to heritage-rich neighborhoods and Waterfront Park on the banks of the Willamette.

DOWN BY THE RIVERSIDE

Old Town And Skidmore

The tile-roofed clock of the **Union Station** on N.W. 6th Ave. has been a beacon since the 1890s when passenger trains first rolled into the red brick terminal. This is the second oldest operating major passenger terminal in the U.S., the oldest big city depot west of St. Louis. Inside, check out the ornate high ceilings, marble floors, and vintage photographs. While Portland has always had a rep as a port city, much of the shipboard cargo arrived or departed behind a locomotive. By the late 19th century it was served by no less than three major rail lines. Theory has it that the city decided to build Union Station on top of the lakefront landfill donated by prominent sea captain John Couch rather than have several different depots controlled by the rail lines.

If you walk southeast from Union Station, you pass through **Chinatown/Old Town,** a compact area of restaurants, galleries, and exotic Asian grocery stores. In 1890 Portland had the largest Chinatown on the West Coast. They came to work on the railroad and in eastern Oregon gold mines. Back then, opium and gambling dens and dens of negotiable affection characterized the

the China Gate

THEO TRIMMEL

neighborhood. Perhaps the most notorious corner of Old Town/Chinatown was S.W. 2nd and Couch, the location of Erickson's Saloon. Here sailors would partake at a bar that stretched 684 feet around. Occasionally, bartenders would conspire with work contractors to drug a seaman's drink. When unconscious, the sailor would then be transported to a waiting ship by means of underground tunnels that extended down to the waterfront, later waking to find himself "hired" and at sea. (Rumor has it that one is being opened up for visitors. Check POVA for details). Today, the area puts its best foot forward two blocks west at the Chinatown gates. The gargoyled gate at 4th Ave. and Burnside is always good for a photograph. Notice that the male statue is on the right with a ball under his foot, while the female has a cub under her paw. Also note the red lamp posts. These are traditional Portland gas-light posts, but they have street names on them written in Chinese. Accupuncture houses, herbal shops, and traditional groceries keep the old ways alive next to the galleries of Portland's contemporary art scene. In spring, the cherry blossoms on 5th and Davis become the highlight of Chinatown. Overlapping this neighborhood are the museums, galleries, restaurants, and shops of **Old Town.** Many of the buildings here date from the 1880s, despite the fact that Portland's beginnings stretch four decades earlier. This is because an 1872 fire razed much of what was then the commercial district. Cast-iron

buildings with Italianate flourishes went up in the wake of the fire. While a large number of these foundry facades were torn down in the 1940s to make way for a Willamette River bridge and a waterfront freeway, a few (more than in any other place in the U.S. except New York City's Soho district) survive in Old Town and the adjoining **Skidmore Historic District.** Old Town runs predominantly north of W. Burnside between Front and 4th Avenues.

Skidmore spills over just south of Burnside. These neighborhoods are adorned with antique street signs, newly touched-up "old brick," and lots of iron and brass. Despite this ambience, the sights and sounds of traffic and panhandlers on W. Burnside might intrude upon your reveries of 19th-century Portland. Nonetheless, these street people would fit right into the historical fabric of a century ago, when shanghaiied seamen and unemployed loggers were commonplace here. In fact, the term "skid row" is said to have originated in Portland or Seattle. This expression came from the "skid roads," paths on which logs were slid downhill to waterfront mills. After logging booms went bust, lumberjacks and other folks down on their luck would hit the skids in these parts of town. If you're not careful in the Old Town/Skidmore districts after sunset, you too might end up "history."

A little south of the Burnside Bridge is the **Skidmore Fountain,** S.W. 1st Ave. and S.W. Ankeny St., named for a man who intended that it provide refreshment for "horses, men, and dogs." Local brewery owner Henry Weinhard offered to fill the fountain with beer for its grand opening, but the city leaders declined, fearing the horses would get drunk. Just south of the fountain, read the Ankeny Block placard on the wall for a good, concise description of Portland's architectural evolution. Despite the spouts and animal troughs, the 1888 bronze-and-granite fountain is still purely decorative. It does serve, however, as a portal to **Saturday Market,** 108 W. Burnside, between Bill Natio Parkway and S.W. 1st Ave. at Burnside and Ankeny, tel. (503) 222-6072, and to **Waterfront Park,** a mile-long oasis of greenery along the Willamette. At the north end of Waterfront Park, north of the Burnside Bridge, are granite boulders with inscriptions pertaining to the history and contributions of Japanese-Americans in the Northwest. Ranked as the largest continuously operating open-air handicrafts market in the United States, Saturday Market is an outdoor potlatch of homegrown edibles, arts, crafts, and excellent street performers. The market takes place every Saturday and Sunday from April through Christmas in the shadow of the Burnside Bridge. On Saturday the hours are 10 a.m.-5 p.m.; on Sunday the market operates 11 a.m.-4:30 p.m.

The 26 food booths here are a street-grunter's delight. Particularly recommended are Cajun shrimp, elephant ears (deep-fried whole-wheat slabs immersed in butter, cinnamon, and sugar), the soul food at **My Brother's Place** ("If my sauce don't send you, you have nowhere to go"), and the seafood crepes at **Nutritious Delicious Crepes.** The handicrafts range from exquisite woodwork (at reasonable prices) and feather jewelry to homemade fire-starter kits and juggling toys. What's astonishing is the high quality that's been maintained here for over two decades. Travelers on a budget should note that prices at food booths drop as closing time approaches (particularly at the Hawaiian Noodle Stand).

Across S.W. 1st Ave. and cobblestoned **Ankeny Square** is the **New Market Theater,** constructed in 1872 as a theater and produce market. Today it houses the American Advertising Museum.

Two blocks south of the market, **Failing Building,** 235 S.W. 1st Ave. and Oak St., typifies the influences and use of cast iron so popular during the 1880s. Today it houses McCormick and Schmick's restaurant. Writer Gideon Bosker asserts you can trace the evolution of American architectural style on a stroll through Portland. This is easy to believe if, from the Failing Bldg., you walk three blocks east to S.W. Front Ave. and turn left to a prime location of elegant restorations. Prior to Portland's era of expressways and bridge building, this whole neighborhood was filled with cast-iron facades and Italianate architecture.

Waterfront Park and Yamhill Historic District

From the Skidmore District, head east to Waterfront Park. En route to **RiverPlace,** an attractive area of restaurants, specialty shops,

Food and local color are found at Yamhill Market.

FRANK LONG

and boating facilities, you'll pass joggers and the **Salmon Street Springs Fountain.** This is often the centerpiece for one of Portland's many festivals and provides a refreshing shower on a hot day. The fountain water's ebb and flow is meant to evoke the rhythms of the city. Tom McCall Waterfront Park is named for the governor credited with helping to reclaim Oregon's rivers. In the early 1970s it replaced Harbor Drive, a freeway that impeded access to the scenic Willamette River.

From the waterfront meander through the **Yamhill Historic District** back to the intersection of S.W. 5th and Washington.

WASHINGTON PARK AND VICINITY

From 5th and Washington board the colorfully painted Tri-Met bus no. 63/Zoo/OMSI (Washington Park). The route includes Washington Park—the hillside home of the International Rose Test Garden, the Japanese Gardens, and the Washington Park Zoo. In addition, there's the Oregon Museum of Science and Industry Annex, a historic carousel, the World Forestry Center, the Hoyt Arboretum, and nearby, the Pittock Mansion (see "Other Sights" following). Clear days can feature views of Mt. Hood and other Cascade peaks from some of these Washington Park aeries. To the rear of Pittock Mansion, you can see Mt. Rainier over 150 miles away on the northeast horizon when the conditions are right.

Northwest District—From Washington Park
You can then head a mile downhill on foot or by bus to the Northwest District, north of Burnside between N.W. 18th and N.W. 27th Avenues. In the heart of the neighborhood, N.W. 23rd Ave., Victorian homes have been remodeled into boutiques to join stylish shopping arcades, bookstores, restaurants, and theaters. Given the profusion of brew pubs and coffee spots here, it's easy to see how northwest Portland has the reputation as "latte-land" and "beervana." An impression of growing gentrification is especially defined on N.W. 21st and N.W. 23rd Avenues, where, at last count, each street boasted almost two dozen dining spots. The area encompassed by these thoroughfares is also ref-

ered to as Nob Hill. On N.W. 21st alone, several eateries have earned accolades from the likes of The New York Times and Bon Appetit. The neighborhood's artsy shops and cafe society also attract strollers en masse, creating a people-watchers paradise. If you continue north for another mile, you'll see **Forest Park** looming over industrial northwest Portland, the largest park within a city in the United States.

The Pearl
Moving east down Burnside you come to a neighborhood which is affectionately referred to as the Pearl, north of Burnside to Marshall, N.W. 8th Ave. to N.W. 15th Avenue. Here, old warehouses have been turned into art galleries, high-priced condos, and antique showrooms. The soon-to-be renovated North Park Blocks neighborhood, vintage trolleys, and a Union Station train museum will add more polish to the Pearl in the next few years. First-Thursday-of-the-month gallery walks feature hors doeuvres and 8 p.m. closing time at some of these establishments. Pick up the free RAZ shuttle to galleries at 2nd and Ash stopping at about a dozen galleries in half hour increments. During the daytime, we highly recommend the **Little Wing Cafe,** 529 N.W. 13th Ave., tel. (503) 228-3101, for a quick bite if you're on the go in the Pearl in daylight hours. On the southern fringe of the Pearl, **Powell's Books** (see "Entertainment" following) is on 10th Ave. and Burnside.

At this point, you've surveyed enough of downtown Portland to get a feel for what goes on west of the Willamette. There are other Portlands worth visiting on the other side of the river. Three excursions by mass transit offer a gourmet taste of this realm.

International Rose Test Gardens
You can get to the Rose Garden by bus no. 63. By car from downtown, go west on Burnside about a mile past N.W. 23rd, hang a fishhook left at the light onto Tichener. Follow the hill up to Kingston and make a right. Follow Kingston a quarter-mile into Washington Park and park at the tennis courts. Just below the tennis courts is the Rose Garden, and the Japanese Gardens sign and access road should be visible up the hill from where you parked. Another way to reach Washington Park is by taking US 26 to zoo exit.

WASHINGTON PARK

MACLEAY PARK

PITTOCK MANSION

N.W. PITTOCK

PITTOCK ACRES PARK

N.W. IRVING

BARNES RD.

MONTE VISTA TER.

N.W. BEUHLA VISTA TER.

N.W. HERMOSA BLVD.

N.W. IMPERIAL

N.W. SANTANITA TER.

N.W. MAYWOOD DR.

TO N.W. 23rd AVE.

W. BURNSIDE ST.

S.W. TICHNER

S.W. CHAMPLAIN DR.

S.W. KINGSTON

S.W. PARKSIDE

S.W. MARCONI

S.W. WRIGHT

LEWIS AND CLARK MONUMENT

S.W. PARK PL.

S.W. RUTLAND TER.

S.W. HAMPSHIRE

S.W. VIEW

S.W. BENNINGTON

S.W. MURRAY LN.

S.W. FAIRVIEW

JAPANESE GARDENS

INTERNATIONAL ROSE TEST GARDEN

S.W. CANYON RD.

S.W. CASCADE

S.W. CASCADE

WASHINGTON

S.W. EVERGREEN LN.

FAIRVIEW BLVD.

HOYT ARBORETUM

PARK

26

KINGSTON

TO INTERSTATE 405

VIETNAM VETERANS MEMORIAL

WORLD FORESTRY CENTER

S.W. KNIGHTS BLVD.

S.W. CANYON RD.

MUSEUM OF SCIENCE AND INDUSTRY ANNEX

WASHINGTON PARK ZOO

26

0   0.2 mi

0   0.2 km

© MOON PUBLICATIONS, INC.

Drive past the zoo and World Forestry Center. Make a right and follow the road over the hill and through the woods down to the Rose Garden. The Rose City's welcome mat is out at this four-acre garden overlooking downtown. With more than 400 species and over 10,000 rose plants it's the largest rose test garden in the country. "Rose test" refers to the fact that the garden is one of 24 offical testing sites for the All American Rose selctions, a group of leading commercial rose growers and hybridizers in the U.S. The blossoms are at their peak in June, commemorated by the Rose Festival (see "Events" following), but even if you're down to the last rose of summer, there's always the view of the city backdropped by (if you're lucky) Mt. Hood. The best vantage point for the latter is the east end of the garden along the Queen's Walk, where the names of the festival beauty-contest winners are enshrined (since 1907).

If you enter from the parking lot west of the restrooms near the center of the garden, look for the rose labeled "Fragrant Cloud" to the left of the walkway at the beginning of the row. As its name suggests, this is *the* place to stop and smell the roses. On the right-hand side of the walk is the all-star lineup of award winners. This floral fantasia can be enjoyed from dawn to dusk at no charge. And while I promised you a rose garden, leave the roses behind, because the fine for picking flowers runs a steep $250 per flower.

Japanese Gardens

From the Rose Garden head west up the steps that go past the parking lot and tennis courts on the way to the Japanese Gardens, off Kingston Ave. in Washington Park, tel. (503) 223-4070. You can walk up the short but steep road that leads to the Japanese Gardens, or hop the free open-air shuttle that climbs up the hill every 10 minutes or so. The Japanese Gardens so moved the Japanese ambassador in 1988 that he pronounced it the most beautiful and authentic landscape of its kind outside Japan. Ponds and bridges, sand and stone, April cherry blossoms, and a snowcapped Fu-jiyama-like peak in the distance help East meet West here. This is always an island of tranquil-ity, but connoisseurs will tell you to come during the fall-foliage peak in October. Many people in Japan feel these gardens are at their best when it's raining. In any case, it's open daily in summer 10 a.m.-6 p.m. and thereafter, Sept. 16-April 4, it's open daily 10 a.m.-4 p.m. The gardens are closed on Thanksgiving, Christmas, and New Year's Day. Admission is $5 for adults, $2.50 for students and seniors; under age three gets in free.

Washington Park Zoo

After the Japanese Gardens, you can catch the Zooliner train, which goes four miles to the zoo. The train costs $2 for ages 12-64 (discounts for seniors) and runs 10:30 a.m.-6:15 p.m. at 40-minute intervals. Figure on 35 minutes for a roundtrip. The ride itself is worth your time if only because the Zooliner is a 30-year-old steam engine. But that's not all. The forested ridge defining the route features 112 species of birds, 62 kinds of mammals, and hundreds of plants. During a brief stopover, you may see the five major mountain peaks of the Cascade Range: Rainier, St. Helens, Adams, Hood, and Jefferson. The train may not run when the weather is rainy or attendance is low.

The Washington Park Zoo, 4001 S.W. Canyon Rd., tel. (503) 226-1561, itself predates the Rose Garden (1887 versus 1917), and it exerts almost as ubiquitous a presence within the city. This is evident from a huge elephant prominently painted on a building near the Burnside Bridge and an array of zoo animals depicted on the multicolored bus no. 63. The city is justly proud of the zoo's award-winning elephant-breeding program and the nation's largest chimpanzee exhibit. Also noteworthy are a colony of Humboldt penguins from Peru and an Alaskan tundra exhibit featuring grizzlies, wolves, and musk-oxen. The latter exhibit is supplemented by polar bears swimming in pools of simulated Arctic ice. Whenever possible, animals are kept in enclosures that re-create their natural habitats. The most recent example is the African Grasslands exhibit, which houses impalas, zebras, giraffes, and a black rhinoceros. You also shouldn't miss the zoo's **Elephant Museum,** which takes a lighthearted look at pachyderms. Along with elephant jokes, elephants in literature and art are depicted with dioramas and masks. A look at the ivory trade injects a somber note into the proceedings. The exhibit is completed by the zoo's collection of the world's largest and most prolific herd of captive Asian elephants. In 1994, Rose Too was born, allowing zoogoers the rare treat to watch a baby elephant grow up. In this vein, it should be mentioned that the zoo also specializes in breeding rare and endangered species, such as orangutans and red pandas. At this writing, the arrival of the new Oregon exhibit with its focus on indigenous species, is eagerly anticipated.

There are several food service outlets at the zoo. The major restaurant is the Africafe, which offers a good selection of moderately priced cafeteria food. The chance to dine overlooking a glassed-in aviary is the big attraction, however.

Compounding the impression that it's all happenin' at the zoo are the concerts in the amphitheater (discussed in the section on concert venues later in this chapter.)

The zoo is open 9:30 a.m.-5:30 p.m. April-Memorial Day, 9:30-6 p.m. June-Labor Day, and 9:30-4 p.m. the rest of the year. Admission is $5.50 for adults, $4 for seniors 65 and over, and $3.50 for kids 3-11 years old. Since many of the animals are nocturnal, it's usually best to get to the zoo early in the morning. But if you go late in the day on the second Tuesday of every month, you can enjoy the zoo at a reduced price. Just be prepared to jog, given just two hours to enjoy the expanse of the exhibits here.

World Forestry Center

Just over from OMSI Annex is the World Forestry Center, 4033 S.W. Canyon Rd., tel. (503) 228-1367, which offers exhibits on the natural processes of trees, the types of forests in the world, fighting forest fires, silviculture, and timber-industry activities. Also featured is the Jessup Wood Collection, within which are displayed examples from the 505 trees native to North America. Dioramas, films, and mechanized exhibits are complemented here by lectures, shows, and special events. The center's most well known (and after five minutes, most boring) attraction is a 70-foot talking tree. Worth more of your time is the second floor rainforest exhibit. Perhaps the best way to understand the mixed conifer forests of the Pacific Northwest is by taking in "The Old Growth Forest: Treasures in Transition." Spotted owls and clearcut logging are some of the issues covered in this acclaimed exhibit. The exhibit on petrified wood is also noteworthy. The museum is open daily 9 a.m.-6 p.m. in summer, in winter daily 10 a.m.-5 p.m. (closed Christmas Day). Admission is $3; children and seniors are $2.

On site is a steam engine that began hauling logs in the Coast Range in 1909, and an old growth stump of impressive girth. Also, don't miss the unique wooden items sold in the gift shop.

Pittock Mansion

Up Burnside from the turnoff to the Rose Garden is the turnoff for the Pittock Mansion, tel. (503) 823-3624, on the righthand side of the road. From here, it's a quarter-mile drive up steep and curving switchbacks. Situated at nearly the

Pittock Mansion

JOAN SELL

highest point in the west hills, 1,000 feet above sea level, this French Renaissance mansion completed in 1914 also stands above the rest of the grand edifices in the city for other reasons. *Oregonian* founder Henry Pittock spared little expense in furnishing his 22-room shack with such accoutrements as modern showers with multiple shower heads, a central cleaning system, room-to-room telephones, and a Turkish smoking room. The antique furniture, access to Forest Park trails, and fair-weather views of the Cascades also make this place a fixture on many itineraries. It's also a movie location and TV backdrop favorite, most recently for *Imaginary Crimes* starring Harvey Keitel (1994), as well as *Good Morning America* and several evening magazine shows. Lunch and afternoon tea are available in the Gate Lodge, the former caretaker's cottage behind the mansion. Lunch is served at 11:30 a.m., between 1 p.m., and 2:30 p.m. tea and dessert are served. For $7-10 you get soups, salads, and sandwiches on the lunch menu (reservations required). Regular tours are conducted (1-5 p.m.) daily except Sunday, and the grounds are open to the public until dark. The mansion is especially nice to visit when it's bedecked in Christmas finery. Be that as it may, the summer flowers surrounding the structure and the vistas in back of the mansion may well offer the most compelling reasons to come up here. On clear days, the view of several snow-capped Cascades volcanoes backdropping the cityscape to the east attracts locals as much as tourists. In fact, the picnic tables overlooking this view may well offer Portland's premier al fresco dining venue. On rare cloudless days, you can look north over the Columbia River to see Mt. Rainier 150 miles away. Admission is $4.50 adults, $4 seniors, and $2 youngsters ages 6-18. Mass-transit access from downtown is provided by bus no. 77 to N.W. Barnes and Burnside St., at which point you'll have to walk the steep half mile up Pittock Avenue. In the north corner of the Pittock parking lot, there's a trailhead that leads two miles down to Cornell Rd. through an old-growth forest. A left on Cornell takes you to the excellent **Audubon Bookstore** at 1515 Cornell. Afterwards, you can veer down the hill along Balch Creek to Macleay Park.

For the sake of orientation, it might help to think of Pittock Acres Park at the top of the hill as a connecting link in Portland's Park network. Macleay Park sits to the north, Forest Park to the west, and Hoyt Arboretum to the south.

EASTSIDE SHOPPING

Lloyd Center

Go to any Gresham-bound MAX (Metropolitan Area Express) station in downtown Portland (pick-up points include Skidmore Fountain-Ankeny Square and N.W. 1st Avenue and Davis St. in Old Town). Purchase "one-two" zone tickets and head to Lloyd Center. This mall was the world's largest shopping center in 1960 and today boasts over a hundred retail outlets, a newly domed ice-skating rink, **Lloyd Ice Pavilion,** tel. (503) 288-6073, and one of the largest theaters in the city, **Lloyd Cinemas,** 4510 N.E. Multnomah, tel. (503) 248-6938, with 10 screens and a futuristic neon interior. The vibrant restaurant scene of nearby Broadway also Despite these attractions, the journey might be better than the destination. The MAX route goes over the Steel Bridge, from which there are great views of the city and river traffic (and on clear days, Mt. Hood) as well as the Rose Garden Arena and the spires of the convention center. The new Rose Garden Arena and the OMSI campus on the eastern shore of the Willamette promise to increasingly shift the focus from the current westside downtown power base.

Hawthorne District

Hop a no. 5 Hawthorne Tri-Met bus from S.W. 5th Transit Mall or from Union Station. This neighborhood, from S.E. 17th to S.E. 55th Avenues along Hawthorne Blvd., recalls the high gourmet ghettos of Berkeley, California, and Cambridge, Massachusetts. Stores purveying records, fine coffees, secondhand clothing, antiques, crafts, and books join cafes and galleries along Hawthorne Boulevard.

A dense concentration of these establishments can be found between 32nd and 39th Avenues. Beyond the Hawthorne District looms **Mt. Tabor.** This extinct volcano has drive-up views of Mt. Hood, the downtown, and the Willamette Valley. There are also old growth conifers and enough deciduous trees to create brilliant fall colors. If you don't have a car, a no.

15 Mt. Tabor bus will get you close enough to hike the trail to these panoramas. If you're picnicking on the slopes, try Hawthorne Blvd.'s best bakery (also voted number one in Seattle), **Grand Central,** 2230 S.E. Hawthorne, for chewy baguettes, scones, pies, and cakes.

North of Hawthorne is N.E. Belmont, and south of Hawthorne is S.E. Clinton, and both are the heirs-apparent to hip-strip status. Belmont features a Gen-X diner (the Paradox), a theater, and first-rate espresso bars. On the other side of Hawthorne, the block defined by S.E. 26th and Clinton have stores purveying artsy videos and antiques. Add the **Clinton Street Theater,** 2522 S.E. Clinton, with a menu of music, film, theater, dance, and performance art as well as such hipster havens as Dots Cafe (famous for cheddar cheese fries and sixties flea market decor) and La Cruda (Mexican food with American hippie flourishes) and you have an exciting Bohemian barrio.

SELLWOOD

Antique hunters will be drawn from downtown to Sellwood in the southeast of Portland. Once a separate city, it annexed itself to Portland in 1890. Over 30 antique stores are spread along 13 blocks with names like Den of Antiquity and Gilt. This shopper's paradise is clustered around S.E. 13th Ave. between Tacoma and Bybee Streets. As with the Hawthorne District, many of the stores open after 11 a.m. Most Sellwood stores are closed Sunday and Monday. At lunchtime, **Gino's,** 8057 S.E. 13th Ave., tel. (503) 233-4613, serves standout pasta dishes, burgers, soups, and salads in a charming 100-year-old building. Expect to pay around $5 for lunch. Just look for the sign indicating its affiliated watering hole, the Leipzig Tavern. For dinner, take the Neapolitan night train to **Assaggio,** 7742 S.E. 13th, tel. (503) 232-6151, whose old world ambience and adventurous moderately priced (most of the 20 pastas on the menu are under $10), forays into Ital-

ian cuisine rate special mention (particularly for vegetarians). An adjoining wine bar (with great hors d'oeuvres at $2/plate) makes waiting a pleasure at this small restaurant that only accepts reservations for parties of six or more.

Somewhat further removed from Antique Row is the **Iron Horse,** 6034 Milwaukie Ave., tel. (503) 232-1826, a combination neighborhood pub/restaurant with surprisingly decent Mexican food. Several streets over, **Papa Haydn,** 5829 Milwaukee Ave., tel. (503) 232-9440, Portland's doyen of desserts, dispenses pricey-but-worth-it decadence. Its larger northwest outlet, 701 N.W. 23rd., tel. (503) 228-7317, adds a substantial menu of Northwest cuisine that maintains the standards of its after-dinner creations. Try the autumn meringue, a chocolate mousse and meringue creation that has become the Portland standard by which to judge all other dessert fantasies.

Walk off dinner at **Sellwood Park,** S.E. 7th Ave. and Sellwood Boulevard. The western extremity of this park sits on a tree-lined bluff above the Willamette. Tennis courts, picnic tables, and access to Oak Bottoms Wildlife refuge make this park a delight in spring and summer. Below the bluff is Oak Park where a pool and roller rink on the Willamette's eastern shore add to the recreational menu. To drive to Oaks Park from downtown, take McLoughlin Blvd south to Tacoma St. exit. Take a left (heading west) to 7th St., turn right on 7th, and then take the first left onto Spokane. Follow the signs to Oak Park.

In late August, the **River Rocks Festival** takes place outdoors here, celebrating Portland's wetlands with topflight entertainment, environmental booths, and a beer garden. To get to the Sellwood area from the Convention Center, take bus no. 70; from downtown, take bus no. 40. Driving from downtown, take Naito Parkway (S.W. Front Ave.) south to Macadam. Cross the Sellwood Bridge and head east a quarter mile to antique row (shortly after crossing the bridge, a left on S.E. 6th will take you over to another Sellwood Park entrance).

OTHER SIGHTS

SOUTH PORTLAND

South Park Blocks Area

The **Oregon History Center,** 1230 S.W. Park Ave., tel. (503) 222-1741, unfurls a pageant of Oregon's patrimony with interactive exhibits, artifacts, paintings, historical documents, and vintage photos. The extensive collection of photographs, maps, documents, and artifacts from the center's second-floor library is currently being catalogued onto an electronic database linked to the Internet, and is accessible by the public via research terminals within the exhibit galleries and library. The center's hours are Tues.-Sat. 10 a.m.-5 p.m., Sunday noon-5 p.m., closed Monday. The museum's admission allows patrons to use the photo archives (a real treat) and library, $6 adults, $3 students and $1.50 kids 6-18. Consult local media outlets to keep up on revolving exhibts here.

Across the street, the **Portland Art Museum,** 1219 S.W. Park Ave., tel. (503) 226-2811, designed by famed architect Pietro Belluschi, can complete a perspective on the Northwest coastal Native Americans. The masks and totem poles displayed here are not merely ornamental but are intimate parts of tribal ritual. The totem animals represent archetypal presences in native belief systems and are rendered with loving detail. Northwest themes are also breathtakingly displayed in the following works: Albert Bierstadt's historic painting of Mt. Hood (European and American Collection), the raven sculpture and Lelooska's totem pole (Axel Rasmussen Collection of Northwest Coast Native Art), and the Wasco horn bowl (Elizabeth Cole Butler Collection of Native Art).

The Asian art wing is in the process of expansion. Four galleries will illuminate different eras of Chinese and Korean art. A greater presence is also forecast for Northwest Native American works. Traditionalists can revel in the museum's collection of works by Picasso, Monet, Degas, Calder, Brancusi, Stella, and Renoir. Perhaps the two most touted acquisitions of the museum are Monet's painting, *Water Lilies,* and

Brancusi's sculpture, *The Muse.* In recent years, blockbuster exhibits such as The Imperial Tombs and China, Wyeth's Helga pictures, a Monet retrospective, and The Splendors of Ancient Egypt have put Portland Art Museum on the map for west coast culture vultures. Art Museum hours are Tues.-Sun. 10 a.m.-5 p.m., staying open late until 9 p.m. the first Thursday of each month. Admission is $6 adults with discounts for seniors students. On the median mall of the South Park blocks in front of the museum, the first Northwest Indian Art Market is slated to take place on Memorial day weekend 1998. Inspired by the Santa Fe Indian art market, it could become a regular event on the city's cultural calendar. Contact POVA for more details. .

The Old Church

Lovers of Victoriana can take in the Old Church (1882) by heading west on Clay St. en route to US 26. The interior of the Old Church shows off the craftsmanship of a bygone era. Vaulted ceilings, hand carved pews, and filigree woodwork framing stainglass windows bring together Baroque, Gothic, Renaissance, and Classical motifs. While there are no longer church services, Portlanders enjoy weddings and community activities as well as free brown bag concerts each Wednesday at 1 p.m. In addition, the Portland Opera company previews its productions here and a theater group and jazz series regularly stage shows in this unique venue. Back on the South Park Blocks, you'll find several other picturesque older churches among the theaters, museums, and PSU buildings.

Council Crest

A viewpoint considered to be among Portland's preeminent vistas can be enjoyed from atop a butte in a ridgetop neighborhood in the post West Hills. At 1073 feet above sea level, this is the highest point within the city limits. The Council Crest is home to such Portland luminaries as award-winning film director Gus Van Sante. To get there from Burnside, take a left (go west) on Vista (23rd), a left on Greenway, then take the right fork, Council Crest Way, into the park. This 1073 foot bluff looks out on snow-capped volcanoes and 3,000 square miles of territory. As you circle the summit, out to the west the panorama of the Tualatin Valley and Washington County is worth a gander, particularly at sunset. On the eastern side, steps lead up to an observation platform with arrows indicating locations of five Cascades peaks (check out the echo here). Even if they are not visible, the view of downtown and the rest of the city to the east is breathtaking.

The Skyline from Council Crest

From atop Council Crest you'll note the two tallest buildings in the Portland skyline. In case you're wondering which of the two bank towers is the highest in Portland, consider the following "stats," then decide upon your frame of reference. The Wells Fargo First Interstate Tower, the whitish building in the center of the city, has 40 stories. Sitting to the north is a big pink structure, the 42-story U.S. Bancorp tower. Number crunchers might take interest in the fact that the top of the Wells Fargo tower is still a tad higher (despite a shortfall of two stories) when the slope of downtown Portland is taken into account.

RIVERSIDE MUSEUMS

Oregon Museum Of Science And Industry

It's often been said that even though Portland's downtown is west of the Willamette, her future is on the eastern shore. The transfer of the **Oregon Museum of Science and Industry**'s main campus from Washington Park to the other side of the river paved the way for the Blazer arena project (see "Recreation" following) and the exponential growth of restaurants and nightspots here.

OMSI, 1945 S.E. Water Ave., tel. (503) 797-4000, is a hands-on interactive museum where you can pilot a ship from its bridge, gain insight on cardiology from a walk through a giant heart, or coordinate the Gemini space capsule's movements from Mission Control. The showcase of OMSI's new 18.5-acre campus, however, is the Omnimax theater (adults $5.50, discounts for seniors and kids). Here you can be transported into such exotic locales as a volcano or space

through the medium of 70-mm film projected onto a four-story-high domed screen. Incredibly vivid acoustics help complete the "you are there" effect in what may be the most intense audiovisual experience ever created. Astronomy and laser shows at the Murdock Sky Theater (adults $6.50, discounts for seniors and kids) and six exhibit halls containing interactive displays make OMSI the perfect entree into the world of science and technology for all ages and levels of sophistication. Particularly enjoyable is the "Nature's Fury" exhibit where visitors can sit inside an earthquake room and feel the simulated effects of a tremor. Trekkies will relish the opportunity to see the bridge of the starship *Enterprise,* assuming that this popular exhibit isn't on loan to some other institution. If you're not claustrophobic, the USS *Blueback,* a decommissioned Navy sub at OMSI available for tours, is interesting from both a technological and human perspective (i.e., how could people live in such close quarters?). Admission is $3.50, $2 with an Omnimax ticket.

The museum is open seven days a week 9:30-7 p.m. daily except on Thursday when it remains open until 8 p.m. These times are likely to change, so call first to reconfirm. General admission is $8-9.50 (discounts for seniors and kids) and is also likely to change (prices were in transition at presstime) ditto for a $15.50 package price that includes general admission, Omnimax, and Blueback admissions. A dining area with a river-view outdoor patio offers sandwiches, salads, pizza, espresso, and other simple, tasty fare. A gift shop selling glow-in-the-dark star maps, kaleidoscopes, and other quality educational toys is also worth a look.

To get there from I-5, take the exit onto Water Avenue. From the Marquam Bridge, take exit 300-B. From I-405 and the Hawthorne Bridge, look for brown signs next to the highway directional markers. Tri-Met's no. 6 bus will pick people up downtown on S.W. Salmon and 5th Ave. and drop them off in front of OMSI. This bus can also be caught at the Oregon Convention Center MAX station.

American Advertising Museum

The American Advertising Museum, the New Market Theater, 5035 S.E. 24th Ave., tel. (503) 226-0000, could just as easily be called the Museum of Modern Americana. The displays trace the early history of advertising up through the best campaigns of all time. Everything from Burma-Shave billboards to Will Vinton's California Raisins guide your journey through this visual and auditory feast. Hours are Mon.-Fri. by appointment only, Sunday noon-5 p.m. Admission is $1 for children and $2 for adults.

Oregon Maritime Center and Museum
On the west side of the river is the Oregon Maritime Center and Museum, 113 S.W. Front Ave., tel. (503) 224-7724. The Waterfront Park location is appropriate, given the Willamette River docking facilities which used to be here. Handmade ship models, Spanish pieces of eight, sternwheelers, and navigational instruments fill this little monument to Portland shipping tradition. Also, don't miss the sea stories told by the "watchstanders" aboard the sternwheeler tug Portland moored across Waterfront Park on the Willamette adjacent to the Battleship Oregon Memorial mast. At any given time, members of the crew will be on the deck of this steam-powered half-century old vessel, eager to share their stories. It was the last remaining steam-powered sternwheel tug in any major harbor in the world when it was retired in 1981. It was put into service in the 1994 movie Maverick, a fact well-documented on the second floor of the museum. The hours are Wed.-Sun. 11 a.m.-4 p.m. April-Oct. Thereafter, these hours apply only to Friday through Sunday. The admission is $4 adults, $2 ages 8-17.

Police Historical Museum
The Police Historical Museum, 111 S.W. 2nd Ave., tel. (503) 796-3019, makes the history of law enforcement and the Portland Police Department an entertaining, if kitschy, excursion into the annals of crime control. An outdated display on drugs and their slang names, a home-made-weapons exhibit (including jerry-built but nonetheless efficient guns fabricated in prison) joint uniforms, badges, and old jail cells in this arcane assemblage. Most fascinating are the old opium pipes seized in Chinatown raids during the 1920s. The museum is located in the Justice Center Building on the 16th floor, room 1682. It's open Mon.-Thurs. 10 a.m.-3 p.m. and is free. Because this museum is located on the 16th

floor of the busy Justice Center, there's usually a long wait for an elevator. Picture I.D. is required to gain entrance to the building. Just up from the Justice Center on S.W. 4th and Main, check out the bronze elk. Set in a fountain which had been a trough for horses and pioneers, it now serves as the city's most aesthetic traffic divider.

THE OUTER EDGES

Crystal Springs Rhododendron Garden
To the south of the city near the **Reed College** campus (distinguished for producing the highest number of Rhodes Scholars in the United States) is the Crystal Springs Rhododendron Garden, S.E. 28th Ave. at Woodstock Blvd., tel. (503) 796-5193. Come in April and May to see 600 varieties of rhodies as well as azaleas on seven acres broken up by an island on a spring-fed lake. Even without the 2,500 species of flowers here, birdwatching and fall foliage encourage a visit. An interpretive sign overlooking the lake provides information about the habitat and diet of commonly seen waterfowl and aquatic birds here. From March till Labor Day a $2 admission fee is charged on weekends and holidays. Otherwise, it's free. To get there, take the no. 19 Woodstock bus (on the Beaver line) and get off at the Reed College entrance. From there, ask any student to point the way.

Sauvie Island
At the confluence of the Willamette and Columbia rivers is the rural enclave of Sauvie Island. Horse-back riding, swimming, U-pick farms (raspberries, peaches, pumpkins, strawberries, and apples), and birdwatching on the Pacific Flyway (eagles, great blue herons, geese, and sandhill cranes) are some of the activities that can be enjoyed a scant 20 minutes from downtown (take I-5 north to the Fremont Bridge, then cross the bridge and look for signs to US 30 northwest to St. Helens, Linnton, and Sauvie Island). Mid-January is one of the only chances to see bald eagles feeding here. Call (503) 292-6855 to join a guided birdwatching excursion, $10, here at that time. In addition, anglers come to Sauvie's lakes and sloughs for panfish and bass, and the Columbia side's sand beaches (check out **Walton Beach** at the end of N.W. Reeder Rd. for

swimming) for sturgeon, salmon, and steelhead; bikers come for the 12-mile "hill-less" biking loop, and wildlife aficionados come to the northern half to sight red foxes and black-tailed deer. Nearby is Collins Beach, a nudist hangout. For more information, call (503) 621-3488.

The more sedate can enjoy fall foliage and the **James Y. Bybee House,** Howell Park Rd., Sauvie Island, tel. (503) 621-3344. This 1858 farm was built by Oregon Trail pioneers and is furnished with pieces from that period. If you're not edified by reading Sauvie Island's written history dating back to Lewis and Clark, the Bybee House also features a collection of old farming implements and an orchard with 115 species of apples brought by the pioneers. The house is open Wed.-Sun. noon-5 p.m. In late September, the Bybee House is open for the Wintering In Festival (see "Events" following). Combining this event with a bike ride through the island's pumpkin patches, yellow-leafed cottonwood trees, and river views is a wonderful way to herald the coming season. There is no admission charge, although Sauvie's $2.50-a-day parking fee might destroy the island-out-of-time ambience. The island is open for day use 4 a.m.-10 p.m.

The Grotto

The Grotto, N.E. 85th and N.E. Sandy Blvd., tel. (503) 254-7371, is a Catholic shrine whose hand-hewn cavern surrounded by lushly landscaped grounds can induce a profound sense of peace, no matter what the religious orientation of the visitor. Within the ivy-covered, fern-lined grotto is an impressive marble pieta. Outside the 30- by 50-foot enclosure, old-growth firs tower over the 110-foot cliff housing the shrine. Roses, camellias, rhododendrons and azaleas, and a cliffside view of the Columbia River also make this worth the 20-minute pilgrimage from downtown Portland (take Tri-Met bus no.12). The Grotto is open daily 9 a.m. till dusk, and while admission is free, there's a nominal charge to take the elevator to the upper level. This cliffside aerie offers views, floral displays, and walking paths. A new glass-enclosed meditation room at the top with comfortable chairs facing the river also justifies the admission price. On clear days, the meditation room offers perhaps the best long-distance view of Mt. St. Helens to be had within the city limits. In the foreground, the sight of planes taking off and landing at the airport can also empty the mind of mudane concerns.

ENTERTAINMENT AND RECREATION

ENTERTAINMENT

Book Lovers' Portland

While Portland lacks the population base of larger cities, Portlanders buy more books per capita than people in most other parts of the country. In bookstore sales per household Portland ranks ahead of New York City. As such, Portland has seen the recent incursion of such excellent megastores as **Barnes and Noble,** N.E. Broadway and 3rd Ave. and other outlets, **Tower Books,** N.E. Halsey and 102nd Ave., and **Borders,** S.W. Morrison and 3rd Ave. and other outlets. Despite the wide-ranging selection of these and other chains, Portland's independent bookstores are the heart and soul of this city of book-lovers.

Powell's Books, 1005 W. Burnside, tel. (503) 228-4651 or (800) 878-7323, is a Portland institution as well as the largest independent book-store in the world. Over a million new and used books are housed in a labyrinth of hallways that take up a city block. A helpful staff and maps of the stacks help locate whatever you might be looking for in 50 sections ranging from automobiles to Zen. Hours are Mon.-Sat. 9 a.m.-11 p.m., Sunday 9 a.m.-9 p.m. To make it even more appealing, there is the **Ann Hughes Coffee Room,** tel. (503) 228-4651, at the west side of the store, which sells espresso drinks, pastries, salads, soups, and snacks. The Coffee Room is a favorite place for singles to make connections. The *New York Times* and other papers on library-style posts and the chance to look over prospective book purchases while sipping coffee makes Ann Hughes (and Powell's) a bastion of civilization in a neighborhood dominated by old warehouses and a brewery. Free parking in a special garage on the side of the store and authors reading their works several nights a week enhance this impression.

bookworm paradise

THEO TRIMMEL

Other landmarks for bibliophiles include an incredible library, a complete periodical store, and used book stores specializing in rare editions. **Portland Public Library,** 801 S.W. 10th, tel. (503) 223-7201, is an architecturally stunning renovation of a 1913 building designed by Alfred Doyle (architect of the Benson Hotel and U.S. Bank) that houses an accessible (60% open stacks) collection of books, CDs, videos, and periodicals. There's even a Starbucks coffeehouse on-site. This is the most used public library per capita in the nation. Unfortunately, the library's hours are in flux due to budget cutbacks.

Rich's Cigar Store, 820 S.W. Alder St., tel. (503) 228-1700; and 706 N.W. 23rd, tel. (503) 227-6907, stocks out-of-town newspapers and magazines from around the world. Finally, Hawthorne Blvd. from 19th to 43rd Avenues features the highest concentration of used-book stores anywhere in town.

Readings and Lectures
Of the many literary events going on in this city, Literuption and Portland Arts and Lectures are the most well-known events on the circuit. **Literuption,** at Masonic Temple on the South Park Blocks, tel. (503) 223-7692, features several dozen Northwest writers doing readings, as well as bookstore booths. Lectures run 10 a.m.-6 p.m. on a weekend in March.

Portland Arts and Lectures, Schnitzer Hall, 1037 S.W. Broadway, tel. (503) 241-0543, provides a forum for prominent literati, scientists, and other intelligentsia in a half-dozen presentations autumn through winter. The series, $60, is usually sold out, but single tickets, $15, are sometimes available. Call (503) 248-4496 for more information.

Theater
Portland's concentration of first-rate theater as well as opera, dance, and other kinds of stage productions is fast becoming one of the West Coast's worst-kept secrets. With equal doses of tradition and eclectic dynamism, the curtain rises on the most diverse schedule to hit the footlights in any city of comparable size.

Headquarters for much of this activity is the **Portland Center for the Performing Arts,** 1111 S.W. Broadway, tel. (503) 248-4496. Four stages grace this facility: 3,000-seat **Civic Auditorium,** 2,776-seat **Arlene Schnitzer Hall,** 900-seat **Intermediate Theater,** and 350-seat **Dolores Winningstad Theater.** Each theater has features suited to different kinds of productions. The Schnitzer Hall is a sumptuously restored 1928 vaudeville-and-movie house. The Winningstad is a high-tech Shakespearean courtyard theater with wraparound balconies. The Intermediate is the crown jewel here, with elegant cherry paneling, teal velour upholstery, and a stage as large as the seating area. Civic Auditorium at 3rd and Clay is designed to accommodate larger audiences. On the way to the stage, the aisles are pitched at such an incline that women should think twice about wearing high heels. While lacking the aesthetic flair of the other theaters, the acoustics and vantages of the stage here are top-notch.

In addition to newspaper listings, the following numbers may be helpful: **Oregon Symphony,** tel. (503) 228-1358; **Oregon Ballet,** tel. (503) 222-5538; **Portland Opera,** (503) 241-1802. Over a dozen theatrical troupes are significant presences in Portland's cultural scene. Here are some you might want to be aware of: The **Portland Repertory Theater,** Two World Trade Center, 25 S.W. Salmon St., tel. (503) 224-4496, is Portland's oldest equity theater group. Count on mainstream plays. **Artist's Repertory,** 111 S.W. 10th Ave., tel. (503) 294-7373, specializes in revivals, dramas and ensemble pieces. What you get here can be often characterized as high quality off-Broadway. Be sure to call first, they are in the process of relocating. **Stark Raving The-**

THEO TRIMMEL

the Intermediate Theater at the Portland Center for the Performing Arts

ater, 4319 Hawthorne, tel. (503) 232-7022, stages thought-provoking and sometimes avant-garde productions that run the gamut from Euripides to contemporary local playwrights. The theater building in back of a coffeehouse that seats only 40 or so has been part of its chain since its inception. A larger performace venue is being contemplated that'll strive to retain intimacy while expanding seating capacity and theatrical capabilities. One aspect that will be missed should they move will be Common Grounds (which the theater currently adjoins), a classic coffeehouse with comfy couches, extensive periodicals as well as good food and drink.

The **Oregon Stage Company,** Interstate Firehouse Cultural Theater, 5340 N. Interstate, tel. (503) 823-2000, emphasizes plays with ethnic flavor. The theater also houses an art gallery. **Paula Productions,** 527 Pine, tel. (503) 238-9692, is another small performance venue specializing in original, often idiosyncratic fare. Recently, they did a musical based on Gilligan's Island. **Imago Theatre,** 27 S.E. 8th Ave., tel. (503) 231-9581, is an internationally acclaimed troupe that employs multimedia visuals, masks, puppets, dance, and animation to achieve dramatic resonance. Located in an old Masonic hall, it's intimate for the audience and spacious enough for the ambitious visual effects and movement of this cutting edge troupe. Ticket prices for the smaller eastside venues generally run $10-15. The westside Repertory theaters are usually double that.

Galleries

More than 30 gallery owners coordinate show openings the first Thursday of every month with many offering complimentary refreshments. A free monthly, *First Thursdays,* maps out gallery locations and summarizes their exhibitions and is available free at Powells and other culturally-oriented locales. Another free weekly, *Our Town,* also has excellent gallery coverage (as well as reviews of restaurants and other aspects of the cultural scene) and sponsors a shuttle throughout the gallery districts (The Pearl, Old Town, etc.) operated by RAZ, tel. (503) 246-3301. The shuttle focuses on such artsy areas as the conflagration of galleries around S.W. 11th, 12th and Glisan, or the area close by Saturday Market near the Burnside Bridge. Two popular First Thursday stops are **Gango,** 205 S.W. 1st Ave., which boasts lots of space and live guitar music, and **Laura Russo,** 805 N.W. 21st Ave., on restaurant row.

An annual Indian Art Market along the lines of Santa Fe's Native Art Mart is being planned for Portland's South Park Blocks, with the first of what will hopefully be an annual affair taking place Memorial Day weekend 1998. Contact POVA (see "Information") for details.

Art Theaters
Besides venues for music and dancing, Portland has a handful of places which may be termed "art theaters," whose diverse cultural offerings provide some of the most stimulating entertainment in the city. Two of the best are described below.

The **Aladdin Theater,** 3017 S.E. Milwaukie Blvd., is a 1920s burlesque house that has been elegantly gussied up to host such eclectic shows as author Ken Kesey doing a reading, performance artist Laurie Anderson, and folksinger Arlo Guthrie. This is the city's only nonsmoking concert club.

In a similar vein, the **Clinton Street Theatre,** 2522 S.E. Clinton St., tel. (503) 385-8899, features avant garde fare. Here, you might find a tapdancing saxophonist, an international political activist giving a speech, or the *Rocky Horror Picture Show.*

Comedy
Music and laughs, they're all here in the Rose City, but in varying degrees. To put it more bluntly, jazz is hot, comedy is usually not. In any case, whether it's cooling your heels or dancing to hot jazz, there's no shortage of nightspots. Portland's major comedy club, **Harvey's,** 426 N.W. 6th Ave., tel. (503) 241-0338, might suffer from poor acoustics and a lack of intimacy if you sit in the back, but the talent is there; besides, it's just about the only game in town. There's a cover charge of $8-10. A reasonably priced menu and a full bar are available at this club. A location near Chinatown offers dining alternatives and proximity to Greyhound and Amtrak make it a convenient retreat for travelers.

Live Music—Festivals
Portland is fortunate to have a critical mass of talented musicians. Notable among the tuneful offerings from this community is one of the West Coast's most vibrant jazz and blues scenes, more opportunities to hear classical music than are currently available in Seattle (especially see Chamber Music Northwest in Events), and plenty of places to suit fans of country, rock, and folk music.

Many nationally known jazz players (i.e. drummer Mel Brown and bassist Leroy Vinnegar) as well as a talented coterie of bluesmen (Robert Cray) were spawned from this milieu. In addition to homegrown talent, Portland has become a prime stop for touring practioners of these quintessentially American art forms. While jazz and blues can be heard in stadiums, coffee houses, brewpubs, and dance halls (see listings in Friday *Oregonian* Arts and Entertainment section and in *Willamette Week*), several summertime outdoor festivals are especially good places to get an earful.

The **Waterfront Blues Festival,** tel. (503) 282-0555, is the largest festival of its kind on the West Coast. Taking place the first weekend in July at Waterfront Park, many famous artists attend. The $3 admission and donations go to the Oregon Food Bank.

The **Mt. Hood Jazz Festival,** P.O. Box 696, Gresham OR, 97030, tel. (503) 666-3810, is *the* event for jazz and blues connoisseurs. The best artists in the world converge the first weekend of each August at Mt. Hood Community College in Gresham 20 minutes east of downtown Portland. Buying tickets in advance (about $30 per day) through Ticketmaster is advisable due to frequent sell-outs. If lawn chairs or picnic-style blankets are not your perch of preference, the covered west grandstand provides protection from the sun as well as offering views of Mt. Hood.

For outdoor concerts, it's all happening at the zoo throughout the summer during the early evening hours on weekends. Crowds spread out on the lawn below the stage to hear first-rate, often big-name talent, usually at a lower price, $5-7, than they would pay elsewhere in the city to see acts of such caliber. Because these events take place in the early evening and are free with zoo admission, it's not uncommon to see throngs of dancing children below the stage.

A higher-priced version of same is enacted at the Rose Garden amphitheatre in Washington

Park in September. Nationally prominent acts of diverse genres perform in what is probably one of the more scenic and acoustically superior venues in the state. Tickets go on sale at Ticketmaster outlets in late June.

On a weekend in mid-October, the **North by Northwest Festival** takes place at several of the downtown clubs listed in the next paragraph. This annual coming out party frequently connects talent to record companies and gives Portland a peak at acts that it might not ordinarily get to see. The music festival is mostly rock and its sub-genres and was inspired by the South-by-Southwest Festival in Austin, Texas. For more information, call *Willamette Week,* tel. (503) 243-2122.

Live Music—Clubs

In addition to festivals and large stadium concerts in the Rose Garden Arena, The River Queen, and Champoeg State Park Outdoor Amphitheatre, live music and dancing can be enjoyed at a wide variety of nightspots. The following suggestions scratch the surface of an ever expanding club scene. As Portland enjoys a national reputation for jazz and blues, special emphasis have been given to those venues featuring these genres. The Portland "Food" section should be referred to for other ideas on where to kick up your heels or listen to live music. Better yet, consult *Willamette Week* (new edition each Wednesday) and *The Oregonian* (Friday A&E section).

La Luna, 215 N.E. 9th Ave., tel. (503) 241-5862, is perhaps Portland's most active nightclub when it comes to live blues, alternative rock, and its offshoots. Downstairs, a spacious room with a beer bar close to the action on the stage is supplemented by a burrito/coffee concession off to the side. Upstairs, the "Living Room" has booths, a beer bar, and billiards. Tickets for "name" acts should be booked through Ticketmaster. "Queer Night" happens on Mondays, and is a relaxed affair (as opposed to being exclusively a pick-up scene) that is comfortable for everyone regardless of sexual orientation.

Berbati's Pan, 231 S.W. Ankey St., tel. (503) 248-4579, has established itself as a major presence in the downtown club scene. Thanks to Tuesday night appearances of jazz legend Leroy Vinnegar and a roster of diverse but always danceable music, complemented by great Greek

food from the adjoining restaurant and a full bar, this spacious, comfortable nightspot (not to mention pool, ping pong, huge dance floor and a killer sound system) has held its own against such longtime Old Town counterparts as **Satyricon,** 125 N.W. 6th Ave., tel. (503) 243-2380, and **Key Largo,** 31 N.W. 1st Ave., tel. (503) 223-9919.

The latter two establishments are frequently cited as the birthplace of "grunge" and currently host blues and new wave acts. Each feature enough good food to keep you rockin' all night. Key Largo's outdoor courtyard is especially appreciated when it gets steamy. Key Largo departs from formula more than Satyricon, featuring everything from world beat to Latin jazz. As such, it attracts more of an age-spread than Satyricon whose "punk" ethos seems to appeal more to the younger set.

Jazz de Opus, 33 N.W. 1st Ave., tel. (503) 223-9919, is another club that has carved a niche in Old Town. This is *the* place to come and hear jazz every night of the week (Sunday 8:30 p.m.-12:30 a.m.—every other night 9 p.m.-1 a.m.). While there's no cover, there's a $2/drink minimum on drinks as well as a $.50 surcharge while musicians are playing. Bar food is noteworthy here, as this club is the lounge to Opus Too, an excellent restaurant.

Jimmy Mak's, 300 N.W. 10th, tel. (503) 295-6542, parlays a great jazz and blues line-up with microbrews and homemade Greek food. The **Green Room,** 2280 N.W. Thurman St., tel. (503) 228-6178, is a comfy blues club with live music Tues.-Sat. Beginning around 8:30 p.m. There's no cover and 5-8 p.m. pints of beer are $2 and appetizers are half-price.

Despite a fancy restaurant on the 30th floor of a bank building running counter to the prevailing stereotype of a crowded, smoky, jazz club, **Atwater's,** 111 S.W. 6th Ave., tel. (503) 275-3600, live jazz on Thursday, Friday, and Saturday evening is an event worth dressing up for and you needn't be intimidated by the pricey fare on the main menu. If you're mostly here for the music, then order appetizers, light meals, and desserts priced from $2-9 while nationally prominent homegrown acts (Leroy Vinnegar, "Tin Pan Alley" vocalist Rebecca Kilgore, and piano accompanist Dave Frishberg and pianist Andre Kitaev) perform, backdropped by breathtaking views of the city.

A quality late-night music and microbrew haunt is the **Laurelthirst Pub,** 1958 N.E. Glisan, tel. (503) 232-1505. Mostly acoustic and low voltage electric acts can be heard Tues.-Sun. between 9 p.m.-1 a.m. A skilled kitchen staff and a pool table also explain the following here. **Brasserie Montmartre,** 626 S.W. Park Ave., tel. (503) 224-5552, frequently serves up live jazz and gourmet pub grub late into the night in a stylish decor evocative of its name.

Every Wednesday from 5:30 p.m.-7:30 p.m. come to **Portland Art Museum's Grand Ballroom,** 3rd floor, 1219 S.W. Park Ave., tel. (503) 226-2811, to hear the best area musicians. These gigs generally run fall through spring and cost $6 a ticket. The new state-of-the-art sound system supplies a different weekly soundtrack to the visual feast here. This smoke-free venue also hosts nationally known talent in its Showman Presents series. For the schedule, consult local listings, call the Art Museum, or boot up http://www.showman. com.

Finally, live music fans should be aware that top flight jazz talent often performs at wineries (i.e. Montinore, Sokol Blosser) and upscale hotels (i.e. the Heathman, the Governor). Consult local listings.

Dancing Alternatives

Here's a few alternatives where you can dance to something other than Portland's predominant blues and rock.

In addition to being a place where you can boogie to the foregoing, **McMenamins Crystal Ballroom,** 1332 W. Burnside, tel. (503) 225-0047, hosts a Sunday ballroom event (with lessons beginning at 4 p.m.) in a majestic 1914 restored dance hall. It's worth noting that in the sixties, Marvin Gaye, James Brown, Etta James, Ike and Tina Turner, the Allman Brothers, and more, gave the vintage moveable dance floor here a workout. Prior to that, the likes of Jinny Dorsey and Glen Miller established the Crystal Ballroom's Big Band cachet. Pictures on the wall attest to this legacy.

Latin dance fans will appreciate weekend live music and salsa lessons at **Sandoval's,** 133 S.W. 2nd Ave., tel. (503) 223-7020. If you need sustenance, Sandoval's tamales are the best in town. In addition, the restaurant's community-conscious stance has made the place a favorite with like-minded celebs (Carlos Santana, Los Lobos, and Tracy Chapman, among others) who might be spotted there when they have a gig in town.

Finally, **Jubitz Ponderosa,** 10205 N. Vancouver Way, tel. (503) 283-1111, is a place to do your boot-scootin' boogie and Texas two-step to live bands. Just take I-5 north to exit 307 and veer right on the frontage road onto Vancouver Way.

Cinema

The *Oregonian* offers a free 24-hour news and information service called **Oregonian Inside Line,** tel. (503) 225-5555. Dial FILM (3456), the category prompt to access film listings for all the cinemas in town. In addition, each theater has its own extension, which you can access directly. A complete list of extensions is published in the Sunday *Oregonian's* "TV Click" section. (See "Media" under "Information and Services" in the "Practicalities" section following for more details on this service.) Adults can expect to pay $6.50 for a movie after 5 p.m. at most ACT III (a chain that controls 85% of Portland's movie screens) movie theaters. Prior to that, half-price matinees are in effect. A similar price range prevails at most of the "independent" movie houses listed below. At some theaters, seniors and students are privy to half-price discounts during evening shows.

In addition to the February festival of the Northwest Film and Video Center (admission) in the **Portland Art Museum** (see below) and the 10-screen **Lloyd Cinemas,** 1510 N.E. Multnomah, tel. (503) 287-0338, Portland offers a wide variety of theaters and an equally diverse choice of cinematic experiences.

The **Movie House,** 1220 S.W. Taylor, tel. (503) 222-4595, offers wine, cheese (card tables and chess upstairs), and art flicks. And at **Mission Theater and Pub,** 1624 N.W. Glisan St., tel. (503) 223-4031, you can settle into old couches with your pint of microbrew, a burger, or a thick sandwich, to watch old Marx Brothers and 1940s classic movies for $1 (and newer flicks, too). It's more a tavern than a movie house, but by the second or third mug, you won't care. It's open 5 p.m.-midnight. The McMenamin brothers also combine film, beer, and food at the **Bagdad Theatre and Pub,** 3710 S.E. Hawthorne, tel. (503) 230-0895, and the **Power**

Station, 2126 S.W. Halsey St., tel. (503) 669-8754. These places tend to focus on recent hit movies. Adults only except for Sunday matinees at the Bagdad. Cult films, classics along with good eats are available at the **Auberge Restaurant,** 2601 N.W. Vaughn St., tel. (503) 223-3302, on Sundays at 8:30 p.m. Bogart, Hitchcock, and company go well with this restaurant's Sunday menu—particularly a signature cheeseburger, free popcorn, and some of the best mixed drinks in town.

The marble staircase of **KOIN Center Cinema,** S.W. 3rd at Clay, tel. (503) 243-3515, leads to six screens showing art films and high-quality Hollywood releases. **Cinema 21,** 616 N.W. 21st. Ave., tel. (503) 223-4515, is an old movie house in the artsy Northwest District showing foreign, experimental, and new-wave movies, as well as documentaries, cult favorites, and revivals.

A well-preserved screen gem is the **Roseway Theater,** 7229 S.W. Sandy Blvd., tel. (503) 281-5173, featuring modern films as well as musicals of the '40s and '50s and a real pipe organ. Another oldie but goody is the **Hollywood Theatre,** N.E. 41st and Sandy Blvd., tel. (503) 248-6977. Enter beneath art deco obelisks to enjoy fading first-run flicks for $1.50.

Film buffs revel in Porland's February **Northwest Film Center Film Festival.** This is the place to catch films that will later go onto national acclaim. Tickets run around $6. Call (503) 221-1156 for more information.

Finally, the **Broadway Metroplex,** 1000 Broadway, tel. (503) 248-6960, combines a downtown location, plush interiors, quality munchies (featuring an outlet of highly regarded Starbuck's coffee), along with several screens showing first-run movies.

RECREATION

Spectator Sports

Portland is a town more for athletes than devotees of spectator sports. Nonetheless, the two stadia in the Rose City draw huge crowds.

In a city where NBA basketball borders on obsession (thanks to the Blazers' NBA record for consecutive playoff appearances and the fact that it's the only pro sports team for almost 200 miles), the new **Rose Garden Arena** located at the east end of the Broadway Bridge, and its accompanying shops-and-restaurant complex can be expected to increase the traffic considerably on the Willamette's eastern shore. (If you MAX out to the complex, exit the train at the Rose Quarter transit center.)

The Rose Garden's high seating capacity (20,339) and enhanced views have given Portland an exciting arena for basketball and concerts. The proximity of the Memorial Coliseum and the Oregon Convention Center will enable the city to attract world-class athletic events, industrial shows, and conventions.

The Rose Garden's elliptical contours with seating aligned in a gentle grade offers better sightlines than those found in most other arenas in the world. In addition, the large size of the venue relative to the number of seats provides more generous leg room than the knees-in-your-mouth seating arrangement found in your typical sports stadium. State-of-the-art acoustics put the finishing touches on your enjoyment. (The arena was nominated as the best new arena concert venue of 1996 by an industry group. Computerized acoustic panels have made this stadium a wonderful place to hear everyone from Garth Brooks to Eric Clapton.)

While most **Trail Blazer** seats are reserved for season ticket-holders, some are available at Ticketmaster outlets or through the arena box office. Then, of course, there are always the overpriced offerings of ticket brokers advertised in the *Oregonian* or scalpers who may be found beyond a four-block radius of the Rose Garden. It's best to call the Blazer ticket line, tel. (503) 231-8000, or write their corporate offices, 700 N.E. Multnomah, Suite 600, Portland 97232, well in advance.

Blazer tickets, according to one study, averaged out to the highest in the league at $47.49. Nonetheless, Blazer management keeps a significant amount of low-priced tickets available for many games, $5-15, and also offers non prohibitive family packages (four games for $20).

The Blazer's former home, the **Memorial Coliseum,** located at 1401 N. Wheeler, tel. (503) 235-8771, now hosts the women's pro-hoop team the **Portland Power.** The tickets are cheap and the crowds lively. In the winter you can also find the **Winter Hawks** hockey team of the Western Hockey League playing at the Coliseum.

Multnomah Kemp Greyhound Park, N.W. 223rd and Glisan St., P.O. Box 9, Fairview 97024, tel. (503) 667-7700, is the only place to see greyhound racing on the West Coast. It's located southeast of Portland near Gresham. The **Multnomah Kennel Club**'s glass-enclosed facility offers beautiful views of Cascade peaks and excellent dining facilities along with pari-mutuel wagering. Evening post time is 7:30 p.m., matinee post time is 1 p.m. The season runs from May through September. The best way to get here is by MAX. Ride it to the Gresham City Hall or Central Station, then board the Tri-Met no. 82 Eastman bus directly to the track. While the bus isn't free, the driver will give you a free pass to the races.

The sport of kings is on display at **Portland Meadows,** 1001 N. Schneer Rd., tel. (503) 284-9144, Friday through Sunday. A glass-enclosed grandstand with complete food service ensures comfort October-April. Rock concerts are sometimes staged here.

Hiking

Portland is famous for having more park acreage per capita than any other major American city, with one twelfth of the city's area devoted to public-accessed recreational venues. Within these holdings, the city has more urban wilderness than any other municipality in the country. As whole books have been written about these retreats, we will confine ourselves to just a few hikes and refer the reader to the **Portland Audubon Society Bookstore,** 5151 N.W. Cornell Rd., tel. (503) 292-6855, (just off the MacLeay Park to Pittock Mansion Trail), which has maps of more than 200 urban wildlife habitat sites in Portland, and *A Pedestrian's Portland* by Karen and Terry Whitehill (Mountaineers Books, $10.95). The book outlines 40 walks in greater Portland, which the authors divide into six areas.

Without doubt, the part of Portland most conducive to a walk on the wild side is up in the hills behind the Northwest neighborhood. The largest urban wilderness in the country, **Forest Park** is accessible off I-5 (heading north) by taking the Fremont Bridge into northwest Portland and making a left onto Nicolai St. or Vaughn Street. Turn left onto 27th Ave. and follow it to Thurman Street. Make a right on Thurman and follow it to its end to reach the portal of Forest Park. The paved walk-way at the edge of the wilderness has numerous side trails to forested hillsides. Despite scenic beauty, the smells and sounds of Portland's industrial northern extremity can occasionally pierce the tranquility here. Thus, weekends and holidays are recommended for excursions into this preserve. Nonetheless, what other city has a park in which bear, elk, deer, and cougar have been sighted? What other city park has old-growth trees and wild scenic areas? The park is 8.5 miles long, 1.5 miles wide.

A scenic adjunct is **MacLeay Park,** which can be reached via the Forest Park route and a turnoff onto Upshur Rd. (instead of Thurman), following it to its end. The Audubon Society Headquarters and bookstore is located on Cornell Rd. a half mile from the trailhead. The gentle uphill trail here follows a deep gully paralleling a creek. (See "Pittock Mansion" under "Washington Park and Vicinity," above).

Another way to reach MacLeay and Forest parks is via the 14-mile **Wildwood Trail,** which heads north through the Hoyt Arboretum and Pittock Acres before plunging downhill into the parklands below. The trail begins on Canyon Rd. near the zoo, OMSI, and Forestry Center. Or you can drive to the **Arboretum Visitor Center,** 4000 S.W. Fairview Blvd.; open 10 a.m.-4 p.m. daily, or the Pittock Mansion to begin your descent into MacLeay and Forest parks. The park itself is open daily 6 a.m.-10 p.m.

The arboretum is the gem of the Wildwood Trail and covers 214 acres and seven miles of trails, including a one-mile tour through one of the country's largest collections of conifers. On Saturday and Sunday Oct.-April at 2 p.m., guided tours highlight foliage season. Prime time to come is during the **Fall Festival of Color** weekend around October 20. Events begin at 9:30 a.m. with a guided one-mile loop (for independents, a comprehensive trail map is available for 50 cents) through more than two dozen species of deciduous trees. Prize species include the endangered Brewer's weeping spruce and the Dawn redwood. This tree had been considered extinct for five million years until a remote stand was found in China. Hoyt's Dawn redwood bore the first cones produced in this hemisphere in 50 million years.

The Wildwood Trail is part of a proposed larger network of trails to loop the city. This was originally the brainchild of the Olmsted brothers (of Yosemite Valley and Central Park fame) at the turn of the century. Their proposed 40-mile loop concept has expanded to a 140-mile matrix. Now the goal is to complete a hiking/biking path connecting parks along the Columbia, Sandy, and Willamette rivers. To find out more, contact the **40 Mile Loop Land Trust,** tel. (503) 241-9105, or pick up a map of the loop at Powell's Travel Bookstore at Pioneer Courthouse Square, tel. (503) 228-1108. A map of the trail system is available from the **Portland Parks Dept.,** 1120 S.W. 5th Ave., 4th floor, tel. (503) 823-2223.

On the other end of town, another potential component of the loop beckons urban walkers in search of rural pleasures. Snaking along the east bank of the Willamette River between the Sellwood and Ross Island bridges, the **Oak Bottoms Wildlife Refuge** is a birdwatcher's paradise. Great blue and green herons find this wetland a prime habitat. In winter, a dozen species of waterfowl can be found. Summertime residents include warblers, orioles, swallows, and woodpeckers. Whenever you go, look for wood ducks joining such permanent denizens as beavers and muskrats.

A ridge along Sellwood Blvd. frames Oak Bottoms and offers good views. You can hike into it at the north end of Sellwood Park at S.W. 7th Ave. and Sellwood Boulevard. The parking lot at the 5000 block of S.E. Milwaukie Blvd. also offers access. After you descend, a loop trail encircles the wetlands, paralleling the bluff on the east side and following the railroad tracks to the west.

Audubon Old Growth Sanctuaries

The aforementioned Audubon Bookstore is also a good place to get directions to the city's oldest treasures. While the size of the groves of centuries-old trees aren't large, the fact that these 500-year old gigantic vegetables are minutes away from the downtown core is compelling. The impression of a time machine voyage is also compounded when you consider that of the 19 million acres of old growth that once covered the Northwest, only 10% still remains. The Audubon Society sponsors Old Growth walks, generally in min-November. Recent flood damage threatens the survival of this resource, so take advantage of the opportunity to see giant Douglas fir and Western red cedar that were alive when Columbus sailed across the ocean.

Sports

Tennis courts, cycling paths, and lakes for swimming and sailing abound in Portland parks, Portland Parks, 1120 S.W. 5th Ave., Room 502, tel. (503) 796-5193. Free swimming pools can also be located by calling this number.

Runners enjoy numerous events, including the well-regarded **Portland Marathon** and the **Cascade Runoff.** To find out about these and other events call the **Runner's Hotline,** tel. (503) 223-7867. The **Oregon Runner's Club,** P.O. Box 549, Beaverton 97025-0549 or (503) 626-2348, is the second-largest club in the country and is glad to recommend the best places to run. Joggers interested in low-impact exercise will appreciate the bark-o-mulch track at Kaiser Hospital's Interstate complex, 3325 N. Interstate Avenue. From downtown, cross the Broadway Bridge and turn left on Interstate and drive several miles. The track is located near the northernmost building in the three building complex.

Bipeds in less of a hurry can pick up a free annotated walker's map at Powell's Books, 1005 W. Burnside, tel. (503) 228-4651. Bikers can procure the *From Here to There by Bike* map at many bookstores in town, and *Getting There by Bike,* published by Metro (a government agency) is sold at bike shops. A major problem is crossing the Willamette River. The Hawthorne and Burnside bridges are best, although bikes must share sidewalks with pedestrians. Provisions to let bicycles on many selected Tri-Met bus routes (bike racks are on board, with $5 passes available at Pioneer Square) will help you get out of the armchair and onto the road. Rent bikes from **Fat Tire Farm,** 2714 N.W. Thurman St., tel. (503) 222-3276. Repair bikes at the **Bicycle Repair Collective,** 4438 S.E. Belmont, tel. (503) 233-0564.

Several years ago, *Bicycling* magazine selected Portland as the most bike-friendly major city (out of 226 cities) in the U.S. Recent evidence of this has been the establishment of covered bike parking, showers, locker space downtown, (tel. 503-823-7671 for info), and increased numbers of bike lane on commuter thoroughfares. Cyclists are currently excited about the 16.8 mile springwater corridor that runs from S.E. Portland through Gresham to Boring. Much of this bike thoroughfare is on reclaimed rail line. Views of Mt. Hood abound throughout much of the route. Along the way, easy access to Leach Botanical Gardens, Powell Butte, and other worthy detours are available. Contact **Portland Parks and Recreation,** 1120 S.W. 5th Ave., room 1302, Portland 97204, tel. (503) 823-2223.

Cyclists looking for organized 30- to 100-mile rides at a touring pace should hook up with the **Portland Wheelmen Touring Club Hotline,** tel. 282-PWTC. Also of interest are **Portland Parks and Recreation,** 1120 S.W. 5th Ave., Portland 97204, tel. (503) 823-5132, "Rides on the Wild Side" bike tours. Cost is $5 a ride except for the slough ride, $9, that includes lunch. Pre-registration for all rides is required. For more information contact the **Office of Transportation Bicycle Program,** 1120 S.W. 5th Ave., Room 730, Portland 97204, tel. (503) 823-7082. Finally, be on the lookout for yellow bikes downtown. These will be available free of charge for pickup and drop-off at designated places as an adjunct to mass transit. A pilot program of this kind resulted in lots of missing two-wheelers several years ago, but the city has enough confidence in new security measures that 1,000 communal bikes are slated to hit the streets before the millenium.

For golfers, Portland has more publicly owned gold courses per capita than any city in the U.S. Twenty 18-hole courses are within 20 miles of the city, but only half are public. Two of the three of the best are Heron Lakes and Eastmoreland. **Heron Lakes,** 3500 Victory Blvd., tel. (503) 289-1818, designed by Robert Trent Jones and 15 minutes from downtown. To get there, take exit 3078 off of I-5, head south of the expo center, and look for signs. The route here included the floodplain of the Vanport flood that obliterated a whole town in the late 1940s. **Eastmoreland Golf Course,** 2425 S.E. Bybee Blvd., tel. (503) 775-2900, is located near the Crystal Springs Rhododendron Garden and also features a driving range. Portland public courses average around $20 for 18 holes. **Pumpkin Ridge,** US 26, N. Plains exit, tel. (503) 647-4747, was *Golf Digest*'s number one public, number two private course in 1992. On weekdays, greens fees for their public course, Ghost Creek, are $60, or $75 on weekends.

Whitewater enthusiasts may want to note there are four columns of ads in the Yellow Pages under Rafts and Raft Trips. Local companies renting rafts (and usually kayaks as well) include **River Trails,** tel. (503) 667-1964, **Polzel,** tel. (503) 761-0188, and **Alder Creek,** tel. (503) 285-0464. In like measure, those interested in salmon fishing in the Willamette near downtown can also access fishing guides and boats from the Yellow Pages. The spring chinook run can be a highlight, assuming no restrictions have been enacted.

Portland Parks and Recreation, tel. (503) 823-3189 for information, oversees the city's 115 tennis courts. The best public courts in terms of surface and surrounding environment are located up the hill from the Rose Garden in Washington Park. They are free of charge. To get there from downtown, take Burnside west up the hill. About a mile past N.W. 23rd, hang a sharp left (feels almost like a U-turn) at the light onto Tichner. Take the next right onto Kingston, and proceed for a minute or so to the parking lot adjacent to the tennis courts.

Skaters can follow in the tracks of Portland personality Tonya Harding and hit the ice at **Lloyd Center,** Weidler St./Multonmah Blvd. between N.E. 13th and N.E. 15th Streets, tel. (503) 288-6073, and **Clackamas Town Center,** 12000 S.E. 82nd Ave., tel. (503) 786-6000. For a couple bucks skate rental, you too can cut double axles in these practice venues. Call ahead for hours.

U-pick and Farmer's Markets

The *Tri-County Farm Fresh Produce Guide,* tel. (503) 324-4990, lists dozens of U-pick outlets and farm-fresh fruit stands in the Clackamas (Washington), and Multnomah County areas. Addresses, phone numbers, hours, and maps are available in this free guide. Pick one up at Powell's Travel at Pioneer Square or at the main store. The best months to find produce items are also annotated in the guide. The **Ripe and Ready Hotline,** tel. (503) 226-4112, can further help you locate outlets.

Here are several Portland-area markets: **Portland Farmer's Market,** Albers Mill parking lot, 1200 N.W. Naito Pkwy., tel. (503) 231-2880, Look for famous local chefs giving cooking demonstrations here in summer months.

Beaverton Farmer's Market, S.W. 15th St. and Hall Blvd., behind the Fire Station, and **Saturday Market** (see "Down By the Riverside" under "Getting Oriented: Portland Neighborhoods," above). These markets operate on weekends, usually 8 a.m.-1 p.m. through October.

Finding the Portland market can be difficult. The easiest way is to get on Naito Pkwy. and head north till your view of the sky is blocked by the Broadway Bridge. Then look for the Albers Mill building, with its name emblazoned near the top of the edifice.

During the week, farm-fresh produce is available at **People's All Organic Farmers Market,** 3029 S.E. 21st Ave., Wednesday 2-7 p.m., May through the first hard frost, and at **Portland Farmers Market,** Pioneer Courthouse Square, Wednesday 11 a.m.-3 p.m., July through the end of November.

Our favorite outlet for fresh produce is the Hollywood Farmer's Market, located in the Bank parking lot on N.E. 44th Ave. and Tillamook, just north of Sandy Blvd. and minutes from downtown. This is a more easily accessible market than the Albers Mill downtown market which many find difficult to locate. It's also a smaller affair, but you can still find homemade goat cheese, live music, gourmet wild mushrooms, fresh berries, master gardener consultations, and children's activities. Hours are 8 a.m.-1 p.m., and may change seasonally.

EVENTS

The **Portland Rose Festival,** tel. (503) 228-9411, has been the major wingding here for nine decades. The Rose Queen and her court (chosen from local high school entrants), sailors and prostitutes, and floats from several parades clog Portland's traffic arteries during this 24-day citywide celebration each June. Air shows, a hot-air balloon classic, the Indy World Series car race, and a traditional rose show round out the big doin's. The flier available at POVA has more information about what is essentially a small town festival done with big town flair. Even if parades and crowds are not your thing, the spirit of civic pride here is genuine and appealing. Portlanders camp out along the parade route in the same places year after year, some-

times several days in advance just to catch a coveted glimpse at the floats passing by.

The key to enjoying festival events is avoiding traffic and parking hassles. A $3.25 Tri-Met pass is good for unlimited rides on MAX or the bus all day long, for the passholder and up to three kids, six and under. As for traffic, be especially wary of the waterfront. Such festival features as food booths and carnival rides in Tom McCall Park, as well as military ship displays on the Willamette, draw crowds reminiscent of lemmings to the sea. Another good reason to come to the waterfront is the chance to see the dragon boat races. These brightly painted ceremonial canoes from China have been taken up in earnest here. With 16 paddlers and a coxswain, teams compete on the Willamette River. Call the Rose Festival information line for more details.

Two of the more colorful offshoots of the June fête are the **Grand Floral Parade** and the **Festival of Flowers** at Pioneer Courthouse Square. In the latter event, all manner of colorful blossoms fill the square to overflowing. This bouquet is on display during the first week of the several-week celebration. As for the Grand Floral Parade, this usually begins the Saturday following the opening of the festival. The floats combine the beauty of flowers with high-tech wizardry in aesthetically whimsical creations. You can reserve seats in the Coliseum for, $7.50-15, but save your money and station yourself on an upper floor along the parade route or visit the floats at Oregon Square between Lloyd Center and the Convention Center during the week following the parade. Any lofty perch is sufficient for taking in all the hoopla, drill teams, Rose Queen, and equestrian demonstrations. This procession is the second-largest all-floral parade in the United States. **Gray Line,** tel. (503) 285-9845, features a package that spares you the hassles of parking and traffic as well as offering great parade seats and breakfast at the Coliseum, all at a very fair price. The Starlight Parade is another winner. Parade route restaurants such as Bucks Cafe on Burnside set up tables outside to take in the festivities. The parades and the flower displays prove that in Rose Festivals, as in life, the best things are free.

Also in June (through mid-July) is **Chamber Music Northwest,** Reed College Commons,

3203 S.E. Woodstock Ave., tel. (503) 229-6400, presenting concerts for five weeks nightly except Sunday. Music begins at 8 p.m. and people picnic beforehand. Enjoy strawberry shortcake at intermission. Tickets to this nationally acclaimed series range $12-27. In addition to the concerts at Reed, performances take place at Catlin Gabel School. To get there from downtown, head west on Burnside. This will become Barnes Rd. where you'll see a sign for the school about five miles west of the Rose Garden turnoff near St. Vincent's Hospital.

In July, check out the **Multnomah County Fair,** Oak Park in Sellwood, tel. (503) 222-2223. The prize bulls, cowpokes, and carnival midway may still be there, but the fair has ventured into the great beyond of multicultural diversity. In the Fair's present incarnation you're likely to find an authentic American Indian powwow, Mexican folk ballet, and a photo exhibit with well-known professionals. In addition, you'll be able to enjoy Latin combos and jazz groups as well as an array of international cuisines alongside the expected country music and cotton candy. The usual hours are Wed.-Sat. noon-11 p.m., Sunday noon-9 p.m., admission is $5, students 6-12 years old are $2. Funding problems threaten the survival of this longtime tradition.

An August festival, **The Bite,** Tom McCall Waterfront Park, tel. (503) 248-0600, lets you sample local culinary specialties of Portland restaurants, with the proceeds going to the Special Olympics. Live music is also featured. Another palate-pleasing August affair is the **Oregon Brewers Festival** described in the Food section of the General Introduction.

Cinco de Mayo celebrates the Mexican Revolution and hispanic pride at Waterfront Park the first weekend (including Thursday and Friday) in May. This has become the largest celebration of its kind in the country. Mariachis, folk dance exhibitions, a large selection of Mexican food, and fireworks displays are included in the festivities. Portland was ranked eighth in a 1997 survey as a city hospitable to hispanics. This is Oregon's largest minority and their presence is evident in the recent proliferation of taquerias, some of which have a presence at the festival. Admission is $4.

The **Wintering-In Festival** at Howell Territorial Park, Sauvie Island, tel. (503) 222-1741, happens near the autumnal equinox. Enjoy fresh farm produce, crafts, and music at the restored pioneer homestead (see "Sauvie Island," above).

In October, watch the salmon spawn at Oxbow Park in the Sandy River Gorge outside Gresham. Old-growth walks, an eight-km run, and a barbecue as well as arts and crafts round out this fête. To get there from downtown, take I-84 east to the Wood Village exit. Turn south on Division and east on Oxbow Parkway, then follow the signs to Oxbow Park. There's a $6 fee per vehicle and a $7 additional charge for lunch and activities. Festival goers will tell you that a rainy day seems to encourage salmon-spawning activity. Call (503) 248-5050 for more information. Anglers are kept busy with spawning runs of coho, fall, and spring Chinook salmon, and winter and summer steelhead trout. Hours are 10:30-5 Sat.-Sun.

The day after Thanksgiving, a Christmas tree is lit in Pioneer Square and a skating rink installed. Skate rentals are available and a small admission is charged. The best Christmas lights display is on Peacock Lane in southeast Portland near beautiful Laurelhurst Park, 29th and Stark; check at the visitor and convention bureau for more details.

The **Grotto's Festival of Lights,** N.E. 85th and Sandy Blvd., tel. (503) 254-7371, is a Christmas event with 100,000 lights including animated lighting displays, narrated fiber-optic displays, and other illuminated depictions of the life of Christ. This is the largest choral festival in the Pacific Northwest and is set amid gorgeous surroundings, making a very special holiday event. Admission is $4.50.

Finally, a Portland event that's sure to please is the annual parade of Christmas ships. Boats with lights creating images of a fire engine, Santa's sleigh, angels, and other fanciful designs parade on the Columbia and the Willamette. Portlanders line waterfront parks and restaurants to enjoy this spectacle which usually runs for about a week with the last night occuring December 23rd.

Tours

In a guide for independent travelers a listing of tours may seem out of place, but sometimes there are organized outings that provide insights unavailable elsewhere.

One such perspective is provided by a harbor cruise on a sternwheeler. This mode of transport

OREGON TOURISM DIVISION

The sternwheeler
Columbia Gorge *cruises*
Portland Harbor and the
Columbia River.

opened up the Willamette a century ago, and the 599-passenger **Columbia Gorge** and the smaller **Cascade Queen,** tel. (503) 223-3928, today. The Cascade Queen handles the cruises in Portland Harbor (departing from Riverplace Marina) and the Columbia Gorge does the trips in Cascade Locks in the region for which it is named. River cruises on the Willamette visit the Willamette greenway, an untouched area south of the city. Downriver trips pass city lights and ships bound for Pacific Rim ports. The Cascade Queen departs Riverplace Marina May 1-Sept 30, 3-5 p.m. Trips last about 2 hours and prices range from $12 for adults to $6 for ages 4-12.

There are a half dozen other sightseeing outfits plying the Columbia and Willamette, with several more reportedly about to enter the fray. As such, we refer the reader to the Sunday *Oregonian* travel section ad page for more information. We've confined our coverage to the Cascade Sternwheelers because of its longstanding niche in a market that will inevitably experience a thinning of the ranks in the coming years.

Ecotours of Oregon, 1906 S.W. Iowa St., tel. (503) 245-1428 or (888) TOURS-33, http://www.Ecotours-of-Oregon.com/Ecotours/, runs tours emphasizing ecological understanding while having a good time. Door-to-door van transport from anywhere in the Portland area,

lunch, and commentary are included in itineraries that run $45-60 per person per day. Packages about whalewatching, Indian culture, Mt. St. Helens, and old growth trees typify the refreshing focus of this small company. Trips are usually confined to vans of six with a professional naturalist-historian guide.

Another riverside perspective is available courtesy of the **Willamette Shore Trolley,** 2511 S.W. Moody St., tel. (503) 222-2226, an authentic vintage streetcar. The 30-mile roundtrip journey between Portland and the southern suburb of Lake Oswego lets you enjoy lush forest and parklands on the west bank of the Willamette that would otherwise be inaccessible. The east bank of the river is clearly visible, as are many interesting homes. Roundtrip fare is $5 for adults, $3 for ages 3-12. The trolley operates daily in summer and on weekends during winter.

The enclosed heated cars are best appreciated during winter, a season when the leaves are off the trees so views are unobstructed. Tours begin near Naito Pkwy. and Harbor Place and end up at 311 N. State St. in Lake Oswego. A vintage trolley runs at Christmastime in other parts of the city as an adjunct to existing mass transit. Call Tri-Met for details. Plans are also underway to connect RiverPlace to Union Station with a trolley line.

Close by Powell's Bookstore is a touring opportunity of special interest on a hot day. The **Blitz-Weinhard Brewery,** 1133 W. Burnside St., tel. (503) 222-4351, has free tours Mon.-Fri. Oct.-May at 12 p.m., 1:30 p.m., and 3 p.m. This is the oldest continuously operating brewery in the United States. Just register at the reception desk. The highlight of the brewery tour is of course the tasting room. Henrys makes excellent root beer as well.

Finally, there is **Gray Line of Portland,** P.O. Box 17306, 21320 N. Suttle, Portland 97217, tel. (503) 285-9845 or (800) 422-7042. Gray Line in most cities runs competent tours with experienced drivers. Portland's outfit is no exception. In addition to day-trips to such locales as Mt. Hood, the coast, and the Columbia River Gorge, three- and seven-hour city tours depart all year-long from Union Station. Half-day trips such as the Multnomah Falls/Columbia Gorge tour (about $20 per person) and full day trips like the Mt. Hood Loop (about $40 per person) are highly recommended. Skiers will want to inquire about their buses up to Mt Hood Meadows. Free weekly roundtrip shuttles to Chinook Winds Casino in Lincoln City on the coast is another interesting offering of this company. A trip to Mt. St. Helens is in the process of being formulated, call for details.

If you're interested in events and destinations that run the gamut from Crater Lake to the Pendleton Roundup, request their *Great Getaways* brochure detailing multi-day packages and daytrips all over the state. While calling to reserve is handy, consider stopping by their downtown offices (separate from the previous address and phone) in Union Station at S.W. 6th and Hoyt by the Broadway Bridge. They're located beyond the Amtrak ticket window near the Package Express. Not only will you be able to talk direcltely to a helpful ticket agent, but you'll also be able to pick up brochures and a free Portland tour map, an info-filled user-friendly layout of the city. Finally, be aware that Gray Line does free hotel pick-ups in conjunction with their tours in selected locations.

PRACTICALITIES

ACCOMMODATIONS

Portland poses no problem for those seeking accommodations at a good dollar value. A Hostelling International hostel, a traditional city-center landmark, a budget motel just over the bridge from the urban core, a high end-but-worth-it all suites hotel, a midtown "apartel," and personality-rich yet affordable B&Bs exemplify some of these alternatives.

Due to soaring occupancy rates, six new hotels are planned for the downtown business district in the next several years. Even half this number would help ease the current "room squeeze" that befalls many visitors April-October. With the projected Embassy Suites, West-in, Marriot, and the other developers serving upscale travelers and conventioneers, the pressure on other sectors of the market would be eased. Even still, travelers of all descriptions need to reserve well in advance for June, July, and August.

Some Surprises
The **Hostelling International,** 3031 S.E. Hawthorne Blvd., tel. (503) 236-3380, is the least-expensive, $13 members, $16 nonmembers, and one of the best-located places to stay in Portland. It's situated in among the restaurants and shops of the Hawthorne neighborhood and on the bus line, from downtown take bus no. 5 to 31st Ave.; from the airport take no. 12, then transfer to no. 5. Kitchen privileges and lots of restaurants nearby also recommend it. Make reservations for this large, rambling white hostelry in summer due to the influx of folks from other countries. A spacious screened-in back porch provides a cool place to sleep in July and August. A $1 all-you-can-eat pancake breakfast and a summer-time BBQ, $2, are appreciated extras here. It should also be mentioned that a day-use fee of $3 is invoked and some chores are required.

Adjunct services for hostel guests and other members of the traveling public are provided by **Hostelling International,** 1520 S.E. 37th Ave., Portland 97214, tel. (503) 235-9493. Guidebooks and a variety of day packs are sold here, free pamphlets are available, and resource people are on hand to provide assistance. Hostelling International also organizes van tours of the region, as well as recreational activities like skiing and whitewater rafting. The goods and services here are very reasonably priced.

Despite moderate rates, the **Mallory Hotel,** 729 S.W. 15th Ave. at Yamhill, Portland 97295, tel. (503) 223-6311 or (800) 228-8657, at first glance suggests a luxury lodging, with a lobby boasting ornate plaster, crystal chandeliers, and an elegant, skylit interior. The dining room's marble pillars and chandeliers sustain the four-star facade along with the elaborate jungle motif of the Driftwood Room Lounge. A location not far from the boutiques of the Northwest district and South Park Block cultural attractions also recommend it. With an address like this, the Mallory's free parking is also especially appreciated. Only the rather plain rooms might justify low prices of around $75 for a double. And if you're lucky enough to score one of the king-sized suites for $105, you'll probably walk away shaking your head in disbelief at this lodging value. A sister hotel, the **Imperial,** 400 S.W. Broadway, tel. (503) 228-7221 or (800) 452-2323, is another good buy in a comparable price range (rooms start at $85). The Imperial shares a location with hotels that charge double it own rate, close by the best of downtown shopping, galleries, and Pioneer Square.

The **Mark Spencer Hotel,** 409 S.W. 11th Ave., Portland, tel. (503) 224-3293 or (800) 548-3934, should be considered one of the best moderately priced, big city lodging values. For $72-109 you get a downtown location complete with tastefully furnished rooms with kichenettes near Powell's Books and Jake's Crawfish.

Hojo's Inn, 3939 N.E. Hancock, tel. (503) 288-6891, sits tucked away off Sandy Blvd. in Portland's Hollywood district. This motel (formerly the Jade Tree) recently became part of the Howard Johnson's chain, an East Coast outfit known for supplying the basics and then some at affordable prices. Proximity to restaurants,

PORTLAND ACCOMMODATIONS

5th Avenue Suites Hotel, 506 S.W. Washington, tel. (503) 222-0001 or (800) 711-2971, $140-225, pets, clean, spacious, and luxurious suites.

Best Western Pony Soldier Inn/Airport, 9901 N.E. Sandy Blvd., tel. (503) 256-1504 or (800) 634-7669, $90-99, restaurant/lounge, laundry, continental breakfast.

Clarion Hotel Airport, 6233 N.E. 78 Court, tel. (503) 251-2000 or (800) 994-7878, $70-100, covered pool, river view, laundry, continental breakfast.

Columbia River Doubletree, 1401 N. Hayden Island Dr., tel. (503) 283-2111 or (800) 222-TREE, $90-175, pool, restaurant/lounge, river views, cookies w/ check-in.

Comfort Inn/Convention Center, 431 N.E. Multnomah St., tel. (503) 233-7933 or (800) 228-5150, $50-125, covered pool, pets, continental breakfast.

Comfort Suites/Portland Airport, 12010 N.E. Airport Way, tel. (503) 261-9000 or (800) 216-5927, $60-80, covered pool, fireplaces, roomy units.

Courtyard by Marriott/Tigard, 15686 S.W. Sequoia Pky., tel. (503) 252-3200 or (800) 321-2211, $80-95, covered pool, laundry, continental breakfast.

Days Inn/City Center, 1414 S.W. 6th Ave., tel. (503) 221-1611 or (800) 899-0248, $75-150, restaurant/lounge, pool, laundry.

Econo Lodge Airport Inn, 9520 N.E. Sandy Blvd., tel. (503) 252-6666, $50-95, laundry, continental breakfast.

Econo Lodge Convention Center, 305 N. Broadway, tel. (503) 284-5181 or (800) 553-2666, $45-60.

Holiday Inn Convention Center, 1021 N.E. Grand Ave., tel. (503) 235-2100 or (800) 343-1822, $65-125, restaurant/lounge, weightroom.

Holdiay Inn Express, 9707 S.E. Stark, tel. (503) 252-7400 or (800) HOLIDAY, $60-80, weightroom, continental breakfast, new building.

Holiday Inn Express Airport, 11938 N.E. Airport Way, tel. (503) 251-9991 or (800) HOLIDAY, $65-110, laundry, continental breakfast, new building.

Holiday Inn/Portland Airport, 8439 N.E. Columbia Blvd., tel. (503) 256-5000 or (800) HOLIDAY, $80-250, restaurant/lounge, covered pool, laundry.

Quality Inn Hotel/Portland Airport, 8247 N.E. Sandy Blvd., tel. (503) 256-4111 or (800) 246-4649, $75-85, restaurant/lounge, pool, laundry, continental breakfast.

Ramada Inn/Portland Airport, 6221 N.E. 82nd Ave., tel. (503) 255-6511 or (800) 272, 6232, $75-105, restaurant/lounge, weightroom.

Doubletree Hotel Downtown, 310 S.W. Lincoln St., tel. (503) 221-0450 or (800) 222-TREE, $125-175, restaurant/lounge, live music, pool, laundry.

Doubletree Hotel Jantzen Beach, 909 Hayden Island Dr., tel. (503) 283-4466 or (800) 222-TREE, $85-175, restaurant/lounge, river view, pool, nice complex.

Doubletree Hotel Lloyd Center, 1000 N.E. Multnomah St., tel. (503) 281-6111 or (800) 222-TREE, $140-185, restaurant/lounge, pool, weightroom, laundry.

Doubletree Hotel Coliseum, 1225 N. Thunderbird Way, tel. (503) 235-8311 or (800) 222-TREE, $85-110, restaurant/lounge, pool, pets, river view.

Residence Inn by Marriott, 1710 N.E. Multnomah St., tel. (503) 288-1400 or (800) 331-3131, $90-155, pool, pets, kitchenettes, laundry, continental breakfast.

Rodeway Inn, 1506 N.E. 2nd Ave., (503) tel. 231-7665 or (800) 228-2000, $45-60, pets, laundry, continental breakfast.

Sheraton Portland Airport Hotel, 8235 N.E. Airport Way, tel. (503) 281-2500 or (800) 325-3535, $120-140, restaurant/lounge, covered pool, weightroom.

Super 8 Motel of Portland, 11011 N.E. Holman, tel. (503) 257-8988, tel. (800) 800-8000, $60-70, pets, laundry.

The Riverside, 50 S.W. Morrison, tel. (503) 221-0711 or (800) 899-0247, $110-140, restaurant/lounge, river view, nice downtown location.

movies, shopping, and the bus line (15 minutes from downtown on the no. 12 bus) comes along with clean, large, well-appointed rooms which range $45-60. Recent downside feedback about upkeep since the last edition will hopefully alleviate such problems as lingering tobacco odors and poor ventilation in the public areas here.

The opulent **White House Bed and Breakfast,** 1914 N.E. 22nd, Portland 97212, tel. (503) 287-7131, gives you the presidential treatment. Located just off Broadway near an avenue of shops and restaurants, only 5-10 minutes from Lloyd Center and downtown, this lovingly restored 1912 lumber baron's mansion has rates ranging from $100-125, double occupancy. The innkeeper's baked scones and other goodies at breakfast and tea, together with the complimentary sherry nightcap, impart the touch of home.

Another B&B in Northeast Portland's Irvington neighborhood is the **Portland Guest House,** 1720 N.E. 15th, tel. (503) 282-1402. The broad tree-shaded avenues of this area and its proximity to excellent restaurants on Broadway would alone dictate mention of this alternative to downtown hotels. While the high-ceiling Victorian elegance and summer blueberries from the garden for breakfast are enticements to many, it's the room tariff that often closes the deal, $45 single, $55-85 double. The owner says there's always quite a run on the single rooms from small business people traveling on their own nickel, so be sure to book well in advance. The availability of rooms with private baths as well as easy access to the bus line compel further consideration of this B&B.

The **5th Avenue Suites Hotel,** 506 S.W Washington, tel. (800) 711-2971, is the latest big player in the luxury hotel sweepstakes. At $135 a double, it's less expensive than its downtown counterparts with more spacious rooms and such extras as complimentary wine every evening in the lobby. It is arguably the most central location in town and has an affordable restaurant, The Red Star Grill, emphasizing gourmet interpretations of American food. Everything combined, the 5th Avenue Suites Hotel is a winning formula.

In the same price range, is the **Portland Hilton,** 921 S.W. 6th Ave., tel. (503) 226-1611. Business travelers will appreciate newly remodeled rooms, generous corporate rates, frequent flyer plan compatibility, a complete business center, a state-of-the-art health club, and a miracle-working concierge. An exceptional rooftop restaurant (see Alexander's in "Food" section) and a location in the heart of the theater district across the street from Niketown are other extras that rate thumbs up with the modern-day road warrior.

Eclectic Lodging Choices

For those who enjoy rural serenity within commuting distance of downtown, there's camping in **Milo McIver State Park,** 24101 South Entrance Rd., Estacada 97013, tel. (503) 695-2261. Set on the banks of the Collowash River (five miles northwest of Estacada), you're 25 miles from downtown Portland, but this retreat seems farther away, particularly when you're gazing at the knockout sunset view of Mt. Hood here. To get there, take I-84 east to I-205 south and follow the exit to ORE 224/Estacada. The road forks right at the town of Carver to go 10 miles to the campground. There are 44 hookup sites, flush toilets, showers, firewood, and a laundromat here, as well as fishing for winter steelhead and late-fall salmon. Other recreation includes hiking and horse trails and a boat ramp. Mt. Hood ski slopes are an hour east of the park. Bagby Hot Springs (no charge, but lock your car) and the trail to it through an old-growth forest are other attractions within an hour's drive off ORE 224. Campground fees are $12 per night with no reservations, and it's open year-round.

Another camping option about 35 miles east of Portland off I-84 is Ainsworth State Park, tel. (503) 695-2261. Picnic tables, fire rings, flush toilets, and an RV camp enhance a prime location near the trails and waterfalls of the Columbia River Gorge. The nightly rate is $18 on a first-come, first serve basis. You can get there via The Columbia Gorge Scenic Highway (see Introduction to Columbia River Gorge chapter) or by taking exit 35 off I-84 East.

Finally, if your funds are low and you just need a place to bed down for the night that is hygenic and safe, try **Warner Pacific College dormitories.** The college rents out dorm rooms June 15-Sept. 1 for $12 s, $22 d per night. The campus is in the 2200 block of S.E. 68th St. and asks for advance reservations by phone, tel. (503) 775-4366. Overnight guests must supply their own bedding on otherwise bare mattresses. In addition, they request no smoking, drinking, or pets in their dorms, and they are separated by sex.

FOOD

Portland's renaissance has resulted in the highest number of restaurants per capita of any city in the country. Perhaps more impressive is the fact that you can have a singular dining experience for much less than you'd pay for a gourmet outing in either Seattle or San Francisco. Even the traditionally overpriced bland food served in many hotel dining rooms can often turn out to be affordable and tasty. In like measure, downtown street carts serve what is often gourmet fare at fast food prices. Also noteworthy are local chains of ethnic fast food as well as a profusion of microbreweries and gourmet coffee outlets. The following cross section leaves the description of many upscale restaurants to such dining guides as *Portland's Best Places* (Sasquatch Press) and the pages of *Bon Appetit* magazine. What's left are places with personality and a sense of fun geared to the budget of the average traveler.

Ethnic Eateries
According to news analysis from the previous decade, Portland has the highest percentage of white to minority citizens of any large U.S. city. This is changing however, if the increase in the number of ethnic eateries here is any indication.

Large portions of ribs, Hawaiian stir-fry, and a blast of hot-sweet flavors served in a bustling friendly atmosphere has made **Noho's Hawaiian Cafe**, S.E. Clinton and 26th, tel. (503) 233-5301, the dining hub of an up-and-coming "hip strip" of antique shops, quirky restaurants, and an avant garde theater. Huge-portioned entrees averaging $6-10 (priciest entree is butterflied shrimp with oyster sauce, $11.95) and occasional live music explain the lines of waitlist diners that extend out the door on weekend nights. The last Sunday of each month boasts the longest lines when Noho's dish up the house specialty, Kahlua pig. Noho's has another outlet in Corvallis near the OSU campus.

While not for the faint of palate, the dim sum at **Fong Chong,** 301 N.W. 4th, tel. (503) 220-0235, is one of the more exotic low-cost dining adventures in the city. It all begins at 11 a.m. every day, when carts of steaming Cantonese delicacies come whooshing down the aisles. Even if the mumbled explanations of the barely bilingual staff don't translate, the array of crepes and buns stuffed with chicken, shrimp, pork, and other fillings are so varied and cost so little (averaging $1.85 per plate) that you can't miss. After 3 p.m. the restaurant reverts to unadventurous Cantonese fare. The adjoining Asian grocery is always fascinating.

Across the bridge to the northeast, near Lloyd Center, **Saigon Kitchen,** 835 N.E. Broadway, tel. (503) 281-3669, improves upon Fong Chong's functional decor and replicates the bountiful servings and reasonable prices. Although Vietnamese flavors predominate, Thai dishes like beef in coconut juice and basil leaves and ginger chicken are highlights. The $4.50 lunch specials Mon.-Fri. are an especially good value. Dinner combination plates in the $8-10 range might include such uncommon specialties as squid in garlic sauce or charcoal chicken with lettuce, mint, cilantro, rice papers, and peanut sauce. Another exotic mainstay is coconut lemongrass soup (at $7.45 feeding several people) This restaurant has always been the darling of Portland's alternative weeklies, which rightfully extol its spring rolls. A serving of three of these at lunch comes to your table all chopped up and ready for dipping into the restaurant's hot-sweet fish sauce—a wonderful light meal in the $4 range.

Chang's Mongolian Grill, 1 S.W. 3rd Ave., tel. (503) 243-2700, among a half dozen other outlets, is based on an intriguing concept that can best be described as Chinese-style burritos cooked to order. Each outlet of the chain features a colorful Genghis Khan mural backdropping a stagestruck chef who cooks your hand-picked ingredients on a large domed grill. Mooshu pancakes with plum sauce and other condiments are stacked tableside for you to wrap the just-cooked fixin's, and you can return to the grill for as many fresh veggies, thin-sliced raw meats, and fish as you like. Pickled cabbage, soup, and tea come with the meal. All-you-can-eat lunches cost $6.50 and dinners cost $8.50.

While pan-Asian places seem to abound all over town, purists may prefer to journey to the source, the neighborhood between N.E. 50th and N.E.70th along Sandy Blvd., the vortex of Portland's southeast Asian business community. Here, at **Zien Hong,** 5314 N.E. Sandy Blvd., tel. (503) 288-2743, and **Yen Ha,** 6820 N.E. Sandy Blvd., tel. (503) 287-3698, Vietnamese, Chinese, and Thai influences assert themselves in the cuisine of each kitchen. Extensive menus, low prices, and high quality distinguish both restaurants. Zien Hong's soups, $4, are meals in themselves, and Yen Ha's meat dishes (the house specialty is bo nuong vi— marinated beef grilled tableside for $11.95) are particularly noteworthy. Zien Hong's late-night hours are especially appreciated on the east side of the Willamette River, where most restaurants close by 10 p.m.

Several other restaurants nearby are dedicated to pho, a Vietnamese beef noodle soup. For just a few bucks, you get a big bowl (other soups and entrees are also usually offered) that's sure to satisfy. **Pho 54,** 6852 N.E. Sandy Blvd., comes recommended. In any case, Portland's large Vietnamese community has graced the Rose City with some of the best purveyors of this cuisine outside Saigon, so sayeth *New Yorker* food philosopher Calvin Trillin.

Sushi in Portland ranges from elaborate eateries catering to Japanese businessmen to gourmet sections of supermarkets. A good sushi bar for the neophyte is **Yoko's,** 2878 S.E. Gladstone, tel. (503) 736-9928. Located in the southeast not far from Reed College, this is sushi creatively put together for American palates. We recommend the Oregon Roll (eight pieces of smoked salmon, cucumber, lettuce, and sushi rice wrapped up in dried seaweed for $3.50) and the spicy tuna roll (eight pieces of spicy tuna, cucumber, daikon radish, and sushi rolled up in seaweed for $3.65) as good places to start. At night, dinner entrees supplement the sushi menu.

The **Bangkok Kitchen,** 2534 S.E. Belmont, tel. (503) 236-7349, is the kind of place Portlanders have up their sleeve to catch visiting Thai-food aficionados by surprise. No one would ever guess that behind the walls of a fifties diner facade, authentic Thai food is served, drenched in hot-sweet fish sauce and a peanut-and-chili-

pepper blend that'll make you cry out in both pain and ecstasy. Don't specify "hot" here unless you're still on novocaine after a dental appointment. With minimal caution, however, you can enjoy one of the best restaurant values in Oregon. We recommend the whole fish cooked in chili paste. You'll pay the market price for this specialty which generally exceeds the $8-10 entree price range that prevails here.

A few blocks down (facing Morrison St.), the "hot zone" is still in force at **Sweetwater Jam House,** 3350 S.E. Morrison St., tel. (503) 233-0333. The restaurant's Carribean-inspired fare is not only hot on the tastebuds, but Sweetwater's recipe of bright colored decor and a muted reggae soundtrack have encouraged many a rain-soaked Portlander to burn a path to this oasis from winter-time dreariness. If such specialties as conch fritters and curried goat don't conjure visions of Bahama beachfronts, then try the Island Skewer (chicken shish kebabs in a pineapple-ginger marinade on coconut rice). The "fall-off-the-bone" ribs have a piquant sauce worthy of any beach barbecue. Add such accompaniments as plantain, cassava, yam, and an assortment of deliciously dangerous rum-based drinks, and you can experience a Carribean vacation without packing your bags. In any case, leave room for habanero cream custard at the end of your meal.

A small northern Indian restaurant on the corner of 11th Ave. and S.W. Morrison has become the talk of Portland's cost-conscious gourmets. The $5.95 buffet lunch at **India House,** 1038 S.W. Morrison St., tel. (503) 274-1017, lets you load up your plate with a variety of vegetable curries, samosas (triangular potato pastries with flaky crust), tandoori chicken, basmati rice, and salads.

Indian food connoisseurs will tell you this cuisine is distinguished by the diner's being able to taste a number of individual spices in one dish, a quality in ample evidence in many India House specialties. You'll even notice this fanfare of flavors in a kind of bread served here. Naan is an unleavened bread cooked in a tandoor oven, a superhot barbecue pit lined with clay. The toasty texture and slight mesquite aftertaste come through with your first bites, and thereafter, the complexities of other flavors assert themselves. The Keema naan, for example, is redolent with cumin and mustard seed, beneath flecks of lamb and butter on top. You can cool your tongue off with the Darjeeling tea and rice pudding for dessert, well-chosen accompaniments to finish off this budget banquet.

Jarra's, 1435 Hawthorne, tel. (503) 230-8990, was Portland's first introduction to Ethiopian food and its mouth-burning stews known as wat. This may be the hottest food in the state, but the flavors of lamb, beef, and chicken assert themselves through the peppers. The spongy enjera bread that accompanies your meal also manages to soak up some of the heat. Dinner will cost less that $9 here, but be prepared to buy an extra drink to cool off your tastebuds.

A good way to judge a Mexican restaurant is by its chiles rellenos. If a place can make this popular dish with a light, crisp batter so as not to mute the taste of the chile pepper and melted cheese, chances are it can pull off the whole enchilada in fine style. **Chez Jose,** 8502 S.W. Terwilliger Blvd., tel. (503) 244-0007, passes this test and probably meets any other standard you might use to judge a Mexican restaurant. You'll also appreciate such touches as being asked if you prefer your order hot or mild, as well as the use of Oregon's famous Tillamook cheddar along with the traditional Monterey jack in many recipes. Best of all, a sumptuous combination plate here can feed two people for around $8. If you want to stray from the old reliables of Mexican food, try such entrees as squash enchilada with peanut sauce, or marinated prawns with chile and honey sauce. For a few bucks more you can order a serving of Mexican chocolate ice cream with a cinnamon aftertaste that recalls the flavor of hot chocolate south of the border. Another branch of Chez Jose is located at N.E. 22nd and Broadway.

Dozens of Mexican taquerias have recently arrived on the scene, serving the true stuff in classic down-home style. **La Sirenita,** 2817 N.E. Alberta St., tel. (503) 335-8283, and **Mi Ranchito,** 2839 N.E. Alberta St., tel. (503) 331-1774, a few doors down attract a largely Spanish-speaking clientele who crave such specialties as birria (shredded goat meat) tacos and machaca burritos containing seasoned, stringy beef with scrambled eggs, tomato, onion, refried beans, and cheese. There's also the more conventional Mexican dishes you'd find in other Mexican restaurants (tacos, enchiladas, chiles rellenos, etc.) except the food's better, portions larger, and the prices lower. Farther east, hikers might spice up their trip with stops at **El Burrito Loco,** 3126 N.E. 82nd Ave., tel. (503) 252-1343, **Taqueria Chavez,** 5703 S.E. 82nd., tel. (503) 777-2282, and **Iguana Feliz,** 10820 N.E. Sandy Blvd, tel. (503) 257-9875.

Maya's Taqueria, 1000 S.W. Morrison, tel. (503) 226-1946, offers well-rendered Mexican fast food ranging from chiles rellenos to chicken mole enchiladas, $6-8. The Mexican beer and refrescos and the best array of salsas in Portland also make this elaborate taco stand seem closer to the Guadalajara marketplace than to Pioneer Courthouse Square. On warm days, sit outside to people-watch and admire the Mexican-style murals. **Santa Fe Taqueria,** 831 N.W. 23rd Ave., tel. (503) 226-0406, is Maya's outlet in the stylish Northwest barrio. **Aztec Willie's** carries the banner for Maya's on Broadway, across from Ron Paul's on N.E. 15th, with a price range around $5-8 for entrees.

South-of-the-border flavors are also served up at **Macheesmo Mouse,** 723 S.W. Salmon St., has a cooking style that's heart-smart and nutritious. Many items list calorie count and come with brown rice and whole-grain tortillas. Thanks to fresh salsa and the Cajun flavors of the restaurant's own Boss Sauce, healthy fast food never tasted so good. This is one of Portland's best bets for a satisfying meal in the $5 range. Macheesmo Mouse has these other outlets as well: 811 N.W. 23rd Ave., tel. (503) 274-0500; 3500 S.E. Hawthorne Blvd., tel. (503) 232-5688; 1200 N.E. Broadway, tel. (503) 249-0002.

A few blocks off N.E. Burnside you'll find the best Tex-Mex food in the city. Behind the hole-in-the-wall facade of a neighborhood beer joint, **Esparza's Cafe,** 2725 S.E. Ankeny St., tel. (503) 234-7909, welcomes you with mahogany booths and a "Back in the Saddle Again" decor. Begin your meal here with nachos—slivers of chicken under melted cheese and jalapeño peppers, all of which appear to have been proportioned and positioned on each individual chip to maximize flavor. While other *antojitos* (traditional appetizers and snacks) demonstrate similar flair, it's the brisket in chile colorado sauce, scrambled huevos rancheros, and diced nopalito cactus lightly dusted with cornmeal that'll evoke El Paso-

Juarez for those who have been there. If you haven't, forgo Otis and Aretha on the jukebox for a norteño polka to accompany Esparza's flavors of the *frontera*. Dinner entrees run $8-12.

Cafe Azul, 112 N.W. Ninth Ave., tel. (503) 525-4422, is not just another taqueria. Chances are you've never had Mexican food like this before. Tinga pie (a chicken and vegetable pastry seasoned with herbs, currants, and smoked chipotle chilies) and cochinita pibil (marinated pork tacos with stringy red onions doused in orange juice) typify what may be best described as gourmet interpretations of peasant fare. Little known ingredients, often indigenous to Central and Southern Mexico, spice up complex moles (a chocolate-based BBQ sauce), stews, and other dishes in a menu that changes with the seasons. Such Northwest "takes" on this theme as wild mushroom empanada use the regional bounty of fresh produce to full advantage. Reassuringly familiar accompaniments like cinnamony Mexican hot chocolate, guacamole, and flan may help you get your culinary bearings here, but most of the time only your tastebuds will be your guide. In like measure, your server will encourage wine instead of the beer that traditionally complements Mexican food. The end result is a memorable meal created by a chef trained at the venerable Chez Panisse.

Until this decade, Portland was the Bermuda Triangle for lovers of Italian food. Unless you wanted to spend upwards of $40 per person at **Genoa,** 2832 S.E. Belmont, tel. (503) 228-1464, the top Italian restaurant in the Northwest according to Zagat and *Gourmet* magazine, there was a shortage of first-rate pasta houses geared to the budget of the average traveler. Thanks to a resurgence led by **Pazzo,** 627 S.W. Washington, tel. (503) 228-1515, Italian food has finally carved out a niche. Pazzo's insistence on local fresh produce, meats, and fish has resulted in such creative dishes as smoked salmon ravioli in lemon cream with asparagus, $15, and a pizza appetizer with roasted garlic and cambozola cheese, $6. Celebrities in town for a movie shoot and locals in search of something more than just spaghetti and meatballs typify the clientele. Great desserts and low-priced gourmet take-out items can be found at **Pazzorria Bakery** next door.

Look for more of the same in Portland's version of Little Italy, the Nob Hill district, encompassing the blocks between N.W. 21st and N.W. 23rd Avenues. **Il Fornaio,** 115 N.E. 22nd Ave., tel. (503) 248-9400, has an ambitious menu (pasta entrees $10-20) backed up by an on-site bakery (excellent for breakfast) in this airy outpost of Italian regional specialties. **Basta's,** 410 N.W. 21st, tel. (503) 274-1572, and **Caffe Mingo,** 807 N.W. 21st Ave., tel. (503) 226-4646, serve up heartier peasant fare that'll deliciously stretch a dollar (budget gourmets will especially appreciate Caffe Mingo's wine list) and your stomach while you rub elbows (literally) with an interesting cross section of Portlanders.

Delfina's, 2112 N.W. Kearney, tel. (503) 221-1195, the originator of this neighborhood love affair with Italian food, is more refined and slighty pricier version of the foregoing. Baguettes from all these downtown eateries are often seen gracing picnic spreads of locals who've discovered that Portland's westside Italian restaurants have the best "in-house" bakeries in town.

Paparazzi's, 2015 N.E. Broadway, tel. (503) 281-7701, features almost two dozen pasta dishes, neopolitan pizza (thin crust, light toppings), great minestrone soup, and the friendliness of a neighborhood trattoria (main dishes $7.50-15). **Il Piatto,** 2348 S.E. Ankey, tel. (503) 236-4997, is another attractive, moderately priced intimate neighborhood place. However, Il Piatto stands out for its artful decor and such culinary flights of fancy as house-made black ravioli filled with rock shrimp, fennel, and spinach smothered in a sauce of spicy roasted corn, peppers, carmelized red onions, white wine and parmesan cheese. White bean salad with proscuitto-wrapped prawns is another popular item whenever it appears on the menu.

Pizza styles from Chicago, New York, and other locales are represented in the Pacific Northwest. Out-of-towners can expect to pay $2.25 a slice on the average and get a greater variety of toppings than what's usually seen elsewhere.

Pizza in Portland means **Escape From New York,** 622 N.W. 23rd Ave., tel. (503) 227-5423, if you're an east coast purist who likes foldable crust, copious cheese, and conventional toppings. If you're not averse to paying a little more for your pizza (from $2.75/slice), head to one of **Pizzicato's** half-dozen outlets around town, 705 N.W. Alder, tel. (503) 226-1007, 28 N.E. Burnside, tel. (503) 236-0045, where exotic condiments on the order of lamb, sausage, chanterelle and shitake mushrooms, and rock shrimp make a meal out of a slice. For price, selection, and a stimulating campus ambience, **Hot Lips Pizza,** 1909 S.W. 6th, tel. (503) 224-0311, near Portland State University is a good choice. On the eastside, **It's a Beautiful Pizza,** 3341 S.E. Belmont, tel. (503) 233-5444, has psychedelic decor, live music, and some of the best pies in the city (from $2.50/slice). These also might be the most filling slices around.

Another place for pizza is the **Bridgeport Brew Pub,** 1313 N.W. Marshall St., tel. (503) 241-7179. The malt-based pizza crust with olives, chorizo, yellow peppers, and eggplant washed down by Blue Heron or Coho Pacific ale can only be described as quintessential Portland. For $3 you can sample seven distinct beers made by Oregon's first microbrewery. On warm days, the outdoor loading dock that serves as the brewery's "picnic area" feels like a millionaire's patio after the second glass.

At the edge of Old Town is a Portland institution. Joie de vivre is in the air when you step into **Alexis,** 215 W. Burnside, tel. (503) 224-8577, but it's not just the retsina, Greek music, and folk dancing that keep people coming back. This is the best Greek food in Oregon. Appetizers like calamari or saganaki (fried cheese) might start your meal here. You can spend an evening just ordering appetizers and enjoying the crusty bread, but it would be a shame to forgo such entrees, $9-13, as the moussaka and oregano chicken. On weekends this moderately priced taverna features belly dancing and an atmosphere that'll bring out the Zorba in anyone.

Portland is starting to see many quality middle eastern restaurants, but we'd like to recommend an "old reliable." **Al Amir,** 223 S.W. Stark, tel. (503) 274-0010, a long-time dinner favorite, is located on the periphery of Old Town in the dark paneled elegance of the former home of Portland's archbishop (circa 1879). Its down-to earth prices belie the fancy digs. The menu emphasizes Lebanese specialties, and there's live jazz 10 p.m.-1 a.m. Friday. The lentil soup with plenty of cumin, baba ghanoush (an eggplant dip), lamb kabobs, and rich, garlicky hummus are standouts. A mezza plate, $15, lets you sample a variety of items including hummus, baba ghanoush, and tabouleh.

Garbonzo's, 2074 N.W. Lovejoy St., tel. (503) 227-4169, is the place to go for late-night middle eastern food. Falafel, spinach pie, and other specialties are prepared a la carte (averaging $4) or come with such "salads" as hummus and tabouleh (w/ entree, around $7). The most expensive item on the menu is lamb kebabs with salads, $8.50. For a lighter meal, Garbonzo's lentil soup with an order of tabouleh is recommended. Eastside diners can also enjoy this healthy fare at 3343 S.E. Hawthorne, tel. (503) 239-6087. These places are open till 3:30 a.m. Fri-Sat. nights, and till 1:30 a.m. the rest of the week.

Eye-Openers

Although lunch is also served at the **Bijou Cafe,** 132 S.W. 3rd Ave., tel. (503) 222-3187, it has built its reputation on breakfast (mostly in the $6 range). While fried cinnamon bread and red snapper hash, $7.25, are morning mainstays in this airy cafe, ordinary breakfast food like scrambled eggs, hash browns, muffins, and oatmeal are done perfectly here with the freshest and most nutritious ingredients. As for the latter, Bijou patrons appreciate the restaurant's emphasis on organic produce and whole-grain products for no more than it would cost to eat at a highway truckstop.

La Patisserie, 208 N.W. Couch, tel. (503) 248-9898, is a second-floor walk-up coffee-house whose windows overlook Old Town, one of the best people-watching neighborhoods in the city. You can also enjoy a tasty and sumptuous breakfast for little more than $5.

Step into tradition at **Zell's,** 1300 S. E. Morrison, tel. 239-0196, a longtime eastside favorite. A late Sunday repast of German pancakes washed down by Zell's excellent Irish coffee is guaranteed to put a spring in your step. Also recommended are the salmon Benedict and any of the blackboard specials. Later on, lighter appetites will appreciate the spinach salad with smoked salmon. Entrees average $7.50.

The three-course, Jewish-style Sunday brunch has helped establish **Bread and Ink,** 3610 S.E. Hawthorne, tel. (503) 239-4756, as *the* gathering place in the Hawthorne neighborhood. If lox, borscht, and the like are not your weekend repast of choice, there's always an assortment of homemade breads and imaginative omelettes to sustain you. Later on in the week, lunchtime diners line up for a massive burger topped with Gruyère cheese and Bermuda onion. Breakfast can run in the $7-11 range.

Portland's most famous breakfast haunt is the **Original Pancake House,** 8600 S.W. Barbur Blvd., tel. (503) 246-9007. This Wed.-Sat. operation has spawned many imitations, but the Original is still the greatest. If you're without a car, take bus no. 38 from downtown. The restaurant opens at 7 a.m., but be there early on weekends. Latecomers should bring a book because waits for seating can be excruciatingly long. Once at the table, the famous apple pancake is a Frisbee-sized cinnamon-laced delight for the growing boy or girl. Lighter appetites can choose from among 20 varieties including the Tahitian Maiden's dream (with fruits and liqueurs) and our favorite, the fresh (local) strawberry pancake in season underneath a dollop of whipped cream. There's also four gourmet omelettes on the menu. Despite the Fifties knotty pine walls, expect to pay around $8 for breakfast—not bad for a place James Beard and Art Buchwald once ranked as among the top ten restaurants in the nation.

Not far from the Original Pancake House is **Marco's,** 7910 S.W. 35th, tel. (503) 245-0199, located in a cluster of antique shops, boutiques, and cafes known as Multnomah Village. Intriguing omelette combinations for $6, wonderful home-fries, and a culinary approach that keeps nutritional concerns foremost makes the 12-minute trip by car (exit 296 off I-5) or 20 minutes by bus (lines 41 and 45) from downtown worth it. After breakfast, go around the corner to Annie Bloom's books for regional titles and a wide-ranging selection. Later on, come back to Marco's for lunch or dinner, saving room for coconut mango cheesecake.

At the **Cadillac Cafe,** 914 N.E. Broadway, tel. (503) 287-4750, if the Fleetwood-fin-shaped logo and shocking-pink color scheme don't wake you up in the morning, the first-rate breakfast will. The thematic continuity of the restaurant's decor, along with fresh flowers and clean architectural lines, bespeak the same attention to detail that greets northeast neighborhood breakfast-goers and lunchtime devotees of the menu's expertly prepared "comfort food." Here you'll find a light omelette batter that doesn't overwhelm the taste

of the ingredients inside, as well as perfectly done hash browns. We recommend an early arrival to get a seat for Henry's North American (sweet Italian sausage scrambled with eggs, spinach, and Swiss cheese) and hazelnut custard French toasts. Breakfast here is in the $6-8 range.

The **Hawthorne Cafe,** 3354 S.E. Hawthorne, tel. (503) 232-4982, carries the banner for a neighborhood long known for its Bohemian feel and ethnic flair. Therefore, it shouldn't be surprising that this restaurant serves up hearty breakfasts and lunches whose nutritional concerns are reminiscent of the '60s—but with the tastiness of Mediterranean cuisine. The latter comes courtesy of such garnishes as the restaurant's homemade hummus and strips of seasoned lamb known as "gyro." Moderate prices and cozy mini-dining rooms also make this place a winner. If you're playing "peek-at-the-boutiques" on N.W. 23rd, the cafe has an outlet, 1310 N.W. 23rd, tel. (503) 222-7840, here that serves the same good food as its flagship with the noteworthy addition of a tree-shrouded patio—as nice a space for an al fresco breakfast in warm weather as exists in the city. If you're making the scene at "Trendy-Third" and Pettygrove and the Hawthorne is too crowded, or you're in the mood for something lighter and ready to go, try the **Marsee Bakery,** tel. (503) 295-5900. Chances are if you've already had the pleasure at Marsee's airport store or at one of its "baker's half dozen" other outlets, you might come here regardless. In addition to an array of baked goods, there's first-rate soup, salads, and sandwiches. After your snack, head back across the street to the **New Renaissance Bookstore** where inspirational and human potential titles can feed the soul.

It's often charged that breakfast in America suffers from a lack of creativity. One bite of corned beef hash, challah French toast, or blue corncakes at **Shaker's,** 1212 N.W. Glisan, tel. (503) 221-0011, lets you measure what we've lost in the era of Egg McMuffin. Egg dishes come with fresh-baked scones ready to be smeared with the homemade preserves placed on every table. For quality of food and ambience, breakfast here is one of the best dollar values, $5-7, in town.

For several decades breakfast at **The Stepping Stone Cafe,** (503) 222-1132, N.W. 24th and Quimby, has meant quality eats served in the formica'd confines of a well-kept fifties hash house. This re-invented corner cafe serves up hearty three egg omelettes for prices more commonly seen in Mexican bus stations than in Portland's trendy Northwest district. Breakfast served everyday until 2 p.m. Closed Monday.

Food Fetishes

The **Doris Cafe,** corner of Russell and MLK, tel. (503) 287-9249, is Portland's most established outpost of soul food. This is more a Sunday dinner with the family kind of place than a ribs joint. The ribs, however, are excellent. There's also plates heaped up high with fried and barbecued chicken or catfish accompanied by black-eyed peas, okra, and red beans and rice. Whatever you choose, begin with corn bread and end with the peach cobbler or sweet potato pie. Dinners usually run $8-13. Next door, **Steen's Coffeehouse,** 2603 N.E. Martin Luther King Jr. Blvd., tel. (503) 284-2026, frequently features live jazz or blues until 10 p.m. On weekends, there's usually a jam session that begins around 4 p.m.

Regarding barbecue, the current buzz in Portland is that **Tennessee Red,** 2133 S.E. 11th Ave, tel. (503) 231-1710, is the man. Whether you like Texas style beef brisket or North Carolina pork loin, this small ribs joint operated by an hombre who has cooked for heads of state won't fail to please. The house ribs are brine-marinated, spice-rubbed, and then wood-smoked the way Red learned to do it in Memphis. Red's moderate prices make it easy to savor it all and still have enough left over for a takeout order.

While not explicity ethnic, **Ron Paul's,** N.E. Broadway and 15th, tel. (503) 284-5347, features many entrees inspired by international cuisines. The Northwest ingredients meld well with the menu of light entrees and creative salads derived from traditional recipes spanning the globe. The bakery take-out counter at the restaurant's N.E. Broadway, N.W. 23rd St., and downtown outlets have become so popular that the owner has opened up an express take-out deli, 507 S.W. Broadway, tel. (503) 221-0052. Ron Paul's is the prototypical Portland eatery where locals come for affordable gourmet dining in an attractive setting or just for the ultimate caffeine high. Ron Paul's legendary Black Angus

cookies or pot du creme accompanied by what might be the most flavorful cup of strong black coffee you'll find at any restaurant in Portland.

Kornblatt's, 628 N.W. 23rd, tel. (503) 242-0055, may be the only Oregon outpost of Jewish "deli" food that would be recognizable to east coast transplants jaded from too many Portland-style five-grain bagels. By contrast, Kornblatt's sticks to what works in New York. Here the "Nova" is thin sliced, the whitefish salad is smoky, the noodle pudding ("kugel") is heavy with cinnamon, and the pickles are extra sour—all they should be. The kitchen's performance is occasionally uneven on cooked meat dishes however. Dinner prices range from $8-12, sandwiches average $5-7, and good bargains can be found in the day-old basket.

With legions of joggers and bikers as well as a leading medical research university, naturopathic college and chiropractic school, Portland is known for its health-conscious population. The five stores of **Nature's Northwest** add to this reputation. In addition to an incredible array of produce and natural food products, Nature's flagship outlet on 24th and Fremont, the new megastore on 30th and Division, 3000 Division St. Portland, tel. (503) 233-4340, and other outlets boast a selection of takeout gourmet items, many of which have a decidedly "un-gourmet" price.

For a great meal for less than $5, try **Good Dog, Bad Dog,** 708 S.W. Alder, tel. (503) 222-3410. The Oregon Smokey, $4, is a spicy introduction to Northwest cuisine. Choose from 10 meaty sausages at this budget diner's dream.

Old Wives' Tales, 1300 E. Burnside, tel. (503) 238-1470, is a restaurant whose wholesome multi-ethnic vegetarian cuisine demonstrates that "moderately priced and nutritious" doesn't have to mean boring. The addition of chicken and fresh seafood, along with beer, wine, and espresso, to the offerings of this onetime "health food" restaurant has enabled it to make the transition to the epicurean tastes of the '90s. The best salad bar in town, famous Hungarian mushroom soup, fresh seafood hash, and cozy backroom booths are other reasons to come. An all-you-can-eat soup/salad bar option for $7.50 is a health-conscious option for the truly famished.

For over 50 years, the **Ring Side,** 2165 W. Burnside, tel. (503) 223-1513, served predominantly steak and prime rib until menu changes in the last decade made some concessions to the culinary trends of the "heart smart" nineties. Caesar salad (with a seafood option) as well as grilled salmon and halibut (also consider the lamb chops and chicken livers) now come highly recommended for those who can forsake the legendary prime rib, $20, and one of the best hamburgers, $7, in town. Epicurean taste trends and health regimens may come and go, but when all is said and done, it's still the plump Walla Walla sweets that put the restaurant's name up in lights. These delicately buttered yet crisp onion rings, $4.50, with a hint of spice are as much an American classic ("The best I've ever had," quoth James Beard) as the Hemingway-esque decor of faded boxing photos and hunting trophies, flaming red booths, and big stone fireplace. In 1996 The American Academy of Restaurants rated this place among the top ten restaurants in the country.

Scenes

While Portland is still, for the most part, an early-to-bed, early-to-rise town, it is steadily becoming more hospitable to creatures of the great American night. Wee small hour hangouts, where people come to see and be seen, where drinks are flowing and the energy palpable, are good places to rub elbows with the locals and enjoy the cutting edge of Portland's newly emerging urbanity.

The **Bistro Montage**, 301 S.E. Morrison, tel. (503) 234-1324, is the salvation of Portland night owls in search of quality eats in an atmosphere that confirms there's intelligent life in the universe. In addition to such bayou classics as jambalaya (try it with smoked mussels, frog legs, or Andouille sausage) and blackened catfish, intriguing variations on macaroni-and-cheese redefine the meaning of budget gourmet. Imagine pasta platters teaming with Cajun gravy and/or combinations of parmesan cheese, peppers, garlic, and hot sausage all for $3-8. In like measure, simple dishes like the red bean soup and red hot sausage omelette are excellent ways to beat the late-night blahs. This is a place that charmingly flaunts its view "that the customer is not always right" in everything from its refusal to serve decaf coffee (and only Rainier beer) to the way the Chopin nocture dinner soundtrack might give way to Nine-Inch Nails and Bob Marley late into the night. Open Sun.-Thur. 11:30 a.m.-2 a.m.,

Fri.-Sat. 11:30 a.m.-4 a.m.

The Pearl District took on a new luster when **Bima**, 1338 N.W. Hoyt, tel. (503) 241-3465, stylishly filled the confines of an old warehouse with exotic Gulf Coast cuisine on the order of Pecan-crusted catfish with chipotle polenta cake and greens, $13.50—good bar food can be had here for half-this price, complemented by vintage cognacs, ports, and other temptations from a well-stocked bar. Even though the cozy booths and dim-lit bar are more intimate than the Montage's "last-supper style" of seating, there's still a buzz of electricity in the air that hits you when you walk in the door of Portland's most architecturally interesting restaurant. If the flamboyantly talented pianist Thomas Lauderdale and his band Pink Martini happen to be appearing here, it'll be a night to remember. Come back for late lunch (2 p.m.-5 p.m.) when any item on the bar menu is half price, $1.75-3.50.

The combination of a darkly urbane cafe and a bright Pan-Asian culinary motif has made **Saucebox**, 214 S.W. Broadway, tel. (503) 241-3393, the quintessence of Portland late-night cool. Whether you're enjoying the mango-mint inflected Vietnamese salad rolls, the Thai curries, or a coconut lime ricky cocktail, Saucebox is an inexpensive way (starters $3-10, entrees $6-11, desserts $3-4) to impress that expensive date. An after-hours cocktail scene (DJs spinning tunes and dancing Tues.-Sat.) also helps empty the mind of mundane daytime concerns.

The nocturnal favorite of Portland's subcultural elite, **Fellini**, 125 N.W. 6th Ave., tel. (503) 243-2120, adjoins new wave nightspot Satyricon (where Kurt Cobain supposedly met Courtney Love). No matter what your musical tastes are, creative vegetarian entrees such as the Abe Vigoda (a kind of scalloped potatoes alfredo), light, crisp calamari, chanterelle mushrooms with a lemon coconut curry sauce over sticky rice, great burgers and gyros, a full bar, and low prices, $3-7, will put enough spring in your step to dance the night away. Open Mon.-Thurs. 11:30 a.m.-2:30 a.m., Friday 11:30 a.m.-4 a.m., and Saturday 8 p.m.-4 a.m.

Another place serving till 4 a.m. on weekends, **The Brazen Bean's**, 2075 N.W. Glisan St., tel. (503) 294-0636, small-plates-and-dessert (small plates $6) formula works well for romantic interludes or a snack after a late-night movie.

The welcoming ambience even extends to smokers, a group usually treated like lepers in Portland, who can enjoy coffee and dessert (chocolate fondue for $2-6) in their own section of the restaurant.

Hotel Dining Rooms

The two most venerated hostelries in Portland are the **Heathman,** S.W. Broadway at Salmon St., tel. (503) 241-4100, and the **Benson Hotel,** S.W. Broadway and Oak St., tel. (503) 228-2000. In like measure, their dining rooms enjoy a reputation for serving some of the finest cuisine in the region. As in most establishments of this ilk, dinner can be on the costly side, but this doesn't mean you have to totally deny yourself the opportunity to break bread in these hallowed halls.

In contrast to dinner, where checks can exceed $40 per person, breakfast at the Benson's London Grill is not appreciably more expensive than many places in town, and the few extra bucks are worth it. The experience begins the moment you step into the hotel. The Russian walnut lining the Benson lobby, together with the marble fireplace and staircase, bespeak the glory that was Simon Benson's Portland in 1916. Benson's legacy also includes the Columbia Gorge Hotel and Scenic Highway as well as dozens of ornate drinking fountains he put up around the city to promote a teetotaling outlook.

Downstairs from the Benson lobby, the chandeliered and mahogany-paneled **London Grill** continues Simon Benson's insistence on ex-

cellence. Whether it's the open-face shrimp omelette with goat cheese and herbs or the vegetable frittata, the scrumptious food, first-rate service, and plush surroundings give a taste of Portland at its best. Better yet, it shouldn't run you too much more than $7. For several times that price, try the Sunday brunch here. This Portland tradition lets you enjoy three meals in one, with items ranging from standard breakfast fare to spicy Chinese noodles, braised veal tips, and sushi. It's all good, but save some room for the chocolate petits fours. After brunch cross the street to take in the U.S. Bank building. This building is considered by many people to be Portland's most beautiful with 54 feet-high Corinthian Columns rich in terra cotta nuance. This building, the Central library, and the Benson itself are all part of the early 20th century architectural legacy of Alfred Doyle.

The Heathman Hotel's interior also exudes the understated Old World elegance of the Benson, with generous use of teak paneling and marble. However, the prices in its trendy **Heathman Restaurant,** 1009 S.W. Broadway, tel. (503) 241-4100, extolled by the late James Beard, will appeal more to the expense-account traveler than to explorers on a budget. Nonetheless, low-priced, $2.50-2.95, tasty soups and rolls are served in the lounge during lunch. Afterward, in the darkly paneled grand court, Heathman elegance can also be experienced at afternoon tea, 2-4:30 p.m. A magnificent chandelier and two wall-sized 18th century harborscapes also evoke

the Benson Hotel

THEO TRIMMEL

a mood of old-world hospitality. Ten teas from around the world, finger sandwiches, scones, pastries, strawberries, and chocolates are served on English bone china in what has become a Portland tradition. It may be of interest to note the Heathman was named one of the top 10 restaurants in America by *Nation's Restaurant News.* Reservations are appreciated.

At night the Heathman bar has jazz, and while it's spendier than many spots in River City, you'd be hard-pressed to find better mixed drinks, appetizers, and atmosphere anywhere else in Oregon. And to affordably sample the delights of award-winning chef Pierre Boulot, reserve a spot at the prix fixe, $21, early dinner special in The Heathman Dining Room between 5 p.m. and 6:30 p.m.

The **Heathman Bakery and Pub,** 901 S.W. Salmon St., tel. (503) 227-5700, also serves Northwest cuisine in the style of its parent restaurant, but at a fraction of the cost (the restaurant is also called B. Moloch, after the caricaturist whose work adorns the walls). The specialty here is gourmet pizza, but pasta-seafood concoctions and dishes boasting such local ingredients as hazelnuts, chevre, Oregon lamb, game pâté, and homemade sausage, as well as the in-house Widmer microbrew and seafood chowder, $3.25 a bowl, are also parts of the restaurant's identity. Lest this sound like the kind of place where only yups come to sup, enough moderately priced items and an informal atmosphere are guaranteed not to scare you away. And if you're willing to stand in line long enough, it's possible to get some of the best bread in the city at a low price when the Heathman Bakery has $1.50 per loaf specials.

Food aficionados, history buffs, and downtown explorers will all find something to appreciate at the newly renovated **Governor Hotel,** S.W. 10th at Alder, tel. (503) 224-3400 or (800) 554-3456. Built in 1909 during one of the city's exponential growth spurts, the old Governor has emerged from its facelift with its sparkling terra-cotta facade and old-style charm intact.

Inside, high ceilings, arts-and-crafts-style furnishings, and the lobby's sepia-toned mural depicting scenes from the Lewis and Clark Expedition all contribute to the turn-of-the-century sense of taste, proportion, and sanity. Even if your budget won't stretch to include a night or two at the Governor (rooms begin at $185), stop by the Celilo Lounge in the lobby for a drink (live music nightly, usually jazz). For an occasion, have a meal at the hotel's **Jake's Grill,** an offspring of its famous parent restaurant but with less emphasis on seafood than its bloodlines might suggest. Voted one of the top 100 restaurants in America by *Conde Nast,* Jake's dinner menu is not exclusively pricey steaks and chops, $17-25, and seafood, $14-25. Expertly prepared, affordable comfort food like chicken pot pie, $9, and meat loaf, $11, also lend credence to this restaurant's high rating. These and other entrees cost less at lunch time. Almost two dozen other "cafe-meals" sandwiches and entree salads in the $8 range enhance this egalitarian image. Gourmet breakfasts in the $6-8 range compound an impression of bourgeois elegance in a culinary landmark. After dining here, wander across the street to the Galleria with its cluster of first-rate shops, including Made in Oregon and the Fossil Cartel. For decor, location, and panache, the Governor embodies Portland downtown style.

Finally, if you have a reason to splurge, try **Alexander's,** 921 S.W. 6th Ave., tel. (503) 226-1611, on the 23rd floor of the Portland Hilton. Even though the tab for two is occasionally equivalent to the price of a decent motel room, views of the snowcapped Cascades backdropping Portland's cityscape and the exquisite presentation of the food can render material concerns irrelevant. As for what to order, consult the personable maitre d'hotel, Joseph, for special insights into what's good that evening (we recommend the hot and sweet prawns). While the entrees skillfully walk a tightrope between nouvelle and traditional, the desserts can only be described as the cheapest legal high you can get.

Seafood

Jake's Famous Crawfish, 901 S.W. 12th St., tel. (503) 226-1419, is not just famous for those lobsterlike denizens of the Oregon freshwater deep. It is also renowned for the widest-ranging seafood menu in the Northwest and one of the most extensive Oregon wine lists. The largest privately owned fine art collection in the region also graces the mahogany-paneled confines of Jake's. Nevertheless, it's the local crawfish (available May-Sept.) that let the restaurant make a name for itself. Other specialties include clam chowder, smoked salmon and sturgeon, steamed butter clams, spring chinook salmon, bouillabaisse, and the best Irish coffee in town. You can also get a good steak and meat loaf here. For the best luck, order one of the two dozen or so specials off the "fresh sheet", $10-20. Whatever you decide on, leave room for chocolate-truffle cake. Getting reserved seating in this 100-year-old plus landmark is often difficult, but not enough to deter dozens of reservationless people who might wait over an hour for an opening. Besides taking advantage of $2 per plate barfood, a cost-effective way to enjoy Jake's cuisine minus the wait is to partake at Jake's Backstage located in the lobby of the Performing Arts Center. Open 6-8 p.m. on performance nights, this dinner buffet includes such popular Jake's dishes as cedar plank salmon, au gratin potatoes, and truffle cake. Vegetarian selections are also available. The full buffet is $9.95 with a dessert-only alternative.

McCormick and Schmick's, 235 S.W. 1st Ave., tel. (503) 224-7527, has venerable roots—it's the offspring of century-old Jake's restaurant and enjoys a location in the historic Failing Building. Be that as it may, this restaurant's "fresh sheet" is the way to go when it comes to ordering. Expect to pay around $20 per person for dinner. Better yet, for $1.95, plus $2 drink minimum, enjoy a bar menu 1:30-6:30 p.m. and 9:30 to closing that might feature Greek or Caesar salad, shrimp stir fry, Cajun cheeseburger, pizza, and more.

Salty's on the Columbia, 3839 N.E. Marine Dr., tel. (503) 288-4444, is a great choice for Columbia Gorge-bound travelers. The river frontage and fish-on-ice displays that greet you set the mood for a seafood feast. Bills can run high, so save this one for an occasion, or take advantage of their lower-priced Blue Heron Cafe located on the upper level. Many fresh specials supplement the menu, which offers such imaginative dishes as a Caesar salad garnished with bits of blackened smoked salmon. Rich desserts and a nautical-theme bar well stocked with Northwest microbrews also recommend this place. If it's warm, the outdoor seating above the river is a special treat. When you emerge from the restaurant, fair-weather views of Mt.

Hood can provide the finishing touch to your dining pleasure.

Oldies but Goodies

Portland abounds in classic dollar-wise spots that have been around for years. Here are several traditional standbys.

Huber's, 411 S.W. 3rd, tel. (503) 228-5686, bills itself as the oldest restaurant in town dating back to 1879. Spanish coffee served with a flame-juggling flourish and the best turkey dinner in town are claims to fame here, but the draw for many patrons is the chance to dine surrounded by tropical hardwoods, stained glass, and the glory that was Portland in the 19th century. While spiked coffee drinks are in the $6 range here, many entrees don't go higher than $8, making Portland's oldest dining tradition eminently affordable.

With a WW II-vintage B-17 plane in the parking lot and good old American food at inexpensive prices, it's no wonder that nostalgic seniors crowd the **Bomber,** 13515 S.E. McLoughlin Blvd., Milwaukee, tel. (503) 659-9306, for breakfast, lunch, and dinner. Inside, walls depicting aviation and war-time scenes and a menu with perfectly made chicken-fried steak, $6.95, BLT's, $3.50, and other comfort food make getting a seat difficult. Other than that, there's every reason to take a sentimental journey down McLoughlin Blvd. (ORE 99E) and head 15 minutes south to this shrine to Rosie the Riveter.

Dan and Louis Oyster Bar, 208 S.W. Ankey, tel. (503) 227-5906, is a 1902 treasure trove of maritime memorabilia and antiques as well as oyster stew made with prized Yaquina Bay oysters (see Newport Introduction). The restaurant owner's ancestors helped start the oyster farm on the coast that made these bivalves famous at the turn of the century. You can enjoy this legacy today along with other fresh Oregon seafood (most entrees are under $10). Couple a weekend meal here with a visit to nearby Saturday Market.

Coffeehouses

Portland's coffee houses are a regional "take" on the Viennese tradition of cafe society—homes away from home to spend an idle hour reading a paper, gabbing with the 'regulars,' or writing the great American novel while sipping rich European-style brewed drinks made from whole bean coffee.

While **Starbucks** on the corner of 37th and Hawthorne embodies the "clean, well-lighted place" and excellent coffee you'll find nationwide at these outlets, Portlanders come here for their daily fix for other reasons. With windows peering out on the neo-Moorish contours of the Bagdad Theatre across the street and people-watching par excellence, this a good place to hang out on a wet, bone-chilling winter day to dream wistfully of brighter days to come. When reveries become reality in Spring, outdoor seating lets you become part of Portland's livelier street scenes. A muted soundtrack of soft jazz and a staff that flavors your morning mocha with just the right amount of sweetness here can even coax a smile at 7 a.m.

Coffee People, a Portland-based chain that recently went national also has quality brewed drinks, and an approach ("Good coffee, no backtalk") that's especially popular with high-octane urbanfolk. The outlet on the corner of N.W. 23rd and Hoyt is a good place to sip Black Tiger, a Turkish coffee-like grind that produces the most intense caffeine high in the city.

Torrefazione also distinctively creates brewed awakenings. If you like Italian dark roasts and aesthetic flourishes running the gamut from hand-painted china to Florentine architecture, then the Italian accents on the corner of N.E. 15th and Weidler (among other outlets) will make you feel at home.

Another Northwest trend is the proliferation of java joints where you stand in line for coffee then sit down to go on-line at a computer terminal. Here are some coffee houses for those who like their Internet chat rooms caffeinated: **Java Jae's,** 1203 N.W. 23rd Ave., tel. (503) 224-8562, http://www.java-jae's.com, and **Millenium Cafe,** 2633 S.E. 21st. St., tel. (503) 235-9945, http://www.millenium-cafe.com. Resident "geeks" help the uninitiated at these establishments.

Cafe Lena's, 2239 S.E. Hawthorne Blvd., tel. (503) 238-7087, Tuesday poetry nights (9-11 p.m.) and nightly folk/blues acoustic entertainment carry on the coffeehouse legacy of the Beat era poets and musicians whose pictures festoon the walls. This is *the* place to come for humble fare with gourmet flair. Whether its potatoes with veggies and cheese, a baguette with sundried tomatoes and olive tapenade, or peanut butter cheesecake, well-rendered espresso drinks and $5-7 meal prices make it all go down easily.

The **Little Wing Cafe,** 529 N.W. 13th Ave., tel. (503) 228-3101, is easy to miss amid the loading docks of surrounding Pearl District warehouses. Once inside, an array of cookies (especially the biscotti and big round vanilla sugar cookies filled with chocolate), European pastries, sandwiches, and coffee drinks fueled by Torrefazione's excellent Italian roast awaits. This is the perfect place to cool your heels after gallery-hopping or to warm your bones on a dreary winter day.

The **Pied Cow,** 3244 S.E. Belmont, tel. (503) 230-4866, is a coffee house set in a striking old Victorian home. Outside, a tree-shaded yard with tables fill up during warm weather. Most of the year however, the tastefully garish interior with multiple alcoves provides shelter from the storm. Add the Pied Cow selection of espresso drinks and baked treats and you have the perfect setting to revive the grand old art of conversation.

Novel Java, 3729 S.E. Hawthorne, tel. (503) 232-8118, is set inside Powell's Bookstore on Hawthorne so you can peruse prospective purchases while enjoying house-roasted java. At 75 cents a cup with a free refill, this is premium coffee at truckstop prices. If you're too depressed by winter weather to read, drown your sorrows in the Mindblower, a black and white mocha.

As you approach **Rimsky-Korsakoffee House,** 707 S.E. 12th Ave., tel. (503) 232-2640, the old red house gives no indications (not even a hand-lettered sign bearing its name!) that this is Portland's favorite artsy hangout and coffeehouse. Only the lines extending out the door on a crowded weekend might convey that the place is something special. Folks come for mocha fudge cake washed down by espresso drinks, live classical music, as well as people and ideas in creative ferment. The atmosphere of a refined house party reigns here 7 p.m.-midnight on weekdays and 7 p.m.-1 a.m. on weekends. Expect a surprise in the upstairs bathroom.

Brewpubs

Brewpubs are built around microbrews and pub grub with personality. The bastions of brews described below helped create Portland's identity as "Munich on the Willamette."

Portland's preeminent brewpubmeisters are the McMenamin brothers. With dozens of establishments throughout western Oregon and such unusual brews as raspberry-flavored Ruby Tuesday and Mars Bars Ale (as well as more traditional creations—try their India Pale Ale) this brewpub chain has been a major catalyst to the current popularity of craft beers. The typical McMenamins is set in an old home or a rathskellar-like tavern, very often with a decor of Grateful Dead concert posters, album covers, and classic prints of romantic themes. While a glass or a pitcher of suds will set you back a little more than an equivalent amount from your local tavern, the quality and selection make quaffing here a good value. On the menu, gourmet pizza, black bean soup, and Greek salad are notable, $4-7, but it's the burgers, $7, that have the biggest following.

Several Portland McMenamins feature movie theaters (see "Cinema" under "Entertainment" above). The **Edgefield Power Station,** 2126 Halsey St. Troutdale, tel. (503) 669-8610, parlays a theater, gourmet restaurant, a B&B/hostel, $20-75, gardens, and an art gallery with the brewpub experience. A similar formula is available closer to downtown Portland at **The Kennedy School,** 5736 N.E. 33rd, tel. (503) 223-0109, in an exclusively B&B setting, $45-115. It's worth a trip if only just to look at the art that graces the interiors of these places. On occasion, Edgefield features the Hammerhead package, good for lodging/meal discounts. Edgefield is located at the beginning of the Columbia River Gorge just off I-84. Link up at http://www.McMenamins.com to reserve Edgefield and Kennedy School and find out about music and movies at all McMenamin outlets.

The **Widmer Brewery and Gasthaus,** 929 N. Russell St., tel. (503) 281-3333, is revered by beer lovers throughout the country as the birthplace of Oregon's most popular microbrew, Widmer hefeweizen. Distributed nationally in bottles, the Gasthaus is the place to enjoy this wheat beer straight from the tap, still cloudy with sediment. The elegant back bar and a mix of wood and brick throughout the restaurant impart a feeling of warmth here complementing homestyle German cooking with Northwest ingredients. To get here, follow N.E. Interstate near the Broadway Bridge and Rose Garden Arena a half-mile down to the corner of Russell Street.

In addition to the Bridgeport and Portland Brewing brewpubs mentioned elsewhere in this book, these pioneer craft beer makers each have other outlets worth checking out. With a picture window on the Pearl District, a wood-paneled barroom, excellent Reuben sandwiches, the critically acclaimed McTarnahan's amber, and no cover blues/rock Wed.-Sat. nights, **Portland Brewing's Flanders St. Pub,** 1339 N.W. Flanders, tel. (503) 222-3414, is a favorite among brewpub connoisseurs. Bridgeport's **Hawthorne St. Ale House,** 3632 S.E. Hawthorne, tel. (503) 233-6549, expands upon the pizza menu of its Northwest Portland outlet with a menu featuring everything from grilled eggplant sandwiches to empanadas, foods that go with our personal favorite, Blue Heron Ale, $1.65 10 oz. pints, $2.75 20 ounces. Taste a bit of Portland at the **Rose and Raindrop Public House,** 532 S.E. Grand St., tel. (503) 238-6996, where a large selection of microbrews, derivative recipes (ale-marinated steelhead) as well as great pub grub (such happy hour items as smoked salmon Caesar salad and fried oysters are on a bar menu beginning at $2.25) express the regional bounty against a backdrop of classic turn-of-the-century decor.

McCormick and Schmick's **Harborside Pilsener Room,** 0309 S.W. Montgomery, tel. (503) 220-1865, has one of the better happy hour (4-6 p.m. daily) menus, $1.95, as well as some of the best river frontage in the city. With 30 microbrews and an outlet of Full Sail Brewery on display behind glass paneled walls you might even be able to ignore feeling "under-dressed" in this upscale hangout.

Produce Row Cafe, 204 S.E. Oak St., tel. (503) 232-8355, has dozens of beers on tap for a good price and hundreds of bottled domestic and imported beers. Huge sandwiches, $5-7, are also a good value, and one feeds two people. The cafe straddles the warehouses beneath Martin Luther King Jr. Blvd. and is open Mon.-Fri. 11 a.m.-1 a.m., Saturday noon-1 a.m., and Sunday 2 p.m.-midnight. Live music takes place weekends on the outside patio. A fall treat is hard pear cider on tap.

Dining on the Edge

Portland's growth curve in the last decade has spawned an accompanying increase in population and sophistication in its suburban bedroom communities. Such "edge cities" as Beaverton and Gresham now rank among the seven most populated areas in the state and have no shortage of upscale eateries catering to the moneyed minions of the Silicon Forest. Here are some places geared more to the budget of the average traveler.

The **Rock Creek Tavern,** 1000 Old Cornelius Pass Rd., Hillsboro, tel. (503) 645-3822, is a brewpub eatery set on rustic grounds in rural Washington County northwest of the high tech industrial parks near I-5. It's hard to believe that less than 10 minutes away from these "big box-style" chip plants is a 1930s hunting lodge with a decidedly old world ambience. Inside the stately old wooden tavern, an ornate fireplace, stained glass, and artwork welcome you to a menu filled with innovative burgers, billowing salads, and other pub grub in the $6-8 range (food prices go down after 10 p.m.) House-made McMenamin's microbrews on tap, $2.75 pint, $6.75 pitcher, live music, and an outdoor patio also contribute to the classic brewpub experience. To get there from downtown Portland, go west on US 26 to Hillsboro where a highway sign on US 26 indicates the exit to the "Historic Rock Creek Tavern."

Swagat, 4325 S.W. 109th Ave., Beaverton, tel. (503) 626-3000, features southern Indian food with its crepe-like dosas filled with a spicy vegetable curry, crispy tempura-like spinach pakoras, and tasty breads. Vegetarians will appreciate the meatless entrees on the dinner menu here. Despite a lack of ambiance and at-times overly laid back service, the $5.95 lunch buffet, reasonably priced dinners (main courses $7-12 or prix fixe $9-12) attracts everyone from high-tech execs to local Indian families to this popular restaurant off the Beaverton/Hillsdale highway. Downtown Swagat fans can partake at the corner of N.W. 21st and Lovejoy.

Sayler's Country Kitchen, 4655 S.W. Griffith Dr.; Beaverton tel. (503) 644-1492, is a solid steak-and-potatoes family restaurant. Unfortunately, it's better known for its 72-ounce top Sirloin dinner which is free if you can finish it, $45 if you can't. You're probably better off paying around $14 for Sayler's regular sirloin dinner. It comes with a relish tray, choice of soup or salad, rice and potatoes, plus ice cream. Similar options exist for filet, fried chicken and seafood.

After packing 'em in for four decades, Sayler's can be counted on for good dollar value. Afterwards, visit the nearby **Washington County Visitor Center and Convention Bureau** (see the special topic Escape to Washington County for additional travel and dining tips).

When Rose's restaurant on N.W. 23rd closed a few years ago, long-time worshippers at the original shrine to football-sized cinnamon rolls and one-feeds-two deli sandwiches bemoaned the passing of a 40-year tradition. Thankfully, eastside **Rose's,** 122 St. and N.E. Glisan, tel. (503) 254-6543, survived the demise of its downtown flagship much to the delight of nearby Gresham as well as Columbia Gorge and Mt. Hoodbound motorists. The faithful from all over Portland still swear by $2.95 breakfast specials and legendary lunch-time creations like the Nosher (half-a-dozen deli meats piled high with condiments between slabs of Rose's home-baked breads—$8.95 to feed a minimum of two people). Dinner-time favorites like pot roast, $9.85, and a memorable version of strawberry shortcake also stand out in an extensive and reasonably priced menu. If you're just too full for dessert, you can always get an almond croissant or rum ball from their takeout bakery next door.

GETTING THERE AND GETTING AROUND

In Portland, streets are named and run east and west, avenues are numbered and run north and south, and boulevards exist in the netherworld of thoroughfares that go in many directions. Adding to the confusion, Martin Luther King Blvd., Portland's main route in town before the Interstates, used to be called Union and the old name survives in some quarters. As it heads south, it becomes McLoughlin Boulevard. Broadway (in effect, 7th Ave.) is Portland's only undefined arterial, having an east-west orientation when it has the prefix N.E.; with the prefix S.W. or when it's just plain Broadway, it runs north-south. Finally, no rules of logic seem to apply in the west hills when it comes to finding your way. Despite these idiosyncrasies, Portland is, for the most part, easily navigable.

Newcomers should note that the Willamette River determines east-west and Burnside Street delineates north-south address prefixes. Also, N.W. Portland streets proceed in alphabetical order from Burnside moving north with streets keyed to names of early settlers. Back in midtown, Naito Parkway (also called Front Avenue, paralleling the Willamette) is in effect, "Zero Avenue," with numbers going up as you move west away from the river. These avenues are all one way. Traffic along 5th and 6th Avenues is largely restricted to mass transit.

By Car

Portland sits on or near the routes of Interstates 5, 405, 205, and 84. I-5 runs from Seattle to San Diego and I-84 goes east to Salt Lake City. I-405 circles downtown Portland to the west and south. I-205 bypasses the city to the east. US 26 heads west to Cannon Beach on the coast and east to the Cascades.

The parking situation in Portland has its good news and bad news. First the bad news. Even though parking meters and day parking proliferate in the city, it's often hard to find an empty spot. The good news is many of the parking garages accept merchant validation stamps (on the garage receipt) for free parking. As for parking on the street, parking is free 6 p.m.-8 a.m. on weekdays and all day Sunday.

A reliable cab company is **Broadway Taxi,** tel. (503) 227-1234. Cabs charge $2 upon pickup and each additional mile is $1.50. A trip from the airport to downtown runs about $23. It can be difficult to hail a cab here, so it's best to give them a call or catch one in front of a hotel.

Finally, keep in mind that gas prices in Portland could well be higher than those found in other U.S. cities. Without self-service gas stations or oil refineries in the state, this trend should unfortunately continue.

By Bus and Train

The **Greyhound** bus station, 550 N.W. 6th Ave., tel. (800) 231-2222, has storage lockers available for 75 cents a day.

The **Green Tortoise,** 616 S.W. College St., tel. (800) 867-8647, goes to Seattle Tuesday and Saturday (and Thursday and Sunday June 1-Oct. 1) at 4 p.m. for $15 and to San Francisco at 12:30 p.m. Sunday and Thursday (plus Tuesday and Friday June 1-Oct. 1) for $49 (plus $4 for dinner and hot tub at a southern Oregon en-

campment). Departures are from the University Deli on 6th and College across from the Cheerful Tortoise. Eugene departures cost $10 and leave the same day as the San Francisco runs.

Amtrak runs Coast Starlight trains north and south to Seattle and L.A. respectively. Trains depart for San Francisco at 3:05 p.m., arriving at 8:50 a.m. the next day. One-way fare is $135. For reservations, call (800) USA-RAIL. Several Portland city buses (nos. 31-35, 54, or 56-59) will take you to Amtrak. Pick up any one of them at the downtown transit mall. The following Tri-Met bus routes access Greyhound and Amtrak terminals (numbers 1, 5, 14, 32, 33, 35, 54, 56, 57, 58, and 59).

By Air

Portland International Airport, (airport city code PDX), for general information call (503) 231-5000, ext. 411, is among America's fastest growing airports, setting traffic records in each month 1992-1997. This increase has spurred massive expansion set to culminate just before the millenium. In the interm, transitional arrangements unfortunately render definitive listings about long and short-term parking impossible. Please contact the information number for updates.

The PDX airport is served by more than a dozen major airlines. Portland and Seattle are linked by commuter flights on **Horizon,** tel. (800) 547-9308, every half-hour during the day. **Air B.C.,** tel. (800) 663-0522, connects PDX to Vancouver B.C. every two hours. **United Express,** tel. (800) 241-6522, competes with Horizon in the Pacific Northwest and with **Southwest,** tel. (800) 435-9792, in California. Portland is the west coast hub of **Delta Airlines,** tel. 242-1919 or (800) 221-1212, with daily flights to Hong Kong, Korea, and Japan. Delta also provides the only nonstop serivce to New York City.

However, as the book comes to press, it appears that two "no frills" airlines, **Western Pacific** and **Air Portland** are targeting PDX for cross-country service. These new entities plan earlier and less expensive flights to New York city airports. Another entry into the nonstop cross country sweepstakes from Portland to Newark, New Jersey is **Continental,** (800) 525-0280.

The #12 Tri-met buses from downtown run 5 a.m.-12:30 a.m. and leave from S.W. 6th Ave. and Main Street. From the airport, buses depart every 15 minutes, 5:30 a.m.-11:30 p.m. Catch no. 12 outside the baggage claim. It arrives downtown 40 minutes later via Sandy Boulevard.

Other ways of getting to town include free hotel courtesy shuttles and the RAZ bus, tel. (503) 246-3301, which stops at the Greyhound station as well as many hotels en route, $8.50 one-way. It runs 5:00 a.m.-midnight. Call RAZ for the exact arrival/departure schedule or ask hotel personnel or the airport information desk on the first floor near the main terminal's baggage claim.

To drive to the city from PDX, follow the signs to downtown. This would take you first to I-205 South which would then flow into I-84 East. About 10 minutes later, you'll flirt briefly with I-5 south before quickly exiting onto the Morrison Street Bridge. This will take you across the river where the first cross street encountered is S.W. 1st Avenue.

To drive to the city, if you follow the signs to downtown they first go to I-205, then I-84 and I-5, which brings you to the Willamette River. Take the Morrison Street Bridge across the river to downtown.

Perhaps the most unusual feature of PDX is its affordable high-quality concession shops, including such Oregon mainstays as Powell's Books, Nike, the Real Mother Goose (a combination gallery and crafts store purveying woodwork, jewelry, and singular art pieces), Made In Oregon (Northwest gourmet food, crafts, books, etc.), and Norm Thompson (the Northwest's answer to L.L. Bean), plus a food court with such Portland mainstays as Marsee Bakery, Macheesmo Mouse, and Coffee People. You'll be glad to know each store must keep its prices identical to those at downtown outlets. As *Oregonian* writer David Sarasohn put it, "This is the image we want to show the rest of the world. Literate yet playful, athletic but epicurean, and on all occasions wearing natural fibers."

Finally, storage facilities at PDX include lockers (C and D concourses) that charge 50 cents a day, and D.J.'s Baggage Service (across the hall from Continental and American baggage claims, tel. (503) 281-9464, with nightly rates starting at $2 a suitcase. Lockers can accommodate only smaller items.

Europeans interested in air connections to and from Oregon should note that a Delta connection through Cinncinati now makes it possible to fly from Portland to Frankfurt, Germany.

Sightseeing Northwest Volcanoes

Savvy air passengers on the San Francisco-Portland-Seattle corridor can enjoy special perspectives on Cascades range volcanoes, assuming the clouds cooperate. For northbound flights, request a seat on the right side of the plane. Conversely, request seats on the left side for southbound trips. Flying into Portland from Seattle offers a look at Mt. Rainier and Mt. St. Helens that can be particularly unforgettable. Of all the carriers flying this route, Alaska Airlines seems most attuned to the sightseeing priorities of volcano-watchers, even supplying route maps in their in-flight magazine denoting the peaks along with capsule commentary. On weekend trips, Alaska's pilots attempt some narration. Northbound voyages from the Golden State afford vistas of California's Cascades giants Mt. Lassen and Mt. Shasta as well as Oregon's own Mt. McLoughlin, Crater Lake, the Three Sisters, Mt Jefferson, and Mt. Hood. Clear winter mornings and the crisp days of early October tend to offer the best viewing.

Public Transportation

Begin your orientation to the Tri-Met bus system at Pioneer Square. The Tri-Met office, 1 Pioneer Courthouse Square, 701 S.W. 6th Ave., tel. 238-RIDE, is open 9 a.m.-5 p.m. weekdays. Information can be obtained from Tri-Met drivers, hotel front desk clerks and concierges, or any branch of Willamette Savings. Or you can call these numbers: recorded information for call-a-bus, tel. (503) 231-3199, or bicycle commuter service, tel. (503) 239-3044. Adult fares range from $1.05 (basic fare) to $1.35 (long trips) Seniors ride anywhere for 50 cents. These fares also apply to MAX, the light-rail train that does not make as many stops. MAX runs every 15 minutes. To ride it to its easternmost extremity, Gresham (17 miles from downtown), takes 45 minutes and costs $1.35. Ditto to Hillsboro, the western terminus. Buy tickets from machines at MAX stations before boarding. Tri-Met buses require exact change, and you can purchase tickets at the Tri-Met office or aboard the area bus.

Passengers in the downtown area can ride free anywhere in "Fareless Square." This 300-square-block area is defined by I-405 to the south, N.W. Hoyt St. to the north, and the Willamette River to the east. Thirty-one shelters (color-coded by their region) make up Transit Mall. Southbound buses pick up passengers on S.W. 5th Ave.; northbound travelers board on S.W. 6th Avenue.

A one-day pass is a good way to get oriented to Portland and environs. Purchase one at Tri-Met service centers (or some credit unions, banks, and supermarkets like Safeway and Albertson's) or at "Tri-Met Central" beneath Pioneer Courthouse Square. In addition, bus drivers can issue a transfer good for all day and all zones, which is the equivalent of a one-day pass. Between Tri-Met's 74 lines and MAX, you can ride from Gresham in the east to Hillsboro in the west and from Vancouver, Washington, in the north to Wilsonville and Oregon City to the south. From the downtown core, the popular northeast part of town is accessible via these lines: no. 8 Irvington, no. 9 Broadway, no. 10 N.E. 33rd, and no. 12 Sandy Blvd., which turns around at the airport. Two lines are your keys to northwest Portland: no. 13 to Montgomery Park (or farther north to MacLeay and Forest Parks) and no. 17, which travels all the way to Sauvie Island. As for other parts of town, remember that bus lines numbered in the 70s are crosstown lines—you can't pick these up at the Transit Mall downtown, but they link various neighborhoods and cut across many of the lines downtown. The line that offers the most to visitors is the no. 63, nicknamed Art, the Cultural Bus. This moving mural runs 6:24 a.m.-7:08 p.m. with service to the following attractions: the zoo and other Washington Park sights, the Convention Center and Coliseum, Lloyd Center, POVA, the Center for the Performing Arts, the Oregon History Center and the Portland Art Museum.

The first step in setting up your own personalized mass-transit tour is picking up a schedule at one of the Tri-Met service centers or bus-information racks scattered around town. For the ultimate aid in figuring where you want to go and when, pay $2.50 for a complete Tri-Met guide, which includes a map (or you can purchase the map alone for $1), schedules, and the lowdown on attractions in various neighborhoods.

INFORMATION AND SERVICES

Portland's visitor-information resources are far-reaching and extensive. Begin at **Portland Oregon Visitors Association,** 26 S.W. Salmon St. Portland, OR, 97218, tel. (800) 345-3214. This facility sits across Front Ave. from Waterfront Park's beautiful fountain. Hours are Mon.-Fri. 9 a.m.-5 p.m., Saturday 9 a.m.-4 p.m., and Sunday 10 a.m.-2 p.m. In addition to knowledgeable personnel, POVA has the most complete collection of printed traveler-information pamphlets in the state. While Portland is naturally the focus of most of these publications, materials about every part of the state fill the racks here. The best free **maps** of the city are available nearby from Powell's at Pioneer Square and from Hertz on the corner of S.W. 6th Ave. and Salmon, tel. (503) 249-5727.

Several travel agencies rate a mention for cheap fares and helpful travel tips. **Council Travel,** 1715 S.W. Morrison, tel. (503) 228-1980 or (800) 228-2854, and **ASA University Travel,** 1503 S.W. Broadway, tel. (503) 224-6659, serve the student community and are up on all the deals. For travel in the Northwest and an ecotourism orientation, **Journeys,** 1526 N.W. 23rd, tel. (503) 226-4849, is tops. Journeys also has a storefront at Powell's Travel store in Pioneer Square.

A local **events hotline,** tel. (503) 233-4444, can supplement the media sources identified below to update you on what's going on, where, and at what time. Other useful numbers include a **Crisis Line,** tel. (503) 223-6161, **Women's Crisis Lines,** tel. (503) 235-5333, **Men's Resource Center,** tel. (503) 235-3433, **Drug Counseling and Intervention,** tel. (503) 320-9654, **Health Help Center,** tel. (503) 288-5995, and the **Aging Services Division,** tel. (503) 248-3464.

A convenient part of town for the traveler to take care of essentials is the Hollywood District north of Sandy Blvd. (US 30) around N.E. 42nd. A mini-mall off N.E. 42nd and Hancock features a bank, a laundromat, and an excellent coffee shop, **Sweet Indulgences,** 1925 N.E. 42nd Ave., tel. (503) 249-0686. Across the street is a post office subcontractor who has weekend hours when the "official" post office outlets are closed.

The hours of the main **post office,** 715 N.W. Hoyt St., Portland 97208, tel. (503) 294-2124, are Mon.-Fri. 8:30 a.m.-8 p.m. and Saturday 8:30 a.m.-5 p.m. The Pioneer Courthouse might be more convenient to use if you're in mid-town Portland.

The **Multnomah County Library** has 15 branches throughout the city with books, films, records, and at some branches, videos available for borrowing. The central branch, 801 S.W. 10th Ave., tel. (503) 223-7201, is a top-notch research facility with a newspaper and periodical section that's well organized and voluminous and 60% open stacks.

Medical care downtown can be most conveniently accessed through **Good Samaritan Hospital,** 1015 N.W. 22nd Ave., tel. (503) 229-7711. This hospital's **Convenience Care Center,** tel. (503) 229-8000, located on-site offers quicker, less costly care than the main Emergency Room, open 9 a.m.-9 p.m.during the week, 10 a.m.-9 p.m. weekends.

Media

The *Oregonian,* 1320 S.W. Broadway, tel. (503) 221-8327, Portland's only daily, is joined by 16 alternative or community papers that circulate around the city. The *Oregonian's* "Arts and Entertainment" section comes out each Friday. The Wednesday *Outdoors* insert covers the state sea level to ski level. Finally, the **Oregonian Inside Line,** tel. (503) 225-5555, is a free 24-hour news and information service from the *Oregonian.* Extensions covering restaurants, theaters, cinemas, live music venues, coastal and mountain getaways, public transport, guided hikes, and the Portland Theatre Alliance exemplify the scope of this service. Look for a full list of extensions in the Sunday "TV Click."

Of all the free weeklies, most useful to the traveler is *Willamette Week.* This publication's excellent cultural listings and restaurant reviews make it a valuable resource. It comes out every Wednesday and can be found at cafes, bookstores, and restaurants in the greater Portland area. Also noteworthy is its heavily patronized singles ads.

PDXS is another alternative weekly worth looking at, particularly for its critques of local media. The best community papers are *Northwest Examiner* serving N.W. 215th and N.W. 23rd (good information on galleries and restaurants and the *Southeast Examiner* serving the "hip strips" (Clinton St., Hawthorne St., and Belmont St.) with news, reviews, and commentary.

Willamette Week comes out each Wednesday and has the premier entertainment listings in the city, along with news, reviews, and comments about a wide range of subjects relevant to visitors. Restaurants, artistic and theatrical presentations, sports, and the local political scuttlebutt are often dealt with in an irreverent, even sardonic, tone.

Our Town also has extensive listings, as well as some reviews and articles aimed at a more mainstream audience. Their sponsorship of The First Thursday shuttle makes thm privy to news from Portland's art world.

As for radio, Portland's nearly three dozen radio stations have something for everybody. Noteworthy on the AM band are a preponderance of call-in talk shows. For the most diverse programming, try KPSU (1450 on the AM dial), the college radio station. Everything from political discussions to the gamut of musical genres can be found here. The FM band concentrates more on music, though several listener-subscriber stations do their part to revive the grand old art of conversation with interviews and news commentary. KBOO (90.7 FM) features eclectic community-based programming. KOPB (91.5 FM) offers classical music and National Public Radio news shows.

Internet fans will find the **Citysearch Portland Web site,** http://www.citysearch.com, to be an easy-to-use directory to the community. Restaurants, hotels, cultural attractions, etc. are continually updated and supplemented by high-viz graphics and maps. The listings go beyond the usual electronic Yellow Pages format with content-laden blurbs written by savvy locals.

Most of the Welcome Centers Oregon has established at key entry points to the state are open May-October. By contrast, Portland's Welcome Center, containing a far-reaching collection of travel information on the state, is open year-round. Strategically located close to Oregon's Columbia River border with Washington just off I-5, a visit to this information outlet at Jantzen Beach Mall can be coupled with a stop at such traveler friendly stores as Barnes and Noble and REI outdoor store. Close by is an outlet of Chang's Mongolian Grill. Take I-5 exit 308 and look for the Welcome Center in the rest area at the north end of the complex. **The American Automobile Association (AAA),** 600 S.W. Market St., tel. (503) 222-6734, sells a good selection of travel books and maps and are glad to answer questions.

DAY-TRIPS FROM PORTLAND

THE WINE COUNTRY

Although the vinifera grape thrives throughout the interior valleys of western Oregon from the Columbia River to the California border, what the national media calls the "wine country" usually includes only those vineyards west and southwest of Portland. This is where the rich soil and long, warm, gentle growing season have created conditions that sustain the largest concentration of vineyards in the Northwest. The slow-cooling fall days engender a complexity in the regional product by inhibiting high sugar concentrations while maintaining the natural acidity of the grape. In summer, Oregon's northern latitude makes for long sunny days without excessive heat, a condition which bodes well for the harvest. These factors combine to produce wines delicate in flavor, low in alcohol, and crisp in finish, despite a tendency toward fruitiness.

A free monthly publication, *Oregon Wine,* Oregon Wine Press, 644 S.E. 20th Ave., Portland 97214, is available in retail outlets throughout western Oregon and can help plan a foray to vineyards throughout the state. In addition, wine and restaurant reports and vintner interviews provide useful information. For portability, accuracy and engaging chatty descriptions of Oregon wineries, we highly recommend *Northwest Wines: A Pocket Guide to the Wineries of Washington, Oregon and Idaho* (Seattle 1996-sec-

ESCAPE TO WASHINGTON COUNTY

First, the Oregon Trail led pioneers to the Willamette Valley, a land "where crops never failed." Getting the crops to markets and to Columbia River ports via Portland, however, necessitated another frontier thoroughfare, the Tualatin Plank Road. Today, a different sort of promised land has grown up around the Plank Road: Washington County. Given the million-dollar deals cut in high-tech boardrooms (Intel, headquartered in Hillsboro, is Oregon's largest employer with 9,000 employees, and the Nike headquarters here, the region between Portland and the Coast Range summit may be more aptly termed "Oregon's tomorrow country."

But equally prominent is the county's identity as a retreat from Portland's urban stress. Despite a population glut around Beaverton, most of the county is decidedly rural. You can enjoy a bacchanal 10 minutes from downtown Beaverton, at **Ponzi Vineyards,** Vandermost Rd., Beaverton, tel. (503) 628-1227; hike Coast Range trails one-half hour away, contact the **Tillamook State Forest Office** in Forest Grove, tel. 357-8005; or follow a primrose path through botanical displays and U-pick farms, contact the **Washington County Visitor's Association,** 5075 Griffiths Dr., Suite 120, Beaverton, tel. (503) 544-5555 or (800) 537-3149. Other Washington County escapes include the 10-mile bike trail around human-made Hagg Lake, seven miles southwest of Forest Grove, tel. (503) 359-5732; and **Pumpkin Ridge golf course,** N. Plains exit on US 26, 15 miles west of Portland, tel. (503) 647-4747, *Golf Digest*'s 1992 choice for the best public course in the country. After 18 holes, cool down with microbrews in the homey confines of a 142 year-old estate at McMenanims **Cornelius Pass Roadhouse,** 4045 N.W. Cornelius Rd., tel. 640-6174, or at one of the world-class wineries in the county. Two tasting rooms of note around Forest Grove are Montinore, whose red and white wines took gold medals in their respective categories at the 1994 Oregon State Fair, and Momokawa, the Northwest's only producer of premium sake. Vineyard and scenic loops annotated by brochures are available from the Visitor's Association.

As anyone who has toured Washington County's award-winning wineries or enjoyed its rural splendor can tell you, the time to visit "tomorrow country" is today. To avoid rush-hour traffic on the Sunset Highway (US 26), follow Burnside St. and Barnes Rd. out of downtown along a beautiful winding route through the West Hills across the county line. Paradoxially, this itinerary parallels the old Tualatin Plank Road, one of Oregon's preeiminent pathways to economic opportunity in the old Oregon Territory 150 years ago.

YAMHILL COUNTY VINEYARDS

ond edition; Sasquatch Books) by Paul Gregutt, Dan McCarthy, and Jeff Prather.

Despite these publications and other literature about wine, it's easy to be overwhelmed. As such, the following wine country ramble concentrates on what most people are looking for—the pick of the harvest. In Oregon that means Yamhill County pinot noir. This vintage has bested the vaunted red wines of Burgundy in numerous competitions; recently a 1992 Rex Hills pinot noir as did a 1989 Argyle Brut (made from pinot noir grapes) graced the White House table. The fact that the world's leading pinot noir festival is held in Yamhill County's McMinnville each year also reflects the exalted status of this wine-growing region.

Despite this status, tasting rooms in Oregon are often no-frills, makeshift affairs, but can impart a personal touch which is sometimes lacking with other more slick promotion-oriented wineries. Oregon vintners are quick to explain this lack of glitz by saying they prefer to put their money into the product. After a day along the trails of the pinot noir, you'll happily drink to that!

Getting Started

Before you go, pick up the *Discover Oregon Wineries* pamphlet at the Portland Convention and Visitors Center, Salmon St. across from Waterfront Park, or by contacting the **Oregon Winegrowers Association,** P.O. Box 6590, Portland 97228-6590, tel. (503) 233-2377. This pamphlet includes directions to the state's vineyards, their hours of operation, and a description of each location's offerings.

Yamhill County wineries and tasting rooms generally are open May-Oct., 11 a.m.-5 p.m. Those that do not have these hours can usually be visited around Thanksgiving, when there is an open house in the region. In any case, it's always a good idea to call in advance to confirm hours and other details. Blue-and-white signs on ORE 99W and its offshoots help point the way to such pantheons of pinot as Rex Hill, Knudsen Erath, Sokol Blosser, Yamhill Valley, and Amity. All these places have tasting rooms open to the public and accommodate visitors for more of the year than many of their counterparts.

On the Trail of Pinot Noir

If you look at a globe, you'll notice that ORE 99W west of Portland shares a latitude in common with the great wine-making regions of the world. While Oregon's Yamhill County (located on the northern cusp of the Willamette Valley) is not yet Burgundy or the Loire Valley of France, its early-ripening grapes, notably the pinot noir and chardonnay, regularly vie with the world's best in international competitions. This began in 1983, when an Oregon pinot noir beat out dozens of French pinot noir burgundies. Yamhill Valley Vineyards came in first, Sokol Blosser second, and Adelsheim third. The French vineyard Domaine Drouhin took fourth, thereafter buying a vineyard in Yamhill County. The state also gained attention for its truth-in-labeling law, which mandates that the varietal grape named on the bottle must be 90% of the pulp used to make the wine in question; other states require just 75%.

Regarding uniqueness, two wines you'll find here and nowhere else outside Oregon (in the U.S.) are the riesling-like Muller-Thurgau (most comparable to Blue Nun) and the chardonnay of the '90s, pinot gris. Finally, keep in mind that 1994 was the banner year for Oregon pinot noir. This vintage has a spicy, fruity, almost zinfandel-like character. Try it with grilled fish and vegetables.

Good wine and good food go together, which explains the creation of some surprisingly sophisticated restaurants and bed and breakfasts in this very rural area. Of late, a profusion of espresso places, art galleries, and other outgrowths of "big city" culture have sprung up alongside the wine country's grange halls and feed stores. Yamhill wine touring has also become popular since downtown Portland sits a mere 30 to 40 miles away from the state's greatest concentration of wineries. Just take I-5 south of the city and go west on ORE 99W, and within 45 minutes you'll find yourself in the midst of filbert orchards and grape stakes. In terms of distance, this might evoke wine-touring routes from San Francisco to the Napa and Sonoma valleys, but the similarity ends there. Don't expect extensive tours of Oregon wineries, and on-site restaurants are seldom seen—nor is there the weekend traffic of Yamhill's California counterparts. This might change, however, with the April 1994 *Life* magazine projection of Oregon's wine country becoming one of America's top new family vacation spots.

Yamhill County Bacchanal

Your Yamhill County bacchanal starts two miles east of Newberg where **Rex Hill Vineyards,** 30835 ORE 99W, Newberg 97132, tel. (503) 538-0666, highlight pinot noir, pinot gris, chardonnay, and riesling. Rex Hill won the prestigious Humphrey Edward Jones award in London for a world championship in 1991 as well as the San Francisco International Competition 1994 gold medal with a '92 pinot noir reserve. Persian rugs, antiques, an ornately carved front door, and a lit fireplace extend a warm welcome to visitors. Try the winery's excellent 1993 pinot gris, a varietal you probably won't have the chance to taste outside of Oregon. Hours at Rex Hill are 11 a.m.-5 p.m. daily, April-Dec., Fri.-Sun. 11 a.m.-5 p.m. Feb.-March. Veritas is open June-Aug. 11 a.m.-5 p.m. daily. On Friday evening Rex Hill frequently hosts surprise events with hors d'oeuvres, Friday-only prices, and other promotions in its lavish tasting room. If you're looking for a first-rate yet affordable overnight, inquire about the winery's Partridge Farm Bed and Breakfast, 4300 E. Portland, Newberg 97132, tel. (503) 538-2050. It is located a half-mile west of Rex Hill on ORE 99W near Newberg.

*Yamhill County
wine country*

After leaving Rex Hill, should your designated driver need a pick-me-up, hit the brakes at **Coffee Cottage,** 808 N.E. Hancock, Newberg, tel. (503) 538-5126. In addition to first-rate java and snacks, there's an in-house bookstore and occasional live music. Covered-and-heated outdoor seating also recommend this spot. In the middle of town, right across from Tina's restaurant, is the state's leading producer of sparkling wine in the tradition of champagne. Enjoy the **Argyle**'s, 691 ORE 99W, Dundee, tel. (503) 538-8520, Victorian farmhouse tasting room open daily 11 a.m.-5 p.m., closed major holidays. Given the fact that sparkling wines are produced from pinot noir, chardonnay, and riesling grapes (Oregon specialties), Oregon bodes well to become the Epernay/Reims of the New World.

Oregon's best-known and, until recently, greatest-producing winery (35,000 cases annually) is **Knudsen Erath,** 17000 N.E. Knudsen Lane, Dundee 97115, tel. (503) 538-3318. Its wood-paneled tasting room sits high in the Red Hills of Dundee, where it commands an imposing view of local vineyards and the Willamette Valley. To get there, go two miles north from the center of Dundee until you see a blue state highway sign marking the turnoff near the junction of ORE 99W and 9th Street. Ninth St. turns into Worden Hill Rd., a thoroughfare

destined to be lauded as the glory road of Oregon wine, given the legacy of Knudsen Erath. Appropriately, the road looks out over vistas dominated by grapevines. The winery's 1987 pinot noir vintages have garnered medals in competitions all over the world. In 1995, the *Seattle Times* called the 1994 pinot gris, $10, here "Oregon's best wine for the money." The tasting room is open 10 a.m.-6 p.m. daily in summer, 11 a.m.-5 p.m. Oct. 15-May 15, and offers cabernet sauvignon, gewürztraminer, chardonnay, and riesling. Beautiful picnic sites also attract visitors and their August Festival features food, music, and musical entertainment. Admission—$6. Close by is **Lange Vineyard,** 18380 N.E. Buena Vista, tel. (503) 538-6476, a good place to try pinot gris. Oregon-style pinot gris is medium-bodied, bright, and acidic, with citrusy overtone—really good with grilled salmon.

The intersection of Sokol Blosser Lane and ORE 99W sits about two miles west of Dundee. Sokol Blosser Lane leads to a winery of the same name. In addition to its pinot noir, the **Sokol Blosser** chardonnay is especially recommended at the tasting room. Robert Parker in *The Wine Spectator* raved about the latter varietal here. The vineyard is open daily May-Oct., 10:30 a.m.-5:30 p.m.; Nov.-April, the hours are

11 a.m.-5 p.m. Free tours of the vineyard are given every hour, and an array of Oregon gourmet food products is on sale here. A free brochure explaining viticulture through the seasons and labeled grape plantings are other features visitors may appreciate. Sokol Blosser's manicured fields framed by white oaks and madrone make a pleasing view from the tasting-room picture window. Top talent is brought in for charming outdoor musical events in the Sokol Blosser summer concert series. This event has showcased Joan Baez, Los Lobos, and other internationally known performers in recent years. While cruising the wine country around Sokol Blosser and Knudsen Erath, antique collectors can pull off ORE 99 into the town of Lafayette, 748 3rd Ave on ORE 99W, tel. (503) 864-2720, where seven days a week Oregon's largest antique display can be found in the old schoolhouse, mill, and auditorium. Imagine 10,000 square feet of antiques spread over three floors in a 1910 building. The mall promises that it won't sell reproductions. Besides traditional antiques, this is the place for folks interested in American pop culture; items on the order of early Disney-related merchandise, 60s rock posters, and trading card memorabilia. The admission is $5/day.

You'll find that the **Yamhill Valley Vineyards,** Oldville Rd., off ORE 18, tel. (503) 843-3100 or (800) 825-4845, tasting room is set amid an oak grove on a 9,300-acre estate and features a balcony overlooking the vineyard. This winery's first release, an '83 pinot noir, first distinguished itself at a 1985 tasting of French and Oregon vintages held in New York City. This wine was also selected as the best vintage wine in Oregon at the 1990 state fair. Yamhill's 1988 Willamette Valley estate-bottled chardonnay took a silver medal there. *Wine Enthusiast* rated Yamhill Valley's '94 pinot noir the 4th best in America. Riesling and gewürztraminer are also available for tasting May-Dec. Tues.-Sun. 11 a.m.-5 p.m., Jan.-April weekends only 11 a.m.-5 p.m.

Another Yamhill County winery is **Amity Vineyards,** 18150 Amity Vineyards Rd. S.E., Amity 97101, tel. (503) 835-2362. The tasting room is located on a 500-foot hill looking out over southern Yamhill County to the Coast Range, making for some beautiful sunset views. There are many award-winning varietals here to sam-

ple. Also noteworthy is the state's first chemical-free organic wine. It's open noon-5 p.m. daily June-Oct., noon-5 p.m. weekends only Nov.-May. It's closed Dec. 24-Jan. 31.

Not far from Amity is the monastery of the **Brigttine monks,** 23300 Walker Lane, Amity 97101, tel. (503) 835-8080 or 836-9622. Their chocolate truffles and fudge are highly regarded, and rooms are rented for spiritual retreats.

Amity wines are also featured at the **Lawrence Gallery,** tel. (503) 843-3787, in Sheraton, nine miles southwest of McMinnville on ORE 18. There are also several dozen other Oregon wines available for tasting here, as well as the work of a multitude of Oregon artists and craftspeople. Five acres of sweeping lawns and gardens surrounding this renovated century-old building make it even more of a reason to stop. Outdoor art pieces proliferate these elegant landscape at every turn. The Fresh Palate Cafe is also on-site, open daily for wine-friendly lunches and Sunday brunch.

Food, Lodging, and Events

The wine country is home to some of the leading purveyors of gourmet fare in the Northwest. In contrast to the budget-conscious choices that typify most of the restaurant recommendations in this book, we've selected two wine country eateries that are "justifiable splurges." Given the natural pairings of good wine and good food, to do any less would be a disservice to our readers.

Make reservations well in advance to dine at one of the best Italian restaurants in the state, **Nick's Italian Cafe,** 521 3rd St., McMinnville, tel. (503) 434-4471. The low-key atmosphere of McMinnville's downtown might at first make you wonder about such an assessment, but any trepidations will be quickly dispelled by the aromas of Nick's hearty fare and a wine list which is both extensive and distinctive. As a host to many wine-country functions, Nick is privy to special releases found nowhere else. The latter are fitting accompaniments to such unique culinary interpretations as lasagna with pine nuts, local mushrooms, and dried tomatoes; green vegetarian spinach ravioli with parmesan; and minestrone with pesto. The less adventurous will be pleased by the restaurant's famous grilled salmon, beef from Nick's own herd, as well as pastries and desserts made on the premises. A five-course, fixed-price dinner goes for $29 and is highly recommended. With Nick's daughter coordinating the restaurant service, his jazz collection forming the audio backdrop for your meal, and his mother's dessert recipes providing the grand finales, every aspect of your dining enjoyment has been well planned. Dinner is not served on Monday. Another unpretentious gem of a restaurant, **Tina's,** 760 ORE 99W, Dundee, tel. (503) 538-8880, is located even closer to Portland. As you're heading west on ORE 99 look for a little blue concrete structure on the right-hand side of the road across from Argyle Winery and the Dundee fire station. Tina's uses the freshest Oregon ingredients to create simple yet elegant fare. For budget diners, this place is a justifiable splurge, and big city sophisticates will recognize good dollar value with one bite of the pan-fried oyster with a lemon thyme mayonnaise or grilled rabbit with morel mushrooms. Don't expect menus here. Do expect to find local produce in season along with Willamette Valley lamb, pork, game hen, and rabbit as well as fresh fish from the nearby Pacific. The desserts are out of this world.

Should you care to extend your stay in the wine country, there is no shortage of bed and breakfasts to accommodate you. Before leaving Portland, consult *Oregon Wine* for a hostelry that can meet your specs.

The Mattey House, 10221 N.E. Mattey Lane, McMinnville 97128, tel. (503) 434-5058, combines Old World charm and proximity to wineries. Set in the middle of wheat fields and orchards at the edge of McMinnville, this 1892 Victorian mansion with Ionic columns, a fireplace with a carved wood and marble hearth, and big windows looks inviting at the end of a day of wine touring. While some of the rooms may be small or lack private baths, individual phones, or TV, you can't beat the Mattey House for coziness and refinement. Antique furnishings, period wallpapers, and old photographs set the mood for afternoon wine and cheese in the living room. A breakfast of homemade breads and jellies, made with fruits and berries from the innkeeper's own orchard together with gourmet egg dishes get your Yamhill bacchanal off to a great start. This fusion of vinticulture and Victoriana begins at $75 a night. To get there, turn off ORE 99W between McMinnville

and Lafayette onto Mattey Lane and drive until you get to a large oak tree near the house.

Of all the events in the Yamhill wine country and its counterparts, no fête can boast the world-class status of the **Annual International Pinot Noir Celebration,** International Pinot Noir Celebration, P.O. Box 1310, McMinnville 97128, tel. (503) 472-8964. More than 50 American and international pinot noir producers are on hand for symposiums, tastings, and winery tours. Meals prepared by internationally known chefs are also a highlight. The three-day event takes place at the end of July on the Linfield College campus in McMinnville. While the cost of registration, $350, is prohibitive for many, tickets to the final tasting can be purchased separately for $30. This epicurean delight takes place on the last day and features a tasting of more than 50 esteemed vintages from around the world.

While harvest festivals, concerts, and other events effectively complement tasting and touring, a drive through the region from mid-September into early October could well offer the biggest treat for the senses. At this time, the sight of multihued grape leaves creates a festive fall feeling, while intoxicating aromas of fermentation fill the air.

A HISTORY TOUR LOOP

Champoeg State Park

Below Yamhill County, just southeast of Newberg on ORE 219, is Champoeg (pronounced "sham-poo-ee" or "cham-poo-ee-eck"), often touted as the birthplace of Oregon. The name means "field of roots" in Chinook, referring to the camas coveted by Native Americans, who boiled it to accompany the traditional salmon feast.

Champoeg State Park commemorates the site of the 1843 vote to break free from British and Hudson's Bay Company rule and establish a pro-American provisional government in the Oregon country. To get there from Portland, drive south on I-5 until you see signs for exit 278. This exit directs you to a rural route that goes five miles to the park visitor center, tel. (503) 678-1251. The 568-acre park is equidistant from Portland and Salem along the Willamette River.

The visitor center has exhibits detailing how the Calapooya Indians, explorers, French Canadian fur traders, and American settlers lived in the Willamette Valley. It's open every day 9 a.m.-5 p.m., and there is no admission charge. The grounds also have several historic buildings. Adjacent to the visitor center is the Manson Barn, built in 1862. The Old Butteville jail (1850) and one-room schoolhouse have also been moved to Champoeg to help evoke frontier life. Just west of the park entrance is a replica of the 1852 house of pioneer Robert Newell, tel. (503) 678-5537. Particularly interesting is the second floor, which showcases Indian artifacts and a collection of inaugural gowns worn by the wives of Oregon governors. The house is open Feb.-Nov., Wed.-Sun. noon-5 p.m. Admission is $1.50 for adults, 50 cents for children. The **Pioneer Mother's Museum** replicates the dwellings in the Willamette Valley circa 1850. A collection of guns and muskets 1775-1850 is also displayed. Admission is 75 cents. In addition, there's also a day use fee of $3.

During July, Thurs.-Sun., the **Champoeg Historical Pageant,** tel. (503) 678-1649, traces Oregon life from settlement to statehood. The spirited drama entitled *Doc* traces the life of Champoeg founder Robert Newell. Showtime is 7:30 p.m., preceded by history exhibits, music, and a picnic supper 5:30-7:30 p.m. The show takes place at the Champoeg State Park amphitheater under the stars. Admission is $7, seniors $6, and students $5. Recently, this amphitheater has been hosting big-time musical talent during the summer. Rock concerts and other events are listed in *The Oregonian* A&E section on Wednesday.

French Prairie Loop

Before leaving Champoeg State Park, pick up a brochure at the visitor center outlining the French Prairie Loop, a 40-mile byway for car and bicycle touring. History buffs, thrift shoppers, and antique aficionados will enjoy the chance to indulge their passions on this drive. French-Canadian trappers settled here in the 1820s and '30s to help the Hudson's Bay Company establish a presence in the Willamette Valley. During the 1849 California gold rush, wheat and produce from this area were shipped to granaries and warehouses in the area of present-day Portland and on to San Francisco.

The 1843 conference at Champoeg marked the beginning of American rule in Oregon Country (from a mural in the state capitol).

OREGON STATE HIGHWAY DIVISION

Churches and buildings dating back to the 19th century have earned **St. Paul,** one of the towns on the loop (ORE 219), National Historic District status. The Northwest's oldest Catholic church, St. Paul's (circa 1846—some parishioners claim ancestral links with the French-Canadian trappers, who were Oregon's first permanent white settlers), had a million-dollar reconstruction as the result of a March 26, 1993 earthquake. The church was rebuilt with its original bricks and was reinforced with concrete. Each July 4th weekend, an Oregon tradition takes place here with the highly regarded St. Paul rodeo, fireworks display, and chicken barbecue. Besides staging the July 4th rodeo with one of the largest purses in the world, attracting top riders and ropers on the circuit, a highly respected Western art show is on display at the fairgrounds. Call (800) 237-5920 for details.

On the east side of the loop, **Aurora,** at the junction of ORE 219 and ORE 99, also enjoys

National Historic District status. Oregon's legacy as a haven for utopian communities began here with a Prussian immigrant, Dr. William Keil. He started up a communal colony for Oregon Trail pioneers, naming the town that grew out of it after his daughter. The Aurora colony fused Christian fundamentalism with collectivist principles, garnering distinction for its thriving farms and the excellence of its handicrafts. Despite Aurora's early success, a smallpox epidemic in 1862 and the coming of the railroad (which undermined Willamette River trade in the next decade) provided the catalysts for the town's demise. Keil himself died in 1877, and the struggling colony disbanded a few years later.

The Old Aurora Colony Museum, tel. (503) 678-5754, consists of five buildings, including two of the colony's homesteads, the communal wash house, and the farm equipment shed. Admission is $2.50 for adults and $1 for children; children under six are admitted free. The entry fee admits you to a slide show explaining the history of the colony and a tour of five historic buildings. Each season has different hours of operation. Call for times. Old tool buffs will particularly enjoy the guided tour. Other items of interest include a musical instrument collection and a recording left over from the colony band, as well as quilts and an herb garden. After the tour, you can take an Aurora walking tour (ask for the free pamphlet) of 33 structures close to the museum to increase your understanding of the site's history.

The museum is easily located by turning east as you enter town. After one block, you'll see the Old Aurora Colony Museum, 212 2nd St., Aurora), housed in a former ox barn. Tours are at 11 a.m., 1 p.m., and 3 p.m. Tues.-Sat. and at 1 and 3 p.m. on Sundays. Sometimes colony descendants are on hand to answer questions or demonstrate historical objects such as an ingenious spinning wheel devised by William Keil. The past also lives on in Aurora thanks to two-dozen clapboard and Victorian houses, as well as 18 antique shops, all clustered along ORE 99E.

OREGON CITY

History
Farther north from Canby on ORE 99E, the road attractively parallels the Willamette River. Jagged rock bluffs on one side of the highway contrast with the smooth-flowing river framed by stately cottonwood and poplar trees. More variety is added by islands in the channel and the broad expanse of 40-foot **Willamette Falls** in Oregon City. As the terminus of the Oregon Trail and the only seat of American power in the territory until 1852, this town is the site of many firsts. Leading off the list is Oregon City's status as the first incorporated city west of the Rockies. Other claims to fame include the West's first mint, paper mill, and newspaper, and the world's first long-distance electric power transmission system. The Oregon territorial capital also was the site of the state's first Protestant church and Masonic lodge.

Ironically, a representative of British interests in Oregon country is credited with starting up Oregon City. John McLoughlin, the Canadian-born chief factor of the Hudson's Bay Company, encouraged French-Canadian trappers to cross the Columbia River from Fort Vancouver and settle here in the northern Willamette Valley, inspiring the name French Prairie. To further the development of this British beachhead, McLoughlin built a flour mill near Willamette Falls in 1832. He moved down to Oregon City himself in the 1840s and became an ardent supporter of American settlers who wanted Oregon to be independent of England and part of the United States.

McLoughlin's flour mill was the precedent for other uses of water power here. It also helped attract pioneers who came over the Cascades via the Barlow Road extension of the Oregon Trail. As a result, Oregon City became a manufacturing center. Its river port thrived due to Willamette Falls impeding the movement of merchant ships farther south on the river. Although the development of the railroad and the city of Portland diminished Oregon City's importance, its glory days live on today thanks to National Historic District status. Buildings that date back to the mid-19th century exemplify Queen Anne, Federal, and Italianate architectural styles.

Orientation
Basalt terraces divide the city into three levels. Downtown is wedged between the river and a 100-foot bluff. A municipal elevator provides transportation between the commercial traffic in

the lower part of town and the historic building on the bluff. Years ago, the McLoughlin House was originally situated on the river but later was moved to the heights to make room for "progress."

Sights

Heading north on ORE 99E from Willamette Falls, look for the Tumwater turnoff on the east side of the highway for the **Clackamas County Historical Society Museum,** 211 Tumwater Dr., Oregon City, tel. (503) 655-5574. Gazing south back at the falls from the elevated perspective of the museum parking lot is a fitting prelude to the exhibits in the collection. The latter is amply recounted with diaries, artifacts, and historic photos on the second floor of the building. Prior to seeing these items, you'll encounter a time line which correlates world events over thousands of years to the geologic, political, and social growth of Oregon. This imparts a larger perspective to what you'll see in the exhibit hall. Signposts for your journey through the ages include Indian baskets and arrowheads, a horse-drawn carriage, and the world's first kidney dialysis machine (invented locally). The county collection serves as a valuable complement to the End of the Trail Visitor Center and historic homes just north of here. The admission is $3 for adults, with discounts for kids, seniors, and families. Hours are Mon.-Fri. 10 a.m.-5 p.m., Saturday, Sunday, and holidays 1-5 p.m.

Ten minutes north on ORE 99E you'll come to a somewhat-the-worse-for-wear rendition of the old territorial capital city. To re-experience the glory that was 19th-century Oregon City take a right turn off ORE 99E (McLoughlin Blvd.) onto 7th St. and follow it to the base of the cliff. At 7th and Railroad Streets, you'll see an immense gray elevator scaling the 90-foot escarpment (operates Mon.-Sat. 7 a.m.-7 p.m. free of charge) backdropping the lower section of town. Take a left-hand turn when you exit the elevator, and a few minutes' stroll northeast along the clifftop will have you peering across a street at the backyard of an Oregon City landmark.

The **McLoughlin House,** 713 Center St., tel. (503) 656-5146, between 7th and 8th Streets is an impressive clapboard-style home of the Father of Oregon. To spare it flood damage, the building was moved from its original site near the river to this location. Behind it are steps leading back to the lower section of town. The admission, $3 for adults, discounts for seniors and kids, may seem a tad steep to view an unexciting collection of original and period furnishings, but the docent's ghost stories and historical insights can make it all come alive. In addition, the grounds are lovingly landscaped with rhododendrons, azaleas, and roses. The building is open Tues.-Sat. 10 a.m.-4 p.m., Sunday 1-4 p.m., closed on holidays and during January.

End of the Trail Interpretive Center

The End of the Trail Interpretive Center, 1726 Washington St., tel. (503) 657-0988, showcases Oregon City's claim as the terminus of the Oregon Trail. This status is also claimed by The Dalles (a city in the Columbia River Gorge). Without belaboring the merits of each claim, it suffices to say that Oregon City was at the end of the Barlow Trail, a spur route over Mt. Hood from The Dalles for pioneers understandably leery of the raft trip down the Columbia River. Hours are Mon.-Sat. 9 a.m.-5 p.m., Sunday hours are similar but may vary. The center is closed in January.

This new large-scale interpretive center was built to commemorate the 150th anniversary of the Great Migration of 1843. To get there coming from Portland, take I-205 south to the Park Place exit, turn south on 213 and follow the signs to Abernethy Green. Organizers have selected an area often identified as the end of the Barlow Road section of the trail to set up these facilities. To find them, just follow Washington St. north to its intersection with Abernethy Rd. or ask one of the locals for directions to Kelly Field. From I-205, you should be able to see three connected buildings in the shape of giant covered wagons.

Visitors first enter a gallery filled with artifacts from pioneer days displayed in the period setting of a Missouri provisioner's shop. The first building also features storytellers dressed in period clothing explaining the items taken on the trail by the pioneers. The second gallery will showcase a 17-minute presentation on the Oregon Trail. This interpretive center's video presentation about the Oregon Trail also happens to be an excellent introduction to the whole state and the modern-day fruition of pioneer dreams. After the video a corridor with displays of Oregon

Trail artifacts leads to a gift shop and three-dimensional model of the End of the Oregon Trail. Open Mon.-Sat. 9 a.m.-5 p.m.; admission is $4.50 for adults, $2.50 for ages 12 and under and 65 and over.

Another way to take in the history of Oregon City and the Oregon Trail is at the pageant held Tues.-Sat. at 8 p.m. at the Interpretive Center's outdoor amphitheater, mid-July through the beginning of August. Tickets are $10 with discounts for seniors, students, children, and families. Call (503) 657-0988 or 656-1619 for more information.

John Inskeep
Environmental Learning Center

John Inskeep Environmental Learning Center, Clackamas Community College, 19600 South Molalla Ave., Oregon City 97045, tel. (503) 657-6958, ext. 2351, located three miles north of Kelly Field on ORE 213, is pioneering efforts of a different sort. The 80-acre environmental-study area showcases alternative technologies and recycling against a backdrop of ponds, trails, and wildlife. Exhibits on aquaculture, birds of prey, and wetlands are included in this environmental education center's portrayal of Oregon's ecosystems. The exhibits are supplemented by one of the largest telescopes in the Northwest (open Wednesday, Friday, and Saturday 7:30-10:30 p.m., $2 admission). Tours and interpretive programs are available at the center on Sunday afternoons. Hours of the entire complex are 9 a.m.-dusk daily with a $2 admission charge.

The center has a special outreach program in February. Every Saturday during the month 3-4:30 p.m. learn about beavers, spring chinook salmon, herons, waterfowl, and wildlife on the center's 37-foot *Envirotrekker*. This vessel is moored in Oregon City's sportcraft boat marina.

For more information, call (503) 657-6958, ext. 2351, Tues.-Sat., or consult the *Oregonian's* "Arts and Entertainment" listings on Friday during February. Adjacent to the Inskeep Environmental Learning Center is the **Home Orchard Society Arboretum,** displaying Oregon's array of fruit-bearing plants.

Food

Even though Portland restaurants are 15 minutes away via I-205 and I-84, for good food and an atmosphere in keeping with Oregon City's heritage, try the **Fellows House,** 416 S. McLoughlin Blvd, tel. (503) 656-2089, a restaurant in a restored 1867 ship captain's home located on the river on ORE 99 a mile south of downtown. Between 7 a.m. and 3 p.m. enjoy hearty breakfast fare and such lunchtime sandwich creations as Dungeness crab with melted cheddar, avocado, onion, tomato, and lettuce topped by the inn's special sauce on fresh sourdough bread, $8.

McAnultys and Barrys, 812 Main St., tel. (503) 656-3817, is a good place for a sandwich—create your own or choose from a wide variety of creative combinations. Quality bar food, espresso drinks, and microbrews also recommend this reasonably-priced (Reubens for $2.35) downtown eatery. A pricier alternative in the same genre with a riverfront location is the Oregon City' **McMenamin's** outlet, 102 9th St., tel. (503) 655-8032. For light breakfast, sandwiches, and Japanese bento, the **Blue Mountain Deli,** next to the courthouse, 723 Main St., tel. (503) 650-4813, is perfect for an eat 'n run meal (less than $5). Pastries, milkshakes, and ice cream are tasty after-thoughts.

Information

For more information on Oregon City, call (800) 424-3002.

THE COLUMBIA RIVER GORGE

Portlanders with only a day to show out-of-towners what Oregon is all about often head east to the Columbia Gorge. In the 70 miles between Troutdale and The Dalles, the state's pioneer history, rainforest-to-desert diversity, orchard country, and hydropower extolled in Woody Guthrie's "Roll On Columbia" paint a holistic mural-come-to-life of the Oregon experience. The majesty of the river, together with dozens of waterfalls coming off the huge basalt cliffs, provide the kind of scenery inadequately enshrined in calendar art and coffee-table books.

HISTORY

Artifacts and petroglyphs found in the Columbia Gorge date human presence there back 10,000 years. Further historical perspective is lent by the fossilized remains of mastodons, camels, and ancient horses unearthed near The Dalles. The Caucasian presence began with the arrival of the American Navy's Captain Gray in 1792 (although the recent discovery of Kennewick Man, a 9,300 year old carcass with Caucasian features makes this arguable). His ship, the *Columbia Rediviva,* was the inspiration for the name of the river. Prior to this time, British mariners Cook (in 1778) and Vancouver (in 1792) navigated past the river's five-mile mouth at Astoria but failed to note it, probably because of bad weather. All of these explorers were motivated by a desire to find a sea route connecting the Atlantic and the Pacific. Upon hearing of Gray's voyage of discovery, Vancouver dispatched Admiral Broughton to establish a British presence on the river. Broughton proceeded to name Mounts Hood, Adams, and Rainier after British naval officers on his excursion up the Columbia. The next major incursion was that of Lewis and Clark (in 1805) who, despite coming by land from the east, were also drawn here in part by the search for the Northwest Passage.

Their journals described "great quantities of salmon" and "a large number of Indians" along the river. It's a good bet that the native population they observed included not just the local residents, because the shores of the Columbia have traditionally hosted gatherings of tribes. As a result, an intermingling of cultures took place, which might have been manifested in a Gorge tribesman wearing a Yurok (California) headband, Kwakiutl (British Columbia) sandals, and a Hudson's Bay Company blanket. Even

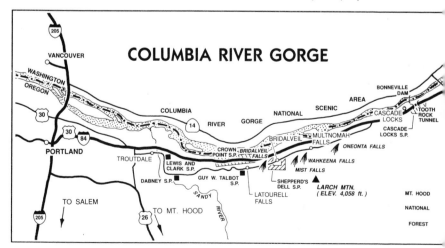

TED LONG ISHIKAWA

Engineer Samuel Lancaster emulated the dry masonry techniques of Charlemagne's legions.

their Chinook dialect became saturated with French and English expressions.

The subsequent decades saw further erosion of the Indian culture. The coming of the trappers during the first part of the 19th century, the missionaries in the 1830s, and the Oregon Trail migrants in the 1840s brought infectious diseases and depleted the salmon as well as other resources in the Columbia Gorge. Steamship transport in the 1850s and the completion of the Union Pacific tracks several decades later facilitated future incursions into this sacred Indian domain.

Lancaster's Vision

The modern era began with the building of the Columbia Gorge Scenic Highway whose roadbed was first laid in 1913. When the project was finished several years later, it was the only paved road in the Northwest, as well as the first designated scenic highway in the country. It was financed by Sam Hill, heir to a railroad fortune, who wanted to build a road to his Maryhill estate on the Washington side of the river. Backed by prominent Portland citizens such as lumber magnate Simon Benson, the project also attracted the support of a national group called the Good

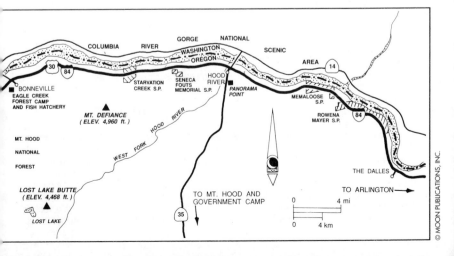

© MOON PUBLICATIONS, INC.

Roads Committee. Hill recruited engineer Samuel Lancaster for the task and took him abroad to study the classic roads of Europe. Such inspirations as Bingen-on-the-Rhine in Germany and the Axenstrasse in Switzerland are reflected in the hairpin turns and scenic overlooks of Lancaster's road. Other touches included the dry-masonry (without mortar) building techniques of Charlemagne's legions, Florentine viaducts, ornate tunnels, and stone benches. Much of the route was beveled into the steep basalt cliffs in order to highlight a view on every curve.

During the highway's construction, civic groups and convict labor joined road crews to give form to Lancaster's vision. Once completed, it became a tradition for middle-class families from Portland to pile into the Model T for Sunday drives on the Columbia Gorge Scenic Highway. By the '30s, the 73.8-mile thoroughfare became so crowded that a state study called for a speedier route. Interstate 84 was the result several decades later. While the riverside route of the interstate didn't lack for aesthetic appeal, Lancaster would have been appalled to see the ensuing neglect and desecration of the old road. Today only one-third of his route remains intact, with the rest consigned to gravel pits and garbage dumps, or simply abandoned. Both state and federal governments have earmarked millions to restore the road to its former glory by the year 2010. The Columbia Gorge National Scenic Area Act passed by Congress in 1986 also made provisions for bicyclists, pedestrians, and people in wheelchairs. Thus, the road that started the American love affair with motor touring could well be breaking new ground by the 21st century.

A Dam Site Better

Tapping the hydropower potential of the river stimulated Roosevelt to initiate the Bonneville Dam and power project in the '30s. This was the first of many dams on the river, and the undertaking yielded benefits immediately. Besides employing thousands during the Depression, the WPA project supplied cheap power to Kaiser's shipyards and Boeing Aviation during World War II. Another Bonneville by-product was the creation of a 370-mile navigable channel from the Pacific Ocean to Idaho, enhancing commerce at the port of Portland. In the decades that followed, aluminum plants and other industries dependent on cheap power came to the Northwest, thanks to Columbia's hydropower. Today the river generates 80% of the region's kilowatts.

Roll on Columbia

The blessings conferred upon the Northwest by the river extend beyond the Columbia's usefulness as an artery of transport and commerce, a major salmon and sturgeon fishery, a source of irrigation water for the surrounding orchard country, and the generator of electricity for the western United States. The scenic beauty of the waterway and the gorge it occupies have forever drawn admirers of Mother Nature's handiwork. In recent years this influx has increased exponentially due to the popularity of windsurfing and other forms of outdoor recreation.

To ensure that the Gorge doesn't become loved to death or overdeveloped, the government created the Columbia Gorge Scenic Area in 1986, an experiment in preserving nature's beauty as well as the region's livelihood. Since there's not enough land for a national park, given the river valley's steep contours filled to the brim with 50,000 residents, this alternative environmental jurisdiction was instituted to monitor and support economic growth in appropriate areas. Many residents fear the federal government's Columbia Gorge Commission will put a damper on business expansion in the areas outside the dozen small towns here. Already, restrictions on recreation and controversies over Indian fishing rights have caused the commission to lock horns with the quintessential dilemma facing Oregon and the whole Northwest: the fact that one person's conservation is very often another's unemployment.

THE LAND

As the only sea-level break in the Cascade Mountains, a range extending from western Canada into California, the Columbia River flows 1,214 miles from its source in British Columbia to its mouth at Astoria. In so doing, it carries a quarter-million cubic feet of water per second to the Pacific. This is 10 times the flow of the Colorado, but to motorists driving east from Portland, the river

Multnomah Falls in the Columbia River Gorge, America's second-highest cascade

appears placid. Now only Woody Guthrie songs and old photos in Columbia Gorge museums and roadside cafes hint at the river's force before the dams reduced the whitewater to what often seems like a hybrid windsurfing pond cum shipping canal. While the four hydroelectric projects along the waterway turned darkness to dawn, the Columbia in an earlier incarnation strutted its stuff in a manner more befitting the second-largest and most powerful river on the continent. The power of waterfalls located near Cascade Locks and The Dalles motivated their selection as dam sites, and before damming, much of the mile-wide channel of the Columbia in through the Gorge was too rough for the safe passage of commercial vessels. But even if we were able to gaze upon a Columbia flowing from the mountains to the sea unimpeded by dams or shipping locks, it couldn't begin to approximate what transpired here after dozens of Ice Age inundations.

Missoula Floods

About 15,000 years ago near the end of the Pleistocene epoch, an ice lobe from Canada backed up the water of a lake in the area of present-day Idaho and Montana. When the lake waters rose high enough to breach and wash away the dam, 500 cubic miles of water powered across eastern Washington into Oregon. This cycle was repeat-ed at least 40, and possibly 100, times or more over a period of several thousand years. Flood waters were 1,000 feet deep where The Dalles is today; they crested almost 750 feet high at Crown Point and covered the Portland area under 400 feet of glacial runoff. These so-called Missoula Floods scoured away the valley walls, changing the V-shape of the river valley to its present U-shape, and forming cliffs and waterfalls on the Oregon side of the waterway.

Diverse Bioregions

The resulting contours of the Gorge have formed a conduit for weather systems east and west of the Cascades. The meteorological mix of air masses has created a high concentration of amazingly diverse microclimates between Portland and The Dalles. Consider that only 50 miles separate the wet, damp conditions at Bonneville (75-inch average annual precipitation) from the arid grasslands at Celilo (12-inch average annual precipitation). Several thousands of feet between the highest and lowest elevations in the Gorge also help define one of the greatest ranges of plant habitats per square mile to be found anywhere in the world. In Oneonta Gorge alone there are 12 plant species found nowhere else. *Wildflowers of the Columbia,* by Russ Jolley, published by the Oregon Historical Society

THE MYTHIC LEGACY OF THE COLUMBIA GORGE

Modern-day history books include Lewis and Clark and the Oregon Trail pioneers in their writings about the Columbia River Gorge. Future tomes on the region will add Woody Guthrie, D.B. Cooper, and perhaps Bigfoot to the Who's Who of area notables. While their relationship with the only sea-level cleft in the Cascades was transitory, each of these gorge travelers has carved out a permanent niche in the psychic landscape of the Pacific Northwest.

Perhaps the most tangible remnants of this legacy are the 26 tunes penned by Woody Guthrie here during one month in the spring of 1941. He had been hired by the federal government (for $266.60) to write songs to help sell the public on the Bonneville Dam's goal of harnessing the river for irrigation, flood control, and cheap electricity. Out of this effort came such standards as "Roll on Columbia" ("your power is turning our darkness to dawn") and "Pastures of Plenty." Considering his forebears in the Columbia Gorge, it's altogether fitting that the folksinger laureate of our country reached his creative peak in this storied landscape.

Despite Guthrie's predominant themes of social justice and environmental grandeur, a song about the heist of the century might have been forthcoming had this troubadour been writing after November 24, 1971. On that day, D.B. Cooper bailed out of a Boeing 727 over southwestern Washington with $200,000 in cash—the result of the world's first successful airplane hijacking/extortion. It all began when someone calling himself Dan Cooper (later misidentified to a UPI reporter as "D.B." by the FBI) commandeered a Portland-to-Seattle flight by handing the stewardess a note about a bomb he said would explode unless he received a large sum of money and some parachutes. To underscore his threat, he opened his briefcase to reveal a foreboding network of wires and sticks. After his request was complied with at the Seattle airport, the flight headed back toward the Oregon border, where he jumped out of the plane and into history. He also might have jumped into the Columbia River if a small portion of the money recovered along its banks in 1980 is any indication. Some years later, a diver found what he claimed was Cooper's parachute not far from this site. In any case, the derring-do of this modern-day Jesse James was the high-tech equivalent of a stage robbery committed at a full gallop. With only unconfirmed sightings of the mysterious Mr. Cooper over the last two decades, all that remains

Press, identifies 744 of the area's more than 800 species of flowering shrubs and wildflowers. Plants usually found at 4,000 feet elevation will grow at 1,600 feet above sea level in the gorge due to the contours of the cliffs. The region's combination of sun and shade, heat and cold, moisture and dryness, humus soil and rock, as well as the juxtaposition of grassland and forest, provide a textbook introduction to most of the bioregions of the American Northwest. Two good places that showcase the interesting plant communities of this region are the aforementioned Oneonta Gorge and Rowena Crest. Each is on the old highway and detailed in this chapter. Oneonta Gorge features such endemics as Howell's Fleabane, a blue flower in the aster family and a rare form of mountain primrose. Rowena Crest is close enough to the interface of the west and dry east that its late May wildflower peak season showcases the greatest variety of species in an easily accessible locale.

THE COLUMBIA GORGE SCENIC HIGHWAY

With a near-total absence of hotels as well as places to camp and eat, the most spectacular section of the Columbia River Scenic Highway is best treated as a day-trip. Beyond Multnomah Falls, creature comforts abound in nearby Cascade Locks and Hood River.

The Columbia Gorge takes on a different aspect when you depart I-84 and enter the Columbia River Scenic Highway (ORE 30) at exit 22 at Corbett, 15 miles from downtown Portland. It's possible to get on the Scenic Highway earlier in Troutdale and enjoy a pleasant drive (en route grab a bite at Tad's Chicken and Dumplings), but you are away from the Columbia River. Thus, if time is of the essence, ignore the first signs for the Scenic Highway you'll see on I-84. Pull off instead at the **Royal Chinook Inn,** 2605 N.E. Corbett Hill Rd., of this crime is the poetic justice of its Old West backdrop to stir imagination and wonder.

Another secret the Columbia Gorge might share if it could talk would be the whereabouts of the abominable snowman, a.k.a. Bigfoot or Sasquatch. Indian tribes of the region regarded this creature as a fact of life and celebrated its presence in art and ritual. Whether it exists outside the mind or not, the King Kong of the Northwest forests has attracted to the region everyone from hunters and academics to curiosity seekers and *National Enquirer* reporters. Although the notion of a half-man, half-ape eluding human capture seems implausible at first, a brief look at some of the evidence might convince you otherwise. As recently as the winter of 1991, reports from a remote area of the Blue Mountains (whose chief drainage is the Columbia River) spoke of more than 60 miles of tracks left in the snow by a large five-toed creature. Scientists on the scene were of the opinion that the pattern of the prints and the gait could not have been fake. A similar conclusion was reached in 1982 about a plaster cast of footprints taken from the same mountain range. A Washington State University professor detected humanlike whorls on the toe portions of the prints, which he said showed that the tracks had to have been made by a large hominid. Reports and evidence of actual encoun-

ters abound in the annals of the Northwest, compelling the U.S. Army Corps of Engineers to list it as an indigenous species, accompanied by a detailed anatomical description. Skamania County, whose southern border is the Columbia River shoreline, declared the harming of these creatures a gross misdemeanor punishable by a year in jail and a thousand-dollar fine.

The unwavering belief of Bigfoot adherents among the scientific community and the native insistence that it's a living entity has naturally met with skepticism. No matter what you believe, it's not inconceivable that a creature somewhat like ourselves could avoid detection for so long, given the recent discoveries of primitive tribes in the Amazon and in the Philippines. To keep up on Bigfoot sightings and learn what's been known or speculated about the Northwest's missing link, http://www.teleport.com/~tbrp/ is the Bigfoot Research Project page.

In any case, Bigfoot, Woody Guthrie, and D.B. Cooper all possess a mythic aura that will last as long as people gather round the campfire to sing songs and tell stories. And in the flickering firelight, there might be a shadow or an echo of someone or something that'll give you pause. It's all happened many times before here in the Columbia River Gorge.

Corbett 97019, tel. (503) 695-2297, for a look at vintage photos from the era before the dams tamed the torrents and before motorists were able to speed through the region at 65 miles per hour. The Royal Chinook's walls are festooned with shots of Indian anglers clustered around Celilo Falls (currently The Dalles Dam), Model Ts in the foreground of a waterfall, and other poignant images from days gone by. This is also the only restaurant for the next 12 miles of the scenic drive, until Multnomah Falls (whose visitor center also displays vintage photos). Their specialty is both fresh and smoked local salmon.

From the cafe wend your way to the top of the hill. If you bear left and follow the signs for Crown Point and Multnomah Falls, you'll soon experience America's first auto-tour route in all its glory.

Larch Mountain

If you take the road marked Larch Mountain instead, you'll go 14 miles to an overlook fea-

turing views of the snowcapped Cascades and the Columbia all the way west to Portland. There are also picnic tables and trailheads to the Gorge below, with gorgeous beargrass blossoms in June. Later, huckleberries in August and mushrooms after the first rains await foragers.

To enjoy one of Oregon's classic sunset experiences, head to the northeast corner of the Larch Mountain parking lot around sunset (look for a small wooden Viewpoint sign). From here, a gently rolling quarter-mile paved path takes you through forests of larch and noble fir. The trail's last 100 yards involve a steep climb up to an elevated outcropping 4,658 feet above sea level. This is **Sherrard Point,** site of a former fire lookout tower. To the east, across miles of treetops, is Mt. Hood. To the south is Mt. Jefferson's symmetrical cone. To the north, Mounts St. Helens, Rainier, and Adams are visible. To the east, the Columbia River becomes bathed in reddish glow during sunset. A short time later, the lights of Portland take back the night.

An ambitious hike involving a car shuttle between trailheads lets you trek from Larch Mountain down to Multnomah Falls Lodge. This trail drops 4,000 feet in 6.8 miles. To reach the descent route from Larch Mountain viewpoint, retrace your steps along the path back toward the parking lot. At about halfway, veer right up the spur trail that crests on a hill. From this hilltop head west a short distance toward a picnic area where the trail down to the gorge begins. Within the first quarter-mile the sound of target-shooters practicing in an area just off the trail may occasion misgivings. While there's no danger, these weekend warriors destruction of tree stumps and disturbance of the peace have many hikers distressed and up in arms. The Forest Service is evaluating controls on the situation.

Vista House

As the Columbia Gorge Scenic Highway winds through the hills from Corbett, you'll catch glimpses of the gorge below. You also might notice the distinctive outline of an octagonal structure, particularly if you pull off at Portland Women's Forum viewpoint and look across the gully. This is the Vista House Visitor Center at Crown Point, 725 feet above the Columbia, opened in 1916 in honor of the highway's completion. The outside observation deck up the steps from the main rotunda showcases 30 miles of the Columbia River Gorge. Samuel Lancaster is paid homage with a plaque outside Vista House that aptly describes his route as possessed of "poetry and drama." Photos of the various stages of the road's construction are displayed in the main rotunda, as are wildflower cuttings to study; four miles down the road at Shepperd's Dell you can find some of the region's endemic plants. Downstairs is the visitor center's bookshop and wallboard of printed materials about the Gorge, both past and present. On weekends, a "mountain man" spins yarns about local wildlife and life in the region. Vista House hours are 9 a.m.-6 p.m. daily, April-October.

Waterfalls

Between Troutdale and The Dalles there are 77 waterfalls. From Vista House, the next 11 miles feature a waterfall a mile, the largest concentration of tall waterfalls in the United States, though Oregon's Silver Falls State Park runs a close second. The highest are Multnomah at 620 feet and Latourell at 249 feet. While all of the cataracts are beautiful and distinctive, the three most majestic falls are, by Lancaster's design, the most visible and accessible from the road. These include the two just mentioned as well as Wahkeena Falls.

Latourell Falls is the first of the big three seen by motorists. A paved 150-yard trail takes you down to Latourell's base, where the shade and cooling spray create a microclimate for fleabane, a delicate bluish member of the aster family, and other flowers normally common to alpine biomes. The filmy tendrils of water against the columnar basalt formations on the cliffs make Latourell a favorite with photographers. Foragers appreciate maidenhair fern and thimbleberries, but hopefully not enough to ever denude the slope. Another trailhead begins in the middle of the parking lot and climbs around and above the falls, though bushes obscure the overhang from which the water descends. You'll probably be more inclined to stop after 50 yards and take in the distant perspective of Latourell from across the canyon.

The next waterfall is not visible from the road, so park your car in the lot of **Bridal Veil Falls State Park,** tel. (503) 695-2661 for information, and put on your walking shoes. A short two-thirds of a mile round trip hike will take you to the observation platform at the base of this impressive cascade on the north side of the highway (where you will initially be hiking downhill). In addition to tree-shaded picnic tables and bathrooms that are open all year, the park features the largest camas patch in the Columbia River Gorge.

The only place to stay on the waterfall route of the Scenic Highway is adjacent to the park, **Bridal Veil Bed and Breakfast,** Bridalveil 97010, tel. (503) 695-2333 or 284-8901 from Portland. It's a homey country inn with a knotty pine interior, antique quilts, historical photos, and the kind of furniture you used to find in Grandma's house. The combination of queen beds, breakfast out on the front porch, and the nearby trails and waterfalls of the Scenic Highway all make this worth the $75 per couple rate, $65 for singles. There are also quaint cottage rooms available on the property featuring private baths and lots of windows and skylights. The inn makes an ideal fall getaway amid a riot of color. Incredibly, this place is only 30 minutes from Portland, making it a great alternative to big city lodging. To get there from Portland, take exit 28 off of I-84. Turn right at the fork (heading west) on the old highway toward the Vista House. Since there is no exit 28 going west on I-84, you must instead take exit 35, Scenic Highway/Ainsworth Park (past the Bonneville Dam exit), and stay on the old highway. You will see the inn on the south side of the road.

Wahkeena Falls, whose name means "Most Beautiful," is a 242-foot series of cascades that descends in staircase fashion to the parking lot. To the right of the small footbridge abutting the road is the beginning of the two-mile **Perdition Trail.** This steep path affords views of both Wahkeena and Multnomah falls. Higher up are panoramic vistas of the Columbia River and Gorge. This trail is especially striking in October, when the cottonwoods and the bigleaf and vine maples sport colorful fall foliage. Hikers should also be on the lookout for poison oak, which grows below the 800-foot level in the Gorge. A picnic area is north of the Scenic Highway across from the falls. At this writing, the wooden staircase to the upper level of this trail has not been replaced after the fires of October 1991. See the Angel's Rest hike at the end of this section if you're looking to hit the trail on the Scenic Highway. In the Cascade Locks Hiking section, the famous Wahkeena to Multnomah Loop hike is described.

Multnomah Falls pours down from the heights with an authority worthy of the prominent Indian chief for whom it is named. The half-mile-long uphill trail to the bridge should be attempted by anyone capable of a small amount of exertion. Here you can bathe in the cool mists of the upper falls and appreciate the power of Multnomah's billowy flumes. The more intrepid can reach the top of the falls and beyond, but the view from the parking lot should be edifying. Placards detailing forest canopies and their understories at different elevations and other aspects of the ecosystem are on display in the first 100 yards of the trail. On the way up keep an eye out for such indigenous species as the Larch Mountain salamander and Howell's daisy. If you hear a whistle at higher elevations, it might be a pika.

OREGON TOURISM DIVISION

Oneonta Gorge is a cool, moist, and green enclave just down the road from the Multnomah Falls.

Look for the image of an Indian maiden's face on the rock behind the falls. Legend has it that she threw herself over the falls as a sacrifice to head off an epidemic. Now when the breeze blows through the water, a silvery stream separates from the upper falls, framing the maiden's form as a token of the spirits' acceptance of her gesture. These and other area falls emanate from melting snows forming creeks on Larch Mountain. The legacy of water in the gorge originated with the previously mentioned Missoula Floods. But today, the major inundation here is human, between one and two million visitors yearly, making Multnomah Falls the most visited place in the state.

The falls area also has a snack bar as well as **Multnomah Falls Lodge,** tel. (503) 695-2376. A magnificent structure, the lodge was built in 1925 and is today operated by a private concessioner under the supervision of the U.S. Forest Service. A cheery solarium adjacent to a high-ceilinged dining room built from native wood and stone makes a casually elegant setting to begin or end a day of hiking. On warm days the outside patio here is delightful. WPA-commissioned paintings and vintage photos of the Cascades and Columbia Gorge scenes and a menu with such indigenous fare as Caesar salad with Columbia River smoked salmon, $11, also effectively articulates the surroundings. Particularly recommended is the mini loaf of home-baked wheat bread and soup for lunch, $6.50. The giant pecan roll makes a nice budget breakfast. The microbrews and huckleberry tarts available with your meals will also help forestall hunger pangs along the trail.

Up from the Ashes—Angel's Rest Hike

In early October 1991, massive fires engulfed portions of the Mt. Hood National Forest off the Scenic Highway. At the time, it was feared that massive erosion from the devastation of the trees and the understory would do in the network of trails in and around the route of the waterfalls. However, only one trail, the Perdition, is still out of service on its upper levels.

For a good perspective on the fire as well as a great view of the gorge between Portland and Bonneville, Angel's Rest Trail no. 415 is recommended. To get there off I-84 take eastbound exit 28 and follow the exit road a quarter mile to its junction with the Scenic Highway. At this point hang a sharp right as if you were going to head up the hill toward Crown Point, but pull over into the gravel parking area on the north side of the highway instead. The trailhead is on the south side of ORE 30. The steep 2.3-mile path to the top of this rocky outcropping gains 1,600 feet and takes you from an unburned forest through vigorous new brush growth beneath live evergreens with singed bark. This gives way to charred conifers as you near the summit. Scientists hope these snags and new openings in the forest can breed more biodiversity in the ecosystem. At any rate, the lack of foliage on the branches of burnt trees has opened new vistas of the Columbia Gorge below.

From the top you can enjoy a balcony-seat view overlooking the action. The stage in this case juts out over the Columbia River with sweeping views toward Portland; to the northeast the snowcapped carapace of Mt. Adams plays peekaboo behind a series of smaller ridges.

Recreation

Swimming is safe at historic and scenic **Rooster Rock State Park,** exit 25 off of I-84 near Troutdale. On summer weekends a three dollar parking charge is leveled on each car. West of the parking area is the monolith for which the park is named. Lewis and Clark labeled the cucumber-shaped promontory on November 2, 1805. Playing fields and a gazebo front a sandy beach on the banks of the Columbia here. The water in the roped-in swimming area is shallow but refreshing. A mile or so east is one of the only nude beaches officially sanctioned by the state (the other one, near downtown Portland, is Collins Beach on Sauvie Island). Windsurfers might want to call (503) 695-2220 for information on wind conditions and weather prior to going to Rooster Rocks. Scenes from the 1994 movie *Maverick* starring Mel Gibson, Jody Foster, and James Garner were shot near here.

Information and Services

A four-color, shaded relief map details natural, cultural, scenic, and recreational opportunities in the Columbia River Gorge. It includes major travel routes, recreational sites, and visitor information. Send $3 to Scenic Area Headquarters, 902 Wasco Ave., Hood River OR, 97031, to obtain this resource.

For visitor information of all kinds, the **Gorge Information Service,** tel. (800) 222-8611 in Oregon, (800) 222-8660 outside of Oregon, has the answers. For advice on lodging, windsurfing, weather, sports, and updates on trail conditions for mountain biking and other activities, check out the Gorge Web site, http://www.gorge.net/rec.htm.

Vista House at Crown Point State Park on the Columbia River Scenic Highway east of Troutdale and west of Multnomah Falls, P.O. Box 204, Corbett 97019, tel. (503) 695-2230, offers visitors a *Columbia Gorge Sights and Services* pamphlet, a regional map, and a handbill reviewing the geologic evolution of the Columbia Gorge. Vista House is open April-Oct., 10 a.m.-6 p.m. daily. The only place to get gas along the route of the waterfalls is at the Corbett Store.

The **Multnomah Falls Information Center,** P.O. Box 68, Bridalveil 97019, tel. (503) 695-2376, has a ranger on duty to recommend campgrounds and hikes. Ask here about such nearby jaunts as Horsetail Falls, Triple Falls, and Oneonta Gorge (the latter is where a stream cuts through nearly 200 feet of basalt a mile east of Multnomah Falls). Be sure to request the Short

TED LONG ISHIKAWA

Locals call Vista House the "million dollar restroom."

Hiking Loops Near Multnomah Falls map for a visual depiction of this network of trails. The center's hours are daily 10 a.m.-6 p.m., June-September. Thereafter, hours vary greatly so call ahead. The information desk is located at the end of a complex featuring restrooms and the Multnomah Falls Lodge Restaurant and Giftshop. This Forest Service facility offers exhibits on the geology and animals of the Columbia Gorge, the cultural history of the area, and a scale model of the region. Particularly interesting are vintage photos of the old highway. Afterwards, you can head out the side door for the trailhead up to Multnomah Falls.

A Portland-based group, **Friends of the Columbia Gorge,** P.O. Box 40820, Portland 97240-0820, tel. (503) 241-3762, offers "Columbia River Gorge Guided Tour" tapes and a map for $21.95. This group also sponsors a free guided hike on weekends in the middle of June; walks are geared to different levels of exertion.

If you're going to the gorge with youngsters, a well-done audio tape is **Columbia Gorge Driving Tours,** sold at Powell's Bookstore and the Oregon History Center in Portland—or you can order by mail by calling (503) 730-7495. For $15, you get a suprisingly entertaining, informative run-down of history, geology, and local color. The entertaining narration is kept simple enough for kids to relate to, but will satisfy older travelers as well.

Another good place for information is **Skamania Lodge,** tel. (800) 221-7117, located on the

Washington side of the gorge. Just drive over the Bridge of the Gods (see "Cascade Locks" following) and make a right. Look for a sign on the left-hand side of WA 14 a few miles later. This Salishan property includes a Forest Service information desk, tel. (800) 221-7117, in the lobby as well as a bookstore operated by Northwest Interpretive Association (NWIA). The NWIA also has excellent facilites in such heavily visited areas as the Bonneville Dam and Mt. Hood Information Center, as well as a mobile unit near Wahkeena Falls during the summer. Or stop in at the nearby **Columbia Gorge Interpretive Center,** tel. (509) 427-8211, located across WA 14 from the entrance to the lodge. This facility tells the story of the gorge with recreations of structures from the gorge past like a fishwheel and an Indian pit house. In addition, a movie about the Missoula flood and artifacts also make this place the quickest, most enjoyable way to get the picture in the gorge. Hours are 10 a.m.-5 p.m. Labor Day-Memorial Day, 10 a.m.-7 p.m. Memorial Day to Labor Day. Admission is $5 for adults, $4 for seniors and students, and $3 for kids 6-12.

While you're on the other side of the gorge, you might also want to take in **Carson Hot Springs,** P.O. Box 370, Carson, WA 98610, tel. (509) 427-8292, a funky, old-but-charming resort hotel east of Stevenson. The healing waters, reasonably priced rooms, and good restaurant make it a worthwhile detour.

Meanwhile, back in Oregon at the **Hood River Ranger Station,** 6780 ORE 35S, Mt.

Hood-Parkdale, tel. (503) 352-6002, you can find a wide variety of information. Check out the progress of the new bike trail east of Hood River on the old highway, the possibility of staying overnight in a fire lookout, and other relatively new attractions in this part of the gorge. Ranger station hours are Mon.-Fri. 7:30 a.m.-4:30 p.m. Also administered by this office are campgrounds and trails along ORE 35 south of Hood River on the eastern flank of Mt Hood.

CASCADE LOCKS

The sleepy appearance of modern-day Cascade Locks belies its historical significance. The town is perched on a small bluff between the river and I-84, and its services and creature comforts are mostly confined to its main drag, Wa Na Pa Street. Before the shipping locks that inspired the burg's utilitarian name were constructed in 1896 to help steamboats navigate around hazardous rapids, boats had to be portaged overland.

Two events which took place outside the city limits, however, gained the town a permanent place in history books. The first of these claims to fame may not have existed at all, but many reputable scientists now believe that an ancient natural bridge once spanned the Columbia's mile-wide channel. According to native oral histories, this formation was destroyed by lava flows from the eruption of two nearby volcanoes. What are believed to be geologic remnants of this event lie just upstream from a modern structure called the Bridge of the Gods in honor of the Indian landmark. The span was raised in 1938 to compensate for a heightened river level due to the Bonneville Dam.

The second event, the construction of the Bonneville Dam in the late '30s, inaugurated boom times in the nearby town of Bonneville. Thousands of workers patronized area businesses and set up temporary residence in the area. The dam created 48-mile Lake Bonneville, which submerged the shipping locks. Today you can see Indian dip-net fishermen by the 1896 locks site in the town's riverfront Marine Park. Look for natives selling whole fresh salmon, walleye, and steelhead late August into September, weekends 10 a.m. to dusk. Bring wax paper and or a cooler with ice to help the fish keep till you're back in camp. Call (888) BUY-1855 for more information. Sales are cash only.

Boom times are gone now, but this little town with a dazzling river view and down-to-earth people is a refreshing change of pace from the big city to the west as well as the burgeoning tourist scene and industrial parks of its neighbors to the east. Reasonably priced food and lodging, a historical museum, the Bonneville Dam, and sternwheeler tours together with superlative hiking trails nearby also make for a nice stopover, as long as you don't come during winter. Most of the 75-inch annual precipitation falls at that time, along with ice storms and gale-force winds. Two funnel clouds were even sighted outside of town during the Columbus Day storm of 1962. Such violent weather is not completely devoid of benefits, however. The rains fostered the growth of massive Douglas firs near here which led to a once-thriving timber industry. Nowadays, the winds account for the Columbia Gorge's status as the windsurfing capital of the world, and the tourist economy's ripple effects are starting to be felt in Cascade Locks.

SIGHTS

Bonneville Dam

The Bonneville Dam, write: Public Information, U.S. Army Corps of Engineers, P.O. Box 2946, Portland 97208, can be reached via exit 40 off I-84. The signs lead you under the interstate through a tunnel to the site of the complex, Bradford Island. En route to the visitor center you drive over a retractable bridge above the modern shipping locks. On the other side are the powerhouse and turbine room. Downriver is the second-largest exposed monolith in the world (Gibraltar is first). This 848-foot lava promontory abutting the shoreline is known as **Beacon Rock,** a moniker bestowed by Lewis and Clark. Beyond the generating facilities is a bridge, underneath which is the human-made fish-diversion canal. These fishways cause back eddies and guide the salmon, shad, steelhead, and other species past turbine blades. You'll want to stop for a brief look at the spillways of the 500-foot-wide Bonneville Dam, especially if they're open. While Bonneville isn't anywhere near the largest or the most powerful dam on the river, it was the first project on the leading hydroelectric waterway in the world. Along with its potential for generating 40% of America's power needs, the Columbia's storage of irrigation water and its dam-related recreation sites make the river the most valuable resource in the Northwest—too valuable to be diverted for drinking water in southern California, despite pleas from Los Angeles politicians.

Benefits notwithstanding, the downside of damming is graphically illustrated by the sight of Indian fishermen enacting a weary pantomime of their forefathers by the Bonneville spillways. The **visitor center,** tel. (503) 374-8820, is open 9 a.m.-5 p.m. year-round. Ask the Army Corps of Engineers personnel at the reception desk about tours of the power-generating facilities and about public campgrounds, boat ramps, swimming, and picnicking areas. The reception area has exhibits on dam operations, pioneer and navigation history on the Columbia, and fish migration. A long elevator ride will take you down to the fish-viewing windows, where the sight of lamprey eels—which accompany the mid-May and mid-September salmon runs—and the fish-counting procedures are particularly fascinating. The fish-counting practice helps determine catch limits on the popular species. Outside the facility there's access to an overlook above the fish ladders. A walkway back to the parking lot is decorated with gorgeous roses from spring into fall.

Retrace your route back to the mainland from Bradford Island and turn right, following the signs to the fish hatchery. This facility is open every day 7:30 a.m.-5 p.m. Visit during spawning season (May and September) to see the salmon making their way upriver. At this time head to the west end of the hatchery, where steps will lead you down to a series of canals and holding pens. So great is the zeal of these fish to spawn they occasionally leap more than a foot out of the water. Inside the building you can see the beginnings of a process that produces the largest number of salmon fry in the state. Here fish culturists sort the fish and extract the bright red salmon roe from the females.

These eggs are taken to the windowed incubation building, where you can view trays holding millions of eggs that will eventually hatch into salmon. Once these fry grow into fingerlings, they are moved to outdoor pools where they live until release into the Columbia River by way of the Tanner Creek canal. The whole process is annotated by placards above the windows inside the incubation building.

The salmon and trout ponds and the floral displays are worth your attention at certain times of the year, but the sturgeon pools to the rear of the visitor center are always something to see. Biologists say the Columbia River white sturgeon, with bony plates instead of scales, has remained unchanged for 200 million years. The record size of a Columbia River sturgeon ever caught was 12 and a half feet long. More often than not, however, a big one is lucky to reach half that size. Despite being the largest freshwater species in North America, this river-bottom scavenger was largely ignored until the gourmet feeding frenzy of the last two decades put a premium on domestic sources of caviar. When *New York Times* food columnist Craig Claiborne pronounced the Columbia's product superior to that of the Caspian Sea, its notoriety was established. In addition, fresh-cooked Columbia River sturgeon is a specialty in the finest dining rooms in the state. The Bonneville Dam visitor center and fish hatchery are both free of charge.

The Marine Park

Down by the river is the Cascade Locks Marine Park (exit 44 off I-84 East). Look for it on your left going east on Wa Na Pa St.; just follow the signs. Here the sternwheeler *Columbia Gorge,* call for reservations in Portland, tel. (503) 223-3623, makes it possible to ride up the river in the style of a century ago. River legends and scenic splendor accompany you on a two-hour narrated cruise. There are several interesting packages of varying themes and duration. This 145-foot, 330-ton replica carries 599 passengers on three decks. Sightseeing cruises depart June 13-October 10 for these excursions; The Lewis and Clark Expedition leaves at 10 a.m.-12 p.m., the Oregon Trail Adventure departs at 12:30-2:30 p.m., and Steamboatin' U.S.A. sets sail at 3-5 p.m. The fare is $12 for adults, $6 for kids 4-12. Brochures with sched-

BARGES

There once was a little girl who lived in Portland and whose bedroom window looked out over the Columbia River. She loved to watch the boats going up and down the waterway, especially the big barges at night. She spent a lot of time looking out of her window, because she was a very sick little girl. She always wondered where the boats were going and what kind of adventures they would have during their voyages, and she'd dream of going along with them some day. Sadly, she passed away from leukemia at the tender age of 10. But before she departed, she left behind a little song that she made up while watching the barges ply the river. Her friends taught the song to their music teacher, who was able to teach it to other teachers in the school district. "Barges" quickly caught on and spread across the Northwest and to points beyond. Soon the Girl Scouts of America picked up on the song and made learning it an integral part of achieving a Mariner's Badge.

Nowadays, children on opposite sides of the globe in Europe and Japan sing it. "Barges" is a very special gift that shows us how to see the world through children's eyes.

arr. by Ted Long Ishikawa

2. Out of my window looking in the night, I can see the barges flickering light
   Starboard glows green and port is glowing red, you can see them flickering ahead
   Barges I would like to go with you , I would like to sail the ocean blue
   Barges are there treasures in your hold, do you fight with pirates brave and bold

ules and rates are available at the Multnomah Falls Visitor Center, tel. (503) 695-2376. An outdoor deck, an inside galley (brunch cruises offered) and competent narration have made these trips popular for years.

Port of Cascade Locks also houses the ticket office as well as an information center and gift shop, which sells an excellent local hiking trails map for $1.25. Historical photos of early sternwheelers and 50-cent showers for hikers also make this facility particularly worthwhile.

About a quarter mile west of the visitor center, **Cascade Locks Historical Museum,** P.O. Box 307, Cascade Locks 97014, tel. (503) 374-8535, is housed in an old lockkeeper's residence and exhibits Indian artifacts and pioneer memorabilia. Information about the fish wheel, a paddlewheel-like contraption that conveyor-belted salmon out of the river and into a pen is especially fascinating. This diabolical device was perfected in Oregon in the early 20th century and was so successful at denuding the Columbia of fish that it was outlawed. June-Sept. the museum is open Mon.-Wed. noon-5 p.m., Thurs.-Sun. 10 a.m.-5 p.m. In May it's open weekends 10 a.m.-5 p.m. Outside the museum is the diminutive Oregon Pony, the first steam locomotive on the Pacific coast. Its maiden voyage dates back to 1862 when it replaced the 4.5 mile portage with a rail route around the Cascades. Close by in the Cascades Locks Marina, natives sell salmon, walleye and steelhead on Sept. weekends and have an event the second weekend in Sept. with dancing, drumming, and storytelling. Call (888) BUY-1855 for details.

Take a walk over to the old locks. Built in 1878 to circumnavigate the steep gradient of the river, they were completed in 1896. By the time the Cascade shipping locks were completed, however, river traffic had unfortunately decreased due to cargo being sent by train, so the effects of altering the river flow here were negligible.

HIKES

Eagle Creek Trail

Since the Eagle Creek Trail is highly recommended by a lot of people, try to avoid peak-use times like summer weekends. This trail begins at Eagle Creek Campground (see "Camping" under "Practicalities," below) and goes 14 miles to Wahtum Lake, where it intersects the Pacific Crest Trail. Along the trail are seven waterfalls, one of which features a perspective from behind the cascade itself. Ideally, this is a two-day backpack, but if you prefer a day-trip, consider Eagle Creek Trail no. 440 about two miles to Punchbowl Falls. It can be reached from the Eagle Creek Campground via exit 41 off I-84. Fifteen minutes west of this exit is exit 44 for Cascade Locks. The four-mile roundtrip to the falls is an easy hike. If you can, come in February when tourists are scarce and stream flow is high.

From Punchbowl Falls continue 1.5 miles to High Bridge. Tall trees, spring wildflowers, basalt outcroppings, and nice views into Eagle Creek's whitewater cleft make the journey almost as compelling as the destination. High Bridge is 80 feet above this particularly beautiful section of the creek. The trail continues on the other side of the gorge several more miles to 100-foot high Tunnel Falls, where you can walk through a tunnel behind the falls.

Wildflowers spring up in April and linger on into August in the higher elevations. To locate such Columbia Gorge endemics as Oregon Fleabane and Howell's daisy, bring along Russ Jolley's *Wildflowers of the Columbia*. Many of these one-of-a-kinds are species left over from a previous glacial period that have adapted because of the shade and moistness of the south side of the Gorge. Almost two dozen varieties of fern, trillium, beargrass, yellow arnica, penstemon, monkeyflower, and devil's club are among the more common species here. This hike is 13 miles roundtrip and is best undertaken on a weekday in spring to catch the blooms and avoid the crowds.

As a prelude to hiking Eagle Creek or one of several other trails in the area, you might want to wander an informative interpretive loop of less than a mile. Just cross the footbridge on the approach road to the Eagle Creek Trailhead over to the other side of the river. After crossing the bridge, follow the markers which describe the region's mixed-conifer forest at various elevations. At trail's end, you might want to take on the steep two-mile trail to Wauna Point. While not as visually arresting as other area jaunts, the view of the Columbia River and its Gorge at the summit makes the effort worthwhile.

Elowah Falls/McCord Creek Trails

You want a hike that takes in the beauties of the Columbia River Gorge but doesn't involve a time-consuming drive from Portland or a long arduous trek. There are trailheads between Crown Point and Multnomah Falls that meet these criteria, but it's a good bet you're going to have a lot of company. To avoid the crowds while taking in spectacularly varied gorge landscapes, try **Elowah Falls/McCord Creek** trails.

From Portland, take I-84 past Multnomah Falls to exit 35, Ainsworth State Park. As you come off the access road you'll have a choice of left turns. Take Frontage Rd. with signs for Dodson. Drive about two miles to the small parking lot of John Yeon State Park, named for one of the major benefactors of the Columbia Gorge Scenic Highway. In the western corner of the lot is the trailhead. Follow it a half mile up the hill, bypassing the spur to the campground and the Nesmith Point Trail. When you reach a junction of two trails, turn right for Upper McCord Creek and left for Elowah Falls.

The Upper McCord Creek trail leads to a mossy glade framing a creek at the top of a waterfall just under a mile from the junction. En route, the trail narrows to a ledge blasted out of a cliff. From behind a railing, gaze hundreds of feet down at the Columbia in the foreground of 12,306 ft. Mt. Adams. Across the gully, layered basalt strata indicate successive lava flows. This is a good place to look for osprey riding the thermals before they dive down to the Columbia for a fish. The trail continues to a view of dual cascades descending the rockface. These are the feeder streams of Elowah Falls. A short while later, recline on the shady banks of Upper McCord Creek.

Retrace your steps to where the trail forks and descend a half mile from the junction to Elowah Falls. This several-hundred-foot-high feathery cascade is set in a steep rock amphitheater amid hues of green that conjure the verdant lushness of Hawaii. Elowah Falls was chosen to grace the cover of *Oregon III,* a famous coffee-table book of Ray Atkeson photos (Portland: Graphic Arts, 1983).

The Wahkeena-Multnomah Loop

This is a hike of about five miles with panoramic river views, perspectives on four waterfalls, and ancient forests. Begin this trail at Wahkeena Falls so you can end with a meal at Multnomah Falls Lodge as well as finishing your survey of gorge waterfalls with the most majestic one of all. As such, it might be worth the extra trouble of parking your car first at the Multnomah Falls lot and walking less than a mile back to Wahkeena trailhead. This way, your car can be easily accessed after dinner.

To get there drive I-84 to exit 28, Bridalveil Falls. Several miles later you'll come to the Wahkeena Falls lot. If you take the trail to the right of the bridge, in about a mile you'll come to Fairy Falls, so named for its ethereal quality. Just past Fairy Falls leave trail no. 420 for the Vista Point Trail no. 419 to see panoramas from 1,600 feet above the river. There's also a revealing look at the singed trunks left over from the fires of October 1991. Old growth Douglas fir usher you through higher elevations on this trail. Rejoin trail no. 420 a mile east of where no. 419 began. Once you get past the first mile-and-a-half of this trail's initial steep ascent, the rest of the route is of moderate difficulty. As you begin your descent, you might become confused by a lack of signs at the junction of no. 420 and the Larch Mountain Trail. Hang a sharp left on no. 441 to head west and down along Multnomah Creek. At the rear of this gorge is pretty Ecola Falls. There are several other cascades along the route. When you hit the blacktopped section of no. 441, you have the option of hanging a left to enjoy views from the top of the falls a short distance away or making a direct ascent. In any case, at the end of the hike, we recommend dinner followed by an evening spent on the Multnomah Falls bridge. The falls are subtly lit, casting an interesting shadow in the rockface behind the falls. If you didn't elect to park at Multnomah Falls, end your day by hiking back on trail #442 above US 30. It may be necessary to walk back along the narrow shoulder of US 30 due to seasonal rockslide damage.

PRACTICALITIES

Accommodations

This town of 820 people features several reasonably priced hotels. Throughout the Columbia Gorge there is a five percent room tax. Canadian travelers frequenting the region here can find some of the best exchange rates between the border and Reno.

The best lodging bargain in the Gorge may be the **Scandian Motor Lodge,** P.O. Box 217, Cascade Locks 97014, tel. (503) 374-8417, next door to the Cascade Inn. (See "Food"). Rooms average around $43-50, depending on the time of year and the number of people. Add $5 more for the rooms with a sauna. These units boast a warm Scandinavian decor with wood paneling, air-conditioning, and a nearby restaurant and lounge, as well as an adjacent laundromat. This retreat fills fast in summer.

If the best view of the Columbia from a hotel room on the Oregon side is important to you then you'll pay $89-124, $65-99 in winter, at the **Best Western Columbia River Inn,** 735 Wa Na Pa St., tel. (503) 374-8777 or (800) 595-7108.

The high end rooms have hot tubs and all rooms have microwaves and refrigerators. You can get a "mountain view" room for $79 in summer, but that would be tantamount to being in Bordeaux and forgoing the wine. With the Charburger next door and the Marine Park down the street, this property has an excellent location.

Camping

There's no shortage of options for campers in this area. Keep in mind the eastern Gorge is Portland's backyard and at times can be very crowded so avoid peak times whenever possible. In addition to first come-first serve Ainsworth State Park detailed in Portland Accommodations, there are several other sites worth considering. These have been chosen on the basis of location (e.g. near attractions or a prime trailhead) or for special amenities.

While the **Eagle Creek Campground,** (800) 452-5687, can be noisy and crowded, it's an ideal base camp for hiking as its location is close to several trailheads. There are sites for tents and RVs up to 22 feet long, with picnic tables, fire grills, flush toilets, sanitary services, and firewood available. It's located between Bonneville Dam and Cascade Locks off I-84 and is open mid-May to October. The fee is $12. At the seven-mile point of the Eagle Creek Trail (see "Hiking," above) there's a primitive free campground, but it fills up on summer weekends.

Herman Horse Camp, write Mt. Hood National Forest, Troutdale 97060, tel. (503) 695-

2276, is only one-half mile east of Cascade Locks, near the Pacific Crest Trail. It's a half mile from Herman Creek and is one of three campgrounds in the area. A full array of services including a laundromat, a store, a cafe, and showers are nearby, supplementing the seven tent and RV sites. Piped water, fire grills, picnic tables, and stock-handling facilities are also welcome additions here. It's open mid-May to October, with no reservations or fee required. There are trails here for hiking and horse-packing. Other attractions include the historic Forest Work Center and nearby rock walls, where visitors can admire the handiwork of the Civilian Conservation Corps. There's also a trail leading to Wyeth campground, a favorite of windsurfers. **Cascade Locks Marine Park,** P.O. Box 307, Cascade Locks 97014, tel. (503) 374-8619, has campsites available close to the center of town. The museum and the sternwheeler are housed in the complex, as are tennis courts. Whatever amenities are not available on-site are within walking distance. It's open all year and the fee is $12.

Finally, two miles east of town near the banks of the Columbia is the Cascade Locks **KOA Kampground,** Box 660, Cascade Locks, OR 97014; information tel. (541) 374-8668, reservation tel. (800) KOA-8698. Open from March 21-Oct. 20, this private campground features the basics plus a spa (hot tub/sauna), hot showers, and a heated swimming pool for $17 per couple, $3 each extra person. Kamping Kabins that come in one room (queen bed and a bunk bed) or two room (queen bed and two sets of bunks) varieties cost $30 and $35 per night respectively (bring your own linens, pillows, towels, sleeping bag, etc.). Kabins fill up quickly, especially on weekends, so reserve well in advance. To get there, take US 30 east from town, and turn left onto Forest Lane. Proceed 1.2 miles down and you'll see the Kampground on the left.

Food

Forget health food and haute cuisine until you get to Hood River. In Cascade Locks, you get downhome country cookin'—and lots of it—at a decent price.

The Charburger, 714 Wa Na Pa St., tel. (503) 374-8477, is located near the Bridge of the Gods at the beginning of town. This is a great place if you're on the go and don't want to spend a fortune for a quick bite. In addition to an extensive salad bar and a bakery, there is a cafeteria line specializing in "home-baked" (and it tastes that way) chicken, omelettes cooked to order, and other wholesome but unexotic dishes. Prices for a meal seldom exceed $6. Other options include a takeout window as well asTex-Mex specialties, and a Sunday brunch downstairs. The restaurant's Hood River outlet, 4100 Westcliff, Hood River, tel. (503) 386-3101, is also located at the west end of that town.

The **Cascade Inn,** in front of the Scandian Motor Lodge, tel. (503) 374-8340, is a neighborhood meat-and-potatoes kind of place where a luncheon crowd of loggers, tradespeople, and secretaries wolf down such overstuffed sandwiches as the Millworker—two beef patties, cheese, bacon, lettuce, tomato, onions, mayonnaise, and relish on a bun. This might not be a "heart-smart" alternative, but you'll leave feeling full, and the space inside your wallet should not decrease substantially either. There's a lounge next door.

East Wind Ice Cream, located between the Charburger and Marine Park, is a traditional stop for families on a Columbia River Gorge Sunday drive.

Events

The last weekend in June, the sternwheeler *Columbia Gorge* is welcomed back to Cascade Locks. Free rides on the boat, dozens of food and craft booths, a salmon bake, and races all bring out the community in force. Call (503) 374-8313 for more information.

July 4th fireworks here are ranked among the state's best displays. The multi-colored explosions are set off on Thunder Island below the Bridge of the Gods over the Columbia River. Watch from the city park where the Volunteer Fire Department puts on a high-quality salmon bake. Better yet, book Cascade Sternwheeler's package (including the salmon dinner for around $30) to take in the fireworks from aboard the riverboat. A DJ spins tasteful renditions of patriotic songs amid the rockets red glare. You can book this from Portland through Gray Line, tel. (800) 422-7042 or (503) 285-9845.

Horseback Riding

Mt. Shadow Ranch, tel. (503) 374-8592, is located at Wyeth off exit 51 (near Herman Horse Camp). Their 23 acres front the Columbia River with the 2,000-foot facade of a mountain behind it. The ranch has a special permit to conduct guided rides in the Mt. Hood National Forest.

Information and Services

In addition to the previously mentioned Marine Park Visitors Center, the **Port of Cascade Locks Tourism Committee,** P.O. Box 355, Cascade Locks 97014, tel. (503) 374-8619, ask for Tahoma, can provide help in planning your visit.

The **state police** can be reached at (800) 452-8573.

HOOD RIVER AND VICINITY

In the past, Hood River was known to the traveling public primarily as the start of a scenic drive through the orchard country beneath the snowcapped backdrop of Mt. Hood, Oregon's highest peak. Since the early '80s, however, well-heeled adherents of windsurfing have transformed this town into a Malibu-in-the-making. Instead of the traditional dependence on cherries, apples, peaches, and pears, Hood River now rakes in up to $25 million annually from the invasion of "boardheads." A good percentage of this subculture tends to be yuppies able to "drop out" here for extended periods to the tune of $50-100 a day for basic creature comforts (this figure and the preceding one according to a University of Oregon study from the late eighties). By the spring of 1997 an estimated 35 companies with sailboarding ties—board and sail makers, designers of harnesses and clothing—made Hood River their base.

The abundance of civilized amenities in the midst of spectacular surroundings complements ideal conditions for this sport. The fury of the winds derives from the heat of the eastern desert drawing in the westerlies. The confining contours of the Gorge dam up these air masses and precipitate their gusty release. Because prime time to "catch a blow" is midday, this is also the best time to find a parking spot downtown. The notion that affluent young people in bathing garb would rescue Hood River from cutbacks at Jantzen apparel, Diamond fruit packers, and other economic mainstays seems the stuff of fantasy—like riding the wind on the great River of the West. City center features an unnaturally high concentration of ethnic eateries, sports-equipment shops, and boutiques for a town of 4,500 people. The main thoroughfare, Oak Street (which becomes Cascade Street as you head west), is set on a plateau between the riverfront marine park to the north and streets running up the Cascade foothills to the south. New brick facades dress up old storefronts, and attire of multihued wetsuits and sandals predominates.

The scenic highlights of Hood River are the orchards during the end of the April Blossom Festival and the leaves during color season in October. For a view of the Hood River Valley that does justice to these events, drive to the end of town on Oak Street and turn right on ORE 35. Head south till you see the sign for **Panorama Point** one mile up the road on the left. Vistas here afford a distant perspective on the orchards below Mt. Hood that have forever served as a visual archetype of the Pacific Northwest.

SIGHTS

Columbia Gorge Hotel
To ease the culture shock of going from the Scenic Highway and the sternwheeler to the brave new world of windsurfing in Hood River, stop first at the Columbia Gorge Hotel, 4000 West Cliff Dr., Hood River 97031; local tel. (503) 386-5566, elsewhere (800) 345-1921, http://www.gorge.net/lodging/cghotel. Take exit 62 off of I-84 and go over the bridge to the north side of the highway and follow Westcliff Drive west to this postcard from the past. The hotel is a lovingly rendered homage to the Jazz Age of the Roaring Twenties, when it was graced by visits from presidents Coolidge and Roosevelt, Rudolph Valentino, Clara Bow, and the big bands. Built by lumber magnate Simon Benson (who was also a patron of the Scenic Highway) in 1921, the grounds feature a 207-foot waterfall and the neo-Moorish outlines of a hotel nicknamed the "Waldorf of the West." Glittering

chandeliers in the lobby, large wing chairs around the fireplace, and fresh-cut bouquets in the dining room bespeak the refinement of an earlier era.

Rates here are high (expect to spend $150-275 a night during peak season, although winter rates are close to half that), but a more romantic retreat would be hard to come by. Spacious rooms with heavy wooden beams, brass beds, fluffed-up pillows, and period furniture clearly demonstrate what was meant by the "good ol' days." The readers of Conde Nast travel agree, voting the hotel to a list of the top 500 hotels in the world.

The dining room looks east at the Columbia rolling toward the hotel from out of the mountains and west toward alpenglow from the sunsets. Local mushrooms, fruits, and wild game as well as Columbia River salmon and sturgeon are featured prominently here. There is also the "world famous farm breakfast." Imagine four courses running the gamut of American breakfast food served with such theatrical flourishes as "honey from the sky"—Hood River Valley apple blossom honey poured from a height of several feet above the table onto hot, fresh-baked biscuits. This symbolizes the 207 foot-high Wah Gwin Gwin ("Rushing Water") Falls that descend the precipice in back of the hotel. As they say at the hotel, "You don't just get a choice—you get it all."

Hood River Museum
To learn the history of the region, drive back to the junction of Oak St. and ORE 35, then cross I-84 toward the river. At the intersection turn left and follow the signs to Marina Park and the Hood River Museum, tel. (503) 386-6772. To get there off I-84, take exit 64 and follow the signs. Exhibits trace life in the Hood River Valley from prehistoric times to the founding of the first pioneer settlement in 1854. Thereafter, the area's development as a renowned fruit-growing center is emphasized. Native American stone artifacts, beadwork and basketry, pioneer quilts, and a Victorian parlor set the time machine in motion. The contributions of the local Finnish and Japanese communities, along with WW I memorabilia, introduce the first half of the 20th century. Photos and implements related to fruit harvesting and packing methods round out the historical collections on the first floor. Upstairs,

the "dry" view of the gorge as seen from Rowena Crest.

REBECCA SINGER

antique logging equipment, dolls, and remnants of a presentation by local schoolchildren for the Lewis and Clark Exposition in 1905 are on display. At the center of the museum is an attractive open-air courtyard planted with Columbia Gorge flora. From April to autumn, the museum is open Wed.-Sat. 10 a.m.-4 p.m., Sunday noon-4 p.m. Other months, it's open Monday and Tuesday by appointment. Admission is free.

Columbia River Views
Back in town drive up to the offices of United Telephone between Oak and State Streets. The lot is restricted to staff vehicles, so park elsewhere and walk to what has to be the most scenic employee parking anywhere. Unimpeded views of the Columbia River, the mouth of the White Salmon River and its deep gorge, the south face of an extinct volcano, and the western flank of Mt. Adams are all laid out before you.

The last leg of the Columbia River Scenic Highway can be reached by driving 15 minutes east on I-84 to **Mosier.** At the far end of this small town is a sign pointing the way to the final section of Lancaster's artful thoroughfare. While not as spectacular as the earlier route of the waterfalls, this section of ORE 30 still provides a picturesque, restful alternative to the interstate.

Hikers and bikers will especially relish the six miles of ORE 30 between Hood River and Mosier. This section is off-limits to cars and features old growth trees and a tunnel with "windows" overlooking spectacular gorge views. Engineers hope to have the entire highway from Troutdale to The Dalles open in time for the old road's 100th anniversary in 2013.

Rowena Crest
The highlight of the drive is Rowena Crest. Almost nowhere else can you see both the dry eastern and wetter western faces of the Columbia River Gorge with such clarity and distinction. The dark Columbia River basalt cliffs are derived from massive lava flows 15 million years ago. The terracing of the region was due to the action of the Missoula Floods upon Columbia Plateau fault scarps. More information on the geology and ecosystem is available from a free pamphlet in the drop box on the north side of the highway, courtesy of the **Tom McCall Nature Preserve.** This 2,300-acre sanctuary on part of Rowena Crest was created by the Nature Conservancy and has trails on the hillsides that are open to the public.

These cliffs represented the beginning of the last hurdle facing Willamette Valley-bound Oregon Trail pioneers. After Rowena, the Gorge cliffs rose up so high that the pioneers were forced to either build rafts and float the then-hazardous rapids on the river, or to follow the Barlow Trail around the south flank of Mt. Hood.

Today, Tom McCall Nature Preserve is the site of a mid-May pilgrimage by wildflower lovers. Because the preserve lies in the transition zone between the wet west and the dry east four endemics and several hundred species flourish here. Included in the spring display are yellow wild sunflowers, purple blooms of shooting stars, scarlet Indian paintbrush, and blue-flowered camas. While the flowers are enticing, be careful of ticks and poison oak. And of course, as with any nature preserve or public park, love the flowers but leave them behind for the next person to enjoy.

South on ORE 35 and the Dee Highway (ORE 281)

Contact the Hood River Ranger Station, 6780 ORE 35, Parkdale 97041, tel. (503) 352-6002 locally, (503) 666-0701 from Portland, about sightseeing the northeastern flank of Mt. Hood. Offshoots from ORE 35 and the Dee Highway (ORE 281) provide access to such mountain meccas as Lost Lake and Cloud Cap.

To get to Lost Lake, turn right off Cascade St. near the City Park onto 13th Street. This will turn into ORE 281 and will take you to Lost Lake in about 14 miles. The well-known view of **Lost Lake** with Mt. Hood in the background is a calendar-photo-come-to-life. The lake offers hiking trails, camping, a limited number of cabins, fishing, rowboats for rent, and a small store. Autumn huckleberry season is the best time to come. In any event, avoid summer weekends and be prepared for mosquitoes in spring and early summer. In July and August, the rangers have campfire programs on Saturday night. Cabins are $40 per night—the largest sleeps seven—and campsites begin at $12. Call (503) 386-6366 at least two weeks in advance to reserve campsites and cabins. Come prepared; the closest fuel is in Parkdale. A half-mile long boardwalk through an old growth cedar grove is a highlight at Lost Lake. It's part of the Lakeshore Trail, an annotated nature walk. Pick up a map with natural history captions that correspond to numbered posts along the route. About two miles down, the old growth trail begins through a thick forest of eight-foot thick cedars.

The Parkdale Lava beds are located outside of town. Pull off ORE 35, then take Baseline Rd. to Lava Bed Drive. Explanatory placards annotate the most recent expression of Mt. Hood's volcanic origins.

Hutson Museum

South of Hood River is the Hutson Museum, Baseline Dr. and Clear Creek Rd., tel. (503) 352-6808. If you're in Parkdale riding the Mt. Hood railroad or en route to Lost Lake or the Parkdale Lava beds, this place is worth a stop if only for the rock and mineral collection. There are also native artifacts, pioneer hand tools, and information on Bigfoot. The latter comes courtesy of Project Big Foot, tel. (800) BIG-FOOT, headquartered in Parkdale. Open Tues.-Sun. 11 a.m.-5:30 p.m. April-Sept., weekends only Oct.-November.

Cloud Cap is an 1891 mountaineers' clubhouse whose historic edifice and magnificent mountain and forest views make it a favorite with sightseers and photographers. Tillie Jane and Cloudcap Saddle campgrounds are located close by, open only during the summer months. Tillie Jane is a good base from which to explore the Cooper Spur area, and its counterpart offers scenic views and unspoiled high-country beauty. Nearby you can access the Timberline Trail (see "Hiking and Camping" under "Mt. Hood" in The High Cascades chapter). To get there, take ORE 35 24 miles south of Hood River to Cooper Spur Road. After passing Cooper Spur Ski Area, follow the signs until coming to Cloud Cap at the end of a gravel-and-dirt road 10 miles from ORE 35.

ACTIVITIES AND RECREATION

Windsurfing

Windsurfing and vineyard-hopping complement nearby Columbia Gorge hiking and auto touring, as well as Mt. Hood skiing. Regarding the latter, the "gorge route" from Portland (I-84 and ORE 35) to Mt. Hood ski slopes is becoming a popular alternative to the more direct US 26. Local wags insist that the lighter traffic can save as much as an hour on weekends, not to mention the scenic appeals of this route. While this is hard to believe, on cold winter days the crystal paradise created by iced-over waterfalls off I-84 make it a worthy scenic detour.

As for windsurfing, neophytes, adepts, and their fans congregate around the **Hood River Marina,** exit 64 off I-84. This complex offers a complete package: swimming beach, picnic shelter, concessions, exercise course, and jogging trail. **Rhonda Smith's Windsurfing Center** offers rentals at $25 a half-day, $30 to $40 for a full day and $150-200 per week, depending on the equipment and location. Lessons, including equipment, start at $20 per hour. A private launch area and rescue service round out the package.

Another good place to watch windsurfing is **Riverfront Park** at The Dalles. To get there, take exit 87 off of I-84. Hood River has the highest density of shops in the world geared to this sport. They rent equipment and give lessons. For information about windsurfing, wind, and weather, call 387-WIND (-9463) or pick up a copy of *Northwest Sailboard,* P.O. Box 918, Hood River 97031. This magazine is available all over town.

In Hood River, the following schools cater to beginners: **Big Winds,** tel. (503) 386-6088, **Front St. Sailboards,** tel. (503) 386-4044, **Gorge Surf Club,** tel. (503) 386-5434, and **Hood River Windsurfing,** tel. (503) 386-5787. Most of these academies of aerodynamics offer lessons through mid-October.

Regarding fall windsurfing, adepts will tell you it's the best. It's less crowded, the water's warm, and winds are lighter at school sites. It easier to find parking and rigging space at launching areas, and there's a quality of light upon the water with enough clear days to add aesthetic appeal. Best of all for beginners is the availability of individualized instruction during fall. While conditions are generally good at most locations along the river during the season, the best places are said to be in the east end of the gorge, notably around Three Mile Canyon and other launch sites in the Arlington, Oregon, and Roosevelt, Washington areas.

Skiing

Off ORE 35 on the east side of Mt. Hood is **Cooper Spur,** tel. (541) 352-7803. Day and night skiing and cross-country skiing are offered. Low prices, $8-12, and a laidback atmosphere make this place a favorite with families and beginners.

Winetasting

Tasting and tours are offered at the **Hood River Vineyard,** 4693 Westwood Dr., Hood River 97031, tel. (503) 386-7772, open 11 a.m.-5 p.m. daily. The microclimate here is similar to that

which produces Germany's Rhine wines. In addition to the rieslings, chardonnays, gewürztraminers, and other white-wine varietals produced here, the area is famous for fruit wines and award-winning pinot noir. Sweet wines, like Anjou pear, marionberry, and zinfandel are done with great flair. The cabernet sauvignon from **Flerchinger Vineyard,** 4200 Post Canyon Dr., tel. 800 (503) 516-8710, took "best of show" at the prestigious Newport Seafood and Wine competition. The winery also produces chardonnay, riesling and merlot. Open daily 11 a.m.-5 p.m. Because it's a little obscure, here's directions to the winery. As with the previous vineyard, take exit 62. Turn right on Country Club road which'll have you heading west for a brief time right after exiting the freeway. A left onto Post Canyon Drive will take you south to the winery.

Biking

The Gorge Scenic Area has supervised the creation of a hiking/biking corridor on the Old Columbia River Highway south of town. Old growth trees and great Columbia River views are highlighted. Mountain bikers can get trail information at Waucoma Bookstore and the chamber of commerce. For the inside scoop, pick the brains of friendly staff at **Discover Bikes,** 1020 Wasco St., Suite E., tel. (503) 386-4820.

Lookout Mountain Hike

Perhaps the best place to appreciate the transition from western alpine conifer forests to eastern high deserts is Lookout Mountain in the Badger Creek Wilderness. This aptly named 6,525 foot peak is the second highest peak in the Mt. Hood National Forest. To get there look for Junction 44, known locally as the Dufur cutoff. It comes up a little south of Cooper Spur Rd. on the east side of ORE 35 not far from Robinhood campground. Follow it to Forest Service Rd. 4410, marked by a sign after a hilly five mile drive. This route will take you to a parking area opposite the trailhead to High Prairie Trail no. 493. Remember that there are no signs most of the six miles on Forest Service Rd. 4410 to the trailhead, but if you bear left at the outset and ignore all the secondary roads, you'll eventually see a sign indicating the final sharp left turn to the trailhead parking area. The 20-minute walk to the top on trail no. 493 takes you where there used to be an old fire spotter's cabin. Directly west looms Mt. Hood. Turn 180 degrees and you face the sagebrush and wheatfields of eastern Oregon. To the south, there's the Three Sisters and Broken Top. West and north of those peaks, Mt. Jefferson's tricorn hat rises up. The body of water to the southwest of Lookout Mountain is Badger Lake. To the north, views of Mounts Adams, St. Helens, and Rainier (on a clear day) will have you reeling with visual intoxication. On most days you can expect cool, windy weather, and there are yellow jackets in August and early September. As with a hike anywhere in Oregon, be sure to wear bright colors during hunting season. On the way down, there are several unsigned spur trails that loop back onto #493. As long as you keep moving downhill north and west, you'll get back to the parking lot.

Horseback Riding

Fir Mountain Ranch, 4051 Fir Mt. Rd., Hood River, tel. (503) 354-2753, rents horses for trail rides and has a bed and breakfast. Horse rental rates start at $20 per hour and views of Mounts Hood, Adams, and St. Helens along the trail add visual appeal. The ranch is located five miles south of Hood River off ORE 35.

In-Town Pursuits

Hood River Golf, 1850 Country Club Rd., Hood River 97031, tel. (503) 386-3009, has nine holes and beautiful views of Mt. Hood, Mt. Adams, elk, and geese. It's open daylight to dark. Come in fall if only to see the spectacular foliage. Contact the chamber of commerce, tel. (503) 386-2000, for other courses in the area.

Two worthwhile shopping stops are **Waucoma Bookstore,** 212 Oak St., Hood River 97031, tel. (503) 386-5353, and the **Fruit Tree,** 4140 Westcliff Dr., Hood River 97031, tel. (503) 386-6688. The bookstore's selection evidences taste and an appreciation of titles relevant to the locale. You can also pick up some gourmet coffee, listen to beautiful music, or browse through a selection of unique cards and pottery. The Fruit Tree is located on the river side of I-84 on the way to the Columbia Gorge Hotel, across from Charburger, and is the perfect place to find a gift box of Oregon jams, smoked salmon, hazelnuts, and other goodies. They help coordinate shipping right from the store and also have fresh local pro-

duce. Try the apple cider. You won't get big discounts on the produce, but it's first rate. For fresh locally grown produce, homemade treats, flowers, and crafts, head to Jackson Park, May and 13th Streets, across from the hospital, every Saturday mid-June through mid-October 9 a.m.-2 p.m. This event is called **Farmers in the Park.** Another outlet for produce is the **River Bend Organic Farm and Store,** 2363 Tucker Rd., tel. (503) 386-8766 or (800) 755-7568, located minutes away from downtown south of Hood River on the way to O'Dell. Call for directions. In addition to organic produce, there's homemade apple cider, huckleberry preserves, spiced peaches, and other homemade products. Antiques and an old timey feel also make this place special. A walk in the gardens outside the store munching a cracker with River Bend's pumpkin butter is our definiton of Mother's Day bliss. Riverbend Store can be found just across Tucker Rd. Bridge on ORE 281.

PRACTICALITIES

Accommodations

It's hard to find a room in the spring and the summer in Hood River, and the prices reflect it. (By the way, remember to add an eight percent Hood River room tax.)

Just west of town, however, there are two reasonably priced alternatives in the $40-50-a-night range. The **Vagabond Lodge,** 4070 Westcliff Dr., tel. (503) 386-2992, and the **Meredith Gorge Motor Lodge,** 4300 Westcliff Dr., tel. (503) 386-1515 or (800) 537-5938, have standard motel rooms, many with river views. Proximity to Hood River's **Charburger Restaurant,** 4100 Westcliff Dr., tel. (503) 386-3101, is another plus if you like better-than-average American road food at Cascade Locks (rather than Hood River) prices. Closer to town, you can still do it on the cheap at the somewhat funky **Lone Pine Motel,** 2429 Cascade St., tel. (503) 386-2600. Despite the fact that some of its rooms abut the Safeway parking lot (a WalMart is also close by), it's quiet at night and kitchen units are available. Rates run $25-50. Also of interest to budget travelers is a nearby drive-in. A quarter-mile east of the motel on Cascade St. in the parking lot of Zeman's music store (past the

Cascade Plaza) is a trailer dispensing "killer" tacos and burritos during the summer months. This is where migrant workers come to fortify themselves between gigs in the fields but downtown office workers have discovered it as well. **El Rinconcito** is a street-grunter's delight where you can feel full for less than $3.

Bed and Breakfasts

The visitor information bureau, tel. (503) 386-2000, http://www.gorge.net/hrccc, has a complete listing of the two dozen bed and breakfasts in the area that they'll gladly send upon request. Most cost above $60 per day, however, and may soon run higher. Here are several good values.

The **Inn at the Gorge,** 1113 Eugene St., tel. (503) 386-4429, is run by a windsurfer for windsurfers. What this means can be summarized thusly: instructions on riding the winds, group and off-season rates, private baths and a complete kitchen in each unit, as well as complimentary transfers to and from bus/train terminals are all offered. Even if you're not a boardhead the included large and tasty breakfast served at this 1908 Victorian would be reason enough to give this place a look. Rates begin at $65.

State Street Inn, 1005 State St., tel. (503) 386-1899, is the place locals recommend to parents and friends. Overlooking the snow-capped eminence of Mt. Adams, this gable-roofed English-stone house is the perfect complement to the scenic beauties of the area. Four rooms share two baths, and a first-rate breakfast is included. A $65-85 price range makes this an especially good value.

Spectacular views from every window can be found at the **Beryl House Bed and Breakfast,** 4079 Barrett Dr., tel. (503) 386-5567. With a location four miles from town in the Hood River Valley orchards, it's not surprising to also find a hearty farm breakfast awaiting you each morning. What is surprising is the budget-friendly charge of $55 for a night here. Four rooms share two baths in this antique and art-filled 1910 farmhouse. With a location half-way between Flerchinger and Hood River vineyards, this B&B is especially recommended for oenophiles. In addition, guests benefit from the innkeeper's expertise on local restaurants and windsurfing.

If the notion of a vintage 1910 hotel appeals to you but you're not prepared to pay Columbia Gorge Hotel prices (see "Sights," above), the **Hood River Hotel,** 102 Oak St., tel. (503) 386-1900, might be your window on the river and on the past. This is not to say that it's cheap, with most of the rooms going for $70-90 (with complimentary continental breakfast), but this graceful rendering of memory lane enjoys river views as well as proximity to downtown dining and shopping. If you miss having TV in your room, the high-ceilinged oak-paneled first floor with adjoining lounge and dining area provides an inviting place to revive the grand old art of conversation. Pasquale's Ristorante, opened by the hotel, has decent Italian cuisine, reasonably priced breakfasts, and outside seating in nice weather.

Camping

It's best to consult the **Hood River Ranger Station,** 6780 ORE 35, Parkdale 97401, tel. (503) 352-6002 local, or tel. (503) 666-0701 in Portland, for Mt. Hood area campgrounds if you can't find a place at some of the following local sites.

Tucker Park, 2440 Dee Hwy., Hood River 97301, tel. (503) 386-4477, is a county park campground set along the banks of the Hood River, four miles south of town on ORE 281. Despite a location off the tourist trail, there's a store, cafe, laundromat, and ice machines within one mile. From April through November, five tent and 29 RV sites go for $10 a night, with picnic tables, electricity, piped water, flush toilets, primitive showers, firewood, and a playground.

Viento Park, tel. (503) 235-2205, is eight miles west of Hood River on the river side of I-84. From mid-April to late October you'll pay $10 a night for five tent sites and 58 RV sites. Electricity, picnic tables, and piped water are provided. As with the other Columbia Gorge state parks, no reservations are accepted.

Sunset Campground is located behind the only laundromat, on the west end of Cascade St. in Hood River. In addition to laundry facilities, restrooms and showers can be found in the open area planted with trees which serves as the campsite. There are 16 tent spaces and hookups for seven RVs. Sunset is a first-come, first-served facility, but call (503) 386-6098 for more information.

BOB RACE

Food

The brie-and-chablis set that blows into town during peak windsurfing season has brought sophisticated tastes and higher prices to Hood River. However, it's still possible to get a decent meal without paying a fortune. Best of all, there's not a town of this size anywhere else in Oregon with as much consistently good coffee or as many places catering to vegetarians. For that matter, there aren't too many small towns of a few thousand people anywhere in the world with their own coffee roasters (Hood River Coffee Co.), a fresh pasta company (Justa Pasta), several wineries (Flerchinger, Hood River) a microbrewery (Full Sail/White Cap), and some of the finest fruit in the country. The only thing to keep in mind is that most restaurants here close early, so plan accordingly.

Hood River Bagels, 13 Oak St., tel. (503) 386-2123, purveys a product that gets nods of approval from even east coast transplants.

Andrew's Pizza and Bakery, 1070 Oak, tel. (503) 386-1448, gets our vote as the best pizza, $2/slice, in the Gorge. The extravagant toppings and by-the-slice options are appreciated as are primo coffee and microbrews to wash it all down. In the morning, fresh-baked scones and cinnamon rolls are other highlights. Next door, foreign flicks and art films are shown, generally on weekend nights. Another pizza place worth putting on the brakes for can be found south of town at **Santacroce's,** 4780 ORE 35, tel. (503) 354-2511, open for dinner only. This place is perfect for those coming back from Lookout Mountain, Cloud Cap, and other excursions in and around the east slopes of Mt. Hood. Several more food-on-the-go options include the **New York Sub Shop,** 1020 Wasco St., tel. (503) 386-5144, where one feeds two, and the breakfast burritos at the **River View Deli,** 202 Cascade St., tel. (503) 386-9404.

Locals swear by **Bette's Place,** at the Oak Mall, 416 Oak St., tel. (503) 386-1880, for breakfast. Favorite ways to start the day here include eggs Benedict, strawberry waffles, hotcakes, cinnamon rolls, or fresh fruit plate. This family restaurant also specializes in chicken dumplings every other Sunday; seafood, vegetarian fare, and orders to go are available. It's open every day except Wednesday (breakfasts $5-7). At **The Mesquitery,** 12th and B Streets, tel. (503) 386-2002, wood-smoked and barbecue flavors issue forth a wake-up call to your taste buds at lunch and dinner. Particularly recommended is pollo vaquero ("chicken cowboy-style"), mesquite-grilled chicken doused in rust-colored pico de gallo sauce and rolled up in a taquito. The menu also features ribs and fish in a restaurant where the spice (as well as the price) is always right, $10-12 range. This small restaurant is about a half-mile south of downtown on the way to Parkdale. Close by, **Big City Chicks,** 303 13th, tel. (503) 386-2111, also spices up the local restaurant scene with an ethnic-accented menu. Set in an older home done up in an art deco theme, the restaurant specialized in spicy dishes from all over the world. On warm evenings, dine out on the lawn. Main courses, $7-12, such as ginger plum chicken with couscous from Morrocco, raspberry salmon from France, and other selections from the 40+-item dinner menu are bound to fuel some travel fantasies.

To make your evening an occasion, try **Stone Hedge Inn,** 3405 Cascade Dr., tel. (503) 386-3940. This turn-of-the-century house surrounded by a wooded area and gardens has a warm paneled interior that's conducive to leisurely dining. Even "light" dinners (portions are huge) here can range $13-18, but the elegantly presented steak, lamb, duck, and seafood dishes are the best in town. What everyone talks most about, however, is the selection of delectable desserts. Chocolate cheesecake and strawberries coated in white and dark chocolate with Grand Marnier are two such memorable confections. Call ahead for reservations and directions to this romantic hideaway at the end of a long, serpentine dirt road. It's open Wed.-Sun. from 5 p.m. If you're entering town via exit 62, look for it just past the gas station on the opposite (right) side of the road.

Another fine dining option is the **Riverside Grill,** 1108 E. Marina Way, tel. (503) 386-2200, at the Best Western Hotel that sits on a bluff above the Columbia. Just drive to the end of Oak Street, make a left to cross over the freeway and when you emerge from a tunnel you're there. Northwest cuisine and nice views of windsurfers will run you about $20 for dinner, but breakfast and lunch are half that price, the food just as good and the view better. Picnickers and natural food fans are referred to Wyeast Naturals, 110 5th St., tel. (503) 386-6181. You can also enjoy sandwiches and fruit smoothies here. If you're still not full, walk up to the corner of 5th and Oak to **Mike's Ice Cream,** 504 Oak, for a huckleberry or espresso milkshake. This place is closed in winter, open in April and serves highly regarded Prince Puckler's Ice Cream from Eugene.

For evening musical entertainment, barbecued burgers, Cajun oysters, and vegetarian munchies washed down by Hood River's award-winning microbrew, Full Sail Ale, head for **White Cap Brew Pub,** 506 Columbia St., tel. (503) 386-2247. Add the panoramic view from the outdoor deck and you have the most laid-back atmosphere in town. Ask about brewery tours and tastings too. To enjoy beers from other microbreweries, head to the **Sixth Street Bistro,** 6th and Cascade, and the **Big Horse Brewpub,** 115 State St., tel. (503) 386-4111, where Big Horse Ale, live music, and dancing make it a local hot spot.

Finally, fans of Mexican street food should keep an eye out for a white trailer in a parking lot just east of Cascade Mall, in the lot next to Zeman's Music 1819 W. Cascade St. on the south side of the highway. **El Rinconcito** (the Little Corner) serves up tacos with birria (goat meat), carnitas (pork), and other down-home specialties. If you hanker for flavors of the frontera, you won't get more (or better) food for the money anywhere in the gorge. It's usually open only in summer.

Events

The most popular events in Hood River County highlight windsurfing and the seasons of blossom, harvest, and foliage in the orchards.

April 20-21, the **Hood River Blossom Festival** celebrates breathtaking views of the valley's orchards in bloom. Arts and crafts, dinners, and the seasonal opening of the Mt. Hood Railroad (see "Information and Services," below) also can be enjoyed. Contact the Hood River Chamber of Commerce for more details.

Special events during the Hood River Blossom Festival include an orchard tour aboard the Mt. Hood Railroad.

MT. HOOD RAILROAD

The fall counterpart of this fête is the **Hood River Harvest Fest.** On October 20 and 21, the valley welcomes visitors for two days of entertainment, crafts, fresh locally grown produce, and colorful foliage. Admission is free and the apples and pears are ripe. Hood River is the winter pear (d'anjou) capital of the world and produces Bartletts, comice bosc, and other varieties at different times of the year. Cherries, peaches, and apples round out this horn of plenty. Newton pippin apples are another renowned Hood River product. The 15,000 acres of orchards are still the leading economic factor in the county, with Diamond Packing the leading pear shipper in the United States.

Apple Jam in late August books top performers for concerts by the marina. In years past, Scott Cossy, Nicolette Larsen, and such local talents as Tom Grant and Curtis Salgado were featured. Call (503) 386-2000 for details.

Two premier windsurfing events take place on the Columbia in July. The **Columbia Gorge Pro-Am** is the world's largest slalom windsurfing event and traditionally falls between the second and ninth of July. Peak season is April-Sept. for this sport. **Hood River Windsurfing,** tel. (503) 386-5787, has all the information.

The **Gorge Cities Blowout** is a spectacular 20-mile open-water race from Cascade Locks to Hood River, July 12-15. Call Michael Clark at (503) 667-7778 for more details.

Also in July, the **Timberland Gorge Games,** tel. (503) 386-7774, http://www.gorgegames.com, is an olympics for outdoor extreme sports including mountain biking, windsurfing, snowboarding, rock climbing, kiteskiing, paragliding, outrigger canoeing, a 10K trail run, and other activities that take advantage of the magnificent setting provided by this cleft in the Cascades. Top musical acts, clinics, and events for the family round out the Gorge Games.

Information and Services

The **Hood River Valley Visitors Council/Chamber of Commerce,** Port Marina Park, Hood River 97031, tel. (503) 386-2000 or (800) 366-3530, http://www.Gorge.net/hrccc, has an extensive array of maps and pamphlets about the area. Take exit 64 off of I-84 and follow the signs to get here. Down the road is the **post office** (Hood River 97031).

Greyhound, 1205 B St., tel. (503) 386-1212, services the community. **Hood River Taxi and Transportation,** 315 Oak St., tel. (503) 386-3355, offers in-city taxi service Sun.-Thurs. 7 a.m.-midnight, Saturday 7 a.m.-3 a.m., as well as group van tours. A travel agency that can line you up with home rentals, airline reservations, windsurfing rentals/lessons, and bed and breakfasts is **Gorge Central Reservation Service,** 220 Eugene St., tel. (503) 386-6109. **Hood River County Transit,** 1020 Wilson St., tel. (503) 386-4202, is the local public bus system.

Club Wet Inc., P.O. Box 697, Hood River 97031, tel. (503) 386-6084, has regular flights between Seattle and Hood River. Call ahead for reservations and ticketing. The average flight time is one hour. Also at the Hood River airport is **Scenic Flites Northwest,** tel. (503) 386-1099 local, or (503) 256-3086 from Portland, which offers a three-quarter-hour Gorge flightsee for $45 per person. **Air Columbia,** tel. (503) 490-1779, has helicopter flights that are featured at the Blossom Festival and by appointment. These tours require a two person minimum and charge $125 per person for a 55-minute trip to Beacon Rock or to Mt. Hood and Timberline Lodge. To get to the airport, take exit 62 off I-84 onto West Cascade to 13th. Go past the hospital and shopping center, where 12th becomes Tucker Road. Follow the airport signs past the drive-in to the airport.

Hood River Memorial Hospital, 13th and May Streets, tel. (503) 338-7889, is open 24 hours a day with a physician-staffed emergency room. **Care Corner,** 12th and May, tel. (503) 386-1111, offers immediate care for illnesses and injuries. This facility refers more serious cases to Hood River Memorial.

For a recent send-up of vintage Americana, the **Trail Twin Indoor/Outdoor Theater,** 1655 Tucker Rd., tel. (503) 386-1666, is a drive-in featuring first run movies nightly from March until the first snow, $6/car. The **U.S. Forest Service** office, 902 Wasco Ave., tel. (503) 386-2333, has hiking information. Be sure to ask about the newly renovated section of the scenic highway just opened to hikers and bikers. Old growth trees and classic tunnels with rock windows in the basalt walls are highlights.

The **Mt. Hood Railroad,** 110 Railroad Ave., tel. (503) 386-3556, ext. 804, has tours in 1910-era passenger cars that traverse the scenic 20-

mile valley between Mt. Hood and the Columbia River. (See "By Train" under "Getting There and Around" in the On the Road chapter.)

Public restrooms are located below City Hall on State Street. **West Side Laundromat,** 1911 W. Cascade St., tel. (503) 386-5650, has extra large capacity machines and is located near Safeway and a pizza place. Radio station 104.5 FM has wind readings 7:20 a.m.-9:50 a.m. at half hour intervals. You can also get ski and road reports. 92.7 FM tunes into the eclectic programming of community radio.

THE DALLES

It hits you shortly after leaving Hood River. Scrub oak gives way to sage and the grasslands of eastern Oregon. And then, just as suddenly, you come upon the traffic and acrid air of an urban environment. You've come to The Dalles, a place Lewis and Clark in 1805 called the "Trading Mart of the Northwest." Instead of seeing an Indian potlatch on the Columbia, however, the modern visitor will see 10,000 souls living in the industrial hub of the Gorge. While the cherry orchards and wheat fields south of town and the aluminum plants and timber mills by the river are more what The Dalles is about these days than tourism, a complete perspective on the history of Oregon is impossible without a day-trip here.

Shortly after you enter town on exit 82 (City Center exit), stop off at the **chamber of commerce,** corner of 2nd and Portland Streets, 404 W. 2nd St., The Dalles 97058, tel. (800) 255-3385, and pick up their pamphlets, *The Dalles: Historic Gateway to the Columbia Gorge* and *Walking Tours to Historic Homes and Buildings.* Take a gander at the restored Wasco County Courthouse next door, which was moved from its original location. This court presided over much of the country west of the Rockies in the mid-1800s. The following overview in conjunction with these publications can annotate your day-trip here. As the walking tour showcases churches, homes, and government buildings built between 1859 and 1929, let's look at those parts of town whose history dates back before that time. Our itinerary will conform to historical chronology.

Seufert Park

Although the visitor center is at the west end of The Dalles, begin your travels six miles east of town off I-84 on exit 87 with the Seufert Park interpretive center, staging area for the free train

which tours The Dalles Dam. (For information on this complex, call (503) 296-6616 or (800) 255-3385. The train and tour take about an hour and run April 14-June 4, Wed.-Sun. 10 a.m.-5 p.m., with the last train departing at 4 p.m. From June 5 to September 3, the hours are 9 a.m.-6 p.m. with the last train departing at 5 p.m. Tours run on the half-hour. On the trip, be on the lookout for the petroglyphs on display. These were unearthed during construction. You'll immediately notice that the dam's longest arm runs parallel to, rather than across, the river. This is because the trough through which the Columbia runs here is so narrow that there wouldn't be room for navigation locks, generators, fish ladders, and spillways with a conventional design. In addition to detailing the workings of the world's fourth-largest hydroelectric project (largest dam on the lower Columbia), displays and commentary recount the historical importance of this location as a gathering place and gateway for native peoples and pioneer travelers. Just upstream from here was Celilo Falls, where Indians armed with spears and dip nets pursued salmon for centuries. Today native fishermen will sell you salmon, steelhead and walleye for low prices here on certain weekends in September. Call (888) BUY-1855 for more information. Although The Dalles Dam ended the fishing frenzy by submerging the falls in 1957, reminders in the form of artifacts and customs recall its spiritual and mercantile significance in the native tradition. Archaeological finds here of objects originating in places as far away as the Great Lakes hint at the draw exerted by this bartering mecca. Photos portraying Indians spreading their 20-foot-long dip nets from precarious platforms above the falls will also help the imagination.

Finally, you might be treated to this same sight on the Columbia today, albeit with lower water and reduced catch levels. If you can be in this area the first weekend of April, the Visitor Information Bureau can direct you to where the age-old native ritual of welcoming the first salmon upstream takes place. The public is welcome to join the Indians free of charge for fry bread, huckleberries, and salmon cooked over an open fire and served with boiled roots and venison. The Celilo Village is located 12 miles east of The Dalles on a shelf at the foot of a bluff overlooking I-84. Just take the Celilo exit off I-84. Look for the ceremonial lodge located a short distance southwest of the exit. This was the site of the Indian fishing village described by Lewis and Clark. It went into decline with the coming of the dams, particularly The Dalles project. Today, it's cut off from the river by railroad tracks and the freeway.

Not surprisingly, the Seufert Park interpretive center's emphasis is on the coming of the white settlers. The arrival of Meriwether Lewis and William Clark was the seminal event in defining another role for the river—transportation for westbound travelers in the Oregon country. French voyagers who had passed through at the behest of fur-trapping concerns called these waters near Celilo Falls "La Grande Dalle de la Columbia" ("The Big Trough of the Columbia"). From this point, the river was not considered safely navigable. As time went on, the area and the town became known as The Dalles. Oregon Trail emigrants loaded their wagons onto boats after portaging them overland around La Grande Dalle de la Columbia. These portages were later abetted by the first railroad tracks in Oregon, constructed by the Oregon Steamship Navigation Company. Thus, the region near the modern dam site has been a focal point for Oregon native civilizations as well as for a pioneer transportation and trade route. Today, the dam itself is the northern terminus of the world's largest intertie power system. Several other important landmarks are back on the other end of town.

Rock Fort

To further stimulate your reverie of the early explorers and for the sake of historical chronology, your next stop might be Lewis and Clark's Rock Fort. Coming from the west, take exit 82 and drive a mile to a sign indicating the road (Weber St.) to the port area. Head left a mile and make a right at the UPS building on W. 1st Street. As you drive east past the warehouses, several signs will reassure you that you'll be at the dynamic duo's overnight bivouac shortly. The undeveloped gravel lot surrounded by big stones overlooking the river contrasts with the warehouses and billboards nearby. Unlike the more impressive Rooster Rock, Beacon Rock, and other Lewis and Clark landmarks, this site will call more upon your imagination to ward off the sights, smells, and sounds of the surrounding industrial park. A visit to the mural "Lewis and Clark at Rock Fort," 401 E. 2nd St., should help fill in any gaps in your visualization of the two explorers on the banks of the Columbia.

City Park and Fort Dalles

For another less-than-thrilling walk on hallowed ground, proceed to The Dalles City Park at 6th and Union Streets. Pioneer Ezra Meeker placed a marker on this site in 1906 to commemorate the end of the original Oregon Trail. In 1845 Samuel Barlow opened the first overland route to the Willamette Valley here, extending the initial route. Barlow Road aficionados should pick up the U.S. Forest Service brochure to guide them over much of this pioneer thoroughfare. The **Dalles Visitor and Convention Bureau,** tel. (800) 225-3385, puts out a driving-tour pamphlet which also outlines how to traverse the northernmost portions of the route.

In this park you'll also note the Victor Trevitt House. An interesting postscript on this pioneer printer and politico is supplied at the Memaloose rest stop halfway between The Dalles and Hood River on the west side of I-84. Behind the restroom overlooking Memaloose Island on the Columbia is a historical placard mentioning that Trevitt's grave was put on the island among native burial sites at his own request, so high was his esteem for his red brothers. "Memaloose" means "to die" in Chinook, and this island experienced a death of sorts a half-century ago. At the time, water backed up by the Bonneville Dam submerged this sacred site, reducing it to its current half-acre size. Given the decimation of the Indian population and the salmon runs, this event can be viewed as adding insult to injury.

As the final prelude to the walking tour, visit Fort Dalles at 15th and Garrison Streets; for information write: City of The Dalles Museum Commission, P.O. Box 806, The Dalles 97058, tel. (503) 296-4547. Unlike the preceding points of interest, there's an actual structure here housing memorabilia. Admission is $2 for adults. The Surgeon's Quarters, dating back to 1856, serves as a museum for armaments, period furniture, and other pioneer items. In 1850, Fort Dalles was established in response to the massacre of missionaries Dr. Marcus and Narcissa Whitman. The Whitmans had attempted to impose the white man's ways on the Indians with unfortunate results. For instance, the natives could not understand the concept of private property and felt that Whitman's whipping of those who inadvertently took what they considered to be communal property was unduly harsh. The last straw occurred when a measels vaccine administered by Whitman to Indian and white children killed the native children while the white children were cured. The Indians were further confused and understandably angry when they were told that their offspring's adverse reactions were due to a lack of immunities. Their violent retaliation incited Congress to establish the only military post between Fort Vancouver and the Rockies. The Surgeon's Quarters is the one remaining part of this complex.

Several years later, the establishment of Wasco County in 1859 made The Dalles the seat of a 130,000-square-mile bailiwick stretching from the Cascades to the Rocky Mountains. This was the largest county ever formed in the United States. Hours are daily 10 a.m.-5 p.m. March-Oct.; Nov.-Feb.; Monday, Thursday, Friday noon-4 p.m. and Saturday 10 a.m.-4 p.m. Coming from the west take Exit 83 off I-84, go east on 6th to Trevitt and follow the signs. Admission $3 adults, discounts for children and seniors.

Now you're ready to take on the walking tour described in the pamphlet, with an understanding of the rich heritage of this gateway to the Gorge and the Oregon Country.

Columbia Gorge Discovery Center and Wasco County Historical Museum

To the Native Americans, it was the great gathering place. To Lewis and Clark and the Oregon Trail pioneers, it was the only pass traversing the Cascades Range at sea level. To connoisseurs of the Pacific Northwest's rich historical mosaic and varied landscapes, the Columbia River Gorge is a journey to the source.

The Columbia Gorge Discovery Center and Wasco County Historical Museum, 4500 Discovery Dr. N., Crates Point, 3 miles west of The Dalles ORE 30, tel. (503) 296-8600, coalesce the rich historical, geological, biological, and cultural legacies of this region. The Discovery Center addresses the region as a whole, articulating a 40-million-year time line with scale models and videos (as well as simulated "hands-on" experiences) that begins with the cataclysms that created the gorge on through its native occupation, to the coming of the pioneers and subsequent domination by the White Man. Along the way, native plants and animals are given attention along with such diverse activities as roadbuilding, orchards, and windsurfing.

A short walk away, the Wasco County Historical Museum reviews 10,000 years of Native American life, early explorers, and industry. Especially interesting are exhibits showcasing such arcane chapters of county history as the race between two competing railroads to build a million-dollar-a-mile route up the Deschutes River Canyon and the reign of Indian guru Bhagwan Sri Rajneesh. As with the Discovery Center, technology is effectively employed to tell the story of a county that saw some of the most critical early chapters of Oregon history.

Situated on a bluff above the Columbia on ORE 30, the museums are accessed via exit 82 off I-84. After turning right onto ORE 30, folow a winding road to the parking lot. Both exhibit halls are open 10 a.m.-6 p.m. daily. A single admission fee pays for both venues, $6.50 adults, $5.50 seniors, $3 ages 6-16.

Murals

Historical murals are appearing in many towns with Oregon Trail heritage, and The Dalles is no exception. *Decision at Dalles,* by Don Crook, shows pioneers setting out on the Columbia River route to the Willamette Valley. Look for this 70-foot-high mural at the corner of 2nd and Federal Streets. *Lewis and Clark at Fort Rock,* by Robert Thomas, can be found at 401 E 2nd St. on the side of Tony's Town and Country Clothing. *The Dalles: Trade Center for 10,000,* by Roger Cooke, is a third mural nearby depicting the gathering of the tribes along the Columbia described by Lewis and Clark. More murals are projected for this town so rich in history and memory.

Windsurfing

Besides its historical significance, The Dalles is gaining a reputation as the best place in the gorge to learn windsurfing. The bowl-like contours of Riverfront Park mute the power of the winds while isolating the area from the Columbia's stiff current and keeping the waves down. With wind currents that always seem to blow you back toward shore, beginning windsurfers can venture out with a greater feeling of security here than elsewhere in the area.

Bed and Board

A box lunch from the **Dobre Deli,** 308 E. 4th St., tel. (503) 298-8239, is a substantial and cost-effective way to sustain your foray along the path of Lewis and Clark and the Oregon Trail. For those who elect to stay over, **Williams House Bed and Breakfast,** 608 W. 6th, The Dalles 97058, tel. (503) 286-2889, is highly recommended. In addition to affordable Victorian elegance, the innkeepers can alert you to local attractions. This 1899 mansion with wraparound porches is stunningly landscaped with a creek running through it. Rates for the two guest rooms and a full suite run $70-90.

After visiting St. Peters Church, the century-old Gothic revival landmark, you can smooth your reentry into the 20th century with a cup of espresso across the street at **La Crema,** 221 W. 4th Street. In addition to highly regarded Captain Beans coffee from Portland, this coffeehouse also serves first-rate cookies and scones.

Another place to grab a bite in the shadow of history is at the **Baldwin Saloon,** 1st and Court Streets, tel. (503) 296-5666. This 1876 building (it was a restaurant then, too) is a repository of turn-of-the-century oil paintings adorning the restaurant's brick walls. The 18-foot mahogany bar and the pendulum clock can also ensure a historical reverie. Try the fresh oysters (pan-fried, $12), homemade soups, smoked salmon mousse, chicken liver pate, breads, and desserts here.

Bookstore

Klindt's Booksellers, 315 2nd St., tel. (503) 296-3355, represents another bit of history in The Dalles. Established in 1870, it is the oldest bookstore in Oregon, complete with original wood floors, a high ceiling, and oak and plate-glass display cases.

Other Activities

A visit to the restored **Granada Theater,** 223 E. 2nd St., tel. (503) 298-6800, will let you enjoy music and movies in a theater that dates back to the days of vaudeville. **Sorosis Park** serves as a backyard for the locals to enjoy tennis courts, picnic areas, and just plain beautiful views. To get there, take Trevitt St. south and follow the signs.

Information

Additional information on this area can be had by calling (800) 98-GORGE.

osprey

BOB RACE

BOB RACE

THE WILLAMETTE VALLEY

This 25- to 40-mile-wide and 120-mile-long fertile river valley bordered by rainforested mountain ranges was the object of Oregon Trail pioneer dreams. Here they found a land where crops never failed, a place that offered a second chance, a stage upon which to play out the most cherished economic, civic, educational, and cultural impulses of civilization. One hundred fifty years after the emigrants' epic march across the continent, diversified agriculture, esteemed universities, and cosmopolitan cities fill the Willamette Valley landscape. Covered bridges and historic homes are also here to remind us of the taming of the frontier.

Horn of Plenty

Prior to the coming of the white settlers, the Calapooya Indians had subsisted for centuries on game, berries, camas (a lily-like perennial with a sweet bulbous root) and wapato tubers, and fish. They had never cultivated the soil or logged, save for burning to provide browse for deer and soils for grasses, roots, and berries. But centuries of setting fire to the valley had cleared the land of a lot of trees and exposed rich alluvial soils ideal for farming.

The first Europeans who came here in the second decade of the 1800s also declined to take advantage of the prime farmland, preferring instead to reap easy money from the fur trade. It fell to the Oregon Trail influx in the mid-19th century to break ground for the present-day agricultural colossus. Today the valley boasts national leadership in everything from berry to prune production. It has carved an identity as the primary source of such specialty crops as English holly, bearded iris, and lily bulbs. Coveted green beans, the highest-yielding sweet corn in the U.S., and domination of world markets in grass seed and hazelnuts compound the impression of pastures of plenty.

But you don't have to go to the farm to experience the Willamette Valley's abundance. It's possible to walk down certain streets in many valley towns during the fall and sample the bounty from pear, plum, and walnut trees as well as blackberry bushes. In the spring, cherry trees in public places provide the snacking treat of choice.

Now, as then, the valley is the population center of Oregon. Between 1970 and 1990, half a million people came here to stay. Another 700,000 new pioneers are projected by the end of the year 2012. Eugene and Salem are the state's second- and third-largest cities, and the region as a whole, including Portland, accounts for over 75% of the state's residents despite occupying only 11% of the area. Nonetheless, you seldom get the feeling of being in a big metropolis south of Portland, thanks to bike routes, parks, and land-use planning based on environmental imperatives.

The Willamette River

This progressive orientation is embodied in the history of the Willamette River. After the Willamette served as the transport route for valley produce to Portland en route to gold rush-era San Francisco, prosperity and people coalesced around its shores. By the 1960s, 20 municipalities and over 600 industrial plants along the river had so befouled the waters that Governor Tom McCall described it as an "open sewer." The next decade's Willamette Greenway legislation put $50 million and the efforts of industry toward a cleanup. The results were the first significant salmon spawning runs in 40 years and a spate of riverfront parks and recreation areas.

The coast fork of the river originates south of Cottage Grove; the Middle Fork comes out of the Cascades near Oakridge. They meet each other and the McKenzie River near Eugene, flowing north to Portland and meeting the Columbia. The surrounding valley extends from Cottage Grove to Portland. (Since the northern Willamette Valley is within the orbit of Portland, it is treated in "Portland and Vicinity," above.) Farther south, Salem, Corvallis, and Eugene have carved a distinct identity as the Emerald Empire.

SALEM AND VICINITY

The used-car lots and fast-food outlets encountered on the way into Salem off I-5 contrast with the inspiring murals and displays in the capitol building. It's comforting to be reminded in the state house of Oregon's pioneer tradition and proud legacy of progressive legislation. Close by, the tranquil beauty and museums of historic Willamette University also provide a break from the Xerox-copy drabness of a town dominated by gray buildings housing the state's bureaucracies.

HISTORY

The Calapooyan name for the locality of Salem was Chemeketa, or "Place of Rest." Connotations of repose were also captured by the Methodist missionary appellation "Salem." This is an anglicized form of the Arabic *salaam* and the Hebrew *shalom,* meaning "peace." The surrounding croplands along with Willamette River transport and waterpower quickly enabled Salem to become the New Jerusalem envisioned by Oregon Trail pioneers. Over the years, the city forged an economic destiny in government, food processing, light manufacturing, and wood products. Today, it has a population of almost 111,000 people.

People of the Central Valley

Even if you don't have time for in-depth exploration, you'll probably find the diverse ethnic makeup of the north-central valley fascinating. In the town of **Woodburn,** located eight miles northwest of Mt. Angel, for example, local school classes are taught on a multilingual basis to accommodate the large concentration of Mexican migrants and Russian Old Believers here. The latter fled religious persecution in the 1960s by traveling to Brazil and New Jersey and then to the Willamette Valley. A small museum devoted to their history is located on the grounds of the Mt. Angel Abbey. Down in the town of Mt. Angel, signs in Spanish and German add further evidence of a rich cultural mix. It was German Catholics who settled Mt. Angel, an influence reflected by the Bavarian feel here. In addition, many residents proudly point to French-Canadian backgrounds bespeaking their connections to the region's first pioneers.

If you're arriving from the Portland area you can take in the cultural variety of Woodburn and Mt. Angel by getting off I-5 at the Woodburn exit and following a marked tour route several miles east of the freeway. From I-5 drive past several miles of fast food outlets and turn right on Settlemeier (look for the City Center signs) just past the French Prairie school. A quarter mile south, make a left onto Hayes St. that will take you a few blocks to the old downtown of Woodburn. Here you'll find Salvador's Bakery at 1st and Hayes Streets, a Mexican-style panaderia or self-serve bakery. This part of Woodburn also boasts several excellent Mexican restaurants, notably La Michoacana across 1st Street from Salvador's. A few blocks south is a thrift store with signs in Russian, Spanish, and English.

SIGHTS

Mission Mill Museum

In 1840-41 the site of the Jason Lee House and Parsonage moved from the Willamette River upstream to Mill Creek, laying the foundations for the present-day cityscape. These structures along with the Boon Home were part of a Methodist mission to the Indians. The reconstructed Thomas Kay Woolen Mill (take exit 253 off I-5) dating back to 1889 is also on the four-acre site of what is now called Mission Mill Museum, 1313 S.E. Mill St., tel. (541) 585-7012. Tours led by guides in period costumes begin at 10 a.m., noon, and 2 and 4 p.m. The oldest frame house in the Northwest and water turbines converting fleece into wool fabric are interesting, but those with limited time might prefer to come here just to obtain brochures about Salem and vicinity in the reception area in front.

The museum is open daily 10 a.m.-4:30 p.m., except Thanksgiving, Christmas and New Year's Day. To gain admission to the historic houses and the mill, adults pay $5, seniors $4.50, students 12-18 pay $4, and children under six get in free. To get to the museum from I-5, exit at ORE 22, go west on Mission St. for two miles to the 13th St. overpass, turn north onto 12th St., and go west onto Mill Street. If you arrive by Amtrak, Mission Mill is within walking distance.

Willamette University

Not far from the museum is Willamette University, 900 State St., tel. (541) 370-6300, the oldest institution of higher learning west of the Mississippi. It began as the Oregon Institute in 1843, a school that Methodist missionary Jason Lee founded to instill Christian values among the settlers. Over the years, Willamette University has turned out its share of Oregon politicos, including longtime senators Mark Hatfield and Bob Packwood. It also has to be one of the prettier campuses in the nation.

The campus is one of Salem's many oases of greenery that soften the hard edge of a city dominated by government buildings and nondescript downtown thoroughfares. Campus landscape architecture features a Japanese garden, ornate fountains, and a grove of five sequoias six feet in diameter. When you stand in the middle of these redwoods, you should be able to discern a star pattern formed by their

a quiet Willamette Valley country lane

BRUCE BUSH

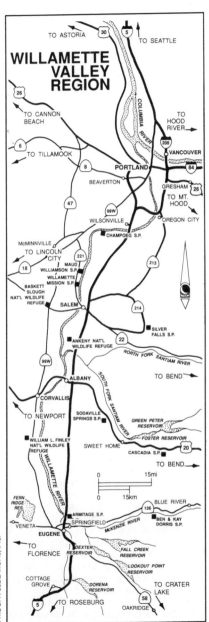

WILLAMETTE VALLEY REGION

TO ASTORIA
30
5
TO SEATTLE
26
TO CANNON BEACH
6
TO TILLAMOOK
8
26
COLUMBIA RIVER
TO HOOD RIVER
205
VANCOUVER
PORTLAND
84
BEAVERTON
GRESHAM
26
TO MT. HOOD
47
99W
WILSONVILLE
OREGON CITY
CHAMPOEG S.P.
McMINNVILLE
TO LINCOLN CITY
221
18
MAUD
WILLIAMSON S.P.
WILLAMETTE MISSION S.P.
213
BASKETT SLOUGH NAT'L WILDLIFE REFUGE
SALEM
214
SILVER FALLS S.P.
ANKENY NAT'L WILDLIFE REFUGE
22
MOON
NORTH FORK SANTIAM RIVER
99W
ALBANY
SOUTH FORK SANTIAM RIVER
TO BEND
CORVALLIS
TO NEWPORT
SODAVILLE SPRINGS S.P.
GREEN PETER RESERVOIR
WILLIAM L. FINLEY NAT'L WILDLIFE REFUGE
FOSTER RESERVOIR
SWEET HOME
20
CASCADIA S.P.
TO BEND
WILLAMETTE RIVER
0   15mi
0   15km
BLUE RIVER
126
FERN RIDGE RES.
ARMITAGE S.P.
BEN & KAY DORRIS S.P.
SPRINGFIELD
McKENZIE RIVER
VENETA
EUGENE
TO FLORENCE
DEXTER RESERVOIR
FALL CREEK RESERVOIR
LOOKOUT POINT RESERVOIR
COTTAGE GROVE
DORENA RESERVOIR
TO CRATER LAKE
5
TO ROSEBURG
58
OAKRIDGE

© MOON PUBLICATIONS, INC.

canopies, giving rise to the name "star trees." This grove, which sits between the state capitol and Collins Hall (home of the science departments), has beside it an Oregon rock of ages. Found atop Ankeny Hill in Salem, the granite boulder floated down from northeastern Washington on an ice raft during the same Missoula Flood that shaped the Columbia River Gorge 25,000 years ago. This glacial erratic stands as a reminder that the Willamette Valley is largely composed of Lake Missoula sediments. In Collins Hall, crystals and exhibits on Oregon glacial activity join an impressive taxidermic array of Oregon wildlife. There's no admission charge and it's open during university hours. Finally, if you're hungry, the food court at the student union, Goudy Commons, is exceptional, reasonably priced, and with enough variety to suit all tatses.

State Capitol

If visiting the State Capitol building, 900 N.E. Court St., tel. (541) 378-4423, strikes you as the kind of saccharine excursion best reserved for a first-grade class trip, you're in for a pleasant surprise. The marble halls of Oregon government are adorned with attractive murals, paintings, and sculptures of the seminal events in this state's inspiring history. These incidents are given eloquent voice by on-site tour guides whose commentary is sure to fill in any gaps in your understanding of this pioneer saga. The Capitol is located on Court Street between W. Summer and E. Summer Streets, just north of the Willamette University campus.

Atop the Capitol dome is a gold-leafed bronze statue of a bearded, axe-wielding pioneer. Massive marble sculptures flank the main entrance—*Covered Wagons* on the west side and *Lewis and Clark by Sacajawea* on the east. Maps of the Oregon Trail and the route of Lewis and Clark are visible on the backs of the statues. The symbolism is sustained after you enter the double glass doors to the rotunda. Your eyes will immediately be drawn to an eight-foot-diameter bronze state seal, set into the floor, which juxtaposes an eagle in flight, a sailing ship, a covered wagon, and forests. The 33 marble steps beyond the cordoned-off emblem lead up to the House and Senate chambers, and symbolize Oregon's place as the 33rd state to enter the

SALEM

© MOON PUBLICATIONS, INC.

Union. Four large murals adorning the rose travertine walls of the rotunda illustrate the settlement and growth of Oregon: Robert Gray sailing into the Columbia estuary in 1792; Lewis and Clark at Celilo Falls in 1805; the first white women to cross the continent being welcomed by Dr. John McLoughlin in 1836; and the first wagon train on the Oregon Trail in 1843. Bronze reliefs and smaller murals symbolic of Oregon's industries also are here. The best part of the Capitol building is the legislative chambers, up the sweeping marble staircases.

Near the ceiling in the Senate and House chambers are friezes depicting an honor roll of people who influenced the growth and settle-ment of Oregon. Included are Thomas Jefferson, who sanctioned the Lewis and Clark expedition, and Thomas Condon, native son and naturalist extraordinaire. Also among the names are those of six women, headed by Lewis and Clark's interpreter-guide Sacajawea. The biggest surprise in the array might be John Quincy Adams, who determined the southern boundary of Oregon when he was secretary of state. In both legislative chambers look for forestry, agricultural, and fishing symbols woven into the carpets; murals about the coming of statehood are behind the speakers' rostrums.

Among the many architecturally eye-catching features to be found in the Capitol are the rotunda's black marble, the House chamber walls and furnishings of golden oak, black walnut room appointments in the Senate, a walnut-paneled governor's office, and bronze door-knobs inlaid with the state seal throughout the building. There is also a carved myrtlewood table inlaid with a mosaic of the Capitol building in the reception area outside the governor's suite between the House and the Senate. All this was paid for with part of the $2 million it took to build the Capitol in 1938.

If you don't want to roam independently, free half-hour building **tours** are given on the hour weekdays 9 a.m.-4 p.m., and Saturday 10 a.m.-3 p.m., with a lunch break on all days noon-1 p.m. Sunday tours are given on the hour at 1, 2, and 3 p.m.

A tower at the top of the Capitol dome gives a superlative view of the valley and surrounding Cascade peaks and is worth the 121-step walk from the fourth floor. It's open from Memorial Day to August but is closed off during this time when the temperature reaches 90°. Tours run Memorial Day through August and other times of the year by appointment, tel. (541) 986-1388 for tour information. Also worth a look in the building is the ongoing exhibit of outstanding Oregon artists in the governor's ceremonial office upstairs. Downstairs is a fine gift shop of Oregon-made crafts, food, and other indigenous items. You'll also find the **Oasis Cafe,** tel. (541) 371-6483, an offshoot of the Off Center Cafe (see "Practicalities" following). On the west side of the building (Court St. entrance) is an indoor visitor information kiosk.

To get to the State Capitol building from I-5, take exit 253 to ORE 22 west. Take the Willamette University/State Offices exit and follow the signs for 12th Street/State Offices. Turn left onto Court Street.

State Archives Building

At the entrance to the Capitol Mall on N. Sumner St., another softly arched marble building has become a popular destination, but not just for the purposes of soaking in Oregon's pioneer and political traditions. The luxurious interior decor of the new State Archives building is viewed by Oregonians as a symbol of bureaucratic extravagance in an era of belt-tightening for everyone else. They come here and glare at $127-a-square-yard carpet covering $180-a-square-yard travertine limestone floors, all illuminated by light fixtures costing $5,000 apiece.

Overpriced adornments notwithstanding, the quilt of Oregon historical scenes on the second floor and other thematic objets d'art are both aesthetic and inspiring. In this vein, anyone who goes to look at the archives themselves will come away with a special perspective on pioneer history. It's hard not to get chills as you read the scrawled accounts of a meeting of early state leaders, or first-hand descriptions of settler life. Original documents relating to the Oregon Territory as well as the first copy of the state Constitution also highlight this paper trail. It's all summed up quite well by the words below a glass mural of the pioneers in the reception area: "To think we came all that way, risked everything, used our bodies as plows, and arrived here with our lives."

Capitol Grounds

At each end of the Capitol building are parks featuring giant sequoias, magnolias, and camper-down elms. Between the Capitol and the State Executive Building on the corner of Court and

The statue of a bearded, axe-wielding pioneer stands tall on top of the capitol rotunda.

Cottage Streets is **Wilson Park.** Lush lawns, a gazebo for concerts, and a wide variety of trees, including sequoia, Port Orford cedar, Asian cedar, blue spruce, mountain ash, dogwood, and incense cedar, invite a picnic. Two large multicolored rose gardens bloom through much of the year to garnish your spread, and a trio of bronze beavers make the perfect lunch companions. Also to the west of the building are the beautiful E.M. Waite Memorial Fountain and a replica of the Liberty Bell. To the east is **Capitol Park,** where you can admire Corinthian columns salvaged from the old Capitol (destroyed by fire in 1935) and statues of Dr. John McLoughlin, Reverend Jason Lee, and the circuit rider. The latter honors horseback evangelists to the pioneers during the era of missionary zeal.

The oldest government building in Salem is the **Supreme Court Building,** 1147 State St., dating back to 1914. It's located to the east of the Capitol on the southern half of the block across Waverly St., facing State St. and bounded by 12th Street. The building's facade is white terracotta, and the marble interior has tile flooring. Visual highlights include an ornate stairwell and a stained-glass skylight in the third-floor courtroom framing a replica of the Oregon state seal. Above all, don't miss the public restrooms. Tastefully appointed in marble, oak, and tile, these facilities were described in· *Oregon* magazine as "doing justice to public needs."

South of the legislative building and the campus are some other places that encourage a step back in time. The historic **Deepwood Estate,** 1116 S.E. Mission St., tel. (541) 363-4825, features tours of an elegant 1894 Queen Anne-style home with hand-carved woodwork, gorgeous stained-glass windows and a well-marked nature trail. English formal gardens here evoke a more genteel era, and the Pringle Creek Trail's native flora and the public greenhouse's tropical plants have a timeless appeal. Parking is at 12th and Lee Streets near the greenhouse. The Deepwood Estate is open May-Sept., noon-4:30 p.m. every day except Saturday. Winter hours are Sunday, Monday, Wednesday, Friday 1-4 p.m., and the grounds are closed on holidays. Admission is $2.50, with discounts for children and seniors. Sit in Deepwood's pagoda-like gazebo with the scent of boxwood heavy in the air on a spring afternoon and you'll soon forget the hue and cry of political proceedings at the Capitol.

Bush House and Park

Bush House Museum, 600 Mission St., tel. (541) 363-4171, is located in Bush Pasture Park off Mission, High, and Bush Streets. This 1877 Victorian, with many original furnishings, is the former home of pioneer banker and newspaper publisher Asahel Bush, who once wrote about his competitor, "there's not a brothel in the land that would not have been disgraced by the presence of the *Oregonian.*" Even if you're not big on house tours, the Italian marble fireplaces and elegant walnut-and-mahogany staircase are worth a look. The museum is open Sept.-May, Tues.-Sun. 2-5 p.m., and June-Aug., Tues.-Sun. noon-5 p.m. The last tour begins at 4:30 p.m. Adults pay $2, with discounts for students and seniors. The house is part of the 80-acre Bush Pasture Park. Besides being a sylvan retreat for picnickers and sports enthusiasts, the park is home to the **Bush Barn Art Center,** write c/o the Bush House Museum, tel. (541) 581-2228. Located next to the Bush House, this center features two galleries with monthly exhibits. On the grounds you'll also find the Bush Conservatory Greenhouse and rose gardens. The Bush Barn hours are Tues.-Fri. 10 a.m.-5 p.m., Saturday 1-5 p.m. The conservatory is open Mon.-Fri. 8 a.m.-4 p.m., Saturday 2-4:30 p.m. Both have free admission. To get there from I-5 take exit 253 and drive two miles west on ORE 22 (Mission St.). Turn south on High Street and enter the park on Bush St., one block south of Madison.

Gilbert House Children's Museum

If you liked Portland's OMSI and Eugene's WISTEC (Willamette Science and Technology Center), the Gilbert House, 116 N.E. Marion St., tel. (541) 371-3631, should more than sate your inquiring mind or those of your kids. Inspired by A.C. Gilbert, a Salem native whose many inventions included the Gilbert Chemistry Set and the Erector Set, this hands-on exposition takes in art, music, drama, science, and nature. Whether you're designing a card or bookmark in the craft room, putting on a puppet show, or disassembling a parking meter, the outlets for creativity here are adaptable to any mood or mind-set. If you don't have participatory inclinations, you can still enjoy fascinating exhibits like the one dedicated to A.C. Gilbert, whose Olympian athletic exploits and proficiency as a world-class magician were overshadowed by his inventions. As you might expect, even the gift shop here is a winner. Museum hours are Tues.-Sat. 10 a.m.-5 p.m. and Sunday noon-4 p.m. Admission is $4 per person, $3 seniors. To get there, drive to the riverfront between the two ORE 22 bridges. Take the Front St. bypass and enter the riverfront via Court St. on the south or Union St. on the north. Park in the lot just north of the Marion St. bridge.

Honeywood Winery

Of the half-dozen local vintners, Honeywood Winery, 1350 S.E. Hines St., tel. (541) 362-4111 or (800) 726-4101, is the largest and the most easily reached, with a location close to Mission Mill Village. It also bills itself as Oregon's oldest winery, having begun in 1933. Honeywood produces a full line of fruit (Honeywood's Grande Peach won a Gold Medal at the 1997 state fair and its raspberry and marionberry took Silver) and varietal wines and offers free tasting Mon.-Fri. 9 a.m.-5 p.m., Saturday 10 a.m.-5 p.m., and Sunday 1-5 p.m., all year long. Salem's wine country is largely clustered along ORE 22 (north of the highway) in a region known as the Eola Hills. Ask the folks at the Honeywood tasting room for information.

The Reed Opera House Mall

At the corner of Court and Liberty is the Reed Opera House Mall. This one-time venue of minstrel shows and other pioneer cultural activities still retains a brick facade and long windows but has new tenants—the boutiques and restaurants of a tastefully rendered shopping mall. After you admire the restoration, which helped this atrium gain admittance to the National Register of Historic Places, peek inside a shop that does justice to the creative traditions of the frontier—**Made In Salem**, 189 N.E. Liberty St., tel. (541) 399-8197. This is a crafts co-op of four dozen local artisans. Creations made from stained glass, Oregon's exotic woods, and many other media are featured, along with artists working on-site. It's open Mon.-Thurs. 10 a.m.-6 p.m., Friday 10 a.m.-9 p.m., Sunday noon-3 p.m.

The Enchanted Forest

Seven miles south of Salem off I-5 on exit 248 is the Enchanted Forest, 8462 Enchanted Way, Turner 97392, tel. (541) 363-3060, one man's answer to Walt Disney. An enterprising Oregonian has single-handedly built a false-front western town, a haunted house, and many more attractions. Whether it's the old woman who lived in the shoe, the seven dwarves' cottage, or Alice in Wonderland's rabbit hole, these and other nursery-rhyme, fairy-tale re-creations will get thumbs up from anyone under 99 years of age. It's open daily 9:30 a.m.-9 p.m., March 15-Sept. 30. Adults pay $5.50 and ages 3-12 pay $4.75, with admission to the bobsled ride and haunted house each $1 extra. The newest attraction is an old English village featuring a life-sized Gepetto and Pinocchio telling stories punctuated by animated characters popping their heads out of windows, a pie with 20 blackbirds, etc. If you're here the third weekend in September, take in the Harvest Festival at the nearby **Willamette Valley Vineyards,** 8800 Enchanted Way, Turner, tel. (800) 344-9463. November and December holiday festivals also feature wine sampling, music, and food—take exit 248 (Sunnyside Turner) off I-5 then left Delaney, then go south on Enchanted Way.

Gardens

Both **Schreiner's Iris Gardens,** 3625 N.E. Quinaby Rd., Salem 97303, tel. (541) 393-3232, and **Cooley's Gardens,** 11553 N.E. Silverton Rd., Silverton 97381, tel. (541) 873-5463, bill themselves as the world's largest iris growers. Both claims are correct based on different criteria, but the important thing to remember is that from mid-May through the first week of June these are the places to visit to take in the peak blossom seasons. Schreiner's is seven miles north of Salem next to I-5, and Cooley's is on the way to Silver Falls State Park. Both places can be visited 8 a.m.-dusk.

Arts

Salem is full of studio tours, downtown art tours, and a First Friday gallery walk (6-9 p.m.) where openings are often fêted with complimentary food and drink. The latter together with theater and musical events (Salem is the Oregon Symphony's home away from home) can be accessed for tickets and information at the Mid-Valley arts council, 265 N.E. Court St., tel. (541) 364-7474, ticket office tel. (541) 370-7469. The Friday *Statesman Journal*'s "Rain or Shine" section also gives complete cultural listings.

Shopping

Salem has the only Nordstrom department store, (503) 371-7710, between Portland and San Francisco.

PRACTICALITIES

Accommodations

Coming into town off the interstate you'll see cut-rate motels advertised with loud billboards. Need we say more? If you think so, please consult the accompanying chart.

Food

Salem is blessed with an unusually large number of Mexican restaurants for a city this size in the Northwest. Many of these establishments boast regional specialties from the state of Jalisco that cater to the large influx of agricultural workers who've come to the Willamette Valley from northwestern Mexico. Some ubiquitous entrees in these places include carne asada and camarones al mojo de ajo. Carne asada is grilled beefsteak, often tough but flavorful. Camarones al mojo de ajo, $10, is shrimp coated with garlic and butter. An example of a typically unpretentious but tasty "estilo Jalisco" restaurant is **La Estrellita,** 3295 N.E. Silverton Rd., tel. (541) 362-7032 among other outlets. With a name that translates as "The Little Star," this place shines with the aforementioned specialties as well as such other classics as camarones à la diabla (shrimp cooked in red sauce with onions and mushrooms) and chile verde (chunks of pork, green pepper, onions, and spices in a green tomatillo sauce). Dinners run $8-10 and can be washed down by a dozen different kinds of Mexican beer. La Estrellita's north Salem location makes it a perfect stopover en route to Silver Falls State Park. It can also supply sustenance to those attending events at the nearby Oregon State Fairgrounds.

Dahlia's, in the Reed Opera House, 189 N.E. Liberty St., tel. (541) 363-5414, is convenient to downtown shopping and culture while managing to be elegant and informal. The menu ranges from haute cuisine to hamburgers, and while it's expensive for Salem, you're guaranteed to have a good meal in this European-style bistro. The menu is suffused with ethnic influences complemented by the fresh ingredients of Northwest cuisine. This is a good place for an occasion, with plenty of indoor foliage, skylights, and glass to keep things bright, open, and cheery. For dinner, try beef medallions Madagascar, $15.

Off Center Cafe, 12th and N.E. Center St., 1741 N.E. Center, tel. (541) 362-9245, has a clientele and a vegetarian-influenced menu that appear to have been imported from the hip college eateries of Eugene. In any case, breakfasts (Tues.-Sun.), lunches (Tues.-Fri.), and dinners (Fri.-Sun.) are tasty and filling. Great coffee, a soda fountain, and scrumptious fruit pies also make this an inexpensive retreat from the ordinary. Coffee-lovers will also take note that the top three leading coffee purveyors in Salem (according to a *Statesman Journal* reader poll) are within a couple of blocks of each other on Court Street. The poll-winning Beanery and the runner-ups Governors Cup and Starbucks also feature an assortment of pastries. **Allan Brothers Beanery,** 545 Court St., tel. (541) 399-7220, has light breakfasts, homemade pastries (cheesecake is recommended), soups, salads, quiche, spanakopita, and lasagna. All of the above are less that $5 and of high quality. The coffee, hot chocolate, and vast array of other drinks has set the standard for the lower Willamette Valley for several decades. Another hangout conducive to conversation is **Boone's Treasury,** 888 N.E. Liberty, tel. (541) 399-9062. You can down microbrews and enjoy live blues and jazz amid the brick confines of the old treasury building.

Two places to kill hunger pangs in a hurry are **Los Baez,** 12920 N.E. Lancaster Dr., tel. (541) 371-3867; and 2920 S.E. Commercial St., tel. (541) 363-3109, and **North's Chuckwagon,** 694 N.E. Lancaster Dr., tel. (541) 581-7311. Los Baez is the home of the legendary Wally Burrito, more than a meal in itself with chicken, beef, pork, cheese, refried beans, guacamole, and sour cream wrapped in a flour tortilla and topped with green enchilada sauce. It might not be *estilo* Jalisco, but it's one of the best deals you'll find north of the border.

North's Chuckwagon is an all-you-can-eat buffet with food that's good and ample enough to attract long-haul truckers. In addition, the prices here are in line with the budget of fixed-income retirees. The fare at lunch is not substantially different from the selection at dinner, but it's a buck cheaper.

If you're looking for a spread with more exotic cuisine, try **Queen of Sheba**, 498 N.E. Church St., tel. (541) 585-7466, for an Ethiopian-style lunch buffet, $4.95. Mon.-Friday. After ladling lentils, spicy stewed beef, or vegetables onto your plate at the steam table, return to your seat and take matters into your own hands—literally. Injera, a spongy sourdough bread, is used to scoop up these fillings (silverware upon request). The pastel-colored latticework canopy and white-washed walls also make this small restaurant seem a continent away from the Meier and Frank parking lot across the street.

Eola Hills Winery, 501 S. Pacific Highway 99W, Rickreall, tel. (541) 623-2405, has a brunch that covers a 40-foot-long table with omelettes, pastas, crepes, pan-fried oysters, Belgian waffles, home-baked pastries, soup, salads, and special weekly entrees prepared fresh to your order. You can choose from many types of fresh pastas with a variety of sauces and from dozens of ingredients for your omelette. This all can be washed down by award-winning wines or sparkling Blanc de Noir Champagne. This gala affair takes place every Sunday, 9:30 a.m.-1 p.m., amid oak and stainless steel wine kegs and the innovative strains of a jazz pianist. Reservations are a must given a price in the $8-18 range (the high end based on adults 21 and over) and its local reputation as the best brunch in Salem. To get there, take ORE 22 west from downtown Salem to ORE 99 and head south a short distance to the winery.

On the other side of the gustatory spectrum, picnickers and backpackers should note that **Sunrise Market**, 3195 Liberty Rd., tel. (541) 375-2105, and **LifeSource Natural Foods**, 2649 Commercial St. S.E., both carry a wide selection of natural foods. **Helitrope**, 2060 Market St. N.E., tel. (541) 362-5487, is one of the oldest natural food stores in the state as well as one of the best.

If the walls of her restaurant can be believed, local politicos and other celebrities seek out **Jackie's Ribs**, 3403 S.E. Commerical St., tel. (541) 399-7464. One bite of a Jamaican roast pork sandwich—spicy pork spilling out of a Kaiser roll—or any of the other moderately

---

SALEM ACCOMMODATIONS

Best Western Pacific Highway Inn, 4630 N.E. Portland Rd., tel. (503) 390-3200 or (800) 832-8905, $60-80, wheelchair access, cable TV, pool, restaurant/lounge, nonsmoking rooms.

City Center Motel, 510 S.E. Liberty St., tel. (503) 364-0121 or (800) 289-0121, $40-55, cable TV, pets, nonsmoking rooms, complimentary continental breakfast.

Execulodge, 200 S.E. Commercial St., tel. (503) 363-4123, $65-80, cable TV, pool, restaurant/lounge.

Quality Inn Hotel and Convention Center, 3301 N.E. Market St., tel. (503) 370-7888 or (800) 248-6273, $70-120, wheelchair access, pets, covered pool, restaurant/lounge, laundry, nonsmoking rooms, live entertainment.

Salem Grand Motel, 1555 State St., tel. (503) 581-2466, $45-85, wheelchair access, cable TV, pets, pool, nonsmoking rooms, very close to Capitol complex and Willamette University.

Salem Super 8 Motel, 1288 N.E. Hawthorne, tel. (503) 370-8888 or (800) 800-8000, $50-60, wheelchair access, pets, covered pool, laundry, nonsmoking rooms.

Shilo Inn, 1855 N.E. Hawthorne, tel. (503) 581-9410 or (800) 222-2244, $85-100, cable TV, pets, pool, nonsmoking rooms, complimentary continental breakfast.

State House Bed and Breakfast, 2146 State St., tel. (503) 588-1340 or (800) 800-6712, $50-80, cable TV, meals available, laundry, nonsmoking rooms, river view.

Tiki Lodge, 3705 N.E. Market St., tel. (503) 581-4441 or (800) 438-8458, $40-60, cable TV, pool, pets, kitchenettes, laundry, restaurant/lounge, nonsmoking rooms.

priced sandwiches and rib platters confirms the judgment of the wallboard kudo-givers and then some. The other outlets in Salem and Portland might have better locations than the parent restaurant's nondescript storefront on Commercial St., but they would be hard-pressed to equal the down-home friendliness of this place.

If the ribs make you thirsty, you're not far from the Salem branch of the McMenamin's brewpub empire, the **Thompson Brewery and Public House,** 3575 S. Liberty Rd., tel. (541) 363-7286. And if you're just looking for a casual brewpub meal, the restaurant's pizza, appetizers, burgers, sandwiches, or salads washed down by McMenamin's ales, beers, or their own Edgefield wines are guaranteed to please. Set in a charming old house that'll make you forget south Salem's commercial sprawl, the brewery is open Mon.-Sat. 11 a.m.-1 a.m., Sunday noon-midnight.

Everyone knows that a half hour after you've eaten a large Chinese meal, you're always hungry enough for dessert. Perhaps this inspired the location of **Gerry Frank's Konditorei,** 310 S.E. Kearney St., tel. (541) 585-7070, across from **Kwan's Cantonese Cuisine,** 835 S.E. Commercial, tel. (541) 362-7711. These restaurants flank two sides of Commercial St. near its intersection with Kearney, so it's a good bet that many diners have enjoyed such Kwan's delicacies as steamed salmon or Dungeness crab in black bean sauce, then topped it off with a slice of baklava or Black Forest cake at the Konditorei. In any case, it was Gerry Frank who brought Chef Kwan from Hong Kong to Salem, blessing this corner of Commercial St. with a delicious union of opposites. And while you're downing a second piece of torte at the Konditorei (open till midnight Fri.-Sat.), you can console yourself that the meal you just finished at Kwan's had no MSG and was prepared with organic vegetables (when available) and purified water.

Camping

Many of the Salem and vicinity excursions are close to campsites. **Silver Creek Falls State Park,** 20024 Silver Falls Hwy., Sublimity 97385, tel. (541) 873-8681, lets campers escape the valley's summertime heat. There are 53 tent sites and nine sites for trailers or motor homes up to 35 feet long. Rates are $16-19. From mid-

April to early October this facility operates with electricity, piped water, and picnic tables. Showers, firewood, and a laundromat are available. In addition to hiking, swimming, and biking, there are stables near the park's entrance.

On the way to Breitenbush Hot Springs, **Cleator Bend,** write: Willamette National Forest, ORE 22, Detroit 97360, tel. (541) 854-3366, offers a campground close enough to the Breitenbush Hot Springs Retreat Center and facilities to permit day use there. Nearby, the Breitenbush River has good fishing. There are nine sites for trailers or motor homes up to 16 feet long, as well as picnic tables and fire grills. Fees are $3 a night from mid-May to late September. On Forest Service Rd. 46, you'll pass several other campgrounds between ORE 22 and the retreat center.

Cove Creek is a campground located near recreation mecca Detroit Lake. With 63 sites, flush toilets, pay showers, ($1.25 in quarters only) a boat launch, and other amenities, the $16 nightly fee is well worth it. Campsites are loacted in a lush second growth Douglas fir forest against a slope. Because there are no individual RV hookups, dump sites, or phones, Cove Creek is more for car campers, backpackers, and outdoor recreationists than people looking for a place to park a rig long-term. The campground is located east of Detroit off Blowout Road. With no reservations, a sign on the highway will announce if the site has reached capacity. For more information, contact the Detroit Ranger Station, tel. (541) 854-3366.

Recreation and Activities

Salem's recreational mix belies its reputation for being a town dedicated to legislation and little else. Cultural life revolves around the **Pentacle Theatre,** P.O. Box 186, Salem 97303, tel. (541) 364-7121, located five miles west of downtown Salem. From the government buildings, follow the signs marked "ocean beaches" and "Dallas." Signs on the right-hand side of the highway, at N.W. 52nd Ave., direct you up the hill and to the theater. This large, attractive wooden building hosts an award-winning 10-play season.

The **Elsinore Center for the Arts,** 142 High St., S.E. Salem, tel. (541) 581-4642, is a vintage theater and emerging downtown cultural venue. Check the *Statesman Journal* for what's scheduled. Other than the L.B. Day amphitheater at the fairgrounds hosting big name acts and brewpubs featuring live music, only the **Grand Theater,** 191 High St., N.E. Salem, tel. (541) 362-7174, fills the niche for an all ages rock club. There's a balcony bar for patrons over 21 with shows offered Thurs.-Sat. Portland rock bands are usually on the bill.

Those who prefer more active pursuits should head to **Leierer's Outdoor LTD,** 934 E. Hylo Rd., tel. (541) 581-2803. This store offers canoe rentals on the Salem waterfront each weekend. One-day guided Santiam and Willamette river trips are also available. Rafting and kayaking equipment can be rented from **Santiam Whitewater Outfitters,** 1595 N.E. Cottage St., tel. (541) 585-2628. They also provide guide service.

The **Salem Golf Club,** 2025 Gold Course Rd., tel. (541) 363-6652, is one of the best public courses in the state. Another alternative is **Santiam Golf Course,** ORE 22 and Golf Club Rd., Stayton, tel. (541) 764-3485. If you drive 15 minutes east on ORE 22 you can look forward to combining a round of golf with a walk in the country. Low greens fees and a full-service restaurant and bar add to the pleasure.

U-pick farms are a delight from spring through fall in and around Salem. Cherries, strawberries, apples, peaches, plums, and blackberries are some of the bounty available. Early in June, the Salem *Statesman Journal,* tel. (541) 399-6622, puts out a list of local outlets in the area (what's available where and when) entitled "Oregon Direct Market Association." The *Statesman Journal* is sold throughout the Willamette Valley, central coast, and central Oregon, and their "Rain or Shine" section features entertainment listings and reviews every Friday that cover the week to come. Although these listings focus on Salem, considerable attention is also given to events throughout the Willamette Valley, central Oregon, and the coast.

Fruit stands abound as well in the newspaper's U-pick guide. Many concessions, such as **Bauman Farms,** 12989 Howell Prairie Rd., tel. (541) 792-3524, have both self-service harvest as well as over-the-counter sales. In addition, several dozen other agricultural products are available here, ranging from 10 berry varieties to pumpkins. Items such as fresh home-pressed apple cider and holiday gift packs round out the array. To get to Bauman's take ORE 99E one mile south of Woodburn to Howell Prairie Road. Following the signs, go about a half mile to reach the stand. Bauman's array of produce is perhaps only exceeded by **Zielinski's E.Z. Orchards,** 5400 Hazel Green Rd., Salem.

The **Oregon State Fair,** 2330 N.E. 17th St., tel. (541) 378-3247 or (800) 833-0011, is an annual celebration held in Salem during the 11 days prior to Labor Day. The fair showcases Oregon agriculture, industries, tourist attractions, natural resources, government, and cultural activities. Big-name entertainment, amusement-park rides, an international photography show, and a horticultural exhibit are also included in this blend of carnival and commerce. The best way to get there off I-5 are via exits 253 or 258. Admission is $6 for adults (13 and up), children under 6 admitted free. The traditional free admission for seniors is presently under review. Parking is $3; entertainment tickets for musical events will run you an extra $5-15. This is the largest agricultural fair on the west coast. It is also host to one of the 10 largest horse shows in the nation. While there's no shortage of worthwhile events, family fun (rides, food, etc.) can come with a hefty price tag.

The Salem Art Association, c/o Bush House Museum, 600 Mission St., tel. (541) 581-2228, puts on the **Salem Art Fair and Festival** for several days in the third week of July. The event includes 200 artists, performing arts, food, children's activities, a five-km run, an Oregon authors' table, wine and cheese tasting, and art-techniques demonstrations. We recommend you take advantage of the free shuttle between South Salem High School and the Pringle parkade.

Getting Around

Salem's State and Center Streets run east-west, while Commerical and Liberty Streets run north-south. East and West Nob Hill Streets run southeast. With a profusion of one-way streets and thoroughfares that end abruptly, it's important to keep your bearings. One helpful frame of reference is supplied by remembering that Commerical St. runs north-south along the Willamette River on the western edge of town.

Salem provides a lot of ways to get in and out of town. The **Greyhound** station, 450 N.E. Church St., tel. (541) 362-2428, is open daily

6:45 a.m.-8:45 p.m. **Amtrak,** 13th and Oak Streets, tel. (541) 588-1551, sits across from Willamette University and is close to Mission Mill Museum. If you are looking for a reasonably priced shuttle to or from Portland International Airport that goes almost everywhere north of Eugene in the Willamette Valley, **Valley Shuttle,** tel. (800) 532-2622, is recommended. The Salem **airport,** tel. (541) 588-6314, is a few miles east of downtown. Flights to Portland and the coast are provided by **Horizon Airlines,** tel. (800) 547-9308. A Salem-to-Portland airport shuttle is run by **Hut Limousine Service,** tel. (541) 362-8059. For short hops to town, there's Salem **Yellow Cab,** tel. (541) 362-2411. Or rent a car at **National,** 745 N.E. Liberty St., tel. (541) 585-4226 or (800) CAR-RENT.

Mass-transit bus service in town means **Cherriotts,** 216 High St., tel. (541) 588-2877. Terminals are in front of the courthouse. Fares run $.75-1.00, depending on the length of your trip, and originate from High Street. Especially appreciated is the Free Zone. Unlimited free rides are permitted within most of the State Capitol Mall as well as to hundreds of downtown shops and restaurants. The zone is defined by the Willamette River on the west, 12th St. on the east, Union to the north, and Mission to the south. Hours of service are Mon.-Fri. 6 a.m.-6:15 p.m. (with buses every half hour during rush hours). On Saturday, they run every hour 7:45 a.m.-6:15 p.m.

The **Green Tortoise** departs Salem/Brooks exit 263 at the Pilot Station, going south on Sunday and Thursday at 1:45 p.m. and north on Monday and Friday at 12:30 p.m. Call (800) 867-8647 for schedule information.

Information and Services

The **visitor center,** 1313 Mill St., tel. (541) 581-4325 or (800) 874-7012, is in the first building of the Mission Mill complex and has pamphlets and brochures covering Salem and the whole state of Oregon. It's open Mon.-Fri. 9 a.m.-5 p.m. Ask about the Marion County Historical Society's Heritage Tree program if you're interested in pioneer plantings and trees of great size. Golfers will want information on the new and highly regarded Creekside golf course. Check here too about First Thursdays (of the month) gallery walks. For generic Willamette Valley information, call (800) 526-2256.

The **post office,** 1030 25th St., Salem 97301, is open Mon.-Fri. 8 a.m.-5 p.m. Other useful numbers include the **Salem Hospital Memorial Unit,** tel. (541) 370-5701, and the **Women's Crisis Center,** tel. (541) 399-7722.

Cyclists and other outdoor recreationists would do well to procure the Salem Bike Map at local and sporting goods stores, $2. The full-color map depicts bike-friendly rural routes outside the city as well as urban bike lanes, inclines and traffic volume. Inset maps show trails within Silver Creek Falls and Champoeg State Parks and Willamette Mission Park. You can have the map shipped for $4 by writing Salem Public Works, 555 Liberty St. S.E., Rm 325, Salem OR, 97301 or calling (541) 588-6211.

DAY-TRIPS FROM SALEM

Silver Creek Falls State Park

If Silver Creek Falls State Park, 22024 Silver Falls Hwy., Sublimity 97385, tel. (541) 873-8361, were in California instead of the remote foothills east of the Willamette Valley, it would probably be designated a national park and be flooded with visitor facilities and people year-round. Instead, one of Oregon's largest and most spectacular state parks remains relatively quiet except during the summer. At that time, hordes seeking relief from the valley heat head up to this cool enclave of waterfalls, 26 miles northeast of Salem. They come to see 10 major waterfalls 30 to 178 feet in height cascading off canyon walls in a forest filled with gargantuan Douglas fir, ferns, and bigleaf and vine maple. There are also yew, chinquapin, and hemlock. The best time to come is during fall foliage season when there are few visitors, just before icy roads and trail closures inhibit travel. The freezing east winds of autumn sometimes make the falls here appear like ice sculptures. In spring, the mid-April blooming of trilliums and yellow wood violets on the canyon bottom is another highlight.

To get there from Salem, drive east on ORE 213, an extension of Silverton Rd. (easily accessed from the State Fairgrounds), 20 miles to Silverton and follow the signs to the park. Before heading into the park, a stop in Silverton is recommended. This rural town of 6,500 is the future home of **Oregon Gardens,** a botanical display that will eventually be 250 acres—five times the size of Victoria B.C.'s fabled Butchart Gardens. With a dream team of landscape architects as well as millions of dollars and the state's dynamic nursery industry (the #1 agricultural entity in 1994) behind them, the gardens will give Silverton another world-class tourist attraction in addition to Silver Creek Falls State Park. The gardens were slated to open provisionally in 1998 with a formal opening two years later.

While it might take a decade or two to be classed with the world's pre-eminent botanical displays, the seeds being planted in the hill-and-pond landscape off ORE 213 west of town are already breaking ground in other ways. Silverton is starting to prepare itself for the anticipated tourism onslaught with such outgrowths as a top-drawer restaurant, the **Silver Grille** 206 E. Main, tel. (541) 873-4035, where the world travels and deft culinary touch of the restaurateurs meet the agricultural bounty of the region; as well as the hoppin' blues joint, **Macs** 206 Water St.; a first-run movie theater, corner of Water and Main Streets; and Norman Rockwell murals on the Masonic Lodge Wall a few blocks east of the Silver Grille. The main drag in town, Water Street (a.k.a. ORE 214, The Silver Creek Falls Highway) heads south out of town toward the park. En route, a stop at the Chamber of Commerce outdoor information kiosk, 421 S.Water St., is recommended to pick up a Silverton directory/map and a park folder. The big "do" in Silverton is **Homer Davenport Days,** usually held the first weekend in August, when locals enjoy crafts, food, music, and the spectacle of neighbors racing furniture down Main Street. Most of the action takes place at Coolidge-McClain park Friday evening and Saturday 10 a.m.-8 p.m. For information, write P.O. Box 781 Silverton or call (541) 873-5211.

Should you decide to stay in town, here are some cost-effective options. In addition to the campground previously mentioned, the **Nordic Hotel,** 310 Water St., tel. (541) 873-5058, and the **Egg Cup B&B,** 11920 Sioux St. are both clean, well-located and inexpensive.

Traveling south and eventually east of Silverton en route to the park on ORE 214, the road climbs up into gently undulating hills past Christmas tree farms and nursery stock. A dearth of signs and a distance that seems longer than the posted 15 miles from town will have you second-guessing these directions until you come to the North Falls parking lot. While North Falls is a few miles north of the visitor services and facilities of Silver Creek Falls state park headquarters at the day use area, you can park your car at the trailhead here without having to make your way through the admission kiosk and shopping mall-sized parking lot down the road. Serious hikers will want to take on the seven-mile **Silver Creek Canyon Trail,** which heads down into a fern-lined basalt gully going past all the falls. The profusion of trees and moisture gives the air a special freshness here, and when the sun hits some of the 10 falls just right you can see rainbows. A two car shuttle is recommended if you plan to hike the whole loop.

The highlights of this 1930s-vintage, Civilian Conservation Corps trail are 177-foot-high South Falls and 136-foot North Falls. The opportunity to walk behind these waterfalls attracts a lot of visitors who follow the trail through a basalt overhang in the cleft of each cliff. Both North Falls and South Falls are easily reached from the North Falls parking lot and day use area respectively, so you don't have to hike the whole loop to see both of them. Bikers and horseback riders also enjoy specially designated trails in this 8,300-acre paradise. To get to the day use area from North Falls parking lot drive several miles south up the hill (on ORE 214) stopping off en route to look back at a spectacular view of North Falls after a mile or two. At the day-use area, a $3 per vehicle day-use fee is collected at the entrance to the parking lot. The day use area features a museum, thick forests with trails, picnic areas, retreat cabins, and the state's largest campground (see Salem Camping).

In the museum, vintage photos from the area's incarnation as a logging site founded by land speculator James "Silver" Smith (so named for his penchant of carrying around a sack of silver dollars) and wildlife exhibits give a nice orientation. A short distance from the museum is a viewpoint and trailhead on 177-foot South Falls. As with North Falls, the trail is a steep ascent of about a quarter-mile.

If you plan to visit the park from Portland, leave I-5 at Woodburn and follow rural ORE 214 south through Mt. Angel and Silverton. From

Salem, the ORE 213 routing outlined previously is both efficient and pleasant but you can also approach the park further south by taking ORE 22 east out of Salem and following the signs northeast to the park from Sublimity. This route is longer but it'll enable you to do a Salem-to-Silver Creek Falls loop on different roads, taking in more varied landscapes in the process.

Mount Angel Abbey and Oktoberfest

Four miles northwest of Silverton off ORE 214 is a retreat of a different sort. High above the rest of the Willamette Valley is the Mt. Angel Abbey, St. Benedict 97373, tel. (541) 845-3025 or 845-3030. From miles away, the neo-Gothic outlines of St. Mary's steeple beckons the outside world to this monastery. The Benedictine abbey sits on a 300-foot hill overlooking cropland and Cascades vistas. From the bluff, look northward at Mt. Hood, Mt. St. Helens, Mt. Adams, and, according to locals, Mt. Rainier on exceptionally clear days. Further inspiration can be gained from an ancient manuscript library and views of the Willamette Valley southern expanses from the meditation patio of the Retreat House.

For a meditative retreat, you can stay at the Abbey for $50 per day for lodging and meals. While the creature comforts are ascetic, the peace of the surroundings and the beauty of the monks' rituals will make the cares of the world go away no matter what your spiritual orientation (or lack thereof). Weekend retreats begin Friday at 7:30 p.m. and end on Sunday at 1 p.m. For further information and reservations write Mt. Angel Abbey Retreat House, St. Benedict, or call (541) 845-3045. On the way up to the abbey, stop in to enjoy the serenity of St. Mary's Church established by Father Odematt who came here from Europe in 1883 to start a colony of German Catholics.

Mt. Angel's other claim to fame is **Oktoberfest,** which takes place in mid-September down in the town itself. Over the quarter century of its existence, many hundreds of thousands have come to enjoy weingarten and the beer garden, $2 admission, and enjoy the oompah-pah of German traditional music. The biggest ethnic folk festival in the Northwest offers monastery tours, stage shows, art displays, yodeling, and street dancing amid beautiful surroundings. The biggest attraction of all, however, is the food.

Stuffed cabbage leaves, strudels, and an array of sausages are the stuff of legend in the Willamette Valley. In this vein, don't miss the Benedictine sister's coffee cafe and the old world farmer's market. Call (541) 845-9440 for details or write P.O. Box 1054, Mt. Angel 97362. Mt. Angel's location an hour south of Portland makes it an excellent day-trip. Just take the Woodburn exit 272 off I-5 and follow the Silver Falls tour route signs. If you're approaching the Abbey from Salem off I-5, take the Chemawa exit and follow the signs. The abbey's mid-summer Bach Festival is frequently sold out, featuring professional musicians in an idyllic setting. Call for details months in advance.

Bikers relish the foothills and farmland around Mt. Angel, which are nearly devoid of traffic. Fall color is exceptional here, and a varied topography ensures an eventful ride whatever the season. Lowland hop fields and filbert orchards give way to Christmas-tree farms in the hills. On the way up, pumpkin and berry patches also break up the predominantly grassy terrain. This region is also known for its crop of red fescue, a type of grass seed grown almost nowhere else except the northern Willamette Valley. Back in Mt. Angel, recover from your ride at the excellent restaurant at **Mt. Angel Brewing Company,** 210 Monroe St., tel. (541) 845-9624, in the middle of town. Wash down the hearty fare with homemade root beer or such excellent microbrews as Ale Mari.

Nurseries abound in the area as well. If you were to take exit 271 off I-5 near Woodburn (en route to Molalla), a trip to the **Wooden Shoe Bulb Company**'s 17-acre tulip farm, tel. (541) 634-2243 for more details, in late March and early April would colorfully illustrate Oregon's rites of spring. Just turn right at the flashing yellow light onto Meridian Rd. and go 1.5 miles. After making a left on Newman Rd., look for the field ablaze in color on the right. When it's clear, the sight of Mt Hood backdropping the tulip fields is unforgettable. Afterwards you can head south through the town of Monitor and reach Mt. Angel via a delightful rural route.

Breitenbush Hot Springs

Salem residents have traditionally taken to the hills via ORE 22 along the North Santiam River to enjoy the fishing and camping at **Detroit Lake** as well as skiing at Hoodoo Ski Bowl (see "Skiing the Cascades" in the "Introduction" to The High Cascades chapter). Lately, the traffic to the mountains includes those seeking a different kind of renewal. Breitenbush Hot Springs Retreat and Conference Center, P.O. Box 758, Detroit 97342, tel. (541) 854-3314 or in Salem, tel. (541) 371-3754, offers mineral-springs baths, trails forested with old growth, as well as a wide variety of programs aimed at healing body, mind, and spirit.

Whether or not new-age bodywork and meditation appeal to you, the peace and beauty of the Breitenbush complex will enchant and edify. Set in the Cascade foothills, this onetime Indian encampment's artesian-flow hot springs have attracted people for healing throughout the ages. The pools, set variously in forest and meadow, have curative effects thanks to 30 freely occurring minerals including the salutary chemical lithium. Music, storytelling, theater, and superb vegetarian cuisine are also part of the experience. Finally, a special sanctuary with a vaulted glass pyramid roof lets you watch the stars or winter storms through the canopy of trees.

The retreat cabins are spartan but sufficient. All have electricity and heat, and most have indoor plumbing. Rates range between $40 and $75 per person (bring your own bedding or pay $7 extra) and include three sumptuous vegetarian meals and use of the facilities and waters during your stay. Large tents on platforms are also available June-Oct. for $35-45 per person. Day-use fees for hot springs and other facilities are $15 for a full day and $8 for a half-day. Individual meals for daytime visitors are $5, all-you-can-eat, and the food is sure to make converts of those who still think of vegetarian fare as mostly rice and slime. Just bring your own coffee if you're used to one for the road.

Nearby Breitenbush are such remarkable natural areas as Breitenbush Gorge, Opal Creek, Bull of the Woods, and Jefferson Park; for more information contact the Detroit Ranger Station at (541) 854-3366.

On site you'll find the Spotted Owl Trail near the entrance of Breitenbush parking lot. In addition to this and other trails (get maps at the reception desk), sacred sweat-lodge ceremonies conducted by Native Americans are offered free of charge. Pre-registration is required, however, and participants are financially responsible for all

other Breitenbush services and facilities used (hot springs and cabins). Write or call Breitenbush for more details and a catalog listing workshops, seminars, speakers, and lodging.

To get to Breitenbush from Salem, take ORE 22 to the town of Detroit. Turn at the gas station, the only one in town, onto Forest Service Rd. 46. Drive 10 miles to Cleator Bend Campground. Go 100 feet past the campground and take a right over the bridge across Breitenbush River. Follow the signs, taking every left turn after the bridge, to the Breitenbush parking lot.

Opal Creek

The old growth forests and emerald pools of Opal Creek have been an environmental battleground for years. Its 31,000 acre watershed has been called the most intact old growth ecosystem on the West Coast (including a grove of thousand-year-old, 250-foot-high red cedar). This fact has forestalled timber company claims on the area to an extent, but complete protection is still a point of contention among federal legislative bodies. Along with the incredible beauty of the park, its uncertain future compels a visit.

To get there from Salem, take ORE 22 for 19 miles east to Mehama. At the second flashing yellow light (at the corner with Swiss Village), turn left off ORE 22 onto Little North Fork Santiam River Rd. past the State Forestry office and go about 20 miles toward the Elkhorn Recreation Area. Stay on ORE 22 until Forest Service Rd. 2209 (mostly gravel) and be sure to veer left, uphill, at the Y intersection of the road. About six miles past the Willamette National Forest sign, a locked gate will bar your car from proceeding farther down Rd. 2209. Park and hike in about three miles along a flat mining road through a large grove of trees to a sign indicating Opal Creek trail. Cross the bridge over the opalescent waters of the North Fork of the Little Santiam River. The trail veers left on the opposite bank through a moss-dripping fern-covered old growth forest. Douglas fir, ponderosa pine, and red cedar flank the path. About a mile later, the trail veers back down to the river at the sign indicating Opal Pool. Here, a cascade cuts through white limestone, coming to rest in the placid green waters of a small circular translucent pool. Continue another 1.5 miles to a grove of 1,000-year-old red cedar. While the entire area is not old growth, about 7,250 acres is made up of anciet trees that can reach 1,000 years in age and 10 feet in diamter. The rest of the forest is made up of younger trees. Former U.S. Senator Mark Hatfield prevailed upon Congress in 1996 to grant wilderness status to this gem.

For a fascinating account of the environmental conflicts here, read *Showdown At Opal Creek* by David Seideman (New York: Carrol and Graf Publishers, 1993).

Mount Jefferson

After a soak in the pools at Breitenbush, your muscles will be primed to hike up Mt. Jefferson, Oregon's second-highest peak, 10,495 feet above sea level. This snowcapped symmetrical volcanic cone dominates the Oregon Cascades horizon between Mt. Hood to the north and the Three Sisters to the south. Unlike Mt. Hood, Mt. Jefferson is rarely visible to motorists approaching from the west.

Twelve miles east of Detroit on ORE 22 turn left; follow Forest Service Rd. 2243 (Whitewater Creek Rd.) 7.5 miles to the Whitewater Creek trailhead. Then it's an easy 4.5 mile hike to Jefferson Park. This is the northern base of the mountain and features a plethora of lakes and wildflowers. The alpine meadows here are full of purple and yellow lupine and red Indian paintbrush in July. On the way up, wild strawberries and red huckleberries can provide a delectable snack. For a special experience during the summer, start up the trail after 5 p.m. on the night of a full moon and enjoy this trail bathed in soft lunar light.

Above Jefferson Park, the ascent of the dormant volcano's cone is a precarious endeavor and should only be attempted by the best in the business. You'll reach the bottom of Whitewater Glacier at 7,000 feet. Thereafter, climbing routes steepen to 45 degrees and snow and rock ridges destruct upon touch. Near the top, the rocks aren't solid enough to allow use of ropes or other forms of climbing protection, forcing what climbers refer to as "death moves," particularly because going down is even more dangerous than going up. Even if you head up the more sedate south face you can expect difficulties due to the instability of the final 400 feet of rock on the pinnacle.

Those who elect not to make the ascent may run into other problems. Sometimes the mosquitoes in Jefferson Park are bloodthirsty enough to pierce thick clothing. On occasion, the area is so crowded with day-use visitors and folks moving along the Pacific Crest Trail nearby that this place seems more like a city park than a mountain wilderness. No matter . . . the sight of Mt. Jefferson in alpenglow at sunset or shrouded in moonlight will make you forget the intrusions of humankind or the elements.

big leaf maple

ANNIE LONG LARSEN

CORVALLIS AND VICINITY

The name "Corvallis" refers to the city's pastoral setting in the "Heart of the Valley." But this appellation tells just part of the story. The influence of Oregon State University looms so large here that it might as well be called "College Town, U.S.A." In fact, Cascadia, the quintessential college town in Bernard Malamud's novel *A New Life,* was modeled on Corvallis. Everything from the coffeehouses and used-book stores to the pizza joints and network of biking trails seems to owe its existence to the ivy-covered walls of academe here.

Beyond the campus neighborhood, the vast acreage of Oregon State University's agricultural extension complex contains facilities ranging from lambing barns to experimental forests in the Coast Range. Agriculture and engineering are emphasized in Oregon State University's course offerings, attracting a less flamboyant student body than the more liberal arts oriented University of Oregon in Eugene. As such, the Corvallis institution is sometimes characterized as "Oregon Straight" or "Moo U." Call it what you will, the campus is essential to the economic base of the city, supplying recruits for local companies as well as assistance to agricultural endeavors.

After gazing upon the grass-seed farms surrounding the town or at the sprawling Corvallis division of the electronics industry giant Hewlett Packard, it's evident that the university is the straw that stirs the drink for this city of 50,000. But it doesn't stop there. The university planted the seeds to create multinational engineering giant CH$_2$M Hill and the Hatfield Marine Science Center in Newport, as well as establishing fertile ground for other start-ups that have taken root beyond the confines of the Willamette Valley.

Corvallis is not so much a place to sightsee as a place to live. While it lacks a Golden Gate Bridge or a Space Needle, this community was selected as the second-best "micropolitan" city in the country (according to the *Rating Guide to Life in America's Small Cities,* Prometheus Books, 1990) based on environment, economics, education, housing, transportation, sophistication, recreation, public safety, and urban proximity. In a similar vein, the Runzheimer 1996 cost-of-living index rated Corvallis among the ten least expensive cities to live in the U.S.

Aesthetic beauty, tranquility, and Corvallis's central location in the heart of the valley also recommend it as a base from which to explore the bird sanctuaries, the Coast Range, and nearby historic communities. In town, you'll be struck by the abundance of stately old trees, some dating back to the first pioneers who came here in 1847. Streets with wide bike lanes—Corvallis leads Oregon with 8.2% of its work force commuting by bicycle—and scenic routes for cyclists that parallel the Willamette and Mary's rivers also contribute to the feeling of an idyllic time warp here. This is especially the case in summer, when many students leave town.

CORVALLIS SIGHTS

Campus and Downtown

In springtime, the daffodil-lined approach to Corvallis on ORE 99W is made even more glorious by the Coast Range and its highest mountain, **Mary's Peak** (4,097 feet), to the west over the hay meadows. Much of the winter, this summit is obscured by rain or fog. Your first stop should be the 500-acre Oregon State campus (follow the signs to Jefferson or Monroe Streets, tel. (541) 737-0123, home to 15,200 students. The parklike campus of this 1868 land-grant institution is the hub of activity in town, with a slew of eateries, bookstores, and craft boutiques on its periphery. Cultural activities on campus include lectures, concerts, theater productions, films, and art exhibits. Many are free and open to the public. Get an activities calendar at no cost by writing the Office of University Relations, Oregon State University, Corvallis 97331.

Come to Oregon State at the end of February through mid-March and you can watch ewes giving birth in the lambing barns at the Sheep Center. Visitors are welcome during daylight hours every day except Thursday morning when a class is held there. To get to the center from downtown Corvallis, head west on Harrison Blvd.

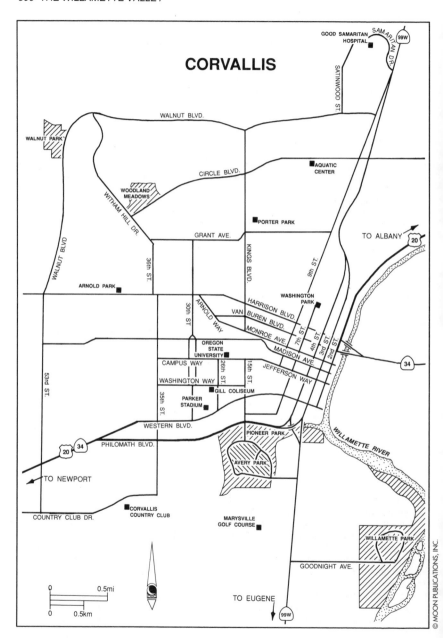

CORVALLIS

GOOD SAMARITAN HOSPITAL

SAMARITAN DR.

99W

SATINWOOD ST.

WALNUT BLVD.

WALNUT PARK

CIRCLE BLVD.

AQUATIC CENTER

WOODLAND MEADOWS

WITHAM HILL DR.

PORTER PARK

GRANT AVE.

WALNUT BLVD

KINGS BLVD.

TO ALBANY

20

36th ST.

ARNOLD PARK

30th ST.

ARNOLD WAY

9th ST.

WASHINGTON PARK

HARRISON BLVD.

VAN BUREN BLVD.

7th ST.

4th ST.

3rd ST.

2nd ST.

MONROE AVE.

53rd ST.

OREGON STATE UNIVERSITY

26th ST.

15th ST.

MADISON AVE.

34

CAMPUS WAY

JEFFERSON WAY

WASHINGTON WAY

35th ST.

PARKER STADIUM

GILL COLISEUM

WESTERN BLVD.

PIONEER PARK

WILLAMETTE RIVER

20 34

PHILOMATH BLVD.

AVERY PARK

TO NEWPORT

COUNTRY CLUB DR.

CORVALLIS COUNTRY CLUB

MARYSVILLE GOLF COURSE

WILLAMETTE PARK

0   0.5mi

0   0.5km

GOODNIGHT AVE.

TO EUGENE

99W

© MOON PUBLICATIONS, INC.

to the 53rd St. intersection. Continue west through the intersection on N.W. Oak Creek Rd. A sign 1.8 miles farther along will indicate the road to the center; this one-lane road has turnouts allowing you to yield to oncoming traffic.

While the notion of one of these fleecy specimens on a dinner plate might strike visitors here as akin to eating Bambi, this facility's research has helped establish Oregon lamb as a gourmet product. Thanks to a diet of nutritious grasses indigenous to Northwest soils, Oregon lambs are larger and richer in flavor than their better-publicized New Zealand counterparts. The barns are open every day during daylight hours. While there are no formal guides, student staffers and yellow informational fliers will help answer questions. The sight of a newborn standing and walking a few minutes after birth is amazing to first-time visitors.

The campus also maintains 11,500 acres of woodlands, notably **McDonald Experimental Forest** and **Peavy Arboretum,** entrance eight miles north of Corvallis on ORE 99W, which feature hiking trails as well as the chance to see the rare Fender's blue butterfly. The latter had been thought extinct for the last 50 years until a habitat was rediscovered here in 1990. This ecosystem serves primarily as a living laboratory for the university's Forestry Department. For more information on the campus-managed forests, check the forest research office on campus, tel. (541) 737-4452.

The university facility to visit is the **Horner Museum,** in the basement of Gill Coliseum on 26th St. off Washington St. and Western Blvd., on the southwest portion of the campus, tel. (541) 754-2951. Taxidermic displays of regional animals, mineral exhibits, and pioneer and Indian artifacts highlight Oregon's oldest and largest state-owned collection of human and natural history. Although the focal point of the exposition is Oregon, the "Other Worlds" exhibits expand the scope of what many refer to as "Oregon's Smithsonian." The hours and admission at this museum are in transition, so call ahead. Before you leave the Horner, pick up the museum's pamphlets about Oregon history. These can aid you in exploring this part of the Willamette Valley.

The major historic landmark in the city is the **Benton County Courthouse,** near 4th, 5th, and Monroe, the oldest functioning courthouse in the lower Willamette Valley. You can't miss its large white clocktower. Also downtown is the **Corvallis Art Center,** 7th and Madison Streets, tel. (541) 654-1551, located in the renovated 1889 Episcopal church near Central Park. It sells local crafts and hosts weekly lunchtime concerts. Hours are Tues.-Sun. noon-5 p.m.

Houses, Heritage, and Hospitality
Oregon's greatest concentration of historic homes and covered bridges is around Corvallis, making it more than just another college town. In addition to the surrounding heritage-conscious

Oregon State University, Corvallis

HENNING LARSEN

communities, artifact collections and pageantry also liven up the historical landscape of Linn and Benton counties.

Six miles west of Corvallis on ORE 34 is the town of **Philomath,** with the **Benton County Historical Society,** 1101 Main St., Philomath 97370, tel. (541) 929-6230. Looms, carriages, printing presses, and other pioneer-history exhibits are mildly diverting here, but the real star is the 1867 Georgian-style brick structure housing the collection. Just look for the imposing building on the right-hand side of the highway on your way to the coast. Hours are Tues.-Sat. 10 a.m.-4:30 p.m., Sunday 1-4:30 p.m. Admission is free.

Wine

South of Corvallis in the Coast Range, **Tyee Winery,** 26335 Greenberry Rd., Corvallis, tel. (541) 753-8754, is located seven miles off ORE 99W south of town on the way up into the Coast Range. As such, it can be incorporated into such nearby trips as Finley Wildlife Refuge, Mary's Peak, or Alsea Falls. Pinot gris, pinot noir, chardonnay, and gewurtztraminer are featured here. Tyee won the 1997 Oregon State Fair's best red wine award. After winetasting, you can enjoy a picnic on the grounds of this historic farmsite or a one and a half mile loop to beaver ponds. Open July-Sept. on Fri.-Mon. noon-5 p.m., May-June on Sat.-Sun. noon-5 p.m., closed Jan.-April.

ALBANY

Twelve miles east of Corvallis on US 20 is Albany, which has more historic homes than any other city in Oregon. More than 350 Victorian houses here are left over from Albany's golden age, 1849 to the early 20th century, when steamships and railroads exported Willamette Valley produce and flour. Wheat was the primary crop. In 1910, 28 trains departed this former commercial hub daily. The **Albany Visitors Association,** Two Rivers Mall 300 S.W. 2nd Ave., Albany 97321, tel. (800) 526-2256, and an information gazebo at the corner of 8th and Ellsworth Streets have maps and pamphlets about the three historic districts covering 100 blocks here. The visitors association is open daily from mid-May to December 31 and Mon.-Sat.

January 1 to mid-May. Ask about Christmas trolley tours. While you're here, be sure to get directions to the **Monteith House,** 518 W. 2nd Ave., tel. (541) 928-0911, a wonderful example of a pioneer home (the oldest pioneer frame building in Albany, dating back to 1849), and the Albany Regional Museum, whose exhibits on the Calapooya tribe and Albany's pioneer and Victorian eras can provide a good orientation. Since the house and trolley tours listed below have admissions and schedules that are subject to change, be sure to clarify these matters beforehand. Finally, taped messages on radio station 1610 AM can also update you on events and attractions here within a five-mile radius of town.

Two Albany residential districts were rivals; the Hackleman District, Ellsworth to Madison Streets and 2nd to 8th Avenues, was a working class neighborhood that at one time featured a furniture factory and a railroad station. These houses are practical but rich in Victorian nuance. The adjoining Monteith District, Elm to Ellsworth Street and 2nd to 12 Avenues, was where wealthy merchants and businessmen lived, and the houses here are more grand and opulent.

Pick up another pamphlet that lays out a self-guided **covered bridge tour.** These canopied crossings protected the wooden trusses from rain, extending the life of the bridges by several decades. By the late '30s, many of the 300 or so covered bridges in the state had fallen into disrepair or were replaced by modern steel and concrete spans. Statewide, 48 remain, with 30 in the Willamette Valley. The Albany Visitors Association pamphlet lays out a tour of eight bridges reachable by a 20- to 30-minute drive from the Albany-Corvallis area. All of these are within an eight-mile radius of **Scio,** a town 13 miles northeast of Albany on ORE 226.

To get to Scio, head north on I-5 for about 10 or 15 minutes, then take exit 233 and follow the signs east to ORE 226. Of all the bridges in this loop don't miss the bright red paint job of the Shimanek Bridge and the creekside splendor of the Larwood bridge. In Scio itself is a small pioneer museum that survives on love and pennies. The hodgepodge of Oregon Trail memorabilia, wood carvings, 19th century newspapers and family heirlooms in this oddly curated assemblage can be more affecting than the slicker, high tech displays you'll encounter elsewhere in the state should you be fortunate to get a docent whose grandfather came across this frontier thoroughfare. It's usually just open weekends in summer but check at the Albany VCB for hours. This place survives exclusively on donations . Oregon's version of "The Bridges of Madison County" is a full day tour looping from the Albany/Corvallis area. Visitor services are at minimum so take advantage of state rest areas on the Interstate and the A&W Root Beer Stand in Scio.

The **Fire Museum,** 120 S.E. 34th St., tel. (541) 967-4302, is another place in town you might want to tour independently. Call the fire department for hours and be sure to check out the 1907, steam-driven, horse-pulled engine. Tree lovers will want to ask at the visitors association or information gazebo for the flier on old plantings around town. These include copper beech, catalpa, elm, and sycamore trees in various gardens, and the old-fashioned rose and herb gardens near the gazebo.

Prime time for a stroll down Albany's memory lane is during the Christmas holiday season. In December, annual old-fashioned **parlor tours** let you revel in eggnog, snapping fires, and frontier hospitality as a guest at a number of Victorian homes. Visitors are welcomed by hostesses at each home and are permitted to walk through the parlor and other open rooms. Entertainment and homemade refreshments are part of the festivities. Tickets are available at the United Presbyterian Church, 330 S.W. 5th Ave., and cost $7.50 for adults, $5 for seniors, children 12 and under admitted free. Historical district hay-wagon and trolley caroling tours are part of the package and can get you in the holiday spirit.

In summer, exterior house tours and trolley tours take place every Sunday in July and August, 1-5 p.m. These are conducted by guides dressed in Gibson-girl costumes. Tours leave in horse-drawn carriages from the information gazebo and are well worth the admission price for fans of Victoriana. A summer interior tour is held on the last Saturday in July, 11 a.m.-5 p.m., and costs the same as the Christmas parlor tours. Visitors are invited to walk through the gardens and complete interiors of several homes; background anecdotes are supplied by guides. Old-fashioned quilts and dolls complement the tour, as do many people in turn-of-

the-century dress strolling the avenues. At all times of the year, more than a dozen antique shops also lure visitors here. A list of these stores is available at the information gazebo. **Flinn's Parlor,** 222 1st Ave., S.W. downtown Historical District, tel. (541) 928-9638, has a dinner theater presentation and a well-regarded tour service.

BROWNSVILLE AND VICINITY

A more down-home version of the pioneer experience awaits in Brownsville. Drive south on ORE 99E (or I-5) and take exit 216; ORE 228 will take you five miles east into this small town located between the Calapooia River and the Cascade foothills. This 1846 settlement began to prosper in 1862 with a woolen mill and, shortly thereafter, the coming of the railroad. Today, the **Linn County Historical Museum,** 101 Park Ave., Brownsville 97327, tel. (541) 466-3390, is located in a turn-of-the-century train depot flanked by freight cars and a circus train. Inside these structures are displays focusing on the lifestyle of the area's first settlers (a barbershop, kitchen, post office, etc.), the Calapooya tribe, and local natural history. Kids will especially relish the vintage covered wagon and 50 miniature horse-drawn wagons, sleighs, carriages, and carts. After viewing exhibits, pick up a self-guided tour brochure Mon.-Sat. 11 a.m.-4 p.m., Sunday 1-5 p.m. May-September. Donations suggested.

The museum also coordinates wagon-ride interludes into the past. Known as **Carriage Me Back Days,** these excursions reenact daily life from days of old. This pageant takes place the third weekend of April. Check here too about tours of the **Moyer House,** 204 N. Main St., an elegant 1881 Italianate home of a successful mill owner/door manufacturer. The home's high-ceilinged interior features a Carrera marble fireplace, ornate wood trim, hand-painted floral patterns, stencils on the ceilings, and oil-painted outdoor scenes on the upper panels in the bay windows. The 1881 grand piano in the south parlor is another must-see. The distinctive cupola perched atop the roof housing a glass observatory will catch your eye from a distance. Come in June to see the strangely twisted wisteria tree on the front lawn in full bloom. May 1-Sept. 30, Tues.-Sat. 11

WILLAMETTE BIRD SANCTUARIES

The federal government established several bird sanctuaries between Salem and Eugene in the mid-1960s because of the encroachment of urbanization and agriculture on the winter habitat of the dusky Canada goose. This species now comes to **Baskett Slough National Wildlife Refuge** (NWR), west of Salem, **Ankeny NWR**, southwest of the capital, and **Finley NWR**, south of Corvallis, each October after summering in Alaska's Copper River Delta. Refuge ecosystems mesh forest, cropland, and riparian environments to attract hummingbirds, swans, geese, sandhill cranes, ducks, egrets, herons, plovers, sandpipers, hawks and other raptors, wrens, woodpeckers, and dozens of other avian ambassadors. A pamphlet, *Birds of Willamette Valley Refuges,* details the best months to birdwatch, frequency of sightings, and locations of hundreds of kinds of birds. It can be obtained by writing the Refuge Manager, Western Oregon Refuges, 26208 Finley Refuge Rd., Corvallis 97337, tel. 757-7236. Migrating waterfowl begin showing up in the Willamette Valley in mid-October. By mid-March, large numbers of Canada geese, tundra swans, and a variety of ducks descend on the refuge.

In the interest of maintaining the sanctity of the birds' habitat, the refuges restrict birders by closing some trails in winter; other trails farther from feeding grounds are kept open year-round. While Finley and Baskett refuges along ORE 99W are

more user-friendly to hikers than Ankeny, Ankeny Hill exit, off I-5, six miles south of Salem, then drive Buena Vista Road through the refuge, it's still advisable to pick up refuge maps in the drop boxes at each locale to find your way.

A hike that can be enjoyed any time of year is Finley NWR's one-mile **Woodpecker Loop.** A variety of plant communities exists here, due to Calapooyan field-burning followed by pioneer logging and cattle grazing. Its location on the border between the Coast Range and the Willamette Valley also contributes to the diversity. Forests of oak and Douglas fir, and a mixed-deciduous grove combine with marshes to provide a wide range of habitats. Look for the rare pileated woodpecker in the deciduous forest. The loop's trailhead is reached by taking ORE 99W to Refuge Road. Look for the footpath on the right after driving three miles. A drop box has a pamphlet with pictures and information on the birds, wildlife, and plant communities here.

Another trail that's always open is the one-mile **Baskett Butte Loop.** Along with birdwatching, Willamette Valley views can be enjoyed here from an elevated perch. From the junction of ORE 22 and ORE 99W, drive north on 99W almost two miles, turn left onto Colville Road, then drive one mile to the trailhead on the right. The path climbs gently above the Morgan Lake trailhead.

BOB RACE

a.m.-4 p.m., Sunday 1-5 p.m.; Oct. 1-April 30 Thurs.-Sat. 11 a.m.-4 p.m., Sunday 1-5 p.m. Should you decide to stay over in the area, **Kirk's Ferry Bed and Breakfast,** 203 Washburn St., tel. (541) 466-3214, offers all the amenities, including breakfast, in an 1892 antique-filled home in the $50 range. You can also get a room for $35 at **Pioneer Villa Hotel,** intersection of I-5 and ORE 228, tel. (541) 369-2801. The best places to grab a bite are the **Brownsville General Store,** corner of N. Main and Standard, and **Silky's Espresso,** 122 Spaulding.

Brownsville and vicinity has other worthwhile attractions. A **pioneer cemetery** on the east end of Kirk St. shelters the grave of the last Calapooya Indian, and some headstones here date to 1846, when Brownsville was established. What ended up being Oregon's third-oldest continuously operating settlement began as a ferry stop on the Calapooia River. A collection of rocks, Indian arrowheads, and woodcarvings is housed in an interesting stone structure at the **Living Rock Studio,** 911

W. Bishop, tel. (541) 466-5814. The highlight is the series of colorful Biblical scenes made from translucent stone, but don't miss out on the second-floor logging exhibit. The suggested donation is $2, and the hours are Mon.-Sat. 10 a.m.-3 p.m.

The state's oldest yearly celebration takes place here in June with the **Pioneer Picnic.** Another event of interest is the **Antique Fair** on the third weekend of August, where food, entertainment, and treasures from old farmsteads are featured. Northeast of Brownsville between Sweet Home and Lebanon is the **Council Tree,** a huge Douglas fir that served as the site of the annual gathering of the Calapooyas. This 400-year-old tree can be reached by taking ORE 228 to Sweet Home and heading north a few miles on US 20 to Liberty Rd., which goes a mile to the turnout.

Northeast of town, the **Quartzville Creek** recreational corridor has gold-panning opportunities. Follow US 20 seven miles and turn left to the access road that goes 27 miles to Quartz Creek. A week's panning here is not likely to produce a quantity large enough to fill a tooth, but the pleasant surroundings and primal thrill of finding "color" in your pan is sure to get you hooked. The Sweet Home area is famous among rockhounds for petrified wood and agates. Finally, Brownsville and vicinity might evoke a feeling of déjà vu, having provided big-screen backdrops for such recent films as *Isn't It Shocking, The Flood, The Body,* and *Stand By Me.*

Sweet Home Recreation and Camping

About 14 miles east of Sweet Home off US 20 is **Cascadia State Park,** for information, contact Armitage Park, P.O. Box 7515, Eugene 97401, tel. (541) 686-7592, near the banks of the South Santiam River. Rocks here form great swimming holes. A nearby waterfall, a cave with petroglyphs, an old-growth Douglas fir, and a hand pump to draw up mineral water are other appeals. Also on US 20 are superlative boating and fishing on Green Peter and Foster Lake reservoirs. No reservations are required for Cascadia's 26 tent sites and trailer spaces. Such amenities as piped water, flush toilets, and firewood are available, and a store is located within a mile. It's open mid-April to late October, $9 a night.

Natural Attractions

The pastures of Lebanon and Brownsville east of Corvallis are good places to spot bald eagles. Venture out to the fields (beginning in February) when sheep are lambing to see America's symbol soaring above the newborns. In the winter, grass seed farms outside Albany, Coburg, and Junction City attract tundra swans.

West of Corvallis, two spots have drawn seekers of natural beauty and solitude for millennia. Mary's Peak and Alsea Falls are each a short drive from ORE 34, a scenic route to Waldport, which branches off of US 20 southwest of Philomath.

Mary's Peak, for information write: Siuslaw National Forest Supervisor's Office, 4077 Research Way, P.O. Box 1148, Corvallis 97333, tel. (541) 757-4480, sits about 12 miles southwest of Corvallis. From I-5, take ORE 20 into Corvallis, then ORE 34 to Philomath. From here it's nine miles west to the road's Coast Range Summit (1,230 ft.). A sign north of the highway points the way to a 10-mile drive to the top of the Coast Range's highest peak (4,097 ft.) on FS 30, the only road on the peak's south side. Along the way, pretty cascades, interesting rock outcroppings, and over-the-shoulder views of the Cascades on the eastern horizon intensify your anticipation of this mountaintop Calapooyan vision-quest site. When you get to the parking lot at the end of the road, the view is impressive—but don't stop there. If it's a clear day, take the short walk across the meadows to either of the two summit lookouts for perspectives on Mounts Hood and Jefferson, the Three Sisters to the east (reportedly eight Cascades peaks in total are potentially visible from here), and the Pacific Ocean at the base of the Coast Range to the west.

In the foreground of the Cascades, agricultural plots patchwork the verdant Willamette Valley, site of 83% of Oregon's prime farmland. For most of this century, huge smoke plumes rrose off the valley floor in August, making it look like a war zone. And it was, in a sense. Despite no shots being fired, you're looking at what had been until very recently, an environmental battleground. The state's 275-million-dollar-a-year grass-seed industry burns the fields here in order to kill off such diseases as ergot and nematodes. The fire also eradicates weeds that compete with rye grass and would otherwise have to be sprayed with herbicides. Field-burning also recycles nutrients back into the soil.

Nonetheless, the respiratory distress inflicted upon valley residents has compelled several serious attempts to ban the practice. When smoke from grass-seed fields was implicated in a 20-car pileup on I-5 in 1989, the antiburning campaign gained impetus. While farmers have been able to head off opposition by pointing to the agricultural benefits and cost-effectiveness of field-burning, they also have been working with opponents to find alternative uses for the straw. There is optimism on both sides that creating new uses for the excess straw, and expanding existing ones, will eventually eliminate the need to burn the fields. Using the straw to fuel power plants, and to make paper, composition firewood, fiberboard, composting materials, kitty litter, and animal feed are some of the possibilities being considered. The latter use has already resulted in a 20-million-dollar annual export market with Japan, which uses the baled straw to fatten livestock. In 1997, the Willamette Valley saw the first significant large-scale reductions in field burning in history.

The outlook is not so sanguine for opponents of clearcutting on the flanks of Mary's Peak. The Forest Service claims its hands are tied, despite potential damage to the watershed when erosion on denuded slopes spills into streams. The summit, thanks to being a federally designated botanical area, remains untouched. A biome unique to the Coast Range exists up here, with such flora as alpine phlox, beargrass, iris, tiger lily, Indian paintbrush, purple lupine, and the blue-green noble fir. Exceptionally large species of this fragrant tree grow on the Meadows Edge Trail. This trail connects to a primitive car camping area with 16 sites (open March 21-Oct. 31, $3 per night) two miles below the summit. It's part of a nine-mile network of trails around the upper slopes of the mountain. You'll also find hemlock, fir, and grand fir. In terms of wildlife, local creeks are home to the unique Mary's Peak salamander, and the surrounding woods host bald eagles, redtail hawks, spotted owls, and Clark nutcrackers—seldom seen west of the Cascades. There are also squirrels and, very occasionally, black bears. Mary's Peak is a prime viewing spot (when it's clear) in Western Oregon for the Perseid meteor shower in August. Snow, an infrequent visitor to most Coast Range slopes, can often be found here in winter, even at lower elevations. In fact, the road is sometimes impassable without chains from late fall till early spring (road conditions and snow report information line, tel. (541) 750-7007. A snow-park permit is required for day use, Nov. 15-April 15. Contact the Alsea Ranger Station, P.O. Box 18591, Alsea 97327, tel. (541) 487-5811, for more information.

Farther down ORE 34 is the town of **Alsea**. The adjoining Lobster Valley area drew many countercultural refugees here in the '70s, a portion of whom have remained to become farmers and craftspeople. The work of some of these

CORVALLIS ACCOMMODATIONS

Best Western Grand Manor Inn, 925 S.W. Garfield, (541) 758-8571 or (800) 528-1234, $75-100, heated pool, sauna, exercise room, in-room refrigerators.

The Harrison House B&B, 2310 N.W. Harrison Blvd., (541) 752-6248 or (800) 233-6248, www.proaxis.com/~harrisonhouse/, $55-85, nonsmoking inn that caters well to visitors.

Jason Inn Motel and Restaurant, 800 N.W. 9th St., tel. (541) 753-7326 or (800) 346-3291, $40-80, cable TV, pets, pool, restaurant/lounge, nonsmoking rooms, live entertainment.

Model Motel, 1480 S.W. 3rd St., tel. (541) 752-8756, $30-65, cable TV, pets, kitchenettes, restaurant/lounge, nonsmoking rooms.

Ramada Inn, 1550 N.W. 9th St., tel. (541) 753-9151 or (800) 2-RAMADA, $75-100, wheelchair access, cable TV, pool, restaurant/lounge, laundry, nonsmoking rooms.

Shanico Inn, 1113 N.W. 9th St., tel. (541) 754-7474 or (800) 432-1233, $45-60, wheelchair access, cable TV, pets, pool, nonsmoking rooms.

Super 8 Motel, 409 N.W. 2nd St., (541) 758-8088 or (800) 800-8000, $55-65, pets, covered pool, laundry

local artisans, including pottery, baskets, and hand-tied fly-fishing lures, is sold at **Farmer's Kitchen and Herb Garden,** 185 W. Main, tel. (541) 487-4384. The gardens that surround the rustic dining room here provide herbs and edible flowers for the restaurant. The greenness of the valley surrounded by Coast Range foothills recalled the lower alpine regions of Europe enough to inspire the nickname "Little Scotland."

South of here, a paved-over logging road through the tall timbers of the Coast Range can take you back to the Willamette Valley on a remote scenic byway. Look for a sign that says Alsea Falls, South Fork Road/Monroe. There's also a campground with 16 sites, piped water, pit toilets, picnic tables, and fire rings for $9 per night. You'll follow the Alsea River much of the way until you come to the sloping parking lot near Alsea Falls on the east side of the road. A short trail leads you to a picturesque cascade, ideal for a picnic. The road continues through once-active logging towns into farming country and the Finley Wildlife Refuge south of Corvallis (see the special topic "Willamette Bird Sanctuaries"). From here, ORE 99W goes north to Corvallis or south to Junction City and Eugene. Midway between Alsea Falls and Finley Reserve, stop at the Wild Rose Deli located in the Alpine Market in the tiny town of Alpine. Homemade pies and picnic lunches are recommended.

PRACTICALITIES

Accommodations
The accommodations chart covers Corvallis lodgings, which are pretty much what you'd expect for a midsized Willamette Valley college town—lots of garden-variety motels with an occasional upscale unit for visiting parents of university students.

Bed and Breakfasts
Bed and breakfasts can provide a dollar-wise alternative to an impersonal hotel room. There are some good choices in the Corvallis area.

Lilla's Bed and Breakfast and Cafe, 206 S.W. 7th Ave., Albany, tel. (541) 928-9437, is a century-old house rich in Victorian nuance. The rates are $45-55 for two, including a full breakfast. Lilla's is also reputed to be a good place to have Sunday brunch or dinner (not included with lodging).

The **Hanson Country Inn,** 795 S.W. Hanson St., tel. (541) 752-2919, gives you the feeling that you're way out of town despite being within walking distance of campus. Antiques, canopy beds, 1920s woodwork, and a book-lined library warm up the interior. On the outside, a hillside overlooking the Hanson farm has a feeling of tranquility. Add private bath and an

late spring in the Willamette Valley, a prime camping time

OREGON DEPT. OF TRANSPORTATION

included breakfast and it's hard to believe that the rates run $65-75.

Camping

Camping in this part of the Willamette Valley can be delightful, especially in late spring and early autumn.

In Corvallis, your best bet from April to late October is **Willamette City Park,** Corvallis Dept. of Parks and Recreation, P.O. Box 1083, Corvallis 97339, tel. (541) 757-6918. To get there drive a mile south of the city on ORE 99W, then go a half mile east on S.E. Goodnight Rd. to the park. For $7 a night, you can enjoy one of the 25 sites for tents and RVs serviced by vault toilets, piped water, and a small outdoor kitchen. If you need civilized comforts, a store, cafe, and laundromat are a mile away. Trails to the nearby Willamette River yield birdwatching and fishing opportunities in this 40-acre park.

Food

Bombs Away Cafe, 2527 N.W. Monroe Ave., tel. (541) 757-7221. This always-filled-to-capacity 65-seat restaurant has walls lined with colorful murals, and the sidewalk outside is lined with waiting-list hopefuls anxious to sample finger food made with the freshest ingredients and organic produce. Other reasons for the queue include prices that run $3-13. Try the duck chichimangas, jalapeño fries, green chili or chicken tamales. Regarding tamales, our favorite is the duck tamales with peanut chipotle sauce. Microbrews and Oregon wines are available on tap.

The **Albany Farmer's Market,** Water and Broadalbin Streets, Albany, is a short drive from Corvallis. Saturday 9 a.m.-noon, June through Thanksgiving, enjoy the Willamette Valley's bountiful harvests of corn, fruit, garlic, peppers, or whatever else happens to be in season. There are also cut flowers on sale as well as such regional specialties as the mild-tasting large-cloved elephant garlic, marionberries (a hybrid blackberry with a tart taste developed by Oregon State University), and dried jumbo Brooks prunes. Best of all, you're buying direct from the grower at a fraction of supermarket cost. Corvallis also has a Farmer's market that takes place Saturday 9 a.m.-1 p.m. from the end of May through the end of October. It's located at the Riverfront Park "Green Lot," First St. between Madison and Mon-

BOB RACE

roe. Look for excellent goat cheese here along with bounty described earlier.

Another Albany tradition is **Novak's Hungarian Paprikas,** 2835 Santiam Hwy., Albany, tel. (541) 967-9488. Authentic kolbasz (a spicy sausage), stuffed cabbage, and chicken paprika exemplify the earthy Eastern European fare. Try chocolate cake with apricot preserves for dessert. Lunch and dinner are served Sun.-Fri., dinner only on Saturday, 4-9 p.m. At dinner, there's a light menu for $7 and a Hungarian menu, $8-14.

If you're on the go in Albany, The Two Rivers Mall, 300 W. 2nd St., features several restaurants. Of these, **Pastabilities** next door to the Visitor Information office is recommended, serving moderately priced Italian food, salads, espresso, and dessert. After your repast, **Rainbow's End Bookstore** in the same complex has a good selection of regional titles.

Another place guaranteed not to go against the grain is the **New Morning Bakery,** 219 S.W. 2nd, tel. (541) 754-0181; and 1870 S.W. 3rd, tel. (541) 757-1821. Try their honey cinnamon rolls or choose from over a dozen varieties of cookies. New Morning salads, pasta dishes, and sandwiches can provision a picnic. It's close enough to Riverfront Park on the Willamette for a picnic, which is a good idea given New Morning's limited seating. Take along some Italian flat bread or French bread for your outing. Oregon-made jams, homemade soups, Italian pastry, cheesecake, and other desserts are also available. Black bean enchiladas and cheesecake (choose from 10 varieties) make a wonderful lunch.

Perhaps the best place to provision a picnic is **First Alternative Co-op,** 1007 S.E. 3rd, tel. (541) 753-3115, which you'll encounter as you come into town via ORE 99W from the south. The organic-produce section is a marvel, and the largely volunteer staff can give excellent leads on what's happening in the area. Across from the co-op, **Papa's Pizza** is a better-than-average chain. The best pie in town, however, is at **Woodstock's Pizza Parlor,** 1045 N.W. Kings Blvd., tel. (541) 752-5151. Next door is Suds n' Suds, a laundromat. Add a convivial bar and a beer garden and you have all that's needed for a smooth transition into the 21st century.

Another spot for those who place a premium on wholesome fare is **Nearly Normal,** 109 N.W. 15th, tel. (541) 753-0791, whose mismatched kitschy decor does justice to its name (inspired by a character in a Tom Robbins novel). Low prices and huge helpings reflect the predominantly student clientele, who savor egg and stir-fry dishes, burritos, and falafels. There's live music on Wednesday, Thursday, and Saturday, and an entertaining waitstaff every day of the week. Price range is $5-8.

The **Gables,** 1121 N.W. 9th, tel. (541) 752-3364, is full of students and parents on graduation day enjoying prime rib, fresh seafood, lamb chops, and other traditional standbys. This is the most expensive place in town (entrees $12-23, though early-bird specials can make things more affordable), but the understated homelike elegance and venerable cuisine make it perfect for an occasion. To get there, follow Harrison to 9th; the restaurant is located a half mile west of ORE 99W.

Thanks to river frontage and a varied menu that is at once upscale yet affordable, **Michael's Landing,** 603 W. 2nd, tel.(541) 754-6141, is one of Corvallis's most popular restaurants. While Italian, cajun, and Asian flavors occasionally assert themselves here, the menu seldom strays from beef, chicken, and seafood. What does stand out is the finesse of an experienced chef.

Prices run $12-17 but a Mon.-Sun. early dinner special (4-5:45 p.m.) features eight entrees for several dollars less than this price. Locals tout the prime rib as the best in town. Lunch runs $5-8 with croissant sandwiches, $6-8, a popular option. Sunday Brunch (9:30 a.m.-1 p.m.) is also well-attended thanks to outdoor seating and a variety of entrees.

Events

Of the many events in Corvallis, the premier celebration has to be the **Corvallis Fall Festival.** This gathering of exceptional artists and craftspeople is now in its second decade. Non-stop varied entertainment and a block of food concessions, including an Oregon wine garden, backdrop this hotbed of creative ferment 10 a.m.-6 p.m. the last weekend in September. Contact the chamber of commerce for more information about this event that takes place in Central Park, between 6th and 8th, Monroe and Madison. The Corvallis chamber can also update you on an artwalk the first Wednesday of each month.

Every Wednesday **Vistas and Vineyards** meets at the Old World Deli/Oregon Trail Brewery, 341 S.W. 2nd St., tel. (541) 752-8549, 8:30-9 a.m. for free classes on watercolor, pastel, and other mediums at one of a half dozen scenic area wineries and several scenic lookouts. The classes take place rain or shine and are taught by professionals. The meeting place, Old World Deli, is located just past the post office on the east side of 2nd Street. The Deli/Brewery incidentally serves up a variety of sandwiches, salads, lasagna, soups, and chili. Five Oregon Trail Brewery beers are always on tap in the deli including the 1994 Great American Beer Festival Silver-medal winning brown ale. For additional information, contact Corvallis Visitor and Convention Bureau, tel. (541) 757-1544.

The **Peacock Tavern,** 125 S.W. 2nd, tel. (541) 754-8522, is where Corvallis rocks out to live music Wed.-Sun. There generally a $2 cover and such Oregon blues stars as Lloyd Jones, Paul De Lay, and Curtis Salgado perform here. Next door, the Corvallis drama scene coalesces around the **Majestic Theater,** 115 S.W. 2nd, tel. (541) 757-6977, a 1913 restored Vaudeville house. For culture vultures there's also the **OSU International Film Series,** tel. (541) 737-2450, that's staged in Gilfillan Auditorium, corner of Orchard Ave. and 26th Street. First run flicks are at **Ninth Street Cinema World,** 1750 9th St., tel. (541) 758-7469.

The Oregon State University **basketball** season at Gill Coliseum, 26th and Washington, tel. (541) 754-2951, is a favorite wintertime activity here. Football is played at nearby Parker Stadium.

Two area musical events held each summer are the **Memorial Day Bluegrass Festival** at Airlie Winery north of Corvallis, tel. (541) 838-0013, and the **Oregon Jamboree,** P.O. Box

430, Sweet Home 97386, tel. (541) 367-3800, Oregon's largest country music event. In years past, Merle Haggard, Wynonna Judd, and other big names have appeared for this event, organized to help timber-dependent communities cope economically with the era of limits in Oregon forests.

Da Vinci Days, for information write: P.O. Box 1536, Corvallis 97339, tel. (800) 334-8118, held in late July focuses on the creative spirit embodied by the genius for whom the festival is named. Sculpt, play chess on a computer, take part in a drama, or just sit and listen to music, as Corvallis's vibrant artistic and scientific community shares its inspirational bounty. New vaudeville acts and food booths also showcase the region's creativity. Kinetic sculpture races—these must be seen to be believed—lectures by scientists, and interactive exhibits impart an intellectual air to the proceedings. The festival takes place on the Oregon State University campus and in Central Park, between 9th and 11th Streets, beginning 6 p.m. Friday and continuing 10 a.m.-11 p.m. Saturday and 10 a.m.-6 p.m. Sunday. Admission is $5 for adults, $3 for kids. Because festival events are spread out all over town, a car or a bike is necessary to take full advantage of it all.

On the first full weekend of June, **Lebanon** celebrates its **Strawberry Festival,** for information write: 104 Park St., Lebanon 97355, tel. (541) 258-7164. This town southeast of Albany off US 20 has become famous for its annual *Guinness* world-record-sized strawberry shortcake, whose 17,000 pieces are dished out at the climax of the event. Oregon berries are coveted by gourmet ice cream makers but their short shelf life makes their presence at out-of-state markets a rarity.

On the third weekend in June, the 100-year-old **Brownsville Pioneer Picnic** features an old-time fiddlers jamboree and a tug-of-war involving large local teams. Also on the agenda are a parade, carnival, crafts fair, foot race, and tour of historical homes (for information see "Brownsville and Vicinity," above). The three-day celebration is held near the spot where a ferry plied the Calapooia in 1846, now part of 10-acre Pioneer Park, located off Main St. at the end of Park Avenue. This event begins every morning with a wagon-train breakfast.

Albany's **World Championship Timber Carnival** takes place July 1-4. Contact the visitors association for more information. Admission is $7 for adults and $5 for children to see three days of logging-related competition. While such events as speed-climbing, springboard-chopping, and log-rolling have little place in the increasingly mechanized world of modern timber management, they're still fun to watch.

Getting Around
Pacific Air, tel. (541) 754-8005, offers six flights a day Monday through Friday between Corvallis and Salem as well as three flights on Saturday and four on Sunday roundtrip flights between Corvallis and Portland each week on an eight-seater Piper Chieftain. The flight averages 23 minutes. **Greyhound** and **Valley Retriever,** 153 N.W. 4th, tel. (541) 757-1797, operate every day, with routes north, south, and west to the coastal town of Newport. The **Green Tortoise** departs Corvallis/Lebanon exit 228 on ORE 34 (behind the AM/PM Mini-Mart) for points north at 2 p.m., or south at 2:30 p.m. Call (800) 867-8647 for schedule information and to set up a "flag stop" (see Green Tortoise information in General Introduction). Albany's **Greyhound,** 108 4th Ave. S.E., tel. (541) 926-2711, has service to Klamath Falls and Bend as well as Willamette Valley locations. **Corvallis Transit,** 501 Madison, tel. (541) 757-6988, operates city buses with a one-way fare on weekdays of 50 cents. To get back and forth between Corvallis and Albany, catch the **Linn Benton Loop System** buses, tel. (541) 967-4318, buses by the University at the corner of 15th St. and Jefferson Ave. The fare is 85 cents. Buses stop outside Albany's City Hall on Broadway and 2nd. **Amtrak** is at 110 W. 10th St. in Albany, tel. (541) 928-0885. Corvallis is laid out logically, so it's easy to get anywhere within 15 minutes.

With 47 miles of bike trails and 13 miles of paved bike paths, it's not surprising that the city has garnered kudos from national media for its commuter-friendly traffic arteries. Recreational bikers sing the praises of the Corvallis-to-Philomath bike path. It begins along the Willamette River in downtown Corvallis and continues eight miles through rural Benton County before ending in Philomath.

Information and Services

The **Corvallis Area Chamber of Commerce,** 420 N.W. 2nd, Corvallis 97330, tel. (541) 757-1505, has a driving-tour brochure of the area. Better yet, contact the helpful folks at the **Corvallis Visitor's Information Center,** 420 N.W. 2nd, Corvallis 97330, tel. (541) 757-1544. They can direct you to such locally favorite attractions as a recently renovated covered bridge on the university campus and Avery Park Rose Gardens. The latter boasts floral beauty framed by towering redwoods.

Suds and Suds, 1035 N.W. King Blvd., tel. (541) 758-5200, has the dual distinction of being both a tavern and a laundromat, hence its bubbly name.

The main **post office,** 311 S.W. 2nd, Corvallis 97330, is open 9 a.m.-5 p.m. weekdays. The **Parks and Recreation Department,** tel. (541) 757-6418, can steer you recreational facilities in and around the area, including an indoor rock-climbing gym, tennis courts, and city parks. **Trysting Tree Golf Course,** ORE 34 and N.E. Electric Rd., tel. (541) 752-3332, is located across the river from downtown Corvallis. **Good Samaritan Hospital,** 3600 Samaritan Dr., tel. (541) 757-5111, has 24-hour emergency-room service.

To catch up on local events, read the *Corvallis Gazette Times,* P.O. Box 368, Corvallis 97339, tel. (541) 753-2641. KOAC (550 on the AM dial) is an excellent public radio station with a top-notch news team and classical music offerings. It serves much of western Oregon and can be picked up in remote coastal and mountain communities.

Corvallis has many fine bookstores. Among them, the **Book Bin,** 351 N.W. Jackson, tel. (541) 752-0040; and 2305 Monroe, tel. 753-TEXT, and **Avocet Used Books,** 614 S.W. 3rd, have good selections of regional titles.

EUGENE AND VICINITY

The pioneers who established Eugene's townsite in the mid-1800s were motivated by visions of material prosperity derived from thick forests and good soil for farming. By contrast, many of the modern immigrants over the last few decades haven't come here primarily to get rich. The local job market, even when big timber is booming, is cyclical at best. Instead, a gardenlike setting, good schools, and a recreational and cultural mix unsurpassed by any other city of comparable size explain Eugene's present-day allure.

The Willamette River curves around the northwest quarter of the community and abundant trees and flowers dot the cityscape. From an elevated perch you can see the Coast and Cascade ranges beckoning you to beach and mountain playgrounds little more than an hour away. In town, a world-renowned Bach Festival and other big-time cultural events are showcased in the Hult Center, praised by the *Los Angeles Times* as having the best acoustics on the West Coast. The University of Oregon campus provides another forum for the best in art and academe, while its Hayward Field track has been the site of the U.S. Olympic Trials several times.

Outdoor gatherings such as Saturday Market and the Oregon Country Fair bring the community together in a potlatch of homegrown edibles, arts, and crafts. You'll also see Eugenians outside, indulging in such local passions as jogging, biking, basketball, and gardening. Less evident to those passing through might be the huge network of environmental organizations and other outlets of political and social activism (Eugene has more human-services organizations per capita than any other city in the United States). When the approximately 120,000 people who live in Eugene are combined with neighboring Springfield's population of 41,000 they make up the second-largest residential/commercial center in the state. Visitors from rural Lane County flock to the Eugene/Springfield area on weekends to shop at Valley River Center, see a movie, attend a convention, or simply go "garage saleing." This place seems to have more flea markets than just about anywhere!

Eugene has also earned the reputation as the timber capital of the world. Situated between the Willamette and Siuslaw national forests, the area is the major point of origin for domestic lumber sales. The mill-choked municipality of Springfield may at first seem like Eugene's ugly half-sister, but

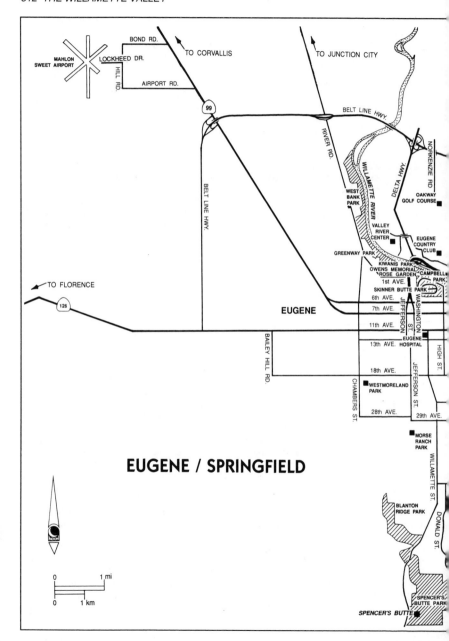

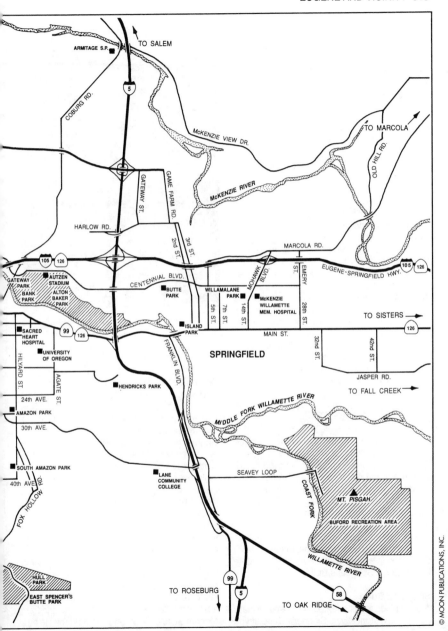

TO SALEM
ARMITAGE S.P.
COBURG RD.
5
McKENZIE VIEW DR.
TO MARCOLA
OLD HILL RD.
GAME FARM RD.
GATEWAY ST.
McKENZIE RIVER
HARLOW RD.
2nd ST.
3rd ST.
MARCOLA RD.
105 126
EUGENE-SPRINGFIELD HWY.
105 126
GATEWAY PARK
BANK PARK
AUTZEN STADIUM
ALTON BAKER PARK
CENTENNIAL BLVD.
BUTTE PARK
WILLAMALANE PARK
MOHAWK BLVD.
EMERY ST.
McKENZIE WILLAMETTE MEM. HOSPITAL
28th ST.
SACRED HEART HOSPITAL
99 126
5th ST.
7th ST.
14th ST.
ISLAND PARK
MAIN ST.
TO SISTERS
126
32nd ST.
UNIVERSITY OF OREGON
HILYARD ST.
AGATE ST.
FRANKLIN BLVD.
SPRINGFIELD
42nd ST.
JASPER RD.
TO FALL CREEK
24th AVE.
HENDRICKS PARK
AMAZON PARK
30th AVE.
MIDDLE FORK WILLAMETTE RIVER
SOUTH AMAZON PARK
40th AVE.
FOX HOLLOW RD.
LANE COMMUNITY COLLEGE
SEAVEY LOOP
COAST FORK
MT. PISGAH
BUFORD RECREATION AREA
HULL PARK
EAST SPENCER'S BUTTE PARK
TO ROSEBURG
99
5
WILLAMETTE RIVER
58
TO OAK RIDGE

© MOON PUBLICATIONS, INC.

the traveler can appreciate some good dining spots and city parks there, and the town is also the gateway to the scenic McKenzie River National Recreation Area. In addition to economic fluctuations caused by the timber industry, the region's fortunes rise and fall with the University of Oregon, the single largest employer and a leading recipient of federal grants. Economic diversity is well under way however, with software and publishing companies as well as Eugene/Springfield's new Sony plant and Hyundai's controversial computer chip factory coming into the area. And in nearby Lorane, the King Estate winery bodes well to dominate Oregon's wine industry with a capacity to produce as much pinot noir as all other state wineries combined.

The activities of another economic mainstay, the multimillion-dollar grass-seed industry, contribute to summertime air-quality emergencies with field-burning and allergy-causing pollens. Air pollution—from this source as well as wood stoves, automobiles, and industrial emissions—constitutes the major noticeable excess in a town noted for a health-conscious, progressive outlook. More often than not, a cleansing rain saves the day for those with sensitive respiratory systems.

In an era when expressions like "livability" and "quality of life" exist primarily as media buzzwords, these elusive entities have taken tangible form in Eugene, Oregon.

SIGHTS

The two areas of visitor interest are minutes south of the Willamette River. The campus, in Eugene's southeast quadrant, and the downtown (bounded by 5th and 10th Avenues, and Charnelton and High Streets) are only a five-minute drive apart from each other. Serious walkers can manage the two-mile distance without trouble.

The major north-south thoroughfare is Willamette St., which can be followed from downtown five miles south to Eugene's favorite hiking haunt, Spencer's Butte.

Skinner's Butte

A good place to get oriented in Eugene, visually as well as historically, is Skinner's Butte. If you

The Eugene Skinner cabin sits under a canopy of fall foliage at Skinner's Butte.

look north from most anywhere downtown you'll see this landmark. A beautiful park fronting the Willamette River is located at the butte's northern base. It's reachable by following the Scenic Drive signs to the river via High Street. This riverfront site served as a dock for pioneer sternwheelers and was where founding father Eugene Skinner ran a ferry service for farmers living north of the river. The town tried to become a major shipping port, but the upper Willamette was uncharted, as well as too shallow and meandering. In addition, sunken logs, gravel bars, and submerged trees and rocks made steamboat navigation difficult. As a result, Ben Holladay's Oregon and California Railroad became Eugene's most effective mode of transport in 1871.

Eugene Skinner, like so many Oregon Trail-era migrants, wanted to take advantage of the federal government's 640-acre land giveaway offer to pioneers, so he staked a claim from the banks of the Willamette to present-day 8th Ave. and from Monroe St. to the river on Hilyard Street. He built his shelter on 2nd and Lincoln Streets and later opened up Lane County's first trading post.

By following the Scenic Drive signs from the park or driving north on Lincoln St. (you can also walk up from the south side in 15 minutes), you can get to the top of the butte and enjoy the vantage point from which Eugene Skinner surveyed the landscape in June 1846. Calapooya Indians called this promontory Yapoah, meaning "High Place," and used it for ceremonial dances. While a population of 261,000 (in the greater Eugene/Springfield area) has grown up in the once-pristine valley below, you can still see the Cascade and Coast ranges on a clear day, as well as pockets of greenery throughout the city. You can also spot another good reference point in your orientation, **Spencer's Butte,** looming above the southern hills four miles away.

Another historic house in the Skinner's Butte area is the 1888 **Shelton McMurphey House** (perhaps the inspiration for the name of local author Ken Kesey's main character in *One Flew Over the Cuckoo's Nest*) on the lower south slope of the butte. The aqua-colored Victorian is the most eye-catching of some 2,000 designated historical properties in the city. During the second week of May the interior of this and other landmarks in the east Skinner's Butte neighborhood may be toured 1-4 p.m. at no charge. Contact the Eugene/Springfield Visitors and Convention Bureau for more information, tel. (800) 547-5445.

Fifth Street Public Market

The past and the present happily coexist a few blocks from the butte's south flank at the Fifth Street Public Market, 296 E. 5th Ave., tel. (541) 484-0383, an old-time feed mill converted into an atrium. This rustic structure houses an impressive collection of crafts boutiques, specialty stores, and restaurants surrounding an open-air courtyard. This courtyard is a favorite haunt of sun worshippers, people-watchers, and street performers. Note: Though the market bears the word street in its title, it is actually located on E. 5th Ave. and High Street.

For a more downhome version of the public market, head to the area near 8th Ave. and Oak Street each Saturday from the first weekend in April until mid-December (when a Christmas Fair at the Lane County Fairgrounds takes over). The **Saturday Market,** P.O. Box 427, Eugene 97440, tel. (541) 686-8885, features open-air food and crafts booths in operation 10 a.m.-5 p.m., accompanied by "new vaudeville" and musical performers. While the latest incarnation of this traditional gathering is not the bargain basement it used to be in the '70s, the good vibes and creative spirit of the community are still in ample evidence. The small farmer's market set up across 8th Ave. from the crafts area has always been a good place to get fresh inexpensive produce. Open Saturday 9 a.m.-5 p.m. from April-Nov. and Tuesday 10 a.m.-4 p.m. from April through mid-October. In addition, should the rig-

Saturday Market, a Eugene institution

ors of travel be getting you down, pay a visit to **Green Journey,** (541) 935-0629. Tucked away toward the rear of the farmer's market, these botanical wizards sell rare and medicinal herbs and can be counted on for excellent travel tips.

Hult Center For The Performing Arts

While you're walking between the two markets, you might look west past the Eugene Hilton and notice another imposing building close by. This is the Hult Center for the Performing Arts, 1 Eugene Center, tel. (541) 687-5000 for the box office, tel. (541) 687-5087 for tour information, on Willamette St. between 6th and 7th Avenues. In addition to its status as a top-flight performance venue, this place is worth a look for aesthetics alone. From the frog and troll statues that greet you at the 6th Ave. entrance to the high-ceilinged interior bedecked with masks, artistic touches abound.

Hult Center talent is showcased beneath interlocking acoustic panels on the domed ceiling and walls of the 2,500-seat **Silva Concert Hall,** simulating a giant upside-down pastel-colored Easter basket. The **Jacobs Gallery** exhibits local artwork, providing another feast for the eyes. Even the bathroom tile here is done up in a visually pleasing theatrical motif. Free guided one-hour tours are offered every Thursday and Saturday at 1 p.m. or by special arrangement. Call for reservations or arrange for one at the front desk. The lobby and ticket office are open Mon.-Fri. 11 a.m.-5 p.m., Saturday 11 a.m.-3 p.m., and one hour prior to performances.

Campus

From downtown head a few blocks south to 13th Ave. then east to the University of Oregon campus (visitor information available at Oregon Hall, Agate and 13th, tel. (541) 346-3814, bounded by Franklin Blvd., 11th and 18th Avenues, and Alder and Moss Streets. With an enrollment around 17,000 students, plus multi-million-dollar federal endowments placing the school in the upper echelon of American university funding, you might be expecting a bureaucratic, impersonal feeling here. Instead, the grounds of the campus are graced by architecturally inviting buildings dating back to the school's creation in the 1870s, as well as 400 varieties of trees. **Deady Hall,** the oldest building

Deady Hall, the oldest building on the University of Oregon campus

on campus, was built in 1876. This campus has often been selected by Hollywood to portray the ivy-covered halls of academe, most notably in the comedy *Animal House.* The quiet and tranquility of the campus are sustained by a ban on vehicular traffic beyond 13th Ave. and Kincaid Street. You can get a free **campus tour** weekdays 10:30 a.m. and 2:30 p.m. from Oregon Hall. You're better off, however, just picking up the free map and setting your own pace.

If you wander the north part of the University of Oregon complex toward Franklin Blvd., you'll see majestic and rare trees (including a Chinese dawn redwood) dotting the landscape between the schools of law and journalism. Interesting outdoor sculptures also liven up a stroll of the campus.

A must on any campus tour is the **Museum of Art,** next to the main library, tel. (541) 346-3027. The highlight is a second-floor nationally renowned Asian collection (don't miss the jade), but the revolving paintings and photography exhibits on the first floor are also usually worthwhile. A secret hideaway on the first floor is a courtyard that could have been taken out of a charming older neighborhood in Paris. You might also stop at the excellent crafts shop to the left of the door as you enter the museum. Consult the Eugene *Register Guard* for information about the Mus Evening program, a weekly after-work social with drinks and espresso that always features a lecture, museum tour, poetry reading, or music performance. There's no admission charge to the museum and the hours are Wed.-Sun. noon-5 p.m. year-round. If you're so inclined, call the museum office about their free one-hour tours.

Oregon prehistory is showcased in the **Natural History Museum,** 1680 E. 15th Ave., tel. (541) 346-3024, with artifacts from digs in eastern Oregon and bird and mammal fossils from around the state. A portion of Thomas Condon's fossil collection displays the curiosities culled from the earth by the man known as Oregon's first geologist and the discoverer of the John Day Fossil Beds. There's also a set of sagebrush sandals (from the collection of those found by Dr. Luther Cressman dated at 9,000 years of age), 15-million-year-old shell fossils, and a whale vertebra and mammoth tusks. Other cultures make up the focus of exhibits here. A $1 donation is requested, and the hours are Wed.-Sun. noon-5 p.m. To get there from Hayward Field on Agate St., go east on 15th and look for a fish sculpture on your right (in front of an attractive wooden building) across the street from the dorms. Pick up the *Trees of Eugene* tour pamphlet at the information desk to annotate a scenic and historic jaunt through Eugene's leafy glades.

Next to the Museum of Art is the **University of Oregon Library.** On the second floor, the **Oregon Collection,** tel. (541) 346-3468, has books and periodicals about the state in open stacks—a great place to plan trips or learn about the region. The nationally famous map library on the first floor can also augment the trip-planning process with their extensive collection of all sorts of maps, helpful staff, and well-tuned photo copying machines.

PARKS

Hendricks Park

Beyond the campus and downtown, Eugene and vicinity has five parks that rank among its preeminent attractions (other parks are mentioned below in "Activities and Recreation"). About two miles east of the campus on a forested ridgeline is Hendricks Park, home to 850 naturally occurring rhododendrons and azaleas and around 10,000 hybrids. There are several ways to get to the park, the easiest being to turn from Fairmount Blvd. onto Summit Drive. Or take Lane Transit bus no. 27/Fairmount, disembark at Summit Dr., and hike on up the hill a quarter mile. Two parking lots accommodate cars—one near the picnic area of stoves and tables, the other at the upper entrance on Sunset Boulevard. The rhododendron gardens are in their glory during May, with 15- to 20-foot-high plants in shades of pink, red, yellow, and purple. Even though the display declines by late June, it's always a great place to stroll. Gorgeous views of the city can be enjoyed from the west end of the garden, and tree-shaded footpaths lead to benches located in secluded cul-de-sacs on the hillside.

The Rose Garden

Another floral display is located at the Owens Memorial Rose Garden at the end of Jefferson St., along the banks of the Willamette River. Another way to get there is to walk downriver on the bike path in back of the Valley River Inn until you get to the footbridge. On the other side of the river are the gardens. Thirty varieties of roses peak in June and last until fall. Along with 3,000 roses and magnolia blossoms in spring, tremendous old cherry (unfortunately, the cherry tree is ailing and may not make it to the millenium) and oak trees also command attention. To get there from I-5, take I-105 west and take the West Eugene offramp. Turn right at the bottom of the ramp onto Madison and follow it north toward the Willamette River. One block to your right is Jefferson St. and the entrance to the Rose Garden, 300 N. Jefferson, tel. (541) 687-5347. The park is open 10 a.m.-11 p.m.

Ridgeline Trail

The South Hills Ridgeline Trail is only minutes from downtown Eugene and offers wildlife-watching opportunities (look for deer, tree frogs, garter snakes, and all kinds of birds) and more species of fern than perhaps any other single spot in Oregon. In addition, old-growth Douglas fir and the lovely and increasingly hard-to-find calypso orchid grow here. A pamphlet listing all the trailside flora and fauna and their months of bloom is put out by Eugene Parks and Recreation Cultural Services, 22 W. 27th Ave., Eugene 97401, tel. (541) 687-5333. The trail is seldom steep and has some spectacular views of the city through clearings. A spur route leads up to the highest point in Eugene, **Spencer's Butte** (elevation 2,052 feet), via a steep and often muddy trail. (If you like seclusion, however, this route might be preferable to the ones outlined in the next paragraph.) The Ridgeline Trail can be reached from several points, including Dillard Rd.; near the corner of Fox Hollow and Christenson Roads; near Willamette and 52nd; off Blanton Rd. near 40th; and the Spencer's Butte parking area (see below).

Spencer's Butte

The Spencer's Butte parking lot is nearby. Just drive south on Willamette St. until you see the signs on the left side of the road. According to one legend, the butte was named after a 19th-century English trapper killed by Indian arrows. The Calapooyans called it "Chamate," meaning "Rattlesnake Mountain." An 1848 account (from Batterns DeGuerre's *Ten Years In Oregon*) of the view from the summit reads as follows:

On one hand was the vast chain of Cascade Mountains, Mt. Hood looming in solitary grandeur far above its fellows; on the other hand was the Umpqua Mountains, and a little farther on, the coast ridge. Between these lay the whole magnificent panorama of the Willamette Valley, with its ribbon streams and carpetlike verdure.

The view today has all of the above, but there are some differences. Below the north summit you look down on Eugene/Springfield, with Fern Ridge Reservoir in the northwest toward Junction City. Beyond the reservoir you can sometimes see Mary's Peak. Other Cascade mountains not noted in the previous account but sometimes visible from the butte include Mt. Jefferson, Mt. Washington, the Three Sisters, and Mt. Bachelor. To the southeast, Creswell and the hills around Cottage Grove are visible.

The two main trails to the top vary in difficulty. If you bear left immediately after leaving the parking lot, you'll come to the route known among the locals as The Face. This trail is shorter in distance than its saddleback counterpart but much steeper and littered with boulders and, sometimes, muddy spots. It can be scaled in 40 minutes by anyone in reasonable health.

The main trail is a straight shot from the parking lot, looping up and around the steep hills. These inclines are broken up by flat stretches. Allow about an hour for the ascent. Signs caution against rattlesnakes, falling limbs, and poison oak, the latter being the most likely problem. The three shiny leaves of the notorious plant can be seen in many places along the trail, particularly on the flanks of the summit. A mixed-conifer forest featuring old-growth Douglas fir with an understory of numerous ferns and wildflowers will usher you along. Die-hard hikers equipped with boots or other durable footwear will enjoy "shooting the butte" in the snow. A "snow shoot" leads you up into a winter wonderland with trails wreathed by old-growth fir dusted with snowflakes.

Mount Pisgah

Mount Pisgah, Friends of Mt. Pisgah, P.O. Box 5601, Eugene 97405, tel. (541) 747-3817, features a mile hike to a marvelous viewpoint and an arboretum on the lower slopes. The arboretum (plants and bird lists are often available at the visitor center, open weekends) sponsors such events as a fall fair dedicated to area mushrooms and a spring wildflower show and plant sale (dates vary, so call ahead). Mount Pisgah can be reached by following E. 30th Ave. from Eugene past Lane Community College to the I-5 interchange. Cross the bridge over the freeway, turn left, and take the next right onto Seavey Loop Road. You'll cross the Coast Fork of the Willamette River and then turn left onto a gravel road (look for the Mt. Pisgah signs) that leads to the trailhead; the arboretum is just beyond the parking lot.

The path to the 1,514-foot-high Mt. Pisgah summit has a dearth of trees, enabling hikers to enjoy vistas of the Willamette Valley on the way up. At the top an unforgettable perspective of the valley in the foreground and the Three Sisters and other Cascade peaks in the distance awaits. A monument is on the summit, honoring author Ken Kesey's son and other members of the ill-fated University of Oregon wrestling team who perished in a van accident (Oregon's most celebrated author lives two miles to the east in Pleasant Hill). This memorial consists of a sculpture with a relief map depicting the mountains, rivers, towns, and other landmarks in the Eugene area. Supporting the map are three five-sided bronze columns upon which the geologic history of Oregon over the past 200 million years is portrayed, using images of more than 300 fossil specimens.

Those making the climb in August will find blackberry bushes for browsing along the way. If you're perspiring from the climb, when you're back on the valley floor head south of the trailhead to the adjoining **Buford Recreation Area** for a dip in the cool waters of the Willamette River. The banks of the Coast Fork here also have a great profusion of white oak, blackberry bushes, and poison oak.

ACTIVITIES AND RECREATION

Eugene's identity is rooted in its reputation as "Tracktown, U.S.A.," and also in its superlative Parks and Recreation Department. In 1988, *Money* magazine ranked Eugene the sixth-best place to live in the nation, and *Self* magazine called the city America's best place to work out. Both articles cited Eugene's recreational priorities as positive factors in the rankings. The *Self* article described in depth the 100 miles of bike paths, backcountry cycling minutes from downtown, and track events. Finally, Eugene ranked as the second healthiest place to live in the country, according to the *50 Healthiest Places to Live and Retire in the U.S.* (New York: Ballantine Books). In this book, medical writer Norman Ford cited the city's bike paths, natural food stores, and abundance of cultural and recreational pursuits as noteworthy in this designation.

But wait, there's more. Hiking trails, whitewater rafting, golf courses, and other outdoor pursuits are complemented by more sedate activities like winetasting, scenic drives, and museums. The following listings scratch the surface of this array. More detailed information can be culled from the Eugene/Springfield Convention and Visitors Bureau or Eugene Parks and Recreation (see "Information and Services," below).

Highbrow Haunts
Maude Kerns Art Center, 1910 15th Ave., tel. (541) 345-1571, is near the University of Oregon campus. Set in an old church, this gallery is dedicated to contemporary art of nationally known as well as regionally prominent artists. The center is open Mon.-Sat. 10 a.m.-5 p.m., Sunday 1-5 p.m. Admission is free. This gallery and others downtown are the focal points of a first Friday of the month gallery walk. It takes place 5:30-8:30 p.m.; contact Lane County Convention and Visitors Association for details, tel. (541) 484-5307. These galleries have open houses with food and drink combining art appreciation (exhibiting artists on hand to talk about their work) with conviviality. Falling rents downtown have enabled a large concentration of galleries to develop here. Art connoisseurs will also relish beautiful murals in Eugene and all over Lane County. Pick up the pamphlet "Muralizing in Lane County" at the Visitor Convention Bureau for descriptions and locations of these wall length works of art.

EUGENE SPRINGFIELD CONVENTION AND VISITOR'S BUREAU

Alton Baker Park offers miles of biking along the Willamette River.

Hinman Vineyards, 27012 Briggs Hill Rd., tel. (541) 345-1945, is a perfect place to spend a summer afternoon. The winery is 15 miles southwest of downtown near Crow and is open noon-5 p.m. daily. Drive west on 11th Ave., turn left on Bertelson Rd., then right on Spencer Creek Road. A left down Briggs Hill Rd. takes you to the tasting room, located on a hillside overlooking a valley. The ride out here is a favorite of the local biking community who continue on into the Coast Range via Vaughan Road (ask directions at the winery for the Crow Valley Store that sits opposite Vaughan Road). While at the vineyard, also ask to sample Hinman's award-winning gewürztraminer if you like wines with a distinctive tang. If available for tasting, pinot gris (a wine described as the "chardonnay of the 90s") is also a connoisseur's delight. The '92 vintage won Zefiro's (Portland's leading restaurant) 1994 pinot gris competition as well as numerous other awards. Oregon is the only state in the nation to produce this wine, whose affinity for seafood has made it a coveted addition to wine lists in sophisticated restaurants elsewhere.

La Velle Vineyards, 89697 Sheffler Rd , tel. (541) 935-9406, makes a wonderful stop on the way out to the coast with a location just off ORE 126 near Elmira. In addition to secluded tables with umbrellas to enjoy La Velle's pinots and rieslings with your picnic lunch, there's also works of local artists on display in the winery itself. A trail to a hillside on the grounds lets you see the snowcapped Three Sisters on a clear day.

The Lane County Historical Museum, 740 W. 13th Ave., tel. (541) 687-4239, can be found next to the fairgrounds. Just look for the steam donkey on the front lawn. There are other 19th-century logging vehicles and period rooms on display. The Oregon Trail exhibits are among the most interesting. Hours are Wed.-Fri. 10 a.m.-4 p.m., Sat. noon-4 p.m. A nominal admission is charged.

Water, Water, Everywhere

Alton Baker Park along the Willamette, and the **Millrace Canal,** which parallels the river for three or four miles, provide escapes from Eugene's main downtown thoroughfares. The millrace is easily accessed from the University of Oregon campus by crossing Franklin Boulevard. Rent canoes or kayaks from **EMU Waterworks Company,** 1395 Franklin Blvd., tel. (541) 346-4386, run by University of Oregon students. The rental rates are $3.60 an hour on the millrace, $14 a day off the millrace with a $30 deposit. Hours are Mon.-Fri. 12:30-dusk; Sat.-Sun. 11 a.m.-dusk, March-October. Enter Alton Baker Park below the Ferry Street Bridge. In addition to running and biking paths, there's also **Autzen Stadium,** home football field for the University of Oregon Ducks (and occasionally a venue for rock concerts), and the nearby **Willamette Science and Technology Center,** 2300 Leo Harris Parkway, tel. (541) 687-3619. WISTEC's raison d'être is to stimulate scientific understanding and curiosity in everyday life. Permanent exhibits here have an OMSI-like (see "Sights" in the Portland and Vicinity chapter) flavor, and are complemented by a new set of scientifically thematic expositions every three months. The latter have included such topics as Chaos, Illusions, Imagery, and Bicycles. WISTEC's hands-on orientation reaches its apex during the summer thanks to these traveling exhibits. Admission is $6 per family, $3 for adults, and $2 for children. Hours are Mon.-Fri. 11 a.m.-5 p.m., Saturday noon-5 p.m.

The excellent Lane Service District **Planetarium** is connected to WISTEC. Its 45-minute presentation is highly recommended (call ahead for times). Planetarium admission is $3 for adults, $2.50 for students/seniors, and $1 for children. The WISTEC/Planetarium complex is reached from I-5 by taking I-105 west to the Coburg Rd. exit and following the signs to Autzen Stadium (look for Centennial Blvd. and the Leo Harris Parkway).

Farther west on the Willamette is the **Riverhouse Outdoor Program** office, 301 N. Adams St., tel. (541) 687-5329, headquarters of the Parks Department outdoor program and a roped-off swimming area.

Reservoirs beyond downtown Eugene provide a wide range of recreation. For information contact the U.S. Army Corps Public Information, P.O. Box 2946, Portland 97208-2946. The one closest to town is **Fern Ridge Lake.** Camp, picnic, swim, water-ski, sail, or watch wildlife here. In addition, fishing for crappie, cutthroat trout, largemouth black bass, and catfish is excellent in early spring. This lake was formed when the Long Tom River was dammed in 1941. Its southeast shore was designated a wildlife refuge in 1979. To reach the lake drive 10 miles west of downtown on W. 11th Ave. (ORE 126) toward Veneta, or take Clear Lake Rd. off of ORE 99W. Marinas on the south or north shores are especially coveted by sailboaters and windsurfers. The lake is drained in winter to allow for flood control, but the resulting marsh (and wildlife refuge) hosts tree frogs, newts, ospreys, rare purple martins (in spring), black-tailed deer, red foxes, beavers, muskrats, minks, pond turtles, and great blue herons. The wildlife area is closed to the public Jan. 1-March 15 for the protection of wintering birds. Regarding birds, there are 250 species found here including tundra swans, northern harriers, Canada geese, mergansers and peregrine falcons. Perhaps the most eye-catching are the egrets because of their white plumage and large size. To get there, make a right off ORE 126 onto Territorial Rd. and look for a sign on the right. This section of Territorial Rd. is also part of the Old Applegate Trail, the southern counterpart to the Oregon Trail.

Dorena Reservoir is 30 minutes south of Eugene and has camping, fishing, and boating. The Army Corps dammed the Row River to create the facility, which can be reached by driving south on I-5 or ORE 99 for 20 miles to Cottage Grove. Then head under the bridge below I-5's Cottage Grove exit (exit 174) and pick up Row River Rd. (this goes up into the mountains, so check snow conditions), which goes eight miles east to Dorena Lake. Several miles up Row River Rd., pick up Layng road and go 1.5 miles to Currin Bridge. Another 1.2 miles south down Layng Rd. is Mosby Creek Bridge. More covered bridges are close by. In addition, Dorena Reservoir is the gateway to the **Bohemia mining district** (see "Events," below) where there are old abandoned mines. Check the Cottage Grove Pioneer Museum, Birch and H Streets, tel. (541) 942-3963, for more information on these attractions or contact the Cottage Grove Chamber of Commerce, 710 Row River Rd., P.O. Box 487, Cottage Grove 97424, tel. (541) 942-2411, two miles east of the ranger station in Cottage Grove, tel. (541) 942-5591, which has a map of a 70-mile Bohemia driving loop ("Tours of the Golden Past"), as well as updates on snow conditions. Ask also about the "rails to trails" loop that follows the tracks of an old mining train

ANGELA ENGLERT

An angler tries his luck at Dorena Lake.

from Cottage Grove to Culp Creek—perfect for mountain biking, mushroom hunting (especially after the first rains of fall), and birding. For more information on this 14.1 mile route contact the Bureau of Land Management, Eugene District, 2890 Chad Dr., P.O. Box 10226, Eugene 97440, tel. (541) 683-6121. While you're in the area, the **Cottage Restaurant,** 2915 Row River Rd., tel. (541) 942-3091, is recommended for home-made soups, vegetarian dishes, fudge pie, and cheesecake. For lunch, their large salads (try artichoke hearts, Gruyère cheese, and cashews on chicken) and sandwiches are the best in the area (inexpensive to moderate). In town, the Book Mine, 702 Main St. Cottage Grove, tel.(541) 942-7414, is one of the best book-stores between Eugene and Ashland.

An hour to the east of Fall Creek Reservoir off ORE 126 is **Cougar Reservoir and hot springs.** From Eugene go 42 miles on ORE 126 to the town of Blue River, then four miles down Forest Service Rd. 19 (paved) up to the west side of Cougar Reservoir. The springs can be reached by hiking to the end of a short trail. This trail overlooks a steep drop-off, so be careful. The several pools in this tranquil forest setting can be overcrowded on weekends.

Off the Beaten Track
Along with the well-known hiking areas described above, the nearby Cascade and Coast ranges also have some recently developed hidden gems, thanks, paradoxically, to such extractive industries as logging and gravel. The industrial "cat" trails which once cut swaths through these forests are today maintained (and sometimes paved over) by the Forest Service for access to natural wonders. Two such places are Kentucky Falls and a grove of the tallest trees in the Northwest.

Picturesque **Kentucky Falls** is set in an old-growth forest on the upper slopes of the Coast Range. To get there from downtown Eugene, drive 35 miles west on ORE 126 to the Whiteaker Creek Recreation Area on the south side of the road, approximately six miles west of the Walton Store and post office. The route to Kentucky Falls winds through the clearcut lower slopes of 3,700-foot-high **Roman Nose Mountain.**

From Whiteaker Creek Recreation Area drive one mile south and make a right turn. Then after one mile bear left on Dunn Ridge Rd. (Forest Service Rd. 18-8-28). In about seven miles the pavement ends and you'll turn left on Knowles Creek Rd. and go 2.7 miles. Make a right onto Forest Service Rd. 23 (gravel) and proceed 1.6 miles until you make a right onto Forest Service Rd. 919. Continue for 2.6 miles to the Kentucky Falls trailhead, marked by a sign on the left side of the road. An old-growth Douglas-fir forest on gently rolling hills for the first half mile gives way to a steep descent into a lush canyon. The upper falls is visible a little over a mile down the trail. You'll hear the water before you actually get a full cross section of a broad cascade pouring out from over the rim of this green canyon. On your drive back to ORE 126, retrace your route carefully to avoid veering off on a hair-raising spur route to Mapleton.

A chance to see what may be the **Northwest's tallest trees** is possible northeast of **Lowell.** This recently discovered grove's 500-year-old Douglas firs average close to 300 feet in height. The tallest tree has been measured at 322 feet, which places it in the rarefied atmosphere of the giant sequoia. Be sure to take along a forest map from the Lowell Ranger Station, Lowell 97452, tel. (541) 937-2129, or the Forest Service headquarters in Eugene, 211 E. 7th Ave., tel. (541) 687-6521.

To get there from Eugene, take ORE 58 to Lowell. From Lowell, follow Jasper-Lowell Rd. two miles to the Unity Covered Bridge and turn right onto Big Fall Creek Road. Proceed down Big Fall Creek Rd. for 11 miles, to where it becomes Forest Service Rd. 18. Turn left onto Forest Service Rd. 1817 and continue on for 10 miles until you reach Forest Service Rd. 1806, at which point you will turn left. Go down 1806 for three miles and then turn left onto Forest Service Rd. 427. The trailhead is a half mile down the road on the left-hand side, but park on the right.

Sports Facilities and Outdoor Programs
The University of Oregon and Eugene Parks and Recreation provide the community with a smorgasbord of recreational facilities and programs.

University sport facilities are open to the public year-round for $3 per day. Covered tennis courts and racquetball courts are found on 15th Ave., east of the physical education building. There are also gyms, weight rooms, a swimming pool, and more racquetball courts inside the physical education building. Pick up schedule information at the physical education building on the corner of University and 15th or at the University of Oregon recreation desk, 103 Gerlinger Hall, tel. (541) 346-4113.

Headquarters for the **University of Oregon Outdoor Program,** tel. (541) 346-4365, http://www.uoregon.edu/~opwww, is located in a southeast-corner basement room of the Erb Memorial Union, corner of 13th and University, festooned with maps, photos, and bulletins covering every sport from biking to bungee jumping. The program sponsors more whitewater activities than any other group in town, as well as backpacking trips outside the state to supplement area hikes. Outings are run on a cooperative shared-expense basis with the participants customizing the trip to their needs. In addition to these activities, you can also connect with people on your own through the office exchange bulletin board. The Outdoor Program also has camping equipment to loan for free. In addition, it's an excellent resource center for statewide travel information, with books, maps, pamphlets, and videos about Oregon wilderness locales and outdoor activities. (You're privy to all this and more for a $8 membership fee.) This program is a community resource not just limited to U. of O. students.

Eugene Parks and Recreation, 22 W. 7th Ave., tel. (541) 687-5333, puts out free seasonal publications about their offerings, which include bus tours, hikes, arts and special-interest classes, as well as a heavy dose of fitness activities. These are largely coordinated through four community centers wherein staffed recreational facilities and bulletin boards offer programs for all ages. Sports equipment is rented inexpensively out of these offices. Especially popular are the pools and fitness centers at **Echo Hollow,** 1560 Echo Hollow Rd., tel. (541) 687-5525, and **Sheldon,** 2445 Willakenzie Rd., tel. (541) 687-5314. The drop-in user fee is $2, and a one-month pass is available for $25. These pools have fitness centers equipped with weights and exercise paraphernalia. Consult Parks and Recreation literature or call for the schedule.

Lane County Ice, Lane County Fairgrounds, 13th and Monroe, Eugene, tel. 687-4ICE, offers ice-skating lessons and open public skating. Admission is $3 and adult skate rental is $3, $2 for students.

There are more than 15 bike sales and repair shops in Eugene's Yellow Pages. Eugene and Springfield together boast 120 miles of on-street bike lanes, limited access streets, and off-street bikeways. **Collins Bike Shop,** 60 E. 11th, tel. (541) 342-4878, enjoys a central location.

Golf

Laurelwood Golf Course, 2700 Columbia St., Eugene, tel. (541) 687-5521 for information, or (541) 484-4653 for tee times, is a city-owned golf course. Greens fees (around $12) and rentals are reasonable, and there's a 250-yard driving range here.

Of the many courses in Lane County, **Tokatee,** 54947 ORE 126, Blue River, tel. (541) 822-3220 or (800) 452-6376, is the best. In fact, *Golf Digest* on more than several occasions rated it among the top 25 courses in the nation (in 1991 this magazine rated it the best in the state), and

Back Nine rated it the best public course in the Pacific Northwest. To get there, drive 47 miles east of Eugene on the McKenzie Highway (ORE 126). The 18 holes here are set in a mountainous landscape patrolled by elk and other forest creatures in the shadow of The Three Sisters. Greens fees are $26 for 18 holes. It's always a good idea to call ahead for reservations.

Tennis, Jogging, Horseback Riding, and Rock Climbing

Of the many public tennis courts throughout Eugene, the best-lit facilities are at the University of Oregon and at 24th and Amazon Parkway near Roosevelt Middle School.

Near the Amazon courts, runners will enjoy the bark-o-mulch trail that follows Amazon Creek in a one-mile loop. This is a good spot to catch such world-class athletes as Mary Slaney, and Marie Mutola doing interval training. The best jogging of all, however, is found at the four-mile **Prefontaine Trail** along the Willamette River east of Alton Baker Park. Named after Steve Prefontaine, whose world-record times and finishing kicks used to rock the Hayward Field grandstands before his untimely death in 1975, this soft path meanders along the river not far from the university. To get there, follow the bike path from Alton Baker Park east toward Springfield. Another route is the road behind Oregon West Fitness, 1475 Franklin Blvd., that's closed off to motorized traffic. This leads to the footbridge that takes bikers, hikers, and joggers to the Prefontaine Trail, Willamette bike path, Autzen Stadium, and other facilities found along the Willamette River Greenway. Exercise equipment can break up your run on the "par course" section of the Prefontaine Trail. Regarding the Willamette River Bike Trail, this six-mile pathway runs east/west on both sides of the river, taking in parts of Skinners Butte Park and Alton Baker Park.

If you're more interested in taking to the trails on your trusty steed, **Bow Wow Ranch,** 33435 Van Duyn Rd., tel. (541) 345-5643, is located off I-5 at exit 199, four miles north of Beltline Highway. Rentals and lessons are also available at **Pruitt's Equestrian Center,** 83260 Rattlesnake Rd., Crow, tel. (541) 726-1545, southwest of Eugene. Call ahead for schedule and reservations.

Some of the best urban climbing to be found anywhere is at "The Columns." This basalt cliff is located on public land against the west side of Skinner's Butte in downtown Eugene. There is parking at the base of "The Columns" but it's best to ride your bike here by following the road rimming the Butte. Climbing is free.

ENTERTAINMENT

Keeping up with Eugene's multifaceted entertainment offerings involves previewing the listings put out by two local newspapers, *Eugene Weekly* and the daily *Eugene Register Guard.* Calling the University of Oregon ticket office for athletic event information, tel. (541) 346-4461, and reading the bulletin boards on the ground floor of the Fifth Street Public Market or at Sundance Natural Foods can supplement these sources.

Spectator Sports

Each spring, the University of Oregon track team, a perennial contender for the best team in the nation, has meets at **Hayward Field,** Agate and 15th Avenue. This site has hosted such world-class events as the NCAA Finals and the United States Olympic Trials in addition to the University of Oregon schedule. Track fans come here each June to enjoy the **Twilight Meet,** and the Prefontaine Classic in which the elite of the sport compete. Tickets to all sporting events will usually cost you a little more than seeing a first-run movie, but at least the money goes toward a fine educational institution.

Fall means Duck football at **Autzen Stadium,** Centennial Blvd. on Day Island. To get there, head north on Ferry Street. Just after crossing the Willamette River, take a hard right on Centennial Boulevard. In winter, the townsfolk cram into **MacArthur Court,** a funky anachronism from 1923 located just south of the physical education building on University Street. Even if you're not a fan, you're bound to get caught up in the frenzied decibels of "quacker backers" who support a team known for its never-say-die attitude. Mac Court, or "the pit" as it's more popularly known, is the oldest college fieldhouse in the nation. The proximity of the fans to the playing floor and the unbelievable decibel level of team supporters has rattled some of the nation's best teams enough to enable the often lowly Ducks to pull off major upsets.

In summer, the **Eugene Emeralds** play ball at Civic Stadium, 2077 Willamette St., tel. (541) 342-5367, for honor, glory, and a chance to break into the big leagues. Even if you don't catch a future hall-of-famer on the way up, enjoy the best concession food you'll ever taste at a ballpark. Barbecued chicken along with hot dogs and burgers are grilled outside, and microbrews are on hand to help wash it all down. Tickets cost $3.50 for adults, $2 for kids. Come Fourth of July to see the best fireworks display in town shoot out the top of this WPA-built stadium (or watch it free from Amazon Park or College Hill).

Dancing and Music

If you tire of watching other folks in action, the best spot for frenetic dancing in town is the **W.O.W. Hall,** 291 W. 8th Ave., tel. (541) 687-2746. This old Wobblie (International Workers of the World) meeting hall has remained as a monument to Oregon's activist past in labor history. Despite having all the ambience of a junior-high-school gym, it hosts some surprisingly famous rock and blues performers. The W.O.W. bills itself as having the best hardwood dance floor in the Pacific Northwest. In any case, it's probably the most crowded and features an interesting cross section of Eugenians. Beer and wine are served downstairs. Another dancing and intimate (600 seat) concert venue is the **Mill Camp,** 215 Q St., Springfield, tel. (541) 747-0877. Old-time lumber camp decor and good food recommend this place no matter who's playing.

Dancing to live bands at the **Erb Memorial Union Ballroom,** 13th and University, tel. (541) 346-4000, tickets tel. (541) 346-4362, is a Eugene tradition. Local-guy-who-made-good Robert Cray and other nationally known performers have played here. The dance floor is more spacious than the W.O.W. Hall's but can actually exceed its downtown counterpart in BTUs generated by the mass of writhing bodies.

Concerts frequently take place within the cavernous enclaves of Autzen Stadium, the home field to the Oregon Duck football team. A good sound system has made it possible for tens of thousands of concert attendees to enjoy such bands as the Grateful Dead and U2.

The **Eugene Hilton Ballroom,** 66 E. 6th Ave., tel. (541) 342-2000, also hosts big names running the gamut of popular music. For more sedate listening, the **Hult Center** (see "Sights," above) is next door to the Hilton. The Eugene Symphony and other estimable local groups like the Chamber Singers perform here along with a wide-ranging array of headliners from the world of music and comedy. The Hult Center's summer series, **Eugene Festival of Musical Theater,** 834 Pearl, Suite 240, tel. (541) 345-0028, features classic theater and mainstream comedies. At Christmastime, the *Nutcracker* is always a treat.

Live jazz in the basement of **Jo Frederigo's,** 295 E. 5th Ave., tel. (541) 343-8488, is made more enjoyable by crayons, paper, and one of their famous Long Island iced teas. Decent Italian food is served upstairs.

Down the block, the **Oregon Electric Station Restaurant and Lounge,** 5th and Willamette, tel. (541) 485-4444, hosts live jazz and rhythm-and-blues acts. This historic landmark features excellent dinner (best prime rib in town) and lunch entrees, a full bar, as well as a back room with couches, wing chairs, and the ambience of an English club. But you never forget you're in Tracktown U.S.A. thanks to a wall festooned with photos of Alberto Salazar and Steve Prefontaine.

In the same neighborhood, **Allan Brothers Coffeehouse and Bakery,** 152 W. 5th Ave., tel. (541) 342-3378, has live folk and blues at night and the same excellent coffee as its Corvallis outlets. This spacious coffeehouse is in a charming old building across from the Lane County Jail and attracts everyone from off-duty cops to madmen playing speed chess. Home-baked goodies and breakfast (try the red potato homefries), lunch, and dinner entrees can be ordered at the counter.

Another coffeehouse hangout is the **Coffee Corner,** 28th and Oak, tel. (541) 342-7238. The entertainment might be limited to an occasional magician or pianist, the coffee prices may be a tad higher than elsewhere, but there's a bright cheery ambience thanks to windows on all sides and a staff that dispenses good vibes along with cups of ambition. In addition to quality java, this place is quietly one of the better places to eat in town. The Mexican scramble for breakfast, $5.50, is filling, and the fresh fish, quiche, homemade soup and desserts during the rest of the day are top-notch.

Close by is **Java Joe's,** 26th and Willamette, tel. (541) 484-9504. Quality coffee, microbrews, pastries, and simple breakfasts are currently available here with expansion imminent. Late night hours, a more diverse menu, and a large backroom hosting live music and poetry readings will soon make this place a hot spot. In 1994, Bend-based **Cafe Paradiso,** corner of Olive St. and W. Broadway, tel. (541) 484-9933, came to Eugene, bringing mellow tunes to a 3,000-square feet venue with live artists Friday and Saturday nights. Board games, light fare, and espresso are also available in the cafe's living room ambience.

Closer to campus is **Taylor's College Side Inn,** 894 E. 13th Ave., situated directly opposite the academic buildings and the university bookstore. Quality blues acts frequently take the stage here, but local bands of different genres also show up. A dance floor, a big-screen cable hookup, espresso drinks, and a selection of microbrews are other enticements. In addition, expensive but substantial burgers, sandwiches, soups, and breakfast fare will help you bop till you drop. The $2 or $3 cover is well worth it. Another time-tested campus hangout is **New Max's Tavern,** 550 E. 13th Avenue. Reggae and new-wave acts often pop up, with $2 or $3 asked at the door. There's also Tuesday night comedy, Wednesday night acoustic acts and Saturday night open mike.

The "in" place to go out to is **Good Times Cafe and Bar,** 375 E. 7th Ave., where a $3 cover lets you enjoy name blues acts. Out in Felony Flats, **Sam Bond's Garage,** 407 Blair, tel. (541) 343-2635, has live music and microbrews at $2.25/pint. **Doc's Pad,** 165 W. 11th, tel. (541) 683-8101, is a Gen X "meet" market where the drinks are strong, the music loud, and the pub grub tasty and cheap. On the mall in midtown, the **Wild Duck,** 169 W. 6th Ave., tel. (541) 485-3825, features big-name acts in a more mainstream setting than the other clubs mentioned.

Theaters

While there's no shortage of movie houses in this town, the real screen gems are usually found at the university (consult the *Oregon Daily Emerald,* the University of Oregon student newspaper, which is distributed free at Fifth Street Market, the University of Oregon Bookstore, and Sundance Natural Foods) and the **Bijou Theatre,** 492 E. 13th Ave., Eugene, tel. (541) 686-2458. The university series favors cult films and classics (*Yellow Submarine, The Last Wave, The Bicycle Thief, King of Hearts,* etc.) and a $3 admission helps you forget the oppressiveness of the lecture halls that serve as theaters. For about twice the price, the Bijou is the place to see foreign films, art flicks, and less commercial mainstream movies. This old converted church is intimate and has great munchies and late-night presentations.

If you want first-run motion pictures, chances are you can find whatever you're looking for at **Movies 12,** Gateway Mall, 2850 Gateway St., Springfield, tel. (541) 741-1231. A dozen features, a $6 admission for adults, $3 for children, and discounted admissions before 6 p.m. make this Eugene's leading movie house.

ACCOMMODATIONS

A few bed and breakfasts and an youth hostel provide the best values for the dollar in town. Seniors, however, can use various discount cards (AARP et al.) to offset the high prices of such upscale accommodations as the Valley River Inn (who also have special packages at a good value) and the Eugene Hilton. Otherwise, you just have a choice of cheap motels on E. Broadway, moderately priced ones on Franklin Blvd., as well as others detailed in the accomodations chart. The best bets for the budget traveler are the campsites and rustic digs east of town on the McKenzie River Highway (see "ORE 126: The McKenzie River Highway" in The High Cascades chapter). As with many Oregon towns, add a 7% room tax to the room tariffs listed below.

Backpackers passin' thru the big city, prospective students checking out the U, or just about any dollar-wise traveler will appreciate the Hummingbird Hostel, 2552 Willamette St., tel. (541) 349-0589. For $13-16 for communal rooms with bunk beds or $34 for a private room (add a small charge for linens and towels), you can enjoy the hospitality of a spacious historic home with a comfortable living room, large dining area and patio. With some of Eugene's best food shopping close by, it's possible to take full advantage of excellent kitchen facilities assuming you can resist equally compelling area dining. An LTD 24 or 25 bus goes from downtown to the corner of 24th and Willamette a few blocks away. Check in between 4 p.m. and 10 p.m. Check out at 10 a.m. Reservations suggested.

Well-located, moderately priced **B & G's B & B,** 711 W. 12th, tel. (541) 343-5739, is a good place to break the motel mold. The garden, skylight, and Scandinavian decor soften the hard edges of too many nights on motel row. A full breakfast featuring organically grown foods is also included.

Visiting parents of University of Oregon students, college lecturers, and folks willing to spend a little extra for quality, head for the **Campus Cottage Bed and Breakfast,** 1136 E. 19th Ave., tel. (541) 342-5346. Bedroom amenities like down comforters, antiques, and fresh flowers are in keeping with rates of around $85 a night. The three bedrooms have private baths, and guests can also enjoy a living room with a fireplace, an outside deck, two cats, and a dog. A full breakfast of special egg dishes, fresh fruits, and pastries is included. As its name implies, the Campus Cottage is located one block south of the University of Oregon.

The **Lorane Valley B&B,** 86621 Lorane Hwy., tel. (541) 686-0241, is the perfect blend of best-of-the-country-but-close-to-the-city. Perched on a grassy knoll overlooking the Larane Hwy., it's hard to believe you're just minutes away from downtown. About the only thing that might deter first-time guests is a steep road up to this aerie that looks more treacherous than it really is. Peaceful summer nights with cricket lullabies and morning breakfast highlighted by Dutch babies overflowing with whipped cream make this a favorite during the Bach Festival and Graduation, so reserve well in advance, $70-90.

Twenty minutes south of Eugene, **Ivanoff's Inn,** 3101 Bennett Creek Rd., Cottage Grove, tel. (541) 942-3171, is a more moderately priced alternative for those seeking the best of the country near the city. To get to Bennett Creek Rd., take the Cottage Grove exit off I-5. This will run into ORE 99, which leads into River Rd. in a quarter mile. Bennett Creek is an eighth of a mile down on the right. Beautiful trees and lush greenery line Bennett Creek Rd., which is paralleled by the Hidden Valley Golf Course on

EUGENE ACCOMMODATIONS

Angus Inn Motel, 2121 Franklin Blvd., tel. (541) 342-1243, $50-70, cable TV, wheelchair access, pool, restaurant/lounge, exercise room, nonsmoking rooms.

Barron's Motor Inn, 1859 Franklin Blvd., tel. (541) 342-6383 or (800) 444-6383, $50-85, cable TV, wheelchair access, pets, restaurant/lounge.

Best Western Greentree Motel, 1759 Franklin Blvd., tel. (541) 485-2727 or (800) 528-1234, $60-90, cable TV, wheelchair access, pets, restaurant/lounge, pool.

Best Western New Oregon Motel, 1655 Franklin Blvd., tel. (541) 683-3669 or (800) 528-1234, $60-85, cable TV, wheelchair access, pets, restaurant/lounge, covered pool, laundry, nonsmoking rooms.

Campus Inn, 390 E. Broadway, tel. (541) 343-3376 or (800) 888-6313, $55-75, cable TV, wheelchair access, pool, pets, nonsmoking rooms.

Franklin Inn, 1857 Franklin Blvd., tel. (541) 342-4804, $45-55, cable TV, restaurant, kitchenettes, pets, nonsmoking rooms, complimentary continental breakfast.

Gateway Motel, 3540 Gateway St., tel. (541) 726-1212, $60-90, wheelchair access, pets, restaurant/lounge, pool, laundry, live entertainment, nonsmoking rooms.

Motel Six, 3690 Glenwood Drive, tel. (541) 687-2395, $35-50, cable TV.

Pacific Nine Motor Inn, 3550 Gateway St., Springfield, tel. (541) 726-9266 or (800) 344-0131, $35-45, cable TV, wheelchair access, pool, continental breakfast.

Phoenix Inn, 850 Franklin Blvd., (541) 344-0001 or (800) 344-0131, $65-105, covered pool, continental breakfast, laundry, close to UO campus.

Doubletree Inn Eugene, 205 Coburg Rd., tel. (541) 342-5201 or (800) 222-TREE, $80-125, cable TV, wheelchair access, pets, restaurant/lounge, pool, live entertainment, nonsmoking rooms.

Doubletree Inn Eugene/Springfield, 3280 Gateway St., tel. (541) 726-8181 or (800) 222-TREE, $80-125, pets, cable TV, pool, restaurant/lounge, tennis courts, nonsmoking rooms.

Shilo Inn, 3350 Gateway St., Springfield, tel. (541) 747-0332 or (800) 222-2244, $60-100, cable TV, wheelchair access, pets, restaurant/lounge, pool, laundry, nonsmoking rooms, complimentary continental breakfast.

Timbers Motel, 1015 Pearl St., tel. (541) 343-3345 or (800) 643-4167, $35-70, cable TV, microwave and refrigerator.

Valley River Inn, 1000 Valley River Way, tel. (541) 687-0123, $98-150, wheelchair access, restaurant/lounge, pool, sauna, jacuzzi, nonsmoking rooms, river view.

---

one side and hills leading up to the Willamette National Forest on the other. Ivanoff's is set on five hilly acres with forested trails. These appealing surroundings are only a five minute drive from Cottage Grove downtown shopping and close to covered bridges and the Bohemia mining country. Three rooms (one with private bath) range from $60 to $70 a night. This includes a full breakfast featuring Swedish specialties. Ask the innkeepers to direct you to the Creswell Dairy Queen, renowned for broasted chicken, peanut butter pie, shakes, and beef from a local herd. For an evening of fine dining, we recommend **The Covered Bridge,** 401 E. Main Cottage Grove, tel. (541) 942-1255. Back in Eugene, the **Campbell House,** 252 Pearl St., tel. (541) 343-1119, is a 14-room Victorian in the historic east Skinner Butte neighborhood (prices begin at $78 with included breakfast). Proximity to the Fifth Street Market, and the river, as well as the sophistication of a European-style pension, make this antique-filled 1892 gem a good lodging choice. A library, afternoon tea, and beautifully landscaped grounds are appreciated touches of refinement.

Ask any local what the best place in town is and the answer will probably be **The Valley River Inn.** With front and back doorways on Eugene's prime shopping area and the Willamette River respectively, this upscale hostelry offers the tranquility of nature close to modern convenience. River views, a first-rate restaurant, a crackling fire in the lobby, proximity to riverside hiking and biking as well as pool and spa facilities add to the allure. The most cost-effective way to experience all of the above is the "B&B" package offering an overnight, breakfast for two, and bicycles for $99.

Eugene-Area Camping

If you're looking for campsites in the covered-bridge country above Cottage Grove try **Baker Bay,** which has 54 sites at $10 per night. Sailboards and small boats are for rent. Located approximately 18 miles from Eugene; get there by I-5 south to Mosby Creek Rd. (take the Cottage Grove exit), turn left, then left again on Row River Rd., then take the right fork. You can get more information by calling (541) 942-7669.

Near the quaint town of Coburg north of Eugene is a **KOA Kampground,** tel. (541) 343-4832. Take the Coburg exit off I-5 and head west and you'll find the KOA a mile or so down the road. Twelve bucks a night buys a tent site for two people, $14.50 is the charge for a vehicle hookup.

Between the coast and the Oregon Country Fair grounds, **Triangle Lake Park,** tel. (541) 927-6189, has three sites for $5 a night. Proceed 25 miles west from the fairgrounds on ORE 126. Take a right onto Poodle Creek Rd., then a left on ORE 36 to Triangle Lake. You'll find the campsites just after the lake.

Whiteaker Creek near Kentucky Falls (see "Off the Beaten Track" under "Activities and Recreation," above) has 30 sites at $4 per night. Take ORE 126 30 miles west of Eugene. Turn left one mile past Wildcat Creek Bridge six miles east of Mapleton.

Close to the Oregon Country Fair is **Fern Ridge Shores,** tel. (541) 935-2335, located in a quiet family park 12 miles west of Eugene. Take Jeans Rd. off ORE 126 near Veneta. Unlike the other previously mentioned sites, reservations are not accepted. Campsites go for $12 per night; hookups are $14.

RVers, Oregon Country Fair-goers, rock concert attendees, and Scandinavian Fair visitors have been taking advantage of a new county park on the shores of Fern Ridge Reservoir six miles northwest of Eugene, contact Lane County Parks, 3040 N. Delta Hwy., Eugene 97401, tel. (541) 341-6940. The 50 sites with hookups and water can be accessed by taking Clear Lake Road off of ORE 99 to its intersection with Territorial Road. Space availability is on a first-come first-served basis in this shaded campground rich in amenities and recreation. It's open April 15-Oct. 15 and costs $14 per night.

EUGENE CUISINE

While there are a number of good restaurants in Eugene, you'll probably be more impressed by the staggering array of locally made gourmet products and natural foods available at markets here. Whether it's Toby's tofu pâté or Euphoria chocolate truffles, it's not hard to find exotic munchies right on the grocer's shelves. Even less arcane local fare offers surprises as one taste of Nancy's honey yogurt, Humble bagels, Prince Puckler's ice cream, Genesis juice, or Metropol French bread will confirm. As you might have guessed, many of these delectables come free of chemicals and often with nutritional concerns foremost. Produce labels in many Eugene specialty food stores intone "fresh," "home grown," and "organic" with the constancy of a mantra, and meat and poultry markets carry products that are rabinically pure. Not surprisingly, two of the nation's leading granola producers are headquartered here.

Two of the leading purveyors of Eugene cuisine began as hippie health-food stores several decades ago. Today, **Sundance Natural Foods,** 748 E. 24th, tel. (541) 345-6153, and the **Kiva,** 125 W. 11th, tel. (541) 342-8666, stock more than just grains, sprouts, and vitamins, and feature some of the best selections of wine and organic produce in the state. Sundance's fresh salad bar and hot buffet is a good deal for anyone who enjoys large helpings of creative healthful entrees for $3.95 (buffet discounted after 10 p.m.). Such relatively recent arrivals upon the scene as **Friendly Foods,** 2757 Friendly, tel. (541) 688-3944, and **Oasis Fine Foods,** flagship store is on 2489 Willamette, tel. (541) 345-1014; the new "superstore" is on 2580 Willakenzie Blvd., tel. (541) 334-6382; have expanded the largely vegetarian stock of their hippie forefathers with more meat and takeout items. The Oasis superstore features a hot foods deli and salad bar to complement one of the largest natural foods inventories on the West Coast. In addition to a great selection of wines, microbrews, and fresh juices, there's also a Metropole bakery outlet just in case you get the urge for something that's not whole grain.

Campus Area

The eateries on the campus periphery are a cut above those found in most college towns. Start the day at **Campus Glenwood,** 1340 Alder, tel. (541) 687-0355, or at the southside **Glenwood,** 2588 Willamette St., tel. (541) 687-8201. The menus are standard American breakfast fare, with a few entrees paying deference to eclectic college-town tastes. What they have in common are large portions in the $5 range. Try the turkito, a turkey burrito with melted cheese that comes with hash browns, or various tofu dishes. Many folks will tell you that the huevos rancheros are the best in town and the eggs Benedict, $5.25, frequently sells out on weekend mornings. You can also get good and reasonably priced lunches (like the veggie burger) and dinners (seasonal specials like fresh salmon). The campus outlet is open until 3 a.m. (the only nongreasy spoon in town open this late) and won a newspaper reader's poll for having the best dinner in town for under $8.

If your tummy can only handle coffee and a croissant in the morning, head to **Espresso Roma,** 825 E. 13th Ave., tel. (541) 484-4848. If hunger pangs should set in, this restaurant has a breakfast special for early arrivals. There is also a delightful outside courtyard that fills up when the rain stops.

An oriental lunchtime favorite is the combination lunch (dim sum on Sunday) at **China Blue,** 879 E. 13th Ave., Eugene, tel. (541) 343-2832; and 2307 N.W. 9th St., Corvallis, tel. (541) 757-3088. Sumptuous lunch specials frequently go for less than $4. **Sy's New York Pizza,** 1211 Alder, tel. (541) 686-9598, would make his mentor, Original Ray's of New York, proud with a by-the-slice operation that lines 'em up at lunch and dinnertime.

Also in the shadow of the campus is one of the best restaurants in town, the **Excelsior Cafe,** 754 E. 13th Ave., tel. (541) 485-1206. Set in a charming old colonial home, the menu changes

monthly, highlighting what's in season. It can be spendy, but lighter "bistro dinners" and hors d'oeuvres let you appreciate the restaurant's innovative approaches to seafood, veal, game, and salads at cheaper prices. While lunch and dinner are served here every day, there's also a Sunday brunch, and service till 2:30 a.m. on Saturday. The menu changes with the seasons, but you can always find "gourmet" pizzas, $7.25, along with entrees, $14-18 dinner main courses, garnished with such Willamette Valley signature ingredients as goat cheese, elephant garlic, filberts and Oregon blue cheese. Despite a reputation for fine food, it's the desserts and cozy bar that are the biggest draws here on week nights.The Excelsior also offers 14 bed-and-breakfast rooms for $75-125 per night. Rates include a $10 meal credit redeemable at breakfast, lunch, or dinner.

Up the street from the Excelsior, **Napoli,** 686 E. 13th Ave., tel. (541) 485-4552, serves gourmet pizza, soups, pasta, and an array of baked goods and desserts (try the cannoli or, if they have it, the tiramisu). Omelettes and frittatas give breakfast an Italian flair. This airy plant-filled cafe with sloping glass walls and classical music is the perfect place to sip espresso and talk (breakfast runs aound $7).

Rennie's Landing, 1214 Kincaid, tel. (541) 687-0600, serves breakfast, gourmet burgers, homemade soups, beer, and wine. Late-night and predawn hours, a second-floor outside deck, and a location right across from the University of Oregon campus make this a favorite with the campus crowd—particularly after Duck games.

Farther away from campus, the McMenamin brothers have two **brewpubs.** One is on the corner of Agate and 19th, the other at 1243 High St., tel. (541) 345-4905. Each repeats the successful formula of the establishments discussed in the Portland and Vicinity chapter. The High Street pub is ensconced in a comfy converted old house, with a tree-shaded brickwork back patio that makes the perfect hangout on a hot afternoon.

The **Gazebo Restaurant,** 1646 E. 19th Ave., tel. (541) 683-6661, has a bright, cheerful ambience and Middle Eastern specialties. While this is a great place for an intimate dinner, you can get the same dish for a slightly cheaper price at lunch. The owner buys a brand of basmati rice available exclusively from a single distributor in L.A., and you'll taste the difference in the many rice-based dishes here. The same care goes into every other aspect of this oasis of moderately-priced elegance. Appetizers such as stuffed grape leaves and baked garlic with camembert are beyond the realm of the ordinary. Among the entrees, lamb Tandoori is recommended. And if baklava is not your dessert of choice, there's always Prince Puckler's Ice Cream across the street.

Chances are many U of O alums still remember **Track Town Pizza's,** 2511 W. 11th, tel. (541) 484-2799, campus branch phone number. This pie's status as the staff of life for late-night cramming sessions owes to the diverse toppings, fresh ingredients, and a delivery time in keeping with Eugene's obsession with record-setting performance.

Fifth Street Market Eateries

A local newspaper once gave the nod to **Terry's Diner,** Fifth Street Market, E. 5th Ave., tel. (541) 683-8190, for the best burgers and best omelettes (thanks to the lemon in the eggs, which makes them extra fluffy) in town. Old advertising billboards and jukebox tunes from the '50s, thick malts that come in the metal mixing container, and laugh-a-minute waitresses stylishly reinvent the all-American diner for those born too late. Terry's is open for all meals until 10 p.m. except Sunday, when it closes at 6 p.m. A short distance away is the **Metropole,** Eugene's number one purveyor of gooey desserts (especially eggnog blackbottom pie). In addition, you can't miss with quiches, sandwiches, and other takeout fare there. There is a walk-up window close by in the public area.

Upstairs in the market is **Mekala's,** tel. (541) 342-4872. Despite elegant decor and exotic Thai dishes (try the duck, any of the salads, pad thai, any of the curries, and coconut ice cream for dessert), prices are reasonable. Two long favorites are tom kah gai (coconut cream soup with vegetables, chicken, lemon grass, peppers, and ginger-like galangka root—$7.50) and Tiger Cries (a light flavorful salad with tender strips of seasoned beef—$8.95). Because few people smoke in Eugene, request the smoking section for intimate dining and a window on 5th Ave., a people-watching perch extraordinaire.

Downstairs in the market, **Casablanca,** tel. (541) 342-3885, has Middle Eastern cuisine with pita sandwiches, babbaghanoush, hummus, and other regional specialties. This restaurant was voted Eugene's favorite lunch spot in a local poll. This is a good place for lunch in the $6 range. A few blocks down near Amtrak, **Cafe Navarro,** 454 Willamette, tel. (541) 374-0943, brings Carribean accented cuisine to Eugene. Dishes flavored with coconut milk, citrus juices, and cilantro can be the perfect antidote to Eugene's dreary winters. Breakfast is a highlight here featuring Challah French toast with mango syrup, wholewheat pancakes with pureed banana, and other creative fare. Main course breakfasts runs $4-8, dinners $7-14.

The Fifth Street Market may lack a microbrewery, but a block west, the **Steelhead Brewery and Cafe,** 199 E. 6th Ave., tel. (541) 686-2739, gives suds connoisseurs a nearby place to quaff the city's best local brew. If the results of the 1994 Great American Beer Festival are any indication, this sobriquet is an understatement. Out of 570 imports and domestic brews in the contest, judges found Steelhead Stout and Steelhead Amber best in their respective categories. The paneled walls, comfortable seating, and quality pub fare are other enticements to pass an hour or two here. The varied menu can include the following: calzone, pizza, burgers, sandwiches, pastas, soups, vegetarian entrees, and salads—in particular try the black bean chili or calamari salad with honey sesame dressing (main courses $4-8).

Downtown Dining

In the heart of downtown are two other popular restaurants. **Anatolia,** 992 Willamette, tel. (541) 343-9661, features Greek and Indian food par excellence. Spicy curries and vindaloo chicken are complemented by saganaki (fried cheese), spanakopita (spinach cheese pie), and gyro sandwiches. The best baklava in town with a shot of ouzo or retsina can finish off a richly flavored and moderately priced repast (top dinner price entree $12). Folks who remember Poppi's, a fabled Greek taverna in the campus district forced to close when Sacred Heart hospital expanded, will especially relish Monday nights here when the menu of one of Eugene's all-time favorite restaurants is re-created. Anatolia's is quickly gaining the following of Poppi's, so get there early.

Dominating the first floor of the Atrium building, **De Frisco's**, 99 W. 10th Ave., tel. (541) 494-2263, has built its reputation on the more than 20 microbrews, imports, and domestic beers it has on tap. A pool table and big-screen TV, a wall paneled with books, and live jazz on Wednesday night also explain De Frisco's enthusiastic following. A variety of hearty soups and barbecued-chicken sandwiches are lunchtime mainstays here (moderate).

A few blocks east is downtown's gourmet gulch. Two places stand out from the pack. **Cafe Zenon**, 898 Pearl St., tel. (541) 343-3005, has a multiethnic menu that is constantly changing. Despite this challenge, the Zenon manages to pull off dishes ranging from Italian to Thai in fine style. The only problems you'll run into are getting in—reservations aren't taken and there's often a wait—and getting out without stopping at the eye-popping dessert display (dinner main courses $11-15). When there's a wait at Cafe Zenon, **Full City Coffee** several doors down can be counted on to sustain you with the best coffee in a town famous for its daily grind.

Across the street from Cafe Zenon is a spacious two-story Italian restaurant, **Ambrosia**, 174 Broadway, tel. (541) 342-4141. Antique furnishings and stained glass set the stage for Old World cuisine prepared to suit contemporary tastes. The individual-size gourmet pizzas (cooked slowly in a wood-burning oven), a wonderful squid-in-batter appetizer, and northern Italian specialties will make spaghetti and meatballs seem like old hat here. Ambrosia restaurant was honored by *Wine Spectator* for having one of the most outstanding wine lists in the world (main courses $10-14).

Many Eugene restaurants trace a lineage back to street carts and Saturday Market. The most successful of these is **Tres Hermanas**, West Broadway and Olive Streets on the mall, tel. (541) 342-4058, whose curbside enterprise used to be a downtown legend. The legend lives on today in the sister's bright airy restaurant where such embellishments on traditional Mexican food such as jalapeno jelly and smoked salmon quesadillas will catch your tastebuds by surprise. A menu of fajitas, tacos, and the like round out a menu rich in fresh ingredients and subtle flavors. A good lunch can be had here for $6, with dinners generally running between $8-13. Tres Hermanas runs a taqueria at Jiffy Mart, 3443 Hilyard, tel. (541) 342-4552, a deli with the best array of beer (foreign, domestic, and microbrew) that we've seen anywhere. Fish and shrimp tacos and chicken burritos typify the fare. It's open Mon.-Fri. 5-8 p.m.

Some of the best restaurant values are located on the fringes of downtown. On 5th Ave., the **Keystone Cafe**, 395 W. 5th Ave., tel. (541) 342-2075, is also known for huge portions, low prices, and its support of community activism. Home-style breakfast features eggs and potatoes and whole-grain pancakes. Highly recommended is the Mexican chorizo (a spicy sausage) made by a local butcher shop specializing in chemical-free meat.

The best natural food/juice bar in town is **Andrew Smash**, tel. 683-5667, 840 Willamette Street.

Perhaps the busiest neighborhood during lunchtime is around Willamette and 16th. The biggest reason for this is the **French Horn**, 1891 Willamette, tel. (541) 343-7473. For $3, the restaurant's soup of the day with fresh French bread is the salvation of scores of people with little time and a taste for home cooking. Hot entrees and salads with homemade mayonnaise round out the menu. At breakfast, the $2.50 scrambled eggs come with your choice of additional ingredients (bacon, cheese, spinach, etc.), each 25 cents. The French Horn's baked goods are also scrumptious. Across the parking lot is **Newman's**, tel. (541) 344-2371, walk-up fish and chips window. Here you can get gourmet renditions of salmon, halibut, and cod with chips for $3-5.

The large white colonial building down the street is the **Vets Club**, where you can sit in the same dimly lit vinyl booths where such visiting literati as William S. Burroughs, Gregory Corso, and Hunter S. Thompson have raised a glass with local writer Ken Kesey. Drinks here are inexpensive and quite strong. There's a bar menu Mon.-Sat. 11 a.m. to closing, and live blues and jazz Wednesday., Friday, and Saturday 9 p.m.-1 a.m.

A block south from the Vets Club on the corner of Willamette is **Euphoria Chocolate Co.**, 6 W. 17th Ave., tel. (541) 343-9223, a chocolatier of national repute. Their Grand Marnier truffle and other confections are sold around town. Come here after holidays and buy the bite-size Santas, hearts, and bunnies at reduced price.

Tino's, corner of 15th and Willamette, tel. (541) 342-8111, has been a Eugene tradition for almost a half century thanks to a pizza with a thick crust, copious amounts of freshly grated cheese, and a good assortment of fresh toppings. One prominent local marathoner "carbo-loads" here with a vegetarian pizza, $13, accompanied by a pitcher of beer. If you don't feel up to pigging out on a pizza or one of Tino's excellent calazones, $7, veggie or sausage, order up a half size pasta—try the alfredo or marinara sauces on spaghetti.

Eleven blocks south on Willamette, **Pizza Pete's,** 2673 Willamette, tel. (541) 484-0996, is another Italian place that's particularly popular with the college crowd. Tuesday nights, the all-you-can eat spaghetti bash featuring four different sauces and bottomless baskets of garlic bread for $3.50 lines 'em up all evening long. The house record is seven plates of spaghetti.

Beyond Downtown

Hilda's, 400 Blair Blvd., tel. (541) 343-4322, specializes in south-of-the-border—south meaning clear down to Tierra Del Fuego. Churrasco (an Argentinian steak dish) and Sancocho (a hearty Colombian stew) exemplify this gourmet fare. In summer, enjoy it all on Hilda's tree-shaded patio with a glass of sangria. Dinner will run you around $15, more than you'd pay in South America, but there's no better way to go there vicariously.

Not far from Hilda's in a neighborhood locals call Felony Flats is the **New Day Bakery,** 345 Van Buren, tel. (541) 345-1695, serving filbert croissants, first-rate coffee, and the best turkey sandwiches in town. Next door is the Red Barn, one of Eugene's quality natural foods groceries.

Not far from Felony Flats is another secret of Eugene budget gourmets. **La Tiendita,** 764 Blair Blvd., tel. (541) 683-5531, serves up locally renowned tamales and other south-of-the-border specialties adjacent to a store devoted to Latino foodstuffs. This modest restaurant has become Eugene's favorite outpost of Mexican food (with forays further south). Low prices, $6-8, huge portions, and down-home Mexican and El Salvadoran specialties (try the pupusas) have enabled this center of Eugene's Latino community to pave the way for a slew of imitators around town. Vegetarians will appreciate tofu tacos with a side of beans and rice.

A few blocks down from La Tiendita is another Mexican place. However, it'd be a mistake to classify **Ay Chihuahua,** 541 Blair Blvd., tel. (541) 345-6992, as just "another" Mexican place. This is Mexican food as close to what you'd find in Mexico and exists in Eugene. The Spanish-speaking clientele is especially heavy on weekends for the traditional Sunday repast, menudo (tripe, $6). Other dishes follow suit—inexpensive, filling, tasty, and authentic Mexican fare served with a minimum of pretense. Daily specials here can often be an exciting maiden voyage into this culinary realm. Pipian, a chicken dish popular in southern Mexico and Guatemala has a crunchy coating of pumpkin and sesame seeds and is one dish that'll keep you coming back for more.

The **Valley River Inn,** 1000 Valley River Way, Valley River Center, tel. (541) 687-0123, has a riverside outdoor deck at Sweetwaters that might offer Eugene's most delightful dining experience on a warm summer night. The extensive menu draws largely on regional ingredients put together creatively to best bring out the flavors of mountain, valley, and coast. Asian accents assert themselves at lunch with yakisoba noodle shrimp salad, $7, and at dinner with dishes like halibut, cilantro, coconut milk and lime, $14.50. The lightly cooked vegetables, sautéed seafood, and other healthful fare seem to go with the Willamette River kayakers and shoreside joggers who whoosh by the dining patio. You can sip Oregon wines by the glass or microbrews here if the moderate-to-upscale dinner prices are beyond your budget. Whatever you decide to do, take a sweater—it cools down fast here at night. A grand finale to any evening here is the marionberry cobbler. Main courses are $12-20. On Sundays, there's a brunch that won the local newspaper reader's poll as the best in town.

For Italian neighborhood dining, **Mazzi's,** 3377 E. Amazon, tel. (541) 687-2252, a chain with other outlets in Portland, Anchorage, and Corvallis. Though you might think it's just another formula pizza joint, the only thing cliché about the restaurant are the red-checkered tablecloths. You immediately sense quality when you sample a handful of Parmesan cheese from the bottle on your table. Instead of the usual heavily salted stale-tasting condiment-from-a-can that passes for cheese, these tasty morsels are as fresh as the hot sourdough French bread accompanying every meal. The best deal for dinner is the $10.95 pasta special—a large salad, minestrone soup, spaghetti and ravioli, with spumoni ice cream for dessert. Although we know it's not the case, everything here seems homemade from scratch. Except perhaps for a pizza crust that's too doughy, Mazzi's is every traveler's Italian-food fantasy.

A few blocks from Mazzi's is **Chef's Kitchen,** 3443 Hilyard, tel. (541) 687-2433, where cuisines of many lands are prepared with a deft touch. Entree specialties range from Hungarian Stroganoff and chicken scallopini to ahi with papaya, ginger, sherry, and raspberry liqueur. Mushrooms show up with great frequency here as do specials with a Pacific Rim flair (entrees $9-13). A pleasant, informal decor with works of local artists on the walls complements the relaxed fine dining. This place is especially popular as a gourmet takeout option.

Finally, if you're driving to the coast on US 126, stop off at the bakery/cafe **Our Daily Bread,** 88170 Territorial Rd., Veneta, tel. (541) 935-4921. Moderately priced homemade soups and sandwiches, desserts and espresso served in the confines of a converted church will get your excursion off to a good start. To get there, follow West 11th (which becomes ORE126) to its intersection with Territorial Rd. 11 miles west of Eugene, make a left and drive about .25 miles and look for the church-like structure on your right.

EVENTS

There is a lot happening in this south Willamette Valley hub of culture and athletics. Several events, however, best impart the flavor of the area.

Oregon Bach Festival
Of all the kulturfests in the Willamette Valley, only one enjoys international acclaim. The Oregon Bach Festival, 1257 University of Oregon, Eugene, 97403-1257, ticket tel. (541) 682-5000, takes place over two weeks from late June into early July under the baton of famed Bach interpreter Helmuth Rilling from Germany. *New York Times* critic Harold Schonberg once rated the festival the best of its kind in the country, and an influx of renowned visiting opera and symphonic virtuosi guarantees this will remain the case. Over two dozen separate concerts are featured, with musical styles ranging from the baroque era to the 20th century. The centerpieces of the festival, however, are Bach works like the *St. Matthew Passion,* numerous cantatas, and the Brandenburg Concertos.

Ticket prices in 1997 were as follows; choral-orchestral $17-37, chamber music and guest artists $13-22, and other programs ran free—$12. Performances take place in the Hult Center and at the Beall Concert Hall at the University of Oregon

last-minute arrivals to the Oregon Bach Festival

Music School. Free events, including "Let's talk with the conductor," mini-concerts, and children's activities also take place at these venues during the festival. Particularly recommended is the festival's Discovery Series—six concertos preceded by a short lecture-demo by Helmuth Rilling. Each 5 p.m. concert features a different Bach church cantata. Free noon concerts in the Hult lobby are also popular. The schedules are available at the University of Oregon Music School and are also published in the *Eugene Register Guard* and *Eugene Weekly*. Better yet, contact the Festival offices directly, tel. (800) 457-1486; http://music1. uoregon.edu/obf/obfhome.html. A scheduled series of brunches, lunches, and dinners with the musicians also adds a special touch to the festival.

Art in the Vineyard

Appealing to lowbrow and highbrow alike is Art in the Vineyard (for information contact the Maude Kerns Art Gallery or the Eugene-Springfield Visitors and Convention Bureau, or call (541) 223-8309, which generally takes place over the several days of the July 4 weekend in Alton Baker Park. This event brings together art, music, and wine in a tranquil park near the Willamette River. One hundred artists' booths and the offerings of a dozen vineyards frequently grace the affair, along with live music (jazz, country, blues, and folk) and food concessions. An admission of $2-5 is charged to yet another Eugene outdoor celebration of its cultural richness.

The Northwest Microbrew Festival

In addition to wine-lovers, Eugene has its share of beer connoisseurs. This group turns out in force for the largest winter microbrew festival in the country, the Northwest Microbrew Festival; for infomation call (541) 485-3907 or (800) 284-6529. Taking place at the Lane County Convention Center in February, the focus is on education with presentations on beer styles, home brewing and the like complemented by the food court, live entertainment and beer tasting.

Oregon Country Fair

Just after the Bach Festival in mid-July, the Oregon Country Fair takes place (see the special topic "Oregon Country Fair") as the second major cultural event of the summer. There's no such thing as free love, but for $7-10 (kids 12

and under free, 55 and above are half price) you can buy a 1967 experience with a price to match. This annual fantasyland is staged among the trees west of Noti on ORE 126; for more information, contact the fair at P.O. Box 2972, Eugene 97402, tel. (541) 343-4298. Gates open at 11 a.m. and close at 7 p.m.

The best way to avoid traffic is to take the free shuttle from 13th and Monroe in Eugene, which goes directly to the wooded fair site near the Long Tom River. This shuttle departs from the County Fairgrounds parking lot. Bus service usually begins around 10:30 a.m., with the last departure from the fair site at 7 p.m. Car access to the fair is open 10 a.m.-6 p.m. Car access may be limited in the future. Due to the popularity of this event, mandatory advance ticket purchase prior to arrival on-site has been instituted. Purchase tickets through **Fastixx,** tel. (800) 992-8499, at the Hult Center or at the UO Erb Memorial student union. Of special interest are the archaeology projects at the fair that detail the oldest known human presence documented in western Oregon, dating back 10,000 years.

Other Events

The fall is ushered in with the **Eugene Celebration.** This two-week fête in late September and early October includes such events as the mayor's Fine Art Show, readings by Oregon authors at the Hult Center, the Fifth Avenue Jazz Festival, and the coronation of the Slug Queen. Street performers all over town and food booths in the parking lot on 8th Ave. and Willamette also help the community put its best foot forward. Contact the Eugene/Springfield Visitors and Convention Bureau for more details, tel. (800) 547-5445.

The university sponsors the **Willamette Valley Folk Festival,** tel. 686-INFO, in the spring, which has attracted the likes of Tom Paxton and blues harpist James Cotton. Call for the schedule of the upcoming concerts. It generally takes place behind the student union on the second weekend of May. The event is free but bring cash to enjoy Eugene's amazing array of street food vendors. Music lovers also revel in the city's "Concerts in the Parks" festival during the summer. A series of free concerts is also held in Alton Baker Park's Cuthbert Am-

OREGON COUNTRY FAIR

Time warp: 1969-1990s

If you've been too busy to follow the growth of the '60s counterculture, put on your paisley and follow an eclectic caravan of handpainted schoolbuses, Volkswagen beetles, Volvos, and BMWs to the Oregon Country Fair.

After buying your ticket at the gatehouse, join the crowds of tie-dyed, fringed, and lovebeaded fairgoers. Entering, you wander through a kaleidoscope of natural fabrics, graceful ceramics, stained glass, rainbow candles, and thousands of other variously sculpted wares. Machine-manufactured items are simply unavailable. Every aspect of the fair, its booths and its participants, is, in a sense, art.

What? Two hours gone by already? You need a cup of espresso and a piece of torte if you're going to make it through this day. Or perhaps you want a **Ritta's** burrito bulging with avocado, salsa, and sprouts. The choices are mouthwatering: get fried rice, sushi, blazing salads, or even a tofuless tofu burger (100% ground beef), and more.

All fed and ready for a little entertainment? Overwhelmed by the constant parade of costumed stilt walkers, strolling musicians, winged "country fairies," children in face paint, bare-breasted men and women, and other ambient wonders? Not far from any burnout point is a stage.

Shady Grove is a quiet venue for acoustic folk, classical, new age, and other music.

The **Daredevil, W.C. Fields,** and **Energy Park** stages host contemporary New Vaudeville stars and other rollicking performers.

See the **Royale Famille du Canniveaux** debut a unique musical comedy.

Marvel as the **Reduced Shakespeare Company** performs *Romeo and Juliet* backwards in one minute flat.

Shake your head and mutter as **Up For Grabs** juggles circular sawblades and/or small children.

But wait, there's more. Try **The Circus** with its parade, orchestra, and veteran virtuosos. Ogle snake charmers and belly dancers at the **Gypsy Stage.** Or dance to the national and international stars of rock 'n' roll, reggae, and alternative music on the **Main Stage.**

Starting to sound less like a "hippie fair" and more like a well-catered and -established art convention? Don't worry; there's always a sojourn into geo-socio-political-eco-consciousness at **Community Village.** Several booths here and in **Energy Park** teach and demonstrate the latest in new and matured '60s activism and environmental awareness.

Tired already? So are we, but there's a whole year to rest up and reminisce before the next Oregon Country Fair.

To get there, head west from Eugene on ORE 126 and follow the signs. For additional information, contact the Oregon Country Fair, P.O. Box 2972, Eugene 97402, tel. (541) 343-4298.

The Oregon Country Fair is where Renaissance-era arts and crafts meet '60s activism and whimsy.

MARIA THOMAS

phitheatre mid-July to late August. Nancy Griffith, David Grisman, and Robert Cray typify the national names appearing here. Call (541) 687-5000 for tickets and information. Lower profile groups grace Amazon and Westmoreland Parks as well as several other venues throughout the city. Contact Lane County Convention and Visitors Association for a schedule and more information, tel. (541) 484-5307.

On the second weekend in August, the **Junction City Scandinavian Festival,** Greenwood St., between 5th and 7th, Junction City, celebrates the town's Danish founders. Folk dancing, traditional crafts, and food make up the bulk of the activities. Skits of Hans Christian Andersen folk tales are enacted during the four-day event, along with guided bus tours into the city's Scandinavian past. The latter are hour-long tours and take you by Scandinavian pioneer farmsteads built in the 1800s. Tour tickets are available at the information windmill for $2.50. Swedish, Finnish, Norwegian, and Icelandic ethnicities also exert a presence in this festival. Junction City is 12 miles northwest of Eugene off ORE 99. Contact the local chamber of commerce, P.O. Box 3, Junction City 97484, tel. (541) 998-6154, for more information on the festival. They can also tell you how to get to the mid-March **daffodil display** on Ferguson Road west of Junction City.

In the other direction from Eugene, **Bohemia Mining Days,** contact the Cottage Grove Chamber of Commerce, 710 Row River Rd., P.O. Box 587, Cottage Grove 97424, tel. (541) 942-2411, convenes in mid-July. The five-day event is highlighted by the Prospector's Breakfast, gold-panning demonstrations, a half-marathon, a bake-off, a flower show, an ugly-dog contest, and other competitions. Many of the events take place at re-created **Bohemia City** on ORE 99. Don't miss the Grand Miner's Parade, which happens on Saturday afternoon. Floats, horse teams, drill teams, and color guards make their way from Harrison Ave. to Row River Rd. with colorful costumes and the kind of enthusiasm last seen around here after turn-of-the-century lucky strikes. A small admission is charged on some days. Another event taking place in the summer outside Eugene is Springfield's **Filbert Festival.** Held at Island Park by the river, this assemblage of food and crafts booths and top

music acts is augmented by bungee jumping, a timber sports competition, and Native American cultural displays. To find out more about the late August fête contact the Lane County Convention and Visitors Association, tel. (541) 484-5307.

PRACTICALITIES

Information and Services

The following list scratches the surface of Eugene's many service institutions and information outlets. A bevy of literature befitting Oregon's second-most-populated area can be obtained at the **Eugene/Springfield Visitors and Convention Bureau,** 115 W. 8th Ave. Suite 190, Eugene 97401, tel. (800) 547-5445.

Eugene Parks and Recreation has the following switchboard numbers: tel. (541) 687-5333 for general information, (541) 687-5360 for athletics, (541) 431-5850 for arts, and (541) 687-5311 for disabled recreation.

The **University of Oregon Switchboard,** 795 Willamette St., tel. (541) 346-3111, is a multipurpose referral line. Rides, housing, and emergencies can be taken care of Mon.-Fri. 8 a.m.-5 p.m.

The main **post office** is located at 5th and Willamette, tel. (541) 341-3611, and is open Mon.-Fri. 8 a.m.-5 p.m., Saturday 9 a.m.-noon.

Sacred Heart Hospital, 1255 Hilyard, tel. (541) 686-6962, is one of the leading institutions of its kind in the state. Emergency-room care is available 24 hours daily. A cheaper alternative is the **Whitebird Clinic,** 341 12th Ave., tel. (541) 342-8255.

Across the street from Sacred Heart, the **Smith Family Bookstore,** 768 E. 13th, tel. (541) 345-1651; and 525 Willamette St., tel. (541) 343-4717, is an excellent used-book store. The **University of Oregon Bookstore,** 13th and Kincaid, and the **Bookmart,** 865 Olive, tel. (541) 484-0512, have the best selection of new titles and periodicals.

The **Eugene Public Library,** 100 W. 13th, tel. (541) 687-5450, has the most user-friendly periodicals section in the state.

Eugene's network of outdoor clubs and environmental organizations is extensive enough to preclude a thorough listing, but the vortex of the environmental community, the **University of**

Oregon Survival Center, Suite 1, Erb Memorial Union, University of Oregon campus, tel. (541) 346-4356, can steer you to the right adventure.

Club Wash, on the corner of 13th and Patterson, is a place to do laundry and cope with insomnia. Video games, munchies, espresso, a suntanning booth, and a big-screen TV offer ambience. Best of all, the machines, which do a load for less (75 cents) than most coin-operated washers, won't clean you out.

Getting Around

Amtrak at 4th and Willamette, tel. (541) 485-1092, offers once daily service both north to Portland and south to Sacramento/San Francisco on the Coast Starlight. The southbound train, $104, leaves at 4:52 p.m., northbound, $24, departs at 12:05 p.m. **Greyhound** at 9th and Pearl, tel. (800) 231-2222, and **Green Tortoise,** which picks up passengers in front of the University of Oregon library at 14th and Kincaid, tel. (800) 867-8647, are the other major modes of long-distance public transport. Tortoise fares are the lowest to San Francisco, $39, and L.A., $59. The northbound bus leaves at 1:15 p.m., the southern route departs at 3:45 p.m. Ten Greyhound buses a day let you head south to San Francisco or north to Portland from Eugene. Samples fares from Eugene to Portland are $13 one-way, $22 round trip. Greyhound also links Eugene up with the coast and Bend. Finally, travelers should note that Amtrak runs several express buses a day between Portland and Eugene, $11.50 one-way.

Around town, **Lane Transit District,** tel. (541) 687-5555, has canopied pavilions displaying the bus timetables downtown. Their business office on 10th and Willamette has pocket-sized schedules. Fares are around $1 (children and seniors half price) and about a third less on weekends. Bike racks are on all buses. The **ride board** on the bottom floor of the Erb Memorial Union at the University of Oregon has a list of rides available for those willing to share gas and driving. **Emerald Taxi,** tel. (541) 686-2010, is fast, reliable, and reasonably priced.

If you're in your own car, remember (1) the campus is in the southeastern part of town; (2) 1st Ave. parallels the Willamette River; and (3) Willamette St. divides the city east and west. The downtown mall, which encompasses the area between 6th through 11th Streets (north to south) and Pearl through Charnelton (east to west) allows through traffic north or south via Olive street. Navigation is complicated by many one-way roads and dead ends. To avoid getting stuck, be on the lookout for alleyways that allow through traffic .

The Eugene **airport,** tel. (541) 687-5430, is a 20-minute drive northwest from downtown. Just get on the Delta Highway off Washington St. and follow the signs. There is no bus service to the airport. Alaska, tel. (800) 426-0333, American, tel. (800) 433-7300, Northwest, tel. (800) 225-2525, United and United Express, tel. (800) 241-6522, and USAir, tel. (800) 428-4322, all operate flights in/out of Eugene. Transfers to Portland are available through Horizon, (800) 547-9308. This new airport has food service on the second floor. The Sunday *Register Guard* lists the lowest airfares to and from Eugene. Finally, Eugene has the seventh best complex of bike lanes in the country according to a 1993 *Bicycling* magazine survey.

Media

Public radio stations are all clustered near the bottom of the FM dial, with the dominant presence being KLCC (89.7 FM). The station's programming ranges from new-wave jazz and "Blues Power" (1-5 p.m. Saturday afternoons) to a dynamic news department. The University of Oregon station KWAX (90.1 FM) can be heard in eastern Oregon and on the coast and provides continuous classical music. Perhaps the most popular AM radio station in the area is KUGN's (590 AM) talk radio format.

Eugene Weekly, 1251 Lincoln St., tel. (541) 484-0519, has the best entertainment listings in Eugene. At the beginning of each season, the magazine's *Chow* edition will point you in the direction of Eugene gourmet restaurants. At all times, environmental articles and reviews by David Johnson are a highlight. This publication is available free at commercial establishments all over town.

A rundown of Eugene's ever-expanding list of live music venues, concert dates, reviews, etc. is available in a free monthly, *Northwest Independent Music News,* available in commercial outlets around town as well as selected venues throughout the state.

Travelers should especially look for columnist Mike Thoele in the *Eugene Register Guard,* 975 High St., tel. (541) 485-1234. His coverage of offbeat Oregon locales, personalities, and local color convey what is special about Oregon, contributing to the newcomer's sense of place as well as to Oregonians' understanding of their own state. While the column appears sporadically, you can catch up on Thoele's previous columns in an anthology, *Footprints Across Oregon* (Portland: Graphic Arts Center Publishing Co., 1988).

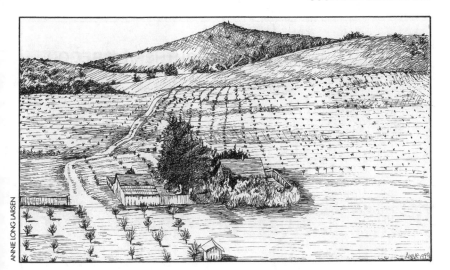

ANNIE LONG LARSEN

SOUTHERN OREGON

South of the Willamette Valley and west of the Cascades is a corridor of the state most residents call southern Oregon. To be more precise, this label refers to cities along Interstate 5 below Cottage Grove as well as towns in the shadow of the Siskiyou Mountains' eastern flank. What the Coast Range is to the Willamette Valley, the Siskiyous' rugged V-shaped canyons, wild rivers, and serpentine rock formations are to southern Oregon. The outstanding features of this region include world-class kulturfests, the biggest chunk of remaining wilderness on the Pacific coast, and California retirees who've come in search of cheap real estate and more sun than they'll see anywhere else west of the Cascades.

Initially it was gold finds on the Rogue River that drew prospectors into the territory in the 1850s. Around this time settlers following the Applegate Trail, a southern alternative to the Oregon Trail, also migrated here. A stagecoach line in the 1870s and a railroad a decade later established commerce with California markets. Forest products, orchard crops, and precious metals went south on these modes of transport until interstate trucking supplanted the iron horse in the 1930s.

Recently, attention has been focused on the northern part of the Siskiyou range and its 440,000 acres of old-growth Douglas fir. Many timber company contracts to clearcut these trees are being contested by environmental groups. The environmentalists claim the forest represents one of the world's most botanically diverse regions—with eight different soil types and more living matter per hectare than any other forest on the planet. As always, timber companies see the trees as a renewable resource and suggest that logging would create minimal damage to the ecosystem.

The region is no stranger to activism and aberration in general. Back-to-the-land refugees came into the tiny hamlet of Takilma on the east fork of the Illinois River to pursue alternative lifestyles decades ago and are still keeping the dream alive. So-called survivalists have chosen the Rogue Valley as the place to make their last stand in the Armageddon they say is inevitable. Several religious and new-age communities have also established themselves here.

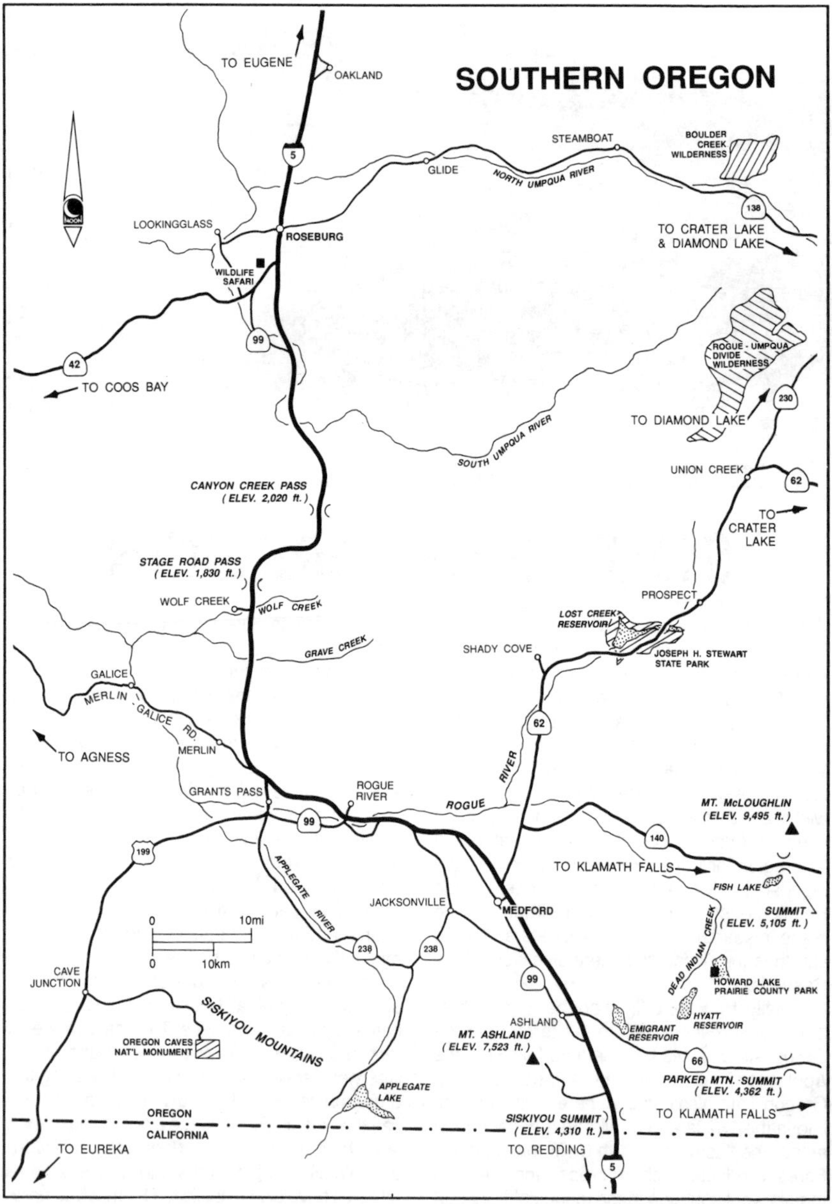

SOUTHERN OREGON

TO EUGENE
OAKLAND
5
STEAMBOAT
GLIDE
NORTH UMPQUA RIVER
BOULDER CREEK WILDERNESS
138
LOOKINGGLASS
ROSEBURG
TO CRATER LAKE & DIAMOND LAKE
WILDLIFE SAFARI
99
ROGUE - UMPQUA DIVIDE WILDERNESS
42
TO COOS BAY
TO DIAMOND LAKE
230
SOUTH UMPQUA RIVER
UNION CREEK
CANYON CREEK PASS (ELEV. 2,020 ft.)
62
TO CRATER LAKE
STAGE ROAD PASS (ELEV. 1,830 ft.)
WOLF CREEK
WOLF CREEK
PROSPECT
GRAVE CREEK
LOST CREEK RESERVOIR
SHADY COVE
GALICE
JOSEPH H. STEWART STATE PARK
MERLIN
GALICE RD.
MERLIN
62
RIVER
TO AGNESS
GRANTS PASS
ROGUE RIVER
ROGUE
RIVER
MT. McLOUGHLIN (ELEV. 9,495 ft.)
99
140
199
TO KLAMATH FALLS
APPLEGATE RIVER
FISH LAKE
JACKSONVILLE
SUMMIT (ELEV. 5,105 ft.)
MEDFORD
0   10mi
0   10km
238
238
99
DEAD INDIAN CREEK
HOWARD LAKE PRAIRIE COUNTY PARK
CAVE JUNCTION
EMIGRANT RESERVOIR
HYATT RESERVOIR
OREGON CAVES NAT'L MONUMENT
SISKIYOU MOUNTAINS
ASHLAND
MT. ASHLAND (ELEV. 7,523 ft.)
66
PARKER MTN. SUMMIT (ELEV. 4,362 ft.)
APPLEGATE LAKE
TO KLAMATH FALLS
OREGON
CALIFORNIA
SISKIYOU SUMMIT (ELEV. 4,310 ft.)
TO EUREKA
TO REDDING
5

© MOON PUBLICATIONS, INC.

Adding to this eclectic mix are over 100 high-tech companies (the "silicon orchard"), white-water rafters, anglers, as well as culture vultures drawn to southern Oregon's Shakespeare Festival in Ashland and the Peter Britt Music Festival in Jacksonville. Travelers enjoy this dynamic region, where Oregon's past, present, and future come together.

The Siskiyous
The Siskiyous are 130 million years old, the third oldest mountain range in the country. In contrast to the volcanic ooze of the Cascades, the rocks here never actually melted. Thus, instead of basalt, you find schist, granite, and feldspar. Scientists theorize the Siskiyous (also

known as the Klamaths) were once an island that annexed itself to the coastline of what was to become southern Oregon and northern California. These mountains boast exceptional floral diversity thanks to the existence of a climatic transition zone where the cool air of the Northwest and warmer drier air of California each have an influence. In addition, every type of forest is represented here.

With a huge chunk of unexplored, unmapped backcountry, there exists an aura of mystique to this range. This fact is underscored by the preponderance of Bigfoot sightings over the years. An excellent book on the natural history of this region is *The Klamath Knot* by David Rains Wallace (San Francisco: Sierra Club Books, 1983).

ASHLAND

With the possible exceptions of Stratford-upon-Avon and its Shakespeare presentations, and Oberammergau, Germany, and its passion play, there is no town so closely identified with a cultural event as Ashland and the Oregon Shakespeare Festival. You can immediately sense this is not just another timber town from a Tudor-style McDonald's, vintage Victorians, and some of the highest property prices you'll encounter anywhere in the state. The newcomer will also be struck by the dearth of neon and obtrusive signs in this population center of 18,000 people. Theater tickets are the coin of the realm here, with contemporary classics and off-off-Broadway joining presentations of the Old Bard.

Blessed with a bucolic setting between the Siskiyous and the Cascades, Ashland embodies the spirit of the Chautauqua movement of a century ago, which was dedicated to bringing culture to the rural hinterlands. Up until the 1930s, however, entertainment was mostly confined to the traveling vaudeville shows that came into the Ashland/Jacksonville area to entertain the residents of a gold-rush country in decline. Then Southern Oregon University started up the Shakespeare Festival under the direction of Professor Angus Bowmer. Such noted thespians as George Peppard, Stacy Keach, and William Hurt have graced Ashland's stages early in their careers, and the festival has garnered its share of Tonys and other awards. Today, the Oregon

Shakespeare Festival is the only classic repertory theater in the country and has the largest audience of any kind of theater in the United States (1996 attendance was over 351,000).

Ashland's tourist economy is also sustained by an auspicious location roughly equidistant between Portland and San Francisco. Closer to home, day-trips to Crater Lake, Rogue River country, and the southern Oregon coast have joined the tradition of "stay four days, see four plays" as a major part of Ashland's appeal.

SIGHTS AND DAY-TRIPS

Lithia Park
The centerpiece of Ashland is Lithia Park. Recognized as a National Historic Site, the park was designed by John McLaren, landscape architect of San Francisco's Golden Gate Park. It's set along Ashland Creek where the Takelma Indians camped and the region's first flour mill was created. Ashland, Ohio natives built the mill here in 1854, orginally calling it Mill Creek. (Some academic scholars suggest Ashland was named after the birthplace of Henry Clay, Ashland, Kentucky.) The park also was the site of Ashland's Chautauqua. A walk through 100-acre Lithia Park along Winburne Way's beautiful tree-shaded trail is a must on any itinerary here. This footpath and a scenic drive through

The Oregon Shakespeare Festival's outdoor Elizabethan stage

HANK KRANZLER

the park start west of the Lithia Fountain. Redwoods, Port Orford cedar, and other species line the drive, which takes you along Ashland Creek to the base of the Siskiyous. The park owes its existence to Jesse Winburne, who made a fortune from advertising on the New York subways and tried to develop a spa around Ashland's Lithia Springs, which he said rivaled the venerated waters of Saratoga Springs, New York. Although the spa never caught on due to the Depression, Winburne was nevertheless instrumental in landscaping Lithia Park with one of the most varied collections of trees and shrubs of any park in the state. Winburne was also responsible for piping the famous Lithia water to the plaza fountains so all might enjoy its beneficial minerals. While many visitors find this slightly sulfurous, effervescent water a bit hard to swallow, many locals have acquired a taste for Ashland's acerbic answer to Perrier and happily chugalug it down.

The hub of the park in the summer months is the Bandshell, where concerts, ballets, and silent movies are shown. Children love to play at the playgrounds or feed the ducks in the ponds. Big kids enjoy tennis, volleyball, horseshoes, or traversing one of the many trails in the park. Every Tuesday on Water St. next to Ashland Creek the **Farmer's Market** is held. Rogue Valley farmers, craftspeople, and ranchers sell arts and crafts, fruit and produce, and dried flowers.

Pick up the *Woodland Trail* guide at the plaza's visitors center kiosk. The gentle mile-long loop takes you from the plaza past a beautiful Japanese garden to the upper duck pond where mallards, wood ducks, and the endangered western pond turtle can be seen on the pond's island. A highlight for birdwatchers is in winter when there are 100-200 wood ducks here and ouzels that dive below the surface of Ashland Creek for fish.

Another way to enjoy the park is by taking a nostalgic ride through it in a horse-drawn carriage. **Lithia Carriage Company,** tel. (541) 482-5319, offers 25-minute excursions that begin at the information booth on the plaza near the park entrance. Fall is an especially nice time of year, with red maple leaves and yellow oaks backdropped by evergreens.

Schneider Museum of Art

The Schneider Museum of Art, Southern Oregon State College campus, Ashland, tel. (541) 482-6245, features contemporary art forms from national and international artists. Hours are Tues.-Fri. 11 a.m.-5 p.m., Saturday 1-5 p.m.

Recreation

Jackson Hot Springs, ORE 99, tel. (541) 482-3776, is two miles north of Ashland on the old highway and has a naturally heated public swimming pool as well as private mineral baths. The

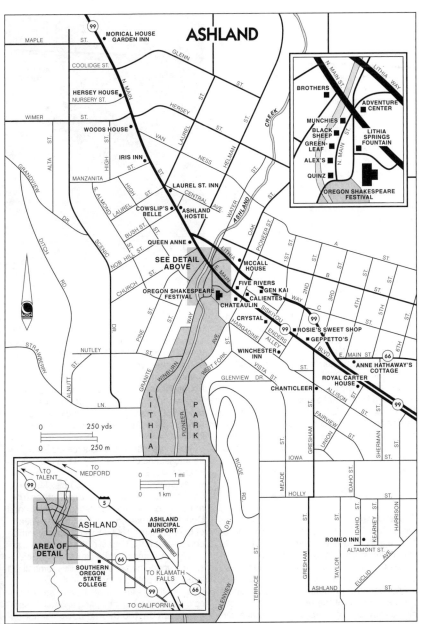

commune that owned the property recently disbanded, and the hot spring was put up for sale. Be sure to call first to see if the new owners allow guests.

Lighted **tennis courts** are found in Lithia Park, Hunter Park (on Summit St.), and on the Southern Oregon State College campus.

Meyer Memorial Pool, Hunter Park, Summit St., Ashland 97520, tel. (541) 488-0313, includes a wading pool for infants and toddlers under age five, as well as a large swimming pool for grown-ups. The season kicks off with a splash Memorial Day weekend with lap and open swimming sessions Saturday and Sunday 1-6 p.m. Summer hours start mid-June with open swimming Mon.-Fri. 1:30-4:45 p.m., Monday and Wednesday 7:30 a.m.-8:45 p.m., and the regular weekend hours of 1-6 p.m. Admission is $2 per session.

Day-Trips

Six miles east of Ashland on ORE 66 is **Emigrant Reservoir.** In addition to water-skiing, sailing, fishing, and swimming, a 270-foot twin flume waterslide, $5 for 10 rides, plus $5 admission, open Mon.-Thurs. 10 a.m.-7 p.m., Fri.-Sun. 10 a.m.-8 p.m., tel. (541) 776-7001, rental Hobie Cats, and sailboards add to the fun in the sun. Sailing lessons and boat rentals are available from the lake's **Hobie House Marina,** tel. (541) 488-0595.

East of Ashland 20 miles on Dead Indian Rd. is **Howard Prairie Lake Resort,** tel. (541) 482-1979. This 4,500-foot-high, six-mile-long lake has facilities for all water sports, horseback riding, and golf. A general store, restaurant, lodging, and 250-acre campground are also found at this retreat.

ASHLAND DRAMA

Shakespeare

While Lithia Park is the heart of Ashland, Shakespeare is the soul of this community. The festival began when Angus Bowmer, an English professor at Ashland College, decided to celebrate Independence Day weekend in 1935 with a Shakespeare production. The city fathers were so unsure of the reception they asked him to allow boxing matches on the stage dur-

HANK KRANZLER

Sir John Falstaff is a basket case in The Merry Wives of Windsor.

ing the day prior to the performance. By the time he retired as artistic director of the festival in 1971, his Fourth of July dream had grown into an internationally acclaimed drama company with three theaters, one named in his honor. Nowadays, the Oregon Shakespeare Festival contributes more than $24 million annually to the local economy, and over four million people have purchased tickets over the last 60 years.

The three festival theaters are located at the southeast end of Lithia Park. Take the Shakespeare steps up the small hill by the Lithia water fountains to get to the complex known as the Festival Courtyard. The **Elizabethan Theater,** built on the site of Ashland's Chautauqua Dome, was modeled after the Fortune Theatre of London, circa 1600. This outdoor summer-only theater is the largest of the three and is primarily the domain of the Bard. While Shakespeare under the stars is incredibly romantic ("I knew she would be my wife after we saw the play together"—true story), it can also get very cold after sunset in the spring and fall. In summer, even on 100 degree days, it's not uncommon for it to cool down to the low sixties after intermission. Dress warmly and consider investing a few bucks in the rental lap blankets and pillows for extra comfort. This theater closes by mid-October and the Festival itself ends October 30.

The second-largest playhouse is the 600-seat **Angus Bowmer.** This indoor complex has excellent acoustics, computerized sound and lighting, and nary a bad seat in the house. The echoes of Shakespeare's immortal prose fill this hall during the wetter winter months when the outdoor stage is closed. Finally, the 150-seat **Black Swan** is the actors' and directors' theater, where modern works and experimental productions are the norm. This theater is small enough to stage plays that might be overwhelmed by a larger venue. Call (541) 482-4331 for performance times, dates, and ticket availability (closed on Monday). June 8-Sept. 5, the box office is open 4:30-8:30 p.m.; in spring and fall it operates 4:30-8 p.m.

Tickets

Getting tickets to the **Oregon Shakespeare Festival,** 15 South Pioneer St., P.O. Box 158, Ashland 97520, tel. (541) 488-5406, for information tel. (541) 482-2111, is as much a part of the show as the performance. Due to tremendous popularity, seats will sell out months in advance, especially for the comedies. Your best strategy is to plan ahead and order well in advance. All seats are reserved, with the best seats up front (but not too close) commanding top dollar and prices decreasing for seats farther from the stage. Ticket prices range $9.50-34 for the Elizabethan Theater, and $26 for the Angus Bowmer and Black Swan. Once purchased, there are no refunds. If you are unable to get tickets ahead of time, your best bet is to get to the Shakespeare Plaza an hour or two before the show with a sign stating what show you want to see. If you are lucky, you will score tickets from someone with extras. Avoid bidding wars with other would-be theatergoers, as ticket scalping is frowned upon here. Otherwise, be at the ticket window at 6 p.m. for any available seats that will then be released. There are usually standing-room-only tickets, $10, if all else fails. And remember, there is no late seat-ing at any of the theaters. As of the 1992 season, the rear third of the Elizabethan Theater's seats were roofed to improve acoustics and restrict street noise.

For a behind-the-scenes look at the action, backstage tours are given by the actors and actresses and lend an interesting inside perspective to the magic of the theater. Included in the tours are visits to the Exhibit Center (a museum with changing displays relating to current shows) and dressing rooms, and an opportunity to handle props from actual productions. The two-hour tours depart from the Black Swan Theatre during the festival season every performance day at 10 a.m. The charge is $7-10, half price for those under 11. Call (541) 482-4331 for more information. Advance reservations are required.

Finally, catch the free **Green Show** before the play. It begins at 7 p.m. (6:30 p.m. in September) on the plaza outside the Elizabethan Theatre and features elaborately costumed dancers, jugglers, and medieval musicians. Humorous asides, flirtatious Renaissance dancing, magic tricks and other hijinks help liven things up. Although every aspect of the show has been researched for authenticity, there is a whimsical air to the proceedings making it accessible to everyone. The Green Show serves as an appetizer to the main course, often relating directly to the show it precedes in the Elizabethan Theatre. It ends at 7:30 p.m. with a second show at 7:45 p.m. in a small stage to the rear of the Elizabethan Theatre. A 32-page *Guide to the Green Show* sells for $2 at the Tudor Guild booth, detailing the historical antecedents of the show's instruments, music, dances, and scripts.

That's Show Biz

Shakespeare isn't the only act in town. Some of the other local companies include the **Actor's Workshop,** the **Lyric Theatre, Studio X, Children's Theatre,** the **Oregon Cabaret Theatre,** and **Southern Oregon State College** productions. Ashland is also home to the **State Ballet of Oregon,** which gives many summer performances. The **Ashland Visitor Information Center,** tel. (541) 482-3486, has complete information on all the goings-on, as does the

Southern Oregon Reservation Center, tel. (541) 488-1011 or (800) 547-8052.

A few miles north of Ashland is the town of Talent. The **Minshall Theatre** melodrama has been a popular favorite there for over 20 years, mainly because audience participation is openly encouraged. Here you get to cheer for the hero and boo and hiss the villain, and a splendid time is guaranteed for all.

SPORTS AND RECREATION

Skiing

Perched high atop the Siskiyou range and straddling the California-Oregon border is 7,523-foot-high **Mt. Ashland,** tel. (541) 482-2897 for information, (541) 482-2754 for the snow report, http://www.mind.net/snow. To get there, take the Mt. Ashland exit off I-5 and follow the road for a few miles to the complex. While Mt. Ashland is 15 miles away from downtown Ashland by road, it's only eight miles away by nordic ski trail. Skiers of all levels enjoy the 23 different runs, 100 miles of cross-country trails, and breathtaking vistas. The vertical drop here is 1,150

OREGON STATE HIGHWAYS

The 7,525-foot-high Mt. Ashland is Oregon's southernmost ski area.

feet. An average of 325 inches of snow falls on the mountain, making it possible to ski Thanksgiving through Easter. Ski at night Thursday through Saturday, $14. The weekend and holiday lift rate is $26, $20 on weekdays.

It is a good idea to check with the Southern Oregon Reservation Center (see "Information and Services" following) about available ski packages. Also, the spring and fall are good times to come to Ashland, as the rates are lower than during the peak summer tourist season. Many proprietors include free Mt. Ashland lift tickets with the price of the room. When the snow has melted off, the walk to the top of Mt. Ashland is an easy one, with good views of the Siskiyous and 14,162 ft. Mt. Shasta in California. It's prudent to bring along a sweater, as it can get fairly windy.

Mt. Ashland Inn

Skiers, hikers, and anyone who can savor views of Mounts McLoughlin and Shasta from within the confines of a three-story cedar lodge will appreciate Mt. Ashland Inn, P.O. Box 9444, 550 Mt. Ashland Rd., Ashland 97520, tel. (541) 482-8707 or (800) 830-8707, http://www.mtashlandinn.com; e-mail mtashinn@teleport.com. Flourishes such as stained glass, oriental rugs, an ornate fireplace, and Windsor chairs impart a cozy charm. The $180 Mt. McLoughlin suite has views of Shasta out one window and McLoughlin out the other. Another knockout view can be had from the Skylakes Suite, $180, as well as a jacuzzi for two with a rock waterfall, river rock gas fireplace, microwave, refrigerator, and other luxurious amenities. There are also four other rooms with the lowest going for $95 per night. Paul Bunyan-like breakfasts, included in the room costs and emphasizing locally produced foodstuffs, fuel hikes and cross-country ski trips on the nearby Pacific Crest Trail. The inn's 7,500-foot elevation also makes for excellent stargazing from its comfortable deck.

Adventure Center

The **Bear Creek Bike and Nature Trail** crisscrosses through town before going down the valley to Medford along Bear Creek. If you like to ride a bike but are not big on pedaling, contact the Adventure Center, 40 N. Main, tel. (541) 488-2819 or (800) 444-2819, http://www.raftingtours.com, e-mail raftingtours.com, for information about their Mt. Ashland downhill bike cruise. This half-day morning or picnic-lunch ride descends 4,000 feet on 16 miles of quiet paved roads through the countryside to Emigrant Reservoir. The three-hour morning cruise departs at 8 a.m., costs $55, and includes fruit, pastries, and drinks. The four-hour picnic cruise departs at 11 a.m., costs $59, and includes a great lunch in a beautiful mountain glade. Bicycles, safety equipment, roundtrip transfer from Ashland, and an experienced guide are provided. All you have to do is steer! The Adventure Center also has mountain bikes for rent that include helmet, lock, and maps for $6 an hour, $20 for a half day, $25 for a full day, and $30 for overnight

The Adventure Center also functions as a clearinghouse for over 60 outfitters and recreational organizations that will help you plan trips (short or long) for any size party. There's never a charge for this service, and they also offer group discounts. Adventure Center rafting trips include all gear (e.g. wet suits, splash jackets, booties, etc.), guides, and transfer from Ashland. The four-hour half-day trip, $59 includes snack, runs 8 a.m.-noon or 1-5 p.m., and the longer whitewater picnic trip, $99 includes lunch, runs 8 a.m.-4 p.m. Rated one of the best floats in southern Oregon, the all-day, $110 all meals, upper Klamath River trip runs 7 a.m.-5:30 p.m. (times vary, call to confirm). Horseback riding, cross-country skiing trips, kayaking, rock climbing, jet boating, and hot air ballooning round out the Adventure Center's array of recreational options.

Mountain Biking

One of the more popular local bike rides is the **Lithia Loop Mountain Bike Route.** The 28 mile ride is strenuous, gaining 3,000 feet in elevation the first six miles. Caution is in order the last seven miles of descent. To avoid the steep ups and downs, you can drive up to the top and ride the fairly level 15 mile stretch. The Lithia Loop is mostly within the Ashland watershed, the source of the city's water supply, and it may be closed to all entry during midsummer and fall.

The Mt. Ashland ski area parking lot is the begining of the **Siskiyou Crest Mountain Bike Route.** The 31 mile roundtrip ranges from moderate to difficult and wends along the crest of the Siskiyou Mountains with incredible views of Mt.

Shasta. The route ends at Dutchman peak, where you'll find one of the few cupola-style fire lookouts left in the Pacific Northwest. This particular lookout was built in 1927. Please note, bicycles are not allowed on the nearby Pacific Crest Trail.

For directions and additional information about these and other mountain bike trails in the area, contact the Ashland Ranger District, 645 Washington, Ashland 97520, tel. (541) 482-3333.

Horseback Riding

Graduate from a two-wheeled coast to a four-legged gallop with the many horseback-riding packages offered by **Mountain Gate Stables**, tel. (541) 482-8873; rates start at $20. To get there, take Ashland St. (ORE 66) two miles east of the Ashland Hills Inn. Short trail rides take in scenic views of the mountains and valleys, and longer rides deep into the woods of the Greentree Mountains include saddlebag lunches prepared by the Greentree Restaurant. And in the event of inclement weather, you can always practice your walk, trot, and canter in the arena. Another option features an overnight stay in creekside cabins at Buckhorn Springs, 2200 Buckhorn Springs Rd., tel. (541) 488-2200, a century old mineral springs resort. If you'd rather drive than ride, room rates in the lodge are $70-100, cabins are $60-150, and their three-bedroom house goes for $175-275, depending on season and number of guests. Open April-December. The meals at Buckhorn are prepared on the premises using the freshest and most organic ingredients available, many out of their own garden. If you're a little saddle-sore, a licensed massage therapist is also available. Call ahead for reservations and additional information on availability of all packages.

Circle Stables, 1275 Old Highway 99, Ashland, tel. (541) 482-7463, mirrors Mountain Gate Stables' offerings with one-, two-, and four-hour rides, $20-70. The four-hour trip includes a lunch you choose from their menu prior to departure. The overnight rides, $99, include all meals prepared by a camp cook, a campfire sing-along, and a night in a tent or under the stars. To get there, take ORE 66 six miles from I-5 and turn right onto Old Highway 99. It's about a half mile to the stables.

About a half hour from Ashland up ORE 66 is **Greensprings Outback,** 11476 ORE 66, Ashland, tel. (541) 488-5062, where you can ride the

Pacific Crest Trail, the historic Applegate trail, and many other wilderness trails that wend through this beautiful mountainous area. While their rates are a little higher than their nearby counterparts, $20-45 for one- to three-hour rides, the scenery makes it well worth it. As you traverse the old growth forests and mountain meadows, there are opportunities to view deer, elk, eagles, osprey, bears, cougars, and even wild horses. Three-hour dinner rides, $60, and the all-day ride, $85, are timed to take maximum advantage of the animals coming out at dusk. Customized overnight trips from 3-10 days, $100 per person per day, are available that include everything except your sleeping bag and personal gear. Most of the camps are set up near a mountain lake or stream with time for fishing, hiking, or just plain relaxing. Winter attractions include sleigh rides with hot drinks and a campfire. Call ahead for reservations and trip departure times.

Equipment and Golf
You can rent outdoor-recreation equipment at reasonable rates from **Ashland Mountain Supply,** 31 N. Main St., tel. (541) 488-2749.

A few miles outside of Ashland on ORE 66 is **Oak Knoll Golf Course,** 3070 ORE 66, tel. (541) 482-4311. Get into the swing of things before the play; at $10 for nine holes and $15 for 18 holes, even if you triple bogey, you can't miss. For weekend rates, add a dollar or two onto the greens fee.

PRACTICALITIES

Bed and Breakfasts
The warm traditions of England are represented in Ashland not only by Oregon's leading Shakespeare festival but also by the town's numerous bed and breakfasts, the most of any locale in the state (as well as the most per capita in the country). Although they cost a bit more than plastic, carbon-copy motel units, you get so much more for your money. In addition to such extras as fresh flowers in your room, antique brass beds with down comforters, and complimentary evening aperitifs, hearty morning meals are usually included. The superficially high price of many of these establishments can sometimes be split between couples traveling together.

Another plus is that most of these inns are within easy walking distance of the theaters. Chances are good you will be home from the show long before many other patrons of the arts are getting to their parked cars. Many of the properties are small, with usually only a handful

ASHLAND ACCOMMODATIONS

Ashland Motel, 1145 Siskiyou Blvd., tel. (541) 482-2561 or (800) 460-8858, $40-60, pets, pool.

Ashland Super 8, 2350 Ashland St., tel. (541) 482-8887 or (800) 800-8000, $50-70, pets, covered pool, laundry facilities.

Best Western Heritage Inn, 434 Valley View Rd., (541) 482-6932 or (800) 528-1234, $50-125, pets, covered pool, laundry.

Columbia Hotel, 262 E. Main, tel. (541) 482-3726, $45-75, European-style inn.

Hillside Inn, 1520 Siskiyou Blvd., tel. (541) 482-2626 or (800) 326-9903, $65-75, wheelchair access, pool.

Knight's Inn Motel, 2359 Ashland St. (I-5 exit 14), tel. (541) 482-5111 or (800) 547-4566, $60-70, cable TV, pool.

Palm Motel, 1065 Siskiyou Blvd., tel. (541) 482-2636, $50-150, wheelchair access, pool.

Rodeway-Ashland Valley Inn, 1193 Siskiyou Blvd., (541) 482-2641 or (800) 547-6414, $75-90, pets, pool, wheelchair access.

Stratford Inn, 555 Siskiyou Blvd., tel. (541) 488-2151 tel. (800) 547-4741 $95-135, wheelchair access, covered pool.

Timbers Motel, 1450 Ashland St., tel. (541) 482-4242, $55-65, kitchenettes, pool.

Vista Motel, 535 Clover Lane (I-5 exit 14), tel. (541) 482-4423, $45-55, pets, pool.

Windmill's Ashland Hills Inn, 2525 Ashland St., tel. (541) 482-8310 or (800) 547-4747 $65-250, free theater shuttle, many amenities.

of rooms. This fact, together with their popularity, mandates advance planning and reservations. The odds of strolling in off the street during summer and finding accommodations at an Ashland bed and breakfast are remote. Most innkeepers suggest reserving a year in advance. June-Sept. weekends demand an even greater window of time and usually require a two-night minimum stay. Off-season rates are 10-30% less than peak.

One way to find a place to bunk is to call one of the bed and breakfast associations. The **Ashland B&B Reservation Network,** tel. (541) 482-BEDS or (800) 944-0329, http://www.opendoor.com/ABBN/, of 25 inns assures you easy access to excellent-quality accommodations. Open daily 9:30 a.m.-7 p.m. Free referrals and brochures. As the network members are so fond of saying, "nobody does it bedder." The **Ashland B&B Clearinghouse,** tel. (541) 488-0338 or (800) 588-0338, also offers one-call reservations for over 50 bed and breakfasts, 14 houses, and four old hotels for a total of over 1,000 possible rooms. Ask for their free Ashland guide. Open Mon.-Sat. 9 a.m.-9 p.m. Both the **Oregon B&B Guild,** tel. (800) 983-4667, http://www.insite.com/obbg/, the **Oregon B&B Directory,** Box 1283, Grants Pass 97526, tel. (800) 841-5448, http://www.moriah.com/inns, e-mail inns@moriah.com, can not only help you find quality lodgings in Ashland, but can assist with B&B reservations throughout Oregon.

Chanticleer, 120 Gresham, tel. (541) 482-1919 or (800) 898-1590, $80-160, rules the roost with six romantic rooms replete with fluffy comforters and private baths. Their gourmet breakfasts are the talk of Ashland. A full cookie jar on the kitchen counter and the green Adirondack chairs in the garden will also linger in your mind long after you leave. Bedside "librettos" of the Shakespeare plays currently in repertory help sustain the mood while you are there.

The six rooms of the **Anne Hathaway's Cottage,** 586 E. Main, tel. (541) 488-1050 or (800) 643-4434, http://www.opendoor.com/AnnesBed, e-mail AnnesBed@opendoor.com, $75-205, four blocks from the theaters, have fresh-cut flowers, down comforters, firm beds, and private baths in all rooms. Their two-room J.T. Currie Suite can comfortably accommodate four, and is good for families. The **Hersey House and Bungalow,** 451 N. Main, tel. (541) 482-4563 or (888) 3-HERSEY, http://www.mind.net/hersey, e-mail herseybb@mind.net, $75-135, is an elgantly restored Victorian with antique furniture and private baths. The bungalow is a separate guest cottage with its own private entrance that includes a fully equipped kitchen, living room, and two bedrooms making it well suited for families and groups up to six. Room rates depend upon season and number of guests. The **Iris Inn,** 59 Manzanita, tel. (541) 488-2286 or (800) 460-7650, e-mail irisinnbb@aol.com, $60-105, is a cheerful Victorian with a fitting decor. Full breakfast in the morning, cold drinks during the day, and wine and sherry at night and to the classical atmosphere. After a walk through the Iris's gardens, you'll probably agree with Shakespeare: "Of all the flowers, methinks a rose is the finest."

The McCall House, 153 Oak St., tel. (541) 482-9296 or (800) 808-9749, http://www.mccallhouse.com, e-mail mccall@mccallhouse.com, $75-180, is a restored Italianate built in 1883 by Ashland pioneer John McCall. A National Historic Landmark, this nine-room inn is a block away from restaurants, shops, theaters, and Lithia Park. **Adam's Cottage,** 737 Siskiyou Blvd., tel. (541) 482-5405 or (800) 345-2570, $60-110, built in 1900, offers four nonsmoking rooms and suites. Children are welcome here, and a babysitter is available.

The Morical House Garden Inn, 668 N. Main, tel. (541) 482-2254 or (800) 208-0960; e-mail moricalhse@aol.com, $90-160, is a restored seven room 1880s farmhouse with a picture postcard view of Grizzly Mt. and the foothills of the Siskiyous. Wooden floors, stained glass windows, and antiques sustain the "good old days" theme despite no shortage of modern conveniences. The two acres of gardens provide organic produce for breakfast in season, including blackberries, raspberries, strawberries, apples, pears, and cherries as well as a wide variety of herbs and flowers. Many species of birds and butterflies are attracted to the gardens, which are tastefully accented by a waterfall and stream meandering through the grounds. Particularly striking are the giant granite boulders scattered about the property, glacial eratics from the last ice age. Given all this, it's sometimes hard to remember that you are only a few blocks away from downtown theaters and shopping.

Although **Romeo Inn,** 295 Idaho St., tel. (541) 488-0884 or (800) 915-8899, $95-180, is eight blocks from the Festival Courtyard, the large bedrooms of this Cape Cod style house with king beds and private baths, the afternoon tea, and the patio with a heated pool and jacuzzi make it worth the walk. The **Royal Carter House,** 514 Siskiyou Blvd., tel. (541) 482-5623, $70-90, has spacious rooms with private baths, antiques, and a special breakfast made from farm fresh ingredients and local organic produce fit for a king. A book-lined library, a bottomless cookie jar, and a well stocked refrigerator enhance the royal treatment.

Two blocks south of the Shakespeare theaters is the critically acclaimed **Winchester Inn,** 35 S. 2nd St., tel. (800) 972-4991, http://www.mind.net/winchesterinn, e-mail ashlandinn@aol.com, $105-200, offering 18 rooms with personality and private baths. Bay windows, private balconies, and English gardens add further distinction. Exotic gourmet delicacies are featured at breakfast (included), and dinner.

Breakfast is served out on the patio surrounded by a half acre of English terrace gardens at the **Woods House,** 333 N. Main, tel. (541) 488-1598 or (800) 435-8260, http://www.mind.net/woodshouse/, e-mail woodshse@mind.net, $75-120. In addition to the six rooms with private baths in the main home, the adjacent carriage house has two-rooms that can comfortably sleep six.

Close by the galleries and shops of the newly thriving Historic Railroad District is the **Peerless Hotel,** 243 4th St., tel. (541) 488-1082 or (800) 460-8758, http://www.mind.net/peerless. What had been a brick boarding house for railroad workers is today an art-filled, skylit lodging with five well appointed rooms and two suites. A full breakfast, health club access, and bicycles for touring Ashland make the $65-175 (for up to four people) a good dollar value.

On the outskirts of town on the edge of Weisinger's vineyard is **Weisinger's Vineyard Cottage** 3150 Siskiyou Blvd., tel. (800) 551-WINE, http://www.weisingers.com, e-mail john@weisingers.com, $110-150. A full kitchen, spacious living and sleeping area, and a large deck with a hot tub highlight this romantic country getaway. This is a special treat for wine connoisseurs with a tasting room, vineyard, and wine shop on the premises (see "Winetasting," below).

Families and couples traveling together will appreciate the space and privacy afforded at the **Oak Street Cottages,** 171 Oak St., tel. (541) 488-3778, $195-260. Located a block away from Lithia Park and the theaters, each cottage has a full service kitchen, dining room, and large living room. Enjoy eating outside on your own private patio equipped with a picnic table and barbecue. These units can comfortably accommodate 6-10 people.

A few blocks up Main St. from the theaters is the **Laurel Street Inn,** 174 N. Main; (541) 488-2222 or (800) 541-5485, $85-175. A massive rock wall blocks out the traffic noise from the main drag, compounding the beauty of their extensive gardens. A bountiful breakfast can be served out on the deck under the shade of a towering redwood. All rooms have private bath and many amenities.

The rooms at the **Cowslip's Belle,** 159 N. Main, tel. (541) 488-2901 or (800) 888-6819, http://www.cowslip.com/cowslip, e-mail stay@cowslip.com, $95-135, are very cute, and the innkeepers go out of their way to make your stay enjoyable. They can help make arrangements for your pets to stay at the North Pole, a good kennel in the area.

The **Queen Anne,** 125 N. Main, tel. (541) 482-0220 or (800) 460-6818, $75-140, is also located on Main St. close to theaters and shopping. This inn has tastefully decorated rooms with private baths, a full country breakfast, and friendly proprietors who treat you like a family guest instead of an income source. Enjoy an afternoon beverage here out on the sunporch while surveying a lovely half acre English garden with a rock waterfall.

Finally, you'll bathe in naturally occuring hot spring water at the **Lithia Springs Inn,** 2165 W. Jackson Rd, tel. (541) 482-7128 or (800) 482-7128, http:/www.ashlandinn.com, e-mail lithia@mind.net, $85-385, and you won't find anything better for making soft, younger-looking skin and taking the stiffness out of sore muscles (especially after a long drive or hard day skiing). Located a couple of miles from downtown, it's close enough for access to Ashland culture, yet far enough away for some real peace and quiet. Seven acres of working gardens provide fresh food and flowers for breakfasts and decoration. Their 3,000-book library has all kinds of interesting tomes, and a secret bookcase in the living room hides an entrance to another room. Twelve of the 14 rooms have whirlpools fed from the hot springs. There are eight cottage suites, two theme suites, and four regular rooms available for guests to enjoy. Most of the one and two room cottages adjacent to the lodge feature a fireplace, refrigerator, wetbar, and double jacuzzi. Be sure to book well in advance to take advantage of this unique property, as demand for rooms here is always high.

Dollar-Wise Choices
Offering 35 beds and family rooms, the **Ashland Hostel,** 150 N. Main St., tel. (541) 482-9217; e-mail ashostel@cdsnet.net, is a two-story 1902 house near the Pacific Crest Trail and only three blocks from the Elizabethan Theater and Lithia Park, and two blocks from the Greyhound station. Reservations are absolutely essential, especially from March-October. Touring bicyclist and Pacific Crest Trail hikers are eligble for a small discount. Family/couple rooms are available, $12-15. The hostel also has a coin laundry. Another dollar-wise choice in this high priced town is the **Columbia Hotel,** 262 and a half E. Main, tel. (541) 482-3726. This well kept 1910 with the grand piano in the lobby has rooms running from $40-90.

Food
Ashland's creative talents are not just confined to theatrical pursuits. Some of Oregon's better restaurants are around Main Street. Even the humbler fare served in Ashland's unpretentious cafes and burger joints can be memorable. The city also has a five percent restaurant tax, a surcharge seen nowhere else in the Beaver State.

The **Greenleaf Restaurant,** 49 N. Main, tel. (541) 482-2808, has patio on the second floor that makes a wonderful spot to enjoy an evening snack. Healthful fare with Mediterranean flair, espresso, and a good selection of desserts pull in the evening crowds, just as the omelettes, frittatas, and fruit smoothies attract devotees of healthy breakfasts. Try the okonomiyaki, a Japanese-style pancake made with fresh vegetables. The **Back Porch Barbecue,** 88 N. Main, tel. (541) 482-4131, lives up to its name. In addition to chicken, ribs, and the like, live music on summer weekends and tables outside the build-ing along the creek round out the cookout motif. The only buffet champagne brunch in town is at the **Ashland Hills Inn,** 2525 Ashland St., tel. (541) 482-8310. A seafood bar and an abundant array of salads, pastries, and entrees are featured 11 a.m.-2 p.m. The brunch is held outside on the patio in warm weather.

Only a half block from the theaters, **Calientes,** 76 N. Pioneer St., tel. (541) 482-1107, serves "heart smart" Mexican cuisine, $6-12, without all of the MSG, salt, and lard. Known for large portions of delicious food at reasonable prices, no one leaves here hungry. The black bean soup is a safe bet, and the chile rellenos (three kinds—try the one with chorizo) hold their own against the competition. Camarones caliente, $12.95, is the most expensive item on the menu, most of the entrees run under $10. **Omar's,** 1380 Siskiyou Blvd., tel. (541) 482-1281, Ashland's oldest restaurant, is noted for its seafood. You'll also be impressed by the restaurant's chicken Dijon, steaks, and moderate prices, $9-20. The map on the back of their takeout menu is better than the ones supplied by governmental agencies.

Another good choice for Mexican food is **Munchies,** 64 N. Main. The food is made mostly from scratch and has no MSG or lard. They also make their own vegetarian refried beans and offer eight different vegetarian specials, all for under $8. **Michael's Fine Hamburgers,** 457 Siskiyou Blvd., tel. (541) 482-9205, not only has the best burgers in town, $4-8, but Texas-style barbecue and chili as well. **Geppetto's,** 345 E. Main, tel. (541) 482-1138, is the place to go for Italian cuisine. Nothing fancy, just real food prepared and served by real people at real prices, $6-12. This Ashland institution serves breakfast all day, and it's open till midnight. **Brothers Restaurant and Deli,** 95 N. Main, tel. (541) 482-9671, specializes in gourmet soup and sandwiches, $6-10. New York meets the Northwest in a tasty marriage of deli delights and indigenous ingredients; open for breakfast, lunch, and dinner.

Rosie's Sweet Shop, 303 E. Main, tel. (541) 488-0179, originally a drugstore soda fountain in the early 1900s, still serves shakes, malts, ice cream sodas, and freezes the old fashioned way. No greasy burgers and oily fries here, only sandwiches piled way too high with your choice of fillings and garnishes, $4-7. Get the half size or split a whole so you can save room for their super sundae or belly-busting banana split. **Gen Kai Japanese Restaurant,** 180 Lithia Way, tel. (541) 482-9632, has authentic Japanese homestyle food—the Ishikawa family favorite. Tables surround a small indoor rock fountain, and Japanese-style seating is also available. The vegetable yaki soba is excellent, $9, as is their famous bento, $11. Japanese food for lunch on the fly can be had at **Bento Express,** 3 Granite Street. Vegetable pot stickers and vegetable curry as well as chicken, beef, and shrimp bento arrangements go for around $4.

The menu at **Crystal,** 212 E. Main, tel. (541) 482-1721, is as elaborate as the huge chandelier that looms over the dining room. A Paris-trained chef prepares sumptuous entrees, artful soups, and elegant desserts. **Alex's,** 35 N. Main, tel. (541) 482-8818, serves lunch, $5-15, and dinner, $8-18, placing an emphasis upon regional ingredients in a changing menu. Steak with Tulelake horseradish is a favorite. Go there early to get one of the two tables upstairs on the balcony above the street.

Chateaulin, 150 E. Main St., tel. (541) 482-2264, looks the most Shakespearean, with its dark wooden interior and lighted stained-glass behind the bar. Traditional French and nouvelle cuisines, $15-24 for dinner, are offered from a weekly menu. Chateaulin's bistro menu average half the cost of their regular offerings and are filling enough to sustain you through the presentations at the Elizabethan Theatre (some of which end after 11 p.m.). Whether it's crepes stuffed with portobello mushrooms, spinach, goat cheese, and garlic or escargot served with country pate, the hearty fare here manages to fuse a medley of delicate flavors. Chateaulin's adjoining gourmet food and wine shop also offers custom picnic lunch baskets (order 24 hours in advance). If you go there after the play for one of their 25 specialty coffee drinks, be careful what you say about the performance—Hamlet or Falstaff may show up wearing blue jeans.

Located in Talent is **New Sammy's Cowboy Bistro,** 2210 S. Pacific Highway, tel. (541) 535-2779; bring cash (no credit cards) and plan ahead (way ahead). With only six tables, New Sammy's fills up fast. Don't be put off by the exterior (gas station upgrade) or the interior decor (it's been described as "looking like Pee Wee Herman's playhouse"); the restaurant uses only organically grown food, and everything is homemade. Open Tues.-Sun., dinners cost $30-40 per person including wine and dessert. No sign, but there's a neon star on the roof.

The best lunch (11 a.m.-3 p.m.) buffet in town is at **Five Rivers,** 139 E. Main St., tel. (541) 488-1883, featuring over a dozen entree items for around $6. Dinner features an abundance of curry dishes that are mild or wild enough for all palates, $5-8, as well as other Indian delicacies. There are also many vegetarian selections available here.

An eclectic mix of food, drink, and patrons can be found at the **Black Sheep,** 51 N. Main St., tel. (541) 482-6414, http://www.mind.net/sheep, e-mail flock@theblacksheep.com. Open 11 a.m.-half past midnight, lunch and dinner creations, $5-14, with a decidedly English flair are available here. Wash them down with large selection of ports, sherries, malt scotches, and microbrews. Minors are permitted while dining 11 a.m.-11 p.m.

Finally, we like the concept at **Quinz,** 29 N. Main St., tel. (541) 488-5937. Instead of the structured meal format where each individual is forced to consume exclusively from their own plate, Quinz places an emphasis upon small plates and shareables, so that everyone can sample a bit of everything. This makes for a more sociable milieu to enjoy upscale, $4-13, casual dining. Foods of Greece, Spain, Italy, and the Pacific Northwest are all represented here, and an outstanding selection of wines by the glass complements the menu. A risotto with rock shrimp or a plate smoked salmon on toast points won't set you back more than $5, but tastefully prove that less is more.

Healthy Picnic Fare

One of the best alternative groceries in southern Oregon is the **Ashland Community Food Store,** 237 N. 1st, tel. (541) 482-2237. Open Mon.-Sat. 8 a.m.-9 p.m., Sunday 9 a.m.-9 p.m., a great variety of organic produce and organic bulk foods can be found here. **Cantwell's,** 310 Oak, tel. (541) 488-2120, deli offers sandwiches for under $4 and creative salads that can easily outfit a picnic. A clean and modern laundromat is also on the premises.

Nightlife

Allann Brothers, 1602 Ashland St., tel. (541) 488-0700, is a cozy coffeehouse with live music Friday and Saturday night. Gourmet coffee drinks, soups and sandwiches, and fine desserts are available. **The Vintage Inn,** 31 Water St., tel. (541) 482-1120, is right next door and features a potpourri of nightly entertainment. Jazz, classical, folk, and bluegrass are some of the musical strains you may hear here. Something always used to be happening at the **Mark Antony Hotel,** 212 E. Main. Unfortunately, at press time it was closed. As the tallest building in town it is a local landmark that one hopes will be reopened soon. Nearby **Canario's Coffee House,** 11 N. 1st, tel. (541) 488-4883; open 7 a.m.-10 p.m., offers an interesting deli menu backed up by a full service coffee bar. The cheapest beer in town can be found at the **Players Tavern,** 41 N. Main St., tel. (541) 482-9701. Late-night food can be procured at the **Copper Kitchen,** 2510 ORE 66, I-5 exit 14, tel. (541) 488-0111. This 24-hour restaurant's food is a cut above the typical truckstop fare.

Galleries

The **Hansen Howard Gallery,** 82 N. Main, has 52 local artists in a bright, airy corner shop at the north end of downtown. The **Fourth St. Garden Gallery and Cafe,** 265 4th St., is also worth a look for paintings, glass, and pottery. It's located in a thriving commercial strip by the railroad tracks.

Winetasting

The climate of southern Oregon is ideal for many bordeaux varietals such as cabernet sauvignon, sauvignon blanc, and merlot. The country cottage tasting room at **Ashland Vineyards,** 2275 E. Main, tel. (541) 488-0088, gives you the opportunity to sample the local product. Open 11 a.m.-5 p.m. daily except Monday (by appointment only Jan.-Feb.), winery tours, a picnic area, and wine for sale are also offered.

Nearby is **Weisinger's Vineyard,** 3150 Siskiyou Blvd, tel. (541) 488-5989 or (800) 551-WINE. Weisinger's makes cabernet sauvignon, gewürztraminer, pinot noir, chardonnay, sauvignon blanc, and Italian varieties and has received national and international awards. Perched upon a knoll, the view of the valley, vineyard, and surrounding mountains from the tasting room heightens the experience. In addition to wines, deli foods, soft drinks, and gifts also may be purchased. A beehive displayed in the tasting room is set up so you can see the queen and her subjects hard at work. Open daily 11 a.m.-6 p.m. June-Sept., Wed.-Sun. 11 a.m.-5 p.m. April-May and October, Fri-Sun. 11 a.m.-5 p.m. Nov.-Feb., and Thurs.-Sun. 11 a.m.-5 p.m. in March.

Events

The **Feast of Will** celebrates the opening of the Shakespeare Festival. It usually takes place mid-June at Lithia Park. Contact the box office for tickets to this bacchanal. The **Rogue Valley Growers and Crafters Market** takes place under the Lithia St./Siskiyou Blvd. overpass a half-block north of the plaza Tuesday 8:30-1:30 a.m. from May-October.

Getting There and Getting Around

Greyhound, 91 Oak St., tel. (541) 482-2516, serves Ashland with a handful of daily north- and southbound departures. Local connections between Medford and Ashland are possible through **Rogue Valley Transportation,** tel. 799-BUSS. The no. 10 bus leaves every half hour 5 a.m.-8 p.m. The **Green Tortoise,** tel. (800) 867-8647, departs the Copper Skillet Restaurant, 2510 Hwy 66, off I-5 exit 14 going north at 5:15 a.m. Monday and Friday, headed south at 11:45 p.m. Sunday and Thursday. Be sure to call to arrange a "flag stop." Contact **Ski Ashland,** P.O. Box 220, Ashland 97520, tel. (541) 482-2897, for information on the Mt. Ashland daily bus to and from Medford and Ashland. Twenty-four-hour **taxi** service is available from **Ashland Taxi,** tel. (541) 482-3065. **Executive Rent-a-Car,** Butler Ford, 1977 ORE 99, tel. (541) 482-2521, picks up and delivers anywhere in the Bear Creek Valley. Used cars for $15 a day plus mileage are available through the **Ashland Hills Inn,** 2525 Ashland St., tel. (541) 482-8310.

Information and Services

Ashland Visitor Information Center, 110 E. Main St., Ashland 97520, tel. (541) 482-3486, offers brochures, play schedules, and other up-to-date information on what's happening. The chamber has two booklets in particular (available for a small fee) that will help you appreciate the unusual variety of trees and shrubs in Lithia

Park: *Woodland Trails* and *Lithia Park—The History.* Another excellent source of information is the **Southern Oregon Reservation Center,** P.O. Box 477, Ashland 97520, tel. (541) 488-1011 or (800) 547-8052. This agency specializes in arranging Shakespearean vacation packages with quality lodging, choice seats for performances in all three theaters, and other tour and entertainment extras.

Ashland is famous for having one of the more dynamic Elderhostel programs in the country. Seniors bed down at Southern Oregon State dorms and take Shakespeare classes at the university to enhance their appreciation of the plays. To find out about the offerings of this hostel as well as the programs of its counterparts in Sandy near Mt. Hood, Corvallis, and Lakeview, write **Elderhostel,** 75 Federal St., Boston, MA 02110-1941, tel. (617) 426-8056, or call (541) 552-6677.

Regional books, out-of-town papers, and a delightful bakery-cafe upstairs make **Bloomsbury Books,** 290 S. Main, tel. (541) 488-0029, a place worth knowing about. Upstairs, a cafe is a good place to peruse prospective purchases. The **Oregon Welcome Center** offers travel information ranging the whole state. Traveling I-5, take exit 14. At the stop sign, turn left onto Ashland Street. Go over the freeway overpass and get into the left-hand turn lane and turn left onto Washington St. The center is located at the Ashland Ranger District—watch for "Tourism Information" signs.

The **post office,** Lithia Way and 1st St., tel. (541) 482-3986, is open during regular business hours; for **police** call (541) 482-5211 or 911. **Ashland Community Hospital,** 280 Maple St., tel. (541) 482-2441, has 24-hour medical service.

MEDFORD AND VICINITY

In the 1850s, gold discoveries drew people and commerce to the Rogue River Valley. The seat of the prosperity was Jacksonville, a major stagecoach stop whose boom went bust in the 1880s when the new railroad line bypassed the town for a train station known as Middle Ford. Middle Ford's name became shortened to Medford, and the town was incorporated in 1885.

Today, along with a resource-based economy revolving around agriculture and timber products, Medford is becoming established as a retirement center. Proximity to Ashland's culture, Rogue Valley recreation, and Cascade getaways, as well as rainfall totals half those recorded in the Willamette Valley, are some of the enticements. Unfortunately, if the current population of 50,000 grows much larger, the already poor air quality here will become worse. Already smog alerts brought on by heat and inversions have some folks calling the city "Dreadford."

Call it what you will, but for cost of living, proximity to mountains and coast, and employment opportunities, there is no better place to live in southern Oregon than Medford.

SIGHTS

Table Rocks

About 10 miles northeast of Medford are two eye-catching basaltic buttes, Upper and Lower Table Rock. They are composed of sandstone with erosion-resistant lava caps deposited during a massive Cascade eruption about four to five million years ago. Over the years, wind and water have undercut the sandstone. Stripped of their underpinnings, the heavy basalt on top of the eroded sandstone is pulled down by gravity, creating the nearly vertical slabs that we see today.

The Table Rocks were the site of a decisive battle in the first of a series of Rogue Indian wars in the 1850s. Major Philip Kearny, who later went on to distinguish himself as the great one-armed Civil War general, was successful in routing the Indians from this seemingly impervious stronghold. A peace treaty was signed here soon afterward by the Rogue (Takelma)

Indians and the American government. For a time, this area was also part of the Table Rock Indian Reservation, but the reservation status was terminated shortly thereafter.

For nearly a century, the Table Rocks were the domain of vultures and rattlesnakes until the **Lower Table Rock Preserve** was established in 1979. This 1,890-acre preserve is near the westernmost butte, which towers 800 feet above the surrounding valley floor. Established by the Nature Conservancy and later turned over to the government, the preserve protects an area of special biologic, geologic, historic, and scenic value. Pacific madrone, white oak, manzanita, and ponderosa pine grow on the flank of the mountain, while the crown is covered with grasses and wildflowers. Newcomers to the region will be especially taken by the madrone trees. This glossy-leaved evergreen has a "skin" that peels in warm weather to reveal a smooth, coppery orange bark. It's found mostly in the Northwest and was noted by early explorers as fuel for long, slow, hot-burning fires.

Park checklists show that over 140 different kinds of plants reside here, including dwarf meadow foam, which grows no place else on earth. One reason is that water doesn't readily percolate through the lava. Small vernal ponds collect on top of the butte, nurturing the wildflowers that flourish in early spring. The wildflower display reaches its zenith in April. A dozen different kinds of flowers cover the rock-strewn flats with bright yellows and vivid purples.

Hikers who take the two-mile trail to the top of horseshoe-shaped Lower Table Rock are in for a treat. Be on the lookout for batches of pale lavender fawn lilies peeking out from underneath the shelter of the scraggly scrub oaks on the way up the mountain. You'll want to walk over to the cliff's edge, which will take you past some of the "mima mounds" or "patterned ground" that distinguishes the surface of the butte. How the mounds were formed is a matter of scientific debate. Some scientists believe they represent centuries of work by rodents, others think they are accumulated silt deposits, while still others maintain that they have been created by the action of the

MEDFORD

TO CRATER LAKE &
KLAMATH FALLS

62

JACKSON COUNTY
EXPO PARK

5

TO GRANTS
PASS

99 TO ROGUE RIVER

BEAR CREEK

MEDFORD - JACKSON
COUNTY AIRPORT

AIRPORT RD.

AIRPORT RD.

TABLE ROCK RD.

ROGUE VALLEY BLVD

CRATER LAKE AVE.

McANDREWS RD.

ROGUE VALLEY BLVD.

JACKSON ST.

HAWTHORNE
PARK

E. MAIN

OAKDALE

GRAPE ST.

238

238

COTTAGE ST.

238

W. MAIN

JACKSONVILLE HWY.
TO JACKSONVILLE

ST.

8th ST.

AVE.

10th ST.

ST.

RIVERSIDE AVE.

SISKIYOU BLVD.

BEAR CREEK

MURPHY RD.

ROSS LN.

COLUMBUS

UNION PARK

MONROE

KENYON ST.

ROGUE VALLEY
MEDICAL CENTER

HAMILTON

DAKOTA AVE.

STEWART AVE.

BARNETT RD.

FICHTER
MAIN WARING
PARK

VETERANS
PARK

MILES
FIELD

TO ASHLAND

99

5

TO ASHLAND

0   0.75mi
0   0.75km

© MOON PUBLICATIONS, INC.

wind. However they got there, the mounds are the only soil banks on the mountain that support grasses, which are unable to grow on the lava. Lichens and mosses manage to grow on the lava, however, painting the dull black basalt with luxuriant greens and fluorescent yellows during the wetter months.

The trail up Upper Table Rock is a little over a mile but much steeper than the Lower Table Rock trail. Clay clings to the slopes of Upper Table Rock, making the going both sticky and slippery during the wet season. The trail affords wonderful vistas of the Rogue River and Sams Valley to the north. Two benches along the way are good places to stop and rest, savor the view, and scrape the heavy clay off of your shoes.

The trail reaches the top of the butte on the far eastern side. The ponds up here are smaller and fewer than on Lower Table Rock, but the mima mounds are more clearly defined. Upper Table Rock also shows less wear and tear from human activity, and the flower show is just as spectacular. Long black strips of hexagonal basalt look as though they were formed by tanks marching across the butte while the lava was cooling. You'll find that this irregular, knobby surface is difficult to walk on, but the colorful mosses and lichens love it. Also look for the tiny bouquets of grass widows, lovely purple flowers that dangle on long, graceful stalks. The odd-looking building off to the west is a navigation device maintained by the Federal Aviation Administration. It's easy to get disoriented out here, with hundreds of acres to explore. The point where the trail heads back down the mountain is marked by two large trees, a ponderosa pine and a Douglas fir, accompanied by a smaller cedar.

To get to the Table Rocks, take ORE 62 northeast out of Medford. Turn left on Table Rock Rd. and follow it until you reach Wheeler Road. Look for small directional signs pointing the way. The parking area and trailhead are located on the west side of Wheeler Road. Table Rock Rd. is also accessible from the north via ORE 234. The **BLM,** 3040 Biddle Rd., tel. (541) 770-2200, has additional information on the Table Rocks.

Harry and David's Country Store

About a mile south of Medford on ORE 99 is the country store of famous fruit purveyors Harry and David Holmes, 1314 Center Dr., Medford

97501, tel. (541) 776-2277. Harry and David took over their family's Bear Creek Orchards in 1914. Bear Creek Orchards was recognized for the size and quality of its pears, which were shipped to the grand hotels of Europe. But their lucrative export market collapsed during the Depression, so the brothers decided to sell their fruit by mail. To establish a new reputation domestically, they headed for both seaboards. Each carried sample gift boxes of fruit, which they personally delivered to high rollers like David Sarnoff, Walter Chrysler, Leland Stanford, and Alfred P. Sloan. Their first foray was an immediate success, and their mail-order business was born.

Today, Harry and David's is one of the world's leading shippers of food and fruit gifts. You'll find food, gifts, and fun in new 17,000 square-foot store. Strolling through the aisles, you can enjoy many free samples of the merchandise. The fruit-stand section of the store offers farm-fresh fruit, vegetables, and produce. You can also find "rejects" from Harry and David's Fruit-of-the-Month Club that are nearly as good as the mail-order fruit but are too small or blemished to meet their high quality standards.

The gourmet-foods section features their complete line of freshly made baked goods, smoked meats and fish, and cheeses. Again, be on the lookout for products with slight imperfections that go for a fraction of the cost listed in the store catalog. The jams and fruit spreads in particular are less expensive here.

For visitors unable to make it south from the Portland area, there is an outlet store east of the city. Take the Troutdale exit off I-84 into the Columbia Outlet Mall, and look for it on the west side of the complex.

To the north of Harry and David's is Jackson and Perkins Co., the world's largest private rose grower. The two have merged under the auspices of the Bear Creek Corporation.

Jackson and Perkins

The history of Jackson and Perkins, 1310 Center Drive, Medford, tel. (800) 292-4769, began in 1872 on the east coast where the company first began wholesaling nursery stock. Their mail-order business started at the 1939 World's Fair in New York. Many customers who had ordered roses appreciated having them shipped and re-

The Antelope Creek "Kissing Bridge" is located near Butte Creek Mill in Eagle Point.

STUART WARREN

quested the same service the following year. From this nucleus, their reputation quickly spread, and orders for their roses came in from all over the country.

Jackson and Perkins moved to California's San Joaquin Valley in 1966 to take advantage of the 262-day growing season. The roses are raised in California, then harvested and sent to the Medford plant where they are prepared for nationwide shipment. The company's annual catalogues offer bulbs, seeds, and plants of all kinds, as well as their award-winning roses. Take a walk down the primrose path of their 43,000-square-foot Test and Display Garden (next to the warehouse) May-Oct. to enjoy the colorful sights and sweet smells of the floral displays.

Rising Sun Farms

Another local food producer to make it big on the national circuit is **Rising Sun Farms**, 5126 S. Pacific Hwy, Talent, tel. (800) 888-0795. The flavors of the Pacific Northwest are represented in their cheese tortas, vinaigrettes, marinades, and mustards. Good "emergency food" can be found in the form of their pestos. Made from core ingredients of organically grown basil, exra virign olive oil, almonds, and sea salt, their half dozen varietes can turn a motel hotplate meal into a fine dining experience.

Grist for the Mill

About 15 minutes away from Medford on ORE 62 is Oregon's last original water-powered grist-

mill that's still in operation, the **Butte Creek Mill,** P.O. Box 561, 402 Royal, Eagle Point 97524, tel. (541) 826-3531. To get there, take ORE 62 about 10 miles north to Eagle Point and follow the signs to the mill. Built in 1872, the foundation pillars were hand-hewn with an axe, and wooden pegs and square nails hold up the rest of the structure. The two 1,400-pound millstones were quarried in France and assembled in Illinois. From there, they were shipped around the Horn and then transported over the mountains by wagon. Genuine stone-ground products are available in the mill shop, including 12 kinds of flours, four kinds of meal, four cracked grains, six cereals, four mixes (pancake, waffle, cornbread, and biscuit), and other grain products. A variety of health-food products rounds out the nutritious collection of edibles here. Open Mon.-Sat. 9 a.m.-5 p.m. daily (except major holidays).

Adjacent to the mill is the **Oregon General Store Museum.** This museum is a re-creation of a typical late-1800s general store. Home remedies, giant coffee grinders, pickle barrels, and other common goods of the day are exhibited. A working music box, antiques and collectibles, and old advertising signs add to the decor. Open 11 a.m.-4 p.m. on Saturday, donations are eagerly accepted.

Just down the street from the mill is the **Lost Creek Covered Bridge.** The 39-foot long bridge was built in 1919 and exhibits a queen post truss design with a shingle roof and flying buttress braces. The rough wooden floor is composed of diagonal planks. Lost Creek was so named because during its thousand foot drop in elevation over a distance of two miles, it disappears beneath a lava flow for a while before resurfacing again. It is closed to vehicular traffic, but you can get a good picture of the bridge by walking across it to the east side of Lost Creek.

Ridin' the Rails
Just about anyone who likes trains will enjoy **Medford Railroad Park,** tel. (541) 770-4586 or 779-7979, on Berrydale Ave. off Table Rock Rd., a few blocks away from the Rogue Valley Mall. The park features miniature steam trains that run the second and fourth Sundays of each month, April-Oct., 11 a.m.-3 p.m. Locomotives and other railway equipment are faithful reproductions of full-size trains, except that one inch here equals a foot out in the real world. Coal, wood, oil, and propane fire the steam boilers that propel the trains around a mile-long track. Passengers are carried in small cars across bridges, culverts, and over a small grade. Full-size cars, cabooses, a hopper car, and locomotives are also on display. Admission is free.

Crater Rock Museum
In 1952, Delmar Smith held a meeting in his home for a local mineral society. Over forty years later, he now gives tours of the new Crater Rock Museum, 2002 Scenic Ave., Central Point, tel. (541) 664-1355, created mostly by the efforts of the Roxy Ann Gem and Mineral Society. While small in size, the museum offers a selection large in scope. Showcased is an impressive array of gems, minerals, fossilized rock, petrified wood, agates, crystals, and moss agates— many of them collected in Oregon. Many examples of the state rock, the thunder egg, and the state gem, the Oregon sunstone, are also prominantly displayed. Marvel at the uncut amethyst cathedral formations or the seashells of the world collection that features a specimen close to two feet in length. The museum also boasts an excellent Early American Indian artifacts collection, many of them found in the Rogue Valley. Of note are the Indian effigies, small fired clay figurines. The building also houses a library with over 450 geology reference books, and their gift shop has maps and directions to good rock

hounding sites. Open daily 9 a.m.-5 p.m.; admission is free, donations accepted.

To get there from the south, take exit I-5 exit 32 and go west on Pine Street to ORE 99. Head north on 99 to Scenic Ave. where you will make a right (east). Proceed down Scenic Ave. and you will see the museum. If coming from the north, take I-5 exit 35 and go south on ORE 99 until you get to Scenic Ave. where you will take a left (east). From either direction, look for the signs and the flashing yellow caution light in the middle of ORE 99 that marks Scenic Avenue.

SPORTS AND RECREATION

Take Me Out To The Ball Game
Medford's **Miles Field,** tel. (541) 770-5364, located about a mile south of town near the Armory on ORE 99, is the home turf of the Medford Athletics baseball team, a farm club of the Oakland Athletics. Here you get the opportunity to watch budding hopefuls round the bases on their way up to the bigs, and might-have-beens shuffle back unnoticed to the dugout. Jose Canseco, home-run slugger and American League rookie-of-the-year in 1985, used to play here. While it's not exactly major-league action, you can sit closer to the field and the admission, $4-10, is definitely minor. The season runs from mid-June through Labor Day. Call ahead to see what team is in town.

Golf
Near Miles Field is **Bear Creek Golf Course,** 2325 South Pacific Hwy., tel. (541) 773-1822. This is a compact nine-hole course that's both a challenge and a bargain at $7 a round. If you would rather go for a regulation-sized course, **Cedar Links Golf Course,** 3144 Cedar Links Dr., tel. (541) 773-4373, in northeastern Medford has 18 holes waiting for you. To get there, take ORE 62 north toward White City. Turn right on Delta Waters Rd., right again on Springbrook Rd., and then left on Cedar Links Drive. The greens fee is $12 for nine holes and $18 for 18 holes; add a dollar or two more on weekends.

Splish Splash
When the mercury heats up into the 90s and 100s during the summer, it's time to cool off in

one of Medford's several public swimming pools. **Jackson Pool,** 815 Summit, tel. (541) 770-4586, is a popular family place to get wet. In addition to the 100-foot-long waterslide, a concession stand sells ice cream, soft drinks, and other snacks. The swimming season starts June 11 and runs into early September. An open recreational swim is held Mon.-Wed. 1-3 p.m. and also on Friday. Thursday evenings are reserved for family swims, 7:30-9:15 p.m. Admission is $2 for adults, $1 for ages 18 and under. **Hawthorne Pool,** 505 E. Main St., tel. (541) 770-4586, features an open swim Sun.-Fri. 1-3 p.m. and 3:30-5:30 p.m.

Biking and Jogging

Bear Creek, which runs through the city, is a greenway that attracts joggers, bikers and walkers. The latter groups also indulge their passions along the Old Stage Road (especially heading into or leaving Jacksonville). For bicycle rentals try Siskiyou Cyclery, 1259 Siskiyou Blvd., Medford.

Medford's Bear Creek Park is a recreation mecca. Kids love the majestic castle playground, and sports enthusiasts revel in acres of open space. To get there from I-5 take exit 27 off I-5 at the Barnett Road-Jacksonville interchange. Go east on Barnett Rd., and turn left on Highland Drive. The park's main entrance is located next to the fire station on Siskiyou Blvd. near the corner of Highland and Siskiyou. It's open 6:30 a.m.-10:30 p.m.

PRACTICALITIES

Bed and Breakfasts

A romantic bed and breakfast with a parklike ambience is the **Greenwood Tree,** 3045 Bellinger Ln., tel. (541) 776-0000, http://www.greenwoodtree.com, e-mail grwdtree@cdsnet.net, $95-125. The rooms and suites have private baths and are decorated with antiques, Persian rugs, and fabric art collections.

A lavish breakfast and afternoon tea served in the parlor, on the porch, or out in the garden, as well as chocolate truffles on your pillow at night, further enhance the atmosphere. Outside this hand-hewn and hand-pegged building dating back to the Civil War, you'll find a willow swing in a three-story barn, a hammock suspended between enormous 300-year-old oaks, and a gazebo beneath shady apple trees overlooking the rose garden.

Holly Street Suites, 304 Holly St., tel. (541) 779-4716, http://www.aaaabb.com, e-mail hollyhouse.dfisse@cyberforce.com, has three historic structures boasting antiques and Victorian woodwork. The five-room Waverly cottage is a turn-of-the-century showplace coupling red cedar and gold-leaf carvings with modern conveniences. One bedroom features a king-sized canopy bed, while the other has a double bed.

MEDFORD ACCOMMODATIONS

Cedar Lodge Motor Inn, 518 N. Riverside Ave., tel. (541) 773-7361 or (800) 282-3419, $35-50, pool, pets, nonsmoking rooms.

City Center Motel, 324 S. Central Ave., tel. (541) 773-6248, $45-60, pool.

Horizon Motor Inn, 1154 E. Barnett Rd., tel. (541) 779-5085 or (800) 452-2255, $75-150, wheelchair access, pool, lounge.

Motel 6, 950 Alba Dr., tel. (541) 773-4290, $35-45, pool.

Pine Tree Inn Motel, 525 S. Riverside Ave., tel. (541) 772-6133, $50-70, pool, nonsmoking rooms.

Pony Soldier Motor Inn, 2340 Crater Lake Hwy. (ORE 62), tel. (541) 779-2011, $70-90 wheelchair access, pets, pool.

Shilo Inn of Medford, 2111 Biddle Rd., tel. (541) 770-5151, $70-80, wheelchair access, pets.

Sierra Inn Motel, 345 S. Central Ave., tel. (541) 773-7727, $50-70, kitchenettes.

Doubletree, 200 N. Riverside Ave., tel. (541) 779-5811 or (800) 222-TREE, $80-125, everything.

Valli Hai Hotel, 1034 Court St., tel. (541) 772-6183, $35-45, cheap and funky.

Windmill Inn of Medford, 1950 Biddle Rd., tel. (541) 779-0050 or (800) 547-4747, $55-90, wheelchair access, pool.

LA BURRITA

If you are an aficionado of Mexican food, make sure that you plan for a lunch or dinner at La Burrita. The original La Burrita Restaurant is on ORE 238 between Jacksonville and Medford, and outlets of this popular establishment have recently opened up in Medford and Grants Pass. But as with many replicas, the copies never seem to be quite as good as the original, so visit the *genuine* La Burrita, 2715 Jacksonville Hwy.—same as ORE 238—tel. 770-5770, if possible.

Half of this restaurant is a store that carries authentic Mexican foodstuffs and beverages, and this is also where you order your meal. The chiles rellenos here are among the best in Oregon, and generous two-item combination plates with rice, beans, and chips go for around $5. The accompanying home-made salsa is hot enough for most people, but if you really want to do the Oregon version of the ""Mexican Hat Dance," ask for the extra-hot salsa: this legendary green mixture is pure ground jalapeños. The dining room is also a throwback to old Mexico, with Day-Glo felt paintings on the walls that are so bad they're good. Enjoy your food along with the toe-tapping gay-sad strains of a distant accordion, *gracias* to the Norteño music that is always playing in the background. This is where the migrant workers come to fortify themselves and socialize in between gigs in the fields and orchards. The place may be funky, but it's got great food at great prices, as well as being a bite-sized slice of southern Oregon life.

BOB RACE

The Holly House has two suites accessed by private entrances as well as kitchen and dining rooms with such refinements as an African mahogany wet bar and an antique wood cookstove, king- and queen-sized beds and room service breakfast. Rates range from $40-70; additional guests are $10 each. Reservations are advised; the Waverly Cottage has a two-day minimum-stay requirement on weekends and holidays.

Hidden away in the foothills of the Siskiyou Mountains, equidistant between Jacksonville and Medford, is the **Carpenter Hill Inn,** 846 Carpenter Hill Rd., Medford, tel. (541) 535-4147, $75-225. Built in 1909 by Edward Carlton, heir to Western Union, it was *the* rendezvous point for high society in southern Oregon. Notables included President Theodore Roosevelt, Clark Gable, and William Randolph Hearst.

In its present bed-and-breakfast incarnation, it is a retreat from the cares of the modern world. Sun yourself by the Olympic-size pool or enjoy the spa while observing the native wildlife including redwing hawk, deer, and pheasant. Visit the stables of the Egyptian show horses or pick exotic Japanese plums, pears, or apples in the orchard. Take a walk through the English gardens in the early evening and then partake of a wine and cheese tasting. For a rendition of the good life, reserve early, especially summer weekends (two-night minimum).

To get there, take ORE 99 south from Barnett Rd (I-5 exit 27) and go past Harry and David's. Go west onto South Stage Rd. toward Jacksonville. Turn left at the first street, Voorhies Rd., which will eventually turn into Carpenter Hill Road. Proceed west on Carpenter Hill Rd., turn right to 846, and follow the driveway up to the inn.

Food
The **Alpine Restaurant,** 1011 Spring St., tel. (541) 772-2481, offers cuisine that reflects the traditions of old Germany. Open for breakfast, lunch, and dinner. The German apple pancake is a popular way to start the day; for dinner try some sauerbraten served with red cabbage and spaetzle (homemade German noodles). Dinners are accompanied by soup, salad, and fresh-baked bread.

A family restaurant where you can find some elegance on a budget is **Apple Annie's,** 1021 S. Riverside, tel. (541) 776-0711; and 900 Alba Dr., tel. (541) 779-4472. Many specialty items are featured on the menu here, as well as some of the more traditional favorites. Breakfast specials like the French-toast combo (two pieces of French toast, two breakfast meats, and one egg) and the deluxe pancake sandwich (two eggs, two meats, and two pancakes) go for $4. Dinner specials range $6-12.

Deli Down, 406 E. Main St. #6, tel. (541) 772-4520, makes its own pasta every day. Specialties include pasta salads, meat pastries, overstuffed sandwiches, all-you-can-eat pasta bar, and homemade cheesecake. You'll find the restaurant in the Main St. Market. "Dagwood-style" sandwiches can also be found at **Zach's Deli,** 1310 F Center Dr., tel. (541) 779-8272.

If your taste buds are set for border food, **Mexicali Rose,** corner of 4th and Fir, 17 W. 4th St., tel. (541) 779-4289, can satisfy your cravings. Large dinners replete with rice and beans (be sure to ask for the special black beans) range $7-10. The Super Nachos is a perfect complement to the list of Latin American import beers or giant margaritas you find on the menu.

A great place for families is **Home Town Buffet,** 1299 Center Dr., tel. (541) 770-6779. You'll find large spreads of fruits and veggies, salads, hot entrees, and fresh baked muffins and desserts at a price you can afford. Breakfast is $5.69, lunch $5.19, and dinner runs $6.99. Discounts for children 2-10 are 45 cents per year of age for lunch and 50 cents per year of age for dinner. The restaurant started out here in Medford, and now has reached national prominence with over 50 outlets. Open Mon.-Sat. 11 a.m.-9 p.m. for lunch and dinner, and 11 a.m.-9 p.m. Sunday for breakfast and dinner.

A good spot for breakfast or lunch downtown is **C.K. Tiffin's,** 226 E. Main, tel. (541) 779-0480. Their health conscious menu, $3-6, includes several vegetarian items like garden-burgers, tostadas, burritos, and chili. Soups, salads, sandwiches, and some specialty items are also featured at very reasonable prices. Open Mon.-Fri. 7:30 a.m.-3:30 p.m.

For a break from the ordinary, head to **Samovar Restaurant and Bakery,** 101 E. Main, tel. (541) 779-4967, for some traditional Russian and Middle Eastern cuisine. The samovar, a Russian teapot, is the symbol of hospitality and friendship, and this establishment provides a fitting bridge between our two cultures. The owners, Gogi and Jennia, came to Oregon from Russia. Gogi's pastries are from secret family recipes passed down from generation to generation. Jennia, a medical doctor, uses her expertise to prepare healthy and nutritionally balanced foods. They both place a premium on natural ingredients, and the proof is in the tasting. Blinichiki (Russian-style blintzes), golubtei (stuffed cabbage), and piroshki (small meat or cheese pies) are just a few of the delectables on the menu here. Open for breakfast and lunch Mon.-Sat. 7:30 a.m.-3 p.m., dinner, $7-14, Tues.-Sat. 5-9 p.m.

The Wild Plum, 1528 Biddle Rd., tel. (541) 772-5200, features fresh salads, soups, and sandwiches as well as light and full dinners. You may go "plum crazy" trying to decide which one of their 33 flavors of pie to enjoy. A favorite with loggers and truckers, **Withams,** 2339 Biddle Rd., tel. (541) 772-9307, has inexpensive daily lunch and dinner specials that include soup or salad. The food's pretty good, and the price is right, even though you might think you're on the set for *Convoy.*

Shopping

You can find many brand-name items at 20-70% off retail price at the **Pear Tree Factory Stores,** I-5 exit 24, 205 Fern Valley Rd; information tel. (541) 535-1194. Twenty different companies offer a wide range of goods from clothing, accessories, and sportswear to books and housewares. There's also a huge diner that serves pretty good food.

On Thursday 8:30 a.m.-1:30 p.m. during April-Nov. at the Medford Center, corner of Jackson St. and Biddle Rd. next to Sears, is the **Rogue Valley Growers and Crafters Market,** for information write P.O. Box 4041, Medford 97501, tel. (541) 855-1326. This open-air market features fresh produce (much of it organic), plants, fresh-cut and dried flowers, baked goods and specialty foods, and locally handcrafted items.

You can find the wares of over 400 artists and craftspeople at the **Crafters Market,** 1233 Court St., tel. (541) 779-4667, a kind of outlet store/clearinghouse for artisans. Country and

Americana motif crafts, dried and silk flowers, quilts, jewelry, furniture, woodwork, stained glass, clothing, ceramics, and many one-of-a-kind originals are all for sale at artist-direct prices. Open weekdays 10 a.m.-6 p.m., Saturday 10 a.m.-5 p.m., and Sunday noon-5 p.m.

Events

The **Jackson County Fair** is held at the county fairgrounds just north of town the third weekend of July. Admission is $6 for adults, $2 for children, and parking is an additional $2. Frequent shuttle-bus departures provided by **Rogue Valley Transportation,** 3200 Crater Lake Ave., Medford, tel. (541) 799-2988, relieve you of fighting the crowds for limited parking spaces. The buses leave from downtown Medford, Poplar Square, Crater High School, and other points around town. The trip back from the fair is free, and the shuttles run approximately every 15 minutes.

Cowboys, ranchers, and farmers all come in with their families for fun and top-name entertainment. Country music seems to dominate the stage, with performers like Ricky Skaggs, Waylon Jennings, and Charley Pride drawling out their tunes. If the kids are going to spend the day at the midway, consider purchasing their ride tickets in advance and saving 50% off the regular "one price for all rides" (except Saturday). Check with the Southern Oregon Visitors Association (see "Information and Services," below) for presale ticket outlets.

Free rides on a 40-foot sternwheeler are offered on the south pond. Professional fishing guides will teach kids tricks of the trade at Huck Finn's Fishing Pier, also located on the pond. And in addition to the normal selection of jams, fruits, and vegetables, fly-tying and contemporary collections (like baseball cards) are other judged categories that are worth a closer look.

Tiny countercultural Ruch, Oregon, 20 minutes northwest of Medford on ORE 238, has hosted a barter fair for the last two decades despite the county government's view that it's an unsavory hippie powwow. The reality is that 15,000 people get together the second weekend of October in a peaceful harvest festival of food and crafts. While the event can give the superficial appearance of flower power preserved in amber, fair-goers can expect a fully clothed, drug-free gathering.

The **Pear Blossom Festival** takes place the second weekend of April with arts and crafts exhibits, a parade, and a 10K run. The real attraction is the panorama of the orchards in bloom against a backdrop of snow-capped Mt. McLoughlin.

Getting There and Getting Around

The **Greyhound,** 212 Barnett Rd., tel. (541) 779-2103, has a half dozen buses dock daily. **Rogue Valley Transportation,** 3200 Crater Lake Ave., tel. (541) 799-2988, provides connections to Jacksonville, Phoenix, White City, Talent, and Ashland. Most buses depart Medford at 6th and Barnett, Mon.-Fri. 8 a.m.-5 p.m., Saturday 9 a.m.-5 p.m., no service Sundays. Linkages to Eagle Point and White City are courtesy of **Cascade Bus Lines,** but call (541) 664-4801 for the schedule, as it fluctuates. **Courtesy Yellow Cab,** tel. (541) 772-6288, has 24-hour service in the Medford area. A wheelchair van, senior-citizen discounts, and special rates on airport transfers are all available on request. Call the **Green Tortoise,** tel. (800) 867-8647, to set up a "flag stop" at the Pilot Station at exit 33 off I-5. The northbound coach departs Monday and Friday at 6 a.m., the southbound at 11 p.m. on Thursday.

Medford/Jackson County Airport, administrative office tel. (800) 882-7488, is the air hub for southern Oregon and is served by United, Horizon, and other carriers. Three rental-car agencies are at the airport: **Budget,** tel. (541) 773-0488, **Avis,** tel. (541) 773-3003 or (800) 831-2847, and **Hertz,** tel. (541) 773-4293 or (800) 654-3131. The local Ford and Toyota dealerships also have rental programs: **Crater Lake Ford, 2611 Biddle Rd., tel. (541) 770-3600, and** Toyota Rent-a-car, 326 N. Bartlett, tel. (541) 770-7164.

Information and Services

The **Southern Oregon Visitors Association,** 304 S. Central Ave., tel. (541) 779-4691 or (800) 469-6307, and the **Log Cabin Information Center,** 88 Stewart Rd., tel. (541) 776-4021. tel. (800) 469-6307, have all kinds of useful maps, directories, and information for the asking. If you are driving north on I-5, you'll see the Log Cabin Visitor Center accessible by the Barnett Rd. exit. Both offices are open Mon.-Fri. 9 a.m.-

5 p.m. Additional information on recreational sites and parks in the Medford area can be acquired from the **Bureau of Land Management** office, 3040 Biddle Rd., tel. (541) 770-2200. The **Medford Library**, 413 W. Main, tel. (541) 776-7287, has one of the best collections of books, magazines, and periodicals in southern Oregon.

The **post office**, 333 W. 8th, Medford 97501, tel. (541) 776-3604, is open Mon.-Fri. 8:30 a.m.-5 p.m. and can help with passport information in addition to selling stamps and envelopes. **Providence Hospital**, 1111 Crater Lake Ave., tel. (541) 773-6611, has 24-hour emergency care. This is where the flying angels of Air Medivac speedily bring in people from remote areas for immediate treatment. From basic home health services to intensive care, the staff of **Rogue Valley Medical Center**, 2825 Barnett Rd., tel.

(541) 773-6281, is ready around the clock to help you when you need help. **Medford Physicians and Surgeons Clinic**, 1025 E. Main St., tel. (541) 773-6271, offers 24-hour pediatrics, surgery, and cardiology care as well as specialists for a host of other ailments.

The **police**, tel. (541) 770-4783, or 911 for emergencies only, and state police, 2700 N. Pacific Hwy., tel. (541) 776-6111, or 911 for emergencies only, can help out in case there's trouble.

Out of a half dozen coin-operated laundries in Medford, **B.J.'s Homestyle Laundromat**, 1712 W. Main, tel. (541) 773-4803, is the most pleasant establishment. With games, television, and a snack bar, it's almost like doing your laundry at home. Open seven days a week 8 a.m.-9 p.m., an attendant is always on duty, and dry-cleaning and drop-off washing services are available.

JACKSONVILLE

Oregon's pioneer past is tastefully preserved in Jacksonville. Located five miles west of Medford and cradled in the foothills of the Siskiyou Mountains, this small town of 2,100 residents retains an atmosphere of tranquil isolation. With about 90 original wooden and brick buildings dating back to the 1850s, it was the first designated National Historic Landmark District in Oregon and the third of eight such sites in the nation.

In early 1852, two itinerant prospectors, Cluggage and Poole, were returning to a northern California mining camp with supplies from the Willamette Valley. They camped by a creek in the area for a night's rest. The next morning, they found a good-sized gold nugget in a hoofprint made by one of their pack animals in what became known as Rich Gulch. They continued to California with their goods for the other miners, but in the excitement of their discovery, the secret slipped out. They hurriedly backtracked their way to southern Oregon and staked their claims along Rich Gulch and Daisy Creek. Within a matter of weeks, the mining camp population grew from two to 2,000. Tents, wooden shacks, and log cabins were hastily erected, and the town of Table Rock City was born. The name was changed to Jacksonville the following

year, in honor of President Andrew Jackson and the town's namesake county.

The town grid was surveyed in September 1852 into 200-foot-square blocks. California and Oregon Streets were then, as now, the hubs of business and social life in Jacksonville. But the city's tightly packed wooden structures proved to be especially prone to fire. Between 1873 and 1884, three major fires reduced most of the original buildings to ashes. These harsh experiences prompted merchants to use brick in the construction of a second generation of buildings, and the practice was furthered by an 1878 city ordinance requiring same. Most of the building blocks were made and fired locally. To prevent them from returning to the earth during the damp seasons, the porous bricks were painted to protect them from the elements; cast-iron window shutters and door frames further reinforced the structures.

Boomtown Jacksonville was the first and largest town in the region and was selected as the county seat. It was even nominated and briefly considered as the state capital. The prominence of Jacksonville was made manifest with the 1883 erection of a 60-foot-high courthouse with 14-inch-thick walls. But like the gold finds that quickly played out, Jacksonville's exuberance began to subside when the Oregon and California Railroad bypassed the town in the early 1880s in favor of the nearby hopeful hamlet of Medford. Businesses were quick to move east to greet the coming of the iron horse, and Jacksonville's stature as a trading center diminished. When the county seat was finally moved to Medford in 1927, Jacksonville's heady days had long since vanished.

During the Depression, families with low incomes took up residence in the town's unmaintained buildings, taking advantage of the cheap rents. Amateur gold mining enjoyed a brief comeback, with residents digging shafts and tunnels in backyards, but it was not enough to revive the derailed economy. However, the following decades saw a gradual resurgence of interest in Jacksonville's gold-rush heritage. The Southern Oregon Historical Society was created after World War II, and individuals began to take interest in the many unaltered late-1880s buildings and restore them to their former glory. The **Beekman Bank** was one of the first structures to be spruced up, and the prominent **United States Hotel** was rehabilitated in 1964. The restoration movement was rewarded when the National Park Service designated Jacksonville as a National Historic Landmark in 1966.

Today, Jacksonville paints a memorable picture of a western town with its historic buildings, excellent museum, and a beautiful pioneer cemetery. In addition, a renowned music festival, colorful pageants, and a rich local folklore all pay tribute to Jacksonville's golden age.

Jackson County Museum

A good place to start your explorations is at the museum, 206 N. 5th St., tel. (541) 773-6536. This imposing two-story brick-and-stone Italianate building was completed in 1883 and served as the county administration building until 1927, when the county seat was moved to Medford. For more than two decades, the structure didn't have any permanent tenants but then became the Jackson County Museum and headquarters of the Southern Oregon Historical Society in 1950.

Nowadays, in addition to pioneer artifacts, a mock-up of Peter Britt's photo studio, and interesting old pictures, the museum also has a good walking-tour map of the other historical sites in the city. Admission is $2. The stucco building next door to the courthouse used to be the county jail, but today it serves as the children's museum. Kids of all ages will enjoy the hands-on experience of seeing old-fashioned toys close up. A small bookstore is located here as well, specializing in local and regional historical publications.

Historic C.C. Beekman House Living History Program

At the Beekman House, corner of California and Laurelwood Streets, tel. (541) 773-6536, costumed interpreters will help introduce you to the friends and family of pioneer banker Cornelius Beekman. The 20 minute guided tours, $3 adults, $2 children ages five and under, charmingly set the time machine in motion.

Mansion By Mail

The **Jeremiah Nunan House,** 635 N. Oregon St., tel. (541) 899-1890, also known as the Catalogue House because it was ordered from Knoxville, Tennessee by a wealthy merchant, is one old Victorian that even house-tour weary guidebook writers would recommend. Located just east of town, this 1892 three-story mansion features immense bird's-eye maple doors, 23 stained glass windows, and a kitchen restored to look as it did when it originally was built. The fir floors and paneling of oak, cherry, fir, pine, and walnut further enhance the impression of turn-of-the-century elegance. While there's plenty of antique furniture in the house, only the wrought-iron chairs and a table on the gazebo-style porch can be traced back to the Nunans. Guided tours point out nuances of the decor while sharing interesting tidbits about 19th-century life. Particularly intriguing are rumors and legends of the Nunan family, whose lives were plagued by infant mortality and suicide. The $7,792 house, complete with its wallpaper and carpets, was shipped in 14 box cars and assembled in six months. You can see it Memorial Day through Labor Day, though hours and days are in flux. Call to confirm. Thirty-minute tours run 10:30 a.m.-5 p.m., on the hour and half hour, admission $5, discounts for children and seniors. Also visit the Christmas Store in the mansion's carriage house.

Peter Britt Gardens

Peter Britt came to Jacksonville not long after gold was first discovered in Rich Gulch in 1851. After briefly trying his hand at prospecting, he redirected his efforts toward painting and photography. The latter turned out to be his specialty, and for nearly 50 years he photographed the places, people, and events of southern Oregon (Britt was the first person to photograph Crater Lake). He also incorporated new techniques and equipment in his studio as photographic advances were developed. You'll find his ambrotypes, daguerreotypes, stereographs, and tintypes on display at the Jackson County Museum.

The Swiss-born Peter Britt was also an accomplished horticulturalist and among the first vintners in southern Oregon. In addition to experimenting with several varieties of fruit and nut trees to see which grew best in the Rogue River Valley, he kept the first weather data records of the region. Another testimonial to his love of plants is the giant redwood tree you see on the western edge of the Britt Gardens, S. 1st and W. Pine Streets, which he planted 130 years ago to commemorate the birth of his first child, Emil.

His house was a beautifully detailed Gothic revival home that was built in 1860 and then enlarged in the 1880s. Unfortunately, it was destroyed by fires in 1957 and 1960 and can now be remembered only through photographs. The stone-and-mortar wall visible today marks the site of the original foundation. Some of the remaining plantings are part of the original gardens, and many others were lovingly put in place in 1976 by Robert Lovinger, a landscape architecture professor from the University of Oregon. The Peter Britt Music Festival was held on the grounds of the estate from 1962 until 1978, when the new Britt Pavilion was built just south.

A short half-mile hike begins 15 yards uphill from the Emil Britt redwood tree. A fairly level path follows the abandoned irrigation ditch that used to divert water from Jackson Creek to the Britt property. Soon you will notice Jackson Creek below the trail, as well as several overgrown sections of a nearly forgotten logging railroad bed. This is a particularly nice walk in the spring when the wildflowers are in bloom and the mosses and ferns are green.

BRITT
FESTIVALS
Jacksonville, Oregon

Peter Britt Music Festival

On a grassy hillside amid majestic ponderosa pines near the Britt homesite, a small classical music festival began in 1962. Over 30 years later, the scope of the **Britt Festival,** offices at 614 Medford Center, Medford 97504, tel. (541) 773-6077 or (800) 88-BRITT, http://www.mind.net/britt, has developed into a musical smorgasbord encompassing such diverse styles as jazz/folk/country/bluegrass/and dance, in addition to the original classical repertoire. Mel Tormé, B.B. King, Bobby McFerrin, Jean-Pierre Rampal, and Joshua Redman, are just a few of the big-name artists who have performed here over the years.

The festival runs from the last week of June through the first week of September (the bulk of the performances fall in August), with a series of nearly 40 concerts. Tickets range from $15-25 for general admission. Concert-goers often bring along blankets, small lawn chairs (allowed only in designated areas), wine, and a picnic supper to enjoy along with entertainment on balmy summer evenings.

Reserved seating was added in 1987, a move many thought would destroy the intimate ambience. However, these seats are built somewhat down into the ground, so the patrons on blankets and lawn chairs behind them are still able to see the action, while those with bad backs and tired bones are able to enjoy the show, too. The reserved seats run $3-5 more than general admission. A large area in front of the seats is for those who like to sit on the grass or on blankets.

Wherever you decide you might like to sit, be sure to order your tickets well in advance to avoid having to stand outside. Like the Oregon Shakespeare Festival, the shows sell out months in advance, especially for the well-known performers.

Tours and Tastings

During the summer, **Trolley Tours,** tel. (541) 535-5617, offers 50-minute narrated tours every hour on the hour 10 a.m.-4 p.m. A motorized trolley car picks up passengers at the corner of 3rd and California Streets for an informative and entertaining excursion into Jacksonville's pioneer past. Adult fares are $5, children under 12 are $2.50 **Jacksonville Carriage Service,** tel. (541) 664-8636, offers five different horse-drawn tours to choose from that depart from the historic Orth Building, 105 S. Oregon. If you'd rather go on your own, many local businesses sell a two-hour walking/driving tour cassette created by Ruth Goldschmidt that details approximately 90 historical buildings and sites.

For a taste of some of the Pacific Northwest's best, head for the **Gary West Tasting Room,** 690 N. 5th, tel. (541) 899-1829. Here you can sample fine food and wine for free. After the tastings, you'll have a better idea of what to choose from in their store. Oregon wines, hickory-smoked meats and jerky, and cheeses are some of the goodies you'll want to take home with you. The Tasting Room packs special Britt Festival picnic baskets, too. You may also sample wine at the **Village Wine and Art Gallery,** 130 W. California St., tel. (541) 899-1001.

About eight miles southwest of Jacksonville in the Applegate Valley is **Valley View Winery,** 1000 Upper Applegate Rd., tel. (541) 899-8468. While the microclimate and the soil types allow for a great diversity of grape varieties, Valley View concentrates mainly on cabernet sauvignon, merlot, and chardonnay. They must be doing something right, because their Barrel Select bottlings have graced the last three U.S.

Presidents' tables, and their award-winning wines are found in many restaurants and wine shops throughout Oregon. Call ahead to confirm open times, which change with the season.

Pioneer Days

The Wild West returns to life in mid-June in Jacksonville with the town's annual Pioneer Days. A parade in old-time regalia down the main streets of Jacksonville kicks off the party. Following the parade, a street fair featuring arts, crafts, and food booths is held along California St. for the rest of the day. A street dance follows in the afternoon with live music, as well as an old-time fiddlers' performance. Children's games and activities are also scheduled for the afternoon. One of the most popular is the haystack search, in which tots grub around in the straw for over $200 in hidden currency. Later in the day another fun annual event called the Ugly Legs Contest takes place. Contestants wear paper sacks over their heads so they are judged solely on how bad their legs look. Mud, sandals, worn-out sneakers, and other cosmetic/artistic touches are allowed. Other special events are also planned for seniors, and bingo games are held all day long. Call the chamber of commerce, tel. (541) 889-8118, for details.

Farmer's Market

The **Jacksonville Farmer's Market,** 4th and California Streets, takes place 9 a.m.-2 p.m. on Saturday from May-October. Look for local peaches and nectarines in the summer, apples and pears in the fall.

PRACTICALITIES

Bed And Breakfasts

The **Jacksonville Inn,** 175 E. California St., tel. (541) 899-1900 or (800) 321-9344, http://www.mind.net/jvinn; e-mail jvinn@mind.net, $80-235, lies in the heart of the commercial historic district. In addition to eight air-conditioned rooms furnished with restored antiques and private baths (breakfast included), the inn has an excellent dining room with gourmet fare and an extensive wine list with well over 700 selections. The Inn also offers three deluxe cottages replete with antiques, fireplace, king canopied beds, fruit and champagne, $200-235, breakfast included. Reservations are highly recommended, especially during the summer. Access to mountain bikes to explore the area also comes with the room. A block down California St. is the **McCully House Inn,** 240 E. California St., tel. (541) 899-1942, http://www.wave.net/upg/ mccully, $105. Built in 1861 in the classical revival style, this mansion has four beautifully decorated bedrooms with private baths. European and American antiques, Oriental rugs, delicate lace curtains, and a magnificent square grand piano (tuned a half step lower than today's A-440) add to the historical ambience. A full "country continental" breakfast is included with the price of your room. Local and international flavors are blended together with fresh ingredients for lunch and dinner (also available to nonguests). For a taste of the surrounding countryside, try the organic vegetables with wild mushrooms and wilted greens followed by a fruit "taco" for dessert. For the full gourmet treatment, go with such dishes as baked eggplant roll with three cheeses and basil marinara or flambeed jumbo scallops with brown rice and brandied peaches. Enjoy your meal in the dining room, on the patio, or outdoors in the garden. A full service bar and coffee drinks round out your dinning pleasure. Call ahead for dinner reservations.

The **Touvelle House,** 455 N. Oregon St., tel. (541) 899-8938 or (800) 846-8422, http://www.wave.net/upg/touvelle, e-mail touvelle@wave.net, offers five rooms and one suite (all with private baths) for $75-135. Each room has its own theme and feature touches like antiques, handmade quilts, and tasteful interior decorations. Out back by the carriage house is their heated swimming pool and spa. Common areas include a library and a large living room. A full three course breakfast is included, and other goodies like fruit and cookies are available for snacking anytime.

The **Orth House,** 105 W. Main St., tel. (541) 899-8665 or (800) 770-7301, http://www.medford.net/orthbnb, e-mail orthbnb@medford.net, $85-135, was built in 1880 and is listed in the U.S. National Register of Historic Homes. Large rooms with clawfoot tubs and period furnishings help to recall a bygone era with the benefit of modern air conditioning. Full country breakfast and afternoon tea and treats are included.

A half mile out of old-town Jacksonville is the **Stage Lodge,** 830 N. 5th St., tel. (541) 899-3953 or (800) 253-8254, $70-135. The modern rooms here are large, clean, and comfortable, with a country feeling. One of the best reasons to book this reasonably priced, charmingly rustic lodging in August is the fact that it's within walking distance of the Britt Festival.

Food

The Jacksonville Inn, 175 E. California St., tel. (541) 899-1900 or (800) 321-9344, has consistently been rated one of the top restaurants in Oregon by the food press. Distinctive cuisine, served à la carte or table d' hôte, is prepared by master chefs for your enjoyment. While the gold-rich mortar sparkles in the walls of the dining room and lounge, the menu is what offers some real treasures. Steaks, seafood, and specialties of the inn like veal, duck, and prime rib are among the offerings in a Victorian atmosphere of red brick and velvet. A selection of vegetarian dishes is also available. A connoisseur's wine cellar of over 700 vintages further enhances your gourmet meal. Open every day for lunch and dinner; reservations are suggested. A seven-course dinner (fixed price $20) featuring stuffed hazelnut chicken is frequently touted as a gourmet's dream meal.

The **Bella Union Restaurant and Saloon,** 170 W. California St., tel. (541) 899-1770, is another popular spot in town. Soups, salads, chicken, steaks, pasta, and pizza are some of the items, $6-14, you'll find on the menu here. Vegetarians have many choices to choose from. When the weather is right, the patio in back of the restaurant is a pleasant place to eat lunch or enjoy a beer. Picnic baskets, take out sandwiches, and salads are also available, a good choice if going to a Britt concert. Be sure to call in your order by 2 p.m.

Mexican food in downtown Jacksonville can be found at **La Fiesta,** 150 S. Oregon St., tel. (541) 899-4450. Located in the Orth building, built in 1872, this place is noted for its large portions of gourmet south-of-the-border fare. Open for lunch, $5-7, and dinner, $7-12, several vegetarian selections can be also found on the menu here.

Lighter fare can be procured from the **Good Bean Company,** 165 S. Oregon St., tel. (541) 899-8740. Snack items from the display case help enhance a cup of Jacksonville's best java. Another local coffeehouse is the **Gold Rush Cafe,** 157 W. California St., tel. (541) 899-9127. Breakfast here features omelettes, quiche, stuffed croissants, and pancakes. Lighter soups, salads, and sandwiches are available the rest of the day. Scones, biscotti, croissants, and cookies supplement your caffeine fix with a good sugar rush. Try the lemon bar (tart yet sweet) with an "Ice Cap," an espresso with cold, frothed milk over ice. **Pony Espresso,** 545 N. 5th St., tel. (541) 899-3757, also features a full service espresso bar as well as sandwiches, pizza, quiche, and other light lunch items, $4-7. The nachos, $5, here come with the works, and when combined with one of their caffeineated concoctions, are perfect for an afternoon pick me up.

Information and Services

The Jacksonville **library,** 170 S. Oregon St., tel. (541) 899-1665, is open Mon.-Tues. noon-6 p.m., Wed.-Thurs. 11 a.m.-5 p.m., Friday 10 a.m.-4 p.m. The **Jacksonville Chamber of Commerce,** P.O. Box 33, 185 N. Oregon St., Jacksonville 97530, tel. (541) 899-8118, http://www.wave.net.upg/jvillechamber/, e-mail jvillechamber@wave.net, is open 10 a.m.-4 p.m. daily and has the scoop on events and activities. The Jacksonville **post office,** 175 N. Oregon St., Jacksonville 97530, tel. (541) 899-1563, is open 8:30 a.m.-5 p.m. weekdays. Public transportation connecting Jacksonville with Medford is available on the 30A and 30B buses. Call 799-BUSS for scheduling information. Public restrooms can be found on 3rd Street between California and C Streets.

GRANTS PASS AND VICINITY

The banner across the main thoroughfare in town proudly proclaims: It's the Climate. But while the 30-inches-a-year precipitation average and 52° yearly mean temperature might seem desirable, the true allure of Grants Pass is the mighty Rogue River, which flows through the heart of this community. More than 25 outfitters in Grants Pass and the surrounding villages of Rogue River and Merlin specialize in fishing, float, and jetboat trips. Numerous riverside lodges, accessible by car, river, or footpath, yield remote relaxation in the shadow of the nearby Klamath-Siskiyou Wilderness.

It was the climate that attracted back-to-the-land refugees of the '60s to nearby Takilma, a planned utopian community. More recently, survivalists, in expectation of nuclear Armageddon, have established a network of shelters in the area. They believe that forests filled with game and foraging opportunities coupled with prevailing winds that will keep radioactive fallout away improve their odds . . . good luck!

The climate is also responsible for the once-thick forests in the surrounding mountains, timber source for the numerous mills which in turn provided many jobs. However, decades of overcutting by the lumber companies has dramatically diminished the supply of sawtimber, resulting in mill shutdowns and high unemployment rates. In response, the economic base has been gradually shifting away from wood products and now keys on the natural beauty of the area, the recreational opportunities, and of course, the benign weather.

SIGHTS

Palmerton Arboretum

Six miles down ORE 99 in the town of Rogue River is the Palmerton Arboretum. Originally a five-acre nursery, the park features plant representatives from around the globe, including Japanese pines and Mediterranean cedars in addition to redwoods and other trees native to the Northwest. A real treat in the spring, the ornamental arboretum offers over 40 species of mature trees complemented by several kinds of azaleas and rhododendrons. Admission is free. While you're there, be sure to see **Skevington's Crossing,** a 200-foot-high swinging suspension bridge over Evans Creek that connects the arboretum to Anna Classick city park.

MeadowView Country Gardens

A mile and a half from town, seven acres of civilized beauty is found at **MeadowView Gardens,** 2315 Upper River Rd. Loop, tel. (541)

GRANTS PASS

TO ROSEBURG

HILLCREST DR.

SOUTHERN OREGON HOSPITAL

MIDLAND AVE.

WASHINGTON BLVD.

9th ST.

JOSEPHINE GENERAL HOSPITAL

A ST.

DIMMICK ST.

E ST.

F ST.

SWIMMING POOL

EAST E ST.

EAST F ST.

4th ST.

6th ST.

7th ST.

9th ST.

M ST.

MILL ST.

ROGUE RIVER

BOAT LANDING

RIVERSIDE PARK

BAKER PARK

PARK ST.

JOSEPHINE COUNTY FAIRGROUNDS

E. PARK ST.

ROGUE RIVER HWY.

TO JACKSONVILLE

TO OREGON CAVES

TO MEDFORD

TO ROGUE RIVER

0   0.5mi

0   0.5km

© MOON PUBLICATIONS, INC.

471-8841. Here you get the opportunity to see a variety of colorful flower and herb gardens and a working organic vegetable farm. You can buy "just picked" certified organic produce and learn about the bio intensive techniques used to grow the vegetables without the use of all those nasty chemicals. Many Oregon chefs claim that organic produce tastes better than the commercial stuff, and you can test that assertion for yourself at the MeadowView tea garden. Even if you forgo lunch, be sure to at least sample their sumptuous lemon tart with afternoon tea. To get there, head west on G Street and look for the rose sign.

The Caveman

It's hard to miss the 18-foot-high statue of the Caveman near the north Grants Pass exit 58 off of I-5. Sporting a simulated mammoth-skin, a dinosaur bone club, and looking like he just strode in off the set of the *Flintstones,* he's been the offical greeter of Grants Pass since 1972. Spawned by a seminotorious local civic group called the Oregon Cavemen who also parade around in skins, drink sabertooth tiger "blood," and eat raw meat during their secret initlation rites, the Caveman cost $18,000 to build. While many locals have lambasted the city's mascot as portraying a backward, redneck image for

Grant's Pass, it's worth noting that over a dozen businesses and the local high school have proudly embraced the Caveman appellation.

Wildlife Images Rehabilitation and Education Center
Originally a rehab station for injured birds of prey, Wildlife Images, 11845 Lower River Rd., tel. (541) 476-0222, has expanded into an outreach program to aid all kinds of injured or orphaned wildlife as well as to educate the public. Bears, cougars, raccoons, and many other indigenous creatures have been helped by this organization. Once the animals are well enough to survive in the wild, they are released. Guided tours (by reservation only at 11 a.m. and 1 p.m. daily) allow groups to view the wildlife currently at the facility. Admission is free, but this nonprofit organization relies upon donations to continue its important work. To get there from 6th St. downtown, head south, turn right onto G St., continue to Upper River Rd., and then onto Lower River Road.

Oregon Vortex
About 10 miles south of Grants Pass on I-5 is the House of Mystery at the Oregon Vortex, 4303 Sardine Creek Rd., Gold Hill 97525, tel. (541) 855-1543. Called the "Forbidden Ground" by the Rogue Indians because the place spooked their horses, it is actually a repelling magnetic field where objects tend to move away from their center of alignment and lean in funny directions. For example, a ball at the end of a string does not hang straight up and down, and people seem taller when viewed from one side of the field as opposed to the other. Visitors may bring balls, levels, cameras, or any other instrument they wish to test the vortex for themselves. Guided tours through the house built on this curious site are about $6 for adults, $4.50 for children ages 5-11. Open March 1-Oct. 14, 9 a.m.-4:45 p.m., except on Sunday and sometimes Thursday.

Wolf Creek Tavern
Approximately 20 miles north of Grants Pass on I-5 in Wolf Creek is Oregon's oldest hostelry, the Wolf Creek Tavern, tel. (541) 866-2474. Originally a hotel for the California and Oregon Stagecoach Line, this historic property is now owned by the state and operated as a restaurant

and hotel. Legend has it that President Rutherford B. Hayes visited the tavern in the late 1880s and One-Eyed Charlie (see the special topic "The Legends of One-eyed Charlie and Black Bart") used to chew the fat in the dining room. You can also view the small room where author Jack London stayed and wrote part of his famous novel, *The End of the Story*. The staff wears early-19th-century clothing in keeping with the ambience of this famous roadhouse.

Some of the food in the restaurant is a little more modern, with such fare as hamburgers, hot dogs, and grilled-cheese sandwiches on the menu, mainly to keep the kids happy. However, other entrees are typical of those you might have found a hundred years ago when taking a road trip through southern Oregon, and they are quite good. And should the lure of tradition pall, fans of haute cuisine can enjoy such dishes as prime rib or filet of sole wrapped around curried bay shrimp. Lunch, $3-8, dinner, $6-12, and Sunday brunch are served; the restaurant is open seven days a week. Afterward, you might want to relax in the "ladies' parlour" or "gentlemen's tap room" or stroll amid the apple trees and roses on the lawn outside. Wolf Creek's boardinghouse had its heyday when it was a halfway house on the Portland-Sacramento stagecoach route, but it continues to serve roadweary travelers with rooms that range from $55 to $90 (room tax and continental breakfast included with room). The period furniture imparts atmosphere, while the beds and private baths here are modern enough to be comfortable.

Travelers might also find it useful to know that the Wolf Creek General Store (I-5 exit 76) is also open 24 hours. The Green Tortoise, tel. (800) 867-8647, stops there going northbound Monday and Friday at 6:45 a.m., and southbound Sunday and Thursday at 11:00 a.m. Be sure to call in advance to set up a "flag stop."

Three miles east of Wolf Creek is the 1890s-era ghost town of Golden. You'll note two churches (no saloon) in a town built upon dreams spawned by a nearby strike that ultimately yielded 1.5 million dollars.**2

Big Pine
About an hour outside of Grants Pass is the tallest ponderosa pine in the world. Standing a whopping 246 feet high and sporting a 57-inch diameter,

THERE'S GOLD IN THEM THAR HILLS

Geologists estimate that the prospectors of the 1850s and commercial mining operations that followed found only 25% of Oregon's potential take. With the wild gyrations of the timber-dependent economy, and gold fetching several hundred dollars a troy ounce, it's no wonder that many out-of-work loggers and other people have taken to gold panning in the waterways of southern Oregon.

Almost all streams in Coos, Curry, Douglas, and Jackson counties are good sources of color. "Color" refers to the flecks and bright chips of metal sometimes called gold dust; larger odd-shaped lumps of gold are nuggets. The gold originally comes from veins in the mountains, where it is washed out by winter weather. Spring floods and heavy rains carry the gold downstream. The density of gold causes it to settle in obstructions (like moss), in quiet water behind boulders, or at the base of waterfalls. These deposits of gold can vary from fine gold flecks to a bonanza of nuggets.

But before you head for the hills, you will need some basic equipment. Specially designed gold pans with flaring sides three to four inches deep are available at many hardware stores. Widths range from six inches to two feet; pick one that is comfortable for you to handle. Keep in mind that a pan full of water and gravel can get pretty heavy! Your pan must also be "blued" before panning, otherwise the layer of oil on it will stick to the gold and cause the stuff to float out with the other lighter materials. Heat the pan on your stove until it is a deep blue color and the oils are burned off. Other useful tools include tweezers, a small vial or two, a trowel, and a small shovel or pick.

Panning takes finesse, but with practice it quickly becomes easier. Put some dirt from a likely location in your pan with some water. Pick out the larger pieces of rock and gravel or squeeze out the moss and discard. Swirl the pan gently around from side to side. This causes the gold to sink to the bottom, making it possible to scoop out more gravel from the top. Tilt the pan at a slight angle, and the gold will now fall to the bottom of the lower edge. Remember that gold is 19 times heavier than water and also heavier than most other minerals contained in the gravel of streams. Continue to dip, shake, and remove sand until you have only a small amount left. This is the stage where you have to be extra cautious not to wash away your gold. When you have taken out as much sand as possible, you will have (if you hit pay dirt) small strands of black sand and gold in your pan. Extract the color with tweezers, grab a beer, and start the process all over again. With some work and a little luck, you'll soon be singing the old refrain, "We're in the money!"

Big Pine lives up to its name with an estimated volume of 12,500 board feet of wood. This 300-year-old giant lives in a grove of large pines, cedars, and Douglas firs at **Big Pine Campground.**

To get there, take the Merlin exit off I-5 just north of Grants Pass if you're traveling south, or exit 61 if you're traveling north, and proceed toward Galice (this Merlin-Galin road goes 100 windy miles to Gold Beach on the coast). Just beyond Morrison's Lodge, a luxurious getaway on the Rogue River, turn left onto Taylor Creek Rd. 25. Big Pine Campground is about 10 miles farther. Another routing option is via US 199. About 20 miles south of Grants Pass on US 199, take Onion Creek Rd. on the north side of the highway and follow it 20 miles to Big Pine.

The campground features 12 picnic sites and 14 campsites. Picnic tables, fire rings, and vault toilets are provided. Water is available from a hand pump between campsites seven and nine. A small playground and primitive softball diamond are tastefully incorporated into the grounds. Many trails take hikers to Big Pine and beyond for a short hike or an all-day adventure. A lazy creek meanders through the area, with alders, hazelnuts, and an array of colorful wildflowers growing along its banks. Deer and other wildlife are frequently spotted grazing in the fragrant meadows nearby. Foragers can pick their fill of blackberries in July and August. Cost is $16-19 a night.

THE OREGON CAVES

About 30 miles southwest of Grants Pass are the Oregon Caves. Take US 199 to Cave Junction (stopping at the **Rolling Pin Bakery,** 203 N. Redwood, for first-rate baked goods, and then wind your way 20 miles up ORE 46. The last 13 miles of this trip are especially exciting. Remember that there are few turnouts of sufficient size to enable a large vehicle to reverse direction. A beautiful old-growth Douglas fir forest lining the road might help divert the faint-of-heart from the nail-biting turns on ORE 46.

The cave itself—as there is really only one, which opens onto successive caverns—was formed over the eons by the action of water. As rain and snowmelt seeped through cracks and fissures in the rock above the cave and percolated down into the underlying limestone, huge sections of the limestone became saturated and collapsed—much as a sand castle too close to sea level always caves in. When the water table eventually lowered, these pockets were drained of water and the process of cave decoration began.

First, the limestone was dissolved by the water and carried in solution into the cave. When the water evaporated, it left behind a microscopic layer of calcite. This process was repeated countless times, gradually creating the beautiful formations visible today. When the minerals are deposited on the ceiling, a stalactite begins to form. Limestone-laden water that evaporates on the floor might leave behind a stalagmite. When a stalactite and a stalagmite meet, they become a column. Other cave sculptures you'll see include helicites, hell-bent formations that twist and turn in crazy directions; draperies, looking just like their household namesakes but cast in stone instead of cloth; and soda straws, stalactites that are hollow in the center like a straw, carrying mineral-rich drops of moisture to their tips.

Discovered in 1874, the Oregon Caves attract thousands of visitors annually. During the Depression, walkways and turnoffs were built to make the cave more accessible. Unfortunately, tons of waste rock and rubble were stashed into nooks and crannies in the cave, instead of being transported out. This had the ironic effect of obscuring the very formations intended for display. However, the National Park Service started to remove the artificial debris in 1985, exposing the natural formations once again. Little by little, the cave is returning to the way it looked before the "improvements" were started.

The River Styx, another victim of Depression-era meddling, is enjoying a similar resurrection.

This stream used to run through the cave but was diverted into pipes to aid trail and tunnel construction. The pipes ended up buried beneath tons of pulverized rock, and now the Park Service is hard at work undoing the work of humans to let the stream flow where Nature intended.

Tours of the cave are conducted year-round by National Park Service interpreters. Their presentations are both informative and entertaining, and you will leave the cave with a better understanding of its natural, geologic, and human history. Admission is $6 for adults and $4 for children ages 6-11. Children under six must be able to pass ability requirements (like walking up many stairs, total vertical climb of 218 feet) as well as being a minimum of 42 inches tall. A babysitting service is available in the "Kiddy Kave." The tour (limited to 16 persons) takes a little over an hour and requires some uphill walking. Remember that during summer you can sometimes wait an hour in line to go on a tour. Also, from October through April, fewer tours are offered. Good walking shoes and warm clothing are recommended. It may be warm and toasty outside, but the cave maintains a fairly consistent year-round temperature of 41°. Passageways can be narrow, ceilings low, and the footing slippery. Tour times can be obtained by calling (541) 592-3400 or 592-2100.

Oregon Caves Chateau

From mid-March through early December, the six-story Oregon Caves Chateau, P.O. Box 128, Cave Junction 97523, tel. (541) 592-3400, http://www.crater-lake.com/caves, offers food and accommodations. Located about 50 miles west of Grants Pass on US 199, the six-story chateau stands at an elevation of 4,000 feet. Built in 1934, this artistically rustic building blends in with the forest and moss-covered marble ledges. Indigenous wood and stone permeate this building so that you never lose a sense of where you are. The rooms feature views of Cave Creek canyon, waterfalls, or the Oregon Caves entrance. Rates range $75-100 per night for two to four people. Special "lovers' retreat" weekend packages including discount dinners and cave admissions are also available, but make reservations early, as the number of packages is limited. For a more unique experience, we recommend the sixth floor. The rooms might be smaller but they have more character and extend out at odd angles from this uniquely configured building. The Pendleton blankets, toll painted chairs, and wooden bed frames add to the historical nuance.

The chateau has been nicknamed the "Marble Halls of Oregon," and you can see the huge marble fireplace in the fourth floor lobby for yourself while you thaw out after your spelunking expedition. The food at the chateau is surprisingly good (breafast $2-5, lunch $5-8, main dinner courses $8-18), and having Cave Creek running through the center of the dining room definitely adds to the unique atmosphere. Downstairs, an old fashioned 1930s style soda fountain dishes up the classic American fare of burgers, fries, and shakes (whipped up fresh and served in the tin).

For a nice after-dinner hike, take a walk down the Big Tree trail. It's a three mile round trip from the Chalet to see this huge Douglas fir tree, estimated to be more than 1,000 years old. With a circumference of 38 feet, seven inches, it is among the largest standing trees in Oregon. The trail wends its way through virgin forest that has tan oak, canyon live oak, Pacific madrone, chinquapin, and manzanita as well as Douglas fir and Ponderosa pine. The hike is not that difficult, and the solitude and views of the surrounding mountains are as inspiring as the Big Tree. For a shorter jaunt that's just under a mile, try the Cliff Nature Trail. Placards will help you identify the plantlife as you traverse the mossy cliffs, and there are also some good vistas of the Siskiyou Mountains. Camping is also available nearby at Caves Creek Campground, $16 per night.

Bed and Breakfast in the Trees
Out n' About Treehouse Institute and Treesort, 300 Page Creek Rd., Cave Junction 97523, tel. (541) 592-2208 or (800) 200-5484, is a unique lodging option that's worth driving a bit out of your way from the Oregon Caves. After all, how many bed and breakfasts do you find in a treehouse? Located in Takilma near Cave Junction, this comfortable rural retreat captures the whimsy of the '60s along with the creature comforts of the '90s. Some well-appointed rooms here are bolted to 100-year-old white oak, 18 feet above the ground. Should you have misgivings about the structural integrity of these accommodations, be advised that the innkeeper gathered nearly

11,000 pounds of his friends to stand on the several units simultaneously—135 times the weight requirements of the local code. Those desiring a more down-to-earth lodging option can stay in a peeled-fir cabin with a cozy woodstove. For the deluxe treatment, reserve a 300-square foot structure of rewood and Douglas fir that features a sink, tub, fridge, queen-sized futon, loft, and a 200-foot deck with mountain views. The "treepee," a teepee done up in Out 'n' About style, and is always popular with the kids. Horseback trail rides, trips to the best Illinois River swimming holes, and whitewater rafting trips can be arranged through the management. Or, swim in the river that runs through the property. Rates range between $75-125 and include a continental breakfast. Pets are allowed on prior approval only, inquire when making your "treeservation."

The Josephine County Commissioners have imposed draconian restrictions on this enterprising innkeeper. Despite adhering to the spirit of building codes (the uniqueness of a treehouse makes it difficult to adhere strictly to the written letter of the law), this establishment has had to constantly battle with the powers that be to stay open as a hotel. Thus, guests here can expect being asked to join a foundation, enroll in a school, and purchase T-shirts in lieu of payment for lodging. This thinly disguised ruse has kept Out 'n' About open despite this duress. In recent years, the B&B has added classes in crafts, performing arts, country living, and equestrian studies that have all been enthusiastically welcomed by visiting families. Successful completion of your core curiculum classes in treehouses, treeology, or treeminology, and will make you a full-fledged "treemusketeer."

Hostel
Fordson Home Hostel, 250 Robinson Rd., Cave Junction 97523, tel. (541) 592-3203, is located about 10 miles away from Oregon Caves. A remarkable collection of antique farm equipment, one of the world's largest Douglas firs, strangely contorted trees in a natural vortex (water runs uphill, people can't stand up straight), and Bigfoot sightings reported in the area add intrigue to your stay here. If you need more than mystique, there are bicycles available for guests, swimming in a nearby river, freshly prepared homegrown organic vegeta-

bles, and a nearby winery. There's also laundry facilities, RV hook-ups, and a camping area, $2. This HI hostel is located seven miles from Cave Junction on country roads. A call in advance for reservations is required (space is limited) and young children and pets are not allowed in this budget lodging in the $15 range. Students, backpackers, and bicyclists are elgible for a discount of $2, as well as a discount of $2 if guests want to go to the Oregon Caves.

Wine Tasting
You can sample some of the local product at **Foris Vineyards,** 654 Kendall Rd., tel. (541) 592-3752, and **Siskiyou Vineyards,** 6220 ORE 46, tel. (541) 592-3727. Both wineries offer tours and tastings 11 a.m.-5 p.m. year round, although their operating hours tend to be reduced in winter. Siskiyou Vineyards is on the way to the Oregon Caves. You can combine a lunch at their picnic grounds along with a tasting after your forray into the bowels of the earth.

Camping
Near the Oregon Caves, camping is available at **Grayback,** Illinois Valley Ranger District, P.O. Box 389, Cave Junction 97523, 12 miles from Cave Junction on ORE 46. There are 25 tent sites and 16 vehicular sites close to Sucker Creek. Electricity and piped water are provided, with a store, laundromat, and showers within a mile. Closer to the caves is **Cave Creek,** same address as above. Just take ORE 46 four miles south of the caves to Forest Service Rd. 4032. Piped water and pit toilets are provided, and showers are available five miles away. You'll also find a ranger station and informative campfire programs here on summer evenings. Both campgrounds charge $10.

Food
Down by the Oregon Caves is **Miller's Wild River Deli and Brewery,** 249 US 199N, Cave Junction, tel. (541) 592-3536. Pizza dough, sandwich rolls, and croissants are made from scratch and then topped/stuffed with fresh ingredients. A salad bar, soup, and southern style fried chicken round out the menu (meals range $5-10). Enjoy their handcrafted European-style beers and ales along with their beer-battered potato chips and onion rings.

The vegetarian **Grayback Cafe,** 120 Cedar Flat Rd., Williams, tel. (541) 846-6900, is located in Williams, about 20 miles south of Grants Pass on the back road to the Oregon Caves. They also have ribs, chicken, and regular burgers (dinners range $5-12).

ROGUE RIVER TRIPS

There are about as many ways to enjoy the Rogue as there are critters in and around it. Some people prefer the excitement and challenge of maneuvering their own craft down the treacherous rapids. Oar rafts (which a guide rows for you), paddle rafts (which you paddle yourself), and one-person inflatable kayaks are the most widely used boats for this sort of river exploration. The 40-mile section downstream from Graves Creek is open only to nonmotorized vessels, and river traffic is strictly regulated by the U.S. Forest Service. For more information,

DON STEVENS/GRANTS PASS VISITORS AND CONVENTION BUREAU

One of the most popular ways to see the Rogue is by kayak.

stop at the Rand Visitor Center, 14335 Galice Rd., Merlin 97534, tel. (541) 479-3735. The limited float permits (25 a day) are prized by rafters around the world, as the Rogue not only has some of the best whitewater in America but also guarantees a first-rate wilderness adventure. And yet, it can be a civilized wilderness. Hot showers, comfortable beds, and sumptuous meals at several of the river lodges tucked away in remote quarters of this famous waterway welcome boaters after a day's voyage. Excellent camping facilities are available for those who want to experience nature directly.

But you don't have to risk life and limb in a fancy inner tube to see the Rogue, because several local companies offer jetboat tours. On a jetboat, powerful engines suck in hundreds of gallons of water a minute and shoot it out the back of the boat through a narrow nozzle, generating the necessary thrust for navigation. With no propeller to hit rocks and other obstacles, these 20-ton machines can carry 40 or more passengers in water only six inches deep. This makes the jetboat an ideal way to enjoy the beauty of the Rogue and at the same time keep your feet dry. Finally, many outfitters charter drift boats to secret fishing holes for anglers to try their luck landing supper.

Fishing on the Rogue

The upper Rogue River is renowned for one of the world's best late-winter steelhead fisheries. Numerous highways and backroads offer easy access to 155 miles of well-ramped river between Lost Creek Reservoir east of Medford and Galice west of Grants Pass. With fall and spring chinook runs and other forms of river recreation, it's no accident that the Rogue Valley is home to the world's top three aluminum and fiberglass driftboat manufacturers. Add rafters, kayakers and plenty of bank anglers and you can understand why peak salmon and steelhead season is sometimes described as "combat fishing." Contact southern Oregon visitor information outlets for rules, regulations, and leads on outfitters.

Float Trips

Paul Brooks Raft Trips, P.O. Box 638, Merlin 97532, tel. (541) 476-8051, offers a one-day guided trip that gives you the choice of oar raft, paddle raft, or inflatable kayak. Enjoy an excellent lunch at one of the river lodges. **Eagle Sun Inc.,** P.O. Box 611, Ashland 97520, tel. (541) 482-5139, has half-, full-, and multiday trips on oar or paddle rafts. Their adventures range from the mild to the wild, and child care can be arranged through their office.

Galice Resort and Store Raft Trips, 11744 Galice Rd., Merlin 97532, tel. (541) 476-3818, offers full-day raft or inflatable-kayak trips as well as river craft rentals. Many outfitters include a meal and/or overnight stay here. Lodging accomodations range $50-150 for primitive cabins to a house with full service kitchen. Another river retreat with attractive packages is **Morrison's Rogue River Lodge,** 8500 Galice Rd., Merlin, tel. (541) 476-3825 or (800) 826-1963, located about 16 miles from Grants Pass. Everything from one-day floats and excursions to two- to four-day trips are available. The longer excursions include either stays at other river lodges or camping along the great green Rogue. Transportation back to Morrison's is included, or your car can be shuttled to meet you at the end of the trip downriver for $50. You can spend extra time at Morrison's before or after your trip with their American Plan lodging package, which includes breakfast, dinner, and room for $80-130 per person/day.

Noah's World of Water, P.O. Box 11, Ashland 97520, tel. (541) 488-2811, has been providing quality rafting and fishing trips since 1974. They have half-day and one- to four-day excursions that vary from exciting whitewater rafting highs to kinder, gentler floats. From late March to early October, they depart Ashland for the Rogue three times daily, and a roundtrip transfer from your lodging is included in the price.

Orange Torpedo Trips, P.O. Box 1111-S, Grants Pass 97526, tel. (541) 479-5061 or (800) 635-2925, has half-day and one- to three-day raft or inflatable-kayak (also affectionately known as orange torpedoes because of their color and shape) adventures. They also offer a unique VIP two-day package that combines the best on the river: jetboat tour, wagon ride, gourmet dining, lodging, wildlife park, and float trip all rolled into one. **Rough and Ready Explorations,** 358 Murphy Creek Rd., tel. (541) 862-2420, intineraries include day trips, dinner trips, and two day trips for $50-200. If you want some real excitement, reserve (well in advance) for their full-moon trips.

Otter River Trips, 12163 Galice Rd., Merlin 97532, tel. (541) 476-8590, caters to families, offering one-day whitewater-rafting trips. They also operate fishing excursions year-round and special gold-panning trips. **River Adventure Float Trips,** P.O. Box 841, Grants Pass 97526, tel. (541) 476-6493, has summer raft and fall fishing trips that vary from a half day to several days. **River Trips Unlimited, Inc.,** 4140 Dry Creek Rd., Medford 97504, tel. (541) 779-3798, has been guiding trips on the Rogue for over 30 years. They have one- to four-day raft, Tahiti, or summer-run steelhead fishing trips that include meals and overnight stays at some of the river lodges. **Rogue River Raft Trips,** 8500 Galice Road, Merlin, OR, 97532, tel. (541) 476-3825 or (800) 826-1963; e-mail mlrrrt@chatlink.com, also offers a multitude of modes and packages to enjoy the river wild.

Rogue/Klamath River Adventures, P.O. Box 4295, Medford 97501, tel. (541) 779-3708 or (800) 231-0769, has one- to three-day whitewater-rafting and inflatable-kayak trips that give you the option of camping out under the stars or roughing it in style at a river lodge.

Rogue/Klamath Whitewater Co., 1202 E. Main St., Medford 97504, tel. (541) 772-8467, has personalized high-quality trips for the lowest available rates. Exciting half-, full-, and two-day overnighter raft, inflatable kayak, and guided salmon-fishing trips are among the offerings. **Rogue Wilderness, Inc.,** P.O. Box 1647, Grants Pass 97526, tel. (541) 336-1647, is here to tailor-make just about any length of trip you may care to take. Whitewater rafting, inflatable kayaking, and salmon and steelhead fishing are some of the available options.

Ferron Fun Trips, 585 Rogue Rim Dr, Merlin, tel. (541) 474-2201, has put together a variety of packages reflecting the Rogue's diversity. In addition to guided rafting, fishing, and whitewater trips, they offer a mountain-bike adventure above the Rogue on Bear Camp Mountain; an excursion to the working Last Chance Mine, where you get a chance to pan for gold; and a two-day wildlife expedition that combines hiking with rafting the Rogue. Boat rentals are available here, too.

For more information on scenic whitewater-rafting and fishing trips, contact the **Rogue River Guides Association,** P.O. Box 792, Medford 97501, tel. (541) 772-5194, the previously mentioned Rand Visitor Center, or the **Visitors Information Center,** P.O. Box 1787, Grants Pass

---

THE CHRISTMAS FLOOD OF 1964

Passing through the serene Rogue River Valley today, little can be seen of the ravages of the Christmas Flood of 1964. The autumn of that fateful year seemed to augur the coming of a peaceful winter in Rogue country. With the white snow on the mountains and a ring around the harvest moon, the only thing that seemed missing was ol' Saint Nick himself, riding through the night sky.

But then the rains came—slowly at first. Then little by little, almost imperceptibly, the downpour transformed into a deluge. The warm rains quickly melted the snowpack, and the swollen streams spurred the foaming Rogue on its course to the sea. Logjams and abnormally high tides contributed to record-high water levels.

Whole towns had to be evacuated from the onslaught of water. Many families saw their hopes and dreams wash away, with their tears, in the rain—victims of the impartial hand of nature. The inundation was not confined to the Rogue, as the killer storm turned almost every western Oregon river into a frighteningly efficient generator of destruction. Governor Hatfield declared the region a disaster area. The damage statewide was in the millions of dollars, and many lives were lost by the time the muddy waters receded a week later. In hope of averting similar castastrophies in the future, the Army Corps of Engineers constructed Lost Creek Reservoir on the upper Rogue not long afterwards.

And while time has healed the effects of the Christmas Flood of 1964, you can still find high-water marks here and there in the valley. Tacked high up on trees and bridges, perched over 100 feet above the now placid waters of the Rogue, they serve as a silent reminder of the magnitude of this great disaster. Unfortunately, the February 1996 floods made these memories a little too real for the many people who have settled along the Rogue in the last few decades.

97526, tel. (800) 547-5927. These information outlets can also supply tips on riverside hiking. The Rogue trails out of Grants Pass aren't as remote as their Gold Beach counterparts, and litter can sometimes mar the route. Nonetheless, the fall color in certain areas along the Rogue, and a profusion of swimming and fishing holes, can add a special dimension to your hike.

Jetboat Trips

Hellgate Excursions, 953 S.E. 7th, Grants Pass 97526, tel. (541) 479-7204 or (800) 648-4874; e-mail trips@hellgate.com, is the premier jetboat operator on this end of the river. Their trips begin at the dock of the Riverside Inn, 971 S.E. 6th St., Grants Pass, and proceed downriver through the forested Siskiyou foothills. En route, black-tailed deer, ospreys, and great blue herons are commonly seen. If you're lucky, a bald eagle or black bear might also be sighted. The scenic highlight is the deep-walled Hellgate Canyon, where you'll look upon what are believed to be the oldest rocks in the state. The rugged beauty here provided the backdrop for John Wayne and Katherine Hepburn in *Rooster Cogburn*. Trips including a champagne brunch, $33 for adults, kids 4-11 $20, and a weekday lunch of barbecued chicken and ribs, $38 for adults, kids $24, at a wilderness lodge are two popular additions to this itinerary. Another option is to tack on an extra foray into Grave Creek Whitewater beyond Hellgate at a price slightly higher than the regular luncheon cruise (lunch is available but not included). Finally, you can also forgo lunch on the river and just see the canyon for $22, children 4-11 $12. These excursions run May 1-Sept. 30 and feature commentary by your pilot, who knows every eddy in the river. Be sure to call ahead for reservations, as space on all of their runs books up fast.

Another section of the Rogue between the town of Rogue River and Gold Hill can be toured by jetboat with **Jet Boat River Excursions,** 8896 Rogue River Hwy., Rogue River, tel. (800) 296-0803. Their two-hour scenic trip departs each morning at 9 a.m. and takes in rapids and beautiful backcountry scenery. The fare for adults is $20; children 4-11 are $12. The one-hour trip goes at noon and 2 p.m. and is about half the price of the two-hour trip. Later, a four-hour evening cruise (adults $36, kids 4-11 $18)

stops at the Rogue Riviera Supper Club for dinner (recommended) and affords good opportunities for wildlife viewing after the meal on the return trip back to Rogue River. Daily departure is at 4:30 p.m. Both trips are available May 1-Sept. 1. After September, call for updates as times change. After your journey, a slice of pie (peanut butter pie is recommended) at the local hotspot, Karen's, 8993 Rogue River Highway, Rogue River, tel. (541) 582-3402, hits the spot.

EVENTS

Boatnik Festival

The Boatnik Festival starts on Memorial Day weekend at Riverside Park in Grants Pass. A carnival, parade, and softball tournament are featured, but the top event is the whitewater boat races. Over two dozen modified speedboats and jetboats compete in a 46-mile course on the Rogue River. Warm-ups begin on Memorial Day morning, followed by the race at 1 p.m. The competition starts at the boat docks in Riverside Park.

Josephine County Fair

The Josephine County Fair normally takes place in mid-August at the fairgrounds in Grants Pass. In addition to the usual fair attractions such as the carnival, concessions, and 4-H livestock, entertainers like Johnny Cash and Three Dog Night perform for enthusiastic crowds. A popular annual competition held here is the four-wheel tractor pull, in which souped-up farm vehicles attempt to drag a bulldozer (with its blade down) 100 yards as fast as possible.

Rooster-Crowing Contest

The nearby city of **Rogue River,** southeast of Grants Pass on I-5, has something to crow about. On the last day of June, the Rogue River Rooster Crow is held at the Rogue River Elementary School grounds, beginning with a parade and followed by live music and entertainment. A street fair featuring arts, crafts, and food is also set up on the premises. But the big event takes place early in the afternoon. Farmers from all over Oregon and northern California bring their roosters to strut their stuff and wing out songs to the enthusiastic crowds. A fowl tradition since 1953, the rooster to crow the most times in his allotted time period wins the prize for his proud owner.

Grants Pass Downs

Horse-racing aficionados will appreciate Grants Pass Downs. The season opens Memorial Day weekend with races on weekends through the Fourth of July. Place your bets on your favorite steeds to place, win, or show, $2 minimum. The cash-sell betting is all computerized, allowing for more exotic bets like the quiniela and the trifecta. The latter are "wheel" bets, in which you get to choose one of every possible combination of two or three horses, $1 minimum, to win. Even if you're not the betting sort, it's a kick watching the horses thunder around the bend and down the home stretch.

Growers' Market

Farmers markets are an Oregon tradition, particularly in the southern part of the state. Grants Pass is said to have the largest one of all, boasting produce, crafts, prepared foods, and strolling entertainers at 4th and F Streets. For more information, contact Growers Market, P.O. Box 576, Grants Pass 97526, tel. (541) 476-5375. It's open Saturday 9 a.m.-1 p.m., from mid-March till Thanksgiving, and also on Tuesday at the same times, beginning in June. To get there, head south on 6th Street then right on F St. for one block.

Rogue Valley Morel Picking

Gourmet mushroom picking can be a fun pastime and/or a money-making proposition in various parts of Oregon. Here in the Rogue Valley, morels, a cone shaped fungus with deeply crenulated caps and short hollow stems are one of several coveted varieties that fare especially well. The fact that they're easily identifiable, fry up great in omelettes, and come out in spring make them especially popular among the residents of this region. Although usually found in forest in such areas as the foothill below Mt. McLoughlin, morels also can be harveted from backyard orchards here in Rogue Valley fruit country. The combination of night temperatures above freezing, high humidity, and daytime conditions between 46-60° are optimum to bring this fungus to fruit. They often pop up in the wake of forest fires or in landscapes disturbed by logging and road building. If it's warm, these mushrooms can be found in late March. When spring conditions hit the lower slopes of the Cascades in the months to follow, pickers usually aren't far behind in pursuit of what many people consider to be the most savory mushroom of all. For a list of mycology associations who are able to supply tips and information, consult the sidebar on edible mushrooms in the General Introduction.

PRACTICALITIES

Bed And Breakfasts

Situated about 20 minutes outside of Grants Pass and well within the wild and scenic section of the Rogue River is the **Doubletree Ranch,** P.O. Box 253, Grants Pass 97526, tel. (541) 476-2946. Originally homesteaded 100 years ago, this 160-acre, four-generation working ranch offers cabins for $60-70 per night with breakfast included. The rugged beauty of the ranch grounds served as the set for a recent feature film starring Dan Haggarty entitled *Spirit of the Eagle.*

Martha's Inn, 764 N.W. 4th St., tel. (541) 476-4330 or (800) 261-0167, $50-90, in the historical district of Grants Pass, is a restored Victorian farmhouse built in 1912. Open May through September, their spacious rooms with private baths, a/c, TV and VCRs, are tastefully decorated. Good coffee, tea, and fresh-squeezed orange juice accompany a full breakfast highlighted by seasonal berries and produce.

You'll find the look and feel of the British isles at the gabled **Ivy House,** 139 S.W. I St., tel. (541) 474-7363. Anglophiles are sure to appreciate the full English breakfast, replete with bangers and a sturdy cup of tea (or coffee if you must). Rooms (with private bath) are comfortable, featuring touches of the empire like down quilts (eiderdowns), lace curtains, and the traditional morning tea and biscuits in bed. Afternoon tea, $3-5, is available that includes biscuits, jam tarts, crumpets, sausage rolls, and fresh scones. Luncheons can also be arranged with the usual British fare of curries, Cornish pastries, shepherd's pie, and Lancashire hotpot, $4-7, as well as the Ploughman's lunch, $6. Room rates, $60-75, are quite reasonable for the experience, advance reservations are required.

GRANTS PASS ACCOMMODATIONS

IN TOWN

Best Western Inn at the Rogue, 8959 Rogue River Hwy, tel. (541) 582-2200 or (800) 238-0700, $60-80, river view, continental breakfast, laundromat.

Flamingo Inn, 728 N.W. 6th St., tel. (541) 476-6601, $35-50, pool, pets, kitchenettes.

Golden Inn, 1950 N.W. Vine St., tel. (541) 479-6611, $40-50, pool, food, pets.

Knight's Inn Motel, 104 S.E. 7th, tel. (541) 479-5595 or (800) 826-6835, $40-50, laundromat, pets.

Motel 6, 1800 7th St., tel. (541) 474-1331, $35-50, pool and air conditioning.

Motel de Rogue, 2600 Rogue River Hwy., tel. (541) 479-2111, $45-65, on the river.

Redwood Motel, 815 N.E. 6th St., tel. (541) 476-0878, $55-70, playground, pool, pets.

Rogue River Inn, 6285 Rogue River Hwy. (old Hwy. 99), tel. (541) 582-1120, $45-85.

Shilo Inn of Grants Pass, 1880 N.W. 6th, tel. (541) 479-8391 or (800) 222-2244, $60-90, pool, pets.

Uptown Motel, 1253 N.E. 6th, tel. (541) 479-2952, $40-50, pets.

ROGUE RIVER RETREATS

Morrison's Rogue River Lodge, 8500 Galice Rd., tel. (541) 476-3825, $150-240, the super-deluxe treatment.

Paradise Ranch Inn, 700 W. Monument Dr., tel. (541) 479-4333, $90-125, reservations recommended.

River Shore Resort, 2520 Rogue River Hwy., tel. (541) 476-6203, $65-95, reservations required.

Riverside Inn Resort, 971 S.E. 6th St., tel. (541) 476-6873, $75-275, home port of Rogue Jetboat Excursions.

Rogue Valley Resort, 7799 Rogue River Hwy., tel. (541) 582-3762, $60-90, reservations required.

A few miles away from the town of Rogue River is the **Home Farm B&B,** 157 Savage Creek Rd., tel. (541) 582-0980, $60-80, a comfortable farmhouse built in 1944. All rooms have private baths and are decorated in their own motifs. The honeymoon suite in the barn is large and airy and affords a lovely view of the wooded hills from the sleeping loft. Their large country-style breakfasts are accompanied by fruit, juice, and beverages. Savage Rapids Park on the Rogue River is a three-minute walk away from your door, and nearby trails into the woodlands provide other hiking opportunities.

About 15 minutes north of town a couple of miles off I-5 exit 66 is **Flery Manor,** 2000 Jumpoff Joe Creek Rd., tel. (541) 476-3591, $75-125. Canopied beds, unique furnishings, and a quiet secluded setting give this country manor a gentile air. All rooms have nice little touches like plush robes, fresh flowers, and morning coffee/tea service. The breakfast features a health conscious menu, where the house specialties are always accompanied by fresh fruit and juices. With a private balcony, double jacuzzi, and fireplace, the Moon-light Suite is the right prescription for a romantic hideaway, and is well worth the $125/night rate. Reservations are a must.

The **Paradise Resort,** 7000 Monument Dr., tel. (541) 479-4333, is reminiscent of a New England Inn. You'll find clean and tastefully apportioned guest rooms and cottages at this 310 acre playground. A continental breakfast is included with lodging at rates that run from $70-125. Golf, tennis, swimming (heated pool), bicyling, and other activities are among the recreational possibilities here. The sense of isolation is compounded by the absence of telephones and televisions in the rooms. The resort's Black Swan restaurant features upscale dining, including several vegetarian entrees, $8-18. Call ahead for reservations and directions.

Finally, tucked away in the quiet ponderosa of the Rogue River Valley about 15 minutes away from Grants Pass is the lovely **Pine Meadow Inn,** 1000 Crow Rd., Merlin, tel. (541) 471-6277 or (800) 554-0806, http://www.cpros.com/~pmi; e-mail pmi@cpros.com, $80-110. This large country home atop a wooded knoll was designed and built specifically to be a B&B. As such, you'll be sure to enjoy the extra soundproofing and oversized private bathrooms in each of the four large sunny bedrooms. Downstairs, French doors open out to the backyard herb and English cutting gardens landscaped with a koi pond and waterfall. The wraparound porch has inviting wicker chairs to relax in while enjoying morning coffee or evening tea with a book from their extensive library. Beneath the pines awaits a hot tub. Given the innkeeper's backgrounds in health care, they places a premium on healthy breakfasts by providing fresh fruit and home-baked breads along with their house specialties. After your stay here, you'll understand exactly why Meryl Streep wanted to rent out the entire house for the summer when *The River Wild* was being filmed on the Rogue.

Campgrounds

Many fine campgrounds are found along the banks of the Rogue River near Grants Pass. The privately owned and operated RV parks in the KOA genre tend to be more expensive than their public counterparts but also offer more amenities like swimming pools, laundromats, and other conveniences. They range from about $10 to $20 a night and are found along ORE 99 between Gold Hill and Grants Pass. The four county parks listed below cost $15 for hookup sites, $9 for tent sites. Contact the **Josephine County Parks Dept.**, Rogue River 97537, tel. (541) 474-5285, for reservations and additional information.

Indian Mary Park is the showcase of Josephine County parks. To get there, go about eight miles east of Merlin on the Merlin-Galice Road. Located on the banks of the Rogue River, this campground has 89 sites, several with sewer hookups and utilities, as well as showers, flush toilets, and piped water. A boat ramp, beautiful hiking trails, a playground, and one of the best beaches on the Rogue make this one of the most popular county campgrounds on the river.

Griffen Park is a smaller campground with 24 sites for tents and trailers. To get there, take the Redwood Highway (US 199) to Riverbanks Rd., then turn onto Griffen Rd. and follow it about five miles to where it meets the Rogue. The park has a boat ramp, showers, flush toilets, piped water, and RV dumping facilities.

Schroeder Park is another complete campground near town. Located on Schroeder Lane off Redwood Ave., the park has 31 sites, some with hookups and utilities. Showers, flush toilets, and a boat ramp make this a favorite spot for fishing enthusiasts. In addition to a picnic area and an excellent swimming hole, a rope tied to a huge cottonwood on the opposite bank of the river near the park is waiting for any swingers who like to make a big splash.

Whitehorse Park is six miles west of Grants Pass on Upper River Road. Purchased by the county in 1958 from the Rogue Rovers Trail Club, this park has 44 campsites, many with hookups and utilities. Showers, piped water, lighting, and good hiking trails developed by the previous owners are found here. The river channel shifted away from the park in the wake of the Christmas flood of 1964, but it's only about a half-mile walk to a fine beach on the Rogue.

The only state park in the area is **The Valley of the Rogue.** Located about halfway between Medford and Grants Pass off of I-5, the park is set along the banks of its namesake river. The Rogue supports year-round salmon and spring steelhead runs. Although there are 97 sites for trailers and motor homes, and 77 tent sites, this place fills up fast, so reservations are recommended during the warmer months. This is also one of the few inland parks that have yurts (circular tent cabins with heat) to rent for the night, $30-45. Hookups, utilities, showers, laundromat, and some wheelchair-accessible facilities make this campground worth the $17-a-night fee.

Food

Although it's not the gourmet capital of Oregon, Grants Pass is a town where many travelers pull in for a bite. Its proximity to Rogue River recreation and fishing, together with a wide range of resonably priced dining alternatives, explain this popularity.

The Skinny Spot, 126 N.E. F St., tel. (541) 479-6234, is one of the few restaurants in Oregon that caters to those with special dietary needs. Restricted-calorie, low-cholesterol, and minimal-sodium-and-sugar items are emphasized on their menu. **Erik's,** 1067 Redwood Spur, Grants Pass, tel. (541) 479-4471, is for the serious eater. The 22-foot-long salad bar is a meal in itself, and there's a hot dinner buffet,

$6.50, where you can fill any extra space left on your plate. A wide range of steak, seafood, chicken, and pasta dinners is also available.

R-Haus, 2140 Rogue River Hwy., tel. (541) 476-4287, a local favorite dinner spot, is a formal dining room in a turn-of-the-century house. Check to see what the nightly early-bird, $7-11, specials are. The waitresses dress in Victorian style at **Yankee Pot Roast,** 720 N.W. 6th, tel. (541) 476-0551. Light dinners are around $9, other dinner selections range $10-16. Slow-cooked pot roast simmering in heavy gravy might be the star of the menu, but don't overlook the halibut, homemade soup, and biscuits. Pies made with local berries make a spectacular dessert.

The menu at **China Hut,** 1434 N.W. 6th, tel. (541) 476-3441, features interesting entrees such as vegetarian chow yuk, Mandarin pineapple duck, and ma po tofu. Even if you don't always understand the lingo, don't worry; all you really need is a big appetite to finish their large portions. Lunch specials run $3-5, dinner specials $5-9. The **Hong Kong,** 820 N.W. 6th, tel. (541) 476-4244, restaurant has a family-pack dinner to go that at arround $10 for two people is one of the best deals in town. **Pongsri's,** 1571 N.E. 6th, tel. (541) 479-1345, is a Thai restaurant (with some Chinese dishes) hidden away in a nondescript shopping mall near the Visitor Center. You'd never guess that such exotic dishes as Tom Ka Gai (a coconut cream soup flavored

I-5 ROAD FOOD

Travelers with many miles to cover generally would rather not spend time looking for a restaurant in a strange town. To help you avoid the inevitable fast-food alternatives, here are three stars along the southern Oregon section of I-5 that offer good, quick, and accessible road food.

If you take the Quines Creek exit (no. 86), you'll find **Heaven on Earth Restaurant and Bakery,** tel. (541) 837-3596, on the east side of the interstate. No matter what time of day or night you enter this always-open restaurant, expect the aroma of freshly baked cinnamon rolls to greet you. Your eyes will fasten on the display tables where giant cinnamon rolls, apple and marionberry pies, and other pastries are arrayed. While the menu can be characterized as elaborate truckstop fare, the restaurant's daily special will hold its own anywhere. Homemade soup, chili, or stew in a sourdough bread bowl served with salad and a dessert (about $7) rates a nod for freshness, taste, and presentation. If it's too late for dinner, breakfast is served anytime here. While you're waiting for your meal, spread some homemade apple butter on a cracker; you'll probably want to buy a jar on your way out to take the taste of home with you.

On the west side of the Rice Hill exit (no. 148) you'll find the **K 'n' R Drive Inn,** tel. (541) 849-2750, a favorite stop for families with hungry kids. One look at the two-pound serving of fries or the ice-cream dispensed in one-pound portions, and you'll understand why. For $1.25 you can get a cone with 6-8 ounces of such flavors as black-

berry rebel and espresso madness. The menu's standard road-food fare is ample and tasty, but it's really the 33 flavors of Umpqua ice-cream that have enshrined K 'n' R in the food fantasies of many Oregon travelers. The ice-cream tastes homemade, and the amount you get for your money is as reminiscent of the Eisenhower era as the drive-in's '50s-like facade.

On first appearance alone, the **Creswell Dairy Queen,** tel. (541) 895-2116, on the west side of the Creswell exit might be dismissed as another roadside chain by those from outside the area. But what other DQs include shrimp cocktails, peanut butter pie, and broasted chicken on their menus? Since 1972 this family restaurant has served entrees several octaves above normal fast food—but at fast-food prices. Fresh Fircrest Farms chicken, raised in Creswell, are broasted to perfection and served with soup or salad, potato or rice, vegetable, and a small ice-cream sundae for around $7. Compounding the impression that this is the reigning monarch of Dairy Queens, long-time patrons say that the restaurant's beef is from a local herd. The homemade peanut butter pie, rich in flavor and not too sweet, is also excellent. Seniors (60 years or older) get a 10% discount.

These comfort food outposts along the Interstate fuel southern Oregon travelers the same way that stagecoach depots along this route dispensed frontier hospitality over a century ago. Then, as now, local specialties were the order of the day, served efficiently and without pretense.

with ginger-like galangka root) is on the menu here as well as nearly two dozen vegetarian dishes. Lunch specials for $3.50 also pull in the locals, entrees range $6-8.

Herb's La Casita, 515 S.E. Rogue River Hwy., tel. (541) 476-1313, has a little bit of everything, featuring a full menu of Mexican and American dishes, 24-hour breakfasts and entertainment ranging from karaoke to dancing. **Maria's Mexican Kitchen,** 105 N.E. Mill, tel. (541) 474-2429, uses handmade tortillas and a special family recipe to make some of the best burritos around.

Aficionados of the old-time soda fountain will appreciate the **Grants Pass Pharmacy,** 414 S.W. 6th St., tel. (541) 476-4262. Decent sandwiches, $3-5, and phosphate drinks for a quarter are featured here. Local old-timers meet there every afternoon, and it's the kid's first stop after school.

The **Wild River Brewing and Pizza Company,** corner E and Mill Streets, tel. 471-RIVR, is the sister of the Cave Junction outlet and features wood-fired pizza, $14-20 for a large, pastas, $6-8, burgers, and sandwiches, $4-7, as well as a full service espresso bar. All breads used for sandwiches are baked right on the premises. If you're only there for the beer, five brews are offered year-round and are complemented by four seasonal ones. One of the best ways to sample the local product is via the 75 cent taster glasses. Free brewery tours are also offered. Open daily from 11 a.m. until closing.

Another place to find a great selection of microbrews on tap is at the **Laughing Clam,** 121 S.W. G St., tel. (541) 479-1110. This nonsmoking eatery and alehouse is kid-friendly, you can bring the family up until 9 p.m. The moderately priced menu, $5-15, offers a wide range of salads, sandwiches, pastas, and burgers in addition to well rounded dinner offerings. Several meatless items are featured in all categories. Their appetizers break away from the ordinary pub grub. One example is the onion anemones, sweet Northwest deep-fried onion dipped in beer batter, accompanied with chili mayonnaise. They look kind of like flowers when you get them, and put ordinary onion rings to shame. Oregon wines are featured exclusively here, so check out the house wine specials to taste some of the best of the state.

A small and intimate place for French cuisine is **Legrand's,** 323 N.E. E St., tel. (541) 471-1554. Open for dinner, $10-20, you'll find delicious continental fare on the menu here. For dinner, order a half plate of brie and pate for starters, then follow up with one of Legrand's veal, chicken, seafood, or pasta creations that are equally pleasing to both eye and palate. If you don't have time for a sit-down meal, stop in for some take-out from their bakery to outfit your own gourmet creations.

Sunshine Natural Foods, 128 S.W. H St., Grants Pass, tel. (541) 474-5044, has a cafe and market catering to those seeking sustenance that's fresh, homegrown, and organic. The soup and salad bar at lunch is always a winner in the $4-6 range.

Shopping

If you would like to take home some Oregon products like Rogue Gold cheese from nearby Central Point, Taylor's sausage, or Oregon beer cookies, visit the **Oregon Outpost,** 137 S.W. G St., tel. (541) 474-2918. Here you'll find a wide selection of Oregon-made T-shirts, wines, jams/preserves and much more, as well as one-of-a-kind items created by the craftspeople of the Rogue Valley. The folks here are genuinely friendly and helpful and point the way to area attractions. **Wild Berry's Community Market,** 106 E. Main, tel. (541) 582-3075, offers a good selection of organic foods and produce, bulk foods, music, and alternative products. There is also a deli on the premises.

Information and Services

The **Grants Pass/Josephine County Visitor Information Center/Chamber of Commerce,** 1995 N.W. Vine, Grants Pass, 97526, tel. (541) 476-7717 or (800) 547-5927, http://www.chatlink.com/~gpcoc, e-mail gpcoc@chatlink.com, is open 8 a.m.-5 p.m. daily in summer, weekdays in winter. For Rogue River backpacking/biking information, the Siskiyou National Forest Service, P.O. Box 440, 200 N.E. Greenfield Rd., Grants Pass 97526, tel. (541) 479-5301, and the BLM, P.O. Box 1047, Medford 97501, can be of assistance.

Three Rivers Community Hospital and Health Center, 715 Dimmick, tel. (541) 476-6831, offers ambulance service around the clock. **Three Rivers–Northwest,** 1505 N.W. Washington, tel. (541) 479-7531, is a participating member of Blue Cross health service and also features 24-hour emergency care. The **police,** tel. (541) 474-6370, and state police, tel. (541) 474-3175, are only a phone call away.

The **post office,** 132 N.W. 6th, Grants Pass 97526, tel. (541) 479-7526, is open 8:30 a.m.-5 p.m. weekdays.

Greyhound, 460 N.E. Agness Ave., tel. (541) 476-4513, offers access to the I-5 corridor and the coast. The **Green Tortoise,** tel. (800) 867-8647, picks up off I-5 at Denny's Restaurant (exit 58) at 6 a.m. going northbound on Monday and Friday, and at 11 p.m. going south on Sunday and Thursday. Be sure to call in advance to set up a "flag stop."

A pleasant air-conditioned and carpeted laundromat is **Maytag Laundry and Dry Cleaners,** 1620 Williams Highway Plaza, tel. (541) 479-1743. Located on the south side of Safeway in the Plaza, it's open seven days a week 7:30 a.m.-10 p.m. **Auto Rental Center,** tel. (541) 479-2403, and **Mock Ford,** (541) 479-2560, feature new and used rental cars. **Classic Auto,** 414 N.E. F St., tel. (541) 476-8938, provides some nonsmoking cars and free pick up and delivery anywhere within the city limits.

Blind George's, G street between 5th and 6th, is a newsstand and smokeshop on the main drag. It's also a local institution, as vintage photos of old-time Grants Pass attest. This is the place to come to get travel information, local gossip, and out-of-town newspapers. In addition to its array of printed media, its buttery, crunchy popcorn is justifiable famous. Blind George's is a good place to pick up a copy of the highly esteemed *Grant's Pass Courier.*

The place to go for mountain bike rentals and information on area bike trails is **Bill's Bikekraft,** 1515 Redwood Ave., tel. (541) 476-4935. Mountain bikes rent for $15 per day, $8 per half day. If you want to go on an extended trip, the overnight rate is $18 and the weekly rate is $60. Car racks and trailers are also available for rent. A cash deposit is required.

About 15 minutes north of Grants Pass is **Red Mountain Golf Course,** 324 N. Schoolhouse Creek Rd., tel. (541) 479-2297. This small but challenging executive course of 2,245 yards is a bargain to play. Greens fee is $5 for nine

holes, $9 for 18, and $13 for all day Mon.-Fri.; add a dollar for weekends. To get there from Grants Pass, take the Merlin exit, go under the freeway, and take a right on Monument Drive. When you see Antler's Store on the left, look for N. Schoolhouse Rd. just ahead to the right. Proceed down N. Schoolhouse Rd. until you reach the course.

Cave Junction and Beyond

Should you care to explore the Illinois River Valley and US 199 beyond Cave Junction, contact the Illinois River Valley Cooperative Visitor Center, 201 Cave Hwy., Cave Junction, 97525, tel. (541) 592-2631, open daily 9 a.m. to 4 p.m. You can also consult **Siskiyou National Forest Illinois Valley Ranger Station,** 26568 Redwood Hwy., Cave Junction, 97525, tel. (541) 592-2166. Botany buffs will especially want to get the lowdown on the Kalmiopsis Wilderness (ask for directions to Babyfoot Lake), the redwoods located in California's Smith River drainage, and the fall harvest of chanterelle, morel, and matsutake mushrooms. If you're seeking relief from the summertime heat in the local's favorite swimming hole, get directions to "the forks." This is where the east and west forks of the Illinois River meet and can be accessed a mile south of Cave Junction at Illinois river State Park. Wine fanciers should get directions to Foris, Siskiyou, and Bridgeview vineyards. Outdoor recreationists will appreciate information on everything from fishing in Lake Selmac and rafting the challenging Illinois River to horsepacking and hiking in the surrounding Siskiyous.

After you cross the California border about 20 miles southwest of Cave Junction, the road begins to wind its way through the Smith River Canyon. The is the Redwood Country, and the combination of the wild blue-green Smith River (the only major river on the West Coast that runs unimpeded by dams from the mountains to the sea) and the oldest, largest living things known to humankind make this drive a thrill a minute.

To get to the southern Oregon coast via this route, allow several hours to get to Brookings. Wintertime rainfall that can average over 100 inches annually and the never-ending sumertime procession of slow moving vehicles and slides on this mostly two lane highway are other inconveniences. As such, it's worth pulling off the road in **Jedediah Smith National Park** on the California side of US 197 (an extension of ORE 199). There is a day use fee of a few dollars to get into the park. Proceed directly down to the picnic area along the banks of the Smith River and park your car. There you will find picnic tables (great place for lunch) and bathrooms. Best of all, there is an excellent nature trail beginning there that loops through the grove. A pamphlet can be procured for a quarter (on the honor system—show some class and ante up) that articulates upon the natural features delineated by numbered markers along the trail. Feel how your footsteps make no sound, so thick is the forest floor from hundreds of years of redwood needles and cones. Be sure to see the myrtlewood trees along the trail, as well as the giant root wads from fallen redwoods. Surprisingly, these towering giants have no single tap root, but instead have many shallow roots that radiate out in all directions, interlocking with their brethren for protection from stormy weather. It takes only 15-25 minutes to walk the loop, and presents an outstanding experience for children.

ROSEBURG AND VICINITY

Many people passing through the Roseburg area might quickly dismiss it as a rural backwater. A closer look, however, reveals many more interesting layers beneath the mill-town veneer. While about half of the folks here rely upon the woods as a workplace (and this fact is reflected in the no-nonsense cafes and businesses meeting their needs), growing pockets of refinement are found in between the pickup trucks and lumber mills. An award-winning museum, Oregon's only drive-through zoo, and some fine restaurants are a few examples of culture in the hinterland.

And yet, the true allure to Roseburg is not really in town, but in the surrounding countryside. The Mediterranean climate of the Umpqua Valley has proven ideal for producing world-class wines and contributes to wonderful winetasting tours. The beautiful North Umpqua River to the east offers rafting, camping, hiking, and fishing. In addition to catching trout, salmon, and bass, anglers come from all over to enjoy one of the world's last rivers with a native run of summer steelhead. Numerous waterfalls along the river and the frothy whitewater make the Indian word Umpqua ("Thunder Water") an appropriate name. And if you are really interested in a closer look at a lumber mill, you can visit the world's largest particleboard plant.

In short, there's more here than a hasty visual appraisal would suggest, and it's worth more time than it takes to top off a tank of gas and wolf down a hamburger. Check it out—you'll be glad you did.

SIGHTS

Art and Culture
The **Douglas County Museum of History and Natural History,** P.O. Box 1550, Roseburg 97470, tel. (541) 440-4507 or (800) 452-0991, is located at the Douglas County Fairgrounds (exit 123 off I-5). This nationally acclaimed museum has four wings of exhibits that range from a million-year-old saber-toothed tiger to 19th-century steam-logging equipment. Eight thousand year old Indian artifacts, a re-creation of the 1882 Dillard Oregon and California Railroad depot, an imaginative forest-industry exhibit, and an extensive collection of historical photos make your visit both entertaining and educational. Open Tues.-Sat. 10 a.m.-4 p.m., Sunday noon-4 p.m., admission is $3.50 for adults. $1 for kids.

The **Umpqua Valley Arts Center,** 1124 W. Harvard, tel. (541) 672-2532, has two galleries. The main gallery features monthly rotating shows of local, regional, and Northwest artists. The Gift Gallery offers one-of-a-kind gifts made by a wide variety of Oregon artists.

Flower Power
The **Lotus Knight Memorial Gardens** are in Riverside Park. Located between Oak and Washington Streets on the banks of the South Umpqua River, these gardens are a feast for the eyes with colorful azaleas and rhododendrons in the spring. Open daily 5 a.m.-10 p.m. South of Roseburg about 15 minutes, near the town of Myrtle Creek, is **Beneschoen Gardens,** with a good collection of rhododendrons, azaleas, azaleas-dendrons, and other rare and unusual plants. Over 150 varieties of azaleas are featured here. Peak blooms for both parks occur from late April to early May.

Something Fishy
The **Winchester Fish Ladder** is just off I-5 at exit 129 on the north bank of the North Umpqua River. Here visitors can watch salmon and steelhead in their native environment as they swim by the viewing window at Winchester Dam. The North Umpqua and the Columbia are the only rivers in Oregon that offer this attraction. Spring chinook and summer steelhead migrate upriver May through August, and coho, fall chinook, and more summer steelhead swim on by from September through November. From December through May, winter steelhead is the primary species seen going through the fish ladders and on past the window. The Umpqua River offers the largest variety of game fish in Oregon.

Mill Tours

The world's largest particleboard plant, **Roseburg Forest Products,** tel. (541) 679-3311, ext. 392, south of Roseburg in nearby **Dillard,** offers tours by appointment only (24 hour advance notice required) Wednesday and Friday at 1:30 p.m. This plant runs around the clock, seven days a week, producing this versatile building material. You'll see the entire process, from wood chip to finished product, accompanied by a cacophony of bells and whistles. The tour lasts about two hours, with some uphill walking and stair climbing. No open-toe shoes or high heels

are allowed. Visitors must be 10 years of age or older. Contact the Roseburg Visitors and Convention Bureau for information on other local mill tours. As you drive down I-5 outside of town you'll see enormous piles of Roseburg Forest Products lumber on the east side of the highway; their size bespeaks this company's one-time status as Oregon's largest privately held, for-profit company (1991 and 1992 figures).

Wildlife Safari

Tucked away in a 600-acre wooded valley is Wildlife Safari, Safari Rd., Winston 97496, tel.

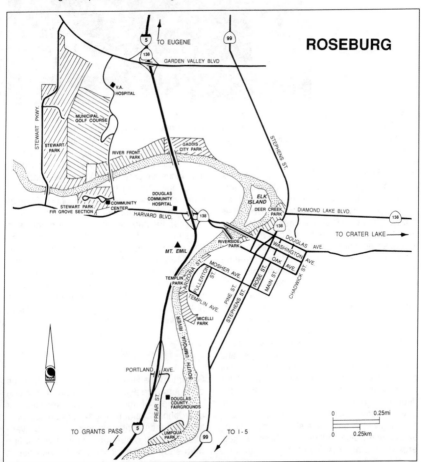

Camels smile at passing motorists at Wildlife Safari.

OREGON STATE HIGHWAYS

(541) 679-6761 or (800) 355-4848, Oregon's drive-through zoo. To get there, take exit 119 off I-5 and follow ORE 42 for four miles. Turn right on Lookingglass Rd. and right again on Safari Road. Families with kids can expect to pay $25-30 in admission here. Once inside the park gates, the brightly colored birds and exotic game animals transport you to other lands, with an oddly appropriate Oregon backdrop. Be that as it may, every possible step has been taken at Wildlife Safari to re-create African and North American animal life zones. Lest this conjure the image of lions, tigers, and bears eating Bambi and company for supper before your very eyes, rest assured that these critters are kept apart from their natural prey. Similar precautions are taken with humans. People must remain inside their vehicles except in designated areas, and windows and sunroofs must be kept closed in the big cats' and bears' areas.

The first loop takes you to see the tigers and cheetahs. These giant felines loll lazily about or catch catnaps in the tall grass. The next link takes you through the heart of "Africa," where the deer and the antelope play. Wildebeests, zebras, and other creatures scamper freely about, seemingly oblivious to the slow parade of cars and people watching them. Elephants, rhinoceroses, and other African big game are also

represented here. Soon you are in "North America." Bears, bighorn sheep, pronghorns, moose, and buffalo are just a few of the animals that live down in the valley. Perhaps the most popular attraction is the petting zoo, where children get "hands-on" experience. When the weather is good, play sheik or sultan and take a memorable ride on the camel or the elephant. Open at 8:30 a.m. in the summer and 9 a.m. the rest of the year, the park closes at dusk regardless of the season. With 600 animals including America's largest (and cutest) collection of cheetah cubs, this is one safari that appeals to all ages. Speaking of cheetahs, this is one of the few places where they are successfully bred in captivity. After your "safari," pull into the White Rhino restaurant, serving good food within view of lions, giraffes, and white rhinos.

WINERIES

Several in the Roseburg vicinity offer tastings and tours. The dry, Mediterranean climate and rich variety of soils in the area are ideal for chardonnay, pinot noir, gewürztraminer, riesling, zinfandel, and cabernet sauvignon varietals. A good wine-tour pamphlet with a fine map showing the location of the wineries is available from the Roseburg Visitors and Convention Bureau.

Hillcrest Vineyard, Callahan Ridge Winery

Hillcrest Vineyard, 240 Vineyard Ln., tel. (541) 673-3709, in business since 1963, is one of the oldest vineyards in Oregon. Their first batch was a humble 240 gallons, but production has since grown to over 20,000 gallons annually. The winery is noted primarily for its rieslings but also produces cabernet sauvignon, pinot noir, and small quantities of other varieties. Open 11 a.m.-5 p.m. daily. Callahan Ridge Winery, 340 Busenbark Ln., tel. (541) 673-7901, open daily 11:30 a.m.-5 p.m. for tastings, tours, and sales, is the Umpqua Valley's newest vintner. They offer a very dry gewürztraminer, white zinfandel, and white riesling, as well as barrel-aged chardonnay and a late-harvest gewürztraminer. The tasting room hours are daily 11:30 a.m.-5 p.m., April-October.

Girardet Wine Cellars

Down the road from Davidson Winery is Girardet Wine Cellars, 895 Reston Rd., tel. (541) 679-7252. Philippe Girardet, from a town at the headwaters of the Rhone River in Switzerland, brings European wine-blending techniques to Oregon. This process produces unique chardonnay, pinot noir, cabernet sauvignon, and riesling wines. Tastings, tours, and sales daily noon-5 p.m., May-Sept.; Saturday noon-5 p.m., Oct.-April. The winery is closed Dec. 20-Jan. 30.

Henry Winery, La Garza Cellars

The Henry Winery, 687 Hubbard Creek Rd., Umpqua 97486, tel. (800) 782-2686, has produced a string of award-winning varietals from chardonnay, gewürztraminer, and pinot noir grapes. Their 1984 pinot noir won the double gold award at the prestigious San Francisco Expo National Wine Competition, proving that Oregon wines can compete with California's best. Recent newcomers to their outstanding lineup include pinot noir blanc and Muller-Thurgau. In addition to tasting and tours daily from noon to 5 p.m., lunch at their shaded picnic tables near the vineyard and the Umpqua River can heighten your enjoyment of the fruit of the vine. La Garza Cellars, 491 Winery Lane, tel. (541) 679-9654, can be reached by taking exit 119 (south of Roseburg). Take a left about 100 feet past the first stoplight onto Winery Lane, and continue on until you get to the vineyard. Winery tours and a gourmet restaurant are enhanced by beautiful surroundings. Open daily 1-5 p.m.

SPORTS AND RECREATION

Two area golf courses are open to the public. **Sutherlin Knolls,** tel. (541) 459-4422, is 12 miles north of Roseburg to the west of Sutherlin on ORE 138. Golf nine holes for $9, 18 holes for $16. For a dollar or two more, you can use an electric golf cart. A coffee shop and lounge provide sustenance and lubricants to keep you

---

DOUGLAS COUNTY

A good look at just about any local mountainside tells the story of Douglas County. For years, the economy here has revolved around *Pseudotsuga menziessi* ("false hemlock"), the Douglas fir. Named after David Douglas of the English Botanical Society, who visited Oregon in the 1820s to research Northwest flora and fauna, the Douglas fir has enabled the county to perpetually rank near the top of the state's timber-production levels. This distinction has given it the nickname of the "Lumberjack County."

After all of this fanfare, you probably think that Douglas County is named after David Douglas, right? Wrong! It's really named after Illinois Senator Steven A. Douglas, who gained fame for debating Abraham Lincoln in 1858 on the "peculiar institution" of slavery. Although Lincoln lost the senatorial election to Douglas, the debates helped Lincoln gain national prominence and polarized the issue, which James Madison called "a firestorm in the night." Douglas's notoriety out west, however, was due more to his ardent advocacy of Oregon statehood in Congress. It was no small honor to choose his name to grace this county where stagecoaches passed en route to Jacksonville gold country, where California-bound steamships plied the Umpqua, and where Oregon's most esteemed pioneer family, the Applegates, chose to settle.

putting happily around. **Roseburg Municipal Golf Course,** 1005 Stewart Park Dr., Roseburg 97470, tel. (541) 672-4592, is closer to town. It costs $8 for nine holes, $13 for 18 holes; add two dollars on weekends. In addition to power carts, a lighted driving range, and rental golf clubs, a complete pro shop offers lessons and any peripherals you may need.

Tennis buffs will find free courts at the Douglas County Fairgrounds, Roseburg High School, and Umpqua Community College. Twelve lighted courts are located at Stewart Park off Stewart Parkway, but they require fees and reservations, tel. (541) 673-8650. The YMCA, tel. (541) 440-9622, is also located in Stewart Park and has racquetball and basketball courts as well as an indoor swimming pool. Umpqua Community College, tel. (541) 440-4600, ext. 686, has a pool, $1.50, that's open to the public during the summer 1-4 p.m. and 7-9 p.m. Roseburg also has two bowling alleys and two movie theater complexes.

DOUGLAS COUNTY FISHING

The Umpqua River system is home to a dozen species of popular eating fish that range from the big chinook salmon to the tiny silver smelt. Visit the Oregon Department of Fish and Wildlife Web site for additional information on the Umpqua, http://www.dfw.state.or.us. Other "fishy" sites include All Things Salmon, http://www.riverdale.k12.or.us/salmon.htm, and the State of Oregon Salmon page, http://www.das.state.or.us/salmon. The following overview will help you decide where and when to go and what to take when you're out to land some supper.

Chinook Salmon
Spring chinook enter the North Umpqua River from March to June, work their way upstream during July and August, and spawn from September to October. The average size is about 15 pounds, though occasionally people hook some big ones two to three times that weight. You'll need a stout rod, sturdy reel, drifting eggs or sand shrimp for bait, and some type of spinner.

Fall chinook are mainly found in the warmer South Umpqua River. Their migration starts in midsummer and peaks in September when the rains increase water flow and lower the river's temperature. Bait and tackle for fall chinook fishing are pretty much the same as spring chinook gear.

Steelhead
The best fishing for summer steelhead on the North Umpqua is from June to October; the fish spawn from January to March. This fish averages only six to eight pounds, but it will make you think that you are trying to reel in a chinook by the way it struggles. Fly-fishing for summer steelhead is extremely popular—so much so that the 31-mile stretch from Rock Creek upriver to Soda Springs is for fly-angling only. Elsewhere on the North Umpqua, spin-casting with drift eggs, plugs, lures, or shrimp is allowed. There are no summer steelhead on the South Umpqua because there are no deep pools for them during the hot summer months.

Winter steelhead are found in both the North and South Umpqua rivers. They begin their migration upriver in November, so December and January are the best fishing months. The fish spawn from February to April. The success of the winter steelhead runs is in great part determined by the weather, which affects important variables like water temperature, level, and color. Generally speaking, if it's cold and wet (but not too wet), the fishing tends to be better. This makes it important to dress warmly in appropriate rain gear so you don't turn as blue as the fish you're trying to catch.

Coho and Sockeye Salmon
Coho, alias "silvers," are found throughout the Umpqua River system. The coho life cycle lasts about three years. Each spends its first year in fresh water, heads for the ocean to spend one to two years, and then returns to fresh water to spawn. The adults weigh an average of 7 pounds each. At this writing, the status of this fishery is in question.

Far more rare in the Umpqua River system are crimson sockeye, affectionately nicknamed "reds" by local guides and everyone else. These river denizens usually weigh about ten pounds; eggs are the preferred bait. Possessing more oil than the chinook, the sockeye is regarded as the number-one salmon for quality and flavor.

THE GOATS OF MOUNT NEBO

There's a saying that only a dude or a fool will predict the weather. But the folks here in Roseburg were once able to tell with 93% accuracy if it was going to rain. Their system was simple enough. A basalt mountain called Mt. Nebo that rises up from the west bank of the South Umpqua River near downtown had been home to a herd of goats for as long as anyone could remember. When the goats came down from the top of Mt. Nebo, that meant it was going to rain.

In the early 1960s, Mother Nature's barometer had to make way for the wheels of progress. Road-building crews blasted out huge chunks of Mt. Nebo to make room for Interstate 5. The goats endured this incursion into their domain and still managed to faithfully make their pilgrimage down from the mountaintop when inclement weather was imminent. But almost two decades later, the highway engineers decided that the freeway entrance at the base of Mt. Nebo was too dangerous and needed more work. So in 1977, the men and machines once again assaulted the goats' territory.

This time, the citizenry of Roseburg came together to protect their weather soothsayers. They circulated petitions to "save our goats" and sent them to Salem with an emotional plea to the governor to halt the construction, but to no avail. With their turf dynamited into oblivion and the gentle grassy glade turned into a steep cliff, the goats departed for points unknown. For years, Mt. Nebo survived in the form of an ugly rock escarpment echoing with the 24-hour roar of traffic, while the plaintive bleating of the goats of Mt. Nebo was only a fading memory.

In 1997, prison laborers terraced a half-mile path up the mountain and planted over 1000 brilliant red roses donated by Medford's Jackson and Perkins (this project was inspired by local initiative and contributions of the citizens of Roseburg). Expect Mt. Nebo to blossom from springtime to the first frost. Many citizens here feel that this mountain of roses will help restore some of the civic pride and local color that was lost along with the goats of Mt. Nebo.

Rainbow Trout

You'll find this brightly speckled fish in nearly all rivers and streams of the Umpqua River system where the water is relatively cool and gravel bars clean. They don't like warm water and avoid the lower South Umpqua and Cow Creek for this reason. Rainbows do like the riffles at the entry or exit of pools. This is the most common game fish in the water, mainly because the rivers, lakes, and streams of the Umpqua are routinely seeded with over 100,000 legal-size (eight inches or longer) rainbows. The fishing season opens in April, with the best fishing in early summer when the fish are actively feeding. The best baits are salmon eggs, worms, or small flies; lures

BOB RACE

can also be used with success. The most popular tackle is spin-casting gear with a light leader.

Brown and Brook Trout

In the rapids of the upper North Umpqua you'll find browns, particularly around Soda Springs. Browns seem to like faster-moving water than rainbows. The average size is about a foot long, but sometimes 20-inchers are landed. Midsummer is the best time to fish for browns. Worms and salmon eggs prove effective, but the best lure is one that resembles a small fish.

High in the icy blue upper reaches of the North Umpqua is a small population of brook trout. The adult brook averages about six inches, which is also the legal minimum size, so light tackle is best. Mid to late summer is when the brook trout are biting, and they go for eggs and worms.

Smallmouth, Largemouth, and Striped Bass

The smallmouth is the most numerous of the three bass species commonly found in the Umpqua River system. The largest concentration of them is near Elkton, and they average between one and two pounds. The best time to fish for this species is when the water warms up to a high 50s-low 60s temperature range during spring and summer. Spinning gear with three-pound test line and a four-inch plastic worm are the most popular, with smaller deep-diving plugs right behind. So plentiful are small-mouth bass on the Umpqua that the river has its own set of guidelines that are more generous than the regulations governing other Oregon waterways. You are allowed 12 bass a day with no more than five over 17 inches.

Largemouth bass are found mainly in valley lakes and reservoirs. These fish average two pounds, with some big ones now and then tipping the scales at four pounds. The bait, tackle, and regulations are the same as for smallmouth. The key difference is that anglers should have a boat to keep moving with the school.

Striped bass are found in the main Umpqua and seem to roam back and forth from brackish to sweet water continuously. The striped bass is the largest of the bass species found here, and the Umpqua has produced some world-record catches of the fish over the years. You'll need a boat to fish for "stripers" as the guides call them, as well as a stout rod, 20- to 30-pound test line, and a variety of bait. Minnow or eel imitations are good for trolling, herring or smelt work for bottom fishing, and hooks or plugs are best for surface casting.

Shad

Commerical fishing interests have been fishing for shad in the Umpqua River since the 1920s. Since 1964, about 60,000 shad a year are taken from the Umpqua. Shad eggs or roe are considered a delicacy, particularly on the East Coast.

Smelt

Smelt are found on the lower Umpqua near Reedsport around Dean Creek. They have no set timetable for their migrations, moving about the ocean and into the river whenever they deem it necessary. Smelt are usually caught with a small mesh net.**2

PRACTICALITIES

Bed and Breakfasts

The Wood's Bed and Breakfast, 428 Oakview Dr., Roseburg 97470, tel. (541) 672-2927, $60-80, is located six miles northwest of town near scenic River Forks Park. Their guest suite overlooks a pond on their seven-acre wooded

ROSEBURG ACCOMMODATIONS

Best Western Douglas Inn Motel, 511 S.E. Stephens St., tel. (541) 673-6625 or (800) 528-1234, $50-70, restaurant.

Best Western, Garden Villa Motel, 760 N.W. Garden Valley Blvd., tel. (541) 672-1601, $50-70, pool, pets, nonsmoking rooms.

Budget 16 Motel, 1067 N.E. Stephens St., tel. (541) 673-5556 or (800) 414-1648, $45-55, pool.

Dunes Motel, 610 W. Madrone, tel. (541) 672-6684 or (800) 260-9973, $45-60, lounge, pets.

Holiday Motel, 444 S.E. Oak, tel. (541) 672-4457, $45-65, pool, pets.

Motel Orleans, 427 N.W. Garden Valley Blvd., tel. (541) 673-5561, $45-80, pool, restaurant, lounge.

Pine Motel, 2821 N.E. Stephens St., tel. (541) 672-4063, $40-60, kitchenettes, pool.

Roseburg Travelodge, 315 W. Harvard, tel. (541) 672-4836 or (800) 578-7878, $45-65, pool.

Rose City Motel, 1142 N.E. Stephens St., tel. (541) 673-8209, $40-50, cable, pets.

Shady Oaks Motel, 2954 Old 99, tel. (541) 672-2608, $30-40, air-conditioning.

Sycamore Motel, 1627 S.E. Stephens St., tel. (541) 672-3354 or (800) 524-9999, $40-50, restaurant.

Town House Motel, 525 N.E. Stephens St., tel. (541) 672-4526, $40-50, cable, pets.

Vista Motel, 1183 N.E. Stephens St., tel. (541) 673-2736, $40-50, Showtime, HBO, pets.

Windmill Inn of Roseburg, 1450 N.W. Mulholland Dr., tel. (541) 673-0901 or (800) 547-4747, $65-90, everything.

spread. Judy Wood, the hostess, has published her own cookbook, and gourmet meals are always featured.

The Gothic-revival-style **Hokanson's Guest House,** 848 S.E. Jackson St., tel. (541) 672-2632, $60-80, was built in 1882 on land once owned by Aaron Rose, the founder of Roseburg. Listed in the National Register of Historic Places, each bedroom in the building has a private bath with a claw-foot tub and period furnishings. Hokanson's Hi-Ho Restaurant is five blocks away. Another classic home from the era when lumber was king is the **House of Hunter,** 813 S.E. Kane St., tel. (541) 672-2335 or (800) 540-7704, $55-95. Two rooms have private baths; two other rooms share a bath. Each room boasts an English wardrobe closet, a handmade quilt, and turn-of-the-century furnishings. Telephone and TV can be hooked up to your room upon request. This turn-of-the-century home in Roseburg's historic neighborhood also has proximity to restaurants, galleries, and antique shops. A sumptuous breakfast and little touches like flowers and sherry have helped the innkeepers create an impressive amount of repeat business.

Campgrounds

Armacher County Park, tel. (541) 672-4901, $10-15, is five miles north of town off I-5 on exit 129. The park is situated on the North Umpqua and has 10 tent sites and 20 RV/trailer sites with full hookups. A bathhouse and picnic area are also found here. **Twin Rivers Vacation Park,** 433 Rivers Forks Rd., tel. (541) 673-3811, $6-15, is six miles out of town (via I-5, take exit 125) where the north and south forks of the Umpqua converge. Water, electricity, waste disposal, and a coin-op laundry are available at this 85-site park. **Fairgrounds RV Park,** 210 Frear St., tel. (541) 440-4505, $14-18, has 50 hookups, water, and a drive-through dump station. **U-Haul RV Center,** 1182 N.E. Stephens, tel. (541) 672-6864, has a dumping station for self-contained vehicles.

Food

Roseburg is not exactly the fine-dining capital of Oregon. Most of the folks here are more interested in getting a big plate of food than titillating their palates. Since there is no shortage of fast-food joints, greasy spoons, and truck-driver restaurants, let's focus instead upon a few unique eateries in town. From mid-May through October, the **Douglas County Farmers Market,** parking lot of Roseburg Valley Mall on Stewart Parkway and Garden Valley Blvd., is a great place to partake of lost flavors each Saturday 9 a.m.-1 p.m.

A highly regarded Tex-Mex establishment is **La Hacienda,** 940 N.W. Garden Valley Blvd., tel. (541) 672-5330. You'll know the place when you see it. In front of the cream-colored stucco building with green and orange stripes are tall arches of typical Spanish design. The food inside is equally inviting. In addition to the usual assortment of tacos, tostadas, and tamales, you'll find some dishes that break away from the Mexican-food norm. The shrimp and chicken fajitas are good, as are the combination dinners and seafood dishes. One of the latter you may care to try is langostinos Jalisco, prawns sautéed in butter, garlic, and white wine. A big basket of chips with green tomatillo salsa or the more traditional red salsa comes with your meal. La Hacienda also features a wide selection of Mexican beers to enhance your lunch, $5-10, or dinner, $7-15.

If you're in the mood for some good, cheap, and plentiful Italian cuisine, head for **Momma's Home Cookin',** 834 N.W. Garden Valley Blvd., tel. (541) 672-4361. Spaghetti, linguine, fettuccine, canneloni, and manicotti are among the "pastabilities." Momma's also features calzone as well as a full line of pizzas. Open seven days a week for lunch and dinner. You'll find good deli sandwiches at **Between the Buns,** 214 S.E. Jackson, tel. (541) 672-8633. "Dagwood-style" sandwiches piled way too high with fillings come at a low price that makes them easy to swallow. Open Mon.-Fri. 11 a.m.-5 p.m.; call the night before to order a picnic lunch.

Brutke's Wagon Wheel, 227 N.W. Garden Valley Blvd., tel. (541) 672-7555, is the place to go for prime rib. The chef's prime rib recipe dates back over 30 years and accounts for over a third of the food sales at the restaurant. But if you don't fit the beefeater's shoes, chicken and "heart smart" entrees are also featured on the menu. The restaurant has a colorful, homey atmosphere. You might see loggers wearing flannel shirts and denims while other folks sport more formal attire. It's not uncommon for couples to come by here for a special occasion and families to drop in for a good, wholesome meal. Open Mon.-Fri. for lunch and dinner, Sat.-Sun. for dinner only.

Umpqua Brewing Company, 328 S.E. Jackson, tel. (541) 672-0452, serves pub grub and hearty microbrews in an old-timey atmosphere. Sit at the counter in the pre-dawn hours at **Mom's Place,** 634-S.E. Cass, tel. (541) 672-8459, to get a sense of Roseburg's timber past and present. Cork-booted timber "fellers" in work-blackened demims and thermos-toting, hard hatted millworkers shovel down gargantuan portions at a price that makes Mom's the workingman's friend.

Cafe Espresso, corner of Douglas and Jackson, 368 S.E. Jackson, tel. (541) 672-1859, has a bright, many-checkered decor and a varied lunch menu. Daily specials, $3.50-7, on the order of quiche and lasagna washed down by caffeinated cups of premium brew are especially appreciated in a town low on good coffeehouses. Breakfast is also served here.

New Day Quality Grocery, 210 S.E. Jackson, tel. (541) 672-0275, has organic produce, bulk foods and herbs, spices, and teas. Open Mon.-Sat. 9:30 a.m.-6:30 p.m., Sunday 9:30 a.m.-5 p.m.

Events

Roseburg's big event is the **Douglas County Fair,** held annually at the fairgrounds the second week of August. Besides the usual assortment of 4-H prize bulls, mom's marmalade, and grandma's-secret-recipe apple pie, the bright lights of the midway rides, food booths, and horse and stock-car races add to the festive atmosphere. In the afternoon, big-name singers entertain the crowds with toe-tapping country music. While it's seven days of fun, and well worth seeing if you're in the neighborhood, high temperatures compel an early start. In September, a wine, art, and cheese fest attracts vintners, artisans, and food booths. Contact the Roseburg Visitors and Convention Bureau for specifics.

In December, the **Umpqua Valley Festival of Lights** is noteworthy for fanciful creations (including an eight-foot high waving Santa and a 36-foot high American Flag) and the sheer size of the display. Contact the Roseburg Visitors and Convention Bureau, tel. (800) 444-9584, for details on both festivals.

There are also nature trails and wildlife viewing at Stewart Park. The park hosts free concerts during Roseburg's **Music on the Halfshell** series in the summer. The park's bandshell is near the banks of the South Umpqua and hosts such urbane entertainers as David Grisman and B.B. King.

Getting There and Getting Around

The **Greyhound/Trailways** bus depot, 835 S.E. Stephens, tel. (541) 673-5326, is open weekdays 7:30 a.m.-6:30 p.m., Saturday 8 a.m.-5 p.m. Routes connect Roseburg with California, the Willamette Valley, and Washington, as well as the Oregon coast. The **Green Tortoise,** (800) 867-8647, departs from the Tom Tom restaurant (just off I-5 exit 125) at 11:15 a.m. Sunday and Thursday for northbound destinations, and at 5:15 p.m. Monday and Friday headed southbound. Be sure to call in advance to arrange for a "flag stop."

Pal Auto Rental, 1410 S.E. Stephens, tel. (541) 673-5210, features new and late-model car rentals at reasonable rates. **The Mobile Tune,** 1400 S.E. Stephens, tel. (541) 673-5210, has vehicles ranging from compacts and economy cars to luxury sedans and pickup trucks in addition to trailers and RVs. **Roseburg Sunshine Taxi Express,** tel. (541) 672-2888, can chauffeur you around the city.

Information and Services

The **Roseburg Visitors and Convention Bureau,** 410 S.E. Spruce St., tel. (541) 672-9731 or (800) 444-9584, has all kinds of useful information free for the taking. One particularly useful pamphlet is a driver's guide to historic places. And while the staff is courteous and can offer decent travel-planning suggestions, they are tight-lipped when it comes to specific recommendations on food and lodging. If you're here for a while ask about U-pick opportunities on Garden Valley Road.

The **Douglas County Library,** 1409 N.E. Diamond Lake Blvd., tel. (541) 440-4305 or (800) 441-2706, located just behind the courthouse. Hours are Monday noon-8 p.m., Tues.-Wed. 10 a.m.-8 p.m., Thurs.-Fri. 10 a.m.-6 p.m., Saturday 10 a.m.-4 p.m. . The **Douglas County Museum Lavola Bakken Research Library,** Douglas County Fairgrounds, tel. (541) 440-4507, is a reference library on the first floor of the museum. It has a good collection on the historical and cultural development of Douglas County, as well as information on the county's botany, geology, and zoology.

The **Starlight Indoor/Outdoor Drive-In,** 400 Grant Smith Rd., tel. (541) 679-6341, is open every day of the year (even Christmas!). Current films are shown, $6/car, and are usually double features.

Douglas Community Hospital, 735 W. Harvard Blvd., tel. (541) 673-6641, offers a 24-hour physician-staffed emergency room treating everything from colds to major trauma. **Harvard Urgent Care Clinic,** 1813 W. Harvard Blvd., Suite 110, tel. (541) 673-1503, is the place to drop in for minor medical problems.

The Roseburg **police,** 774 S.E. Rose, tel. (541) 673-6633 or 911 for emergencies only, and the state police, tel. (541) 440-3333, are always available should any trouble occur. The **post office,** 519 S.E. Kane, Roseburg 97470, tel. (541) 673-5326, is open Mon.-Fri. 8:30 a.m.-5 p.m. If you're recycling your dirty clothes, **Wash and Dry Laundry,** 1820 N.E. Stephens, tel. (541) 673-7701, and **Clothes Hamper Launderette,** 2428 W. Harvard Blvd., tel. (541) 672-0240, both feature coin-operated machines.

OAKLAND

Many travelers drive by the exit marked Oakland on I-5 joking that maybe they made a wrong turn somewhere and ended up in California. But the curious who venture a few miles off the freeway to explore this National Historic Landmark discover that *this* Oakland is an interesting voyage into Oregon's past. Established in the 1850s, this hamlet today gives little indication of the caprices of fate and fortune it has experienced in its 140-year history.

Oakland was a stopover point for the main stagecoach line linking Portland and Sacramento until the Oregon and California Railroad came to town in 1872. With these two transportation linkages, Oakland thrived as a trading center for outlying hop fields and prune orchards. In the early 1900s, millions of pounds of dried prunes were shipped all over the world from Oakland. In the 1920s and '30s, raising

turkeys became the prominent industry in the area, and Oakland became the leading turkey-shipping center in the western United States. During the '40s through the '60s, the lumber industry dominated the local economy. Today, livestock ranching, farming, and tourism are the economic mainstays.

While not as built-up as its counterpart restoration farther south in Jacksonville, Oakland still provides a good place to pull off the interstate and reflect on the passing of time in a onetime boomtown turned rural hamlet.

Sights
Old Town Oakland is a good place to start your tour, because this is where it all began. An excellent free history and walking-tour pamphlet is available at city hall, 117 3rd Street. The original wooden buildings were destroyed by fires in the 1890s, and most of the brick and stone structures in the historical district date back to this era of reconstruction. There are many antique stores, art galleries, and curio shops to browse through as well. The **Oakland Museum,** 136 Locust, is worth visiting. The exhibit in the back re-creates Oakland during its boom times. Open daily 1-4:30 p.m.; closed on holidays; admission is free.

Accommodations
Tolly's Beckley House, 338 S.E. 2nd, tel. (541) 459-9320, is a Queen Anne-style house dating back to 1890. Such touches as the antique-furnished suites and an included Tolly's Restaurant breakfast make the $70-100 rate well worth it.

Food
The **Lamplighter Inn,** 126 Locust, tel. (541) 459-4938, opens at 6 a.m. for breakfast and serves basic American food like omelettes, sandwiches, and burgers. The lounge in the back of the restaurant is the hot spot in town, where locals come to tilt glasses and play video poker. Even if you're not in the mood for a drink, go inside and check out their huge Maxfield Parrish-like painting of a naked women petting a swan. It is based on William Butler Yeats's 1923 poem "Leda and the Swan." Leda was ravished by Zeus in the form of a swan, and subsequently gave birth to Helen of Troy. Oakland is noteworthy for these leftover touches of refinement from its golden age, which seem almost incon-

THE LEGENDS OF ONE-EYED CHARLIE AND BLACK BART

While it has been a century since southern Oregon has heard the pounding hoofbeats and grinding axles of an approaching Portland-to-Sacramento stagecoach, the West's first organized interstate transportation system hasn't been forgotten. Such stageline stopovers as Wolf Creek Tavern, north of Grants Pass, and Jacksonville, west of Medford, have been commemorated with National Historic Landmark and National Historic District status. In addition to these evocations of the era, the stories of two romantic figures, Black Bart and One-Eyed Charlie, help to bring back a time when the Wild West lived up to its name.

One-Eyed Charlie was a stagecoach driver, a job that commanded considerable respect back in 19th-century Oregon. A look at the roadbeds of such wagon-route remnants as I-5 between Grants Pass and Roseburg and ORE 238 north of Jacksonville might help you to understand why. Hostile Indians, ruthless highwaymen, and inclement weather plagued these frontier thoroughfares. Even without such hazards, bouncing along for days on end on a buckboard carriage, minus shock absorbers and air-conditioning, required considerable fortitude.

Of all the men on the Oregon-to-California line, One-Eyed Charlie was the driver of choice whenever Wells Fargo needed to send a valuable cargo. Despite a salty vocabulary, an opinionated demeanor, and a rough appearance, all of which might have rankled some passengers, no one was better at handling the horses or dealing with adversity.

When the stage would roll into Portland or Sacramento, One-Eyed Charlie would collect his paycheck and disappear for a few days. It was said he was a heavy drinker and gambler during his sojourns deep into the seamy frontier underworld. When it came time to make the next trip through, however, he'd be back at the helm, sober and cantankerous as ever.

One day, One-Eyed Charlie's hard-drivin' hard-drinkin' life caught up with him. When the coroner was preparing the body for burial, he made a surprising discovery. One-Eyed Charlie was really One-Eyed Charlene! Shock waves reverberated up and down the West Coast at the realization that a woman had been best at what was considered exclusively a man's domain. But the real kicker was that she had voted in the 1860 and 1864 presidential elections for Abraham Lincoln, over half a century before a woman could legally vote! As the voting records have been lost, legal scholars have been unable to prove or debunk the persistent legend of One-Eyed Charlie.

Another personality from the stagecoach era, the outlaw Black Bart, has also become part of Western folklore. Between 1875 and his capture in 1883, he robbed 28 stagecoaches of their gold shipments. Known as the Gentleman Bandit due to his polite treatment of passengers, Black Bart had a penchant for verse. One of his finer efforts read:

I've labored hard and long for bread,
for honor and for riches.
But on my corns too long you've tread,
you fine-haired sons of bitches.
Let come what will, I'll try it on, my
condition can't be worse.
And if there's money in that box, tis
munney in my purse."

But the Gentleman Bandit's chivalrous ways proved to be his undoing. A handkerchief much like one he offered to the ladies when he helped them off of the stage was found at the scene of a robbery. The initials "CB" were embroidered on the corner. Traced by its laundry mark to San Francisco, the owner was identified as Charles Bolton, an employee of Wells Fargo Bank. This explained why Black Bart was able to know the arrival time of gold shipments. After completing four years of a six-year sentence at San Quentin, Charles Bolton was let out for good behavior. He disappeared shortly thereafter, but will forever be remembered as the Gentleman Bandit for his refinement and the fact that he never shot anyone.

gruous against its present-day small-town facade. You may recognize Main Street Oakland if you saw the movie *Fire in the Sky.*

Fancier fare is found across the street at **Tolly's,** 115 Locust, tel. (541) 459-3796, "where sodas flow and friendships grow." Lunch is served 10 a.m.-6 p.m. and features deli, croissant, and Scandinavian sandwiches (like the Svensk Farsk Frukt, which is cream cheese, peanut butter, dried apricots, prunes, and bananas, guaranteed to give you that "get up and go" feeling), as well as creative entrees and salads. We recommend prawns Dijon. Elaborate gourmet dinners, $8-17, are served 5:30-10 p.m. (except Monday) and are complemented by a fine wine list and mellow piano music. Whichever meal you are having, be sure to save some room for the homemade desserts proudly shown off in the lobby display case. The well-illuminated upstairs room is the nicest place to sit. Here, you can admire the sturdy 25-foot-long, 4- by 20-inch Douglas fir roof supports that tell of another era when lumber was king.

Information and Services
The small but quaint **Oakland Public Library,** 100 N.E. 7th, is in the historic Washington School Building (1910). Open Monday 2-8 p.m., Tuesday 10 a.m.-2 p.m., Wednesday 10 a.m.-noon and 2-6 p.m., and Friday 1-5 p.m. The **post office,** 109 Locust St., Oakland 97462, is open Mon.-Fri. 8:30 a.m.-5 p.m., closed one hour for lunch. The **chamber of commerce** is at city hall, 117 3rd Street. The **police** can be reached at (541) 440-4471, and for **emergency medical care,** dial 911. For general visitor information on Oakland, call Cindy Whitaker of the **Oakland Business Association,** tel. (541) 459-4688.

Events
Each year, on the second weekend of September (after labor Day), the main street of Oakland is vacated for two days to accommodate booths offering wine tasting, food, and arts and crafts while jazz holds forth in the city park. This is the **Umpqua Valley Wine, Art and Jazz festival,** a three-decade old kulturfest that left Roseburg in the mid-nineties for this small town. A lamb barbecue attended by the winemakers and music that spans all jazz genres and often includes blues makes this event a "must" if you're in the area. Call (541) 459-4688 for details.

BOB RACE

THE HIGH CASCADES
INTRODUCTION

The Cascades comprise one of the most magnificent natural playgrounds in the world. This collage of green forest and black basalt outcroppings is topped by extinct volcano cones covered with snow. Plenty of lakes, rivers, and waterfalls provide a pleasing contrast to the earth tones here. There are over 160 parks in the High Cascades, providing easy access to hiking, camping, climbing, and other recreational pursuits. Many of these parks are linked by the Pacific Crest Trail, which traverses the entire range border to border. The famous thoroughfare is the backbone of an extensive network of footpaths that wind through this spectacular region. In addition, six national forests, six federal wilderness areas, and Oregon's only national park, Crater Lake, are also found in the Oregon Cascades. Add to this list the bevy of luxury resorts, nine developed ski areas, hundreds of miles of cross-country skiing and snowmobiling trails, as well as numerous waterways teeming with fish, and you have all the accoutrements for roughing it in style.

THE LAND

What fault scarps are to the California landscape, lava fields and snowcapped volcano cones are to Oregon. While remnants of the state's not-so-distant volcanic past abound, the most impressive and dramatic examples are found in the High Cascades, a chain of icy peaks stretching from northern California to British Columbia. The Oregon Cascades lie in the heart of this great range, and many have been named after former military commanders and heads of state. Given their stature and commanding presences, Mounts Hood, Jefferson, and Washington rate such distinction. Mount Hood (11,235 feet) is the tallest in the state, and many others top out at over 10,000 feet. Oregon's peaks are part of the great Ring of Fire which encircles the Pacific and includes Cotopaxi (Ecuador), Fuji (Japan), and Krakatoa (Indonesia), as well as the Cascades' notorious sister volcanoes, Lassen (California) and St. Helens (Washington).

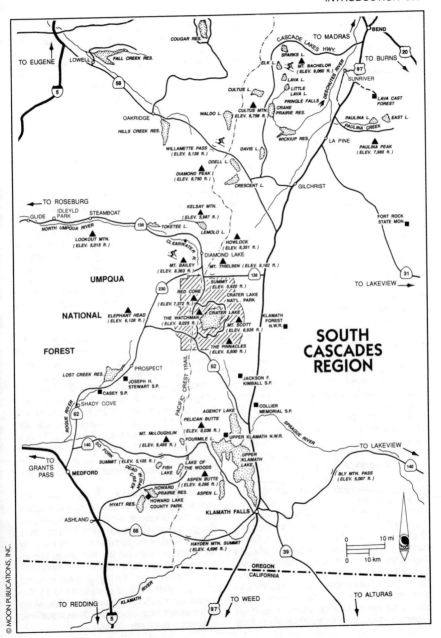

SOUTH
CASCADES
REGION

They are linked by the theory of continental drift and plate tectonics. According to the theory, the landmasses force the ocean floor to slip underneath the continental plate. This creates heat-generating friction, causing rocks to melt. The resulting hot, soupy subterranean mass feeds inland volcanoes with magma and molten rock, 20-plus miles beneath the earth's surface.

When water is added to this hellish brew, the melting point of the rocks is lowered by 1,000° F or more. Water also acts as the major explosive agent of volcanic eruptions, primarily due to the steam created in the reaction. Eventually, the vapors can no longer be confined, and the plugged vent is pierced by the tremendous pressures of the steam and other gases produced from the magma. The lighter materials are ejected first—ash, cinders, and pyroclastic debris, and oftentimes the earth spits up mouthfuls of its fiery interior as well. Once the water supply is spent, the lava usually becomes too viscous to flow, and the vent is once again sealed up by the cooling rock to start the process anew.

The Cascade Range is approximately 25 million years old, perhaps the youngest mountain range in the contiguous 48 states. However, geologists are uncertain when the Cascade volcanoes began to form. Guesstimates date their formation at several million years ago, during the Pleistocene epoch. And while the mountains appear to be dormant, keep in mind that nature's clock is unpredictable. Although the odds of Oregon becoming a Pompeii in our lifetime seem remote, the recent worldwide increase in earthquakes and volcanic eruptions suggests that the earth's internal burners are heating up again, and one of Oregon's slumbering giants may awaken soon. One group of geologists in late 1996 included Newberry volcano outside Bend on their list of volcanoes in the the continental U.S. most likely to erupt.

There are four major types of volcanoes, and all of them are found in the Cascades. Cinder cones, like Lava Butte and Black Butte, are formed by the explosive ejection of ash and particles of lava and rarely exceed 1,200 feet in height. Shield volcanoes, like Mt. Washington and Three Fingered Jack, form gently sloping domes that tend to be wider than they are high. Erosion is responsible for their present ragged-edged appearance. Plug-dome volcanoes, like Beacon Rock in the Columbia River Gorge, are the result of lava cooling until it's too thick to flow beyond the vent, creating a massive dome. Finally, there are composite volcanoes, making up the bulk of the majestic Cascades, which are formed layer by layer from ash, cinders, and lava.

CLIMATE

The Cascades, never more than 100 to 150 miles from the Pacific, effectively divide the state into dramatically different biomes. The moisture-laden westerlies dump prodigious amounts of precipitation on western Cascade slopes, up to 150 inches a year in some locations. Having thus purged themselves, the clouds then pass over the east side of the range, retaining what little moisture they have left. While the wet-siders are busy picking the moss out from between their toes and enduring the seemingly endless succession of rainy days, the dry-siders enjoy an average of 200 days of sunshine and about 12 inches of precipitation a year.

When it's not raining in the Cascades, it's usually snowing. Willamette Pass, for example, gets an average of 300 inches of snow a year. Crater Lake, oftentimes the coldest place in the Cascades, has recorded a chilly -21° F and averages 44 feet annual snowfall. Mount Hood has experienced over 100 feet of snowfall in a year. The snow nourishes glaciers on the major peaks left over from the last ice age, 11,000 years ago, and feeds rivers, lakes, and streams with summer runoff as well. The snowpack also makes for some of the finest skiing in the Northwest.

Lest you think folks living on the western Cascades' flanks are confined to their log cabins all year by the lavish amounts of precipitation, the good news is that the weather is pleasant and dry most of the summer and into the early fall. Summer temperatures also usher in conditions favorable for a variety of outdoor pursuits. The flip side of the benign weather is that it brings higher numbers of visitors and dry, tinderbox conditions to the forest. The latter, along with frequent thunderstorms, makes forest fires a recurring seasonal menace.

FLORA AND FAUNA

Flora

The wet western slopes of the Cascades are dominated by the state tree, the Douglas fir. This towering evergreen requires abundant moisture and plenty of sunshine. The drier east side is comprised mostly of ponderosa and lodgepole pine forests. The trees often meet with almost no transition zone, because the changes in rainfall are so marked on Cascade summits. However, in southern Oregon, where precipitation levels are generally lower, pine trees have stolen over the crest into the Klamath, Rogue, and Umpqua river basins.

Fires and humans can have more effect on the natural balance of a forest than fluctuations in weather. The changes in ground cover, shade, and soil make conditions more favorable for one species of tree over others. The aggressive Oregon oak is one such example, an easily established tree that can quickly challenge the kingdom of the Douglas fir. The oak's reign, however, is often cut short by the bitter cold, deep snow, and dry summers. Eventually,

Bear grass, a common sight in the Cascades, blooms under Mt. Hood's shadow.

OREGON TOURISM DIVISION

the Douglas fir is able to usurp the oak and regain its former rule over the forest.

The lodgepole pine is the primary benefactor in the southern Cascades, where frequent summer lightning storms take their annual toll of other species. The tough little cones of this tree endure fires and other adversities such as climatic extremes and barren soils, sprouting when favorable conditions return. The tree colonizes an area rapidly, growing up straight, true, and fine. As their name implies, these forthright trees were often used in the construction of lodges by the Indians and pioneers. But the lodgepole pine usually meets the same fate as the Oregon oak, sooner or later choked out by the larger and longer-lived climax species like Douglas fir, cedar, balsam fir, Engelmann spruce, white pine, and hemlock.

And the lodgepole pine is not entirely free of competition for turf in the wake of a fire. Oftentimes low brush quickly moves in, firmly establishing its territorial dominance over young pine seedlings. The tenacious manzanita, sticky laurel, and varieties of ceanothus, currants, and other miscellaneous shrubs generically labeled as buckbrush or snowbrush are the predominant examples of this type of chaparral.

Wild rhododendrons, dogwoods, and myriad wildflowers are the smile of spring in the Cascades as Old Man Winter releases his frozen grip upon the land. Summer foragers can find blackberries, huckleberries, and salmonberries, as well as many exotic types of mushrooms, in the damp recesses of the forest. Fall color from hardwoods is limited on Cascade slopes. Bright splashes of gold are provided by ash, aspen, cottonwood, tamarack, and bigleaf maple, but the heavy hitters are the brilliantly colored Douglas and vine maples. The vine maples in particular can make the otherwise lackluster fall foliage of the Cascades come alive with vivid reds and yellows.

Fauna

The Cascades are Oregon's forest primeval. The black bear, wolf, mountain lion, lynx and bobcat compete with each other as well as with humans in the hunt for beavers, deer, elk (wapiti), and snowshoe hares. The smaller predators such as foxes, weasels, and martens prey upon chipmunks, squirrels, porcupines, and rats.

Other commonly encountered forest creatures include the coyote, raccoon, and skunk. A half-dozen species of bats add to the diversity of mammals present in the Cascades. Indeed, this is where the wild things are.

The mountains are also home to a wide range of amphibians and reptiles. Generally speaking, most amphibians, such as frogs and salamanders, are found in cool and damp habitats west of the Cascades, whereas their cold-blooded reptilian fellow travelers (especially the lizard) prefer the warm and dry eastern flank. However, there always seem to be exceptions to every rule. Several of these critters are found on both sides of the Cascades, seemingly oblivious to the inherent climatic discrepancies.

The most widespread example of Cascade herpetofauna is the Pacific tree frog, *Hyla regilla*. It has been found on both sides of the range at elevations up to 7,000 feet. One secret to the frog's success is its versatility in using available breeding water for egg laying and larval development. While many mountain pools are strictly temporary or seasonal, they nonetheless allow enough time for the rapid growth and subsequent proliferation of the species. Also, the frogs are able to adapt to their terrestrial existence. During the dry summer months, tree frogs absorb moisture from the night air through their skin. The moisture is collected in their bladder and then excreted through the skin during the day to keep the frog cool. Furthermore, the frogs seem to have enough sense to take refuge during extreme weather conditions in abandoned rodent burrows or rock or log crevices and sit it out.

A handful of other species of frogs and toads also hop around the Cascades. If you are camping near a Cascade lake in the summer, you may be surprised at how loudly the frogs croak at night. While this deep-throated chorus may leave some campers tossing and turning on their air mattresses, others will undoubtedly rest assured that the frogs are also busy consuming an inordinate amount of insects, especially the pesky mosquito.

Visitors to the high country come upon many a giant Pacific salamander in mountain waterways. Common in high to low elevations, the timing of their metamorphosis into adults coincides with the seasonal fluctuations of their home stream. In addition to the Pacific giant, six other species of salamanders also call the Cascades home.

Reptiles prefer to slink around the warmer and drier east side. Over a dozen species of snakes and lizards are common to the Cascades. The most dangerous member of the family is *Crotalus viridis*, the western rattlesnake. Able to strike with blinding quickness and inject potentially lethal amounts of venom into its victim, this diamond-headed snake should be avoided at all costs. They like to sun themselves in warm open spots and can be difficult to spot until you step on them, as they tend to coil up. Listen for the telltale rattle of the snake's tail, and give them a wide berth. Baby rattlers, while smaller than the adults, are just as deadly, and more dangerous to wilderness adventurers because their rattles have not yet developed enough to make any noise. And while you may be tempted to smash a rattlesnake to smithereens with a handy rock or tree branch, keep in mind that these reptiles effectively police the exponential growth of rodent populations.

The Cascades have over 70 species of birds, ranging from the great horned owl to the hummingbird. The successional stages of forest management in the mountains play an important role in the habitat and territory of many species. When an area is first logged over, the grasses and small shrubs that grow soon afterward are favorite haunts of the state bird, the western meadowlark. The mountain quail prefers thicker brush and small trees, the second phase of forest regeneration. The mixed deciduous woods that comprise the next stage make the ideal habitat for warblers. Finally, when the conifers have once again become the climax species of the forest, sharp-shinned hawks will move in. Thus, changes in habitats often increase certain species of birds at the expense of others.

SKIING THE CASCADES

The Cascades are a haven for winter sports that range from Alpine and Nordic skiing to snowmobiling and snowshoeing. There are nine developed ski areas and hundreds of miles of backcountry trails for these wintertime recreational pursuits. And while other ski areas in Colorado, Idaho, and California have been hard-hit by drought, Oregon is still blessed with an abundant annual snowpack that makes for nearly year-round skiing. It is no wonder that ski pros like Billy Kidd and the famous Mahre brothers hold racing camps in Oregon, or that the Cascades are the official training ground for the U.S. Olympic Ski Team. While the Cascades don't have the mystique of the Rockies, the greater challenge here is due to the variability of conditions. Other advantages of Oregon skiing include proximity to major cities and the longest season in the country.

Mount Hood

In addition to being the state's highest mountain, Mt. Hood also boasts the most ski areas, five in all. A popular destination for families and beginners is **Cooper Spur,** P.O. Box 977, Hood River 97032, tel. (541) 352-7803. Located on the northeastern flank of the mountain, 24 miles south of Hood River on ORE 35, it usually offers protection from storms and prevailing westerlies, yet has more than enough snow for a good time and is affordable for families. Call (541) 386-5900 for hours (which fluctuate with the season) and the snow report. You can also find out about the Cloud Cap auto tour, an 11-mile scenic loop in the area. Nordic skiers appreciate the Tilly Jane Trail here. Also on the east side is **Mt. Hood Meadows,** P.O. Box 470, Mt. Hood 97028, tel. (541) 337-2222, http://www.ski-hood.com, the peak's largest ski area. Ten miles from Government Camp on ORE 35, hundreds of acres of groomed slopes and seven double chairlifts plus one triple and one quad ensure plenty of room for all, though this place is so popular at times you might have to wait. The construction of a new four seat chairlift should ease congestion on the two mile long access road from Oregon 35 to the ski area. Massive construction projects over the past few years partially explain Oregon's highest-priced lift tickets here. Call 227-SNOW for the hours of operation and snow report. It's often sunny here on the east slope of the mountain when on the west side it's snowing and raining.

Ski Bowl

Ski Bowl, P.O. Box 280, 87000 E ORE 21, Government Camp 97028, tel. (541) 272-3206, is only 53 miles away from metropolitan Portland on ORE 26 and features the most extensive night skiing in the country. The upper bowl also has some of the most challenging skiing to be found on the mountain. Within the complex are venues for snowboarding, bungee jumping, and mountain biking. Call 222-BOWL for the current hours of operation and the snow report. A mile farther down ORE 26 is **Summit Ski Area,** P.O. Box 385, Government Camp 97028, tel. (541) 272-0256 or 621-3684, the place for families, beginners, and people who just like to play in the snow. You can ski on beginners' slopes or rent an inner tube for $5-10 to barrel down the gently sloping surrounding hills. Several other good sliding hills are close by. To get to Summit, drive through the town of Government Camp off US 26. Beyond the stores and concessions you'll see a large parking lot on the left-hand side of the road with a structure housing a burger joint and equipment rental.

The only noncommercial developed sliding hill in the Mt. Hood National Forest is at Little John Sno-Park, located nine miles north of Mt Hood Meadows on ORE 35.

Timberline

The undisputed king of the mountain is Timberline, Timberline Ski Area, Timberline Lodge 97028, tel. (541) 272-3311. Located 60 miles east of Portland on ORE 26, the skiing starts where the trees end. With the highest vertical drop of any ski area in Oregon (3,600 feet) as well as the highest elevation accessible by chairlift (8,600 feet), 60% of Timberline's ski runs are in the intermediate-level category. Given this terrain, it should come as no surprise that the U.S. Olympic Ski Team trains here on Palmer Glacier during the summer months. Call (541) 222-2111 for the current operating hours and the snow report. This is the mountain's only year-round ski area. Timberline has the longest ski season in the nation. Recent improvements to the Palmer Chairlift has made this experience better than ever.

Attractive midweek ski packages include lodging at the hall of the mountain king, **Timberline Lodge,** http://www.teleport.com/-timlodge. This National Historic Site was built in the 1930s as a Works Progress Administration project (for more information see Mt. Hood Chapter). Billed as the most magnificent wooden structure ever built, the lodge also features fine dining and a heated outdoor swimming pool. For lodging reservations and information on special packages, call (541) 231-5400 from Portland, (800) 452-1335 from the rest of Oregon, and (800) 547-1406 from Nevada, northern California, Idaho, Utah, and Washington. For ski information here, call (541) 231-7979

Here, at 6,000 feet, the frequently wet Cascade snow is less sloppy. While it's not as light as powder, the 31 runs are so well groomed that Timberline snow is easily navigable. The chairlifts (six in winter, two in summer) are mostly obscured by trees or topography, so you get a feeling of intimacy with the natural surroundings when you're schussing downhill. You can go up two lifts, enjoying a nearly two-mile-long run that drops 2,500 feet vertically. At the top of the Palmer chairlift is a sign that tells the story of scout Joel Palmer, who climbed the mountain to this elevation to help pioneer the Barlow Road section of the Oregon Trail.

Though the first fresh snow usually comes in November or December, several years ago there were flurries on the Fourth of July, underscoring Timberline's claim of offering the only lift-serviced summer skiing in the United States. Skiers can pay around $30+ for a one-day summer lift ticket at Timberline. The two summer chairs run daily through Labor Day. The upper Palmer lift, highest on the mountain, is open only from late spring through fall, when conditions are safe for skiing on the Palmer glacier. The Magic Mile chair, directly below the Palmer, is open to the 7,000 foot level for sightseers as well as skiers. The price for nonskiing sightseers is about 20% of what skiers pay for lift tickets. Remember that summer temperatures on Mt. Hood can vary from below freezing to 90° F. Along with sun cream, dark glasses, and other warm-weather gear, bring layered ski apparel to adapt to varied conditions.

Transportation direct from Portland airport to Timberline can be arranged through **Mt. Hood Express,** tel. (541) 250-4379. This van service ranges from $15 per person for six to as high as $60 for one person. G.I. Joe's (a sporting goods store) and Grayline in Portland also frequently sponsor ski buses up to the resorts on Mt. Hood.

Hoodoo Ski Bowl

The state's oldest ski area, Hoodoo Ski Bowl, P.O. Box 20, ORE 20, Sisters 97759, tel. (541) 342-5540, http://www.hoodoo.com, has the additional distinction of also being the least expensive. Located between Salem and Bend on ORE 20, this family-oriented resort is evenly divided into beginner, intermediate, and advanced terrain and also offers night skiing. Hours are Tues.-Sun. 9 a.m.-4 p.m.; night skiing Wed.-Sun. 4-10 p.m. For the updated operating hours and snow report, call (541) 345-7416 from Eugene, (541) 585-8081 from Salem, (541) 752-8887 from Corvallis, or (800) 944-LIFT. Contact the **Sisters Ranger District,** Deschutes National Forest, Sisters, 97759, tel. (541) 549-2111, of the McKenzie Ranger District, Willamette National Forest, McKenzie Bridge 97413, tel. (541) 822-3381, for information on cross-country skiing from snow-park areas.

Willamette Pass

Willamette Pass, 69 miles southeast of Eugene on ORE 58, write: 1899 Willamette St., Suite 1, Eugene 97401, tel. (541) 484-5030, http://www.willamettepass.com, has some of the most challenging runs in the state as well as a multitude of beginner and intermediate trails. You'll find some of the steepest runs in the state here, as opposed to open chutes or powder bowls at other ski areas. Since Willamette Pass plows its own parking lot, you will not need a snow-park permit here. Hours before January 1: Wed.-Sun. 9 a.m.-4 p.m. After January 1: Wed.-Sat. 9 a.m.-9 p.m., Sunday 9 a.m.-4 p.m. Call 345-SNOW for the ski report.

Mount Bachelor

The Northwest's largest and most complete ski area is Mt. Bachelor, P.O. Box 1031, Bend 97709, tel. (541) 382-3224 inside Oregon or (800) 829-2442 outside Oregon, http://www.mbachelor.com. Located 22 miles southwest of Bend on Century Dr., 12 ski lifts, including five high-speed quads, and trails that range from beginner to expert, make for some of the most popular skiing in the state. This is the winter training grounds for the U.S. Olympic Ski Team. With a top elevation over 9,000 feet and steady northwest air flow, skiing here can run well into the summer months. Call (541) 382-7888 for the hours of operation and the snow report. *Ski* magazine ranks Mt. Bachelor among the top five ski resorts in North America. However, avoid skiing here after

1 p.m. in May and June, when conditions become slushy. If you must ski then, choose the westside snowfields, which hold up better in the late afternoon light. Across the lot from Oregon's biggest Nordic area, skiers can take advantage of the most complete Nordic Center, tel. (541) 382-2607, in the state. Finally, while there may not be enough snow in summer to ski, you can still ride the chairlift to the peak of this volcano for an unsurpassed view of the surrounding countryside.

Mount Bailey
Limited to only 12 skiers a day, Mt. Bailey Snowcat Skiing, Diamond Lake Resort, Diamond Lake 97731, tel. (541) 793-3333, is a unique backcountry adventure for the experienced skier. Located north of Crater Lake on ORE 138, Mt. Bailey does not have crowds and lines but does have virgin slopes of powder and dynamite scenery. Snowcat skiing tours begin at 7 a.m., by reservation only. Diamond Lake Resort is southern Oregon's most complete winter resort, with downhill and cross-country skiing, skating, sledding, and snowmobiling.

Information
From Portland you can hear road- and ski-condition reports on KINK FM 102 at 6:30 a.m., 7:30 a.m., 12:15 p.m. Mon.-Fri., Dec.-March. Or call (541) 226-3102 for road information. For daily **bus** transportation from Portland to Mt. Hood skiing events, contact T.I. Joe's Ticketmaster in Portland, at various outlets.

HEALTH

Tick Talk
While relevant Cascade health hazards have already been discussed in the On the Road chapter of this book (see "Health and Help"), a few words about ticks are also in order. The deer tick, found throughout the Cascades, has been fingered in the spread of Lyme disease. First discovered in Lyme, Connecticut, in 1975, this strain of disease is now extant in western Oregon.

The first sign of an infected bite is a rash called erythema chronicum migrans. It starts at the site of the bite and gradually enlarges, clearing up at the center while staying red around the edges. The rash is accompanied by flulike symptoms, and it spreads all over the body in one out of two cases.

The second stage of the illness affects only about 15% of those infected, but the consequences are no less severe. Inflammation of the nerves and covering tissues of the spinal cord-brain can often result in headaches and memory and concentration problems. The heart can also be affected, resulting in decreased heart function and fainting spells.

The last stage occurs weeks to years after the bite. It is characterized by aching joints, and the knees appear to be particularly vulnerable. It is suspected that the illness also can contribute to arthritis in the victim's future.

The good news is that the disease can be cured with a 10-day dosage of tetracycline. If you see the telltale red rash days or weeks after your romp in the woods, see a doctor. A prescription for prevention would be to lay the insect repellent on real thick.

bighorn sheep

BOB RACE

KLAMATH FALLS

"One person's conservation is another's unemployment." This bromide underscores life in Klamath County, which had one of the highest unemployment rates and lowest per-capita incomes in the state, largely due to cutbacks in logging.

Klamath Falls, or K Falls as locals call it, is the county's population hub, with 17,000 people. It's used to hard times after witnessing the decline of its previous economic base, the railroads. In an attempt to build a viable future, the Salt Caves Dam Project was proposed on the Klamath River.

This hydropower project was cancelled after a decade of legal battles over its alleged negative effects on fish populations. The latter paralleled the restrictions put on the ponderosa pine logging (at one time, Klamath Falls milled the most in the U.S.). Just when it seemed that Klamath Falls was doomed to economic oblivion, help came from unexpected quarters. High-tech and secondary wood products companies relocated here, and the development of Klamath Lake's blue-green algae into a multimillion dollar business (a high-protein food source) gave a boost to sagging spirits and fortunes. The establishment of the Klamath Tribes Casino, 22 miles north of Klamath Falls at US 97, OR 62 junction, is also viewed as a potential economic impetus.

The biggest hopes for the future here center on K Falls as a place to live. Interest in Klamath Falls as a retirement community was sparked by an American Chamber of Commerce poll in the early nineties showing that the cost of living here was the lowest among western cities surveyed. Recreational incentives for relocation include a dry climate with 280 days of sunshine, cold but not damp winters (less cold and rainy than Bend), and the fact that it's a paradise for the outdoorsperson. Klamath River trout are legendary (average size 21 inches) and such draws as world-class whitewater rafting and the region's status as the preeminent North American winter roost of the bald eagle also could spur an influx of new population. Finally, gold medal decathlete Dan O'Brien's comments about growing up here stirred civic pride while letting the world know that K Falls is a good place to raise children.

THE LAND

Many people get a glimpse of Klamath Falls by passing through on Amtrak. Unfortunately, this isn't the way to appreciate the richness of nature here. The town is located in the transition zone between the wet western slopes of the Cascades and the Great Basin desert to the east. As such, the area boasts an incredible diversity ranging from sage and juniper to pine forests and wetland flora. The town itself overlooks the southern end of gigantic Upper Klamath Lake where it empties into smaller Lake Ewana by the mile-long Link River. The lake's outlet was once the site of the falls for which the city is named, but now the outlet is blocked by a dam. Two lakeside parks here are good places to enjoy a picnic or some birdwatching.

Hunters and the Hunted

Fall hikers in the remote forests of northern Klamath County looking for some peace and quiet in this largely undeveloped backcountry should be aware others are out there looking for something too. Hikers are likely to encounter matsutake mushroom pickers, because the moisture-rich conifer forests of the south Cascades are the prime breeding ground for Oregon's 16 million dollar annual crop of this delicacy. Members of picking crews frequently use shotgun blasts to signal each other that they've hit paydirt, understandably upsetting those who've taken to the hills for the peace of nature. Add the rifle retorts of fall hunters to the commotion caused by several thousand pickers, and you might just want to consider another locale for your fall camping trip.

SIGHTS

Favell Museum

A fine collection of Indian artifacts and western art is found at the Favell Museum, 125 W. Main St.,

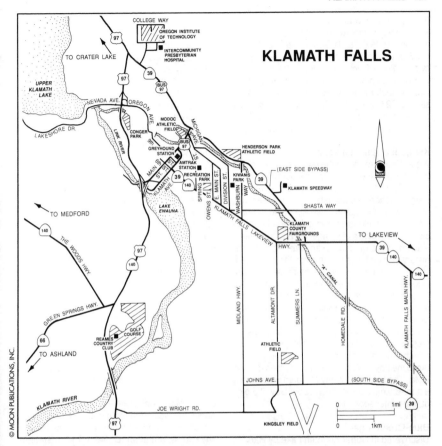

Klamath Falls 97601, tel. (541) 882-9996. Here you'll find beautiful displays of Indian stonework, bone and shellwork, beadwork, quilts, basketry, pottery, and Northwest coast carvings. A collection of over 60,000 mounted arrowheads, including an exquisite fire-opal arrowhead, also helps get the point across that this is no ordinary museum. Other exhibits of note include the Cougar Mountain Cave Collection, the Nicolarsen Cache Find, and Monte Sherman's silver treasure from an abandoned wagon train. Another attraction is the collection of miniature working firearms, ranging from Gatling guns to inch-long Colt .45s, displayed in the museum's walk-in vault.

If artifacts aren't your bag, you're bound to appreciate one of the best collections of western art in the state. Oils, acrylics, and watercolors are featured here, as well as bronzes, dioramas, photography, taxidermy, and woodcarvings. Over 300 artists are represented, including eight from Oregon. Thirteen of the artists are members of the Cowboy Artists of America. The museum's gift shop and art gallery specializes in limited-edition prints and original western art. Open Mon.-Sat. 9:30 a.m.-5:30 p.m.; admission is $4 for adults, $3 for seniors, $2 for children 6-16, and kids under age six get in free.

Baldwin Hotel Museum

Travel back in time to the early 1900s thanks to the Baldwin Hotel's, 31 Main St., tel. (541) 883-4207, original fixtures and furnishings—the legacy of a talented woman photographer whose father built the place. A video presentation in the lobby complements guided tours, $4 adults, $3 seniors, $2 kids ages 6-16, of digs once occupied by presidents Teddy Roosevelt, Taft, and Wilson. It's open Tues.-Sat. 10-4, June-September.

Klamath County Museum

A good background on the region can be gained from a visit to the free Klamath County Museum, 1451 Main St., tel. (541) 883-4208. The natural-history section has exhibits on fossils, geology, minerals, and indigenous wildlife of the Klamath Basin. The exploration and settlement area depicts the hardships of pioneer life and the events leading to the Modoc Indian War. The general history section takes you through the world wars and on up memory lane to the present. Those who really want to revel in local history can make an appointment to pore through the museum's research library, which includes one of the largest regional collections of primary sources on Captain Jack and the Modoc Indian War. During the summer, a restored 1906 trolley will give you free transportation from the Klamath County Museum to the Favell Museum and the historic Baldwin Hotel. The Klamath County Museum is open daily 9 a.m.-6 p.m., June through Labor Day, 9-5 p.m. during winter season.

Blue-Green Algae

Discovered in Upper Klamath Lake by Harvard graduate Daryl J. Kollman, blue-green algae, *Aphanizomenon flosaquae,* has been touted by Cell-Tech (a leading manufacturer of this product; call 800-800-1300, ask for PR Dept.) to have more chlorophyll and protein than any other edible organism known to man. Cell-Tech harvests blue-green algae from Upper Klamath Lake and processes it within an hour, using low temperature techniques that help perserve minerals, amino acids, and valuable enzymes. The lake itself is rich in natural nutrients and low in toxins, producing an algae superior to those grown in a man-made controlled environment. While the research on blue-green algae is incomplete, preliminary data suggests that it may enhance mental clarity, improve digestion and elimination, strengthen the immune system, and increase and sustain energy levels.

Mares Eggs Springs

Not far west of Klamath Falls off of ORE 140W is Mares Eggs Springs. This shallow pond, about an acre in size, is one of the few places on earth where *Nostoc amlissimum gard,* also known as mares eggs, grow. This blue-green unicellular algae is actually groups of minute cells that are joined together in chains by a gelatinous substance, forming a spherical colony in a rusty green sac. When the colony, or mares egg, reaches maturity, it breaks up into small fragments which in turn form new colonies. The mares eggs found in this locale can range in size from a pinhead to an extra-large potato.

Nostoc thrive here in the cold, clear water. Snowmelt and icy springs feed this pond, and temperatures never exceed 40°. Mares eggs have also been called witch's butter, star jelly, and spittle of the stars. They are considered a delicacy in China and Japan.

To get to Mares Eggs Springs, take ORE 140W to the first paved road past the Rocky Point turnoff, marked To Fort Klamath. Turn right and go past a marsh to a wooded area. The pond is on the right and marked by a sign, but look carefully because it can be easy to miss if you are not paying attention.

Collier Memorial State Park

About 30 miles north of Klamath Falls on US 97 is Collier Memorial State Park, tel. (541) 783-2471 for information. Donated to the state in 1945 by Alfred and Andrew Collier as a memorial to their parents, this 146-acre park documents the history of logging's technological improvements (there is no charge for these day use facilities). The first building at the south end of the parking lot in the park's Pioneer Village is the logger's homestead cabin, stocked with a wide variety of tools and artifacts on display inside. Near the homestead cabin is the blacksmith shed, representative of the type of shop found in early logging camps. The next building houses an assortment of logging machinery including log wagons with wheels made of cross-cut sections of logs bound in iron, and chain-drive trucks with hard rubber tires. Also on display are steam-propelled devices including tractors, a narrow-gauge locomotive, and a one-person handcart. Don't miss the over 200-foot-long, 16-feet-wide **Clatsop Fir,** a fallen tree that was mature when Columbus landed in the New World. The tree could supply enough wood for several four-bedroom homes. For better or worse, it's probably the largest Douglas Fir ever cut. Across from the museum are 18 tent sites and 50 spaces for full hookups. Reservations are not necessary for camping, but space for the day use area can be reserved with Reservations Northwest, tel. (800) 452-5687. The park is open April 15-Oct. 29, and the campground fee is $14-17. Nearby are a nature trail and fishing spot.

Thunderbeast Park

About 40 miles north of Klamath Falls on US 97 is Thunderbeast Park. For the price of admission, $4 for adults, $3 for students, free for kids under age five, you can see life-sized replicas of the giant mammals that roamed western Oregon 50 million years ago. Two-horned rhinoceroses, zebralike horses, and large saber-toothed tigers are just a few of the critters that haunt this place. The size and shapes of these animals are based upon skeletons from the American Museum of Natural History in New York, and their outward appearances are based on paintings from nationally known paleontol-ogists. Placards placed in front of each exhibit give the name and a concise history of the animal. While some are quick to scoff at the park as a hokey tourist trap, many people, especially youngsters, enjoy this well-presented glimpse into the past, when the land was semitropical.

KLAMATH BASIN WILDLIFE REFUGES

The Klamath Reclamation Project

One hundred years ago, about 185,000 acres of the Klamath Basin consisted of shallow lakes and marshes. These wetlands used to be a fall stopover for over six million waterfowl migrating south for the winter. In addition to the wide variety of birds winging their way through the territory, large concentrations of marsh birds like pelicans, cormorants, egrets, and herons resided here as well. The fertile web of life created by the wetlands further supported a host of other animals like mink, otter, beaver, deer, bear, and elk. Lunker trout and other fish grew fat in the nutrient-rich waters, providing an abundant food source for the largest concentration of osprey and bald eagles in the contiguous United States.

But our national bird didn't get to rule the roost for long. Many people believed that keeping the wetlands in their natural state was a waste of space. In 1905, the U.S. Bureau of Reclamation

OREGON DEPT. OF TRANSPORTATION

Oregon's largest lake, Upper Klamath, is also home to large bird populations.

began to pull the plug on many of the lakes and marshes here with the initiation of the Klamath Reclamation Project. The drained land was converted to irrigated agricultural endeavors, which now support a major facet of the basin's economy. However, while this was good for ranchers and farmers, it was not so good for the birds. Faced with a habitat reduced over 75%, the peak fall concentrations of migratory Pacific Flyway waterfowl have dwindled over 80%.

Fortunately, some of the basin's original habitat has been protected as national wildlife refuges that are managed by the **U.S. Fish and Wildlife Service,** 1400 Miller Island Rd. W, Klamath Falls 97603, tel. (541) 883-5732. There are currently six such refuges, three in Oregon and three more just across the state line in California. Coniferous forests, grassy meadows, marshes, open water, sagebrush and juniper grasslands, and cliffs and rocky slopes are some of the habitats found in the parks. This variety of terrain and vegetation supports an abundant population of wildlife; park checklists show 411 different species present at the refuges.

bald eagle

Fall is the best time of year to observe waterfowl migrations. Starting in late August with the arrival of pintails and white-fronted geese, the numbers of ducks and geese swell to nearly one million by early November. Canada, Ross's, and snow geese, mallards, green-winged teals, tundra swans, and pigeons are some of the other major migratory species represented. August and September are also good times to view marsh birds like cormorants, egrets, grebes, gulls, herons, pelicans, and terns. The latter group generally moves out of the basin by late October.

Eagles

From December through February, the Klamath Basin is home to the largest wintering concentration of bald eagles in the lower 48 states. The thousands of winter waterfowl that reside here provide a plentiful food source for these raptors. By January, 700-800 eagles coming from as far north as Southeast Alaska's Chilkat River, Saskatchewan, and the Northwest Territories congregate here. While bald eagles can and do take live birds, they feed primarily on waterfowl that have died from hunting injuries, diseases like fowl cholera, or natural causes.

In addition to a readily available food supply, the eagles require night-roosting areas. The **Upper Klamath National Wildlife Refuge** (just south of Crater Lake) and the **Bear Valley National Wildlife Refuge** (between Keno and Worden) both have mature stands of timber that can support the weight of up to 300 eagles a night. The eagles prefer trees on northeastern-facing slopes that protect them from the cold southwest and westerly winds. They also like trees that have large open-pattern branches that give them easy landing and takeoff points. However, the eagles *don't* like it when people bother them. Hence, the roosting areas are closed from early November through March 30.

The good news is that there are still ample viewing opportunities of our national bird, especially when it is very cold. When ice covers the shallow lakes and marshes, the waterfowl are forced to congregate in the few areas of remaining open water. With the food source concentrated like this, it doesn't take long for an eagle to swoop down out of the sky and grab some supper. Contact the Fish and Wildlife office for the latest information on the best eagle-watching locations. A good sighting can be had driving to Bear Valley at sunrise. To get there, drive one mile south of Worden on US 97. Turn right on Keno Worden Rd. after the grain silos, cross the railroad tracks, and take an immediate left on the gravel road. Travel about a mile and pull off the road. From here you can sometimes see up to 100 bald eagles soar from their roosts at the top of the ridge to their daytime feeding area on the lake to the east. Bring binoculars, warm clothing, and a camera with a telephoto lens.

A world-renowned eagle conference, for information write: Klamath Basin Eagle Conference, 4647 Miller Island Rd., Klamath Falls 97603; or Ralph and Charlotte Opp, 5803 Es-

BOB RACE

tate Dr., Klamath Falls 97603, tel. (541) 882-8486, is held in February with lectures, a film festival, art and photography shows, road racing, field trips, and workshops. The highlight is a predawn field trip to the nearby Bear Valley roost. It's sponsored by the Audubon Society at Oregon Institute of Technology at Klamath Falls. The conference fee is $25.

Get a free map and bald-eagle brochure by sending a stamped, self-addressed envelope to: Klamath Basin National Wildlife Refuges, Route 1, Box 74, Tule Lake, CA 96134, tel. (916) 667-2231. Ask them to include information on local accommodations and restaurants. The nearest motels are in Merrill, or Tule Lake and Dorris, both across the border in California.

Water Birds

March through May is when waterfowl and shorebirds stop over in the basin on their way north to their breeding grounds in Alaska and Canada. They rest and fatten up during the spring to build up the necessary strength and body fat to carry them through their long migration. This time of year is also the nesting season for thousands of marsh birds and waterfowl. The **Klamath Forest National Wildlife Refuge** north of Klamath Falls on US 97 is a good place during spring to observe sandhill cranes, shorebirds, waterfowl, and raptors.

The summer months are ideal for taking the self-guided auto tour routes and canoe trails. Descriptive leaflets are available for both attractions from the Oregon Fish and Wildlife office. Among the most prolific waterfowl and marsh bird areas in the Northwest, over 4,500 ducks, 2,600 Canada geese, and thousands of marsh and shorebirds are raised here each year. You may also see American white pelicans, *Pelecanus erythrorhynchos,* at the Upper Klamath National Wildlife Refuge during the summer. Unlike the brown pelican found on the Oregon coast, white pelicans prefer freshwater or estuarine areas. Another distinction that separates them from their seabound counterparts is that they paddle and dip their bills for food, whereas brown pelicans will dive into the water for fish.

The refuges are open during daylight hours, except when nesting and hunting seasons dictate schedule modifications. Overnight camping is not permitted at any of the refuges.

SPORTS AND RECREATION

With all the lakes, rivers, and mountains in the region, there's no shortage of fishing, rafting, golfing, and other recreational opportunities. Here's a short list of some local attractions.

Fishing

Three local guides can get you outfitted and on the water angling for the elusive big one. **John's Guide Service,** 23120 Alpin St., Klamath Falls, tel. (541) 356-2111 or (800) 233-8223, **Ed Miranda's Guide Service,** 26408 Rocky Point Rd., Klamath Falls, tel. (541) 356-2266, and **Darren Roe Guide Service,** 27338 Rocky Point Rd., Klamath Falls, tel. (541) 356-2244 all offer trips on the Klamath Lakes (lake rainbow trout record is 25 pounds, 10+ pounders pulled out regularly) and the nearby Wood and Willamson rivers, which are both noted for their runs of wild trout. Rates for all three outfitters are roughly the same; half day trip for 1-2 people runs $150, full day trips cost $200 for one person, $250 for two. Contact the outfitter for specific details on their individual reservation deposit policies.

Sailing

One way to get out onto Oregon's largest lake is to rent a sailboat or take a chartered tour through **Meridian Sail Center,** Pelican Marina, Dock C, 928 Front St., tel. (541) 884-5869. Tours cost $35/pp, or $150 for a private charter trip. Sailboat rentals are $35 half-day, $60 full day. Sailing instruction is also available. Call ahead for the sailing report and to make reservations. **Klamath Lake Touring Company,** tel. (541) 882-8150, also offers lake tours with similiar rates that emphasize the natural history, geography, and native peoples of the area.

Whitewater Rafting

Just under an hour west of Klamath Falls is what's known as Hell's Corner of the Upper Klamath River. From May-Oct., one or two day adventures through this remote, secluded canyon are offered by **Cascade River Runners,** Box 86, Klamath Falls, 97601, tel. (541) 883-6340 or (800) 884-2113. With several class IV+ rapids, the Upper Klamath provides some of the best spring and summer rafting in the state. Day trips, $98 adult, $89 youth, take on 18 miles of whitewater, and two day campout voyages, $255 adults, $225 youth, charge through 24 miles of unforgettable turbulence. Call for reservations and additional trip information (i.e group discounts).

You can also arrange a raft trip in the Klamath Falls region through Ashland's **Adventure Center,** tel. (800) 444-2809.

Golfing

There are several area courses open to the public. **Harbor Links,** 601 Harbor Isle Blvd., tel. (541) 882-0609, and **Shield Crest,** 3151 Shieldcrest Dr., tel. (541) 884-1493, both offer 18-hole courses with greens fees in the $20-25 range. Rental golf clubs are also available at these two establishments for around $10. Smaller 9-hole **Round Lake,** 4000 Round Lake Rd., tel. (541) 884-2520, is a bargain at $7 and club rental at $4.

Entertainment

The region's cultural hub is the **Ross Ragland Theater,** 218 N. 7th, Klamath Falls, tel. (541) 884-5483. In addition to local productions, the Klamath Symphony, and other community organizations, country stars, internationally acclaimed guest artists, and touring Broadway troupes grace the stage of this 800-seat auditorium. Call the theater or check the daily *Herald & News* to see what's scheduled.

PRACTICALITIES

Accommodations

Klamath Falls has long considered the crossroads of southeastern Oregon. John. C. Fremont led mapping expeditions for the U.S. Government in 1843 and 1846, blazing the way for settlers to arrive via the Applegate Trail. With the arrival of the railroad decades later, Klamath Falls status in southeastern Oregon also grew. The development of Highway 97, ORE 140, and ORE 66 in the 20th century infused additional growth to the city. However, most people over the years just stopped for food and shelter, and then pushed on to where ever they were headed. But while the word has recently gotten out that the region offers much more

than a pit stop, you can still find quality accommodations at reasonable rates that continue to meet the needs of the traveling public at the crossroads of southeastern Oregon.

Bed and Breakfasts

The **Boarding House Inn B&B,** 1800 Esplanade Ave., Klamath Falls, tel. (541) 883-8584, remains true to its heritage as a boarding house for railroad workers, but with many comfortable modern refinements. The period furnishings, antiques, and fixtures of a half century ago impart a sense of visiting grandmother's house, and at a price she would undoubtedly approve. The two bedrooms, $45, come with walk-in closets, full kitchens, and private bath. The two suites, $65, offer the same amenities plus a larger kitchen and living room. There's also a library stocked with old tomes for guests to read over with tea or coffee in the evening. Breakfast is yet another highlight here, as the owner was trained at the California Culinary Academy in San Francisco, and he produces elaborate meal presentations worthy of a five-star rating. Exceptional dinners are also available here. It's no wonder then that space books up here fast, and that advance reservations are always necessary.

Ten minutes from town on the south shore of Upper Klamath Lake adjacent to 400-acre Moore Park is **Thompson's B&B,** 1420 Wild Plum Ct, tel. (541) 882-7933; e-mail tompholl@aol.com. Their location on the lake and a huge deck overlooking the water make it an ideal place to spot all manner of wildlife. They've been in the business for nearly two decades, and know how to take care of people right. From the commons room stocked with goodies (popcorn, candy, drinks), microwave, and refrigerator to the full American breakfast, everything here is geared to please the guests. Rent a sailboat from **Meridan Sails,** tel. (541) 884-5869, at the marina a block away, $35/half day, to get a closer look at the aquatic wildlife, and then return to the B&B for evening aperitifs. Location and the comfort factor make the $65-75 rate a good dollar value. Payment in cash or check only, $25 deposit required, 48 hour cancellation notice policy.

On the eastern section of the Crater Lake Highway (ORE 62) about a half hour from Crater Lake is **Sun Pass Ranch,** 52125 ORE 62, Box 499, Fort Klamath OR, 97626-0499, tel. (541)

KLAMATH FALLS ACCOMMODATIONS

Doubletree, 3612 S. 6th St., tel. (541) 882-8864, $70-100, pool, pets, laundry.

Best Western Klamath Inn, 4061 S. 6th St., tel. (541) 882-1200 or (800) 528-1234, $55-75, pets, covered pool, continental breakfast.

Best Western Olympic Inn, 2627 S. 6th St, tel. (541) 882-9665 or (800) 600-9665, $70-100, pool, continental breakfast.

Cimarron Motor Inn, 3060 S. 6th, tel. (541) 882-4601 or (800) 742-2648, $50-60, pets, continental breakfast, laundromat, pool.

Comfort Inn, 2500 S. 6th, tel. (541) 884-9999 or (800) 228-5150, $55-125, covered pool, continental breakfast, laundromat.

Hill View Motel, 5543 S. 6th St., tel. (541) 883-7771, $45-70, restaurant/lounge, pets.

Maverick Motel, 1220 Main St., tel. (541) 882-6688, $45-55, pool, continental breakfast.

La Vista Motor Lodge, ORE 97 or P.O. Box 761, Klamath Falls 97601, tel. (541) 882-8844, $35-50, pool, laundry, continental breakfast.

North Entrance Motel, 3844 ORE 97, tel. (541) 884-8104, $40-60, covered pool, pets.

Oregon Motel 8, 5225 ORE 97, tel. (541) 883-3431, $35-45, pool, kitchenettes, laundry.

Quality Inn 100 Main St., tel. (541) 882-4666 or (800) 732-2025, $65-95, pool, laundry, continental breakfast

Super 8 Motel, 3805 ORE 97, tel. (541) 884-8880 or (800) 843-1991, $50-65, wheelchair access, restaurant, laundry.

Shilo Inn Klamath Falls, 2500 Almond St., tel. (541) 885-7980 or (800) 222-2244, $90-130, pets, covered pool, laundry, continental breakfast.

Value 20 Motel Klamath Falls, 124 N. 2nd St., tel. (541) 882-7741, $35-50, wheelchair access, river views.

381-2259. This combo B&B/Guest Ranch is located in the heart of what some locals call the Sky Lakes wilderness. Close by the ranch, a wide variety of wildlife can easily be spotted. To help you get to see all those wild critters out there, they offer mountain bike rentals, back country pack trips with horses, and even hiking expeditions with llamas. Fishing, rafting, and canoeing are also among the offerings. Room rates are $65-75 double occupancy, $10/extra person, advance reservations required.

Finally, decent one, $70, and two bedroom, $90, cabins with fully equipped kitchen, private bath, and outdoor barbecue are featured at **Rocky Point Resort,** 28124 Rocky Point Rd., tel. (541) 356-2287. Guest rooms in the lodge are also available, $55. You can rent everything from a kayak to a whaler at their marina to explore the waters of Klamath Lake. A restaurant is on site too. Call ahead for advance deposit information and room availablity.

Campgrounds

Most of the campgrounds you'll find in the vicinity of Klamath Falls are privately owned. These facilities cater mostly to RVs with electric, water, and sewer hookups, as well as other creature comforts like swimming pools, laundromats, and recreational halls. These properties also tend to be in prime locations, which accounts for rates that are steeper than those of their public counterparts. Fortunately, there are several places to pitch a tent in both types of parks without having to deal with someone parked right next to your sleeping bag in a 40-foot-long mobile home.

On the north end of Upper Klamath Lake adjacent to the Upper Klamath National Wildlife Refuge lies **Harriman Springs Resort and Marina,** Harriman Route, Box 79, Klamath Falls 97601, tel. (541) 356-2323. The campground features six tent and 17 RV sites with hookups. Flush toilets, showers, firewood, and a laundromat are also available. Open from April to late October, the fee is $10 per night. To get there, go 27 miles northwest of Klamath Falls on ORE 140W and take a right onto Rocky Point Road. Proceed another two miles and you will see the resort on the right.

Another mile down Rocky Point Rd. is **Rocky Point Resort,** Harriman Route, Box 92, Klamath Falls 97601, tel. (541) 356-2287, also in close proximity to the Upper Klamath National

Wildlife Refuge. This resort has five tent and 28 RV sites with hookups and rustic cabins. Flush toilets, showers, firewood, a laundromat, recreation hall, and other summer-camp trappings are available. Open April to mid-November, the camp charges $14 per night. Ask about canoe rentals for trips on the Upper Klamath Canoe Trail. For more information about the trail, contact the **U.S. Fish and Wildlife Service, Klamath Basin National Wildlife Refuge,** P.O. Box 74, Tule Lake, CA 96134, tel. (916) 667-2231.

Several other campgrounds are also found on Upper Klamath Lake. The best deal around is **Hagelstein County Park,** County Parks Dept., Klamath Falls 97601, tel. (541) 882-2501. This small park accommodates only five tent campers and five RVs in sites featuring picnic tables and fire grills, with flush toilets and water nearby. In addition to being the only campground on the east shore of the lake, it's the least expensive campground in the area. Open April to late November, reservations are recommended. To get there, head north of Klamath Falls for nine miles and look for the signs on the left side of the road.

About four miles north of Klamath Falls on US 97 on the southeastern shore of Upper Klamath Lake is **Mallard Campground,** Route 5, Box 1348, Klamath Falls 97601, tel. (541) 882-0482. Here you'll find 10 tent and 43 RV sites with hookups. Showers, flush toilets, laundromat, and pool are also on the premises. Open all year, $14 per night.

Approximately seven miles farther north of Mallard Campground on US 97 is **KOA Klamath Falls,** 3435 Shasta Way, Klamath Falls 97601, tel. (541) 884-4644. Set along the shore of Upper Klamath Lake, the park features 18 tent and 73 RV sites with hookups. In true KOA style, flush toilets, showers, a pool, laundromat, recreation hall, and other amenities are available. Open all year, $17-21 per night.

Food

Klamath Falls is a small, unpretentious town. Despite being the second-largest city east of the Cascades, Klamath Falls offers few opportunities for gourmet grub. Locals suggest that visitors come here for the birds, not necessarily for the food. Fowl jokes aside, sandwiched in between the obligatory fast-food joints are a flock of noteworthy eating establishments.

You can get just about anything you want at **Alice's,** 1012 Main St., tel. (541) 884-1444, restaurant. Open for breakfast, lunch, and dinner, Alice's recalls a San Francisco bill of fare at moderate prices. Pasta, steaks, seafood, and fresh baked goods are complemented by good coffee, espresso, and imported beers and wines. Several vegetarian meals are also available here. On campus square near the Oregon Institute of Technology, **Renaldo's Cafe Espresso,** tel. (541) 884-3846, has baked specialties, gourmet desserts, light lunch fare, $3-5, and blended coffee drinks. The Kona cappuccino shake is ideal to both pick you up and cool you down on a hot day.

Cactus Jack's, 2636 Biehn St., tel. (541) 883-2777, country-and-western ambiance and wood-fired rotisserie should please range riders and city slickers alike. Cacti, succulents, and cowboy motif decor set the mood and ribs, steaks, and pork loin do the rest. On Sunday, Wild Boar pork chops are featured. There's also chicken and turkey, shrimp dishes, homemade sandwiches, and a full bar. For lunch, we're partial to taters—Klamath Basin spuds topped with onions, peppers, herbs and spices, choice of meat, and covered with melted cheese, $5.50. Dinner prices for just a few entrees exceed $11, and the portions are huge. After dinner, take in a movie at the Pelican Cinema, tel. (541) 884-5000, across the street

For something Italian, try **Fiorella Italian Ristorante,** 6139 Summers, tel. (541) 882-1878. Open for dinner Tues.-Sat., the restaurant specializes in pasticcio (Venetian-style lasagna). Seafood and vegetarian meals are also found on the menu, as well as imported beers and wines. Dinner entrees here range $9-17. **Molatore's,** 100 Main St., tel. (541) 884-6298, open for breakfast, lunch, and dinner, also features Italian cuisine, with moderately priced steak and seafood rounding out the offerings.

If you're in the mood for some Chinese food, head for **Wong's,** 421 Main St., tel. (541) 884-6578. In addition to an assortment of Chinese combination dinners and vegetarian dishes, you can also find American-style steak and seafood here. **King Wah,** 2765 Pershing Way, tel. (541) 882-0489, specializing in Cantonese cuisine and thick-cut steaks, is another option for Asian fare. Dinners for both establishments range $6-12.

For a meal you're sure to remember, try the **Mongolian Grill**, 610 Main, tel. (541) 884-6863. Here, you get to be the chef, only you don't do the cooking. Over a dozen veggies, chicken, beef, and shrimp are presented salad bar style. Grab a plate, $5 one time through, $7 all-you-can-eat, choose your ingredients, and then top it off with one of 10 different freshly made sauces (like peanut, ginger, teriyaki, and etc.). Present your custom arrangement to the kitchen help, and they will grill it up for you to perfection. Eighteen microbrews are available on tap, and there's also dance floor featuring live bands on Saturday nights. All of this makes the grill one of Klamath Falls hot spots. Open Mon.-Thurs. 11 a.m.-9 p.m., Fri.-Sat. 11 a.m.-10 p.m., and closed on Sunday.

The best burgers in town are at **Blondies**, 210 Spring, tel. (541) 883-3127. Fresh, never-frozen beef with your choice of condiments stacked up high on fresh buns made daily onsite keep the handful of booths in this small trailer always full. In fact, those homemade buns are so popular with locals that they are sold individually. The ultimate gut bomb on hamburger hill is Blondie's Super Deluxe. Dynamite dogs and multi-tiered sandwiches are also avaliable. Most menu items range from $2-6. Open Mon.-Fri., 11 a.m.-7 p.m., Saturday 11 a.m.-5 p.m.

Open Tues.-Sat. for dinner only, **Chez Nous**, 3927 S. 6th, tel. (541) 883-8719, offers continental cuisine, steak, pasta, and seafood, and an extensive wine list. The food is excellent, the ambiance classical. All entrees are full-course meals (soup, salad, potato/rice, vegetables, and bread included). This is the place in town to go to impress your date, but be prepared to pay for it (entrees are $13-20). In contrast, economical meals, $1-5, on the fly can be had at **Hobo Junction**, 7th and Main, tel. (541) 882-8013. Soups, salads, sandwiches, and specialty hot dogs are featured here. The real attraction here is the smoked baked potato that comes with a variety of toppings.

When it comes to pizza in Klamath Falls, the locals swear by **McPherson's Old Town Pizza Company**, 722 Main, tel. (541) 884-8858 and 6200 S. 6th, tel. (541) 883-2918. Pizzas come in four sizes from individual, $3-4, to large, $15-18, and in three kinds of crusts (thick, thin, or pan), but it is the thin crust pizza which accounts for over 75% of their sales that comes recommended. You'll find one of the best lunch buffet deals in town here that includes pizza, chicken (regular and barbecue), lasagna, spuds, soups, desserts, and a huge salad bar for $5.25. This feast for the common man is available Mon.-Fri. 11:30 a.m.-1:30 p.m. and Sat.-Sun. noon-2 p.m. A more elaborate dinner version is featured 5:30-7:30 p.m. Monday and Tuesday for $7.25.

Finally, the region's best Mexican food is found about a half-hour north of town on US 97 at **Los Chiles**, mile post 255, tel. (541) 783-2202. Look for a small building on the east side of the highway with a gravel parking lot. Every menu item field tested by Oregon Handbook's tasting team met with rave reviews—we even had to go back the next day for an encore! With salsa, Mexican rice, and beans (no lard) made fresh daily on the premises, a firm foundation exists for the rest of the menu items. The tacos are filled with freshly grilled meat (beef, pork, chicken, or fish) accompanied by onions, tomatoes, lettuce, and cilantro for $1.50 each. The taquitos, $3.75 for a half dozen, come on a bed of lettuce with guacamole, sour cream, olives, onion, green onion, and tomato. The burrito grande, $4, was yet another home run. Do call ahead before heading out from town to make sure they'll be open for you, as hours fluctuate with the seasons.

Information and Services

The **post office**, 317 S. 4th, tel. (541) 884-9226, is open 9 a.m.-5 p.m. weekdays. You can find additional information about the region by visiting the **Klamath County Library**, 126 S. 3rd, tel. (541) 882-8894. The **police**, 5th and Walnut, tel. (541) 883-5336 or 911 for emergencies only, and **state police**, 2525 Biehn, tel. (541) 883-5711, are always on call to assist. You can find the hard stuff at the **State Liquor Store**, 4309 S. 6th, tel. (541) 884-3313. For health problems, the men and women of **Merle West Medical Center**, 2865 Dagget Ave., Klamath Falls 97601, tel. (541) 882-6311, or 883-6176 for emergencies only, can help put all the pieces together again.

Amtrak, S. Spring and Oak Streets, tel. (541) 884-2822, can connect you with northern and southern destinations via the *Coast Starlight*. **Greyhound**, 1200 Klamath Ave., tel. (541) 882-4616, can also take you to California and the

Willamette Valley. The **Klamath Falls airport** is serviced by United Express, tel. (800) 241-6522, and **Horizon,** tel. (541) 884-3331, to/from Portland and other airports. **Hertz,** tel. (541) 882-0220 or (800) 654-3131, and **Avis,** tel. (541) 882-7273 or (800) 831-2847, both have outlets near the airport on Rand Way.

The **Klamath County Tourism Department,** P.O. Box 1867, 1451 Main, Klamath Falls 97601, tel. (541) 884-0666 or (800) 445-6728, can provide an excellent pamphlet on the self-guided loop tour. Look for this visitor center in Veteran's Park, just off US 97 at the entrance to the city. After stocking up on brochures, head back outside and watch the waterfowl.

Over 2.2 million acres of Klamath County is publicly owned. The **Klamath Ranger District** office, 1936 California Ave., Klamath Falls OR, 97601, tel. (541) 885-3400, can give/send you outdoor recreational information on the Winema National Forest and other surrounding natural areas of interest. The **Bureau of Land Management,** 2795 Anderson Ave., #25, Klamath Falls OR, 97601, tel. (541) 883-6916, can also be of assistance in this regard.

You'll find the **Oregon Welcome Center** located on US 97 about halfway between Klamath Falls and the California/Oregon border. They have a broad collection of brochures and information about locales all over the state.

BOB RACE

ORE 62: THE CRATER LAKE HIGHWAY

Many locals who live near the Crater Lake Highway sport bumper stickers on their vehicles that read, "I Survived Highway 62." The challenges of successfully navigating this precipitous and circuitous thoroughfare, with its horrific winter weather and slow-moving summer crowds, help give it a killer reputation. Even so, there always seems to be traffic on this winding conduit between Crater Lake and southern Oregon. This isn't surprising when you consider the scenic appeals of the Rogue River and Cascade Mountains. Add excellent fishing on the Rogue below Oregon's largest fish hatchery, Cole Rivers, along with the swimming, boating, and rafting opportunities, and you too will be taking to the hills along Highway 62.

HIKES

Many choice hikes are found along the 50-mile stretch of the Rogue River Trail from Lost Creek Lake to the river's source at Boundary Springs just inside Crater Lake National Park. Tall waterfalls, deep gushing gorges, and a natural bridge are all easily accessible. Those interested in more than just a short walk from the parking lot to the viewpoint can design hikes of two to 18 miles with or without an overnight stay. Travelers with two cars can arrange shuttles to avoid having to double back.

Mill Creek Falls

One of the more scenic recreation spots is owned by Boise Cascade, a timber conglomerate. Boise Cascade has constructed a botanically marked nature trail system through its land to a series of three waterfalls in an impressive, rock-choked section of the Rogue River called the Avenue of the Giant Boulders. To give you an idea how spectacular this deep and narrow gorge strewn with volcanic monoliths is, the Avenue of the Giant Boulders was actually lit up during the 1920s. The largest of the three waterfalls is Mill Creek Falls, which plunges 173 feet down into the river. Signs along the highway and Mill Creek

Drive (formerly the old Crater Lake Highway, a scenic loop out of the community of **Prospect**) direct visitors to the trailhead. Boise Cascade has also posted a large map that further details the trail routes. The trail is short, but steep. Wear shoes you don't mind getting wet and that have good traction, as you may have to scramble over some of the boulders and wade through some small ponds along the way.

Takelma Gorge

A particularly wild section of the river is found at Takelma Gorge. Located one mile from River Bridge Campground on the upper Rogue River, the trail offers vistas of sharp, foaming bends in the river with logs jammed in at crazy angles on the rocks, and ferns growing in the mist of the waterfalls. Although the river's course is rugged, the grade on the trail is an easy one.

Natural Bridge

Even if you're in a hurry, you should take 15 minutes to get out of your car and stretch your legs at the Natural Bridge. Located a quarter mile from Natural Bridge Campground, a mile west of Union Creek on ORE 62, here the Rogue River drops into a lava tube and disappears from sight, only to emerge later a little way downstream. A short paved path takes you to a human-made bridge that fords this unique section of the river. Several placards along the way explain the formation of the Natural Bridge and other points of interest.

Rogue River Gorge

Just outside of **Union Creek** on ORE 62 is the spectacular Rogue River Gorge. The narrowest point on the river, the action of the water has carved out a deep chasm in the rock. A short trail with several well-placed overlooks follows the rim of the gorge. Green mossed walls, logjams, and a frothy torrent of water are all clearly visible from the trail. Informative placards discuss curiosities like the living stump and the potholes carved in the lava rock by pebbles and the action of the water.

THE HOODOOS OF GODFREY GLEN

The approach to Crater Lake on ORE 62 passes by many eerie rock formations called hoodoos, which were formed after Mt. Mazama erupted and hot gases bubbled up through ash deposits hundreds of feet thick. In some places, the hot gases helped solidify this ash into a brittle rock. The effects of water and ice have been at work ever since, breaking the rock down into smaller sandlike particles. The areas on top of the hoodoos are more exposed to the elements and therefore contain the most sandy ash. A brief look at the physics of hoodoos will help explain why these formations are dangerous and best explored with extreme caution.

The slope of the sand is defined by a balance of mass, gravity, and friction. An applied external force like water or snow will increase the sand's total mass until it's greater than the force of the friction holding it in place. When this happens, gravity will pull the sand down the slope to compensate. The sand will also move to reach an equilibrium if the slope is increased—as for instance when the underlying rock breaks off.

Due to this natural equilibrium, the fate of a person standing on the sandy slope hangs in the balance. The individual's mass translates into a force pointing down the slope that works against the static friction force going up the slope. If the total downward force is greater than the resistance of the static friction force, the sand will shift. With movement, the total resistance of the static friction decreases and becomes a constant called kinetic friction. This is bad news if you happen to be sliding down the top of a hoodoo, because once the force of the static friction is overcome, reversing the downhill process becomes virtually impossible. The acceleration from your movement, and the additional force exerted attempting to stop, are greater than the kinetic friction force that could save you.

A walk along the Godfrey Glen trail takes you over the top of many hoodoos. Currently, the trail does not have fences or walls, in keeping with the National Park Service's credo of maintaining a natural state. The hoodoos are stark and beautiful, and the temptation to take an extra step for a better look is understandable. However, be advised that some curious unfortunates have taken that last fatal step, but you need not follow their footprints toward the relentless conclusion to this cold equation. Children and teenagers in particular should be closely monitored along the cliffside trails in Crater Lake National Park. Enjoy the park safely, and avoid testing Newton's laws on the hoodoos of Godfrey Glen.

National Creek Falls

Another short hike for hurried motorists is National Creek Falls. An easy half-mile walk down a trail bordered by magnificent Douglas firs leads to this tumultuous cascade. To get there, take ORE 230 to Forest Service Rd. 6530. Follow the road until you reach the trailhead marked by a sign.

Boundary Springs

A two-mile hike down a cool and shady trail takes you to the source of the mighty Rogue River, Boundary Springs. Situated just inside Crater Lake National Park, it's a great place for a picnic. About a mile down the path from the trailhead, hang a left at the fork to get to Boundary Springs. Once at the springs, you'll discover small cataracts rising out of the jumbled volcanic rock that's densely covered with moss and other vegetation. While the temptation to get a closer look is great, the vegetation here is extremely fragile, so please refrain from walking on the moss. To get there, take ORE 230 north from ORE 62 to the crater rim viewpoint, where parking can be found on the left-hand side of the road.

In the fall, take ORE 62 from Medford and turn east onto ORE 140 to enjoy the golden hues of larch and aspen. En route, you might stop at Fish Lake or Lake of the Woods resorts. From here you can take scenic Westside Rd. to Fort Klamath. Crater Lake lies a scant six miles from here.

RAFTING AND FISHING

Rafting Trips

Both **Adventure West,** tel. (541) 878-4019, and **Noah's White Water,** tel. (541) 488-2811, offer guided trips on the upper Rogue. However, an-

TED LONG ISHIKAWA

the narrow confines of the Rogue River Gorge

other way to do this mild, 10 mile section of the Rogue river from the hatchery back to town is to do it yourself. It takes about a half-day to float downstream, and many people like to enjoy a picnic along the way. **Rogue Rafting Co.,** Shady Cove, across from Shady Cove Park, tel. (541) 878-2585, and **Ragin Water Raft,** 21873 ORE 62, Shady Cove, tel. (541) 878-4000, can get you set up. Equipment ranging from inflatable kayaks, tahitis, water guns, and various sized rafts that can accomodate up to 12 people are available. Life vests, paddles, and a shuttle service from Shady Cove up to Cole Rivers Fish Hatchery are provided at no extra charge. Rogue Rafting Co. can even outfit you with an ice chest and dry bags to carry your riverbank feast.

Fishing Trips

The fish runs on the Rogue River are second only in size to the ones on the Columbia. Nearly three million fish are reared and released into the Rogue from the Cole Rivers Fish Hatchery, located 153 miles from the mouth of the Rogue. Close to a half million salmon and steelhead are caught annually on the Rogue. The following guide services can provide you with all you need to land your own catch: **Fishing Outfitters,** tel. (541) 773-5145, **Longbrake Guide Service,** tel. (541) 826-6794, **Native Run,** tel. (541) 474-0018, **River Trips Unlimited,** tel. (541) 779-3798, **Slusser River Guide,** tel. (541) 476-8047, **Strieby's Guide Service,** tel. (541) 773-4967, and **Swisher Guide Service,** tel. (541) 535-5177.

PRACTICALITIES

Camping

For those who like roughing it in style with all of the amenities in their RVs, a couple of well-maintained trailer parks in the Rogue country can accommodate large vehicles. **Fly-Casters Campground and Trailer Park,** P.O. Box 1170, Shady Cove 97539, tel. (541) 878-2749, $14-18 per night; and **Shady Trails RV Park and Campground,** P.O. Box 1299, Shady Cove 97539, tel. (541) 878-2206, $14 per night; are both located about 23 miles north of Medford on ORE 62. Situated on the banks of the Rogue

River, these parks feature hookups and picnic tables. Flush toilets, bottled gas, gray wastewater disposal, and showers are also available. A grocery store and restaurants are in the nearby town of **Shady Cove.** Both these parks are good home bases for RV owners who like to fish and hike.

Five miles below Lost Creek Lake on ORE 62 is **Rogue Elk County Park,** Jackson County Parks and Recreation, 10 South Oakdale, Medford 97501, tel. (541) 465-2241. This campground features 20 sites for tents and RVs (15 feet maximum) with picnic tables and fire grills. Piped water and vault toilets are also on the premises. Open July to late October, the camp fee is $10 per night. The kids will enjoy swimming in Elk Creek, which, in addition to being adjacent to the campground, is warmer and safer than the Rogue. A rope swing tied to a tree adds to the fun at the swimming hole.

Along the shore of Lost Creek Lake is **Joseph Stewart State Park,** 35251 ORE 62, Trail 97541, tel. (541) 560-3334. Here you'll find 50 tent and 151 RV sites (40 feet maximum). Electricity, sewer hookups, fire grills, and picnic tables are provided. Flush toilets, water, gray wastewater disposal services, showers, and firewood are also available. Bike paths, a beach, and barbecue grills make this a family-friendly locale. Boat-launching facilities for Lost Creek Lake are located nearby. Open all year, the fee is $16-20 per night. Eight miles of hiking trails and bike paths crisscross the park. Lost Creek Lake also has a marina, beach, and boat rentals.

If you want to get away from the highway, head for **Abbott Creek,** Rogue National Forest, Prospect Ranger Station, Prospect 97536, tel. (541) 560-3623. One of the few backwoods camps in the area that has potable water, it's seven miles northeast of the town of Prospect on ORE 62 and three miles down Forest Service Rd. 68. Situated at the confluence of Abbott and Woodruff creeks and not far from the upper Rogue River, this campground has nine tent and 12 RV sites (22 feet maximum) with picnic tables and fire grills. Hand-pumped water and vault toilets are also available. Open from late May to late October, the camp charges $11 per night.

Set along the bank of Union Creek where it merges with the upper Rogue River is **Union Creek,** Rogue National Forest, Prospect Ranger Station, Prospect 97536, tel. (541) 560-3623. Located 11 miles northeast of Prospect, you'll find 72 tent and RV sites (16 feet maximum) with picnic tables, fire grills, piped water, and pit toilets. Open from late May to early September, the fee is $14 per night. Many fine hikes on the Rogue River Trail (see "Hikes," above) are within close proximity of the campground.

A half mile past Union Creek Campground on ORE 62 is **Farewell Bend,** Rogue National Forest, Prospect Ranger Station, Prospect 97536, tel. (541) 560-3623. Located near the junction of ORE 62 and ORE 230, the camp has 61 tent and RV sites (22 feet maximum) with picnic tables and fire grills. Piped water and flush toilets are also within the campground boundaries. Open from late May to early September, the fee is $14 per night. This campground is situated along the banks of the upper Rogue near the Rogue River Gorge (see "Hikes," above).

A nice little campground tucked off the highway and yet fairly close to the Rogue River and Crater Lake National Park is **Huckleberry Mountain,** Rogue National Forest, Prospect Ranger Station, Prospect 97536, tel. (541) 560-3623. To get there, go about 18 miles northeast of Prospect on ORE 62 and then four miles down Forest Service Rd. 60. There you'll find 15 tent and RV sites (21 feet maximum) with picnic tables and fire grills. Water and vault toilets are also available. Open July to late October, the campground is free of charge (14-day maximum stay). This campground is at an elevation of 5,400 feet, so be sure to have the proper gear to ensure a comfortable visit (see "Camping and Hiking" under "Outdoor Activities" in the On the Road chapter).

Accommodations

The accommodations you'll find on ORE 62 are rustic and simple, catering mainly to anglers and lovers of the great outdoors. The abundance of excellent campgrounds and RV parks also explains the dearth of lodgings.

The **Maple Leaf Motel,** 20717 ORE 62, Shady Cove 97539, tel. (541) 878-2169, has kitchenettes, cable TV, and a picnic and barbecue area to grill the day's catch or some burgers if the fish weren't biting. Rates range $40-55. The **Two Pines Motel,** P.O. Box 182, 21331

ORE 62, Shady Cove 97539, tel. (541) 878-2511, features kitchenettes with cable TV and runs $25-45 per night. The **Royal Coachman Motel,** P.O. Box 509, Shady Cove 97539, tel. (541) 878-2481, has kitchenettes, cable TV, and HBO for $40-70 per night. Rooms with decks overlooking the river run $50-80.

The **Prospect Hotel and Motel,** 391 Mill Creek Rd., Prospect 97536, tel. (541) 560-3664 or (800) 944-6490, gives you a choice between something old and something new. The hotel, built in 1889 and listed on the National Register of Historic Places, has several small but comfortable rooms with bath. The rooms are named after local residents and famous people who have stayed at the hotel, including Zane Grey, Teddy Roosevelt, and Jack London. Because the hotel is small and old, no children, smoking, or pets are permitted. Rates are $70 a night per room. The adjacent motel features clean, spacious, and modern units that range $60-90 (rates 10% less in winter), with some kitchenettes available. You can smoke and bring the kids and family dog along, too.

Not far away from Prospect on the Crater Lake Highway is the **Union Creek Resort,** Prospect 97536, tel. (541) 560-3339 or 560-3565. Built in the early 1930s, the Union Creek is listed on the National Register of Historic Places. Open year-round, it has rooms available in your choice of the original lodge, cabins, or housekeeping cabins. The lodge rooms, paneled in knotty pine, range $50-75, have washbasins in them and lodge guests all share the bathrooms down the hall. The stone fireplace in the lobby is built of opalized wood from Lakeview, Oregon. The sleeping cabins with bath range $55-80. The housekeeping cabins with bath and kitchen range $70-95. The **Union Creek Country Store,** located at the resort, carries groceries and other essential items. Fishing licenses and snow-park permits can also be purchased here.

Food

ORE 62 parallels an old stagecoach road between Fort Klamath and the Rogue Valley. While the ruts in the road are gone, the tradition of frontier hospitality lives on in the establishments along this much-traveled mountain pass.

The finest restaurant on this section of the Rogue River is **Beldi's.** From the cloth napkins to the crystal wineglasses, you're assured a first-class dinner from start to finish. The dining room is perched on a bluff overlooking the river, further enhancing the visual appeal of the meal presentation. Chicken, veal, steak, and seafood dinners range $12-25. Be sure to call ahead, tel. (541) 878-2010, for reservations.

About halfway between Medford and Crater Lake in the vicinity of Prospect are a few eateries worth a mention. The **Prospect Cafe,** 31 Mill Creek Rd., Prospect, tel. (541) 560-3641, is open for breakfast, lunch, and dinner seven days a week. Breakfast with two eggs, hash browns, toast, and jam costs around $3. Omelettes are cooked the way you like them with your choice of a dozen fillings. Best buys include the Mini Logger (one hotcake, one egg, two strips of bacon, and two links) and the Timber Feller (two hotcakes, two eggs, two strips of bacon, and two links).

While the names of the sandwiches on the menu (like Cougar Catch and Beefy Bobcat) match many of the stuffed critters adorning the walls, lunch is basic lumberjack fare, and lots of it. All sandwiches are accompanied with fries and choice of potato, coleslaw, or green salad.

Dinner entrees range $7-14 and include soup and salad, vegetable, choice of potato, and fresh baked bread. Be sure to ask about the nightly special.

The dinner house at the **Prospect Hotel,** 391 Mill Creek Rd., Prospect, tel. (541) 560-3664, also comes recommended. This fine establishment serves breakfast, lunch and dinner from Memorial Day through Labor day and Sunday brunch on weekends. Dinner entrees range $9-19. One very special treat you can enjoy year-round here is huckleberry pie. Local residents forage through the forest in search of huckleberries and bring them to the hotel, which pays them $15 a pound. The best time of year for this delectable dessert is during the fall huckleberry harvest when the berries are fresh, but the hotel freezes vast quantities of them to ensure this trademark dessert year-round. In our opinion, this is the best huckleberry pie you'll find anywhere. Full of berries, rich in flavor, and not overly sweet, a generous slice accompanied with a good strong cup of coffee costs under $3. Be sure to ask for it warm to accentuate the delicate flavor. You can purchase an entire pie for under $15 to take with you. The huckleberries are also used in their compote to top pancakes, waffles, and French toast.

Beckie's, Union Creek Resort, tel. (541) 560-3339, is an intimate place to stop for a bite to eat. One half of the building is an old log cabin; the other half is a modern design with plenty of windows. Breakfast runs $4-8 with all the trimmings. The lunch menu features sandwiches and burgers in the $3-6 bracket. Dinners that include chicken, pork, or steak entrees range $8-15. There's also the ever-present huckleberry pie. If you simply want to cool off on a hot day, the thick soda fountain-style shakes or malts at the ice-cream parlor next door to the restaurant will do the trick.

Information

The following phone numbers can help plan your foray into the Rogue River National Forest. **Prospect Ranger Station,** tel. (541) 498-2531, **Rogue River National Forest Service,** Medford, tel. (541) 858-2200, and the **Oregon Tourism Commission,** tel. (800) 543-7842. The latter entity can send you a helpful publication entitled *Off the Beaten Freeway: A Guide to Oregon's Scenic Byways* that has some useful tips on this region as well as the rest of the state.

CRATER LAKE

High in the Cascades lies the crown jewel of Oregon, Crater Lake. America's deepest lake (1,932 feet) glimmers like a polished sapphire in a setting created by a volcano blowing its top and collapsing thousands of years ago. Crater Lake's extraordinary hues are produced by the depth and clarity of the water and its ability to absorb all the colors of the spectrum except the shortest light waves, blue and violet, which are reflected and refracted skyward. Kodak used to send their apologies along with customers' photographs of Crater Lake, because they thought that they had goofed on the processing, so unbelievable are the colors of the water. In addition to a 33-mile rim drive around the main attraction, Oregon's only national park also features 210 campsites, dozens of hiking trails, and boat tours on the lake itself. Admission to the park is $10 per car plus $5 per individual. Before you start carrying on about the rate, just be glad that the Congress didn't sell the park to Disneyland to lessen the National Debt.

If you're seeing Crater Lake for the first time, drive into the area from the north for the most dramatic perspective. After crossing through a red pumice desert where the barren landscape is punctuated only occasionally by grapeleaf fern, you climb up to higher elevations overlooking the lake. In contrast to this subdued ap-

*Oregon's crown jewel,
Crater Lake*

JOAN SELL

proach, the blueness and size of the lake can hit with a suddenness that stops all thought. On a clear day, you can peer south across Crater Lake and discern the snowy eminence of Mt. Shasta over 100 miles away in California.

THE LAND

Geologically speaking, the name Crater Lake is a misnomer. A crater is an elliptical or circular depression in the surface of the earth that is surrounded by an inward-facing rim. Many craters are volcanic in origin, their walls formed by ash and lava fragments that were expelled explosively from the volcano's vent. Technically, however, Crater Lake lies in a caldera, which is produced when the center of a volcano caves in upon itself; in this case, the cataclysm occurred 6,600 years ago with the destruction of formerly 12,000-foot-high Mt. Mazama.

Klamath Indian legend has it that Mt. Mazama was the home of Llao, King of the Underworld. The chief of the world above was Skell, who sometimes would stand upon Mt. Shasta, 100 miles to the south. A fierce battle between these two gods took place, a time marked by great explosions, thunder, and lightning. Burning ash fell from the sky, igniting the forest, and molten rivers of lava gushed 35 miles down the mountainside, burying Indian villages. For a week the night sky was lit by the flames of the great confrontation. The story climaxes with Skell's destruction of Llao's throne, as the mountain collapsed upon itself and sealed Llao beneath the surface, never again to frighten the Indians and destroy their homes. Although the lake became serene and beautiful as the caldera filled with water, the Indians believed that only punishment awaited those who foolishly gazed upon the sacred battleground of the gods.

The aftereffects of this great eruption can still be seen. Huge drifts of ash and pumice hundreds of feet deep were deposited over a wide area—up to 80 miles away. The pumice deserts to the north of the lake and the deep, ashen canyons

to the south are the most dramatic examples. So thick and widespread is the pumice that water percolates through too rapidly for plants to survive, creating reddish pockets of bleakness in the otherwise green forest. The eerie gray hoodoos in the southern canyons were created by hot gases bubbling up through the ash, hardening it into rocklike towers. These formations have withstood centuries of erosion by water that has long since washed away the loosely packed ash, creating the steep canyons visible today. **Wizard Island,** a large cinder cone that rises 760 feet above the surface of the lake, and the **Phantom Ship,** located in the southeastern corner, offer evidence of volcanic activity since the caldera's formation. Ash deposits have been found in Saskatchewan, Canada that have been traced back to the Mazama eruption.

The lake is confined by walls of multicolored lava that rise 500 to 2,000 feet above the water. Although it does not have a drainage outlet, Crater Lake is not saline because it is fed entirely by snow and rain, and the surrounding volcanic rocks are nearly salt-free. And yet, the level of the lake fluctuates only one to three feet a year, as evaporation and seepage keep it remarkably constant. Another surprise is that while Crater Lake often records the coldest temperatures in the Cascades, the lake itself has only frozen over once since records have been kept. The water stays around 38° F, although scientists have discovered hot spots 1,400 feet below

RECORD SNOWFALLS

Crater Lake is famed for massive snow accumulation. Roads are frequently closed due to drifts until the beginning of July, and 50-foot annual deposits are common. If this fails to impress, consider some of the following Crater Lake snow jobs: In the winter of 1932-33, the lake saw the most snow ever recorded in the state during a calendar year, 879 inches. The most snow to fall in 12 consecutive months fell here between April 1948 and March 1949, a grand total of 931 inches. The most snow that ever fell on an Oregon locale in one storm, 119 inches, occurred here March 16-25, 1975. The most snow ever recorded in Oregon in one month was at Crater Lake in 1933, 256 inches. Finally, and more recently, the 33-inch total racked up on November 17, 1994 has to be among the highest one-day accumulations.

the lake's surface that are 66°. Rainbow trout and kokanee (a landlocked salmon) were introduced to the lake many years ago by humans. Due to the lack of proper food, these fish are too small and scrawny to make good eating, but they nevertheless manage to eke out a meager existence in the frigid waters. Some types of mosses and green algae grow more than 400 feet below the lake's surface, a world record for these freshwater species. Another distinction was Crater Lake's selection as the purest lake in the world by scientists who determined that the water's clarity extended down 142 feet in 1997.

HISTORY

Accounts differ on who "discovered" Crater Lake, but most sources agree that it was John Wesley Hillman, a prospector looking for the Lost Bucket Mine. He christened his find Deep Blue Lake. Successive discoverers named it Blue Lake, Lake Majesty, Great Sunken Lake, and finally, Crater Lake. Peter Britt first photographed it in the 1880s, bringing widespread attention to the lake. This, coupled with the tireless work of William Gladstone Steel, culminated in Crater Lake's establishment as a national park in 1902.

SIGHTS

Visitor Centers
The new visitor center is located below Rim Village near park headquarters and is a good place to start. Open daily from summer into fall (depending on snowfall), the center provides information, maps, and publications, as well as backcountry permits and first aid. If the lake is socked in by lousy weather, you can still see it anyway: excellent films about Crater Lake are shown in the center's theater every half hour and by special arrangement. For additional information, contact the superintendent, Crater Lake National Park, P.O. Box 7, Crater Lake 97604, tel. (541) 594-2211.

The original visitor center is on the rim. A rock stairway behind the small building leads to Sinnott Memorial and one of the best views of the lake. Perched on a rock outcropping, accompanying interpretive placards help you iden-

tify the surrounding formations as well as flora and fauna. As you drive north from Rim Village you'll notice reddish earth a few miles later, indicative of poor soil. Water percolates down in these pumice deserts, inhibiting plant growth. If you look skyward a mile north from Rim Village, you'll note a fire lookout cabin on the highest peak on the west rim of the lake.

Boat Tours
There are over 100 miles of hiking trails in the park, and yet only one leads down to the lake itself. This is because the 1.1-mile-long **Cleetwood Trail** is the only part of the caldera's steep, avalanche-prone slope safe enough for passage. The trail drops 700 feet in elevation and is recommended for those in good physical condition. There is no alternative transportation to Cleetwood Cove dock, located at the end of the trail, where the Crater Lake **boat tours,** tel. (541) 594-2511, begin. These narrated excursions depart on the hour 10 a.m.-4:30 p.m. late June to mid-September and cost $12 for adults, $6 for children under 12 (free for kids under 18 months). Allow one hour from Rim Village to drive 12 miles and hike down to the boat's departure point. Dress warmly because it's cooler on the lake than on terra firma.

In addition to cruising around the lake and giving you a close look at the Phantom Ship and other geologic oddities, the tour includes a 10-minute stop on Wizard Island. Passengers electing to hike the steep, one-mile spiral path to the top of the island volcano can catch a later boat back to the dock. However, keep in mind that boats have limited space, which means your return trip could be as late as 5 p.m., depending upon availability. And while it's a great place for a picnic, please be careful to leave this unique island in an unspoiled condition for future visitors. Allow three hours for the whole experience. It takes one hour to reach the point of embarkation and two hours for the tour itself. Tickets are sold at the dock on a first-come first-served basis.

Hikes
July and August are the most popular months. Colorful flowers and mild weather greet the summer throngs. One of the best places to view the mid-July flora is on the **Castle Crest Wildflower**

Trail. The trailhead to this half-mile-long loop trail is a half mile from the park headquarters. Stop there for directions to the trailhead as well as a self-guiding trail booklet that will tell you about the ponderosa pine, Shasta red fir, mountain hemlock, lodgepole pine, and rabbit brush along the trail. Wildlife in the area include elk, deer, foxes, pikas, marmots, and a variety of birds. Peak wildflower season is usually around the last two weeks of July.

A suitable challenge of brawn and breath is the **Garfield Peak Trail.** The trailhead to this imposing ridge is just east of Crater Lake Lodge. It is a steep climb up the 1.7-mile-long trail, but the wildflower displays of phlox, Indian paintbrush, and lupine, as well as frequent sightings of eagles and hawks, give ample opportunity for you to stop and catch your breath. The highlight of the hike is atop Garfield Peak, which provides a spectacular view of Crater Lake 1,888 feet below.

When snow again buries the area in the wintertime, services and activities are cut to a minimum. However, many cross-country skiers, snowshoe enthusiasts, and winter campers enjoy this solitude. Park rangers lead snowshoe hikes (weather permitting) at 1 p.m. weekends, daily during Christmas week. Ski and snowshoe rentals are available at Rim Village.

Winter trekkers should be aware that there are no groomed cross-country trails. Thus, it's imperative to inquire about trail, avalanche, road, and weather conditions at the visitor center (open 8:30 a.m.-4:30 p.m. daily). Circumnavigating the lake, which is visited by frequent snowstorms, takes two to three days, even in good weather. Only skilled winter hikers should attempt this 33-mile route that requires a compass and maps to traverse unmarked routes and avalanche paths. There are no overnight accommodations in the area mid-October through June (and you are not allowed to sleep in your vehicle), necessitating a long drive out of the park for any creature comforts. Prior to setting out on any extended journey, pick up a permit and some free advice at the visitor center. You might also inquire about a hike to the top of Mt. Scott (8,926 feet), the highest peak in the area. Lake views and perspectives on 12 Cascade peaks are potential rewards at the end of the 2.5-mile trek.

A Mushrooming Problem

The harvest of wild matsutake mushrooms (which can fetch in excess of $100/pound from U.S. mushroom brokers for export to Japan) bring in bands of poachers armed with knives and guns to Crater Lake National Park in late summer and early fall. If you're hiking in the pine forests in the east and north sides of the park where the mushrooms tend to grow, be very careful not to surprise these miscreants. It is illegal to exploit natural resources in our National Parks. This fact, coupled with the competition of various factions coverging on this mycological resource make these ruffians a dangerous lot to be avoided. Unfortunately, some innocent bystanders have wandered into backwoods turf wars and become victims of such violent exchanges. Currently, park rangers are leveling $500 to $5,000 fines and/or six months in jail on these poachers in an attempt to control the problem. Clear out of an area immediately if you hear gunshots, see suspicious groups, or observe anyone else that doesn't fit the description of the average backpacker. Don't be a hero, just report any unusual activity to park rangers, and the Feds will take care of the rest.

PRACTICALITIES

Campgrounds

Mazama Campground, eight miles south of the rim, has 198 sites, restrooms, and a dump station. **Lost Creek Campground,** located on the eastern section of Rim Dr., has 12 sites, water, and pit toilets. Neither campground has showers or hookups. They are opened when the snow melts, and closed for the season when the snow returns. Contact the park superintendent, tel. (541) 594-2211, for more information. Foot traffic in the backcountry is light, so you can set up camp wherever you like in the remote areas surounding Crater Lake.

Accommodations and Food

One of the nicest things about 183,180-acre Crater Lake National Park is that it's not very developed. The services are concentrated on the southern edge of the lake at **Rim Village;** lodgings are open May-Sept. only. From May 19 to October 14, accommodations in the park at

Mazama Cabins, tel. (541) 954-2511, are found next to Mazama Campground. Each room features two queen beds and a bath, and two are designed for wheelchair access. Be sure to call ahead for reservations.

But you can still get a hot meal at the **Cafeteria** and the **Watchman Deli Lounge.** The Cafeteria is open all year, serving traditional breakfasts, with lunch and dinner offerings including a salad bar, cook-to-order entrees, and deli sandwiches. The Watchman Deli Lounge is located upstairs above the Cafeteria and is open from noon to 11 p.m., mid-June through Labor Day. The Watchman menu includes hamburgers, deli sandwiches, pizza, and snacks, as well as microbrews, espresso, wine, and spirits. There's also surprising good entrees that you'd find in a full-service restaurant. Service can be slow but there's a great view from the 2nd floor window that can make up for a multitude of sins. Even though it's called a lounge, families are always welcome. The adjoining gift shop is stocked with postcards and knickknacks. A small grocery section there sells various foodstuffs and beverages in case you've run out of peanut butter and beer.

In 1995, the **Crater Lake Lodge,** tel. (541) 830-8700, (800) 575-1540, reopened (May-Sept.) to full capacity—71 rooms—after years of restoration. The lodge is situated on the rim south of the Sinnott Overlook and is hewn of indigenous wood and stone. The massive lobby boasts a picture window on the lake and has a decor echoing back to its 1915 origins. The stone fireplace is large enough to walk into and serves as a gathering spot on chilly evenings. Many of the rooms have expansive views of the lake below. Others face out toward upper Klamath Lake and Mt. Shasta, 150 miles away in California. Amid all the amenities of a first-class national park hotel, it's nice to be reminded of the past by such touches as antique wallpaper and old-fashioned bathtubs (rooms 401 and 201 offer views of the lake from clawfoot tubs). Rates are $105-130 for one to two people; loft suites spanning two floors for four people are $180. This marriage of past and present in such a prime location has proven so popular it's imperative to reserve many months in advance. The 72-seat dining room, $20-25 for gourmet Northwest cuisine in a classic setting, gives preference to reservations made by hotel guests. Call (541) 830-8700 for reservations or write: Crater Lake Lodge Company, P.O. Box 97, Crater Lake 97604.

Getting There and Getting Around

The only year-round access to Crater Lake is from the south via ORE 62. To reach Crater Lake from Grants Pass, head for Gold Hall and take ORE 234 until it meets ORE 62. As you head up ORE 62 you might spot roadside snow poles in anticipation of the onset of winter. This highway makes a horseshoe bend through the Cascades, starting at Medford and ending 20 miles north of Klamath Falls. The northern route via ORE 138 (Roseburg to ORE 97, south of Beaver Marsh) is usually closed by snow mid-October through July. The tremendous snowfall also closes 33-mile-long Rim Drive, although portions are opened when conditions permit. Rim Drive is generally opened to motorists around the same time as the northern entrance to the park.

The quickest route from Portland is I-5 to Eugene; ORE 58 east across Cascades to US 97 south. At Chiloquin, take ORE 62 through Fort Klamath into the south entrance of the park.

ORE 138: THE UMPQUA HIGHWAY

One of the great escapes into the Cascade Mountains is via the Umpqua Highway. This road runs along the part of the Umpqua River coveted by Zane Grey and Clark Gable as well as legions of less ballyhooed nimrods during steelhead season. The North Umpqua is a premier fishing river full of trout and salmon as well as a source of excitement for whitewater rafters who shoot the rapids. Numerous waterfalls, including Watson Falls, feed this great waterway and are found close to the road. Tall timbers line the road through the Umpqua National Forest, and many fine campgrounds are situated within its confines. Mountain lakes like Toketee Reservoir, Lemolo Lake, and Diamond Lake offer boating and other recreational opportunities. The Umpqua National Forest also boasts challenging and yet accessible mountain trails up the flanks of Mt. Bailey (8,363 feet) and Mt. Thielsen (9,182 feet). And when snow carpets the landscape in winter, you can go cross-country skiing, snowmobiling, and snowcat skiing on Mt. Bailey free from the crowds at other winter sports areas.

This place is still so wild primarily because of the rugged terrain. The first road was built in the 1920s, a crude dirt trail that ran from Roseburg to Steamboat. Travelers of the day who wanted to get to the Diamond Lake Lodge spent three days traversing this road by car, then had to journey another 20 miles on horseback to reach their final destination. The North Umpqua Road was expanded to Copeland Creek by the Civilian Conservation Corps during the Depression, but the trips to Diamond and Crater Lakes were still limited to a trailwise few.

It wasn't until the late 1950s, when President Dwight D. Eisenhower pushed for development of the nation's interstate freeways and state highways, that road improvement began in earnest. Douglas County responded to the president's call by allocating $2.76 million toward federal matching funds to construct the Umpqua Highway. The all-weather thoroughfare was completed in the summer of 1964, opening up the North Umpqua basin to timber interests, sportspeople, and tourists.

The economy of Douglas County feeds upon the timber of the Umpqua National Forest. Approximately three-fourths of all workers in the county are directly or indirectly dependent on the timber industry. Timber receipts from federal lands generate $60 million annually for county coffers, providing money for roads, schools, and other services. But with over a quarter-million truckloads of logs rolling out of the Umpqua National Forest each year, it's no wonder that the timber boom is going bust. The dwindling supply of trees after 25 years of unabated cutting, and huge cutbacks in the allowable harvest of old-growth timber due to endangered species like the spotted owl, mean that the lumberjack county is in for a major transition in the near future.

The good news is that many unspoiled areas were spared the lumberman's axe and are easily accessible to the traveler. Come and enjoy a beautiful green section of the Oregon Cascades on a road less traveled.

SIGHTS

Colliding Rivers

Just off of ORE 138 on the west side of the town of **Glide** is the site of the colliding rivers. The Wild and Umpqua rivers meet head-on in a bowl of green serpentine. The best time to view this spectacle is after winter storms and when spring runoff is high. If the water is low, check out the high-water mark sign from the Christmas Flood of 1964. Water levels from that great inundation were lapping at the parking lot, a chilling reminder that *umpqua* means "thundering water" in Chinook.

Waterfalls

Visitors can get an unusual perspective of **Grotto Falls** because there's a trail in back of this 100-foot cascade. If you venture behind the shimmering water, watch your step because the moss-covered rocks are very slippery. To get there, take ORE 138 for 18 miles east of Roseburg to Glide. Follow Little River Rd. to the Coolwater Campground where you'll find

*Numerous Indian rock
paintings are found in
the Umpqua region.*

FRANK LONG

the turnoff to Forest Service Rd. 2703 nearby. Take it for five miles until you reach the junction of Forest Service Rd. 2703-150. Proceed down Forest Service Rd. 2703-150 for another two miles until you reach the trailhead. It's only a short hike in to view Grotto Falls.

About 10 miles west of the town of **Steamboat** is 50-foot-high **Susan Creek Falls,** whose trailhead sits off ORE 138 near the Susan Creek picnic area. A one-mile trail winds through a rainforestlike setting to the falls. The cascade is bordered on three sides by green mossy rock walls that never see the light of the sun and stay wet 365 days a year. Another quarter mile up the trail are the **Indian Mounds.** One of the rites of manhood for Umpqua Indian boys was to fast and pile up stones in hopes of being granted a vision or spiritual powers. Also called the Vision Quest Site, you can see many different stacks of moss-covered stones in an area protected by a fence.

Four miles west of Susan Creek Falls is **Fall Creek Falls.** Look for the trailhead off of ORE 138 at Fall Creek. A good walk for families with young children and for older people, the mild one-mile trail goes around and through slabs of bedrock. Halfway up the trail is a lush area called **Job's Garden.** Stay on the Fall Creek Trail and in another half mile you'll come to the falls. It's a double falls with each tier 35 to 50 feet in height. Back at Job's Garden, you may care to explore the Job's Garden Trail, which leads to the base of columnar basalt outcroppings.

During fish-migration season, it's fun to venture a little way off of ORE 138 at Steamboat and go up Steamboat Creek Rd. 38 to see the fish battle two small waterfalls. The first, **Little Falls,** is a mile up the road. It's always exciting to see the fish miraculously wriggle their way up this 10-foot cascade. Four miles farther down Steamboat Creek Rd. is **Steamboat Falls.** A viewpoint showcases this 30-foot falls, but not as many fish try to swim up this one because of the fish ladders nearby.

Back on ORE 138 about three miles east of Steamboat is **Jack Falls.** Look for the trailhead sign and follow the trail along the brushy bank of Jack Creek to a series of three closely grouped falls ranging 20-70 feet in height.

Two big waterfalls are another 19 miles down ORE 138 near the Toketee Ranger Station. To get to **Toketee Falls,** follow Forest Service Rd. 34 at the west entrance of the ranger station, cross the first bridge, and turn left. There you'll find the trailhead and a parking area. The half-mile trail ends up at a double waterfall with a combined height of over 150 feet. The word *toketee* means "graceful" in the Indian dialect, and after viewing the water plunge over the sheer wall of basalt you'll probably agree it's aptly named.

Double back to ORE 138 and take Forest Service Rd. 37 near the east entrance of the Toketee Ranger Station. This road will take you to the trailhead of **Watson Falls,** a 272-foot-high flume of water. A moderate half-mile trail climbs through tall stands of Douglas fir and western hemlock and is complemented by an understory of green salal, Oregon grape, and ferns. A bridge spans the canyon just below the falls, giving outstanding views of this towering cascade. The cool spray that billows up to the bridge always feels good on hot days after the hike uphill.

Another falls worth a visit is **Lemolo Falls.** *Lemolo* is an Indian word meaning "wild and untamed," and you'll see this is the case with this thunderous 100-foot waterfall. To get there, take Lemolo Lake Rd. off of ORE 138, then follow Forest Service Roads 2610 and 2610-600 and look for the trailhead sign. The trail is a gentle one-mile path that drops down into the North Umpqua Canyon and passes several small waterfalls on the way to Lemolo Falls.

Umpqua Hot Springs
The Umpqua Hot Springs is mostly unknown and far away enough from civilized haunts not to be overused, and yet it's accessible enough for those in the know to enjoy. The springs have been developed with wooden pools and a crude lean-to shelter. It's best to go midweek, as weekends tend to have more visitors, forcing you to wait your turn for a soak. To get there, go north from the Toketee Ranger Station and turn right onto County Rd. 34, just past the Pacific Power and Light buildings. Proceed down 34 past Toketee Lake about six miles. When you cross the bridge over Deer Creek, which is clearly noted by a sign, you will be a little less than a half mile from the turnoff. The turnoff is a dirt road to the right that goes a mile and ends at a small parking area. Please note that in wet weather this road may be impassable, and it is not recommended for low-slung cars in any season. From the parking area, it's a half mile down the blocked road to the hot springs trailhead and another half mile to the pool.

SPORTS AND RECREATION

The North Umpqua has several distinctions. First, it is known as one of the most difficult North American rivers to fish. No boats are permitted from 15 miles in either direction of Steamboat, and no bait or spinners are allowed ei-

ther. This puts a premium on skillful fly-fishing. You can wade on in and poke around for the best fishing holes on the North Umpqua, one of the few rivers with a native summer run of steelhead—or better yet, hire a guide.

Fishing Outfitters
"Fishing is our only business," proclaims the sign at **Umpqua Angler,** 420 S.E. Main, Roseburg 97470, tel. (541) 673-9809, and their staff is always eager to help you sink your hooks into some supper. This full-service shop features licensed and insured guides for spring and fall salmon as well as summer and winter steelhead. They have all kinds of fishing equipment, bait and tackle, and boats and boat supplies. If you have trouble with your rod and reel, this is the place to bring it in for repairs. Open at 7 a.m. seven days a week.

One of the decisions fishing-guide shoppers have to make is to choose from Gary, Larry, or Jerry. **Gary's Guide Service,** 607 Fawn Dr., Roseburg 97470, tel. (541) 672-2460, has been in the fishing business for over 20 years and can teach you tried-and-true secrets of the trade. Licensed, bonded, and insured, all equipment is provided for fly- or drift-fishing for salmon and steelhead on the North Umpqua. **Larry's Guide Service,** 12736 N. Umpqua Hwy., Roseburg 97470, tel. (541) 673-3099, can help you get out on the river year-round to fish for salmon, steelhead, and striped bass. The drift-boats are large and heated; bait, tackle, and safety equipment are all provided. Rates are $150 for full-day trips; call ahead for reservations and additional information. **Jerry's Guide Service,**

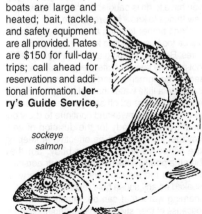

sockeye salmon

BOB RACE

tel. (541) 672-8324, mimics Gary's and Larry's offerings. Jerry Phelps, a teacher, naturalist, and guide with a master of science degree, offers an educational and entertaining fishing experience.

Bill Conners Guide Service, P.O. Box 575, Glide 97443, tel. (541) 496-0309, offers trips on the North Umpqua River for winter steelhead Jan.-April, for chinook salmon May-June and Sept.-Oct., and for summer steelhead June-October. He uses drift boats and gives you a choice of fly-, bait, or lure fishing. Call ahead for rates and reservations.

Rafting

It's no secret that the fishing is excellent on the North Umpqua River. And yet, the river has only recently been "discovered" and gained popularity with whitewater rafters and kayakers. But fishing and floating are not always compatible, so guidelines for boaters and rafters have been established by the Bureau of Land Management and the Umpqua National Forest. The area around Steamboat has the most restrictions, mainly because of the heavy fishing in the area that boaters would disturb. Be sure to check with the Forest Service, tel. (541) 498-2531, prior to setting out to make sure that you are making a legal trip. A good way to get started rafting and avoid the hassle of rules, regulations, and gear is to go along with an experienced whitewater guide. They provide the safety equipment, the boats, and the expertise; all you have to do is paddle. There are, however, a few things to know before you go.

Don't bother to bring a camera; your hands will be too busy paddling to have time to take pictures. Besides, keeping a camera dry in a raft is not an easy task and often requires special protective equipment. Short pants are preferable, because a little water that splashes up on your leg can be brushed off easily, whereas soaked jeans will remain wet and continue to draw out heat from your body for the duration of your voyage. Ponchos can be effective at keeping the water off of your upper body, but they breathe poorly. This means that your perspiration from the exertion will get you nearly as soaked as any souse hole (exhilarating pools of foaming water that can be equally dangerous because of their strong eddies). Another thing to remember is to wear a pair of worn-out sneakers that you don't really care about and leave the Gucci sandals at home. There always seems to be a little bit of water in the bottom of the boat, and shoes are always required for safety reasons. Finally, a hat and liberal layers of sunscreen are recommended to protect your skin from the ravages of the mountain sun.

In addition to rafting, inflatable kayak trips are offered by outfitters. Inflatables are easier for the neophyte to handle than the hardshell type, though these craft expose you to more chills and spills. Whatever your mode of floating the river, expect more than a dozen Class III or IV rapids, and plenty of Class IIs, as well as oldgrowth trees and osprey nests. Best of all, this world-class river is still relatively undiscovered. Spring and summer are the best times to enjoy the North Umpqua, although it's boatable year-round. Boaters are allowed on the river between 10 a.m. and 6 p.m. only, leaving the morning and evening for fish.

Rafting Outfitters

North Umpqua Outfitters, P.O. Box 1574, 368 N.E. Garden Valley Blvd., Roseburg 97470, tel. (541) 673-4599, offers raft, kayak, and drift-boat trips. Half-day raft trips are $40 per person; full-day raft trips with lunch are $60 per person. This company operates the North Umpqua Kayak School, which gives classes on how to paddle safely, to roll and handle surfing waves, and survive souse holes. Half- and full-day kayak lessons include all necessary equipment. Half- and full-day drift-boat trips are available for those who like to troll their fishing line in the water on their way downstream. They also rent boats, rafts, kayaks, and the appropriate accoutrements. If you make your reservation in advance, you are given a discount, and you can also knock off 10% on certain packages if you bring in their brochure, available at the Roseburg Visitors and Convention Bureau at 401 S.E. Spruce St., tel. (541) 672-9731. Other outfitters are the **Adventure Center,** tel. (541) 482-2897, in Ashland, **Orange Torpedo Trips,** tel. (541) 479-5061, in Grants Pass, and **Oregon Ridge and River Excursions,** tel. (541) 496-3333.

You can combine rafting and mountain biking with **Oregon Ridge and River Excursions,** P.O. Box 495, Glide, tel. (541) 496-3333. Their popular two- or three-day overnighter trip mountain bikes down the trail along the North Umpqua River and takes in some whitewater paddle rafting, too. They also offer raft and kayak packages. Snacks, great outdoor cooking, and comfortable camping are provided. Call for rates and reservations.

If you want to rent your equipment, a good place to check out is **North Umpqua Equipment Rental Sales and Service,** 14168 ORE 138, Roseburg 97470, tel. (541) 673-5391. You'll find it 12 miles east of Roseburg on ORE 138 next to the Whistlers Park Mercantile Store. They feature one- and two-person inflatable kayaks (also called "orange torpedoes") and whitewater rafts for two to six people.

Hikes

Over 570 miles of trails crisscross the one-million-acre **Umpqua National Forest.** With elevations that range from 1,000 to over 9,000 feet, there are hikes to please families and mountain climbers alike. Wildlife and wildflowers, mountain lakes and mountain peaks, old-growth forest and alpine meadows are some of the attractions visitors see along the way.

If you're camping along the North Umpqua River, many pleasant day-hikes are possible on the **North Umpqua Trail.** Slated to be completed by the late 1990s, this projected 76-mile thoroughfare will stretch from Rock Creek just east of Idleyld Park all the way up to the Pacific Crest Trail at Windigo Pass. The trail connects many of the campgrounds and has many access points from ORE 138. Check with the Umpqua National Forest Ranger Station, Diamond Lake Ranger District, HC 60, P.O. Box 101, Idleyld Park 97447, tel. (541) 498-2531, for a map and brochure to plan your expedition along this beautiful walkway.

One completed segment of the North Umpqua Trail is the **Panther Trail.** This gentle one-mile hike begins near Steamboat at the parking lot of the former ranger station. Many wildflowers are seen late April through early June on the way up to the old fish hatchery. One flower to look for is the bright red snow plant, *Sarcodes sanguinea,* which grows beneath Douglas firs and sugar pine trees. Also called the carmine snowflower or snow lily, the snow plant is classified as a saprophyte, a plant that contains no chlorophyll and derives nour-

ishment from decayed materials. Growing 8-24 inches in height, the red flowers are crowded at the crown of the stem.

A **five-mile hike** that ranges from easy to moderate is found on the south slope of 8,363-foot-high Mt. Bailey. Bring plenty of water and good sturdy hiking shoes because the last half mile of the ascent is steep, with many sharp rocks. To get to the trailhead, take ORE 138 to the north entrance of Diamond Lake. Turn off onto Forest Service Rd. 4795 and follow it five miles to the junction of Forest Service Rd. 4795-300. Proceed down 4795-300 another mile until you see the trail marker.

The easy two-mile **Diamond Lake Loop** takes hikers through a mix of lodgepole pine and true fir to Lake Creek, Diamond Lake's only outlet. There are many views of Mt. Bailey along the way, as well as some private coves ideal for a swim on hot days. But while the grade is easy, keep in mind that the elevation is nearly a mile high and pace yourself accordingly. To get to the loop, take Forest Service Rd. 4795 off of ORE 138 on the north entrance to Diamond Lake and look for the trailhead sign on the west side of the road.

For those who like to climb mountains for reasons other than just because they are there, the **Mt. Thielsen Trail** offers a million-dollar view from the top of the mountain. This four-mile moderate-to-difficult trail winds to the top of Mt. Thielsen's spire-pointed 9,182-foot-high volcanic peak. Bring along water and quick-energy snacks; hiking boots are also recommended due to the sharp volcanic rocks that could easily damage ordinary shoes. Extra care should be taken getting up and down the last 200 feet, since the rocks weaken from ice and erosion during the winter and are prone to crumbling underfoot. If you make it to the top, be sure to enter your name in the climbing register found there. Then take a look at the view, which stretches from Mt. Shasta to Mt. Hood, and forget all the silly preoccupations that plague us mortals. You'll find the trailhead on the east side of ORE 138 one mile north of the junction of ORE 230.

Mount Bailey Snowcat Skiing

Located 80 miles east of Roseburg off of ORE 138 in the central Cascades is Mt. Bailey, tel. (541) 793-3333. Snowcats transport no more than 12 skiers up the mountain from Diamond Lake Resort to the summit of this 8,363-foot-high peak. Experienced guides then lead small groups down routes that best suit the abilities of each group. The skiing is challenging and should only be attempted by those who can ski advanced runs at major ski areas in various snow conditions. Open bowls, steep chutes, and tree-lined glaciers are some of the types of terrain encountered during the 3,000-foot drop in elevation back to the resort.

The prices may also seem steep at $160 a day, but it's worth it given the pristine beauty of the area, dearth of crowds, and superlative skiing. You can save some money with the Powder Pass—six days of skiing for the price of five. Other attractive packages include overnight lodging in fireside cabins at Diamond Lake Resort as well as an "alpine lunch" of breads, meats, cheeses, vegetables, homemade pie, and coffee served up on the mountain. Only a limited number of skiers can be booked, so be sure to call ahead for reservations.

Slip Slidin' Away
If you fit the bunny hill category, you might enjoy inner-tubing at **Sliding Hill,** tel. (541) 793-3333, near Diamond Lake Resort. A rope tow takes "tubers" to the top of the hill seven days a week, 9 a.m.-5 p.m., for nonstop thrills and spills on the way back down. The hill has a ticket system similar to other ski lifts, with full-day, half-day, and two-hour passes available. Passes including an inner tube cost $10 for the full day, $8 for the half day, and $6 for two hours. A $5 refundable deposit is required for the equipment, and many sizes of inner tubes are available. If you bring your own inner tube, you can save a dollar or two.

Cross-Country Skiing
Over 56 miles of designated Nordic trails are found in the Diamond and Lemolo lakes area along the upper reaches of ORE 138. The trails range in elevation from 4,200 feet to over 8,000 feet at the top of Mt. Bailey. Some of the trails are groomed, and all of them are clearly marked by blue trail signs. Contact the **Umpqua National Forest,** Diamond Lake Ranger District, HC 60, P.O. Box 101, Idleyld Park 97447, tel. (541) 498-2531, and request maps and information on these trails.

The **Nordic Center,** tel. (541) 793-3333, at Diamond Lake Resort has equipment, waxes, and rentals, and is open 8 a.m.-5 p.m. daily. It costs $12 per day for a rental package including skis, boots, and poles. Lessons are also available. A great option to cross-country buffs is to take a snowcat from Diamond Lake to the north rim of Crater Lake for $70 per person. You have the option to ski the 10 miles back to Diamond Lake (mostly downhill) with a guide, or ride back on the snowcat for an additional $50. A hearty lunch is included in the package.

Motorized Snow Trails
Approximately 133 miles of designated motorized snow trails are concentrated around the Lemolo and Diamond lakes area. The trails are usually open in late November, when snow accumulations permit, and range from 4,000 to over 8,000 feet in elevation. Many of these trails are groomed on a regular basis, and all are clearly marked by orange trail signs and diamond-shaped trail blazes pegged up on trees above the snowline. Contact Umpqua National Forest (see "Cross-country Skiing," above) for maps and additional information.

One of the more exotic runs is into Crater Lake National Park. Snowmobiles and ATVs (all-terrain vehicles) must register at the north entrance of the park and stay on the road. The trail climbs up about 10 miles from the park gates to the north rim of the lake. Be aware that the mountain weather here can change suddenly, creating dangerous subzero temperatures and whiteout conditions. Also, watch for Nordic skiers and other people sometimes found on motorized-vehicle trails.

Snowmobile Tours
If you've ever wanted to ride on one of these motorized snow broncs, then this is the way to go. Each person is furnished with his or her own snowmobile and fuel. A half-dozen tours are available ranging from $50 for the one-hour, 17-mile ride around Diamond Lake to $150 for the eight-hour, 100-mile trip to Crescent Lake. The most popular trip is the Crater Lake rim tour. It costs $75 and takes four hours to cover the 50 miles of snowbound terrain. A hearty lunch is included. Make your reservations at the **Diamond Lake Resort Hilltop Shop,** tel. (541)

793-3333. The only catch to the offer is that you must be a guest of the resort, due to the clauses in the liability insurance policy carried by the concessionaire.

PRACTICALITIES

Camping on the Little River

If the thought of a campground with good shade trees and a waterfall with a swimming hole sounds idyllic, head for **Cavitt Creek Falls,** Bureau of Land Management, 777 N.W. Garden Valley Blvd., Roseburg 97470, tel. (541) 672-4491. To get there, head east of Roseburg on ORE 138 to Glide, take Little Creek Rd. (County Rd. 17) for seven miles, then continue three miles down Cavitt Creek Road. Eight sites for RVs (20 feet maximum) with picnic tables and fire grills are provided, with piped water, pit toilets, and firewood available on the premises. Open May to late October, Cavitt Creek runs $10 per night.

Another campsite five miles up Little River Rd. is **Wolf Creek,** North Umpqua Ranger District, 18782 ORE 138, Glide 97443, tel. (541) 496-3532, which features five sites for tents and RVs (16 feet maximum) and three tent-only sites. Picnic tables, fire grills, vault toilets, and piped water are provided. Open mid-May to late October, the fee is $4 per night. The grounds also have a group picnic site with a pavilion sheltering 14 picnic tables, plus barbecue grills, flush toilets, and chlorinated water. This facility is booked on a reservation-only basis for $50 per day. A softball field, horseshoe pits, and swimming in the Little River make this a fine place for family get-togethers.

An easy way to keep your cool is at **Coolwater,** North Umpqua Ranger District, 18782 ORE 138, Glide 97443, tel. (541) 496-3532. Seven tent and RV sites (16 feet maximum) with picnic tables and fire grills are available; vault toilets and well water from a hand pump are also on the grounds. Open mid-May to late October, the campground is available free of charge. To get there, follow Little River Rd. 15 miles out of Glide. There are many good hiking trails nearby, including **Grotto Falls, Wolf Creek Nature Trail,** and **Wolf Creek Falls Trail.**

One of the best deals on the Little River is at **White Creek,** North Umpqua Ranger District, 18782 ORE 138, Glide 97443, tel. (541) 496-3532. Open from mid-May to late September, this small five-site campground accommodates tents and RVs (31 feet maximum) free of charge. Picnic tables and fire grills are provided, and piped water and vault toilets are available. Situated on the confluence of White Creek and Little River, a good beach and shallow water provide excellent swimming for children. The only catch to this oasis of tranquility is that your stay is limited to two weeks at a time. To get there, take Little Creek Rd. 17 miles to Red Butte Rd. and proceed a mile down Red Butte Rd. to the campground.

Tucked away at an elevation of 3,200 feet on the upper reaches of the Little River is **Lake in the Woods,** North Umpqua Ranger District, 18782 ORE 138, Glide 97443, tel. (541) 496-3532. Here you'll find nine sites for tents and RVs (16 feet maximum), with picnic tables, fire grills, vault toilets, and hand-pumped water. Open from June to late October, the camp charges $8 per night. Set along the shore of four-acre, human-made Little Lake in the Woods, motorized craft are not permitted in this eight-foot-deep pond. Two good hikes nearby are to **Hemlock Falls** and **Yakso Falls.** To get there, head 20 miles up Little River Rd. to where the pavement ends; proceed another seven miles until you reach the campground.

North Umpqua River Camping

Set along the bank of the North Umpqua River 15 miles east of Roseburg on ORE 138 is **Whistler's Bend,** P.O. Box 800, Winchester 97495, tel. (541) 673-4863. Picnic tables and fire grills are provided at this county park, as are piped water, flush toilets, and showers. No reservations are necessary, and the fee is $10 per night. The fishing is good here, and even though it's fairly close to town, it doesn't usually get too crowded.

About 30 miles east of ORE 138 is **Susan Creek,** Bureau of Land Management, 777 N.W. Garden Valley Blvd., Roseburg 97470, tel. (541) 672-4491. This campground has 33 tent and RV sites (20 feet maximum) with picnic tables and fire grills. Flush toilets, piped water, and firewood are also available. Open May to late October, the fee is $9 per night. Situated in a grove of old-growth Douglas fir and sugar pine next to the North Umpqua River, a fine beach and swimming hole complement the setting.

Within easy access to great fishing (fly-angling only), rafting, and hiking, **Bogus Creek,** Diamond Lake Ranger District, HC 60, P.O. Box 101, Idleyld Park 97447, tel. (541) 498-2531, offers you the real thing. Here you'll find five tent sites and 10 tent and RV sites (20 feet maximum) with picnic tables and fire grills. Flush toilets, iodinated water, and gray wastewater sumps are available. Open May 1-Oct. 31, the fee is $9 per night. As the campground is a major launching point for whitewater expeditions and within a few miles of Fall Creek Falls and Job's Garden Geological Area (see "Waterfalls" under "Sights," above), it's hard to beat the feeling here.

About 38 miles east of Roseburg on ORE 138 near Steamboat is **Canton Creek,** Diamond Lake Ranger District, HC 60, P.O. Box 101, Idleyld Park 97447, tel. (541) 498-2531. Take Steamboat Creek Rd. off ORE 138 and proceed 400 yards to the campground. This campground features 12 sites for tents and RVs (16 feet maximum) with the standard picnic tables and fire grills, plus piped water, flush toilets, and gray wastewater sumps. Open from mid-May to late October, Canton Creek costs $9 per night. Close to good fly-fishing on the North Umpqua, this site gets surprisingly little use.

Horseshoe Bend, Diamond Lake Ranger District, HC 60, P.O. Box 101, Idleyld Park 97447, tel. (541) 498-2531, is 10 miles east of Steamboat. There are 34 sites for tents and RVs (22 feet maximum) with picnic tables and fire grills. Flush toilets, piped water, gray wastewater sumps, a laundromat, and a general store are also available. Open mid-May to late September, the fee is $12 per night. Located in the middle of a big bend of the North Umpqua covered with old-growth Douglas firs and sugar pines, this is a popular base camp for rafting and fishing enthusiasts.

Campsites at Diamond Lake

Several campgrounds are in the vicinity of beautiful 5,200-foot-high Diamond Lake; boating, fishing, swimming, bicycling, and hiking are among the popular recreational options here. The trout fishing is particularly good in the early summer, and there are also excellent hikes into the Mt. Thielsen Wilderness, Crater Lake National Park, and Mt. Bailey areas. While technically no reservations are necessary, the campgrounds here can fill up fast, so it's always a good idea to book a space ahead of time. For the campgrounds listed below, contact Diamond Lake Ranger District, HC 60, P.O. Box 101, Idleyld Park 97447, tel. (541) 498-2531.

Though ORE 138 twists and turns most of the 80 miles from Roseburg to Diamond Lake, many people head straight for **Broken Arrow.** This 142-site campground with standard picnic tables and fire grills has plenty of room for tents and RVs (30 feet maximum); flush toilets, piped water, and gray wastewater sumps are available. Open from early May to late September, the fee is $10-18 per night, depending upon the site. Premium lakeshore sites command top dollar.

The next campground bears the name of its raison d'être, **Diamond Lake.** Here you'll find 160 campsites for tents and RVs (22 feet maximum) with picnic tables and fire grills. Piped water, flush toilets, and firewood are also available. Open May 15-Oct. 31, the fee is $14 per night. Numerous hiking trails lead from the campground, including the Pacific Crest National Scenic Trail. Boat docks, launching facilities, and rentals are nearby at Diamond Lake Lodge.

On the east shore of Diamond Lake is **Thielsen View.** It features 60 tent and RV sites (30 feet maximum) with picnic tables and fire grills. Piped water, vault toilets, gray wastewater sumps, and a boat ramp are also available. It's open late May to late September, and the fee ranges $6-12 per night, depending upon the site. As the name implies, this campground has picturesque views of Mt. Thielsen.

Accommodations

The number of lodgings on the North Umpqua is limited to a few properties that range from rustic lodging to full-service resorts. The abundance of campgrounds and wilderness getaways accessible via the Umpqua Highway partially explains the dearth of motel units. In short, most people come here to get close to nature's teachings and leave the trappings of civilization behind. However, if the weather takes a turn for the worse or you'd rather rough it in style, you have several options that will give you shelter from the storm.

STEAMBOAT INN

In the late 1800s, a steamboat chugged up the Umpqua River from Reedsport to Roseburg. Based upon this sole voyage, the Umpqua is still listed as a navigable river by the U.S. Coast Guard and all river traffic is regulated. While no vessels made it to the area 38 miles upriver from Roseburg that's called Steamboat today, the name comes from the common practice of unscrupulous gold speculators who would overestimate the value of holdings to buyers and after the sale would catch the first available steamboat out of the region.

The gold mines are worked out now, but the real treasure of the North Umpqua can still be found at the **Steamboat Inn,** Steamboat 97447, tel. (541) 496-3495 or 498-2411. This is the premier dining and accommodations property on the river. The inn is extremely popular and there are only 17 units, so reservations are a must. The two new riverside suites are an outstanding value at around $200 per night. The grounds are beautifully maintained and blend in with the natural surroundings. Pets are allowed on prior approval only. It's an ideal getaway from civilization, near the hiking trails, waterfalls, and fishing holes for which the Umpqua is famous.

The $85-95 room rate is the best investment in peace of mind that you can make. The breakfast specialty is the sour cream roll-up. This delectable concoction is a big pancake stuffed with homemade jam and sour cream. Omelettes, French toast, hotcakes, and eggs are other featured eye openers, and homemade cinnamon rolls and bran muffins round out the offerings. The health conscious will enjoy the homemade granola with yogurt and fresh fruit. Lunch features burgers, sandwiches, soups, and salads.

The special Fisherman's Dinner, $30, is served nightly during the summer and on weekends the rest of the year. The elaborate presentation begins about a half-hour after dusk with champagne and hors d'oeuvres. There is no set menu for the Fisherman's Dinner, only lots of good things designed around the guests' preferences. The entree of the day (vegetarian entrees are available upon advance request), freshly baked bread, vegetables, and other dishes are served up family style on the inn's big wood-slab tables. An elegant dessert and hot beverage conclude the meal. Reservations are required for the Fisherman's Dinner.

Near Idleyld Park is the **North Umpqua Resort,** P.O. Box 177, Idleyld Park 97447, tel. (541) 496-0149. Situated on ORE 138 along the north bank of the Umpqua, the place is not fancy, but it is at least clean. The rooms range from $40 to $80, and good fishing can be had from the private bank of the property on the river. About four miles east of Idleyld Park is the **Dogwood Motel,** HC 60, P.O. Box 19, Idleyld Park 97447, tel. (541) 496-3403. Here you'll find clean modern units with or without kitchenettes located on tidy, well-kept grounds. Room rates range $45-60.

Near the summit of the Cascade Mountains about 75 miles east of Roseburg and 13 miles from Diamond Lake is **Lemolo Lake Resort,** write HC 60, P.O. Box 79 B, Idleyld Park 97447, tel. (541) 496-0900. Formed by a Pacific Power and Light dam, Lemolo Lake has German brown trout, as well as kokanee salmon, eastern brook trout, and rainbow trout. The lake is sheltered from wind by gently sloping ridges, and there are many coves and sandy beaches along the 8.3 miles of shoreline. Water-skiing is permitted on the lake. Boats and canoes can be rented, and many miles of snowmobiling and cross-country skiing trails are nearby.

The resort itself has cabins, both housekeeping and standard, and rooms available. Each Swiss-chalet housekeeping cabin is equipped with a furnished kitchen, bathroom with shower, and wood-burning stove. They can sleep up to five and they cost $80 per night. The Swiss-chalet standard cabins (with bathroom but no kitchen) sleep six in two double and two single beds for $70. Rooms with two double beds go for $65 and rooms with one double bed cost $55.

Diamond Lake Resort, Diamond Lake, tel. (541) 793-3333 or (800) 733-7593, offers lodgings, restaurants, groceries, a service station, a laundromat, and showers. Two-bedroom cabins rent for $85-145; rooms and studios average 60% less than that. Lodgings here are popular as base camps for a Crater Lake excursion. This is a rustic mountain resort with enough modern amenities to suit the tenderfoot.

Food

If you've got a craving for some junk food, the **Colliding Rivers Drive-In,** 19162 ORE 138, Glide, tel. (541) 496-3205, can satisfy you. Nothing fancy: burgers, chicken, and spuds. For the ultimate gut bomb, try the Overload, a three-quarter-pound hamburger with bacon, cheese, and ham for $7. Chicken dinners with spuds and dinner rolls rival the colonel. Sixteen flavors of ice cream offer a sweet alternative to fried food.

Munchies, 20142 ORE 138, Glide, tel. (541) 496-3112, features Mexican food made mostly from scratch with no lard or MSG. They make their own vegetarian refried beans and offer eight vegetarian specials on the menu. Omnivores will enjoy the Munchie burrito, a large tortilla stuffed with beef or chicken and beans and topped with melted cheeses, lettuce, onions, olives, tomatoes, salsa, sour cream, and guacamole. The large burrito will fill you up in a hurry. Burgers, sandwiches, and breakfasts served all day can be found here, as well as homemade pie. Open seven days a week 9 a.m.-9 p.m.

Another option in Glide is **The Red Barn,** 20641 ORE 138, Glide, tel. (541) 496-0246. Breakfast here ranges $2-6, and lunches featuring burgers or sandwiches come with fries or chips and potato or green salad. Vegetarians will enjoy the garden veggie sandwich with Swiss cheese, lettuce, tomato, cucumber, alfalfa sprouts, and cream cheese that comes garnished with cottage cheese or potato salad. Moderately priced, $7-15, steaks, poultry, and seafood are the primary dinners featured, including salad, fries, rice or baked potato, and a light dessert. Lighter fare is available as well, and the best seats in the house are in the back room overlooking the Umpqua River. Open Mon.-Thurs. 7:30 a.m.-8:30 p.m., Fri.-Sat. 7:30 a.m.-4 p.m., and Sunday 7:30 a.m.-8:30 p.m.

In nearby Idleyld Park is **Dave and Ellen's,** P.O. Box 177, Idleyld Park, tel. (541) 496-0855. This full-service restaurant makes its food from scratch and piles your plate high with lots of it. Breakfast ranges $3-7, lunches $3-8, and dinners $7-15. Homemade rolls and stir-fried vegetables accompany all dinners.

Information and Services

The **post office,** 18404 ORE 138, Idleyld Park 97447, tel. (541) 496-3412, is open Mon.-Fri. 8 a.m.-1 p.m. and 2-5 p.m. Get additional information on hikes, campgrounds, and fishing from the **Forest Service,** North Umpqua District Ranger Station, 18782 ORE 138, Glide 97443, tel. (541) 496-3532.

ORE 58: OAKRIDGE AND VICINITY

Halfway between Eugene and the Cascades' summit on ORE 58 lies the town of Oakridge. Originally a Southern Pacific railway stop called Hazeldel, Oakridge changed its name in 1912 to fit the topography. Known also as the "Gateway City to the national forest," lumber, secondary wood products (furniture, toys, etc.), recreation, and tourism support this small community (pop. 4,000) tucked away in a foothill valley of the Cascades. The surrounding Willamette National Forest turns out billions of board feet of lumber each year, but it still retains some of the finest wilderness areas in Oregon.

There are over 100 lakes and streams near here, waiting for just about any nimrod to pull out his or her quota of rainbow, German brown, cutthroat, and Dolly Varden trout from the cool waters. A short drive from town are Waldo Lake and Diamond Peak Wilderness Area, as well as summer sailing and water-skiing at Odell Lake. Winter sport enthusiasts can find excellent downhill skiing at Willamette Pass, which features 18 runs, four chairlifts, a rope tow, and a day lodge. There are plenty of beautiful trails available for Nordic skiers too. If you like to fish, hike, camp, sail, ski, mountain bike, or just hang out in the woods, it's all only minutes away from Oakridge.

SIGHTS

The **Oakridge Pioneer Museum,** 76433 Pine St., tel. (541) 782-2666 or 782-2703, is open Saturday 1-4 p.m., or by special request. Pioneer artifacts ranging from tools to toys are on display. Two colorful exhibits in particular recreate the 1880s—a grocery and a typical kitchen of the early Oregon settlers. A large collection of old dolls and children's toys fills up a showcase that today's kids still find fascinating. The Chain Saw Tree, an interesting presentation on the evolution of the saws that conquered the forest, is also worth taking a look at.

McCredie Hot Springs is found 10 miles southeast of Oakridge on ORE 58 near mile marker 45. A short walk down to Salt Creek brings you to a small hot spring adjacent to the river. This location allows the visitor to enjoy the rush of simultaneously hot and cold water. Depending on how you position yourself, you can take a bath at any temperature you choose. There are plans to develop McCredie Hot Springs into a resort, so it is recommended you partake of this experience while it's still in its natural state.

Another primitive hot springs in the area is **Meditation Pool,** Wall Creek. It's really more like a warm spring, as the water ranges from 104° to about 90°, depending upon weather conditions. It's a short easy hike in, and the soak is worth the effort. To get there, turn north onto Rose St. from ORE 58 in Oakridge. Turn right onto 1st St., proceed east, and 1st St. will eventually become Forest Service Rd. 24 paralleling Salmon Creek. About 10 miles out of Oakridge, look for Forest Service Rd. 1934 on the left (north) side of the road. Approximately a half mile down Forest Service Rd. 1934 you'll see a trailhead sign (the kind with no name, only two figures hiking) on the west (left) side of the road. Follow the path along Wall Creek about a third of a mile up to the creekside pool. East of Oakridge on ORE 58 on the south side of the highway is Greenwater rest area, a beautiful place to take in the laidback charm of the upper Willamette River.

Westfir Covered Bridge

A short distance out of Oakridge on the Aufderheide National Scenic Byway is the Westfir Covered Bridge. This bright red span has the distinction of being the longest covered bridge in Oregon (180 feet) as well as the tallest covered bridge west of the Mississippi. Furthermore, it is likely that it is also the heaviest span of any wood construction bridge due to its Howe trusses, extension rods, and cords. You can see what remains of the Hines Company mill on the opposite side of the bridge; in its heyday it employed 750 people and operated around the clock. You can get a good picture of the bridge from the road as you approach the town of Westfir.

a Cascades creek
in winter finery

OREGON TOURISM DIVISION

Salt Creek Falls

About 20 miles southeast of Oakridge, just west of Willamette Pass on the way to Odell Lake on ORE 58 is Oregon's second highest waterfall, Salt Creek Falls. You'll find the pullout on the south side of the highway. The short walk to the viewing area of the 286-foot high cascade provides a great photo opportunity. Trails access both the top and the bottom of the falls for those interested in taking a closer look at this raw display of hydropower. Restrooms and a picnic area, all wheelchair accessible, are available at the falls. There are also interpretive placards along the trail to supplement the information kiosk. This waterfall is considered the headwaters of the Willamette River.

HIKES

Fall Creek National Recreation Trail

The Fall Creek National Recreation Trail is about 30 miles southeast of Eugene. To get there, take ORE 58 about 15 miles to Lowell, then go north for two miles to the covered bridge at Unity Junction. Take a right onto Forest Service Rd. 18 (Fall Creek Rd.), and stay to the left of the reservoir. Follow the road for 11 miles to Dolly Varden Campground, where the trail starts.

The 14-mile-long Fall Creek Trail is ideal for short day-hikes or longer expeditions; several national forest entry/exit points crop up along the way. Another plus is the low elevation of the trail, which makes it accessible year-round. Strolling through the wilderness, you will pass many deep pools, whitewater rapids, and over a dozen small streams. Giant Douglas firs, bigleaf maples, vine maples, dogwoods, and red alders are some of the predominant vegetation you'll see along the way. In the spring, visitors are treated to shooting stars, trillium, bleeding heart, and other vibrant wildflowers.

There are five campgrounds en route and three other spur trails that merge into the Fall Creek Trail. **Bedrock Campground** is a particularly popular spot for swimming. Those without a fear of heights can jump off the bridge into the deep waters of the creek 40 feet below, or perhaps attempt a dive off of the adjacent rock escarpment.

Larison Creek Trail

The Larison Creek Trail (Trail 3646) is less than 10 minutes away from Oakridge. To get there, take ORE 58 to Oakridge. Turn onto Kitson Springs County Rd. and proceed for a half mile. Turn right on Forest Service Rd. 21 and follow it three miles to the trailhead, which you'll find on the right side of the road.

Multicolored mosses cover the valley floor, and its walls simulate a brush-stroked backdrop to stands of old-growth fir. Further contrast is supplied by waterfalls and swimming holes. The mild grade and low elevation of this trail make it accessible year-round.

Tufti Creek Trail

Another good hike close to Oakridge is the Tufti Creek Trail (Trail 3624). To get there, take ORE 58 to Oakridge. Turn onto Kitson Springs County Rd. and proceed for about a mile. Turn left onto Forest Service Rd. 23 and follow it for six miles. This will take you along the northeast

bank of Hills Creek Lake and on past Kitson Hot Springs (which is also worthy of investigation). Look for the trailhead sign on the right, about a mile past the hot springs.

This short and friendly half-mile trail winds through large Douglas firs and cedars and overlooks Hills Creek Gorge. There are many small waterfalls and deep swimming holes along the way. This trail is also accessible year-round.

Waldo Lake Wilderness—An Introduction

The Waldo Lake Wilderness is a 37,000 acre gem 70 miles southeast of Eugene via ORE 58. The centerpiece of this alpine paradise is 10

WILLAMETTE NATIONAL FOREST

In the middle of Oregon's Cascade Range is the Willamette National Forest, Supervisor's Office, 211 E. 17th, Eugene 97440, tel. (541) 687-6521. Encompassing over 1.6 million acres of land stretching from the Mt. Jefferson area east of Salem to the Calapooya Mountains northeast of Roseburg, this enormous forest is about the size of New Jersey.

Eight wilderness areas take up one-quarter of its land, and seven major Cascade peaks lie within its boundaries. In addition to three national recreation trails (Fall Creek, McKenzie River, and South Breitenbush Gorge) and the famed Pacific Crest Trail, over 1,300 miles of developed trails weave throughout Willamette National Forest.

Recreational opportunities abound. Two developed ski areas, Willamette Pass and Hoodoo Ski Bowl, serve schussers. Near each ski park are snowmobile areas, at Waldo Lake and Big Lake respectively. Cross-country skiing is also available on many of the National Forest Service roads and trails. Precipitation in the Willamette National Forest ranges 40-150 inches a year, providing the Willamette and McKenzie rivers with excellent conditions for whitewater rafting, drift-boat fishing, canoeing, and kayaking. Dozens of lakes and reservoirs round out the boating picture with sailing, rowing, and water-skiing. Big-game hunters can stalk black bear, Roosevelt elk, and deer (black-tailed deer west of the Cascades, mule deer east). Anglers can try their luck catching dinner in one of the forest's many lakes, rivers, and streams.

And yet, this playground in the woods is also the workplace for a significant percentage of the population in the six counties that occupy the Willamette National Forest. The area is usually the

top timber producer of all 159 national forests in the United States. Supplying approximately eight percent of the total cut on National Forest Service lands in the country, the Willamette National Forest generates over $130 million annually in timber receipts. In addition to providing a steady source of employment for thousands of people, 25% of the forest's timber revenues go to local coffers to help fund public schools and roads.

Besides the Douglas fir, another Willamette Forest tree has become a source of revenue. The discovery that the Pacific yew tree yields taxol, effective against some kinds of cancer, has focused the eyes of the country here. Just look for a small twisted tree with sparse dark needles, moss-laden branches, peeling reddish bark, and sprouting burls in damp, shady areas. From April to the fall, a small red berrylike growth decorates yew branches. Birds and deer love them but they're poisonous to humans. The fact that the yew thrives in the shade of an old-growth forest has thrust this species into the middle of debates over the importance of preserving the biodiversity of this ecosystem.

Four major highways lead to the Willamette National Forest: ORE 58 (the Willamette Highway), ORE 126 (the McKenzie Highway), US 20 (the Cascadia Highway), and ORE 22 (the Santiam Highway). Whichever route you choose to follow, William Cullen Bryant's words should apply: ". . . Go forth, under the open sky, and list to Nature's teachings . . . the hills rock-ribbed and ancient as the sun—the vales stretching in pensive quietness between; the venerable woods—rivers that move in majesty, and the contiguous woods where rolls the Oregon . . ."

mile-high Waldo Lake

TED LONG ISHIKAWA

square-mile Waldo Lake (third largest in Oregon) whose waters were once rated the purest in the country in a nationwide study of 30 lakes. In 1997, however, Crater Lake got the number one spot as the purest lake in the world with 142 feet visibility. Regardless, peering down into the green translucent depths of this lake, it's possible to see rocky reefs and fish 50-100 feet below. Canoeing, sailing, trout fishing and windsurfing (no motorized craft allowed) on the lake complement hiking, and cross-country skiing to give you different ways to experience the lake and surrounding region. Add wildlife watching highlighted by the early September rutting season of Roosevelt elk and you'll quickly understand why Waldo Lake is a favorite with Cascades connoisseurs.

To best savor it all, visit the area between late August and mid-October to avoid a plague of summer mosquitoes and early winter snowfall. Whenever you go, expect a lack of crowds, views of 8,744-foot Diamond Peak in the distance, as well as first-rate trails and campgrounds. There's even one Forest Service campground, **Rhododendron Island,** that is accessed only by boat.

While the Rigdon Lakes hike and the Waldo Lake campgrounds in this chapter are a good introduction to this magical realm, there's many more great spots out there waiting to be enjoyed. Your best source for maps, information, and recreational tips is the **Oakridge Ranger Station,** 46375 ORE 58, West Fir, OR 97492, tel. (541) 782-2291.

Rigdon Lakes

A more ambitious hike is up to Rigdon Lakes (Trails 3590 and 3583). To get there, follow ORE 58 for 24 miles southeast of Oakridge. Take a left on Forest Service Rd. 5897. Follow it 10 miles to North Waldo Campground; the trailhead is to the right of the restrooms. This three-mile walk starts at North Waldo Lake Campground on Trail 3590. The trail is mild and scenic, paralleling the north shore of Waldo Lake for about two miles until the Rigdon Trail junction (Trail 3583). Head north (turn right) at the trail intersection for another mile to get to the first of the three Rigdon lakes, which has several peninsulas that are ideal for a picnic and several small islands that might tempt swimmers who don't mind cold water. A hike afterward up to the top of Rigdon Butte is highly recommended. You will have to bushwack, as there is no clear trail, but it is not a difficult climb if you follow the saddle of the ridge. From this vantage point, you can see all three Rigdon lakes as well as many other nearby Cascade landmarks. If you want to take a closer look at the two other Rigdon Lakes, they're only another mile or so down Trail 3583 from the first lake.

PRACTICALITIES

Accommodations

There are some reasonable lodging options in the area. The **Arbor Inn,** 48229 ORE 58, tel. (541) 782-2611 or (800) 505-9047, $30-40, is a small clean motel with microwaves and refrigerators in all rooms, some kitchenettes are also available. Pets are allowed here on prior approval only. **Silver Star Motel**, 47487 ORE 58, tel. (541) 782-2602; and the **Best Western Oakridge Inn**, 47433 ORE 58, tel. (541) 782-2212 or (800) 528-1234, which has 30 nice units that during the June 1-Oct. 30 summer season range $45-70. Winter rates are about $5 less.

Odell Lake, 30 miles southeast of Oakridge on ORE 58, deserves a special mention. There are two resorts, several summer homes, and five campgrounds around this 3,582-acre lake. Located in a deep glacial trough, the lake probably filled with water about 11,000 years ago when a terminal moraine blocked the drainage of Odell Creek. Due to the depth of the lake and the nearly perpetual west-to-east winds that blow through Willamette Pass, the water averages a cold 39° F. Those breezes, however, help to keep the pesky mosquitoes and other obnoxious insects away and make for some of the best sailing in the Cascades. The premier property on Odell Lake is the **Odell Lake Lodge**, P.O. Box 72, Crescent Lake 97425, tel. (541) 433-2540. To get there, take the East Odell exit off of ORE 58 and follow the road a couple of miles. The hotel rooms range $50-80 a night, with the cabins going for $75-125. Skiers may want to take advantage of large cabin 12, which comfortably houses as many as 16 people for $205 a night. Since the lodge is extremely popular, reservations are strongly recommended, as much as a year in advance for weekends.

Moorages are available for rent, as are canoes, powerboats, and sailboats. The lodge has a complete tackle shop to help outfit you to catch the kokanee and mackinaw that inhabit the icy waters, and rental equipment is also available if you didn't bring your own. The restaurant at the lodge will cook your bounty for you and serve it along with soup or salad, potatoes, vegetables, and bread for around $8 per person. The lodge also maintains its own system of trails, which provide good biking in the summer and cross-country skiing in the winter. The owners of the resort have put together an area map to guide you to various waterfalls. Bikes and ski equipment can be rented from the lodge. In addition to these outdoor pursuits, basketball, volleyball,

badminton, and horseshoes round out the fun. Tots and toddlers will enjoy the sandbox, the toy library, and the swings. Every Sunday afternoon features Cajun food and live music.

Across the lake from the lodge is **Shelter Cove Resort**, West Odell Lake Rd., Cascade Summit, tel. (541) 433-2548, which features eight cabins complete with kitchens, $80-150, 69 campsites with picnic tables and electricity, $10-17, and 65 moorages, $5-10, in the marina. The General Store handles everything from groceries, tackle, and boat rentals to snow-park permits and fishing/hunting licenses. The September to October displays of Odell Lake's landlocked salmon spawning are unforgettable. Contact the Rigdon Ranger Station, tel. (541) 782-2283, to reserve the 14-by-14 foot fire lookout cabin atop the 240-foot tower. At 5,800 feet elevation it has views of Diamond Peak, Three Sisters, and Mount Bachelor. It rents for $25 per night when not being used in summer as a fire lookout.

Bed and Breakfasts

In the former office building of Hines Lumber Company in Westfir across the street from the covered bridge is the **Westfir Lodge**, 47365 1st St., Westfir, tel. (541) 782-3103. The building has been tastefully converted into seven guest rooms with English-style bathrooms (each room has its own private bath, but it's across the hall from the bedroom). The house is full of curious Asian antiques, and the pantry used to be the company vault. A full breakfast (try the English bangers, a mild sausage) is included in the tariff, which is $45 for a single, $65 for double occupancy.

Campgrounds

Blue Pool Campground, on the banks of Salt Creek, is 10 miles from Oakridge on ORE 58. During the summer, water is available for flush toilets and general use. Each of the 18 sites features a picnic table and a fireplace grill. It costs $10 for a family per site, or $18 for two families on one site. A Golden Age passport grants the holder a 50% discount. Contact the Oakridge Ranger Station, 46375 ORE 58, Westfir 97492, tel. (541) 728-2291, for information.

Six miles west of Oakridge on the banks of the Willamette River and not too far from Lookout Point Lake is **Black Canyon Campground**.

Open May through late October, there are 72 sites for tents, trailers, or motor homes up to 22 feet long for $11 a night. Picnic tables and fireplace grills are standard; piped water, firewood, and vault toilets are also available. Boat docks and launching facilities are nearby on the south end of Lookout Point Lake. For additional information, write to Willamette National Forest, 46375 ORE 58, Westfir 97492, tel. (541) 782-2291.

There are two very nice campgrounds up at Waldo Lake called **Shadow Bay** and **North Waldo.** To get there, take ORE 58 for 24 miles southeast of Oakridge. Take a left on Forest Service Rd. 5897. It is five miles to Forest Service Rd. 5896, which takes you to Shadow Bay, and 10 miles down Forest Service Rd. 5897 to North Waldo. Both campgrounds charge $12.

Since there are 150 campsites between the two campgrounds, this usually ensures enough views of this mile-high lake for everyone to enjoy. Open June to late September, the fee is $12 a night. Boat docks and launching facilities are available, plus good sailing and fishing at Waldo. Many trails lead to small backcountry lakes from here; this is a good place to establish a base camp. Contact the Oakridge Ranger District for additional information.

If you want to get away from the traffic of ORE 58 and don't mind bouncing down Forest Service roads for over half an hour, you might consider **Blair Lake Campground.** To get to Blair Lake, head east out of Oakridge on County Route 149 for one mile. Turn left onto Forest Service Rd. 24 and go eight miles until you hit Forest Service Rd. 1934. It's another seven miles down Forest Service Rd. 1934 to Blair Lake. For further information, contact Willamette National Forest, 46375 ORE 58, Westfir 97492, tel. (541) 782-2291.

On the shore of little Blair Lake, a picturesque setting at 4,800 feet with nine tent sites awaits the determined explorer. Open June through mid-October, the fee is $7 per night, no reservations necessary. Picnic tables and fireplace grills are provided, with piped water, firewood, and pit toilets available. Boat docks are nearby, but no motorized craft are permitted on the lake.

Food

Sandwiched in between the roller rink (where the tri-state competition is annually held) and the bowling alley is **Village Cafe,** 47961 ORE 58, tel. (541) 782-2935. Standard American cuisine is the order of the day. Nothing terribly fancy, but nothing that terrible either.

After a hard day skiing, head on down the hill to **Timber Jim's,** 45727 ORE 58, tel. (541) 782-4310. This restaurant can best be described as the house that Jack built—lumberjack, that is. Huge rough-hewn wooden beams provide the roof support, the walls are paneled with latticework, and thick slabs of wood provide tables and benches for eating. "Misery whips" (two-person crosscut saws), pictures of logging crews from over 50 years ago, and other lumber paraphernalia round out the decor. A barroom piano sits proudly in the middle of the room, and sing-alongs after ski parties are not uncommon. Big Jim serves beer and wine, and the salad bar is decent. Try the Logger's Favorite pizza with the works. Dinners range from $5 for spaghetti to $12 for steak and prawns.

Latecomers or early risers should remember that the **Sportsman Cafe,** 48127 ORE 58, tel. (541) 782-2051, is open 24 hours a day (except Christmas Eve and Day). This is where you can hear many a fish story about the day's catch or the big one that got away. If the fish weren't biting, you can still find something good on the menu to get your hooks into. Dinners range $5-12 and come with salad, fries, and toast.

For variety, health, and taste, **New China Restaurant,** 48017 ORE 58, tel. (541) 782-4716, is probably the best place in town. You'll find all of your favorite Chinese dishes on the menu at reasonable prices. Open for lunch and dinner, they also have an assortment of American-style foods if the kids are being finicky. If you're in the mood for a home-cooked meal, try **Manning's Cafe,** 47460 ORE 58, tel. (541) 782-4816. They offer a selection of dinners for around $7 that satisfy lumberjack-sized appetites, and on cold days their hearty homemade soups thaw out a chill. The Mannings make their own bread and rolls that come with soup and dinner as well as delicious homemade pies and cakes for dessert.

If you're in an eat and run mode, **A&W,** 47841 ORE 58, tel. (541) 782-3662, is always a safe call. In addition to standard fast food, their trademark root beer is featured. Cool off on a hot day with a root beer float. Make sure that you get it in a chilled glass mug that turns the beverage into a half solid, half liquid concoction.

Information and Services
The **chamber of commerce,** 44284 ORE 58, Oakridge 97463, tel. (541) 782-4146, offers a wide assortment of information on the area.

The **post office,** 48264 E. 1st, Oakridge 97463, tel. (541) 782-2730, is open during business hours. To get there, turn at the town's only traffic light, cross over the bridge, and go right. The post office is about a half mile down. The **Oakridge Medical Clinic,** 47815 ORE 58, tel. (541) 782-2221, offers family and emergency medicine. Hours are Mon.-Fri. 9 a.m.-5 p.m., Saturday 9 a.m.-noon. For after-hours emergencies, call 911. The **Liquor Store,** 48019 ORE 58, tel. (541) 782-3405, is open Mon.-Sat. 11 a.m.-7 p.m., closed on holidays.

Mountain bike rentals and repairs, guided and/or catered biker/hiker trips, and cross-country ski rentals are all available through **Pathfinders,** 47470 ORE 58, tel. (541) 782-4838. While you're here pick up *Mountain Bike Ride Guide-*

Lane County Oregon by Keith Nelsin and Dan Geiger (published by the University of Oregon Outdoor Program, Eugene, 1993, and take advantage of the trail network around Oakridge. Recently the 500 miles of single track trails have been discovered by acolytes from as far away as southern California. They load their bikes on Amtrak for $5, get off in Eugene, head up to Oakridge and are on a trail shortly thereafter. One of the best mountain bike trails in the area is the 21-mile loop around Waldo Lake. Additional information on biking, hiking, camping, and the Aufderheide National Scenic Byway (see "ORE 126: The McKenzie River Highway," below) can be obtained from the Oakridge Ranger Station, 46375 ORE 58, Westfir, tel. (541) 782-2291. Oakridge also hosts a mountain bike festival called the **Fat Tire Festival,** call (541) 782-4288 for information. Usually held the fourth weekend of July, guided mountain bike tours and one or more races challenge all skill levels. Live entertainment and a barbecue dinner provide the finishing touches for this popular rally.

ORE 126: THE McKENZIE RIVER HIGHWAY

The best way to get to this scenic road from the Willamette Valley is to take I-105 east from I-5 near Eugene. Take a left at the end of the interstate near the outskirts of Springfield and you will be on the McKenzie River Highway. There are four lanes for a couple of miles, and this is one of your best chances to ease by any slow-moving vehicles. However, beware of the highway patrol, which often patrols the road here—it's easy to end up with a ticket!

In any case, just past where the four lanes merge into two, the McKenzie River Recreation Area begins. For the next 60 miles, you will not see any major population centers, as most of the towns consist of little more than a post office. However, you will see beautiful views of the blue-green McKenzie River with heavily forested mountains, frothy waterfalls, jet-black lava beds, and snowcapped peaks as a backdrop. The river was named for Donald McKenzie, a member of Astor Pacific Company, who explored the region in 1812.

The first 15 miles of the McKenzie River Highway pass through many fruit and nut orchards (primarily apples, cherries, and filberts), Christmas-tree farms, and berry patches (blueberry, raspberry, and marionberry). McKenzie River farmers enjoy plentiful water supplies from the McKenzie diversion canal, as well as fertile soils and a mild climate. Walterville is located in the middle of this agricultural section of the McKenzie Recreation Area.

The Leaburg Dam on the right signals your entry into the middle section of the McKenzie, where there are many vacation homes. A total of six dams on the McKenzie provide power, irrigation, and what the Army Corps of Engineers calls "fish enhancement." A favorite haunt of fishing enthusiasts, the mellow waters of the middle McKenzie teem with trout, steelhead, and salmon. You'll notice many driftboats parked in driveways. These boats have bows at both ends to prevent water inundation from either front or back. Mild whitewater rafting and drift-

Oregon produces most of the world's supply of filberts.

TED LONG ISHIKAWA

boat fishing are popular here, and there are many local guides and outfitters ready to help you float your expeditions.

The Willamette National Forest boundary is near Blue River. Huge, old-growth Douglas firs usher the clear blue waters of the McKenzie through the mountains. In addition to the McKenzie River National Recreation Trail, waterfalls, mountain lakes, and lava formations are all a short trek from the road. In addition to the myriad recreational opportunities, hot springs, quality accommodations, fine dining, and a dearth of crowds give you the southern Cascades at their finest.

SIGHTS

Proxy Falls

To get to Proxy Falls, follow the old McKenzie Pass (ORE 242) from the new McKenzie Pass (ORE 126) for 10 miles. Look for a small hiker-symbol sign on the right-hand side of the road. This is the only marker for the trail to a spectacular pair of waterfalls, Upper and Lower Proxy Falls.

An A-plus trail, it's an easy half-mile walk to Upper Proxy. The trail goes through a lush forest that changes with the season. There are giant rhododendrons that bloom in late spring, tart huckleberries in summer, and brilliant red foliage from the vine maples in the fall. Take a left at the first fork in the trail. This will take you to

Upper Proxy Falls. A particularly good view of the falls can be obtained near the giant Douglas fir at the base of the pool.

Now that you've seen Upper Proxy Falls from the bottom up, check out Lower Proxy Falls from the top down. Go back to the fork in the trail and take a left. In less than a half mile, you will suddenly be on a ridge looking across a valley at Lower Proxy falls. A good time to photograph both of these falls is around midday, when the sun's angle best illuminates the water.

Dee Wright Observatory

The Dee Wright Observatory, 57600 McKenzie River Hwy., tel. (541) 882-3381, on ORE 242 (closed in winter) is about halfway between ORE 126 and Sisters. Built in the early '30s as a Civilian Conservation Corps project, it was christened after the building's supervisor, who died prior to its completion. The tower windows line up with views of Mt. Jefferson, Mt. Washington, and the Three Sisters, as well as the eight-mile-long, half-mile-wide lava flow that bubbled out of nearby Yapoah a little less than 3,000 years ago.

Unfortunately, the Dee Wright Observatory was struck by lightning in September of 1989, and the building suffered heavy structural damage from the ensuing fire. Built mostly out of lava rock, the supporting timbers sustained the bulk of the damage. With tight state and federal budgets and the estimated high price tag for repairs, the fate of this historic landmark remains unclear.

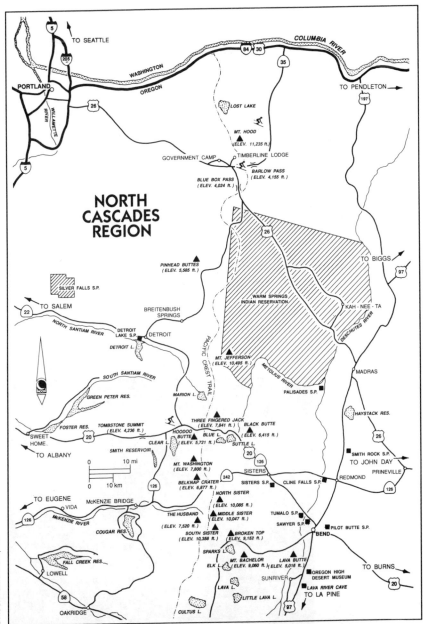

NORTH CASCADES REGION

However, all was not lost: the half-mile-long **Lava River Trail** next to the observatory offers a fine foray into the surrounding hills of rolling black rock. In addition to helpfully placed and concise interpretive placards explaining the lava formations, the trail is wheelchair-accessible. But while the walk is easy enough, the 5,300-foot elevation can sometimes make it seem a little more difficult.

Koosah Falls

This cascade is about 20 miles from McKenzie Bridge on ORE 126. The visitor facilities here have recently been improved and now provide wheelchair access and excellent views of this impressive 70-foot-high falls on the McKenzie. The blue water bounces and bubbles over and through a basalt formation that flowed into the McKenzie thousands of years ago. If you look carefully, you can see many small springs flowing from crevices at the base of the falls. The blue water may have inspired the name Koosah, which comes from the Chinook word for sky.

Sahalie Falls

Another beautiful waterfall is only a half mile farther east on ORE 126 from Koosah Falls. On the trail from Koosah Falls giant cedar and fir trees line the path. It is only a few yards from the parking lot to the viewpoints of the falls. Also

the result of a lava dam from the Cascade Range's not-so-distant volcanic past, here the river tumbles 100 feet into a green canyon. These are the highest falls on the McKenzie river—Sahalie means "high" in the Chinook dialect. It's said that this waterfall churns out the highest volume of water of any falls in the state. Anyone who might want to take a shower is welcome to hike the slippery, unimproved trail to the base of the roaring cascade. Most people, however, are content to enjoy the view from benches and observation posts along the paved path. The Disney movie *Homeward Bound* featured these waterfalls in a scene portraying a family cat being swept over the top.

Sawyer's Cave

This ice cave is on the right just past the junction of ORE 126 and US 20, near mile marker 72. You'll need a flashlight and a sweater to explore Sawyer's Cave; watch your head and watch your step. Classified as a lava tube, it's the result of a lava flow that cooled faster on the top and sides, forming a crust. Underneath, the hotter lava continued to drain downhill, leaving the lava tube behind. There are also small stalactites hanging down from the ceilings, formed from lava drippings. The basalt rock is a poor heat conductor, and like a natural refrigerator it keeps the coolness of winter and

Koosah Falls thunder on the McKenzie.

BRUCE BUSH

night inside the cave. Ice can be found on the floor of the cave during the hottest summer months.

Aufderheide National Scenic Byway

One of the nation's first 50 National Scenic Byways, the 58-mile long Aufderheide Drive links ORE 126 to ORE 58. You'll find the Auferheide turnoff (Forest Service Rd. 19) at milemarker 45.9 about five miles east of Blue River. The road winds along the south fork of the McKenzie River, crests over the pass, and then follows the north fork of the middle fork Willamette River down to Oakridge and ORE 58. Sights along the way include the Delta Old-Growth Grove Nature Trail, Terwilliger (Cougar) hot springs, the spectacular Willamette River Gorge, and the Westfir covered bridge. A copy of a cassette tape tour can be borrowed from the Blue River Ranger Station, tel. (541) 822-3317, or the Oakridge Ranger Station, 46375 ORE 58, Westfir, tel. (541) 782-2291, and dropped off at either station upon completion of your trip. The tape highlights cultural, geological, and historical points of interest along the way.

Terwilliger (Cougar) Hot Springs

If you'd like to try a hot springs in a natural setting, head for Terwilliger Hot Springs. Located in a forested canyon at the end of a quarter mile long trail, hot water bubbles up out of the earth at 116° and flows down through a series of log and stone pools, each one a few degrees cooler than the previous one. A series of access steps and railings have also been built to help you get to the various soaking ponds. The local custom is optional clothing, so don't be surprised to see people parading around in their birthday suits. To get there, take the Aufderheide Drive from ORE 126 up toward Cougar Reservoir. The trailhead for the hot springs on the west side of the road is marked by a sign just past milepost seven. You can park in a large lot on the east side of the road about a tenth of a mile past the trailhead. Parking alongside the road is prohibited (and enforced) from sunset to sunrise one mile from the trailhead. The trail from the parking lot to the spring overlooks a steep drop-off, so be careful. The several pools in this tranquil forest setting can be overcrowded on weekends.

HIKES

McKenzie River National Recreation Trail

The McKenzie River National Recreation Trail runs for 26 miles. It starts just outside the small town of **McKenzie Bridge** and goes to the Old Santiam Wagon Road, about three miles from the junction of ORE 126 and US 20. But don't let that scare you. There are enough access points to let you design treks of three, five, eight, or more miles along this beautiful trail. It is hard to say which section of the footpath is the best, as each portion has its own peculiar charms; the following highlights give you a sample of what to expect.

Start at the top of the McKenzie River Trail at the **Old Santiam Wagon Road.** Completed in the early 1860s, this was the first link of the route from the mid-Willamette Valley to central and eastern Oregon. Way stations were established a day's journey apart to assist the pioneers along their weary way. While most of these primitive establishments are no more, some of the historic buildings have survived and are still used today by packers. There isn't much left of the Old Santiam Wagon Rd. either, as much of it was destroyed with the construction of ORE 126. However, a seven-mile stretch remains from ORE 126 through the rugged lava country to the Pacific Crest Trail. A short walk on this former road to the promised land helps you to appreciate both the hardiness of the pioneers and the comforts of modern travel.

From the Old Santiam Wagon Rd., the McKenzie River Trail surveys many remarkable volcanic formations. Lava flows over the last few thousand years have built dams, created waterfalls, and even buried the river altogether. At the northern end of **Clear Lake,** you can see the remains of an ancient forest preserved for nearly 3,000 years in the lake's cool waters. When nearby Sand Mountain erupted, the lava dammed up the McKenzie River and created Clear Lake. Koosah and Sahalie falls were also created by lava dams, and the view of these whitewater cascades from the McKenzie River Trail is much different than the accessible version from the highway. Another interesting sight is the **Tamolitch Valley,** where the McKenzie gradually sinks beneath the porous lava, disappearing altogether until it reemerges three miles later at Tamolitch Pool. This area is accessible only on the National Recreation Trail.

If at all possible, arrange your McKenzie outing with friends and take two cars. This way you can have a car stationed at the beginning and ending segments of your hike, and thus avoid doubling back. Also keep in mind that hikes starting at the upper end of the trail take advantage of the descending elevation. Mountain bikes are allowed on all sections of the McKenzie River Trail.

Delta Old-Growth Grove Nature Trail

You'll find this half-mile loop trail on the west side of the Aufderheide Byway not far from ORE 126. This is an excellent opportunity to explore an old-growth ecosystem. In addition to 650 year old conifers, you'll observe other layers of life from shrubs and ground cover plants to fish, mammals, birds, and amphibians. Many plant species are clearly marked along the trail of this living laboratory and are explained in detail in a pamphlet called *Delta Old-Growth Grove, Ancient Provider* available from the National Forest Service.

Robinson Lake Trail

The quarter-mile-long Robinson Lake Trail takes you to a heart-shaped lake with some fishing and swimming. To get there, turn off ORE 126 onto Robinson Lake Road. Be on the lookout for logging trucks and rocks on the gravel road. Follow the signs marked Forest Service Rd. 2664. At the unmarked junction, go straight onto the red pumice road (Forest Service Rd. 2664, and continue until you reach the parking lot. It takes about 10 minutes to drive the four miles in. The trail is in good condition; the left fork takes you to the center shore of Robinson Lake. The shallow lake warms up considerably during the summer, making a swim all the more inviting.

RAFTING

McKenzie River Adventures, P.O. Box 567, Sisters 97759, tel. (541) 549-1325 or 822-3806 evenings, has half-day, full-day, and two-day whitewater rafting trips May-September. The half-day (four-hour) trip (lunch included) is $50 per person, $35 per child; the full-day (six-hour) trip (lunch included) is $80 per person, $50 per child; and the two-day overnight (meals included) is $200 per person, $150 per child. The cruises range from seven to 18 miles and take in some Class-II and -III rapids. Reservations are recommended.

Jim's Oregon Whitewater, 56324 ORE 126, McKenzie Bridge 97413, tel. (541) 822-6003, charters whitewater rafts April-Sept. and fly-fishing driftboats April-October. The half-day whitewater-rafting trip (lunch included) costs $50 per person, the full-day (lunch included) is $66 per person, and the two-day overnighter (meals included) is $200 per person. For those interested in some serious fly-fishing, it's $200-230 per boat (one to two people) per day. Price includes all gear and tackle; you'll need to provide Oregon fishing license and tags, food, and beverage. Reservations are recommended.

Spencer Outfitters and Guide Service, 656 N. 71st St., Springfield 97478, tel. (541) 747-8153; or P.O. Box 116, Vida 97488, tel. (541) 896-3941, charters whitewater rafting trips May-September. The full-day (lunch included) trip is $65. Full-day fishing trips cost $200 per boat with a maximum two guests per boat; evening charters are $125 per boat. Food, tackle, and rain gear are provided on all fishing charters.

Larger parties interested in a mellow float on the McKenzie might want to consider going with **McKenzie Pontoon Trips,** 37855 Shanandoah Loop, Springfield, tel. (541) 741-1905. These large crafts, which can be described as catamarans without the sail, offer a smoother ride than their smaller inflatable counterparts. The price for a full-day trip is $50 per person and includes lunch at one of the riverside lodges. Groups of 10 or more receive a 10% discount. Reservations are required.

Oregon Whitewater Adventures, 660 Kelly Blvd., Springfield, tel. (541) 746-5422, offers guided half-day trips (no lunch) for $40, full-day trips for $60, and a two-day overnighter for $150. All necessary gear and transportation back to your car are included. Group discounts are also available. Simular full-day guided trips are also available through **Wild Water Adventures,** tel. (541) 895-4465 or (800) 289-4534, $50 for the lower McKenzie and $60 for the upper.

FISHING

Sure it's crowded, but scenic beauty and the chance to bag a five trout limit lines 'em up on one of the state's best trout streams. Unless you can get a driftboat, access is limited. On weekends, driftboats and rafters vie for space. You can cast worms or spinners, though you're better off using flies when you're fishing off of a boat for rainbows April-October. Consult the *Oregon Guides And Packers Directory* for guides, P.O. Box 10841, Eugene 97440, tel. (541) 683-9552. The best pools tend to be west of Blue River, but it's harder to get to them because of private landholdings. Be sure to check for rules and regulations before you go fishing, the **Dept. of Fish and Wildlife,** tel. (541) 726-3515, can give you the information you need.

GOLF

If you like to play golf, you should plan your vacation around a visit to **Tokatee Golf Club,** 54947 ORE 126, Blue River, tel. (541) 822-3220 or (800) 452-6376. Consistently rated among the top 25 courses in America by *Golf Digest,* Tokatee is a marriage of golf and wilderness beauty that creates a unique and satisfying experience. Good for all levels of experience, every hole has its own challenge. No houses are on the fairways to obstruct the knockout views of the forested mountains and the Three Sisters Wilderness. Another nice point is that you are allowed to walk and enjoy the magnificent setting (rental carts are also available if you'd rather drive the greens). Open March to mid-November, greens fees are $15 for nine holes, $28 for 18; children under 17 get $5 off, and students with a current ID are also entitled to a generous discount.

MOUNTAIN BIKING

In the upper sections of the McKenzie, most of the usable trails gain elevation rapidly due to the steep terrain and make for very challenging biking. The most popular route is the McKenzie River Trail. The best description of routes

open to mountain biking is a pamphlet available from the Blue River Ranger District called *Bike routes: Oakridge/Upper Willamette.* Bike rentals, $5 an hour, $20 a day, and additional information are also available from **McKenzie Bridge Store,** 91837 Taylor Rd., McKenzie Bridge, tel. (541) 822-3221.

PRACTICALITIES

Accommodations

Fry's Double JJ Motel, ORE 126, Vida 97488, tel. (541) 822-5304, is a small family operation that rents out two housekeeping cabins. Depending upon the time of year and the number of people, the units range $30-55. **Sleepy Hollow Motel,** 54791 ORE 126, Blue River 97413, tel. (541) 822-3805, is located within walking distance of one of the finest public golf courses in the country, Tokatee. This property is open April 1-Nov. 1. The motel has 14 air-conditioned units that range $45-85, $5 each additional person. Reservations are recommended.

The Cedarwood Lodge, ORE 126, McKenzie Bridge 97413, tel. (541) 822-3351, is tucked away in a grove of old cedars just outside of the town of McKenzie Bridge. The lodge has nine vacation housekeeping cottages that feature fully equipped kitchens, bathrooms (with showers), fireplaces (wood provided), and portable barbecues. Rates vary from $60 to $100 for two people, depending on the cabin and the season, $10 each additional person. Minimum three-day advance reservations are required July-Sept. and holidays.

The historic **Log Cabin Inn,** ORE 126, McKenzie Bridge 97413, tel. (541) 822-3432, is an excellent bed and breakfast. The inn was built in 1906, and President Hoover, Clark Gable, and the Duke of Windsor are among the many notables who have stayed here over the years. With its homey decor, wraparound porch, and cedar-paneled dining hall, the Log Cabin Inn would make a wonderful label on a bottle of maple syrup. There are also nine guest cottages, each one of them boasting a fireplace, a porch, and a view of the McKenzie River. For $4 per person, the inn will bring a continental breakfast to your cabin in the morning for you to enjoy along with the scenery. The Log Cabin's restaurant features game and salmon. Room rates range $70-80 double occupancy, each additional person $5. Reservations required. The inn is located at mile post 51 near the intersection of ORE 126 and ORE 242.

Belknap Lodge and Hot Springs, P.O. Box 1, McKenzie Bridge 97413, tel. (541) 822-3512, offers rooms, cabins, and camping. The lodge rooms range $60-90 per couple, $10 each additional person. In the lodge rooms you can enjoy the hot spring water in the privacy of your own tub. The five cabins range $45-75, $5 each additional person. Camping sites are $7 per person per day, or $30 per person per week. The main attraction on the property is **Belknap Springs.** The water (which contains 26 different minerals) is gently filtered piping hot into a swimming pool on the south bank of the McKenzie. The property is clean, the scenery is beautiful, and the price is right. For $5, you can use the mineral pool facilities, just what the doctor ordered to ease the aching muscles from that killer hike or the ski marathon. But don't wait too long to fill this prescription—the pool closes at 9 p.m. If you forget your towel, you can rent one.

Both **Heaven's Gate Cottages,** 50055 ORE 126, Vida, tel. (541) 822-3214, and **Woodland Cottages,** 52560 ORE 126, Blue River, tel. (541) 822-3597, offer housekeeping cabins right on the McKenzie. While the cabins at either place are sandwiched between the highway and the river, the unspoiled riverside view more than compensates for the traffic (which drops off considerably by nightfall). One Heaven's Gate cabin called Blue Moon is right over a good fishing hole and nightlights illuminate the rapids for your contemplation. A fireplace adds an additional romantic touch. Woodland Cottages also feature large sun decks on each cabin that are ideal for appreciating the tranquility of the river. Their cabins accommodate two to four occupants, and one unit will sleep six. Both establishments' cabins may be old, small, and semi-rustic, but their riverside location helps overcome a multitude of sins.

Surrounded by 14 acres of private forest along the McKenzie River is **Loloma Lodge,** 56687 ORE 126, McKenzie Bridge, tel. (541) 822-3830, which offers cottages, a cabin, and two vacation homes that are good for families. The housekeeping cottages in particular are lovely, clean,

and fairly modern. Located on the banks of the McKenzie, they afford magnificent views both from the inside looking out through big bay windows or from the lounge chairs on the deck. Accommodating one to four people, rates range $100-150 with a three night minimum stay required. A coin-operated washer and dryer on the premises are available for guest use.

You know when you cross over the McKenzie on the 165-foot-long Goodpasture covered bridge (circa 1938), the most photographed bridge in Oregon, that you're headed for someplace special. A great place for families, including pets, and those who want to get away from the noise of the McKenzie highway is the **Wayfarer Resort,** 46725 Goodpasture Rd., Vida, tel. (541) 896-3613, featuring over a dozen cabins on the McKenzie and glacier-fed Marten Creek, $75-125 per night. Accommodating one to six people, the cabins have porches with barbecues overlooking the water, full kitchens, and lots of wood paneling. Two larger units, the Homestead, $175, and the Octogon, $200, can sleep eight and are fully equipped with all the amenities. The Octagon features a deluxe kitchen, wet bar, washer/dryer, and a jacuzzi. Children can enjoy fishing privileges in the resort's private trout pond while the folks play on the all-weather tennis court. All guests are welcome to supplement their menus with pickin's from the Wayfarer's organic gardens and berry patch. In the summer, advance reservations are a must for this popular retreat.

Campgrounds

The following campgrounds are under the jurisdiction of the Willamette National Forest (McKenzie Ranger District, McKenzie Bridge 97413, tel. (541) 822-3381. Contact the office for reservations and additional information. All are open late May to early September. Many of these campsites connect with the beautiful McKenzie River National Recreation Trail. The fishing is also quite good on the McKenzie and the many lakes and reservoirs within this bailiwick. Its prime location halfway between Eugene and Bend also helps make the area a popular vacation spot during the summer, so advance reservations are recommended.

A mile west of McKenzie Bridge on ORE 126 is **McKenzie Bridge Campground.** As the name implies, this 20-site multi-use park is along the banks of its namesake river. The fee is $10 a night. Piped well water, vault toilets, and a boat launch are provided. East of McKenzie Bridge about three miles on ORE 126 is **Paradise Creek Campground.** Although there are 54 tent/RV (up to 22 feet) campsites, flush toilets, and piped water, only 20 of the sites are in premium riverside locations. The summer trout fishing here can be very good, and the fireplace grills and wooden tables make it easy to cook and eat a fresh-caught meal. Welcome to paradise! The fee is $12 a night and reservations are recommended.

Olallie Campground is 11 miles outside of McKenzie Bridge on ORE 126 and has 17 multi-use sites. Olallie is situated on the banks of the McKenzie River; boating, fishing, and hiking are some of the nearby attractions. Piped water, vault toilets, and picnic tables are provided. The fee is $7 a night. A couple more miles past Olallie on ORE 126 is **Trailbridge Campground.** Located on the north shore of Trailbridge Reservoir, piped water, vault toilets, and picnic tables are provided at this 24-site multi-use campground. Boat docks are close by, and the reservoir is noted for its good trout fishing.

Another ideal campground for boating enthusiasts is **Lake's End** on nearby Smith Reservoir. One of the few boat-in campgrounds in Oregon, the only way to reach this park is via a two-mile sail across the lake. To get there, take ORE 126 for 13 miles northeast of McKenzie Bridge and turn right on Forest Service Rd. 1477. Follow the road for three miles to the boat ramp, and bon voyage! Be sure to take along plenty of water, because the campground does not provide any. You will, however, find picnic tables, vault toilets, and plenty of peace and quiet away from the cars and traffic of the other mainstream parks. There is no fee for this escape from the ordinary.

On the south shore of Clear Lake, 14 miles northeast of McKenzie Bridge on ORE 126, is **Coldwater Cove Campground.** Piped water, vault toilets, and picnic tables are provided at this 34-site multi-use park. The fee is $12 a night. **Crocket Lodge,** no phone, is adjacent to the campground and has a store, cafe (serving breakfast 6:30-10 a.m. and lunch 11 a.m.-2 p.m.), and cabins, as well as boat docks, launches, and

rentals. Keep in mind that small electric fishing-boat motors are the only mechanical means of propulsion allowed here by the Forest Service.

A handful of campgrounds dot ORE 242, the old McKenzie Pass, but only **Alder Springs** has piped water. This remote campground with seven tent sites charges $7 a night. Also on ORE 242 is privately owned **Camp Yale,** 58980 ORE 242, McKenzie Bridge, tel. (541) 822-3691. Open all year, 11 full hookups (water, sewer line, and electricity) for $16, five with electricity only for $14, and several tent sites for $10 are featured. Modern restrooms with hot water showers are on site. Camp Yale also offers the only public dump station between Springfield and Sisters.

Food
It's easy to zip by the tiny restaurant near Vida called the **Village Cafe,** tel. (541) 822-3891. But if you have a sweet tooth, be on the lookout for mile marker 35 and a small red building nearby with a sign on top that reads Mom's Home-made Pies. This place has established quite a reputation, as the hundreds of business cards pinned to the ceiling will attest. The food is simple and straightforward: hamburgers, hot dogs, grilled cheese sandwiches, and the like. However, Mom's pies are the attraction that keeps the parking lot full and the customers coming back for more.

About 15 minutes up the road near McKenzie Bridge is the **Rustic Skillet,** 547771 ORE 126, McKenzie Bridge, tel. (541) 822-3400. Open for breakfast, lunch, and dinner, it can be likened to a fancy truck stop—just good ol' American food. Lest this sound like damning with faint praise we should add the menu is diverse for its genre. Kids (young and old alike) will enjoy a complimentary round of miniature golf with their meal. In town, **McKenzie Pizza,** McKenzie Bridge, tel. (541) 822-3669, offers pizza, soups, and sandwiches. Their vegetarian sandwich with avocado, mushrooms, carrots, cucumber, tomato, grated cheese, and sprouts with your choice of bread is a winner.

If you're in the mood for a good lunch or dinner served with a generous helping of historical ambience, head for the **Log Cabin Inn,** see "Accommodations," above. Built in 1906, the inn's cedar-paneled dining room reflects the soft hues of a different era. Their sandwiches cost between $3 and $7 and are served with potato salad. For a couple of bucks extra, you can wash lunch down with a glass of smooth port. Dinners range $7-20 and feature salmon and game dishes with all the trimmings. Whatever meal you choose to take in, try the beer-cheese soup, and save some room for one of their homemade cobblers or pies (especially the marionberry).

Getting There
The best way for car-less travelers to get to the McKenzie National Recreation Trail from Eugene is via Lane Transit District, tel. (541) 687-5555. Their route 91 bus starts at downtown Eugene and heads up the McKenzie River Highway, making a three-hour roundtrip for only 75 cents. The bus is equipped to carry a couple of mountain bikes. The terminus point is the McKenzie River Ranger Station at McKenzie Bridge. On weekdays the bus makes two roundtrips in the morning and two in the afternoon; on Saturdays there's one morning and one afternoon trip.

Information and Services
Additional information on attractions and services can be acquired from the **McKenzie River**

Chamber of Commerce, P.O. Box 1117, Leaburg, 97489, tel. (541) 896-3330. Wilderness permits, camping, hiking, and mountain biking information are available at the **Blue River Ranger Station,** Blue River, tel. (541) 822-3317, or **McKenzie Ranger Station,** McKenzie Bridge, tel. (541) 822-3381. For medical help, contact the **McKenzie River Clinic,** tel. (541) 822-3341. Open Mon.-Fri. 9 a.m.-noon and 1-5 p.m., a physician is on call 24 hours a day.

The National Forest Service has a $5 pamphlet called *Daytripper* that tells about seasonal drives in the state with a lot of information on ORE 126 and ORE 242; write U.S. Forest Service Willamette District 211, East 7th St., Eugene 97401. You can also contact the Bend Chamber of Commerce, tel. (541) 382-3221, for their McKenzie-Santiam brochure.

The **Blue River Coin Laundry,** 91217 Blue River St., is open 8 a.m.-9 p.m. For groceries, hardware, fishing tackle, or almost anything else between Sisters and Springfield, **Harbick's Country Store,** 91808 Mill Creek Rd., McKenzie Bridge, is *the* place for one-stop shopping. Located 45 miles east of Springfield, it's also ideally located to refuel your rig or fuel up on espresso and deli items. There's even an ATM machine at this outpost of civilization.

SISTERS AND VICINITY

Sisters, established in 1888 when nearby Camp Polk was deactivated, is named after its backdrop to the south, the Three Sisters. These over-10,000-foot-high peaks were the last major obstacle for the pioneers to circumnavigate on their journey to the fertile Willamette Valley. The emigrants named the mountains after some of the virtues that helped propel them through the hardships of the frontier: faith, hope, and charity. Over the years, no one could agree upon exactly which mountain was named what, so the Oregon legislature settled the dispute by labeling the mountains as the North, Middle, and South Sisters.

In any case, while most of the Old Santiam Wagon Rd. has long since been replaced by asphalt and forest overgrowth, the 19th-century flavor has been preserved in the town of Sisters. Wooden boardwalks, 1880s-style storefronts, and plenty of good ol'-fashioned western hospitality grace this small town of about 1,000. Some

people are quick to lambast the thematic zoning ordinances of Sisters as cheap gimmicks to lure tourists, while others seem to enjoy the lovingly re-created ambience. As well as being a food, fuel, and lodging stop, Sisters is also a jumping-off point for a wealth of outdoor activities. Skiing at Hoodoo Ski Bowl, fly-fishing and rafting on the Metolius River, and backpacking into the great Three Sisters Wilderness are just a few of the popular local pursuits. Nearby luxury resorts such as Black Butte Ranch, an annual rodeo, and North America's largest llama ranch add to the appeal of this vintage-1888 village.

SIGHTS

Dick Patterson's Arabian Ranch
Dick Patterson's Arabian Ranch, 15425 US 20, Sisters 97759, tel. (541) 549-3391, is located

BRUCE BUSH

the Three Sisters Wilderness, backyard to the vintage town of Sisters

just outside the city limits. In addition to a large herd of these fine-looking horses, the ranch is also home for over 500 llamas. These critters are used as pack animals on expeditions into the mountains, as well as for pets and wool production. Sheep ranchers in particular like to have a llama or two around their livestock because predators such as wolves and coyotes abhor their scent. The Pattersons do not give guided tours of the ranch. However, they will try to accommodate people who would like to visit and see the animals, provided they call ahead and make an appointment.

Llama Treks
It's easy to fall in love with llamas. Their regal manner, soft dark eyes, and gentleness engender an immediate connection. In addition, outfitters who rent them out for guided trips (or solos) point out that their padded feet hardly leave a trace on the trail. Two area outfitters, **Last Camp Llamas,** 4555 N.W. Pershall Way, Redmond 97756, tel. (541) 546-6828, and **Oregon Llamas,** P.O. Box 6, Camp Sherman, tel. (541) 595-2088, make their animals available for $30-40 a day with a minimum of two llamas. Remember to procure a Forest Service permit for overnights in the Three Sisters, Mt. Washington, and Mt. Jefferson wildernesses if you elect to go by yourself. These permits (obtainable from ranger stations) specify grazing etiquette for your animals. An orientation class offered by the outfitter for those traveling independently will review such procedures before you hit the trail.

Metolius River
About 10 miles from Sisters is the second-largest tributary of the Deschutes River, the Metolius. To get there, take the Camp Sherman Hwy. off of US 20 five miles west of Sisters. This road will take you around Black Butte. On the north face of this steep, evergreen-covered cinder cone lies the source of the Metolius. Known simply as "the Spring," the water wells up out of the earth at a constant 48° F. The warm, spring-fed waters of the upper Metolius are ideal for insect egg and larval development, which in turn provides an abundant food source for rainbow, brown, brook, and bull trout, kokanee salmon, and whitefish. Consequently, some of the best fly-fishing in the state is found on the upper Metolius. This was no secret to the Indians. The name Metolius derives from the Indian word for "white fish," after the lightly colored salmon found in the river. A beautiful riverside trail follows the Metolius as it meanders through the Ponderosa trees past many excellent fishing holes. Driftboats are used to tackle the harder-to-reach places along this 25-mile-long waterway.

Other streams merge with the Metolius, lowering the water temperature to an average of 35° F. While the fishing isn't as good as in the warmer upper reaches, the whitewater rafting is actually better downstream. The increased water volume coupled with steeper flow gradients provide plenty of exciting rapids for river-runners to splash around in. The Metolius was designated a National Wild and Scenic River in 1988, creating a 4,600 acre corridor within the unique 86,000 acre Metolius Conservation Area.

Five miles downstream from Camp Sherman is the **Wizard Falls Fish Hatchery.** Open every day for visitors, over two and a half million fish, including Atlantic salmon, brook and rainbow trout, and kokanee salmon, are raised here annually.

Hoodoo Ski Bowl

A little over a half hour west of Sisters on ORE 126 is one of Oregon's most family-oriented skiing areas, Hoodoo Ski Bowl, tel. (541) 342-5540. Generally operating from Thanksgiving to Easter (snow conditions permitting), it's open Tues.-Sun. 9 a.m.-4 p.m. Hoodoo features 17 ski runs serviced by three chairlifts and a rope tow. The maximum vertical drop is 1,035 feet, and the runs are fairly evenly divided between advanced, intermediate, and beginner levels of difficulty. The rates at this 55-year-old ski bowl are equally attractive. Adult all-day passes are $18, and seniors (65 and over) and children under six accompanied by a paying adult ski free. The rates on the rope tow are $9 per day. The "sno-fone", tel. (541) 354-7416 from Eugene, (541) 585-8081 from Salem, (541) 753-8887 from Corvallis, has the latest information on weather and snow conditions.

Inexpensive lodging is found across the highway from the ski area at **Santiam Lodge,** tel. (541) 342-5540. Built by the Civilian Conservation Corps during the Depression, this facility offers dormitory-style accommodations for groups of 15-75. A fully equipped kitchen, dining room, and large lounge with a fireplace are upstairs; the rooms and bathrooms are downstairs. The rates are quite reasonable—as little as $25 per night per person. "Lodging and three meals" packages start at $45, and reduced rates on lift tickets and rental equipment are also available to groups making advance reservations. After a weekend at Santiam Pass, there will be no doubt "Hoodoo" you love.

PRACTICALITIES

Accommodations

Sisters Motor Lodge, 600 W. Cascade, Sisters 97759, tel. (541) 549-2551, is within easy walking distance of the shops and boutiques of Sisters. Bedrooms and kitchenettes go for $60-85 a night, and you can bring the dog along, too. The **Best Western Ponderosa Lodge,** 505 ORE 20, P.O. Box 218, Sisters 97759, tel. (541) 549-1234 or (800) 528-1234, is a new, ranch-style resort motel. Rooms, $65-85, feature private balconies with views of the mountains and the adjacent Deschutes National Forest, as well as dial-direct phones and cable TV. Other amenities include a spa, heated pool, and free continental breakfast.

The **Fourth Sister Lodge,** P.O. Box 591, Sisters 97559, tel. (541) 549-6441, offers bedrooms and bedroom suites, $60-140. Each of the bedroom suites has a fully equipped kitchen, a dining room, and a large living room with a fireplace, as well as one or two bedrooms. The recreation room in the center of the lodge complex has a sauna, spa, and swimming pool. Reservations are requested two weeks in advance, but since this popular property fills up fast, extra lead time is advised.

Lake Creek Lodge, Sisters 97759, tel. (541) 595-6331 or (800) 595-6331, is located in the nearby Metolius Recreation Area. This full-service resort has individual houses and cottages that range $110-175 depending upon the unit and number of people. Tennis, swimming, and fishing are some of the many activities available here. Dinner is served family style in the pine-paneled main lodge and features a different entree each day, complemented by homemade breads, salads, and desserts. The establishment caters especially well to families; pets are allowed on prior approval only.

Another Metolius retreat can be found at **Cold Springs Resort,** Cold Springs Resort Ln., HCR 1270, Camp Sherman 97730, tel. (541) 595-6271. Open from mid-April to mid-October, the cabins here, $85-125, feature naturally pure artesian well water. A footbridge across the Metolius connects the resort to Camp Sherman, where groceries, a church, and a cafe are within easy walking distance. Pets are allowed here for $5 per night but must be kept on a leash at all times and never left unattended.

The **Metolius River Lodge,** P.O. Box 110, Camp Sherman 97730, tel. (541) 596-6290 or (800) 595-6290, is a 12-unit complex featuring six pine-paneled cabins. The latter vary in price, $60-110, depending on room configuration and accoutrements. The most coveted pair have decks extending over the river, and the majority have fireplaces. The price includes continental breakfast brought to your door and all the firewood you need.

Wedged in between giant Ponderosa pines and the banks of the Metolius are the 12 elegant cabins of the **Metolius River Resort,** P.O. Box 1210, Camp Sherman, tel. (541) 595-6281 or (800) 81-TROUT. These beautiful wooden structures, built in 1992, are bright and airy with lots of windows. The cabins are two stories high with over 900 square feet of living space and comfortably sleep 4-6 people. Featuring a fully equipped modern kitchen, full bath, river rock fireplace (stocked with all the firewood you'll need), and a riverview deck, it's a bargain at $120-160 per night double occupancy (additional persons $10 extra). Reservations made well in advance are a must if you want to stay here. You'll find the resort behind the Kokanee Cafe.

Northwest of Sisters about 18 miles is the **Blue Lake Resort,** 13900 Blue Lake Dr., Sisters 97759, tel. (541) 595-6671, $65-125. Situated in the Deschutes National Forest at 3,500 feet, the resort offers accommodations that range from cabins and A-frames to townhouses and condos. All units have kitchens with utensils, dishes, and appliances. Their marina has boats, canoes, kayaks, and paddleboats for rent. It's a beautiful spot to relax and enjoy a lake that rivals Crater Lake in color. This lake occupies an ancient volcanic crater a half-mile west of Suttle Lake. Access to Blue Lake is via a well-marked Forest Service road that circles Suttle Lake on its southern shore.

Bed and Breakfasts

Near the Sisters airport are two fine bed and breakfasts, the **Conklin House,** 69013 Camp Polk Rd, Sisters, tel. (541) 549-0123 or (800) 549-4262, and the **Cascade Country Inn,** 15870 Barclay Dr., Sisters, tel. (541) 549-INNN

or (800) 316-0089. The Conklin House has a country decor and old-fashioned warmth that spells "welcome home" to the visitor. Relax by the pool, fish in the trout ponds, barbecue on the back porch, or even catch up on some laundry during your stay. Rooms with shared bath are $70-90; private bath $90-110. Groups of three to seven can stay in the dormitory for $30 per person. All rooms include a full country breakfast which can be substituted with a Mexican breakfast or picnic basket upon prior request. Complimentary refreshments are served in the evening. The sunny, beautifully decorated rooms at the Cascade Country Inn range $100-125 a night; their dorm room costs $35 per person (minimum three). Homemade quiches, muffins, and fresh fruits are typical fare for breakfast. Evening refreshments and the use of the inn's mountain bikes are also included in their tariff. Reservations for both establishments are recommended, especially on weekends during the ski season and summer.

Near Camp Sherman you'll find the **Metolius Inn,** Forest Service Rd. 503, Camp Sherman, tel. (541) 595-6445, which features two large bedrooms, each with private bath and patio. Full breakfast is included in the $80 per room rate, and they will accommodate special dietary considerations if notified in advance.

Food

The **Ranch House,** 310 S.E. Hood St., Sisters, tel. (541) 549-8911, specializes in sandwiches and take 'n' bake pizza and also has a good selection of domestic and imported beers and wines. The **Gallery Restaurant,** 230 W. Cascade, Sisters, tel. (541) 549-2631, offers chuckwagon dinners that range $7-14. Surprisingly tasteful paintings on Old West themes as well as flintlocks and other ancient armaments pay homage to the area's pioneer past. Many eastern Oregonians will tell you that **Papandrea's,** 325 S.W. Hood, Sisters, tel. (541) 549-6081, makes the best pizza in the state. While such claims are highly subjective, outlets in Bend and Oregon City attest to this small chain's dedicated following.

The hot spot in town is undoubtedly the **Hotel Sisters and Bronco Billy Saloon.** Built in 1912, the upstairs rooms of this historical structure have been refurbished into intimate mini-dining rooms. Barbecued ribs are the specialty of the house, but you can also find fresh seafood, steaks, chicken dishes, and Mexican fare here, $7-17. In one corner of the building, on the other side of the western-style saloon doors, is Bronco Billy's. This funky watering hole must look much the same as it did 80 years ago. A racy painting that used to grace the local brothel is proudly displayed behind the bar, and cowboy hats on most heads complete the picture of a town whose Old West ambience gets better with age. For the price of a beer, you can get one of the local Stetson-hatted good ol' boys to tell you the inside scoop on where to go and what to do in this neck of the woods.

In nearby Camp Sherman, a special treat awaits at the **Kokanee Cafe,** tel. (541) 595-6420. Dinners served Mon.-Sat. 5-9 p.m. feature an excellent variety of expertly prepared chicken, pasta, steak, seafood, and fish entrees. Burgers and grilled cheese sandwiches are offered if the kids don't go for the good stuff. Vegetarian dishes include Bow Tie Pasta with oyster mushrooms, artichoke hearts, and sun-dried tomatoes in a light cream sauce and that famous Oregon-made staple, the gardenburger. Their special salad made with 14 different kinds of organic greens is alone worth the trip. Owned and operated by sixth-generation Oregonians, they place a premium on Northwest-grown products and organic meat and produce whenever possible. Dinners range $12-25 for entrees; burgers and lunch prices are around $6. Dinner reservations are crucial during the summer and fishing season, given the small size of the building. On Sunday, the Kokanee is open 9 a.m.-9 p.m. serving breakfast, lunch, and dinner. Full breakfasts are featured, but you'll find more Kokanee trout and salmon on the menu than bacon and eggs. The Kokanee is generally open April-October. During this time, the restaurant rents out two rooms upstairs for around $50.

Campgrounds

A handful of campgrounds open only in summer are near Sisters on the old McKenzie Highway, ORE 242. **Cold Springs,** Contact Sisters Ranger Station, tel. (541) 549-2111, $9, is five miles west of town on ORE 242. This campground, 3,400 feet in elevation, has 23 sites for tents and small trailers (22 feet maximum). Picnic tables, fire

grills, pit toilets, and water are provided. It's a pretty spot, near the source of Trout Creek.

Six miles farther down the road is **Whispering Pine,** same contact. No fees are charged at this primitive campground with six tent sites, mainly because there is no water available. Another six miles up the pass at 5,200 feet is **Lava Camp Lake,** same contact. Two tent sites and 10 RV sites (22 feet maximum) are available at this rustic campground. There is no fee, but there's also no water. The main allure is its close proximity to the Pacific Crest Trail and the Three Sisters Wilderness.

Shopping

A small but interesting complex of stores are clustered together downtown. An exceptional jewelry and rock shop, a decent bookstore with natural history titles and a quilter's fantasy of a fabric store are standouts. Also don't overlook Applejack's Natural Foods on the eastern end of town.

Events

The annual **Sisters Rodeo** opens the second weekend of June. In addition to the normal assortment of calf-roping and bronco-bucking, country dances, a "buckaroo breakfast," and a 10-km Stampede Run round out the fun. A quilter's fair takes place each summer that can attract over 20,000 in a weekend. Contact the **Sisters Chamber of Commerce,** P.O. Box 476, Sisters 97759, tel. (541) 549-0251, for the schedule of events.

Services

The Sisters **post office,** 160 1st St., Sisters 97759, tel. (541) 549-3561, is open for service Mon.-Fri. 9 a.m.-5 p.m. The office is also open Saturday, but without window service. The **liquor store,** 216 Cascade, tel. 549-98 41, is open Mon.-Sat. 10 a.m.-6 p.m., Oct. 1-May 31; Mon.-Sat. 10 a.m.-7 p.m., June 1-Sept. 3rd. Public restrooms are found at the corner of Washington and Spruce. The **police,** 150 N. Fir, tel. (541) 548-2302, are unobtrusive in this town. The **library,** 291 E. Main, tel. (541) 549-2921, has good books about the region by Raymond Hatton. Three miles outside of Sisters, a **laundromat** is found at the KOA campground, 67667 US 20, Bend 97701, tel. (541) 549-3021, which is open 9 a.m.-10 p.m. all week long. Detailed information about the geology, natural history, wildlife, wilderness areas, and numerous recreational opportunities in the Metolius Recreation Area can be obtained by calling the Sisters Ranger Station, tel. (541) 549-2111.

For guided trips, contact the High Cascades Stable/Pack Station, tel. (541) 549-4972, and the Llama Association, P.O. Box 5534, Sisters 97708. Other information is available from the Sisters Chamber of Commerce, tel. (541) 549-0251.

BEND AND VICINITY

Since 1980, Deschutes County has been the state's fastest-growing population center (from 42,400 to over 94,000 in twenty years and expected to double again over the next two decades), largely due to its hiking trails, fishing streams, golf courses, whitewater runs, and ski slopes. Proximity to all this recreation has made the city of Bend Oregon's number-one destination for the active traveler. While the resulting increase in traffic and prices can sometimes make you forget you're in Oregon, Bend's location between the eastern flank of the Cascades and the desert provides respite from what the locals call "Californication." The boom in real estate can be appreciated by the fact the average price for a three-bedroom, two-bath house was $60,000 in 1987. Four years later, the price had jumped 50%. By 1995, that same house boasted an average market value of $174,825. Not surprisingly, *Money* magazine tapped this city of 45,000 as one of 10 places in the U.S. where in the '90s home values could be expected to appreciate significantly.

The seeds of growth were planted several decades ago when a onetime military encampment a dozen miles south of town was transformed into the Sunriver Resort community. Black Butte Ranch, the Inn of the Seventh Mountain, and other destination resorts soon followed. South of the city is some of the best skiing in the state on Mt. Bachelor; to the north, world-class rock-climbing routes at Smith Rock State Park and famed fishing holes on the Metolius River await. Add Cascade hiking, Deschutes River rafting and fishing, and other nearby locales for rockhounding, golf, horseback riding, and water sports, and you'll understand why it's often hard to find a place to bed down for the night here on weekends.

FRANK LONG

the Deschutes River

HISTORY

Situated at a point on the Deschutes River where travelers got their last look at the river, this area was originally referred to as "Farewell Bend" by the pioneers. A ranch by the same name grew up here in the late 19th century. This outpost and the other small ranches that located here to take advantage of the region's good water eventually took on the name Bend. With the coming of the railroad in the 1900s, timber and agriculture, with the larger harvest due to the irrigation projects, had the transportation to support the creation of a stable economic base.

SIGHTS

Drake Park

The Deschutes River has a dam and diversion channel just above downtown Bend. It provides valuable irrigation water for the farmers and ranchers of the dry but fertile plateau to the north, and creates a placid stretch of water called Mirror Pond that is home to Canada geese, ducks, and other wildlife. Drake Park is on the east bank of this greenbelt and is a nice place to relax, have a quiet lunch, or maybe toss a Frisbee around.

However, you had better be careful where you step, as the birds leave behind numerous land mines. The folks living in those nice houses on the west bank of Mirror Pond got tired of scraping the guano off of their shoes, but unfortunately for them, they were legally unable to do anything against their fowl neighbors due to the birds' protected status. They came up with a rather ingenious solution to the geese and their offensive droppings. The residents chipped in $1500 to buy a pair of swans from Queen Elizabeth's Royal Swannery in England. Since geese and swans do not get along, the citizens reasoned that the blue-blooded swans would chase away the common Canada geese. While the geese are still here, you will notice that they tend to congregate in Drake Park,

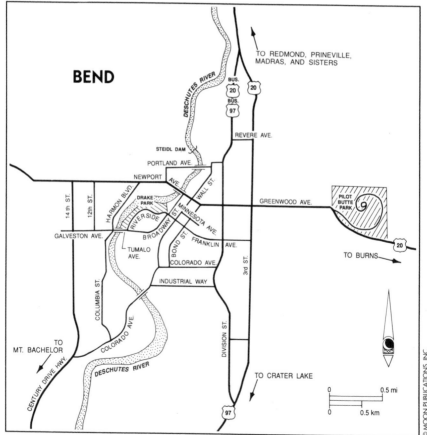

while the swans have a decided preference for the private estates.

Pilot Butte

On the east side of town is Pilot Butte. A road spirals its way up to the top of this 511-foot-high volcanic remnant. You can enjoy a sweeping view of nine snowcapped Cascade peaks and their green forests. It is also pretty at night, with the twinkling lights of the city below and the stars above. Full moons are especially awesome, illuminating the ghostly forms of the mountains in icy, light-blue silhouettes.

Pine Mountain Observatory

Another peak experience worth investigating is the Pine Mountain Observatory, tel. (541) 382-8331, located about 40 miles east of Bend on US 20. Take the road out of Millican to the top of 6,395-foot-high Pine Mountain to reach the installation. Three Cassegrain telescopes with 15-, 24-, and 32-inch mirrors are used by University of Oregon teachers and students to unlock the secrets of the universe. On this 6,300-foot mountain the friendly astronomers will often allow visitors an intriguing peek at the neighboring stars and planets. Call ahead for information and weather conditions before making the trip. Generally, the public visits after April on weekends. Wear warm clothes and take a flashlight. A donation of $2 per person is suggested.

A Mountain of Glass

Farther down US 20 you ease into the Great Basin desert and such attractions as the Sagehen Nature Trail (see "Sights" under "Burns and Vicinity" in the Southeastern Oregon chapter), located 70 miles from the Pine Mountain Observatory turnoff, and the Glass Buttes. Located 36 miles past the observatory, the latter attraction is one of the world's largest obsidian outcroppings, a mountain of volcanic glass, gently rising 2,000 feet above the surrounding countryside. The **Bureau of Land Management**, 185 E. 4th St. P.O. Box 500, Prineville 97745, tel. (541) 447-4115, can provide you with more information. From here the next big town is Burns, 55 miles to the east.

Newberry Volcano National Monument

The West's newest national monument enshrines the obsidian fields, deep mountain lakes, and lava formations left in the wake of a massive series of eruptions. While lacking the visual impact of Crater Lake, this preserve is more accessible and less crowded than its southern Cascade counterpart. Beyond Newberry Crater itself, the monument extends north 25 miles along a volcanic fracture zone to Lava Butte. A 1981 U.S. Geological Survey probe drilled into the caldera floor found temperatures of 510° F, the highest recorded in an inactive Cascade volcano. For more information on all the geologic features encompassed in the area between Newberry Crater and the Lava Butte, contact the following: Deschutes National Forest, 1645 Hwy. 20E, Bend 97701, tel. (541) 338-2715; Lava Land Visitor Center 58201 S. Hwy. 97, Bend 97707, tel. (541) 593-2421; and Newberry National Volcanic Monument, Fort Rock Ranger District, Suite A 262, Bend 97701, tel. (541) 388-5667.

Lava Lands Visitor Center, Lava Butte

About 11 miles south of Bend on US 97 are the Lava Lands Visitor Center, tel. (541) 593-2421, and Lava Butte. The center has some interpretive exhibits that explain the region's volcanic history, as well as a small but good selection of local geology books and an assortment of free pamphlets on local attractions; their bulletin board has the latest activities and goings-on posted. Guided walks are offered here during the summer that give a good perspective on the lava lands. Open 9 a.m.-5 p.m. daily from June-Sept., 9 a.m.-5 p.m. Wed.-Sun in spring and fall; closed from Columbus Day to May 1.

After your orientation, cruise on up to the top of 500-foot-high Lava Butte, located just behind the visitor center. During the summer, to get to the top you must take the shuttle, which leaves the parking lot every half hour; adults $1, children 50 cents. The rest of the year you can take your own vehicle up, although the road is not recommended for trailers and RVs. The observation platform on top of this fire lookout (established in 1928) offers the best viewpoint. Be sure to talk with the resident lookout, and have him or her explain how to work the Osborne fire finder. Nearly a mile above sea level, the butte affords a commanding panorama of the Cascade Range. On a clear day you can see most of the major peaks, with Mounts

Jefferson and Hood looming prominently on the northern horizon. These snowcapped turrets backdrop a 10-square-mile lava field. You can venture out into this eerie landscape by taking the trail that starts from the visitor center and makes its way to the Phil Brogan lookout. From July-August on Saturday evenings, a park naturalist gives an hour and a half presentation on top of Lava Butte. After sunset, the forest takes on a different character as the creatures of the night make their presences known. As darkness continues to envelope the area and celistian objects come into view, the emphasis shifts to a tour of the constellations and planets. Be sure to call ahead for starting times of this excellent attraction for families.

A short trail circumnavigates the 150-foot-deep crater on Lava Butte and is complemented by informative placards that help you interpret this otherworldly environment. From the trail you can see how the lava flow from the butte changed the course of the Deschutes River. You can also see the "kipukas," small islands of green trees surrounded by a sea of black lava. Along the trail, look for some of what geologists call splatter. You'll know it when you see it, because it looks exactly like what it sounds like. Pick up a couple of red pumice rocks for the children, who will be fascinated by the way the stones float in the bathtub.

Lava River Cave

About 12 miles south of Bend on US 97 is Oregon's longest known lava tube, the Lava River Cave. Located a mile south of Lava Butte; call (541) 593-2421 for information. Open from mid-May to mid-September, the admission is $2.50, and lantern rentals (available at the Lava Lands Visitor Center) are also $2.50. The cave is a cool 40° F year-round, so dress warmly. Since the walking surface is uneven, flat-heeled shoes are recommended. Bring a flashlight to guide you through this lava tube or rent one at the entrance for $1 (lanterns come recommended—no batteries to die out one mile deep in darkness). The trail is an easy 2.4-mile roundtrip from the parking lot.

The first chamber you enter is called the Collapsed Corridor. Volcanic rocks that fell from the roof and walls lie in jumbled piles. Freezing water in cracks pries a few rocks loose each winter, which is why the cave is usually closed during the cold months. Stairs take you out of the Collapsed Corridor into a large void called Echo Hall. Here the ceiling reaches 58 feet high and the cave is 50 feet wide. Conversations return from the opposite side of the hall as eerie noises in the dark. The lateral markings you see etched on the walls here show the various levels of past volcanic flows.

At Low Bridge Lane, watch your head because the ceiling dips down to five feet. Look for the "lavacicles" in this and other areas of the cave. (This term comes from a geologist's 1923 publication on the cave called *The Lava River Tunnel*.) Two kinds of them are found here: the hollow cylindrical "soda straws" were formed by escaping gases, and the other cone-shaped formations were created by remelted lava dripping down from the ceiling.

The next curiosity you'll come across is a cave inside the cave, the Two Tube Tunnel. Two tubes running for 95 feet intermittently connect. The smaller tube was formed

CENTRAL OREGON— WHERE EAST MEETS WEST

It's a paradox in Oregon that one goes east to reach what feels like the West. Driving from lush wet western Oregon to the sage-covered cowboy country east of the Cascades changes your perspective like a fun-house mirror. In a transformation so abrupt it can be blinding, the muted light and thick forest canopy part to reveal chaparral, buff-colored desert flora, or green lollipop-shaped junipers. This growth is lower to the ground and more spread out than the fir and hemlock of western Oregon, enlarging your field of vision. The low humidity here gives a clarity to starry night skies and so sharpens the outlines of distant objects that mountains 50 miles away seem within easy walking distance. The marked contrasts between conditions on each side of the Cascades are best appreciated when there's an opportunity to observe a stormfront approaching from the west. Darkened cloud masses on the crest of the Cascades can often be seen from a central Oregon vantage point bathed in sunlight.

when the level of the lava flow dropped; and the cooling lava created a second roof and tube inside the existing cave.

The terrain changes again in the Sand Gardens. Rain and snowmelt carry volcanic ash down through cracks and openings in the cave and deposit them here. The process continues today with the nearly constant dripping water carving out spires and pinnacles in the sand. These formations take hundreds of years to grow, so please stay behind the fenced-off area. The sand gets thicker and thicker until it completely blocks off the lava tube, forcing an abrupt about-face. The walk back to the light of the sun affords a different perspective on this remarkable natural attraction.

It is important to avoid littering the cave, collecting samples, or doing anything else to mar this national treasure. Don't light flares, paper, or cigarettes, because the fumes kill off insects, a food source of the cave's bat population. Roosting bats should not be disturbed, because waking them from hibernation results in certain death for these winged mammals. Incidentally, bat droppings support this cavernous ecosystem, and elsewhere, bat guano is harvested commercially and used for detoxifying wastes, improving detergents, and producing antibiotics. Bats can catch hundreds of mosquitos within an hour, and are also important pollinators. There are nearly 50 species of bats living in North America, and if left alone, they pose little threat to humans. In short, "Leave nothing but footprints, take nothing but pictures, and kill nothing but time."

A couple miles south of Lava River Cave is the Lava Cast Forest. Take US 97 and go nine miles on the cinder road (Forest Service Rd. 9720). From there, follow a self-guided trail through an unreal world created when lava enveloped the trees 6,000 years ago.

Benham Falls

Four miles down Forest Service Rd. 9702 from the Lava Lands Visitor Center is Benham Falls. Give other cars a wide berth and plenty of following distance, as the road's pumice and fine dust are hard on paint jobs and engines. The road leads to a small picnic area in a grove of giant ponderosa pines on the bank of the Deschutes River. With tables, pit toilets, fire grills, and plenty of shade, this is a nice place for a picnic. Be sure to tote your own fluids, though, because there is no water. Day use only, no fees and no camping.

The hike to the falls is an easy one-mile jaunt downstream. Take the footbridge across the river, and enjoy your stroll past a spectacular section of untamed whitewater. While the water in the Deschutes is much too cold and dangerous for a swim (except perhaps on very hot days), it's always ideal for soaking your feet a little after you've completed your hike. Benham Falls was created when magma from Lava Butte splashed over the side, flowing five miles to the Deschutes. When the molten rock collided with the icy water, the churning rapids and crashing waterfall were created here.

Cascades Lakes Highway

The Cascades Lakes Highway (a.k.a. Century Drive or ORE 46) is an 89-mile drive leading to more than half a dozen lakes in the shadow of the snowcapped Cascades. These lakes feature boating, fishing, and other water sports. Hiking, birdwatching, biking, skiing, and camping also attract people. From downtown, drive west off of US 97 south onto Franklin, which becomes Galveston, to Century Drive (14th St.). Turn left one mile from downtown. The route is well-marked and the road climbs in elevation for a significant portion of the drive.

If you just want a gourmet taste of this realm, we recommend a shortened version of the loop. The following tour can be enjoyed in several hours, even allowing for several stops. IBy contrast, driving the entire loop necessitates a whole day with only limited time spent out of the car.

Begin by taking US 97 south 13 miles to the Sunriver cut-off. Shortly after making a right turn, you'll come to a fork where you'll go left. (You might first want to procure a map at the Sunriver Lodge concierge desk by driving straight a quarter mile to the main lodge, then doubling back to the fork.) This left fork begins a loop that'll take you through Sunriver property and the Deschutes Forest to the first stop of Little Lava Lake. The drive to the lake is about 10 miles. The Deschutes River begins its 252-mile course to the Columbia from here. A gorgeous view of the South Sister looms to the northwest, and cabins, a store, and a boat ramp provide the creature comforts. Despite the view of the mountain from the store's porch, in the summer your attention could be diverted by the hummingbirds who flock to a hanging feeder. From Lava Lake, head back to the main road to continue west along the shores of Elk Lake, a favorite of windsurfers and sailboaters. The cabins are also popular, as are pictures taken from the lake's beach picnic grounds on the southernmost tip of shoreline. Here you have the full length of Elk Lake before you, backdropped by the South Sister and Mt. Bachelor mountains. Not far away, the red volcanic cinder highway contrasts with the black lava flows en route to aqua-tinted Devil's Lake. From the northern end of this lake, on the other side of the highway, you'll find Devil's Pile, a conglomeration of lava flows and volcanic glass where Apollo 11 astronauts reportedly culled a rock to deposit on the lunar surface. The road winds around to the Mt. Bachelor Summit ski lifts (see "Mount Bachelor Summit Chair lift" under "Sports and Recreation," below). From the deck in front of the sport shop/cafeteria complex, you can see the Three Sisters and Broken Top in a view reminiscent of the Swiss Alps. You might want to hike the short trail to Todd Lake (see "Camping" under "Sports and Recreation," below); canoe Sparks Lake in the shadow of Broken Top and South Sister; or visit the Ray Atkeson Memorial, dedicated to Oregon's "photographer laureate." All are located between Devil's Pile and the ski lifts. From Mt. Bachelor it's a 15-minute drive back to Sunriver.

High Desert Museum

Six miles south of Bend on US 97 is the High Desert Museum, 59800 South US 97, Bend 97702, tel. (541) 382-4754. If a quick look at the rave reviews in their guest book doesn't immediately convince you that you're in the right place, confirmation of same is sure to come as you prowl the corridors and outdoor off-the-trail exhibits. This award-winning center for natural resources, native animals, and cultural history of the intermountain, western high desert is well worth the price of admission (adults $6, seniors $5, children ages 6-12 $3, and kids under five free). Along the many trails that wind through the 150-acre facility, visitors can observe river otters at play, porcupines sticking it to each other, and birds of prey dispassionately watching over the

whole scene. Replicas of a sheepherder's cabin, a settler's cabin, forestry displays, and other historical interpretations are also along the museum walkways.

Inside the museum's main building, unique exhibits, slide and movie shows, galleries, and pioneer history demonstrations are presented. The "desertarium" is a special delight full of native plants and populated by 37 small critters whose nocturnal lifestyles often keep them from view in the wild. Bats, lizards, mice, toads, snakes, and owls reveal that the desert is more alive than its superficially barren landscape might suggest. The **Earle A. Chiles Center** exhibit on the Spirit of the West features eight "you are there" life-sized dioramas. This walk through time begins 8,000 years ago beside a still marsh and takes you to a fur brigade camp, into the depths of a gold mine, and down Main Street of a boisterous frontier town. The **Spirit of the West Gallery** has representative arts and artifacts of the early American West, as well as tools, clothing, and other personal belongings from the 19th century. The Bounds collection of Indian artifacts and the Hall of Plateau Heritage balance out the museum's coverage of the peoples of the high desert, while the Changing Forest exhibit addresses old-growth life cycles and other issues of forest ecology. Also of interest is the newly opened **Birds of Prey Center.** The **Henry J. Casey Hall of Plateau Heritage,** an 8,000 square-foot venue, showcases the Doris Swayze Bounds Native American artifact collection as well as other Native Americana.

As you might gather, the scope and interactive nature of this facility make it appealing for people who don't usually like museums. With the addition of the Silver Stage Trading gift shop and the Rimrock Cafe, the museum offers visitors a worthwhile diversion outside of Bend. Hours are 9 a.m.-5 p.m. daily, closed Thanksgiving, Christmas, and New Year's Day.

Newberry Volcano

Lava Butte is one of over 400 cinder cones in a family of over 1,000 other smaller volcanoes that together comprise Newberry Volcano. This vast shield volcano covers 500 square miles. In the five-mile-diameter caldera of this mountain, which blew its top 1,300 years ago, lie two alpine lakes called Paulina and East lakes.

Composed of rocks ranging from basalt to rhyolite, the black obsidian flow that's found at Newberry Volcano has been the source of raw material for Indian spearpoints, arrowheads, and hide scrapers for thousands of years. Prized by the original inhabitants of the area, the obsidian tools were also highly valued by other Indian nations and were a medium of exchange for blankets, firearms, and other possessions at the Taos Fair in New Mexico. These tools and other barterings helped to spread Newberry Volcano obsidian all across the West and into Canada and Mexico. Centuries later, NASA sent astronauts to walk on the volcano's pumice-dusted surface in preparation for landing on the moon. Additional interest came when a 9,500 year-old circular structure called a "wickiup" was excavated at Paulina Lake in 1992. If you are curious about other archaelogical findings in the area and would "dig" looking for prehistoric artifacts, contact the **Archaeological Society of Central Oregon,** c/o Central Oregon Environmental Center, 16 N.W. Kansas, Bend OR, 97701.

Paulina and East Lakes

South from Bend 27 miles on US 97 is the turnoff to Paulina and East Lakes. The 16-mile paved but ragged County Rd. 21 twists and turns its way up to the lakes in the caldera of Newberry Crater. Several campgrounds and two resorts are located along the shores of these lakes, which are noted for their excellent trout fishing. Be sure to take the four-mile drive (summer only) to the top of 7,985-foot-high Paulina Peak, the highest point along the jagged edge of Newberry Crater, on Forest Service Rd. 500. Towering 1,500 feet over the lakes in Newberry Crater, the peak also allows a perspective on the forest, obsidian fields, and basalt flows in the surrounding area. To the far west, a palisade of snow-clad Cascade peaks runs the length of the horizon.

Fishing in the area is said to be best in the fall. In Lake Paulina, fisherfolk can troll for kokanee, a gourmet's delight, as well as brown and rainbow trout. Paulina's twin, East Lake, features a fall run of German brown trout (the Oregon state record German brown was caught here in 1993, weighing in at a hair over 27 pounds) that move out of the depths to spawn in shoreline shallows.

Paulina Lake Resort, tel. (541) 536-2240, books up early with a dozen three-bedroom log cabins going for $70-140 a night. Hearty lunches and dinners, $3-15, can be had in the resort's log-paneled dining room. Boat rentals and a general store are also on-site. During winter, the resort is open to snowmobilers, giving access to over 330,000 acres of designated snowmobile areas. **East Lake Resort,** tel. (541) 536-2230, offers 11 cabins with housekeeping facilities for $65-95 per night. A snack bar, general store, and boat rentals are on-site, and the nearby RV park has a laundry, public showers, and pay phones. Each year, 225,000 trout are planted in East Lake, and in 1990, Atlantic salmon

The Paulina Peak drive is one of the highest in the state.

TED LONG ISHIKAWA

were introduced here. The cold water and abundant freshwater shrimp make for excellent-tasting fish. Camping is also available; contact the Bend Ranger Station for details. Paulina Resort is open in the summer for fishing and Dec.-March for cross-country skiing and snowmobiling. East Lake Resort is open mid-May through mid-October.

SPORTS AND RECREATION

Camping
With the Three Sisters Wilderness and the Deschutes National Forest flanking the western edges of Bend, there are many wonderful spots to enjoy camping out under the stars. But for those who want to stay within a two-mile radius of civilization, four decent RV parks can be found near Bend. **Bend Keystone,** 305 N.E. Burnside, Bend 97701, tel. (541) 382-2335, $16, **Crown Villa,** 60801 Brosterhous, Bend 97701, tel. (541) 388-1131, $16-28, **John's Trailer Park,** 61415 US 97S, Bend 97701, tel. (541) 382-6206, $17, and **Bend Kampground,** 63615 US 97N, Bend 97701, tel. (541) 382-7738, $15-25, offer all of the major amenities. However, while a swimming pool, recreation room, and cable TV hookups are pleasant enough, they can ultimately take the spotlight away from the main attraction: around Bend, nature is the star.

Tumalo State Park, tel. (541) 382-2601, $15 tents, $18 hookups, provides a middle ground between the rugged wilderness and tamed RV parks. Located five miles northwest of Bend off of US 20 along the banks of the Deschutes River, 68 tent sites and 20 sites for RVs up to 35 feet long are available here. Showers, flush toilets, hookups, utilities, and a laundromat are also accessible. Open mid-April to late October.

A more secluded setting is **Tumalo Falls,** contact Deschutes National Forest, 1230 N.E. 3rd St., Bend 97701, tel. (541) 388-5664. Located 16 miles west of town down Forest Service Roads 4601 and 4603, this small campground is situated along Tumalo Creek. Many fine hiking trails are in the area, including a short one to 97-foot-high Tumalo Falls. However, the facilities are primitive—pit toilets and no water.

Another exceptionally beautiful but equally rustic National Forest Service campground is

Todd Lake, also contact the Forest Service for more information. To get there, take Century Dr. toward Mt. Bachelor. About a mile or two past the ski area, take the first Forest Service Rd. on the right. While this road eventually arrives at Sisters, it is not recommended for passenger cars. However, you will have to venture less than a mile on a well-maintained section to reach the parking area for Todd Lake. It's a short walk up the trail to the campsites at this 6,200-foot-high alpine lake. While tables, fire grills, and pit toilets are provided, you will need to pack in your own water and supplies, as no vehicles are allowed. It's a good thing, because the drone of a Winnebago generator into the wee hours of the night would definitely detract from the grandeur of this pristine spot. You'll find good swimming and wading on the sandy shoal on the south end of the lake, and you can't miss the captivating views of Broken Top to the north.

Heading north from Bend, outdoor recreationists needn't put away their gear. Between Redmond and Madras is a park that offers hiking, boating, fishing, water-skiing, and bird-watching. **Cove Palisades State Park,** tel. (541) 546-3412, is located 14 miles southwest of Madras, off ORE 97. Towering cliffs, Cascade vistas, gnarled junipers, and Lake Billy Chinook with its 72-mile shoreline create a stunning backdrop for outdoor activities. The lake was created when Round Butte Dam backed up the waters of the Deschutes, Metolius, and Crooked rivers. Two overnight campgrounds offer all the amenities: Deschutes Camp has 87 full hookup sites and 94 tent sites; the Crooked River camp, perched right on the canyon rim, has 93 sites with electricity and water. Campsites are available May-Oct. and cost $15-19; reserve sites through Oregon State Parks—this is an extremely popular campground.

Farther away from the city is **Lapine State Park,** P.O. Box 5309, Bend 97708, tel. (541) 536-2428 after Labor Day; before Labor Day tel. (800) 452-5687 in Oregon, tel. (541) 284-7388 outside of Oregon. Look for a sign on the west side of the highway marking the three-mile-long entrance road located eight miles north of Lapine off US 97. With 14 campsites, swimming, canoeing, and trout fishing, this place fills early on a first-come, first-served basis. This area also has one of the taller ponderosa pines in Oregon (191 feet) and close proximity to the Cascade Lakes Drive, the High Desert Museum, and an array of volcanic phenomena. Open from mid-April to late October depending upon snowfall, such amenities as flush toilets, firewood, showers, and a laundromat are available. Fees run $15 for a full hookup site, $18 for an electricity-only hookup.

Horsing Around

Several public stables in the vicinity of Bend offer horseback rides that satisfy everyone from the dude to the experienced equestrian. Whether it be a mild-mannered pony for young children or a lively steed for the wannabe buckaroos, you'll find appropriate mounts and trail rides for all ages and skill levels.

Black Butte Stables, P.O. Box 8000, Black Butte 97759-80000, tel. (541) 595-2061, at Black Butte Ranch has several packages that take you down trails in the shadow of the Three Sisters. The Big Meadow pony ride for children is $7 for 15 minutes and $10 for a half hour. The one-hour Big Loop trail ride costs $22; the one-hour Gobblers Knob ride costs $29; the Hole-in-the-Wall Gang ride costs $35; and the four-hour Reata Trail ride (for experienced riders only) costs $65. The full-day Black Butte Posse ride costs $95. Given a couple days' advance notice, the proprietors will provide breakfast or a barbecue at the end of the one- and two-hour rides.

Reservations are suggested for the short rides and are required for the half-day, full-day, and meal rides. Riding lessons are also available.

Located 15 minutes west of Sisters on ORE 126 is **Blue Lake Corrals,** tel. (541) 595-2648. The half-hour pony ride for children on Jeepers costs $10. The one-hour Crater Rim ride, $20, takes you through alpine meadows to the top of the crater that holds 314-foot-deep Blue Lake. The 2.5-hour Waterfall Wonders ride, $35, incorporates views of several waterfalls as well as Three Fingered Jack. The two-hour Lakes Loop trip, $27, meanders through the forest past three crystal-clear mountain lakes. The two-hour Twilight ride, $29, offers cooler temperatures, lovely sunsets and skyscapes, and views of wildlife coming out of the woods to feed. Reservations are requested at least one hour before the trail rides.

Blue Lake Corrals' two longer rides, the Discovery Trail (five hours) and Cache Mountain Trail (eight hours), both cost $75. Inquire, too, about their pack trips into the Three Sisters and Jefferson wilderness areas.

Five miles west of Redmond at the Eagle Crest Resort is **Eagle Crest Equestrian Center,** P.O. Box 1194, Redmond 97756, tel. (541) 923-2072. The half-hour kids' pony ride on Geronimo costs $6. The one-hour Juniper Trail ride takes you through the junipers and sagebrush of the high desert and costs $17. The two-hour Cline Butte ride, $30, goes to the top of Cline Butte, where you get a good view of the interface between Cascade and desert life zones. The half-day Skyline Trail ride takes you out into the wilds of the desert, where you and your guide blaze your own trails (reservations required). Wagon rides, cookout rides, and riding lessons are also available.

About 15 miles south of Bend on US 97 at Sunriver Resort is **Sunriver Stables,** P.O. Box 3254, Sunriver 97709, tel. (541) 593-2538. The 15-minute Smallest Buckaroo pony ride costs $7. A good ride for beginners is the half-hour Bald Eagle Loop, $15, which goes along the Deschutes River. The one-hour Nature's Cove ride, $25, takes in views of the Deschutes River, wildlife, and wildflowers. The two-hour Ramsey Ridge ride climbs to a panoramic viewpoint overlooking the resort. For those who want to do some serious riding, you can create your own ride (three hours minimum) into the Deschutes National Forest for $40 for the first two hours, then $15 per additional hour. Private lessons and surrey, covered wagon, and sleigh (winter only) rides are also available.

Fishing

With over 100 mountain lakes and the Deschutes River within an hour's drive of Bend, your piscatorial pleasures will be satisfied in central Oregon. The high lakes offer rainbow, brown, and brook trout as well as landlocked Atlantic and coho salmon. The Deschutes River is famed for its red-sided rainbow trout and summer steelhead. You will need appropriate fishing gear like chest waders, rod 'n' reel, and fishing license/steelhead tags. All gear and permits are available locally.

A full-service pro shop with everything for the fly fisher is **The Fly Box,** 1293 S.E. 3rd St.,

Bend 97701, tel. (541) 388-3330. Custom-tied flies and a full selection of fly-tying tools and materials provide you with the goodies to keep the fish biting. Fly-fishing classes, fishing guide services, and equipment sales, rentals, and repairs can also be found here.

Lacy's Whitewater and Wild Fish, 57 Pinecrest Court, Bend 97701, tel. (541) 389-2434, offers guided float trips on the Deschutes and John Day rivers. Stable water temperatures from the spring-fed river and abundant water hatches of baetis, midges, stoneflies, salmon-flies, goldenstones, mayflies and caddisflies keep the fish here in top condition. The wild red-sided trout of the Deschutes River are there all year, and the summer steelhead are found in the river July-December. The John Day River is noted for being the only river in the state that hosts an all-wild run of summer steelhead.

High Desert Drifter, 721 N.W. Ogden, Bend 97701, tel. (541) 389-0607, also offers guided fly-fishing float trips on the Deschutes River. The full-day trip that includes lunch, the necessary river-boater pass, and Warm Springs Indian Reservation fishing permit costs $250 for one person, $300 for two, and $420 for three. Multiday trips including all meals run $450 for two days, $600 for three days, $800 for four days, and $1000 for five days.

Women who like fishing but don't care to hang out with a bunch of crude and rude fishermen will enjoy **Trout Magic**'s, Box 321, Bend 97709, tel. 383-FISH, women-only fishing trips (sorry fellas, can't tag alone on this one, even if you're one of the "good guys"). The company owner, Raven Wing, has been fishing here for over a decade and she is also a teacher at Central Oregon Community College. Groups of two to six are taken out on these popular outings. Rates vary with the number of people in your group (the more people you have, the more money you save).

Families are catered to by **Garrison's Fishing Service,** Box 4113, Sunriver OR, 97707, tel. (541) 593-8394, which features pontoon boats with padded swivel chairs that cruise the lakes and rivers of Central Oregon looking for the big ones. Full day rates are $150 for the first person, and $75 for each additional individual in your party.

All of these outfitters require completion of a trip application form and a deposit. It's always a good idea to plan your reservations well in advance, especially during the fall fishing season.

Whitewater Rafting

The Deschutes River offers some of the finest whitewater in central Oregon. The numerous lava flows have diverted the river to create tumultuous rapids that attract raft, kayak, and canoe enthusiasts. From short rafting trips to multiday adventures, you'll find many options available to enjoy the exciting Deschutes River. You will need swimwear, footwear, sunblock, and sunglasses for all rafting trips. It's also advisable to have a set of dry clothes handy at the end of the voyage.

Cascade River Adventures, P.O. Box 71, Bend 97709, tel. (541) 389-8370; from Sunriver, tel. (541) 593-3113, features several rafting packages. The two-hour Mini Expedition, $34 adults, $28 children ages 6-12, floats through a three-mile section of the Deschutes River with some challenging rapids. Six daily departures from Bend include transfer to and from the river. The all-day trip, $80 adults, $70 children, takes in 12 action-packed miles of whitewater, including some exciting Class IV rapids like Box Car, Oak Springs, and Elevator. A barbecue cookout lunch and plenty of drinks are included. The transfer pick-up point for the day-trips is at the Bend office at 8 a.m. and returns around 6 p.m.

The Inn of the Seventh Mountain, 18575 Century Dr., Bend 97701, tel. (541) 389-2722, offers a short two-hour raft trip, $28 adults, $22 children, down a three-mile section of the Deschutes that takes in some Class I-IV rapids. With names like Pinball Alley and the Souse Hole, you can be assured of a good ride! Transfer between the Inn and the river is included. A full day trip on the lower Deschutes taking on 14 miles of raging whitewater is also offered, $75, that includes a continental breakfast, transportation, and cookout lunch.

Rapid River Rafters, 60107 Cinder Butte Rd., Bend 97702, tel. (541) 382-1514 or (800) 962-3327, http://www.websinc.com/rrrafters, e-mail rapidrr@transport.com, offers a series of full- and multiday packages on the Deschutes River. The one-day trip, $75-80, takes in 17 miles of the river from Harpham Flat to Lone Pine. An all-you-can-eat hot barbecue chicken lunch is included. The two-day trip, $215, floats 44 miles of exciting whitewater from Trout Creek to Sandy Beach. The three-day trip, $325, runs 55 miles from Warm Springs to Sandy Beach. On all of the multiday trips, the camping and meal preparations at pleasant riverside locations are taken care of by your guides. Season runs from late April to early October, and camping equipment is available for rent if you don't have your own.

Sun Country Tours, P.O. Box 771, Bend 97709, tel. (541) 382-6277 or (800) 770-2161, http://www.sunriver.com/rafting, e-mail suncountry@empnet.com, is based at the Sunriver Resort. Their two-hour, three-mile whitewater adventure takes in Class I-IV rapids on the Deschutes River. It costs $28 for children 8-12 and $34 for adults. The full-day trip, $80 adults, $70 children, runs 13 miles through a dozen minor rapids and seven major ones including Wapinitia, Train Hole, and Oak Springs. A hearty barbecue lunch is included. Multiday packages 29-55 miles in length are also available. The two-day trip costs $225, the three-day costs $350, and the four-day costs $415. All meals on multiday trips are included, and the transfer from Sunriver to Maupin is also part of the day-trip packages.

If you would rather shoot the rapids on your own, you can rent canoes, kayaks, and rafts from **Bend Whitewater Supply,** 55 N.W. Wall St., Building C, Bend 97701, tel. (541) 389-7191. This locally owned and operated full-service whitewater store can provide you with everything necessary for a safe and enjoyable whitewater experience. Bend Whitewater Supply also offers canoe and kayak lessons from the "never ever before" who have never tried it to advanced paddlers who want to learn more "rodeo style" and technique.

Mount Bachelor Summit Chairlift

Even when ski season is over, Mt. Bachelor Summit Chair Lift, tel. (541) 382-3224 in Oregon or (800) 829-2442, http//www.mtbachelor.com, and the Sunrise Lodge Lift are in operation. The view from the top of 9,065 foot Mt. Bachelor takes in many of the Cascade lakes and peaks. The lift runs 10 a.m.-4 p.m. daily, Memorial to Labor Day and costs $10 adults, $5 children ages 7-12. Try to time your journey to the top

with the ranger talks offered at 11:30 a.m. and 2:30 p.m. seven days a week. Lunch is served daily in the mid-mountain Pine Marten Lodge 10 a.m.-4 p.m. Mountain bike rentals are available from the Mt. Bachelor Ski and Sport shop at West Village. Bikes are allowed on the cross country trails, but not on the chairlift.

The peak's natural history is conveyed by a three mile trail where white bark pine and pumice grape-fern grow. The purplish fern is found in only four other alpine plant communities in Oregon, most notably in the pumice desert on the northwest side of Crater Lake. You can get to Sunrise Lodge and Lift via the Cascades Lakes Highway (see "Sights," above). Many consider the perspective from Mt. Bachelor's 9,065 feet summit to be *the* alpine view in the state.

Juniper Aquatic and Fitness Center

One of the finest aquatic and fitness centers east of the Cascades is found at Juniper Aquatic and Fitness Center, 800 N.E. 6th St., Bend 97701, tel. (541) 389-7665. Part of the Bend Metro Park and Recreation District, the center is located in 20-acre Juniper Park and features two indoor pools and a large 40-yard outdoor pool providing plenty of space for splashing around. Serious swimmers can enjoy frequent lap swims and adults-only swim times daily. An aerobics room, weight room, jogging trail, and tennis court offer other exercise options. A sauna and jacuzzi provide you with yet another way to sweat it out. Call ahead to see what's on the schedule for the day's activities.

Cycle Coasting

If you like to bike but would rather have gravity do all of the work, consider the Paulina Plunge with **High Cascade Descent,** 333 Riverfront, Bend 97702, tel. (541) 389-0562. They provide quality 15- and 18-speed mountain bikes, helmets, experienced guides, and the shuttle transfer from Bend and back. The action starts at Paulina Lake, where you begin your coast down forested trails alongside Paulina Creek. You'll pass by 50 waterfalls on your 3,000-foot descent, as well as abundant wildlife and varied vegetation. A deli-style lunch (vegetarian meals available upon request) and numerous opportunities for photography and fishing round out the fun. The tour costs $40 per person, $35 for children under 12. Large groups of over 10 people can receive discounts if they book trips in advance. If you have your own bicycle, you can deduct $5 from the tour price. This popular trip is offered June-October.

Equipment Rentals
For skis, boots, poles, and snowboards, **Bend Ski and Sport,** 1009 N.W. Galveston, tel. (541) 389-4667, can get you outfitted. Clothing, kid's skis, car racks, stunt kites, and many other accessories are also available here. For snowmobiles, **Fantastic Recreation Rentals,** 1972 N.E. Third St., tel. (541) 389-5640, and **Pauline Tours,** 53750 US 97, LaPine, tel. (541) 536-2214, can help you prepare for an arctic express adventure with both rentals and tours. Snowmobile maps and other information can be procured from the **Oregon State Snowmobile Association,** Box 435, LaPine, OR 97739, tel. (541) 536-3668.

Baseball
Double A baseball can be enjoyed each spring and summer at Vince Genna Stadium, 401 S.E. Roosevelt, tel. (541) 382-8011. This small west-facing park where the sun goes down behind Broken Top and the Three Sisters hosts the Bend Bandits.

Birdwatching
About an hour and a half south of Bend near Fort Rock is **Cabin Lake Campground,** De-schutes National Forest, tel. (541) 388-2715, an exceptional spot for viewing a wide variety of birds and wildlife. There is no lake at Cabin Lake, but the Forest Service has built two small ponds that blend in with the natural surroundings. Permanent wildlife viewing blinds made of logs, built and donated by the Portland Audubon Society, are adjacent to this small 12 site campground, and give close visual access to these ponds. In fact, the blinds are so close that binoculars aren't really needed. Since there is little water in this 3,000 foot-high meeting of desert and mountain biomes, both mountain and desert birds are regularly attracted, usually in large quantities. The Red Crossbill, a member of the finch family that is increasingly rare, is a regular visitor to this avian oasis. The Pinyon Jap is another fairly uncommon bird that can be seen here with frequency. Woodpeckers, including Lewis' woodpecker, common Flicker, White-headed woodpecker, and Hairy woodpecker are also often sighted here. Park checklists show the California Quail, bluebirds, chickadees, flycatchers, sparrows, warblers, and the Western Tanager making appearances, too. Best viewing times are in the morning, but birds can usually be seen all day long.

Mushing the Trail
A unique opportunity is available through **Oregon Trail of Dreams,** tel. (541) 382-2442 or (800) 829-2442, to ride in an Iditarod sled behind a team of trained huskies through the spectac-

Mt. Bachelor as seen from Sunriver

TAUK TOURS

ular winter scenery of the central Cascades. This is actually a winter training camp for professional sled dog teams preparing to run in the Iditarod and Yukon Quest races, which are both over 1,000 miles long and take nearly two weeks to complete. Many of these huskies were featured in Disney's movie *Iron Will*. While here in Oregon, they run seven days a week regardless of weather. As such, you will also need to be appropriately dressed as conditions dictate to undertake a dog sled ride.

A good introduction is the standard trip, $60 adults, $30 children under 80 pounds, which includes an hour and a half of orientation and trail time as well as the chance to help care and feed the dogs after the trip. You can circumnavigate Mt. Bachelor on the five hour, 26 mile long Marathon trip, $350 per 350 pounds, adults only. For those who want to take it to the max, there's the 65 mile trip from Mt. Bachelor to the Odell Lake Lodge. Lunch, snack, and overnight accommodations are included, $700 per 350 pounds, ages 13 and up, mid-week only.

The beginning of all rides starts with an atmosphere of excitement and anticipation. The dogs are pumped up with enthusiasm and ready to run as the mushers make their last checks of the equipment and harnesses. When the word is finally given to start, hold on tight. Snow flies everywhere as the huskies madly paw their way down the trail, their happy howls echoing through the forest, as you soak it all up in the wake of their exhileration. Later on, the dogs settle into their rhythm, and the ride becomes more serene, giving you time to enjoy the majestic vistas of Broken Top, the Three Sisters, and Mt. Bachelor. It's similar to a snowmobile ride without all the noise, and it's one of those once-in-a-lifetime opportunities that's well worth taking. Reservations are required, advance booking is recommended.

Llamas
Central Oregon is the heart of the state's thriving llama industry. Here are a couple of ranchers who welcome visitors to see this interesting creature up close.

The **Ultimate Llama,** 2381 Smith Rock Way, Terrebonne, tel. (541) 923-1603; e-mail ultimate@bendnet.com, offers hikes with llamas. It's fun, easy, and a great introduction to these mild-mannered animals. **Rancho Paraiso Llamase,** 19345 Dusty Loop, Bend, tel. (541) 388-7333, http://www.teleport.com/~rgr/ranches/rp., e-mail rgr@teleport.com, will also be happy to show you around. In courtesy to both ranchers, please be sure to contact them in advance before visiting.

Golf
Central Oregon has recently gained recognition for world-class golfing. And no wonder. With a dozen courses and six more slated for construction, you can find just about every kind of golf challenge here. The warm sunny days, cool evenings, and spectacular mountain scenery make every shot a memorable one.

Two well-groomed courses, Big Meadow and Glaze Meadow, are found at **Black Butte Ranch,** tel. (541) 595-6689. Big Meadow is more open and forgiving, while Glaze Meadow demands precise shots. Both have tall trees and lush fairways from tee to green. This course was recently named by *Golf Digest* as one of Oregon's top 10 golf courses. Greens fees are $24 for nine holes and $40 for 18 holes. Reservations for weekdays must be made at least one day in advance, while weekend bookings must be made no later than the Monday before.

Crooked River Ranch, tel. (541) 923-6343, a nine-hole par-32 course, is wide open with few trees, but that doesn't detract from the challenge or the scenic vistas. Rates are $10-12 for nine holes and $18 for 18 holes. Weekend reservations must be made by Thursday.

A blend of open and tight holes can be found on the popular course at **Eagle Crest Resort,** tel. (541) 923-4653. The two nine-hole segments of this par-72 course differ in character. The first set allows you to swing away, while the second places a premium on club and shot selection. The stand of 1,000-year-old junipers in mid-fairway and excellent greens add to the challenge and enjoyment. The greens fees are $17 for nine holes and $28 for 18 holes for registered guests, $20 and $34 for visitors. Weekend reservations must be made by Thursday.

Eighteen new holes opened up recently at the **Inn of the Seventh Mountain,** tel. (541) 382-8711. Designed by Robert Muir Graves, the course's strategically placed trees, lakes, and sand traps have already given this place the reputation as the "mean green" golf course of central Oregon. The 18 holes here are spoken in the same breath as Sunriver's North Course and Black Butte's Glaze Meadows—fast company indeed. The greens fees are $25 for nine holes, $40 for 18 holes.

A true desert course found in Redmond that requires shot accuracy is the **Juniper Golf Club,** tel. (541) 548-3121. This is an 18-hole par-72 course that snakes through the juniper and lava of the high desert. The prevailing winds and abundance of rocks off of the fairway challenge the golfer's shot-making abilities. Rates are $11-13 for nine holes and $20-25 for 18 holes. Reservations are required at least one day in advance.

Sixty miles north of Bend is the well-maintained 18-hole par-72 course at **Kah-Nee-Ta Resort,** tel. (541) 553-1112, ext. 371. While shorter than many other resort courses in the area, it's nonetheless both a challenge and a delight to play. In addition to water to contend with from the Warm Springs River that meanders through the course, several holes have elevated greens that require blind shots to reach. The greens fees are $15 for nine holes and $27.50 for 18. Reservations can be made at any time.

A beautiful course in Bend with tight fairways, large greens, sand, and "water, water everywhere" is **Mountain High Golf Club,** tel. (541) 382-1111. Two tricky par-four dogleg holes, three par-fives, and the necessity of placing shots over and around the junipers add to the test. Rates are $20 for nine holes and $30 for 18. Reservations can be made anytime for weekdays, but must be made at least four days in advance for weekends.

About 45 miles north of Bend on US 97 at the Madras Golf and Country Club is **Nine Peaks,** tel. (541) 475-3511. This short par-36 nine-hole course is flat and more forgiving than most courses in the area. The name comes from the nine Cascade peaks that provide a stunning visual backdrop. Rates are $7-9 for nine holes and $12-16 for 18. Reservations are required at least one day in advance.

A course popular with seniors, women, and beginners is found at **Orion Greens,** tel. (541) 388-3999, in Bend. This short executive course with no homesites lining the fairways can be deceptively tough. Water comes into play on four holes and accuracy is a must. Rates are $10 for nine holes and $17 for 18. Reservations are required at least one day in advance.

The hilly, rocky terrain of **River's Edge,** tel. (541) 389-2828, in Bend makes it both beautiful and an extreme challenge. This testy nine-hole par-36 course has tiered greens and one of the region's most demanding water holes. Shot accuracy is more important here than at any other course in the vicinity. Rates are $14 for nine holes and $22 for 18 on weekdays, $15 for nine holes and $25 for 18 on weekends. Reservations are required one week in advance.

Three distinct 18-hole courses are found at **Sunriver Resort,** tel. (541) 593-1221, 15 miles south of Bend on US 97. The South Course is long, with fast greens that require a soft touch. The North Course, the premier course in the area, has been rated among the top 25 in the country and is the site of the annual Oregon Open. Water, abundant bunkers, and constricted approaches to the greens make club selection and shot accuracy very important. The new crosswater course is touted by the management as the best course north of Pebble Beach. It won *Golf Digest*'s 1997 award for the best new resort course. The rates for either course are $24 for nine holes and $40 for 18 for registered guests, $30 for nine holes and $50 for 18 for visitors. The restaurant here gets good word-of-mouth from the locals.

Prineville Meadows Course, west of the city on US 26, adds another public course to the region's already formidable array of places to putter around.

Tours

A great way to explore central Oregon in depth is through **Wanderlust Tours,** 143 S.W. Cleveland Ave., Bend, tel. (541) 389-8359 or (800) 962-2862; e-mail wanderlust@empnet.com, with their focus on the area's geology, history, flora, fauna, and local issues. Day-trips to Crater Lake, the lava lands, the Deschutes River, and the Cascades Lakes Highway are featured. Your guide, Dave Nissen, knows the area as well as anyone in the state, and the small groups (14 passenger van), creative itineraries, and informal atmosphere merit a hearty recommendation. Dave's ecotourism packages have rated special notice in Oregon media, and it's clear that he runs the best tour company east of the Cascades. Especially noteworth is the fact that Wanderlust offers Crater Lake trips, $54 per person, minimum four passengers. As no public transportation exists to what is frequently suggested as the 8th wonder of the world, this itinerary takes on special significance. An array of hikes and adventures that key upon the mountain to desert variety of central Oregon are also offered, $26-44. Snowshoe tours, $22-125, are available in winter, and special moonlight trips can be arranged too. All day trips include lunch, vegetarian meals available upon request. Call or write for their brochure, reservations are advised as space is limited.

ACCOMMODATIONS

Bend has exploded into the largest full-fledged resort town in the state. On holidays or ski weekends, it's hard to find a decent room if you don't have reservations, and it's bound to get worse. Nonetheless, a profusion of cut-rate motels just off the main drag makes it possible to put a roof over your head without putting a dent in your pocketbook. One place where price won't ever be an inhibiting factor, $12-17, is Bend's **Cascade Hostel**, 19 S.W. Century Drive, Bend 97702, tel. (541) 389-3813 or (800) 299-3813, located on the road to Mt. Bachelor ski slopes. Added inducements to stay here include a free ski shuttle and 10% discounts on both Powder House ski rentals and hot tubbing at Soaks Unlimited. Reserve at least 24 hours in advance by phone or three weeks in advance with a deposit equal to a night's stay, family/couple rooms are available. To get to the hostel from downtown take Franklin off 3rd St. This becomes Galveston and goes to Century Drive (14th St.). From here turn left and look for the sign. When calling to reserve ask about shuttle service on Resort Bus Lines from the Chemult Amtrak station. Another good dollar value is **Bend Riverside Motel**, 1565 N.W. Hill St., tel. (541) 389-2363 or (800) 284-2363, offering rooms from $50-110 per night. Some of their suites overlook the river and have fireplaces and kitchens.

BEND ACCOMMODATIONS

Bend Super 8 Motel, 1275 US 97, tel. (541) 388-6888 or (800) 800-8000, $55-75, wheelchair access, covered pool, laundry.

Best Western Entrada Lodge, 19221 Century Dr., tel. (541) 382-4080 or (800) 528-1234, $50-90, pool, jacuzzi, pets, restaurant.

Best Western Inn & Suites, 721 N.E. 3rd St., tel. (541) 382-1515 or (800) 528-1234, $55-90, pool, jacuzzi, pets.

Cascade Lodge Motel, 420 S.E. 3rd St., tel. (541) 382-2612 or (800) 852-6031, $40-60, pool, pets, restaurant.

Cimarron Motel, 201 N.E. 3rd St., tel. (541) 382-8282 or (800) 304-4050, $40-50, pool, pets, river view.

Dunes Motel, 1515 N.E. 3rd St., tel. (541) 382-6811, $50-100.

Hampton Inn, 15 N.E. Butler Market Rd., (541) 388-4114 or (800) 426-7866, $55-85, pets, pool, continental breakfast.

Motel West, 228 N.E. Irving, tel. (541) 389-5577, $35-45, kitchenettes, pets.

Mt. Bachelor Village Resort, 19717 Mt. Bachelor Dr., (541) 389-5900 or (800) 452-9846, $80-300, river view, pool, resort atmosphere.

Pine Ridge Inn, 1200 S.W. Century Dr., (541) 389-6137 or (800) 600-4095, $100-225, river views, continental breakfast, resort atmosphere.

Riverhouse Resort, (541) 389-3111 or (800) 547-3928, $65-100, clean, pets, nice kitchen/suites available.

Shilo Inn Suites, 3105 O.B. Riley Rd., (541) 389-9600 or (800) 222-2244, $80-135, pets, covered pool, continental breakfast, laundry.

Sonoma Lodge, 450 S.E. 3rd St., tel. (541) 382-4891, $35-50, pets.

Westward Ho Motel, 904 S.E. 3rd St., tel. (541) 382-2111 or (800) 999-8143, $35-75, covered pool, fireplaces, pets.

Central Oregon Resorts

There are several premier resorts in Deschutes County that have helped transform it from a primarily agricultural area to the Aspen of the Northwest. Golf, horseback riding, tennis, swimming, biking/jogging/hiking trails, saunas, and hot tubs grace these all-year playgrounds, along with first-rate lodgings and restaurants. Ski packages and other special offers are also available at each establishment. While all of them feature recreation amid pleasant surroundings, subtle distinctions among them bear mention.

Located 31 miles west of Bend on US 20, **Black Butte Ranch,** P.O. Box 8000, Black Butte Ranch 97759, tel. (541) 595-6211 or (800) 452-7455, sits on the plain of the seven peaks. Ponderosa pines, lush meadows, and aspen-lined streams round out the metaphor of mountains' majesty. Over 16 miles of trails thread through the 1,800 acres of forested grounds. Accommodations range from deluxe hotel-type bedrooms to one- to three-bedroom condominium suites and resort homes. Rates for these digs range $80-280. A nationally rated golf course, bike trails, tennis courts, and other facilities also explain why this resort has won the *Family Circle* "Resort of the Year" award twice. In January 1997, Black Butte was voted to the prestigious "gold list" of *Conde Naste's* top hotels and resorts of the world.

Eagle Crest Resort, P.O. Box 1215, Redmond 97756, tel. (541) 923-2453 or (800) 682-4786, is five miles west of Redmond. This relative newcomer to the central Oregon resort scene offers hotel rooms, two-bedroom suites, and condos in the $80-235 range. The terrain and vegetation are representative of the high desert, and backdropped by views of eight Cascade peaks. Ask about ski and golf packages. This is a low-key, family oriented place.

Another great place for families is **The Inn of the Seventh Mountain,** P.O. Box 1207, Bend 97709, tel. (541) 382-8711 or (800) 452-6810. It is located five miles outside of Bend on Century Drive in the Deschutes National Forest. Bedroom units, fireside studios, and condos are available in the $60-270 range. Their outstanding recreation department plugs the kids into nonstop fun, leaving the parents free to enjoy grown-up pursuits. Ice skating, cross-country skiing, and snowmobile trips are available during the winter months, and rafting, swimming, tennis, golf, horseback riding, and more are offered during the summer. Ask about their ski packages.

A location close by the Deschutes River recommends the inn as a base for rafting (see "Sports and Recreation," above) and one of the prettiest fall bike rides in Oregon. The whitecaps of the blue Deschutes River and the strewn black lava rock accompany you on the 8.5-mile jaunt to Benham Falls. Add three waterfalls, volcano views, meadows, lava fields, and sage brush flats and you can imagine the visual intoxication of the ride. To get to the starting point, go five miles west of Bend on Century Drive. Turn south just before the golf course at a sign pointing to Meadow picnic area, then drive on a gravel road one mile to a parking area by the Deschutes River.

Yet another place to bring the family is **Kah-Nee-Ta Resort,** P.O. Box K, Warm Springs 97761, tel. (541) 553-1112 or (800) 554-4786. Located at the bottom of a canyon about a dozen miles off US 26 from the town of Warm Springs, Kah-Nee-Ta basks in 300 days of sunshine a year. The 1,000-foot elevation and 12-inch annual rainfall enable golfers to play its championship course year-round. It's even snow-free in February. Owned by the Confederated Tribes of Warm Springs, this arrow-shaped hotel is the centerpiece of the 600,000-acre reservation, which includes a working ranch and wild horses. Lodging possibilities include authentic Indian tipis from $55; hotel rooms, suites, and cottages range $115-200. The hot mineral baths and spring-fed olympic-sized swimming pool are among the highlights here. There are also bike rentals, tennis, horseback riding, and hiking. Such native-inspired dishes as salmon cooked outside in the traditional way (with roots and wild herbs) and bird-in-clay (a game hen stewing in its own juices inside a clay mold for $19) also impart a unique flavor to a vacation here. There is also a gaming resort on site. Day vistors can also take advantage of Kah-Nee-Ta's venerated hot spring pool and baths (included in overnight room rate) for $5. The kids are sure to enjoy the 140 foot water slide, $2.

The Northwest's most complete resort, **Sunriver Lodge,** P.O. Box 3609, Sunriver 97707, tel. (800) 547-3922, not only has proximity to Mt. Bachelor skiing, Deschutes river canoeing/whitewater rafting, and hiking/horse trails in the Deschutes National Forest but also boasts golf courses, pools, tennis courts, and 30 miles of biking routes. An on-site astronomical observatory and nature center, which features live animal displays and botanical gardens, together with Sunriver's shopping mall, compound the impression of a recreation mecca with something for everybody. Larger parties will find the spacious lodge suites (limit four persons to a suite) to be well worth the $165-180 asking price. Each of these units features a floor-to-ceiling fireplace, a fully equipped kitchen, a sleeping loft, and tall picture windows which open up to a patio. During the summer, complimentary bicycles and a two-hour float down the Deschutes in a canoe are included with room rental. In 1997, this resort won *Family Circle*'s Resort of the Year award.

Condo rentals, $140-250, at Sunriver that sleep from four to ten people are available through **Mountain Resort Properties,** tel. (541) 593-8685 or (800) 346-6337, and **Deschutes Realty,** tel. (800) 423-5443. All units have a fully equipped kitchen, linens, washer/dryer, TV, barbecue, and telephone as well as access to swimming and tennis at Sunriver. Since these are privately owned units, other ammenities like VCR, hot tub, sauna, bicycles will vary. Most of these condos do not allow pets or smoking, but there are a couple of exceptions; inquire when making reservations. Another good source for ranch resort rentals is found at the **Deschutes River Ranch,** 20210 Swalley Rd., Bend, tel. (541) 382-7240 or (888) 377-4242, $150-185. There are 22 three bedroom ranch vacation homes offered here (two night minimum stay) on the river that are fully equipped with all the appliances you need to set up housekeeping. The lodge facilities offer an exercise room, spa, solar heated swimming pool as well as volleyball, basketball, softball, and children's playground.

Tucked away in a small valley nine miles west of Bend is **Rock Springs Guest Ranch,** 64201 Tyler Rd. Bend, tel. (541) 382-1957 or (800) 225-3833, http://www.rocksprings.com. Guests here stay by the week (Sat.-Sat.) on the American Plan, where all meals, lodging, horseback riding, and all other ranch activities are included in one flat rate $1,430 adults, $1,065 ages 6-16, $865 ages 3-5. Only 50 guests are allowed per week, ensuring a high degree of personal service. Food is ample and delicious, and those with special dietary preferences will be accommodated adequately. Cookies, fruit, and beverages are always available for guests in the lodge dining room. Guests get their own cabins that are clean and well furnished. A proactive recreation program supervised by well qualified conselors keeps the kids on the go all day long with croquet, badminton, volleyball, basketball, and horseback riding. The horseback riding program is outstanding, and is the forte of the ranch. Riders are matched up with steeds appropriate to their level, and will enjoy rides catered to all levels of experience that grow more challenging as the week progresses. After a day in the saddle, it's great to relax in their spa to work out the kinks. If your family likes to horse around, this is the place to do it.

Bed and Breakfasts

Close to downtown Bend, Drake Park, and Mirror Pond is the **Lara House,** 640 N.W. Congress, tel. (541) 388-4064 or (800) 766-4064, $75-125. This large three story house was built in 1910 and features six large bedrooms with private bath. All rooms are furnished with antiques and reflect individual grace and charm. A delicious homemade breakfast is served in the bright solarium overlooking the colorful gardens and Drake Park. A large hot tub helps loosen aching musles after a long day skiing, hiking, or other prototypical Bend outdoor sports. Call ahead for reservations.

Originally an early 1900s hotel and boarding house, the **Mill Inn B&B,** 642 N.W. Colorado, Bend, tel. (541) 389-9198, $40-70, was extensively remodeled in 1990 into a contemporary 10-bedroom inn. Most of the rooms feature private baths, and some room sets adjoin to accommodate families (the Locker Room has four bunks, a bargain at $15/person). All rates include a full breakfast, and ski and golf packages are available. Add access to a washer/dryer, refrigerator, and hot tub, and you'll understand why advance booking is a necessity here.

Two other B&Bs in country-like settings in Bend are **The Country Inn The City,** 1776 N.E. 8th St., tel. (541) 385-7639, $40-60, and the **Gazebo,** 21679 Obsidian Ave., tel. (541) 389-7202, $40-60. Both of these properties feature a full breakfast; call for reservations and directions.

FOOD

The scenery around Bend feeds the soul, and restaurants here do the rest. While area restaurants run the gamut from fast-food franchises to elegant dinner houses, many travelers also want something in between those extremes. Some alternatives for every budget are listed below.

Beef and Brew, Bend River Mall, tel. (541) 388-4646, is a good dinner house, $8-17, for choice beef, seafood, and a tall cool one. Reservations are recommended. For a healthy, low-fat, low-cholesterol vegetarian breakfast, $4-8, or lunch, $4-10, with many organic items available, **Cafe Santé,** 718 N.W. Franklin, tel. (541) 383-3530, is the place to go. Even simple foods like soup and salad are highlights here. Decent Chinese cuisine is found at the **Hong Kong Restaurant and Lounge,** 580 S.E. 3rd, tel. (541) 389-8880. A wide selection of Cantonese, Sichuan, and American food, as well as many vegetarian and "health food" dishes, are prepared here.

An Italian fine-dining experience is available at the **Italian Cottage,** 1564 N.E. Division St., tel. (541) 382-5062. You can choose from over 30 entrees, and their pastas and breads are made fresh daily. For some of the largest portions in central Oregon, head down to **Jake's Diner,** 61260 US 97S, tel. (541) 382-0118. Hearty breakfasts are served here 24 hours a day, and the tasty giant cinnamon rolls, $2.50, are a treat. Truckers everywhere in the West sing the praises of this place. Nonetheless, lunch and dinner might disappoint you if you're expecting "cuisine" instead of basic food. Another US 97 shrine to road food is **Dandy's Burgers,** 1334 US 97.

Ernesto's Italian, 1203 N.E. 3rd St., tel. (541) 389-7274, has a good reputation with the locals. Situated in an old church and designed with an open kitchen, the dinner entrees range $8-16. The seafood fettucine has Poseidon's bounty of shrimp, clams, halibut, and other denizens of the Oregon deep.

Mexicali Rose, 301 N.E. Franklin, tel. (541) 389-0149, has the best Mexican food around Bend. Open every evening for dinner, $7-15,; be sure to ask for their special black beans with your entree. Call ahead for reservations because the restaurant is very popular with locals.

The **Pine Tavern Restaurant,** 967 N.W. Brooks St., tel. (541) 382-5581, has been in business since 1919, so they must be doing something right. The restaurant is located in a garden setting overlooking Mirror Pond, and ponderosa pines coming up through the floor enhance the interior ambience. Fresh mountain trout, prime rib, lamb, and hot sourdough scones with honey butter are among the many specialties, $10-20, here. Reservations are recommended. Sunriver's **Meadows Restaurant,** Sunriver Resort, tel. (800) 547-3922, has always been a major culinary presence east of the Cascades. At press time the entire Sunriver lodge complex was closed and under major rennovation. The new Meadows Restaurant will center around a more family-friendly orientation. Creative northwest cuisine in the Sunriver tradition of excellence geared to cater to all age tastes, a more relaxed atmosphere (formally informal dress), and some of the region's best Mt. Bachelor views should make this incarnation a good one.

Finally, located at the Inn of the Seventh Mountain, you'll find a restaurant for the whole family, **Josiah's,** 18575 Century Dr., tel. (541) 382-8711. Dinner entrees range $8-17 and feature some vegetarian items on the menu. One popular dish is Josiah's stew, loaded with cuts of marinated beef, red potatoes, Walla Walla onions, and carrots all stuffed into a warm sourdough bread bowl for about $10. The artichoke dip with green chilis served with red, white, and blue tortilla chips is just the right accompaniment to their selection of microbrews. Children receive a free skating pass for the resort's rink (roller in summer, ice in winter) along with their meal.

Downtown Dining

There are many fine restaurants catering to a wide variety of tastes all within walking distance of each other in the heart of Bend; look for a particularly high concentration near the 900 block of Bond Street, west of US 97. Here's a brief survey of some of what's cookin' downtown.

The place to go for breakfast and lunch is the **Alpenglow Cafe,** 1040 N.W. Bond, tel. (541) 383-7676. Just about everything here is made on the premises; no canned products are used for anything. They make their own breads, muffins, buns, rolls, and pasta, and use fresh and local Oregon staples whenever possible.

A summer seasonal favorite is the berry-stuffed french toast, extra thick slices of the restaurant's own special bread filled with fresh blueberries or raspberries, $7. If you don't mind waiting an extra 10 minutes, try the potato pancakes, $5, chunky potato mixed with cheddar cheese, Deschutes bacon, and spices that comes with sour cream or housemade applesauce. The huevos rancheros and California omelette also rate kudos. Lunches, $5-8, include soups, salads, sandwiches, and gourmet burgers. Open 6:30 a.m.-2:30 p.m., this small but bright establishment fills up fast with patrons in the know. Budget gourmets hit the **Taco Stand,** 221 N.W. Hill St.) where you can have a filling burrito for around a buck. There are also chiles rellenos, enchiladas, red snapper burritos, and chili verde. Just look for the line of customers on Hill Street just off of Division.

Yoko's Japanese Restaurant, 1028 N.W. Bond St., tel. (541) 382-2999, is Bend's preeminent Japanese restaurant and sushi bar. While the teriyaki, tempura, and sukiyaki dinners are prepared to suit American tastes, it's not uncommon to see Japanese visitors here enjoying their native cuisine. When the popular Japanese TV show *From Oregon With Love* was being filmed in central Oregon, this is where the production crews would eat most of their meals. Their Portland outlet near the corner of N.W. 23rd and Glisan sells reasonably priced sushi with an attitude. **Giuseppe's Ristorante,** 932 N.W. Bond St., tel. (541) 389-8899, brings the taste of northern Italy to Bend. Dinner specialties, $9-20, include chicken, veal, and 17 pasta dishes. Microbrews including an Italian Pilsner, McTarnahans, and Bridgeport Coho are available.

Great Harvest Bread Co., 835 N.W. Bond, is a bakery chain with outlets in Eugene and Portland, and will be a hit with those who like hearty whole-wheat breads from stone-ground flour, or such intriguing muffin combinations as oat bran/raspberry/applesauce. Cinnamon rolls, cookies, and other Great Harvest confections are made without eggs, dairy products, or oils. You'll also appreciate the chance to sample these products prior to making a purchase. A winner on the sandwich circuit is the **Desert Deli,** 118 N.W. Minnesota, tel. (541) 382-3559. A complete lunch with sandwich, chips, beverage, brownie, and utensils is around $6. Lunch is all they do here, and they do it right. The Desert Deli also delivers.

Bend also boasts central Oregon's first brewery and brewpub, **Deschutes Brewery and Public House,** 1044 N.W. Bond St., tel. (541) 382-9242. This is the place to come and relax with fresh, handcrafted ales and better-than-average pubfood, $3-6. There are vegetarian burgers, sandwiches, and black bean chili among the offerings. Check the specials board to see which ones of the over 5,000 rotating items are being featured that evening. Large viewing windows in the pub enable you to watch next month's batch being concocted in the brewery. Try the seven-layer dip, $6, best shared with a friend or two, and a glass of Cascade Golden Ale. A family oriented atmosphere is found at **Legends Publick House,** 125 N.W. Oregon Ave., tel. (541) 382-5654. This nonsmoking, kid-friendly place caters well to all ages. A wide selection of American pub fare, $4-14, is available that should please all age groups, and healthy party-portion sized dishes make sure no one leaves hungry. Kids can enjoy the game room while the folks get a chance to discreetly sample some of the microbrews on draft. Open for lunch and dinner Mon.-Fri., dinner only Saturday, and closed on Sunday.

High Tides's parent restaurant is Tidal Raves in Depoe Bay, which brings a renowned legacy of cooking experience to central Oregon. This Bend incarnation, 1045 N.W. Bond, tel. (541) 389-5244, features more creative versions of upscale seafood entrees, $10-18, and the chef will gladly customize gourmet vegetarian dishes to your liking. The jet-fresh Dungeness Crab and rockshrimp casserole baked with white cheddar and penne pasta in a white wine sauce with mushrooms, $13, is a safe bet. Wines, microbrews, gourmet sodas, an espresso cart, and not-too-sweet desserts round out the offerings. Open for lunch (11 a.m.-2:30 p.m., $4-10) and dinner (5-9 p.m.), reservations are accepted.

A local favorite attracting skiers, bohemians, and businesspeople is **Cafe Paradiso,** 945 N.W. Bond, tel. (541) 385-5931. This full service coffee bar also serves light entrees on the order of quiche, pasta, burritos, and home-baked goodies. Open Mon.-Thurs. 8 a.m.-11 p.m., Fri.-Sat. 8 a.m.-midnight, and Sunday 6 p.m.-11 p.m.

Live entertainment takes the stage on Friday nights in this high-ceilinged hangout. Sitting back in the comfy armchairs and couches over one of the cafe's board games or a good book seems to be the pastime of choice on chilly evenings in Bend. When weather permits, sidewalk seating is available.

A Mediterranean flavor predominates at **Hans,** 915 N.W. Wall St., tel. (541) 389-9700. While the menu changes weekly, the grilled (not baked) pizzas, $7-9, are a constant. An international wine list and local microbrews further enhance their varied offerings. Check out the desserts, cakes, and cookies in the glass case to get your Pavlov reflex going. Another alternative for pizza is **Pizza Mondo,** 811 N.W. Wall St., tel. (541) 330-9093, producing Bend's finest hand-tossed, stone baked pies. The Maui Wowie is one of their customer's "faves" with Canadian bacon, pineapple, and crushed Macadamia nuts. Dynamite calzones and a mean Caesar salad that would give Brutus pause add to their diverse pizza selections. Pizza is also available by the slice. Open for lunch and dinner Tues.-Sat.11 a.m.-9 p.m.

For fast, fresh, and healthy grilled fish, chicken, steak, and veggies with a lot of Mexican "Ole," try **Baja Norte,** 801 N.W. Wall St., tel. (541) 385-0611. Open seven days a week 11 a.m.-9 p.m., tacos, quesadillas, tostadas, burritos, and fajitas, $3-6, are all made up from scratch and taste great. We recommend the fish tacos (grilled Mahi Mahi with jack cheese, lettuce, and tropical salsa) as well as the artichoke Quesadilla's (artichoke hearts, jalapeños, and jack cheese garnished with sour cream, guacamole (the real stuff), and Baja salad. Housemade rice and beans can be added for a dollar extra, making any respective item a complete and economical meal.

You can find 111 Thai dishes at **Toomie's,** 119 N.W. Minesota, tel. (541) 388-5590. Open for lunch, $5-7, and dinner, $8-15, a wide variety of rice, noodle, curry, chicken, seafood, pork, beef, and vegetarian dishes are offered. Be forwarned that when they say "look out!" in regards to hot and spicy dishes, they mean it.

Many locals concur that **Cyrano's,** 119 N.W. Minnesota Ave., tel. (541) 389-6276, is one of central Oregon's premier dining experiences. With a reputation built around thick-cut steaks

that are grilled to perfection over red oak, the menu also features fresh seafood and other gourmet specialties, $10-20. If the weather is pleasant, enjoy lunch outside at their sidewalk cafe. Wholesome home-cooked food is available at **D & D Bar and Grill,** 927 N.W. Bond St., tel. (541) 382-4592. Open every day (except Christmas) for breakfast, lunch, and dinner, the Grill has reasonably priced breakfasts, $3-7, and a good selection of hamburgers.

EVENTS

The **Cascade Festival of Music** is held in late summer on the banks of the Deschutes River in Drake Park. In addition to world-class performances of classical, pop, and jazz in the pavilion tent, children's concerts, music workshops, and strolling minstrels round out the pageant. Tickets and information are available through the Cascade Festival of Music office, tel. (541) 383-2202; tickets $5-20.

The **Sunriver Music and Arts Festival,** held in the magnificent log-and-stone structure called the Great Hall at Sunriver Resort, has been pleasing capacity crowds since the festival's inception in 1977. The five-concert series features top performers from around the world. Highlights include the gala pops concert and the gourmet dinner as well as four traditional classical concerts and two children's concerts. Tickets and information are available through the Sunriver Music Festival office, tel. (541) 593-1084.

The Bend Summer Fest brings out food booths, Oregon wine and microbrews, art exhibits, and live music all in one big block party the second weekend in July. Contact the Bend Chamber of Commerce for more details, tel. (541) 382-3221. Tickets runs $7-35.

GETTING THERE AND GETTING AROUND

By Air

With about a dozen flights to/from Portland and several to/from San Francisco daily, access to central Oregon has improved dramatically in the last decade. The air hub of this section of the state is Redmond Air Center, Redmond 97756, tel. (541) 548-5071, located 16 miles north of Bend on US 97. **Alaska Airlines,** tel. (800) 426-0333, has nonstop jet flights out of L.A. and Seattle; **Horizon Air,** tel. (800) 547-9308, services the region from Portland and Seattle; and **United Express,** tel. (800) 241-6522, provides flights to and from Portland and San Francisco. Taxi, limo, and bus transfers connect the traveler to Bend at nominal costs. The terminal has interesting displays on central Oregon attractions. Interactive media and audiovisual aids can even teach locals about their home region.

By Bus

Greyhound, 1068 N.W. Bond St., tel. (541) 382-2151, is open Mon.-Fri. 7:30 a.m.-5:30 p.m., Saturday 7:30 a.m.-noon, Sunday 8 a.m.-noon, and every evening 8:30-9:45 p.m. Bus service connects Bend with Klamath Falls to the south and Biggs, Maupin, and The Dalles to the north. **Resort Bus Lines,** 767 S.E. Glenwood Dr., tel. (541) 389-7755, handles service to most outlying areas not serviced by Greyhound. **Central Oregon Shuttle Service,** tel. (541) 382-0800, serves Bend to and from Portland International Airport. It's reasonably priced (around $30) and offers pick-ups and drop-offs at downtown hotels. **Redmond Airport Shuttle,** tel. (541) 382-1687 or (800) 955-8267, offers door-to-door service to and from the Redmond airport. A free **ski shuttle** run by Mt. Bachelor, tel. (541) 382-2442, links downtown Bend to West Village on the mountain. **Yellow Cab,** tel. (541) 382-3311, can always haul you around if you need a ride. There is no inner city bus service

By Train

The closest you can get to Bend via Amtrak, tel. (800) 872-7245, is Chemult, 60 miles to the south on US 97. Amtrak will assist you in scheduling your transfer to Bend.

By Car

The automobile is still the vehicle of choice for exploring this quadrant of the state. Highways 97 and 20 converge on Bend, much as the Indian trails and pioneer wagon roads did 150 years ago when this outpost on the Deschutes was called Farewell Bend. Portland is three hours away via US 97 and US 26, Salem is two hours away via US 20 and ORE 22, and Eugene is

two hours away via US 20 and ORE 126. Crater Lake National Park is about two hours south down US 97. There are also many loops worth investigating, like the Cascade Lakes Highway, Newberry Crater, and the Lava Lands, as well as other touring corridors.

At press time, plans for the Bend Parkway were getting underway. This road will parallel Division Street and enable traffic to move more quickly through the city. Until its completion, expect some disruption in traffic flow over the next several years. Third St. (US 97) always seems to be glutted during peak travel times so plan accordingly.

You can rent a car for around $30 per day with 50 free miles daily from **Dorn Brothers Rentals,** 148 N. 6th, Redmond 97756, tel. (541) 923-2027 in Redmond, or (541) 382-2783 in Bend. They offer compact and midsize cars, passenger vans, four-by-fours, and pickups. Ski racks are also available. **Hertz,** 1057 S.E. 3rd St., Bend, tel. (541) 382-1711, Redmond Airport tel. (541) 923-1411, or Sunriver tel. (541) 593-1221 ext. 418, and **Budget,** 2060 US 20E, Bend, tel. (541) 389-3031, are two national rental outfits also represented here.

INFORMATION AND SERVICES

The **police,** 720 N.W. Wall St., tel. (541) 388-5530 or 911, and the state police, 63319 US 20W, tel. (541) 388-6300 or 911, are at your beck and call. The **post office,** 2300 N.E. 4th, Bend 97701, tel. (541) 388-1971, is open Mon.-Fri. 8:30 a.m.-5:30 p.m. If you like to make your own cocktails, the **liquor store,** 939 N.W. Bond, tel. (541) 382-6450, is open noon-8 p.m. Warm Springs Indian Reservation's KWSO (91.9 FM) features an intriguing blend of progressive country music, morning chants by tribal elders, and discussions of issues concerning Native Americans.

Cascades East is a free publication distributed at various locations in the region. Natural attractions, restaurants, outdoor recreation, and nightlife are well covered, though more with an eye toward promotion rather than objectivity.

For additional information on the Bend area, the **chamber of commerce,** 63085 US 97N, tel. (541) 382-3221 or (800) 905-2363, is open Mon.-Thurs. 9 a.m.-5 p.m., Friday 8 a.m.-6 p.m.,

Saturday 8 a.m.-5 p.m., and Sunday 11 a.m.-4 p.m. Generic central Oregon information can be obtained at tel. (800) 806-8334. The **Deschutes County Library,** 507 N.W. Wall St., tel. (541) 388-6677, is open Mon.-Sat. 9 a.m.-6 p.m. The Bend and Fort Rock **Ranger Station,** 1230 N.E. 3rd St., tel. (541) 388-5664, is the place to go for permits and information on the vast array of lands in central Oregon managed by the Forest Service.

St. Charles Immediate Care Center, 1302 US 97, tel. (541) 388-7799, can be of assistance for minor medical problems and emergencies. The parent hospital, **St. Charles Medical Center,** 2500 N.E. Nelf, tel. (541) 382-4321, or 382-4321 ext. 7100 for emergencies only, treats major trauma and other health-care problems. To get there from downtown, head toward Pilot Butte bypassing the butte and then bear left. A few miles later you'll see the hospital. If you're out in the boondocks and time is of the essence, **Air Life of Oregon,** tel. (800) 621-5433 or 911, can get you to the medical center in a hurry. The **Bend Memorial Clinic,** 1501 N.E. Medical Center Dr., tel. (541) 382-2811, is another option to remedy minor aches, pains, and ailments.

NORTH OF BEND

North of the Bend-Redmond area, the juniper-and-sage-lined roadsides and the fields of mint and wheat stand in welcome contrast to the malled-over main drags of central Oregon's biggest urban complex. The 500-foot-deep Crooked River Gorge, 15 miles south of Madras off US 97 at Ogden Scenic Wayside, and snow-capped vistas of Oregon's two highest mountains to the northeast (Mt. Hood and Mt. Jefferson) add further variety to the topography.

Petersen's Rock Garden

What began as one man's flight of fancy over the years has metamorphosed into a full-fledged rock fantasy. Petersen, a Danish immigrant farmer, created four acres of intricately detailed miniature castles, towers, and bridges made of agate, jasper, obsidian, malachite, petrified wood, and thunder eggs. There's also the Statue of Liberty, the American flag, and many other compositions hewn out of natural rock. This

rock garden to end all rock gardens, 7930 S.W. 77th St., Redmond 97756, tel. (541) 382-5574, is free of charge and open 365 days a year 8 a.m.-9 p.m. (or till dusk in winter). To get there, take Gift Rd. off of US 97 seven miles south of Redmond and 10 miles north of Bend. Follow the signs; it's only three miles off the highway. There is a very nice museum and gift shop in the rear of the complex featuring many types of rocks, crystals, fossils, and semiprecious gemstones. In the back of the museum is the Fluorescent Room, where little castles made of zinc, tungsten, uranium, and manganese glow in the dark. Free-roaming peacocks, chickens, and ducks are here to remind you this was once a working farm. The staff will help direct rockhounds to promising sites in the vicinity to further their own collections. Admission is $2 for adults, $1 for children 6-16.

Smith Rock State Park

The majestic spires towering above the Crooked River north of Redmond on US 97 are part of this 623-acre state park. Named after a soldier who fell to his death off of the highest promontory (3,230 feet) in the configuration, the park is a popular retreat for hikers, rock climbers, and casual visitors. Seven miles of well-marked trails follow the Crooked River and wend up the canyon walls to emerge on the ridgetops. Because the area is delicate and extremely sensitive to erosion, it's important not to blaze any trails because they may leave visible scars for years. Picnic tables, drinking water, and restrooms can be found near the parking area. The more adventurous can camp out in the park's primitive walk-in camping area, $2 a night. It's located near the park entrance about 100 yards from the **Rockhard Store,** 9297 N.E. Crooked River Dr., Terrebonne—try the huckleberry ice cream, and includes showers and sanitary facilities.

While it's not exactly Yosemite, some of the climbing routes at Smith Rock are as difficult and challenging as any you'll find in the United States. Most of the mountain's 17-million-year-old volcanic rock is soft and crumbly, making descents extra challenging. Chocks, nuts, friends, and other clean-climbing equipment and techniques are encouraged to reduce damage to the rock. On certain routes where these methods would prove impractical, permanent anchors have been placed. Climbers should use these fixed bolts (after testing them first for safety, of course) to minimize impact on the rock face. *Oregon Rock: A Climber's Guide* by Jeff Thomas has listings of all the routes at Smith Rock that do not require mounting of additional fixed protection. Climbers should never disturb birds of prey and their young in the lofty aeries. Finally, pack plenty of water. The Crooked River is contaminated with chemicals from nearby farmlands and isn't suitable for drinking. Discussions are currently underway to build a destination resort in the area. Needless to say, this is a controversial proposition.

As for more down-to-earth concerns, we recommend **La Siesta Mexican Restaurant,** 8320 US 97, Terrebonne, tel. (541) 548-4898. Located on the south side of town in a nondescript crackerbox of a structure, this climber's favorite features such hard-to-find south-of-the-border specialties as nopal cactus, chorizo, and mole sauce. Moderate prices and dishes made from scratch make this an oasis in the culinary wastes of the high desert.

Warm Springs Indian Reservation

The past lives on as more than a memory at the Warm Springs Indian Reservation, which straddles US 26. Within this 600,000 acre bailiwick,

ON THE TRAIL OF THE FIRST OREGONIANS

About five miles south of Warm Springs on US 26, there's an eye-popping view of Mt. Jefferson's snowcapped volcano cone looming across 50 miles of sagebrush. The base of the mountain marks the western extent of the Warm Springs tribe's 1,000-square-mile reservation. You'll find a smaller but equally impressive display of the tribe's wealth at the **Museum at Warm Springs,** P.O. Box C, Warm Springs 97761, tel. (541) 553-3331, located below the viewpoint at the bottom of the Deschutes River Canyon. Audiovisual displays, old photos, and tapes of traditional chants of the Paiute, Warm Springs, and Wasco peoples are aesthetically arrayed here. Each tribe's distinct culture and their coming together to form a thriving social and economic community define the major themes in the Northwest's only tribal museum. Replicas of a Paiute mat lodge, a Warm Springs tepee, and a Wasco plank house, along with recordings of each tribe's language, underscore this cultural richness and diversity. The exhibits, including items culled from a collection of more than 20,000 artifacts, range from a display of primitive prehistoric hand tools to a high-tech, push-button activated Wasco wedding scene. The museum is open daily 10 a.m.-5 p.m. except Thanksgiving, New Year's Day, and Christmas Day; $5 admission, discounts for seniors and children.

Aficionados of Northwest native lore might want to take in the foregoing museum as part of a circuit including two other world-class exhibit halls: the High Desert Museum and the Maryhill Museum. Begin at the **High Desert Museum** (see "Sights"

under "Bend and Vicinity" in The High Cascades chapter), a 90-minute drive south of Warm Springs on US 97, 10 miles south of Bend. Exhibits here will give you an overview of the native peoples of the intermountain West and their land. Start with the "big picture" here, followed by the tribal exhibits at Warm Springs, then continue north on US 26 to ORE 35. Follow ORE 35 to I-84 in Hood River, head east on I-84 to The Dalles, and cross over the Columbia past The Dalles Dam via US 197. Once in Washington, take a right (north) on Highway 14. Keep an eye out for the Horsethief Lake State Park sign shortly and the petroglyphs on the rocks after you arrive on the Columbia's north shore. A little more than 20 miles up the road, near Goldendale, is the **Maryhill Museum,** Maryhill Museum Drive, tel. (509) 773-3733. It's pretty hard to miss this large French chateau-style building surrealistically planted on the sparsely vegetated bluff above the Columbia. The museum is open daily 9 a.m.-5 p.m., March 15-Nov. 15; adults pay $4 admission, seniors $3.50 and children 6-16 $1.50. Built by Sam Hill of Columbia Gorge Scenic Highway fame, the museum includes impressive Rodin plasters and chess sets spanning time and the globe, but the native baskets and clothing steal the show. The ground floor collection of native artifacts pays particular attention to the tribes along the Columbia, completing your perspective on the first residents of the Northwest.

It's best to take two or three days to complete this 170-mile museum circuit to do justice to the tribal legacy on display at all three museums.

you can see the age-old practice of dip-net fishing on the Deschutes, as well as the richest collection of tribal artifacts in the country at a 27,000-square-foot museum. Along with these touches of tradition, the reservation is the embodiment of the modern-day American dream, successfully operating a dam, a resort hotel, and a lumber mill. It's interesting to note that the employees of these enterprises are the descendants of the same Indians who greeted Lewis and Clark on the Columbia in 1805, as well as such Deschutes explorers as Peter Skene Ogden (in 1826), John Frémont, and Kit Carson (both in 1843).

Before heading to the Warm Springs Museum pull into the restaurant just off of US 26 on the west side of the highway. Here you can down some Indian tacos (fry bread) and a piece of wild huckleberry pie while picking up on the tribal gossip in the *Warm Springs* newspaper. Across the lot is a trading post selling craft items made by the confederated tribes. Both are a quarter mile south of the museum.

Richardson's Recreational Ranch
If you're a rockhound, you'll want to visit Richardson's Recreational Ranch, Gateway Route Box 440, Madras 97741, tel. (541) 475-2680. This family-owned and -operated enterprise has extensive rock beds loaded with thunder eggs, moss agates, jaspers, jasper-agate, Oregon sunset, and rainbow agates. If you want to chip agates out of one of the many exposed ledges on the ranch, you will need to brings chisels, wedges, and other necessary hard-rock mining tools. Once you've completed your dig, you drop your rocks off at the office and pay for them by the pound. And if you don't care for dirt under your fingernails, you can always find rocks for sale from all over the world in the ranch's rock shop.

The motto here is "fun for everyone," and you're sure to meet many interesting "rocky fellers" back at the ranch. To get there, take US 97 north of Madras for 11 miles and turn right at the sign near mile marker 81. Follow the road for three miles to the ranch office.

Rajneeshpuram
Throughout its history, north-central Oregon's topographic variety has been paralleled by the diversity of the human landscape here.

The name Madras evokes the mystic East. While this central Oregon town has no such ties, it would have been hard to tell anyone that in the early 1980s. Between 1981 and 1984 the population base of ranchers and farmers was augmented by thousands of red-clad disciples of Indian guru Bhagwan Shree Rajneesh. A 175,000-acre ranch was bought for the faithful near Antelope, a tiny community 30 miles northeast of Madras.

Although the commune demonstrated agricultural and architectural ingenuity, it was the Bhagwan's fleet of 96 Rolls Royces that got the headlines. When the Rajneeshees recruited homeless people to stuff the ballot box in local elections and then sent them away shortly thereafter, they compounded the bad first impression Oregonians had of their new neighbors. Before long, adverse publicity over the community's arsenal of combat weapons and their stated intent to use them alerted authorities to a potential threat. The Rajneeshees turned out to be more of a threat to themselves, with the Bhagwan's second-in-command implicated in everything from plots to murder the guru to the embezzlement of millions. Shortly before the dissolution of Rancho Rajneesh, the guru himself was deported because his vow of silence was inconsistent with a teaching visa. Today, the ranch is being converted into a Christian youth camp.

Shaniko
A half hour northeast of Madras is the ghost town of Shaniko. In its day, Shaniko was the largest wool-shipping center in the United States. The Columbia Southern railroad transported wool, sheep, cattle, gold, and people deep into the remote Oregon outback, and the city at the terminus prospered. Boomtown Shaniko had 13 saloons, stores, hotels, a schoolhouse, and a city hall. But when the railroad's main line was diverted to the Deschutes River, Shaniko's prominence quickly faded.

Today you can still see many old buildings in Shaniko. The water tower provides a remarkable display of the jerry-rigged but nonetheless efficient water-distribution system. The three-room Shaniko schoolhouse (built in 1901) and City Hall, featuring the Constable's office and the jail, are also still standing. If you'd like to overnight here, the moderately priced **Shaniko Historic Hotel**, Shaniko 97057, tel. (541) 489-3441, has been restored and combines the ambience of the past with modern comforts.

MOUNT HOOD

HIKING AND CAMPING

Mount Hood Climbs

Mt. Hood, at 11,235 feet the highest mountain in Oregon, has the additional distinction of being the second-most-climbed glacier-covered peak in the world. Nicknamed the "Fujiyama of America," there are hikes up Mt. Hood that cater to everyone, from beginners to advanced climbers. Another similarity to its Japanese counterpart is that there are only about two months out of the year that are safe for climbing, from May to mid-July. (Many mountaineers feel that the safe climbing season terminates at the end of July.)

Since the summer heat brings on the threat of avalanche danger and rockfall hazards, the time of day of your departure is just as important as the time of year. Most expeditions depart in the wee hours of the morning when the snow is firm and rockfall danger is lessened. Though you won't get as much sleep, you will be able to enjoy beautiful sunrise scenery as you venture to the top of the world—in Oregon, that is.

There are a few short and easy hikes from Timberline Lodge that require basic day-hiking equipment—hiking boots, water, snacks, sunglasses, sunscreen, and warm, waterproof clothing (since the weather can change rapidly, even in midsummer). Those intent upon reaching the top of the mountain, however, had best go prepared. In addition to the previously mentioned supplies, an ice axe, crampons and extra straps, extra clothing and food, first-aid kit, at least a quart of water, CB radio, topographic map and compass, and a 120-foot rope are necessary. Your boots should be waterproof and well insulated, because the final 3,000 feet in elevation is over glaciers and snowfields. Wool is the best material for keeping warm; wool socks (take an extra pair for emergency mittens), mittens, hat, sweater, and pants will keep you warm even when wet. A warm, water-resistant jacket is also a good idea. Remember that this peak breeds clouds and storms, although most accidents occur in warmer weather when the ice and snow are unstable. Summer snow conditions, the 50 degree slope of the final 2,000 feet, and the tiring effects of the climb have contributed to the deaths of at least 10 people over the years.

While the climb looks like only a few miles on the map, it takes 10-15 hours to make the trip

OREGON STATE HIGHWAYS

glacier-covered Mt. Hood, above Trillium Lake

from Timberline Lodge to the top and back. The four primary routes up Mt. Hood—Hogsback, Mazama, Wyeast, and Castle Crags—are all *technical* climbs; there is no hiking trail to the summit. Having the right equipment means little if you don't know how to use it. It takes at least three people to compose a safe party (many solo adventurers here have ended up decomposing), and you should have a competent, experienced leader. Always register at the lodge before climbing and check out when you return.

Most climbing deaths and injuries are avoidable. Dangers like falling ice, rock, and snow, gaping crevasses, and the temperamental mountain weather can all be surmounted with planning, preparedness, and common sense. The ultimate safety device became available several years ago. For $5 (for three days),

climbers can rent a one- by two-inch transmitter at several Portland-area mountain shops. It gives off a signal which will enable search and rescue teams to find you. Be one of the hundreds of thousands of happy hikers who have successfully reached the summit and back, not another unfortunate statistic claimed by Old Man Mountain. Before you go, be sure to register at Timberline's Wyeast Day Lodge for Oregon's most popular alpine challenge. For information on climbing guides (as well as Alpine and Nordic ski instructors), contact the **Mt. Hood Recreation Association,** 68260 E. Welches Rd., Welches 97067, tel. (541) 622-3017.

Know Your Routes

The most common route up Mt. Hood is from the south side, beginning at Timberline Lodge. Once

THAR SHE BLOWS!

In the past, Mt. Hood and Mt. St. Helens in Washington have shared many periods of volcanic activity. Although the 1980 eruption of Mt. St. Helens has given her more name recognition and public awareness than her Oregon counterpart, Mt. Hood is nonetheless a slumbering giant that occasionally snores loudly. Consider that six eruptions were recorded on Mt. Hood in the mid-1800s, with the last one in 1907. According to a carbon-dated four-to six-inch layer of ash found on the northeast and southeast flanks of the mountain, Lewis and Clark just missed the 1804 eruption. And with smoky emissions coming out of Mt. Hood fumaroles in the 1980s, scientists have placed sensitive seismic monitoring equipment to keep tabs on the volcano. In 1980, after the Mt. St. Helens eruption, a geologist pointed out that Mt. Hood usually errupts 20 years after Mt. St. Helens.

While Old Man Mountain still appears to be sleeping, the Portland Office of Emergency Management has drafted contingency plans for worst-case scenarios. Portland is located far enough away to be out of range of most volcanic debris, but its water source would be cut off. Portland relies upon the bountiful Bull Run watershed located on Mt. Hood, and ash and mudflows from a major eruption would have devastating effects upon the city's water supply. Giant mudflows into the Columbia River present another threat; they could precipitate downstream flooding.

The federal government has also gotten involved by developing complex evacuation plans for the foothill communities of Sandy and Hood River. The residents may be lucky enough to escape with their hides intact, but the lush fields and well-groomed orchards on the northeastern side of the mountain would very likely be blanketed with ash and debris and sound the death knell to the local way of life. The loss of this major agricultural resource would have statewide repercussions.

The timber industry would also be hard hit by a major eruption. In addition to thousands of square miles of stumpage destroyed by mud, ash, and lava flows, scientists suggest that there would be a high probability of forest fires as well. Like the fruit growers of the Hood River Valley, the region's loggers would be hard-pressed to eke out a living from the charred ground should the mountain ever blow.

The good news is that the aftereffects of a volcanic eruption are eventually softened with time. In the wake of the Mt. St. Helens blast, insects, vegetation, and wildlife returned to the area within a year or two. Farmers in eastern Washington who saw their crops destroyed in 1980 are now enjoying bumper yields due to the soil's increased fertility. Nonetheless, in an era of worldwide earthquakes and volcanic eruptions, many locals look to the mountain and wonder if it will soon be Mt. Hood's turn to roar.

you've driven to the 6,000-foot level, there's only about 5,000 feet of vertical gain to the summit. The south-face route takes climbers up the "Miracle Mile" from the lodge to the top of Palmer ski lift, passing Silcox Warming Hut along the way. As you near the peak, you can pick up the route known as Hogsback.

Hogsback

Of the four routes to the summit departing from Timberline Lodge, Hogsback is the most climbed. A good trip for beginners, the climb takes an average 10-12 hours roundtrip. The first mile ascends 1,000 feet and ends at the **Silcox Warming Hut.** Built in 1939, this rustic stone-and-timber shelter used to house the upper terminal of the original Magic Mile chair lift. This was the second chair lift built in the country, the first to use steel towers, and the nation's oldest operating chair lift until it was discontinued in 1962. Silcox is now a dorm-style lodging unit with all of the amenities. Call Timberline Sales, tel. (503) 231-5400 in Portland, (800) 547-1406 elsewhere, for more information.

The trail continues up Palmer Glacier and onto White River Glacier. You climb up the glacier between Crater Rock and the Steel Cliffs and soon reach the saddle above Crater Rock. From here you stay on the saddle and head for the chute that leads to the summit. **Mazama** is a variation on Hogsback, and is a good route for your second climb. You cross the saddle above Crater Rock and reach the summit going up the chute on the far left of the rock outcroppings.

Wyeast

An intermediate route for experienced climbers is Wyeast, which averages 12-14 hours roundtrip. About a half mile above Silcox Warming Hut, you would cross over White River Glacier and reach the saddle of the Steel Cliffs. From there you follow the saddle on up to the top. It doesn't go over as much snow, but the rocks on the ridge of the Steel Cliffs are dangerous and require expertise.

Castle Crags

Castle Crags offers an advanced route for experienced climbers. Because this trail goes over Illumination Rock and the Hot Rocks, climbers must go when the ice and rock are solid during

January through April. Adding to the dangers of bona fide rock-climbing is the everpresent threat of winter weather. Disorienting whiteout conditions, frigid cold, and wicked gale-force winds compound the hardships already imposed by the grueling trail. This 12- to 14-hour roundtrip should only be attempted by serious climbers when the weather conditions are right.

Buried Forest Overlook

If the snowbound summit is not for you, an easier one-mile roundtrip hike is the Buried Forest Overlook. This overlook provides a dramatic view of the White River Canyon, where a thick forest was buried during one of the mountain's major eruptive periods about 200-250 years ago. Superheated gases blew down giant trees like matchsticks, and in the next instant, all was buried underneath a mixture of water, ash, and mud. The erosional forces of wind and water have since exposed the remains of the Buried Forest. To get there, follow one of the trails behind Timberline Lodge up the mountain about a quarter mile until you reach the Pacific Crest National Scenic Trail. Turn east (right) onto the Pacific Crest Trail and follow it another quarter mile or so to the overlook. Hood's north face, steep and rock-strewn, is for more accomplished climbers.

Mt. Hood Hiking

Hikes in the **Zigzag Ranger District,** 70220 US 26E, Zigzag 97049, tel. (541) 666-0704, or tel. (503) 622-3191 from Portland, are an excellent introduction to the wealth of recreation options in the Mt. Hood National Forest off US 26. Whether you're driving the whole Mt. Hood Loop (US 26 to ORE 35 to I-84) or just looking for a nice day-trip from the Portland area, the Zigzag District's relatively low elevation and spectacular views of the state's highest mountain can be enjoyed by neophyte hikers or trail-wise veterans.

Coming from Portland, take I-84 to the Wood Village exit and follow the Mt. Hood Loop signs to US 26. After leaving Sandy, you'll notice fruit stands and the **Wasson Brothers Winery** tasting room, 41901 US 26, Sandy, tel. (541) 668-3124, which can help provision a picnic on the slopes. En route to the trailheads, US 26 is often lined with vehicles during winter ski weekends and summer vacation, with less traffic during the best hiking seasons, spring and fall.

The first stop you'll want to make is at the **Mt. Hood Visitor Center,** 65000 US 26E, Welches 97028, tel. (541) 648-4822, located in Mt. Hood RV park on the south side of the highway. This facility will help you get your bearings, with a wealth of pamphlets and an information desk. Pick up the free Forest Service flier *Mt. Hood Hikes* here or a few miles up the road at the Zigzag Ranger Station. Of the 15 trails outlined in the Zigzag District, we've chosen one hike as a maiden voyage into this magical realm. Our criteria include ease of hiking, proximity to Portland, and aesthetic appeal. Unfortunately, the latter qualities have also made the **Ramona Falls Trail** perhaps the most traveled wilderness byway on the mountain. With judicious planning, however, you can avoid peak-use times. To reach Ramona Falls drive 18 miles east of Sandy on US 26 to Lolo Pass Rd., close by the ranger station. This route (Route 18) heads north from the Zigzag store, eventually leading up to Lost Lake, whose views of Mt. Hood have graced many a postcard.

But instead of going all the way to the lake, you will want to go five miles up Lolo Pass Rd. to Forest Service Rd. 1825. From here, you'll take the road about four miles to its end. Once you've parked, all you need to do is follow the trail paralleling the Sandy River. In a little more than a mile you'll come to a bridge over the river with a pretty view of Mt. Hood. On the other side of the river, Trail 797 will get you to Ramona Falls in about two miles. The grade of the slope is gentle throughout, and while much of the trail isn't especially scenic (except for a bridge over the Sandy River, June rhododendrons, and views of Mt. Hood), Ramona Falls itself makes it all worthwhile. Imagine a multitude of cascades coursing over a 100-foot-high, 50-foot-wide series of basalt outcroppings. This weeping wall is set in a grove of gargantuan Douglas firs. The spray beneath this canopy of trees can drop the temperature 20° F, making the place a popular retreat on hot summer days. In the winter the trail makes a great cross-country ski run. In warmer times of the year, Ramona Falls is a popular equestrian trail.

Next, we'd like to recommend a hike to the McNeil Point Shelter. A map and consultation, both available at the Mt. Hood Information Center, is essential for this one, given some tricky trail nuances. With a trailhead not far from Ramona Falls, this will be a nice follow-up to your maiden voyage. To get there, follow the directions in the camping section to McNeil Point Campground, veering right on Forest Service Rd. 1828. Proceed 13 miles until you reach the Top Spur Trailhead #785. A half mile down the hiking trail, take a right on the Pacific Crest Trail and keep right 60 yards up the trail at a four-way intersection. In about 15 minutes or so gorgeous views of Mt. Hood and a spectacular June wildflower display will greet you. The remaining three miles contains some twists and turns that need cartographic clarification from the Forest Service. Your reward will be breathtaking above timberline views of the Mt. Hood National Forest. This excursion is four miles each way and tame enough for weekend warriors. Just start early enough to give yourself sufficient daylight. In addition to Zigzag-area jaunts, you could spend a year hiking all the trails described by the pamphlet in the several other ranger districts around the mountain.

More ambitious trekkers will take on the 36-mile Timberline Trail, a three- to five-day backpack usually begun at Timberline Lodge. If you undertake this loop, you'll finish up back at the lodge to cool off in the showers or swimming pool. While the alpine meadows on the Timberline Trail are beautiful, consult the rangers to see if water in the half-dozen creeks passed en route is too high during the June and July snowmelt seasons.

With almost two dozen trails branching off the Timberline, opportunities for shorter daytrip loop hikes abound. Most of the main trail follows the base of the mountain near timberline at elevations of 5,000 to 7,000 feet. On the northwest side, however, it drops to 3,000 feet and merges with the Pacific Crest Trail. This means that there's snow on the trail for most of the year. Make the trip in the fall to avoid the crowds; in July and August the mountain meadows are ablaze with wildflowers.

Backpackers must camp at least 200 feet from water and 100 feet from any trail, mountain meadow, or obvious viewpoint.

Camping

Set along the banks of the Salmon River is **Green Canyon,** Zigzag Ranger District, 70220

US 26E, Zigzag 97049, tel. (541) 622-3191 or (503) 666-0704 from Portland. This is the same contact for the next six campgrounds. Here you'll find 15 campsites for tents and RVs (31 feet maximum), with picnic tables and fire grills, piped water, pit toilets, and firewood available. Green Canyon is open from May to late September, and the fee is $12 per night, depending upon the site. Nearby a trail that goes through the old-growth forests lining the Salmon River and past several waterfalls. A store and a cafe are about five miles away. To get there, go to Zigzag on US 26 and take Salmon River Rd. (2618) four miles to the campground. Superlative hiking is close by. Trail #742 is accessible at a point two miles down Forest Service Rd. #2618 prior to reaching the campground, and again from the lower end of a gravel parking lot two miles past the campground. The trail leading off to the left at the end of the parking lot is a very easy hike accessing old growth fir and cedar. The Salmon River Gorge, with many waterfalls, volcanic plugs, and forested cliffs, is accessed by a trail several hundred feet above the river. In fall, enjoy red and gold maples; year-round, giant cedars and firs dominate.

Near the replica of the Barlow Road Tollgate is **Tollgate.** Set along the banks of the Zigzag River, this campground has 23 tent sites and nine RV sites (22 feet maximum) with picnic tables and fire grills. Water, pit toilets, and firewood are also available. Open from late May to late September, the campground costs $14 per night. While it's one of the more primitive campgrounds in the area, it's close to the Mt. Hood Wilderness and many hiking trails. Take US 26 one mile past Rhododendron to get there.

Situated on the Clear Fork of the Sandy River, **McNeil** has a good view of Mt. Hood. The campground has 34 sites for tents and RVs (22 feet maximum) with picnic tables and fire grills. Piped water, vault toilets, and firewood are also available. Open May to late September, McNeil charges $9 per night. To get there, turn onto Lolo Pass Rd. (County Route 18) at Zigzag and follow it for four miles. Turn right onto Forest Service Rd. 1825 and follow signs to the campground, about a mile farther. For a beautiful drive, go back to Lolo Pass Rd. and make a right, heading over the pass 25 miles to Dee. It takes about an hour if you drive straight there,

but allow another 15 minutes for photo stops from Lost Lake, located on a spur road. Lolo Pass Road's gravel surface sees a fair amount of log trucks during the week, so be careful. From Dee it takes 25 minutes to reach I-84 to loop back to Portland.

A popular place for a night out in the woods is **Camp Creek.** This campground has 30 sites for tents and RVs (22 feet maximum), with piped water, picnic tables, and fire grills. Flush toilets and firewood are also available. Open from late May to late September, Camp Creek charges $7 per night. Situated along Camp Creek not far from the Zigzag River, the campground has double campsites that two parties can share. To get there, go three miles east of Rhododendron on US 26 and turn south to the campground.

About a mile down the road from Timberline Lodge is **Alpine.** The high-elevation setting here lives up to its name, with snow remaining on the ground until late in the summer during heavy snow years. There are 16 campsites for tents and trailers (22 feet maximum), plus piped water, picnic tables, and fire grills. Alpine is open July to late September, and the fee is $9 per night. In addition to summer skiing up at Mt. Hood, the Pacific Crest Trail passes by very close to the camp.

Near the junction of US 26 and ORE 35 is **Still Creek.** Here you'll find 27 sites for tents and RVs (30 feet maximum), with picnic tables and fire grills. Piped water, pit toilets, and firewood are also available. Open from mid-June to late September, Still Creek costs $10 per night. The campground has many large trees and is close to the Old Swim Hot Springs Resort, a pioneer cemetery, and Trillium Lake.

A good place for a base camp for those who like to canoe is at **Trillium Lake.** At only 60 miles from Portland, the lake is a great place for city kids. If they're 13 years and under, they don't need a fishing license and may keep up to 10 fish per day. Crayfish also prowl the lake bottom awaiting capture. At night, a new amphitheater hosts campfire programs and nature talks. There are 30 sites for tents and RVs (30 feet maximum), with picnic tables and fire grills. Piped water and flush toilets were installed recently; boat docking and launching facilities are nearby, but no motorized craft are permitted on the lake. The campground is open from late May to late September and costs $9-18 per night, depending upon the site. To get there, take US 26 two miles southeast of Government Camp, then turn right onto Forest Service Rd. 2656. Proceed for one mile to the campground.

A spot that offers good fishing, swimming, and windsurfing is **Clear Lake,** Bear Springs Ranger District, Route 1, Box 222, Maupin 97037, tel. (541) 328-6211. Here you'll find 28 tent and RV sites (22 feet maximum) with picnic tables and fire grills. Piped water, vault toilets, and firewood are also available. Clear Lake is open late May to early September, and the fee is $7-11 per night. Boat docking and launching facilities are nearby, and motorized craft are allowed on the lake. To get there, go nine miles southwest of Government Camp on US 26, then one mile south on Forest Service Rd. 449 to the campground.

A midsized county park called **Toll Bridge,** 7360 Toll Bridge, Parkdale 97041, tel. (541) 352-6300, is located 18 miles south of Hood River on ORE 35. This campground has 18 tent and 20 RV (20 feet maximum) sites with electricity, piped water, sewer hookups, and picnic tables. Flush toilets, showers, firewood, a recreation hall, and a playground are also featured. Open April-Nov. (and weekends during the off-season, weather permitting), $13-20 per night. Set along the banks of the Hood River, this campground includes bike trails, hiking trails, and tennis courts.

Two campgrounds on ORE 35 are **Robin Hood** and **Sherwood,** 15 and 11 miles south of Parkdale respectively. Both are open from Memorial Day to Labor Day and include basic amenities. Fees for each are $9 per night. Both are located on the east ork of the Hood River and offer good hiking. Contact the Hood Ranger District, 6780 ORE 35 Parkdale 97401; in Portland tel. (541) 666-0701, for more information.

If you're taking the back road to Breitenbush, you can bed down in what *Sunset* magazine rated one of the top ten campgrounds in the west, **Twenty Lakes,** reservations tel. (800) 280-2267, information tel. (800) 622-3360. Although this version of the forest primeval doesn't have RV hookups, you'll find 1,270 sites with water, picnic tables, vault toilets, and fire rings. Leashed pets are permitted as are mountain bikes. We prefer Twenty Lakes to Trillium and Lost Lakes

because it can support more campsites, imparting a sense of seclusion. Of the five campgrounds here, **Hoodview** is the most scenic, $10-15. To get there, take US 26 about 39 miles past Sandy. Turn south onto Forest Service Rd. #42 and proceed for nine miles until you reach Forest Service Rd. #57. Go west on #57 for a couple of miles and you'll see signs for the campground.

Sightseeing

The **Philip Foster Farm and Homestead,** 29912 S.E. ORE 211, Estacada, is the end of the historic Barlow Rd, the place that greeted the emigrants after crossing Mt. Hood en route to the Willamette Valley. Just pick up ORE 211 off ORE 26 and head south for six miles to Eagle Creek. This working historical farm features a home, a barn, a blacksmith shop filled with period artifacts, and pioneer gardens of flowers, herbs, and vegetables. There is also an apple orchard containing varieties from the pioneer era. Visitors can have hands-on experience grinding corn, building log cabins, and partaking in other chores typical of the pioneers. The Pioneer Store features Northwest food and crafts as well as history-oriented items. Shady picnic tables make this site ideal for a family outing. Admission is free, but donations are appreciated. Hours are Fri.-Sun. 11-4 p.m. June-Aug.; Sat-Sun. through September.

PRACTICALITIES

Accommodations

Since Mt. Hood is only an hour away from Portland, most people return to the city instead of staying at one of the commercial properties on the loop. But if you do want to make a night of it on Mt. Hood, forgo the ersatz Swiss ski chalets; follow the signs from US 26 and step into history at **Timberline Lodge,** Timberline 97208, tel. (800) 547-1406 from outside Oregon, (541) 231-7979 in-state, 3.6 miles from the summit of Mt. Hood. This is Oregon's Hall of the Mountain King, whose alpine setting and WPA-commissioned interior decor make it a cherished landmark of the Northwest. Room rates ranging between $65 and $180 make it as affordable as a garden-variety ski condo, and numerous bargain ski packages also help lay out the welcome mat.

The Lodge's "chalet rooms" with bunk beds are $65 a night, with $20 charged for each additional guest, children 11 and under stay free. Minutes away from Timberline's 1,100-pound door is a ski lift, your magic carpet to the slopes and, during the summer, to an array of wildflowers and superlative views. Other Timberline claims to fame are pioneer and Indian motifs to match the mountain. Hand-forged wrought-iron light fixtures and handwoven draperies and upholstery complement the 92-foot-high fireplace and floor-to-ceiling windows in the lobby. The lodge also features some 820 pieces of handcrafted furniture and wood carvings. Outside, check out the 750-pound bronze weather vane on the roof, and the famous St. Bernard dogs that greet visitors at the door. You might recognize the building's exterior and one of Timberline's doors from the 1983 movie *The Shining.* During the off-peak ski seasons of spring and summer, enjoy the best views of Mt. Hood from lodge windows that in winter are usually blocked by snow. Finally, listen to FDR's dedication speech in the Exhibition Center on the main entry level and take in the scale model of Mt. Hood in the day lodge (push buttons to call up information).

The food in the award-winning **Cascade Dining Room** is outstanding, particularly the vine-maple-cured salmon. Such ingredients as the locally produced, internationally renowned fruit brandies from Clear Creek distillery, as well as Willamette Valley hazelnuts and wild mush-

HUNGER IN THE SHADOW OF MT. HOOD

Ralph Waldo Emerson once said, "the wilderness makes a wonderful mistress but a difficult wife." Despite extolling the primacy of nature in his writings, it seems the sage of Concord had distinctly urban sensibilities when it came to his palate. But then again, he never had the experience of quelling just-off-the-trail hunger pangs in the Mt. Hood National Forest.

The array of dining alternatives off ORE 26 between Sandy and Timberline Lodge belies the usual stereotype of gorp and camp-store rations found in this kind of environment. Zigzag, Welches, Government Camp, and other towns in the shadow of Mt. Hood profit enough from après-ski business to support everything from high price haute cuisine to casual pub grub. Between these extremes exists what many urban day-trippers are looking for—a restaurant serving distinctive, affordable cuisine in a warm, welcoming milieu.

The **Rendezvous Tap Room and Grill,** 67149 E. ORE 26, Welches, tel. (503) 622-6837, meets those criteria while boasting proximity to many popular trails. Despite a location abutting ORE 26, it's easy for eastbound travelers to miss it in the heavy tree cover on the north (left) side of the highway. Just remember—if you see the sign for the Hoodland Shopping Center, you've gone several miles too far. Chances are your first glimpse of the long tan-and-green building set behind antique wagons will come as you're heading west on ORE

26 after returning from a hike at one of the many trailheads located just east of the restaurant.

Once inside, the alpine motif and friendly hosts Tom and Susie Anderson set a mood appropriate to the surroundings. As for the menu, the chef imbues the ever-changing bill-of-fare with seasonal flourishes showcasing fresh regional produce and seafood. Whatever the season, expect to see such signature dishes as rigatoni topped with alder-smoked chicken, toasted hazelnuts, dried cranberries, and fresh spinach, all in a champagne cream sauce. And if you're just in for a burger, fries, and a microbrew, count on a good, honest meal with such optional dipping sauces as red-pepper pesto. The chanterelles might come from the surrounding forests, and the pasta and bread might come from Portland's Grand Central Bakery, but the desserts are straight from heaven.

There's enough variety here to suit most tastes and budgets. The reasonably priced wine list can change more than once a week, and reflects a connoisseur's eye. It's also a pleasure to read the capsule commentaries on each vintage. How fitting that a restaurant emphasizing Northwest cuisines should be located in the shadow of Mt. Hood, whose snow-capped symmetry has become a symbol of the state. And though our spirits may take flight while skiing the slopes and hiking the trails on Oregon's highest mountain, there's nothing quite so uplifting at day's end as a peak dining experience.

rooms from Mt. Hood National Forest, enhance many dishes here. Spirits can be purchased at the restaurant and in the Ram's Head and the Blue Ox bars. After a long day skiing the challenging slopes here, you'll relish a soak in the outdoor heated pool, especially enjoyable in the middle of a snowstorm or on cold, clear nights under a full moon.

Fernwood at Alder Creek, 54850 ORE 26 E., Sandy, 97055, tel. (503) 622-3570, is an early 1900s log home B&B on a magnificent rushing creek in the woods. Their two rooms have antiques, private baths, and whirlpool tubs. Terrific family-style breakfasts are included in the tariff, $70-80. The vintage editions of *Life* and *Reader's Digest* and a good library here can fill your respites between hiking on a deck close by a gurgling stream.

Food

It doesn't really matter what you've been up to on the mountain. Whether you've been skiing, hiking, climbing, or biking, the end result is usually the same by the time you get down the hill. You're hungry. The Mt. Hood corridor is blessed with several eateries that fit most any mood and pocketbook. From fast food on the fly to leisurely gourmet dining, it's all here on the loop between Sandy and Government Camp.

While it doesn't rate a mention in the dining category, the area produces one gourmet treat that's become world-famous by word-of-mouth. The 80-year-old **Zigzag Mountain Store,** 70171 E. ORE 26, Rhododendron, tel. (541) 622-3200, purveys naturally smoked, slightly hot, slightly sweet strips of prime cut beef jerky at $8/pound. This price didn't keep a massive order from being sent to Desert Storm troops. Nor does it deter scores of travelers en route or from the slopes or trailheads who've heard about it from friends. Since the jerky is not advertised, you'll have to ask for it at the counter.

The **Elusive Trout,** 39333 Proctor Blvd., Sandy, tel. (541) 668-7884, is a well-known gateway eatery on the Mt. Hood highway. Whether you're heading up to the mountain on US 26 (a.k.a. Proctor Blvd.) or returning from a day of skiing or hiking, the pub is a great place to stop. Homemade soup, Mexican entrees, and gourmet burgers complement one of

the best selections of microbrews in the state. Live music and revolving art displays by local artists also liven up this local hotspot. And while there's no shortage of food markets and down-home eateries in Sandy, it's hard to find high quality coffee. Those who take advantage of **The Kaffee Klatch,** 38871 Proctor Blvd., tel. (541) 668-3495, a converted gas station in the center of town, will leave with a spring in their step. Chances are they'll also leave the place with a book in hand from the Kaffee Klatch collection of regional travel books, fiction, and self-help titles. Mexican food and live blues (Wednesday and Thursday) somehow go well after a day on the slopes. **Armadillo Crossing,** 38781 Pioneer Blvd., Sandy, tel. (541) 668-6740, parlays this combination with down-home style.

One mile west of Zigzag on US 26 in Wemme is **The Inn Between,** tel. (541) 622-5400. Open for lunch and dinner, here you can tour the taps (a dozen draft beers are available) and enjoy a steak cooked just the way you like it (because you can supervise how it's cooked yourself). Tuesday night is when steak prices drop to $8 for the 12-ouncer and $7 for the smaller version. If you've got a beef against red meat, the Inn can prepare a feast to suit even the most discriminating of vegetarian palates. Seafood specialties, teriyaki chicken, and gourmet sandwiches are also among the many offerings. For lighter appetites, a variety of salads and delicious homemade soups are also available. On Monday nights, in addition to the football game on the big-screen TV, the Inn features 75 cent tacos that will fill you up in a hurry. If you're only here for the large selection of microbrews, try some barbecued ribs in the Inn's secret zesty sauce, or perhaps the "Macho Nachos" to keep your blood-alcohol level reasonable.

Follow US 26 to the west end of Government Camp and you'll find the **Mt. Hood Brewing Company,** tel. (541) 272-3724. Sandwiches, pasta, chili, and design-your-own pizza can be washed down by microbrews (try their own oatmeal stout), espresso drinks, and local wines. Also in town is the **Huckleberry Inn,** which deserves mention if only for its 24-hour, seven-days-a-week restaurant and, you guessed it, wild huckleberry pie. The inn's $15 per person dormitory rooms also provide welcome respite for rained-out campers on a budget.

The salads, seafood items, and meat dishes (especially the pepper bacon) at the Resort at the Mountains **Highland Restaurant**'s Sunday brunch alone would justify mention of this local favorite, 68010 E. Fairway Ave., Welches, tel. (541) 622-3101. Add reasonable prices and a lush setting in the foothills of Mt. Hood, and you have the ingredients for one of the state's best Sunday repasts. To get there, turn right off ORE 26 just west of the Hoodland Shopping Center and follow the signs.

pika

ANNIE LONG LARSEN

SOUTHEASTERN OREGON
LAKE COUNTY

One of Oregon's three largest counties, Lake County covers 8,340 square miles and yet has only 7,500 people—and about 120,000 head of cattle. In other words, there's lots of elbow room, with the population density working out to about one person per square mile. This land of open spaces and geologic marvels is home to a hardy breed that clings to the traditions of the Old West. Cowboys herd cattle on horseback, itinerant prospectors dig for color in the Quartz Mountains, and homesteaders tend to their farms in the remote outback. The county is called the Gem of Oregon because of the stark beauty of wide-ranging vistas beneath skies of pastel blue, and because the region is the best place to find Oregon's official gemstone, the Plush diamond, a type of spangled glass also called aventurine.

Visitors can climb the ancient citadel of Fort Rock, camp along a high mountain stream in Fremont National Forest, soak their bones in the soothing mineral waters of Hunter Hot Springs, or watch the graceful strides of antelope as they cross the uplands of Hart Mountain National Antelope Refuge. At 4,800 feet in elevation, Lakeview, the county hub, bills itself as the highest town in Oregon. Because of the varied vertical topography and wind drafts, hang gliding has become the local passion. In addition to enjoying outdoor activities year-round, the people of Lake County are an active bunch with a busy calendar of rodeos, fairs, and celebrations.

The climate here is generally cool and semi-arid with 250 days of sunshine a year. Summer temperatures stay in the mid-80s, while winter temperatures drop to the low 30s. Precipitation averages about 16 inches a year. At higher elevations in Lake County, there are as few as 20 frost-free days a year. This area can be a harsh land with little tolerance for the foolish, so take sensible precautions like toting extra water and gas. Despite a low density of creature comforts, you'll enjoy exploring this high desert country loaded to its sandy brim with wonders found nowhere else.

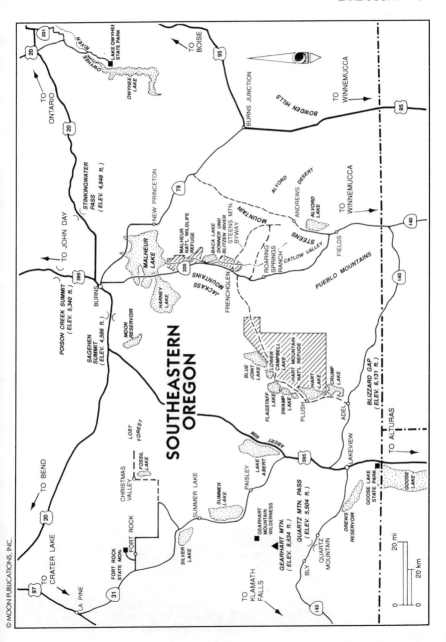

© MOON PUBLICATIONS, INC.

HISTORY

The history of human occupation here has been dated back 13,200 years through Dr. Luther Cressman's exploratory work at Fort Rock Cave. Early desert dwellers who roamed the Great Basin in search of game and food witnessed the eruption of Mt. Mazama 6,000 years ago. Their descendants, the Northern Paiutes, were also hunter-gatherers. This Lake County tribe was known as the "Groundhog Eaters." These indigenous peoples left more petroglyphs and pictographs in Lake County than in all the rest of Oregon and Washington.

The first Europeans to venture into the area were French Canadian trappers working for the Hudson's Bay Company in the early 1800s. Seeking out beaver pelts for the fashion trade back east and in Europe—the guard hairs of North America's largest rodent were used in the manufacture of felt hats, much coveted by the aristocracy of the time—these trappers were eventually joined by American mountain men. It wasn't until 1825 that Peter Skene Ogden, chief trader for the Hudson's Bay Company, made an "official" tour of the area when he sensed the threat of an American incursion. John Frémont and a party guided by Kit Carson marched through here in 1843, naming Summer and Abert lakes.

The journals kept during these expeditions noted broad valleys with grasses "belly-high to a horse." This information attracted a new cast of players to the Great Basin: the cattle and sheep barons. With the passage of the Homestead Act in 1862, homesteaders moved in and started up more modest spreads. The white influx resulted in frequent tensions with the original occupants, which often culminated in bloodletting on both sides. But after the Bannock-Paiute uprising in 1878, the local natives were herded up and banished to a reservation.

This predictable quick fix eased the trouble on the frontier and led to a growth spurt. The town of Lakeview was chartered in 1889; it burned to the ground the following year and was rebuilt with brick and corrugated-iron roofs. Other hopeful hamlets with names like Arrow, Buffalo, and Loma Vista sprang up around the county, thanks to a reactivated Federal Homestead Act in 1909 that sanctioned 320 free acres per settler. Many of these tiny burgs dried up and blew away after the two-year drought of 1918-20. However, the larger communities like Lakeview, Paisley, and Summer Lake held on. With the advent of refrigerated railroad cars, big ranchers prospered, selling beef to our "hamburger nation." Local farmers figured out how to irrigate and cultivate this ornery land, and those tough enough to survive eventually came to terms with life on the dry side. Nonetheless, because riparian rights are still being clarified, many underground water tables are being drained, raising the specter of another prolonged dry spell here.

SIGHTS: LA PINE TO LAKEVIEW

Getting the Big Picture

The Great Basin high desert occupies three very large, lonely counties: Lake (8,340 square miles), Harney (10,281 square miles), and Malheur (9,925 square miles) as well as a small

The 325-foot-high Fort Rock is visible from miles away.

OREGON DEPT. OF TRANSPORTATION

portion of Deschutes County. Equivalent in area to New England minus Maine, the entire high desert region shelters fewer than 45,000 people, most of whom live near Ontario or Vale near the Idaho border.

Lake County has some of the most intriguing geological formations in the Northwest. The following is a tour of a few of these marvels, starting at the junction of US 97 and ORE 31 at La Pine. Evidence of the cataclysmic forces that shaped the Columbia Plateau and the Great Basin are on display in this starkly beautiful part of the state. Ruptures in the ground and wave patterns left by ancient lakes on the flanks of mountains are some of the fingerprints left here by the hand of nature. Many sites described in the following itinerary are annotated in the BLM's *Christmas Valley* brochure, available from the BLM Lakeview office, 1000 E. 9th St., Lakeview 97630, and in a Forest Service brochure available from Fort Rock Ranger District, 1230 N.E. 3rd, Bend 97701. Better yet, refer to pages 101-05 of *Back Country Byways* by Stewart Green (Falcon Press, 1991) for a complete description of the remote routes to these phenomena. A high-clearance vehicle is indispensable in this region if you value your oil pan. At La Pine on US 97, stock up on provisions for your travels into the Great Basin. This town of 13,000 is the second largest in the region. However, the supply for shunpikers is Christmas Valley, a complex of alfalfa farms, a kitty litter factory, and mobile homes spread out over the sagebrush. With several restaurants, two filling stations, two food markets, cut-rate motels, and a golf course near a human-made lake, Christmas Valley makes a good base of operations close by the phenomena described below.

Cracks and Caves

Twenty-six miles down ORE 31 is **Hole-in-the-Ground,** a curiosity located a mile off the highway. Although this 500-foot-deep indentation looks like a meteor crater, scientists believe that molten lava came into contact with water here, causing a massive explosion that quarried out the quarter-acre pit. Astronauts came here in 1966 to experience the lunarlike terrain. About five miles farther down the road is **Fort Rock Cave.** Sandals woven from sagebrush and dated at over 9,000 years old were found here

in 1938 by anthropologist Luther Cressman. These are the oldest human artifacts found in the Northwest.

Not far from the cave is **Fort Rock,** which towers 325 feet above the sagebrush plains. At the base of this tuff ring is an area of wave erosion cut by a long-disappeared lake. Fall and winter here offer wildlife viewing par excellence; large herds of mule deer can be seen mid-November to mid-April, and pronghorn range over the alfalfa fields year-round. Many birds nest in the rocks, and golden eagles, hawks, kestrels, and peregrine falcons soar overhead. **Fort Rock State Park** offers trails and amenities for climbers and sightseers. The nearby town of Fort Rock has an old-time flavor that has been accentuated by the recent restoration of homestead cabins in a pioneer village managed by the **Fort Rock Valley Historical Society,** tel. (541) 576-2327.

An interesting journey down into the bowels of the earth is offered at **Derrick Cave,** located 22 miles north of Fort Rock. This large lava tube is a half-mile long, with rooms up to 40 feet wide and 60 feet high. During the Cuban missile crisis of 1962, the cave was turned into a fallout shelter. Metal doors were installed and provisions for 1,000 people were stockpiled. The supplies were later plundered by vandals and the cave's civil-defense status was eventually dropped.

If you drive six miles north of Christmas Valley on a rough BLM road, you'll come to another break in terra firma that'll keep your imagination working overtime. **Crack-in-the-Ground** is about two miles long, 10-15 feet wide, and up to 70 feet deep. On hot days here, it's nice and cool within this chasm. In fact, the crack is so deep that sometimes cold winter air gets trapped within and ice is preserved into summer. According to geologists, this dramatic fissure has been open for at least 1,000 years; the opening was once larger but lava from nearby volcanoes filled it in to its present dimensions. A BLM picnic area is at one end of this curious landmark.

Five miles northwest of Crack-in-the-Ground (on rough BLM Road 6109C) is Green Mountain Campground and fire lookout, which sits high above the previously mentioned Derrick Cave site. This primitive campground (large enough for three cars but without water or toilets) sits atop a small cinder cone overlooking hundreds of square miles of high desert, lava beds, and forest from 5,190 feet above sea level. In addition to Christmas Valley and Fort Rock Valley, you'll see snowcapped Diamond Peak 70 miles to the west and Wagontire Mountain 50 miles east.

Fossil Lake

Fossil Lake is two miles east of Christmas Valley. During wetter times thousands of years ago, this was a watering hole for camels, several-hundred-pound beavers, flamingos, mammoths, and miniature horses. It was once part of a much larger body of water in the Fort Rock basin that was perhaps 40 miles wide and 200 feet deep. The water and animals disappeared when the climate changed, but their fossilized remains are still unearthed by paleontologists on sanctioned digs. Be aware that it is illegal to remove *any* fossils from the beds without proper authorization. Unfortunately, unscrupulous profiteers have been looting these timeless treasures from the lake and other fossil-rich sites in eastern Oregon. Be sure to notify the authorities immediately if you see any suspicious characters pilfering these valuable relics.

Lost Forest

An unusual sight in this area is located 10 miles northeast of Christmas Valley on a rough but passable BLM road. A 9,000-acre stand of ponderosa pines intermixed with the largest juniper trees in Oregon is all that is left of an ancient grove that dates back thousands of years. Surprisingly, studies of tree rings show that this area has received only nine inches of rain a year for the last 600 years, half the amount normally needed to sustain growth of ponderosa pines. But here, a layer of pumicelike soil beneath the surface traps and retains enough moisture to allow the trees to draw water up through shorter-than-usual root systems. This island of green is 40 miles away from the nearest forest, accentuating the isolation and solitude of these stately sentinels. Many of the junipers here are over a thousand years old. On hot summer days, this place is a welcome source of shade. Any time of year, the sound of the desert wind through the trees can stir contemplation. The final three-mile stretch of the approach to Lost Forest requires high vehicle clearance. To reach the area, drive eight miles east of the Christmas Valley post office, go eight miles

north, and then eight miles east. The forest borders the largest inland sand dunes in the state.

Summer Lake

Summer Lake lies 15 miles beyond Silver Lake. En route to Summer Lake on ORE 31, pull into **Picture Rock Turnout.** Take the trail 80 feet to the southeast. Behind the tallest rock is a pictograph. In the town of Summer Lake, the old **Harris School** is worth a picture. This classic one-room schoolhouse, complete with bell tower, is straight out of *Little House on the Prairie.* The highway also passes through the **Summer Lake Wildlife Area,** home to 170 species of migratory birds. Spring is the best time to see snow geese, avocets, black-necked stilts, and snowy plovers. An eight-mile wildlife-viewing trail around the lake is a recommended diversion at mile marker 70. Pick up a bird checklist from Oregon Fish and Wildlife. Summer Lake Hot Springs, on the southern tip of Summer Lake, is a private operation open seven days a week 9 a.m.-9 p.m. during summer, and Sat.-Thurs. 9 a.m.-6 p.m. the rest of the year. A dip in the concrete pool costs $2 for people six and over, free to children under six.

The region surrounding Summer Lake sits at the interface of desert and mixed conifer forest. Abundant wildlife, geological wonders, Indian sites, and historic structures beckon further investigation. The 20-mile-long and 10-mile-wide lake is surrounded by the mountains of the Fremont National Forest and Winter Ridge. A good base for explorations is **The Inn of the Rising Sun,** 31501 ORE 31 Summer Lake, 97640, tel. (541) 943-3983 or (800) 262-2778. (Previously Summer Lake B&B Ranch.) Situated along the shore of the lake, this reconstructed pioneer homestead is paneled with a variety of wood, including redwood, cedar, oak, pine, fir, and myrtlewood. The feeling of warmth is enhanced by Darrell Seven, the innkeeper, whose flair for interior decorating, gourmet cooking, and sharing of local anecdotes compels a stay here as much as the beautiful outdoor environment does. The latter can be enjoyed from your bed, where views of the lake and the surrounding 8,000-foot mountains will stimulate dreams of your next day's activities. Amenities include a sauna, hot tub, and activities such as arrowhead hunting, world-class birdwatching, cross-country skiing, flyfishing, rock hounding, and candlelight dining, all of which add to the charm of the place. The Inn of the Rising Sun is 110 miles from Bend and 65 miles north of Lakeview. Rates are $50-85 a night. The more expensive rates are for self-contained cabins with jacuzzis and skylights. Daily all-you-can-eat breakfasts for $6 and dinners (Wed.-Sat., $12-16) reflect the same attention to detail as the other creature comforts here.

Paisley

A few miles south of the lake is the cowtown of Paisley. At the **Paisley Ranger Compound** there are several structures built by the Civilian Conservation Corps during the Depression. Check out the pine dugout canoe carved by CCC workers for Forest Service personnel. Trout fishing on the Chewaucan River and deer hunting also draw folks here. Perhaps Paisley's major claim to fame is the ZX Ranch, which at over 1.3 million acres is the nation's largest. The ranch property is 137 miles long and 64 miles wide.

If you're getting a little hungry, there are a couple of eateries in Paisley that will satisfy your cravings. The **Homestead Restaurant,** tel. (541) 943-3187, is the full-service establishment in the locale, serving breakfast, lunch, and dinner. The soup du jour complemented with a sandwich makes a good lunch, and be sure to save room for the homemade cobbler. The local watering hole, **Pioneer Saloon,** tel. (541) 943-3289, doubles as a family eating place. Pizza, steaks, and Mexican food are among the offerings on the menu here. If you need to stay over, the **Miles Motel,** tel. (541) 943-3148, has clean rooms at low prices.

Lakeview

The "big city" of the county (population 1,800, elevation 1,800) is Lakeview, where some interesting repositories of history can be found. The **Schminck Memorial Museum,** 128 S.E. Lakeview, tel. (541) 947-3134, has over 5,000 antiques assembled by the Oregon chapter of the Daughters of the American Revolution. It's open Tues.-Sat. 1-5 p.m. or by appointment. **Indian Village,** 508 N. 1st, tel. (541) 947-2833, boasts one of the West's largest arrowhead collections. The complex also has a restaurant and lounge that features eye-opening specials like scram-

bled eggs with diced mushrooms, toast, and coffee for several dollars. The gift shop offers turquoise and silver jewelry and, oddly enough, is where many working people buy their flannel shirts and cowboy hats. If you're in the mood for something different, cruise 15 miles south of Lakeview on US 395 to **Stringer's.** In addition to fine gifts, they claim to produce the world's only wild-plum wine and wild-plum jam. Look for hang gliders coming off 2,000-foot Black Cap Hill above the east side of Lakeview from May through October.

Abert Rim

Fifteen miles north of Lakeview on US 395 is the Abert Rim, the highest fault escarpment in the United States. The rim rises 2,000 feet above Lake Abert. This unusual body of water has no outlet and is rich in brine shrimp, which attract countless waterfowl and shorebirds. As at Summer Lake, fall is an especially good birdwatching season here. Expect thousands of plovers and other shorebirds. Due to its high alkalinity, it is hazardous to swim in the lake. Below Abert Rim along the east shore of Lake Abert, the slope is covered with boulders, some of which hold petroglyphs. Several are located right off the highway near the geological marker. Forest Service roads lead through the North Warner Mountains to BLM trails up the back side of Abert Rim; obtain routing information on these obscure byways from the Lakeview Ranger Station (see "Information and Services," following). While reaching the rim requires an arduous journey down bumpy back roads and a steep hike up the mountain, the view from the top is spectacular. Just watch for rattlesnakes in the rocks.

Gearhart Mountain Wilderness Area

About 40 miles west of Lakeview off of ORE 140 is the 22,000-acre roadless Gearhart Mountain Wilderness Area. Accessible only on foot or horseback, two major trails take adventurers into a challenging outdoor environment. **Gearhart Trail** (#100) incorporates 12 of the area's 16 miles of improved trails. This trail runs from **Lookout Rock** in the southeast corner of the wilderness, up over the mountain, down to **Blue Lake,** and to a trailhead on North Creek. The **Boulder Springs Trail** (#100A) runs from the west side of the wilderness to a junction with the other trail a half mile from the mountain summit. For maps and more information, contact the U.S. Forest Service ranger stations in Lakeview, Paisley, or Silver Lake (see "Information and Services," following).

While you're in the neighborhood, you might want to visit the **Mitchell Monument,** on ORE 140 between the wilderness area and Bly, which commemorates a tragedy that occurred on May 5, 1945. Reverend Archie Mitchell and his wife were escorting five children on a picnic near Corral Creek when one of the kids discovered a bomb dropped by a balloon from a Japanese plane. Unfortunately, the child triggered the bomb, and all but the good reverend were killed. This is the only recorded incident of World War II fatalities in the 48 contiguous states. Balloon bombs came down all over the western states, but only Oregon recorded civilian deaths due to their detonation.

Hart Mountain National Antelope Refuge

At the far eastern end of the county is a wildlife refuge that stretches across a high plateau rising above Warner Lakes. To get there from Adel, the first town east of Lakeview on ORE 140, go northeast 29 miles to Plush and take the road to the refuge headquarters. The ranger station, tel. (541) 947-3311, has information and a display describing this 275,000-acre sanctuary for pronghorn. In summer, hundreds of these agile tan-and-white animals occasionally gather at sunset along the dirt road south of the refuge. The refuge is also home to bighorn sheep, mule deer, 213 species of birds, and many small mammals. A dunk in the hot springs a short distance from the station is highly recommended to take out the stiffness from bouncing down the dirt roads to get there. A campground is near the hot springs. The refuge is also a popular place for rockhounds searching for agates, fire opals, crystals, and sunstones. Check with the Lake-

view Visitors Association or the ranger at Hart Mountain for more information.

Despite the name of the preserve, you won't find any antelope here. In fact, there are no wild antelope in North America—only pronghorn. Because these animals shed the outer sheaths of their horns each year, they differ from their Asian and African counterparts, which have permanent horns. Male pronghorn have prongs, protrusions extending from their sheaths, to further distinguish them from antelope. The lingering misnomer was bestowed on these Oregon animals by Lewis and Clark. At any rate, many scientists believe that pronghorn could be the world's fastest land mammals over a long distance, barely edging out the cheetah on distances exceeding 1,000 yards. It's said they can cruise at more than 35 miles per hour, maintain 60 mph for half a mile, and reach 70 mph in short bursts.

SPORTS AND RECREATION

In Town

The **Lakeridge Country Club,** ORE 140, tel. (541) 947-3855, has a nine-hole golf course with a pro shop, a putting green, lessons, and cart rentals. **Christmas Valley Golf Course,** Christmas Valley, tel. (541) 576-2333, is another nine-holer next to a 130-acre artificial lake. It's served by a pro shop in the nearby Christmas Valley Lodge. The restaurant is the only full-service dining room in these parts. Even if you're not a golfer, visit the lake at sunset to hear frogs croaking loud enough to be mistaken for a plane taking off at an airport runway.

On Friday, Saturday, and Sunday, the **Alger Theatre,** 22 F St., Lakeview, tel. (541) 947-2023, shows feature films for $5 adults, discounts for kids and seniors.

Fishing

With a name like Lake County, you'd be right in thinking that the fishing holes are plentiful here. Known for excellent trout fishing in the mountain-

KAREN McKINLEY

ous areas, the region is also gaining a reputation for bass, crappie, catfish, and other warm-water fishing. **Crump, Flagstaff, Anderson,** and **Campbell lakes** in eastern Lake County provide the hottest action for crappie.

Friday Reservoir, located between Adel and Plush, is stocked with Lahontan cutthroat trout, and **Rock Creek,** which flows out of the Hart Mountain National Antelope Refuge, has red-banded trout. Off US 395 in western Lake County, **Goose Lake,** half in California, half in Oregon, is also home to the native red-banded trout, but it's hard to fish for this unique subspecies in the shallow water. **Drews Reservoir,** 25 miles west of Lakeview on ORE 140, offers excellent fishing for channel catfish—some as large as 10 pounds. In the northern section of the county, **Thompson Valley Reservoir,** reached by driving south from Silver Lake on County Road 4-12, has yielded large rainbows. The **Chewaucan River,** which flows into Abert Lake, is heavily stocked with trout.

Skiing

Winter sports play a major role in Lake County's recreational schedule. **Warner Canyon Ski Area,** seven miles east of Lakeview on ORE 140, can accommodate almost any level of Alpine or Nordic skier, with 14 runs and three miles of cross-country trails. Thanks to a mile-high base elevation and the dry southeastern Oregon climate, excellent dry powder conditions are common. The area has a day lodge near the base of the hill with a snack bar that serves breakfast and lunch. The season may start as early as mid-December and run through the end of March. During this time the hill is open Thurs.-Fri. 1-4 p.m., Sat.-Sun. 10 a.m.-4 p.m.

Rockhounding

Rockhounding is a popular hobby in Lake County. Best known for its abundance of sunstones (also known as aventurine or Plush di-

amonds), the area also has jasper, agates, petrified wood, fire opal, wonder stones, thunder eggs, and obsidian. To get to the sunstone-hunting grounds, go east on ORE 140 to the Plush junction and turn north. At the first junction take Valley Falls Rd. and follow the signs. Another spot for rockhounding can be reached by taking Hogback Rd. just north of the upper section of the Abert Rim; the Hogback junction is about 50 miles north of Lakeview on US 395. For more information visit the **High Desert Rock Shop,** 244 N. M St., Lakeview.

PRACTICALITIES

Campgrounds

Junipers Reservoir RV Resort, tel. (541) 947-2050, is 10 miles west of Lakeview on ORE 140. This private reservoir with campgrounds is situated on a working cattle ranch that's open April 15-Oct. 31, depending on the weather. Designated as one of six private wildlife-viewing

LAKE COUNTY ACCOMMODATIONS

AA Motel, 411 N. F St., Lakeview, tel. (541) 947-2201, $40-50, modern, air-conditioned units.

Best Western Skyline Motor Lodge, Skyline 414 N. G St., Lakeview, tel. (541) 947-2194, $60-70, covered pool, air-conditioning, laundry, nonsmoking rooms, complimentary continental breakfast.

Desert Inn, Christmas Valley, tel. (541) 576-2262, $40-50, kitchenettes with refrigerators, arrowhead collection.

Hunter's Hot Spring Resort, US 395, Lakeview, tel. (541) 947-2125, $50-90, pool, kitchenettes, restaurant/lounge, live entertainment.

Interstate 8 Motel, 354 N. K St., Lakeview, tel. (541) 947-3341, $40-65, pets, kitchenettes, restaurant, laundry, complimentary continental breakfast.

Lakeside Terrace Motel and Restaurant, Christmas Valley, tel. (541) 576-2309, $40-50.

Lakeview Lodge Motel, 301 N. G St., Lakeview, tel. (541) 947-2181, $40-65, pets, kitchenettes, air-conditioning, nonsmoking rooms.

Rim Rock Motel, US 395, Lakeview, tel. (541) 947-2185, $30-40, pets, air-conditioning, complimentary continental breakfast.

areas in the state, a visit to this spread offers an excellent chance to view longhorn cattle, deer, eagles, ospreys, and coyotes.

Goose Lake Campground is a large facility 15 miles south of Lakeview on US 395. The campground has tent sites, RV hookups, and a boat launch on the shore of the huge lake. **Corral Creek Campground** is a good headquarters for an exploration of the Gearhart Mountain Wilderness, an area of high meadows, cliffs, and worn-down volcanoes. To get to the campsite turn off ORE 140 at Quartz Mountain, 24 miles west of Lakeview, and drive north on Forest Service Rd. 3600. **Wildlife Refuge Campground** is on the Ana River just north of Summer Lake on ORE 31. Birdwatchers like to camp here and walk the dikes of Summer Lake looking for waterfowl and swamp mammals.

Food

Like most parts of the sagebrush side of Oregon, Lake County isn't known for its nouvelle cuisine. Be prepared for basic American food with an emphasis on hearty, home-cooked meals. Here's a list of eateries that won't enchant your palate, but will refuel your tank.

The **Duck Inn** at Hunter's Hot Springs Resort offers steaks, fish, and Italian food (dinner entrees $8-15). Many locals consider the best place in the county to be **Plush West,** 9 N. F St., Lakeview, tel. (541) 947-2353, for steak, lamb, and seafood, $10-18. It's open for dinner only, from 5:30 p.m. In a town known for hang gliding, it shouldn't be surprising to find a restaurant called **The Landing,** right on US 395 in Lakeview. What *is* surprising are the submarine sandwiches on homemade bread, $4-7, that rank with the best in the state. **Eagles Nest,** 117 N. E St., tel. (541) 947-4824, serves a varied menu in a warm welcoming atmosphere. The prime rib here is testimony to the quality of Oregon beef. **Safeway** in Lakeview is also open 24 hours and is a good place to stock up on groceries prior to heading out into the boondocks.

Entertainment and Events

The **Christmas Valley Rodeo** runs the last weekend in May. Local cowboys and cowgirls compete in bareback riding, roping, and races. The following weekend is the **Silver Lake Rodeo** with more of the same. During the last weekend in June, the **Lake County Junior Rodeo** is held at the Lake County Fairgrounds in Lakeview. Finally, the fall **Lake County Round-Up** and fair held Labor Day weekend at the county fairgrounds includes a carnival, several parades, a barbecue, a buckaroo breakfast, and the annual rodeo.

Many of the earliest pioneers in Lake County were Irish immigrants who worked as sheepherders, some of whom turned to cattle ranching. To celebrate St. Patrick's Day, Lakeview merchants hold **Irish Days,** with a parade led by the Grand Leprechaun, usually the town's oldest Irishman. Other popular events are the potato stick races and the cow-chip fling. The community of Paisley prides itself on having some the largest mosquitoes in the state. To raise funds for controlling these pests, the town stages the **Mosquito Festival** in late July. The action includes a parade, a raft race, a turkey shoot, spitting, lying, cussing, and hollering contests, and the crowning of Ms. Quito. You'll also enjoy the relief provided by Paisley's oasis of greenery in the midst of the surrounding sagebrush desert. The U.S. Hang-gliding National Championships were held in Lakeview in 1993. Lakeview's hang-gliding festival takes place in July each year with several hundred recreational pilots, barbecues, swimming, fireworks, and biking and running races. This is the area's biggest event.

Around Christmastime people flock to Christmas Valley's little blue post office to request a timely postal cancellation (done by hand with large franking symbols). Collectors send a letter addressed to themselves with a request for a December 24 or 25 cancellation. Such noel niceties can be obtained by addressing an envelope to Christmas Valley 97641 and enclosing instructions.

In case you're interested, this nondescript alfalfa-farming town got its picturesque name by accident. Southeast of here, John C. Frémont spent Christmas at a lake during one of his mid-19th-century treks and called it Christmas Lake. A turn-of-the-century mapmaker mistakenly affixed this name to a lake adjacent to the present-day town site, which also took on the merry moniker.

Getting There and Around

Buses depart twice a day from the **Red Ball Stage Lines Depot,** 619 Center St., Lakeview, tel. (541) 947-2255, for Klamath Falls and other connecting points. The depot is open 9-11 a.m. for the 9:15 departure (10 a.m. on Saturday), and 4:15-5:15 p.m. for the 5:05 departure. Public **airports** are located in Lakeview, Paisley, Christmas Valley, and Alkali Lake, with private and government strips at Silver Lake, Fort Rock, Adel, and Wagontire. There are no regular commercial flights, but **Goose Lake Aviation,** tel. (541) 947-4222, provides air-taxi service and an air ambulance at the Lakeview landing field.

Information and Services

The **Lake District Hospital and Nursing Facility,** 700 S. J St., Lakeview, tel. (541) 947-2114, has 24-hour emergency services. The **Lake County Chamber of Commerce,** tel. (541) 947-6040, is located at the Lake County Courthouse. The **Lakeview Ranger Station,** US 395N, Lakeview 97630, tel. (541) 947-3334, has information on the nearby wildernesses. The **post office,** 18 S. G St., Lakeview 97630, tel. (541) 947-2280, is open 9 a.m.-5 p.m. The Lakeview **police,** 525 N. 1st St., tel. (541) 947-2029, are here if you have any trouble. **Fire and ambulance** service is available by calling (541) 947-2345. Public radio 91.7 FM serves Burns, Silver Lake, and the rest of the Great Basin, giving a media presence to what are, for the most part, dead air waves.

Finally, should you ever need to call on someone here, be aware that the code of the frontier is fully operative. People gladly help each other out and expect nothing in return. Although the small population in a harsh land is extremely close-knit, people passing through need not ever fear being shunned as outsiders.

BURNS AND VICINITY

Harney County occupies 10,185 square miles of sagebrush, rimrock, and grassy plains that are shared by only 7,100 inhabitants. With an average elevation of 4,000 feet above sea level, this northern edge of the Great Basin has a short growing season, a yearly snowfall of 36 inches, and clear skies at least 250 days per year. The main industries are logging, milling, and cattle ranching, with farming limited to hardy grains and hay. An index of the sparse population density here is the fact that Harney County has one of the few public boarding schools in the United States. Students reside in dorms on campus because most come from ranches located many miles from town.

For travelers, the towns of Burns, Hines, and a few wide spots along US 20 hold few points of interest—just places to refuel your rig and yourself. But off the main thoroughfares traversing the southeastern portion of the state are recreational retreats worthy of closer investigation. The Malheur Wildlife Refuge is nationally recognized as one of the best birdwatching sites in the country; the Steens Mountain Recreation Area is also famous for its stunning scenery; and the Ochoco and Malheur national forests are renowned for their fishing, boating, camping, backpacking, and hiking opportunities.

HISTORY

Oregon's high desert county was first inhabited by Bannock, Northern Paiute, and Shoshone Indians. When French-Canadian trappers arrived in the area, they were promptly ripped off by the natives. After losing horses and supplies, the trappers named the nearby river "Malheur" ("Unhappiness," or "Misfortune"). The surrounding region's alkali flats and parched hills also suggest this moniker.

Explorer Peter Skene Ogden scouted the area in 1826 while leading a fur brigade for the Hudson's Bay Company. He wasn't impressed with the region as a place for settlers, but the Idaho gold rush of 1860 brought prospectors through the area on their way to the gold fields, and they told stories of rich grasslands, plentiful water, and broad forests.

Pony soldiers under the command of Gen. William Harney explored the region in 1848 and again in 1858, opening up southeastern Oregon to settlement. The most noted military adventure was the construction of a wagon road built between Harney County and Eugene. The leader of this work party, Enoch Steen, gave his name to Steens Mountain.

Steens Mountain, rising abruptly above Mann Lake

OREGON STATE HIGHWAYS

In 1878, 2,000 Bannocks, fed up with their loss of territory and poor treatment, took to the warpath. Troops from forts all over the West were sent to fight the natives in a war that dragged on until 1880.

The town of **Burns,** named after the Scottish poet Robert Burns, was founded on January 22, 1884. By 1889 it had a population of 250, which has since grown to over 3,000. A significant boost to the town's economy came in 1924 when a rail line reached Burns. Its sister city, **Hines,** was incorporated in 1930. Named after Chicago lumberman Edward Hines, this town of 1,400 residents is primarily a bedroom community for Burns.

SIGHTS

Sagehen Hill Nature Trail

The Sagehen Hill Nature Trail is 16 miles west of Burns at the Sagehen Rest Stop on US 20. This half-mile nature trail has 11 stations on a route that takes you around Sagehen Hill through sagebrush, bitterbrush, and western juniper. Other plants found along the way include lupine, larkspur, owl clover, and yellowbell. The lucky visitor in early May might also catch the sage grouse courtship ritual. The male will display his plumage and make clucking noises to attract the attention of the females. The puffed-upped necks and bobbing heads of these feathered philanderers are something to see. If these feathered friends are not visible, the views of Steens Mountain (elevation 9,733 feet) to the southeast can make the hike worthwhile.

Harney County Museum

The Harney County Museum, 18 W. D St., Burns 97720, tel. (541) 573-2636, started its career as a brewery and then became a laundry and a wrecking yard. Local pioneer families have donated quilts, furniture, a complete kitchen, a wagon shed, and machinery to the museum. Of special interest are artifacts from Pete French's ranch. The museum is open June-Sept., Tues.-Fri. 9 a.m.-5 p.m., Saturday 9 a.m.-noon. Admission is $1.50 adults, $2 for a family, and 50 cents for children.

Diamond Craters

Diamond Craters have been described by scientists as the most diverse basaltic volcanic features in the United States. To tour these unique formations, drive 55 miles south of Burns on ORE 205 until you reach the Diamond junction. Turn left and begin a 40-mile route ending at New Princeton on ORE 78. On the way you'll see why this area is called "Oregon's Geologic Gem." There are craters, domes, lava flows, and pits that give an outstanding visual lesson on volcanism. To aid your self-guided tour, pick up the *Diamond Craters* brochure at the BLM office in Hines.

Round Barn

While on the road to New Princeton, stop at the Round Barn, a historic structure built by rancher Pete French to break his saddle horses. Located 20 miles northeast of Diamond, the barn is 100 feet in diameter with a 60-foot circular lava-rock corral inside. Twelve tall juniper poles support a roof covered with 50,000 shingles. Hundreds of cowpokes have carved their initials in the posts of this famous corral.

Malheur National Wildlife Refuge

Malheur and Harney lakes, fed by the mountain snow runoff filling the Blitzen and Silvies rivers, have been major avian nesting and migration stopovers since prehistoric times. The contrast between the stark, dry basin land, with its red sandstone monoliths and mesas, and the lush green marshes is startling. These vast marshes (the longest freshwater marsh in the western U.S.), meadows, and riparian areas surrounded by the eastern Oregon desert attract thousands of birds and hundreds of birdwatchers. The refuge is dominated by three fluctuating lakes—Malheur, Mud, and Harney. These are nourished by a scant eight inches of rain a year.

Refuge officials say that 250 species have been counted within its boundaries. Prime birdwatching times are spring and fall. In the spring, the flocks come from the Great Basin south of

---

THE CATTLE KINGS OF EASTERN OREGON

Cattle barons, those early-day entrepreneurs who ran the huge livestock operations of the 19th century, have typically been portrayed as imperious characters in old Western movies. More recently, the crusty but benign Ben Cartwright of television's "Bonanza," has added to our image of these men as two-fisted hardheads who brooked little interference in their affairs. Indians, sheepherders, and homesteaders beware! A quick look at the lives of three eastern Oregon cattle kings confirms some of this stereotype, yet John Devine, Pete French, and Bill Brown were unique individuals with personalities that are still talked about today.

John Devine came to Oregon in 1868 and started snapping up land by the simple method of squatting on it. He grabbed U.S. government land, Indian territory, and acreage ostensibly owned by road companies, which he quickly covered with vast herds of cattle. Part of his holding included the Alvord and the Whitehorse ranches on the east side of the Steens. After the devastating winter of 1889-90, during which he lost 75% of his stock, Devine's fortunes plummeted. He was bought out by another cattle baron, Henry Miller, and held on to only the Whitehorse Ranch until his death in 1901 at the age of 62.

Another rancher whose fate is still debated in this arid country is Pete French, an arrogant, forceful man with a bushy mustache that gave him the appearance of Wyatt Earp. Born in Red Bluff, California in 1849, French moved to Oregon in 1873 to manage the stock ranch of Dr. Hugh Glenn in the Donner and Blitzen Valley. French married the boss's daughter, and after Glenn was murdered by his bookkeeper, French built the French-Glenn Livestock Company into one of the largest spreads in the West. At its peak, the ranch had 100,000 acres on which roamed 30,000 head of cattle and 3,000 horses. Five hundred miles of barbed wire defined this empire stretching from the Donner and Blitzen River to Harney Lake.

While he was developing the P Ranch, French earned the enmity of hundreds of local homesteaders, many of whom were evicted from their squatter's shacks. One of his enemies, homesteader Ed Oliver, rode up to French one day and shot him dead. Oliver was arrested but later acquitted by a jury of settlers.

Bill Brown was a more popular and certainly more eccentric rancher than Pete French. His Gap Ranch, headquartered a few miles east of Hampton, halfway between Brothers and Riley, was at its largest 38,000 acres spread throughout four counties. Bill Brown didn't start out rich and he died penniless. In between he earned and lost a number of fortunes. His first enterprise was running a flock of 400 sheep. During that era he was so hard up he only owned one sock, which he switched from one foot to the other every day. Brown added horses to his holdings with such zeal that by the advent of WW I he owned 25,000 head, many of which he sold to the U.S. Cavalry. After the war, and with the advent of mass production of automobiles, Brown lost his shirt and his land. Many stories have been told about this balding six-footer with a square jaw and a mild manner. He never cussed, drank, or gambled, unless his faith in his store customers could be considered gambling. The operator of a mercantile, Brown was seldom behind the counter, relying instead on the honesty of his customers, who were asked to toss their cash in a cigar box. Another quirk was Brown's legendary habit of writing checks on anything available, from tomato-can labels to wooden slats. Local bankers had no problem cashing the "checks" for Brown's hired help or suppliers.

the refuge. They generally nest for several months here and then head north to Canada. In March, the first Malheur arrivals include Canada and snow geese, and in the vast Malheur Marsh, swans, mallards, and other ducks. Also look for sandhill cranes in the wet meadows. Great horned owls and golden eagles are two other early arrivals. Shorebirds are followed by warblers, sparrows, and other songbirds in spring. Red-tailed hawks can be seen swooping over the sage-covered prairies throughout spring, summer, and fall. In the late spring, ponds and canals at Malheur occasionally host the trumpeter swan, a majestic bird with a seven-foot wingspan. This is one of the few places where you can observe this endangered species nesting. Flocks of pelicans are a summertime spectacle worth catching. See them before they head south to Mexico in the fall. An annual highlight occurs in September and October with the concentration of greater sandhill cranes, Canada geese, and mallard ducks foraging on Blitzen Valley grain fields. The first two weeks of September are particularly nice because hunting season has yet to begin and the aspens have turned golden.

Late spring is a good time to visit before summer's scorching heat and mosquitoes. Beyond the barrackslike Malheur Field Station, where students study desert ecology and wildlife, is a gravel road. If you follow the signs you'll come to the refuge headquarters in a grove of cottonwoods looking out over the huge expanse of Malheur Lake. Here you can pick up maps for the self-guided auto tour of the refuge. A short distance downhill is a small museum where more than 250 bird specimens are beautifully arrayed. Also of interest is the charming park on the edge of the lake.

While the absolute numbers of birds at Malheur are not as great as they are at the Klamath Lakes or along the Oregon coast, the variety here is unsurpassed. Among birders, however, it is the "accidental list" of 55 infrequently sighted species that makes this preserve special. Many of these "exotics" are sighted nowhere else in the region. A total of 312 different species have been sighted here over the last century. *Birds of Malheur Refuge,* by Carol Littlefield (Corvallis: Oregon State University Press, 1994) is recommended for serious birders.

In the late 1800s, settlers enjoyed unrestricted hunting here, and at the turn of the century hunters killed thousands of swans, egrets, herons, and grebes for feathers for the millinery trade. In 1908, Pres. Theodore Roosevelt put a stop to the slaughter by protecting the area as a bird sanctuary. The Blitzen Valley and P Ranch were added to the refuge in 1935. Today, 185,000 acres are protected.

To get to the refuge drive 25 miles south from Burns on ORE 205 and then nine miles east on the county road to Princeton. The last six miles to the refuge headquarters are gravel surfaced. For general information on Malheur, call (541) 493-2612. For details and reservations on dorm rooms or trailers within the refuge, write Malheur Field Station, HC 72, P.O. Box 260, Princeton 97721. These spartan accommodations range between $11 and $20. Most of the time you'll be sharing a bath, and it's necessary to bring your own bedding and a towel. Cafeteria-style meals are available here (breakfast $5.75, dinner $7; reservations required). Call (541) 493-2629 to put dibs on these creature comforts; otherwise you might have to drive 35 miles to Burns for bed and board.

Frenchglen

Named for famous rancher Pete French and his wealthy father-in-law, Dr. Hugh Glenn, the town of Frenchglen was originally known as P Station and was part of the nearby P Ranch. Today, this historic community with its hotel, store, corral, and post office remains essentially the same as it was 50 years ago. To get there, drive about 60 miles south on ORE 205 from Burns.

Steens Mountain

Steens Mountain, named after Maj. Enoch Steen, an Army officer assigned the task of building a military road through Harney County, is one of the great scenic wonders of Oregon. A 30-mile fault block, the mountain rises straight up from the Alvord Desert to a row of glacial peaks. On the western side, huge gorges carved out by glaciers a million years ago descend to a gentle slope drained by the Donner and Blitzen River, which flows into Malheur Lake. Steens Mountain has five vegetation zones ranging from tall sage to alpine tundra. The best way to see the transition is to drive the **Steens Mountain Byway** out of Frenchglen to the top of Steens Mountain. This is the highest road in Oregon, rising 9,000 feet in elevation. The first 15 miles of the road are gravel and the last nine miles are dirt. The latter portion is not recommended for low-slung passenger cars.

Steens Mountain Loop

A good way to see the Steens area is via the Steens Mountain Byway, a 52-mile driving adventure starting and ending at Frenchglen. The route up the highest mountain in the state without conifers or significant tree cover of any kind (save for some beautiful aspens) can be compared to a visit to Alaska's alpine tundra. Multicolored low-to-the-ground wildflowers and a sense of vastness give the feeling of being on top of the world. This impression is accentuated by standing in snow while you look 5,000 feet straight down into the sun-scorched Alvord Desert, which records seven inches of rain annually. Steens Mountain is the highest point in the Great Basin. Below, the Alvord Desert is the "truest" desert landform in Oregon.

The first four miles of the trek lead across the Malheur Wildlife Refuge and up to the foothills of Steens Mountain. **Page Springs,** the first campground on the route, is a popular spot offering campsites along the bank of the Donner and Blitzen River. Approximately 13 miles beyond Page Springs is **Lily Lake,** a good place for a picnic. This shallow lake has an abundance of water lilies, frogs, songbirds, and waterfowl. After Lily Lake, you really start to climb up the mountain to **Fish Lake, Jackman Park** (both with campsites), and viewpoints of Kiger Gorge and the East Rim. **Kiger Gorge** is a spectacular example of a wide, U-shaped path left by a glacier.

The **East Rim** is a dramatic example of earth-shifting in prehistoric epochs. The lava layers that cap the mountain are thousands of feet thick, formed 15 million years ago when lava erupted from cracks in the ground. Several million years later, the Steens Mountain fault block began to lift along a fault below the east rim. The fault block tilted to the west, forming the gentler slope that stretches to the Malheur Lake Basin. At the summit (9,670 feet) you can see the corners of four states on a clear day—California, Nevada, Oregon, and Idaho. A good time to visit is August to mid-September—Indian

summer. Nights are cold but daytime temperatures are more pleasant than summertime scorchers. Later in the fall, red bushes and yellow aspens attract photographers. Some of the aspens are located at Whorehouse Meadow and are indirectly responsible for its name. Lonely shepherds would scratch love notes and erotica in the tree bark, pining away for a visit from the horse-drawn bordellos that serviced these parts. Wildlife-viewing highlights include bighorn sheep, seen around the East Rim viewpoint in summer; hummingbirds, often observed at high elevations; and hawks, which can be spotted anywhere, anytime here, especially from the ridge above Fish Lake.

The area has off-highway vehicle restrictions to protect the environment. Five gates controlling access to the Steens are located at various elevations and are opened as road and weather conditions permit. Normally, the Steens Byway is not open until mid- to late July and is closed by snow in October or November. Gas is available only in Burns, Frenchglen, and Fields. Take reasonable precautions when driving the loop: sudden storms, lightning, flash floods, and extreme road conditions can be hazardous to travelers. The loop returns to ORE 205 about 10 miles south of Frenchglen.

Catlow Valley/Alvord Desert Loop

Another equally ambitious loop is the drive around Steens Mountain along the Catlow Rim and Alvord Desert and back to Burns. Starting at Burns, head south on ORE 205 through the Malheur Wildlife Refuge, past Frenchglen, and up over the divide into the Catlow Valley, which was once a massive inland lake. A side trip to the ghost town of **Blitzen** starts at a right turn (to the west) four miles south of the Steens Mountain Byway. This eight-mile jaunt will take you to the ruins (a half dozen dilapidated buildings) of a little town founded in the late 1800s. Blitzen was named after the Donner and Blitzen River, which flows nearby. *Donner und blitzen* is German for thunder and lightning, the label given this stream by Capt. George Curry, who tried to cross it during a fierce thunderstorm.

The next point of interest on the loop is **Roaring Springs Ranch,** tucked under the west rim of Steens Mountain. Originally homesteaded by Tom Wall, the ranch was sold to Pete French and in later years developed into the largest cattle operation in the county. The dramatic backdrop, well-kept classic ranch building, and the surrounding meadows make Roaring Springs Ranch an ideal Western movie set.

After driving 33 miles through the Catlow Valley you'll come to **Fields,** the largest community on the east side of Steens. Homesteaded by Charles Field, the town was established as a supply station in 1881. Fields now has a gas station, store, cafe, and motel. The cafe next to the tiny motel and store here serves great milkshakes. A root beer shake made with hard ice cream flavored with bananas or oreos tastes great on a hot summer day. Field's original stone cabin is across the road.

From Fields head north into the Alvord Desert, site of the dry Alvord Lake and the Alvord Ranch. Along the way you'll pass through **Andrews,** a small community at the edge of the alkali flats. Another stop worthy of attention, particularly if you're in need of revitalization after your travels, is **Alvord Hot Springs,** a few miles north of Andrews. This rustic spa is recognizable by its corrugated-steel shack on the east side of the road. Two pools of hot mineral water piped in from spring runoff will cook your bones and soak away your aches and pains at no charge. The road continues until it connects with ORE 78, which leads back to Burns or south to Burns Junction. The panorama of the east side of Steens Mountain alone is worthy of a trip, but views of the **Pueblo Mountains** to the south and the Great Basin country to the east are also impressive.

Mickey Hot Springs

A little six- to eight-foot jet of 200° F water on the north end of an ancient dry lake bed is often visible in the spring in the Alvord Desert. Consult the BLM in Hines for directions. This site east of the Steens is fenced in to protect the fragile "plumbing system" of the only counterpart to Old Perpetual, a geyser near Lakeview. Also within the 20-acre complex are hot pools, steam vents, and the only mud pot in Oregon.

Oard's Free Museum

Oard's Free Museum, tel. (541) 493-2535, is located 23 miles east of Burns on US 20. The museum has antique guns, clocks, barbed wire, spinning wheels, and dolls as well as native artifacts, including a Yakima chief's regalia. Hours are 7 a.m.-8 p.m. every day.

Paiute Reservation

If you want a livelier encounter with Native American culture, visit the Burns Paiute Reservation. Contact the tribal headquarters first for information; either call them at (541) 573-2088 or write to HC-71, 100 Pa' Si' Go Street, Burns 97720.

SPORTS AND RECREATION

Golf

Harney County's "Oasis in the Desert" is the nine-hole **Valley Golf Club,** 345 Burns-Hines Hwy., Burns 97720, tel. (541) 573-6251. This challenging course is open to the public, but clubhouse facilities are reserved for members and guests.

Rockhounding

Harney County is rockhound country. Each year, thousands of these enthusiasts flock to this far-flung corner of the state to collect fossils, agates, jasper, obsidian, and thunder eggs. The **Stinking Water Mountains,** 30 miles east of Burns, are a good source of gemstones and petrified wood. Thunder eggs can be dug up four miles south of Oard's Museum on US 20 after getting permission from the Don Robbins family. Contact them through the museum. **Warm Springs Reservoir,** just east of the Stinking Water Mountains, is popular with agate hunters. **Charlie Creek** and **Radar,** west and north of Burns respectively, produce black, banded, and brown obsidians. Be sure to collect only your limit—be a rockhound, not a rockhog. Also keep in mind that it is illegal to take arrowheads and other artifacts from public lands.

Fishing

Rainbow and red-banded trout occur naturally in most streams in this area and many lakes and rivers are also stocked. Good fishing is available on the Donner and Blitzen and Malheur rivers, Emigrant Creek, Chickahominy Reservoir, Delintment Lake, and Yellowjacket Lake. Krumbo Reservoir on the Malheur Wildlife Refuge is a good bet for trout or largemouth bass.

The Frenchglen Hotel is a restored turn-of-the-century hotel.

OREGON DEPT. OF TRANSPORTATION

PRACTICALITIES

Accommodations

If you're seeking shelter in Burns, you'll find that the properties here are generally inexpensive, have air-conditioning to help you beat the heat, and allow you to bring the family dog along, too. The **Orbit Motel**, Hwys. 20/395, Burns 97720, tel. (541) 573-2034 or (800) 235-6155, features a pool, nonsmoking rooms, cable TV, and wheelchair access; their rates range $30-50. It's located a half mile north of Burns. Another bargain is the **Silver Spur Motel,** 789 N. Broadway, Burns 97720, tel. (541) 573-2077, which offers nonsmoking rooms, a weight workout room, a complimentary continental breakfast, and rates of $40-45. You get treated like a king at the **Royal Inn,** 999 Oregon Ave., Burns 97720, tel. (541) 573-5295. Enjoy the tennis courts, two swimming pools, and a decent restaurant (for Burns) without paying a king's ransom. Rates range $45-55. The **Best Western Ponderosa Motel,** 577 W. Monroe, Burns 97720, tel. (541) 573-2047, features a swimming pool, nonsmoking rooms, and large spacious rooms for $40-50.

The **Frenchglen Hotel,** Frenchglen, tel. (541) 493-2825, is 60 miles south of Burns on ORE 205 and is an excellent place to stay while visiting Steens Mountain or Malheur Wildlife Refuge. Built in 1914 as a stage stopover in historic Frenchglen, the hotel has eight smallish rooms (with shared bath down the hall) for $50-60 and

ranch cooks ready to fix you a family-style breakfast, lunch, or dinner. The family-style evening repast here is in the $10-15 range, and you must be there at 6:30 p.m. Their Better Than Sex chocolate cake is aptly named. Watching thunderstorms sweep across Steens Mountain from the hotel's screened-in porch can provide after-dinner entertainment. The hotel's season runs March to November. Breakfasts here, $3-6, are a nice prelude to driving to the top of Steens Mountain. Next door at Frenchglen Mercantile groceries, Southwest Indian art, books, and a mélange of other items are offered. The attached Buckaroo Room features good moderately priced meals (such as Basque chicken, $7) and microbrews. A post office and a BLM information kiosk are also in the Frenchglen complex.

Campgrounds

There are three high-elevation campgrounds along the Steens Mountain Loop Road. **Page Springs,** four miles southeast of Frenchglen, is open all year. Close to the Malheur Wildlife Refuge, the campground is a good headquarters for birdwatching, fishing, hiking, and sightseeing. **Fish Lake** is 17 miles east of Frenchglen and open July 1-Nov. 15. The namesake lake is stocked with eastern brook, cutthroat, and rainbow trout. Aspens surround the campsites, which have toilets, well water, and firepits; firewood is included in the campsite fee. **Jackman Park** is three miles east of Fish Lake and is particularly popular with backpackers who use it as a takeoff point. It has six sites with toilets and potable water. All of these campgrounds cost $4 per night for each vehicle. Write the BLM, Burns District, HC-74, Box 12533, Hwy. 20 West, Hines 97336, tel. (541) 573-5241. As for summertime Steens weather, the 100° F temperatures in the high desert give way to 50-80° daytime temperatures atop the mountain. Nonetheless, be aware that the summit can have severe thunderstorms and lightning. At night, the mercury will often drop below freezing, even on days with high noontime temperatures.

A couple of campgrounds to the north of Burns up in the Malheur National Forest are **Yellowjacket** and **Idlewild.** Yellowjacket is on the shore of Yellowjacket Lake, 30 miles northwest of Burns on Forest Service Rd. 2170. As the name implies, be sure to keep your food under wraps, especially meats, if you want to avoid being visited by the namesake hosts of the lake. Idlewild is 17 miles north of Burns on US 395. There is no charge for overnighting in either spot, but don't expect amenities either.

Food
The culinary highlight of Burns is coffee in the **Safeway** deli (Monroe St.). In other words, B.Y.O. food here. A little west of Burns, a sign in Hines proclaims "Worst Foods of The World— 70's prices." To be blunt, we think it's worth waiting till you get to Frenchglen to eat. The Frenchglen Hotel and the Buckaroo Room in back of the Frenchglen Mercantile both serve food that's tasty and affordable.

Entertainment and Events
In mid-April, the **John Scharff Migratory Waterfowl Conference** held in Burns celebrates the spring return of waterbirds to the region with lectures, movies, slides, and guided birdwatching tours. For information on the festival call (541) 493-2612. Harney County, once the trapping territory of mountain men like Peter Skene Ogden and Joe Meek, has two blackpowder clubs that relive those days with a yearly **Blackpowder Shoot and Rendezvous.** The **Steens Mountain Men** hold their shoot in September and the **Harney Free Trappers** hold theirs in June. These rendezvous attract colorful gatherings of folks in buckskin, talkin', shootin', lyin', and renewing friendships from "afore last winter." For information on dates and locations call Bigfoot at (541)

573-7814 or Silver Fox at (541) 573-7554.

Steens Mountain Days is held in early August. Centered in Frenchglen, the fun includes a 10-km run along the Steens rim, a sagebrush roping contest, a barbecue, a street dance, and a beer garden. During the last weekend in June, the sky is filled with lighter-than-air ships for the **High Desert Hot Air Balloon Rally** at Burns Union High School. Burns is also the site of **Obsidian Days** in mid-June, as well as the **Harney County Fair** and the Rodeo and Race Meet held in early September. First-run flicks can be enjoyed at **Desert Community Theatre,** 68 Broadway, Burns, tel. (541) 573-4220.

During the first week of September, Burns hosts the **Harney County Fair,** tel. (541) 573-7152, an old-fashioned county fair featuring a rodeo, 4-H competitions, and exhibits on canning, wine- and beer-making, and leatherworking. At 4,140 feet in elevation, Burns is sometimes dusted with snow during the fair.

Information and Services
For general information on the region, contact the **Harney County Chamber of Commerce,** 18 W. D St., Burns 97720, tel. (541) 573-2636. For information on recreation, stop by the **Bureau of Land Management** office, 12533 US 20W, Hines 97738, tel. (541) 573-5241. The **Burns and Snow Mountain Ranger District** is also nearby, P.O. Box 12870, US 20, Hines 97738, tel. (541) 573-7292.

If you need the law, call the Burns and Hines City **police,** tel. (541) 573-6028, or the Harney County **sheriff,** tel. (541) 573-7281 (during normal business hours) or (541) 573-6028 (after 5 p.m. weekdays and on weekends). The **post office,** 222 N. Broadway, Burns 97720, tel. (541) 573-2931, is open 9 a.m.-5 p.m. weekdays.

The Burns Airport, 87A, Rural Route HC 71, tel. (541) 573-6139, is five miles from town.

Lindberg's Highland Rock Shop, 1316 Hines Blvd., Burns, tel. (541) 573-5118, might be the best rock shop for certain kinds of specimens in the Northwest. Even if you're not buying, check out the thunder eggs and petrified wood. Also ask to see the glow-in-the-dark rocks and the fireplace hacked out of local treasures in the back of the store. Information on where to look for rocks yourself is also available (pamphlets for sale). A $2 map outlines the rock and gem trails throughout the state.

NORTHEASTERN OREGON

US 26: PRINEVILLE TO SUMPTER

Prineville, the geographic center of Oregon, is a fitting starting point for this route across the north-central section of the state. It's the oldest incorporated town in central Oregon and one of the first "Old West" towns you'll encounter after crossing the Cascades. The sagebrush and Stetson-hatted citizens starkly contrast with Bend's resort-town atmosphere. Coming from the west, you drop down from tall bluffs into the Crooked River Valley and, nearing the city, cruise through hills dotted with juniper. White-and-black magpies dart in front of your car, and red-winged blackbirds observe your passing from their fenceposts. A thriving community and the seat of Crook County, Prineville has a population of 5,000, gets a meager 10 inches of rain a year, and relies on agriculture, wood products, and tourism for its economy. The town is also known as the Gateway to the Ochocos, a heavily wooded mountain range that runs east-west for 50 miles. One of Ore-gon's least-known recreational areas, the Ochocos are still ruggedly pristine. Beyond these mountains stretches the long valley of the John Day River. Also in the vicinity are the famous John Day Fossil Beds, the historic gold-mining camps of Canyon City and Sumpter, and another wild area called the Strawberry Mountain Wilderness.

Just as the fossil beds provide a cross section of the earth's biological history, a trip down US 26 will give you a feel for the leather-tough countryside of central eastern Oregon and the people who settled here: the second-generation pioneers who arrived from the Willamette Valley, the Basques, Scots, and Irish from the old countries, and the Chinese who came to pick over the tailings left by gold miners in a hurry. Their combined heritage is here for the finding, along with night skies unobscured by city lights and diverse wildlife roaming the vast plains and forests.

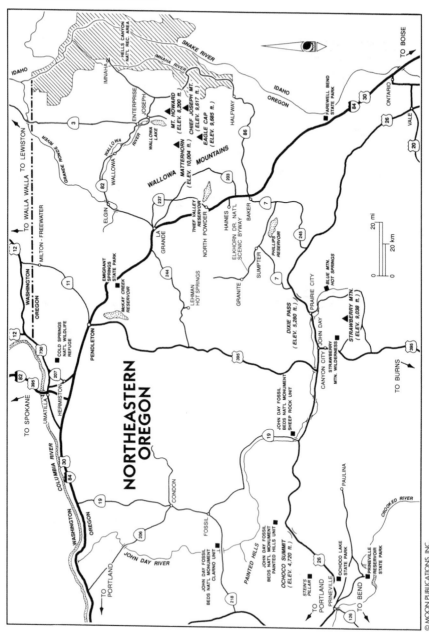

© MOON PUBLICATIONS, INC.

HISTORY

The Ochocos

The Ochoco country, named after a Paiute Indian word for willows, was heavily populated by natives who lived off a bounty of deer, elk, fish, and camas roots. The first significant passage of Europeans other than trappers through the area was the Lost Wagon Train of 1845. Led by Stephen Meek, brother of the Oregon Territory spokesman Joe Meek, the pioneers were seeking a route to the Willamette Valley easier than the arduous trek over the Blue Mountains. Instead, they found hardship, starvation, thirst, and death on a tortuous journey through the deserts of Malheur and Harney counties and along the rugged ridges of the Ochoco Mountains. Their hardships finally ended when they found the Crooked River and followed it north to The Dalles. Somewhere during the trek, members of the party scooped up gold nuggets and kept them in a blue bucket. Though the legend of the Blue Bucket Mine has since captivated fans of Oregon history, its actual site has never been found.

In 1860, Maj. Enoch Steen led an expedition through the region, which resulted in a number of geographic features being named after him, including Steens Mountain and Stein's Pillar. Eight years later, Barney Prine built a blacksmith shop, a store, and a saloon near the bank of Ochoco Creek; the outpost grew into the city of Prineville, the only town in 10,000 square miles. It was settled by the sons of the pioneers who came west in the wagon trains. It was their turn to carve out a life from the wilds.

At the turn of the century, cinnabar, the raw ore in which mercury is found, was discovered in the Ochocos, resulting in an influx of miners. About the same time, a range war broke out between the cattlemen and sheepherders. Groups like the Ezee Sheep Shooters and the Crook County Sheep Shooters Association bragged that they had slaughtered

8,000-10,000 sheep in 1905 alone. Incensed by this lawlessness, the citizens of Oregon moved to stop the killing, but troubles continued for cattle and sheep ranchers and farmers. Harsh winters took their toll on livestock, and the hope that the plains would be receptive to wheat farming didn't work out.

During WW I, many homesteaders gave up and moved to the cities to work for the war effort. In 1917, Prineville made a decision that wound up boosting the local economy. They built a railroad to Redmond, linking their line with the Union Pacific. Used primarily to haul ponderosa pine logs, the railroad remains the only city-owned railroad still in operation in the United States. In the 1950s a new industry was added to the mainstays of logging, ranching, and farming. Gemstones of high quality were discovered in the Ochocos, prompting a rockhound/tourism boom that continues to this day.

One peculiar historical note of interest: for most of its 11-decade existence, Crook County was a bellwether county, giving the majority of its vote to the winner of every presidential race.

ADOPT-A-WILDERNESS PROGRAM

Most of eastern Oregon is public land under the jurisdiction of the Bureau of Land Management. One of the laws that governs the BLM's management of these millions of acres of semiarid steppes is the Federal Land Policy and Management Act (FLPMA) of 1976, which mandates a review of all BLM roadless areas for possible inclusion in the Wilderness Preservation System. Of the five million acres inventoried, the BLM is recommending protection of 1.1 million acres. Conservationists are calling for twice that amount. To convince Congress to meet the conservationists' acreage requests, an Adopt-A-Wilderness Program has been initiated with the goal of preparing a collection of on-site reports called the Sage Alternative.

Sponsored by the Oregon Natural Desert Association, the program invites desert-lovers to pick an area to adopt as their own. The "parents" go on field trips, gather information, take photographs, prepare slide shows, brochures, portfolios, and other profiles as evidence that their small portion of the desert needs to be preserved in its natural state.

To get involved, contact ONDA, P.O. Box 1005, Bend 97709, tel. (541) 385-6908, the central clearinghouse for the program. Then lace up your boots, grab your hat, and get out there!

However, the county lost its distinction as the nation's last election-eve litmus test as a result of its choice of George Bush over Bill Clinton.

John Day Region

A string of communities runs east from Prineville and includes Mitchell, Dayville, Mt. Vernon, John Day, Canyon City, and Prairie City. The early history of this stretch of the John Day Valley centers around the discovery of gold in 1862. According to most estimates, $26 million in gold was taken out of the Strawberry Mountain Wilderness. At the peak of the gold rush, Whiskey Flat, later called Canyon City, was populated by 5,000 miners, which made it larger than Portland at the time. Thousands of Chinese immigrated to the area to work the tailings, or leftovers, from the mines. Their history is well articulated by the docents at the Kam Wah Chung Museum in John Day.

One of the more colorful denizens of Canyon City was the celebrated poet Joaquin Miller, who served as the first elected judge in Grant County. Known as the "Byron of Oregon," this dashing figure dressed like Buffalo Bill and orated his florid sonnets to a baffled audience of miners.

Lastly, the area generated an irony common in history: John Day, the man whose name was attached to a river, a valley, and a town, never saw any of them. A hunter from Virginia, Day was hired to provide meat for the Pacific Fur Company expedition led by Wilson Price Hunt. Thirty miles east of The Dalles, near what was then known as the Mau Hau River, Day and another mountain man were attacked by Indians and left naked and injured. The river soon became known as Day's River; mapmakers later changed it to the John Day River.

OCHOCO SIGHTS

Prineville

A good place to begin your travels in Ochoco country is at the **A.R. Bowman Museum,** 246 N. Main St., Prineville 97754, tel. (541) 447-3715, open Mon.-Fri. 10 a.m.-5 p.m., Saturday noon-5 p.m. This museum's two floors of exhibits and displays are a notch above most small-town historical museums. Fans of the Old West will enjoy the tack room with saddles, halters, and woolly chaps. Rockhounds will be delighted with the displays of Blue Mountain picture jasper, thunder eggs, and fossils. Other classic displays include a moonshine still, a country store, an upstairs parlor of the early 1900s, and a campfire setup with a graniteware coffee pot and a pound of Bull Durham tobacco.

Stein's Pillar

Outside town, the country east of Prineville starts to shift from juniper flats to pine ridges. One landmark that stands out is Stein's Pillar, a 300-foot monolith that rises like a rocky forefinger out of the pines. To get to this impressive column of stone, take the Mill Creek Rd. at Ochoco Lake, six miles east of Prineville. Stein's Pillar will be on your right. The scenic route back to Prineville from the Mill Creek Wilderness on McKay Rd. takes you by some exquisite meadows and clear mountain streams.

Lookout Mountain

Another side trip of note is a visit to the Lookout Mountain Special Management Area. To get there, drive 15.3 miles east from Prineville on US 26, and bear right at the sign for the ranger station. Located in the Ochocos, it's a unique biosphere with 28 plant communities, one of the finest stands of ponderosa pines in the state, lots of elk and deer, a wild mustang herd, and creeks full of rainbow and brook trout. A seven-mile trail starts near the Ochoco Ranger Station 22 miles east of Prineville on Forest Service Rd. 22 at the campground picnic area, and ends at the summit of Lookout Mountain, from which 11 major peaks are visible. Friends of Lookout, a coalition of environmental and recreational groups, invites you to visit the area and lend your support to efforts to secure legislation protecting this unique habitat. June is the time to see one of the best wildflower displays in the state. Check with the Prineville Ranger District, tel. (541) 447-3825, before going.

JOHN DAY FOSSIL BEDS NATIONAL MONUMENT

The next sights as you travel east are among the most prominent tourist stops in eastern Oregon. In the 1860s, self-taught geologist Thomas

Condon discovered what is now known as the John Day Fossil Beds. These archives of stone provide a paleontological record of the over 40 million years and five geologic epochs of life on this planet. The days of 50-ton brontosaurs and 50-foot crocodiles, as well as delicate ferns and flowers, are captured in the rock formations of the three beds, easily visited in a day's excursion. This is the richest concentration of prehistoric mammalian and plant fossils in the world. More than 120 species have been identified here, and help document a period dating from the extinction of the dinosaurs to the beginning of the last great Ice Age. This 14,000-acre monument is divided into three areas: the Sheep Rock unit, located about 40 miles west of John Day; the Painted Hills unit, another 45 miles farther west; and the Clarno unit, found to the northwest about 20 miles from the town of Fossil.

The Painted Hills

The first stop, the Painted Hills, is 50 miles east of Prineville on a spur road off US 26. Turn left at the sign outside Mitchell and go six miles along Bridge Creek to the site. Stop first at the visitor center to get oriented and fill your canteen. Continuing on, you'll soon notice the startling, deep red colors of the hills, complemented by pink, gold, buff, bronze, and black. Although the view from the road is impressive, you really have to get out and hike the trails to literally get the picture. The half-mile **Painted Hills Overlook Trail** provides a view of mineral-bearing clays exposed by erosion. Near the junction with the road and the preceding trail is the 1.5-mile **Carroll Rim Trail** with a spectacular all-encompassing view of the Painted Hills. The **High Desert Trail** is a three-mile loop into the desert for those seeking the quiet and the solitude of the big empty. Enjoy deep yellows, browns, and reds thanks to the multihued volcanic debris that piled up centuries ago. But the most vivid colors of all are found at the **Painted Cove Trail.** Viewing the red mounds up close is a highlight. A printed trail guide is available at the trailhead. Close by, the **Leaf Hill Trail** will lead you to remnants of a 30 million-year-old hardwood forest. While walking on the hill itself is prohibited, there's an exhibit describing how our knowledge of Oregon's most ancient forests emanated from studies of this area. In the modern era,

it's common knowledge among wildflower buffs that the springtime display here is exceptional.

The Clarno Formations

The next beds, the Clarno Formations, are the oldest and northernmost of the three units comprising the national monument. To get to them, take ORE 207 north of Mitchell Service Creek, then ORE 19 to Fossil and ORE 218 to Clarno. Fossil is situated 45 miles north of the Painted Hills. You might want to stop in this little town of 430 to collect fossils and petrified wood since it's prohibited within the monument. Ask the locals to point the way to the high school. A hill behind the high school contains crumbled shale that bears imprints of leaves from an ancient forest. After passing through Fossil, the Clarno Formations are 18 miles farther west. Picnic facilities, drinking water, and restrooms are available. The **Clarno Arch Trail** leads you into the formations at the base of the Eroded Palisades, the Petrified Logs, and the Clarno Arch. The Clarno unit is one of the few places in the world where stems of ancient plants, as well as their leaves, seeds, and nuts, all are preserved in the same location. Fossilized imprints of palm, gingko, and magnolia leaves culled from volcanic mudflows here point to a subtropical forest capable of supporting flowering trees. While the Clarno Formations are the least visually dramatic unit within the monument, they retain a special fascination for paleontologists. Considering that even five-million-year-old fossil beds are considered rare, the 40 million years of diverse plant and animal life that exisited here between 45 and five million years ago takes on greater significance.

A scenic little side loop through the ghost town of **Twickenham** will take you through a canyon with sandstone meadows—just follow the signs through this little wayside. Banded cliffs are so close you can almost reach out and touch them.

Sheep Rock Unit

The third area of the John Day beds, the Sheep Rock unit, can be reached by driving back down ORE 19 to Service Creek, where you turn east and follow the John Day River to Spray and **Kimberly**—the latter famous for its cherry season in late June— and then south for 20 miles. If you're

Sheep Rock looms over the John Day Fossil Beds.

OREGON STATE HIGHWAYS

coming from the Painted Hills, just head to US 26 and continue about 60 miles east to its junction with ORE 19. This road will lead you into the Sheep Rock unit. The **Sheep Rock Overlook Trail** wends through this area. Another 2.3 miles along ORE 19 will bring you to the **Cant Ranch Visitor Center,** headquarters for the National Park Service here, which maintains the John Day Fossil Beds National Monument. Ask to see their excellent orientation film in the back room of this converted farmhouse. Of the exhibits in the front room, the fossils from the Clarno nutbeds are especially worthy of attention. Booklets and informational pamphlets supplement the rangers' interpretive talks. You might also want to visit the small structure in the backyard where scientists extract fossil specimens from stone. Two fascinating trails several miles north of here are the **Island in Time Trail** and the **Blue Basin Trail.** In certain places the ground at Blue Basin is cobalt blue and the creek water is green.

John Day Practicalities
The **John Day Fossil Beds National Monument administrative office,** 420 W. Main, John Day 97845, tel. (541) 575-0271, has information on natural history and places to camp. For further information on camping in the area contact the **Grant County Chamber of Com-**

merce, 281 W. Main, John Day 97845, tel. (541) 575-0547, and request their pamphlet "Selected Local Campgrounds of Grant County." Information about other campgrounds near the John Day Fossil Beds is posted on the bulletin board near the Cant Ranch parking lot.

Of the few campsites available, the most comfortable for Sheep Rock visitors is **Clyde Holliday State Park,** c/o John Day Office of Oregon State Parks, Main St., John Day 97845, tel. (541) 575-2771. In addition to comfortable shaded hookups for $15 and hiker/biker sites for $4 near the John Day River, the park offers films and evening presentations about the fossil beds and other area natural attractions; call (541) 575-2006 for the schedule. The park is located off US 26 between the towns of John Day and Mt. Vernon. And if you've been on the trail too long, the **John Day Trailer Park,** 660 W. Main, John Day, tel. (541) 575-1557, has a **laundromat** and **shower** to get you ready for the next adventure. Hours are 7 a.m.-9 p.m.

Another good base of operations is the **Fish House,** 110 Franklin, Dayville, tel. (541) 987-2124. This bed and breakfast is located six miles west of the fossil beds in a small town with a historical grocery, the century-old Dayville Mercantile on US 26. These pleasant digs are decorated with antique farm tools and fishing gear and go for $35-55. A country breakfast is included. Not far from the bed and breakfast is a restaurant, **The Dayville Diggins.** If you plan to drive to Fossil and beyond from here, top off your tank near the Minit Mart.

If you're looking to camp near Clarno, the nearest public campground is **Shelton State Wayside,** 10 miles southeast of Fossil on ORE 19. Clarno visitors also have an invitation to "sleep in a fossil bed" at **Fossil Motel and Trailer Park,** P.O. Box 282, Fossil 97830, tel. (541) 763-4075. Rates are $25-45. Things are pretty basic, but hey, it's definitely the best place in town.

On a shady hillside close by the Painted Hills, the **Skyhook Motel,** US 26, Mitchell, tel. (541) 462-3569, has rooms with kitchen facilities for $25-35. While in town, check out Wheeler County Mercantile (circa 1876), a classic general store.

Where East Meets West
A must stop in the town of John Day is the **Kam Wah Chung and Company Museum,** 250 N.W. Canton, tel. (541) 575-0028, near the city park and pool. It's open May-Oct., Mon.-Thurs. 9 a.m.-noon, Sat.-Sun. 1-5 p.m. Admission is $2 for adults, $1.50 for seniors, and $1 for children. In addition to the herbal remedies arrayed in cigar boxes labeled with Chinese calligraphy, there are vintage photos, old tools, furnishings, and other artifacts. Even the labels on the old canned goods are fascinating. This was the center of Chinese life in the John Day area, serving as a general store and pharmacy with over 500 herbs. People came from hundreds of miles away for the herbal remedies of Doc Hay, who lived here. The building also served in more limited capacities as an assay office, fortune-teller's studio, and Taoist shrine. It began as a trading post on The Dalles Military Road in 1866-67. The influx of Chinese to the area during the gold rush brought about the outpost's evolution into a center for Asian medicine, trade, and spirituality in 1887 when it was purchased by two Chinese apothecaries. It remained a gathering place for the Chinese community in eastern Oregon until the early 1940s. While it admirably fulfilled this role, the opium-blackened walls, bootleg whiskey, and gambling paraphernalia here evidence the less salutary aspects of the Kam Wah Chung lifestyle. At the time of the 1879 census, eastern Oregon had

960 East Coast emigrants and 2,468 Chinese, proof that the current museum is not some arcane exhibit but rather a window onto the past. In fact, in 1983, scholars from China came to categorize the herbs and religious objects here.

It's the little touches in the faithfully restored building that stay with you. First your eye will be drawn to the metal shutters and outside wooden staircase on this rough stone edifice. Inside, there's a locked and barred herb cage where Ing Hay prepared medicine and where gold dust was weighed. A Taoist shrine graces the room where groceries and opium were dispensed. Finally, the meat cleaver by Doc Hay's bed bespeaks the fear and despair of Chinese life here near the turn of the century. For more information, read *The Chinese Doctor of John Day* by Jerry Barlow and Christine Richardson (Binford and Mort, 1979).

OTHER AREA SIGHTS

Museums
Another repository of local history is the **Grant County Historical Museum** in Canyon City, a couple of miles south of John Day on US 395. The museum is open June 1-Sept. 30, Mon.-Sat. 9:30 a.m.-4:30 p.m., Sunday 1-5 p.m. Centered in the heart of Oregon's mining and ranching country, the facility's wealth of memorabilia depicts the early days of Grant County and includes an extensive rock collection plus Chinese and Native American items.

The **Dewitt Museum,** South Main, Prairie City, is in the old western terminus of the Sumpter Valley Railroad, which operated between Baker and Prairie City from 1909 until 1947. The depot was restored in 1979 and today has 10 rooms full of artifacts from Grant County's early days. Open May 15-Oct. 15, Thurs.-Sat. 10 a.m.-3 p.m.

While not an official museum, the ghost town of **Whitney,** located 12 miles up ORE 7 from its junction with US 26 (about 15 miles east of Prairie City), has a story to tell to those who visit its ruins. Whitney was the terminus for stage lines to the mining and cattle towns of Unity, Bridgeport, and Malheur City. Now abandoned buildings are all that remain of this bustling community of the early 1900s. An interpretive sign just off ORE 7 explains the local history.

Sumpter and Vicinity

Traveling north of Whitney, you come to the **Sumpter Valley Wildlife Area,** a 158-acre site located between Phillips Reservoir and Sumpter on ORE 7. Canada geese, ring-necked ducks, bitterns, and Virginia rails can be seen in the wetlands and gravel dredge remains along the Powder River.

A few miles north of the refuge is Sumpter, a gold-mining town in the Elkhorn Mountains. To get to the historic little town, turn off US 26 at Austin and drive 22 miles on ORE 7 through the Sumpter Valley. The first settlers here were five Southerners who built a stone cabin and christened it Fort Sumter after the South Carolina garrison that was shelled in April of 1861, signaling the start of the Civil War. In 1883, the U.S. Post Office rejected the name, so locals changed it by dropping the "Fort" and adding a "p." The heyday of gold mining in the area was 1900-05, when over 3,000 miners worked the hard-rock mines and dredged the Powder River. By 1905, most of the gold was gone, but dredging continued until 1954. A park is under construction around the dredge and will offer trails, wildlife-viewing areas, and railroad displays. Contact the Baker County Visitors Association for more information. In addition to this park, abandoned digs, mining equipment, and overgrown cemeteries mark a triangular ghost-town loop here along ORE 7, US 26, and I-84.

One of the attractions of the Sumpter area is the **Sumpter Valley Railroad Excursion,** P.O. Box 389, Baker City 97814, tel. (541) 894-2268. Passengers ride in two observation cars pulled by a wood-burning, narrow-gauge steam engine originally used to haul logs and ore in addition to people. A restored 1920 car and an 1890 caboose are also part of the train. The seven-mile run from Phillips Reservoir to Sumpter costs $8 for adults, $6 for children under 16, $20 per family. The railroad is open from Memorial Day weekend through the last weekend in September with four runs daily at 10 a.m., noon, 2 p.m., and 4 p.m. Call or write the railroad to find out about special moonlight rides featuring live entertainment and hobo stew. Construction of a depot within Sumpter Valley Dredge State Park is in the planning stages. The railroad will make a 1.5-mile loop around the dredge. The depot will feature a museum and an auditorium. With the possible exception of the dredge in Fox, Alaska, this is the longest and most accessible gold dredge in the country.

When you're ready to leave Sumpter, you have three travel options. You can retrace your route back to US 26 and continue east to Vale and Ontario or head west toward US 97 and Bend. Another possibility is to drive 19 miles east on ORE 7 to ORE 245, and then north nine miles to Baker. The third choice, the **Elkhorn Drive National Scenic Byway,** takes you northwest from Sumpter through the gold-mining territory to Granite (check out the old wooden schoolhouse here, Oregon's first), across the north fork of the John Day, past Anthony Lake, and on to Baker. Because much of this road is above 5,000 feet in elevation, the loop is open only a few months of the year. The portion south of Anthony Lakes and north of Granite is closed by snow from early November through June or early July. The Elkhorn Byway climbs higher than any other paved road in Oregon (7,392 feet), after passing North Fork John Day Campground and the junction with Blue Mountains Scenic Byway. The craggy granite peaks of the northern Elkhorns—several higher than 8,000 feet—are near this area. Call the ranger district, tel. (541) 523-4476, for more information and road conditions. Of all the locales in the region, shunpikers and ghost-town connoisseurs might want to stop and take a gander at the remains of Granite, Oregon's smallest incorporated town (population 22). Placards here denote a church, a brothel, and a pharmacy. There's also the shell of an old wooden schoolhouse, Oregon's first. The profusion of pioneer graves in the city cemetery also should give pause to anyone given to romanticizing the frontier. In short, unlike many other places identified as "ghost towns," Granite, with its false-fronted buildings of unpainted, splintered boards, looks the part. Hard as it is to believe, this place once had four saloons, a 50-room hotel, several smaller hotels, a boardinghouse, a church, and a wooden jail. Founded in 1862, its mining legacy sustained the town through the 1930s. The need for miners in defense industries at that time compelled President Roosevelt to shut down the mines. Today, people are moving back despite no police or phone service. Instead, regional ties are maintained by visits to the Granite store where miners, retirees, and other residents keep the ghost alive.

SPORTS AND RECREATION

Lakes
Prineville Reservoir, 17 miles south of Prineville on ORE 27, was built for irrigation and flood control and covers 310 acres. A popular year-round boating and fishing lake, it is famous for its huge bass. **Ochoco Lake,** six miles east of Prineville on US 26, is a favorite recreational spot for locals, with year-round fishing, boating, and camping (see "Camping" following).

Golf
Meadow Lake Golf Course and Restaurant, tel. (541) 447-7640, is located a half mile west of downtown Prineville. This is the area's newest public course as well as Prineville's best spot for Sunday brunch—surprisingly reasonable prices. Greens fee is $25. This is a challenging course that has drawn high praise from golf writers.

Or try a round of golf at the **Mountain View Country Club,** tel. (541) 575-0179. Located just west of John Day on US 26, this nine-hole golf course accepts greens fees from non-members.

Rockhounding
The Ochocos are prime rockhound territory, with free public collecting areas operated by the Rockhound Pow-Wow Association. Two good sites are off of US 26. **Whistler Springs** is between mile markers 49 and 50. Turn left on Forest Service Rd. 27 for about six miles, then turn right onto Forest Service Rd. 500 and follow it to the springs. The collection area is near the campground. **White Fir Springs** is a good spot for jasper-filled thunder eggs. To get there, drive to mile marker 41, turn left on Forest Service Rd. 3350, and follow it five miles to the diggings. For more information on rockhounding and where to dig, **Elkins Gem Stones,** 833 S. Main St., Prineville, tel. (541) 447-5547, can help.

Riding the Ranges
Ever dreamed of going on a cattle drive? You can do it for real in the John Day River Valley with the cowboys of the **Cottonwood Ranch,** P.O. Box 334, Dayville 97825, tel. (541) 987-2134. The two-day trip includes chuckwagon dinners and breakfast, a barbecue, a hayride, and camping in tipis. The cost is $250 per person.

PRACTICALITIES

Accommodations
The **Rustlers Roost Motel,** 960 W. 3rd, Prineville 97754, tel. (541) 447-4185, was designed in the Old West style. Art by local artists and antique furniture grace the rooms. Rates start at $39 for a single and $44 for a double. The **Prineville Reservoir Resort,** HC 78, Box 1300, Prineville 97754, tel. (541) 447-7468, is on the shoreline of Prineville Reservoir, 17 miles southeast of Prineville on the Paulina Highway (ORE 27). This resort offers motel accommodations with kitchenettes starting at $60 for a double. Camping units go for $15. The resort also rents fishing boats, paddleboats, and motors. Those driving US 26 to the Painted Hills, Prineville to Mitchell, will enjoy comfort and moderate prices, $35-60, at the **Carolina Motel,** 1050 E. 3rd, Prineville, tel. (541) 447-4132, east of downtown. Housekeeping units, air-conditioning, and a large multiroom family unit are just some of the amenities here.

The **Elliot House Bed and Breakfast,** 305 W. 1st, Prineville 97754, tel. (541) 447-7442, is a classic Queen Anne-style home that was entered on the National Register of Historic Places in 1989. In keeping with the 19th-century flavor of the house, the hosts serve a sumptuous breakfast in the morning and a formal tea at 3 p.m.

If you find yourself in a similar situation in John Day, try the **Dreamer's Lodge,** 144 Canyon Blvd., John Day 97845, tel. (541) 575-0526. There's air-conditioning and a fridge in every room. Rates are $45-50. The lodge is located across from the post ofice, a half block north of the town's only traffic light. Similar comforts and rates are available at the **Gold Country Motel,** 250 E. Main St., Prineville, tel. (541) 575-2100, a half block east of the traffic light. **Bed and Breakfast by the River,** Route 2, Box 790, Prairie City 97869, tel. (541) 820-4470, located on a working ranch by the John Day River, is a good takeoff spot for hiking in the nearby Strawberry Mountain Wilderness, fishing or rafting on the river, or just basking in country hospitality. Rates are $30 and $60 per day for double occupancy.

Camping

For good campsites in the Ochocos, take Ochoco Creek Rd. approximately 10 miles east of Ochoco Lake. Choices include **Ochoco Camp, Walton Lake,** where you can fish, boat, or hike the trail to Round Mountain, **Wildwood,** and **Ochoco Divide.** Open from mid-April to late October, these campsites cost $10 per night. While on this loop, stop at the mining ghost town of **Mayflower.** Founded in 1873, the community was active until 1925. A stamp mill is still visible.

Strawberry Fields Forever

The **Strawberry Mountain Wilderness,** a pocket mountain range southeast of John Day, offers a good system of trails, seven lakes, volcanic rock formations, and if you're lucky, glimpses of bighorn sheep. Set up your base camp at **Strawberry Campground,** eight miles south of Prairie City on County Route 60, then two miles west on Forest Service Rd. 6001. Open from June to mid-October, Strawberry's fees are $7 per night. The campground is next to Strawberry Creek and is the trailhead for jaunts to Strawberry Lake, Strawberry Falls, and Strawberry Mountain. As you might guess, chances are good you'll find some of these wild berries along the way!

If your travels find you in this neighborhood in winter, try the groomed snowmobile and cross-country ski trails, which run from the Austin House in Bates (at the junction of US 26 and ORE 7) to Sumpter, a distance of 23 miles. For more information on the trails, contact this roadhouse, P.O. Box 8, US 26, Bates 97817, tel. (541) 488-2387.

For information on Strawberry Mountain hiking, contact the Prairie City Ranger District at the Malheur National Forest office, P.O. Box 337, Prairie City 97864, tel. (541) 820-3811. Ask about the 11-mile loop circumnavigating 9,000-foot Strawberry Mountain. To do it in style, call **Strawberry Mountain Llamas,** tel. (541) 820-3746.

Food

If you get hungry while in Prineville you can try a folksy little spot called **Barr's Cafe,** 887 N. Main, Prineville, tel. (541) 447-5897. It's open 24 hours, with breakfast served around the clock. Also on Main St. is the **Robin's Nest,** which rates a mention if only for its cafe lattes. The top-of-the-line restaurant in town is the **Ochoco Inn and Cinnabar Restaurant,** 123 E. 3rd, Prineville, tel. (541) 447-3888. You'll find the ubiquitous Western motif in a building built on the site of the Jackson Hotel, which burned in 1922, and the Prineville Hotel, which went up in flames in 1966. The restaurant makes generous bunkhouse deli sandwiches and also features a hazelnut pesto fettuccine dish. The eclectic menu is highlighted by a seven-ounce steak marinated in whiskey, Worcestershire sauce, red wine, and herbs for $9.95. Cheers!

Those heading to the Painted Hills via US 26 are encouraged to stop off at the **Blueberry Muffin Restaurant,** tel. (541) 462-3434, located on the west side of Mitchell just past the turnoff to the John Day Fossil Beds. This is likely to be the only restaurant worthy of the name encountered after leaving Prineville. Expect decent American food, with homemade pies a highlight.

A more traditional approach to beefsteak is favored by the **Grubsteak Mining Company,** 149 E. Main St., John Day, tel. (541) 575-1970. Their best deal is an eight-ounce rib-eye steak for $13, but also check out their lunch specials. The regular lunch menu runs $5-9, dinners average $12-35. Thirteen miles east of John Day you come to **Prairie City,** currently going through a transition into a tourist town similar to Sisters in central Oregon. One of the prime examples of this renovation is **Ferdinand's,** 128 Front St., tel. (541) 820-9359. This colorful watering hole in a refurbished butcher shop built in 1902 has a carving of a bull over the front door, and inside sports a collection of antiques, cougar hides, and old photos on the walls. Be sure to check out the two carved maidens, called the Twin Virgins, over the classic long bar. The figures were sculpted in Milan, Italy, in 1879, and they and the bar furniture made the trip around the Horn, up the Cólumbia River on a sternwheeler, and then to Prairie City by wagon. Ferdinand's has a full menu of surprisingly urbane fare that can be washed down with microbrewery beer and ale from Portland.

Finally, if you have a car full of hungry children, you might want to fill them up in the

Elkhorn Saloon and Family Restaurant, tel. (541) 894-2244, in Sumpter. The claim to fame here is a homemade combo pizza, weighing in at five pounds, for $18.95.

Entertainment and Events

The **Central Oregon Timber Carnival** is held in Prineville during the second week in May with a parade, equipment display, logging show, men's and women's logrolling, and a tug-of-war between loggers and Forest Service workers. For more information call (541) 447-5031. Another popular Prineville get-together is the **Annual Prineville Rockhound Show and Powwow,** P.O. Box 671, Prineville 97754, tel. (541) 447-6760, held in mid-June. The powwow attracts prospectors and rock-hounds from all over the country.

The first week in July is the time and Prineville is the site for the **Crooked River Roundup,** with pari-mutuel horse racing. The restored cars of the Prineville Railroad make special trips during the summer, including a **Fourth of July bar-becue run.** Check with the Prineville Chamber of Commerce for details.

Down the road a ways, Mt. Vernon holds its **Cinnabar Mountain Rendezvous** May 26-28. The rendezvous includes a parade, dance, community potluck, and lumberjack contest. Another midsummer festival is **'62 Days** in Canyon City, just south of John Day on US 395, which celebrates the local discovery of gold in 1862 with a medicine-wagon show, can-can girls, and a reenactment of the opening of historic Sel's Brewery. The **Elkhorn Crest Sled Dog Races** in January and the **Rooster Crowing Contest** in July are two popular Sumpter events. On the first weekend of August the town sponsors the **Old Time Fiddler's Contest.** On Memorial Day, July Fourth, and Labor Day weekend, folks head to the fairgrounds for the **Sumpter Flea Market,** P.O. Box 513, Sumpter 97877, tel. (541) 894-2264. Collectibles, crafts, and food are arrayed in a beautiful mountain setting. This event is legendary among Oregon's bargain hunters.

Getting Around

Prineville Airport, tel. (541) 447-2833, two miles west of Prineville, is a fixed-base operator facility serviced by Rimrock Aviation. The **John Day Airport,** Airport Rd., John Day 97845, tel. (541) 575-1151, has no commercial flights but

does have a charter service. Prineville is served by **Greyhound,** 1825 E. 3rd., Prineville 97754, tel. (541) 447-5516, but no buses serve John Day and vicinity.

Information and Services

For general information, the **Prineville-Crook County Chamber of Commerce,** 390 N. Fairview St., P.O. Box 546, Prineville 97754, tel. (541) 447-6304, is a valuable resource. If you need the law, the **Prineville City Police,** 400 E. 3rd St., tel. (541) 447-4168, the **Crook County Sheriff's Office,** 308 E. 2nd St., Prineville, tel. (541) 447-6398, and the **state police,** 400 E. 3rd St., Prineville, tel. (541) 447-4168, are always ready to serve you. In the next county over, the **John Day Police,** 240 S. Canyon Blvd., John Day 97845, tel. (541) 575-0030, and the **Grant County Sheriff's Office,** 200 S. Canyon City Blvd., Canyon City 97820, tel. (541) 575-1131, are also at your beck and call. Out here in the wide-open spaces, these numbers can sometimes prove useful.

The two newspapers in the area are the *Central Oregonian,* 558 N. Main, Prineville 97754, tel. (541) 447-6205, which publishes twice a week, and the *Blue Mountain Eagle,* 714 E. Main, John Day 97845, tel. (541) 575-0710, circulated weekly on Thursday. The **Book Cover,** 233 S. Canyon Blvd., John Day, tel. (541) 575-5006, is a good place to find regional titles and books for the kids. Radio reception is hard to come by in Grant County except for KJDY 1400 AM in John Day. News, weather, road reports in winter, and Portland Trail Blazer games can liven up the long drives. The **Grant County Chamber of Commerce** is at 281 Main St., John Day, tel. (541) 575-0547 or (800) 769-5664.

The Prineville **post office,** 155 Court, Prineville 97754, tel. (541) 447-5652, is open Mon.-Fri. 6:30 a.m.-5:15 p.m., Saturday 6:30 a.m.-4:30 p.m. The John Day post office, 151 Canyon Blvd., John Day 97845, tel. (541) 575-1306, keeps similar hours.

The Ochoco National Forest is administered from the following offices: **Prineville Ranger District,** 2321 E. 3rd., Prineville 97754, tel. (541) 447-3825; **Paulina Ranger District,** 6015 Paulina Star Route, Paulina 97751, tel. (541) 447-3713; **Big Summit Ranger District,** Box 225K,

Mitchell Star Route, Prineville 97754, tel. (541) 447-3845; **Snow Mountain Ranger District,** Star Route 4, Box 12870, US 20, Hines 97738, tel. (541) 573-7292; and the **Malheur National Forest Office,** 139 N.E. Dayton St., John Day 97845, tel. (541) 575-1731.

Pioneer Memorial Hospital, 1201 N. Elm, Prineville 97754, tel. (541) 447-6254, has 24-hour emergency services. In John Day, medical help is available at the **Blue Mountain Hospital,** 170 Ford Rd., John Day 97845, tel. (541) 575-1311. The **Third St. Shell and Food Mart,** 550 W. 3rd, Prineville 97754, tel. (541) 447-4476, is open 24 hours. The **Laundry and Dry Cleaners,** 250 E. 4th St., Prineville, tel. (541) 447-3126, is also open 24 hours, with dry cleaning available Mon.-Fri. 9 a.m.-5 p.m. In John Day, you can get your clothes clean at the aptly named **Weary Traveler Laundromat,** 755 S. Canyon Blvd., John Day, tel. (541) 575-2076.

ALONG THE OLD OREGON TRAIL

The pioneer trek along the Oregon Trail, a tide of migration starting in 1841 and lasting over 20 years, is one of this country's great epochs, celebrated in novels, films, books, and songs. It's almost the largest voluntary human migration ever recorded. The wagon trains started in Independence, Missouri, as soon as the spring grass was green. Then the race was on to get across the far mountains before the winter snows. Although the first few hundred miles were easy traveling across the plains, the hardships were not long in coming. Indian attacks, cholera, exhaustion, drownings, and in some cases, bad directions gave this 2,000-mile journey the nickname "The Longest Graveyard." Some historians believe that by 1859, at least 30,000 immigrants had died on the Oregon Trail. This would amount to an average of one unmarked grave for every 100 yards between Independence and Oregon City. By some estimates, over 300,000 people made the trek from the Midwest to Oregon between 1841 and the turn of the century. In 1843, some 900 immigrants traveled the Oregon Trail, a number that swelled to 17,500 just 10 years later. When it was all over, about 50,000 pioneers followed the trail to the end and settled in Oregon Country—present-day Oregon, Washington, and Idaho. But these numbers tell only part of the story.

At Fort Hall in eastern Idaho, there was a fork in the trail and a sign that read To Oregon. It was here that the pioneers had to make a key decision. They could head south to California and the gold fields shining with the promise of instant wealth, or they could continue west to Oregon, where the fertile Willamette Valley offered its own allure as a New Jerusalem for serious farmers and homesteaders. Some older Oregonians can recall a childhood version of the story, which claimed that the California road was marked by a pile of gold-painted rocks, in contrast to the To Oregon sign. The implication was that people who could read—or who were more interested in domestic pursuits than adventure—would head to Oregon. While this intepretation is not seriously accepted by historians, it remains a source of good-natured humor between the two states.

Those who did choose Oregon crossed the Snake River near Ontario, the Malheur River at Vale, and followed the wagon ruts north to lose sight of the Snake at Farewell Bend. The route is now paralleled by I-84 through Baker, La Grande, Pendleton, and on down the Columbia River Gorge to Portland. The towns along this modern Oregon Trail reflect the heritage of the pioneer era. The character and tenacity of those who chose Oregon over California can be seen in the sunburned, wind-creased faces of these sagebrush citizens. The following section offers a tour of this region, starting with Ontario and traveling northwest. Keep in mind that pioneer diaries substantiate that the mountains of eastern Oregon proved a more significant obstacle to west-bound emigrants than even the Rockies.

Located midway between Portland and Salt Lake City in Oregon's far east, Ontario is where "Oregon's day begins." It's the biggest city in Malheur County, with a population of 9,750. Ontario ships over five percent of the nation's onions and provides a good portion of the sweet russet potatoes used for French fries. Other local crops include sugar beets, peppermint, grains, and ornamental flowers. This abundance

*Leslie Gulch
in Malheur County*

derives from a location on the fertile plain at the junction of the Snake and Malheur rivers.

Baker, set in a valley between the Wallowas and the Blue Mountains, is the jumping-off spot for Hells Canyon, the deepest gorge in the world. Ranchers still drive their herds down the highways here, and folks wave howdy to passersby. It's a friendly place that has held on to its pioneer spirit.

La Grande is located in the Grande Ronde Valley, which the indigenous peoples called Copi Copi (the "Valley of Peace"). Home of Eastern Oregon State College, La Grande enjoys a brisk economy based on beef ranching, wheat farming, and timber. Tourism is on the rise as well. In addition to being the gateway to Wallowa Lake and the northern flank of the Wallowa Range, the region has a rich history, which is detailed at a new Forest Service visitor area along a section of trail in the Blue Mountains between Pendleton and La Grande on I-84.

HISTORY

Ontario, the town at the beginning of the Oregon section of the Oregon Trail, began as a cattle-shipping depot. The 1883 completion of the Oregon Short Line Railroad connected it to the Union Pacific and markets in the east. In 1939, reservoirs began irrigating the Snake River Valley, turning it into a rich agricultural region. During WW II, relocation centers for Japanese-Americans were built here. The only crime these citizens had committed was having the wrong ancestry. Stripped of their rights by a single executive order signed by President Roosevelt, about 5,000 Americans of Japanese ancestry were forced to liquidate their property and move into prisonlike barracks in remote sections of the West. This serious breach of constitutional freedoms remains one of the saddest chapters in American history. It's also worth noting that many of these unjustly incarcerated pariahs fought in the European theater of war in some of the most decorated units in the American Armed Forces.

In any case, a good percentage of the internees stayed in the area and now are well represented in the local business and agricultural communities. As in the Columbia Gorge, Japanese surnames grace many a ranch or farmstead in eastern Oregon. An influx of Hispanic migrant workers who came to work the crops in the '50s and '60s also stayed to start new lives, adding yet another ethnic flavor to a cultural stew that also contained Paiute Indians and Basques. All of the above will be celebrated in the **Four Rivers Cultural Center,** at Treasure Valley Community College, at the junction of I-84, ORE 20, US 26, and Idaho 95, tel. (541) 889-8012, featuring a museum, theater, convention center, and formal Japanese garden, all slated to be completed in 1998.

Baker, the next major town up the line, was named after Col. Edward Baker, Oregon's first senator and a one-time law partner of Abraham Lincoln. Baker City got its charter in 1874 and soon became known as the "Queen City," for all roads led to this commercial center. In 1861, it became the hub of the eastern Oregon gold rush and its population swelled to 6,600, making it bigger than Boise. Stop by the U.S. National Bank there and check out the 80.4-ounce **Armstrong gold nugget,** found in 1913. It's a remnant from the days when this wealthy, raucous frontier boomtown was the biggest and most important in the region. It boasted the finest hotel between Salt Lake City and Portland and even had a high school, the second in the Pacific Northwest.

Pioneer cattleman Herman Oliver recalls his visits to Baker as a young boy. He remembers the trolley car that ran the length of Main Street for a nickel. When the conductor reached the end of the line, he pulled a pin holding the horse and led the animal to the other end of the trolley and hooked it up for the return trip. Today, this frontier-era cattle, lumber, and gold-mining crossroads recaptures its 120 years of history with stone and brick buildings, many of which date from betwen 1880 and 1915. Local historians say the town's architectural styles include Italianate, classic revival, Victorian, and Carpenter Gothic. East of town, along ORE 7 and its offshoots, ghost towns like Granite and McEwen give new meaning to Gertrude Stein's description of another place: "There's no there there." The route, which follows the twisty contours of the Powder River, is particularly pretty when the deciduous trees take on fall hues.

La Grande, the third city on the Oregon Trail, is in a valley where the Nez Percé once gathered for their summer encampments until the Oregon Trail cut through their territory. More than a few of the pioneers were impressed with the possibilities of the Grande Ronde country. They stayed to build a town that became the market center for a broad stretch of wheat and grass-seed farms. Lumber from the Blue Mountains and livestock that fattened easily on lush fields of tall grass also helped the Oregon Trail pioneers' dreams come true. Located alongside the Grande Ronde River (which flows into the Snake), this town is where I-84 hooks up with ORE 82, the road to the Wallowas.

SIGHTS

Vale and Oregon Trail Sites

Vale, the seat of Malheur County, is located on the Malheur River at the spot where the wagons crossed the river, 28 miles west of Ontario on US 20/26. If you're intrigued by the drama of the pioneers, this little town offers an abundance of historical insight as well as evocative murals of historical scenes. On your visit to Vale, look north to **Malheur Butte** at mile marker 254. This long-extinct volcano was used as a lookout point by Indians watching for the wagon trains. The next historical site is **Malheur Crossing** on the east edge of Vale. The pioneers stopped here to take advantage of natural hot water from underground thermal springs to bathe and do their laundry.

The **Keeney Pass Oregon Trail Historic Site,** on the southern outskirts of Vale, has a display of the deep ruts cut into the earth by ironclad wagon wheels. This exhibit marks the most-used route of the wagon trains as they passed through the Snake River Valley on their way to Baker Valley to the north. From the top of this pass you can see the route of a whole day's journey on the trail to Oregon, 150 years ago. Ponder the fact that one pioneer in 10 died on this arduous transcontinental trek as you gaze out at the Snake River crossing near Old Fort Boise to the southeast. In June and July, Indian paintbrush and penstemon add a dash of color to the sagebrush and rabbitbrush that surround the ruts in the trail. Another site of interest is the **Stone House,** one block east of the Courthouse on Main Street. Built in 1872, it replaced a mud hut way station on the trail.

Oregon Trail Interpretive Center

Six miles east of Baker is the 23,000-square-foot Oregon Trail Interpretive Center, P.O. Box 854, Baker 97814, tel. (541) 523-6391. The center is open 9 a.m.-6 p.m. from summer into early fall. Between November 1 and May 31, the center is open 10 a.m.-4 p.m. Admission is $5, discounts for seniors and children.

The museum is perched atop Flagstaff Hill overlooking a picturesque section of this famous frontier thoroughfare. The exhibit halls are arranged to simulate the route and experiences of pioneers on the 547-mile section of the trail within state borders. While there are impressive artifacts as well as thought-provoking historic photos and video presentations, rather too much emphasis is placed on passive viewing. By contrast, the life-sized dioramas of Oregon Trail scenes, backdropped by taped renditions of immigrant voices and wagon wheels, make you feel like part of the great migration. Theatrical entertainment, paintings, living-history exhibits, and aptly chosen pioneer diary entries recount the crossing of the Blue Mountains and the Cascades, or rafting down the Columbia into the Willamette Valley. The museum's interpretive loop articulates the immigrant's state of mind—whether it's awe giving way to boredom across the Oregon prairie, emotional duress on a perilous river crossing, or adjusting to settlement at journey's end—as much as the physical obstacles of the trail. Attention is given also to the pioneers' effect on Native American lands and cultures.

Outside the museum, your historical reverie is sustained by living-history exhibits and the chance to stand in the actual ruts left behind by pioneer wagons at **Virtue Flat,** a two-mile walk from the center. Here, surrounded by the 10,000-foot Elkhorn Mountains to the west, the Blues to the south, and the craggy Eagle Cap to the northeast, the "land at Eden's gate" becomes more than just another florid phrase from a pioneer diary.

Prior to departing the Oregon Trail Interpretive Center, check out the raised relief map of northeastern Oregon. Besides getting the lay of the land, you can call up information on area attractions by pushing a button.

Oregon Trail Regional Museum
The Oregon Trail Regional Museum, Campbell and Grove Streets, Baker 97814, tel. (541) 523-9308, is open daily 9 a.m.-4 p.m. May-October. It's located across from Geiser Pollman Park, and admission is by donation. In addition to exhibits depicting the great migration, the museum houses an extensive collection of seashells and corals as well as one of the most comprehensive exhibits of rocks, minerals, and stones in the country. In conjunction with the museum, from June through September the Baker City Trolley conducts city tours. The hour-long narrated tour describes the gold-rush era and the interplay between con men, ranchers, and miners.

Historical homes and buildings are also the focus of this horse-drawn excursion into Baker's past. Tours are conducted at 3, 4, and 5 p.m. Friday and Saturday.

Crossroads Center
Crossroads Creative and Performing Arts Center, 2020 Auburn Ave., Baker 97814, tel. (541) 523-3704, is in the old Carnegie Library. It has monthly exhibits, a gift shop, and an Arts and Crafts Fair held July 17-19. While you're at the Crossroads Center, ask for a pamphlet describing the **Baker's Dozen,** a tour of the town's historical homes.

Eastern Oregon Museum
The Eastern Oregon Museum, 3rd and School, Haines 97833, tel. (541) 856-3568, is open every day 9 a.m.-5 p.m. April 15-Oct. 15 and has an outstanding collection of farming, mining, and pioneer artifacts. Afterwards, hit the **Haines Steakhouse** for dinner.

Geographical Center of the United States
According to local wags, the geographical center of the United States shifted dramatically with the addition of Hawaii and Alaska, to a spot 12 miles north of Medical Springs, where ORE 203 meets Catherine Creek.

Hot Lake
Hot Lake Mineral Hot Springs was considered "Big Medicine" by the western tribes that camped near its healing waters. In 1810, Astor Pacific Fur Company trappers described elk crowding around this spring. Thereafter, the lake, located five miles east of La Grande on ORE 203, became a popular spot for explorers and emigrants. In 1864, Samuel Newhart built a hotel and bathhouse here. A hospital was added at the turn of the century, and it soon became known as the Mayo Clinic of the West, a polite euphemism for one of the Northwest's first "fat farms." During that era, the healing waters here were thought to give relief from arthritis and rheumatism. The resort is not currently in operation.

North Powder Elk
North Powder Elkhorn Wildlife Management Area is a winter elk feeding station open for visits (by permit) Dec. 1-April 15, but viewing is

possible from nearby county roads in late afternoon and evening. To get there, go west 10 miles from exit 285 off I-84. Viewpoints are one mile south of the headquarters on River Rd. and two miles north of headquarters on Tucker Flat Road. These Rocky Mountain elk are somewhat smaller than the Roosevelt elk commonly seen on the west side of the Cascades. Call (541) 523-9308 for information on tours out to this area.

Elgin Opera House
This 1912 restored two-story brick house with perfect acoustics hosts movies, plays, live theatre, and other entertainment. First run flicks are shown Friday, Saturday, and Sunday. Call (541) 437-2520 for event listings. To get there, take ORE 82 17 miles northeast of La Grande.

Deadman's Pass
Deadman's Pass, at exit 228 on I-84, led emigrants out of the Blue Mountains into the Umatilla Valley. This was the last big hump they had to cross before the raft trip down the Columbia. The name comes from three incidents during the Bannock Indian War of 1878 in which seven men were killed. Look for a sign directing you up a trail to a sampling of still-visible wagon ruts.

Ladd Marsh Nature Trail
Birdwatchers will enjoy the chance to observe more than 32 species of ducks, geese, swans, and other birds, six miles southwest of La Grande along Foothill Road. Take exit 268 from I-84. This is one of the largest remaining wetlands in Northeast Oregon.

The Blue Mountain Crossing
If you take exit 248 off I-84 west of La Grande, you'll come to several trailheads located near restrooms and a covered shelter. Here are some of the nation's best-preserved tracks of the Old Emigrant Road. Colorful ceramic panels depict the pioneer's struggle through the tall tress and over the rugged Blue Mountains. Your walk along these shady trails will be enhanced when you consider that over 90% of the 2,170-mile route has been destroyed by human activity in the guise of progress. The interpretive center is open during daylight hours (follow the gravel roads about three miles toward the hamlet of Kamela).

In downtown La Grande, Birmic Park on the south side of town was an area used for wagon encampments prior to Oregon Trail pioneers crossing the Blue Mountains. The park is located on B Ave. and Bekeler and is decorated with an abstract pioneer art memorial and a life-size wrought-iron pioneer play wagon.

SPORTS AND RECREATION

The country through which the Oregon Trail passes is filled with recreational choices. **Ontario-Shadow Butte Golf Course,** tel. (541) 889-9022, is an 18-hole municipal course with pro shop and lounge, two miles west of Ontario. **Bully Creek Reservoir,** 30 minutes' drive west of Ontario near the small town of Vale, has boat-launch facilities, picnic and camping areas, swimming, and water-skiing. The fishing includes crappie, bass, trout, and perch. **Anthony Lakes Ski Area,** tel. (800) 762-7941, is between Baker and La Grande, 18 miles west of North Powder and Haines on I-84. Open the day after Thanksgiving until mid-April, daily 9 a.m.-4 p.m., this ski resort offers a chairlift, Nordic trail system, day lodge, ski shop, and ski lessons. All-day tickets are $16.50; children under 10 pay $11. This is Oregon's first and highest (7,000 feet in elevation) ski area. It offers pristine dry powder and a family-oriented environment. For updates on snow conditions, call (541) 886-3277.

Camping
Of the many campsites in the Wallowa-Whitman National Forest, here are four of the best. **Grande Ronde Lake Campground** along the shore of the lake has all the amenities and good trout fishing as a bonus. The fee is $9 per night. To get there drive 17 miles northwest of Haines on ORE 411, then eight miles west on Forest Service Rd. 73. The camp is one-half mile northwest on Forest Service Rd. 43. **Sherwood Forest Campground** is a small site on the banks of the Grande Ronde River. There is no fee for this campground, which is open late May through late November. Go nine miles northwest of La Grande on I-84 (exit 252), then 13 miles southwest on ORE 244. This road meanders along the river and its valley, where ponderosa pine and aspen are broken up by meadows and farm-

land. From there, drive six miles south on Forest Service Rd. 51. After camping, you might want to follow ORE 244 up to **Lehman Hot Springs,** tel. (541) 427-3015, and thereafter to its junction with US 395. En route you'll pass through Ukiah, often Oregon's coldest place. Therefore, we advise a soak in Lehman Hot Springs prior to arrival in this little mountain town. Each of the three chambers in Lehman's giant swimming pool is calibrated to an increasing degree of hotness, with the hottest level being scorching. This area used to be a historic gathering place for the Nez Perce. Call (800) 848-9969 for more information on this drive as well as other activities in the Wallowa Whitman Forest.

A third site, **Hilgard Junction State Park,** is also on the Grande Ronde River, at the foot of the Blue Mountains. Fees for this 18-site (no hookups) campground are $9 per night. To get there drive eight miles west of La Grande on I-84 to Starkey Road. This campground is very popular during deer- and elk-hunting seasons and is on the original route of the Oregon Trail. This site above the steep slopes of the Grand Ronde Valley gave the pioneers pause. Information placards detail how their wagons maneuvered over this precipitous terrain. The fourth site is **Emigrant Springs State Park,** tel. (541) 988-2277, a large facility with flush toilets, a laundromat, and a playground, right off I-84 near the Umatilla Indian Reservation between Pendleton and La Grande. The fee is $13 per night. This park has a display on the Oregon Trail and is a good spot to stop while traveling on the interstate, thanks to its laundromat, showers, piped water, and other amenities. There are 33 tent sites and 18 fuel hookups in a wooded area.

Outdoor Recreation

Sport Springs, between Westin and Elgin on ORE 204, tel. (541) 556-2164, has excellent powder that makes up for a 550-foot vertical drop. Lift tickets are $16 and you can rent skis at **Anson Ski Shop,** 112 Depot St., tel. (541) 963-3660. The Grande Ronde is one of Oregon's least known quality rafting experiences to out-of-staters. **Tilden River Tours,** tel. (541) 437-9270, takes you into the spectacular enclaves of the Grande Ronde River canyon south of Elgin (en route to the Snake) on a trip you'll never forget. Anglers will want to try their luck at Red Bridge

State Park on ORE 244. Check first with Oregon Fish and Wildlife officials about regulations governing endangered steelhead and salmon.

PRACTICALITIES

Accommodations

These lodgings, ranging from affordable to fancy, should make your own trek along the Oregon Trail far more comfortable than it would have been 150 years ago. Baker City is the hub, with 11 motels (455 motel rooms) plus two bed and breakfasts and three RV parks. Closer to the other end of the scale, the Geiser Grand Hotel in downtown Baker, the showplace of Oregon's gold country in 1889, is being restored and will be managed by Portland's venerable Heathman Hotel (expected rate $75 a night with breakfast amid Viennese chandeliers, mahogany columns, and a skylight 40 feet above the dining room). Meanwhile, Baker also has other worthy lodging alternatives from which to choose. The **Fireside Motel,** 1737 N. Oregon, Ontario 97914, tel. (541) 889-3101, will run you $35-65. The **Tapadera Motor Inn,** 1249 Tapadera Ave., Ontario, tel. (541) 889-8621, ranges $40-50 per night.

The **Grant House Bed and Breakfast,** 2525 3rd St., Baker 97814, tel. (541) 523-4364, charges $55-75. This large, four-story inn boasts an outdoor hot tub and five sleeping chambers, including the Gore Vidal and Cybill Shepherd rooms. The **Sunridge Inn,** 1 Sunridge Lane, Baker 97814, tel. (541) 523-6444, has a heated pool and private patios and is this town's high-priced spread with rates of $75. The **Western Motel,** 3055 10th St., Baker 97814, tel. (541) 523-4646, is a more economical choice, with rates of $26-33. If you don't feel like dining in their restaurant, you can whip up something in your own kitchen. **Stange Manor,** 1612 Walnut, La Grande 97850, tel. (541) 963-2400, is a Georgian colonial mansion built by a timber baron. Period furniture, large individually decorated rooms, and views of the mountains make this a steal at $70-95. Each of the four rooms has a bath. Other appreciated features are the cozy dining room fireplace, bikes available to guests, and home-cooked delicacies for breakfast.

The **El Dorado Inn,** 695 Campbell St., Baker 97814, tel. (541) 523-6494, is a bargain at $40-

49. Amenities include a 24-hour restaurant and an indoor pool and jacuzzi. To get there, take the city center exit of I-84. The hotel is conveniently located near the Greyhound station and the Baker City Visitor and Convention Bureau.

The **Union Hotel,** 326 N. Main, Union 97883, tel. (541) 562-5417, will take you back to another era, with a room and bath for around $40. The town of Union is 11 miles southeast of La Grande on ORE 203, and shows off lots of great old brick buildings and old-time atmosphere. The town museum has a great exhibit entitled "Cowboys Then and Now." The **Moon Motel,** 2116 Adams Ave., La Grande 97850, tel. (541) 963-2724, is the most affordable lodging in town, with rates of $30-40. The **Broken Arrow Lodge,** 2215 Adams Ave., tel. (541) 963-7176, is in the same range and offers a few spaces for RVs.

Food

Not too many recommendations on this route, but here are a few worth tucking in your napkin for. **Cafe du Jour,** 257 S. Oregon St., Ontario, is famous for muffins, brownies, and other baked goods. The **Front St. Cafe,** 1840 Main St., Baker City, tel. (541) 523-7526, is a good bet for lunch. Burgers, home fries, 14 varieties of salad, and good coffee can fortify your wanderings along the Oregon Trail. **Mamacita's,** 110 Depot, La Grande, tel. (541) 963-6223, has tasty Mexican food at moderate prices. The Guadalajara tostada and *arroz con pollo* are particularly good values. Flan and Kahlua pie are recommended for dessert. **Ten Depot Street,** 10 Depot St., La Grande, tel. (541) 963-8766, might be a harbinger of things to come. Such interesting plates as teriyaki tofu, Oregon-raised lamb chops, and a delicious salmon pâté will evoke bistros west of the Cascades. To complete the effect they also serve Portland microbrewery beer and ale. Dinner can sometimes run over $20 here in this converted old Mason's Lodge. A lot of people will tell you that the state's best fast food is available at **Nells In 'n' Out,** 1704½ Adams Ave., La Grande, tel. (541) 963-5733. Creative variations on shakes and floats, hand-curled French fries, and a full array of burgers are highlights.

Ten miles north of Baker City is the well-regarded **Haines Steakhouse,** ORE 30, tel. (541) 856-8639. Open Wed.-Mon. for dinner, you can sup on charcoal-grilled steak (there's also fish, chicken, and barbecued steak), garlicky potato salad, and smoky baked beans, if you're still hungry after a trip to the well-stocked salad bar. Antiques and cowboy Americana decorate the restaurant, enhancing what may be described as first-rate chuckwagon fare. Stetson-hatted diners and log-cabin style booths will get you in the mood for all this frontier hospitality. The restaurant's blond-wood false front stands out in this town of stone and brick structures like a Conestoga wagon on an open prairie.

Entertainment and Events

Like every town in America, each town on our route has a special festivity in which the locals whoop it up in their own way. The **Obon Odori Festival** celebrating Ontario's Japanese heritage is held the third week in July at the Buddhist temple. On the schedule are tours of the temple, a dinner featuring Asian cuisine, arts-and-crafts displays, and an evening of dancing with audience participation.

The **Vale Rodeo** is a four-day fête that takes place July 1-4. It's highlighted by the Suicide Race, an event held at nearby Vale Butte in which cowboys race their horses off a steep slope into the arena. The **Miner's Jubilee,** the big wingding in Baker, is traditionally celebrated during the third week in July. On the bill are a fiddle festival, an arts and crafts fair, bed and raft races, a cowbelles' breakfast, and the World Championship Porcupine Sprint Race. On the Fourth of July in Haines, a wide spot on ORE 30 between Baker and North Powder, they have a competition to name the oldest working cowhand in the Northwest. If you think you qualify call (541) 856-3211. La Grande's major celebrations of the year are the **Oregon Trail Days and Rendezvous** in mid-August and **Blue Mountain Days** in late June, which features a parade, rodeo, and motorcycle rally.

Health

Ontario's hospital is **Holy Rosary Medical Center,** 381 S.W. 9th, tel. (541) 889-5331. It has 24-hour emergency service. **St. Elizabeth Hospital,** 3325 Pocahontas Rd., Baker, also has a 24-hour emergency room. **Grande Ronde Hospital,** 900 Sunset Dr., La Grande, tel. (541) 963-8421, has an air ambulance service called Blue Mountain Aeromedical, tel. (800) 426-5554.

Getting Around

There is very little public transit in this land of large distances and small population. Here's what is available: **Greyhound** has terminals in Baker, 515 Campbell, tel. (541) 523-5011, and in La Grande, 2108 Cove Ave., tel. (541) 963-5156. Check in the La Grande terminal about Wallowa Stage Lines' once daily service to Joseph and Enterprise. You'll pay less than $10 for the two-hour trip. If you need wheels, call **Designated Driver Cab Co.,** tel. (541) 963-8960, or rent a rig from **Tamarack Ford,** tel. (541) 963-2161. **Grande Ronde Transportation Company,** 1901 Jefferson, La Grande 97850, tel. (541) 963-6119, has a bus charter service. **La Grande Aviation,** Route 2, Box 2546, La Grande 97850, tel. (541) 963-6572, will fly you where you want to go.

Information and Services

Useful information to aid your explorations along the old Oregon Trail is available from several **chambers of commerce,** including: the Malheur County Chamber of Commerce, 173 S.W. 1st St., Ontario 97914, tel. (541) 889-8012; the Vale County Chamber of Commerce, 272 N. Main, Vale 97918, tel. (541) 473-3800; the Baker County Chamber of Commerce, 490 Campbell St., Baker 97814, tel. (541) 523-5855; and the La Grande-Union County Chamber of Commerce, 2111 Adams, La Grande 97850, tel. (800) 848-9969. Better yet, contact the **Baker City Visitor and Convention Bureau,** 490 Campbell St., Baker City 97814, tel. (800) 523-1235, or call the **Eastern Oregon/Oregon Trail information phone,** tel. (800) 332-1843.

The 1100 block of Washington St. in La Grande features **Sunflower Books,** with adjacent coffee shop, a beautiful mural, and each Saturday morning June through September on the front lawn, the Blue Mountain Produce Market. Also worth noting is eastern Oregon's most complete bookstore, **Betty's Books,** 1813 Main St., Baker, tel. (541) 523-7551.

You can find a **post office** in Baker, 1550 Dewey Ave., Baker 97814, tel. (541) 523-4237, and in La Grande, 1202 Washington, La Grande 97850, tel. (541) 963-2041. The **state police** have offices in Baker, 1050 S. Bridge, tel. (541) 523-5866, and La Grande, 3014 Island Avenue, tel. (541) 963-7174. The **local police** also have offices in Baker, tel. (541) 523-3644, and La Grande, tel. (541) 962-1017. The *Baker City Herald,* P.O. Box 807, Baker City 97814, publishes a good annual travel guide to the local area. It's available free at area museums and tourist facilities. If you'd like it in advance, send $1.35 with your address and request to the newspaper.

BOB RACE

THE WALLOWAS

Acclaimed as the "Switzerland of America," the Wallowa Mountains and the broad valley to the north are not just another spectacular alpine region. Thanks to the outdoor-recreation boom and a publicity mill fueled by magazines like *Outside* and *Backpacker,* these mountains have become the new hot mecca for lovers of life on the wild side. Come now, before the word gets out about this backpackers' paradise where snowcapped Teton-like spires and blue-green glacial lakes are still relatively unvisited.

Ask most Oregonians who have been there and they will tell you that the Wallowa range is one place in Oregon "you gotta see—you just gotta." With 17 of the state's 29 mountains over 9,000 feet and 50 glacial lakes sprinkled throughout 300,000 acres, the Eagle Cap Wilderness is a recreational area that should figure prominently in your travel plans. Campers and cross-country skiers are regularly treated to glimpses of bighorn sheep, mountain goats, elk, and mule deer, as well as snow-streaked limestone peaks rising above meadows dotted with an artist's palette of wildflowers. But you don't have to go far into the backcountry to get away from it all here. With a population of only 7,000 in the county, and no traffic lights or cellular phone service, Oregon's northeastern corner offers plenty of places to hide. If you still need convincing, check out the handmade sign at the valley entrance: Deer and Elk Skins, Buy or Trade.

The Wallowa Valley is formed by the drainages of the Wallowa, Minam, and Grande Ronde rivers. The area's economy is fueled by the traditional eastern Oregon triad of timber, farming, and cattle ranching. Enterprise is the commercial center of it all, while Joseph is the hub of a growing arts community and the gateway to Wallowa Lake, a recreational haven at the end of the road. After a visit to this "larger-than-life" countryside, it is easy to see how it sustained the proud and indomitable Nez Percé, the native people who once roamed its river canyons, glacial basins, and grassy hills.

The Land
Topped by 10,004-foot Matterhorn and 9,933-foot Sacajawea peaks, the Wallowas are the wettest place east of the Cascades. The higher reaches of the range may receive 60 inches of precipitation annually. These upper elevations crest in the **Eagle Cap Wilderness Area** and descend gradually to the south toward Baker City. The mountains' two million acres extend east from La Grande past the Snake River into western Idaho. To the north, they nudge Hells Canyon country. The Wallowas are one of the West's oldest mountain ranges; seashells in limestone and greenstone outcroppings here attest to the range's 200 million years in age. It's theorized that these mountains were once part of tropical islands in the mid-Pacific. Due to continental drift, the range attached itself to an ancient coastline, much like the Klamaths did in southern Oregon. A different link has been established with the Austrian Alps since the Wallowas contain similar fossilized corals, mollusks, algae, and sponges.

HISTORY

The Wallowa Valley, set apart by deep river canyons and mountain ranges, is the ancestral home of the Nez Percé, a tribe known for its horse-raising skills and fierce independence. These regal people, astride their spotted Appaloosas, first encountered Europeans when mountain men wandered onto their land. At first they were friendly, feeding and caring for the Bonneville Party, which had struggled up out of the Snake River Canyon in 1834. Later, when a dry spell in the Grande Ronde Valley to the south prompted homesteaders to give the Wallowas a try, the two cultures clashed.

A tense era followed, in which various drafts of different treaties added to the confusion. The settlers later successfully lobbied the United States government to evict the natives, which led to the Nez Percé War of 1877. Chief Joseph and his people fought a running battle that covered 1,700 miles and ended with their surrender in the Bear's Paw Mountains, 50 miles from the Montana-Canada border. Meanwhile, back at the ranch in the Wallowa Valley, the toughest of the settlers endured the winters, droughts, and other hardships of life on the frontier. One bachelor, in an attempt to ease his loneliness, sent the following note to a friend in Missouri: "Send at once C.O.D. a good-looking maid or widow, 30 years or under. Widow with a few children preferred."

In 1908, a passenger train steamed into Wallowa on a newly laid track from Elgin, thus expanding a route that had previously seen only horses and wagons. Not much has changed since those early days. The people of the Wallowa Valley believe that they inhabit paradise, and they seem to enjoy sharing it with visitors drawn by its natural beauty and vivid history.

SIGHTS

Wildlife

Two wildlife-viewing areas await you as you sweep down into the Wallowa Valley. The **Spring Branch Wildlife Area,** a woodland marsh, is two miles east of Wallowa on ORE 82, on the north side where the road leaves the Wallowa River. The eight-acre viewing area, managed by the Oregon Department of Fish and Wildlife, has beaver dams and lots of waterfowl, including the black tern, an insect-eating bird found in eastern Oregon marshes. The **Enterprise Wildlife Area** is two miles west of Enterprise off ORE 82. To get there, turn south on Fish Hatchery Rd. to this 32-acre site located just before the fish hatchery. Walk down the dike that goes through a grove of trees to view marsh wrens, snipe, mink, beavers, and muskrats.

Culture in the Hinterland

If you have an afternoon to spare in **Enterprise,** the Wallowa County Centennial Committee has organized a **walking tour** for you. Stop by the chamber of commerce booth in the Enterprise Mall and pick up their brochure. It has descriptions and locations of many of the historic buildings in the area, like the Wallowa County Courthouse, the Enterprise Hotel, the Oddfellows Hall, and a number of private homes. After an hour of edification and exercise, take a break at the **Bookloft-Skylight Gallery,** 107 E. Main, Enterprise, tel. (541) 426-3351, just across the street from the county courthouse. This gathering spot for artists and community activists sells best-sellers and local-history books and offers monthly shows of guest artists, as well as freshly brewed coffee and home-baked cookies.

Joseph

Cruising farther into the valley, you reach the lively community of Joseph, named after the famous Nez Percé chief. The town's 1,000 residents populate the north end of Wallowa Lake, which is cradled at its southern tip by the Eagle Cap Wilderness area. A must-stop for history buffs is the **Wallowa County Museum** on Main St., tel. (541) 432-6095. Open from the last weekend in May to the third weekend in September, hours are daily 10 a.m.-5 p.m. Built in 1888, the museum building has served as a bank, a newspaper office, a private hospital, and a meeting hall. Its current incarnation as a museum started in 1960. The theme of the museum is Wallowa history, including displays of pioneer life and the Nez Percé tribe, the valley's original inhabitants. Near the museum during summer, a reenactment of the Great Joseph Bank Robbery takes place every Wednesday and Saturday at 1 p.m. As an ironic historical aside, one of the original robbers later became the bank's president.

Joseph is also the center of a blossoming art community in the Wallowas. Galleries here and in Enterprise showcase watercolor and oil paintings, sculpture, pottery, and photographs. Take a walk down Main St. and you'll find a number of art galleries and antique stores. World-famous bronzes by David Lee Manuel as well as Native American artifacts, John Wayne mementos, and Civil War memorabilia fill the attractive log confines of the **Manuel Museum,** tel. (541) 432-7325, also known as the Nez Percé Crossing Museum. The **Gene Hayes Gallery** specializes in the outdoors and the Old West. **Eagle Mountain Gallery and Valley Bronze,** 307 W. Alder St., tel. (541) 432-7551, also on Main, is a casting foundry that uses the lost-wax casting process to create monumental sculptures. Daily tours of the foundry and monument building are offered.

Other galleries include the **Wallowa Lake Gallery, Wild Goose Antiques,** and the **Edge of the Wilderness Gallery.**

Wallowa Lake

The brightest gem in the Wallowas setting is Wallowa Lake, which at 5,000 feet in elevation is the highest body of water in eastern Oregon.

CHIEF JOSEPH

The Nez Percé Indians had lived in peace with white explorers and neighboring tribes of the Northwest for generations. They gave the Lewis and Clark Expedition much needed horses and promised that they'd never make war on the white man. But with the incursion of miners and settlers, and because of misunderstandings surrounding the annexation of Indian land through a series of treaties never signed by Chief Joseph, tension increased to the breaking point. White disregard of native property spurred on some rash young Nez Percé to retaliate. The ensuing 11-week conflict, during which the Nez Percé engaged ten separate United States military commands in 13 battles (the majority of which the Nez Percé won), guaranteed Chief Joseph's fame as a brilliant military tactician. However, after many hardships, Chief Joseph surrendered with the following words to Generals Miles and Howard on October 5, 1877, only 50 miles from the sanctuary of the Canadian border.

Tell General Howard I know his heart. What he told me before, I have in my heart. I am tired of fighting. Our chiefs are killed. Looking Glass is dead. Too-hool-hool-suit is dead. The old men are dead. It is the young men who say yes and no. He who led on the young men is dead. It is cold and we have no blankets. The little children are freezing to death. My people, some of them, have run away to the hills and have no blankets, no food; no one knows where they are, perhaps freezing to death. I want to have time to look for my children and see how many I can find. Maybe I shall find them among the dead. Hear me, my chiefs. I am tired; my heart is sick and sad. From where the sun now stands, I will fight no more forever.

In 1879, Chief Joseph spoke to the Department of Indian Affairs in Washington D.C., detailing the broken promises of the government, the suffering of his people, and the unjust treatment of the Indians by white society.

I have heard talk and talk, but nothing is done. Good words do not last long unless they amount to something. Words do not pay for my dead people. They do not pay for my country, now overrun by white men. They do not protect my father's grave. They do not pay for all my horses and cattle. Good words will not give me back my children. Good words will not make good the promise of your War Chief General Miles. Good words will not give my people good health and stop them from dying. Good words will not get my people a home where they can live in peace and take care of themselves. I am tired of talk that comes to nothing. It makes my heart sick when I remember all the good words and all the broken promises. There has been too much talking by men who had no right to talk. Too many misrepresentations have been made, too many misunderstandings have come up between the white men about the Indians. If the white man wants to live in peace with the Indian he can live in peace. There need be no trouble. Treat all men alike. Give them the same law. Give them all an even chance to live and grow. All men were made by the same Great Spirit Chief. They are all brothers. The earth is the mother of all people, and all people should have equal rights upon it. You might as well expect the rivers to run backward as that any man who was a free man should be contented when penned up and denied liberty to go where he pleases. If you tie a horse to a stake, do you expect he will grow fat? If you pen an Indian up on a small spot of earth, and compel him to stay there, he will not be contented, nor will he grow and prosper. I have asked some of the great white chiefs where they get their authority to say to the Indian that he shall stay in one place, while he sees white men going where they please. They cannot tell me.

I only ask of the government to be treated as all other men are treated. If I cannot go to my own home, let me have a home in some country where my people will not die so fast. I would like to go to Bitter Root Valley. There my people would be healthy; where they are now they are dying. Three have died since I left my camp to come to Washington.

When I think of our condition my heart is heavy. I see men of my race treated as outlaws and driven from country to country, or shot down like animals.

I know that my race must change. We cannot hold our own with the white men as we are. We only ask an even chance to live as other men live. We ask to be recognized as men. We ask that the same law shall work alike on all men. If

the Indian breaks the law, punish him by the law. If the white man breaks the law, punish him also.

Let me be a free man—free to travel, free to stop, free to work, free to trade where I choose, free to choose my own teachers, free to follow the religion of my fathers, free to think and talk and act for myself—and I will obey every law, or submit to the penalty.

Whenever the white man treats an Indian as they treat each other, then we will have no more wars. We shall all be alike—brothers of one father and one mother, with one sky above us and one country around us, and one government for all. Then the Great Spirit Chief who rules above will smile upon this land, and send rain to wash out the bloody spots made by brothers' hands from the face of the earth. For this time the Indian race are waiting and praying. I hope that no more groans of wounded men and women will ever go to the ear of the Great Spirit Chief above, and that all people may be one people.

ANNIE LONG LARSEN

This classic moraine-held glacial lake is a few miles south of Joseph on ORE 82 at the east end of the Wallowa Valley. The lake is ringed with lodges, amusement rides, a large state park with an overnight campground, packhorse corrals, boat launches, and marinas. It is also home to the **Wallowa Lake Monster,** a creature with a gentle disposition and a length varying 30-100 feet, depending on the sighting. Reports of the critter go back several centuries to Native American tales and are also the current focus of the Monster Observation and Preser-

vation Society (MOPS). Around the lake you'll find cottonwood, larch, spruce, and fir.

A real treat for visitors is a ride in the **Mt. Howard Gondola.** Open during the summer 10 a.m.-4 p.m., the gondola route is the steepest and longest in North America, lifting passengers from the edge of Wallowa Lake up 3,200 feet to the 8,200-foot summit of Mt. Howard. As the lift floats upward, the pastureland and wheatfield views near Wallowa Lake give way to forests of lodgepole pine, tamarack, and quaking aspen. On top stay on the trails through the fragile alpine tundra so as not to damage the tiny and rare plants here. The 15-minute trip in the closed gondola car costs $9 for adults, $8 for seniors, and $5 for children 10 and under. It operates daily June-Aug., and half days in May and September. The ride ends at a snack bar and gift shop on top of the peak. But forget about the snacks, knick-knacks, and trinkets; the best reason for taking the trip is the view of 26 mountain peaks, including the Wallowa Range, Snake River country, and Idaho's Seven Devils area. The eight peaks of Eagle Cap Wilderness are mirrored into the lake below, and the gorges of the Snake and Imnaha rivers stretch to the east.

ROAD TRIPS

Joseph Canyon Viewpoint

Thirty miles north of Wallowa Lake via ORE 3 from Enterprise is Joseph Canyon Viewpoint, overlooking the canyon that served as a winter homeland for the Nez Percé. In 1997, a lot of land in this area passed back into Nez Percé hands.

Wallowa Mountain Loop Road

This is a scenic 54-mile drive into Hells Canyon Country. It begins with the Joseph-Imnaha highway through farms and canyons. Turn south on Wallowa Mountain Loop Road to the Imnaha River, then ascend into alpine forests along Dry Creek Rd. to Halfway. You'll come out on the south flank of the Wallowas where *Paint Your Wagon,* starring Lee Marvin, was filmed in the '60s and Disney's *Homeward Bound* was filmed in the early '90s. Turn east for a shoreline view of Snake River Canyon and Hells Canyon at Oxbow (Hells Canyon and Brownlee Dams). This fully paved route can serve as a shortcut to Baker and Boise in summer.

SPORTS AND RECREATION

Hiking and Camping

Most Eagle Cap Wilderness Area trails are long and steep, and most alpine lakes are at least five miles from a trailhead, so opportunities for easy day hikes are few. Camping is the best way to enjoy the area. Before heading out, pick up the Eagle Cap map from a Forest Service office or at local sporting goods stores. Higher elevations are usually free from snow by July 1.

Camping out in the Wallowa Valley and the Eagle Cap Wilderness can be as easy as pulling off ORE 82 just 15 miles east of Elgin and pitching your tent at **Minam State Recreation Area,** $6, or as rigorous as using one of the following three campsites as a jumping-off point for backpacking into the high country.

Boundary Campsite is five miles south of Wallowa on County Route 515, then two miles south on Forest Service Rd. 163. There's no fee for this site set along the banks of Bear Creek, but there's also no water. A trailhead provides access to the dazzling grandeur of the Eagle Cap basin.

The next campsite/trailhead is **Two Pan,** one of the most popular gateways into the Wallowas. To get there, head south from Lostine on County Route 551 for seven miles and down Forest Service Rd. 5202 for 11 miles. This is a rough and rocky washboard grade, so take your time. Firewood and vault toilets are available; there are no fees or water. Trails leave Two Pan for the Lostine River Valley and the glacial lakes at the base of Eagle Cap.

The third campsite is **Hurricane Creek,** three miles southwest of Joseph on Forest Service Rd. 8205. There's no charge for overnight camping, and piped water and firewood are available. The Hurricane Creek trailhead leads to a hike along the east slope of the Hurricane Divide past Sacajawea Peak and the Matterhorn to the glacial lakes basin. An ambitious trek would start at Two Pan and end at Hurricane Creek. The lake basin area south of Joseph can get crowded, especially on July and August weekends.

Then there's always **Wallowa State Park** campground, Wallowa Lake, Rt. 1, Box 323, Joseph 97846, reservation tel. (800) 452-5687, information tel. (541) 432-4185. This is one of 13 Oregon campgrounds that operate on a reservation system (see "Camping and Hiking" under "Outdoor Activities" in the On the Road chapter); reserve seven months in advance or you're outta luck. Lake views, large campsites (89 tent and 121 RV sites), clean bathhouses, and covered kitchen shelters make it worth the $16-20 nightly fee. A marina, a sports field, and the cultural diversions of nearby Joseph (home to the Jazz at

OREGON TOURISM DIVISION

At Eagle Cap you can hike where eagles soar.

the Lake Festival in July) also recommend an early reservation. As one of six outstanding far West parks chosen by *National Geographic,* this site is not what you'd call a secret hideaway.

Skiing

The recreational delights of the Wallowas are not reserved for summer only. The skiing in this alpine wonderland is excellent. **Ferguson Ridge Ski Area,** tel. (541) 426-3493, is a good example. To get there, drive east from Joseph about five miles on the Wallowa Loop Hwy., then follow signs south on Tucker Down Road. This small facility has a rope tow and T-bar that climb from a 5,100-foot base to 5,800-foot-high Ferguson Ridge. Lift tickets are $7 a day; children under 13 pay $5. It's open 10 a.m.-4 p.m. weekends and holidays. The light eastern Oregon powder here, when there's enough of it, makes for good skiing. Nordic skiers can try a mile loop trail or take an eight-mile marked and packed route to Salt Creek Summit.

Another popular spot is **Salt Creek Summit,** about 20 miles southeast of Joseph on Wallowa Loop Highway. The facility has five miles of marked but ungroomed ski trails and a plowed snow park. A European approach to a skiing adventure is a tour of **Wallowa Alpine Huts.** Three-day, two-night hut-to-hut tours of the

Eagle Cap Wilderness are priced in the $250 range. Skiers making the seven-mile trek only have to carry personal gear; bedding and meals are provided, along with woodstoves and saunas at the huts. Also available are lessons, helicopter skiing, and telemark camps. For information contact Alpine Huts, P.O. Box 9252, Moscow, ID 83843, tel. (800) 545-5537.

For cross-country skiers, the **Wallowa Lake Nordic Center,** Wallowa Lake State Park, tel. (541) 426-4611, maintains 13 miles of Nordic ski trails around Wallowa Lake. Finally, **Sacajawea Park Cross-Country Ski Trail** challenges the ambitious. Take Hurricane Creek Rd. west from Joseph to the Hurricane Creek trailhead. This cross-country ski route will take you up into a basin on the northeast side of Sacajawea Peak. After two steep miles through the forest, the trail opens up into a clear area with a view of the surrounding glacial peaks. For more information on this trek call the Eagle Cap Ranger District office at (541) 426-3104.

Outfitters

If your budget allows for a guided adventure into the Wallowa wilds, here are two excellent services. The **Eagle Cap Wilderness Pack Station,** Route 1, Box 416, Joseph, tel. (541) 432-4145, charges fees starting at $7 an hour per person for short trips to lakes and streams in the Eagle Cap high country, and going up to $750 for deluxe excursions to Hells Canyon or along the Imnaha River. **Wallowa Llamas,** Route 1, Box 84, Halfway 97834, tel. (541) 742-4930, will show you a unique way to venture into the wilderness. One surefooted, even-tempered llama will carry 20 pounds of your gear; you carry the rest. The outfit offers trips to Hells Canyon, Imnaha Falls, Eagle Meadows, and across the rugged Wallowas. The expeditions are designed for those with some backpacking experience or anyone in reasonably good shape. Excursions average $75-100 per day for several days or a week.

Fishing

Fishing in this high country is a matter of choosing your favorite game fish. You can catch kokanee (landlocked salmon) and mackinaws in **Wallowa Lake,** trout and steelhead in the streams that flow out of the ice-capped mountains, or bass, crappie, and sturgeon in the **Snake River.** According to experts, the **Imnaha River** is one of the best late-season fishing streams in the Pacific Northwest.

PRACTICALITIES

Accommodations

The following lodgings in the Wallowas reflect the special flavor of this unique outback.

On the Imnaha River 14 miles south of Imnaha is **Diamond W Ranch,** Route 1, Box 466, Imnaha 97842, tel. (541) 577-3157. Rates start at $60 for adults and $30 for children and include meals and horses. The **Flying Arrow Resort,** 59782 Wallowa Lake Hwy., Joseph 97846, tel. (541) 432-2951, not only has a great name but also a swimming pool, hot tub, chocolate shop, bookstore, and village market. Rates range $60-168.

Red's Wallowa Horse Ranch, P.O. Box 26, Joseph 97846, tel. (541) 432-9171, is one of Oregon's best-known retreats. The lodge is tucked away in a high mountain valley with no phones or electricity and is famous for its home cooking and hospitality. You either fly in or arrive by an eight-mile pack trip. Guests stay in the lodge or in log cabins equipped with hot water,

kerosene lamps, and fireplaces. Horseback rides, hiking, fishing, snowshoeing, and cross-country skiing trips can be arranged. Package rates are $75-100 a day for the whole shootin' match. The Forest Service is debating the future of this oasis in the wilderness, so call ahead.

Another accommodation near Joseph is **Eagle Cap Chalets,** Route 1, Box 419, Wallowa Lake Hwy., Joseph 97846, tel. (541) 432-4704. Tucked into the pines, this cluster of cabins and condos has all you need to visit Wallowa Lake in comfort and style. Rates run $52-90. In town, for lodging with fair prices, $40-50, and such little touches as flower baskets and decorative prints, try the **Indian Lodge,** 201 S. Main St., Joseph 97846, tel. (541) 432-2651.

A couple of hostelries on the shore of Wallowa Lake are good bets for those who want comfort rather than campouts. The **Wallowa Lake Lodge,** P.O. Box 1, Joseph 97846, tel. (541) 432-9821, is a renovated 1923 hotel with a room for two in the $70 range in winter and $85 in summer. Eight cabins with fireplaces and kitchens start at $55 in winter and $105 in summer. Despite their considerable charm, some of the 22 rooms recall the closet-sized dimensions of a cruise-ship stateroom. The Nordic center is a five-minute walk away and there are a store and gas station on the grounds. There's a dearth of twin-bed rooms in the main lodge, so reserve early. Even if you don't stay overnight, the dining room is worth a stop for its hazelnut pancakes with marionberry butter. Sitting by the lobby fireplace on a cold morning is also a delight. **Matterhorn Swiss Village,** Route 1, Box 350, Joseph 97846, tel. (541) 432-4071, has rates from $41 to $48. In keeping with the notion that the Wallowas are the Switzerland of America, this facility has six cottages with names like the Alpenhof and Berghof, a gift and sports shop, and water-ski, bike, and windsurfing gear rentals.

Food

Like most frontier outposts in the American West, the Wallowa Valley has lots of standard takeout joints and few eateries worth a special stop. However, the following restaurants will not only keep you going during your visit but give you a few tasty surprises as well.

The **T'N'T Kitchen** in Wallowa, tel. (541) 886-7705, grills a tasty buffalo burger with soup, salad, and fries for under $5. They also sell stuffed buffalo toys in case the kids would rather play with their food than eat it. **Cloud Nine,** 105 S.E. 1st, Enterprise, tel. (541) 426-3790, serves up deli sandwiches, good coffee, and home-made soups in an old firehouse. Sandwiches run $3-5. **A Country Place on Pete's Pond,** P.O. Box 459, Montclair St., Enterprise, tel. (541) 426-3642, is a charming lunch spot on the edge of a five-acre lake. Pete invites you to feed the fish, enjoy the swans, and eat indoors or out on the lawn. A floating bandstand has musical entertainment on some occasions. Their sandwiches run $4-5, are made with homemade bread, and come with fries, salad, or soup.

Another spot in Enterprise with good food is **Sonita's Cafe Olé,** 107 S.W. 1st St., tel. (541) 426-4888. Located in the Enterprise Mall, the cafe has both Mexican and American dishes with combination dinners running $6-15. Specialties include the Burrito Del Mar with shrimp and Monterey jack for $10.95 and chimichangas for $6.95.

Your best bet in Joseph is **Pam's Country Inn Restaurant,** 500 N. Main, tel. (541) 432-1195. Pam's has an ambience reminiscent of a French country inn. Their "country cooking" menu features dinners starting at $6 and house specialties like beef Wellington and chicken teriyaki from $10. Their eight-ounce filet mignon runs $14.95. Close to Wallowa Lake, **Vali's Alpine Delicatessen** features great cinnamon rolls and homemade doughnuts at breakfast (9-11 a.m.) and a different dinner menu each day featuring German and Hungarian specialties. Seatings are at 6 and 8 p.m.; reservations are recommended. Open Tues.-Sun. in summer, weekends only in winter.

Entertainment and Events

Most of the local celebrations here revolve around cowboys and Indians and the arts community. The **Wallowa Valley Festival of the Arts** held at the Joseph Civic Center happens in the third week of April. Along with awards for Northwest artists, there are winetasting parties, a silent auction, and a quick-draw competition. A recent addition to the festivities is a reading by cowboy poets. For information on the festival call the Wallowa Valley Arts Council at (800) 635-2000. The **Wallowa County Fiddlers' Con-**test brings fiddlers from throughout the Northwest to mix it up with music, good grub, and the spirit of the pioneer days. Held in Enterprise on the third weekend in July, the contest is a treat for both the performers and their appreciative audiences. **Jazz at the Lake,** tel. (541) 963-8530, takes place at Wallowa Lake in mid-July with artists from thoughout the U.S. participating. Around the same time in Joseph, a low-key but talent-laden literary gathering known as **Fishtrap,** tel. (541) 426-3623, is held in an old Methodist meetinghouse. Authors writing in different genres attend. In years past William Kitteridge, Ursula LeGuin, Ivan Doig, Sandra Scofield, and Terry Tempest Williams have attended. For more information, write to Fishtrap, P.O. Box 38, Enterprise 97828.

The tiny town of **Lostine** celebrates the **Fourth of July** with artists, craftspeople, and collectors plying their wares in the Lostine Sidewalk Flea Market. People come here from all over the Northwest beginning on Friday 6-9 p.m. and continuing on Saturday noon-9 p.m. Call (541) 963-8530 for details.

Chief Joseph Days is a weeklong cowboy-and-Indian festival hosted by Joseph, the little town near Wallowa Lake. Held in late July, the list of events includes dances, a carnival, a Grand Parade, a ranch-style breakfast, and a three-day rodeo, which has grown to be one of the largest in the Northwest. For tickets and information call (541) 432-1015. Another echo of the Wild West can be witnessed at 1 p.m. every Wednesday, Friday, and Saturday during the summer as four outlaws ride into town and rob the First Bank of Joseph. This dramatic re-creation of a historic robbery is played out on the spot of the original heist. The bank building now houses the Wallowa County Museum.

Alpenfest is a three-day festival held the third weekend after Labor Day in Edelweiss Hall next to the tramway at Wallowa Lake. This gala is a return to the old country and all that's Bavarian, sending echoes into the mountains with music, alpenhorn blowing, and yodeling competitions. Dancing, sailboat racing, and a bounty of Northern European cuisine are also featured. For reservations and information call the Wallowa Lake Tourist Committee at (541) 432-6325.

Hells Canyon Mule Days, held the second weekend after Labor Day at the Enterprise Fairgrounds, is where pack-animal fanciers can get their kicks. The action includes mule races, a parade, a speed mule-shoeing contest, and endurance races.

Getting There and Getting Around
The main road into the valley, ORE 821 through the Minam Gorge, has been divided, easing the six-hour drive from Portland. **Moffit Brothers Transportation,** Lostine, tel. (541) 569-2284, makes a daily roundtrip between La Grande and Wallowa Lake. **Wallowa Valley Stage,** tel. (541) 432-3531, leaves from Paul's Chevron in Joseph. Don't worry about finding this gas station; it's the only one in town.

Two air services operate in Wallowa County. **Joseph Air Service,** Airport Rd., Joseph, tel. (541) 432-6305, and **Spence Air Service,** P.O. Box 217, Enterprise, tel. (541) 426-3288, are both listed in the *Oregon Pilot's Guide* and are available for charter flights. Joseph's shabby airport will be undergoing renovation in the near future. Another option is to take a Horizon flight to Lewiston, Idaho and rent a car for the 85-mile drive west; you eventually hook up with ORE 3. Or fly into Pendleton, 120 miles away by car.

Information and Services
The Wallowa **post office** is at 104 N. Stories, tel. (541) 886-3422, while the one in Enterprise is at 201 W. North, tel. (541) 426-3555. The local office of the **Oregon State Police** is at 522 River, Enterprise, tel. (541) 426-3036. Contact the Wallowa sheriff's office at (541) 426-3131, Wallowa police at (541) 886-2422, Enterprise police at (541) 426-3755, and Joseph police at (541) 432-3832. The only hospital in Wallowa County is the **Wallowa Memorial Hospital,** 410 E. 1st, Enterprise, tel. (541) 426-3111.

The **Wallowa County Chamber of Commerce,** P.O. Box 427A, 107 S.W. 1st St., Enterprise 97828, tel. (541) 426-4622, has a booth in the Enterprise Mall with a full complement of brochures, maps, and other information on the area. Additional information is available from the **Joseph Chamber of Commerce,** P.O. Box 13, Dept. CC, Joseph 97846, tel. (541) 433-1015, and the **Wallowa Lake Tourist Commission,** P.O. Box 853, Dept. V, Joseph 97846. The county has two newspapers, the *Wallowa County Chieftain,* 106 N.W. 1st, Enterprise, tel. (541) 426-4567, and the *Joseph Eagle,* P.O. Box 549, Joseph, tel. (541) 432-5585. If you need to get in touch with the **Forest Service,** the Eagle Cap Ranger District office is at 612 S.W. 2nd, Enterprise, tel. (541) 426-3104; the Wallowa Valley Ranger District is one mile north of Joseph on ORE 82, tel. (541) 432-2171.

Given that two-thirds of the county hereabouts is federal land contained in the Eagle Cap Wilderness, the Wallowa-Whitman National Forest, and the Hells Canyon National Recreation Area, it's a good idea to visit the **Wallowa Information Center,** tel. (541) 426-4978, a half mile west of Enterprise. Exhibits highlighting forests, geology, and wildlife complement an observation deck with views of meadows, farms, and mountains. The center is open Mon.-Fri. 7:30 a.m.-5 p.m.

elk

BOB RACE

HELLS CANYON

Hells Canyon, carved out by the Snake River, is the deepest river-carved gorge in the world, averaging 6,600 feet in depth. A 67-mile stretch of the Snake at the bottom of this canyon is one of the nation's protected Wild and Scenic Rivers. In 1975, Congress established the **Hells Canyon National Recreation Area,** comprising 650,000 acres of stunning vistas, archaeological sites with petroglyphs, and native ruins, as well as a mighty river thundering through rugged canyon lands. For a 40-mile stretch between Oregon and Idaho, the canyon averages just 10 miles in width, contrasting with its 5,500-6,100-foot-depth along the same stretch. It's a hard place to get to, so be sure you check the local weather and road conditions before visiting the area. Also, it's a good idea to pack a snakebite kit. There are rattlesnakes in this country!

There are several ways to get to Hells Canyon from the Oregon side. The first route is easiest and on paved roads. From Baker take ORE 86 for 50 miles east to **Halfway.** Stop here to stock up on groceries and gas and then continue on ORE 86 another 16 miles to Oxbow Dam and then another 20 miles to Hells Canyon Dam. A new visitor center is open on the Idaho side of this dam, adjacent to where rafts put in on the Snake River. This site affords a spectacular view of the canyon. Another paved approach is via ORE 82 through the Wallowa Valley to Enterprise, Joseph, and Imnaha. From Imnaha, one of the most isolated towns in America, take a rough albeit recently improved road for 24 miles to Hat Point Lookout. Once you get there you'll be convinced that the all-encompassing view was worth the hassle.

Sights

The interior of Hells Canyon is a rugged wilderness framed by basalt cliffs. From Idaho's Seven Devils Wilderness to the Snake River in Hells Canyon you'll find areas that replicate most of North America's ecological zones. Cheatgrass, primroses, sunflowers, and prickly pear cactus are included in the canyon's varied botany. Bear, elk, mule deer, bighorn sheep, eagles, otters, and chukhar partridges are frequently seen here.

Many outfitters can steer you to the canyon's pictographs, which some sources place at 10,000 years of age. In addition to Chief Joseph and his Nez Percé tribe, the area was also occupied by miners and pioneers, as turn-of-the-century log cabins and shacks attest.

SPORTS AND RECREATION

In its new 10-year plan, the Forest Service is proposing Hells Canyon tourist developments and further motorization of the rims and canyons. With the increase in snowmobile use and jet boat business on the Snake, controversies endemic to the preservation-versus-use question are to be expected. Throw proposals for more salvage logging and livestock grazing into the mix, and you have the makings of an environmental cause celebre. Whatever happens, the resulting publicity is bound to draw more people in the long run, so the next several years may be prime time to know Hells Canyon as it was.

Backpacking

Before your trip into Hells Canyon, consider what the authors of *Hiking Guide to the Great Northwest* (Seattle: The Mountaineers, 1991) have to say about hiking here: "Hells Canyon is definitely not paradise. Summer temperatures soar above 100°, rattlesnakes abound, and . . . despite the river, drinkable water can be hard to find." Nonetheless, over 900 miles of trails provide hikers with a wide variety of recreational choices in the Hells Canyon Recreation Area. Major trails are maintained but others are difficult to follow. Ticks and poison oak can be problems here, too. Black widow and brown recluse spiders constitute the biggest danger, however. There are 12 campgrounds on the Oregon side of Hells Canyon. Here are a few of the better ones.

Lake Fork Campground is 18 miles northeast of Halfway on Forest Service Rd. 39. There are 10 sites with drinking water, and the fishing is good at nearby Fish Lake. **Indian Crossing** is located 45 miles southeast of Joseph on Forest Service Rd. 3960 and has drinking water as well as a trailhead for backpacking into the Eagle Cap Wilderness. On the northern end of the recreational area, **Buckhorn Springs** is 43 miles northeast of Enterprise and features a great view, spring water, and berry-picking in season.

River Outfitters

Spring and fall are the best seasons for water sports. **Hells Canyon Challenge,** Star Route, Box 25, Lostine 97857, tel. (541) 569-2445, offers an excursion full of excitement and gorgeous views. You start out at the mouth of the Grande Ronde River and then power up the Snake River in a jetboat. The rates average $50-70 for a one-day trip and go up to $150 for a two-day trip for four persons. Other river guides offering trips up and down the Snake are **Hells Canyon Adventures,** P.O. Box 159, Oxbow 97840, tel. (800) (541) 422-3568, and **Anderson River Adventures,** Route 2, Box 192-H, Milton-Freewater 97862, tel. (541) 558-3629. They both have one-day trips for under $100. In addition, Hells Canyon Adventures offers jetboat trips. The **Oregon outfitter's** publication is a good resource in which to locate other outfitters, P.O. Box 10841, Eugene 97440, tel. (541) 683-9552. Those interested in jetboat trips should remember that the Forest Service decided to limit jetboat use to four days a week in peak season on the Snake River. This was done to make it safer for rafters. Call the Hells Canyon NRA, tel. (541) 426-3151, for more information.

Fishing for trout, catfish, smallmouth bass, and, if you're lucky, 100-year-old sturgeon can add to the pleasure of a raft trip. You might also enjoy swimming in 68° water. Trips last three to five days, putting in at Hells Canyon Dam or Dug Bar. Try to go either before May 27 or after September 15 to avoid the crowds. Hire a good guide to deal with rough rapids; the Snake River has sections with Class V whitewater.

Another option is a hike/day-trip offered by **Canyon Outfitters,** P.O. Box 893, Halfway 97834, tel. (541) 742-4110. Boats parallel your hike, allowing you to float when you're tired of walking, or when the trail strays from scenic sections along the river. Expect gourmet food and a lot of local color shared around the campfire at day's end. Trips begin at a Halfway bed and breakfast, where Canyon Outfitters provides transport to the launch point 40 miles below the Hells Canyon Dam. Four days later you're at Pittsburg Landing. The hosts will also arrange trips out of the canyon ranging from horseback to airplane.

PRACTICALITIES

Accommodations

Clear Creek Farm Bed and Breakfast, Route 1, Box 138, Halfway 97834, tel. (541) 742-2233, is in a comfy old farmhouse on 160 secluded acres with a creek and pond for swimming and a great view of the upper Hells Canyon and Eagle Cap Wilderness. Best of all, it's all yours for $45. **Birch Leaf Lodge,** Route 1, Box 91, Halfway 97834, tel. (541) 742-2990, is a turn-of-the-century farmhouse on 42 acres at the foot of the Wallowa Mountains. Rates run $65-75 and include an organic country breakfast. The birding here is exceptional. A special feature of this bed and breakfast is a resident excursion planner who will help you schedule your recreational activities. Particularly recommended is a loop taking in the Oregon Trail Visitor Center at Baker City, and McGraw Point, the only paved Hells Canyon overlook from Halfway, en route north to Joseph. From McGraw Point, reachable by Forest Service Roads 39 and 3465, you can see the Snake River Canyon, the Seven Devils Range, and the McGraw Canyon. Snow impedes access in November.

Reasonably priced rooms can be had at the **Halfway Hotel,** 170 S. Main, Halfway 97834, tel. (541) 742-5722. Some have kitchenettes; all are close to gas, food, and shops.

Food

If you're on your own, it would be prudent to pack a few picnic items. Restaurants are few and far between in this country. But there is a good restaurant in Halfway called **Wild Bill's,** named after the owner. Their dinners run $4.95-12.95 with two specials of the house—chicken teriyaki for $7 and chicken-fried steak made with their homemade gravy for $6.50. Also worth a stop here is **Amador's,** 166 N. Main St. Halfway 97834, tel. (541) 742-5722, which serves surprisingly urbane fare with homemade flair. Pasta dishes are highly recommended. Lunch hours are Tues.-Sat. 11 a.m.-3 p.m.; call for dinner hours. Close by, the **Pine Valley**

Lodge/Halfway Supper Club, 163 N. Main St., Halfway 97834, tel. (541) 742-2025, is one place in town that goes all the way. Candlelit haute cuisine and eiderdown bedding set the local standard for bed and board.

Information
Hells Canyon National Recreation Area Headquarters, P.O. Box 490, Enterprise 97828, tel. (541) 426-3151, has additional information on Hells Canyon.

PENDLETON

The title of Sam Shepard's play *True West* is an appropriate moniker for this outpost on the prairie. People are really at home on the range here, leaving the city streets pretty quiet until a mid-September rodeo draws cowboys, cowgirls, and wannabes from all over the West. The transformation of Pendleton from a refueling and supply stop for surrounding ranchers to "party central" takes place in September during the Round-Up, with brewtaps going full tilt and streets filled with tourists in straw cowboy hats and bright new bandanas. When you're done whooping it up with the local good ol' boys, a town rich in history and memory awaits.

With a population of 15,000, Pendleton is one of the largest towns in eastern Oregon. It's an economic force thanks to vast wheat fields (Umatilla County ranks fifth in the U.S. in wheat production), rows of green peas, famous woolen mills, and tourism from the Pendleton Round-Up. The climate is mild and dry, with an average temperature of 51° and annual rainfall of 13 inches. Locals joke that this is where summer spends the winter. Located on I-84 equidistant from Portland, Seattle, Spokane, and Boise, Pendleton sits pretty much by itself in the midst of wide-open spaces. Residents like it that way.

HISTORY

Pendleton, originally called Goodwin's Station, is situated two miles downriver from the Oregon Trail's crossing at Emigrant Springs State Park. For millennia the ancient homeland of the Umatilla Indians, the area was visited by Lewis and Clark in 1805 and John Jacob Astor's American Fur Company in 1812. No Europeans put down roots until 1843, when Methodist missionaries led by Dr. Marcus Whitman brought a thousand settlers and 1,300 cattle to the region. The town itself, named after Senator George

Hunt Pendleton, was founded in 1868 and incorporated in 1880. At that time, Pendleton consisted of a hotel and five houses. But it grew through the late 1880s into a ripsnorting cattle and farming center with 18 houses of negotiable affection and 32 saloons. It quickly gained the reputation of being the town that couldn't be tamed. The feistiness of the citizens here was demonstrated by the theft of the county seal and records from Umatilla Landing, thus making Pendleton the county seat.

ORIENTATION

Many of Pendleton's streets are named after Confederate generals—a legacy of hundreds of Southern emigrants who drifted west after the Civil War. Still other streets are numbered chronologically, but with confusing directional considerations. This has resulted in two 1st Streets (one southeast, one southwest), two 2nd Streets, and so on—good luck.

Finally, be aware that the stretch of I-84 above Pendleton known as Cabbage Hill is treacherous to drive during icy winters. In addition to the slickness of the surface, sudden blizzards and high winds can result in white-out conditions.

SIGHTS

Round-Up Hall of Fame
The Round-Up Hall of Fame, 13th and S.W. Court Ave., open 10 a.m.-5 p.m. every day during the summer, can be found under the south grandstand area at the Round-Up Stadium. The history of America's biggest rodeo is depicted in photos of past champions and famous bucking broncos along with displays of artifacts. The star of the show is a stuffed horse named War Paint. Admission is free and guided tours are avail-

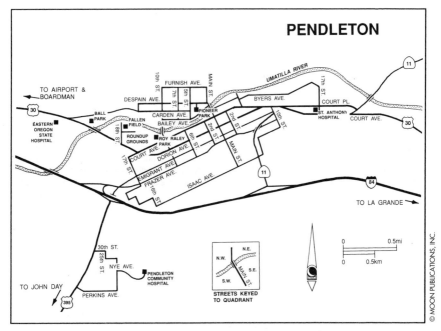

PENDLETON

able. The Pendleton Round-Up itself costs $5-10 and takes place over four days in September (see "Entertainment and Events" following).

Pendleton Woolen Mills
Next to the Pendleton Round-Up, the town is best known for the Pendleton Woolen Mills, 1307 S.E. Court Place, tel. (541) 276-6911, where they make those immortal plaid shirts. After shearing, the wool goes to a scouring mill in Portland where it's graded, sorted, and washed. Then the dried wool returns to the Pendleton mill for dyeing, carding, spinning, rewinding, and weaving.

The business began over in the Willamette Valley in Brownsville when Thomas Kay, a Yorkshire man whose family was in the woolen business in England, started a weaving mill. His descendant, Clarence Bishop, founded the Pendleton facility. Production began in 1909 with Indian-style blankets, which are still going strong, along with men's and women's sportswear. There are several different labels produced by Pendleton. The "Pendleton" label blankets are all wool and

are the most extensively marketed to the public. The "Beaver State" blankets are made with a pure fleece wool filling and are heavier with more intricate designs than the Pendletons; they're also more expensive. The "Cayuse Blanket" is a lower-priced version of the latter. Pendleton carved its lucrative niche by copying traditional designs for blankets used by Native Americans in Arizona and New Mexico. It introduced Western-style woolen shirts in the 1920s.

Tours run Mon.-Fri. at 9 a.m., 11 a.m., 1:30 p.m., and 3 p.m. Large groups are asked to make an appointment. To get to the mills on I-84 going east, take exit 207 through Pendleton on Dorion. Do not cross the viaduct but turn left and proceed four blocks. For additional information, write P.O. Box 969, Pendleton 97801.

Umatilla County
Historical Society Museum
In 1881 the Oregon-Washington Railway and Navigation Company, a subsidiary of the Union Pacific Railroad, constructed the northern branch of its transcontinental railroad through northeast

Oregon, and Pendleton served as an important stop on the route. By 1910, Pendleton had become the second-largest city in eastern Oregon and merited a new railroad depot. The building, P.O. Box 253, 108 S.W. Frazer, Pendleton 97801, tel. (541) 276-0012, an adaptation of the California mission style, boasted multipaneled windows, decorative brickwork, and wide, flaring eaves. The depot no longer serves railroad passengers but instead houses the museum's collection of Oregon Trail pioneer and Indian artifacts. Gold miners, sheep ranchers, and moonshiners are also given attention here in well-captured displays. Particularly interesting is a depiction of native blanket styles used to communicate anger, courtship, and other nonverbal messages enhancing social interaction.

Native Peoples Museum

Providing a much needed balance to the saga of Oregon pioneer migration, the Confederated Tribes of the Umatilla Reservation just outside town are putting together a 43,000-square-foot museum. To get there from I-84, take Exit 216 and drive north for one mile. The museum describes the effects of the white settler's arrival here. Featured are exhibits on tribal life prior to the pioneers' arrival; the impact of the horse (brought to North America by Europeans) on native peoples; and an Oregon Trail retrospective from the point of view of the Cayuse, Umatilla, and Walla Walla tribes. The trail passed right through the current reservation site and meant long-term environmental problems, including diminished salmon runs and the depletion of the Blue Mountains forests. The trail also brought chicken pox and measles, while the railroad that paralleled the trail brought tobacco, syphilis, and tuberculosis. Today, nuclear wastes are transported along I-84, paralleling the ruts where prairie schooners once traveled. In addition to human historical perspectives, an inquiry into the future of the land looks at once-flourishing animal and plant populations that are now extinct, as well as the deleterious effects of newly introduced "exotics" from Europe and Asia. Sharing this 640-acre site at the base of the Blue Mountains is a gaming resort, golf course, RV park, motel, and restaurant. The Interpretive Center will add a living encampment, interpretive trails, and an outdoor amphitheater.

As the museum is still under construction, call the Pendleton Chamber of Commerce Visitors and Convention Bureau, tel. (541) 276-7411, or the **Wildhorse Gaming Center,** tel. (800) 654-WILD, for hours and further information.

Tours

One of the area's liveliest attractions is **Pendleton Underground Tours,** P.O. Box 1072, 37 S.W. Emigrant Ave., Pendleton 97801, tel. (541) 276-0730. This visit to the wild and woolly days of the Old West takes you through the tunnels underneath Pendleton's historic district. The tour starts at S.W. 1st and Emigrant and continues to the old Shamrock Cardroom, filled with the bouncy sounds of honkytonk music. From there, it's on to the Cozy Rooms Bordello, Hop Sing's laundry, and the Empire Meat Company, complete with mannequins. In March and October, for $20 participants can feel like a part of history. After this event you'll understand how the old town of 3,000 once supported 32 saloons and 18 bordellos.

At one time a series of 90 passageways, originally dug as freight tunnels by Chinese workers who weren't allowed to walk above ground, crisscrossed beneath the downtown area. During the Prohibition era, bootleggers, gamblers, opium dealers, and Chinese railroad laborers frequented the businesses that grew up here. Three tours are available; the Underground tour, the Cozy Rooms Bordello tour, or a combination of both excursions. Open Mon.-Sat. 9 a.m.-5 p.m. For each tour, admission is $5 for adults, $3 for kids under 12. The combination tour charge is $9 for adults, $5 for kids. Tours are 45 minutes each and reservations are recommended. To get there from I-84, take exit 209 and turn north into Pendleton. Continue up Emigrant Ave. to S.W. 1st Street. The tour begins on the northeast corner of S.W. 1st St. and Emigrant Avenue.

Hamley's Western Store, 30 S.E. Court Ave., tel. (541) 276-2321, is internationally known for its Western saddles and custom leathercraft. The second floor is a gallery of Native American artists. Stop by and join one of the tours of saddle-making in progress, held Mon.-Sat. 9 a.m.-5:30 p.m.

A good place to learn more about the local scene is **Armchair Books,** 39 S.W. Dorion, tel. (541) 276-7323, a store that specializes in regional titles and authors. There's a good selection of titles concerning Native Americans.

Those interested in Umatilla and Cayuse art should visit the **Collectors Gallery,** 223 S.E. Court, tel. (541) 276-6697, across from the post office.

Murals

Pendleton is graced by wall murals on commercial establishments and government buildings. Check out the one on the north wall of Albertson's market, across S.W. Court Ave. from the Round-Up Station. Depicted is a wagon train emerging from the Blue Mountains, closely watched by Native Americans on horseback. On Main and S.W. Emigrant is an 1880s' street scene, and Frontier Auto Parts' back wall features a tableau of wagons and Native Americans against a Blue Mountain backdrop.

SPORTS AND RECREATION

Lots of sun is conducive to such outdoor activities as golf at **Pendleton Country Club,** seven miles south of town on US 395, and boating and water-skiing on **McKay Reservoir** near the country club. In a little over an hour, fishing enthusiasts can head north and arrive at the Columbia River for salmon, steelhead, and bass, or try the area's reservoirs for bluegills, bass, and catfish. During the winter months, skiing is on tap up at **Spout Springs,** one of the oldest ski resorts in the Northwest. To get there, drive north on ORE 11 to Weston, turn east on Ore 204, and travel a few miles past Tollgate to the ski area. It's located 40 miles northeast of Pendleton and is rumored to hold on to its dry powder longer than any other ski area in the state. Finally, the River Parkway, a paved strip paralleling the Umatilla River through much of downtown, is recommended for walkers and bikers.

PRACTICALITIES

Accommodations

The cost for lodging in this town is reasonable. But if you show up at rodeo time without a reservation or unprepared to pay double the room rate, you might be out of luck. The chamber of commerce has a list of private homes that rent for a little less than a motel room, but they are normally booked well in advance. If you bring a tent, camping is usually available in schoolyards and other special sites set up for the several days of the Round-Up.

A tonic to modern life is a stay at the **Bar M Ranch,** 31 miles northeast of Pendleton on ORE 11. Built on the site of the historic Bingham Springs Resort, the ranch lies at the base of the Blue Mountains in the Umatilla National Forest. A stable of 50 horses, a natural warm springs, a recreation barn, and eight rooms in a hand-hewn log house let you rough it in style. Rates are $545 per week for a single and $505 each for double occupancy, which includes horse rides, meals, and all amenities.

The **Working Girls Old Hotel,** Main at Emigrant, Pendleton, tel. (541) 276-0630, is a bed and breakfast built around a Pendleton historical tradition—the houses of negotiable affection. The city underground tour (see "Tours," above), half price with a room, will supply the details. Antique-filled rooms go for $55-65 and include a continental breakfast. Southeast of Pendleton at **Emigrant Springs Campground,** Oregon State Parks, tel. (541) 378-6305, runs a lodge with two separate cabins open year-round. Rates are $14 per night.

Bed and Breakfasts

Two B&Bs close to downtown rate a special mention. **Swift St. Station,** 602 S.E. Byers, tel. (541) 276-3739, lets you return to the Victorian era with modern comforts, including a five-course breakfast. The **Parker House,** 311 N. Main, tel. (800) 700-8581, pays homage to early-20th-century elegance with oriental rugs and original silk wall coverings. A comfy porch and a fire going in the dining room while you enjoy creative breakfast fare might give you incentive to linger awhile. Rooms go $75-85.

Food

During Round-up, Main St. is cordoned off for fast food, fiddling, and fairground souvenirs. The rest of the year Pendleton offers frontier hospitality at the following places. The **Rainbow Bar and Grill,** 209 S. Main, tel. (541) 276-4120, is a famous saloon/restaurant for rodeo fans and local buckaroos. The walls are covered with photos of Round-Up champions and Indian princesses, and the place was recently mentioned in Craig Lesley's novel *Winterkill,* the tale of a modern-day Indian bronc rider trying to scrape by. The Rainbow serves passable American diner food, which you shouldn't pass up, if only for local color.

The **Harvester Restaurant and Lounge,** 2220 S.E. Court Ave., tel. (541) 276-9046, is home of the giant chicken-fried steak. **Cimmiyotti's,** 137 Main St., tel. (541) 276-4314, is a dark cozy spot evoking an Old West bordello that has both American and Italian cuisine (main courses $9-17). The **Great Pacific Wine and Coffee Co.,** 403 S. Main, tel. (541) 276-1350, offers evidence that "hip" has come to Pendleton. They feature imported cheeses, desserts, croissant sandwiches, microbrews and the area's largest wine selection, an espresso bar, and gourmet products.

The **Circle S,** 210 S.E. 5th, tel. (541) 276-9637, is a Western-style restaurant that serves up a great barbecue sandwich for $3.50. **The Health Nuts,** 1700 S.W. Court Place, tel. (541) 276-2251, is an oasis of natural foods in Pendleton, with a complete selection of whole grains, nuts, yogurt, and organic vegetables in season.

The **Bread Board and Catering Service,** 141 S. Main St., tel. (541) 276-4520, has scrumptious homemade soups and sandwiches—a great place to provision a picnic. In an elegant older home across from City Hall enjoy upscale dining in **Raphaels,** 233 S.E. 4th, tel. (541) 276-8500. As you savor salmon wrapped in spinach topped by huckleberry puree, a visual feast of Native American art will also happily engage your senses.

Wildhorse Gaming Resort

In addition to gambling, this resort offers buffets, a range of accommodations, a planned golf course, and the Native People's Museum described previously. For more information call (800) 654-WILD.

Entertainment and Events

In 1910, Pendleton farmers and ranchers got together to celebrate the end of the wheat harvest. This was the first year of the **Pendleton Round-Up,** which now draws 45,000 rodeo fans

OREGON TOURISM DIVISION

Pendleton Round-Up brings back the glory of the Old West.

in the grand tradition started by legendary rodeo stars like Jackson Sundown and Yakima Canutt. Usually held in mid-September at Raley Park, the fun begins with the **Westward Ho Historical Parade,** including covered wagons, mule teams, buggies, and hundreds of Indians in full regalia. There's also a **Happy Canyon Pageant,** which portrays the Native American culture, the coming of the emigrants, clashes between the two, and the birth of a frontier town. The Round-Up features such classic competitions as bulldogging, calf-roping, and wild-horse races Wed.-Saturday. Kids will enjoy Western-theme carnival rides on Main Street.

A **tipi encampment** of hundreds of Indians (Umatilla, Cayuse, Warm Springs, Blackfoot, and Nez Percé) on the Round-Up grounds and the **cowboy breakfast** of ham, eggs, flapjacks, and coffee served Wed.-Sat. at 6 a.m. in Stillman Park exemplify the traditions here that take the Old West beyond the rodeo ring. The Round-Up is staged primarily by 1,600 unpaid volun-

PENDLETON ACCOMMODATIONS

Chaparral Motel, 620 S.W. Tutuilla, tel. (541) 276-8654, $40-50, cable, wheelchair access, pets, kitchenettes, restaurant, nonsmoking rooms.

Econo Lodge, 201 S.W. Court Ave., tel. (541) 276-5252, $40-60, cable, pets, pool.

Longhorn Motel, 411 S.W. Dorion, tel. (541) 276-7531, $35-60, cable, pets, restaurant, nonsmoking rooms.

Motel 6, 325 Nye Ave., tel. (541) 276-3160, $35-50, clean and basic.

Pioneer Motel, 1807 S.E. Court Ave., tel. (541) 276-4521, $35-50.

Ranch Motel, 7 I-84, Barnhart Exit, tel. (541) 276-4711, $50-85, cable, wheelchair access, pets, pool, restaurant.

Doubletree, 304 S.E. Nye, tel. (541) 276-6111 or (800) 222-TREE, $80-115, cable, wheelchair access, restaurant/lounge, pool, live entertainment, nonsmoking rooms.

Tapadera Motor Inn, 105 S.E. Court Ave., tel. (541) 276-3731 or (800) 722-8277, $55-90, cable, pets, restaurant/lounge, nonsmoking rooms.

Thrifty Motel, 102 S.W. 18th St, tel. (541) 276-1920, $35-50.

Travelers Inn, 310 S.E. Dorion Ave., tel. (541) 276-6231, $45-65, cable, pets, pool, restaurant, laundry.

teers. With over two million dollars filling local coffers during the festivities, it's no surprise that schools and local government offices close during the mid-September pageant.

Tickets for each day run $5-10 depending on location. For information contact Pendleton Round-Up, P.O. Box 609, Pendleton 97801, tel. (541) 276-2553. The **Northwest Cowboy Poetry Roundup,** tel. (541) 276-2321, takes place the end of June at the Convention Center.

If you'd like a different slant on cowboys and Indians, take in the **Tygh Valley All-Indian Rodeo,** tel. (541) 344-3371, 30 miles south of The Dalles, which is held the third week in May.

Information and Services
St. Anthony's Hospital, 1601 S.E. Court Ave., tel. (541) 278-3214, has 24-hour emergency service. The **Pendleton Chamber of Commerce Visitor and Convention Bureau,** 25 S.E. Dorion, Pendleton 97801, tel. (541) 276-7411 or (800) 547-8911, can steer you to local sights and special events. A self-guided walking-tour map of the historic downtown district is helpful in this regard. The tour starts at the corner of Main and Frazer and takes in many historic buildings. If you run into trouble during the Round-Up, the **police** can be reached at (541) 276-4411. The **post office,** 104 Dorion Ave., Pendleton 97801, tel. (541) 278-0203, is down the street and open 8:30 a.m.-5 p.m.

Pendleton Airport, 2016 Airport Rd., tel. (541) 278-0947, is located 3.5 miles west of town center and is served by **Horizon Air,** tel. (800) 547-9308. **Aerowest Aviation,** tel. (541) 276-3835, provides charter rentals. At the airport, **Hertz Rent-a-Car,** tel. (541) 276-3183, is the only such outfit in these parts. **Greyhound,** 320 Court Ave., tel. (541) 276-1551, and **Pendleton Bus Co.,** tel. (541) 276-5621, offer charters and transportation. **Pendleton Cinemas,** 415 W. First St., tel. (541) 278-0479, has three theaters. Bargain matinees begin before 5 p.m.

BOOKLIST

In addition to the titles cited in the text, Oregon-bound travelers would do well to acquaint themselves with these books.

Atlases

Two publications authored by Samuel Dickman make Oregon's cultural and geological landscapes come alive. *Oregon Divided* (Portland: Oregon Historical Society, 1982) and *The Making of Oregon* (Portland: Oregon Historical Society, 1979) address the human history, economics, and topography of each part of the state.

Oregon Geographic Names by Lewis MacArthur (Portland: Oregon Historical Society, 1982) might be a physically weighty tome, but its alphabetic rundown of the history of the place-names here makes for light and informative reading.

The Coast

There are many good books on the coast, but the only one we've found that'll give something beyond what you'll find in conventional guidebooks was written by out-of-staters. East Coast residents and former *Rolling Stone* writers Parke Puterbaugh and Alan Bisbort's *Life is a Beach* (New York: McGraw-Hill Book Company, 1988) portrays Oregon's western edge with humor, insight, and graceful prose.

Oregon Coast Hikes by Paul Williams (Seattle: Mountaineers Books, 1985) is the best regional hiking guide.

Eastern Oregon

The classics for this area are *The Oregon Desert* by E. R. Jackson and R. A. Long (Caldwell, Idaho: Caxton Ltd., 1964) and *Steens Mountain in Oregon's High Desert Country* (Caldwell, Idaho: Caxton, Ltd., 1967). Within the volumes, history and local color fill in the east side's wide-open spaces.

Fiction

The book to read before coming here is *Sometimes a Great Notion* by Ken Kesey (New York:

Viking, 1964). This book is a fictional portrayal of what Mark Twain called the "westering spirit." In the same vein, the original prankster's latest fiction effort, *The Last Go Round* (New York: Viking, 1994) is recommended reading for anyone seeking a little texture about the Pendleton Round-Up. Old photos and background information impart a sense of history, and the tensions among a white, a black, and a Nez Percé contestant during the 1911 rodeo will hold your interest.

General Interest

The hottest new "reads" on the region are *The Good Rain* by Timothy Egan (New York: Alfred A. Knopf, 1990) and *Stepping Westward* by Sallie Tisdale (New York: Holt and Co., 1991). While both books depict the past, present, and future of the Northwest, each work stakes out different bailiwicks in the psychic landscape here. Egan brings the practiced eye of a *New York Times* correspondent to towns along the Columbia and other parts of Oregon and Washington caught in the transition from a resource based economy. The historical perspectives of a 19th-century diarist's entries underscore his descriptions of local color and contemporary issues throughout this book. Tisdale's treatment of similar terrain and themes emphasize a native world view and myths. Fact and fancy are deftly interwoven by this author who is also an award-winning essayist.

Perhaps the best general survey of the state ever done is Judy Jewell's *Oregon* (New York: Fodor's Compass American Guides, 1994). Read this guide before traveling to the state, to complement *Oregon Handbook* as your on-the-road reference. Beautiful color photos and insightful travel tips liven up this literary rendition of Oregon's greatest hits.

Other Northwest vignettes worth perusing are found in the final chapters of the late Supreme Court Justice William O. Douglas's autobiography, *Of Men and Mountains* (San Francisco: Chronicle Books, 1985). Particularly evocative are his descriptions of the Wallowas.

The Best of Oregon by Ken Metzler (Portland: Timber Press, 1986) is a loving look at the state by a longtime Oregon journalist and University of Oregon professor. Also recommended is Michael Thoele's *Footprints Across Oregon* (Portland: Graphic Arts Center Publishing Co., 1988).

Guidebooks

Ralph Friedman is Oregon's King of the Road. Of his half-dozen books, *Oregon for the Curious* (Caldwell, Idaho: Caxton Ltd., 1972) is most recommended. It still is the best mile-by-mile description of the state ever done.

Another writer who can stake a claim as the Dean of Oregon Travel Writers is Mimi Bell, simply on the strength of *Off Beat Oregon* (San Francisco: Chronicle Books, 1983). Charming essays about travel in all four corners of the state will get you out of the armchair and onto the road.

Other excellent supplements to *Oregon Handbook* are penned by William L. Mainwaring for West Ridge Press in Salem, Oregon. His *Exploring Oregon's Central and Southern Cascades* (1979), *Exploring the Oregon Coast* (1985), and *Exploring the Mt. Hood Loop* (1992) outline activities, hikes, camping, history, and local color.

Also recommended are Briget B. McCarthy's self-published *Where to find the Oregon in Oregon: A Guide to Oregon's Local, Natural and Cultural Resources* (1994: Write to 7277 S.W. Barnes Rd., Portland 97225); John Garren's *Oregon River Tours* (Portland: Garren Publishing, 1991); and Karen and Terry Whitehill's *A Pedestrian's Portland: Forty Walks in Portland Area Parks and Neighborhoods* (Seattle: Mountaineers Books, 1989).

History

The best concise history of Oregon can be found in the back of *Oregon Blue Book* (published biannually by the state of Oregon in Salem). Given its heft and cost (around $30), we'd recommend a perusal in a library. This section of Oregon's political "Who's Who" is written by noted historian Terrence O'Donnell. His work in that book as well as in *Portland: An Informal History and Guide* (Portland: Oregon Historical Society, 1964) should disabuse you of any notions you might have that history is boring.

Chinese life in Oregon at the turn of the 20th century is chronicled in Jerry Barlow and Christine Richardson's *The Chinese Doctor of John Day* (Portland: Binford and Mort, 1979).

The grandaddy of them all, the *WPA Guide to Oregon* (Federal Writers' Project, 1941) is the primary inspiration for *Oregon Handbook*. The product of dozens of authors working in the Federal Writers' Project, this post-Depression guidebook still sets the standard for completeness and vividness of description. Although much of the information is dated, its rundown of pioneer history and glimpses of early 20th-century Oregon continue to make it a valuable tool for any modern traveler interested in understanding the Beaver State. Available in many public libraries.

Natural Oregon

Serious birders and naturalists would do well to acquaint themselves with the following wildlife guides. An excellent general resource is James Yuskavitch's *Oregon Wildlife Viewing Guide* (Helena, MT: Falcon Press, 1994), which lists wildlife sites and nearby accommodations. All proceeds from the book go to wildlife site maintenance and publications put out by Defenders of Wildlife. Dennis Paulson's highly regarded *Shorebirds of the Pacific Northwest* (Seattle: University of Washington Press, 1994) also contains detailed birding information on the region. Russ Jolley's *Wildflowers of the Columbia* is an exhaustive study on Oregon's plant species, identifying 744 of the Columbia Gorge's more than 800 species of flowering shrubs and wildflowers.

Photo Essays

The western part of the state is effectively profiled by Marnie McPhee in *Western Oregon: A Portrait of the Land and Its People* (Helena: American Geographic Publishing, 1987). Excellent color photos make the wetside's landscape and cultural geography come alive. In the same series, Mark Hoy's *Backroads of Oregon* (Helena: American Geographic Publishing, 1987) is also a winner.

Insight Guides: Pacific Northwest, edited by Hans Hoefer (Portland: Graphic Arts Center Publishing Co., 1986) and featuring Oregon chapters by state residents (including the *Oregon Handbook* writers), is a cross between a coffee-table book and a guidebook. Despite the relative lack of hard information, lavish illustrations covering the whole state paint an evocative portrait in broad strokes. The book, now published by Houghton Mifflin, is also badly in need of an update.

The preeminent coffee-table books of Oregon photos were done by Ray Atkeson (Portland: Graphic Arts Center Publishing, 1968-1987). The once-costly hard-covered editions of his *Oregon I, Oregon II,* and *Oregon III* are now available in paperback.

Environment
For readers interested in Oregon's environmental movement, we recommend Ernest Callenbach's *Ecotopia* (New York: Bantam, rev. ed. 1983), which argues that northern California should break off from the rest of the state to join Oregon as the single republic "Ecotopia," based on environmental imperatives. Another bioregional manifesto, *The Nine Nations of North America,* divides the continent into nine bioregions on the basis of their cultural, historical, ethnic, economic, and environmental interests. Environmental conflicts among the old growth forests of Opal Creek are detailed in David Seideman's fascinating *Showdown At Opal Creek* (New York: Carrol and Graf Publishers, 1993).

Statewide Hiking and Camping Guides
The best of this genre is undoubtedly *Exploring Oregon's Wild Areas* by William L. Sullivan (Seattle: Mountaineers Books, 1988). Activities for hikers, backpackers, climbers, cross-country skiers, and saddlers are outlined in this well-organized book. Geology and botany are also addressed. Other Sullivan titles covering each region of the state in depth are also first rate.

We also recommend Wendell Wood's *A Walking Guide To Oregon's Ancient Forests* (Portland: Oregon Natural Resources Council, 1992), and Ira Spring and Harvey Manning's *Hiking Guide to the Great Northwest* (Seattle: Mountaineers Books, 1991).

Auto Tapes
The notion of having entertaining commentary while you drive Oregon's scenic highways sounds appealing. Oregon is blessed to have two companies, **Road Tapes,** 872 B St., Ashland, OR 97520, and **Columbia Gorge Driving Tours,** tel. 730-7495, that enable you to share such an experience. At this writing, Road Tapes covers the I-5 corridor and Columbia Gorge Driving Tours guides you through a region of the same name. Each feature professional actors doing the commentary and background music to set a mood. Dramatic reenactments of historical events, native myths, and local color make the miles go quickly. Expect the offerings of these companies to grow in the near future.

INDEX

Page numbers in *italics* indicate information in maps.

ABOUT THE AUTHORS

Stuart Warren

Stuart discovered at an early age that serendipity was getting paid to travel to favorite places. While jobs as a tour director, tour planner, and travel agent let him glimpse this dream, *Oregon Handbook* let him live it. He resides in Portland, Oregon with his son and the cast of characters that hang out on his porch.

Ted Long Ishikawa

Having spent most of his life in Oregon, Ted is always surprised at how many travel treasures he finds during his frequent research trips for *Oregon Handbook*. A Eugene resident for many years, Ted is currently enrolled in chiropractic school in Atlanta, Georgia. Be that as it may, he often finds himself daydreaming over his textbooks about the Pacific Wonderland, anticipating a return to his roots by the end of the century to set up practice. "In the meantime," Ted says, "please enjoy the Oregon experience for me; I trust that *Oregon Handbook* will enhance your visit."

NOTES

NOTES

LOSE YOURSELF IN THE EXPERIENCE, NOT THE CROWD

For 25 years, Moon Travel Handbooks have been the guidebooks of choice for adventurous travelers. Our award-winning Handbook series provides focused, comprehensive coverage of distinct destinations all over the world. Each Handbook is like an entire bookcase of cultural insight and introductory information in one portable volume. Our goal at Moon is to give travelers all the background and practical information they'll need for an extraordinary travel experience.

The following pages include a complete list of Handbooks, covering North America and Hawaii, Mexico, Central America and the Caribbean, and Asia and the Pacific. To purchase Moon Travel Handbooks, check your local bookstore or order by phone: (800) 345-5473 M-F 8 am.-5 p.m. PST or outside the U.S. phone: (530) 345-5473.

"An in-depth dunk into the land, the people and their history, arts, and politics."
—*Student Travels*

"Amazingly detailed in a style easy to understand, the Handbooks offer a lot for a good price."
—*International Travel News*

"Moon Travel Handbooks' line of travel guides adds wisdom to one's wanderings."
—*Excursions*

"Outdoor enthusiasts gravitate to the well-written Moon Travel Handbooks. In addition to politically correct historic and cultural features, the series focuses on flora, fauna and outdoor recreation. Maps and meticulous directions also are a trademark of Moon guides."
—*Houston Chronicle*

"Moon [Travel Handbooks] . . . bring a healthy respect to the places they investigate. Best of all, they provide a host of odd nuggets that give a place texture and prod the wary traveler from the beaten path. The finest are written with such care and insight they deserve listing as literature."
—*American Geographical Society*

"Moon Travel Handbooks offer in-depth historical essays and useful maps, enhanced by a sense of humor and a neat, compact format."
—*Swing*

"Perfect for the more adventurous, these are long on history, sightseeing and nitty-gritty information and very price-specific."
—*Columbus Dispatch*

"Moon guides manage to be comprehensive and countercultural at the same time . . . Handbooks are packed with maps, photographs, drawings, and sidebars that constitute a college-level introduction to each country's history, culture, people, and crafts."
—*National Geographic Traveler*

"Few travel guides do a better job helping travelers create their own itineraries than the Moon Travel Handbook series. The authors have a knack for homing in on the essentials."
—*Colorado Springs Gazette Telegraph*

MEXICO

"These books will delight the armchair traveler, aid the undecided person in selecting a destination, and guide the seasoned road warrior looking for lesser-known hideaways."

—*Mexican Meanderings* Newsletter

"From tourist traps to off-the-beaten track hideaways, these guides offer consistent, accurate details without pretension."

—*Foreign Service Journal*

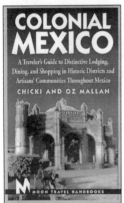

Archaeological Mexico	**$19.95**
Andrew Coe	450 pages, 25 maps
Baja Handbook	**$15.95**
Joe Cummings	380 pages, 44 maps
Cabo Handbook	**$14.95**
Joe Cummings	265 pages, 18 maps
Cancun Handbooks	**$13.95**
Chicki Mallan	270 pages, 25 maps
Colonial Mexico	**$16.95**
Chicki Mallan	300 pages, 38 maps
Mexico Handbook	**$21.95**
Joe Cummings and Chicki Mallan	1,200 pages, 232 maps
Northern Mexico Handbook	**$16.95**
Joe Cummings	590 pages, 68 maps
Pacific Mexico Handbook	**$17.95**
Bruce Whipperman	580 pages, 69 maps
Puerto Vallarta Handbook	**$14.95**
Bruce Whipperman	330 pages, 36 maps
Yucatan Handbook	**$15.95**
Chicki Mallan	470 pages, 62 maps

LATIN AMERICA AND THE CARIBBEAN

"Solidly packed with practical information and full of significant cultural asides that will enlighten you on the whys and wherefores of things you might easily see but not easily grasp."

—Boston Globe

Belize Handbook	**$15.95**
Chicki Mallan	390 pages, 45 maps
Caribbean Handbook	**$16.95**
Karl Luntta	400 pages, 56 maps
Ecuador Handbook	**$16.95**
Julian Smith	450 pages, 43 maps
Costa Rica Handbook	**$19.95**
Christopher P. Baker	780 pages, 74 maps
Cuba Handbook	**$19.95**
Christopher P. Baker	740 pages, 70 maps
Dominican Republic Handbook	**$15.95**
Gaylord Dold	420 pages, 24 maps
Honduras Handbook	**$15.95**
Chris Humphrey	330 pages, 40 maps
Jamaica Handbook	**$15.95**
Karl Luntta	330 pages, 17 maps
Virgin Islands Handbook	**$13.95**
Karl Luntta	220 pages, 19 maps

NORTH AMERICA AND HAWAII

"These domestic guides convey the same sense of exoticism that their foreign counterparts do, making home-country travel seem like far-flung adventure."

—Sierra Magazine

Alaska-Yukon Handbook	**$17.95**
Deke Castleman and Don Pitcher	530 pages, 92 maps
Alberta and the Northwest Territories Handbook	**$17.95**
Andrew Hempstead and Nadina Purdon	530 pages, 72 maps,
Arizona Traveler's Handbook	**$17.95**
Bill Weir and Robert Blake	512 pages,54 maps
Atlantic Canada Handbook	**$17.95**
Nan Drosdick and Mark Morris	460 pages, 61 maps
Big Island of Hawaii Handbook	**$13.95**
J.D. Bisignani	370 pages, 23 maps
British Columbia Handbook	**$16.95**
Jane King and Andrew Hempstead	400 pages, 65 maps

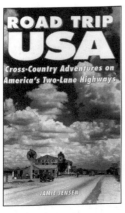

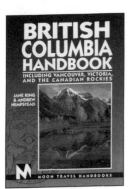

Colorado Handbook	**$18.95**
Stephen Metzger	480 pages, 59 maps
Georgia Handbook	**$17.95**
Kap Stann	370 pages, 50 maps
Hawaii Handbook	**$19.95**
J.D. Bisignani	1,030 pages, 90 maps
Honolulu-Waikiki Handbook	**$14.95**
J.D. Bisignani	380 pages, 20 maps
Idaho Handbook	**$18.95**
Don Root	610 pages, 42 maps
Kauai Handbook	**$15.95**
J.D. Bisignani	320 pages, 23 maps
Maui Handbook	**$14.95**
J.D. Bisignani	410 pages, 35 maps
Montana Handbook	**$17.95**
Judy Jewell and W.C. McRae	480 pages, 52 maps
Nevada Handbook	**$16.95**
Deke Castleman	500 pages, 40 maps
New Mexico Handbook	**$15.95**
Stephen Metzger	360 pages, 47 maps
New York City Handbook	**$13.95**
Christiane Bird	300 pages, 20 maps
New York Handbook	**$19.95**
Christiane Bird	780 pages, 95 maps
Northern California Handbook	**$19.95**
Kim Weir	800 pages, 50 maps
Oregon Handbook	**$16.95**
Stuart Warren and Ted Long Ishikawa	540 pages, 33 maps
Road Trip USA	**$22.50**
Jamie Jensen	800 pages, 165 maps
Southern California Handbook	**$19.95**
Kim Weir	750 pages, 30 maps
Tennessee Handbook	**$17.95**
Jeff Bradley	530 pages, 44 maps
Texas Handbook	**$17.95**
Joe Cummings	620 pages, 70 maps
Utah Handbook	**$17.95**
Bill Weir and W.C. McRae	490 pages, 40 maps
Washington Handbook	**$19.95**
Don Pitcher	870 pages, 113 maps
Wisconsin Handbook	**$18.95**
Thomas Huhti	590 pages, 69 maps
Wyoming Handbook	**$17.95**
Don Pitcher	610 pages, 80 maps

ASIA AND THE PACIFIC

"Scores of maps, detailed practical info down to business hours of small-town libraries. You can't beat the Asian titles for sheer heft. (The) series is sort of an American Lonely Planet, with better writing but fewer titles. (The) individual voice of researchers comes through."

—Travel & Leisure

Australia Handbook	**$21.95**
Marael Johnson, Andrew Hempstead, and Nadina Purdon	940 pages, 141 maps
Bali Handbook	**$19.95**
Bill Dalton	750 pages, 54 maps
Bangkok Handbook	**$13.95**
Michael Buckley	244 pages, 30 maps
Fiji Islands Handbook	**$13.95**
David Stanley	280 pages, 38 maps
Hong Kong Handbook	**$16.95**
Kerry Moran	370 pages, 39 maps
Indonesia Handbook	**$25.00**
Bill Dalton	1,380 pages, 249 maps
Japan Handbook	**$22.50**
J.D. Bisignani	970 pages, 213 maps
Micronesia Handbook	**$14.95**
Neil M. Levy	340 pages, 70 maps
Nepal Handbook	**$18.95**
Kerry Moran	490 pages, 51 maps
New Zealand Handbook	**$19.95**
Jane King	620 pages, 81 maps
Outback Australia Handbook	**$18.95**
Marael Johnson	450 pages, 57 maps
Pakistan Hanbdbook	**$19.95**
Isobel Shaw	660 pages, 85 maps
Philippines Handbook	**$17.95**
Peter Harper and Laurie Fullerton	670 pages, 116 maps
Singapore Handbook	**$15.95**
Carl Parkes	350 pages, 29 maps
Southeast Asia Handbook	**$21.95**
Carl Parkes	1,000 pages, 196 maps
South Korea Handbook	**$19.95**
Robert Nilsen	820 pages, 141 maps
South Pacific Handbook	**$22.95**
David Stanley	920 pages, 147 maps

Tahiti-Polynesia Handbook	$13.95
David Stanley	270 pages, 35 maps
Thailand Handbook	**$19.95**
Carl Parkes	860 pages, 142 maps
Vietnam, Cambodia & Laos Handbook	**$18.95**
Michael Buckley	720 pages, 112 maps

OTHER GREAT TITLES FROM MOON

"For hardy wanderers, few guides come more highly recommended than the Handbooks. They include good maps, steer clear of fluff and flackery, and offer plenty of money-saving tips. They also give you the kind of information that visitors to strange lands—on any budget—need to survive."

—*US News & World Report*

Moon Handbook	$10.00
Carl Koppeschaar	141 pages, 8 maps
Moscow-St. Petersburg Handbook	**$13.95**
Masha Nordbye	259 pages, 16 maps
The Practical Nomad: How to Travel Around the World	**$17.95**
Edward Hasbrouck	575 pages
Staying Healthy in Asia, Africa, and Latin America	**$11.95**
Dirk Schroeder	197 pages, 4 maps

MOONBELT

A new concept in moneybelts. Made of heavy-duty Cordura nylon, the Moonbelt offers maximum protection for your money and important papers. This pouch, designed for all-weather comfort, slips under your shirt or waistband, rendering it virtually undetectable and inaccessible to pickpockets. It features a one-inch high-test quick-release buckle so there's no more fumbling around for the strap or repeated adjustments. This handy plastic buckle opens and closes with a touch but won't come undone until you want it to. Moonbelts accommodate traveler's checks, passports, cash, photos, etc. Size 5 x 9 inches. Available in black only. **$8.95**

THE PRACTICAL NOMAD

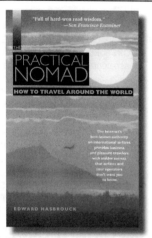

✈ TAKE THE PLUNGE

"The greatest barriers to long-term travel by Americans are the disempowered feelings that leave them afraid to ask for the time off. Just do it."

✈ TAKE NOTHING FOR GRANTED

"Even 'What time is it?' is a highly politicized question in some areas, and the answer may depend on your informant's ethnicity and political allegiance as well as the proximity of the secret police."

✈ TAKE THIS BOOK

With experience helping thousands of his globetrotting clients plan their trips around the world, travel industry insider Edward Hasbrouck provides the secrets that can save readers money and valuable travel time.
An indispensable complement to destination-specific travel guides,
The Practical Nomad includes:

airfare strategies

ticket discounts

long-term travel considerations

travel documents

border crossings

entry requirements

government offices

travel publications

Internet information resources

WHERE TO BUY MOON TRAVEL HANDBOOKS

BOOKSTORES AND LIBRARIES: Moon Travel Handbooks are distributed worldwide. Please contact our sales manager for a list of wholesalers and distributors in your area.

TRAVELERS: We would like to have Moon Travel Handbooks available throughout the world. Please ask your bookstore to write or call us for ordering information. If your bookstore will not order our guides for you, please contact us for a free catalog.

Moon Travel Handbooks
P.O. Box 3040
Chico, CA 95927-3040 U.S.A.
tel.: (800) 345-5473, outside the U.S. (530) 345-5473
fax: (530) 345-6751
e-mail: travel@moon.com

IMPORTANT ORDERING INFORMATION

PRICES: All prices are subject to change. We always ship the most current edition. We will let you know if there is a price increase on the book you order.

SHIPPING AND HANDLING OPTIONS: Domestic UPS or USPS first class (allow 10 working days for delivery): $4.50 for the first item, $1.00 for each additional item.

Moonbelt shipping is $1.50 for one, 50 cents for each additional belt.

UPS 2nd Day Air or Printed Airmail requires a special quote.

International Surface Bookrate 8-12 weeks delivery: $3.00 for the first item, $1.00 for each additional item. Note: We cannot guarantee international surface bookrate shipping. We recommends sending international orders via air mail, which requires a special quote.

FOREIGN ORDERS: Orders that originate outside the U.S.A. must be paid for with an international money order, a check in U.S. currency drawn on a major U.S. bank based in the U.S.A., or Visa, MasterCard, or Discover.

TELEPHONE ORDERS: We accept Visa, MasterCard, or Discover payments. Call in your order: (800) 345-5473, 8 a.m.-5 p.m. Pacific standard time. Outside the U.S. the number is (530) 345-5473.

INTERNET ORDERS: Visit our site at: www.moon.com

ORDER FORM

Prices are subject to change without notice. Be sure to call (800) 345-5473,
or (530) 345-5473 from outside the U.S. 8 a.m.–5 p.m. PST for current prices and editions,
or for the name of the bookstore nearest you that carries Moon Travel Handbooks.
(See important ordering information on preceding page.)

Name: _____ Date: _____

Street: _____

City: _____ Daytime Phone: _____

State or Country: _____ Zip Code: _____

QUANTITY	TITLE	PRICE

Taxable Total_____

Sales Tax (7.25%) for California Residents_____

Shipping & Handling_____

TOTAL_____

Ship: ☐ UPS (no P.O. Boxes) ☐ 1st class ☐ International surface mail
Ship to: ☐ address above ☐ other _____

_____

Make checks payable to: **MOON TRAVEL HANDBOOKS**, P.O. Box 3040, Chico, CA 95927-3040
U.S.A. We accept Visa, MasterCard, or Discover. **To Order**: Call in your Visa, MasterCard, or Discover number,
or send a written order with your Visa, MasterCard, or Discover number and expiration date clearly written.

Card Number: ☐ **Visa** ☐ **MasterCard** ☐ **Discover**

☐ ☐ ☐ ☐ ☐ ☐ ☐ ☐ ☐ ☐ ☐ ☐ ☐ ☐ ☐ ☐

Exact Name on Card: _____

Expiration date:_____

Signature: _____

U.S.~METRIC CONVERSION

1 inch = 2.54 centimeters (cm)
1 foot = .304 meters (m)
1 mile = 1.6093 kilometers (km)
1 km = .6214 miles
1 fathom = 1.8288 m
1 chain = 20.1168 m
1 furlong = 201.168 m
1 acre = .4047 hectares
1 sq km = 100 hectares
1 sq mile = 2.59 square km
1 ounce = 28.35 grams
1 pound = .4536 kilograms
1 short ton = .90718 metric ton
1 short ton = 2000 pounds
1 long ton = 1.016 metric tons
1 long ton = 2240 pounds
1 metric ton = 1000 kilograms
1 quart = .94635 liters
1 US gallon = 3.7854 liters
1 Imperial gallon = 4.5459 liters
1 nautical mile = 1.852 km

To compute celsius temperatures, subtract 32 from Fahrenheit and divide by 1.8. To go the other way, multiply celsius by 1.8 and add 32.

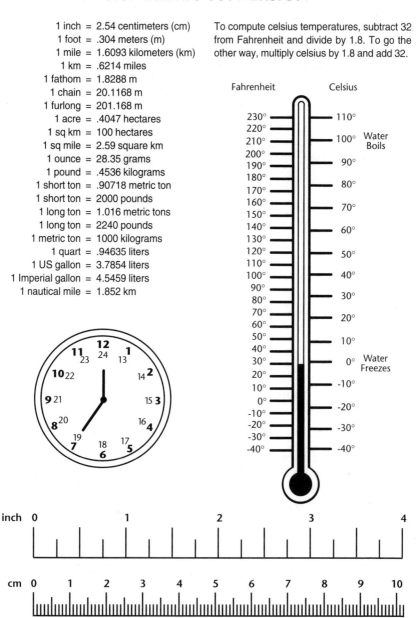